CEAC (TRAN) (handwritten)

CHRYSLER

FRONT WHEEL ~~DRIVE~~ 1981-95 REP~~AIR~~

D0800133

**Covers all U.S. and Canadian models of
Chrysler E-class, Executive Sedan, Laser (1984-86),
LeBaron, LeBaron GTS, Limousine, New Yorker,
Town and Country, TC by Maserati, Dodge Aries,
Daytona, Dynasty, Lancer, Shadow, Spirit,
400 and 600, Eagle Premier, Plymouth Acclaim,
Caravelle, Reliant and Sundance
4-Cylinder Engines Only**

by George B. Heinrich III, A.S.E., S.A.E.

CHILTON *Automotive Books*

PUBLISHED BY **HAYNES NORTH AMERICA, Inc.**

Manufactured in USA
© 1996 Haynes North America, Inc.
ISBN 0-8019-8673-7
Library of Congress Catalog Card No. 96-84178
8901234567 9876543210

Haynes Publishing Group
Sparkford Nr Yeovil
Somerset BA22 7JJ England

Haynes North America, Inc
861 Lawrence Drive
Newbury Park
California 91320 USA

ABCDE
FGHIJ
KLMNO
PQRS 2

5E1

CHILTON'S (vertical text, left margin)

Contents

Contents

SAFETY NOTICE

Proper service and repair procedures are vital to the safe, reliable operation of all motor vehicles, as well as the personal safety of those performing repairs. This manual outlines procedures for servicing and repairing vehicles using safe, effective methods. The procedures contain many NOTES, CAUTIONS and WARNINGS which should be followed, along with standard procedures to eliminate the possibility of personal injury or improper service which could damage the vehicle or compromise its safety.

It is important to note that repair procedures and techniques, tools and parts for servicing motor vehicles, as well as the skill and experience of the individual performing the work vary widely. It is not possible to anticipate all of the conceivable ways or conditions under which vehicles may be serviced, or to provide cautions as to all possible hazards that may result. Standard and accepted safety precautions and equipment should be used when handling toxic or flammable fluids, and safety goggles or other protection should be used during cutting, grinding, chiseling, prying, or any other process that can cause material removal or projectiles.

Some procedures require the use of tools specially designed for a specific purpose. Before substituting another tool or procedure, you must be completely satisfied that neither your personal safety, nor the performance of the vehicle will be endangered.

Although information in this manual is based on industry sources and is complete as possible at the time of publication, the possibility exists that some car manufacturers made later changes which could not be included here. While striving for total accuracy, the authors or publishers cannot assume responsibility for any errors, changes or omissions that may occur in the compilation of this data.

PART NUMBERS

Part numbers listed in this reference are not recommendations by Haynes North America, Inc. for any product brand name. They are references that can be used with interchange manuals and aftermarket supplier catalogs to locate each brand supplier's discrete part number.

SPECIAL TOOLS

Special tools are recommended by the vehicle manufacturer to perform their specific job. Use has been kept to a minimum, but where absolutely necessary, they are referred to in the text by the part number of the tool manufacturer. These tools can be purchased, under the appropriate part number, from your local dealer or regional distributor, or an equivalent tool can be purchased locally from a tool supplier or parts outlet. Before substituting any tool for the one recommended, read the SAFETY NOTICE at the top of this page.

ACKNOWLEDGMENTS

The publisher expresses appreciation to Chrysler Corporation for their generous assistance.

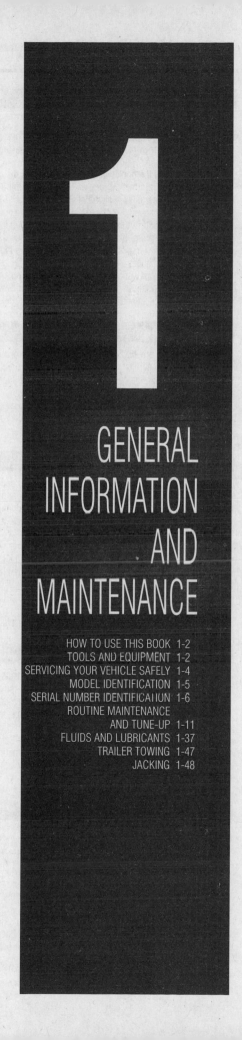

1

GENERAL INFORMATION AND MAINTENANCE

HOW TO USE THIS BOOK

This Chilton's Total Car Care manual, for 1981–95 4-cylinder, front wheel drive Chrysler, Dodge and Plymouth automobiles, is intended to help you learn more about the inner workings of your vehicle while saving you money on its upkeep and operation.

The beginning of the book will likely be referred to the most, since that is where you will find information for maintenance and tune-up. The other sections deal with the more complex systems of your vehicle. Systems (from engine through brakes) are covered to the extent that the average do-it-yourselfer can attempt. This book will not explain such things as rebuilding a differential because the expertise required and the special tools necessary make this uneconomical. It will, however, give you detailed instructions to help you change your own brake pads and shoes, replace spark plugs, and perform many more jobs that can save you money and help avoid expensive problems.

A secondary purpose of this book is a reference for owners who want to understand their vehicle and/or their mechanics better.

Where to Begin

Before removing any bolts, read through the entire procedure. This will give you the overall view of what tools and supplies will be required. So read ahead and plan ahead. Each operation should be approached logically and all procedures thoroughly understood before attempting any work.

If repair of a component is not considered practical, we tell you how to remove the part and then how to install the new or rebuilt replacement. In this way, you at least save labor costs.

Avoiding Trouble

Many procedures in this book require you to "label and disconnect . . ." a group of lines, hoses or wires. Don't be think you can remember where everything goes—you won't. If you hook up vacuum or fuel lines incorrectly, the vehicle may run poorly, if at all. If you hook up electrical wiring incorrectly, you may instantly learn a very expensive lesson.

You don't need to know the proper name for each hose or line. A piece of masking tape on the hose and a piece on its fitting will allow you to assign your own label. As long as you remember your own code, the lines can be reconnected by matching your tags. Remember that tape will dissolve in gasoline or solvents; if a part is to be washed or cleaned, use another method of identification. A permanent felt-tipped marker or a metal scribe can be very handy for marking metal parts. Remove any tape or paper labels after assembly.

Maintenance or Repair?

Maintenance includes routine inspections, adjustments, and replacement of parts which show signs of normal wear. Maintenance compensates for wear or deterioration. Repair implies that something has broken or is not working. A need for a repair is often caused by lack of maintenance. for example: draining and refilling automatic transmission fluid is maintenance recommended at specific intervals. Failure to do this can shorten the life of the transmission/transaxle, requiring very expensive repairs. While no maintenance program can prevent items from eventually breaking or wearing out, a general rule is true: MAINTENANCE IS CHEAPER THAN REPAIR.

TOOLS AND EQUIPMENT

▶ **See Figures 1 thru 15**

Without the proper tools and equipment it is impossible to properly service your vehicle. It would be virtually impossible to catalog every tool that you would need to perform all of the operations in this book. It would be unwise for the amateur to rush out and buy an expensive set of tools on the theory that he/she may need one or more of them at some time.

The best approach is to proceed slowly, gathering a good quality set of those tools that are used most frequently. Don't be misled by the low cost of bargain tools. It is far better to spend a little more for better quality. Forged wrenches, 6 or 12-point sockets and fine tooth ratchets are by far preferable to their less expensive counterparts. As any good mechanic can tell you, there are few worse experiences than trying to work on a vehicle with bad tools.

Two basic mechanic's rules should be mentioned here. First, whenever the left side of the vehicle or engine is referred to, it means the driver's side. Conversely, the right side of the vehicle means the passenger's side. Second, screws and bolts are removed by turning counterclockwise, and tightened by turning clockwise unless specifically noted.

Safety is always the most important rule. Constantly be aware of the dangers involved in working on an automobile and take the proper precautions. Please refer to the information in this section regarding SERVICING YOUR VEHICLE SAFELY and the SAFETY NOTICE on the acknowledgment page.

Avoiding the Most Common Mistakes

Pay attention to the instructions provided. There are 3 common mistakes in mechanical work:

1. Incorrect order of assembly, disassembly or adjustment. When taking something apart or putting it together, performing steps in the wrong order usually just costs you extra time; however, it CAN break something. Read the entire procedure before beginning. Perform everything in the order in which the instructions say you should, even if you can't see a reason for it. When you're taking apart something that is very intricate, you might want to draw a picture of how it looks when assembled in order to make sure you get everything back in its proper position. When making adjustments, perform them in the proper order. One adjustment possibly will affect another.

2. Overtorquing (or undertorquing). While it is more common for overtorquing to cause damage, undertorquing may allow a fastener to vibrate loose causing serious damage. Especially when dealing with aluminum parts, pay attention to torque specifications and utilize a torque wrench in assembly. If a torque figure is not available, remember that if you are using the right tool to perform the job, you will probably not have to strain yourself to get a fastener tight enough. The pitch of most threads is so slight that the tension you put on the wrench will be multiplied many times in actual force on what you are tightening.

There are many commercial products available for ensuring that fasteners won't come loose, even if they are not torqued just right (a very common brand is Loctite®). If you're worried about getting something together tight enough to hold, but loose enough to avoid mechanical damage during assembly, one of these products might offer substantial insurance. Before choosing a threadlocking compound, read the label on the package and make sure the product is compatible with the materials, fluids, etc. involved.

3. Crossthreading. This occurs when a part such as a bolt is screwed into a nut or casting at the wrong angle and forced. Crossthreading is more likely to occur if access is difficult. It helps to clean and lubricate fasteners, then to start threading the bolt, spark plug, etc. with your fingers. If you encounter resistance, unscrew the part and start over again at a different angle until it can be inserted and turned several times without much effort. Keep in mind that many parts have tapered threads, so that gentle turning will automatically bring the part you're threading to the proper angle. Don't put a wrench on the part until it's been tightened a couple of turns by hand. If you suddenly encounter resistance, and the part has not seated fully, don't force it. Pull it back out to make sure it's clean and threading properly.

Be sure to take your time and be patient, and always plan ahead. Allow yourself ample time to perform repairs and maintenance.

Your monetary savings will be far outweighed by frustration and mangled knuckles.

Begin accumulating those tools that are used most frequently: those associated with routine maintenance and tune-up. In addition to the normal assortment of screwdrivers and pliers, you should have the following tools:

• Wrenches/sockets and combination open end/box end wrenches in sizes ⅛–¾ in. and/or 3mm–19mm ¹³⁄₁₆ in. or ⅝ in. spark plug socket (depending on plug type).

➡**If possible, buy various length socket drive extensions. Universal-joint and wobble extensions can be extremely useful, but be careful when using them, as they can change the amount of torque applied to the socket.**

- Jackstands for support.
- Oil filter wrench.
- Spout or funnel for pouring fluids.
- Grease gun for chassis lubrication (unless your vehicle is not equipped with any grease fittings)
- Hydrometer for checking the battery (unless equipped with a sealed, maintenance-free battery).
- A container for draining oil and other fluids.
- Rags for wiping up the inevitable mess.

In addition to the above items there are several others that are not absolutely necessary, but handy to have around. These include an equivalent oil absorbent gravel, like cat litter, and the usual supply of lubricants, antifreeze and fluids. This is a basic list for routine maintenance, but only your personal needs and desire can accurately determine your list of tools.

After performing a few projects on the vehicle, you'll be amazed at the other tools and non-tools on your workbench. Some useful household items are: a large turkey baster or siphon, empty coffee cans and ice trays (to store parts), a ball of twine, electrical tape for wiring, small rolls of colored tape for tagging lines or hoses, markers and pens, a note pad, golf tees (for plugging vacuum lines), metal coat hangers or a roll of mechanic's wire (to hold things out of the way), dental pick or similar long, pointed probe, a strong magnet, and a small mirror (to see into recesses and under manifolds).

A more advanced set of tools, suitable for tune-up work, can be drawn up easily. While the tools are slightly more sophisticated, they need not be outrageously expensive. There are several inexpensive tach/dwell meters on the market that are every bit as good for the average mechanic as a professional model. Just be sure that it goes to a least 1200–1500 rpm on the tach scale and that it works on 4, 6 and 8-cylinder engines. The key to these purchases is to make them with an eye towards adaptability and wide range. A basic list of tune-up tools could include:

- Tach/dwell meter.
- Spark plug wrench and gapping tool.
- Feeler gauges for valve adjustment.
- Timing light.

Fig. 1 All but the most basic procedures will require an assortment of ratchets and sockets

TCCS1200

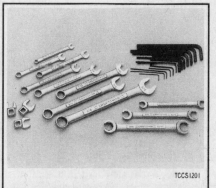

Fig. 2 In addition to ratchets, a good set of wrenches and hex keys will be necessary

TCCS1201

Fig. 3 A hydraulic floor jack and a set of jackstands are essential for lifting and supporting the vehicle

TCCS1202

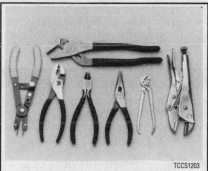

Fig. 4 An assortment of pliers, grippers and cutters will be handy for old rusted parts and stripped bolt heads

TCCS1203

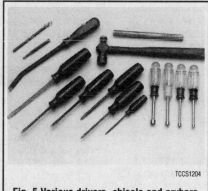

Fig. 5 Various drivers, chisels and prybars are great tools to have in your toolbox

TCCS1204

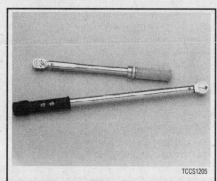

Fig. 6 Many repairs will require the use of a torque wrench to assure the components are properly fastened

TCCS1205

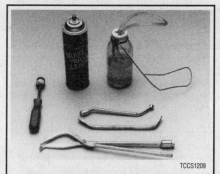

Fig. 7 Although not always necessary, using specialized brake tools will save time

TCCS1209

Fig. 8 A few inexpensive lubrication tools will make maintenance easier

TCCS1210

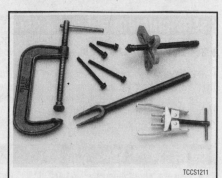

Fig. 9 Various pullers, clamps and separator tools are needed for many larger, more complicated repairs

TCCS1211

Fig. 10 A variety of tools and gauges should be used for spark plug gapping and installation

TCCS1212

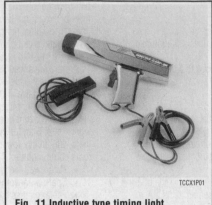

Fig. 11 Inductive type timing light

TCCX1P01

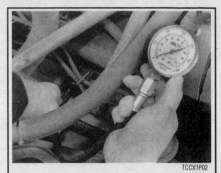

Fig. 12 A screw-in type compression gauge is recommended for compression testing

TCCX1P02

Fig. 13 A vacuum/pressure tester is necessary for many testing procedures

TCCX1P03

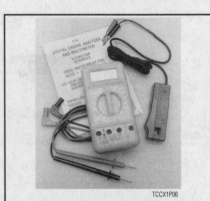

Fig. 14 Most modern automotive multimeters incorporate many helpful features

TCCX1P06

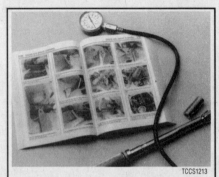

Fig. 15 Proper information is vital, so always have a Chilton Total Car Care manual handy

TCCS1213

The choice of a timing light should be made carefully. A light which works on the DC current supplied by the vehicle's battery is the best choice; it should have a xenon tube for brightness. On any vehicle with an electronic ignition system, a timing light with an inductive pickup that clamps around the No. 1 spark plug cable is preferred.

In addition to these basic tools, there are several other tools and gauges you may find useful. These include:

- Compression gauge. The screw-in type is slower to use, but eliminates the possibility of a faulty reading due to escaping pressure.
- Manifold vacuum gauge.
- 12V test light.
- A combination volt/ohmmeter
- Induction Ammeter. This is used for determining whether or not there is current in a wire. These are handy for use if a wire is broken somewhere in a wiring harness.

As a final note, you will probably find a torque wrench necessary for all but the most basic work. The beam type models are perfectly adequate, although the newer click types (breakaway) are easier to use. The click type torque wrenches tend to be more expensive. Also keep in mind that all types of torque wrenches should be periodically checked and/or recalibrated. You will have to decide for yourself which better fits your pocketbook, and purpose.

Special Tools

Normally, the use of special factory tools is avoided for repair procedures, since these are not readily available for the do-it-yourself mechanic. When it is possible to perform the job with more commonly available tools, it will be pointed out, but occasionally, a special tool was designed to perform a specific function and should be used. Before substituting another tool, you should be convinced that neither your safety nor the performance of the vehicle will be compromised.

Special tools can usually be purchased from an automotive parts store or from your dealer. In some cases special tools may be available directly from the tool manufacturer.

SERVICING YOUR VEHICLE SAFELY

♦ **See Figures 16, 17 and 18**

It is virtually impossible to anticipate all of the hazards involved with automotive maintenance and service, but care and common sense will prevent most accidents.

The rules of safety for mechanics range from "don't smoke around gasoline," to "use the proper tool(s) for the job." The trick to avoiding injuries is to develop safe work habits and to take every possible precaution.

Do's

- Do keep a fire extinguisher and first aid kit handy.
- Do wear safety glasses or goggles when cutting, drilling, grinding or prying, even if you have 20–20 vision. If you wear glasses for the sake of vision, wear safety goggles over your regular glasses.

- Do shield your eyes whenever you work around the battery. Batteries contain sulfuric acid. In case of contact with, flush the area with water or a mixture of water and baking soda, then seek immediate medical attention.
- Do use safety stands (jackstands) for any undervehicle service. Jacks are for raising vehicles; jackstands are for making sure the vehicle stays raised until you want it to come down.
- Do use adequate ventilation when working with any chemicals or hazardous materials. Like carbon monoxide, the asbestos dust resulting from some brake lining wear can be hazardous in sufficient quantities.
- Do disconnect the negative battery cable when working on the electrical system. The secondary ignition system contains EXTREMELY HIGH VOLTAGE. In some cases it can even exceed 50,000 volts.
- Do follow manufacturer's directions whenever working with potentially hazardous materials. Most chemicals and fluids are poisonous.

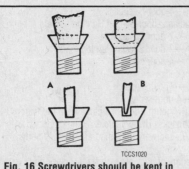

Fig. 16 Screwdrivers should be kept in good condition to prevent injury or damage which could result if the blade slips from the screw

Fig. 17 Using the correct size wrench will help prevent the possibility of rounding off a nut

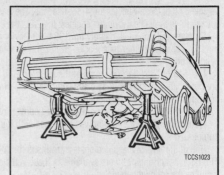

Fig. 18 NEVER work under a vehicle unless it is supported using safety stands (jackstands)

- Do properly maintain your tools. Loose hammerheads, mushroomed punches and chisels, frayed or poorly grounded electrical cords, excessively worn screwdrivers, spread wrenches (open end), cracked sockets, slipping ratchets, or faulty droplight sockets can cause accidents.
- Likewise, keep your tools clean; a greasy wrench can slip off a bolt head, ruining the bolt and often harming your knuckles in the process.
- Do use the proper size and type of tool for the job at hand. Do select a wrench or socket that fits the nut or bolt. The wrench or socket should sit straight, not cocked.
- Do, when possible, pull on a wrench handle rather than push on it, and adjust your stance to prevent a fall.
- Do be sure that adjustable wrenches are tightly closed on the nut or bolt and pulled so that the force is on the side of the fixed jaw.
- Do strike squarely with a hammer; avoid glancing blows.
- Do set the parking brake and block the drive wheels if the work requires a running engine.

Don'ts

- Don't run the engine in a garage or anywhere else without proper ventilation—EVER! Carbon monoxide is poisonous; it takes a long time to leave the human body and you can build up a deadly supply of it in your system by simply breathing in a little at a time. You may not realize you are slowly poisoning yourself. Always use power vents, windows, fans and/or open the garage door.
- Don't work around moving parts while wearing loose clothing. Short sleeves are much safer than long, loose sleeves. Hard-toed shoes with neoprene soles protect your toes and give a better grip on slippery surfaces. Watches and jewelry is not safe working around a vehicle. Long hair should be tied back under a hat or cap.
- Don't use pockets for toolboxes. A fall or bump can drive a screwdriver deep into your body. Even a rag hanging from your back pocket can wrap around a spinning shaft or fan.
- Don't smoke when working around gasoline, cleaning solvent or other flammable material.
- Don't smoke when working around the battery. When the battery is being charged, it gives off explosive hydrogen gas.
- Don't use gasoline to wash your hands; there are excellent soaps available. Gasoline contains dangerous additives which can enter the body through a cut or through your pores. Gasoline also removes all the natural oils from the skin so that bone dry hands will suck up oil and grease.
- Don't service the air conditioning system unless you are equipped with the necessary tools and training. When liquid or compressed gas refrigerant is released to atmospheric pressure it will absorb heat from whatever it contacts. This will chill or freeze anything it touches.
- Don't use screwdrivers for anything other than driving screws! A screwdriver used as an prying tool can snap when you least expect it, causing injuries. At the very least, you'll ruin a good screwdriver.
- Don't use an emergency jack (that little ratchet, scissors, or pantograph jack supplied with the vehicle) for anything other than changing a flat! These jacks are only intended for emergency use out on the road; they are NOT designed as a maintenance tool. If you are serious about maintaining your vehicle yourself, invest in a hydraulic floor jack of at least a 1½ ton capacity, and at least two sturdy jackstands.

MODEL IDENTIFICATION

The Chrysler, as well as the Eagle, Dodge and Plymouth, front-wheel drive cars equipped with 4-cylinder engines are grouped according to their body designations. The body models from the Chrysler cars are denoted by a letter. There are 10 letter designated body styles. Since it is often the case that Chrysler, Dodge, Plymouth and Eagle share general car designs, the cars fall into categories together with often only very slight differences between them. The body style can be ascertained from the Vehicle Identification Number (VIN) plate located on the upper edge of the left-hand side of the dashboard (by the windshield). The 5th position (a letter) will read as following (with the exclusion of 1989–95 models):

1981 Vehicles:
- K—Aries and Reliant models (AK body designation)

1982–83 Vehicles:
- C—LeBaron (AK body)
- D—Aries (AK body)
- E—600 (AE or AK body)
- P—Reliant (AK body)
- T—New Yorker (AE body)
- V—400 (AK body)

1984–88 Vehicles:
- J—Caravelle (AE body)
- E—600 and 600ES (AE body)
- T—New Yorker and E Class (AE body)

- P—Reliant (AK body)
- D—Aries (AK body); Shadow (AP body); Lancer (AH body)
- L—Caravelle (AK body)
- V—600 (AK body); Daytona (AG body)
- C—LeBaron, Town & Country and Executive Sedan (AK body); Laser (AG body)
- P—Sundance (AP body)

The vehicles from 1989–95 use their body designation letter as the VIN code. Therefore, a Daytona, which is an AG body, would have the VIN code of G, just as a Sundance model (AP body) has the VIN designation of P.

The AA class (all Chrysler vehicle model designations are preceded by the letter A, therefore, for example, the J class vehicles are actually AJ class vehicles) body designation cars are the 1989–95 Chrysler LeBaron, Dodge Spirit and Plymouth Acclaim. The A bodies are 4-door sedans. The LeBaron was also available as a 2-door coupe or convertible, however these models of the 2-door LeBaron are classified in a different model category (AJ). The Spirit and the Acclaim were available with 4-cylinder engines from 1989–95. The 4-door LeBaron was equipped with the 2.5L 4-cylinder engine from 1992–93.

The AC class body is the 1988–93 Dodge Dynasty 4-door Sedan. The Dynasty came equipped with the 2.5L engine.

The AE class vehicles are the 1983–88 Caravelle, the Caravelle SE, the 600, the 600 SE and the New Yorker. The 1983–84 E-Class is also included in the AE class vehicles. All of these vehicles are 4-door sedans. These vehicles came equipped with all three available 4-cylinder engines: the 2.2L, the 2.5L and the 2.6L.

AG class automobiles, namely the 1984–93 Daytona and 1984–86 Laser models, came as 2-door hatchbacks. Both cars were equipped with all three 4-cylinder engines.

The 4-door hatchback versions of the LeBaron GTS and of the Lancer models are designated as the AH body class vehicles. The AH vehicles were also equipped with all three 4-cylinder engines.

The 1987–93 LeBaron 2-door coupe and convertible is classified as a AJ type body. The 2-door LeBaron was equipped with the 2.2L or the 2.5L engines.

One of the largest class designated groups is the AK body class group. All three 4-cylinder engines were available in these vehicles. The AK group includes the following vehicles:
- 1981–89 Aries and Reliant—2-door coupe
- 1981–89 Aries and Reliant—4-door sedan

- 1981–89 Aries and Reliant—4-door hatchback
- 1983–85 Caravelle—Canadian 2-door Special Hardtop model
- 1982–86 600 and LeBaron—2-door convertible
- 1982–86 600 and LeBaron—2-door Special Hardtop model
- 1982–85 600 and LeBaron—4-door sedan
- 1987–88 LeBaron—4-door sedan
- 1982–88 Town & Country—4-door wagon
- Executive and Limousine—4-door sedan

The Dodge Shadow and the Plymouth Sundance came from the factory as either 2-door or 4-door hatchbacks. These vehicles came equipped with 4-cylinder engines from 1987–95 and were classified as AP class body styles.

The last letter-designated category of body styles is the AQ class body. Chrysler's TC was manufactured by Maserati, but utilized the same 2.2L engine as the other Chrysler vehicles. This vehicle was available with the 4-cylinder engine for only two years from 1989 to 1990.

SERIAL NUMBER IDENTIFICATION

Vehicle

▶ See Figures 19 and 20

The Vehicle Identification Number (VIN) is located on a plate on the top left side of the instrument panel and is visible through the windshield. The VIN consists of 17 characters in a combination of letters and numbers that provide specific information about the vehicle. The VIN code can be broken down as follows:
- Digit 1—Country of manufacture (1=United States, 2=Canada, 3=Mexico)
- Digit 2—Make of vehicle (B=Dodge, C=Chrysler, E=Eagle, P=Plymouth)

Fig. 19 The metal VIN tag is located on the upper driver's side of the dash panel

86731P00

Fig. 20 The VIN can also be found on other ID tags and labels, including this plate in the engine bay

86731P01

- Digit 3—Type of vehicle (3=Passenger car)
- Digit 4—Passenger safety system (A=Air bag, B=Manual seat belts, C=Automatic seat belts, E=Active restraint and passenger air bag, X=Driver's side air bag and passenger's side manual seat belts, Y=Driver's side air bag and passenger's side automatic seat belts
- Digit 5—Body class designation (Refer to model identification earlier in this section for more details)
- Digit 6—Vehicle series (1=Economy, 2=Low, 4=High, 5=Premium, 6=Special/Sport, 7=Performance/Image)
- Digit 7—Body style (1=2-door coupe, 4=2-door hatchback, 5=2-door convertible, 6=4-door sedan, 8=4-door hatchback)
- Digit 8—Engine code (A=1987–93 2.2L SOHC MFI-turbocharged engine, B=1981–82 2.2L carbureted engine, C=1982–84 2.2L carbureted engine, D=1981–82 2.6L carbureted engine OR 1984–94 2.2L SFI engine, E=1984–88 2.2L SOHC MFI-turbocharged engine, G=1982–85 2.6L carbureted engine, J=1989–92 2.5L MFI-turbocharged engine, K=1986–95 2.5L SFI engine, R=1989–90 2.2L DOHC MFI-turbocharged engine, V=1993–95 2.5L Flex Fuel MFI engine
- Digit 9—Check digit (1 through 9, 0, or X)
- Digit 10—Model Year (B=1981, C=1982, D=1983, E=1984, F=1985, G=1986, H=1987, J=1988, K=1989, L=1990, M=1991, N=1992, P=1993, R=1994, S=1995)
- Digit 11—Assembly plant code
- Digits 12 through 17—Sequence assembly number

Engine Identification Number

▶ See Figures 21 and 22

All engine assemblies carry an Engine Identification Number (EIN). The 135 cid (2.2L) EIN is located on the left (engine rear) face of the block directly under the head. The 156 cid (2.6L) identification number is located on the left side of the block (radiator side) between the core plug and the rear edge of the block (models through 1985). In 1986, the 2.6L Mitsubishi built engine was replaced by a 2.5L powerplant developed jointly by Mitsubishi and Chrysler, which is manufactured in the U.S. The 1986–91 2.5L EIN tag is located on the left side of the block between the core plug and the rear face of the block (the "rear" face is the end of the block attached to the transaxle). For 2.5L engines manufactured from 1992–95, the EIN is located on the left (engine rear) face of the block directly under the head.

Engine Serial Number

In addition to the EIN, some engines have a serial number, which must be referred to when ordering engine replacement parts. The serial number on the 2.2L engine is located on the rear face of the block directly below the head. On the 2.6L engine it is located on the right front side of the engine block, adjacent to the exhaust manifold. On the 2.5 liter engine, it is located on the right rear (dash panel) side of the block, near the exhaust manifold stud.

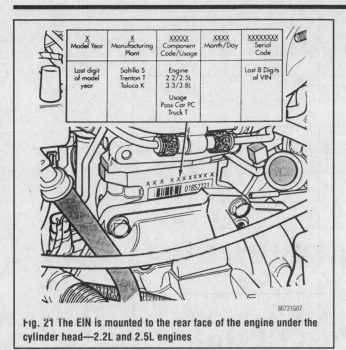

X Model Year	X Manufacturing Plant	XXXXX Component Code/Usage	XXXX Month/Day	XXXXXXX Serial Code
Last digit of model year	Saltillo S Trenton T Toluca K	Engine 2.2/2.5L 3.3/3.8L		Last 8 Digits of VIN
		Usage Pass Car PC Truck T		

Fig. 21 The EIN is mounted to the rear face of the engine under the cylinder head—2.2L and 2.5L engines

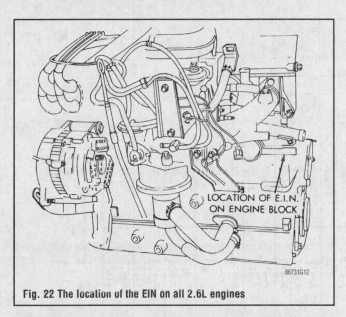

LOCATION OF E.I.N. ON ENGINE BLOCK

Fig. 22 The location of the EIN on all 2.6L engines

Transaxle Identification Number

▶ See Figures 23, 24 and 25

The Transaxle Identification Number is stamped on a boss located on the upper part of the transaxle housing. Every transaxle also carries an assembly part number, which is also required for parts ordering purposes. On the A-412 manual transaxle, it is located on the top of the housing, between the timing window and the differential.

On all other types of manual transaxles, this number is located on a metal tag attached to the front of the transaxle. On automatic models, it is stamped on a pad located just above the oil pan at the rear of the unit.

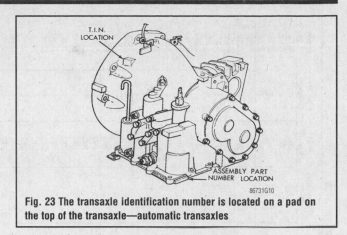

T.I.N. LOCATION

ASSEMBLY PART NUMBER LOCATION

Fig. 23 The transaxle identification number is located on a pad on the top of the transaxle—automatic transaxles

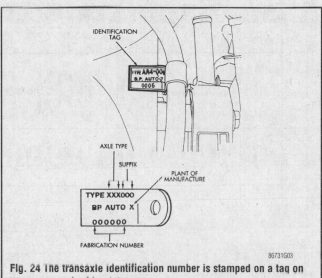

IDENTIFICATION TAG

TYP AA4-00 B.P. AUTO-7 0006

AXLE TYPE

SUFFIX

PLANT OF MANUFACTURE

TYPE XXX000 BP AUTO X 000000

FABRICATION NUMBER

Fig. 24 The transaxle identification number is stamped on a tag on the passenger's side of the case

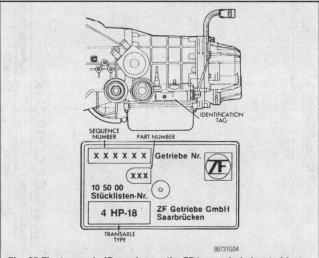

IDENTIFICATION TAG

SEQUENCE NUMBER

PART NUMBER

X X X X X X Getriebe Nr.

XXX

10 50 00 Stücklisten-Nr.

4 HP-18

ZF Getriebe GmbH Saarbrücken

TRANSAXLE TYPE

Fig. 25 The transaxle ID number on the ZF transaxle is located just above the oil pan on the driver's side of the case

ENGINE IDENTIFICATION

Year	Make	Model	Engine Displacement Liters (cc)	Engine Series (ID/VIN)	Fuel System	No. of Cylinders	Engine Type
1981	Dodge	Aries	2.2 (2212)	B	2BC	4	SOHC
	Dodge	Aries	2.6 (2556)	D	2BC	4	SOHC
	Plymouth	Reliant	2.2 (2212)	B	2BC	4	SOHC
	Plymouth	Reliant	2.6 (2556)	D	2BC	4	SOHC
1982	Chrysler	LeBaron	2.2 (2212)	C	2BC	4	SOHC
	Chrysler	LeBaron	2.6 (2556)	G	2BC	4	SOHC
	Chrysler	Town & Country	2.2 (2212)	C	2BC	4	SOHC
	Chrysler	Town & Country	2.6 (2556)	G	2BC	4	SOHC
	Dodge	400	2.2 (2212)	C	2BC	4	SOHC
	Dodge	400	2.6 (2556)	G	2BC	4	SOHC
	Dodge	600	2.2 (2212)	C	2BC	4	SOHC
	Dodge	600	2.6 (2556)	G	2BC	4	SOHC
	Dodge	Aries	2.2 (2212)	B	2BC	4	SOHC
	Dodge	Aries	2.6 (2556)	D	2BC	4	SOHC
	Plymouth	Reliant	2.2 (2212)	B	2BC	4	SOHC
	Plymouth	Reliant	2.6 (2556)	D	2BC	4	SOHC
1983	Chrysler	E-Class	2.2 (2212)	C	2BC	4	SOHC
	Chrysler	E-Class	2.6 (2556)	G	2BC	4	SOHC
	Chrysler	LeBaron	2.2 (2212)	C	2BC	4	SOHC
	Chrysler	LeBaron	2.6 (2556)	G	2BC	4	SOHC
	Chrysler	New Yorker	2.2 (2212)	C	2BC	4	SOHC
	Chrysler	New Yorker	2.6 (2556)	G	2BC	4	SOHC
	Chrysler	Town & Country	2.2 (2212)	C	2BC	4	SOHC
	Chrysler	Town & Country	2.6 (2556)	G	2BC	4	SOHC
	Dodge	400	2.2 (2212)	C	2BC	4	SOHC
	Dodge	600	2.2 (2212)	C	2BC	4	SOHC
	Dodge	600	2.6 (2556)	G	2BC	4	SOHC
	Dodge	Aries	2.2 (2212)	C	2BC	4	SOHC
	Dodge	Aries	2.6 (2556)	G	2BC	4	SOHC
1984	Chrysler	E-Class	2.2 (2212)	D	EFI	4	SOHC
	Chrysler	E-Class	2.2 (2212)	E	MFI-Turbo	4	SOHC
	Chrysler	E-Class	2.6 (2556)	G	2BC	4	SOHC
	Chrysler	Laser	2.2 (2212)	D	EFI	4	SOHC
	Chrysler	LeBaron	2.2 (2212)	E	MFI-Turbo	4	SOHC
	Chrysler	LeBaron	2.2 (2212)	C	2BC	4	SOHC
	Chrysler	New Yorker	2.2 (2212)	E	MFI-Turbo	4	SOHC
	Chrysler	New Yorker	2.2 (2212)	D	EFI	4	SOHC
	Chrysler	New Yorker	2.2 (2212)	E	MFI-Turbo	4	SOHC
	Chrysler	Town & Country	2.6 (2556)	G	2BC	4	SOHC
	Chrysler	Town & Country	2.2 (2212)	G	2BC	4	SOHC
	Dodge	600	2.6 (2556)	C	2BC	4	SOHC
	Dodge	600	2.2 (2212)	D	EFI	4	SOHC
	Dodge	600	2.6 (2556)	G	2BC	4	SOHC
	Dodge	Aries	2.2 (2212)	C	2BC	4	SOHC

86731C01

VEHICLE IDENTIFICATION CHART

Engine Code

Code	Liters	Cu. In. (cc)	Cyl.	Fuel Sys.	Eng. Mfg.
A	2.2	135 (2212)	I4	MFI-Turbo	Chrysler
B	2.2	135 (2212)	I4	2BC	Chrysler
C	2.2	135 (2212)	I4	2BC	Chrysler
C	2.2	135 (2212)	I4	MFI-Turbo	Chrysler
D	2.2	135 (2212)	I4	EFI	Chrysler
E	2.6	156 (2556)	I4	2BC	Mitsubishi
G	2.2	135 (2212)	I4	MFI-Turbo	Chrysler
J	2.6	156 (2556)	I4	2BC	Mitsubishi
K	2.5	153 (2507)	I4	MFI-Turbo	Chrysler
L	2.5	153 (2507)	I4	EFI	Chrysler
P	2.2	135 (2212)	I4	MFI-Turbo	Chrysler
R	2.2	135 (2212)	I4	MFI-Turbo	Chrysler
V	2.5	153 (2507)	I4	FF MFI	Chrysler

Model Year

Code	Year
B	1981
C	1982
D	1983
E	1984
F	1985
G	1986
H	1987
J	1988
K	1989
L	1990
M	1991
N	1992
P	1993
R	1994
S	1995

BC - Barrel carburetor
EFI - Electronic Fuel Injection
FF MFI - Flexible Fuel Multi-port Fuel Injection
MFI - Multi-port Fuel Injection
TBI - Throttle Body fuel Injection

86731C00

TRANSAXLE IDENTIFICATION

Year	Manual Transaxles Model ID	Gears	Automatic Transaxles Model ID	Gears
1981-83	A-460	4 spd	A-404	3 spd
	A-465	5 spd	A-413	3 spd
			A-470	3 spd
1984	A-460	4 spd	A-415	3 spd
	A-465	5 spd	A-413	3 spd
	A-525	5 spd	A-470	3 spd
1985-86	A-460	4 spd	A-413	3 spd
	A-525	5 spd	A-470 ①	3 spd
1987-89	A-520 ②	5 spd	A-413	3 spd
	A-555 ③	5 spd		
	A-525 ④	5 spd		
1990-92	A-523 ②	5 spd	A-413	3 spd
	A-568 ③	5 spd	A-604	4 spd
1993	A-523 ②	5 spd	A-413	3 spd
	A-568 ③	5 spd	41TE	4 spd
1994-95	A-523	5 spd	A-413	3 spd
			41TE	4 spd

① Only 1985
② Except Turbo
③ Turbo Models
④ Shadow and Sundance, 1987-88 only
⑤ Premier models only

86731C07

ENGINE IDENTIFICATION

Year	Make	Model	Engine Displacement Liters (cc)	Engine Series (ID/VIN)	Fuel System	No. of Cylinders	Engine Type
1986	Dodge	Aries	2.2 (2212)	D	EFI	4	SOHC
	Dodge	Aries	2.5 (2507)	K	EFI	4	SOHC
	Dodge	Daytona	2.2 (2212)	D	EFI	4	SOHC
	Dodge	Daytona	2.2 (2212)	E	MFI-Turbo	4	SOHC
	Dodge	Daytona	2.5 (2507)	K	EFI	4	SOHC
	Dodge	Lancer	2.2 (2212)	D	EFI	4	SOHC
	Dodge	Lancer	2.2 (2212)	E	MFI-Turbo	4	SOHC
	Dodge	Lancer	2.5 (2507)	K	EFI	4	SOHC
	Plymouth	Caravelle	2.2 (2212)	D	EFI	4	SOHC
	Plymouth	Caravelle	2.2 (2212)	E	MFI-Turbo	4	SOHC
	Plymouth	Caravelle	2.5 (2507)	K	EFI	4	SOHC
	Plymouth	Reliant	2.2 (2212)	C	2BC	4	SOHC
	Plymouth	Reliant	2.2 (2212)	D	EFI	4	SOHC
	Plymouth	Reliant	2.5 (2507)	K	EFI	4	SOHC
1987	Chrysler	LeBaron	2.2 (2212)	D	EFI	4	SOHC
	Chrysler	LeBaron	2.2 (2212)	E	MFI-Turbo	4	SOHC
	Chrysler	LeBaron	2.5 (2507)	K	EFI	4	SOHC
	Chrysler	LeBaron GTS	2.2 (2212)	D	EFI	4	SOHC
	Chrysler	LeBaron GTS	2.2 (2212)	E	MFI-Turbo	4	SOHC
	Chrysler	LeBaron GTS	2.5 (2507)	K	EFI	4	SOHC
	Chrysler	New Yorker	2.2 (2212)	E	MFI-Turbo	4	SOHC
	Chrysler	New Yorker	2.5 (2507)	K	EFI	4	SOHC
	Chrysler	Town & Country	2.2 (2212)	E	MFI-Turbo	4	SOHC
	Chrysler	Town & Country	2.5 (2507)	K	EFI	4	SOHC
	Dodge	600	2.2 (2212)	D	EFI	4	SOHC
	Dodge	600	2.5 (2507)	K	EFI	4	SOHC
	Dodge	Aries	2.2 (2212)	D	EFI	4	SOHC
	Dodge	Aries	2.5 (2507)	K	EFI	4	SOHC
	Dodge	Daytona	2.2 (2212)	A	MFI-Turbo	4	SOHC
	Dodge	Daytona	2.2 (2212)	E	MFI-Turbo	4	SOHC
	Dodge	Daytona	2.5 (2507)	K	EFI	4	SOHC
	Dodge	Lancer	2.2 (2212)	D	EFI	4	SOHC
	Dodge	Lancer	2.2 (2212)	E	MFI-Turbo	4	SOHC
	Dodge	Lancer	2.5 (2507)	K	EFI	4	SOHC
	Dodge	Shadow	2.2 (2212)	D	EFI	4	SOHC
	Dodge	Shadow	2.2 (2212)	E	MFI-Turbo	4	SOHC
	Plymouth	Caravelle	2.2 (2212)	D	EFI	4	SOHC
	Plymouth	Caravelle	2.5 (2507)	K	EFI	4	SOHC
	Plymouth	Reliant	2.2 (2212)	D	EFI	4	SOHC
	Plymouth	Reliant	2.5 (2507)	K	EFI	4	SOHC
	Plymouth	Sundance	2.2 (2212)	D	EFI	4	SOHC
	Plymouth	Sundance	2.2 (2212)	E	MFI-Turbo	4	SOHC
1983	Chrysler	LeBaron	2.2 (2212)	D	MFI-Turbo	4	SOHC
	Chrysler	LeBaron	2.2 (2212)	E	MFI-Turbo	4	SOHC
	Chrysler	LeBaron	2.5 (2507)	K	EFI	4	SOHC
	Chrysler	LeBaron GTS	2.2 (2212)	D	MFI-Turbo	4	SOHC
	Chrysler	LeBaron GTS	2.5 (2507)	K	MFI-Turbo	4	SOHC
	Chrysler	New Yorker	2.2 (22·2)	E	MFI-Turbo	4	SOHC

ENGINE IDENTIFICATION

Year	Make	Model	Engine Displacement Liters (cc)	Engine Series (ID/VIN)	Fuel System	No. of Cylinders	Engine Type
1984	Dodge	Aries	2.6 (2556)	G	2BC	4	SOHC
	Dodge	Daytona	2.2 (2212)	D	EFI	4	SOHC
	Dodge	Daytona	2.2 (2212)	E	MFI-Turbo	4	SOHC
	Plymouth	Reliant	2.2 (2212)	C	2BC	4	SOHC
	Plymouth	Reliant	2.6 (2556)	G	2BC	4	SOHC
1985	Chrysler	Laser	2.2 (2212)	D	EFI	4	SOHC
	Chrysler	Laser	2.2 (2212)	E	MFI-Turbo	4	SOHC
	Chrysler	LeBaron	2.2 (2212)	D	EFI	4	SOHC
	Chrysler	LeBaron	2.2 (2212)	E	MFI-Turbo	4	SOHC
	Chrysler	LeBaron	2.6 (2556)	G	2BC	4	SOHC
	Chrysler	LeBaron GTS	2.2 (2212)	D	EFI	4	SOHC
	Chrysler	LeBaron GTS	2.2 (2212)	E	MFI-Turbo	4	SOHC
	Chrysler	LeBaron Limo	2.6 (2556)	G	2BC	4	SOHC
	Chrysler	New Yorker	2.2 (2212)	E	MFI-Turbo	4	SOHC
	Chrysler	New Yorker	2.6 (2556)	G	2BC	4	SOHC
	Chrysler	Town & Country	2.2 (2212)	E	MFI-Turbo	4	SOHC
	Chrysler	Town & Country	2.6 (2556)	G	2BC	4	SOHC
	Dodge	600	2.2 (2212)	D	EFI	4	SOHC
	Dodge	600	2.2 (2212)	E	MFI-Turbo	4	SOHC
	Dodge	600	2.6 (2556)	G	2BC	4	SOHC
	Dodge	Aries	2.2 (2212)	C	2BC	4	SOHC
	Dodge	Aries	2.2 (2212)	D	EFI	4	SOHC
	Dodge	Aries	2.6 (2556)	G	2BC	4	SOHC
	Dodge	Daytona	2.2 (2212)	D	EFI	4	SOHC
	Dodge	Daytona	2.2 (2212)	E	MFI-Turbo	4	SOHC
	Dodge	Lancer	2.2 (2212)	D	EFI	4	SOHC
	Dodge	Lancer	2.2 (2212)	E	MFI-Turbo	4	SOHC
	Plymouth	Caravelle	2.2 (2212)	D	EFI	4	SOHC
	Plymouth	Caravelle	2.6 (2556)	G	2BC	4	SOHC
	Plymouth	Reliant	2.2 (22·2)	D	EFI	4	SOHC
	Plymouth	Reliant	2.6 (2556)	G	2BC	4	SOHC
1986	Chrysler	Laser	2.2 (2212)	D	EFI	4	SOHC
	Chrysler	Laser	2.2 (2212)	E	MFI-Turbo	4	SOHC
	Chrysler	LeBaron	2.2 (2212)	K	EFI	4	SOHC
	Chrysler	LeBaron	2.2 (2212)	E	EFI	4	SOHC
	Chrysler	LeBaron	2.5 (2507)	K	MFI-Turbo	4	SOHC
	Chrysler	LeBaron GTS	2.2 (2212)	D	EFI	4	SOHC
	Chrysler	LeBaron GTS	2.2 (2212)	E	MFI-Turbo	4	SOHC
	Chrysler	LeBaron GTS	2.5 (2507)	K	EFI	4	SOHC
	Chrysler	New Yorker	2.2 (2212)	E	MFI-Turbo	4	SOHC
	Chrysler	New Yorker	2.5 (2507)	K	EFI	4	SOHC
	Chrysler	Town & Country	2.2 (2212)	E	MFI-Turbo	4	SOHC
	Chrysler	Town & Country	2.5 (2507)	K	EFI	4	SOHC
	Dodge	600	2.2 (2212)	D	EFI	4	SOHC
	Dodge	600	2.5 (2507)	K	EFI	4	SOHC
	Dodge	Aries	2.2 (2212)	C	2BC	4	SOHC

86731C03
86731C02

ENGINE IDENTIFICATION

Year	Make	Model	Engine Displacement Liters (cc)	Engine Series (ID/VIN)	Fuel System	No. of Cylinders	Engine Type
1989	Dodge	Shadow	2.5 (2507)	J	MFI-Turbo	4	SOHC
	Dodge	Shadow	2.5 (2507)	K	EFI	4	SOHC
	Dodge	Spirit	2.5 (2507)	K	EFI	4	SOHC
	Dodge	Spirit	2.5 (2507)	J	MFI-Turbo	4	SOHC
	Plymouth	Acclaim	2.5 (2507)	K	EFI	4	SOHC
	Plymouth	Acclaim	2.2 (2212)	D	EFI	4	SOHC
	Plymouth	Reliant	2.5 (2507)	D	EFI	4	SOHC
	Plymouth	Reliant	2.5 (2507)	K	EFI	4	SOHC
	Plymouth	Sundance	2.2 (2212)	D	MFI-Turbo	4	SOHC
	Plymouth	Sundance	2.5 (2507)	J	MFI-Turbo	4	SOHC
	Plymouth	Sundance	2.5 (2507)	K	EFI	4	SOHC
1990	Chrysler	LeBaron	2.2 (2212)	C	MFI-Turbo	4	SOHC
	Chrysler	LeBaron	2.5 (2507)	J	MFI-Turbo	4	SOHC
	Chrysler	LeBaron	2.5 (2507)	K	EFI	4	SOHC
	Chrysler	TC Maserati	2.2 (2212)	R	MFI-Turbo	4	DOHC
	Dodge	Daytona	2.2 (2212)	C	MFI-Turbo	4	SOHC
	Dodge	Daytona	2.5 (2507)	J	MFI-Turbo	4	SOHC
	Dodge	Daytona	2.5 (2507)	K	EFI	4	SOHC
	Dodge	Dynasty	2.5 (2507)	K	EFI	4	SOHC
	Dodge	Shadow	2.2 (2212)	C	MFI-Turbo	4	SOHC
	Dodge	Shadow	2.2 (2212)	D	EFI	4	SOHC
	Dodge	Shadow	2.5 (2507)	K	MFI-Turbo	4	SOHC
	Dodge	Spirit	2.5 (2507)	J	EFI	4	SOHC
	Dodge	Spirit	2.5 (2507)	K	MFI-Turbo	4	SOHC
	Plymouth	Acclaim	2.5 (2507)	K	EFI	4	SOHC
1991	Plymouth	Sundance	2.2 (2212)	D	EFI	4	SOHC
	Plymouth	Sundance	2.5 (2507)	K	MFI-Turbo	4	SOHC
	Chrysler	LeBaron	2.5 (2507)	K	MFI-Turbo	4	SOHC
	Chrysler	LeBaron	2.5 (2507)	J	EFI	4	SOHC
	Dodge	Daytona	2.5 (2507)	K	MFI-Turbo	4	SOHC
	Dodge	Dynasty	2.2 (2212)	J	EFI	4	SOHC
	Dodge	Shadow	2.5 (2507)	D	MFI-Turbo	4	SOHC
	Dodge	Shadow	2.5 (2507)	J	MFI-Turbo	4	SOHC
	Dodge	Spirit	2.2 (2212)	A	EFI	4	SOHC
	Dodge	Spirit	2.5 (2507)	J	MFI-Turbo	4	SOHC
	Dodge	Spirit	2.5 (2507)	K	MFI-Turbo	4	SOHC
1992	Plymouth	Acclaim	2.5 (2507)	K	EFI	4	SOHC
	Plymouth	Acclaim	2.2 (2212)	J	MFI-Turbo	4	SOHC
	Plymouth	Sundance	2.2 (2212)	D	EFI	4	SOHC
	Plymouth	Sundance	2.5 (2507)	K	MFI-Turbo	4	SOHC
	Chrysler	LeBaron	2.5 (2507)	J	EFI	4	SOHC
	Chrysler	LeBaron	2.5 (2507)	K	MFI-Turbo	4	SOHC
	Dodge	Daytona	2.2 (2212)	A	MFI-Turbo	4	DOHC

86731C05

ENGINE IDENTIFICATION

Year	Make	Model	Engine Displacement Liters (cc)	Engine Series (ID/VIN)	Fuel System	No. of Cylinders	Engine Type
1988	Chrysler	Town & Country	2.2 (2212)	E	MFI-Turbo	4	SOHC
	Chrysler	Town & Country	2.5 (2507)	K	EFI	4	SOHC
	Dodge	600	2.2 (2212)	D	EFI	4	SOHC
	Dodge	600	2.2 (2212)	E	MFI-Turbo	4	SOHC
	Dodge	600	2.5 (2507)	K	EFI	4	SOHC
	Dodge	Aries	2.2 (2212)	D	EFI	4	SOHC
	Dodge	Aries	2.5 (2507)	K	EFI	4	SOHC
	Dodge	Daytona	2.2 (2212)	A	MFI-Turbo	4	SOHC
	Dodge	Daytona	2.2 (2212)	E	MFI-Turbo	4	SOHC
	Dodge	Daytona	2.5 (2507)	K	EFI	4	SOHC
	Dodge	Dynasty	2.5 (2507)	K	EFI	4	SOHC
	Dodge	Lancer	2.2 (2212)	A	MFI-Turbo	4	SOHC
	Dodge	Lancer	2.2 (2212)	D	EFI	4	SOHC
	Dodge	Lancer	2.2 (2212)	E	MFI-Turbo	4	SOHC
	Dodge	Shadow	2.2 (2212)	D	EFI	4	SOHC
	Dodge	Shadow	2.2 (2212)	E	MFI-Turbo	4	SOHC
	Dodge	Shadow	2.5 (2507)	K	EFI	4	SOHC
	Plymouth	Caravelle	2.2 (2212)	D	EFI	4	SOHC
	Plymouth	Caravelle	2.2 (2212)	E	MFI-Turbo	4	SOHC
	Plymouth	Caravelle	2.5 (2507)	K	EFI	4	SOHC
	Plymouth	Reliant	2.2 (2212)	D	EFI	4	SOHC
	Plymouth	Reliant	2.5 (2507)	K	EFI	4	SOHC
	Plymouth	Sundance	2.2 (2212)	D	EFI	4	SOHC
	Plymouth	Sundance	2.5 (2507)	K	EFI	4	SOHC
1989	Chrysler	LeBaron	2.2 (2212)	A	MFI-Turbo	4	SOHC
	Chrysler	LeBaron	2.5 (2507)	J	EFI	4	SOHC
	Chrysler	LeBaron	2.2 (2212)	K	EFI	4	SOHC
	Chrysler	LeBaron GTS	2.2 (2212)	A	MFI-Turbo	4	SOHC
	Chrysler	LeBaron GTS	2.2 (2212)	D	EFI	4	SOHC
	Chrysler	LeBaron GTS	2.2 (2212)	J	MFI-Turbo	4	SOHC
	Chrysler	TC Maserati	2.2 (2212)	P	MFI-Turbo	4	SOHC
	Chrysler	TC Maserati	2.2 (2212)	R	MFI-Turbo	4	DOHC
	Dodge	Aries	2.2 (2212)	D	EFI	4	SOHC
	Dodge	Aries	2.5 (2507)	K	EFI	4	SOHC
	Dodge	Daytona	2.2 (2212)	A	MFI-Turbo	4	SOHC
	Dodge	Daytona	2.2 (2212)	E	MFI-Turbo	4	SOHC
	Dodge	Daytona	2.5 (2507)	J	MFI-Turbo	4	SOHC
	Dodge	Daytona	2.5 (2507)	K	EFI	4	SOHC
	Dodge	Dynasty	2.5 (2507)	K	EFI	4	SOHC
	Dodge	Lancer	2.2 (2212)	A	MFI-Turbo	4	SOHC
	Dodge	Lancer	2.2 (2212)	E	MFI-Turbo	4	SOHC
	Dodge	Lancer	2.2 (2212)	D	EFI	4	SOHC
	Dodge	Lancer	2.5 (2507)	J	MFI-Turbo	4	SOHC
	Dodge	Shadow	2.2 (2212)	D	EFI	4	SOHC
	Dodge	Shadow	2.2 (2212)	E	MFI-Turbo	4	SOHC

86731C04

ENGINE IDENTIFICATION

Year	Make	Model	Engine Displacement Liters (cc)	Engine Series (ID/VIN)	Fuel System	No. of Cylinders	Engine Type
1992	Dodge	Daytona	2.5 (2507)	J	MFI-Turbo	4	SOHC
	Dodge	Daytona	2.5 (2507)	K	EFI	4	SOHC
	Dodge	Dynasty	2.5 (2507)	K	EFI	4	SOHC
	Dodge	Shadow	2.2 (2212)	D	EFI	4	SOHC
	Dodge	Shadow	2.5 (2507)	J	MFI-Turbo	4	SOHC
	Dodge	Shadow	2.5 (2507)	K	EFI	4	SOHC
	Dodge	Spirit	2.2 (2212)	A	MFI-Turbo	4	DOHC
	Dodge	Spirit	2.5 (2507)	J	MFI-Turbo	4	SOHC
	Dodge	Spirit	2.5 (2507)	K	EFI	4	SOHC
	Plymouth	Acclaim	2.5 (2507)	K	EFI	4	SOHC
	Plymouth	Sundance	2.2 (2212)	D	EFI	4	SOHC
	Plymouth	Sundance	2.5 (2507)	K	EFI	4	SOHC
1993	Chrysler	LeBaron	2.5 (2507)	K	EFI	4	SOHC
	Chrysler	LeBaron	2.5 (2507)	V	FF MFI	4	SOHC
	Dodge	Daytona	2.2 (2212)	A	MFI-Turbo	4	DOHC
	Dodge	Daytona	2.5 (2507)	K	EFI	4	SOHC
	Dodge	Dynasty	2.5 (2507)	K	EFI	4	SOHC
	Dodge	Shadow	2.2 (2212)	D	EFI	4	SOHC
	Dodge	Shadow	2.5 (2507)	K	EFI	4	SOHC
	Dodge	Spirit	2.5 (2507)	K	EFI	4	SOHC
	Dodge	Spirit	2.5 (2507)	V	FF MFI	4	SOHC
	Plymouth	Acclaim	2.5 (2507)	K	EFI	4	SOHC
	Plymouth	Acclaim	2.5 (2507)	V	FF MFI	4	SOHC
	Plymouth	Sundance	2.2 (2212)	D	EFI	4	SOHC
	Plymouth	Sundance	2.5 (2507)	K	EFI	4	SOHC
1994	Dodge	Shadow	2.2 (2212)	D	EFI	4	SOHC
	Dodge	Shadow	2.5 (2507)	K	EFI	4	SOHC
	Dodge	Spirit	2.5 (2507)	K	EFI	4	SOHC
	Dodge	Spirit	2.5 (2507)	V	FF MFI	4	SOHC
	Plymouth	Acclaim	2.5 (2507)	K	EFI	4	SOHC
	Plymouth	Acclaim	2.5 (2507)	V	FF MFI	4	SOHC
	Plymouth	Sundance	2.2 (2212)	D	EFI	4	SOHC
	Plymouth	Sundance	2.5 (2507)	K	EFI	4	SOHC
1995	Dodge	Spirit	2.5 (2507)	K	EFI	4	SOHC
	Dodge	Spirit	2.5 (2507)	V	FF MFI	4	SOHC
	Plymouth	Acclaim	2.5 (2507)	K	EFI	4	SOHC
	Plymouth	Acclaim	2.5 (2507)	V	FF MFI	4	SOHC

NOTE: EFI is used to designate Chrysler Single Point Fuel Injection.

EFI - Electronic Fuel Injection system
FF MFI - Flexible Fuel Multi-port Fuel Injection system
MFI - Multi-port Fuel Injection system
TBI - Eagle Throttle Body Fuel Injection system

DOHC -Dual Overhead Camshaft
OHV - Overhead Valve
SOHC - Single Overhead Camshaft

2BC - 2 Barrel Carburetor

86731C06

ROUTINE MAINTENANCE AND TUNE-UP

Proper maintenance and tune-up is the key to long and trouble-free vehicle life, and the work can yield its own rewards. Studies have shown that a properly tuned and maintained vehicle can achieve better gas mileage than an out-of-tune vehicle. As a conscientious owner and driver, set aside a Saturday morning, say once a month, to check or replace items which could cause major problems later. Keep your own personal log to jot down which services you performed, how much the parts cost you, the date, and the exact odometer reading at the time. Keep all receipts for such items as engine oil and filters, so that they may be referred to in case of related problems or to determine operating expenses. As a do-it-yourselfer, these receipts are the only proof you have that the required maintenance was performed. In the event of a warranty problem, these receipts will be invaluable.

The literature provided with your vehicle when it was originally delivered includes the factory recommended maintenance schedule. If you no longer have this literature, replacement copies are usually available from the dealer. A maintenance schedule is provided later in this section, in case you do not have the factory literature.

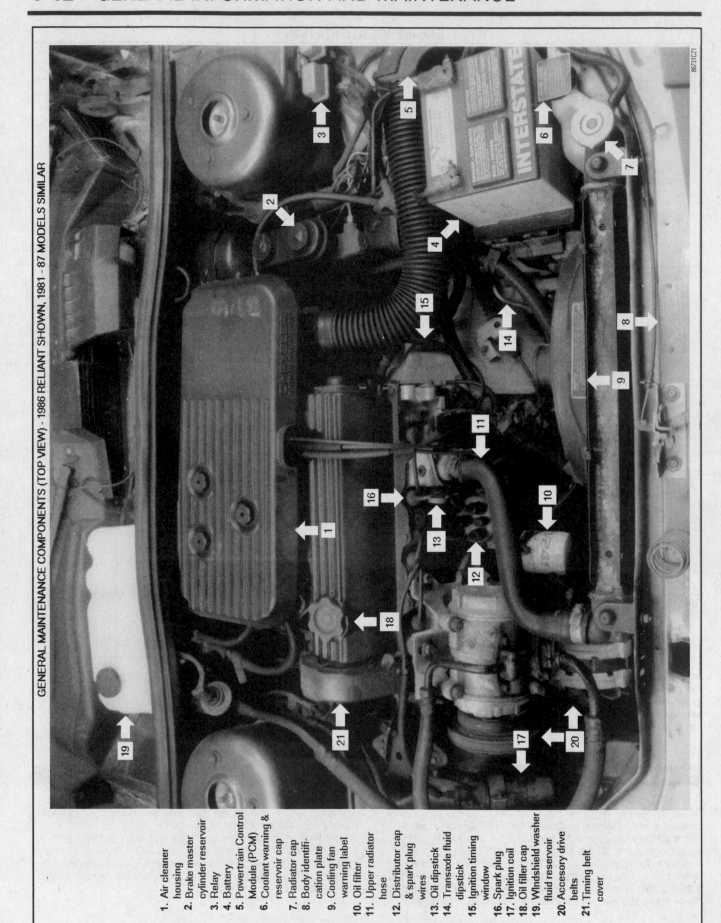

GENERAL MAINTENANCE COMPONENTS (TOP VIEW) - 1986 RELIANT SHOWN, 1981 - 87 MODELS SIMILAR

1. Air cleaner housing
2. Brake master cylinder reservoir
3. Relay
4. Battery
5. Powertrain Control Module (PCM)
6. Coolant warning & reservoir cap
7. Radiator cap
8. Body identification plate
9. Cooling fan warning label
10. Oil filter
11. Upper radiator hose
12. Distributor cap & spark plug wires
13. Oil dipstick
14. Transaxle fluid dipstick
15. Ignition timing window
16. Spark plug
17. Ignition coil
18. Oil filler cap
19. Windshield washer fluid reservoir
20. Accesory drive belts
21. Timing belt cover

GENERAL MAINTENANCE COMPONENTS (BOTTOM VIEW) - 1986 RELIANT SHOWN, 1981 - 87 MODELS SIMILAR

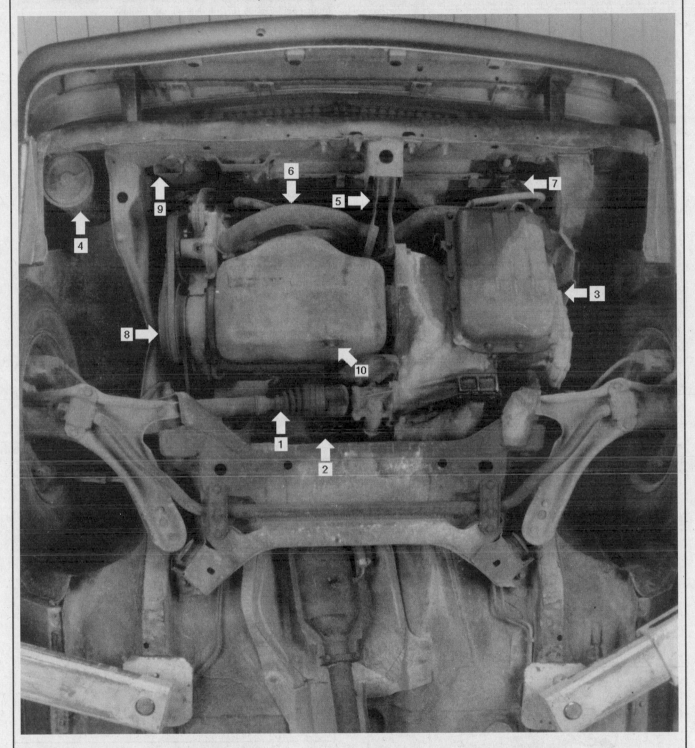

1. Inner CV - joint boot
2. Oxygen sensor
3. Transaxle fluid pan
4. Charcoal canister
5. Lower engine mount
6. Lower radiator hose
7. Radiator draincock
8. Accessory drive belts
9. Horn
10. Oil pan drain plug

86731CZ0

Air Cleaner

An air cleaner is used to keep airborne dirt and dust out of the air flowing through the engine. This material, if allowed to enter the engine, would form an abrasive compound in conjunction with the engine oil and drastically shorten engine life. For this reason, you should never run the engine without the air cleaner in place except for a very brief period if required for trouble diagnosis. You should also be sure to use the proper replacement part to avoid poor fit and consequent air leakage.

Proper maintenance is important since a clogged air filter will allow an ever decreasing amount of air to enter the engine and, therefore, will increasingly enrichen the fuel/air mixture, causing poor fuel economy, a drastic increase in emissions and even serious damage to the catalytic converter system.

SERVICING

Replace the air cleaner filter element with a new one every 30,000 miles (48,000 km)—inspect every 15,000 miles (24,000 km), follow service procedures and replace as necessary—under ordinary driving conditions. If you drive under severe conditions (stop-and-go driving in dusty conditions, extensive idling, frequent short trips, operating at sustained high speeds during hot weather above 90°F/32°C, police, taxi, limousine or commercial type operation, or trailer towing), inspect the filter every 15,000 miles (24,000 km) and replace it as necessary.

When opening up the air cleaner housing to replace the air filter, wipe dust out of the air cleaner with a clean rag. Work carefully, to prevent the entry of dirt, dust, or foreign objects. Also, after you have reassembled the housing, inspect it to make sure the air cleaner is properly installed and sealed tightly. A vacuum leak here could allow dust to enter the engine and cause severely accelerated wear.

REMOVAL & INSTALLATION

2.2L Engines

CARBURETED MODELS

▶ See Figure 26

➡ **Make sure you perform the steps in exactly the sequence described below, or the air cleaner may leak, causing accelerated engine wear.**

1. Unfasten the three hold-down clips on the air cleaner assembly lid.
2. Remove the three wing nuts retaining the air cleaner-crossover cover to the carburetor and bracket.
3. Lift the cover and pull the old element out of the air cleaner assembly.
To install:
4. Install the new filter with the screen upward.
5. Position the cover on top of the air cleaner assembly, aligning the three clips and making sure the element seals all around. Let the three studs stick upward through the holes in the cover.
6. Install both of the plastic wing nuts onto the two studs on the carburetor. Tighten each wing nut finger-tight.
7. Install the third wing nut—the one that fastens the air cleaner to the support bracket—and finger-tighten it.
8. Close the three hold-down clips.

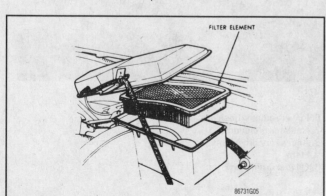

Fig. 26 The air filter orientation in the air cleaner housing—2.2L carbureted engines

1981–85 ELECTRONIC FUEL INJECTED (EFI) MODELS

➡ **The Chrysler single-point fuel injection system is referred to as Electronic Fuel Injection (EFI) throughout this manual.**

1. Remove the clamp fastening the air hose to the throttle body.
2. Unfasten the five clips which hold the top of the air cleaner to the lower housing.
3. Pull the air hose off the throttle body, then lift the cover and hose off the bottom of the air cleaner.
4. Remove the filter from the air cleaner assembly.
To install:
5. Install the new filter by setting it screen side up in the plastic bottom section of the lower air cleaner housing.
6. Install the clamp loosely onto the throttle body hose, then connect the hose to the throttle body.
7. Slide the top of the air cleaner squarely down over the seal of the filter element, making sure it is not pinching the seal anywhere. It should lay flat all around its circumference.
8. Fasten the five hold-down clips, then tighten the clamp around the hose at the throttle body until it is snug.

1986–95 EFI MODELS

▶ See Figure 27

When changing the filter element in this air cleaner, the body of the unit remains mounted on the intake manifold. Only the top cover need be removed unless the crankcase ventilation filter must be serviced.

1. Remove the three attaching thumbscrews, then lift the air cleaner top cover off of the cleaner housing.
2. If necessary, remove the small filter element retaining plate from the air filter.
3. Grab the paper element at two locations on the inside diameter, then lift it out of the air cleaner housing.
To install:
4. Install the new filter by turning the element so that its flat sides line up with those in the housing.
5. Install the air cleaner housing lid so that it sits flat on the housing.
6. Install the three thumbscrews. Be careful to tighten the three fasteners for the top cover in the numbered order shown in the illustration. They should not be extremely tight (the recommended torque value is only 12 inch lbs. or 1.36 Nm).

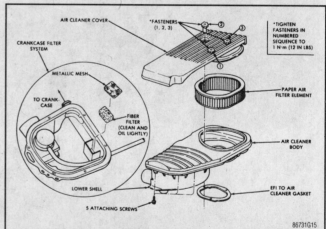

Fig. 27 When installing the thumbscrews, make sure to tighten them in the sequence shown

MULTI-PORT FUEL INJECTED (TURBOCHARGED) MODELS

▶ See Figure 28

1. Unfasten the hold-down clips attaching the top cover of the air cleaner to the main housing.
2. Gently pull the cover off the housing.
3. If the intake hose restricts the movement of the air cleaner cover so that you cannot gain access to the element without putting a lot of stress on the hose, loosen the hose clamp and pull the air intake hose off the housing cover.

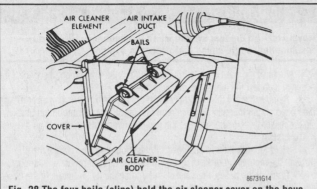

Fig. 28 The four bails (clips) hold the air cleaner cover on the housing, thereby holding the filter in the housing

4. Remove the element, noting that the rubber seal goes in last and fits into the groove around the top, or intake side, of the lower housing.

To install:

5. Install the new element in the air cleaner housing. Make certain that the rubber seal fits into the groove around the top of the housing.

6. Install the top cover over the element so that it fits squarely over the rubber seal, then fasten all of the hold-down clips securely.

7. If necessary, reconnect the intake hose and tighten the clamp securely.

2.5L Engines

EXCEPT FLEXIBLE FUEL AND TURBOCHARGED MODELS

▶ See Figures 27, 29, 30 and 31

When changing the filter element in this air cleaner, the body of the unit remains mounted on the intake manifold. Only the top cover need be removed unless the crankcase ventilation filter must be serviced.

Fig. 29 To remove the air filter, first remove the hold-down thumbscrews . . .

1. Remove the three attaching thumbscrews, then lift the air cleaner top cover off of the cleaner housing.

2. Grab the paper element at two locations on the inside diameter, then lift it out of the air cleaner housing.

To install:

3. Install the new filter by turning the element so that its flat sides line up with those in the housing.

4. Install the air cleaner housing lid so that it sits flat on the housing.

5. Install the three thumbscrews. Be careful to tighten the three fasteners for the top cover in the numbered order shown in the illustration. They should not be extremely tight (the recommended torque value is only 12 inch lbs./1.36 Nm).

TURBOCHARGED AND FLEXIBLE FUEL MODELS

1. Unfasten the hold-down clips attaching the top cover of the air cleaner to the main housing.

2. Gently pull the cover off the housing.

3. If the intake hose restricts the movement of the air cleaner cover so that you cannot gain access to the element without putting a lot of stress on the hose, loosen the hose clamp and pull the air intake hose off the housing cover.

4. Remove the element, noting that the rubber seal goes in last and fits into the groove around the top, or intake side, of the lower housing

5. Wipe the housing clean with a shop rag and inspect the housing, inlet hose and filter element for damage.

6. Hold a shop light on the throttle body side of the air filter element. Inspect the air intake side of the element for visible light. If the shop light is visible through the element, blow the element clean with compressed air and reuse the filter. If the filter saturated with oil or the light is not visible, replace the filter with a new one. If the element is saturated with oil, perform an inspection of the PCV system.

To install:

7. Install the new element in the air cleaner housing. Make certain that the rubber seal fits into the groove around the top of the housing.

8. Install the top cover over the element so that it fits squarely over the rubber seal, then fasten all of the hold-down clips securely.

9. If necessary, reconnect the intake hose and tighten the clamp securely.

2.6L Engines

▶ See Figure 32

1. Unfasten the four clips fastening the air cleaner housing cover in place.

2. Lift the cover off the lower housing (the intake hose is flexible enough to permit this), then remove the filter.

To install:

3. Clean the inside of the air cleaner housing of all dirt, grease and other contaminants before installing the new air filter.

4. Set the new filter in place inside of the air cleaner housing. Make sure that it sits square in the housing.

5. Install the housing cover onto the air cleaner housing. Make sure that it fits securely over the air cleaner filter.

6. Fasten the hold-down clips.

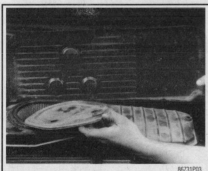

Fig. 30 . . . lift the upper filter cover and small retainer plate off of the filter—2.5L engine

Fig. 31 The air filter element can then be removed from its recess in the lower housing

Fig. 32 The air hose does not need to be disconnected to remove the air filter—the air hose is very flexible

Fuel Filter

✳✳ CAUTION

Never smoke when working around gasoline! Avoid all sources of sparks or ignition. Gasoline vapors are EXTREMELY volatile!

REMOVAL & INSTALLATION

Carbureted Engines

▶ **See Figures 33, 34, 35, 36 and 37**

There are two fuel filters in the carbureted system. One is part of the gauge unit assembly located inside the fuel tank on the suction end of the tube. This filter normally does not need servicing, but may be replaced or cleaned if a very large amount of extremely coarse material gets into the tank and clogs it.

The 2.2L engine uses a disposable filter-vapor separator that is located on the front side of the engine block between the fuel pump and carburetor. On some applications, this filter has not only inlet and outlet connections, but a third connection designed to permit fuel to return to the tank so that vapor, which accumulates in hot weather, will not interfere with carburetion.

The 2.6L engine uses a disposable, canister type filter. This type of filter has only two connections. A few models equipped with 2.6L engines use a filter-reservoir assembly that attaches to the air cleaner and also has three connections, one for the elimination of vapor.

A plugged fuel filter can limit the speed at which a vehicle can be driven and may cause hard starting. The most critical symptom will usually be suddenly reduced engine performance at maximum engine power levels, as when passing.

Remove the filter as follows:
1. Have a metal container ready to catch spilled fuel. Make sure the engine is cool.

✳✳ CAUTION

Never work on the fuel system when the engine is still warm—residual heat could cause fuel vapors to explode.

2. Remove the hose clamps from each end of the filter. Then, disconnect the hoses and collect the fuel in the metal container.
3. Remove the old filter and hoses. On the non-return (two connection) type filter used on 2.6 liter engines, this requires unfastening the mounting bracket. On the reservoir type filter, remove the two mounting nuts inside the air cleaner.

To install:
4. Hold the new filter in position. If it has mounting studs, pass them through the mounting bracket and then install the attaching nuts until snug.
5. Connect the hoses, then install and tighten the hose clamps (if the hoses are difficult to install onto the nipples, you can wet the inside of the hose very slightly). Make sure the clamps are located approximately ¼ in. (6mm) from the ends of the hoses. The hose clamps should also be installed so that they are situated on the inside of the nipples' bulges (located on the ends of the filter connections).
6. Start the engine and check for fuel leaks.

Fuel Injected Engines

▶ **See Figures 38, 39, 40 and 41**

✳✳ CAUTION

Fuel injected engines utilize high pressures in their fuel systems. This pressure is maintained through the action of check valves even when the engine is off. Therefore, you must be sure to work on the fuel carrying parts of injected cars only when the engine has cooled off and only after you have properly relieved the pressure from the fuel system. Failure to do this could cause fire or personal injury.

1. Relieve the fuel system pressure as outlined in Section 5 of this manual.

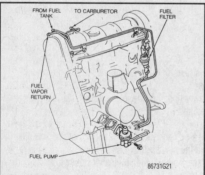

Fig. 33 Engine compartment fuel line routing and fuel filter mounting location—2.2L carbureted engines

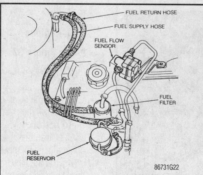

Fig. 34 Engine compartment fuel line routing and fuel filter mounting location—2.6L engines

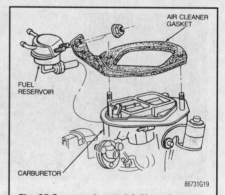

Fig. 35 Some carbureted 2.6L engines are also equipped with a filter-reservoir unit

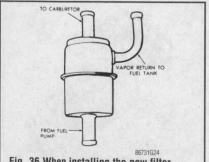

Fig. 36 When installing the new filter, make certain to connect the hoses to the correct filter nipples—2.2L carbureted engines

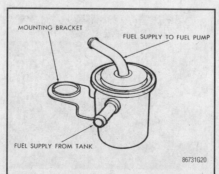

Fig. 37 The fuel filter on 2.6L engines is not equipped with a third outlet for venting fumes back to the fuel tank

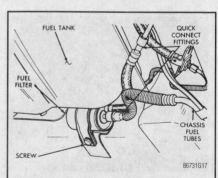

Fig. 38 Vehicles manufactured from 1988–95 utilize special quick-disconnect fittings on the fuel system hoses

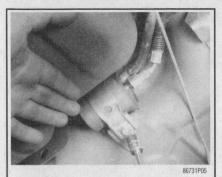

Fig. 39 The fuel filter is mounted under the car, next to the fuel tank—first remove the mounting bolt . . .

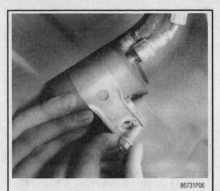

Fig. 40 . . . then lower the fuel filter from its mounting and . . .

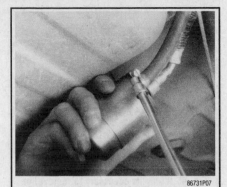

Fig. 41 . . . disconnect the fuel lines from the filter—fuel injected engines

➡The fuel filter is mounted in the rear of the car onto the vehicle body rail next to the fuel tank.

2. Remove the retaining screw that mounts the filter to its retaining bracket so you can reach the hose clamps.

➡For 1991–95 models, refer to Section 5 for procedures concerning the quick-disconnect type fuel lines.

3. Loosen the clamps for both the inlet and outlet lines. Quickly wrap a shop towel around these connections to collect escaping fuel safely. Then, dispose of this towel in such a way as to protect it from heat and the chance of fire.

4. Note the routing of the hoses. The high pressure hose from the tank and pump goes to the inlet connection, which is always located toward the outer edge of the filter. The outlet hose to the engine is labeled on some filters and is always at the center. Pull the hoses off the connections on the filter.

5. Replace the filter, draining fuel into a metal container and disposing of it safely. Inspect the hoses and clamps—replace defective parts as necessary.

➡Chrysler uses and recommends hoses that meet their specifications and are labeled "EFM/EFI18519". Make sure you use either this type of hose or an equivalent, high pressure—up to 55 psi (379 kPa) type of fuel hose available in the automotive aftermarket. Do not use ordinary rubber fuel hose, as this is not strong enough for high pressure use and may not be able to resist the destruction caused by certain types of contamination. Also on vehicles utilizing hose clamps, if the hose clamps require replacement, note that the original equipment clamps have rolled edges to keep the edge of the band from cutting into the hose, due to the necessary use of high clamping forces with a high pressure fuel system. Make sure that you use either an original equipment clamp or a similar type of clamp available in the aftermarket.

To install:

➡For 1991–95 models, refer to Section 5 for procedures concerning the quick-disconnect type fuel lines.

6. Reconnect the hoses, using the proper routing noted earlier. On 1981–87 models, you may want to very slightly wet the inside diameter of the hoses to make it easier to install them onto the filter connections. Slide them onto the filter connections as far as possible, until they are well over the bulges at the ends of the connectors. Install the clamps so they are a short distance away from the ends of the hoses but well over the bulged areas at the ends of the filter connections. Tighten both clamps securely.

7. Install the filter on the bracket with the mounting screw.

8. Start the engine and check for leaks.

PCV Valve

GENERAL INFORMATION

Chrysler Corporation recommends that a PCV valve not be cleaned. A new Mopar or equivalent PCV valve should be installed when servicing is required. Over a period of time, depending on the environment where the vehicle is used, deposits build up in the PCV vacuum circuit. The PCV system should be inspected at every oil change. Service the PCV system if engine oil is being discharged into the air cleaner. Chrysler recommends on replacing the PCV valve with a new one every 60,000 miles (96,000 km), unless the vehicle is driven under severe conditions, in which case, the PCV valve should be changed every 30,000 miles (48,000 km).

REMOVAL & INSTALLATION

▶ See Figures 42 thru 48

To inspect the system, remove the PCV valve from the crankcase vent module, rocker arm cover, or crankcase vent valve hose, then shake it. If the valve rattles, this is a partial indication that it is okay; if there is no sound, it must be replaced and the PCV hose cleaned by spraying carburetor cleaner solvent through it.

If the valve rattles, you should still check the PCV valve with the engine idling. Pull it out of the vent module and place your finger or thumb over the end to stop air flow. You should feel some suction, and the engine speed should

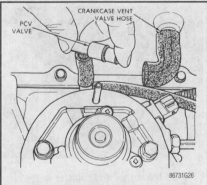

Fig. 42 Check for suction at the PCV valve while the vehicle is idling

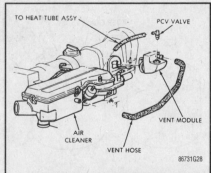

Fig. 43 The PCV valve location and system hose routing—2.2L and 2.6L carbureted engines

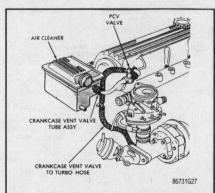

Fig. 44 The PCV valve location and system hose routing—1982–88 2.2L turbo engines

Fig. 45 It may be necessary to remove, or at least loosen, the air cleaner housing—1989 2.5L engine

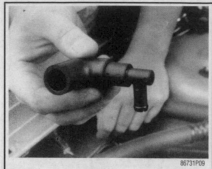

Fig. 46 Chrysler recommends that the PCV valve not be cleaned; it should be replaced instead

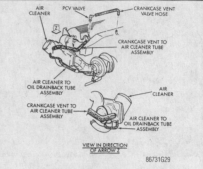

Fig. 47 PCV valve location and system hose routing—1989–95 2.2L turbo, 2.5L turbo and 2.5L flexible fuel engines

drop slightly. If there is no suction, or if the engine idle speeds up and smoothes out considerably, replace the valve. Inspect the PCV hose and clean it by spraying solvent through it, if the inside is coated with gum and varnish.

Check the vacuum at the PCV inlet (from the rocker arm cover to the air cleaner) tube, as well. Disconnect this tube from the air cleaner and loosely hold a piece of paper over the tube. After about a minute, enough vacuum should build up to cause the paper to be sucked against the opening with a noticeable amount of force. This test proves whether or not the suction side of the system is clear.

Regardless of PCV valve or system performance, the valve itself should be replaced at specified intervals. At this time, you should inspect the hoses for clogging and spray a small amount of a safe cleaning solvent designed for this purpose through the hoses to remove any accumulated sludge or varnish. To replace the PCV valve, as follows:

1. Remove the air cleaner assembly for clearance, if necessary.
2. Pull the PCV valve or PCV valve hose out of the rocker arm cover.
3. Disconnect the PCV valve from the second hose by pulling.
4. Remove the PCV valve from the vehicle.

To install:

5. Slide one end of the PCV valve into the hose leading to the intake manifold or throttle body.
6. Insert the other end into the hose, which attaches to the rocker arm cover or slide the PCV valve directly into the rocker arm cover (depends on the specific engine).
7. If necessary, install the air cleaner housing. If not already performed, this would be a great time to inspect the air cleaner filter!

Evaporative Canister

SERVICING

▶ See Figures 49 and 50

The function of the Evaporative Control System is to prevent gasoline vapors from the fuel tank from escaping into the atmosphere. Periodic maintenance is required only on 1981–82 models (all other vehicles have a sealed, mainte-

nance-free charcoal canister). The fiberglass filter on the bottom of the canister must be replaced on these models, but only if the vehicle is driven under very dusty conditions.

To replace the filter:

1. Note the locations of the hoses going to the canister, then disconnect them.
2. Loosen the canister hold-down clamp, then lift the canister out of the mounting bracket.
3. Invert the canister, then remove the bottom of the canister.
4. Pull the used filter out of the canister.

To install:

5. Insert the new filter into the bottom of the canister so that it sits flat.
6. Attach the bottom cover onto the canister, then position the canister in its mounting bracket.
7. Secure the canister in place with the hold-down clamp, then attach the hoses to the applicable ports on the canister.

In spite of the fact that this system requires no periodic maintenance, it is a good idea to quickly look over the hoses when servicing the PCV system. If any of these hoses appears cracked, torn, or rotted, the result could be vacuum leaks, poor engine operation or the annoying smell of fuel vapor. If any of these hoses should require replacement, make sure to use a high quality replacement hose of a material approved for use in fuel bearing applications. Ordinary vacuum type rubber hose will not provide satisfactory life or reliable performance.

Battery

GENERAL MAINTENANCE

All batteries, regardless of type, should be carefully secured by a battery hold-down device. If this is not done, the battery terminals or casing may crack from stress applied to the battery during vehicle operation. A battery which is not secured may allow acid to leak out, making it discharge faster; such leaking corrosive acid can also eat away components under the hood. A battery that is not sealed must be checked periodically for electrolyte level. You cannot add water to a sealed maintenance-free battery (though not all maintenance-free bat-

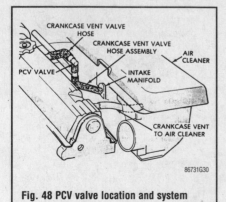

Fig. 48 PCV valve location and system hose routing—2.2L and 2.5L EFI engines

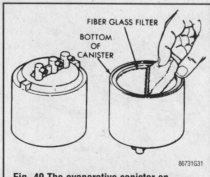

Fig. 49 The evaporative canister on 1981–82 model vehicles is provided with a replaceable fiberglass filter

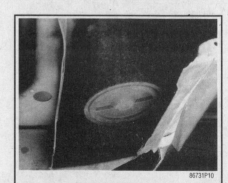

Fig. 50 The evaporative canister is mounted under the right-hand wheel well—later models

teries are sealed), but a sealed battery must also be checked for proper electrolyte level as indicated by the color of the built-in hydrometer "eye."

Keep the top of the battery clean, as a film of dirt can help completely discharge a battery that is not used for long periods. A solution of baking soda and water may be used for cleaning, but be careful to flush this off with clear water. DO NOT let any of the solution into the filler holes. Baking soda neutralizes battery acid and will de-activate a battery cell.

✳✳ CAUTION

Always use caution when working on or near the battery. Never allow a tool to bridge the gap between the negative and positive battery terminals. Also, be careful not to allow a tool to provide a ground between the positive cable/terminal and any metal component on the vehicle. Either of these conditions will cause a short circuit leading to sparks and possible personal injury.

Batteries in vehicles which are not operated on a regular basis can fall victim to parasitic loads (small current drains which are constantly drawing current from the battery). Normal parasitic loads may drain a battery on a vehicle that is in storage and not used for 6–8 weeks. Vehicles that have additional accessories such as a cellular phone, an alarm system or other devices that increase parasitic load may discharge a battery sooner. If the vehicle is to be stored for 6–8 weeks in a secure area and the alarm system, if present, is not necessary, the negative battery cable should be disconnected at the onset of storage to protect the battery charge.

Remember that constantly discharging and recharging will shorten battery life. Take care not to allow a battery to be needlessly discharged.

BATTERY FLUID

♦ **See Figures 51, 52 and 53**

✳✳ CAUTION

Battery electrolyte contains sulfuric acid. If you should splash any on your skin or in your eyes, flush the affected area with plenty of clear water. If it lands in your eyes, get medical help immediately.

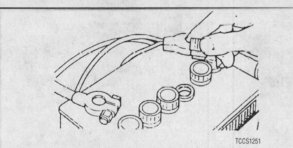

Fig. 51 On non-maintenance free batteries, the level can be checked through the case on translucent batteries; the cell caps must be removed on other models

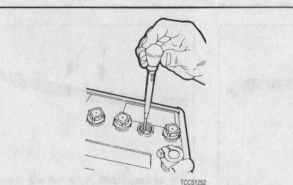

Fig. 52 Check the specific gravity of the battery's electrolyte with a hydrometer

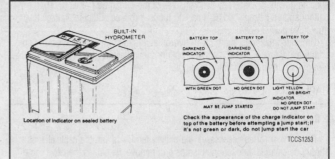

Fig. 53 A typical sealed (maintenance-free) battery with a built-in hydrometer—NOTE that the hydrometer eye may vary between battery manufacturers; always refer to the battery's label

The fluid (sulfuric acid solution) contained in the battery cells will tell you many things about the condition of the battery. Because the cell plates must be kept submerged below the fluid level in order to operate, maintaining the fluid level is extremely important. And, because the specific gravity of the acid is an indication of electrical charge, testing the fluid can be an aid in determining if the battery must be replaced. A battery in a vehicle with a properly operating charging system should require little maintenance, but careful, periodic inspection should reveal problems before they leave you stranded.

Fluid Level

Check the battery electrolyte level at least once a month, or more often in hot weather or during periods of extended vehicle operation. On non-sealed batteries, the level can be checked either through the case on translucent batteries or by removing the cell caps on opaque-cased types. The electrolyte level in each cell should be kept filled to the split ring inside each cell, or the line marked on the outside of the case.

If the level is low, add only distilled water through the opening until the level is correct. Each cell is separate from the others, so each must be checked and filled individually. Distilled water should be used, because the chemicals and minerals found in most drinking water are harmful to the battery and could significantly shorten its life.

If water is added in freezing weather, the vehicle should be driven several miles to allow the water to mix with the electrolyte. Otherwise, the battery could freeze.

Although some maintenance-free batteries have removable cell caps for access to the electrolyte, the electrolyte condition and level on all sealed maintenance-free batteries must be checked using the built-in hydrometer "eye." The exact type of eye varies between battery manufacturers, but most apply a sticker to the battery itself explaining the possible readings. When in doubt, refer to the battery manufacturer's instructions to interpret battery condition using the built in hydrometer.

➡**Although the readings from built-in hydrometers found in sealed batteries may vary, a green eye usually indicates a properly charged battery with sufficient fluid level. A dark eye is normally an indicator of a battery with sufficient fluid, but one which may be low in charge. And a light or yellow eye is usually an indication that electrolyte supply has dropped below the necessary level for battery (and hydrometer) operation. In this last case, sealed batteries with an insufficient electrolyte level must usually be discarded.**

Specific Gravity

As stated earlier, the specific gravity of a battery's electrolyte level can be used as an indication of battery charge. At least once a year, check the specific gravity of the battery. It should be between 1.20 and 1.26 on the gravity scale. Most auto supply stores carry a variety of inexpensive battery testing hydrometers. These can be used on any non-sealed battery to test the specific gravity in each cell.

The battery testing hydrometer has a squeeze bulb at one end and a nozzle at the other. Battery electrolyte is sucked into the hydrometer until the float is lifted from its seat. The specific gravity is then read by noting the position of the float. If gravity is low in one or more cells, the battery should be slowly charged and checked again to see if the gravity has come up. Generally, if after charging, the specific gravity between any two cells varies more than 50 points (0.50), the battery should be replaced as it can no longer produce sufficient voltage to guarantee proper operation.

On sealed batteries, the built-in hydrometer is the only way of checking specific gravity. Again, check with your battery's manufacturer for proper interpretation of its built-in hydrometer readings.

CABLES

▶ See Figures 54, 55 and 56

Once a year (or as necessary), the battery terminals and the cable clamps should be cleaned. Loosen the clamps and remove the cables, negative cable first. On batteries with posts on top, the use of a puller specially made for this purpose is recommended. These are inexpensive and available in most auto parts stores. Side terminal battery cables are secured with a small bolt.

Clean the cable clamps and the battery terminal with a wire brush, until all corrosion, grease, etc., is removed and the metal is shiny. It is especially important to clean the inside of the clamp (an old knife is useful here) thoroughly, since a small deposit of foreign material or oxidation there will prevent a sound electrical connection and inhibit either starting or charging. Special tools are available for cleaning these parts, one type for conventional top post batteries and another type for side terminal batteries.

Before installing the cables, loosen the battery hold-down clamp or strap, remove the battery and check the battery tray. Clear it of any debris, and check it for soundness (the battery tray can be cleaned with a baking soda and water solution). Rust should be wire brushed away, and the metal given a couple coats of anti-rust paint. Install the battery and tighten the hold-down clamp or strap securely. Do not overtighten, as this can crack the battery case.

After the clamps and terminals are clean, reinstall the cables, negative cable last; DO NOT hammer the clamps onto post batteries. Tighten the clamps securely, but do not distort them. Give the clamps and terminals a thin external coating of grease after installation, to retard corrosion.

Check the cables at the same time that the terminals are cleaned. If the cable insulation is cracked or broken, or if the ends are frayed, the cable should be replaced with a new cable of the same length and gauge.

CHARGING

❊❊❊ CAUTION

The chemical reaction which takes place in all batteries generates explosive hydrogen gas. A spark can cause the battery to explode and splash acid. To avoid serious personal injury, be sure there is proper ventilation and take appropriate fire safety precautions when connecting, disconnecting, or charging a battery and when using jumper cables.

A battery should be charged at a slow rate to keep the plates inside from getting too hot. However, if some maintenance-free batteries are allowed to discharge until they are almost "dead," they may have to be charged at a high rate to bring them back to "life." Always follow the charger manufacturer's instructions on charging the battery.

REPLACEMENT

When it becomes necessary to replace the battery, select one with a rating equal to or greater than the battery originally installed. Deterioration and just plain aging of the battery cables, starter motor, and associated wires makes the battery's job harder in successive years. The slow increase in electrical resistance over time makes it prudent to install a new battery with a greater capacity than the old.

Accessory Drive Belts

INSPECTION

▶ See Figures 57, 58, 59, 60 and 61

Except Serpentine Belt

Check the drive belts every 15,000 miles (24,000 km) or 12 months (whichever occurs first). Determine the belt tension at a point half-way between the pulleys by

Fig. 54 Maintenance is performed with household items and with special tools like this post cleaner

Fig. 55 The underside of this special battery tool has a wire brush to clean post terminals

Fig. 56 Place the tool over the terminals and twist to clean the post

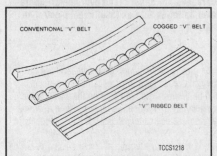

Fig. 57 There are typically 3 types of accessory drive belts found on vehicles today

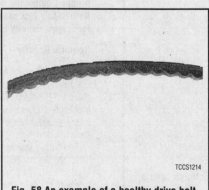

Fig. 58 An example of a healthy drive belt

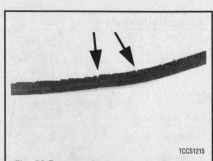

Fig. 59 Deep cracks in this belt will cause flex, building up heat that will eventually lead to belt failure

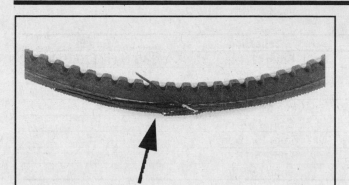

Fig. 60 The cover of this belt is worn, exposing the critical reinforcing cords to excessive wear

Fig. 61 Installing too wide a belt can result in serious belt wear and/or breakage

pressing on the belt with moderate thumb pressure. The belt should deflect about ¼–½ in. (6–13mm) at this point. Note that "deflection" is not play, but the ability of the belt, under actual tension, to stretch slightly and give.

Inspect the belts for signs of glazing or cracking. A glazed belt will be perfectly smooth from slippage, while a good belt will have a slight texture of fabric visible. Cracks will usually start at the inner edge of the belt and run outward. All worn or damaged drive belts should be replaced immediately. It is best to replace all drive belts at one time, as a preventive maintenance measure, during this service operation.

Although it is generally easier on the component to have the belt too loose than too tight, a very loose belt may place a high impact load on a bearing due to the whipping or snapping action of the belt. A belt that is slightly loose may slip, especially when component loads are high. This slippage may be hard to identify. For example, the generator belt may run okay during the day, and then slip at night when headlights are turned on. Slipping belts wear quickly not only due to the direct effect of slippage but also because of the heat the slippage generates. Extreme slippage may even cause a belt to burn. A very smooth,

glazed appearance on the belt's sides, as opposed to the obvious pattern of a fabric cover, indicates that the belt has been slipping.

Serpentine Belt

The 1989–93 2.2L Turbo III engines are equipped with serpentine belts. Check the drive belts every 15,000 miles (24,000 km) or 12 months (whichever occurs first). Inspect the belts for signs of glazing or cracking. A glazed belt will be perfectly smooth from slippage, while a good belt will have a slight texture of fabric visible. Cracks will usually start at the inner edge of the belt and run outward. All worn or damaged drive belts should be replaced immediately. It is best to replace all drive belts at one time, as a preventive maintenance measure, during this service operation.

ADJUSTMENT

❊❊ WARNING

Be careful not to overtighten the drive belts, as this will damage the driven components' bearings.

1981–88 Models

▶ See Figures 62 and 63

Determine the belt tension at a point half-way between the pulleys by pressing on the belt with moderate thumb pressure. The belt should deflect a certain amount (depending on the particular belt—refer to the accompanying chart) at this point. Note that "deflection" is not play, but the ability of the belt, under actual tension, to stretch slightly and give.

EXCEPT ALTERNATOR/WATER PUMP DRIVE BELT

1. Loosen the accessory's slotted adjusting bracket bolt. If the hinge bolt is excessively tight, it too will have to be loosened.
2. Use a strong, wooden prytool to lever the accessory either closer to, or farther away from, the engine to provide the correct tension. Do not use a metal prybar, which may damage the component. Refer to the accompanying charts for the proper deflection of the drive belt.
3. When the belt tension is correct, tighten the adjusting bracket bolts. Check the adjustment, in case the component moved slightly while tightening the bolts.

ALTERNATOR/WATER PUMP DRIVE BELT

On most of the 1981–88 model year engines covered in this manual, the alternator/water pump drive belt is tensioned by a screw type tensioner, which makes precise tension adjustment easy.

1. On 1981–87 models, loosen the locknut, located on the locking screw or lockbolt—located in a slotted portion of the outboard alternator mounting bracket.
2. On 1988 models, loosen the T-bolt, located in the center of the disc shaped portion of the outboard alternator bracket.
3. Tighten or loosen the drive belt tensioning bolt. This bolt is tightened to increase belt tension and loosened to decrease it.
4. When the belt tension is correct, tighten the lockbolt.

Accessory Drive Belt		Gauge	Deflection	Torque
Air Conditioning	New	105 lb.	8mm (5/16 in.)	54 N·m (40 ft. lbs.)
Compressor	Used	80 lb.	9mm (7/16 in.)	41 N·m (30 ft. lbs.)
Air Pump	New	—	5mm (3/16 in.)	61 N·m (45 ft. lbs.)
	Used	—	6mm (1/4 in.)	47 N·m (35 ft. lbs.)
Alternator/Water Pump	New	115 lb.	3mm (1/8 in.)	149 N·m (110 ft. lbs.)
"V" Belt and Poly "V"	Used	80 lb.	6mm (1/4 in.)	108 N·m (80 ft. lbs.)
Power Steering Pump	New	105 lb.	6mm (1/4 in.)	102 N·m (75 ft. lbs.)
	Used	80 lb.	11mm (7/16 in.)	75 N·m (55 ft. lbs.)

Fig. 62 Belt deflection and tensioning specifications—1981–88 2.2L and 1986–88 2.5L engines

Accessory Drive Belt		Gauge	Deflection	Torque
Power Steering Pump	New	95 lb.	6mm (1/4 in.)	149 N·m (110 ft. lbs.)
	Used	80 lb.	9mm (3/8 in.)	102 N·m (75 ft. lbs.)
Alternator	New	115 lb.	4mm (3/16 in.)	—
	Used	80 lb.	6mm (1/4 in.)	—
Alternator/Air Conditioning Compressor	New	115 lb.	6mm (1/4 in.)	—
	Used	80 lb.	8mm (5/16 in.)	—
Water Pump	New	—	8mm (5/16 in.)	—
	Used	—	9mm (3/8 in.)	—

86731G44

Fig. 63 Belt deflection and tensioning specifications—1981–85 2.6L engines

1989–95 Models—Except Turbo III Engines

▶ See Figure 64

Determine the belt tension either by using a belt tensioning tool, such as Special Tool Kit C-4162, or by using a torque wrench in the adjusting openings in the component brackets (refer to the belt routing diagrams for exact locations). The actual tension is different for each belt.

A/C COMPRESSOR BELT

1. Loosen the idler bracket pivot bolt (A) and locking bolts (B).
2. Adjust belt tension by applying 35 ft. lbs. (47 Nm) for a new belt, or 20 ft. lbs. (27 Nm) of force (with a torque wrench) to the square hole (C) on the idler bracket.
3. While holding the tension on the belt with the torque wrench, tighten the locking bolts, then the pivot bolt to 40 ft. lbs. (55 Nm).

POWER STEERING PUMP BELT—ZF AND TC TYPES

1. Loosen locking nut, locking bolt (G) and pivot nut (H).
2. Loosen the adjusting nut (J) to release belt tension.
3. Tighten the adjusting nut (J) to adjust belt tension to 105 lbs. (467 N) for a new belt, or to 80 lbs. (358 N) for a used belt. To accurately measure the belt tension a special tension tool will be needed, such as Chrysler Special Tool Kit C-4162.
4. Tighten the locking nut and bolt (G) to 40 ft. lbs. (55 Nm).
5. Tighten the pivot nut (H) to 20 ft. lbs. (27 Nm).

POWER STEERING PUMP BELT—S TYPE

1. From the top of the vehicle, loosen the locking bolt (G).
2. From under the vehicle, loosen the pivot bolt and pivot nut (H).
3. Adjust the belt tension with a torque wrench installed in the adjusting bracket. Tighten the belt until the torque wrench registers 43 ft. lbs. (58 Nm) for a new belt, or 32 ft. lbs. (43 Nm) for a used belt.

4. While holding the correct amount of tension on the belt, tighten the locking bolt (G) to 40 ft. lbs. (55 Nm). Tighten the pivot bolt and nut (H) to 40 ft. lbs. (55 Nm).

ALTERNATOR BELT

1. Loosen the T-bolt locking nut (E) and adjusting bolt (F).
2. Tighten the adjusting bolt (F) to adjust the belt tension. To measure the belt tension, a belt tension tool will be needed, such as Chrysler Special Tool Kit C-4162. A new belt requires 135 lbs. (600 N) and a used belt will need 80 lbs. (358 N).
3. Tighten the T-bolt locking nut (E) to 40 ft. lbs. (55 Nm).

2.2L Turbo III Engines

▶ See Figure 65

The serpentine belts found on the 2.2L Turbo III engine are adjusted automatically by an idler pulley/tensioner assembly. No belt tensioning is possible or necessary.

REMOVAL & INSTALLATION

✳✳ WARNING

Be careful not to overtighten the drive belts, as this will damage the driven components' bearings.

1981–88 Models

If a belt must be replaced, the driven unit must be loosened and moved to its extreme loosest position, generally by moving it toward the center of the motor. After removing the old belt, check the pulleys for dirt or built-up material which could affect belt contact. Carefully install the new belt, remembering that it is new and unused—it may appear to be just a little too small to fit over the pulley flanges. Fit the belt over the largest pulley (usually the crankshaft pulley at the bottom center of the motor) first, then work on the smaller one(s).

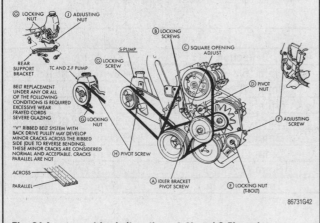

Fig. 64 Accessory drive belt routing—2.2L and 2.5L engines

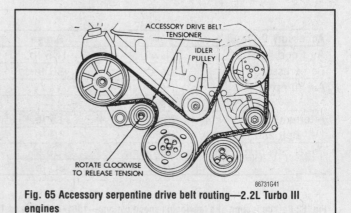

Fig. 65 Accessory serpentine drive belt routing—2.2L Turbo III engines

Gentle pressure in the direction of rotation is helpful. Some belts run around a third or idler pulley, which acts as an additional pivot in the belt's path. It may be possible to loosen the idler pulley as well as the main component, making your job much easier. Depending on which belt(s) you are changing, it may be necessary to loosen or remove other interfering belts to get at the one(s) you want.

When buying replacement belts, remember that the fit is critical according to the length of the belt ("diameter"), the width of the belt, the depth of the belt and the angle or profile of the V shape or the ribs. The belt shape should exactly match the shape of the pulley; belts that are not an exact match can cause noise, slippage and premature failure.

After the new belt is installed, draw tension on it by moving the driven unit away from the motor and tighten its mounting bolts. This is sometimes a three or four-handed job; you may find an assistant helpful. Make sure that all the bolts you loosened get retightened and that any other loosened belts also have the correct tension. A new belt can be expected to stretch a bit after installation so be prepared to re-adjust your new belt, if needed, within the first two hundred miles of use.

EXCEPT ALTERNATOR/WATER PUMP DRIVE BELT

▶ See Figure 66

1. Loosen the accessory's slotted adjusting bracket bolt. If the hinge bolt is excessively tight, it too will have to be loosened.
2. Push the component toward the engine to provide enough slack in the belt so that it will slide over one of the accessory drive pulleys. Remove the drive belt from the accessory drive pulleys and from the vehicle.

To install:
3. Position the new drive belt over the component pulleys. Make sure that it is routed correctly.
4. Adjust the tension of the belt, as described earlier in this section.

ALTERNATOR/WATER PUMP DRIVE BELT

▶ See Figures 67 and 68

1. On 1981–87 models, loosen the locknut, located on the locking screw or lockbolt—located in a slotted portion of the outboard alternator mounting bracket.
2. On 1988 models, loosen the T-bolt, located in the center of the disc shaped portion of the outboard alternator bracket.
3. Loosen the drive belt tensioning bolt until the most possible slack is gained from the component.
4. Slip the belt off of the alternator pulley, then remove it from the other pulleys. Remove the belt from the vehicle.

To install:
5. Route the new belt on the component pulleys. Make certain that it is routed correctly— incorrect routing could cause a components to spin backward, possibly damaging it.
6. Once the belt is correctly positioned on all of the pulleys, adjust the tension as described earlier in this section.

1989–95 Models—Except Turbo III Engines

▶ See Figure 64

A/C COMPRESSOR BELT

1. Loosen the idler bracket pivot bolt (A) and locking bolts (B).
2. Move the idler pulley until the most amount of slack is gained.
3. Remove the drive belt from the A/C compressor pulley, then from the other applicable pulleys.

To install:
4. Position the new belt over the crankshaft pulley, the idler pulley and the A/C compressor pulley. Make certain that it is correctly routed, otherwise it could cause the A/C compressor to be rotated backwards. This could cause damage to the compressor.
5. Adjust the belt tension, as described earlier in this section.
6. While holding the tension on the belt with the torque wrench, tighten the locking bolts, then the pivot bolt to 40 ft. lbs. (55 Nm).

POWER STEERING PUMP BELT—ZF AND TC TYPES

1. Loosen locking nut, locking bolt (G) and pivot nut (H).
2. Loosen the adjusting nut (J) to release belt tension until the maximum amount of slack in the drive belt is gained.
3. Remove the drive belt from the applicable pulleys.

To install:
4. Route the new belt onto the component pulleys. Make certain that it is correctly routed, otherwise damage may occur to the power steering pump.
5. Adjust belt tension, as described earlier in this section. To accurately measure the belt tension a special tension tool will be needed, such as Chrysler Special Tool Kit C-4162.
6. Tighten the locking nut and bolt (G) to 40 ft. lbs. (55 Nm).
7. Tighten the pivot nut (H) to 20 ft. lbs. (27 Nm).

POWER STEERING PUMP BELT—S TYPE

1. From the top of the vehicle, loosen the locking bolt (G).
2. From under the vehicle, loosen the pivot bolt and pivot nut (H).
3. Push the power steering pump toward the engine until the maximum amount of slack in the belt is gained.
4. Remove the drive belt from the components' pulleys.

To install:
5. Position the drive belt onto the accessories pulleys. Make sure that the new belt is correctly routed.
6. Adjust the belt tension, as described earlier in this section.
7. While holding the correct amount of tension on the belt, tighten the locking bolt (G) to 40 ft. lbs. (55 Nm). Tighten the pivot bolt and nut (H) to 40 ft. lbs. (55 Nm).

ALTERNATOR BELT

1. Loosen the T-bolt locking nut (E) and adjusting bolt (F).
2. Tighten the adjusting bolt (F) to loosen the belt tension. Loosen the drive belt until the maximum amount of slack is gained.

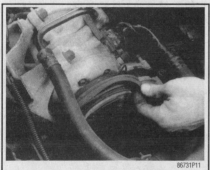
Fig. 66 Once the A/C compressor bolts are loosened, the belt can be removed from the pulley

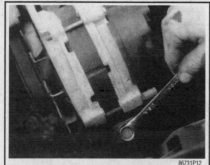
Fig. 67 After loosening the lockbolt, loosen the adjusting bolt to relieve the belt's tension

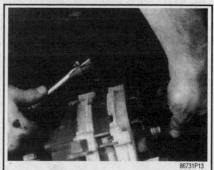
Fig. 68 Once the belt is adequately loosened, remove the belt from the drive pulley

3. Remove the drive belt from the applicable drive pulleys.

To install:

4. Install the drive belt onto the applicable pulleys.
5. Adjust the drive belt tension, as described earlier in this section.
6. Tighten the T-bolt locking nut (E) to 40 ft. lbs. (55 Nm).

2.2L Turbo III Engines

▶ See Figure 65

The serpentine drive belt is provided with a dynamic tensioner to maintain proper belt tension. To remove or install this belt:

1. Raise the front of the vehicle and safely support on jackstands.
2. Remove the right front splash shield.
3. Release tension of the belt by rotating the tensioner assembly clockwise.
4. While holding the tensioner in the rotated position, remove the belt from the various pulleys—make sure to note the route that the belt takes before removal.

To install:

5. Route the belt on the various pulleys except for the tensioner pulley. Once the belt is satisfactorily mounted on the pulleys, rotate the tensioner clockwise and slide the belt onto the tensioner pulley. Make certain that the belt is mounted so that the grooves in the belt are correctly aligned with the grooves in the pulleys.
6. Install the right front splash shield to the underside of the vehicle.
7. Lower the vehicle back to the ground.
8. Start the engine and allow to idle for a few minutes. Shut the engine off and double check the placement of the belt on the pulleys.

Hoses

INSPECTION

▶ See Figures 69, 70, 71 and 72

Upper and lower radiator hoses along with the heater hoses should be checked for deterioration, leaks and loose hose clamps at least every 15,000 miles (24,000 km). It is also wise to check the hoses periodically in early spring

Fig. 69 The cracks developing along this hose are a result of age-related hardening

and at the beginning of the fall or winter when you are performing other maintenance. A quick visual inspection could discover a weakened hose which might have left you stranded if it had remained unrepaired.

Whenever you are checking the hoses, make sure the engine and cooling system are cold. Visually inspect for cracking, rotting or collapsed hoses, and replace as necessary. Run your hand along the length of the hose. If a weak or swollen spot is noted when squeezing the hose wall, the hose should be replaced.

REMOVAL & INSTALLATION

1. Remove the radiator pressure cap.

✼ CAUTION

Never remove the pressure cap while the engine is running, or personal injury from scalding hot coolant or steam may result. If possible, wait until the engine has cooled to remove the pressure cap. If this is not possible, wrap a thick cloth around the pressure cap and turn it slowly to the stop. Step back while the pressure is released from the cooling system. When you are sure all the pressure has been released, use the cloth to turn and remove the cap.

2. Position a clean container under the radiator and/or engine draincock or plug, then open the drain and allow the cooling system to drain to an appropriate level. For some upper hoses, only a little coolant must be drained. To remove hoses positioned lower on the engine, such as a lower radiator hose, the entire cooling system must be emptied.

✼ CAUTION

When draining coolant, keep in mind that cats and dogs are attracted by ethylene glycol antifreeze, and are quite likely to drink any that is left in an uncovered container or in puddles on the ground. This will prove fatal in sufficient quantity. Always drain coolant into a sealable container. Coolant may be reused unless it is contaminated or several years old.

3. Loosen the hose clamps at each end of the hose requiring replacement. Clamps are usually either of the spring tension type (which require pliers to squeeze the tabs and loosen) or of the screw tension type (which require screw or hex drivers to loosen). Pull the clamps back on the hose away from the connection.
4. Twist, pull and slide the hose off the fitting, taking care not to damage the neck of the component from which the hose is being removed.

➡ **If the hose is stuck at the connection, do not try to insert a screwdriver or other sharp tool under the hose end in an effort to free it, as the connection and/or hose may become damaged. Heater connections especially may be easily damaged by such a procedure. If the hose is to be replaced, use a single-edged razor blade to make a slice along the portion of the hose which is stuck on the connection, perpendicular to the end of the hose. Do not cut deep so as to prevent damaging the connection. The hose can then be peeled from the connection and discarded.**

Fig. 70 A hose clamp that is too tight can cause older hoses to separate and tear on either side of the clamp

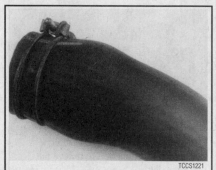

Fig. 71 A soft spongy hose (identifiable by the swollen section) will eventually burst and should be replaced

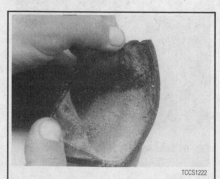

Fig. 72 Hoses are likely to deteriorate from the inside if the cooling system is not periodically flushed

5. Clean both hose mounting connections. Inspect the condition of the hose clamps and replace them, if necessary.

To install:

6. Dip the ends of the new hose into clean engine coolant to ease installation.

7. Slide the clamps over the replacement hose, then slide the hose ends over the connections into position.

8. Position and secure the clamps at least ¼ in. (6.35mm) from the ends of the hose. Make sure they are located beyond the raised bead of the connector.

9. Close the radiator or engine drains and properly refill the cooling system with the clean drained engine coolant or a suitable mixture of ethylene glycol coolant and water.

10. If available, install a pressure tester and check for leaks. If a pressure tester is not available, run the engine until normal operating temperature is reached (allowing the system to naturally pressurize), then check for leaks.

✳✳ CAUTION

If you are checking for leaks with the system at normal operating temperature, BE EXTREMELY CAREFUL not to touch any moving or hot engine parts. Once temperature has been reached, shut the engine OFF, and check for leaks around the hose fittings and connections which were removed earlier.

CV-Boots

INSPECTION

▸ **See Figures 73, 74 and 75**

It is vitally important during any service procedures requiring boot handling, that care be taken not to puncture or tear the boot by over tightening clamps, misuse of tool(s) or pinching the boot. Pinching can occur by rotating the CV joints (especially the tripod) beyond normal working angles.

The driveshaft boots are not compatible with oil, gasoline, or cleaning solvents. Care must be taken that the boots never come into contact with any of these liquids.

➥**The ONLY acceptable cleaning agent for driveshaft boots is soap and water. After washing, the boot must be thoroughly rinsed and dried before reusing.**

Chrysler recommends inspecting the CV-boots at every oil change (every 3,000 miles or 4,800 km). However, a good rule of thumb is that, if the vehicle needs to be raised for any procedure, check the CV-boots. Noticeable amounts of grease on areas adjacent to or on the exterior of the CV joint boot is the first indication that a boot is punctured, torn or that a clamp has loosened. When a CV joint is removed for servicing of the joint, the boot should be properly cleaned and inspected for cracks, tears and scuffed areas on the interior surfaces. If any of these conditions exist, boot replacement is recommended.

For removal and installation procedures, refer to halfshaft procedures located in Section 7.

Spark Plugs

GENERAL INFORMATION

▸ **See Figures 76 and 77**

A typical spark plug consists of a metal shell surrounding a ceramic insulator. A metal electrode extends downward through the center of the insulator and protrudes a small distance. Located at the end of the plug and attached to the side of the outer metal shell is the side electrode. The side electrode bends in at a 90° angle so that its tip is even with, and parallel to, the tip of the center electrode. The distance between these two electrodes, measured in thousandths of an inch or millimeters, is called the spark plug gap. The spark plug in no way produces a spark but merely provides a gap across which the current can arc. The coil produces anywhere from 20,000 to 40,000 volts which travels to the distributor where it is distributed through the spark plug wires to the spark

Fig. 73 CV-Boots must be inspected periodically for damage

Fig. 74 A torn boot should be replaced immediately

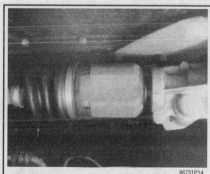

Fig. 75 Also make certain to inspect the inner CV-boots as well—this boot is in perfect condition

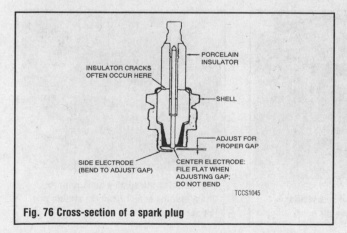

Fig. 76 Cross-section of a spark plug

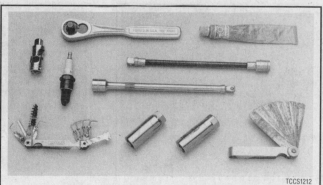

Fig. 77 A variety of tools and gauges are needed for spark plug service

plugs. The current passes along the center electrode and jumps the gap to the side electrode, and, in doing so, ignites the air/fuel mixture in the combustion chamber. Resistor spark plugs are used in all engines and have resistance values of 6,000–20,000 ohms when checked with at least a 1000 volt tester.

SPARK PLUG HEAT RANGE

▶ **See Figure 78**

Spark plug heat range is the ability of the plug to dissipate heat. The longer the insulator (or the farther it extends into the engine), the hotter the plug will operate; the shorter the insulator (the closer the electrode is to the block's cooling passages) the cooler it will operate. A plug that absorbs little heat and remains too cool will quickly accumulate deposits of oil and carbon since it is not hot enough to burn them off. This leads to plug fouling and consequently to misfiring. A plug that absorbs too much heat will have no deposits but, due to the excessive heat, the electrodes will burn away quickly and might possibly lead to preignition or other ignition problems. Preignition takes place when plug tips get so hot that they glow sufficiently to ignite the air/fuel mixture before the actual spark occurs. This early ignition will usually cause a pinging during low speeds and heavy loads.

The general rule of thumb for choosing the correct heat range when picking a spark plug is: if most of your driving is long distance, high speed travel, use a colder plug; if most of your driving is stop and go, use a hotter plug. Original equipment plugs are generally a good compromise between the 2 styles and most people never have the need to change their plugs from the factory-recommended heat range.

REMOVAL & INSTALLATION

▶ **See Figures 79, 80 and 81**

A set of spark plugs usually requires replacement after about 20,000–30,000 miles (32,000–48,000 km), depending on your style of driving. In normal operation plug gap increases about 0.001 in (0.025 mm) for every 2,500 miles (4000 km). As the gap increases, the plug's voltage requirement also increases. It requires a greater voltage to jump the wider gap and about two to three times as much voltage to fire the plug at high speeds than at idle. The improved air/fuel ratio control of modern fuel injection combined with the higher voltage output of modern ignition systems will often allow an engine to run significantly longer on a set of standard spark plugs, but keep in mind that efficiency will drop as the gap widens (along with fuel economy and power).

When you're removing spark plugs, work on one at a time. Don't start by removing the plug wires all at once, because, unless you number them, they may become mixed up. Take a minute before you begin and number the wires with tape.

1. Disconnect the negative battery cable, and if the vehicle has been run recently, allow the engine to thoroughly cool.

2. If necessary, remove the distributor cover for additional access to the spark plug wires.

3. Carefully twist the spark plug wire boot to loosen it, then pull upward and remove the boot from the plug. Be sure to pull on the boot and not on the wire, otherwise the connector located inside the boot may become separated.

4. Using compressed air, blow any water or debris from the spark plug well to assure that no harmful contaminants are allowed to enter the combustion chamber when the spark plug is removed. If compressed air is not available, use a rag or a brush to clean the area.

➡Remove the spark plugs when the engine is cold, if possible, to prevent damage to the threads. If removal of the plugs is difficult, apply a few drops of penetrating oil or silicone spray to the area around the base of the plug, and allow it a few minutes to work.

5. Using a spark plug socket that is equipped with a rubber insert to properly hold the plug, turn the spark plug counterclockwise to loosen and remove the spark plug from the bore.

✳ WARNING

Be sure not to use a flexible extension on the socket. Use of a flexible extension may allow a shear force to be applied to the plug. A shear force could break the plug off in the cylinder head, leading to costly and frustrating repairs.

To install:

6. Inspect the spark plug boot for tears or damage. If a damaged boot is found, the spark plug wire must be replaced.

7. Using a wire feeler gauge, check and adjust the spark plug gap. When using a gauge, the proper size should pass between the electrodes with a slight drag. The next larger size should not be able to pass while the next smaller size should pass freely.

8. Carefully thread the plug into the bore by hand. If resistance is felt before the plug is almost completely threaded, back the plug out and begin threading again. In small, hard to reach areas, an old spark plug wire and boot could be used as a threading tool. The boot will hold the plug while you twist the end of the wire and the wire is supple enough to twist before it would allow the plug to crossthread.

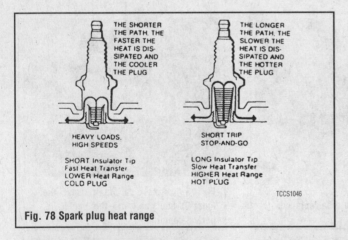

THE SHORTER THE PATH, THE FASTER THE HEAT IS DISSIPATED AND THE COOLER THE PLUG

THE LONGER THE PATH, THE SLOWER THE HEAT IS DISSIPATED AND THE HOTTER THE PLUG

HEAVY LOADS, HIGH SPEEDS

SHORT Insulator Tip
Fast Heat Transfer
LOWER Heat Range
COLD PLUG

SHORT TRIP
STOP-AND-GO

LONG Insulator Tip
Slow Heat Transfer
HIGHER Heat Range
HOT PLUG

TCCS1046

Fig. 78 Spark plug heat range

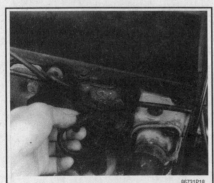

86731P18

Fig. 79 Pull the spark plug cable off of the spark plug terminal

86731P19

Fig. 80 Use a spark plug socket and ratchet wrench to remove the spark plugs

86731P20

Fig. 81 Once the spark plug is removed, the operating condition of the engine can be ascertained

Do not use the spark plug socket to thread the plugs. Always carefully thread the plug by hand or using an old plug wire to prevent the possibility of crossthreading and damaging the cylinder head bore.

9. Carefully tighten the spark plug to 20 ft. lbs. (28 Nm). If the plug you are installing is equipped with a crush washer, seat the plug, then tighten about ¼ turn to crush the washer. If you are installing a tapered seat plug, tighten the plug to specifications provided by the vehicle or plug manufacturer.

10. Apply a small amount of silicone dielectric compound to the end of the spark plug lead or inside the spark plug boot to prevent sticking, then install the boot to the spark plug and push until it clicks into place. The click may be felt or heard, then gently pull back on the boot to assure proper contact.

INSPECTION & GAPPING

▶ **See Figures 82, 83, 84 and 85**

Check the plugs for deposits and wear. If they are not going to be replaced, clean the plugs thoroughly. Remember that any kind of deposit will decrease the efficiency of the plug. Plugs can be cleaned on a spark plug cleaning machine, which can sometimes be found in service stations, or you can do an acceptable job of cleaning with a stiff brush. If the plugs are cleaned, the electrodes must be filed flat. Use an ignition points file, not an emery board or the like, which will leave deposits. The electrodes must be filed perfectly flat with sharp edges; rounded edges reduce the spark plug voltage by as much as 50%.

Check spark plug gap before installation. The ground electrode (the L-shaped one connected to the body of the plug) must be parallel to the center electrode and the specified size wire gauge (please refer to the Tune-Up Specifications chart for details) must pass between the electrodes with a slight drag.

➡**NEVER adjust the gap on a used platinum type spark plug, unless the manufacturer indicates otherwise.**

Always check the gap on new plugs as they are not always set correctly at the factory. Do not use a flat feeler gauge when measuring the gap on a used plug, because the reading may be inaccurate. A round-wire type gapping tool is the best way to check the gap. The correct gauge should pass through the electrode gap with a slight drag. If you're in doubt, try one size smaller and one larger. The smaller gauge should go through easily, while the larger one shouldn't go through at all. Wire gapping tools usually have a bending tool attached. Use that to adjust the side electrode until the proper distance is obtained. Absolutely never attempt to bend the center electrode. Also, be careful not to bend the side electrode too far or too often as it may weaken and break off within the engine, requiring removal of the cylinder head to retrieve it.

Undamaged low mileage spark plugs can be cleaned and reused. After cleaning, file the center electrode flat with a small point file or a jewelers file; a rounded electrode can decrease the energy output by 50 percent. Adjust the gap between the electrodes to the following values based on engines:

- 2.2L and 2.5L engines—0.033–0.038 in. (0.84–0.97mm)
- 2.6L engine—0.035–0.040 in. (0.89–1.02mm)

Always tighten spark plugs to the specified torque. Over-tightening can cause distortion and change spark plug gap. Tighten the spark plugs to 20 ft. lbs. (28 Nm).

On spark plugs with normal wear, the few deposits present will be probably light tan or slightly gray in color with most grades of commercial gasoline. There will not be evidence of electrode burning. Gap growth will not average more than approximately 0.001 in. (0.025mm) per 1000 miles (1600 km) or operation. Spark plugs that have normal wear can usually be cleaned, have the electrodes filed and regapped, and then reinstalled.

Some fuel refiners in several areas of the United States of America have introduced a manganese additive (MMT) for unleaded fuel. During combustion, fuel with MMT coats the entire tip of the spark plug with a rust color deposit. The rust color deposits could be misdiagnosed as being caused by coolant in the combustion chamber. MMT deposits do not affect spark plug performance.

Spark Plug Wires

TESTING

The plug wires carry a very tiny amount of current under extremely high voltage. The conductors inside must offer some resistance to flow of current, or operation of a radio in the car, or even nearby, would be impossible. For these reasons, these wires deteriorate steadily and often produce puzzling and unexpected lapses in performance. The most typical evidence of wire problems is the sudden failure of the car to start on a damp morning.

The wires should be inspected frequently for full seating at the plugs and distributor cap towers. Before inspection, wipe the wires carefully with a cloth slightly moistened with a non-flammable solvent so it will be easier to see cracks or other damage. The insulation and all rubber boots should be flexible and free of cracks. Replace the wires as a set as soon as any such problems develop.

Unfortunately, the invisible conductors inside high quality wires can deteriorate before evidence of poor insulation exists. You can remove such wires and test the resistance if you have an ohmmeter. Measure the length of each wire with a ruler and then multiply the length by the figures given, in order to measure total resistance. Resistance must be 250–600 ohms per inch (25mm) for 1981–90 vehicles and to 250–1000 ohms per inch (25mm) for 1991–95 models, or to 3,000–7,200 ohms per foot (30.5 cm) for 1981–90 models and to 3,000–12,000 ohms per foot (30.5 cm) for 1991–95 models. If you wish to check the cap at the same time, you can run your test between the spark plug end of the plug wire and the contact at the center of the inside of the cap.

If you do not have an ohmmeter, you may want to take you car to a mechanic or diagnostic center with an oscilloscope type of diagnosis system. This unit will read the curve of ignition voltage and uncover problems with wires, or any other component, easily. You may also want to refer to the previous procedures on spark plug analysis, as looking at the plugs may help you to identify wire problems.

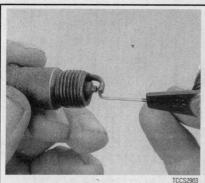

Fig. 82 Checking the spark plug gap with a feeler gauge

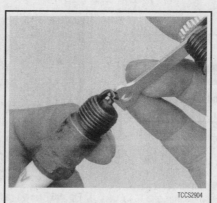

Fig. 83 Adjusting the spark plug gap

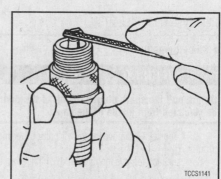

Fig. 84 If the standard plug is in good condition, the electrode may be filed flat— WARNING: do not file platinum plugs

A normally worn spark plug should have light tan or gray deposits on the firing tip.

A carbon fouled plug, identified by soft, sooty, black deposits, may indicate an improperly tuned vehicle. Check the air cleaner, ignition components and engine control system.

This spark plug has been **left in the engine too long,** as evidenced by the extreme gap- Plugs with such an extreme gap can cause misfiring and stumbling accompanied by a noticeable lack of power.

An oil fouled spark plug indicates an engine with worn poston rings and/or bad valve seals allowing excessive oil to enter the chamber.

A physically damaged spark plug may be evidence of severe detonation in that cylinder. Watch that cylinder carefully between services, as a continued detonation will not only damage the plug, but could also damage the engine.

A bridged or almost bridged spark plug, identified by a build-up between the electrodes caused by excessive carbon or oil build-up on the plug.

TCCA1P40

Fig. 85 Inspect the spark plug to determine engine running conditions

REMOVAL & INSTALLATION

▶ See Figure 86

✳ WARNING

Do not pull the spark plug wires off of the distributor cap, they must be released from inside of the cap.

1. If applicable, remove the 2 distributor cover mounting bolts and the distributor cover.
2. Label and remove the ignition coil cable from the ignition coil center tower.
3. Label and remove all of the spark plug cable ends from the spark plugs.
4. Note the spark plug cable routing, then detach the cables from any retainers or brackets.

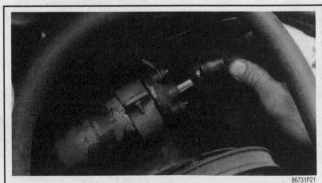

86731P21

Fig. 86 Always remove and install the ignition cables by holding them on the boot, not on the wire itself

5. Matchmark the cap to the distributor housing. Remove the distributor cap from the distributor housing by unscrewing the cap hold-down screws. Lift the cap off of the housing with the spark plug cables attached.

6. From inside of the distributor cap, use a pair of pliers to compress the positive-locking terminal tangs of the spark plug wires. While the tangs are compressed, pull the cable out of the distributor cap from the outside.

To install:

7. Push the spark plug cable terminals into the distributor cap until the positive-locking terminal tangs are fully engaged.

8. Install the distributor cap with the matchmarks aligned, then install the distributor cap hold-down screws until snug.

9. Route the spark plug cables as when removed into any retainers or brackets. Push the spark plug cables onto the spark plugs until fully seated.

10. Install the ignition coil cable so that the end is fully inserted into the ignition coil tower.

11. If necessary, install the distributor cover.

Distributor Cap and Rotor

INSPECTION

Remove the distributor cap and inspect the inside for flash over, cracking of the carbon button, lack of spring tension on the carbon button, cracking of the cap, and burned, worn terminals. Also check for broken distributor cap towers. If any of these conditions are present, the distributor cap and/or cables should be replaced.

When replacing the distributor cap, transfer cables from the original cap to the new cap one at a time. Ensure each cable is installed into the corresponding tower of the new cap. Fully seat the wires into the towers. If necessary, refer to the appropriate engine firing order diagram.

Light scaling of the terminals can be cleaned with a sharp knife. If the terminals are heavily scaled, replace the distributor cap.

A cap that is greasy, dirty or has a powder-like substance on the inside should be cleaned with a solution of warm water and mild detergent. Scrub the cap with a soft brush. Thoroughly rinse the cap and dry it with a clean soft cloth.

Replace the rotor with a new one if it is cracked, the tip is excessively burned or heavily scaled. If the spring terminal does not have adequate tension, replace the rotor with a new one.

REMOVAL & INSTALLATION

▶ See Figures 87 thru 92

1. If equipped, detach the distributor connector from the engine wiring harness connector.

2. If applicable, remove the distributor cover by removing the cover hold-down bolts.

3. Remove the distributor cap retaining screws.

4. Label and disconnect the spark plug cables from the spark plugs and the ignition coil cable from the ignition coil.

Do not pull the spark plug wires off of the distributor cap, they must be released from inside of the cap.

5. Lift the cap off of the distributor. If the distributor cap is found to be defective, remove the spark plug cables as described in the previous inspection procedures or in the spark plug cable procedures located earlier in this section.

6. Note in which direction the distributor spark pick-up (rotor) is pointing, then pull the rotor off of the distributor shaft.

To install:

7. Push the new rotor onto the distributor shaft until it is fully seated on the distributor shaft. Make certain it is pointing in the same direction as when removed.

8. Set the distributor cap back onto the distributor.

9. Tighten the distributor cap retaining screws until they are snug.

10. Connect the spark plug cables to the spark plugs and the ignition cable to the ignition coil.

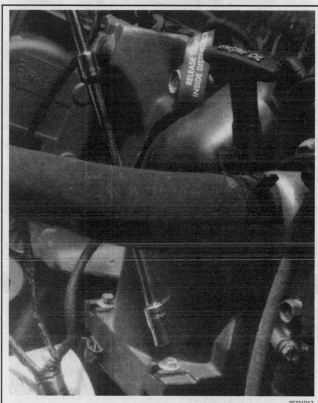

Fig. 87 Remove the plastic distributor cover, then set it aside

Fig. 88 Pull the spark plug cable off of the spark plug terminal by grasping the cable boot

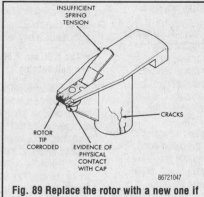

Fig. 89 Replace the rotor with a new one if any of these worn conditions are evident

Fig. 90 After removing the cover, remove the hold-down screws and . . .

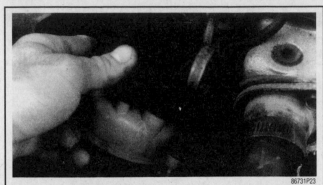

Fig. 91 . . . lift the distributor cap off of the distributor housing—1986 Reliant shown

Fig. 92 The rotor simply pulls off of the distributor shaft—note the direction it points before removal

11. If necessary, install the distributor cover.
12. If equipped, attach the distributor connector to the engine wiring harness.

Ignition Timing

GENERAL INFORMATION

Ignition timing is the measurement, in degrees of crankshaft rotation, of the point at which the spark plugs fire in each of the cylinders. It is measured in degrees before or after Top Dead Center (TDC) of the compression stroke.

Because it takes a fraction of a second for the spark plug to ignite the mixture in the cylinder, the spark plug must fire a little before the piston reaches TDC. Otherwise, the mixture will not be completely ignited as the piston passes TDC and the full power of the explosion will not be used by the engine.

The timing measurement is given in degrees of crankshaft rotation before the piston reaches TDC (BTDC). If the setting for the ignition timing is 5° BTDC, the spark plug must fire 5° before each piston reaches TDC. This only holds true, however, when the engine is at idle speed.

As the engine speed increases, the pistons go faster. The spark plugs have to ignite the fuel even sooner if it is to be completely ignited when the piston reaches TDC. To do this, distributors have various means of advancing the spark timing as the engine speed increases. On some earlier model vehicles, this is accomplished by centrifugal weights within the distributor along with a vacuum diaphragm mounted on the side of the distributor. Later model vehicles are equipped with electronic ignition systems, in which the advance of the ignition timing is controlled by the Powertrain Control Module (PCM).

If the ignition is set too far advanced (BTDC), the ignition and expansion of the fuel in the cylinder will occur too soon and tend to force the piston down while it is still traveling up. This causes engine ping. If the ignition spark is set too far retarded, after TDC (ATDC), the piston will have already passed TDC and started on its way down when the fuel is ignited. This will cause the piston to be forced down for only a portion of its travel. This will result in poor engine performance and lack of power.

Timing marks generally consist of a notch on the rim of the crankshaft pulley and a scale of degrees attached to the front of the engine (often on the engine front cover). The notch corresponds to the position of the piston in the number 1 cylinder. A stroboscopic (dynamic) timing light is used, which is hooked into the circuit of the No. 1 cylinder spark plug. Every time the spark plug fires, the timing light flashes. By aiming the timing light at the timing marks while the engine is running, the exact position of the piston within the cylinder can be easily read since the stroboscopic flash makes the mark on the pulley appear to be standing still. Proper timing is indicated when the notch is aligned with the correct number on the scale.

There are three basic types of timing lights available. The first is a simple neon bulb with two wire connections (one for the spark plug and one for the plug wire, connecting the light in series). This type of light is quite dim, and must be held closely to the marks to be seen, but it is quite inexpensive. The second type of light is powered by the car's battery. Two alligator clips connect to the battery terminals, while a third wire connects to the spark plug with an adapter. This type of light is more expensive, but the xenon bulb provides a nice bright flash which can even be seen in sunlight. The third type replaces the battery source with 110 volt house current, but still attaches to the No. 1 spark plug wire in order to determine when the plug is fired. Some timing lights have other functions built into them, such as dwell meters, tachometers, or remote starting switches. These are convenient, in that they reduce the tangle of wires under the hood, but may duplicate the functions of tools you already have.

➡**Never pierce a spark plug wire in order to attach a timing light or perform tests. The pierced insulation will eventually lead to an electrical arc and related ignition troubles.**

An inductive pick-up timing light should be used with the Chrysler vehicles. The inductive pick-up simply clamps onto the No. 1 spark plug wire, eliminating the adapter. It is not susceptible to cross-firing or false triggering, which may occur with a conventional light, due to the greater voltages produced by electronic ignition.

INSPECTION & ADJUSTMENT

▶ **See Figure 93**

For the correct timing specifications refer to the Vehicle Emission Control Information (VECI) label or the Tune-up Specifications chart in this section. If the VECI label and specifications chart disagree as to the correct ignition timing, always use the information on the VECI label. The VECI label reflects any running changes made by the manufacturer.

On all 2.2 and 2.5L, the timing marks are located on the flywheel with the pointer on an access hole in the transaxle, or on the edge of the access hole with a line on the flywheel. On the 2.6L engines, the timing marks are on a special bracket mounted on the front of the block and there is a notch in the front pulley.

1981–87 Models

▶ **See Figures 94 and 95**

1. Warm the engine to normal operating temperature. Shut off the engine and connect the timing light to the No. 1 spark plug. Do not under any circumstances pierce a wire to hook up a light.
2. Clean off the timing marks and mark the pulley or damper notch and the timing scale with white chalk or paint. The timing notch on the damper or pulley can be elusive. Bump the engine around with the starter or turn the crankshaft with a wrench on the front pulley bolt to get it to an accessible position.

➡**The 2.2L and 2.5L engines have their timing marks on the flywheel and bell housing.**

3. Disconnect and plug the vacuum advance hose at the distributor or, at the spark advance computer vacuum transducer on (carbureted) models that have one in all years through 1987, to prevent any distributor advance. The computer is located in the air intake on the driver's side fender well, with the vacuum transducer's diaphragm clearly in view on top. The vacuum line is the rubber hose connected to the metal cone-shaped canister on the side of the distributor or the top/center of the transducer diaphragm. A short screw, pencil, or a golf tee can be used to plug the hose. On 1986 models equipped with a carburetor switch, connect a jumper wire between the carburetor switch and ground. On 1987 2.2 and 2.5L engines with Electronic Fuel Injection, disconnect the coolant

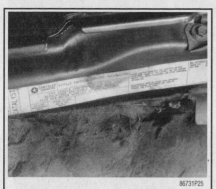

Fig. 93 Always refer to the VECI label located on the underside of the hood

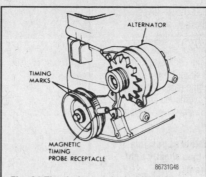

Fig. 94 The timing marks for the 2.6L engine are located on a tab above the crankshaft pulley

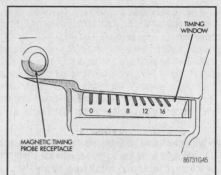

Fig. 95 The timing marks for the 2.2L EFI and 2.5L engines are located at the transmission/engine flange

temperature sensor electrical lead at the sensor, which is located on the thermostat housing.

4. Make sure the idle screw rests against its stop. If necessary, open and close the throttle to make sure the linkage is not binding. Start the engine and adjust the idle speed to that specified in the Tune-up Specifications chart. Since some cars require that the timing be set with the transmission in Neutral, you can disconnect the idle solenoid to lower the idle speed. If the vehicle is not equipped with an idle solenoid, adjust the idle speed screw to lower the idle speed. Adjusting the idle speed is vital, since it prevents any centrifugal advance from affecting the distributor timing.

5. Aim the timing light at the timing marks. Be careful not to touch the fan, which may appear to be standing still. Keep your clothes and hair, and the light's wire clear of the fan, belts, and pulleys. If the pulley or damper notch isn't aligned with the proper timing mark (see the Tune-up Specifications chart or the Vehicle Emission Control Information label on the underside of the vehicle's hood), the timing will have to be adjusted.

➡️ Top Dead Center (TDC) corresponds to 0°; Before Top Dead Center (B or BTDC) may be shown as BEFORE; After Top Dead Center (A or ATDC) may be shown as AFTER.

6. Loosen the distributor base clamp locknut. You can buy special wrenches which will make this task easy. Turn the distributor slowly to adjust the timing, holding it by the body and not the cap. Turn the distributor in the direction of rotor rotation (found in the Firing Order illustrations) to retard, and against the direction to advance.

7. Tighten the locknut. Check the timing, in case the distributor moved as you tightened it.

8. Reconnect the distributor vacuum hose. Correct the idle speed.

9. Shut off the engine and disconnect the light. Reconnect the coolant temperature sensor connector, if necessary.

1988–95 Models

◆ See Figures 95 and 96

1. Set the gearshift selector in Park or Neutral and apply the parking brake. All lights and accessories must be off.

2. Attach an inductive pick-up type of timing light to the No. 1 cylinder spark plug wire.

✳✳ WARNING

Do not puncture cables, boots or nipples with test probes. Always use the proper adapters. Also make sure that the timing light wires are not in the way of any moving engine components, such as the cooling fan.

3. Start the engine and allow it to idle until normal operating temperature is reached.

4. Detach the Engine Coolant Temperature (ECT) sensor connector. The electric radiator fan will turn on and the malfunction indicator lamp (in the instrument panel) will turn ON after disconnecting the ECT sensor.

5. Aim the timing light at the timing marks. Be careful not to touch the fan, which may appear to be standing still. Keep your clothes and hair, and the

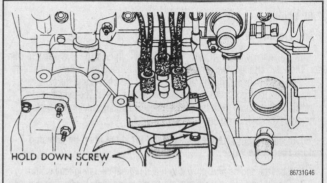

Fig. 96 To adjust the timing, loosen the hold-down screw and turn the distributor

light's wire clear of the fan, belts, and pulleys. If the pulley or damper notch isn't aligned with the proper timing mark (see the Tune-up Specifications chart or the Vehicle Emission Control Information label on the underside of the vehicle's hood), the timing will have to be adjusted.

➡️ Top Dead Center (TDC) corresponds to 0°; Before Top Dead Center (B or BTDC) may be shown as BEFORE; After Top Dead Center (A or ATDC) may be shown as AFTER.

6. Loosen the distributor base clamp locknut. You can buy special wrenches which will make this task easy. Turn the distributor slowly to adjust the timing, holding it by the body and not the cap. Turn the distributor in the direction of rotor rotation (found in the Firing Order illustrations) to retard, and against the direction to advance.

7. Tighten the locknut. Recheck the timing just in case the distributor moved as it was tightened.

8. Shut off the engine and disconnect the light. Reattach the ECT sensor connector. Some fault codes may be set, but they can be cleared immediately only with a special test instrument (DRB-II scan tool). However, as the ignition is turned ON and OFF 50–100 times (some later model years may take less restarts to clear codes) in normal use, they will automatically be cleared by the system.

Valve Lash

ADJUSTMENT

Valve adjustment determines how far the valves enter the cylinder and how long they stay open and closed.

If the valve clearance is too large, part of the lift of the camshaft will be used in removing the excessive clearance. Consequently, the valve will not be opening as far as it should. This condition has two effects: the valve train components will emit a tapping sound as they take up the excessive clearance and the engine will perform poorly because the valves don't open fully and allow the proper amount of gases to flow into and out of the engine.

If the valve clearance is too small, the intake valve and the exhaust valves will open too far and they will not fully seat on the cylinder head when they close. When a valve seats itself on the cylinder head, it does two things: it seals the combustion chamber so that none of the gases in the cylinder escape and it cools itself by transferring some of the heat it absorbs from the combustion in the cylinder to the cylinder head and to the engine's cooling system. If the valve clearance is too small, the engine will run poorly because of the gases escaping from the combustion chamber. The valves will also become overheated and will warp, since they cannot transfer heat unless they are touching the valve seat in the cylinder head.

➡**While all valve adjustments must be made as accurately as possible, it is better to have the valve adjustment slightly loose than slightly tight as a burned valve may result from overly tight adjustments.**

2.2L and 2.5L Engines

The 2.2L and 2.5L engines use hydraulic lash adjusters. No periodic adjustment or checking is necessary.

2.6L Engine

▶ See Figures 97 and 98

The 2.6L engine has a jet valve located beside the intake valve on each cylinder. The valve arrangement on the 2.6L is simple: the intake valves and smaller jet valves are on the left-hand (radiator) side of the engine and the exhaust valves are on the right-hand (firewall) side of the engine. The cylinders are numbered 1 through 4 from the front (crankshaft pulley side) to the back (transaxle) end of the engine.

➡**When adjusting valve clearances, the jet valve must be adjusted before the intake valve.**

1. Start the engine and allow it to reach normal operating temperature.
2. Stop the engine and remove the air cleaner and its hoses. Remove any other cables, hoses, wires, etc., which are attached to the valve cover, and remove the valve cover.
3. Disconnect the high tension coil-to-distributor wire at the coil.
4. While watching the rocker arms for the No. 1 cylinder, rotate the crankshaft until the exhaust valve is closing and the intake valve has just started to open. At this point, the No. 4 cylinder piston will be at Top Dead Center (TDC) on the power stroke.
5. Loosen the locknut on cylinder No. 4 intake valve adjusting screw 2 or more turns.
6. Loosen the locknut on the jet valve adjusting screw.
7. Turn the jet valve adjusting screw counterclockwise and insert a 0.006 in. (0.15mm) feeler gauge between the jet valve stem and the adjusting screw.
8. Tighten the adjusting screw until it touches the feeler gauge.

➡**Take care not to press on the valve while adjusting, because the jet valve spring is very weak. If the adjusting screw is tight, special care must be taken to avoid pressing down on the jet valve when adjusting the clearance or a false reading will result.**

9. Tighten the locknut securely, while holding the rocker arm adjusting screw with a screwdriver to prevent it from turning.
10. Make sure that a 0.006 in. (0.15mm) feeler gauge can be easily inserted between the jet valve and the rocker arm.
11. Adjust the No. 4 cylinder intake valve to 0.006 in. (0.15mm) and its exhaust valve to 0.010 in.(0.25mm). Tighten the adjusting screw locknuts and recheck each clearance.
12. While watching the rocker arms for the No. 2 cylinder, rotate the crankshaft until the exhaust valve is closing and the intake valve has just started to open. At this point, the No. 3 cylinder piston will be at Top Dead Center (TDC) on the power stroke. Adjust the lash on No. 3 cylinder jet valve, intake valve and exhaust valve as detailed in Steps 5 through 11—make sure that the valves are adjusted for cylinder No. 3, not cylinder No. 4.
13. While watching the rocker arms for the No. 3 cylinder, once again rotate the crankshaft until the exhaust valve is closing and the intake valve

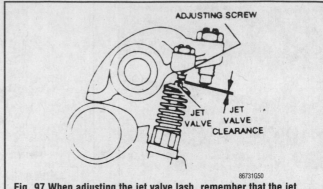

Fig. 97 When adjusting the jet valve lash, remember that the jet valve spring is easy to depress and a false reading is possible

Fig. 98 Once the correct lash is achieved, hold the adjusting screw while tightening the locknut

has just started to open. At this point, the No. 2 cylinder piston will be at Top Dead Center (TDC) on the power stroke. Adjust the lash on No. 2 cylinder jet valve, intake valve and exhaust valve as detailed in Steps 5 through 11—make sure that the valves are adjusted for cylinder No. 2, not cylinder No. 4.
14. And finally while watching the rocker arms for the No. 4 cylinder, rotate the crankshaft until the exhaust valve is closing and the intake valve has just started to open. At this point, the No. 1 cylinder piston will be at Top Dead Center (TDC) on the power stroke. Adjust the lash on No. 1 cylinder jet valve, intake valve and exhaust valve as detailed in Steps 5 through 11—make sure that the valves are adjusted for cylinder No. 1, not cylinder No. 4.
15. Replace the valve cover and all other components. Make sure to apply sealer to the top surface of the semi-circular packing. For more details on installing the rocker arm covers, refer to Section 3.
16. Run the engine and check for oil leaks at the valve cover.

Idle Speed and Mixture Adjustments

Idle speed and mixture adjustments are not considered periodic adjustments by Chrysler. If idle speed or mixture requires adjustment, refer to either the carburetor adjustments or the specific fuel injection throttle body adjustments in Section 5.

GASOLINE ENGINE TUNE-UP SPECIFICATIONS

Year	Engine ID/VIN	Engine Displacement Liters (cc)	Spark Plugs Gap (in.)	Ignition Timing (deg.) MT	Ignition Timing (deg.) AT	Fuel Pump (psi)	Idle Speed (rpm) MT	Idle Speed (rpm) AT	Valve Clearance In.	Valve Clearance Ex.
1981	B	2.2 (2212)	0.035	10B	10B	4.5-6.0	900	900	HYD	HYD
	D	2.6 (2556)	0.035	-	7B	4.5-6.0	-	800	0.006 ⑥	0.010 ⑥
1982	B	2.2 (2212)	0.035	12B	12B	4.5-6.0	900	900	HYD	HYD
	C	2.2 (2212)	0.035	12B	12B	4.5-6.0	900	900	HYD	HYD
	D	2.6 (2556)	0.035	-	7B	4.5-6.0	-	800	0.006 ⑥	0.010 ⑥
	G	2.6 (2556)	0.035	-	7B	4.5-6.0	-	800	0.006 ⑥	0.010 ⑥
1983	C	2.2 (2212)	0.035	10B	10B	4.5-6.0	775	900	HYD	HYD
	G	2.6 (2556)	0.035	7B	7B	4.5-6.0	800	800	0.006 ⑥	0.010 ⑥
1984	C	2.2 (2212)	0.035	10B	10B	4.5-6.0	800	800	HYD	HYD
	D	2.2 (2212)	0.035	6B	6B	4.5-6.0	800 ②	750	HYD	HYD
	E	2.6 (2556)	0.035	12B	12B	14.5	850	850	0.006 ⑥	0.010 ⑥
1985	C	2.2 (2212)	0.035	7B	7B	4.5-6.0	950	800	HYD	HYD
	D	2.2 (2212)	0.035	10B	10B	4.5-6.0	850	750	HYD	HYD
	E	2.6 (2556)	0.035	12B	12B	14.5	950	950	0.006 ⑥	0.010 ⑥
	G	2.6 (2556)	0.040 ③	7B	7B	4.5-6.0	800	800	0.006 ⑧	0-10 ⑥
1986	C	2.2 (2212)	0.035	10B	10B	4.5-6.0	800 ②	800	HYD	HYD
	D	2.2 (2212)	0.035	12B	12B	14.5	900	700	HYD	HYD
	E	2.5 (2507)	0.035	12B	12B	55	900	800	HYD	HYD
1987	K	2.5 (2507)	0.035	12B	15B	55	900 ④	800	HYD	HYD
	A	2.2 (2212)	0.035	12B	12B	14.5	900	800	HYD	HYD
	D	2.2 (2212)	0.035	12B	12B	55	900	800	HYD	HYD
	E	2.5 (2507)	0.035	15B	15B	14.5	900	800	HYD	HYD
1988	K	2.2 (2212)	0.035	12B	12B	14.5	900 ④	800	HYD	HYD
	A	2.2 (2212)	0.035	12B	12B	55	900	800	HYD	HYD
	D	2.2 (2212)	0.035	12B	12B	14.5	900	800	HYD	HYD
	E	2.5 (2507)	0.035	12B	12B	55	800 ④	800	HYD	HYD
1989	A	2.2 (2212)	0.035	12B	12B	55	900	800	HYD	HYD
	D	2.2 (2212)	0.035	12B	12B	14.5	900	800	HYD	HYD
	P	2.2 (2212)	0.035	12B	-	55	900	900	HYD	HYD
	R	2.2 (2212)	0.035	12B	12B	55	900	-	0.012 ⑦	0.016 ⑦
	J	2.5 (2507)	0.035	12B	12B	55	800	800	HYD	HYD
	K	2.5 (2507)	0.035	12B	12B	14.5	800	800	HYD	HYD
	E	2.2 (2212)	0.035	12B	12B	55	900	800	HYD	HYD

① Early Shadow convertible: 14.5 psi / All others: 39 psi
② Canada: 900 rpm
③ Canada: 0.035 in.
④ Canada: 750 rpm
⑤ Non-adjustable; refer to the underhood specifications sticker
⑥ Hot engine
⑦ Cold engine

86731C08

GASOLINE ENGINE TUNE-UP SPECIFICATIONS

Year	Engine ID/VIN	Engine Displacement Liters (cc)	Spark Plugs Gap (in.)	Ignition Timing (deg.) MT	Ignition Timing (deg.) AT	Fuel Pump (psi)	Idle Speed (rpm) MT	Idle Speed (rpm) AT	Valve Clearance In.	Valve Clearance Ex.
1990	C	2.2 (2212)	0.035	12B	-	55	900	-	HYD	HYD
	D	2.2 (2212)	0.035	12B	12B	14.5	850	850	HYD	HYD
	R	2.2 (2212)	0.030	12B	-	55	900	-	0.012 ⑦	0.016 ⑦
	J	2.5 (2507)	0.035	12B	12B	55	900	800	HYD	HYD
	K	2.5 (2507)	0.035	12B	12B	14.5	850	850	HYD	HYD
1991	A	2.2 (2212)	0.035	NA	-	55	NA	NA	HYD	HYD
	D	2.2 (2212)	0.085	12B	12B	39	NA	NA	HYD	HYD
	J	2.5 (2507)	0.085	12B	12B	55	NA	NA	HYD	HYD
	K	2.5 (2507)	0.095	12B	12B	①	NA	NA	HYD	HYD
1992	A	2.2 (2212)	0.095	NA	-	55	NA	NA	HYD	HYD
	D	2.2 (2212)	0.045	12B	12B	39	NA	NA	HYD	HYD
	J	2.5 (2507)	0.045	12B	12B	55	NA	NA	HYD	HYD
	K	2.5 (2507)	0.045	12B	12B	39	NA	-	HYD	HYD
1993	A	2.2 (2212)	0.035	NA	-	55	NA	NA	HYD	HYD
	D	2.2 (2212)	0.035	12B	12B	39	NA	NA	HYD	HYD
	K	2.5 (2507)	0.035	12B	12B	39	NA	NA	HYD	HYD
	V	2.5 (2507)	0.035	-	12B	55	NA	NA	HYD	HYD
1994	D	2.2 (2212)	0.035	12B	12B	39	NA	NA	HYD	HYD
	K	2.5 (2507)	0.035	12B	12B	55	NA	NA	HYD	HYD
	V	2.5 (2507)	0.035	-	12B	39	NA	NA	HYD	HYD
1995	K	2.5 (2507)	0.035	12B	12B	39	NA	-	HYD	HYD
	V	2.5 (2507)	0.035	-	12B	55	-	-	HYD	HYD

NOTE: The Vehicle Emission Control Information label often reflects specification changes made during production. The label figures must be used if they differ from those in this chart.
NOTE: Idle speed on fuel injected models is controlled by the Powertrain Control Module (PCM) and is not adjustable.
B - Before top dead center
HYD - Hydraulic
NA - Not Available

① Early Shadow convertible: 14.5 psi
All others: 39 psi
② Canada: 900 rpm
③ Canada: 0.035 in.
④ Canada: 750 rpm
⑤ Non-adjustable; refer to the underhood specifications sticker
⑥ Hot engine
⑦ Cold engine

86731C09

Air Conditioning System

SYSTEM SERVICE & REPAIR

➡It is recommended that the A/C system be serviced by an EPA Section 609 certified automotive technician utilizing a refrigerant recovery/recycling machine.

The do-it-yourselfer should not service his/her own vehicle's A/C system for many reasons, including legal concerns, personal injury, environmental damage and cost.

According to the U.S. Clean Air Act, it is a federal crime to service or repair (involving the refrigerant) a Motor Vehicle Air Conditioning (MVAC) system for money without being EPA certified. It is also illegal to vent R-12 and R-134a refrigerants into the atmosphere. State and/or local laws may be more strict than the federal regulations, so be sure to check with your state and/or local authorities for further information.

➡Federal law dictates that a fine of up to $25,000 may be levied on people convicted of venting refrigerant into the atmosphere.

When servicing an A/C system you run the risk of handling or coming in contact with refrigerant, which may result in skin or eye irritation or frostbite. Although low in toxicity (due to chemical stability), inhalation of concentrated refrigerant fumes is dangerous and can result in death; cases of fatal cardiac arrhythmia have been reported in people accidentally subjected to high levels of refrigerant. Some early symptoms include loss of concentration and drowsiness.

➡Generally, the limit for exposure is lower for R-134a than it is for R-12. Exceptional care must be practiced when handling R-134a.

Also, some refrigerants can decompose at high temperatures (near gas heaters or open flame), which may result in hydrofluoric acid, hydrochloric acid and phosgene (a fatal nerve gas).

It is usually more economically feasible to have a certified MVAC automotive technician perform A/C system service on your vehicle.

R-12 Refrigerant Conversion

If your vehicle still uses R-12 refrigerant, one way to save A/C system costs down the road is to investigate the possibility of having your system converted to R-134a. The older R-12 systems can be easily converted to R-134a refrigerant by a certified automotive technician by installing a few new components and changing the system oil.

The cost of R-12 is steadily rising and will continue to increase, because it is no longer imported or manufactured in the United States. Therefore, it is often possible to have an R-12 system converted to R-134a and recharged for less than it would cost to just charge the system with R-12.

If you are interested in having your system converted, contact local automotive service stations for more details and information.

PREVENTIVE MAINTENANCE

Although the A/C system should not be serviced by the do-it-yourselfer, preventive maintenance should be practiced to help maintain the efficiency of the vehicle's A/C system. Be sure to perform the following:

• The easiest and most important preventive maintenance for your A/C system is to be sure that it is used on a regular basis. Running the system for five minutes each month (no matter what the season) will help ensure that the seals and all internal components remain lubricated.

➡Some vehicles automatically operate the A/C system compressor whenever the windshield defroster is activated. Therefore, the A/C system would not need to be operated each month if the defroster was used.

• In order to prevent heater core freeze-up during A/C operation, it is necessary to maintain proper antifreeze protection. Be sure to properly maintain the engine cooling system.

• Any obstruction of or damage to the condenser configuration will restrict air flow which is essential to its efficient operation. Keep this unit clean and in proper physical shape.

➡Bug screens which are mounted in front of the condenser (unless they are original equipment) are regarded as obstructions.

• The condensation drain tube expels any water which accumuiates on the bottom of the evaporator housing into the engine compartment. If this tube is obstructed, the air conditioning performance can be restricted and condensation buildup can spill over onto the vehicle's floor.

SYSTEM INSPECTION

Although the A/C system should not be serviced by the do-it-yourselfer, system inspections should be performed to help maintain the efficiency of the vehicle's A/C system. Be sure to perform the following:

The easiest and often most important check for the air conditioning system consists of a visual inspection of the system components. Visually inspect the system for refrigerant leaks, damaged compressor clutch, abnormal compressor drive belt tension and/or condition, plugged evaporator drain tube, blocked condenser fins, disconnected or broken wires, blown fuses, corroded connections and poor insulation.

A refrigerant leak will usually appear as an oily residue at the leakage point in the system. The oily residue soon picks up dust or dirt particles from the surrounding air and appears greasy. Through time, this will build up and appear to be a heavy dirt impregnated grease.

For a thorough visual and operational inspection, check the following:
• Check the surface of the radiator and condenser for dirt, leaves or other material which might block air flow.
• Check for kinks in hoses and lines. Check the system for leaks.
• Make sure the drive belt is properly tensioned. During operation, make sure the belt is free of noise or slippage.
• Make sure the blower motor operates at all appropriate positions, then check for distribution of the air from all outlets.

➡Remember that in high humidity, air discharged from the vents may not feel as cold as expected, even if the system is working properly. This is because moisture in humid air retains heat more effectively than dry air, thereby making humid air more difficult to cool.

Windshield Wipers

▶ See Figures 99, 100 and 101

For maximum effectiveness and longest element life, the windshield and wiper blades should be kept clean. Dirt, tree sap, road tar and so on will cause streaking, smearing and blade deterioration if left on the glass. It is advisable to wash the windshield carefully with a commercial glass cleaner at least once a month. Wipe off the rubber blades with the wet rag afterwards. Do not attempt to move wipers across the windshield by hand; damage to the motor and drive mechanism will result.

To inspect and/or replace the wiper blade elements, place the wiper switch in the **LOW** speed position and the ignition switch in the **ACC** position. When the wiper blades are approximately vertical on the windshield, turn the ignition switch to **OFF**.

Examine the wiper blade elements. If they are found to be cracked, broken or torn, they should be replaced immediately. Replacement intervals will vary with usage, although ozone deterioration usually limits element life to about one year. If the wiper pattern is smeared or streaked, or if the blade chatters across the glass, the elements should be replaced. It is easiest and most sensible to replace the elements in pairs.

If your vehicle is equipped with aftermarket blades, there are several different types of refills and your vehicle might have any kind. Aftermarket blades and arms rarely use the exact same type blade or refill as the original equipment.

Regardless of the type of refill used, be sure to follow the part manufacturer's instructions closely. Make sure that all of the frame jaws are engaged as the refill is pushed into place and locked. If the metal blade holder and frame are allowed to touch the glass during wiper operation, the glass will be scratched.

Tires and Wheels

Common sense and good driving habits will afford maximum tire life. Make sure that you don't overload the vehicle or run with incorrect pressure in the tires. Either of these will increase tread wear. Fast starts, sudden stops and sharp cornering are hard on tires and will shorten their useful life span.

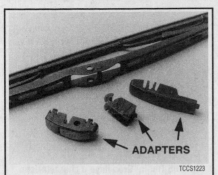

Fig. 99 Most aftermarket blades are available with multiple adapters to fit different vehicles

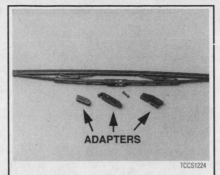

Fig. 100 Choose a blade which will fit your vehicle, and that will be readily available next time you need blades

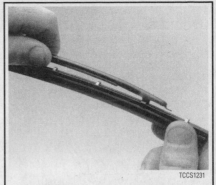

Fig. 101 When installed, be certain the blade is fully inserted into the backing

➡ For optimum tire life, keep the tires properly inflated, rotate them often and have the wheel alignment checked periodically.

Inspect your tires frequently. Be especially careful to watch for bubbles in the tread or sidewall, deep cuts or underinflation. Replace any tires with bubbles in the sidewall. If cuts are so deep that they penetrate to the cords, discard the tire. Any cut in the sidewall of a radial tire renders it unsafe. Also look for uneven tread wear patterns that may indicate the front end is out of alignment or that the tires are out of balance.

TIRE ROTATION

▶ See Figure 102

Tires must be rotated periodically to equalize wear patterns that vary with a tire's position on the vehicle. Tires will also wear in an uneven way as the front steering/suspension system wears to the point where the alignment should be reset.

Rotating the tires will ensure maximum life for the tires as a set, so you will not have to discard a tire early due to wear on only part of the tread. Regular rotation is required to equalize wear.

When rotating "unidirectional tires," make sure that they always roll in the same direction. This means that a tire used on the left side of the vehicle must not be switched to the right side and vice-versa. Such tires should only be rotated front-to-rear or rear-to-front, while always remaining on the same side of the vehicle. These tires are marked on the sidewall as to the direction of rotation; observe the marks when reinstalling the tire(s).

Some styled or "mag" wheels may have different offsets front to rear. In these cases, the rear wheels must not be used up front and vice-versa. Furthermore, if these wheels are equipped with unidirectional tires, they cannot be rotated unless the tire is remounted for the proper direction of rotation.

➡ The compact or space-saver spare is strictly for emergency use. It must never be included in the tire rotation or placed on the vehicle for everyday use.

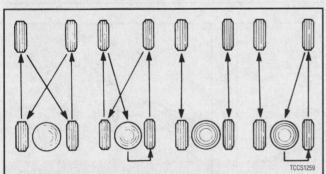

Fig. 102 Common tire rotation patterns for 4 and 5-wheel rotations—if the vehicle is equipped with a space saver spare, use the 4-wheel rotation

TIRE DESIGN

▶ See Figure 103

For maximum satisfaction, tires should be used in sets of four. Mixing of different brands or types (radial, bias-belted, fiberglass belted) should be avoided. In most cases, the vehicle manufacturer has designated a type of tire on which the vehicle will perform best. Your first choice when replacing tires should be to use the same type of tire that the manufacturer recommends.

When radial tires are used, tire sizes and wheel diameters should be selected to maintain ground clearance and tire load capacity equivalent to the original specified tire. Radial tires should always be used in sets of four.

✳ CAUTION

Radial tires should never be used on only the front axle.

When selecting tires, pay attention to the original size as marked on the tire. Most tires are described using an industry size code sometimes referred to as P-Metric. This allows the exact identification of the tire specifications, regardless of the manufacturer. If selecting a different tire size or brand, remember to check the installed tire for any sign of interference with the body or suspension while the vehicle is stopping, turning sharply or heavily loaded.

Snow Tires

Good radial tires can produce a big advantage in slippery weather, but in snow, a street radial tire does not have sufficient tread to provide traction and control. The small grooves of a street tire quickly pack with snow and the tire behaves like a billiard ball on a marble floor. The more open, chunky tread of a snow tire will self-clean as the tire turns, providing much better grip on snowy surfaces.

To satisfy municipalities requiring snow tires during weather emergencies, most snow tires carry either an M + S designation after the tire size stamped on the sidewall, or the designation "all-season." In general, no change in tire size is necessary when buying snow tires.

Most manufacturers strongly recommend the use of 4 snow tires on their vehicles for reasons of stability. If snow tires are fitted only to the drive wheels, the opposite end of the vehicle may become very unstable when braking or turning on slippery surfaces. This instability can lead to unpleasant endings if the driver can't counteract the slide in time.

Note that snow tires, whether 2 or 4, will affect vehicle handling in all non-snow situations. The stiffer, heavier snow tires will noticeably change the turning and braking characteristics of the vehicle. Once the snow tires are installed, you must re-learn the behavior of the vehicle and drive accordingly.

➡ Consider buying extra wheels on which to mount the snow tires. Once done, the "snow wheels" can be installed and removed as needed. This eliminates the potential damage to tires or wheels from seasonal removal and installation. Even if your vehicle has styled wheels, see if inexpensive steel wheels are available. Although the look of the vehicle will change, the expensive wheels will be protected from salt, curb hits and pothole damage.

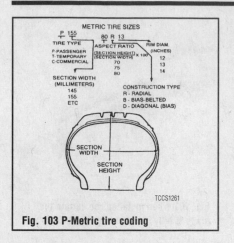

Fig. 103 P-Metric tire coding

Fig. 104 Tires with deep cuts, or cuts which bulge, should be replaced immediately

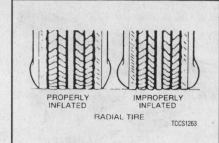

Fig. 105 Radial tires have a characteristic sidewall bulge; don't try to measure pressure by looking at the tire. Use a quality air pressure gauge

TIRE STORAGE

If they are mounted on wheels, store the tires at proper inflation pressure. All tires should be kept in a cool, dry place. If they are stored in the garage or basement, do not let them stand on a concrete floor; set them on strips of wood, a mat or a large stack of newspaper. Keeping them away from direct moisture is of paramount importance. Tires should not be stored upright, but in a flat position.

INFLATION & INSPECTION

▶ **See Figures 104 thru 109**

The importance of proper tire inflation cannot be overemphasized. A tire employs air as part of its structure. It is designed around the supporting strength of the air at a specified pressure. For this reason, improper inflation drastically reduces the tire's ability to perform as intended. A tire will lose some air in day-to-day use; having to add a few pounds of air periodically is not necessarily a sign of a leaking tire.

Two items should be a permanent fixture in every glove compartment: an accurate tire pressure gauge and a tread depth gauge. Check the tire pressure (including the spare) regularly with a pocket type gauge. Too often, the gauge on the end of the air hose at your corner garage is not accurate because it suffers too much abuse. Always check tire pressure when the tires are cold, as pressure increases with temperature. If you must move the vehicle to check the tire inflation, do not drive more than a mile before checking. A cold tire is generally one that has not been driven for more than three hours.

A plate or sticker is normally provided somewhere in the vehicle (door post, hood, tailgate or trunk lid) which shows the proper pressure for the tires. Never counteract excessive pressure build-up by bleeding off air pressure (letting some air out). This will cause the tire to run hotter and wear quicker.

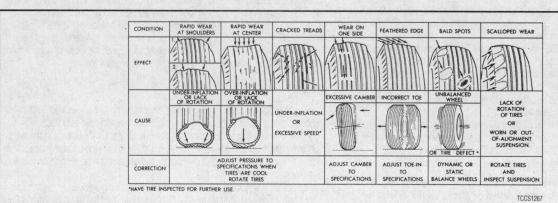

Fig. 106 Common tire wear patterns and causes

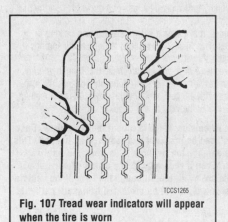

Fig. 107 Tread wear indicators will appear when the tire is worn

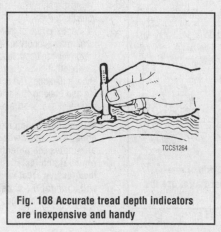

Fig. 108 Accurate tread depth indicators are inexpensive and handy

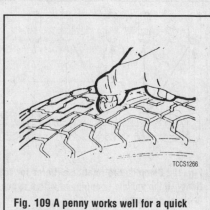

Fig. 109 A penny works well for a quick check of tread depth

✲✲ CAUTION

Never exceed the maximum tire pressure embossed on the tire! This is the pressure to be used when the tire is at maximum loading, but it is rarely the correct pressure for everyday driving. Consult the owner's manual or the tire pressure sticker for the correct tire pressure.

Once you've maintained the correct tire pressures for several weeks, you'll be familiar with the vehicle's braking and handling personality. Slight adjustments in tire pressures can fine-tune these characteristics, but never change the cold pressure specification by more than 2 psi. A slightly softer tire pressure will give a softer ride but also yield lower fuel mileage. A slightly harder tire will give crisper dry road handling but can cause skidding on wet surfaces. Unless you're fully attuned to the vehicle, stick to the recommended inflation pressures.

All automotive tires have built-in tread wear indicator bars that show up as ½ in. (13mm) wide smooth bands across the tire when ¹⁄₁₆ in. (1.5mm) of tread remains. The appearance of tread wear indicators means that the tires should be replaced. In fact, many states have laws prohibiting the use of tires with less than this amount of tread.

You can check your own tread depth with an inexpensive gauge or by using a Lincoln head penny. Slip the Lincoln penny (with Lincoln's head upside-down) into several tread grooves. If you can see the top of Lincoln's head in 2 adjacent grooves, the tire has less than ¹⁄₁₆ in. (1.5mm) tread left and should be replaced. You can measure snow tires in the same manner by using the "tails" side of the Lincoln penny. If you can see the top of the Lincoln memorial, it's time to replace the snow tire(s).

FLUIDS AND LUBRICANTS

Fluid Disposal

Used fluids such as engine oil, transmission fluid, antifreeze and brake fluid are hazardous wastes and must be disposed of properly. Before draining any fluids, consult with your local authorities; in many areas waste oil, etc. is being accepted as a part of recycling programs. A number of service stations and auto parts stores are also accepting waste fluids for recycling.

Be sure of the recycling center's policies before draining any fluids, as many will not accept different fluids that have been mixed together.

Fuel and Engine Oil Recommendations

OIL

Non-Flexible Fuel Models

♦ **See Figures 110 and 111**

Chrysler Corporation recommends the use of a high quality, heavy duty detergent oil with the proper viscosity for prevailing conditions. Oils labeled SG/CC are satisfactory for use in all non-turbocharged engines; however, a higher quality oil, labeled SG/CD is preferred and necessary for turbocharged models.

It's important to recognize the distinctions between these oil types and the additional stresses put on oil used in turbocharged engines. Since the turbocharger bearings receive heat conducted directly from the unit's turbine, which may reach a cherry-red heat, oil passing through these bearings may reach temperatures high enough to cause chemical breakdown. This problem is especially severe right when the engine is shut down. Also, the additional power a turbocharged engine produces translates to higher mechanical loads and oil temperatures within the rest of the engine.

The CD designated oil has chemical additives capable of resisting this breakdown and countering its effects. If your car is turbocharged, it will almost surely pay you to use the better designation.

Oil must also meet viscosity standards. Follow the chart below precisely. Make sure the oil you buy is clearly labeled so as to confirm to both these basic standards.

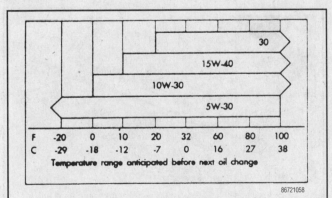

Fig. 110 Oil viscosity recommendations for 1981–88 models

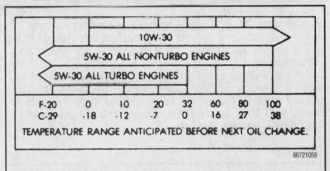

Fig. 111 Oil viscosity recommendations for 1989–95 models

Use only quality oils. Never use straight mineral or non-detergent oils, that is, oils not equipped with special cleaning agents. You must not only choose the grade of oil, but the viscosity number. Viscosity refers to the thickness of the oil. It's actually measured by how rapidly it flows though a hole of calibrated size. Thicker oil flows more slowly and has higher viscosity numbers—SAE 40 or 50. Thinner oil flows more easily and has lower numbers—SAE 10 or 20.

Chrysler recommends the use of what are called "multigrade" oils. These are specially formulated to change their viscosity with a change in temperature, unlike straight grade oils. The oils are designated by the use of two numbers, the first referring to the thickness of the oil, relative to straight mineral oils, at a low temperature such as 0°F (–18°C). The second number refers to the thickness, also relative to straight mineral oils, at high temperatures typical of highway driving (200°F/93°C). These numbers are preceded by the designation "SAE," representing the Society of Automotive Engineers which sets the viscosity standards. For example, use of an SAE 10W–40 oil would give nearly ideal engine operation under almost all operating conditions. The oil would be as thin as a straight 10 weight oil at cold cranking temperatures, and as thick as a straight 40 weight oil at hot running conditions.

Flexible Fuel Models

✲✲ WARNING

If flexible fuel engine oil is not used, engine wear may be increased significantly.

When operating a vehicle on M–85 fuel either full or part time, use on the specific flexible fuel engine oil such as Chryslers MS-9214 or equivalent. Equivalent oils may be labeled Multi-Fuel, Variable Fuel, Flexible Fuel, etc. These engine oils may be satisfactory if met with the Chrysler standards.

If you operate the vehicle ONLY on regular unleaded gasoline, use the oil that meets the standards of Chryslers MS–6395 or equivalent. The quality level of the engine oil must meet the SG or SG/CD API standards. SAE 10W–30 engine oil is preferred for use in the flexible fuel engines.

SYNTHETIC OIL

There are excellent synthetic and fuel-efficient oils available that, under the right circumstances, can help provide better fuel mileage and better engine protection. However, these advantages come at a price, which can be more than the cost per quart of conventional motor oils.

Before pouring any synthetic oils into your vehicle's engine, you should consider the condition of the engine and the type of driving you do. Also, check the manufacturer's warranty conditions regarding the use of synthetics.

Generally, it is best to avoid the use of synthetic oil in both brand new and older, high mileage engines. New engines require a proper break-in, and the synthetics are so slippery that they can hinder this. Most manufacturers recommend that you wait at least 5,000 miles (8000 km) before switching to a synthetic oil. Conversely, older engines are looser and tend to use more oil. Synthetics will slip past worn parts more readily than regular oil. If your car already leaks oil (due to worn parts and bad seals or gaskets), it will leak more with a slippery synthetic inside.

Consider your type of driving. If most of your accumulated mileage is on the highway at higher, steadier speeds, a synthetic oil will reduce friction and probably help deliver fuel mileage. Under such ideal highway conditions, the oil change interval can be extended, as long as the oil filter will operate effectively for the extended life of the oil. If the filter can't do its job for this extended period, dirt and sludge will build up in your engine's crankcase, sump, oil pump and lines, no matter what type of oil is used. If using synthetic oil in this manner, you should continue to change the oil filter at the recommended intervals.

Cars used under harder, stop-and-go, short hop circumstances should always be serviced more frequently, and for these vehicles, synthetic oil may not be a wise investment. Because of the necessary shorter change interval needed for this type of driving, you cannot take advantage of the long recommended change interval of most synthetic oils.

GASOLINE

Non-Flexible Fuel Vehicles

A prime requirement for gasoline is the use of unleaded fuel only. All the vehicles covered in this manual require the use of unleaded fuel exclusively, to protect the catalytic converter. Failure to follow this recommendation will result in failure of the catalyst and consequent failure to pass the emission test many states now require. The use of unleaded fuel also prolongs the life of spark plugs, the engine as a whole, and the exhaust system.

Fuels of the same octane rating have varying anti-knock qualities. Thus, if your engine knocks or pings, try switching brands of gasoline before trying a more expensive higher octane fuel. Fuel should be selected for the brand and octane which performs without pinging.

Your engine's fuel requirements can change with time, due to carbon buildup which changes the compression ratio. If switching brands or grades of gas doesn't work, check the ignition timing. If it is necessary to retard timing from specifications, don't change it more than about 4°. Retarded timing will reduce power output and fuel mileage and increase engine temperature.

Basic engine octane requirements, to be used in your initial choice of fuel, are 87 octane, unleaded. This rating is an average of Research and Motor methods of determination: (R+M)/2. For increased vehicle performance and gas mileage use a premium unleaded fuel, that is, one with a rating of 91 octane. More octane results in better performance and economy in these engines because the ignition system will compensate for their characteristics by advancing the timing.

Gasohol consisting of 10% ethanol and gasoline may be used in your car, but gasoline containing methanol (wood alcohol) is not approved. They can damage fuel system parts and cause operating problems.

Flexible Fuel Vehicles

PRECAUTIONS

✳ CAUTION

Methanol is more toxic than gasoline and can cause serious injury or even death. To help prevent any personal injury, read the following precautions before working around methanol fuel.

- Breathing methanol vapors can seriously effect your nervous system. You could experience headaches, dizziness, and even unconsciousness. Avoid breathing these vapors.

- Swallowing methanol can cause death, blindness, or other serious injury. Symptoms of indigestion, such as nausea, diarrhea are not always immediate and can be delayed.

- Contact with your eyes could result in blindness or blurred vision along with damage to the eye tissue.

- Prolonged skin contact could result in dry skin, an allergic reaction, or absorption through the skin.

- Anyone taking medication for alcoholism treatment might have the same reaction as if alcohol had been consumed if their skin contacts methanol, or if there has been **any inhalation** of methanol fumes.

M–85 is a mixture of approximately 85% methanol and 15% unleaded gasoline. This fuel helps reduce the smog causing conditions of emissions, and reduces dependence on foreign oil.

Engine

OIL LEVEL CHECK

▶ **See Figures 112 and 113**

✳ CAUTION

The EPA warns that prolonged contact with used engine oil may cause a number of skin disorders, including cancer! You should make every effort to minimize your exposure to used engine oil. Protective gloves should be worn when changing the oil. Wash your hands and any other exposed skin areas as soon as possible after exposure to used engine oil. Soap and water, or waterless hand cleaner should be used.

As often as you stop for fuel check the engine oil as follows:
1. Park the vehicle on a level surface (if the vehicle is not level, the reading will not be completely accurate).
2. If the vehicle has been running, stop the engine and allow it to sit for a full ten minutes. If the engine is cold, check the oil before starting it. It does not

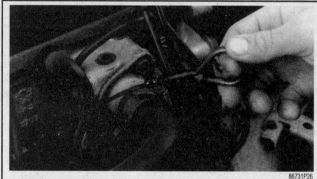

Fig. 112 To inspect the oil level, remove the oil dipstick . . .

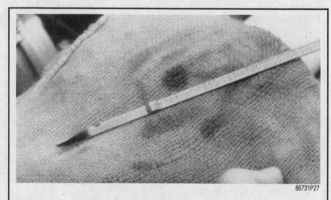

Fig. 113 . . . and inspect the oil level on the end of the dipstick matter whether the oil is hot or cold, as long as it has had time to drain out of the engine itself and into the oil pan.

3. Open the hood and locate the dipstick (it is located on the radiator side of the engine). It consists of a T-handle running into a tube which is connected to the engine. Pull the dipstick out and wipe all the oil off the bottom with a clean rag. If this is not done, you will not get an accurate reading of the oil level.

4. Re-insert the dipstick and make sure it goes all the way into the tube. Then, pull it out and read it on the side with the oil level scale (two lines, two dots, etc.).

a. If the oil level is above the lower line, although the oil level is high enough, you should still add enough oil to bring the level up to the upper mark. Usually the amount of oil needed to bring the level from the lower mark to the upper mark is one quart, however you should fill the oil slowly and check often. It is important not to overfill the engine.

b. If it is right near or at the lower line, add oil slowly (⅓ or ½ quart) and check the level often. Fill the oil up to the upper mark, but do not over-fill.

c. If the oil is below the lower line, add oil, ⅓ or ½ quart at a time, until the level is at the upper mark. A beginning level below the lower line indicates that either you are not checking the oil level frequently enough or that the engine is using too much oil.

➡ **Running the engine with the oil below the lower line may contribute to excessive heat and dirt in the oil, and will leave you with insufficient reserve to allow for normal oil consumption—you could run out on the road. However, you should not add oil to the point where the level is significantly above the upper line. Under these conditions, the rotating crankshaft will cause the oil to foam, which can be damaging to the engine and will sometimes cause valve train noise.**

5. To add oil, unscrew the cap on the valve cover on top of the engine and pour the oil into the engine. Be sure to use only approved oil. Avoid letting any dirt get into the engine, and make sure to reinstall the cap before starting the engine.

➡**Do not overfill the crankcase. This will cause oil aeration and loss of oil pressure.**

OIL AND FILTER CHANGE

▶ **See Figures 114, 115, 116 and 117**

❋❋ CAUTION

The EPA warns that prolonged contact with used engine oil may cause a number of skin disorders, including cancer! You should make every effort to minimize your exposure to used engine oil. Protective gloves should be worn when changing the oil. Wash your hands and any other exposed skin areas as soon as possible after exposure to used engine oil. Soap and water, or waterless hand cleaner should be used.

➡**The manufacturer recommends that the oil filter be changed at every other oil change, after the initial change, which can be effective maintenance. Chilton, however, recommends changing the filter with every oil change to ensure longer engine life by lowering the chance of filter clogging and the increased engine wear this would cause. Further, replacing the filter removes a substantial amount of dirty oil whose additives are depleted—an amount that otherwise remains in the system.**

Always drain the oil after the engine has been running long enough to bring it to operating temperature. It's best to actually drive the vehicle until the temperature gauge reaches normal operating temperature to help ensure the oil will be as warm as possible. Hot oil will flow out of the oil pan more easily and will keep contaminants in suspension so that they will be removed with the oil instead of staying in the pan. You will need a large capacity oil pan—usually about 6 qt. (6.4 l) capacity is best. Just make sure the capacity of the pan is greater than the oil pan and filter as shown in the Capacities chart. You will also need a strap wrench to loosen the filter, and an ordinary set of open-end wrenches. You can purchase tools and supplies at any store which sells automotive parts. It is also necessary for you to have some clean rags available to clean up inevitable spills.

You should also make plans to dispose properly of the used oil. Sometimes a local service station or garage will sell its used oil to a reprocessor. You may be able to add your used oil to his oil drain tank.

1. Warm the engine as described above.
2. Turn the engine **OFF** and remove the oil filler cap.
3. Support the vehicle securely on jackstands or ramps. If you can work under the vehicle at its normal height, this is okay provided the wheels are chocked.

❋❋ CAUTION

Never crawl under the vehicle while it is only supported by a jack designed for tire changing.

4. Place the drain pan under the oil pan. It should be located where the stream of oil running out of the drain hole will run into the pan—not just directly below the drain hole.

5. Loosen the drain plug using a box wrench or a ratchet, short extension and socket. Turn the plug out slowly by hand, using a rag to shield your fingers from the hot oil. By keeping inward pressure on the plug with your fingers as you unscrew it, oil won't escape past the threads and you can remove it without being burned by hot oil.

6. Quickly withdraw the drain plug and move your hands out of the way, but make sure you keep hold of the plug so that it does not drop into the pan. Wipe the plug with a clean rag. Put it in a safe place—one where it won't get kicked or bumped out of sight. As the oil drains, the stream may shift as the level in the pan changes. Keep your eye on the stream and shift the pan as needed.

❋❋ CAUTION

Be careful! The oil can be extremely hot and cause painful burns. Use rubber gloves, if necessary.

7. Allow the oil to drain completely in the pan, then install and carefully tighten the drain plug. Use a new drain plug washer if necessary. Be careful not to overtighten the drain plug, otherwise you will be buying a new pan or a trick replacement plug for stripped threads.

Fig. 114 To drain the engine oil, raise the vehicle and locate the drain plug, . . .

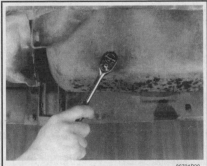

Fig. 115 . . . loosen and remove the drain plug with a wrench or ratchet wrench, and . . .

Fig. 116 . . . allow the used engine oil to drain completely into the catch pan

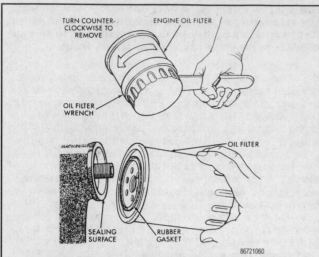

Fig. 117 Before installation, make certain that the rubber gasket has a film of new, clean oil on it

8. Move the pan under the oil filter. Use a strap-type or cap-type wrench to loosen the oil filter. Cover your hand with a rag and spin the filter off by hand; turn it slowly. Keep in mind that it's holding about one quart of dirty, hot oil. Empty the filter into the drain pan.

➡**If the oil filter cannot be loosened by conventional methods, punch a hole through both sides at the mounting base of the filter, insert a punch and use it to break the oil filter loose. After the oil filter is loosened, remove the oil filter from the engine with a oil filter wrench or by hand.**

9. With a clean rag, wipe off the filter adapter on the engine block. Make sure that no lint from the rag remains on the adapter as it could clog an oil passage. Also make sure the rubber gasket from the old filter did not remain on the adapter.

10. Using your finger, apply a film of new oil to the rubber gasket on the top of the new oil filter. Read the directions on the side of the filter, or on the box it came in, to ascertain how tightly it should be installed. Carefully screw the new filter onto the oil filter mounting pad. If the filter becomes immediately difficult to turn, it is probably crossthreaded. Remove the filter and continue to install it until the filter goes on and turns easily. Once the threads do start, turn the filter gently until it just touches the engine block; it will suddenly get harder to turn at this point.

11. You may want to mark the filter at this point so you'll know just how far you turn it. By hand, turn it an additional ½–¾ turn, or as specified by the filter manufacturer. If the filter is turned past this point, the rubber gasket may leak.

12. Wipe the drain plug area on the oil pan and carefully reinstall the drain plug. Just as with the filter, be careful not to crossthread the plug. It will easily turn well past the point where the threads have started if it's not crossthreaded.

13. Lower the vehicle back down to the ground.

14. Pour in oil to the full capacity of the oil pan and filter, as specified in the Capacities chart. Reinstall the filler cap. Just as a precaution, remove the dipstick and check the oil level. If the oil level is slightly over the upper mark on the dipstick, this is all right because the new filter has not yet been filled with oil. After the engine has been run, however, the oil level should have dropped to below the upper mark.

15. Once the engine has enough oil, start the engine, preferably without touching the throttle, as there will be no oil pressure for 10 seconds or more while the oil pump fills the filter and engine oil passages. Allow the engine to idle at the lowest possible speed until the oil light goes out or the gauge shows that oil pressure has been established. If you do not get oil pressure within 15 to 30 seconds, stop the engine and investigate. Once oil pressure is established, leave the engine running and inspect the filter and oil plug for leaks. If there is slight leakage around the filter, you might want to try to tighten it just a bit more to stop the leaks. Usually, if you've tightened it properly, the only cause of leakage is a defective filter or gasket, which would have to be replaced before you drive the truck.

16. Turn the engine **OFF**, allow the oil to drain into the pan, recheck the level, and add oil as needed.

Manual Transaxle

FLUID RECOMMENDATIONS

Some early vehicles may be equipped with the A-412 manual transaxle. This unit can be identified by locating the position of the starter which is found on the radiator side of the engine compartment. If it becomes necessary to add fluid to this unit, SAE 80W-90 gear lube is recommended.

If your vehicle has the A-460 or A-465 manual transaxle (4- and 5-speed transaxles respectively), the starter will be next to the firewall. When it becomes necessary to add fluid to this unit, Dexron®II is recommended. On the A-520 and A-555 manual transaxles used in 1987–88 models, add SAE 5W-30 SG or SG/CC or the equivalent.

On all 1989–95 models, Chrysler recommends Mopar® engine oil, SG or SG/CD SAE 5W-30 or equivalent.

LEVEL CHECK

The manual transaxle should be inspected for oil leaks and proper oil level when under vehicle service is performed. To inspect the transaxle oil level, position the vehicle on a level surface. Remove the fill plug from the transaxle side cover. The oil level should not be below ³⁄₁₆ in. (4mm) from the bottom of the oil fill opening, refer to the following procedures.

The manual transaxle does not require periodic maintenance. The oil should be changed only when water contamination is suspected. If the oil has a foamy or milky appearance, it probably is contaminated. a circular magnet located behind the differential cover collects metallic particles circulating in the oil. For proper service procedures, refer to Section 7.

1. On 1981–85 vehicles, use the right size wrench rather than an adjustable one. If you use an adjustable wrench, fit it very snugly and make sure the movable jaw is on the side toward which you are turning (that is, on the right side, if the wrench handle is below the plug).

2. On 1986–95 cars, just grab the plug with your fingers rather than using a wrench. Loosen the plug and remove it.

3. If a little fluid runs out, the level is okay. If not, feel for the presence of fluid by sticking your finger or a clean object into the hole. The level must be within ³⁄₁₆ in. (4mm) of the bottom of the hole. If necessary, add fluid with a clean syringe. Wipe off the threads, replace the filler plug, and tighten it just snug.

DRAIN AND REFILL

▶ **See Figures 118 and 119**

➡**The manual transaxle does not require periodic maintenance; refer to the vehicle owner's manual for maintenance schedules. The oil should be changed only when water contamination is suspected.**

1. Raise and support the vehicle safely on jackstands.

2. The unit has no drain plug. To drain the fluid, you will need a tube of RTV sealant and a supply of clean rags. Place a drain pan under the rear end cover of the unit (the side away from the engine and clutch).

3. Remove the bolts or studs. Gently pull the cover away from the transaxle and remove it to allow the fluid to drain.

4. Clean the magnet and the inside surface of the cover. Make sure to remove all of the old sealant. Then, use the tube of sealant to form a new gasket on the inside of the cover, as shown in the illustration.

5. Install the cover mounting bolts and tighten them to 40 ft. lbs. (54 Nm) on the A-543 models (1990–95) and on the A-520 manual transaxles used in 1988–89 models, or to 21 ft. lbs. on the A-460/465/525 models. Refill the unit with the approved fluid until it appears at the filler plug, then install and tighten the plug.

Automatic Transaxle

FLUID RECOMMENDATIONS

Dexron® II ATF should be used for all automatic transaxles up through 1986. For 1987–95 models, Chrysler recommends the use of Mopar ATF Plus (fluid

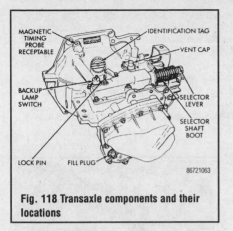

Fig. 118 Transaxle components and their locations

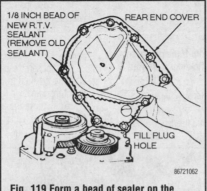

Fig. 119 Form a bead of sealer on the manual transaxle rear end cover

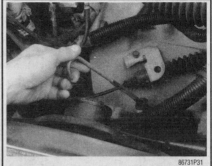

Fig. 120 With the engine idling and at normal operating temperature, remove the transaxle dipstick . . .

type (7176) for optimum transaxle performance. Dexron®II may be used if the Chrysler fluid is not available.

LEVEL CHECK

▶ **See Figures 120, 121, 122 and 123**

Inspect the fluid level on the dipstick at least every 6 months. Low fluid level can cause a variety of conditions because it allows the pump to take in air along with the fluid. As in any hydraulic system, air bubbles make the fluid spongy, therefore, pressures will be low and build up slowly.

Improper filling can also raise the fluid level too high. When the transaxle has too much fluid, the gears churn up foam and cause the same conditions which occur with a low fluid level.

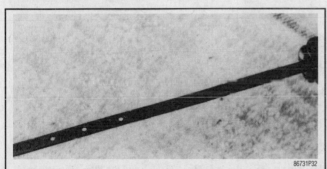

Fig. 121 . . . and inspect the transaxle fluid level against the dipstick hash marks

In either case, the air bubbles can cause overheating, fluid oxidation, and varnishing. This can interfere with normal valve, clutch, and servo operation. Foaming can also result in fluid escaping from the transaxle vent, dipstick handle) where it may be mistaken for a leak.

Along with fluid level, it is important to check the condition of the fluid. When the fluid smells burned, and is contaminated with metal or friction material particles, a complete transaxle overhaul is needed. Be sure to examine the fluid on the dipstick closely. If there is any doubt about its condition, drain out a sample for a double check.

After the fluid has been checked, seat the dipstick fully to seal out water and dirt.

1. To avoid false readings, which could produce under or over full conditions, do not check the level until the fluid is at normal operating temperature.

2. Shift the transaxle into Neutral, apply the parking brake and block the wheels.

3. Operate the engine at curb idle speed.

❊❊ WARNING

When performing underhood operations with the engine running, keep your hands well away from hot or rotating engine components. Do not wear loose articles of clothing which could become entangled in engine components or accessories.

4. Clean the dipstick filler cap and tube before removing the dipstick.

5. Remove the dipstick and inspect the fluid level. The correct level is between ADD and FULL HOT marks on the dipstick.

6. Check the fluid condition. The fluid should be dark red to light red in color and free of dirt or debris.

7. If the fluid is discolored or smells burned but the transaxle operation was OK, flush the cooler and lines and change the fluid and filter. Then road test the car again to confirm proper operation.

8. If the fluid is black or dark brown, burned or turned to sludge, and contains large quantities of metal or friction material particles, transaxle may have to be replaced; especially if the problems were evident during a road test and preliminary diagnosis.

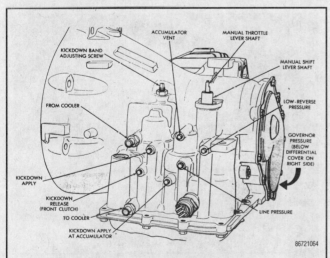

Fig. 122 Torqueflite 3-speed automatic transaxle components—41TE 4-speed automatic transaxles are similar

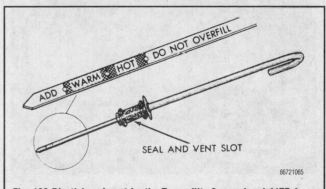

Fig. 123 Dipstick and vent for the Torqueflite 3-speed and 41TE 4-speed transaxles

DRAIN AND REFILL

♦ **See Figures 124 thru 131**

➡**To prevent dirt and water from entering the automatic transaxle after checking or replenishing fluid, make certain the dipstick cap is seated properly.**

On all vehicles refer to Vehicle Owner's Manual or Maintenance Interval Chart for mileage interval to perform the necessary service.

For this procedure a new gasket and transaxle fluid will be needed.

1. Raise the front end of the vehicle with a floor jack and support safely with jackstands.
2. If equipped, remove the splash shield.
3. Place a drain container with a large opening under the transaxle oil pan.
4. Loosen the pan bolts and tap the pan at one corner to break it loose allowing the fluid to drain, then remove the oil pan. Pour any remaining fluid out of the transaxle fluid pan.
5. Remove the transaxle fluid filter by removing the mounting bolts. Pull the filter off of the transaxle.

Fig. 124 To drain the transaxle fluid, raise the vehicle and locate the transaxle fluid pan . . .

Fig. 125 . . . then remove all but 2 of the transaxle mounting bolts

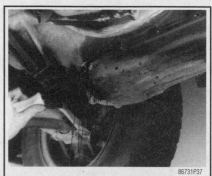

Fig. 126 Loosen the last 2 bolts and separate the pan from the transaxle to drain more fluid

Fig. 127 Remove the remaining bolts and lower the fluid pan

Fig. 128 To replace the filter, remove the filter mounting screws, then . . .

Fig. 129 . . . pull the filter off of the bottom of the transaxle

Fig. 130 Make sure to clean the transaxle-to-fluid pan mounting flange of all oil and gasket material

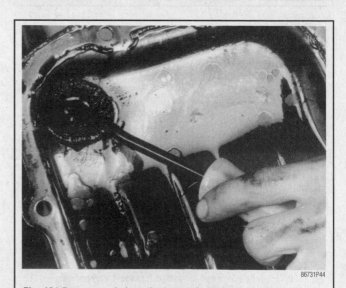

Fig. 131 Remove and clean the transaxle fluid pan magnet

To install:

6. Install a new filter and gasket on bottom of the valve body and tighten the filter retaining screws to 46 inch lbs. (5 Nm).

7. Clean the oil pan and magnet.

8. Reinstall the pan using new MOPAR® Adhesive sealant. Tighten the oil pan bolts to 14 ft. lbs. (19 Nm).

9. If equipped, install the splash shield. Lower the vehicle.

10. Pour four quarts of the correct fluid through the dipstick opening.

11. Start the engine and allow it to idle for at least one minute. Then, with the parking and service brakes applied, move the selector lever momentarily to each position, ending in the Park or Neutral position.

12. Add sufficient fluid to bring the level to ⅛ in. (3mm) below the ADD mark.

Recheck the fluid level after the transaxle is at normal operating temperature. The level should be in the HOT region.

PAN AND FILTER SERVICE

For the transaxle fluid pan and filter procedure, refer to the previously located Drain and Refill procedures in this section.

Cooling System

FLUID RECOMMENDATIONS

The cooling system was filled at the factory with a high quality coolant solution that is good for year-round operation and protects the system from freezing. If coolant is needed, a 50/50 mix of ethylene glycol or other suitable antifreeze and water should be used. Alcohol or methanol base coolants are specifically not recommended. Antifreeze solution should be used all year, even in summer, to prevent rust and to take advantage of the solution's higher boiling point compared to plain water. This is imperative on air conditioned models; the heater core can freeze if it isn't protected.

LEVEL CHECK

▶ See Figure 132

The coolant should be checked at each fuel stop, to prevent the possibility of overheating and serious engine damage. To check the coolant level simply look into the expansion tank.

✳✳ CAUTION

The radiator coolant is under pressure when hot. To avoid the danger of physical injury, coolant should be checked or replenished only when cool. To remove the cap, slowly rotate it counterclockwise to the stop, but do not press down. Wait until all pressure is released (indicated when the hissing sound stops) then press down on the cap while continuing to rotate it counterclockwise. Wear a glove or use a thick rag for protection.

Simply add coolant mixture to the tank until the upper level line is reached. If the system shows signs of overheating and, possibly, a small leak, you may want to check the level in the radiator when the engine is **cold**. If the radiator is not full, replace the cap with a new one, as it has lost the ability to retain vacuum or is of improper design for a coolant overflow tank type of system.

✳✳ WARNING

Never add large quantities of cold coolant to a hot engine. A cracked engine block may result. If it is absolutely necessary to add coolant to a hot engine, do so only with the engine idling and add only small quantities at a time.

Each year, the cooling system should be serviced as follows:

1. Wash the radiator cap and filler neck with clean water.

2. Check the coolant for proper level and freeze protection.

3. Have the system pressure tested. If a replacement cap is installed, be sure that it conforms to the original specifications.

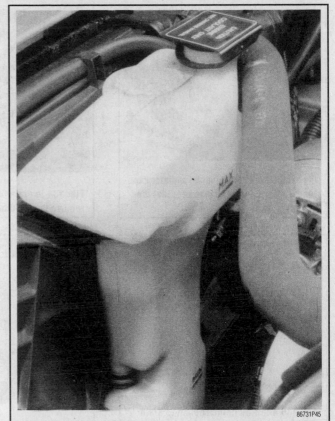

Fig. 132 To initially check the coolant level, use the MAX and MIN marks on the overflow tank

86731P45

4. Tighten the hose clamps and inspect all hoses. Replace hoses that are swollen, cracked or otherwise deteriorated.

5. Clean the frontal area of the radiator core and the air conditioning condenser, if so equipped.

DRAIN AND REFILL

▶ See Figures 133, 134, 135, 136 and 137

Every 2 years, the system should be serviced as follows:

1. Run the engine with the cap removed and the heater on until operating temperature is reached (indicated by heat in the upper radiator hose).

2. With the engine stopped, open the radiator draincock located at the bottom of the radiator, and (to speed the draining) the engine block drains, if so equipped (most of the cars covered in this manual do not have block drains).

3. Completely drain the coolant, and close the draincocks.

4. Add sufficient clean water to fill the system. Run the engine and drain and refill the system as often as necessary until the drain water is as close to colorless as possible.

5. Add sufficient ethylene glycol coolant to provide the required freezing and corrosion protection (at least a 50 percent solution of antifreeze and water). Fill the radiator to the cold level. Run the engine with the cap removed until normal operating temperature is reached.

6. Check the hot level.

7. Install the cap and fill the overflow tank to the HOT line.

FLUSHING AND CLEANING THE SYSTEM

A well maintained system should never require aggressive flushing or cleaning. However, you may find that you (or a previous owner) have neglected to change the antifreeze often enough to fully protect the system. It may have obviously accumulated rust inside, or there may be visible clogging of the radiator tubes.

Fig. 133 Before removing the radiator cap, read all warnings and make sure that the engine is cool

Fig. 134 To drain the cooling system, first remove the radiator cap, then . . .

Fig. 135 . . . loosen the draincock, located on the bottom right-hand corner of the radiator

Fig. 136 Allow all of the coolant to drain into a catch pan—antifreeze is a pollutant, dispose of it properly

Fig. 137 Close the draincock, then refill the cooling system

Fig. 138 Twist the brake reservoir cap off to inspect the fluid level, . . .

There are two basic means of rectifying this situation for the do-it-your-selfer. One is to purchase a kit designed to allow you to reverse-flush the system with the pressure available from a garden hose. This kit comes with special fittings which allow you to force water downward inside the engine block and upward (or in reverse of normal flow) in the radiator. It will have complete instructions.

The other means is to purchase a chemical cleaner. The cleaner is installed after the system is flushed and filled with fresh water and cleans the system as you drive a short distance or idle the engine hot. In all cases, the cleaner must be flushed completely from the system after use. In some cases, it may be necessary to follow up with use of a neutralizer. Make sure to follow the instructions very carefully. These cleaners are quite potent, chemically, and work very well; because of that fact, you must be careful to flush and, if necessary, neutralize the effect of the cleaner to keep it from damaging your cooling system.

If the radiator is severely clogged, it may be necessary to have the tubes rodded out by a professional radiator repair shop. In this case, the radiator must be removed and taken to the shop for this highly specialized work. You can save money on the job by removing and replacing the radiator yourself, as described in Section 3.

Brake Master Cylinder

FLUID RECOMMENDATIONS

Use **only** brake fluid conforming to Federal DOT 3 specifications.

LEVEL CHECK

▶ See Figures 138, 139, 140 and 141

Once every 7500 miles (12,000 km) or 6 months, check the brake fluid level in the master cylinder. The master cylinder is mounted either on the firewall or

Fig. 139 . . . which should come to the bottom edge of the filler hole walls

Fig. 140 If fluid is needed, use a funnel to prevent fluid spills—brake fluid can eat through paint

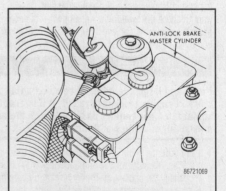

Fig. 141 An Anti-lock Brake System (ABS) master brake cylinder

the brake booster, and is divided into two reservoirs. The fluid must be maintained at the bottom of the split ring.

➡On vehicles with anti-lock brake system, depressurize the system BEFORE, inspecting the fluid level. Turn OFF the ignition and remove the key. Pump the brake pedal at least 50 times to relieve the pressure in the brake system.

Remove the two master cylinder caps and fill to the bottom of the split rings using DOT 3 brake fluid. If the brake fluid level is chronically low there may be a leak in the system which should be investigated immediately.

➡Brake fluid absorbs moisture from the air, which reduces its effectiveness and causes corrosion. Never leave the brake fluid container or master cylinder uncovered any longer than necessary. Brake fluid also damages paint. If any is spilled, it should be washed off immediately with clear, cold water.

Power Steering Pump

FLUID RECOMMENDATIONS

Use only Mopar Power Steering Fluid, or its equivalent.

LEVEL CHECK

▶ See Figures 142, 143 and 144

✳✳ WARNING

Do not overfill the power steering reservoir when adding fluid, as seal damage and leakage can result.

1. Position the vehicle on a level surface with the engine at normal running temperature.

Fig. 142 On 2.2L and 2.5L engines the steering pump is mounted between the engine and firewall

Fig. 143 Remove the power steering dipstick and check the fluid level against the dipstick markings . . .

Fig. 144 . . . then add the correct amount of power steering fluid, if necessary

✳✳ CAUTION

The engine must not be running when inspecting the power steering fluid level, as personal injury can result.

2. Turn the engine OFF and remove the ignition key.
3. Using a rag, clean oil and dirt residue from around the power steering reservoir cap.
4. Remove the reservoir cap or dipstick and wipe off any fluid.
5. Install the cap/dipstick.
6. Remove the cap/dipstick again. Holding the handle or cap above the tip of the dipstick, read the fluid level. Add fluid if the reading is below the cold level mark on the dipstick.

Manual Steering Gear

FLUID RECOMMENDATIONS

The rack and pinion manual steering units used on this car are permanently sealed. The lubricant is replenished only in connection with a major rebuild of the unit not covered by this manual. The power steering gear (rack and pinion unit) should NOT be serviced or adjusted. If a malfunction or oil leak occurs, the complete steering gear should be replaced.

LEAK CHECK

▶ See Figure 145

The manual steering gear is permanently lubricated at the factory and periodic replenishment of lubricant is not needed. However, you should inspect the two rubber boots that seal between the housing and the tie rod ends when checking the engine oil and other fluid levels. Make sure there is no leakage and that the boots are intact. Have the boots replaced if necessary. Check also for leakage where the steering shaft passes into the gearbox. If any leakage is found, replace the entire rack and pinion gear assembly with a new one.

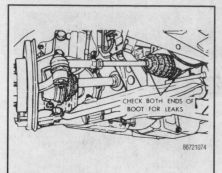

Fig. 145 Periodically check both sides of the boots on the steering gear rack and pinion assembly

Fig. 146 Lubricate the upper and lower ball joints until the seals start to swell—wipe off any excess grease

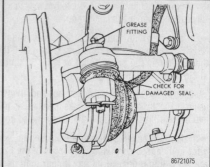

Fig. 147 Along with the ball joints, also grease the tie rod ends every 15,000 miles (24,000 km) or 18 months

Chassis Greasing

♦ **See Figures 146 and 147**

Chassis greasing can be performed with a pressurized grease gun or it can be performed at home using a hand-operated grease gun. Wipe the fittings clean before greasing, in order to prevent the possibility of forcing any dirt into the component. Fill the ball joint or tie rod end with grease until the seal starts to swell. When the lubrication operation is complete, wipe off any excess grease.

Ball joint and steering linkages are semi-permanently lubricated at the factory with a special grease. They should be greased every 15,000 miles (24,000 km) or 18 months, whichever comes first. When greasing is necessary, use only special long life chassis grease such as Mopar, Multi-Mileage Lube or its equivalent.

Body Lubrication and Maintenance

Body hinges and latches should be lubricated, as necessary, to maintain smooth operation of doors and front and rear hoods. Wipe all parts with a clean rag prior to lubrication. Pay particular attention to the smooth operation of hood latch components as failure to operate can produce a safety hazard; inspect and lubricate these with great care. If any problems appear, have them corrected immediately. Lubricate each part with the specified grease:

• Door hinges—Engine oil.
• Door latches, rotors, and strikers—Wheel bearing grease.
• Hood latch, release mechanism, and safety catch (apply sparingly to all contact areas)—Multipurpose lubricant NLGI Grade 2.
• Hood hinges and counterbalance springs—Mopar Multi-mileage Lubricant 4318062 or equivalent.
• Seat regulator and track adjusters—Mopar Spray White Lube 4318066 or equivalent.
• Tailgate (all pivot and slide contact surfaces on hinges, quick release pins, and release handles)—Spray White Lube.
• Tailgate check arms—Engine oil.

Wheel Bearings

➡ **Front wheel drive vehicles are equipped with permanently sealed front wheel bearings. There is no periodic lubrication or maintenance recommended for these units. However, if during servicing the brake system, service to the front wheel bearing is required, refer to Section 7 in this manual.**

The lubricant in the rear wheel bearings should be inspected whenever the hubs are removed to inspect or service the brake system, or at least every 30,000 miles (48,000 km). The bearings should be cleaned and repacked with a High Temperature Multipurpose E.P. Grease whenever the disc rotors are resurfaced.

INSPECTION

Check the lubricant to see that it is adequate in quantity and quality. If the grease is low in quantity, contains dirt, appears dry or has been contaminated

with water, it will appear milky. The bearings must then be cleaned and repacked.

➡ **Do not add grease to a wheel bearing that already has grease packed in it. Relubricate completely. Mixing of different types of greases in wheel bearings should be avoided since it may result in excessive thinning and leakage of the grease.**

REMOVAL, PACKING AND INSTALLATION

♦ **See Figure 148**

For the servicing, removal and installation of the rear wheel bearings utilize to the following procedure:
1. Remove the rear tire and wheel assembly.
2. On the rear disc brake equipped vehicles, remove the caliper and rotor. Support the caliper out of the way with strong cord or wire. **Do not allow the caliper to hang by the hydraulic hose.** For further procedures, refer to Section 9.
3. Remove the grease cap, cotter pin, locknut, nut thrust washer and outer wheel bearing.
4. Carefully slide the hub or drum off of the spindle. Do not drag the inner bearing or grease seal over the stub axle (thread, bearing, and oil seal may be damaged.) Remove the grease seal and inner bearing from the drum or hub. Discard the old grease seal, a new seal should be used when reinstalling the inner bearing.
5. Thoroughly clean all old grease from the outer and inner bearings, bearing cups and hub cavity. To clean the bearings, soak them in an appropriate cleaning solvent. Strike the flat surface of the bearing inner race against a hardwood block several times. Immerse the bearings in solvent between the blows to

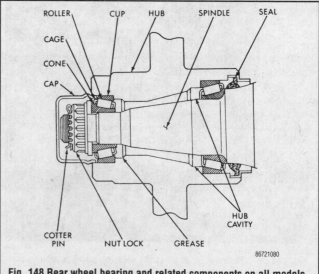

Fig. 148 Rear wheel bearing and related components on all models

jar the grease loose and wash old particles of hardened grease from the bearings. Repeat this operation until the bearings are clean. Bearings can be dried using compressed air, but do not spin the bearings. After cleaning, oil the bearings with engine oil. Insert the bearing into its appropriate cup, apply pressure to the bearing while rotating it to test them for pitting and roughness. Replace all worn or defective bearings with new ones. Bearings must be replaced as a set, both the cup and the bearing need to be replaced at the same time. If the bearings are suitable for further use, remove the engine oil from the bearings using the appropriate solvent, then dry the bearings. Repack the bearings using a Multi-Purpose NLGI Grade 2 EP Grease such as Mopar or equivalent. Make sure to work as much grease as possible into the bearings. Place the bearings in a clean covered container until ready for installation. If a bearing packer is not available, hand pack the grease into all cavities between the bearing cage and rollers.

6. If the bearings and cups are to be replaced, remove the cups from the drum or hub using a brass drift or suitable remover.

7. Install the new bearing cups with a bearing cup installation tool.

8. Install the inner bearing in the grease coated hub and bearing cup, and install new grease seals using the appropriate seal installer.

9. Coat the hub cavity and cup with grease.

10. Before installing the hub or drum assembly, inspect the stub axle and seal surface for burrs or roughness, and smooth out all rough surfaces.

11. Coat the stub axle with Multi-Purpose NLGI Grade 2 EP grease such as Mopar or equivalent.

12. Carefully slide the hub of the drum assembly onto the stub axle. **Do not drag the seal or inner bearing over the threaded area of the stub axle.**

13. Install the outer bearing, thrust washer and nut.

14. Tighten the wheel bearing adjusting nut to 20–25 ft. lbs. (27–34 Nm) while rotating hub or the drum assembly. This seats the bearings.

15. Back off the adjusting nut ¼ turn (90°), then finger-tighten it.

16. Position the locknut over the bearing adjusting nut with one pair of slots in line with the cotter pin hole in the stub axle, and install the cotter pin.

17. Install the grease caps and the wheel and tire assemblies. Tighten the wheel stud nuts to 85 ft. lbs. (115 Nm) on all models. Reinstall the wheel covers, if so equipped.

TRAILER TOWING

General Recommendations

Your vehicle was primarily designed to carry passengers and cargo. It is important to remember that towing a trailer will place additional loads on your vehicle's engine, drive train, steering, braking and other systems. However, if you find it necessary to tow a trailer, using the proper equipment is a must.

Local laws may require specific equipment such as trailer brakes or fender mounted mirrors. Check your local laws.

➡**Trailer towing by convertible models is not recommended by the manufacturer.**

Trailer towing is best performed by vehicles equipped with special towing packages to improve engine and transaxle cooling and to help the suspension system carry the extra weight. However, towing is permitted without these special systems, provided the road conditions are normal (both ascending and descending steep hills must be avoided) and the temperatures are moderate (extreme heat must also be avoided). The sole exception is that towing is **strictly prohibited with a turbocharged engine.** This is because of the tremendous ability of the turbocharged engine to produce high power output, which, in the absence of towing a trailer, can usually be sustained for only very short periods.

The Maximum loads for the V6 engines is a total maximum of 2,000 lbs. (907 kg). The trailer tongue load must not cause the total weight permitted for your car to be exceeded. Note also that, if the trailer weighs more than 1,000 lbs. (454 kg) it must not be towed without its own brakes, as the capacity of the vehicle's brakes will be substantially exceeded.

Check the automatic transaxle fluid level and color. Make sure the fluid level is correct. If the fluid is burnt, replace the fluid and filter. Should the temperature gauge rise above the normal indication while driving on the highway, reduce your speed. If the engine begins to get hot in traffic, put the (automatic) transaxle in neutral and allow the engine to idle and normal idle speed.

Trailer Weight

The weight of the trailer is the most important factor. A good weight-to-horsepower ratio is about 35:1, 35 lbs. of GCW (Gross Combined Weight) for every horsepower your engine develops. Multiply the engine's rated horsepower by 35 and subtract the weight of the car passengers and luggage. The result is the approximate ideal maximum weight you should tow, although a numerically higher axle ratio can help compensate for heavier weight.

Hitch (Tongue) Weight

♦ **See Figure 149**

Figure the hitch weight to select a proper hitch. Hitch weight is usually 9–11% of the trailer gross weight and should be measured with the trailer loaded. Hitches fall into various categories: those that mount on the frame and rear bumper, the bolt-on or weld-on distribution type used for larger trailers. Axle mounted or clamp-on bumper hitches should never be used.

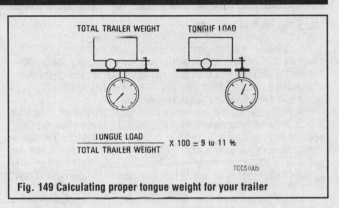

Fig. 149 Calculating proper tongue weight for your trailer

Check the gross weight rating of your trailer. Tongue weight is usually figured as 10% of gross trailer weight. Therefore, a trailer with a maximum gross weight of 2,000 lbs. (907 kg) will have a maximum tongue weight of 200 lbs. (91 kg) Class I trailers fall into this category. Class II trailers are those with a gross weight rating of 2,000–3,000 lbs. (907–1,361 kg), while Class III trailers fall into the 3,500–6,000 lb. (1,588–2,722 kg) category. Class IV trailers are those over 6,000 lbs. (2,722 kg) and are for use with fifth wheel trucks only.

When you've determined the hitch that you'll need, follow the manufacturer's installation instructions, exactly, especially when it comes to fastener torques. The hitch will subjected to a lot of stress and good hitches come with hardened bolts. Never substitute an inferior bolt for a hardened bolt.

Cooling

ENGINE

One of the most common, if not THE most common, problems associated with trailer towing is engine overheating. If you have a standard cooling system, without an expansion tank, you'll definitely need to get an aftermarket expansion tank kit, preferably one with at least a 2 quart capacity. These kits are easily installed on the radiator's overflow hose, and come with a pressure cap designed for expansion tanks.

Another helpful accessory for vehicles using a belt-driven radiator fan is a flex fan. These fans are large diameter units are designed to provide more airflow at low speeds, with blades that have deeply cupped surfaces. The blades then flex, or flatten out, at high speed, when less cooling air is needed. These fans are far lighter in weight than stock fans, requiring less horsepower to drive them. Also, they are far quieter than stock fans. If you do decide to replace your stock fan with a flex fan, note that if your car has a fan clutch, a spacer will be needed between the flex fan and water pump hub.

Aftermarket engine oil coolers are helpful for prolonging engine oil life and reducing overall engine temperatures. Both of these factors increase engine life. While not absolutely necessary in towing Class I and some Class II trailers, they are recommended for heavier Class II and all Class III towing. Engine oil cooler systems consists of an adapter, screwed on in place of the oil filter, a remote filter mounting and a multi-tube, finned heat exchanger, which is mounted in front of the radiator or air conditioning condenser.

TRANSAXLE

An automatic transaxle is usually recommended for trailer towing. Modern automatics have proven reliable and, of course, easy to operate, in trailer towing. The increased load of a trailer, however, causes an increase in the temperature of the automatic transaxle fluid. Heat is the worst enemy of an automatic transaxle. As the temperature of the fluid increases, the life of the fluid decreases.

It is essential, therefore, that you install an automatic transaxle cooler. The cooler, which consists of a multi-tube, finned heat exchanger, is usually installed in front of the radiator or air conditioning compressor, and hooked in-line with the transaxle cooler tank inlet line. Follow the cooler manufacturer's installation instructions.

Select a cooler of at least adequate capacity, based upon the combined gross weights of the car and trailer.

Cooler manufacturers recommend that you use an aftermarket cooler in addition to, and not instead of, the present cooling tank in your radiator. If you do want to use it in place of the radiator cooling tank, get a cooler at least two sizes larger than normally necessary.

➡ **A transaxle cooler can, sometimes, cause slow or harsh shifting in the transaxle during cold weather, until the fluid has a chance to come up to normal operating temperature. Some coolers can be purchased with or retrofitted with a temperature bypass valve which will allow fluid flow through the cooler only when the fluid has reached above a certain operating temperature.**

Handling A Trailer

Towing a trailer with ease and safety requires a certain amount of experience. It's a good idea to learn the feel of a trailer by practicing turning, stopping and backing in an open area such as an empty parking lot.

JACKING

◆ **See Figures 150 thru 163**

The standard jack utilizes special receptacles located at the body sills to accept the scissors jack supplied with the vehicle for emergency road service. The jack supplied with the car should never be used for any service operation other than tire changing. Never get under the car while it is supported by only a jack. Always block the wheels when changing tires.

The service operations in this manual often require that one end or the other, or both, of the car be raised and safely supported. The ideal method, of course, would be a hydraulic hoist. Since this is beyond both the resource and requirement of the do-it-yourselfer, a small hydraulic floor, screw or scissors jack will suffice for the procedures in this guide. Two sturdy jackstands should be acquired if you intend to work under the car at any time. An alternate method of

raising the car would be drive-on ramps. These are available commercially. Be sure to block the wheels when using ramps.

❊❊ CAUTION

Concrete or cinder blocks are not recommended for supporting the car. They are likely to crumble if the load is not evenly distributed. Boxes and milk crates of any description must not be used to support the car!

Jacking Precautions

The following safety points cannot be overemphasized:

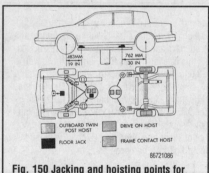

Fig. 150 Jacking and hoisting points for the AC body (1988–93 Dynasty) and AA body models (1989–95 Spirit, Acclaim and some LeBaron)

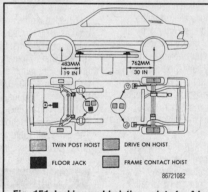

Fig. 151 Jacking and hoisting points for AJ body vehicles (some 1987–93 LeBaron)

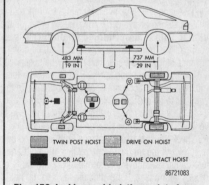

Fig. 152 Jacking and hoisting points for AG body models (Daytona and Laser)

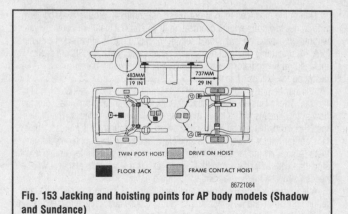

Fig. 153 Jacking and hoisting points for AP body models (Shadow and Sundance)

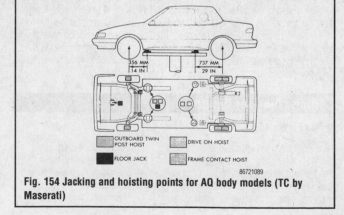

Fig. 154 Jacking and hoisting points for AQ body models (TC by Maserati)

- Always block the opposite wheel or wheels to keep the vehicle from rolling off the jack.
- When raising the front of the vehicle, firmly apply the parking brake.
- When the drive wheels are to remain on the ground, leave the vehicle in gear to help prevent it from rolling.

- Always use jackstands to support the vehicle when you are working underneath. Place the stands beneath the vehicle's jacking brackets. Before climbing underneath, rock the vehicle a bit to make sure it is firmly supported.

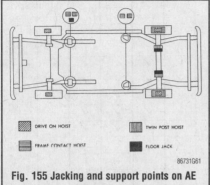

Fig. 155 Jacking and support points on AE body vehicles (New Yorker, E-Class, some Caravelle and some 600)

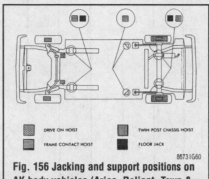

Fig. 156 Jacking and support positions on AK body vehicles (Aries, Reliant, Town & Country, Executive, some Caravelle, some 600 and some LeBaron)

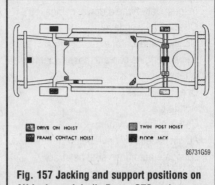

Fig. 157 Jacking and support positions on AH body models (LeBaron GTS and Lancer)

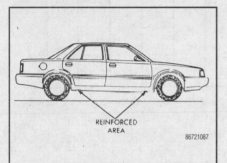

Fig. 158 When using the factory equipped tire changing jack, be sure to position it under the reinforced areas ONLY

Fig. 159 When raising the vehicle, always be certain to use proper jacking points as illustrated in this section

Fig. 160 Use a floor jack to lift the vehicle, then place jackstands under the support rails

Fig. 161 Make sure that the floor jack pad is securely positioned under a structural member of the vehicle

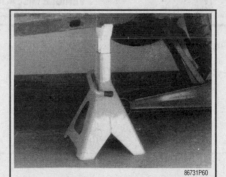

Fig. 162 Make certain that the jackstands are positioned on level, secure ground and . . .

Fig. 163 . . . the jackstand upper mount is situated under a jacking point on the underside of the car

MANUFACTURER RECOMMENDED MAINTENANCE INTERVALS (Normal Service)

TO BE SERVICED		VEHICLE MILEAGE INTERVAL (x1000)												
		7.5	15	22.5	30	37.5	45	52.5	60	67.5	75	82.5	90	miles
		6	12	18	24	30	36	42	48	54	60	66	72	mos
Inspect tire pressure	①													
Inspect battery hold down, cables, etc.	①													
Check & fill fluid levels	①													
Check operation of external lights	①													
Inspect engine coolant, hoses, clamps, etc.		✓	✓	✓	✓	✓	✓	✓	✓	✓	✓	✓	✓	
Change engine oil		✓	✓	✓	✓	✓	✓	✓	✓	✓	✓	✓	✓	
Change oil filter				✓	✓		✓		✓		✓		✓	
Rotate tires		✓	✓	✓	✓	✓	✓	✓	✓	✓	✓	✓	✓	
Check exhaust system		✓	✓	✓	✓	✓	✓	✓	✓	✓	✓	✓	✓	
Adjust accessory drive belts				✓	✓				✓		✓		✓	
Lubricate automatic seat belt track				✓	✓				✓		✓		✓	
Replace air cleaner filter					✓				✓				✓	
Replace spark plugs					✓				✓				✓	
Replace PCV filter					✓				✓				✓	
Flush and replace engine coolant							✓						✓	
Replace ignition cables									✓					
Replace PCV filter									✓					
Replace accessory drive belts									✓					
Lubricate front suspension ball joints & tie rod	②								✓					
Replace timing belt on 2.2L & 2.5L Chrysler													✓	

① Inspect monthly
② Lubricate every 24 / 30,000 after initial lubrication

86731C10

MANUFACTURER RECOMMENDED MAINTENANCE INTERVALS (Severe Service)

Stop and go driving; extensive idling; dusty conditions; frequent short trips; trailer towing;
operating at sustained high speeds during weather above 90° F/ 32° C

TO BE SERVICED	VEHICLE MILEAGE INTERVAL (x1000)																
	3	6	9	12	15	18	21	24	27	30	33	36	39	42	45	48	miles
Change engine oil	✓	✓	✓	✓	✓	✓	✓	✓	✓	✓	✓	✓	✓	✓	✓	✓	
Inspect CV joints and ball joints	✓	✓	✓	✓	✓	✓	✓	✓	✓	✓	✓	✓	✓	✓	✓	✓	
Replace engine oil filter		✓		✓		✓		✓		✓		✓		✓		✓	
Inspect brake linings			✓			✓			✓			✓			✓		
Lubricate steering linkage and tie rods					✓					✓					✓		
Change ATF and Filter; adjust bands, if equipped					✓					✓					✓		
Replace air cleaner element					✓					✓					✓		
Inspect PCV valve								✓								✓	

86731C11

CAPACITIES

Year	Model	Engine ID/VIN	Engine Displacement Liters (cc)	Engine Oil with Filter (qts.)	Transaxle (pts.)			Transfer Case (pts.)	Drive Axle		Fuel Tank (gal.)	Cooling System (qts.)
					4-Spd	5-Spd	Auto.		Front (pts.)	Rear (pts.)		
1981	Aries	B	2.2 (2212)	4.0	4.0	-	15.0 ①	-	2	-	13.0	7.0
	Aries	D	2.6 (2556)	5.0	4.0	-	17.0 ①	-	2	-	13.0	8.5
	Reliant	B	2.2 (2212)	4.0	4.0	-	15.0 ①	-	2	-	13.0	7.0
	Reliant	D	2.6 (2556)	5.0	4.0	-	17.0 ①	-	2	-	13.0	8.5
1982	LeBaron	C	2.2 (2212)	4.0	4.0	-	15.0 ①	-	2	-	13.0	7.0
	LeBaron	G	2.6 (2556)	5.0	4.0	-	17.0 ①	-	2	-	13.0	8.5
	Town & Country	C	2.2 (2212)	4.0	4.0	-	15.0 ①	-	2	-	13.0	7.0
	Town & Country	G	2.6 (2556)	5.0	4.0	-	17.0 ①	-	2	-	13.0	8.5
	400	C	2.2 (2212)	4.0	4.0	-	15.0 ①	-	2	-	13.0	7.0
	400	G	2.6 (2556)	5.0	4.0	-	17.0 ①	-	2	-	13.0	8.5
	600	C	2.2 (2212)	4.0	4.0	-	15.0 ①	-	2	-	13.0	7.0
	600	G	2.6 (2556)	5.0	4.0	-	17.0 ①	-	2	-	13.0	8.5
	Aries	B	2.2 (2212)	4.0	4.0	-	15.0 ①	-	2	-	13.0	7.0
	Aries	D	2.6 (2556)	5.0	4.0	-	17.0 ①	-	2	-	13.0	8.5
	Reliant	B	2.2 (2212)	4.0	4.0	-	15.0 ①	-	2	-	13.0	7.0
	Reliant	D	2.6 (2556)	5.0	4.0	-	17.0 ①	-	2	-	13.0	8.5
1983	E-Class	C	2.2 (2212)	4.0	4.0	4.6	②	-	-	-	13.0	9.0
	E-Class	G	2.6 (2556)	5.0	4.0	4.6	②	-	-	-	13.0	9.0
	LeBaron	C	2.2 (2212)	4.0	4.0	4.6	②	-	-	-	13.0	9.0
	LeBaron	G	2.6 (2556)	5.0	4.0	4.6	②	-	-	-	13.0	9.0
	New Yorker	C	2.2 (2212)	4.0	4.0	4.6	②	-	-	-	13.0	9.0
	New Yorker	G	2.6 (2556)	5.0	4.0	4.6	②	-	-	-	13.0	9.0
	Town & Country	C	2.2 (2212)	4.0	4.0	4.6	②	-	-	-	13.0	9.0
	Town & Country	G	2.6 (2556)	5.0	4.0	4.6	②	-	-	-	13.0	9.0
	400	C	2.2 (2212)	4.0	4.0	4.6	②	-	-	-	13.0	9.0
	400	G	2.6 (2556)	5.0	4.0	4.6	②	-	-	-	13.0	9.0
	600	C	2.2 (2212)	4.0	4.0	4.6	②	-	-	-	13.0	9.0
	600	G	2.6 (2556)	5.0	4.0	4.0	①	-	-	-	13.0	9.0
	Aries	C	2.2 (2212)	4.0	4.0	4.6	②	-	-	-	13.0	9.0
	Aries	G	2.6 (2556)	5.0	4.0	4.6	②	-	-	-	13.0	9.0
	Reliant	C	2.2 (2212)	4.0	4.0	4.6	②	-	-	-	13.0	9.0
	Reliant	G	2.6 (2556)	5.0	4.0	4.6	②	-	-	-	13.0	9.0
1984	E-Class	D	2.2 (2212)	4.0	4.0	4.6	②	-	-	-	14.0	9.0
	E-Class	E	2.2 (2212)	5.0	4.0	4.6	②	-	-	-	14.0	9.0
	E-Class	G	2.6 (2556)	5.0	4.0	4.6	②	-	-	-	14.0	9.0
	Laser	D	2.2 (2212)	4.0	4.0	4.6	②	-	-	-	14.0	9.0
	Laser	E	2.2 (2212)	5.0	4.0	4.6	②	-	-	-	14.0	9.0
	LeBaron	C	2.2 (2212)	4.0	4.0	4.6	②	-	-	-	14.0	9.0
	LeBaron	E	2.2 (2212)	5.0	4.0	4.6	②	-	-	-	14.0	9.0
	LeBaron	G	2.6 (2556)	5.0	4.0	4.6	②	-	-	-	14.0	9.0
	New Yorker	D	2.2 (2212)	4.0	4.0	4.6	②	-	-	-	14.0	9.0
	New Yorker	E	2.2 (2212)	5.0	4.0	4.6	②	-	-	-	14.0	9.0
	New Yorker	G	2.6 (2556)	5.0	4.0	4.6	②	-	-	-	14.0	9.0
	Town & Country	C	2.2 (2212)	4.0	4.0	4.6	②	-	-	-	14.0	9.0
	Town & Country	G	2.6 (2556)	5.0	4.0	4.6	②	-	-	-	14.0	9.0
	600	C	2.2 (2212)	4.0	4.0	4.6	②	-	-	-	14.0	9.0
	600	D	2.2 (2212)	4.0	4.0	4.6	②	-	-	-	14.0	9.0
	600	E	2.2 (2212)	5.0	4.0	4.6	②	-	-	-	14.0	9.0
	600	G	2.6 (2556)	5.0	4.0	4.6	②	-	-	-	14.0	9.0

86731C12

CAPACITIES

Year	Model	Engine ID/VIN	Engine Displacement Liters (cc)	Engine Oil with Filter (qts.)	Transaxle (pts.) 4-Spd	Transaxle (pts.) 5-Spd	Transaxle (pts.) Auto.	Transfer Case (pts.)	Drive Axle Front (pts.)	Drive Axle Rear (pts.)	Fuel Tank (gal.)	Cooling System (qts.)
1984	Aries	C	2.2 (2212)	4.0	4.0	4.6	②	–	–	–	14.0	9.0
	Aries	G	2.6 (2556)	5.0	4.0	4.6	②	–	–	–	14.0	9.0
	Daytona	D	2.2 (2212)	4.0	4.0	4.6	②	–	–	–	14.0	9.0
	Daytona	E	2.2 (2212)	5.0	4.0	4.6	②	–	–	–	14.0	9.0
	Reliant	C	2.2 (2212)	4.0	4.0	4.6	②	–	–	–	14.0	9.0
	Reliant	G	2.6 (2556)	5.0	–	4.6	②	–	–	–	14.0	9.0
1985	600	D	2.2 (2212)	4.0	–	4.6	②	–	–	–	14.0	9.0
	600	E	2.2 (2212)	5.0	–	–	②	–	–	–	14.0	9.0
	600	G	2.6 (2556)	5.0	4.0	–	②	–	–	–	14.0	9.0
	Aries	D	2.2 (2212)	4.0	–	4.6	②	–	–	–	14.0	9.0
	Aries	G	2.6 (2556)	5.0	–	4.6	②	–	–	–	14.0	9.0
	Caravelle	D	2.2 (2212)	4.0	–	4.6	②	–	–	–	14.0	9.0
	Caravelle	E	2.2 (2212)	5.0	–	4.6	②	–	–	–	14.0	9.0
	Caravelle	G	2.6 (2556)	5.0	–	4.6	②	–	–	–	14.0	9.0
	Daytona	D	2.2 (2212)	4.0	–	4.6	17.8 ③	–	–	–	14.0	9.0
	Daytona	D	2.2 (2212)	4.0	–	4.6	17.8 ③	–	–	–	14.0	9.0
	Lancer	E	2.2 (2212)	5.0	–	4.6	②	–	–	–	14.0	9.0
	Laser	D	2.2 (2212)	4.0	–	4.6	17.8 ③	–	–	–	14.0	9.0
	Laser	E	2.2 (2212)	5.0	–	–	17.8 ③	–	–	–	14.0	9.0
	Lebaron	D	2.2 (2212)	4.0	–	4.6	②	–	–	–	14.0	9.0
	Lebaron	E	2.2 (2212)	5.0	–	–	②	–	–	–	14.0	9.0
	Lebaron GTS	D	2.2 (2212)	4.0	–	4.6	17.8 ③	–	–	–	14.0	9.0
	Lebaron GTS	E	2.2 (2212)	5.0	–	4.6	17.8 ③	–	–	–	14.0	9.0
	Lebaron Limo	G	2.6 (2556)	5.0	–	–	②	–	–	–	14.0	9.0
	New Yorker	G	2.6 (2556)	5.0	–	–	②	–	–	–	14.0	9.0
	Reliant	C	2.2 (2212)	4.0	4.0	4.6	②	–	–	–	14.0	9.0
	Reliant	D	2.2 (2212)	4.0	–	4.6	②	–	–	–	14.0	9.0
	Reliant	E	2.2 (2212)	5.0	–	4.6	②	–	–	–	14.0	9.0
	Town & Country	D	2.2 (2212)	4.0	–	4.6	②	–	–	–	14.0	9.0
	Town & Country	E	2.2 (2212)	5.0	–	–	②	–	–	–	14.0	9.0
1986	600	D	2.2 (2212)	4.0	–	4.6	②	–	–	–	14.0	9.0
	600	E	2.2 (2212)	5.0	–	4.6	②	–	–	–	14.0	9.0
	600	K	2.5 (2507)	4.0	4.0	–	②	–	–	–	14.0	9.0
	Aries	C	2.2 (2212)	4.0	4.0	4.6	②	–	–	–	14.0	9.0
	Aries	K	2.5 (2507)	4.0	–	4.6	②	–	–	–	14.0	9.0
	Caravelle	D	2.2 (2212)	4.0	–	4.6	②	–	–	–	14.0	9.0
	Caravelle	K	2.5 (2507)	5.0	–	4.6	②	–	–	–	14.0	9.0
	Daytona	D	2.2 (2212)	4.0	–	4.6	②	–	–	–	14.0	9.0
	Daytona	E	2.2 (2212)	5.0	–	4.6	②	–	–	–	14.0	9.0
	Daytona	K	2.5 (2507)	4.0	–	4.6	②	–	–	–	14.0	9.0
	Lancer	E	2.2 (2212)	5.0	–	4.6	②	–	–	–	14.0	9.0
	Lancer	K	2.5 (2507)	4.0	–	4.6	②	–	–	–	14.0	9.0

CAPACITIES

Year	Model	Engine ID/VIN	Engine Displacement Liters (cc)	Engine Oil with Filter (qts.)	Transaxle (pts.) 4-Spd	Transaxle (pts.) 5-Spd	Transaxle (pts.) Auto.	Transfer Case (pts.)	Drive Axle Front (pts.)	Drive Axle Rear (pts.)	Fuel Tank (gal.)	Cooling System (qts.)
1986	Laser	D	2.2 (2212)	4.0	–	4.6	②	–	–	–	14.0	9.0
	Laser	E	2.2 (2212)	5.0	–	4.6	②	–	–	–	14.0	9.0
	Laser	K	2.5 (2507)	4.0	–	–	②	–	–	–	14.0	9.0
	Lebaron	D	2.2 (2212)	4.0	–	–	②	–	–	–	14.0	9.0
	Lebaron	E	2.2 (2212)	5.0	–	–	②	–	–	–	14.0	9.0
	Reliant	K	2.5 (2507)	4.0	–	–	②	–	–	–	14.0	9.0
	Lebaron GTS	D	2.2 (2212)	4.0	–	4.6	②	–	–	–	14.0	9.0
	Lebaron GTS	E	2.2 (2212)	5.0	–	4.6	②	–	–	–	14.0	9.0
	Lebaron GTS	K	2.5 (2507)	4.0	–	4.6	②	–	–	–	14.0	9.0
	New Yorker	E	2.2 (2212)	5.0	–	–	②	–	–	–	14.0	9.0
	New Yorker	K	2.5 (2507)	4.0	–	–	②	–	–	–	14.0	9.0
	Reliant	C	2.2 (2212)	4.0	4.0	4.6	②	–	–	–	14.0	9.0
	Reliant	K	2.5 (2507)	4.0	–	4.6	②	–	–	–	14.0	9.0
	Town & Country	E	2.2 (2212)	5.0	–	–	②	–	–	–	14.0	9.0
	Town & Country	K	2.5 (2507)	4.0	–	–	②	–	–	–	14.0	9.0
1987	600	D	2.2 (2212)	4.0	–	–	②	–	–	–	14.0	9.0
	600	E	2.2 (2212)	5.0	–	–	②	–	–	–	14.0	9.0
	600	K	2.5 (2507)	4.0	–	–	②	–	–	–	14.0	9.0
	Aries	D	2.2 (2212)	4.0	–	5.0	②	–	–	–	14.0	9.0
	Aries	K	2.5 (2507)	4.0	–	5.0	②	–	–	–	14.0	9.0
	Caravelle	D	2.2 (2212)	4.0	–	–	②	–	–	–	14.0	9.0
	Caravelle	E	2.2 (2212)	5.0	–	–	②	–	–	–	14.0	9.0
	Caravelle	K	2.5 (2507)	4.0	–	–	②	–	–	–	14.0	9.0
	Daytona	A	2.2 (2212)	4.0	–	5.0	②	–	–	–	14.0	9.0
	Daytona	E	2.2 (2212)	5.0	–	5.0	②	–	–	–	14.0	9.0
	Daytona	K	2.5 (2507)	4.0	–	5.0	②	–	–	–	14.0	9.0
	Lancer	D	2.2 (2212)	4.0	–	5.0	②	–	–	–	14.0	9.0
	Lancer	E	2.2 (2212)	5.0	–	5.0	②	–	–	–	14.0	9.0
	Lancer	K	2.5 (2507)	4.0	–	5.0	②	–	–	–	14.0	9.0
	Lebaron	D	2.2 (2212)	4.0	–	5.0	②	–	–	–	14.0	9.0
	Lebaron	E	2.2 (2212)	5.0	–	5.0	②	–	–	–	14.0	9.0
	Lebaron	K	2.5 (2507)	4.0	–	5.0	②	–	–	–	14.0	9.0
	Lebaron GTS	D	2.2 (2212)	4.0	–	5.0	②	–	–	–	14.0	9.0
	Lebaron GTS	E	2.2 (2212)	5.0	–	5.0	②	–	–	–	14.0	9.0
	Lebaron GTS	K	2.5 (2507)	4.0	–	5.0	②	–	–	–	14.0	9.0
	New Yorker	E	2.2 (2212)	5.0	–	–	②	–	–	–	14.0	9.0
	New Yorker	K	2.5 (2507)	4.0	–	–	②	–	–	–	14.0	9.0
	Reliant	D	2.2 (2212)	4.0	–	5.0	②	–	–	–	14.0	9.0
	Reliant	K	2.5 (2507)	4.0	–	5.0	②	–	–	–	14.0	9.0
	Shadow	D	2.2 (2212)	4.0	–	4.6	②	–	–	–	14.0	9.0
	Shadow	E	2.2 (2212)	5.0	–	4.6	②	–	–	–	14.0	9.0
	Sundance	D	2.2 (2212)	4.0	–	4.6	②	–	–	–	14.0	9.0
	Sundance	E	2.2 (2212)	5.0	–	4.6	②	–	–	–	14.0	9.0
	Town & Country	E	2.2 (2212)	4.0	–	–	②	–	–	–	14.0	9.0
	Town & Country	K	2.5 (2507)	4.0	–	–	②	–	–	–	14.0	9.0
1988	600	D	2.2 (2212)	4.0	–	–	②	–	–	–	14.0	9.0
	600	E	2.2 (2212)	4.0	–	–	②	–	–	–	14.0	9.0
	600	K	2.5 (2507)	4.0	–	–	②	–	–	–	14.0	9.0

86731C14

86731C13

CAPACITIES

Year	Model	Engine ID/VIN	Engine Displacement Liters (cc)	Engine Oil with Filter (qts.)	Transaxle 4-Spd	Transaxle 5-Spd	Transaxle Auto.	Transfer Case (pts.)	Drive Axle Front (pts.)	Drive Axle Rear (pts.)	Fuel Tank (gal.)	Cooling System (qts.)
1989	Shadow	D	2.2 (2212)	4.0	-	4.6	④	-	-	-	14.0	9.0
	Shadow	J	2.5 (2507)	4.0	-	4.6	④	-	-	-	14.0	9.0
	Shadow	K	2.5 (2507)	4.0	-	4.6	④	-	-	-	14.0	9.0
	Spirit	J	2.5 (2507)	4.0	-	4.8	④	-	-	-	16.0	9.0
	Spirit	K	2.5 (2507)	4.0	-	4.8	④	-	-	-	16.0	9.0
	Sundance	D	2.2 (2212)	4.0	-	4.6	④	-	-	-	14.0	9.0
	Sundance	J	2.5 (2507)	4.0	-	4.6	④	-	-	-	14.0	9.0
	Sundance	K	2.5 (2507)	4.0	-	4.6	④	-	-	-	14.0	9.0
	TC Maserati	P	2.2 (2212)	4.0	-	-	④	-	-	-	14.0	9.0
	TC Maserati	R	2.2 (2212)	4.0	-	4.6	④	4	-	-	14.0	9.0
1990	Acclaim	J	2.5 (2507)	4.0	-	4.8	④	-	-	-	16.0	9.0
	Acclaim	K	2.5 (2507)	4.0	-	4.8	④	-	-	-	16.0	9.0
	Daytona	C	2.2 (2212)	4.0	-	4.8	④	-	-	-	14.0	9.0
	Daytona	J	2.5 (2507)	4.0	-	4.8	④	-	-	-	14.0	9.0
	Daytona	K	2.5 (2507)	4.0	-	4.8	④	-	-	-	16.0	9.0
	Dynasy	K	2.5 (2507)	4.0	-	-	④	-	-	-	14.0	9.0
	Lebaron	C	2.2 (2212)	4.0	-	4.8	④	-	-	-	14.0	9.0
	Lebacn	J	2.5 (2507)	4.0	-	4.8	④	-	-	-	14.0	9.0
	Lebacn	K	2.5 (2507)	4.0	-	4.8	④	-	-	-	14.0	9.0
	Shadow	C	2.2 (2212)	4.0	-	4.8	④	-	-	-	14.0	9.0
	Shadow	D	2.2 (2212)	4.0	-	4.8	④	-	-	-	14.0	9.0
	Shadow	K	2.5 (2507)	4.0	-	4.8	④	-	-	-	16.0	9.0
	Spirit	J	2.5 (2507)	4.0	-	4.8	④	-	-	-	16.0	9.0
	Spirit	K	2.5 (2507)	4.0	-	4.8	④	-	-	-	16.0	9.0
	Sundance	D	2.2 (2212)	4.0	-	4.8	④	-	-	-	14.0	9.0
	Sundance	J	2.5 (2507)	4.0	-	4.8	④	-	-	-	14.0	9.0
	TC Maserati	R	2.2 (2212)	4.0	-	4.8	④	-	-	-	14.0	9.0
1991	Acclaim	J	2.5 (2507)	4.5	-	4.8	④	-	-	-	16.0	9.0
	Acclaim	K	2.5 (2507)	4.5	-	4.8	④	-	-	-	16.0	9.0
	Caytona	J	2.5 (2507)	4.5	-	4.8	④	-	-	-	14.0	9.0
	Caytona	K	2.5 (2507)	4.5	-	4.8	④	-	-	-	14.0	9.0
	Cynasty	K	2.5 (2507)	4.5	-	-	④	-	-	-	16.0	9.0
	Labaron	K	2.5 (2507)	4.5	-	4.8	④	-	-	-	16.0	9.0
	Labaron	A	2.2 (2212)	4.5	-	4.8	④	-	-	-	14.0	9.0
	Shadcw	D	2.2 (2212)	4.5	-	4.8	④	-	-	-	14.0	9.0
	Shadow	K	2.5 (2507)	4.5	-	4.8	④	-	-	-	14.0	9.0
	Spirit	A	2.2 (2212)	4.5	-	4.8	④	-	-	-	16.0	9.0
	Spirit	K	2.5 (2507)	4.5	-	4.8	④	-	-	-	16.0	9.0
	Sundarce	D	2.2 (2212)	4.5	-	4.8	④	-	-	-	14.0	9.0
	Sundarce	J	2.5 (2507)	4.5	-	4.8	④	-	-	-	14.0	9.0
	Sundarce	K	2.5 (2507)	4.5	-	4.8	④	-	-	-	14.0	9.0

86731C16

CAPACITIES

Year	Model	Engine ID/VIN	Engine Displacement Liters (cc)	Engine Oil with Filter (qts.)	Transaxle 4-Spd	Transaxle 5-Spd	Transaxle Auto.	Transfer Case (pts.)	Drive Axle Front (pts.)	Drive Axle Rear (pts.)	Fuel Tank (gal.)	Cooling System (qts.)
1988	Aries	D	2.2 (2212)	4.0	-	5.0	②	-	-	-	14.0	9.0
	Aries	K	2.5 (2507)	4.0	-	5.0	②	-	-	-	14.0	9.0
	Caravelle	D	2.2 (2212)	4.0	-	-	②	-	-	-	14.0	9.0
	Caravelle	E	2.2 (2212)	4.0	-	-	②	-	-	-	14.0	9.0
	Caravelle	K	2.5 (2507)	4.0	-	-	②	-	-	-	14.0	9.0
	Daytona	A	2.2 (2212)	4.0	-	5.0	②	-	-	-	14.0	9.0
	Daytona	E	2.2 (2212)	4.0	-	5.0	②	-	-	-	14.0	9.0
	Daytona	K	2.5 (2507)	4.0	-	5.0	②	-	-	-	14.0	9.0
	Dynasty	K	2.5 (2507)	4.0	-	-	②	-	-	-	14.0	9.0
	Lancer	D	2.2 (2212)	4.0	-	5.0	②	-	-	-	14.0	9.0
	Lancer	E	2.2 (2212)	4.0	-	5.0	②	-	-	-	14.0	9.0
	Lancer	K	2.5 (2507)	4.0	-	5.0	②	-	-	-	14.0	9.0
	Lebaron	D	2.2 (2212)	4.0	-	5.0	②	-	-	-	14.0	9.0
	Lebaron	E	2.2 (2212)	4.0	-	5.0	②	-	-	-	14.0	9.0
	Lebaron	K	2.5 (2507)	4.0	-	5.0	②	-	-	-	14.0	9.0
	Lebaron GTS	E	2.2 (2212)	4.0	-	5.0	②	-	-	-	14.0	9.0
	Lebaron GTS	K	2.5 (2507)	4.0	-	5.0	②	-	-	-	14.0	9.0
	New Yorker	E	2.2 (2212)	4.0	-	-	②	-	-	-	14.0	9.0
	Premier	Z	2.5 (2458)	5.0	-	-	11.2 ⑥	②	1.78	-	17.0	86
	Reliant	D	2.2 (2212)	4.0	-	5.0	②	-	-	-	14.0	90
	Reliant	K	2.5 (2507)	4.0	-	5.0	②	-	-	-	14.0	90
	Shadow	D	2.2 (2212)	4.0	-	5.0	②	-	-	-	14.0	90
	Shadow	E	2.2 (2212)	4.0	-	5.0	②	-	-	-	14.0	90
	Sundance	D	2.2 (2212)	4.0	-	5.0	②	-	-	-	14.0	90
	Sundance	E	2.2 (2212)	4.0	-	5.0	②	-	-	-	14.0	90
	Town & Country	E	2.2 (2212)	4.0	-	-	②	-	-	-	14.0	90
	Town & Country	K	2.5 (2507)	4.0	-	-	②	-	-	-	16.0	90
1989	Acclaim	J	2.5 (2507)	4.0	-	4.8	④	-	-	-	16.0	9.0
	Acclaim	K	2.5 (2507)	4.0	-	4.8	④	-	-	-	16.0	9.0
	Aries	D	2.2 (2212)	4.0	-	4.6	④	-	-	-	14.0	9.0
	Aries	K	2.5 (2507)	4.0	-	4.6	④	-	-	-	14.0	9.0
	Daytona	A	2.2 (2212)	4.0	-	-	④	-	-	-	14.0	9.0
	Daytona	J	2.5 (2507)	4.0	-	4.6	④	-	-	-	14.0	9.0
	Daytona	K	2.5 (2507)	4.0	-	4.6	④	-	-	-	14.0	9.0
	Dynasty	K	2.5 (2507)	4.0	-	-	④	-	-	-	16.0	9.0
	Labaron	A	2.2 (2212)	4.0	-	4.6	④	-	-	-	14.0	9.0
	Lancer	D	2.2 (2212)	4.0	-	4.6	④	-	-	-	14.0	9.0
	Lancer	J	2.2 (2212)	4.0	-	4.6	④	-	-	-	14.0	9.0
	Lancer	K	2.5 (2507)	4.0	-	4.6	④	-	-	-	14.0	9.0
	Lebaron	A	2.2 (2212)	4.0	-	4.6	④	-	-	-	14.0	9.0
	Lebaron	J	2.5 (2507)	4.0	-	4.6	④	-	-	-	14.0	9.0
	Lebaron GTS	K	2.2 (2212)	4.0	-	4.6	④	-	-	-	14.0	9.0
	Lebaron GTS	A	2.2 (2212)	4.0	-	4.6	④	-	-	-	14.0	9.0
	Lebaron GTS	D	2.2 (2212)	4.0	-	4.6	④	-	-	-	14.0	9.0
	Lebaron GTS	J	2.5 (2507)	4.0	-	4.6	④	-	-	-	14.0	9.0
	Reliant	K	2.2 (2212)	4.0	-	4.6	④	-	-	-	14.0	9.0
	Reliant	D	2.2 (2212)	4.0	-	4.6	④	-	-	-	14.0	9.0
	Reliant	K	2.5 (2507)	4.0	-	4.6	④	-	-	-	14.0	9.0

86731C15

ENGLISH TO METRIC CONVERSION: MASS (WEIGHT)

Current mass measurement is expressed in pounds and ounces (lbs. & ozs.). The metric unit of mass (or weight) is the kilogram (kg). Even although this table does not show conversion of masses (weights) larger than 15 lbs, it is easy to calculate larger units by following the data immediately below.

To convert ounces (oz.) to grams (g): multiply th number of ozs. by 28
To convert grams (g) to ounces (oz.): multiply the number of grams by .035
To convert pounds (lbs.) to kilograms (kg): multiply the number of lbs. by .45
To convert kilograms (kg) to pounds (lbs.): multiply the number of kilograms by 2.2
To convert kilograms (kg) to pounds (lbs.): multiply the number of kilograms by 2.2

lbs	kg	oz	kg	lbs	kg	oz	kg
0.1	0.04	0.1	0.003	0.9	0.41	0.9	0.024
0.2	0.09	0.2	0.005	1	0.4	1	0.03
0.3	0.14	0.3	0.008	2	0.9	2	0.06
0.4	0.18	0.4	0.011	3	1.4	3	0.08
0.5	0.23	0.5	0.014	4	1.8	4	0.11
0.6	0.27	0.6	0.017	5	2.3	5	0.14
0.7	0.32	0.7	0.020	10	4.5	10	0.28
0.8	0.36	0.8	0.023	15	6.8	15	0.42

TCCS1C01

ENGLISH TO METRIC CONVERSION: TEMPERATURE

To convert Fahrenheit (F) to Celsius (°C): take number of °F and subtract 32; multiply result by 5; divide result by 9
To convert Celsius (°C) to Fahrenheit (°F): take number of °C and multiply by 9; divide result by 5; add 32 to total

Fahrenheit (F)		Celsius (C)		Fahrenheit (F)		Celsius (C)		Fahrenheit (F)		Celsius (C)	
°F	°C	°C	°F	°F	°C	°C	°F	°F	°C	°C	°F
-40	-40	-38	-36.4	80	26.7	18	64.4	215	101.7	80	176
-35	-37.2	-36	-32.8	85	29.4	20	68	220	104.4	85	185
-30	-34.4	-34	-29.2	90	32.2	22	71.6	225	107.2	90	194
-25	-31.7	-32	-25.6	95	35.0	24	75.2	230	110.0	95	202
-20	-28.9	-30	-22	100	37.8	26	78.8	235	112.8	100	212
-15	-26.1	-28	-18.4	105	40.6	28	82.4	240	115.6	105	221
-10	-23.3	-26	-14.8	110	43.3	30	86	245	118.3	110	230
-5	-20.6	-24	-11.2	115	46.1	32	89.6	250	121.1	115	239
0	-17.8	-22	-7.6	120	48.9	34	93.2	255	123.9	120	248
1	-17.2	-20	-4	125	51.7	36	96.8	260	126.6	125	257
2	-16.7	-18	-0.4	130	54.4	38	100.4	265	129.4	130	266
3	-16.1	-16	3.2	135	57.2	40	104	270	132.2	135	275
4	-15.6	-14	6.8	140	60.0	42	107.6	275	135.0	140	284
5	-15.0	-12	10.4	145	62.8	44	112.2	280	137.8	145	293
10	-12.2	-10	14	150	65.6	46	114.8	285	140.6	150	302
15	-9.4	-8	17.6	155	68.3	48	118.4	290	143.3	155	311
20	-6.7	-6	21.2	160	71.1	50	122	295	146.1	160	320
25	-3.9	-4	24.8	165	73.9	52	125.6	300	148.9	165	329
30	-1.1	-2	28.4	170	76.7	54	129.2	305	151.7	170	338
35	1.7	0	32	175	79.4	56	132.8	310	154.4	175	347
40	4.4	2	35.6	180	82.2	58	136.4	315	157.2	180	356
45	7.2	4	39.2	185	85.0	60	140	320	160.0	185	365
50	10.0	6	42.8	190	87.8	62	143.6	325	162.8	190	374
55	12.8	8	46.4	195	90.6	64	147.2	330	165.6	195	383
60	15.6	10	50	200	93.3	66	150.8	335	168.3	200	392
65	18.3	12	53.6	205	96.1	68	154.4	340	171.1	205	401
70	21.1	14	57.2	210	98.9	70	158	345	173.9	210	410
75	23.9	16	60.8	212	100.0	75	167	350	176.7	215	414

CAPACITIES

Year	Model	Engine ID/VIN	Engine Displacement Liters (cc)	Engine Oil with Filter (qts.)	Transaxle (pts.) 4-Spd	Transaxle (pts.) 5-Spd	Transaxle (pts.) Auto.	Transfer Case (pts.)	Drive Axle Front (pts.)	Drive Axle Rear (pts.)	Fuel Tank (gal.)	Cooling System (qts.)
1992	Acclaim	K	2.5 (2507)	4.5	-	4.8	④	-	-	-	16.0	9.0
	Daytona	A	2.2 (2212)	4.5	-	4.8	④	-	-	-	14.0	9.0
	Daytona	J	2.5 (2507)	4.5	-	4.8	④	-	-	-	14.0	9.0
	Daytona	K	2.5 (2507)	4.5	-	-	④	-	-	-	14.0	9.0
	Dynasty	K	2.5 (2507)	4.5	-	-	④	-	-	-	16.0	9.0
	Lebaron	J	2.5 (2507)	4.5	-	4.8	④	-	-	-	14.0	9.0
	Lebaron	K	2.5 (2507)	4.5	-	4.8	④	-	-	-	14.0	9.0
	Shadow	D	2.2 (2212)	4.5	-	4.8	④	-	-	-	14.0	9.0
	Shadow	J	2.5 (2507)	4.5	-	4.8	④	-	-	-	14.0	9.0
	Shadow	K	2.5 (2507)	4.5	-	4.8	④	-	-	-	14.0	9.0
	Spirit	A	2.2 (2212)	4.5	-	4.8	④	-	-	-	16.0	9.0
	Spirit	J	2.5 (2507)	4.5	-	4.8	④	-	-	-	16.0	9.0
	Spirit	K	2.5 (2507)	4.5	-	4.8	④	-	-	-	16.0	9.0
	Sundance	D	2.2 (2212)	4.5	-	4.8	④	-	-	-	14.0	9.0
	Sundance	K	2.5 (2507)	4.5	-	4.8	④	-	-	-	14.0	9.0
1993	Acclaim	K	2.5 (2507)	4.5	-	4.8	⑤	-	-	-	16.0	9.0
	Acclaim	V	2.5 (2507)	4.5	-	4.8	⑤	-	-	-	18.0	9.0
	Daytona	A	2.2 (2212)	4.5	-	4.8	⑤	-	-	-	14.0	9.0
	Daytona	D	2.2 (2212)	4.5	-	4.8	⑤	-	-	-	14.0	9.0
	Dynasty	K	2.5 (2507)	4.5	-	-	⑤	-	-	-	16.0	9.0
	Lebaron	K	2.5 (2507)	4.5	-	4.8	⑤	-	-	-	16.0	9.0
	Lebaron	D	2.2 (2212)	4.5	-	4.8	⑤	-	-	-	14.0	9.0
	Shadow	D	2.2 (2212)	4.5	-	4.8	⑤	-	-	-	14.0	9.0
	Shadow	K	2.5 (2507)	4.5	-	4.8	⑤	-	-	-	14.0	9.0
	Spirit	K	2.5 (2507)	4.5	-	4.8	⑤	-	-	-	16.0	9.0
	Spirit	V	2.5 (2507)	4.5	-	-	⑤	-	-	-	18.0	9.0
	Sundance	D	2.2 (2212)	4.5	-	4.8	⑤	-	-	-	14.0	9.0
	Sundance	K	2.5 (2507)	4.5	-	4.8	⑤	-	-	-	14.0	9.0
1994	Acclaim	K	2.5 (2507)	4.5	-	4.8	⑤	-	-	-	16.0	9.0
	Acclaim	V	2.5 (2507)	4.5	-	4.8	⑤	-	-	-	18.0	9.0
	Shadow	D	2.2 (2212)	4.5	-	4.8	⑤	-	-	-	14.0	9.0
	Daytona	K	2.5 (2507)	4.5	-	4.8	⑤	-	-	-	16.0	9.0
	Spirit	K	2.5 (2507)	4.5	-	-	⑤	-	-	-	18.0	9.0
	Spirit	V	2.5 (2507)	4.5	-	4.8	⑤	-	-	-	16.0	9.0
	Sundance	D	2.2 (2212)	4.5	-	4.8	⑤	-	-	-	14.0	9.0
	Sundance	K	2.5 (2507)	4.5	-	4.8	⑤	-	-	-	14.0	9.0
1995	Acclaim	K	2.5 (2507)	4.5	-	4.8	⑤	-	-	-	16.0	9.0
	Acclaim	V	2.5 (2507)	4.5	-	-	⑤	-	-	-	18.0	9.0
	Spirit	K	2.5 (2507)	4.5	-	4.8	⑤	-	-	-	16.0	9.0
	Spirit	V	2.5 (2507)	4.5	-	-	⑤	-	-	-	18.0	9.0

① Overhaul capacity shown. For pan removal only - 6.0 pts.
② Non-fleet models 17.8 pts. Fleet models - 18.4 pts.
③ For pan removal only - 8.0 pts.
④ Overhaul capacity shown. For pan removal only - 8.0 pts.

④ 3 speed - 17.8 pts.
3 speed (fixed) - 18.4 pts.
3 speed (lock-up) - 17.0 pts.
4 speed - 19.8 pts.
4 speed (electronic) - 18.2 pts.
For pan removal only - 8.0 pts.

⑤ 3 speed - 17.6 pts.
3 speed (fixed) - 18.4 pts.
4 speed - 19.8 pts.
Overhaul capacity shown.
For pan removal only - 5.6 pts.

86731C17

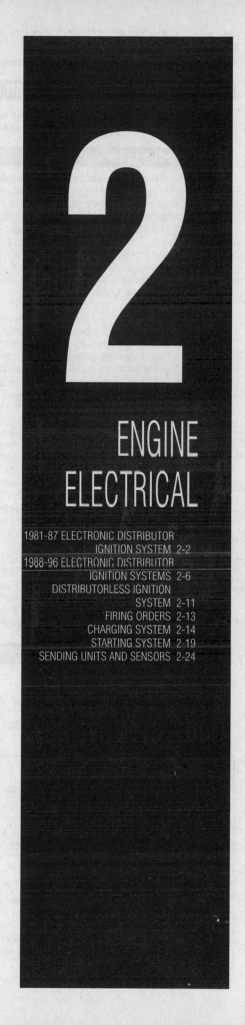

2

ENGINE ELECTRICAL

1981-87 ELECTRONIC DISTRIBUTOR IGNITION SYSTEM

➡For information on understanding electricity and troubleshooting electrical circuits, please refer to Section 6 of this manual.

General Information

2.6L engines utilize a system which consists of the battery, ignition switch, coil, and IC igniter (electronic control unit) built into the distributor, spark plugs and inter-component wiring. Primary current is switched by the IC igniter in response to timing signals produced by a magnetic pickup.

Models using the 2.2L and 2.5L engines are equipped with the "Electronic Fuel Control System". This consists of a Spark Control Computer, various engine sensors, and a specially calibrated carburetor with an electronically controlled fuel metering system. On fuel injected engines, the computer controls the total amount of fuel injected by slightly modifying the pulses that operate the injectors. The function of this system is to provide a way for the engine to burn a correct air-fuel mixture.

On The Spark Control Computer (also known as the Power Module—this component develops into what is known as the Powertrain Control Module, Single Board Engine Controller or the Single Module Engine Controller on newer vehicles) is the heart of the entire system. It has the capability of igniting the fuel mixture according to different models of engine operation by delivering an infinite number of different variable advance curves. The computer consists of one electronic printed circuit board, which simultaneously received signals from all the sensors and within milliseconds, analyzes them to determine how the engine is operating and then advances or retards the timing.

The distributor, on all three engines, is equipped with both centrifugal and vacuum advance mechanisms on 1981-83 models. The centrifugal advance is located below the rotor assembly, and has governor weights that move in and out with changes in engine speed. As speed increases the weights move outward and cause the reluctor to rotate ahead of the distributor shaft, this advances ignition timing. The vacuum advance has a spring loaded diaphragm connected to the breaker assembly. The diaphragm is actuated by intake manifold vacuum. As the vacuum increases, the diaphragm causes the movable breaker assembly to pivot in a direction opposite to distributor rotation, advancing the ignition timing.

On 1984-87 models, the vacuum advance mechanism has been replaced by a vacuum transducer, located on top of the computer. This unit responds to engine vacuum the way the vacuum advance unit does, but produces an electronic signal that is fed to the computer, instead of acting to advance the ignition timing directly. This allows the computer to tailor the advance curve (the amount of advance the distributor provides) to the operating conditions.

Diagnosis and Testing

♦ See Figures 1, 2 and 3

All diagnosis and testing should be perform in order according to the service charts below. Perform all test in the order stated by the diagnosis charts. Battery voltage must be 12 volts before starting all test procedures.

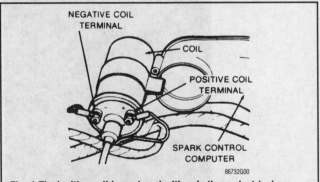

Fig. 1 The ignition coil is equipped with only three electrical connections—the negative terminal, the positive terminal and the coil-to-distributor high tension cable

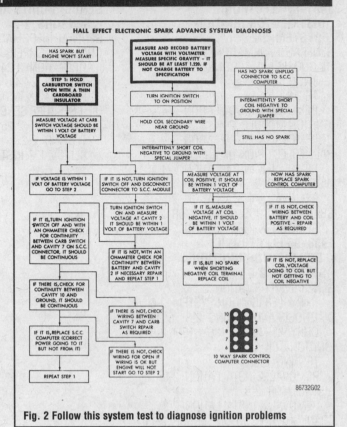

Fig. 2 Follow this system test to diagnose ignition problems

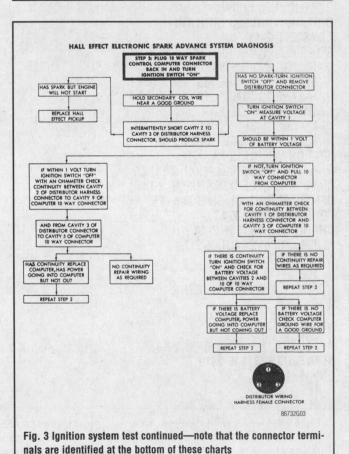

Fig. 3 Ignition system test continued—note that the connector terminals are identified at the bottom of these charts

Ignition Coil

TESTING

▶ **See Figures 4, 5, 6 and 7**

1. Inspect the coil for signs of external leaks and arcing; replace the ignition coil if any are found. Every time an ignition coil assembly is replaced because of a burned tower, carbon tracking, arcing at the tower, or damage to the nipple or boot on the coil end of the coil wire (secondary cable), replace the cable (coil wire). Any arcing at the tower will carbonize the nipple so that placing it on a new coil assembly will invariably cause another coil failure. If coil wire shows any signs of damage, the coil wire (secondary cable) should be replaced since carbon tracking on an old cable can cause arcing and ruin a new coil assembly.

➡ **To perform this test on the coil, you have to fashion or purchase a particular jumper wire tool. You'll need two simple wires several feet long with alligator clips on the ends. A third wire must incorporate a capacitor of 0.33 MicroFarad capacitance. The materials and components needed to make up such jumpers should be available at a reasonable price in a local electronics store. Refer to the accompanying diagram for the make-up of the jumper wire tool.**

2. With a Digital Volt-Ohmmeter (DVOM) measure the battery voltage at the battery terminals and note it. Battery voltage must be at least 12.4 volts to adequately test the coil.

3. Disconnect the coil secondary wire (the high tension cable) from the distributor cap.

4. With the ignition key **ON** and by using the special jumper wire (refer to the accompanying diagram), hold the coil secondary cable approximately ¼ in. (6mm) from a good engine ground with insulated pliers (or similar insulated tool) and momentarily touch the negative (-) terminal of the coil to ground. A strong, blue-white spark should be obtained. If no spark was obtained, proceed with the test, otherwise the ignition is functioning within normal parameters.

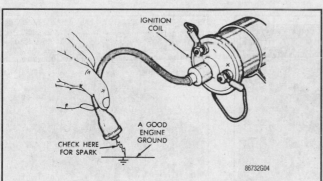

Fig. 4 To test the secondary spark, hold the secondary coil wire (the high tension cable) near a good ground while shorting terminal 2 to terminal 3

5. Turn the ignition key **OFF** and detach the 10-way dual connector from the Spark Control Computer (SCC).

➡ **Do not remove the grease from the 10-way dual connector or connector cavity in the SCC—this grease is used to prevent moisture from corroding the connector terminals.**

6. Inspect the amount of grease in the 10-way dual connector. If there is not at least ⅛ in. (3mm) of grease on the bottom of the SCC connector, apply Mopar® Multi-purpose grease Part No. 4318063, or equivalent, over the entire end of the connector plug before reattaching it.

7. With the ignition key **ON** and by using the special jumper wire (refer to the accompanying diagram), once again hold the coil secondary cable approximately ¼ in. (6mm) from a good engine ground with insulated pliers (or similar insulated tool) and momentarily touch the negative (-) terminal of the coil to ground. A strong, blue-white spark should be obtained. If no spark was obtained, proceed with the test, otherwise the computer output circuit is shorted. Replace the SCC with a new one and try to start the vehicle.

8. Measure the voltage at the ignition coil positive (+) terminal. The voltage should be within one volt of the aforemeasured battery voltage. If the voltage is not as specified, there is a wiring fault between the battery and the coil.

9. If the voltage was within one volt, measure the battery voltage at the ignition coil negative (-) terminal. This should also be within one volt of the battery voltage. If this voltage is within specifications and no spark was produced in Step 4 and Step 7, the ignition coil is faulty and should be replaced with a new one. If the correct voltage is not exhibited at the coil negative terminal, the coil is also faulty and must be replaced with a new one.

10. If the vehicle still does not start, the problem lies elsewhere.

REMOVAL & INSTALLATION

➡ **The ignition coil is either mounted on the right-hand inner fender well, near the A/C compressor pulley or on the left-hand side of the engine, next to the distributor.**

1. Disconnect the negative battery cable.
2. Using a small wrench or socket and ratchet wrench, remove the positive and negative coil terminal attaching nuts. Label, then pull the positive and negative terminal wires from the ignition coil terminal studs.

⚠ WARNING

Do not pull on the ignition cable wire; always pull on the wire boot.

3. Grasp the ignition coil secondary cable (high tension wire) on the boot and pull it from the ignition coil center tower.
4. Remove the ignition coil mounting bracket retaining bolt and remove the coil and bracket from the engine compartment.
5. Slide the ignition coil out of the mounting bracket.
To install:
6. Slide the new ignition coil into the mounting bracket.
7. Position the ignition coil and bracket in place either on the inner fender well or on the left-hand side of the engine.
8. Install the ignition coil bracket mounting bolt until secure.

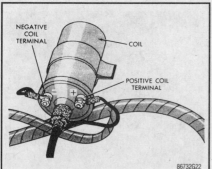

Fig. 5 When testing the ignition coil, make certain to correctly identify the positive (+) and negative (-) terminals

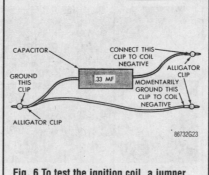

Fig. 6 To test the ignition coil, a jumper wire like the one shown must be fabricated or purchased

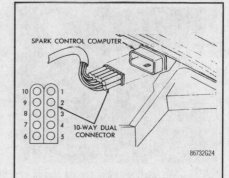

Fig. 7 10-way Spark Control Computer (SCC) connector terminal identification

9. Push the secondary ignition coil onto the ignition coil center tower and make sure that the terminal engages the wire fully.

10. Slide the positive and negative wires eyelets over their respective ignition coil terminal studs, then install the terminal attaching nuts until snug. Make certain that the positive wires are connected to the positive terminal and the negative wires to the negative terminal.

11. Connect the negative battery cable.

Ignition Module

REMOVAL & INSTALLATION

♦ **See Figure 8**

The ignition module, referred to as either the Spark Control Computer (SCC) or Power Module by Chrysler, is mounted on the inner, left-hand fender, next to the battery. The SCC or Power Module is what develops into Chrysler's Powertrain Control Module (PCM).

1. To gain access to the SCC, remove the battery from the vehicle.

2. Disconnect the air inlet hose from the rear end of the SCC. Position the hose aside without disconnecting it from the air cleaner assembly.

3. Detach the 10-way and the 14-way engine wiring harness connectors from the SCC.

➡**Do not remove the grease from the 10-way dual connector or connector cavity in the SCC—this grease is used to prevent moisture from corroding the connector terminals.**

4. If the SCC is equipped with a vacuum transducer (carbureted engines), label and disconnect the vacuum hose from the SCC.

5. Remove the SCC mounting screws and pull the SCC away from the inner fender. Remove the SCC from the vehicle.

To install:

6. Hold the SCC in position against the inner fender, then install the mounting screws until snug.

7. If equipped, attach the vacuum hose to the vacuum transducer.

8. Inspect the amount of grease in the 10-way and 14-way connectors. If there is not at least ⅛ in. (3mm) of grease on the bottom of the SCC connector, apply Mopar® Multi-purpose grease Part No. 4318063, or equivalent, over the entire end of the connector plugs before reattaching them.

9. Push the 14-way and 10-way connectors into their respective ports until the connector tangs engage fully. Give a slight tug backward to ensure that the connector plugs are fully engaged.

10. Slide the air inlet hose over the SCC neck and tighten the clamp until snug.

11. Install the battery and connect the battery cables.

Hall Effect Pick-up Assembly

REMOVAL & INSTALLATION

2.2L and 2.5L Engines

♦ **See Figures 9, 10, 11, 12 and 13**

1. Disconnect the negative battery cable.

2. Remove the distributor splash shield mounting screws (2) along with the pick-up lead connector retainer screw and remove the splash shield.

3. Loosen the two distributor cap retaining screws. Remove the distributor cap.

4. Pull the rotor up off the distributor shaft.

5. Remove the two clips retaining the Hall effect pick-up assembly to the distributor body on 1981–85 models.

6. Pull the Hall effect pick-up lead multi-prong connector out of its retaining clip, then detach it from the engine wiring harness. Then, lift the Hall effect pick-up assembly off of the top of the distributor body.

To install:

7. Position the Hall effect pick-up assembly on the distributor. Route the pick-up wires properly through the hole in the distributor body so they will not

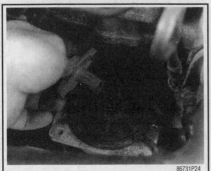
Fig. 8 The SCC 10-way connector is plugged into the SCC right next to the battery in the engine compartment

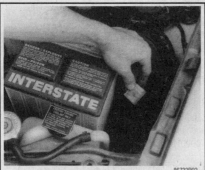
Fig. 9 After removing the cover, remove the hold-down screws and . . .

Fig. 10 . . . lift the distributor cap off of the distributor housing—1986 Reliant shown

Fig. 11 The rotor simply pulls off of the distributor shaft—note the direction it points before removal

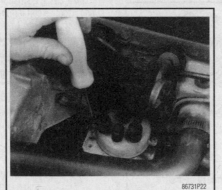
Fig. 12 Detach the distributor pick-up lead connector from the engine wiring harness

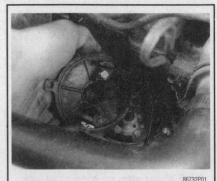
Fig. 13 Lift the pick-up assembly from the distributor housing

be pinched and damaged when the distributor cap is reinstalled. Install the wires to the retaining clip and attach the distributor lead to the engine wiring harness. Make sure the multi-prong connector is securely plugged in and then securely mounted in its retaining clip.

8. Secure the Hall effect assembly with the hold-down retaining clips.

9. Set the distributor cap onto the distributor housing, making sure that the Hall effect pick-up wires are not being pinched.

10. Tighten the distributor cap hold-down screws until snug.

11. Install the distributor cover.

12. Connect the negative battery cable.

2.6L Engine

▶ **See Figure 14**

1. Disconnect the negative battery cable.

2. Unscrew the 2 Phillips type retaining screws and remove the distributor cap. Set the cap aside with the spark plug cables still attached.

3. Remove the two screws retaining the rotor and pull it off of the distributor shaft. Using a box or socket wrench, remove the governor assembly retaining bolt from the upper end of the distributor shaft.

4. Slide the governor assembly upward and off of the shaft. Make sure to keep governor springs either in place or in order for proper installation in the same positions (they are not interchangeable).

5. Remove the distributor pick-up wire retaining clamp screw from the retaining clamp on the side of the distributor.

6. Remove the pick-up/igniter mounting screws from the clip on the side of the distributor. Unplug the pick-up/wiring connector from the harness. Then, remove both the pick-up coil and igniter, keeping them together. Pull the wiring conduit out of the side of the distributor.

7. If you are replacing the breaker assembly or pole piece underneath, remove the two retaining screws and remove them.

To install:

8. If removed, position the breaker assembly or pole piece on the distributor and install the mounting screws until snug.

9. Route the pick-up/igniter wiring through the distributor, then set the pick-up/igniter on the distributor. Install the mounting screws until secure.

10. Secure the distributor pick-up/igniter wiring to the wiring retaining clamp with the screw.

11. Slide the governor down over the distributor shaft, making sure that the springs are mounted in their original positions. Tighten the governor nut until secure.

12. Install the rotor onto the distributor shaft. Make sure to install the rotor retaining screws.

13. Install the distributor cap, then connect the negative battery cable.

Distributor

REMOVAL & INSTALLATION

▶ **See Figures 9, 10, 12, 15, 16, 17 and 18**

Engine Not Disturbed

➡**Use this procedure only if the engine was not disturbed (the crankshaft wasn't rotated).**

1. Disconnect the negative battery cable.

2. Detach the distributor pick-up lead wire at the engine wiring harness connector (two are found on 2.2L turbocharged vehicles). Remove the two retaining screws and remove the distributor splash shield.

3. Remove the two distributor cap retaining screws and remove the distributor cap.

4. Rotate the engine crankshaft (in the direction of normal rotation—clockwise when viewing the engine from the front) until No. 1 cylinder piston is at Top Dead Center (TDC) on the compression stroke. At this point, the timing mark on the crankshaft pulley or flywheel/flex plate will line up with the TDC mark on the timing mark tab or transaxle housing and the distributor rotor will point to the high tension wire terminal for the No. 1 cylinder in the cap simultaneously. If the rotor does not line up properly, turn the engine crankshaft another 360° (one full rotation).

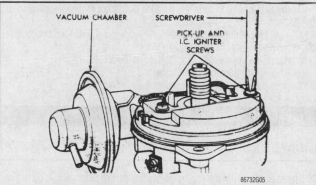

Fig. 14 The pick-up/igniter assembly is secured to the distributor housing by 2 Phillips head screws—2.6L engines

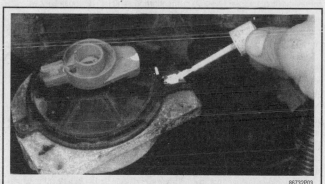

Fig. 15 Before removing the distributor, matchmark the rotor to the distributor housing, then . . .

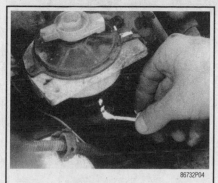

Fig. 16 . . . matchmark the distributor housing to the engine block

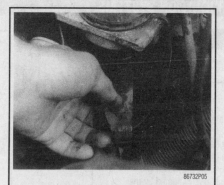

Fig. 17 Remove the distributor hold-down bolt and bracket, then . . .

Fig. 18 . . . lift the distributor out of the engine—all 1981–87 2.2L and 2.5L engines

5. Matchmark the distributor rotor and the distributor housing for installation reference. Also mark the relationship between the body of the distributor and the engine block so that the distributor can be installed in a position where the ignition timing will be almost correct.

6. Remove the distributor hold-down bolt.

7. Carefully lift the distributor from the engine. The shaft will rotate slightly as the distributor is removed because of the curvature in the teeth of the drive gear. Note the angle at which the rotor sits as the shaft stops rotating and also mark it on the distributor housing also.

To install:

8. Before installing the distributor, rotate the rotor so that it points to the second matchmark on the distributor housing (the one made after the distributor was lifted out of the engine).

9. Position the distributor over the distributor hole, so that the distributor-to-engine block matchmark is aligned. Slowly insert the distributor into the engine block. If the distributor drive gear does not immediately engage with the accessory shaft, turn the rotor back and forth very slightly, keeping it as nearly aligned with the second mark as possible. Do this until it engages the drive gear, making it easy to slide the distributor into the block.

10. Once the distributor is seated on the block, verify that the first mark and the rotor tip are aligned. Make sure the distributor seats fully so that the gasket at its base will seal.

11. Install the hold-down bolt to hold the distributor in this preliminary position.

12. Install the distributor cap and spark plug wires. Tighten the distributor hold-down screws until snug.

13. Attach the ignition coil cable to the distributor.

14. Connect the negative battery cable.

15. Adjust the ignition timing, as described in Section 1.

Engine Disturbed

➡Use the following procedure if the engine was cranked or the crankshaft was rotated with the distributor removed.

1. Disconnect the negative battery cable.

2. Detach the distributor pick-up lead wire at the engine wiring harness connector (two are found on 2.2L turbocharged vehicles). Remove the two retaining screws and remove the distributor splash shield.

3. Remove the two distributor cap retaining screws and remove the distributor cap.

4. Rotate the engine crankshaft (in the direction of normal rotation—clockwise when viewing the engine from the front) until No. 1 cylinder piston is at Top Dead Center (TDC) on the compression stroke. At this point, the timing mark on the crankshaft pulley or flywheel/flex plate will line up with the TDC mark on the timing mark tab or transaxle housing and the distributor rotor will point to the high tension wire terminal for the No. 1. cylinder in the cap simultaneously. If the rotor does not line up properly, turn the engine crankshaft another 360° (one full rotation).

5. Matchmark the distributor rotor and the distributor housing for installation reference. Also mark the relationship between the body of the distributor and the engine block so that the distributor can be installed in a position where the ignition timing will be almost correct.

6. Remove the distributor hold-down bolt.

7. Carefully lift the distributor from the engine. The shaft will rotate slightly as the distributor is removed because of the curvature in the teeth of the drive gear. Note the angle at which the rotor sits as the shaft stops rotating and also mark it on the distributor housing also.

To install:

➡This installation procedure is for engines which have been disturbed (the crankshaft was rotated) while the distributor was removed from the engine. If this is not the case with your engine, refer to the previous procedure.

8. Rotate the crankshaft until the No. 1 cylinder piston is at TDC on the compression stroke. This will be indicated by the 0 mark on the flywheel or crankshaft pulley aligning with the pointer on the clutch housing or engine front cover. Now, you must verify that No. 1 cylinder is at Top Dead Center firing position, and not at the top of the exhaust stroke. Do this in one of the two following ways:

a. Remove the rocker arm cover and check the positions of No. 1 valve springs and rockers. The valves should be closed (with springs decompressed as far as possible) and the rockers should be in contact with the base circles of the cams, rather than with the cam lobes. If the camshaft is depressing either the intake or exhaust valves (remember, this only refers to the No. 1 cylinder valves), rotate the engine another 360° until the timing marks are again at Top Dead Center.

b. OR remove the No. 1 Cylinder spark plug and put your finger over the spark plug hole (make sure to create a good seal around the spark plug hole with your finger or thumb) as you crank the engine toward Top Dead Center. As the engine approaches TDC on the compression stroke, you will feel air being forcibly expelled from the cylinder. After this air is felt, rotate the engine so that the TDC marks are aligned. If the engine is approaching Top Dead Center of the exhaust stroke, air will not be forcibly expelled. If this latter situation is the case, turn the engine another 360°, and feel for air pressure.

9. Once the engine is at TDC No. 1 firing position, position the rotor just ahead of the No. 1 cylinder terminal of the distributor cap, at the second mark made earlier, and lower the distributor into the engine. With the distributor fully seated, the rotor should be directly under the No. 1 cylinder terminal in the cap.

10. Install the hold-down bolt to hold the distributor in this preliminary position.

11. Install the distributor cap and spark plug wires. Tighten the distributor hold-down screws until snug.

12. Attach the ignition coil cable to the distributor.

13. Connect the negative battery cable.

14. Adjust the ignition timing, as described in Section 1.

Crankshaft Position Sensor

REMOVAL & INSTALLATION

Refer to Section 4 for the crankshaft position sensor removal and installation procedures.

1988–96 ELECTRONIC DISTRIBUTOR IGNITION SYSTEMS

General Information

CHRYSLER IGNITION SYSTEM

▶ **See Figures 19 and 20**

The engine speed input is supplied to the PCM by the distributor pick-up. The distributor pick-up is a Hall effect device.

All 1988–95 versions of the 2.2L EFI (non-turbocharged), 2.5L EFI, 2.5L MFI Flex Fuel and 2.5L MFI Turbo I engines utilize the Chrysler ignition system. The 2.2L MFI Turbo III engine utilizes a distributorless ignition system, which will be covered later in this section. The Chrysler ignition system is regulated by the Powertrain Control Module (PCM), which is also known as the Single Board Engine Controller (SBEC) or the Single Module Engine Controller (SMEC),

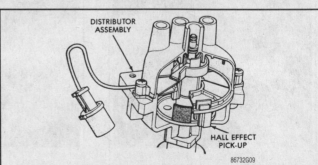

Fig. 19 The internal shutter (interrupter) mechanism of the 2.2L EFI and 2.5L EFI engines

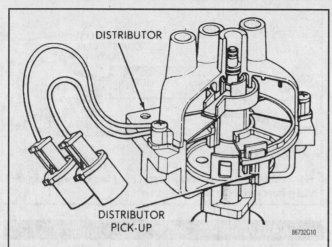

Fig. 20 The distributor for the 2.5L MFI Turbo I and the 2.5L MFI Flex Fuel engines has two pick-up leads, whereas the other distributor has only one

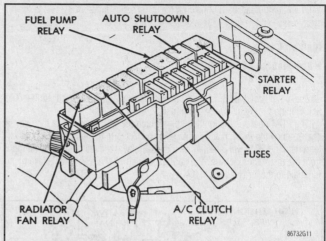

Fig. 21 ASD relay location for the 1992–93 Daytona and LeBaron coupe/convertible models shown. On 1991 the Daytona and LeBaron the ASD relay is located in place of the A/C clutch relay

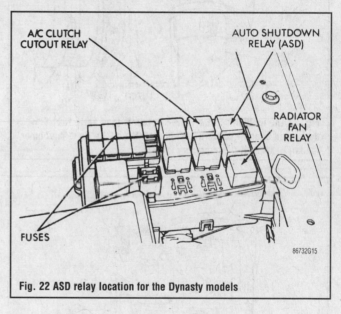

Fig. 22 ASD relay location for the Dynasty models

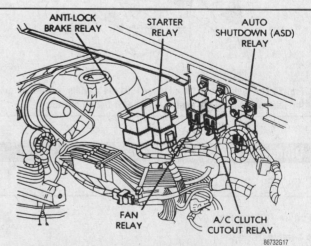

Fig. 23 ASD relay location for the 1991–95 Spirit, Acclaim, Shadow and Sundance models shown, 1988–90 models (except Dynasty) similar

depending on the year of manufacture of the vehicle. The PCM, SBEC and SMEC function in the exact same manner and will be known from here on as simply the PCM. The PCM supplies battery voltage to the ignition coil through the Auto Shutdown (ASD) relay. The PCM also controls the ground circuit for the ignition coil. By switching the ground path for the coil ON and OFF, the PCM adjusts the ignition timing to meet changing engine operating conditions.

During the crank-start period, the PCM advances ignition timing a predetermined amount. During engine operation, the amount of spark advance provided by the PCM is determined by these input factors:

- Coolant temperature
- Engine RPM
- Available manifold vacuum

The PCM also regulates the fuel injection system. Refer to Section 4 for electronic engine controls and components.

A shutter, sometimes referred to as an interrupter, is attached to the distributor shaft. The shutter contains four blades, one per engine cylinder. A switch plate is mounted to the distributor housing above the shutter. The switch plate contains the distributor pick-up (Hall effect device and magnet) through which the shutter blades rotate. As the shutter blades pass through the pick-up, they interrupt the magnetic field. The Hall effect device in the pick-up senses the change in the magnetic field and switches ON and OFF (which creates pulses), generating the input signal to the PCM. The PCM calculates engine speed through the number of pulses generated.

On 2.5L MFI (flexible fuel vehicles) engines, one of the shutter blades has a window cut into it. The PCM determines injector synchronization from this window. Also, the PCM uses the input for detonation control.

Auto Shutdown (ASD) Relay

▶ **See Figures 21, 22 and 23**

The PCM operates the Auto Shutdown (ASD) relay and fuel pump relay through one ground path. The PCM operates the relays by switching the ground path on and off. Both relays turn on and off at the same time.

The ASD relay connects the battery voltage to the fuel injector and ignition coil. The fuel pump relay connects the battery voltage to the fuel pump and oxygen sensor heating element.

The PCM turns the ground path off when the ignition switch is in the **OFF** position. Both relays are off. When the ignition switch is in the **ON** or crank position, the PCM monitors the distributor pick-up signal. From the pick-up signal, the PCM determines engine speed and ignition timing (coil dwell). If the PCM does not receive a distributor signal when the ignition switch is in the **RUN** position, it will de-energize both relays. When the relays are de-energized, battery voltage is not supplied to the fuel injector, ignition coil, fuel pump and oxygen sensor heating element.

On Dynasty, Daytona and LeBaron coupe or convertible models, the ASD relay and fuel pump relay are located in the Power Distribution Center. On LeBaron sedan, Spirit, Acclaim, Shadow and Sundance models, the ASD relay and fuel pump relay are mounted on the driver's side fender well, next to the strut tower.

Ignition Coil

▶ See Figures 24 and 25

The 2.2L EFI, 2.5L EFI, 2.5L MFI Turbo I and 2.5L MFI Flex Fuel engines use an epoxy type coil, which is not oil filled. The windings are embedded in a heat and vibration resistant epoxy compound.

The PCM operates the ignition coil through the ASD relay. When the relay is energized by the PCM, battery voltage is connected to the ignition coil positive terminal. The PCM will de-energize the ASD relay if it does not receive an input from the distributor pick-up. The coil is mounted on the rear of the intake manifold next to the air cleaner.

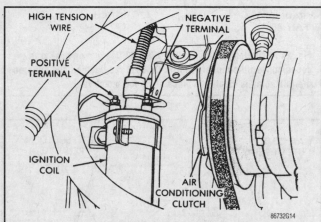

Fig. 24 The ignition coil for 1988–90 models (and early 1991 Sundance and Shadow convertibles) is mounted on the right-hand inner fender, near the A/C compressor

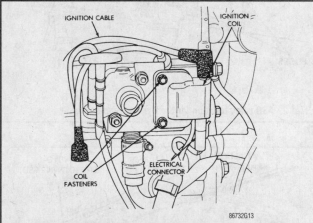

Fig. 25 The ignition coil for all other 1991–95 models is mounted to the left-hand side of the engine block, near the oil dipstick

Diagnosis and Testing

CHRYSLER IGNITION SYSTEM

Failure-To-Start Test

▶ See Figure 26

Before proceeding with this test make certain that spark has been checked for at the coil. Refer to the ignition coil testing procedures. Failure to do this may lead to unnecessary diagnostic time and wrong test results.

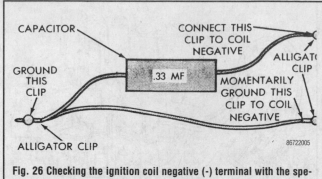

Fig. 26 Checking the ignition coil negative (-) terminal with the special jumper wire—Chrysler ignition system

❉❉ CAUTION

Be sure to apply the parking brake and block the wheels before performing any test with the engine running.

1. Check the battery voltage. It must be at least 12.4 volts to perform the test. If the battery voltage is not at least 12.4 volts, refer to Section 1 for battery charging procedures.

2. Crank the engine for 5 seconds while monitoring the voltage at the coil positive (+) terminal. If the voltage remains near zero during the entire period of cranking, refer to Section 4 for the On-board Diagnostic checks. The checks will test the PCM and the ASD relay.

3. If the voltage is at near-battery voltage and drops to zero after 1–2 seconds of cranking, refer to Section 4 On-board Diagnostic procedures. The problem is likely to be related to the distributor reference pick-up circuit to the PCM.

4. If the voltage remains at near battery voltage during the entire 5 seconds, with the key **OFF**, remove the PCM 60-way connector. Check the 60-way connector for any terminals that are pushed out or loose.

5. Remove the connector from the coil positive (+) and connect a jumper wire between the battery positive (+) terminal and the coil (+) terminal.

6. Using the special jumper wire shown in the illustration, momentarily ground terminal No. 19 of the 60-way connector. A spark should be generated when the ground is removed.

7. If a spark is generated, replace the PCM with a new one.

8. If no spark is generated, use the special jumper wire to ground the coil negative (-) terminal directly.

9. If a spark is produced, inspect the wiring harness for an open circuit condition.

10. If no spark is produced, replace the ignition coil with a new one.

Ignition Coil

TESTING

▶ See Figure 27

The ignition coil is designed to operate without an external ballast resistor. Inspect the coil for arcing. Test the coil primary and secondary resistance.

To measure the primary resistance, connect an ohmmeter between the positive (+) and negative (-) terminals on the coil. To test the secondary resistance, connect an ohmmeter between the positive (+) coil terminal and the high voltage cable terminal on the coil. Then, measure the resistance between the positive (+) coil terminal and the coil case; the resistance for the case should exhibit infinite resistance. For 1990–95 models, the specific resistance values for coils manufactured by specific companies should be as follows:

• Diamond—primary resistance at 70–80°F (21–27°C) should be 0.97–1.18 ohms and the secondary resistance should be 11,300–15,300 ohms

• Toyodenso—primary resistance at 70–80°F (21–27°C) of 0.95–1.20 ohms and a secondary resistance of 11,300–13,300 ohms

For 1988–89 models, the specific resistance values for the ignition coils manufactured by specific companies should be as follows:

• Chrysler Prestolite—primary resistance 1.35–1.55 ohms and a secondary resistance of 9,400–11,700 ohms

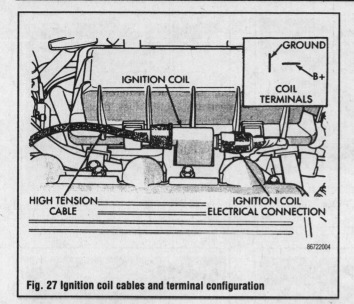

Fig. 27 Ignition coil cables and terminal configuration

- Chrysler Essex—primary resistance of 1.35–1.55 ohms and a secondary resistance of 9,000–12,200 ohms
- Diamond—primary resistance of 1.35–1.55 ohms and a secondary resistance of 15,000–19,000 ohms

Replace any coil with a new one if it does not meet the specifications.

If the ignition coil is replaced with a new one due to a burned tower, carbon tracking, arcing at the tower, or damage to the terminal or boot on the coil end of the secondary cable, the cable must also be replaced with a new one. Arcing at the tower will carbonize the nipple which, if it is connected to a new coil, will cause the coil to fail.

If a secondary cable shows any signs of damage, the cable should be replaced with a new cable and new terminal. Carbon tracking on the old cable can cause arcing and the failure of a new coil.

TESTING FOR SPARK AT COIL

♦ See Figure 28

> ❉ **WARNING**
>
> **Spark plug cables may be damaged if this test is performed with more than ¼ inch (6mm) clearance between the cable and an engine ground.**

Remove the coil secondary cable from the distributor cap. Hold the end of the cable about ¼ inch (6mm) away from a good engine ground. Crank the engine and inspect for spark at the coil secondary cable.

There must be a constant spark at the coil secondary cable. If the spark is constant, have a helper continue to crank the engine and, while slowly moving the coil secondary cable away from the ground, look for arcing at the coil tower.

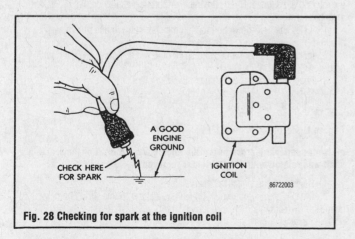

Fig. 28 Checking for spark at the ignition coil

If arcing occurs at the tower, replace the coil with a new one. If the spark is not constant or there is no spark, proceed to the failure-to-start test.

If a constant spark is present and no arcing occurs at the coil tower, the ignition system is producing the necessary high secondary voltage. However, make sure that the spark plugs are firing. Inspect the distributor rotor, cap, spark plug cables, and spark plugs—refer to Section 1. If they are in proper working order, the ignition system is not the reason why the engine will not start. Inspect the fuel system and engine for proper operation.

REMOVAL & INSTALLATION

♦ See Figure 29

The ignition coil is mounted on the thermostat housing on the left-hand side of the engine (radiator side).
1. Disconnect the negative (-) battery cable from the battery.
2. Disconnect the distributor-to-ignition coil high tension cable from the coil.
3. Unplug the wiring harness connector from the coil.
4. Loosen and remove the coil mounting screws, then remove the coil from the vehicle.

To install:
5. Loosely install the ignition coil onto the thermostat housing bracket. Tighten the mounting screws to 85 inch lbs. (9.5 Nm).
6. Attach the wiring harness connector to the coil.
7. Connect the distributor-to-ignition coil high tension cable to the coil.
8. Connect the negative battery cable to the battery.

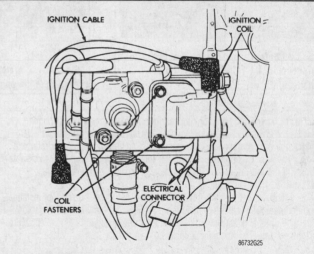

Fig. 29 The ignition coil mounts to the thermostat bracket, next to the oil level dipstick

Distributor

REMOVAL & INSTALLATION

♦ See Figures 30 thru 36

Engine Not Disturbed

➡Use this procedure only if the engine was not disturbed (i.e. the crankshaft wasn't rotated).

1. Disconnect the negative battery cable.
2. Detach the distributor pick-up lead wire at the engine wiring harness connector (two are found on 2.2L turbocharged vehicles). Remove the two retaining screws and remove the distributor splash shield.
3. Remove the two distributor cap retaining screws and remove the distributor cap.
4. Rotate the engine crankshaft (in the direction of normal rotation—clockwise when viewing the engine from the front) until No. 1 cylinder piston is at

Fig. 30 After removing the cover, remove the hold-down screws and . . .

Fig. 31 . . . lift the distributor cap off of the distributor housing—1986 Reliant shown

Fig. 32 Detach the distributor pick-up lead connector from the engine wiring harness

Fig. 33 Before removing the distributor, matchmark the rotor to the distributor housing, then . . .

Fig. 34 . . . matchmark the distributor housing to the engine block

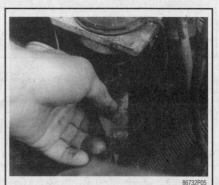

Fig. 35 Remove the distributor hold-down bolt and bracket, then . . .

Top Dead Center (TDC) on the compression stroke. At this point, the timing mark on the crankshaft pulley or flywheel/flex plate will line up with the TDC mark on the timing mark tab or transaxle housing and the distributor rotor will point to the high tension wire terminal for the No. 1. cylinder in the cap simultaneously. If the rotor does not line up properly, turn the engine crankshaft another 360° (one full rotation).

5. Matchmark the distributor rotor and the distributor housing for installation reference. Also mark the relationship between the body of the distributor and the engine block so that the distributor can be installed in a position where the ignition timing will be almost correct.

Fig. 36 . . . lift the distributor out of the engine—all 1981–87 2.2L and 2.5L engines

6. Remove the distributor hold-down bolt.

7. Carefully lift the distributor from the engine. The shaft will rotate slightly as the distributor is removed because of the curvature in the teeth of the drive gear. Note the angle at which the rotor sits as the shaft stops rotating and also mark it on the distributor housing also.

To install:

8. Before installing the distributor, rotate the rotor so that it points to the second matchmark on the distributor housing (the one made after the distributor was lifted out of the engine).

9. Position the distributor over the distributor hole, so that the distributor-to-engine block matchmark is aligned. Slowly insert the distributor into the engine block. If the distributor drive gear does not immediately engage with the accessory shaft, turn the rotor back and forth very slightly, keeping it as nearly aligned with the second mark as possible. Do this until it engages the drive gear, making it easy to slide the distributor into the block.

10. Once the distributor is seated on the block, verify that the first mark and the rotor tip are aligned. Make sure the distributor seats fully so that the gasket at its base will seal.

11. Install the hold-down bolt to hold the distributor in this preliminary position.

12. Install the distributor cap and spark plug wires. Tighten the distributor hold-down screws until snug.

13. Attach the ignition coil cable to the distributor.

14. Connect the negative battery cable.

15. Adjust the ignition timing, as described in Section 1.

Engine Disturbed

➡**Use the following procedure if the engine was cranked or the crankshaft was rotated with the distributor removed.**

1. Disconnect the negative battery cable.

2. Detach the distributor pick-up lead wire at the engine wiring harness connector (two are found on 2.2L turbocharged vehicles). Remove the two retaining screws and remove the distributor splash shield.

3. Remove the two distributor cap retaining screws and remove the distributor cap.

4. Rotate the engine crankshaft (in the direction of normal rotation—clockwise when viewing the engine from the front) until No. 1 cylinder piston is at Top Dead Center (TDC) on the compression stroke. At this point, the timing mark on the crankshaft pulley or flywheel/flex plate will line up with the TDC mark on the timing mark tab or transaxle housing and the distributor rotor will point to the high tension wire terminal for the No. 1. cylinder in the cap simultaneously. If the rotor does not line up properly, turn the engine crankshaft another 360° (one full rotation).

5. Matchmark the distributor rotor and the distributor housing for installation reference. Also mark the relationship between the body of the distributor and the engine block so that the distributor can be installed in a position where the ignition timing will be almost correct.

6. Remove the distributor hold-down bolt.

7. Carefully lift the distributor from the engine. The shaft will rotate slightly as the distributor is removed because of the curvature in the teeth of the drive gear. Note the angle at which the rotor sits as the shaft stops rotating and also mark it on the distributor housing also.

To install:

➡This installation procedure is written for engines which have been disturbed (i.e. the crankshaft was rotated) while the distributor was removed from the engine. If this is not the case with your engine, refer to the previous procedure.

8. Rotate the crankshaft until the No. 1 cylinder piston is at TDC on the compression stroke. This will be indicated by the 0 mark on the flywheel or crankshaft pulley aligning with the pointer on the clutch housing or engine front cover. Now, you must verify that No. 1 cylinder is at Top Dead Center firing position, and not at the top of the exhaust stroke. Do this in one of the two following ways:

a. Remove the rocker arm cover and check the positions of No. 1 valve springs and rockers. The valves should be closed (with springs decompressed as far as possible) and the rockers should be in contact with the base circles of the cams, rather than with the cam lobes. If the camshaft is depressing either the intake or exhaust valves (remember, this only refers to the No. 1 cylinder valves), rotate the camshaft another 360° until the timing marks are again at Top Dead Center.

b. OR remove the No. 1 Cylinder spark plug and put your finger over the spark plug hole (make sure to create a good seal around the spark plug hole with your finger or thumb) as you crank the engine toward Top Dead Center. As the engine approaches TDC on the compression stroke, you will feel air being forcibly expelled from the cylinder. After this air is felt, rotate the engine so that the TDC marks are aligned. If the engine is approaching Top Dead Center of the exhaust stroke, air will not be forcibly expelled. If this latter situation is the case, turn the engine another 360°, and feel for air pressure.

9. Once the engine is at TDC No. 1 firing position, position the rotor just ahead of the No. 1 cylinder terminal of the distributor cap, at the second mark made earlier, and lower the distributor into the engine. With the distributor fully seated, the rotor should be directly under the No. 1 cylinder terminal in the cap.

10. Install the hold-down bolt to hold the distributor in this preliminary position.

11. Install the distributor cap and spark plug wires. Tighten the distributor hold-down screws until snug.

12. Attach the ignition coil cable to the distributor.

13. Connect the negative battery cable.

14. Adjust the ignition timing, as described in Section 1.

Crankshaft Position Sensor

REMOVAL & INSTALLATION

Although an important part of the engine ignition system, the Crankshaft Position Sensor (CPS) is also a major component in the engine control fuel system. For the CPS procedures, refer to Section 4 in this manual.

DISTRIBUTORLESS IGNITION SYSTEM

General Information

♦ **See Figures 37 thru 42**

There is only one 4-cylinder engine covered by this manual which employs a distributorless ignition system. This engine is the 1991–93 2.2L Turbo III engine.

The distributorless ignition system is referred to as the Direct Ignition System (DIS). This system's three main components are the coil pack, the crankshaft sensor, and the camshaft sensor. The crankshaft and camshaft sensors are hall effect devices. These devices use the change in a magnetic field (from an internal magnet) to sense whether a slot is present on the camshaft sprocket or a window is present on the torque converter driveplate. When a slot or window is sensed, the sensors switch (sensor) input voltage from high (5.0 volts) to low (less than 0.3 volts). As the slot or window passes, the input voltage is switched back to high (5.0 volts). These changes in input voltage allow the engine controller to compute engine speed, crankshaft position, and camshaft position.

The ignition system is regulated by the Powertrain Control Module (PCM). The PCM supplies battery voltage to the ignition coil through the Auto Shutdown (ASD) relay. The PCM also controls the ground circuit for the ignition coil. By switching the ground path for the coil on and off, the PCM adjusts the ignition timing to meet changing engine operating conditions.

During the crank-start period the PCM advances ignition timing a set amount. During engine operation, the amount of spark advance provided by the PCM is determined by these input factors:

- Coolant temperature
- Engine RPM
- Available manifold vacuum

The PCM also regulates the fuel injection system.

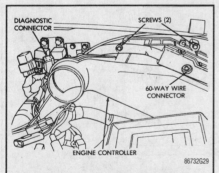

Fig. 37 The Powertrain Control Module (PCM) is mounted on the inner, left-hand fender, next to the battery

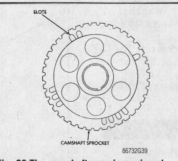

Fig. 38 The camshaft gear is equipped with windows so that the camshaft position sensor can read the angle of the camshaft

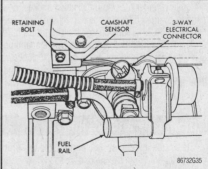

Fig. 39 The camshaft position sensor is located next to the fuel pressure regulator on the cylinder head

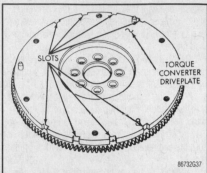

Fig. 40 The CPS uses the slots in the edge of the drive plate to ascertain the positions of the engine's pistons

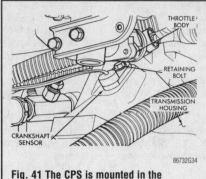

Fig. 41 The CPS is mounted in the transaxle housing, directly below the throttle body

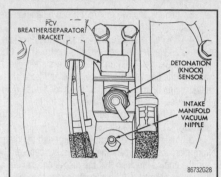

Fig. 42 The 2.2L Turbo III engine's knock sensor is mounted in the intake manifold, directly below the PCV breather

The camshaft position sensor provides fuel injection synchronization and cylinder identification information. The sensor generates pulses that are the input sent to the PCM. The PCM interprets the camshaft position sensor input (along with the crankshaft position sensor input) to determine crankshaft position. The PCM uses the crankshaft position sensor input to determine injector sequence and ignition timing.

The camshaft position sensor determines when a slot or window in the camshaft gear passes beneath it. When metal aligns with the sensor, voltage drops to less than 0.5 volts. When a notch or window aligns with the sensor, voltages jumps to 5.0 volts. As a group of notches or windows pass under the sensor, the voltage switches from low to high then back to low. The number of notches determine the amount of pulses.

The camshaft position sensor is mounted to the top of the timing case cover. The bottom of the sensor is positioned above the camshaft sprocket. The distance between the bottom of the sensor and the camshaft sprocket is critical to the operation of the system.

The crankshaft position sensor senses slots cut into the transaxle driveplate extension. There are 2 sets of slots. Each set contains 4 slots, for a total of 8 slots. Basic timing is set by the position of the last slot in each group. Once the PCM senses the last slot, it determines crankshaft position (which piston will next be at TDC) from the camshaft position sensor input. It may take the PCM up to ⅔ of an engine revolution to determine crankshaft position during cranking.

The PCM uses the camshaft position sensor to determine injector sequence. The PCM determines ignition timing from the crankshaft position sensor. Once the crankshaft position has been determined, the PCM begins energizing the injectors in sequence.

The crankshaft position sensor is located in the transaxle housing, below the throttle body. The bottom of the sensor is positioned next to the driveplate. The distance between the bottom of the sensor and the driveplate is critical to the operation of the system.

The coil assembly consists of 2 coils molded together. The assembly is mounted at the front of the engine. The number of each coil appears on the front of the coil pack.

High tension leads route to each cylinder from the coil. The coil fires two spark plugs every power stroke. One plug is the cylinder under compression, the other cylinder fires on the exhaust stroke. The PCM determines which of the coils to charge and fire at the correct time. The coil's low primary resistance allows the PCM to fully charge the coil for each firing.

The 2.2L Turbo III engine utilizes a detonation sensor (knock sensor). The sensor generates a signal when spark knock occurs in the combustion chambers. The sensor is mounted at the intake manifold behind the PCV breather. The sensor provides information used by the PCM to modify the spark advance and boost schedules in order to eliminate detonation.

Diagnosis and Testing

To test the ignition system perform the test procedures in a particular sequence. Start with the secondary spark test, commence to the coil test (located under the coil procedures later in this section) and finally perform the failure-to-start test. Performing the tests in this order will narrow down the ignition system problem in the easiest manner.

SECONDARY SPARK TEST

✱✱ CAUTION

The Direct Ignition System generates approximately 40,000 volts. Personal injury could result from contact with this system.

Since there are 2 independent coils in the assembly, each coil must be checked individually. Cylinders 1 and 4, and 2 and 3 are grouped together.

1. Remove the cable from the No. 1 spark plug, then insert a clean spark plug into the spark plug boot.

➥Due to the high secondary voltage and risk of electrical shock, it is advisable to wrap a thick, dry cloth around the boot before grasping it.

✱✱ WARNING

Spark plug wire damage may occur if the spark plug is moved more than ¼ in. (6mm) away from the engine ground.

2. Ground the plug to the engine (touch the spark plug metal body to the engine block or other piece of metal on the car).

3. Crank the engine and look for spark across the electrodes of the spark plug.

4. Repeat the test for the three remaining cylinders. If there is no spark during all cylinder tests, refer to the failure-to-start test. If one or more tests indicate irregular, weak or no spark, refer to the coil test.

FAILURE-TO-START TEST

▶ See Figure 43

Before proceeding with this test, refer to the testing procedures for the ignition coil, located later in this section.

1. Using a Digital Volt/Ohmmeter (DVOM) measure the voltage from the

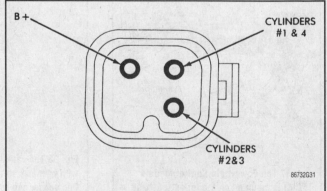

Fig. 43 Ignition coil wiring harness connector terminal identification

negative (-) battery terminal to the positive (+) battery terminal. The voltage should be at least 12.4 volts. This amount of voltage is necessary for an accurate inspection of the system.

2. Detach the ignition coil harness connector and attach the positive (+) lead of the DVOM to the B+ terminal of the harness connector. Connect the negative lead of the DVOM to a good ground.

3. Crank the engine over for approximately 5 seconds while monitoring the voltage at the B+ connector terminal.

    a. If the voltage remains near zero during the entire period of cranking, check the Auto Shutdown (ASD) relay and PCM; refer to Section 4 for more details regarding Diagnosis Read-out Boxes (DRB scan tools) and PCM diagnostics.

    b. If the voltage is at near-battery voltage and drops to zero after 1–2 seconds of cranking, check the camshaft sensor, crankshaft sensor and their circuits. Refer to Section 4 for more information on testing the crankshaft and camshaft position sensors.

    c. If the voltage remains at near-battery voltage during the entire 5 seconds, continue with the test.

➡**The Powertrain Control Module (PCM) is mounted to the left-hand inner fender, next to the battery.**

4. Turn the ignition key **OFF**. Remove the PCM 60-way connector. Check the 60-way connector for any terminals loose from the connector.

Ignition Coil Pack

TESTING

Coil Test

▸ **See Figures 44 and 45**

➡**Coil one fires cylinders 1 and 4; coil two fires cylinders 2 and 3. Each coil tower is labeled with the number of the corresponding cylinder.**

1. Unplug the ignition cables from the coil terminals and the spark plugs. Make certain to label them before removal. Measure the resistance of the cables. Resistance must be between 3,000–12,000 ohms per ft. (30.5 cm) of cable. Replace any cable not within tolerance.

2. Unplug the electrical wiring harness connector from the coil pack.

3. Measure the primary resistance of each coil. At the coil, connect an ohmmeter between the B+ pin and the pin corresponding to the cylinders in ques-

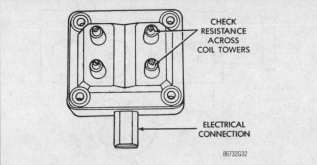

Fig. 45 Secondary resistance should be measured from each tower belonging to the same coil—cylinders 1 and 4 belong to one coil; cylinders 2 and 3 belong to another

tion. Resistance on the primary side of each coil should be 0.5–0.7 ohms. Replace the coil with a new one if the resistance is not within tolerance.

4. Remove the ignition cables from the secondary towers of the coil. Measure the secondary resistance of the coil between the towers of each individual coil. Resistance should be 11,600–15,800 ohms. If the coils' resistances are not within specifications, the coils must be replaced.

REMOVAL & INSTALLATION

1. Disconnect the negative battery cable.
2. Unplug and label the spark plug cables from the coil pack.
3. Detach the electrical wiring harness connector from the coil pack.
4. Loosen and remove the coil mounting screws.
5. Remove the ignition coil from the engine.

To Install:

6. Set the ignition coil back in place and secure with the mounting screws. The mounting screws should be tightened to 9 ft. lbs. (12 Nm).

7. Plug the electrical wiring harness connector back into the coil pack.

8. Attach the spark plug cables to the ignition pack, making certain the cables are attached to the correct coil towers.

9. Connect the negative battery cable.

Ignition Module

REMOVAL & INSTALLATION

The vehicles equipped with direct ignition systems do not have a separate ignition module. The Powertrain Control Module (PCM) controls the functions of an ignition module. For the removal and installation procedures of the PCM, refer to Section 4.

Crankshaft Position Sensor

For removal and installation procedures of the Crankshaft Position Sensor, refer to Section 4.

Camshaft Position Sensor

Refer to Section 4 for removal and installation procedures of the camshaft position sensor.

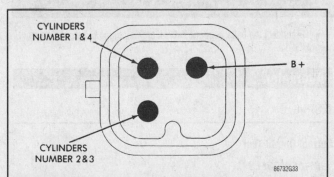

Fig. 44 Primary resistance should be measured from the B+ terminal to the coil terminals, one at a time—resistance should be 0.5–0.7 ohms

FIRING ORDERS

▸ **See Figures 46, 47 and 48**

If a distributor is not keyed for installation with only one orientation, it could have been removed previously and rewired. The resultant wiring would hold the correct firing order, but could change the relative placement of the plug towers in relation to the engine. For this reason it is imperative that you label all wires

before disconnecting any of them. Also, before removal, compare the current wiring with the accompanying illustrations. If the current wiring does not match, make notes in your book to reflect how your engine is wired.

➡**To avoid confusion, remove and tag the spark plug wires one at a time, for replacement.**

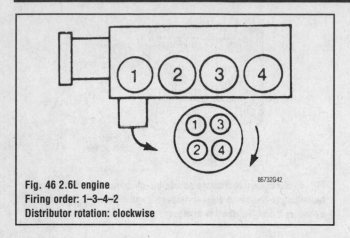

Fig. 46 2.6L engine
Firing order: 1–3–4–2
Distributor rotation: clockwise

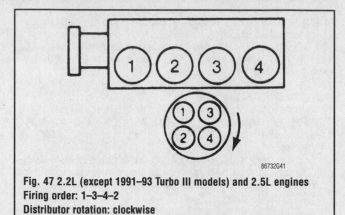

Fig. 47 2.2L (except 1991–93 Turbo III models) and 2.5L engines
Firing order: 1–3–4–2
Distributor rotation: clockwise

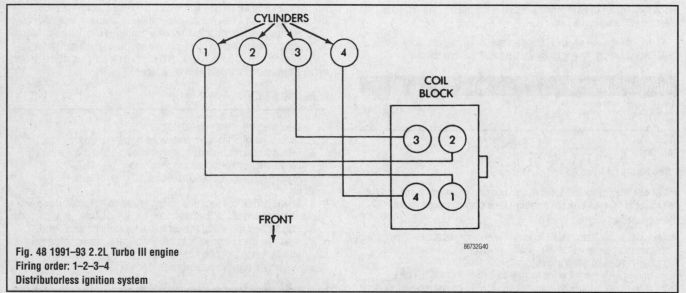

Fig. 48 1991–93 2.2L Turbo III engine
Firing order: 1–2–3–4
Distributorless ignition system

CHARGING SYSTEM

Alternator Precautions

Several precautions must be observed with alternator equipped vehicles to avoid damaging the unit. They are as follows:

• If the battery is removed for any reason, make sure that it is reconnected with the correct polarity. Reversing the battery connections may result in damage to the one-way rectifiers.

• When utilizing a booster battery as a starting aid, always connect it as follows: positive to positive, and negative (booster battery) to a good ground on the engine of the car being started.

• Never use a fast charger as a booster to start cars with alternating current (AC) circuits.

• When servicing the battery with a fast charger, always disconnect the car battery cables.

• Never attempt to polarize an alternator.

• Avoid long soldering times when replacing diodes or transistors. Prolonged heat is damaging to alternators.

• Do not use test lamps of more than 12 volts (V) for checking diode continuity.

• Do not short across or ground any of the terminals on the alternator.

• The polarity of the battery, alternator, and regulator must be matched and considered before making any electrical connections within the system.

• Never separate the alternator on an open circuit. Make sure that all connections within the circuit are clean and tight.

• Disconnect the battery terminals when performing any service on the electrical system. This will eliminate the possibility of accidental reversal of polarity.

• Disconnect the battery ground cable if arc welding is to be done on any part of the car.

Alternator

TESTING

Current Output Test

1986–95 MODELS

▶ **See Figures 49, 50, 51, 52 and 53**

The current output test decides whether the alternator can deliver its rated current output.

1. Before starting any tests, make sure that the vehicle has a fully charged battery. For more information on charging the battery, refer to Section 1.

2. Disconnect the negative battery cable.

3. Detach the output wire from the B+ terminal on the alternator.

4. Connect a 0–150 amp scale (DC) ammeter in series between the B+ terminal and the output wire. Connect the positive lead to the B+ terminal and the negative lead to the output wire.

5. Using a 0–18 volt minimum voltmeter, connect the positive lead to the B+ terminal and the negative lead to a good ground.

6. Connect an engine tachometer to the engine. Refer to the tachometer manufacturer's instructions.

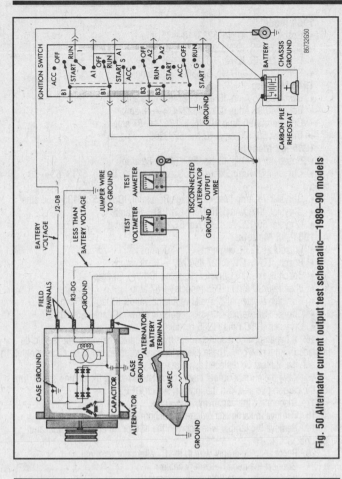

Fig. 50 Alternator current output test schematic—1989–90 models

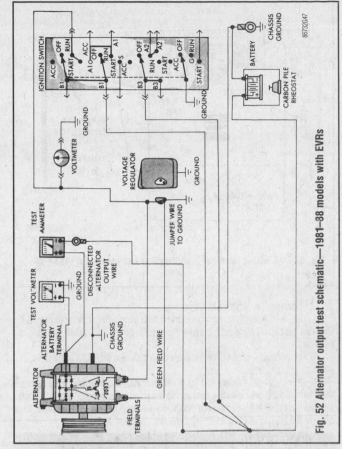

Fig. 52 Alternator output test schematic—1981–88 models with EVRs

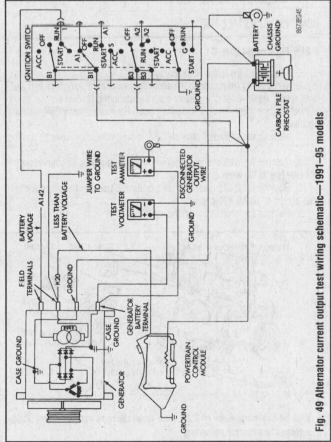

Fig. 49 Alternator current output test wiring schematic—1991–95 models

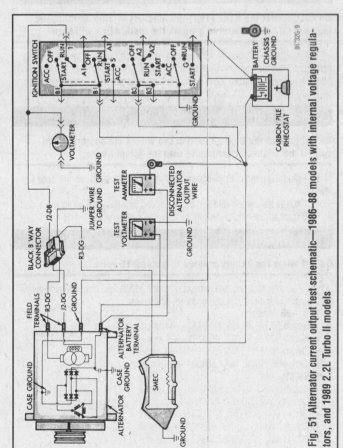

Fig. 51 Alternator current output test schematic—1986–88 models with internal voltage regulators, and 1989 2.2L Turbo II models

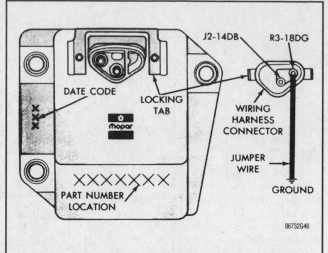

Fig. 53 EVR wiring terminal identification and locations—1981–88 models

7. Connect the negative battery cable.

8. Connect a volt/amp tester equipped with a variable carbon pile rheostat between the battery terminals. Be sure the carbon pile is OFF before connecting the leads.

9. If necessary, remove the fresh air hose between the PCM and the air cleaner.

10. For 1988–95 models and 1986–87 models with internal voltage regulators, full field the alternator by connecting a jumper wire between a good ground and the K20 (1991–95 models) or R3 (1986–90 models) circuit terminal at the back of the alternator (refer to the generator output test diagram).

✳✳ WARNING

Do not connect the A142 (1991–95 models) or blue J2 (1986–90 models) circuit terminal to ground; the fusible link will burn.

11. For 1986–87 models with external voltage regulator, detach the wiring harness connector from the Electronic Voltage Regulator (EVR) on the vehicle. Attach a jumper wire from the EVR wiring harness connector green wire (outside terminal) to ground.

✳✳ WARNING

Do not ground the blue J2 lead of the wiring connector. Do not spread the connector terminals with the jumper wire.

12. Start the engine. Immediately after starting, reduce the engine speed to idle.

13. Adjust the carbon pile and engine speed in steps until an engine speed of 1250 rpm, and a voltage reading of 15 volts is obtained.

✳✳ WARNING

Do not allow the battery voltage to exceed 16 volts.

14. The alternator amperage must meet the MINIMUM output requirements for the particular alternator being tested, as follows:

1991–95 Models:
- Bosch 90 HS, ID No. 4557431—84 amp
- Bosch 90 RS, ID No. 5234231—88 amp
- Denso 75 HS, ID No. 4557301—68 amp
- Denso 90 HS, ID No. 5234031—86 amp

1990 Models:
- Bosch 90 RS, ID No. 5234208—75 amp
- Denso 75 HS, ID No. 4557301—68 amp
- Denso 90 HS, ID No. 5234031—87 amp
- Denso 120 HS, ID No. 5234208—98 amp
- Denso 120 HS, ID No. 5234231—98 amp

1989 Models:
- Bosch 90 RS, ID No. 5233718—75 amp
- Denso 75 HS, ID No. 5233416—68 amp
- Denso 90 HS, ID No. 5233418—87 amp
- Denso 120 HS, ID No. 5233608—98 amp

1988 Models:
- Bosch 35/75 Amp, ID No. 5227469—30 amp
- Bosch 40/90 Amp, ID No. 5227474—40 amp
- Chrysler 40/90 Amp, ID No. 5233474—87 amp
- Chrysler 50/120 Amp, ID No. 5233508—98 amp

1986–87 Models:
- Bosch 40/90 Amp, ID No. 5226600—80 amp
- Chrysler 78 Amp External Voltage Regulator, ID No. 5213763—56 amp
- Chrysler 78 Amp Internal Voltage Regulator, ID No. 5226135—56 amp
- Chrysler 40/90 Amp, ID No. 5227100—87 amp
- Chrysler 50/120 Amp, ID No. 5226457—98 amp

1981–85 Models:
- Mitsubishi (2.6L engines)—63–70 amps
- Bosch, ID No. B120 427 850 MP—78–85 amps
- Bosch w/external Chrysler regulator, ID K1—50 amp
- Bosch 40/90 Amp (1985 models)—87 amp
- Chrysler w/external Chrysler regulator, yellow ID tag—45 amp
- Chrysler w/external Chrysler regulator, brown ID tag—56 amp
- Chrysler 40/90 Amp (1985 models)—96 amp

15. If the amperage reading is less than specified the alternator should be replaced with a new one. These alternators are not intended to be disassembled for service. It must be replaced as an assembly.

16. After the current output test is completed, reduce the engine speed, turn off the carbon pile and turn the ignition switch **OFF**.

17. Disconnect the negative battery cable.

18. Remove the ammeter, voltmeter, tachometer and carbon pile.

19. Remove the jumper wire between the K20 or R3 circuit terminal and ground.

20. Reconnect the output wire to the B+ alternator terminal.

21. Connect the negative battery cable.

22. If necessary, install the fresh air hose.

REMOVAL & INSTALLATION

▶ See Figures 54 thru 61

1. Disconnect the negative battery terminal.

2. If necessary for access to the alternator, remove the A/C drive belt and compressor. Remove the compressor from the mounting bracket and set aside without disconnecting the A/C refrigerant lines. For more information, refer to Section 6.

3. Remove the alternator drive belt. For more information, refer to Section 1.

4. Remove the wire connector hold-down nuts and plug-in connectors from the rear of the alternator housing.

5. Remove the 2 alternator mounting bolts and position the alternator to gain access to all the wire connectors.

6. Remove the alternator from the vehicle.

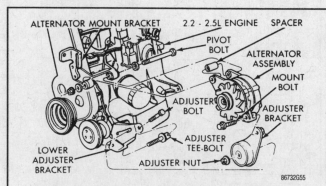

Fig. 54 Exploded view of 2.2L (non-turbocharged versions) and 2.5L engines' alternator mounting

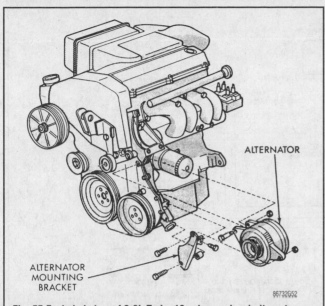

Fig. 55 Exploded view of 2.2L Turbo 16 valve engines' alternator mounting

To install:

7. Position the alternator in the engine compartment so that the wiring connectors can be attached to the rear of the alternator housing. Tighten the alternator field terminal nuts to 25 inch lbs. (3 Nm) and the B+ and ground terminal nuts to 75 inch lbs. (9 Nm)

8. Once the alternator wiring is attached, position the alternator against the alternator mounting bracket.

9. Install and tighten the mounting bolts and nuts to 40 ft. lbs. (54 Nm).

10. Install and properly tension the alternator drive belt. For more information, refer to Section 1.

11. If removed, install the A/C compressor and drive belt. Refer to Section 6 for the proper A/C installation procedures. Properly tension the A/C compressor drive belt, as described in Section 1.

12. Connect the negative battery cable.

Regulator

REMOVAL & INSTALLATION

◗ See Figure 62

➡The alternator on the 2.6 liter engine has an integral regulator; servicing is not possible. The voltage of all 1988–95 alternators is regulated by the Powertrain Control Module (PCM). Servicing of the voltage regulators on these models is not possible. Other alternators on the 2.2L and 2.5L engines may incorporate a separate regulator.

1. Disconnect the negative battery cable.

2. Disengage the engine wiring harness connector from the voltage regulator.

3. Remove the mounting bolts and remove the regulator from the inner fender or from the fire wall, depending on the specific model.

4. This regulator is not serviceable and must be replaced as a unit, if found to be defective.

5. Installation is the reverse of the removal procedure.

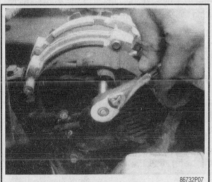

Fig. 56 After removing the A/C compressor, loosen the alternator wiring connectors . . .

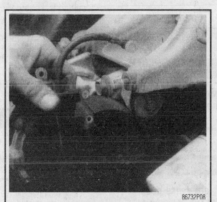

Fig. 57 . . . then pull the wiring connectors off of the alternator

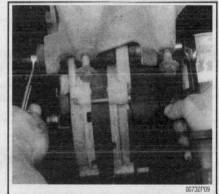

Fig. 58 Remove the adjusting bolt, then loosen the pivot bolt and nut . . .

Fig. 59 . . . remove the nut and washer from the pivot bolt and . . .

Fig. 60 . . . slide the pivot bolt out while holding the alternator from falling

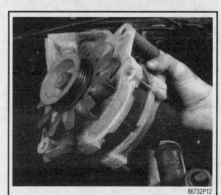

Fig. 61 Remove the alternator from the engine compartment—1986 2.2L engine shown

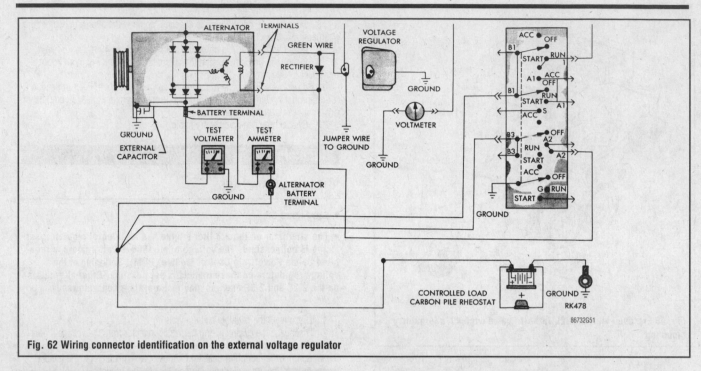

Fig. 62 Wiring connector identification on the external voltage regulator

Battery

➡ For more information on the upkeep and general maintenance of the battery and related components, refer to Section 1.

REMOVAL & INSTALLATION

▶ See Figures 63 thru 71

✳✳ CAUTION

Batteries often develop acid leaks! During all battery handling, thick (not medical or household) rubber gloves should be worn. Failure to do this could result in acid burns!

1. Turn the ignition switch **OFF**.

✳✳ WARNING

Always disconnect the negative battery cable first, otherwise possible sparking or arcing can occur causing damage to the electronic components in the vehicle.

2. Disconnect both of the battery cable terminals, as follows:
   a. Loosen the clamping bolt and nut from the negative battery cable end.

   b. Lift the negative battery cable end from the terminals with a twisting motion. If there is a battery cable puller available, make use of it.
   c. Set the disconnected negative battery cable aside so that it will not accidentally come into contact with the negative terminal post of the battery while the vehicle is being serviced. Tying the cable end to another, remote component should keep it from accidentally touching the battery post. The is most important when servicing the Supplemental Restraint System (SRS), or air bag.
   d. Perform the same for the positive battery cable end.
3. Remove the battery hold-down bolt and clamp. A long extension for the socket and ratchet wrench is necessary to access this hold-down bolt.
4. Carefully lift the battery out of the vehicle.

To install:

✳✳ WARNING

If cleaning the battery with a baking powder/water solution, make certain that no solution leaks down into the battery cells. Baking powder is an alkali and will neutralize the acid in the battery.

5. Clean the battery tray with a mild solution of baking soda and water, using a stiff, bristle brush. If the battery is to be reinstalled, clean it as well, and then wipe it with a rag dampened in ammonia. Clean the battery and cable terminals with a stiff wire brush or a special battery terminal cleaner tool.
6. Carefully set the battery into the battery tray. Make sure that the positive and negative terminals are in the positions as when the battery was removed.

Fig. 63 When removing or disconnecting the battery, always disconnect the negative battery cable first

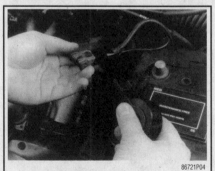

Fig. 64 Wrap the negative battery cable end with electrical tape to prevent accidental conductivity

Fig. 65 Loosen and remove the hold-down nut using a long socket extension or wrench

Fig. 66 Lift the battery cover up and off of the battery

Fig. 67 Remove the loosened hold-down nut and hold-down bracket from the battery tray

Fig. 68 Carefully lift the battery out of the engine compartment

Fig. 69 If necessary, remove the battery tray—note: two bolts are located under the tray

Fig. 70 Unplug and label the vacuum lines from the attached vacuum box . . .

Fig. 71 . . . then remove the battery tray from the engine compartment

7. Locate the battery hold-down stud on the battery tray, then slide the battery away from the hold-down stud until the battery retaining lip (on the opposite side of the battery tray from the hold-down stud) engages the lower lip of the battery case. Install the hold-down clamp and nut. Tighten the nut to 15 ft. lbs. (20 Nm).

8. Gently rock the battery back-and-forth to ensure that it is held securely to the battery tray.

9. Slide the positive battery cable end over the battery positive terminal until flush on the battery case. Tighten the clamping bolt nut until the cable end is securely clamped around the battery terminal. Gently wiggle the battery cable end to ensure that it is adequately tightened to the battery terminal.

10. Install the negative battery cable end in the same manner.

11. Coat the terminals with a petroleum grease or equivalent.

STARTING SYSTEM

▶ See Figure 72

Starter

TESTING

▶ See Figure 73

When testing the starter motor and related components, first utilize the starter motor diagnosis illustration to help pinpoint the specific problem, then commence to the particular testing procedure.

Testing Preparation

Before commencing with the starting system diagnostics, verify:
• The battery top posts, and terminals are clean.
• The alternator drive belt tension and condition is correct.
• The battery state-of-charge is correct.
• The battery cable connections at the starter and engine block are clean and free from corrosion.
• The wiring harness connectors and terminals are clean and free from corrosion.
• Proper circuit grounding.

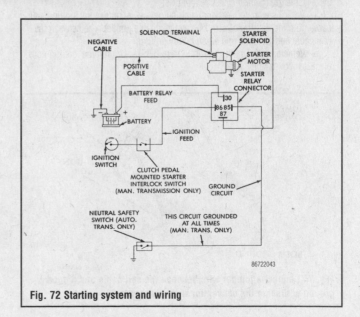

Fig. 72 Starting system and wiring

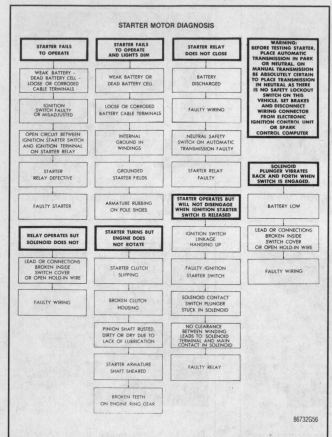

STARTER MOTOR DIAGNOSIS

| STARTER FAILS TO OPERATE | STARTER FAILS TO OPERATE AND LIGHTS DIM | STARTER RELAY DOES NOT CLOSE | WARNING: BEFORE TESTING STARTER, PLACE AUTOMATIC TRANSMISSION IN PARK OR NEUTRAL. ON MANUAL TRANSMISSION BE ABSOLUTELY CERTAIN TO PLACE TRANSMISSION IN NEUTRAL AS THERE IS NO SAFETY LOCKOUT SWITCH ON THIS VEHICLE. SET BRAKES AND DISCONNECT WIRING CONNECTOR FROM ELECTRONIC IGNITION CONTROL UNIT OR SPARK CONTROL COMPUTER |

Fig. 73 Use this flowchart to help pinpoint a problem in the starting system

Starter Feed Circuit

▶ See Figure 74

❊❊ CAUTION

The ignition system must be disabled to prevent engine start while performing the following tests.

1. Connect a volt-ampere tester (multimeter) to the battery terminals.
2. Disable the ignition system as follows:
   a. Vehicles with conventional distributors—Disconnect the ignition coil cable from the distributor cap. Connect a suitable jumper wire between the coil cable end-terminal and a good body ground.
   b. Vehicles with Direct Ignition System (DIS)—Unplug the ignition coils electrical connector.

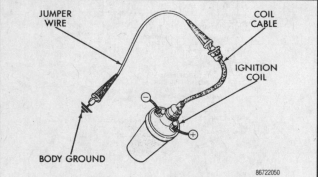

Fig. 74 Connect a jumper wire between the coil cable and a good ground to disable the conventional ignition system

3. Verify that all lights and accessories are Off, and the transaxle shift selector is in Park (automatic) or Neutral (manual). Set the parking brake.
4. Rotate and hold the ignition switch in the **START** position. Observe the volt-ampere tester:
   • If the voltage reads above 9.6 volts, and the amperage draw reads above 250 amps, go to the starter feed circuit resistance test (following this test).
   • If the voltage reads 12.4 volts or greater and the amperage reads 0–10 amps, refer to the starter solenoid and relay tests.

❊❊ WARNING

Do not overheat the starter motor or draw the battery voltage below 9.6 volts during cranking operations.

5. After the starting system problems have been corrected, verify the battery state of charge and charge the battery if necessary. Disconnect all of the testing equipment and connect the ignition coil cable or ignition coil connector. Start the vehicle several times to assure the problem was corrected.

Starter Feed Circuit Resistance

▶ See Figures 74 and 75

Before proceeding with this test, refer to the battery tests and starter feed circuit test. The following test will require a voltmeter, which is capable of accuracy to 0.1 volt.

❊❊ CAUTION

The ignition system must be disabled to prevent engine start while performing the following tests.

1. Disable the ignition system as follows:
   a. Vehicles with conventional distributors—Disconnect the ignition coil cable from the distributor cap. Connect a suitable jumper wire between the coil cable end-terminal and a good body ground.
   b. Vehicles with Direct Ignition System (DIS)—Unplug the ignition coils electrical connector.
2. With all wiring harnesses and components (except for the coils) properly connected, perform the following:
   a. Connect the negative (-) lead of the voltmeter to the negative battery post, and the positive (+) lead to the negative (-) battery cable clamp. Rotate and hold the ignition switch in the **START** position. Observe the voltmeter. If the voltage is detected, correct the poor contact between the cable clamp and post.
   b. Connect the positive (+) lead of the voltmeter to the positive battery post, and the negative (-) to the positive battery cable clamp. Rotate and hold the ignition switch key in the **START** position. Observe the voltmeter. If voltage is detected, correct the poor contact between the cable clamp and post.
   c. Connect the negative lead of the voltmeter to the negative (-) battery terminal, and positive lead to the engine block near the battery cable attaching point. Rotate and hold the ignition switch in the **START** position. If the voltage reads above 0.2 volt, correct the poor contact at ground cable attaching point. If the voltage reading is still above 0.2 volt after correcting the poor contact, replace the negative ground cable with a new one.

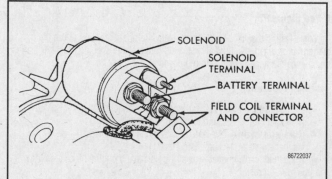

Fig. 75 Bosch starter motor solenoid electrical terminals—all models

3. Remove the heater shield. Refer to removal and installation procedures to gain access to the starter motor and solenoid connections. Perform the following steps:

   a. Connect the positive (+) voltmeter lead to the starter motor housing and the negative (-) lead to the negative battery terminal. Hold the ignition switch key in the **START** position. If the voltage reads above 0.2 volt, correct the poor starter to engine ground.

   b. Connect the positive (+) voltmeter lead to the positive battery terminal, and the negative lead to the battery cable terminal on the starter solenoid. Rotate and hold the ignition key in the **START** position. If the voltage reads above 0.2 volt, correct poor contact at the battery cable to the solenoid connection. If the reading is still above 0.2 volt after correcting the poor contacts, replace the positive battery cable with a new one.

   c. If the resistance tests did not detect feed circuit failures, refer to the starter solenoid test.

Starter Solenoid

1981–87 MODELS AND TC BY MASERATI

▶ See Figure 76

1. Connect a heavy jumper wire on the starter relay connector between the battery terminal (1) and the solenoid terminal (3). If the engine cranks over, the starter solenoid is good. Proceed to the starter relay test.

2. If the engine does not crank or the solenoid chatters, check the wiring and connectors from the relay to the starter for being loose or corroded, particularly at the starter terminals.

3. Repeat the test. If the engine still fails to crank properly, the trouble is within the starter and it must be removed for bench testing.

1988–95 MODELS—EXCEPT TC BY MASERATI

▶ See Figures 77, 78, 79 and 80

1. Battery and circuit tests must be performed before this test. Perform this test before the starter relay test.

⁂ WARNING

Check to ensure that the transaxle is in Park (automatic) or Neutral (manual) with the parking brake applied.

2. Raise and safely support the front of the vehicle on jackstands.
3. Perform a visual inspection of the starter/starter solenoid for corrosion, loose connections or faulty wiring.
4. Lower the vehicle.
5. Locate the starter relay as follows:
• On Dynasty, Daytona, LeBaron coupe/convertible models, the relay is located in the Power Distribution Center (PDC). This center is mounted near the front of the left front strut tower. The position of the starter relay within the center will be shown on the center cover
• On LeBaron sedan, Spirit, Acclaim, Sundance and Shadow models, the relay is located on the front of the left front strut tower
6. Remove the starter relay from the connector.
7. Connect a remote starter switch or a jumper wire between the battery positive (+) post and terminal 87 on the starter relay connector (see the illustration).
8. Try to crank the engine over with the ignition switch:
• If the engine now cranks, the starter/solenoid is good. Refer to the starter relay test
• If the engine does not crank with this test, or the solenoid chatters, check the wiring and connectors from the starter relay to the starter solenoid for loose or corroded connections. Particularly at the starter terminals
9. Repeat the test. If the engine still fails to crank properly, trouble is within the starter or starter mounted solenoid. The starter must be removed and bench tested, refer to the starter bench test.

Starter Relay

TC BY MASERATI

▶ See Figures 81 and 82

1. Position the transaxle gear selector in the Neutral (manual) or Park (automatic) position.

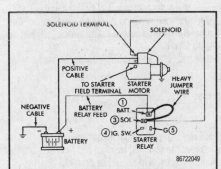

Fig. 76 Connect terminal 1 (battery) and terminal 3 (solenoid) when testing the starter solenoid—TC by Maserati and 1981–87 models

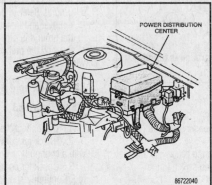

Fig. 77 Starter relay location—1988–95 Dynasty, Daytona and LeBaron (AJ Body)

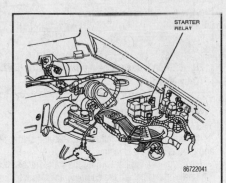

Fig. 78 Starter relay location—1988–95 LeBaron (AA Body), Spirit, Acclaim, Sundance and Shadow

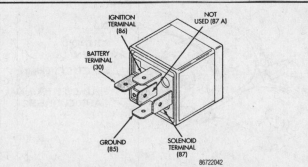

Fig. 79 The starter relay terminal identification—1988–95 models (except TC by Maserati)

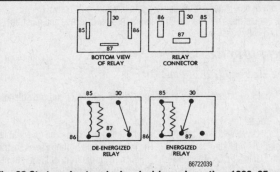

Fig. 80 Starter relay terminal and wiring schematic—1988–95 models (except TC by Maserati)

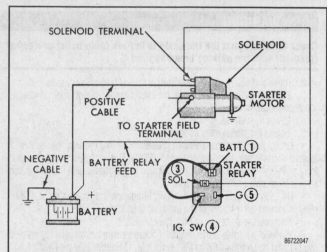

Fig. 81 Connect terminal 1 (battery) and terminal 4 (ignition switch) to test the starter relay—TC by Maserati

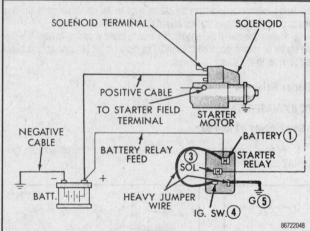

Fig. 82 Add a second heavy jumper wire if a bad ground is found—TC by Maserati

2. Set the parking brake.

3. Do not remove the starter relay connector.

4. Check for battery voltage between the starter relay battery terminal (1) and ground with a test lamp.

5. Connect a jumper wire on the starter relay between the battery (1) and the ignition (4) terminals. If the engine cranks (turn the ignition switch to the **START** position) the relay is good.

6. If the engine does not crank, connect a second jumper wire to the starter relay between the ground terminal (5) and a good ground (such as the engine block). Repeat the test:

• Engine cranks—The starter relay is good. The transaxle linkage is, however, out of adjustment or the safety neutral switch is defective

• Engine does not crank—The starter relay is defective and must be replaced with a new one.

EXCEPT TC BY MASERATI

▶ See Figures 77, 78, 79 and 80

1. Before performing this test, complete the battery, circuit and solenoid tests.

2. Locate the starter relay as follows:
    a. On New Yorker, Dynasty, Daytona, LeBaron coupe and convertible, Imperial and Fifth Ave. bodies—The relay is located in the Power Distribution Center (PDC). This center is mounted near the front of the left front strut tower. The position of the starter relay within the center will be shown on the center cover.

    b. On LeBaron sedan, Spirit, Acclaim, Sundance and Shadow bodies—The relay is located on the front of the left front strut tower.

3. Remove the starter relay from the connector.

4. Connect a jumper wire between the positive (+) battery post and terminal 87 on the relay connector. Try to crank the engine over with the ignition switch:
    a. Engine does not crank: refer to the previous solenoid test.
    b. Engine cranks: continue to Step 5.

5. With the relay remove and the ignition switch **ON**, check for 12 volts at terminal 30 of the relay connector:
    a. 12 volts is NOT present: check for an open circuit. Refer to Section 6 for the vehicle wiring diagrams.
    b. 12 volts is present: the circuit is OK. Continue to Step 6.

6. With the relay still removed, check for 12 volts at terminal 86 with the ignition switch in the **START** (cranking) position:
    a. 12 volts is present: skip to Step 8.
    b. 12 volts is NOT present: go to Step 7.

7. Depending on the transaxle in the vehicle, refer to the following procedures:
    a. Automatic transaxle: the circuit from the ignition switch is open. Refer to Section 6 for the vehicle wiring diagrams. Do not continue to Step 8.
    b. Manual transaxle: unplug the wiring connector from the clutch pedal mounted interlock switch. Connect a jumper wire across the two terminals of this connector. If 12 volts is now present at terminal 86 (with ignition switch in the cranking position), the switch may be out of adjustment or bad. Refer to Section 7 for the clutch procedures. Otherwise, if the 12 volts is still not present at terminal 86, the circuit is open somewhere. Refer to Section 6 for vehicle wiring diagrams and procedures for checking circuits. Do not continue to Step 8.

8. With the relay still removed, check for a ground circuit at terminal 85 of the starter relay connector. If the vehicle is equipped with an automatic transaxle, ground should only be present with the shifter in the Park or Neutral positions only. If the vehicle is equipped with a manual transaxle, a ground must be present at all times.
    a. Manual transaxle: If the ground is not present, the circuit is open or short-circuited. Refer to Section 6 for the vehicle wiring diagrams. However, if the ground is present, refer to Step 8.
    b. Automatic transaxle: If the ground is not present when the shifter is in the Park or Neutral positions, check the neutral safety switch continuity to ground. Refer to Section 6 for the vehicle wiring diagrams and Section 7 for removal and installation procedures of the neutral safety switch. However, if the ground is present, refer to Step 8.

9. If all the preceding circuit tests checked out OK, replace the starter relay with a new one.

Starter Solenoid Bench Test

▶ See Figure 83

1. Disconnect the field coil wire from the field coil terminal.

2. Check for continuity between the solenoid terminal and field coil terminal with a continuity tester. Continuity (resistance) should be present.

3. Check for continuity between the solenoid terminal and solenoid housing. Continuity should be detected. If continuity is detected, the solenoid is good.

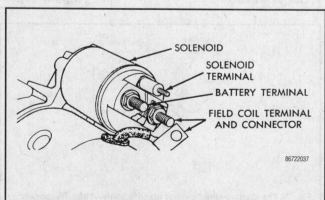

Fig. 83 Bosch starter motor solenoid electrical terminals

4. If continuity is not detected in either test, the solenoid has an open circuit and is defective. Replace the solenoid with a new one.

5. Connect the field coil wire to the field coil terminal.

Starter Motor

With the starter motor removed from the engine, the pinion gear should be tested for freedom of operation by turning it on the screw shaft. The armature should be tested for freedom of rotation by prying the pinion gear with a prytool to engage it with the shaft.

Tight bearings, a bent armature or driveshaft, or a bent frame will cause the armature to catch and not rotate freely.

If the shafts do not rotate freely, the motor should be replaced with either a professionally rebuilt or new motor. Chrysler does not provide disassembly procedures for anything other than solenoid removal (Bosch starters) and gear removal.

No rotation and high current flow conditions indicate one or more of the following:

- Connecting terminal or armature windings shorted to ground.
- Seized bearings (this should have been determined by rotating the armature by hand).

No rotation and no current flow conditions indicate one or more of the following:

- Open armature windings (inspect the commutator for badly burned commutator bars, if disassembled).
- Broken brush springs, worn brushes, protruding insulation between commutator bars, or other causes could prevent good contact between brushes and commutator.

REMOVAL & INSTALLATION

♦ See Figure 84

➡️ **All 1988–95 2.2L and 2.5L engines utilize Bosch starter motors, whereas the earlier engines used either Nippondenso or Bosch starter motors.**

1. Disconnect the negative (-) battery cable.
2. Raise and safely support the front of the vehicle on jackstands.
3. Remove the engine undercovers, if so equipped.
4. On early model 2.2 liter engines it may be necessary to loosen the air pump tube at the exhaust manifold and move the tube bracket away from the starter for added clearance.
5. Disconnect the speedometer cable from the transaxle, if necessary, to gain clearance to remove the starter assembly.
6. Remove the nuts and bolts attaching the starter to the engine/transaxle.

✳✳ CAUTION

Be careful when removing the starter motor mounting bolts, the motor can be quite heavy. Personal injury could result if the starter motor falls from its mounting position.

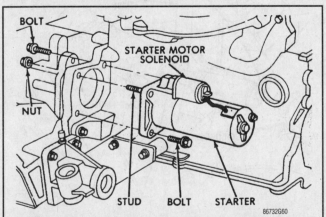

Fig. 84 The starter motor is mounted to the engine with 2 bolts and one nut—make sure they are installed from the correct direction

7. Remove the heat shield and its clamp, if so equipped.
8. Remove the two electrical wire connector terminal nuts and remove the wiring connector from the starter.
9. Remove the starter from the vehicle.

To install:

10. Clean all wire terminals of dirt, grease or corrosion.
11. Attach the electrical wire connectors and secure with the mounting nuts. Tighten the starter solenoid B+ nut to 80 inch lbs. (9 Nm) and the solenoid wire-to-starter nut to 55 inch lbs. (6 Nm).
12. Install the heat shield if one was removed.
13. Hold the starter motor in place, then secure in place with the 3 attaching bolts. Tighten the bolts to 40 ft. lbs. (54 Nm).
14. If applicable, reattach the speedometer cable and the air pump tube. For more information regarding the removal and installation of the air pump tube, refer to Section 3.
15. Install any undercovers which were removed from the vehicle.
16. Lower the vehicle.
17. Connect the negative (-) battery cable.

SOLENOID REPLACEMENT

Bosch Starter Motors

♦ See Figure 85

1. Remove the starter as previously outlined.
2. Disconnect the field coil wire from the solenoid by removing the nut and pulling the connector off. Make certain to retain the nut and washer for reassembly.
3. Remove the 3 solenoid mounting screws.
4. Remove the solenoid by working the plunger stem off the shift fork.

To install:

5. Install the solenoid onto the starter motor, making sure that the plunger correctly engages the solenoid.
6. Install and tighten the 3 solenoid-to-starter motor mounting screws.
7. Slide the field terminal onto the field terminal stud, then install the washer and nut. Tighten the nut to 55 inch lbs. (6 Nm).
8. Install the starter motor onto the vehicle.

Nippondenso Starter Motors

2.2L ENGINE

➡️ **The 2.2L and the 2.6L engines used different Nippondenso starter motors. Only the 2.2L starter motor has a serviceable solenoid; if the solenoid on the 2.6L starter motor is found to be faulty, replace the entire starter motor as a unit.**

1. Remove the starter motor from the vehicle, as described previously in this section.
2. Loosen the field coil terminal nut.
3. Remove the field coil terminal nut from the solenoid terminal.
4. Remove the field coil wire from the solenoid terminal.
5. Remove the 2 solenoid-to-starter housing mounting nuts.
6. Work the solenoid hook off of the shift fork, then remove the solenoid from the solenoid.

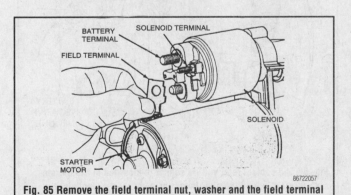

Fig. 85 Remove the field terminal nut, washer and the field terminal itself—Bosch starter motors

To install:

7. Work the solenoid onto the shift fork. Make sure that the solenoid shaft hook is correctly engaged with the shift fork.

8. Install the 2 solenoid-to-starter motor mounting nuts. Tighten until snug.

SENDING UNITS AND SENSORS

General Information

The sending units and sensors covered in this section are not related to engine control. For the sensors and sending units which help control the engine, refer to Section 4.

Coolant Temperature Sensor

OPERATION

The engine coolant temperature sending unit, not to be confused with the engine temperature sensor which is used for the fuel injection system, is a variable resistor. The sending unit decreases its circuit's resistance as the temperature of the engine coolant rises.

The temperature sending unit contains one circuit for the temperature gauge. This circuit has a variable resistor. The wire for this sending unit is yellow with a tracer, and the sending unit is located on the right side of the engine.

TESTING

▶ **See Figure 86**

The sending unit terminal is connected to a variable resistor in the sending unit itself. The resistance of the entire circuit is changed depending on the temperature of the engine coolant. The temperature gauge reads the changes in resistance and converts them into the movement of the gauge needle. The resistance of this circuit should never be infinite (open circuit) and should change smoothly and evenly when heated or cooled.

Perform this test on a cold or cool engine.

1. Disconnect the negative (-) battery cable.

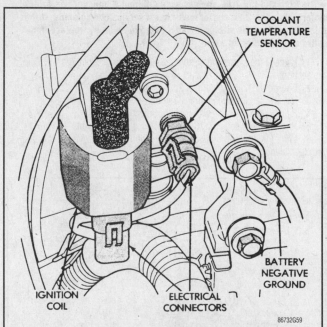

Fig. 86 The coolant temperature sensor is mounted in the thermostat, directly behind the distributor cap and, on later models, the ignition coil

9. Install the field coil wire on the solenoid terminal, then install the field coil terminal nut to the solenoid terminal. .

10. It is a good idea to bench test the starter motor before installing it into the vehicle to ensure that the solenoid is functioning properly.

11. Install the starter motor, as described earlier in this section.

2. Unplug the electrical wiring from the sending unit.

3. Using an ohmmeter, measure the resistance between the terminal and the sending unit's metal body

a. Infinite resistance or zero resistance: the sending unit is bad, replace the sender with a new one.

b. Other than infinite or zero resistance: continue to the next step.

4. Remove the temperature sender from the engine.

5. Position the water temperature sending unit in such a way that the metal shaft (opposite end from the electrical connectors) is situated in a pot of water. Make sure that the electrical connector is not submerged and that only the tip of the sending unit's body is in the water.

6. Heat the pot of water at a medium rate. While the water is warming, continue to measure the resistance of the terminal and the metal body of the sending unit:

a. As the water warms up, the resistance exhibited by the ohmmeter goes down in a steady manner: the sending unit is good.

b. As the water warms up, the resistance does not change or changes in erratic jumps: the sender is bad, replace it with a new one.

7. Install the good or new sending unit into the engine, then connect the negative battery cable.

REMOVAL & INSTALLATION

▶ **See Figure 86**

✳✳ CAUTION

When draining the coolant, keep in mind that cats and dogs are attracted by ethylene glycol antifreeze, and are quite likely to drink any that is left in an uncovered container or in puddles on the ground. This will prove fatal in sufficient quantity. Always drain the coolant into a sealable container. Coolant should be reused unless it is contaminated or several years old.

1. Disconnect the negative battery cable.

2. Drain the cooling system until the coolant level is below the coolant sensor.

3. Detach the electrical connector from the sensor.

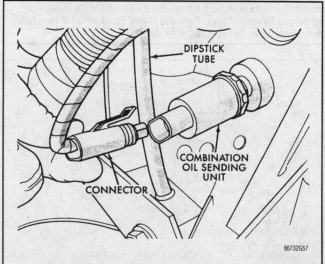

Fig. 87 The oil pressure switch/sending unit is mounted in the bottom of the dipstick side of the engine block

4. Remove the sensor from the engine. On some applications, the coolant sensor threads into the thermostat housing.

5. Installation is the reverse of the removal procedure. Fill and bleed the cooling system.

Oil Pressure Sending Unit

OPERATION

▶ **See Figure 87**

The low oil pressure/check gauges warning lamp (fed by the oil pressure sending unit) will illuminate when the ignition key is turned to the **ON** position without starting the vehicle. In cluster assemblies without tachometers, the low oil pressure lamp will illuminate if the sending unit indicates that the engine oil pressure has dropped below a safe oil pressure level. The sending unit alters resistance in its circuit depending on the amount of oil pressure detected. (The resistance is raised as the oil pressure is increased). Therefore, the range of various resistances is read by the oil pressure/check gauge and translated into a needle position of the oil pressure gauge. When the oil sending unit receives pressure which below a factory set level, the oil pressure warning light illuminates.

In cluster assemblies equipped with tachometers, the check gauges warning lamp illuminates when there is a problem in oil pressure level, high engine temperature or low voltage.

The combination oil unit, which is essentially a combination of an oil pressure switch (for the warning light) and an oil pressure sending unit (for the oil pressure gauge), has two functions:

• Oil pressure switch—The normal closed circuit keeps the oil pressure warning/check gauges lamp on until there is oil pressure.

• Oil pressure gauge—The sending unit provides resistance that varies with oil pressure.

TESTING

Except TC by Maserati

▶ **See Figures 88 and 89**

1. To test the normally closed oil lamp circuit, disengage the locking connector and measure the resistance between the switch terminal (terminal for the wire to the warning lamp) and the metal housing. The ohmmeter should read 0 ohms.

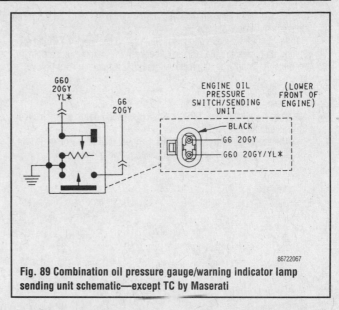

Fig. 89 Combination oil pressure gauge/warning indicator lamp sending unit schematic—except TC by Maserati

2. To test the sending unit, measure the resistance between the sending unit terminal and the metal housing. The ohmmeter should read an open circuit (infinite resistance).

3. Start the engine.

4. Once again, test each terminal against the metal housing:

a. The oil switch terminal-to-housing circuit should read an open circuit if there is oil pressure present.

b. The sending unit-to-housing circuit should read between 30–55 ohms, depending on the engine speed, oil temperature and oil viscosity.

5. If the above results were not obtained, replace the sending unit/switch with a new one.

TC by Maserati

▶ **See Figure 90**

The TC by Maserati vehicles are equipped with separate sending units/switches for the warning indicator lamp on the instrument panel and for the oil pressure gauge.

1. To test the low oil pressure switch, disengage the locking connector and

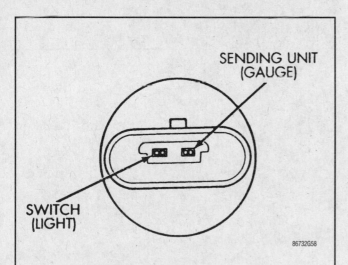

Fig. 88 Identification of the oil pressure switch/sending unit terminals—except TC by Maserati models

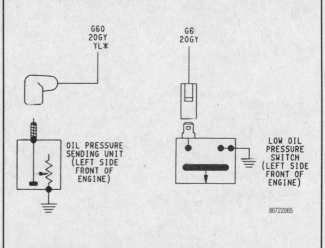

Fig. 90 Oil pressure gauge sending unit and low oil pressure warning indicator lamp switch schematic—TC by Maserati

measure the resistance between the switch terminal and the metal housing. The ohmmeter should read 0 ohms.

2. To test the oil pressure gauge sending unit, disconnect the wiring to the sending unit. Measure the resistance between the sending unit terminal and the metal housing. The ohmmeter should read an open circuit (infinite resistance).

3. Start the engine.

4. Once again, test each terminal against the metal housing:

   a. The oil switch terminal-to-housing circuit should read an open circuit if there is oil pressure present.

   b. The sending unit-to-housing circuit should read between 30–55 ohms, depending on the engine speed, oil temperature and oil viscosity.

5. If the above results were not obtained, replace the sending unit or the switch with a new one.

REMOVAL & INSTALLATION

The oil pressure switch and sending unit is located directly above the oil filter and next to the starter motor on the lower side of the engine block.

1. Disconnect the negative (-) battery cable from the battery.

2. Unplug the oil pressure sending unit wiring harness connector from the sending unit.

3. Unscrew the sending unit from the engine block.

4. Installation is the reverse of the removal procedure.

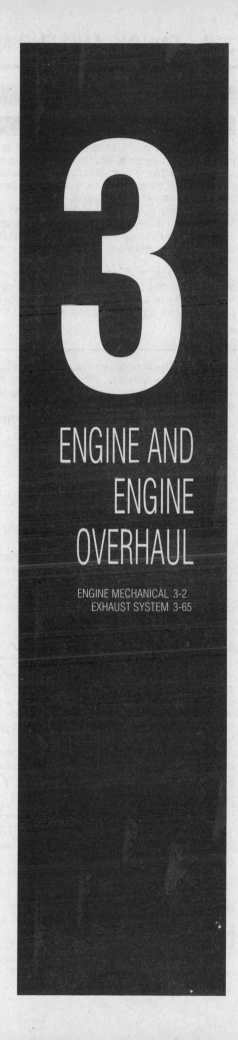

3

ENGINE AND ENGINE OVERHAUL

ENGINE MECHANICAL 3-2
EXHAUST SYSTEM 3-65

ENGINE MECHANICAL

Engine Overhaul Tips

Most engine overhaul procedures are fairly standard. In addition to specific parts replacement procedures and specifications for your individual engine, this section is also a guide to acceptable rebuilding procedures. Examples of standard rebuilding practice are given and should be used along with specific details concerning your particular engine.

Competent and accurate machine shop services will ensure maximum performance, reliability and engine life. In most instances it is more profitable for the do-it-yourself mechanic to remove, clean and inspect the component, buy the necessary parts and deliver these to a shop for actual machine work.

On the other hand, much of the rebuilding work (crankshaft, block, bearings, piston rods, and other components) is well within the scope of the do-it-yourself mechanic's tools and abilities. You will have to decide for yourself the depth of involvement you desire in an engine repair or rebuild.

TOOLS

The tools required for an engine overhaul or parts replacement will depend on the depth of your involvement. With a few exceptions, they will be the tools found in a mechanic's tool kit (see Section 1 of this manual). More in-depth work will require some or all of the following:

- A dial indicator (reading in thousandths) mounted on a universal base
- Micrometers and telescope gauges
- Jaw and screw-type pullers
- Scraper
- Valve spring compressor
- Ring groove cleaner
- Piston ring expander and compressor
- Ridge reamer
- Cylinder hone or glaze breaker
- Plastigage®
- Engine stand

The use of most of these tools is illustrated in this chapter. Many can be rented for a one-time use from a local parts jobber or tool supply house specializing in automotive work.

Occasionally, the use of special tools is called for. See the information on Special Tools and the Safety Notice in the front of this book before substituting another tool.

INSPECTION TECHNIQUES

Procedures and specifications are given in this chapter for inspecting, cleaning and assessing the wear limits of most major components. Other procedures such as Magnaflux® and Zyglo® can be used to locate material flaws and stress cracks. Magnaflux® is a magnetic process applicable only to ferrous materials. The Zyglo® process coats the material with a fluorescent dye penetrant and can be used on any material.

Checking for suspected surface cracks can be more readily made using spot check dye. The dye is sprayed onto the suspected area, wiped off and the area sprayed with a developer. Cracks will show up brightly.

OVERHAUL TIPS

Aluminum has become extremely popular for use in engines, due to its low weight. Observe the following precautions when handling aluminum parts:

- Never hot tank aluminum parts (the caustic hot tank solution will eat the aluminum.
- Remove all aluminum parts (identification tag, etc.) from engine parts prior to the tanking.
- Always coat threads lightly with engine oil or anti-seize compounds before installation, to prevent seizure.
- Never overtighten bolts or spark plugs especially in aluminum threads.

Stripped threads in any component can be repaired using any of several commercial repair kits (Heli-Coil®, Microdot®, Keenserts®, etc.).

When assembling the engine, any parts that will be exposed to frictional con-

tact must be prelubricated to provide lubrication at initial start-up. Any product specifically formulated for this purpose can be used, but engine oil is not recommended as a prelubricate in most cases.

When semi-permanent (locked, but removable) installation of bolts or nuts is desired, threads should be cleaned and coated with Loctite® or another similar, commercial non-hardening sealant.

REPAIRING DAMAGED THREADS

♦ See Figures 1, 2, 3, 4 and 5

Several methods of repairing damaged threads are available. Heli-Coil® (shown here), Keenserts® and Microdot® are among the most widely used. All involve basically the same principle—drilling out stripped threads, tapping the

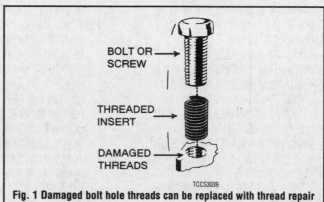

Fig. 1 Damaged bolt hole threads can be replaced with thread repair inserts

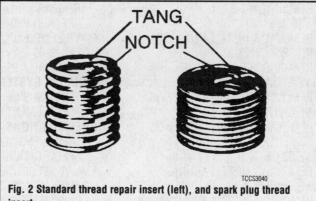

Fig. 2 Standard thread repair insert (left), and spark plug thread insert

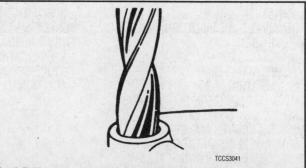

Fig. 3 Drill out the damaged threads with the specified size bit. Be sure to drill completely through the hole or to the bottom of a blind hole

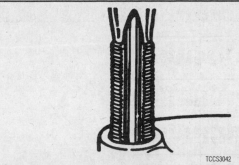

Fig. 4 Using the kit, tap the hole in order to receive the thread insert. Keep the tap well oiled and back it out frequently to avoid clogging the threads

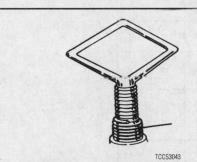

Fig. 5 Screw the insert onto the installer tool until the tang engages the slot. Thread the insert into the hole until it is ¼–½ turn below the top surface, then remove the tool and break off the tang using a punch

hole and installing a prewound insert—making welding, plugging and oversize fasteners unnecessary.

Two types of thread repair inserts are usually supplied: a standard type for most inch coarse, inch fine, metric course and metric fine thread sizes and a spark lug type to fit most spark plug port sizes. Consult the individual tool manufacturer's catalog to determine exact applications. Typical thread repair kits will contain a selection of prewound threaded inserts, a tap (corresponding to the outside diameter threads of the insert) and an installation tool. Spark plug inserts usually differ because they require a tap equipped with pilot threads and a combined reamer/tap section. Most manufacturers also supply blister-packed thread repair inserts separately in addition to a master kit containing a variety of taps and inserts plus installation tools.

Before attempting to repair a threaded hole, remove any snapped, broken or damaged bolts or studs. Penetrating oil can be used to free frozen threads. The offending item can usually be removed with locking pliers or using a screw/stud extractor. After the hole is clear, the thread can be repaired, as shown in the series of accompanying illustrations and in the kit manufacturer's instructions.

Checking Engine Compression

▶ See Figure 6

A noticeable lack of engine power, excessive oil consumption and/or poor fuel mileage measured over an extended period are all indicators of internal

Fig. 6 A screw-in type compression gauge is more accurate and easier to use without an assistant

engine wear. Worn piston rings, scored or worn cylinder bores, blown head gaskets, sticking or burnt valves and worn valve seats are all possible culprits here. A check of each cylinder's compression will help you locate the problems.

As mentioned in the tools and equipment of portion Section 1, a screw-in type compression gauge is more accurate than the type you simply hold against the spark plug hole, although it takes slightly longer to use. It's worth it to obtain a more accurate reading. Follow this procedure:

1. Warm up the engine to normal operating temperature.
2. Remove all the spark plugs.
3. Disconnect the high tension lead from the ignition coil for conventional ignition systems, or detach the ignition coil wiring harness connector on models with Direct Ignition Systems (DIS).
4. Fully open the throttle either by operating the carburetor throttle linkage by hand or by having an assistant floor the accelerator pedal.
5. Screw the compression gauge into the No. 1 spark plug hole until the fitting is snug.

✳✳ WARNING

Be careful not to crossthread the plug hole. On aluminum cylinder heads use extra care, as the threads in these heads are easily damaged.

6. Ask an assistant to fully depress the accelerator pedal. Then, while you read the compression gauge, ask the assistant to crank the engine 4 or 5 times in short bursts using the ignition switch.
7. Read the compression gauge at the end of each series of cranks, and record the highest of these readings. Repeat this procedure for each of the engine's cylinders.

A cylinder's compression pressure is considered within specification if the lowest reading cylinder is within 75% of the highest. The minimum acceptable pressure for these engines is about 100 psi. (689 kPa).

8. If a cylinder is unusually low, pour a tablespoon of clean engine oil into the cylinder through the spark plug hole and repeat the compression test. If the compression increases after adding the oil, it appears that the cylinder's piston rings or bore are damaged or worn. If the pressure remains low, the valves may not be seating properly (a valve job is needed), or the head gasket may be blown near that cylinder. If compression in any two adjacent cylinders is low, and if the addition of oil doesn't help the compression, there is probably leakage past the head gasket. Oil and coolant water in the combustion chamber can result from this problem. If there is evidence of water droplets in the oil film on the engine dipstick, the engine oil appears light brown and "milky" when the oil is drained, or oil is found in the radiator coolant, it is very likely that the head gasket has blown.

VALVE SPECIFICATIONS

Year	Engine ID/VIN	Engine Displacement Liters (cc)	Seat Angle (deg.)	Face Angle (deg.)	Spring Test Pressure (lbs. @ in.)	Spring Installed Height (in.)	Stem-to-Guide Clearance (in.) Intake	Stem-to-Guide Clearance (in.) Exhaust	Stem Diameter (in.) Intake	Stem Diameter (in.) Exhaust
1981	B	2.2 (2212)	45	45	100@1.65	1.650	0.0009-0.0026	0.0028-0.0044	0.3124 MIN	0.3103 MIN
	D	2.6 (2556)	45	45	61@1.59 ③	1.590	0.0012-0.0024	0.0020-0.0035	0.3150 ② MIN	0.3150 MIN
1982	B	2.2 (2212)	45	45	100@1.65	1.650	0.0009-0.0026	0.0028-0.0044	0.3124 MIN	0.3103 MIN
	C	2.2 (2212)	45	45	100@1.65	1.650	0.0009-0.0026	0.0028-0.0044	0.3124 MIN	0.3103 MIN
	D	2.6 (2556)	45	45	61@1.59 ③	1.590	0.0012-0.0024	0.0020-0.0044	0.3150 ② MIN	0.3150 MIN
	G	2.6 (2556)	45	45	61@1.59 ③	1.590	0.0012-0.0024	0.0020-0.0035	0.3150 ② MIN	0.3150 MIN
1983	C	2.2 (2212)	45	45	100@1.65	1.650	0.0009-0.0026	0.0028-0.0044	0.3124 MIN	0.3103 MIN
	G	2.6 (2556)	45	45	61@1.59 ③	1.590	0.0012-0.0024	0.0020-0.0035	0.3150 ② MIN	0.3150 MIN
1984	C	2.2 (2212)	45	45	100@1.65	1.650	0.0009-0.0026	0.0030-0.0047	0.3124 MIN	0.3103 MIN
	D	2.2 (2212)	45	45	100@1.65	1.650	0.0009-0.0026	0.0030-0.0047	0.3124 MIN	0.3103 MIN
	E	2.2 (2212)	45	45	108@1.65	1.650	0.0009-0.0026	0.0030-0.0047	0.3124 MIN	0.3103 MIN
	G	2.6 (2556)	45	45	61@1.59 ③	1.590	0.0012-0.0024	0.0020-0.0035	0.3150 ② MIN	0.3150 MIN
1985	C	2.2 (2212)	45	45	100@1.65	1.650	0.0009-0.0026	0.0030-0.0047	0.3124 MIN	0.3103 MIN
	D	2.2 (2212)	45	45	100@1.65	1.650	0.0009-0.0026	0.0030-0.0047	0.3124 MIN	0.3103 MIN
	E	2.2 (2212)	45	45	108@1.65	1.650	0.0009-0.0026	0.0030-0.0047	0.3124 MIN	0.3103 MIN
	G	2.6 (2556)	45	45	61@1.59 ③	1.590	0.0012-0.0024	0.0020-0.0035	0.3150 ② MIN	0.3150 MIN
1986	C	2.2 (2212)	45	45	100@1.65	1.650	0.0009-0.0026	0.0030-0.0047	0.3124 MIN	0.3103 MIN
	D	2.2 (2212)	45	45	100@1.65	1.650	0.0009-0.0026	0.0030-0.0047	0.3124 MIN	0.3103 MIN
	E	2.2 (2212)	45	45	108@1.65	1.650	0.0009-0.0026	0.0030-0.0047	0.3124 MIN	0.3103 MIN
	K	2.5 (2507)	45	45	100@1.65	1.650	0.0009-0.0026	0.0030-0.0047	0.3124 MIN	0.3103 MIN
1987	A	2.2 (2212)	45	45	108@1.65	1.650	0.0009-0.0026	0.0030-0.0047	0.3124 MIN	0.3124 MIN
	D	2.2 (2212)	45	45	100@1.65	1.650	0.0009-0.0026	0.0030-0.0047	0.3124 MIN	0.3103 MIN
	E	2.2 (2212)	45	45	108@1.65	1.650	0.0009-0.0026	0.0030-0.0047	0.3124 MIN	0.3103 MIN
	K	2.5 (2507)	45	45	100@1.65	1.650	0.0009-0.0026	0.0030-0.0047	0.3124 MIN	0.3103 MIN
1988	A	2.2 (2212)	45	45	114@1.65	1.650	0.0009-0.0026	0.0030-0.0047	0.3124 MIN	0.3124 MIN
	D	2.2 (2212)	45	45	114@1.65	1.650	0.0009-0.0026	0.0030-0.0047	0.3124 MIN	0.3124 MIN
	E	2.2 (2212)	45	45	114@1.65	1.650	0.0009-0.0026	0.0030-0.0047	0.3124 MIN	0.3103 MIN
	K	2.5 (2507)	45	45	114@1.65	1.650	0.0009-0.0026	0.0030-0.0047	0.3124 MIN	0.3103 MIN

86733C11

GENERAL ENGINE SPECIFICATIONS

Year	Engine ID/VIN	Engine Displacement Liters (cc)	Fuel System Type	Net Horsepower @ rpm	Net Torque @ rpm (ft. lbs.)	Bore x Stroke (in.)	Compression Ratio	Oil Pressure @ rpm
1981	D	2.6 (2556)	2BC	84@4800	111@2500	3.59x3.86	8.5:1	50@2000
	B	2.2 (2212)	2BC	92@4500	131@2500	3.44x3.62	8.5:1	45-90@3000
1982	B	2.2 (2212)	2BC	84@4800	111@2800	3.44x3.62	8.5:1	50@2000
	D	2.6 (2556)	2BC	92@4500	131@2500	3.59x3.86	8.2:1	45-90@3000
	C	2.2 (2212)	2BC	94@4800	119@2800	3.44x3.62	9.0:1	45-90@3000
	C	2.6 (2556)	2BC	92@4500	131@2500	3.59x3.86	8.2:1	45-90@3000
	D	2.2 (2212)	2BC	96@5200	119@3200	3.44x3.62	9.0:1	45-90@3000
1983	C	2.2 (2212)	2BC	96@5200	119@3200	3.44x3.62	9.0:1	45-90@3000
	E	2.2 (2212)	MFI-Turbo	142@5600	160@3600	3.44x3.62	8.5:1	45-90@3000
	G	2.6 (2556)	2BC	101@4800	140@2800	3.59x3.86	8.7:1	45-90@3000
1984	C	2.2 (2212)	2BC	96@5200	119@3200	3.44x3.62	9.5:1	25-80@3000
	D	2.2 (2212)	EFI	99@5600	121@3200	3.44x3.62	9.5:1	25-80@3000
	E	2.2 (2212)	MFI-Turbo	146@6200	168@3200	3.44x3.62	8.5:1	25-80@3000
	G	2.6 (2556)	2BC	101@4800	140@2800	3.59x3.86	8.7:1	45-90@3000
1985	C	2.2 (2212)	EFI	97@5600	122@3200	3.44x3.62	9.0:1	25-80@3000
	D	2.2 (2212)	EFI	99@5600	121@3200	3.44x3.62	9.5:1	25-80@3000
	E	2.2 (2212)	MFI-Turbo	146@6200	168@3200	3.44x3.62	8.5:1	25-80@3000
1986	A	2.2 (2212)	MFI-Turbo	174@4800	200@3200	3.44x3.62	8.5:1	25-80@3000
	E	2.2 (2212)	MFI-Turbo	146@6200	170@3600	3.44x3.62	8.5:1	25-80@3000
	K	2.5 (2507)	EFI	100@4800	135@2800	3.44x4.09	8.9:1	25-80@3000
	P	2.2 (2212)	MFI-Turbo	174@4800	210@2400	3.44x3.62	8.1:1	25-80@3000
1987	A	2.2 (2212)	MFI-Turbo	174@4800	200@2400	3.44x3.62	9.0:1	25-80@3000
	D	2.2 (2212)	EFI	93@4800	122@3200	3.44x3.62	9.5:1	25-80@3000
	K	2.5 (2507)	EFI	100@4800	135@2800	3.44x4.09	8.9:1	25-80@3000
	R	2.2 (2212)	MFI-Turbo	174@4800	220@3400	3.44x3.62	7.8:1	25-80@3000
1988	A	2.2 (2212)	MFI-Turbo	174@5200	170@2500	3.44x3.62	9.5:1	25-80@3000
	D	2.2 (2212)	EFI	96@4800	133@3200	3.44x3.62	8.9:1	25-80@3000
	K	2.5 (2507)	EFI	100@4800	135@2800	3.44x4.09	8.9:1	25-80@3000
1989	A	2.2 (2212)	MFI-Turbo	174@5200	174@4800	3.44x3.62	8.1:1	25-80@3000
	D	2.2 (2212)	EFI	93@4800	122@3200	3.44x3.62	9.5:1	25-80@3000
	J	2.5 (2507)	MFI-Turbo	150@4800	180@2000	3.44x4.09	7.8:1	25-80@3000
	K	2.5 (2507)	EFI	100@4800	135@2800	3.44x4.09	8.9:1	25-80@3000
	R	2.2 (2212)	MFI-Turbo	200@5200	210@2400	3.44x3.62	7.4:1	25-80@3000
1990	A	2.2 (2212)	MFI-Turbo	174@5200	220@3400	3.44x3.62	8.1:1	25-80@3000
	D	2.2 (2212)	EFI	93@4800	122@3200	3.44x3.62	9.5:1	25-80@3000
	J	2.5 (2507)	MFI-Turbo	150@4800	180@2000	3.44x4.09	7.8:1	25-80@3000
	K	2.5 (2507)	EFI	100@4800	135@2800	3.44x4.09	8.9:1	25-80@3000
1991	R	2.2 (2212)	MFI-Turbo	224@6000	217@2800	3.44x3.62	8.1:1	25-80@3000
	D	2.2 (2212)	EFI	93@4800	122@3200	3.44x3.62	9.5:1	25-80@3000
	K	2.5 (2507)	EFI	100@4800	135@2800	3.44x4.09	8.9:1	25-80@3000
1992	A	2.2 (2212)	MFI-Turbo	224@6000	217@2800	3.44x3.62	8.1:1	25-80@3000
	D	2.2 (2212)	EFI	93@4800	122@3200	3.44x3.62	9.5:1	25-80@3000
	J	2.5 (2507)	MFI-Turbo	150@4800	180@2000	3.44x4.09	7.8:1	25-80@3000
	K	2.5 (2507)	EFI	100@4800	135@2800	3.44x4.09	8.9:1	25-80@3000
1993	A	2.2 (2212)	MFI-Turbo	224@6000	217@2800	3.44x3.62	8.1:1	25-80@3000
	D	2.2 (2212)	EFI	93@4800	122@3200	3.44x3.62	9.5:1	25-80@3000
	K	2.5 (2507)	EFI	100@4800	135@2800	3.44x4.09	8.9:1	25-80@3000
1994	D	2.2 (2212)	EFI	93@4800	122@3200	3.44x3.62	9.5:1	25-80@3000
	K	2.5 (2507)	EFI	100@4800	135@2400	3.44x4.09	8.9:1	25-80@3000
	V	2.5 (2507)	FF MFI	100@4800	145@2400	3.44x4.09	8.9:1	25-80@3000
1995	K	2.5 (2507)	EFI	100@4800	135@2400	3.44x4.09	8.9:1	25-80@3000
	V	2.5 (2507)	FF MFI	106@4400	145@2400	3.44x4.09	8.9:1	25-80@3000

BC - Barrel carburetor
EFI - Electronic Fuel Injection
FF MFI - Flexible Fuel Multi-port Fuel Injection
MFI - Multi-port Fuel Injection

① Except Shadow - 93@4800 / Shadow - 100@5200
② Except Shadow - 122@3200 / Shadow - 134@3200
③ Manual transaxle - 150@5000 / Automatic transaxle - 152@4800
④ Manual transaxle - 180@2000 / Automatic transaxle - 210@2400

86733C14

CAMSHAFT SPECIFICATIONS
All measurements given in inches.

Year	Engine ID/VIN	Engine Displacement Liters (cc)	Journal Diameter 1	2	3	4	5	Elevation In.	Ex.	Bearing Clearance	Camshaft End-Play
1981	B	2.2 (2212)	1.3750-1.3760	1.3750-1.3760	1.3750-1.3760	1.3750-1.3760	1.3750-1.3760	NA	NA	NA	0.0050-0.0130
	D	2.6 (2556)	1.3390	1.3390	1.3390	1.3390	1.3390	0.4130	0.4130	0.0020-0.0040	0.0040-0.0080
1982	B	2.2 (2212)	1.3750-1.3760	1.3750-1.3760	1.3750-1.3760	1.3750-1.3760	1.3750-1.3760	NA	NA	NA	0.0050-0.0130
	C	2.2 (2212)	1.3750-1.3760	1.3750-1.3760	1.3750-1.3760	1.3750-1.3760	1.3750-1.3760	NA	NA	NA	0.0050-0.0130
	D	2.6 (2556)	1.3390	1.3390	1.3390	1.3390	1.3390	0.4130	0.4130	0.0020-0.0040	0.0040-0.0080
	G	2.6 (2556)	1.3390	1.3390	1.3390	1.3390	1.3390	0.4130	0.4130	0.0020-0.0040	0.0040-0.0080
1983	C	2.2 (2212)	1.3750-1.3760	1.3750-1.3760	1.3750-1.3760	1.3750-1.3760	1.3750-1.3760	NA	NA	NA	0.0050-0.0130
	G	2.6 (2556)	1.3390	1.3390	1.3390	1.3390	1.3390	0.4130	0.4130	0.0020-0.0040	0.0040-0.0080
1984	C	2.2 (2212)	1.3750-1.3760	1.3750-1.3760	1.3750-1.3760	1.3750-1.3760	1.3750-1.3760	NA	NA	NA	0.0050-0.0130
	D	2.2 (2212)	1.3750-1.3760	1.3750-1.3760	1.3750-1.3760	1.3750-1.3760	1.3750-1.3760	NA	NA	NA	0.0050-0.0130
	E	2.2 (2212)	1.3750-1.3760	1.3750-1.3760	1.3750-1.3760	1.3750-1.3760	1.3750-1.3760	NA	NA	NA	0.0050-0.0130
	G	2.6 (2556)	1.3390	1.3390	1.3390	1.3390	1.3390	0.4130	0.4130	0.0020-0.0040	0.0040-0.0080
1985	C	2.2 (2212)	1.3750-1.3760	1.3750-1.3760	1.3750-1.3760	1.3750-1.3760	1.3750-1.3760	NA	NA	NA	0.0050-0.0130
	D	2.2 (2212)	1.3750-1.3760	1.3750-1.3760	1.3750-1.3760	1.3750-1.3760	1.3750-1.3760	NA	NA	NA	0.0050-0.0130
	E	2.2 (2212)	1.3750-1.3760	1.3750-1.3760	1.3750-1.3760	1.3750-1.3760	1.3750-1.3760	NA	NA	NA	0.0050-0.0130
	G	2.6 (2556)	1.3390	1.3390	1.3390	1.3390	1.3390	0.4130	0.4130	0.0020-0.0040	0.0040-0.0080
1986	C	2.2 (2212)	1.3750-1.3760	1.3750-1.3760	1.3750-1.3760	1.3750-1.3760	1.3750-1.3760	NA	NA	NA	0.0050-0.0130
	D	2.2 (2212)	1.3750-1.3760	1.3750-1.3760	1.3750-1.3760	1.3750-1.3760	1.3750-1.3760	NA	NA	NA	0.0050-0.0130
	E	2.2 (2212)	1.3750-1.3760	1.3750-1.3760	1.3750-1.3760	1.3750-1.3760	1.3750-1.3760	NA	NA	NA	0.0050-0.0130
	K	2.5 (2507)	1.3750-1.3760	1.3750-1.3760	1.3750-1.3760	1.3750-1.3760	1.3750-1.3760	NA	NA	NA	0.0050-0.0130
1987	A	2.2 (2212)	1.3750-1.3760	1.3750-1.3760	1.3750-1.3760	1.3750-1.3760	1.3750-1.3760	NA	NA	NA	0.0050-0.0130
	D	2.2 (2212)	1.3750-1.3760	1.3750-1.3760	1.3750-1.3760	1.3750-1.3760	1.3750-1.3760	NA	NA	NA	0.0050-0.0130
	E	2.2 (2212)	1.3750-1.3760	1.3750-1.3760	1.3750-1.3760	1.3750-1.3760	1.3750-1.3760	NA	NA	NA	0.0050-0.0130
	K	2.5 (2507)	1.3750-1.3760	1.3750-1.3760	1.3750-1.3760	1.3750-1.3760	1.3750-1.3760	NA	NA	NA	0.0050-0.0130
1988	A	2.2 (2212)	1.3750-1.3760	1.3750-1.3760	1.3750-1.3760	1.3750-1.3760	1.3750-1.3760	NA	NA	NA	0.0050-0.0130
	D	2.2 (2212)	1.3750-1.3760	1.3750-1.3760	1.3750-1.3760	1.3750-1.3760	1.3750-1.3760	NA	NA	NA	0.0050-0.0130
	E	2.2 (2212)	1.3750-1.3760	1.3750-1.3760	1.3750-1.3760	1.3750-1.3760	1.3750-1.3760	NA	NA	NA	0.0050-0.0130
	K	2.5 (2507)	1.3750-1.3760	1.3750-1.3760	1.3750-1.3760	1.3750-1.3760	1.3750-1.3760	NA	NA	NA	0.0050-0.0130

86733C08

VALVE SPECIFICATIONS

Year	Engine ID/VIN	Engine Displacement Liters (cc)	Seat Angle (deg.)	Face Angle (deg.)	Spring Test Pressure (lbs. @ in.)	Spring Installed Height (in.)	Stem-to-Guide Clearance (in.) Intake	Exhaust	Stem Diameter (in.) Intake	Exhaust
1989	D	2.2 (2212)	45	45	114@1.65	1.650	0.0009-0.0026	0.0030-0.0047	0.3124 MIN	0.3105 MIN
	D	2.5 (2507)	45	45	114@1.65	1.650	0.0009-0.0026	0.0030-0.0047	0.3124 MIN	0.3105 MIN
	J	2.5 (2507)	45	45	114@1.65	1.650	0.0009-0.0026	0.0030-0.0047	0.3124 MIN	0.3103 MIN
	K	2.5 (2507)	45	45	114@1.65	1.650	0.0009-0.0026	0.0030-0.0047	0.3124 MIN	0.3103 MIN
	P	2.2 (2212)	45	45	108@1.65	1.650	0.0009-0.0026	0.0030-0.0047	0.3124 MIN	0.3103 MIN
	R	2.2 (2212)	NA	NA	NA	①	0.0007-0.0017	0.0013-0.0024	0.2752-0.2758	0.2752-0.2758
1990	C	2.2 (2212)	45	45	114@1.65	1.650	0.0009-0.0026	0.0030-0.0047	0.3124 MIN	0.3103 MIN
	D	2.2 (2212)	45	45	114@1.65	1.650	0.0009-0.0026	0.0030-0.0047	0.3124 MIN	0.3103 MIN
	J	2.5 (2507)	45	45	114@1.65	1.650	0.0009-0.0026	0.0030-0.0047	0.3124 MIN	0.3103 MIN
	K	2.5 (2507)	45	45	114@1.65	1.650	0.0009-0.0026	0.0030-0.0047	0.3124 MIN	0.3103 MIN
	R	2.2 (2212)	NA	NA	NA	①	0.0007-0.0017	0.0013-0.0024	0.2752-0.2758	0.2752-0.2758
1991	A	2.2 (2212)	45	45	73@1.41	1.410	0.0011-0.0024	0.0020-0.0031	0.2740 MIN	0.2730 MIN
	D	2.2 (2212)	45	45	114@1.65	1.650	0.0009-0.0026	0.0030-0.0047	0.3124 MIN	0.3103 MIN
	J	2.5 (2507)	45	45	114@1.65	1.650	0.0009-0.0026	0.0030-0.0047	0.3124 MIN	0.3103 MIN
	K	2.5 (2507)	45	45	114@1.65	1.650	0.0009-0.0026	0.0030-0.0047	0.3124 MIN	0.3103 MIN
1992	A	2.2 (2212)	45	45	114@1.65	1.730	0.0011-0.0024	0.0020-0.0031	0.2740 MIN	0.2730 MIN
	D	2.2 (2212)	45	45	114@1.65	1.650	0.0009-0.0026	0.0030-0.0047	0.3124 MIN	0.3103 MIN
	J	2.5 (2507)	45	45	121@1.73	1.730	0.0011-0.0024	0.0020-0.0031	0.2740 MIN	MIN
	K	2.5 (2507)	45	45	114@1.65	1.650	0.0009-0.0026	0.0030-0.0047	0.3124 MIN	0.3193 MIN
1993	A	2.2 (2212)	45	45	121@1.73	1.730	0.0011-0.0024	0.0020-0.0031	0.2740 MIN	MIN
	D	2.2 (2212)	45	45	114@1.65	1.650	0.0009-0.0026	0.0030-0.0047	0.3124 MIN	0.3103 MIN
	K	2.5 (2507)	45	45	114@1.65	1.650	0.0009-0.0026	0.0030-0.0047	0.3124 MIN	0.3103 MIN
	V	2.5 (2507)	45	45	114@1.65	1.650	0.0009-0.0026	0.0030-0.0047	0.3124 MIN	0.3103 MIN
1994	D	2.2 (2212)	45	45	114@1.65	1.650	0.0009-0.0026	0.0030-0.0047	0.3124 MIN	0.3103 MIN
	K	2.5 (2507)	45	45	114@1.65	1.650	0.0009-0.0026	0.0030-0.0047	0.3124 MIN	0.3105 MIN
	V	2.5 (2507)	45	45	114@1.65	1.650	0.0009-0.0026	0.0030-0.0047	0.3124 MIN	0.3105 MIN
1995	K	2.5 (2507)	45	45	114@1.65	1.650	0.0009-0.0026	0.0030-0.0047	0.3124 MIN	0.3104 MIN
	V	2.5 (2507)	45	45	114@1.65	1.650	0.0009-0.0026	0.0030-0.0047	0.3124 MIN	0.3104 MIN

NA - Not Available   MIN - Minimum

① Free length: 1.164 in.   ② Jet valve - 0.1693 in.   ③ Jet valve - 5.5@0.846

36734C12

CRANKSHAFT AND CONNECTING ROD SPECIFICATIONS
All measurements are given in inches.

Year	Engine ID/VIN	Engine Displacement Liters (cc)	Main Brg. Journal Dia.	Crankshaft Main Brg Oil Clearance	Crankshaft Shaft End-play	Thrust on No.	Connecting Rod Journal Diameter	Connecting Rod Oil Clearance	Connecting Rod Side Clearance
1981	B	2.2 (2212)	2.3620-2.3630	0.0003-0.0031	0.0020-0.0070 ②	3	1.9680-1.9690	0.0008-0.0034 ②	0.0050-0.0130 ②
	D	2.6 (2556)	2.3622	0.0008-0.0028	0.0020-0.0070	3	2.0866	0.0008-0.0028	0.0040-0.0100
1982	B	2.2 (2212)	2.3620-2.3630	0.0003-0.0031	0.0020-0.0070 ②	3	1.9680-1.9690	0.0006-0.0034 ②	0.0050-0.0130 ②
	C	2.2 (2212)	2.3620-2.3630	0.0003-0.0031	0.0020-0.0070 ②	3	1.9680-1.9990	0.0008-0.0034 ②	0.0050-0.0130 ②
	D	2.6 (2556)	2.3622	0.0008-0.0028	0.0020-0.0070	3	2.0866	0.0008-0.0028	0.0040-0.0100
	G	2.6 (2556)	2.3622	0.0008-0.0028	0.0020-0.0070	3	2.0866	0.0008-0.0028	0.0040-0.0100
1983	C	2.2 (2212)	2.3620-2.3630	0.0003-0.0031	0.0020-0.0070 ②	3	1.9680-1.9990	0.0008-0.0034 ②	0.0050-0.0130 ②
	G	2.6 (2556)	2.3622	0.0008-0.0028	0.0020-0.0070	3	2.0866	0.0008-0.0028	0.0040-0.0100
1984	C	2.2 (2212)	2.3620-2.3630	0.0003-0.0031	0.0020-0.0070 ②	3	1.9680-1.9990	0.0008-0.0034 ②	0.0050-0.0130 ②
	D	2.2 (2212)	2.3620-2.3630	0.0003-0.0031	0.0020-0.0070	3	1.9680-1.9690	0.0008-0.0034	0.0050-0.0130
	E	2.2 (2212)	2.3620-2.3630	0.0004-0.0023	0.0020-0.0070	3	1.9680-1.9690	0.0004-0.0031	0.0050-0.0130
	G	2.6 (2556)	2.3622	0.0008-0.0028	0.0020-0.0070	3	2.0866	0.0008-0.0028	0.0040-0.0100
1985	C	2.2 (2212)	2.3620-2.3630	0.0003-0.0031	0.0020-0.0070 ②	3	1.9680-1.9690	0.0008-0.0034 ②	0.0050-0.0130 ②
	D	2.2 (2212)	2.3620-2.3630	0.0003-0.0031	0.0020-0.0070	3	1.9680-1.9690	0.0008-0.0034	0.0050-0.0130
	E	2.2 (2212)	2.3620-2.3630	0.0004-0.0023	0.0020-0.0070	3	1.9680-1.9690	0.0004-0.0031	0.0050-0.0130
	G	2.6 (2556)	2.3622	0.0008-0.0028	0.0020-0.0070	3	2.0866	0.0008-0.0028	0.0040-0.0100
1986	C	2.2 (2212)	2.3620-2.3630	0.0003-0.0031	0.0020-0.0070 ②	3	1.9680-1.9690	0.0008-0.0034 ②	0.0050-0.0130 ②
	D	2.2 (2212)	2.3620-2.3630	0.0003-0.0031	0.0020-0.0070	3	1.9660-1.9690	0.0034	0.0050-0.0130
	E	2.2 (2212)	2.3620-2.3630	0.0004-0.0023	0.0020-0.0070	3	1.9660-1.9690	0.0008-0.0031	0.0050-0.0130
	G	2.6 (2556)	2.3622	0.0008-0.0028	0.0020-0.0070	3	2.0866	0.0008-0.0028	0.0040-0.0100
1987	A	2.2 (2212)	2.3620-2.3630	0.0004-0.0023	0.0020-0.0070 ②	3	1.9680-1.9690	0.0008-0.0034 ②	0.0050-0.0130 ②
	D	2.2 (2212)	2.3620-2.3630	0.0003-0.0031	0.0020-0.0070	3	1.9660-1.9690	0.0034	0.0050-0.0130
	E	2.2 (2212)	2.3620-2.3630	0.0004-0.0023	0.0020-0.0070	3	1.9660-1.9690	0.0008-0.0031	0.0050-0.0130
	K	2.5 (2507)	2.3620-2.3630	0.0003-0.0031	0.0020-0.0070	3	1.9680-1.9690	0.0008-0.0034	0.0050-0.0130
1988	A	2.2 (2212)	2.3620-2.3630	0.0004-0.0028	0.0020-0.0070 ②	3	1.9680-1.9690	0.0008-0.0031 ②	0.0050-0.0130 ②
	D	2.2 (2212)	2.3620-2.3630	0.0004-0.0028	0.0020-0.0070	3	1.9660-1.9690	0.0008-0.0034	0.0050-0.0130
	E	2.2 (2212)	2.3620-2.3630	0.0004-0.0028	0.0020-0.0070	3	1.9660-1.9690	0.0008-0.0031	0.0050-0.0130
	K	2.5 (2507)	2.3620-2.3630	0.0004-0.0028	0.0020-0.0070	3	1.9680-1.9690	0.0008-0.0034	0.0050-0.0130
1989	A	2.2 (2212)	2.3620-2.3630	0.0004-0.0028	0.0020-0.0070 ②	3	1.9680-1.9690	0.0008-0.0031 ②	0.0050-0.0130 ②
	K	2.5 (2507)	2.3620-2.3630	0.0004-0.0028	0.0020-0.0070	3	1.9680-1.9690	0.0008-0.0034	0.0050-0.0130

86733C05

CAMSHAFT SPECIFICATIONS
All measurements given in inches.

Year	Engine ID/VIN	Engine Displacement Liters (cc)	Journal Diameter 1	2	3	4	5	Elevation In.	Elevation Ex.	Bearing Clearance	Camshaft End-Play
1989	A	2.2 (2212)	1.3750-1.3760	1.3750-1.3760	1.3750-1.3760	1.3750-1.3760	1.3750-1.3760	NA	NA	NA	0.0050-0.0130
	D	2.2 (2212)	1.3750-1.3760	1.3750-1.3760	1.3750-1.3760	1.3750-1.3760	1.3750-1.3760	NA	NA	NA	0.0050-0.0130
	E	2.2 (2212)	1.3750-1.3760	1.3750-1.3760	1.3750-1.3760	1.3750-1.3760	1.3750-1.3760	NA	NA	NA	0.0050-0.0130
	P	2.2 (2212)	1.3750-1.3760	1.3750-1.3760	1.3750-1.3760	1.3750-1.3760	1.3750-1.3760	NA	NA	NA	0.0050-0.0130
	R	2.2 (2212)	NA	NA	NA	NA	NA	NA	NA	NA	NA
	J	2.5 (2507)	1.3750-1.3760	1.3750-1.3760	1.3750-1.3760	1.3750-1.3760	1.3750-1.3760	NA	NA	NA	0.0050-0.0130
	K	2.5 (2507)	1.3750-1.3760	1.3750-1.3760	1.3750-1.3760	1.3750-1.3760	1.3750-1.3760	NA	NA	NA	0.0050-0.0130
1990	C	2.2 (2212)	1.3750-1.3760	1.3750-1.3760	1.3750-1.3760	1.3750-1.3760	1.3750-1.3760	NA	NA	NA	0.0050-0.0130
	D	2.2 (2212)	1.3750-1.3760	1.3750-1.3760	1.3750-1.3760	1.3750-1.3760	1.3750-1.3760	NA	NA	NA	0.0050-0.0130
	R	2.2 (2212)	NA	NA	NA	NA	NA	NA	NA	NA	NA
	J	2.5 (2507)	1.3750-1.3760	1.3750-1.3760	1.3750-1.3760	1.3750-1.3760	1.3750-1.3760	NA	NA	NA	0.0050-0.0130
	K	2.5 (2507)	1.3750-1.3760	1.3750-1.3760	1.3750-1.3760	1.3750-1.3760	1.3750-1.3760	NA	NA	NA	0.0050-0.0130
1991	A	2.2 (2212)	1.8860-1.8870	1.8860-1.8870	1.8860-1.8870	1.8860-1.8870	1.8860-1.8870	NA	NA	NA	0.0010-0.0080
	D	2.2 (2212)	1.8860-1.8870	1.8860-1.8870	1.8860-1.8870	1.8860-1.8870	1.8860-1.8870	NA	NA	NA	0.0050-0.0130
	J	2.5 (2507)	1.3750-1.3760	1.3750-1.3760	1.3750-1.3760	1.3750-1.3760	1.3750-1.3760	NA	NA	NA	0.0050-0.0130
	K	2.5 (2507)	1.3750-1.3760	1.3750-1.3760	1.3750-1.3760	1.3750-1.3760	1.3750-1.3760	NA	NA	NA	0.0050-0.0130
1992	A	2.2 (2212)	1.8860-1.8870	1.8860-1.8870	1.8860-1.8870	1.8860-1.8870	1.8860-1.8870	NA	NA	NA	0.0010-0.0080
	D	2.2 (2212)	1.8860-1.8870	1.8860-1.8870	1.8860-1.8870	1.8860-1.8870	1.8860-1.8870	NA	NA	NA	0.0050-0.0130
	J	2.5 (2507)	1.3750-1.3760	1.3750-1.3760	1.3750-1.3760	1.3750-1.3760	1.3750-1.3760	NA	NA	NA	0.0050-0.0130
	K	2.5 (2507)	1.3750-1.3760	1.3750-1.3760	1.3750-1.3760	1.3750-1.3760	1.3750-1.3760	NA	NA	NA	0.0050-0.0130
1993	A	2.2 (2212)	1.8860-1.8870	1.8860-1.8870	1.8860-1.8870	1.8860-1.8870	1.8860-1.8870	NA	NA	NA	0.0010-0.0080
	D	2.2 (2212)	1.3750-1.3760	1.3750-1.3760	1.3750-1.3760	1.3750-1.3760	1.3750-1.3760	NA	NA	NA	0.0050-0.0130
	K	2.5 (2507)	1.3750-1.3760	1.3750-1.3760	1.3750-1.3760	1.3750-1.3760	1.3750-1.3760	NA	NA	NA	0.0050-0.0130
	V	2.5 (2507)	1.3750-1.3760	1.3750-1.3760	1.3750-1.3760	1.3750-1.3760	1.3750-1.3760	NA	NA	NA	0.0050-0.0130
1994	D	2.2 (2212)	1.3750-1.3760	1.3750-1.3760	1.3750-1.3760	1.3750-1.3760	1.3750-1.3760	NA	NA	NA	0.0050-0.0130
	K	2.5 (2507)	1.3750-1.3760	1.3750-1.3760	1.3750-1.3760	1.3750-1.3760	1.3750-1.3760	NA	NA	NA	0.0050-0.0130
	V	2.5 (2507)	1.3750-1.3760	1.3750-1.3760	1.3750-1.3760	1.3750-1.3760	1.3750-1.3760	NA	NA	NA	0.0050-0.0130
1995	K	2.5 (2507)	1.3750-1.3760	1.3750-1.3760	1.3750-1.3760	1.3750-1.3760	1.3750-1.3760	NA	NA	NA	0.0050-0.0130
	V	2.5 (2507)	1.3750-1.3760	1.3750-1.3760	1.3750-1.3760	1.3750-1.3760	1.3750-1.3760	NA	NA	NA	0.0050-0.0130

NOTE: Some 2.2L & 2.5L Chrysler built engines use oversize camshaft journals. The specification for these vehicles is 1.3950-1.3960 in.

NA - Not Available

86733C09

PISTON AND RING SPECIFICATIONS

All measurements are given in inches.

Year	Engine ID/VIN	Engine Displacement Liters (cc)	Piston Clearance	Ring Gap Top Compression	Ring Gap Bottom Compression	Ring Gap Oil Control	Ring Side Clearance Top Compression	Ring Side Clearance Bottom Compression	Ring Side Clearance Oil Control
1981	B	2.2 (2212)	0.0006-0.0015	② 0.0110-0.0210	② 0.0110-0.0210	③ 0.0150-0.0550	① 0.0015-0.0031	① 0.0015-0.0037	0.0080 MAX
	D	2.6 (2556)	0.0008-0.0016	0.0100-0.0180	0.0100-0.0180	0.0078-0.0350	0.0024-0.0039	0.0008-0.0024	NA
1982	B	2.2 (2212)	0.0005-0.0015	② 0.0110-0.0210	② 0.0110-0.0210	③ 0.0150-0.0550	① 0.0015-0.0031	① 0.0015-0.0037	0.0080 MAX
	C	2.2 (2212)	0.0005-0.0015	② 0.0110-0.0210	② 0.0110-0.0210	③ 0.0150-0.0550	① 0.0015-0.0031	① 0.0015-0.0037	0.0080 MAX
	D	2.6 (2556)	0.0008-0.0016	0.0100-0.0180	0.0100-0.0180	0.0078-0.0350	0.0024-0.0039	0.0008-0.0024	NA
	G	2.6 (2556)	0.0008-0.0016	0.0100-0.0180	0.0100-0.0180	0.0078-0.0350	0.0024-0.0039	0.0008-0.0024	NA
1983	C	2.2 (2212)	0.0005-0.0015	② 0.0110-0.0210	② 0.0110-0.0210	③ 0.0150-0.0550	① 0.0015-0.0031	① 0.0015-0.0037	0.0080 MAX
	G	2.6 (2556)	0.0008-0.0016	0.0100-0.0180	0.0100-0.0180	0.0078-0.0350	0.0024-0.0039	0.0008-0.0024	NA
1984	C	2.2 (2212)	0.0005-0.0015	② 0.0110-0.0210	② 0.0110-0.0210	③ 0.0150-0.0550	① 0.0015-0.0031	① 0.0015-0.0037	0.0080 MAX
	D	2.2 (2212)	0.0005-0.0015	② 0.0110-0.0210	② 0.0110-0.0210	③ 0.0150-0.0550	① 0.0015-0.0031	① 0.0015-0.0037	0.0080 MAX
	E	2.2 (2212)	0.0015-0.0025	⑦ 0.0100-0.0200	⑦ 0.0090-0.0190	③ 0.0150-0.0078	① 0.0015-0.0031	① 0.0015-0.0037	0.0080 MAX
	G	2.6 (2556)	0.0008-0.0016	0.0100-0.0180	0.0100-0.0180	0.0078-0.0350	0.0024-0.0039	0.0008-0.0024	NA
1985	C	2.2 (2212)	0.0005-0.0015	② 0.0110-0.0210	② 0.0110-0.0210	③ 0.0150-0.0550	① 0.0015-0.0031	① 0.0015-0.0037	0.0080 MAX
	D	2.2 (2212)	0.0005-0.0015	② 0.0110-0.0210	② 0.0110-0.0210	③ 0.0150-0.0550	① 0.0015-0.0031	① 0.0015-0.0037	0.0080 MAX
	E	2.2 (2212)	0.0015-0.0025	⑦ 0.0100-0.0200	⑦ 0.0090-0.0190	③ 0.0150-0.0078	① 0.0015-0.0031	① 0.0015-0.0037	0.0080 MAX
1986	C	2.2 (2212)	0.0005-0.0015	② 0.0110-0.0210	② 0.0110-0.0210	③ 0.0150-0.0550	① 0.0015-0.0031	① 0.0015-0.0037	0.0080 MAX
	D	2.2 (2212)	0.0005-0.0015	② 0.0110-0.0210	② 0.0110-0.0210	③ 0.0150-0.0550	① 0.0015-0.0031	① 0.0015-0.0037	0.0080 MAX
	E	2.2 (2212)	0.0015-0.0025	⑦ 0.0100-0.0200	⑦ 0.0090-0.0190	③ 0.0150-0.0078	① 0.0015-0.0031	① 0.0015-0.0037	0.0080 MAX
	G	2.6 (2556)	0.0008-0.0016	0.0100-0.0180	0.0100-0.0180	0.0078-0.0350	0.0024-0.0039	0.0008-0.0024	NA
1987	A	2.2 (2212)	0.0005-0.0025	⑦ 0.0100-0.0200	⑦ 0.0090-0.0190	③ 0.0078-0.0150	① 0.0024-0.0039	① 0.0008-0.0024	0.0080 MAX
	D	2.2 (2212)	0.0005-0.0015	② 0.0110-0.0210	② 0.0110-0.0210	③ 0.0150-0.0550	① 0.0015-0.0031	① 0.0015-0.0037	0.0080 MAX
	E	2.2 (2212)	0.0015-0.0025	⑦ 0.0100-0.0200	⑦ 0.0090-0.0190	③ 0.0150-0.0550	① 0.0015-0.0031	① 0.0015-0.0037	0.0080 MAX
	K	2.5 (2507)	0.0005-0.0015	② 0.0110-0.0210	② 0.0110-0.0210	③ 0.0150-0.0550	① 0.0015-0.0031	① 0.0015-0.0037	0.0080 MAX
1988	A	2.2 (2212)	0.0005-0.0025	⑦ 0.0100-0.0200	⑦ 0.0090-0.0190	③ 0.0090-0.0550	① 0.0024-0.0031	① 0.0015-0.0037	0.0080 MAX
	D	2.2 (2212)	0.0005-0.0015	② 0.0110-0.0210	② 0.0110-0.0210	③ 0.0150-0.0550	① 0.0015-0.0031	① 0.0015-0.0037	0.0080 MAX
	E	2.2 (2212)	0.0015-0.0025	⑦ 0.0100-0.0200	⑦ 0.0090-0.0190	③ 0.0150-0.0550	① 0.0015-0.0031	① 0.0015-0.0037	0.0080 MAX
	K	2.5 (2507)	0.0005-0.0015	② 0.0110-0.0210	② 0.0110-0.0210	③ 0.0150-0.0550	① 0.0015-0.0031	① 0.0015-0.0037	0.0080 MAX
1989	A	2.2 (2212)	0.0015-0.0026	⑦ 0.0100-0.0200	⑦ 0.0090-0.0190	③ 0.0150-0.0550	① 0.0016-0.0030	① 0.0016-0.0035	0.0080 MAX
	D	2.2 (2212)	0.0005-0.0015	② 0.0110-0.0210	② 0.0110-0.0210	③ 0.0150-0.0550	① 0.0015-0.0031	① 0.0015-0.0037	0.0080 MAX

86733C02

CRANKSHAFT AND CONNECTING ROD SPECIFICATIONS

All measurements are given in inches.

Year	Engine ID/VIN	Engine Displacement Liters (cc)	Main Brg. Journal Dia	Crankshaft Main Brg. Oil Clearance	Crankshaft Shaft End-play	Thrust on No.	Connecting Rod Journal Diameter	Connecting Rod Oil Clearance	Connecting Rod Side Clearance
1989	D	2.2 (2212)	2.3620-2.3630	② 0.0004-0.0028	③ 0.0020-0.0070	3	1.9680-1.9690	② 0.0008-0.0034	② 0.0050-0.0130
	E	2.2 (2212)	2.3620-2.3630	② 0.0004-0.0028	③ 0.0020-0.0070	3	1.9680-1.9690	② 0.0006-0.0034	② 0.0050-0.0130
	J	2.5 (2507)	2.3520-2.3530	0.0028	0.0070	3	1.9690	0.0031	0.0130
	K	2.5 (2507)	2.3620-2.3630	② 0.0004-0.0028	③ 0.0020-0.0070	3	1.9680-1.9690	② 0.0008-0.0034	② 0.0050-0.0130
	P	2.2 (2212)	2.3620-2.3630	② 0.0004-0.0028	③ 0.0020-0.0070	3	1.9680-1.9690	② 0.0008-0.0034	② 0.0050-0.0130
	R	2.2 (2212)	2.3617-2.3627	0.0011-0.0031	0.0020-0.0070	3	1.9695-1.9705	0.0006-0.0016	0.0063-0.0234
1990	C	2.2 (2212)	2.3620-2.3630	② 0.0004-0.0028	③ 0.0020-0.0070	3	1.9680-1.9690	② 0.0008-0.0034	② 0.0250-0.0130
	D	2.2 (2212)	2.3620-2.3630	② 0.0004-0.0028	③ 0.0020-0.0070	3	1.9680-1.9690	② 0.0008-0.0034	② 0.0250-0.0130
	J	2.5 (2507)	2.3620-2.3630	0.0028	0.0070	3	1.9680-1.9690	0.0034	0.0130
	K	2.5 (2507)	2.3620-2.3630	② 0.0004-0.0028	③ 0.0020-0.0070	3	1.9680-1.9690	② 0.0008-0.0034	② 0.0050-0.0130
	R	2.2 (2212)	2.3617-2.3627	0.0011-0.0031	0.0020-0.0070	3	1.9695-1.9705	0.0006-0.0016	0.0063-0.0234
1991	A	2.2 (2212)	2.3620-2.3630	② 0.0004-0.0028	③ 0.0020-0.0070	3	1.9680-1.9690	② 0.0008-0.0034	② 0.0050-0.0180
	D	2.2 (2212)	2.3620-2.3630	② 0.0004-0.0028	③ 0.0020-0.0070	3	1.9680-1.9690	② 0.0008-0.0034	② 0.0050-0.0130
	J	2.5 (2507)	2.3620-2.3630	0.0028	0.0070	3	1.9680-1.9690	0.0034	0.0130
	K	2.5 (2507)	2.3620-2.3630	② 0.0004-0.0028	③ 0.0020-0.0070	3	1.9680-1.9690	② 0.0008-0.0034	② 0.0050-0.0130
1992	A	2.2 (2212)	2.3620-2.3630	② 0.0004-0.0028	③ 0.0020-0.0070	3	1.9680-1.9690	② 0.0008-0.0030	② 0.0050-0.0130
	D	2.2 (2212)	2.3620-2.3630	② 0.0004-0.0028	③ 0.0020-0.0070	3	1.9680-1.9690	② 0.0008-0.0030	② 0.0050-0.0130
	J	2.5 (2507)	2.3620-2.3630	0.0028	0.0070	3	1.9680-1.9690	0.0030	0.0130
	K	2.5 (2507)	2.3620-2.3630	② 0.0004-0.0028	③ 0.0020-0.0070	3	1.9680-1.9690	② 0.0008-0.0030	② 0.0050-0.0130
1993	A	2.2 (2212)	2.3620-2.3630	② 0.0004-0.0028	③ 0.0020-0.0070	3	1.9680-1.9690	② 0.0008-0.0030	② 0.0050-0.0130
	D	2.2 (2212)	2.3620-2.3630	② 0.0004-0.0028	③ 0.0020-0.0070	3	1.9680-1.9690	② 0.0008-0.0030	② 0.0050-0.0130
	K	2.5 (2507)	2.3620-2.3630	② 0.0004-0.0028	③ 0.0020-0.0070	3	1.9680-1.9690	② 0.0008-0.0030	② 0.0050-0.0130
	V	2.5 (2507)	2.3620-2.3630	② 0.0004-0.0028	③ 0.0020-0.0070	3	1.9680-1.9690	② 0.0008-0.0030	② 0.0050-0.0130
1994	A	2.2 (2212)	2.3620-2.3630	② 0.0004-0.0028	③ 0.0020-0.0070	3	1.9680-1.9690	② 0.0008-0.0030	② 0.0050-0.0130
	K	2.5 (2507)	2.3620-2.3630	② 0.0004-0.0028	③ 0.0020-0.0070	3	1.9680-1.9690	② 0.0008-0.0030	② 0.0050-0.0130
	V	2.5 (2507)	2.3620-2.3630	② 0.0004-0.0028	③ 0.0020-0.0070	3	1.9680-1.9690	② 0.0008-0.0030	② 0.0050-0.0130
1995	K	2.5 (2507)	2.3620-2.3630	② 0.0004-0.0028	③ 0.0020-0.0070	3	1.9680-1.9690	② 0.0008-0.0030	② 0.0050-0.0130
	V	2.5 (2507)	2.3620-2.3630	② 0.0004-0.0028	③ 0.0020-0.0070	3	1.9680-1.9690	② 0.0008-0.0030	② 0.0050-0.0130

① No. 1: 0.0005-0.0015 in.
　Nos. 2-5: 0.0005-0.0025 in.
② Service limit: 0.0040 in.
③ Service limit: 0.0150 in.
④ Preferred clearance: 0.0020 in.
⑤ Preferred clearance: 0.0015-0.0020 in.

86733C06

TORQUE SPECIFICATIONS
All readings in ft. lbs.

Year	Engine ID/VIN	Engine Displacement Liters (cc)	Cylinder Head Bolts	Main Bearing Bolts	Rod Bearing Bolts	Crankshaft Damper Bolts	Flywheel Bolts	Intake Manifold	Exhaust Manifold	Spark Plugs	Lug Nut
1981	B	2.2 (2212)	⑩	⑪	⑨	⑫	⑥	17	17	26	80
1982	B	2.6 (2556)	⑪	58	34	87	⑥	13	13	18	80
	C	2.2 (2212)	⑩	②	⑨	⑫	⑥	17	17	26	80
	D	2.6 (2556)	⑪	58	34	87	⑥	13	13	18	80
1983	D	2.6 (2556)	⑪	58	34	87	⑥	13	13	18	80
	C	2.2 (2212)	⑩	②	⑨	⑫	⑥	17	17	26	80
	G	2.6 (2556)	⑪	58	34	87	⑥	13	13	18	80
1984	C	2.2 (2212)	⑩	②	⑨	⑫	⑥	17	17	26	95
	D	2.2 (2212)	⑩	②	⑨	⑫	⑥	17	17	26	95
	E	2.2 (2212)	⑩	②	⑨	⑫	⑥	17	17	26	80
	G	2.6 (2556)	⑪	58	34	87	⑥	13	13	18	95
1985	C	2.2 (2212)	⑩	②	⑨	⑫	⑥	17	17	26	95
	D	2.2 (2212)	⑩	②	⑨	⑫	⑥	17	17	26	95
	E	2.2 (2212)	⑩	②	⑨	⑫	⑥	17	17	26	95
	G	2.6 (2556)	⑪	58	34	87	⑥	13	13	18	95
1986	C	2.2 (2212)	⑩	②	⑨	⑫	70	17	17	26	95
	D	2.2 (2212)	⑩	②	⑨	⑫	70	17	17	26	95
	K	2.5 (2507)	⑩	②	⑨	⑫	70	17	17	26	95
1987	A	2.2 (2212)	⑩	②	⑨	⑫	70	17	17	26	95
	D	2.2 (2212)	⑩	②	⑨	⑫	70	17	17	26	95
	E	2.2 (2212)	⑩	②	⑨	⑫	70	17	17	26	95
	K	2.5 (2507)	⑩	②	⑨	⑫	70	17	17	26	95
1988	A	2.2 (2212)	⑩	②	⑨	⑫	70	17	17	26	95
	D	2.2 (2212)	⑩	②	⑨	⑫	70	17	17	26	95
	E	2.2 (2212)	⑩	②	⑨	⑫	70	17	17	26	95
	K	2.5 (2507)	⑩	②	⑨	⑫	70	17	17	26	95
1989	A	2.2 (2212)	⑩	②	⑨	⑫	70	17	17	26	95
	D	2.2 (2212)	⑩	②	⑨	⑫	70	17	17	26	95
	J	2.5 (2507)	⑩	②	⑨	⑫	70	17	17	26	95
	K	2.5 (2507)	⑩	②	⑨	⑫	70	17	17	26	95
	P	2.2 (2212)	⑩	②	⑨	⑫	70	17	17	26	95
	R	2.2 (2212)	⑬	②	48	⑫	70	17	17	20	95

86733C00

PISTON AND RING SPECIFICATIONS
All measurements are given in inches.

Year	Engine ID/VIN	Engine Displacement Liters (cc)	Piston Clearance	Ring Gap Top Compression	Ring Gap Bottom Compression	Ring Gap Oil Control	Ring Side Clearance Top Compression	Ring Side Clearance Bottom Compression	Ring Side Clearance Oil Control
1989	E	2.2 (2212)	0.0015-0.0026 ⑦	0.0100-0.0200 ②	0.0090-0.0190 ⑧	0.0150-0.0550 ③	0.0016-0.0030 ①	0.0016-0.0035	0.0080 MAX
	J	2.5 (2507)	0.0006-0.0018 ⑧	0.0100-0.0200 ⑦	0.0090-0.0190 ⑧	0.0150-0.0550 ③	0.0016-0.0030 ①	0.0016-0.0035	0.0080 MAX
	K	2.5 (2507)	0.0010-0.0020	0.0100-0.0200 ②	0.0110-0.0210 ②	0.0150-0.0550	0.0015-0.0031 ①	0.0015-0.0037	0.0080 MAX
	P	2.2 (2212)	0.0015-0.0026	0.0100-0.0200 ⑦	0.0110-0.0210 ②	0.0150-0.0550	0.0016-0.0031 ①	0.0016-0.0037	0.0080 MAX
	R	2.2 (2212)	NA	0.0090-0.0190	0.0090-0.0190	0.0150-0.0550	0.0015-0.0031	0.0015-0.0035	0.0080 MAX
1990	C	2.2 (2212)	0.0005-0.0015 ④	0.0100-0.0200 ②	0.0090-0.0190 ②	0.0150-0.0550 ③	0.0016-0.0030 ①	0.0016-0.0035	0.0080 MAX
	D	2.2 (2212)	0.0005-0.0015 ④	0.0100-0.0200 ②	0.0110-0.0210 ②	0.0150-0.0550	0.0015-0.0030 ①	0.0015-0.0035	0.0080 MAX
	J	2.5 (2507)	0.0006-0.0016 ⑧	0.0100-0.0200 ⑧	0.0110-0.0210	0.0150-0.0550	0.0016-0.0031 ①	0.0016-0.0037	0.0080 MAX
	K	2.5 (2507)	0.0010-0.0020	0.0100-0.0200	0.0110-0.0210	0.0150-0.0550	0.0015-0.0031	0.0015-0.0037	0.0080 MAX
	R	2.2 (2212)	NA	0.0090-0.0190	0.0090-0.0190	0.0150-0.0550	0.0015-0.0031	0.0015-0.0016	0.0080 MAX
1991	A	2.2 (2212)	0.0018-0.0028 ①	0.0140-0.0200	0.0140-0.0200	0.0100-0.0200	0.0016-0.0030 ①	0.0016-0.0030	0.0040-0.0200
	D	2.2 (2212)	0.0005-0.0015 ④	0.0100-0.0200 ②	0.0110-0.0210	0.0150-0.0550	0.0015-0.0030 ①	0.0015-0.0030	0.0080 MAX
	J	2.5 (2507)	0.0006-0.0016 ⑧	0.0100-0.0200 ⑧	0.0090-0.0190	0.0150-0.0550	0.0016-0.0031 ①	0.0016-0.0031	0.0080 MAX
	K	2.5 (2507)	0.0010-0.0020	0.0100-0.0200	0.0110-0.0210	0.0150-0.0550	0.0015-0.0031	0.0015-0.0037	0.0080 MAX
1992	A	2.2 (2212)	0.0018-0.0028	0.0100-0.0200 ②	0.0140-0.0200	0.0100-0.0200	0.0016-0.0030 ①	0.0016-0.0030	0.0007-0.0020
	D	2.2 (2212)	0.0005-0.0015 ④	0.0100-0.0200	0.0110-0.0210	0.0150-0.0200	0.0016-0.0030 ①	0.0015-0.0030	0.0080 MAX
	J	2.5 (2507)	0.0006-0.0016	0.0100-0.0200	0.0110-0.0210	0.0150-0.0550	0.0016-0.0031 ①	0.0016-0.0035	0.0080 MAX
	K	2.5 (2507)	0.0010-0.0020	0.0100-0.0200	0.0110-0.0210	0.0150-0.0550	0.0015-0.0031	0.0015-0.0037	0.0080 MAX
1993	A	2.2 (2212)	0.0018-0.0028	0.0010-0.0200 ②	0.0110-0.0200	0.0100-0.0200	0.0016-0.0030 ①	0.0016-0.0030	0.0007-0.0020
	D	2.2 (2212)	0.0005-0.0015	0.0100-0.0200	0.0100-0.0210	0.0100-0.0200	0.0015-0.0030 ①	0.0015-0.0030	0.0080 MAX
	J	2.5 (2507)	0.0010-0.0020	0.0100-0.0200	0.0110-0.0210	0.0010-0.0050	0.0015-0.0031 ①	0.0015-0.0031	0.0080 MAX
	K	2.5 (2507)	0.0010-0.0020	0.0100-0.0200	0.0110-0.0210	0.0010-0.0050	0.0015-0.0031	0.0015-0.0037	0.0080 MAX
1994	D	2.2 (2212)	0.0005-0.0015 ④	0.0100-0.0200 ②	0.0090-0.0190	0.0010-0.0050	0.0015-0.0031 ①	0.0015-0.0035	0.0080 MAX
	K	2.5 (2507)	0.0010-0.0020	0.0100-0.0200	0.0110-0.0210	0.0010-0.0050	0.0015-0.0031	0.0015-0.0037	0.0080 MAX
	V	2.5 (2507)	0.0010-0.0020	0.0090-0.0190	0.0090-0.0190	0.0010-0.0050	0.0016-0.0031	0.0016-0.0035	0.0080 MAX
1995	K	2.5 (2507)	0.0010-0.0020 ④	0.0100-0.0200	0.0110-0.0210	0.0010-0.0050	0.0015-0.0031 ①	0.0015-0.0037	0.0080 MAX
	V	2.5 (2507)	0.0010-0.0020	0.0100-0.0200	0.0090-0.0190	0.0010-0.0050	0.0015-0.0031	0.0016-0.0035	0.0080 MAX

NA - Not Available
① Service limit: 0.0040 in.
② Service limit: 0.0390 in.
③ Service limit: 0.0740 in.
④ Service limit: 0.0027 in.
⑤ Service limit: 0.0050 in.
⑥ Service limit: 0.0030 in.
⑦ Service limit: 0.0380 in.
⑧ Service limit: 0.0370 in.
⑨ Service limit: 0.0037 in.

86733C03

TORQUE SPECIFICATIONS
All readings in ft. lbs.

Year	Engine ID/VIN	Engine Displacement Liters (cc)	Cylinder Head Bolts	Main Bearing Bolts	Rod Bearing Bolts	Crankshaft Damper Bolts	Flywheel Bolts	Manifold Intake	Manifold Exhaust	Spark Plugs	Lug Nut
1990	C	2.2 (2212)	①	②	③	⑫	70	17	17	26	95
	D	2.2 (2212)	①	②	③	⑫	70	17	17	26	95
	J	2.5 (2507)	①	②	③	⑫	70	17	17	26	95
	K	2.5 (2507)	①	②	③	⑫	70	17	17	26	95
	R	2.2 (2212)	⑦	⑧	⑨	⑫	70	17	17	13	95
1991	A	2.2 (2212)	①	②	50	⑫	70	17	18	18	95
	D	2.2 (2212)	①	②	③	⑫	70	17	17	26	95
	J	2.5 (2507)	①	②	③	⑫	70	17	17	26	95
	K	2.5 (2507)	①	②	③	⑫	70	17	17	26	95
1992	A	2.2 (2212)	①	②	50	⑫	70	17	18	18	95
	D	2.2 (2212)	①	②	③	⑫	70	17	17	20	95
	J	2.5 (2507)	①	②	③	⑫	70	17	17	20	95
	K	2.5 (2507)	①	②	③	⑫	70	17	17	20	95
1993	A	2.2 (2212)	①	②	50	⑯	70	18	18	18	95
	D	2.2 (2212)	①	②	③	⑯	70	17	17	20	95
	K	2.5 (2507)	①	②	③	⑮	70	17	17	20	95
	V	2.5 (2507)	①	②	③	⑯	70	17	17	20	95
1994	D	2.2 (2212)	①	②	③	⑯	70	17	17	20	95
	K	2.5 (2507)	①	②	③	⑯	70	17	17	20	95
	V	2.5 (2507)	①	②	③	⑯	70	17	17	20	95
1995	K	2.5 (2507)	①	②	③	⑯	70	17	17	20	95
	V	2.5 (2507)	①	②	③	⑯	70	17	17	20	95

① Step 1: 45 ft. lbs.
Step 2: 65 ft. lbs.
Step 3: 65 ft. lbs.
Step 4: +90 degrees
② Step 1: 30 ft. lbs.
Step 2: +90 degrees
③ Step 1: 40 ft. lbs.
Step 2: +90 degrees
④ Step 1: 22 ft. lbs
Step 2: 45 ft. lbs
Step 3: 45 ft. lbs
Step 4: bolts 1-6; 110 ft. lbs
Step 5: bolt 7; 100 ft. lbs
Step 6: bolts 8-10; 110 ft. lbs

⑤ Steel wheels: 90 ft. lbs.
Aluminum wheels: 63 ft. lbs.
⑥ Tighten fasteners in sequence
to the specified torque:
Fasteners 1,6,7,8: 30 ft. lbs
Fasteners 2,3,4,5: 23 ft. lbs.
Fasteners 9,10: 14 ft. lbs.
⑦ Step 1: 32 ft. lbs.
Step 2: 50 ft. lbs.
Step 3: 65 ft. lbs.
Step 4: Plus 1/4 turn
⑧ Step 1: 32 ft. lbs.
Step 2: 43 ft. lbs.
Step 3: 76 ft. lbs.

⑨ Step 1: 32 ft. lbs.
Step 2: 47 ft. lbs.
⑩ Step 1: 30 ft. lbs.
Step 2: 45 ft. lbs.
Step 3: 45 ft. lbs.
Step 4: +90 degrees
⑪ Cold engine: 69 ft. lbs.
Hot engine: 76 ft. lbs.
⑫ Pulley bolt: 21 ft. lbs.
⑬ With A404, A415 transaxle: 50 ft. lbs.
With A413 transaxle: 65 ft. lbs.
With A470 transaxle: 100 ft. lbs.
With A460, A465 transaxle: 65 ft. lbs.

⑭ Step 1: 40 ft. lbs.
Step 2: +60 degrees
⑮ Step 1: 44 ft. lbs.
Step 2: 59 ft. lbs.
Step 3: +90 degrees
⑯ Pulley bolt: 23 ft. lbs.

86733C01

Engine

REMOVAL & INSTALLATION

▶ See Figures 7, 8, 9, 10 and 11

In the process of removing the engine, you will come across a number of steps which call for the removal of a separate component or system, such as "disconnect the exhaust system" or "remove the radiator." In most instances, a detailed removal procedure can be found elsewhere in this manual.

Fig. 8 The lower engine mount changes very little throughout the models years—1991 Acclaim

It is virtually impossible to list each individual wire and hose which must be disconnected, simply because so many different model and engine combinations have been manufactured. Careful observation and common sense are the best possible additions to any repair procedure. Be absolutely sure to tag any wire or hose before it is disconnected, so that you can be assured of proper connection during installation.

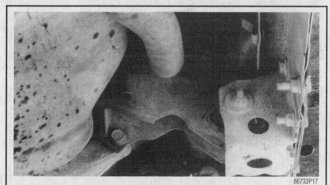

Fig. 7 The lower left-hand engine mount is attached to the front, lower radiator support—1986 Reliant

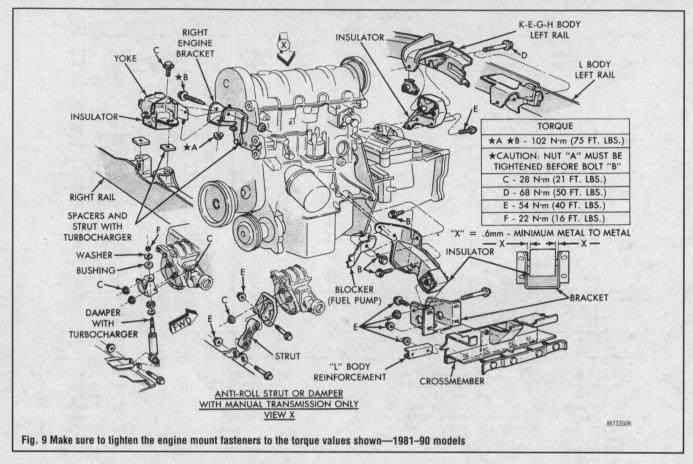

TORQUE	
★A ★B - 102 N·m (75 FT. LBS.)	
★CAUTION: NUT "A" MUST BE TIGHTENED BEFORE BOLT "B"	
C - 28 N·m (21 FT. LBS.)	
D - 68 N·m (50 FT. LBS.)	
E - 54 N·m (40 FT. LBS.)	
F - 22 N·m (16 FT. LBS.)	

"X" = .6mm - MINIMUM METAL TO METAL

ANTI-ROLL STRUT OR DAMPER
WITH MANUAL TRANSMISSION ONLY
VIEW X

86733G06

Fig. 9 Make sure to tighten the engine mount fasteners to the torque values shown—1981–90 models

ENGINE MOUNTS

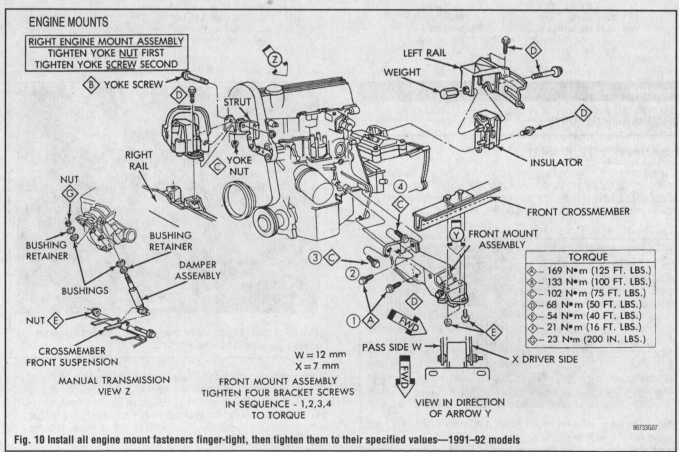

RIGHT ENGINE MOUNT ASSEMBLY
TIGHTEN YOKE NUT FIRST
TIGHTEN YOKE SCREW SECOND

TORQUE	
Ⓐ – 169 N•m (125 FT. LBS.)	
Ⓑ – 133 N•m (100 FT. LBS.)	
Ⓒ – 102 N•m (75 FT. LBS.)	
Ⓓ – 68 N•m (50 FT. LBS.)	
Ⓔ – 54 N•m (40 FT. LBS.)	
Ⓕ – 21 N•m (16 FT. LBS.)	
Ⓖ – 23 N•m (200 IN. LBS.)	

MANUAL TRANSMISSION
VIEW Z

W = 12 mm
X = 7 mm

FRONT MOUNT ASSEMBLY
TIGHTEN FOUR BRACKET SCREWS
IN SEQUENCE - 1,2,3,4
TO TORQUE

VIEW IN DIRECTION
OF ARROW Y

86733G07

Fig. 10 Install all engine mount fasteners finger-tight, then tighten them to their specified values—1991–92 models

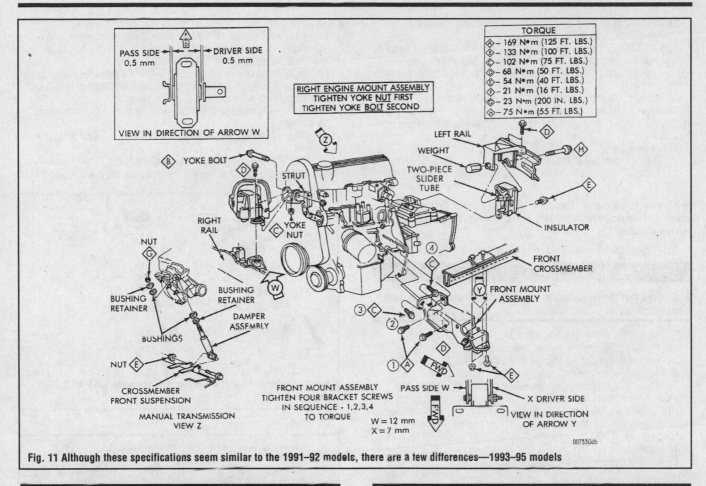

Fig. 11 Although these specifications seem similar to the 1991–92 models, there are a few differences—1993–95 models

---

❊❊ CAUTION

When draining coolant, keep in mind that cats and dogs are attracted by ethylene glycol antifreeze, and are quite likely to drink any that is left in an uncovered container or in puddles on the ground. This will prove fatal in sufficient quantity. Always drain the coolant into a sealable container. Coolant should be reused unless it is contaminated or several years old.

➡The following procedure can be used on all years and models. Slight variations may occur due to extra wires, hoses, etc. because of model-specific options.

1. Relieve the fuel system pressure, as described in Section 5.
2. Disconnect the negative battery cable and all engine ground straps.
3. Mark the hood hinge outlines on the hood and remove the hood. For more information, refer to Section 10.

❊❊ CAUTION

The EPA warns that prolonged contact with used engine oil may cause a number of skin disorders, including cancer! You should make every effort to minimize your exposure to used engine oil. Protective gloves should be worn when changing the oil. Wash your hands and any other exposed skin areas as soon as possible after exposure to used engine oil. Soap and water, or waterless hand cleaner should be used.

4. Drain the cooling system and engine oil. Remove the radiator hoses, fan assembly, radiator and intercooler, if equipped.
5. Remove the air cleaner, duct hoses and oil filter.

❊❊ CAUTION

Do not disconnect the A/C lines unless the A/C system was discharged by a qualified automotive technician using a refrigerant recovery/recycling machine, otherwise A/C system damage or personal injury could be the result.

6. Unbolt the air conditioning compressor from its mount, if equipped, and position it aside without disconnecting the refrigerant lines.
7. Remove the power steering pump mounting bolts and position the pump aside without disconnecting any fluid lines.
8. Label and disengage all electrical connectors from the engine, alternator and fuel system.
9. Disconnect and plug the fuel lines and heater hoses.
10. Disconnect the throttle body or carburetor linkage.
11. Apply the parking brake and block the rear wheels, then raise and safely support the front of the vehicle on jackstands.
12. Disconnect the exhaust system from the exhaust manifold.
13. Remove the starter motor and set it aside. Do not allow it to hang suspended from its wires.
14. Perform the following on vehicles equipped with manual transaxles:
    a. Disconnect the clutch cable from the transaxle.
    b. Remove the transaxle case lower cover.
    c. Support the transaxle with a hydraulic floor jack or a special transaxle holding fixture.
15. If the vehicle is equipped with an automatic transaxle, perform the following:
    a. Remove the transaxle case lower cover.
    b. Matchmark the flexplate to the torque converter for reinstallation.
    c. Remove the torque converter-to-flexplate bolts. The crankshaft must be

turned to access all of the bolts; turn the crankshaft with a wrench on the crankshaft front pulley bolt.

    d. Attach a C-clamp on the front bottom of the torque converter housing to prevent the torque converter from falling out of the transaxle.

    e. Support the transaxle with a hydraulic floor jack or a special transaxle holding fixture.

16. Lower the vehicle and support the transaxle with either a hydraulic floor jack or a special transaxle holding fixture. Attach an engine lifting hoist to the engine and raise the hoist until it just starts to take the weight off of the engine mounts.

17. Remove the right inner splash shield.

18. Remove the engine ground strap.

19. Remove the long through-bolt from the right engine bracket yoke and insulator.

➡️**If removing the engine insulator-to-side rail screws, first mark the position of the insulator on the side rail to insure proper alignment during reinstallation.**

20. Remove the transaxle-to-engine mounting bolts.

❋ WARNING

Make sure that the clutch cable has been disconnected on manual transaxle models.

---

21. Remove the front engine mount bolt and nut.

22. If equipped, remove the manual transaxle damper.

23. Remove the left side insulator (engine mount) through-bolt from inside of the wheel well, or remove the insulator bracket-to-transaxle bolts.

24. Carefully lift the engine from the vehicle with the engine hoist. Make sure that all wires, hoses and other components are completely disconnected and that nothing gets snagged during engine removal. Once the engine is raised high enough to clear the front radiator support, carefully roll the engine hoist and engine from the vehicle.

To install:

25. Lower the engine into the engine compartment. Make sure the lifting device is supporting the full weight of the engine and loosely install all of the mounting bolts until all are threaded. Then tighten all bolts to the torque values shown in the accompanying illustrations.

26. Install and tighten the transaxle-to-engine case bolts to 70 ft. lbs. (95 Nm).

27. Remove the engine lifting hoist and transaxle support.

28. Installation of the remaining components is the reverse of the removal procedure. Make sure all components are tightened securely, and all wiring and hoses are properly connected.

29. Fill the engine crankcase with the proper amount and type of engine oil. Fill the cooling system.

30. Install the hood, as outlined in Section 10.

31. Connect the positive battery cable, then connect the negative battery cable. Make sure that the cables are installed in this order.

32. Start the engine and run until operating temperature is reached. Check for fuel, oil, coolant, or vacuum leaks. If necessary, adjust the transaxle linkage, as described in Section 7.

Rocker Arm (Valve) Cover

REMOVAL & INSTALLATION

Except 2.2L Turbo III Models

▶ **See Figures 12 thru 22**

➡️**Since Chrysler jumps back and forth with its use of a sealing liquid gasket and a standard cork or rubber gasket, check with your local parts professional for the correct sealing component for your engine, if confused or unsure.**

1. Disconnect the negative battery cable.

2. Disconnect the PCV line from the PCV valve.

3. Remove, disconnect or move aside any other lines or hoses which run across the rocker arm cover assembly.

4. On the 2.2L and 2.5L engines, remove the upper timing belt cover retaining nuts and bolts, then remove the upper timing belt cover.

5. Loosen the cover retaining bolts and remove them. Gently rock the cover to free it from the gasket or sealer, then remove it.

6. On 1986 and later models with EFI, remove the air/oil separating curtain located on top of the head just under the valve cover. Be careful to keep the rubber bumpers located at the top of the curtain in place.

7. Pull the old end gaskets from the underside of the rocker arm cover.

To install:

8. Clean the cylinder head and cover mating surfaces. Make certain the rails are flat.

9. If the engine is equipped with the air/oil separating curtain, install it as follows (otherwise, proceed to Step 10). Install the curtain, manifold side first,

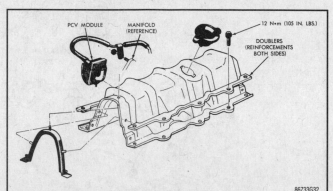

Fig. 12 Exploded view of the rocker arm cover for 1981–85 2.2L engines

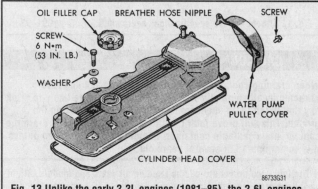

Fig. 13 Unlike the early 2.2L engines (1981–85), the 2.6L engines utilized a rocker arm cover gasket

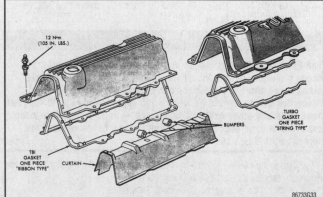

Fig. 14 The 1986–95 2.2L and 2.5L engines (except for Turbo III) used an air/oil separator curtain under the rocker arm cover—note the use of rocker arm gaskets for 1988–90 models

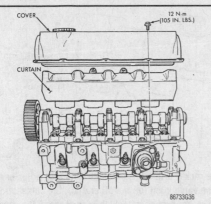

Fig. 15 During installation, make sure that the upper rubber spacers are installed in the curtain and the curtain cutouts are positioned on the intake side

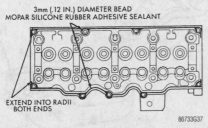

Fig. 16 The 2.2L and 2.5L engines revert back to using liquid gasket in 1991 and continue with its use until 1995—apply the liquid gasket as shown

with the cutouts over the camshaft towers and contacting the cylinder head floor, then press the opposite side (distributor side) into position below the cylinder head rail. The curtain is retained in position with the rubber bumpers.

10. On 1981–87 and 1991–95 2.2L and 2.5L engines, form a gasket on the sealing surface of the head. It is necessary to use an RTV silicone aerobic gasket material (Chrysler Part No. 4318025 or equivalent). Install new end seals; insert the end seal locating tabs into the matching holes in the cover and pull until the barbs on the locating tabs are engaged in the holes.

11. On 1988–90 2.2L and 2.5L engines and all 2.6L engines, install the gasket onto the cam cover (fasten the gasket in place by forcing the tabs through the holes in the cover).

12. Install the reinforcements on both sides of the rocker arm cover, if so equipped. Install the mounting bolts and tighten them alternately from the center out to 105 inch lbs. (12 Nm). Make sure that the 2 mounting studs are installed in the 2 front-most holes (these are used to mount the upper timing belt cover to the cylinder head).

13. Install the upper timing belt cover.

14. Install the hoses, cables or wires which were removed earlier.

15. Connect the negative battery cable.

2.2L Turbo III Models

▶ See Figure 23

➡The 2.2L Turbo III engines utilize two separate rocker arm covers on each bank of valves.

1. Disconnect the negative battery cable.

2. Remove the ignition cable cover retaining fasteners, then lift the cover off of the top of the engine.

3. Remove the upper timing belt cover by removing the upper timing belt cover mounting nuts and bolts.

4. Disconnect the PCV valve hose from the valve.

5. Remove the rocker arm cover hold-down bolts, then lift the rocker arm cover off of the cylinder head. It may be necessary to gently rock the rocker arm cover to free it from the gasket. Remove the second rocker arm cover as well.

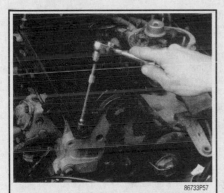

Fig. 17 Remove the rocker arm cover attaching bolts and . . .

Fig. 18 . . . remove the rear camshaft seal, then . . .

Fig. 19 . . . lift the rocker arm cover off of the cylinder head

Fig. 20 Remove the old gaskets and residual material from the rocker arm cover . . .

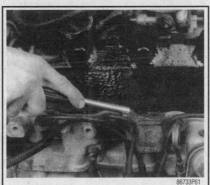

Fig. 21 . . . and from the cylinder head surface

Fig. 22 Lift the inner curtain off of the cylinder head after the gasket material is cleaned off the head

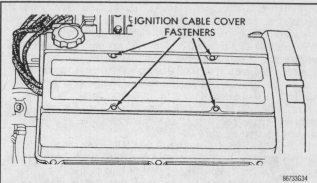

Fig. 23 The ignition cable cover spans the gap between the two rocker arm covers on the 2.2L Turbo III engines

To install:

6. Clean the cylinder head and cover mating surfaces. Make sure that the rails are flat.

✵ WARNING

Do not allow oil or solvents to contact the timing belt as they can be deteriorate the rubber and cause tooth skipping.

7. Install the rocker arm cover with a new rocker arm cover gasket. Tighten the mounting bolts alternately from the center out to 105 inch lbs. (12 Nm). Install the second rocker arm cover in the same manner.
8. Position the ignition cable cover in place, then install the hold-down fasteners. Tighten the fasteners until snug.
9. Attach the PCV hose to the PCV valve.
10. Install the upper timing belt cover.
11. Connect the negative battery cable.

Rocker Arms/Shafts

REMOVAL & INSTALLATION

➡**When disassembling the valve train components, always keep the parts in order so that they can be assembled into their original locations. This is most important when all of the old components are to be reused.**

Except 2.2L Turbo III and 2.6L Engines

▶ **See Figures 24, 25 and 26**

The rocker arms may be removed very easily after camshaft removal. In case they are to be removed as a group for inspection or to proceed further with disassembly, mark each as to location for installation in the same position.

If the rockers are to be removed in order to gain access to a valve or lifter

Fig. 24 Use the special Chrysler tool C-4682-A, or equivalent, to depress the valve springs for rocker arm removal and installation

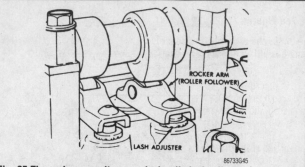

Fig. 25 The rocker arm sits on an hydraulic lash adjuster (on one end) and the valve stem (on the other end); the camshaft lobe pushes the rocker arm down, which in turn opens the valve

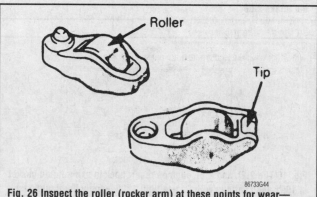

Fig. 26 Inspect the roller (rocker arm) at these points for wear—replace if excessive wear is evident

(camshaft installed), you will need a special tool designed to hook over the camshaft and depress the applicable valve, such as Chrysler Tool C-4682-A or equivalent.

1. Remove the valve cover. Mark the rocker as to its location, unless you expect to remove only one at a time.
2. Rotate the crankshaft, using a wrench on the crankshaft pulley, until the camshaft lobe that actuates the rocker you want to remove is pointing straight up.
3. Install the valve spring compressing tool so that the jaws on its fulcrum fit on either side of the valve cap. Then, clip the hook at its forward end over the adjacent thin section of the camshaft (a portion not incorporating either a cam or a bearing journal).
4. Lift the rocker gently at the lash adjuster end (the end opposite the tool). Pull downward gently on the outer end of the tool lever just until the rocker can be disengaged from the lifter. Pull it out from between the valve and camshaft.
5. Remove the hydraulic lash adjuster from the cylinder head.

To install:

➡**Visually check the roller on the rocker arm and replace if dent, damage or seizure is evident. Check the roller for smooth rotation, replace if its binds or there is an excessive play. Check the valve contact surface for possible damage when performing this repair.**

6. Install the hydraulic lash adjusters making sure that the adjusters are at least partially full of engine oil. This is indicated by little or no plunger travel when the lash adjuster is depressed.
7. If the engine was rotated while the rocker arms were removed from the cylinder head, position the camshaft so that the lobe for the specific valve, on which the rocker arm is to be installed, is pointing straight up (the base circle of the camshaft should be toward the cylinder head).
8. Depress the valve, with the special tool as during removal, just far enough to slide the rocker arm in between the top of the valve stem and the camshaft and still clear the hydraulic lash adjuster. When the rocker is correctly positioned on the valve stem and lifter, gradually release the tension on the tool.
9. Repeat the procedure until all the necessary rockers have been replaced.
10. Check and make sure the locks on the valve springs are in the proper location, then install the valve cover.

2.2L Turbo III Models

▶ See Figures 27, 28, 29 and 30

➡Unlike the other engines covered by this manual, the 2.2L Turbo III engines utilize a rocker arm shaft for each bank of rocker arms.

1. Remove the rocker arm covers, as described earlier in this section.
2. Loosen the rocker arm shaft mounting bolts in the sequence shown in the accompanying illustration. Remove the mounting bolts, then lift the rocker arm shaft with the rocker arms off of the cylinder head. Be careful, the rocker arms will slide off the shaft if given the chance.
3. Before removing the second rocker arm shaft assembly, identify the first rocker arm shaft assembly for installation.
4. Slide the rocker arms off of the shaft, keeping them in order for reassembly.
5. Remove the second rocker arm shaft from the cylinder head in the same manner.

✳✳ WARNING

Check the lash adjuster for loose or missing retainers before continuing the service procedure.

6. Remove the hydraulic lash adjusters from each rocker arm

To install:

7. Slide the rocker arms onto the shaft in their original positions.
8. Install the hydraulic lash adjusters, making sure that the adjusters are at least partially full of engine oil. This is indicated by little or no plunger travel when the lash adjuster is depressed.
9. Position the rocker arm shaft assemblies onto the cylinder head and tighten the mounting bolts in the sequence shown to 18 ft. lbs. (24 Nm).
10. Install the rocker arm covers, as described earlier in this section.

2.6L Engine

▶ See Figures 31, 32, 33 and 34

➡When removing the sprocket from the camshaft, you must maintain adequate tension on the sprocket and chain assembly to prevent the chain from disengaging with the crankshaft timing gear. Use Special Tool C-4852, or equivalent, and a stretch cord.

1. Disconnect the negative battery cable.
2. Remove the rocker arm cover, as described earlier in this section.
3. Loosen the large center bolt holding the camshaft sprocket to the camshaft; do not remove it, just loosen it.
4. Matchmark the timing chain to the camshaft sprocket.
5. Turn the crankshaft pulley clockwise until the timing marks align on both the cylinder head and engine block, and the crankshaft pulley and engine block. This sets the engine at Top Dead Center (TDC) for the No.1 cylinder on its compression stroke. Once this position is established, the engine MUST NOT be rotated during repairs.
6. Position the Special Tool C-4852, or equivalent, over the timing chain gear.
7. Remove the center bolt from the sprocket and remove the small distributor drive gear.
8. Pull the camshaft sprocket with the chain attached out from the camshaft and hang it from the camshaft sprocket holder. Do not allow the chain to come off the camshaft or crankshaft sprockets.

➡If a camshaft gear holding apparatus is not available, removal of the timing chain and covers is necessary.

9. Loosen but do not remove the camshaft bearing cap bolts (not the outer or cylinder head bolts). Start at an inner, or center, bolt and work outward in a circular pattern, loosening each bolt a little at a time.

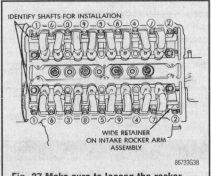

Fig. 27 Make sure to loosen the rocker arm shaft mounting bolts in the order shown

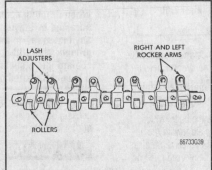

Fig. 28 An underside view of one of the rocker arm shafts and some of the related components

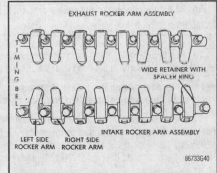

Fig. 29 Make sure to place the rocker arms on the rocker arm shaft in the original order

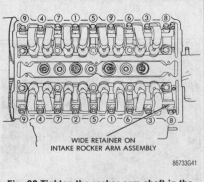

Fig. 30 Tighten the rocker arm shaft in the sequence shown to 18 ft. lbs. (24 Nm)

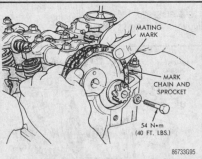

Fig. 31 When removing the camshaft gear, matchmark the timing chain to the gear for reassembly—make sure to retain the distributor drive gear

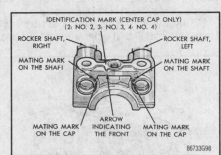

Fig. 32 Identification marks found on the camshaft bearing cap/rocker shaft retaining end caps—install the rocker shafts so that the mating mark on the shafts is aligned with the mating mark on the cap

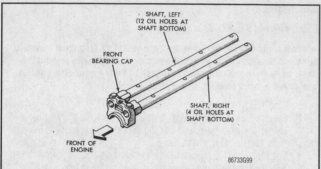

Fig. 33 One way to tell the difference between the right and left rocker shafts is to count the number of oil holes on the bottom of the shaft

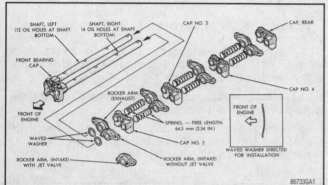

Fig. 34 Exploded view of the rocker arm/shaft assembly—2.6L engine

10. Remove the bolts after all are loosened. Hold the ends so the assembly stays together and remove the rocker shaft assembly from the cylinder head.

➡Before disassembling the rocker shaft assemblies, mark the components as to their original positions for ease of reassembly.

11. Place the assembly on a clean work bench. Remove the bolts (which retain the bearing caps in position on the shafts) 2 at a time along with the associated cap, washers, springs and rockers. Continue until all parts are disassembled. Keep all parts in original order. All parts that will be re-used must be in original positions.

To install:

12. Inspection of parts should include verifying that the pads that follow the cam lobes are not worn excessively and that the oil holes are clear. Replace the rockers and/or shafts, if rockers are loose on the shafts. Replace the rocker arms if excessive wear, nicks or similar damage is found.

13. Install the left and right side rocker shafts into the front bearing cap. The rear end of the left (intake) rocker arm shaft has a notch. Align the mating marks

on the front of each rocker shaft with the mating marks on the front bearing cap. Insert the bolts to hold the shafts in the cap.

14. Install the wave washer so that the rounded side bulges toward the timing chain.

15. Coat the inner surfaces of the rockers and the upper bearing surfaces of the bearing caps with clean engine oil and assemble rockers, springs, and the remaining bearing caps in order. Note that the rockers are labeled for cylinders 2, 3 and 4. While similar in shape, they must be reinstalled in their original position. Use mounting bolts to hold the caps in place after each is assembled. When the assembly is complete, position it on the head and start all mounting bolts into the head until finger-tight.

16. Tighten the attaching bolts for the rocker assembly to 15 ft. lbs. (20 Nm), working from the center outward.

17. Without removing tension from the timing chain, remove the camshaft sprocket from the suspension tool and position it against the front of the camshaft. Make sure the locating tang on the sprocket goes into the hole in the front of the camshaft.

18. Install the distributor drive gear, making certain it is properly seated. Install the sprocket bolt and tighten it finger-tight, then to 40 ft. lbs. (54 Nm).

19. Apply sealant to the flat face of the half-circle plug in the head. Install the rocker arm cover and gasket. For more details, refer to the rocker arm procedure earlier in this section.

20. Connect the negative battery cable.

Thermostat

REMOVAL & INSTALLATION

▶ **See Figures 35, 36, 37, 38 and 39**

✳✳ CAUTION

When draining coolant, keep in mind that cats and dogs are attracted by ethylene glycol antifreeze, and are quite likely to drink any that is left in an uncovered container or in puddles on the ground. This will prove fatal in sufficient quantity. Always drain the coolant into a sealable container. Coolant should be reused unless it is contaminated or several years old.

The thermostat on the 2.2L and 2.5L engines is located in the thermostat housing on the cylinder head, next to the distributor. On 2.6L engines, the thermostat housing is located near the intake manifold.

✳✳ CAUTION

Do not loosen the radiator drain with the system hot and pressurized because serious burns from the coolant and steam can occur.

1. Drain the cooling system to a level below the thermostat.

2. Remove the upper radiator hose clamp, slide the hose clamp away from the end of the hose, then disconnect the hose from the thermostat housing.

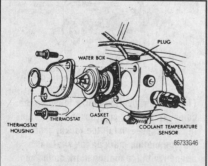

Fig. 35 Exploded view of the thermostat housing, thermostat and gasket—2.2L and 2.5L engines (except 2.2L Turbo III)

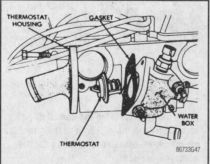

Fig. 36 Exploded view of the thermostat housing, thermostat and gasket—2.2L Turbo III engine

Fig. 37 After draining the coolant, detach the radiator hose from the thermostat housing . . .

Fig. 38 . . . remove the housing, then pull the thermostat out of the water box

Fig. 39 Make sure to clean all old gasket material off of the water box

Fig. 40 To remove the intake/exhaust manifolds, first remove the air cleaner assembly . . .

3. Remove the oil dipstick bracket retaining nut from the thermostat stud. Pivot the oil dipstick bracket away from the thermostat housing.

4. Remove the 2 mounting bolts (one is a stud/bolt), then remove the thermostat housing.

5. Remove the thermostat and discard the old gasket. Clean both gasket surfaces thoroughly.

To install:

6. Lightly coat the gasket with a high-tack type gasket cement to hold the gasket in position on the water box. Position the gasket on the water box so that the bolt holes are aligned. Position the thermostat on the water box, making sure it is properly seated by centering it on top of the gasket. Install the thermostat housing over the gasket and thermostat, then install the 2 mounting bolts. Tighten thermostat housing retaining bolts gradually to 21 ft. lbs. (28 Nm).

7. Reposition the oil dipstick so that the bracket is installed onto the thermostat housing stud. Install the bracket retaining nut and tighten it until snug.

8. Reconnect the upper radiator hose. Install and tighten the hose clamp.

9. Refill the cooling system, start the engine, and check for leaks. After the engine has reached operating temperature, allow it to cool. Then, recheck coolant level in the radiator, refilling as necessary.

Cooling System Bleeding

To bleed air from the 2.2L and 2.5L engines, remove the plug or sensor on the top of the thermostat housing. Fill the radiator with coolant until the coolant comes out the hole. Since the plug is made out of steel and the thermostat housing is aluminum, it is a good idea to apply an anti-seizing compound or Teflon® tape on the plug threads prior to installation. Install the plug and continue to fill the radiator. This will vent all trapped air from the engine.

Intake and Exhaust Manifolds

REMOVAL & INSTALLATION

➡ Of all the 4-cylinder engines covered by this manual, only two (the 2.2L Turbo III and 2.6L) have exhaust and intake manifolds which are totally independent from each other. All other engines share the intake/exhaust manifold gasket—some even share mounting bolts—therefore both manifolds must be removed to replace the gasket, which should be replaced every time one of the manifolds is removed from the cylinder head.

✳✳ CAUTION

When draining coolant, keep in mind that cats and dogs are attracted by ethylene glycol antifreeze, and are quite likely to drink any that is left in an uncovered container or in puddles on the ground. This will prove fatal in sufficient quantity. Always drain the coolant into a sealable container. Coolant should be reused unless it is contaminated or several years old.

2.2L and 2.5L Non-Turbocharged Engines

▶ See Figures 40 thru 46

1981–86 MODELS

1. Disconnect the negative battery cable.

2. Drain the cooling system, as described in Section 1.

3. Remove the air cleaner and hoses.

4. If the engine is fuel injected, depressurize the fuel system, as described in Section 5. Remove all wiring and any hoses connected to the carburetor or injection throttle body and the manifold.

5. Disconnect the accelerator linkage.

6. Loosen the power steering pump mounting bolts and remove the belt. Disconnect the power brake vacuum hose at the manifold.

7. On Canadian cars, remove the coupling hose (connecting the diverter valve and the exhaust manifold air injection tube).

8. Disconnect the water hose from the water crossover.

9. Apply the parking brake, block the rear wheels, then raise and safely support the front of the vehicle on jackstands.

10. Disconnect the exhaust system from the exhaust manifold.

11. Remove the power steering pump, leaving the lines connected, and hang it to one side so the hoses are not stressed.

12. Remove the intake manifold support bracket.

13. Remove the intake manifold-to-head bolts.

14. Lower the vehicle and remove the intake manifold from the cylinder head.

15. Remove the exhaust manifold retaining nuts and remove the exhaust manifold.

To install:

16. Clean all gasket surfaces and reposition the intake and exhaust manifolds using new gaskets. A composition gasket must be installed without any sealant, whereas a steel gasket must be coated with a sealer such as Chrysler Part No. 3419115 or equivalent.

17. Situate the exhaust manifold in position and install the retaining nuts finger-tight. Set the intake manifold into position and install all accessible bolts. Raise the car and support it securely on jackstands.

18. Install all the manifold-to-head bolts finger-tight. Install the intake manifold support bracket. Install the power steering pump, bolting it into position with the mounting bolts just finger-tight.

19. Connect the exhaust pipe at the manifold using a new seal, then tighten the bolts and nuts to 21 ft. lbs. (28 Nm).

20. Lower the car and tighten the manifold nuts and bolts in three stages, starting at the center and progressing outward, to 17 ft. lbs. (23 Nm).

21. Connect the power brake vacuum hose to the manifold. Connect the water hose to the water crossover.

22. On Canadian cars, install the coupling hose (connecting the diverter valve and the exhaust manifold air injection tube).

23. Install the power steering pump belt and adjust the belt tension, as described in Section 1.

24. Connect the accelerator linkage, then install the air cleaner and hoses.

25. Install all wiring and hoses disconnected from the carburetor or throttle body and the manifold.

26. Refill the cooling system, reconnect the battery, start the engine and run it to check for leaks.

Fig. 41 . . . then loosen the intake manifold attaching bolts

Fig. 42 After removing the throttle body, remove the attaching bolts and manifold

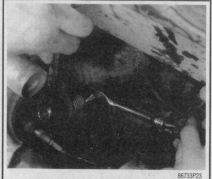

Fig. 43 Detach the front exhaust pipe from the exhaust manifold . . .

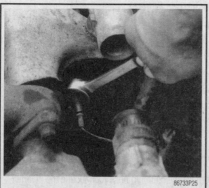

Fig. 44 . . . then remove the oxygen sensor from the exhaust manifold

Fig. 45 Remove the exhaust manifold-to-cylinder head attaching bolts . . .

Fig. 46 . . . then remove the exhaust manifold from the cylinder head

27. Refill the cooling system after the engine has reached operating temperature (air has been bled out) and it has cooled off again.

1987–95 ELECTRONIC FUEL INJECTED (NON-FLEX FUEL) MODELS

◆ See Figures 47 and 48

➡On some vehicles, some of the manifold attaching bolts are not accessible or too heavily sealed from the factory and cannot be removed on the vehicle. Head removal would be necessary in these situations.

1. Disconnect the negative battery cable.
2. Relieve the fuel system pressure, as described in Section 5.
3. Drain the cooling system. For more details, refer to Section 1.
4. Remove the air cleaner and disconnect all vacuum lines, electrical wiring and fuel lines from the throttle body.
5. Disconnect the throttle linkage.

6. Loosen the power steering pump and remove the drive belt.
7. Remove the power brake vacuum hose from the intake manifold.
8. Remove the water hoses from the water crossover.
9. Apply the parking brakes, block the rear wheels, then raise and safely support the front of the vehicle on jackstands.
10. Disconnect the exhaust pipe from the exhaust manifold.
11. Remove the power steering pump from its mounting bracket and set it aside without disconnecting the fluid hoses.
12. Remove the intake manifold support bracket, if equipped.
13. Remove the EGR tube, if equipped.
14. Remove the intake manifold bolts.
15. Lower the vehicle and remove the intake manifold.
16. Remove the exhaust manifold retaining nuts, then remove the exhaust manifold.

To install:

17. Discard the gaskets and clean all gasket surfaces on both manifolds and on the cylinder head.

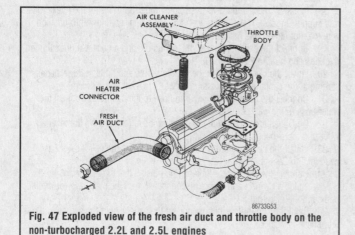

Fig. 47 Exploded view of the fresh air duct and throttle body on the non-turbocharged 2.2L and 2.5L engines

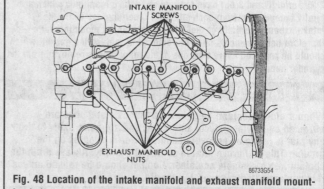

Fig. 48 Location of the intake manifold and exhaust manifold mounting bolts

18. Test the gasket surfaces of the manifolds for flatness with a straightedge. Surface warpage must not exceed 0.006 in. (0.15mm) per foot (30cm) of manifold length.

19. Inspect the manifolds for cracks and distortion; replace the manifolds if any such damage is evident.

20. Install a new combination manifold gasket. Coat a steel gasket lightly with Chrysler Gasket Sealer, or equivalent, on the manifold side. DO NOT coat composition gaskets with any sealer.

21. Install the exhaust manifold assembly. Starting from the middle and working outwards, install the mounting nuts and tighten to 17 ft. lbs. (23 Nm). Install the heat cowl to the exhaust manifold.

22. Install the intake manifold. Starting from the middle and working outward, tighten the bolts to 17 ft. lbs. (23 Nm.).

23. Raise and safely support the front of the vehicle on jackstands.

24. Connect the exhaust system to the exhaust manifold, as described later in this section.

25. Install the EGR tube, if removed.

26. Install the intake manifold support bracket, if equipped.

27. Install the power steering pump.

28. Lower the vehicle and remove the wheel blocks.

29. Install the water hoses to the water crossover.

30. Install the power brake vacuum hose to the intake manifold.

31. Connect the throttle linkage, as described in Section 5.

32. Install all vacuum lines, electrical wiring and fuel lines to the throttle body.

33. Install the air cleaner assembly.

34. Refill the cooling system.

35. Connect the negative battery cable and check for leaks.

1993–95 FLEXIBLE FUEL ELECTRONIC FUEL INJECTED ENGINES

> ※※ **CAUTION**
>
> **Before servicing any flexible fuel system components, refer to the warnings in Section 1. Methanol is more toxic than gasoline and requires extreme care when handling.**

1. Disconnect the negative battery cable.

> ※※ **CAUTION**
>
> **Release fuel system pressure before servicing any fuel system components. Wear methanol resistant gloves and eye protection while servicing the fuel system.**

2. Release the fuel system pressure, as described in Section 5.

3. Remove the air cleaner hose from the throttle body.

4. Remove the accelerator and cruise control cables, if equipped.

5. Disengage the Automatic Idle Speed (AIS) motor and Throttle Position Sensor (TPS) wiring connectors.

6. Disconnect the fuel injectors' wiring connector.

7. Remove the fuel supply and return lines from the fuel tube assembly quick-disconnect from the frame rail, as described in Section 5. Open the fuel tube clip around the fuel tubes.

> ※※ **CAUTION**
>
> **Have shop rags handy to catch any residual fuel leakage when the fuel lines are detached.**

8. Detach the fuel pressure regulator vacuum hose from the regulator.

9. Remove the PCV vacuum harness, brake booster, and vacuum vapor harness from the intake manifold.

10. Apply the parking brake, block the rear wheels, then raise and safely support the front of the vehicle on jackstands.

11. Disconnect the exhaust system from the exhaust manifold.

12. Lower the vehicle.

13. Remove the 8 intake manifold bolts and washers, then remove the intake manifold from the cylinder head.

14. Disconnect the exhaust pipe from the exhaust manifold articulate joint.

15. Disengage the heated oxygen sensor electrical connection.

16. Remove the 8 exhaust manifold retaining nuts and remove the exhaust manifold from the cylinder head.

To install:

17. Discard the gasket and clean all gasket surfaces on the manifolds and cylinder head.

18. Test the gasket surfaces for flatness with a straightedge. the surface must be flat within 0.006 in. (0.15mm) per foot (30cm) of manifold length.

19. Inspect the manifolds for cracks or distortion.

20. Install a new two-sided Grafoil® or equivalent intake/exhaust manifold gasket. DO NOT apply sealer.

21. Set the exhaust manifold in position on the cylinder head, then install and tighten the retaining nuts, starting at the center and progressing outward in both directions. Tighten the nuts to 17 ft. lbs. (23 Nm).

22. Position the intake manifold on the cylinder head, then install and tighten the 8 retaining bolts, starting at the center and progressing outward in both directions. Tighten the bolts to 17 ft. lbs. (23 Nm).

23. Apply the parking brake, block the rear wheels, then raise and safely support the front of the vehicle on jackstands.

24. Attach the exhaust system to the exhaust manifold, as described later in this section.

25. Lower the vehicle and remove the wheel blocks.

26. Install the remaining components in the reverse of the removal procedure.

27. Connect the negative battery cable, then start the engine and check for leaks.

2.2L Turbo I and Turbo II Engines

1. Disconnect the negative battery cable.

2. Apply the parking brake, block the rear wheels, then raise and safely support the front of the vehicle on jackstands.

3. Remove the air cleaner assembly and intake manifold upper plenum-to-cylinder head support bracket.

4. Separate the throttle body assembly from the intake manifold. Detach the EGR tube from the valve.

5. Disengage the PCV, Manifold Absolute Pressure (MAP) and brake booster vacuum supply hoses. Disengage the charge temperature sensor electrical connector.

6. Remove the starter motor. For more information, refer to Section 2.

7. From under the vehicle, remove the 7 bolts to separate the upper intake manifold plenum from the lower intake manifold runner.

8. From above the engine, remove the upper plenum and plenum runner gasket. Cover the lower intake manifold runner opening with a clean shop rag to prevent any debris from falling into the engine.

> ※※ **WARNING**
>
> **Do not allow any debris to enter the runners.**

9. Remove the cowl mounted heat shield and fuel rail, as described in Section 5.

10. Remove the turbocharger, as described later in this section.

11. Remove the 8 lower intake manifold bolt and washer assemblies and remove the lower manifold from the cylinder head.

12. Remove the 8 exhaust manifold bolt and washer assemblies and remove the exhaust manifold from the cylinder head.

To install:

13. Discard the gaskets and clean all gasket surfaces on both manifolds and on the cylinder head.

14. Test the gasket surfaces of the manifolds for flatness with a straightedge. Surface warpage must not exceed 0.006 in. (0.15mm) per foot (30cm) of manifold length.

15. Inspect the manifolds for cracks and distortion; replace the manifolds if any such damage is evident.

16. Install a new Grafoil or equivalent combination manifold gasket. DO NOT coat the gasket with sealer.

17. Position the lower intake manifold against the cylinder head and install the mounting bolts. Tighten the mounting bolts by starting at the center and progressing outward in both directions to 17 ft. lbs. (23 Nm).

18. Position the exhaust manifold against the cylinder head and install the mounting bolts. Tighten the mounting bolts by starting at the center and progressing outward in both directions to 17 ft. lbs. (23 Nm).

19. Install the fuel rail. For more information, refer to Section 5.

20. Install the cowl mounted heat shield.

21. Install a new gasket on the lower intake manifold runner and install the upper manifold plenum. Tighten the plenum-to-lower manifold bolts to 17 ft. lbs. (23 Nm).

22. Install the plenum-to-cylinder head support bracket and tighten the bolts to 40 ft. lbs. (54 Nm).

23. Install the turbocharger, as described later in this section.

24. Install the starter motor. For more information, refer to Section 2.

25. Attach the PCV, Manifold Absolute Pressure (MAP) and brake booster vacuum supply hoses, as well as the charge temperature sensor electrical connector.

26. Install the throttle body assembly to the intake manifold, as described in Section 5. Install the EGR tube to the valve.

27. Install the air cleaner assembly.

28. Lower the vehicle and remove the wheel blocks.

29. Connect the negative battery cable.

30. Start the engine and check for fuel, coolant, oil and vacuum leaks.

2.2L Turbo III Engine

INTAKE MANIFOLD

▶ **See Figure 49**

1. Disconnect the negative battery cable.

2. Relieve the fuel system pressure, as described in Section 5.

3. Drain the cooling system, as described in Section 1.

4. Remove the fresh air duct from the air filter housing. Remove the inlet hose from the intercooler.

5. Remove the radiator hose from the thermostat housing.

6. Remove the DIS ignition coil from the intake manifold.

7. Disconnect the throttle and cruise control cables (if equipped) from the throttle body.

8. Disconnect the intercooler-to-throttle body outlet hose. Disconnect the vacuum hoses from the throttle body and carefully remove the harness.

9. Disconnect the AIS motor and TPS wiring connectors.

10. Remove the PCV breather/separator box and vacuum harness assembly. Remove the brake booster hose, vacuum vapor harness and fuel pressure regulator from the intake manifold.

11. Disconnect the fuel injector wiring harness and charge temperature sensor.

12. Wrap shop towels around the fittings and disconnect the fuel supply and return fuel lines.

13. Remove the intake manifold retaining bolts and remove the manifold from the cylinder head.

To install:

14. Inspect the manifold for damage of any kind. Thoroughly clean and dry the mating surfaces.

15. Install the new gasket and manifold on the cylinder head. Starting at the center and working outwards, torque the bolts gradually and evenly to 17 ft. lbs. (23 Nm).

16. Lubricate the quick connect fuel fittings with oil and connect to the chassis tubes. Ensure they are locked by pulling on them.

17. Install the PCV breather/separator box and vacuum harness assembly. Connect the brake booster hose, vacuum vapor harness and fuel pressure regulator to the intake manifold.

18. Connect the fuel injector wiring harness and charge temperature sensor. Connect the AIS motor and TPS wiring connectors.

19. Connect the vacuum hoses to the throttle body and carefully install the harness. Connect the intercooler-to-throttle body outlet hose.

20. Connect the throttle and speed control cables to the throttle body.

21. Install the DIS ignition coil to the intake manifold.

22. Connect the radiator hose to the thermostat housing.

23. Install the inlet hose on the intercooler. Install the fresh air duct on the air filter housing.

24. Refill and bleed the cooling system. Connect the negative battery cable. Start the engine and check for leaks.

EXHAUST MANIFOLD

1. Disconnect the negative battery cable.

2. Remove the turbocharger assembly.

3. Remove the coolant tube from the cylinder head.

4. Remove the exhaust manifold retaining nuts and remove the manifold.

5. Clean the gasket mounting surfaces. Inspect the manifolds for cracks, flatness and/or damage.

To install:

6. Install a new exhaust manifold gasket. Do not use sealer of any kind.

7. Position the manifold on the studs and install the retaining nuts. Starting at the center and working outwards, torque the nuts gradually and evenly to 17 ft. lbs. (23 Nm).

8. Using a new gasket, connect the coolant tube to the cylinder head.

9. Install the turbocharger assembly.

10. Connect the negative battery cable.

11. Start the engine and check for exhaust leaks.

2.5L Turbo I Engine

▶ **See Figures 50 and 51**

1. Disconnect the negative battery cable.

2. Remove the turbocharger, as described later in this section.

3. Remove the 8 intake manifold bolts and washers, then remove the intake manifold from the cylinder head.

4. Remove the 8 exhaust manifold bolts and washers, then remove the exhaust manifold from the cylinder head.

To install:

5. Discard the gaskets and clean all gasket surfaces on both manifolds and on the cylinder head.

6. Test the gasket surfaces of the manifolds for flatness with a straightedge. Surface warpage must not exceed 0.006 in. (0.15mm) per foot (30cm) of manifold length.

7. Inspect the manifolds for cracks and distortion; replace the manifolds if any such damage is evident.

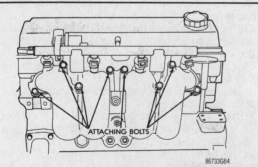

Fig. 49 The mounting bolts for the intake manifold should be tightened from the center of the manifold, progressing outward in both directions

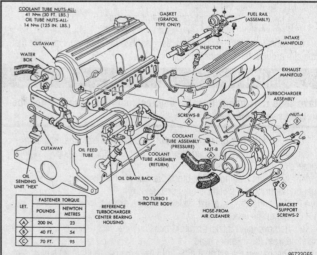

Fig. 50 Exploded view of the intake manifold, exhaust manifold and turbocharger mounting—Tighten all fasteners to the specifications shown

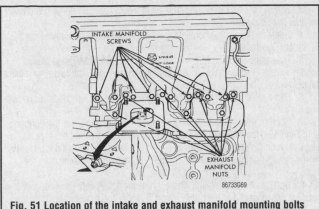

Fig. 51 Location of the intake and exhaust manifold mounting bolts

8. Install a new Grafoil or equivalent combination manifold gasket. DO NOT coat the gasket with sealer.

9. Position the lower intake manifold against the cylinder head and install the mounting bolts. Tighten the mounting bolts by starting at the center and progressing outward in both directions to 17 ft. lbs. (23 Nm).

10. Position the exhaust manifold against the cylinder head and install the mounting bolts. Tighten the mounting bolts by starting at the center and progressing outward in both directions to 17 ft. lbs. (23 Nm).

11. Install the cowl mounted heat shield.

12. Install the turbocharger, as described later in this section.

13. Install the fuel rail onto the intake manifold. For complete instructions, refer to Section 5.

14. Connect the negative battery cable.

2.6L Engine

INTAKE MANIFOLD

1. Disconnect the battery negative cable.

2. Drain the cooling system, as described in Section 1.

3. Disconnect the coolant hose running from the water pump to the intake manifold.

4. Disconnect the carburetor air intake hose and move it out of the way.

5. Label and disconnect all vacuum hoses connected to the intake manifold and carburetor.

6. Disconnect the throttle linkage at the carburetor and move it out of the way.

7. Disconnect the inlet line at the fuel filter, collecting any gasoline that spills out in a metal cup. Then, remove the fuel filter and pump and move them to one side.

8. Remove the mounting nuts and accompanying washers from the manifold attaching studs, and remove the manifold from the engine.

To install:

9. Clean all gasket surfaces and install the intake manifold using new gaskets. Tighten the bolts in three stages to 17 ft. lbs. (23 Nm).

10. Reinstall the fuel pump and fuel filter, as described in Section 5. Connect the inlet line and clamp it securely.

11. Reconnect the throttle linkage to the carburetor and adjust it to eliminate excessive play. For more details, refer to Section 5.

12. Reconnect all the vacuum hoses to the intake manifold and carburetor, according to the labels made earlier.

13. Connect the carburetor air intake hose to the carburetor and clamp it securely.

14. Connect the coolant hose running from the water pump to the intake manifold. For more details regarding cooling system hose clamp tightening and positioning, refer to Section 1.

15. Refill the cooling system with 50/50 mixture of antifreeze and water. For more details, refer to Section 1.

16. Connect the negative battery cable.

17. Start the engine and check for fluid leaks. After the engine reaches operating temperature, shut it **OFF**. When it has cooled, refill the cooling system, if necessary.

EXHAUST MANIFOLD

1. Remove air cleaner.

2. Remove the heat shield from the exhaust manifold. Remove the EGR lines and reed valve, if equipped.

3. Unbolt the exhaust flange connection.

4. Remove the nuts holding manifold to the cylinder head.

5. Remove the manifold.

6. Installation is the reverse of removal. Tighten flange connection bolts to 11–18 ft. lbs. (15–25 Nm). Tighten the manifold bolts to 11–14 ft. lbs. (15–19 Nm).

Turbocharger/Intercooler

REMOVAL & INSTALLATION

✷✷ CAUTION

When draining coolant, keep in mind that cats and dogs are attracted by ethylene glycol antifreeze, and are quite likely to drink any that is left in an uncovered container or in puddles on the ground. This will prove fatal in sufficient quantity. Always drain the coolant into a sealable container. Coolant should be reused unless it is contaminated or several years old.

Many turbocharger failures are due to oil supply problems. Heat soak after hot shutdown can cause the engine oil in the turbocharger and oil lines to "coke." Often the oil feed lines will become partially or completely blocked with hardened particles of carbon, blocking oil flow. Check the oil feed pipe and oil return line for clogging. Clean these tubes well. Always use new gaskets above and below the oil feed eyebolt fitting. Do not allow particles of dirt or old gasket material to enter the oil passage hole and that no portion of the new gasket blocks the passage.

1984–85 Models

1. Disconnect the negative battery cable.

2. Apply the parking brake, block the rear wheels, then raise and safely support the front of the vehicle on jackstands.

3. Drain the cooling system, as described in Section 1.

4. Disconnect the exhaust pipe at the articulated joint and detach the O2 sensor electrical connections.

5. Remove the turbocharger-to-block support bracket.

6. Loosen the clamps for the oil drain-back tube, then move the tube downward onto the block fitting so it no longer connects with the turbocharger.

7. Disconnect the turbocharger coolant supply tube at the block outlet below the power steering pump bracket and at the tube support bracket.

8. Disconnect and remove the air cleaner complete with the throttle body adapter, hose, and air cleaner box and support bracket.

9. Loosen the throttle body-to-turbocharger inlet hose clamps. Then, remove the 3 throttle body-to-intake manifold attaching screws and remove the throttle body.

10. Loosen the turbocharger discharge hose end clamps, leaving the center band in place to retain the deswirler.

11. Pull the fuel rail out of the way after removing the hose retaining bracket screw, 4 bracket screws from the intake manifold, and two bracket-to-heat shield retaining clips. The rail, injectors, wiring harness, and fuel lines should be moved as an assembly.

12. Disconnect the oil feed line at the turbocharger bearing housing.

13. Remove the 3 screws attaching the heat shield to the intake manifold and remove the shield.

14. Disconnect the coolant return tube and hose assembly at the turbocharger and water box. Remove the tube support bracket from the cylinder head and remove the assembly.

15. Remove the 4 nuts attaching the turbocharger to the exhaust manifold. Then, remove the turbocharger by lifting it off the exhaust manifold studs, tilting it downward toward the passenger's side of the car, and then pulling it up and out of the engine compartment.

To install:

16. Lower the turbocharger into the engine compartment and position it against the exhaust manifold. When repositioning the turbocharger on the mounting studs, make sure the discharge tube goes in position so that it is properly connected to both the intake manifold and turbocharger. Apply an anti-seize compound such as Loctite® 771–64 or equivalent to the threads. Tighten the nuts to 30 ft. lbs. (41 Nm).

17. Connect the coolant return tube and hose assembly to the turbocharger and water box. Install the tube support bracket onto the cylinder head and tighten the attaching fasteners to 30 ft. lbs. (41 Nm).

18. Install the heat shield to the intake manifold, then install the 3 attaching screws.

19. Connect the oil feed line to the turbocharger bearing housing, then tighten the oil feed line nuts to 125 inch lbs. (14 Nm).

20. Install the fuel rail onto the intake manifold, as described in Section 5. The fuel rail mounting bolts should be tightened to 21 ft. lbs. (28 Nm).

21. Tighten the turbocharger discharge hose end clamps to 35 inch lbs. (4 Nm).

22. Install the throttle body, then install and tighten the 3 throttle body-to-intake manifold attaching screws to 21 ft. lbs. (28 Nm). Tighten the throttle body-to-turbocharger inlet hose clamps to 35 inch lbs. (4 Nm).

23. Install the air cleaner complete with the throttle body adapter, hose, and air cleaner box and support bracket. Tighten the hose adapter-to-throttle body screws to 55 inch lbs. (6.2 Nm). Tighten the air cleaner box support bracket bolts to 40 ft. lbs. (54 Nm).

24. Connect the turbocharger coolant supply tube to the engine block outlet below the power steering pump bracket and at the tube support bracket. Tighten the coolant tube nut-to-block fastener to 30 ft. lbs. (41 Nm).

25. Connect the oil drain-back tube to the turbocharger, then tighten the hose clamps.

26. Install the turbocharger-to-engine block support bracket. When installing the turbocharger-to-block support bracket, first install screws finger-tight. Tighten the block screw to 40 ft. lbs. (54 Nm) first, then tighten the screw going into the turbocharger housing to 20 ft. lbs. (27 Nm). Tighten the articulated ball joint shoulder bolts to 21 ft. lbs. (28 Nm).

27. Connect the exhaust pipe to the articulated joint (for more details, refer to the end of this section) and attach the O₂ sensor electrical connections.

28. Fill and bleed the cooling system, as described in Section 1. Recheck the level after the coolant begins circulating through the radiator, and check for leaks after you install the pressure cap.

29. Lower the vehicle and remove the wheel blocks.

30. Connect the negative battery cable, start the engine and inspect for fluid leaks. Check the turbocharger carefully for any oil leaks and correct if necessary.

1986–93 Models

▶ See Figure 52

➡ The 2.2L Turbo II engine's intercooler is an integral part of the turbocharger unit.

1. Disconnect the negative battery cable.

2. Apply the parking brake, block the rear wheels, then raise and safely support the front of the vehicle on jackstands.

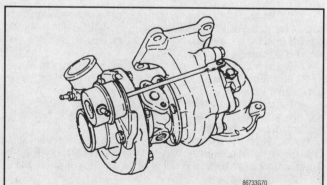

Fig. 52 The turbocharger unit removed from the vehicle—2.2L turbo II model's intercooler is an integral part of the turbocharger

86733G70

3. Remove the air cleaner assembly and intake manifold upper plenum-to-cylinder head support bracket.

4. Separate the throttle body assembly from the intake manifold. Detach the EGR tube from the valve.

5. Disengage the PCV, Manifold Absolute Pressure (MAP) and brake booster vacuum supply hoses. Disengage the charge temperature sensor electrical connector.

6. Remove the cowl mounted heat shield and fuel rail, as described in Section 5.

7. Support the engine from underneath on the oil pan (near the front end of the engine—the pulley end of the engine) with a hydraulic floor jack and a block of wood (to protect the underside of the engine), remove the front engine mount through-bolt and rotate the engine (top) forward and away from the cowl.

8. Unfasten the coolant line where it runs along the water box and turbo housing. Disconnect it at the turbocharger housing and remove the fitting from the turbocharger as well.

9. Disconnect the oil feed line at the turbocharger housing.

10. Remove the wastegate rod-to-gate retaining clip.

11. Remove the 2 upper and 1 lower (driver's side) nuts which retain the turbocharger to the manifold. Disconnect the oxygen sensor electrical lead and vacuum lines.

12. Remove the right side halfshaft, as described in Section 7.

13. Remove the turbocharger-to-block support bracket. Then, separate the oil drainback tube fitting from the turbocharger housing and remove the fitting and associated hose.

14. Remove the 1 remaining nut retaining the turbocharger to the manifold.

15. Disconnect the articulated exhaust pipe joint from the turbocharger turbine housing outlet.

16. Remove the lower coolant line and the inlet fitting, through which coolant passes into the housing.

17. Lift the turbocharger off the manifold mounting studs and lower it down and out of the vehicle.

To install:

18. Position the turbocharger onto the exhaust manifold. Apply an anti-seize compound such as Loctite 771–64® or equivalent on the threads and install 1 lower retaining nut on the passenger's side, tightening it to 40 ft. lbs. (55 Nm).

19. Apply a thread sealant to the lower coolant inlet line fitting and install the fitting into the turbocharger housing. Connect the lower coolant line.

20. Install a new gasket and install the oil drain-back tube fitting into the turbocharger housing. Connect the coolant line to the fitting.

21. Install the turbocharger-to-block support bracket and install the attaching screws finger tight. First, tighten the block screw to 40 ft. lbs. (55 Nm), then tighten the screw attaching the bracket to the turbocharger housing to 20 ft. lbs. (27 Nm).

22. Reposition the exhaust pipe and connect it to the turbocharger housing outlet. Tighten the attaching bolts to 21 ft. lbs. (28 Nm).

23. Install the right side halfshaft, as described in Section 7. Install the right side front wheel.

24. Unfasten the coolant line where it runs along the water box and turbo housing. Disconnect it at the turbocharger housing and remove the fitting from the turbocharger as well.

25. Install the remaining 3 turbocharger-to-intake manifold nuts, tightening them to 40 ft. lbs. (54 Nm). Connect the oxygen sensor electrical lead and vacuum lines.

26. Install the wastegate rod-to-gate retaining clip.

27. Connect the oil feed line to the turbocharger housing.

28. In reassembling the front engine mount, align the mount in the cross-member bracket, install the bolt, and tighten it to 40 ft. lbs. (54 Nm).

29. Install the fuel rail. For more information, refer to Section 5.

30. Install the cowl mounted heat shield.

31. Attach the PCV, Manifold Absolute Pressure (MAP) and brake booster vacuum supply hoses, as well as the charge temperature sensor electrical connector.

32. Install the throttle body assembly on the intake manifold, as described in Section 5. Install the EGR tube on the valve.

33. Install the air cleaner assembly.

34. Connect the negative battery cable.

35. Start the engine and check for fuel, coolant, oil and vacuum leaks.

Radiator

REMOVAL & INSTALLATION

► **See Figures 53 thru 60**

1. Disconnect the negative (-) battery cable.

✳✳ CAUTION

Do not remove the cylinder block or the radiator draincock with the system hot and under pressure because serious burns from coolant can occur.

2. Drain the cooling system.
3. Remove the hose clamps and hoses from the radiator. Remove the coolant reserve system tank-to-filler neck tube.

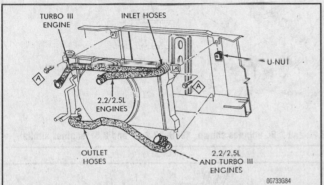

Fig. 53 Hose routing and radiator mounting for 1988–95 models with single fans

4. Remove the automatic transaxle hoses, if so equipped.
5. Remove the fan and fan support assembly by disconnecting the fan motor electrical wiring.
6. Remove the fan shroud retaining clips, located on the top and bottom of the shroud for most of the vehicles (the Dynasty has them only on the top).
7. Lift the shroud up and out of the bottom shroud attachment clips separating the shroud from the radiator. Avoid damaging the fan.
8. Remove the upper radiator mounting screws. Disconnect the engine block heater wire, if so equipped.
9. Remove the air conditioning condenser attaching screws located at the top front of the radiator, if the vehicle is equipped with air conditioning.
10. Lift the radiator free of the engine compartment.

➡**Care should be taken not to damage the radiator cooling fins or water tubes during removal or installation.**

To install:

11. Slide the radiator down into position behind the radiator support.
12. Attach the air conditioning condenser to the radiator, if so equipped, with a force of approximately 10 lbs. (44 N) to seat the radiator assembly lower rubber isolators in the mount holes provided.
13. Tighten the radiator mounting screws to 108 inch lbs. (12 Nm).
14. Connect the automatic transaxle hoses, if so equipped. Tighten the hose clamps to 35 inch lbs. (4 Nm).
15. Slide the fan shroud, fan and motor down into the clips on the lower radiator flange. Install new shroud retaining clips.
16. Install the upper and lower radiator hoses (including the coolant reserve hose).
17. Plug the fan motor electrical connection and attach the negative (-) battery cable.
18. Fill the cooling system with coolant (refer to Section 1 for more details).
19. Operate the engine until it reaches normal operating temperature. Check the cooling system and automatic transaxle (if equipped) for the correct fluid levels. Also check for coolant leaks.

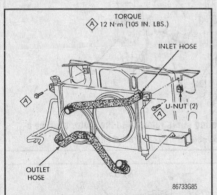

Fig. 54 Hose routing and radiator mounting for 1988–95 models with dual fans

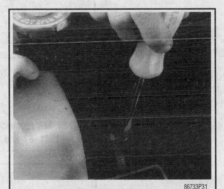

Fig. 55 After removing the cooling fan, disconnect the hoses from the radiator . . .

Fig. 56 . . . then detach the overflow tube from the radiator

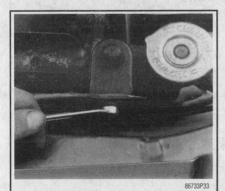

Fig. 57 To unfasten the top of the radiator, either loosen the bracket nut . . .

Fig. 58 . . . and remove the upper holding bracket . . .

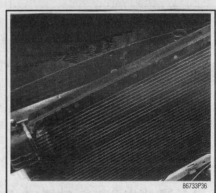

Fig. 59 Carefully lift the radiator up and out of the lower holding rail

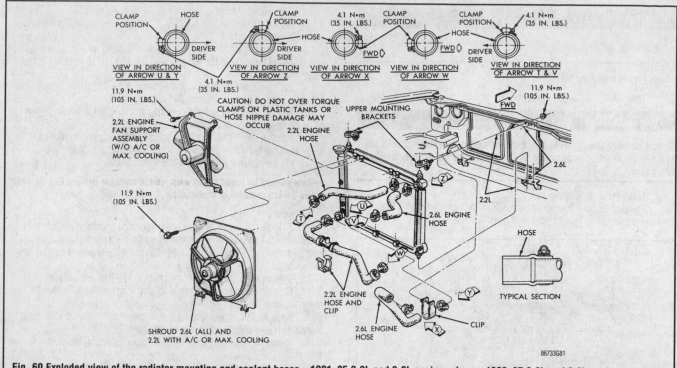

Fig. 60 Exploded view of the radiator mounting and coolant hoses—1981–85 2.2L and 2.6L engines shown, 1986–87 2.2L and 2.5L engines similar

Engine Cooling Fan

REMOVAL & INSTALLATION

▶ See Figures 61 thru 66

All models use electric motor driven cooling system fans. The fan modules include a motor support which may (depending on the model) include a shroud. The module is fastened to the radiator by screws with U-nuts and retaining clips.

The Dynasty models utilize a dual fan module. The dual fan module is a combination of 2 fans (mounted in a one piece shroud) which are simultaneously activated. The dual fan system improves engine cooling and air conditioning performance in hot weather and severe driving conditions, while reducing fan noise and power consumption.

There are no repairs which can be made to the fan. If the fan is warped, cracked, or otherwise damaged, it must be replaced.

1. Disconnect the negative (-) battery cable.
2. Disconnect the electric motor lead.
3. Remove the fan module-to-radiator fasteners and retaining clips.
4. Remove the assembly form the radiator support.
5. To remove the fan from the motor shaft, support the motor and motor shaft on a bench, while removing the fan retaining clip. This will help avoid

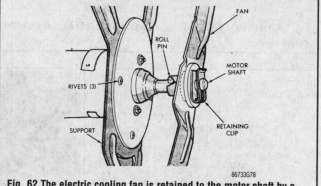

Fig. 62 The electric cooling fan is retained to the motor shaft by a clip—1981–87 and 1989–90 TC by Maserati models

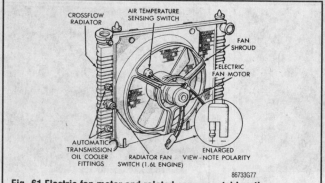

Fig. 61 Electric fan motor and related components' locations—1981–87 and 1989–90 TC by Maserati models

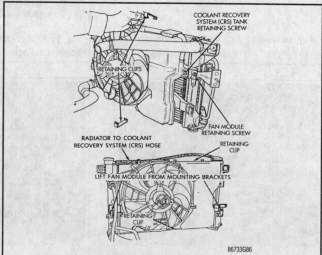

Fig. 63 The cooling fan is mounted on the radiator by retaining clips or screws—1988–95 models (dual fan models similar)

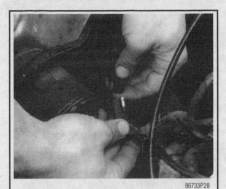

Fig. 64 Detach the electric cooling fan connector . . .

Fig. 65 . . . remove the cooling fan shroud attaching bolts, then . . .

Fig. 66 . . . lift the fan and shroud assembly out of the engine bay

damage to the shaft and motor by excessive force. Surface or burr removal may be required to remove the fan from the motor shaft. Do not permit the fan blades to touch the bench.

To install:

6. Slide the fan onto the motor shaft. Support the motor and shaft as above while installing the fan's retaining clip.

7. Install the assembly into the pocket on the lower radiator tank.

8. Attach the retaining clips and fasteners to the radiator tank.

➡ **The right-side fastener is longer on A/C equipped vehicles.**

9. Connect the fan motor lead to the fan motor.

TESTING

♦ **See Figures 61, 67 and 68**

1981–87 Models

1. Disconnect the negative battery cable.

2. Disengage the electric fan motor connector, then, using 14 gauge jumper wires, attach the fan terminals to a good 12 volt battery. Make sure to attach the positive fan terminal to the positive battery terminal and the negative fan terminal to the negative battery terminal. Refer to the illustrations for the identification of the fan motor wire connector terminals.

3. The fan should turn on and run normally. If the fan does not turn on, double check the jumper wire connections and polarity (negative to negative and positive to positive).

4. If the fan still does not function normally, replace it with a new unit, as described earlier in this section.

5. If the motor is noticeably overheated (i.e. wire insulation is melted, motor is charred, etc.) the system voltage may be too high. The voltage regulator may be defective.

6. After testing, attach the fan motor connector to the wiring harness.

7. Connect the negative battery cable.

1988–95 Models

To check out the electric fan motor, disconnect the fan motor wire connector and connect it with 14 gauge wires to a good 12 volt battery observing the correct polarity. If the fan runs normally, the motor is functioning properly. If not, replace the fan module with a new one using the removal and installation procedures. If the motor is noticeably overheated (i.e. wire insulation melted, motor charred) the system voltage may be too high.

1. For this system diagnostic test, the following tools will be needed:

a. Diagnostic tool DRB II or the equivalent.

b. Volt/ohmmeter.

c. Refer to Section 6 for general circuit testing procedures and wiring diagrams.

2. Run the engine until the normal operating temperature is reached.

3. Check the wiring connectors for proper engagement.

4. Using the diagnostic tool, plugged into the diagnostic connector rearward of the battery, check the On-Board Diagnostics (OBD) in the Engine Controller for fault codes. Refer to Section 4 for more details regarding diagnostic trouble codes.

5. If the fault code 88–12–35–55 is detected, proceed to the next step.

6. With the ignition switch in the **RUN** position, test for battery voltage (single pin connector) at the fan relay. If the voltage reading shows battery voltage, proceed to Step 7. If the voltage is only 0–1 volt, proceed to Step 8.

7. With the ignition switch **OFF**, disconnect the 60-way connector from the Engine Controller (outboard of the battery) and return the ignition to the **RUN** position. Test for battery voltage at cavity **31** of the 60-way connector. If the reading shows battery voltage, replace the Engine Controller. If the voltage reading shows 0 volts, repair the open or short in the **C27** circuit.

8. With the ignition **OFF**, disconnect the 60-way connector from the Engine Controller (outboard of the battery) and return the ignition to the **RUN** position. Test for battery voltage at the single pin connector at the fan relay. If the voltage shows battery voltage, replace the Engine Controller. If the voltage reading is only 0–1 volt, proceed to Step 9.

9. With the ignition in the **RUN** position, test for battery voltage at the wire (**C27**) in the 3-way connector of the fan relay. If the voltage reading shows bat-

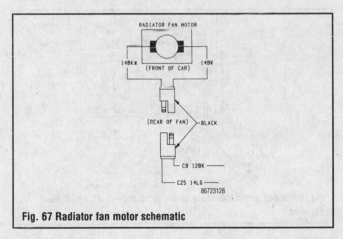

Fig. 67 Radiator fan motor schematic

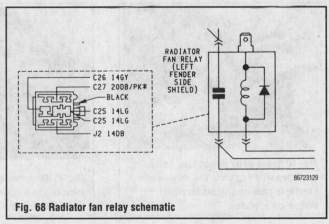

Fig. 68 Radiator fan relay schematic

tery voltage, replace the fan relay. If the voltage reading is 0 volts, repair the open or short in the **C27** circuit.

10. Turn the ignition **OFF**, connect the 60-way connector at the Engine Controller and test the system.

Water Pump

REMOVAL & INSTALLATION

CAUTION

When draining coolant, keep in mind that cats and dogs are attracted by ethylene glycol antifreeze, and are quite likely to drink any that is left in an uncovered container or in puddles on the ground. This will prove fatal in sufficient quantity. Always drain the coolant into a sealable container. Coolant should be reused unless it is contaminated or several years old.

2.2 and 2.5L Engines

See Figures 69, 70, 71 and 72

1. Disconnect the battery negative cable.
2. Apply the parking brake, block the rear wheels, then raise and safely support the front of the vehicle on jackstands.
3. Drain the cooling system through the draincock, located on the bottom right-hand side of the radiator, into a large, clean catch pan.
4. Remove the upper radiator hose.
5. Remove the alternator, as described in Section 2.

Do not disconnect the air conditioner compressor lines during water pump removal. The compressor can be moved far enough out of the way to remove the water pump without disturbing the refrigerant-filled lines. A/C system refrigerant lines require special knowledge for servicing, refer to the A/C system cautions and warnings in Section 1 for further information.

6. On models with non-solid mount compressors, unbolt the air conditioning compressor brackets from the water pump. On solid mount compressors, remove the compressor-to-engine bolts. Secure the compressor out of the way. Suspend the compressor with strong cord or wire so that it will not put stress on the refrigerant lines.
7. Disconnect the bypass hose, heater return hose, and lower radiator hose.
8. Unbolt and remove the water pump assembly. On the 2.2L Turbo III engine, there is a spacer between the water pump and engine block on the lower bolt; make certain to retain this spacer for reassembly.
9. To disassemble the pump, perform the following:
   a. Remove the 3 bolts fastening the drive pulley to the water pump.
   b. Remove the 9 bolts fastening the water pump body to the housing. Then, use a chisel to gently break the bond between the pump and housing.

To install:

10. Assemble the water pump as follows, if necessary:
    a. Clean the gasket surfaces on the pump body and housing. Remove the O-ring gasket and discard it. Clean the O-ring groove.
    b. Either apply RTV sealer to the sealing surface of the water pump body or use a new gasket during assembly. If using sealant, the bead should be 1/8 in. (3mm) in diameter and should encircle all bolt holes. Assemble the pump body to the housing, install the 9 bolts, and tighten them to 105 inch lbs. (12 Nm). Make sure the gasket material has set (as per package instructions) before actually filling the system.
    c. Position a new O-ring in the groove, then situate the pulley on the pump. Install the 3 attaching bolts, and tighten them to 21 ft. lbs. (28 Nm).
11. For 2.2L Turbo III engines, install the coolant deflector into the engine block before installing the water pump on the engine.
12. Position the water pump on the engine and, on 2.2L Turbo III engines, install the spacer.
13. Install the water pump mounting bolts finger-tight.
14. Tighten the top 3 water pump bolts to 21 ft. lbs. (28 Nm) and the lower bolt to 50 ft. lbs. (68 Nm).
15. Install the bypass, heater return and lower radiator hoses. For more information on cooling system hose servicing, refer to Section 1.
16. Install the A/C compressor, as described in Section 6.
17. Install the alternator. For more information, refer to Section 2.
18. Install the upper radiator hose and close the radiator draincock.
19. Lower the vehicle and remove the wheel blocks.
20. Connect the negative battery cable.
21. Fill the cooling system with a 50/50 mixture of water and antifreeze, as described in Section 1.
22. Start the engine, allow the engine to warm up to normal operating temperature, check for coolant leaks, turn off the engine, allow the engine to cool, then refill the cooling system as needed.

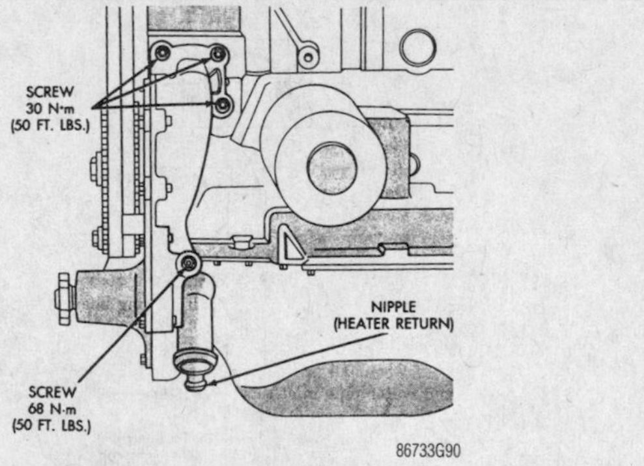

Fig. 69 Water pump mounting screw locations—2.2L and 2.5L engines

2.6L Engine

See Figure 73

1. Disconnect the negative battery cable.
2. Apply the parking brake, block the rear wheels, then raise and safely support the front of the vehicle on jackstands.

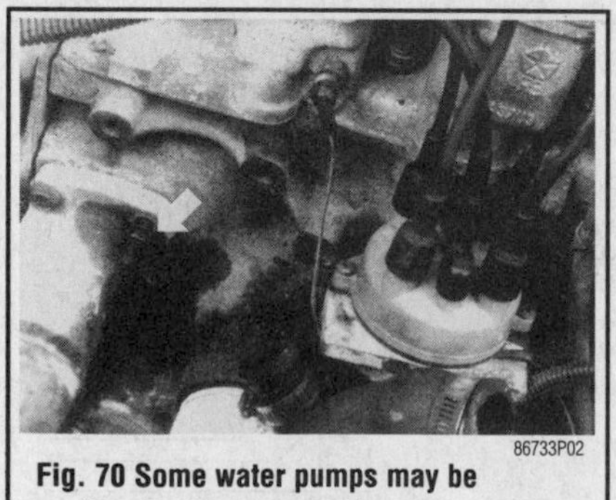

Fig. 70 Some water pumps may be equipped with one attaching stud—make certain to note its original location for proper installation

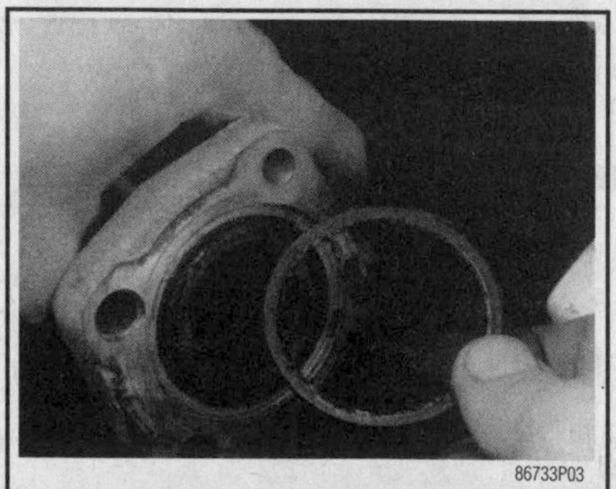

Fig. 71 After removal of the water pump, remove and discard the old gasket—a new one is needed for installation

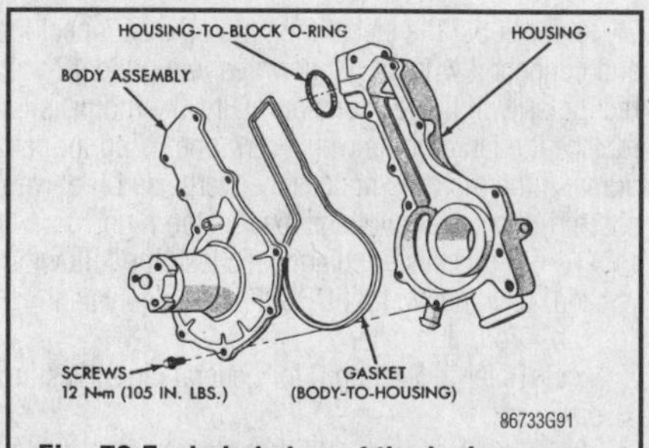

Fig. 72 Exploded view of the body assembly and the housing—earlier models call for sealant, whereas newer models (1988–95) utilize gaskets (shown) between the assembly and housing

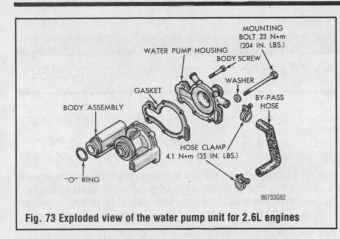

Fig. 73 Exploded view of the water pump unit for 2.6L engines

3. Drain the cooling system through the draincock, located on the bottom right-hand side of the radiator, into a large, clean catch pan.

4. Disconnect the radiator, bypass, and heater hoses from the water pump.

5. Remove the 2 mounting bolts and remove the drive pulley shield.

6. Remove the lockscrew and the 2 pivot screws. Then, separate the pump from the drive belt and remove it from the engine.

7. Remove the bolts attaching the water pump housing to the pump body and separate the pump from the body.

To install:

8. Discard the gasket and clean the gasket surfaces. Discard the used O-ring and clean the O-ring groove.

9. Install a new gasket on the pump body, then position the pump assembly onto it. Install the attaching bolts and tighten them to 80 inch lbs. (9 Nm). Position a new O-ring into the appropriate groove.

10. Position the pump on the engine, install the drive belt, and install the pivot and locking screws finger-tight. Tension the drive belt, as described in Section 1, then tighten all 3 mounting bolts to 17 ft. lbs. (23 Nm).

11. Install the drive pulley cover.

12. Install the radiator, bypass and heater hoses to the water pump, as described in Section 1.

13. Close the radiator draincock, lower the vehicle and remove the wheel blocks.

14. Connect the negative battery cable.

15. Refill the system (make sure that the thermostat is open) with 50/50 antifreeze/water mix. Recheck coolant level after vehicle has cooled.

Cylinder Head

REMOVAL & INSTALLATION

➡ Review the entire procedure before starting this repair. Make sure to locate the correct year, engine and model service procedure for your vehicle.

✷✷ CAUTION

The EPA warns that prolonged contact with used engine oil may cause a number of skin disorders, including cancer! You should make every effort to minimize your exposure to used engine oil. Protective gloves should be worn when changing the oil. Wash your hands and any other exposed skin areas as soon as possible after exposure to used engine oil. Soap and water, or waterless hand cleaner should be used.

1981–88 Engines

EXCEPT 2.6L ENGINE

♦ See Figures 74 thru 80

1. Disconnect the negative battery cable.

Fig. 74 Use a breaker bar to loosen and remove the cylinder head attaching bolts . . .

Fig. 75 . . . then lift the cylinder head off of the engine

Fig. 76 Remove the old gasket from the engine block and . . .

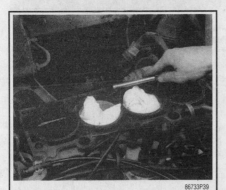

Fig. 77 . . . clean any residual gasket material from the engine block

Fig. 78 Make certain to tighten the cylinder head bolts with a torque wrench

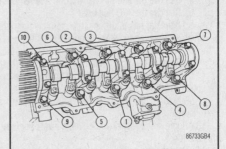

Fig. 79 Tighten the cylinder head bolts in the sequence shown—2.2L and 2.5L except 2.2L Turbo III engines

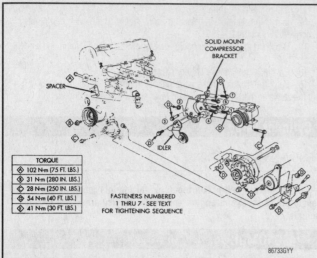

TORQUE

◈ 102 N·m (75 FT. LBS.)
◈ 31 N·m (280 IN. LBS.)
◈ 28 N·m (250 IN. LBS.)
◈ 54 N·m (40 FT. LBS.)
◈ 41 N·m (30 FT. LBS.)

FASTENERS NUMBERED
1 THRU 7 - SEE TEXT
FOR TIGHTENING SEQUENCE

86733GYY

Fig. 80 Exploded view of the solid mount compressor bracket and related torque values

✳ CAUTION

When draining coolant, keep in mind that cats and dogs are attracted by ethylene glycol antifreeze, and are quite likely to drink any that is left in an uncovered container or in puddles on the ground. This will prove fatal in sufficient quantity. Always drain the coolant into a sealable container. Coolant should be reused unless it is contaminated or several years old.

2. With the engine cold, drain the cooling system. If the dipstick bracket attaches to the thermostat housing, disconnect the dipstick bracket from the thermostat housing and rotate it away from the mounting stud to disconnect it without bending it.

3. Remove the air cleaner assembly.

4. Label and then disconnect all lines, hoses and wires from the head, manifold and carburetor or throttle body. Before disconnecting the fuel lines on fuel injected engines, be sure to depressurize the system as described in Section 1.

5. Disconnect the accelerator linkage.

6. Remove the distributor cap.

7. Disconnect the exhaust pipe.

8. Remove the carburetor or throttle body on engines so-equipped.

9. Remove the intake and exhaust manifolds as described earlier. On turbo engines, remove the turbo and then remove the manifolds.

10. Remove the front cover.

11. Remove the timing belt, as described later in this section.

12. If equipped with air conditioning, remove the compressor from the mounting brackets and support it out of the way with wires. Remove the mounting bracket from the cylinder head. Then, if the engine is equipped with the solid mount attached to the engine block and cylinder head, perform the following:

a. Remove the alternator pivot bolt and remove the alternator.

b. Remove the A/C belt idler.

c. If the car has a turbocharger, remove the right engine mount yoke bolt, which secures the isolator support bracket to the engine mount bracket.

d. Now, remove all 5 side mounting bolts—those facing the radiator.

e. Remove the front mounting nut and bolt (both face the fender well).

f. Now, rotate the bracket away from the engine and slide it on the stud until it is free.

g. Now, reinstall the front mounting bolt into the hole to stop the leakage of coolant.

13. Remove the rocker arm cover, gaskets and seals, as described earlier in this section.

14. Remove the cylinder head mounting bolts in the reverse order of the tightening sequence shown in the accompanying illustration.

15. Lift the cylinder head off of the engine block and discard the old gasket.

16. Inspect the cylinder head and engine block. Clean both gasket surfaces thoroughly.

To install:

✳ WARNING

Turbo II engines use a unique head gasket. DO NOT use a Turbo I gasket on a Turbo II engine.

17. Make certain all gasket surfaces are thoroughly cleaned and are free of deep nicks or scratches. Always use new gaskets and seals. Never reuse a gasket or seal, even if it looks good.

18. Position the head on the block, then insert bolt No. 8 and bolt No. 10 (see illustration) to align the cylinder head and gasket with the engine block.

➡ **In the 1986 model year, the 10mm cylinder head mounting bolts were replaced with 11mm bolts marked "11" on the head. Tighten the cylinder head mounting bolts in the order shown to specifications.**

19. For 1981–86 models with 10mm cylinder head mounting bolts, tighten the bolts, in the order shown, to the following torque values:

- Step 1—30 ft. lbs. (41 Nm)
- Step 2—45 ft. lbs. (61 Nm)
- Step 3—Once again to 45 ft. lbs. (61 Nm)
- Step 4—tighten each bolt an additional ¼ turn

20. For 1986–88 models with 11mm cylinder head mounting bolts, tighten the bolts, in the order shown, to the following torque values:

- Step 1—45 ft. lbs. (61 Nm)
- Step 2—65 ft. lbs. (88 Nm)
- Step 3—Once again to 65 ft. lbs. (88 Nm)
- Step 4—tighten each bolt an additional ¼ turn

➡ **Note that on the 1986–88 models using the 11mm bolts, torque must reach 90 ft. lbs. (122 Nm), otherwise replace the bolt.**

21. Install the valve cover, gaskets and seals, as described earlier in this section.

22. If the car is equipped with air conditioning (non-solid mount compressors):

a. Remove the front mounting bolt for the compressor installed to stop coolant leakage.

b. Install the A/C compressor bracket by rotating it into place in reverse of the removal procedure. Install the front mounting nut and bolt and all 5 side mounting bolts.

c. On turbocharged vehicles the right engine mount yoke bolt was removed. Reinstall it to secure the isolator support bracket to the engine mounting bracket. Tighten it to 75 ft. lbs. (102 Nm).

d. Install the A/C compressor drive belt idler pulley assembly.

e. Install the alternator, including the alternator pivot bolt, as described in Section 2.

23. For vehicles with A/C and solid mount compressors, install the solid mount compressor bracket as follows:

a. Position the spacer onto the stud, then install the bracket on the front (2 nut) mounting stud and slide the bracket over the timing belt cover into position.

b. Loosen the assembly bracket-to-engine fasteners (numbered 1 through 7—refer to the accompanying illustration).

✳ WARNING

The bracket fasteners must be tightened in the proper sequence and to the specified torque values.

c. Tighten the fasteners in the following sequence: 1) bolt 1 to 30 inch lbs. (3.3 Nm), 2) nut 2 and bolt 3 to 40 ft. lbs. (54 Nm), 3) bolts 1, 4 and 5 to 40 ft. lbs. (54 Nm), 4) bolts 6 and 7 to 40 ft. lbs. (54 Nm).

d. Install the alternator and compressor to the bracket. Tighten the compressor mounting bolts to 40 ft. lbs. (54 Nm).

24. Make sure all timing marks on the crankshaft, camshaft and engine block are properly aligned. Install and adjust the timing belt, as described later in this section. The timing belt is correctly tensioned when it can be twisted only 90 degrees with the thumb and index finger midway between the camshaft and the intermediate shaft. Check to make sure tension is correct.

25. Install the front cover. Install the intake and exhaust manifolds (with turbocharger, if so equipped). For more information, refer to the intake and exhaust manifolds removal and installation procedures earlier in this section.

26. Reconnect the exhaust pipe, using a new seal, and tighten the fasteners to 21 ft. lbs. (28 Nm).

27. Install the distributor cap and spark plug wires.

28. Attach the accelerator linkage to the carburetor or throttle body, depending on the specific model.

29. Reattach all electrical wiring connectors, fuel and vacuum hoses, and any hoses detached during removal.

30. Install the air cleaner.

31. Connect the negative battery cable.

32. Fill the cooling system, as described in Section 1.

33. Start the engine and allow it to run until it reaches operating temperature, then check for leaks. Shut the engine **OFF**, allow the engine to cool and refill the cooling system as needed.

2.6L ENGINE

♦ See Figure 81

✳✳ CAUTION

The EPA warns that prolonged contact with used engine oil may cause a number of skin disorders, including cancer! You should make every effort to minimize your exposure to used engine oil. Protective gloves should be worn when changing the oil. Wash your hands and any other exposed skin areas as soon as possible after exposure to used engine oil. Soap and water, or waterless hand cleaner should be used.

➡**Do not perform this operation on a warm engine. Remove the head bolts in the sequence shown and in several steps. Loosen the head bolts evenly. Do not attempt to slide the cylinder head off the block, as it is located with dowel pins. Lift the head straight up and off the block.**

1. Disconnect the negative battery cable.

2. Remove the rocker arm cover, as described earlier in this section.

3. Remove the intake and exhaust manifolds. For more information, refer to the procedures earlier in this section.

4. Remove the timing chain cover, timing chain and camshaft sprocket, as described later in this section.

5. Remove the distributor, as described in Section 2.

6. Disconnect the air feeder hoses from underneath the vehicle.

7. If the vehicle is equipped with power steering, unbolt the pump and move aside without disconnecting hoses. Secure the pump in place with strong cord or wire; do not allow it to hang from the fluid lines.

8. Remove the ground wire and dipstick tube bracket from the cylinder head.

9. Remove the exhaust manifold, as described earlier in this section.

10. Remove the cylinder head bolts in several stages (loosen the bolts in the reverse order of the tightening sequence shown). Lift the cylinder head off the engine.

To install:

11. Install the new gasket without sealer and in a position which allows all bolt holes and the outer border of the gasket to align with the bolt holes and outer edge of the block. Lightly oil all of the bolt threads, then install and tighten the cylinder head mounting bolts in the following steps:

- Step 1—finger-tight
- Step 2—35 ft. lbs. (48 Nm)
- Step 3—69 ft. lbs. (94 Nm)

12. Tighten the cylinder head-to-timing chain cover bolts to 13 ft. lbs. (17 Nm).

13. Attach the exhaust manifold to the catalytic converter, as described at the end of this section.

14. Install the ground wire and dipstick tube.

15. Install the power steering pump and belt, then adjust the belt tension. For more information, refer to Section 8 for power steering procedures and to Section 1 for drive belt tensioning procedures.

16. From underneath the vehicle, install the air feeder tubes.

➡**Before installing the timing chain and gear, refer to the timing chain procedures located later in this section.**

17. Make certain that the engine is still at TDC on cylinder No. 1 compression stroke and that all of the timing marks on the pulleys and engine block are aligned. Install the camshaft sprocket, bolt and distributor drive gear. Make certain that the matchmarks made during removal are aligned once the timing chain is installed onto the camshaft sprocket.

18. Reinstall all electrical engine wiring, engine vacuum hoses and carburetor linkage.

19. Install the distributor and spark plug wires, as described in Section 2.

20. Connect the upper radiator hose and heater hoses. For more information on cooling system hose procedures, refer to Section 1.

21. Install the rocker arm cover, as described earlier in this section.

22. Install the fuel pump cover bracket and water pump pulley cover.

23. Reconnect the PCV hose.

24. Install the air cleaner and reconnect all ducting and vacuum hoses securely.

25. Close the radiator draincock, if open, lower the vehicle and remove the wheel blocks.

26. Connect the negative battery cable.

27. Fill the cooling system, then start the engine and check for leaks. When the engine has reached operating temperature, check the ignition timing. When the engine has cooled back off, refill the cooling system, if necessary.

1989–95 Engines

♦ See Figure 82

✳✳ CAUTION

The EPA warns that prolonged contact with used engine oil may cause a number of skin disorders, including cancer! You should make every effort to minimize your exposure to used engine oil. Protective gloves should be worn when changing the oil. Wash your hands and any other exposed skin areas as soon as possible after exposure to used engine oil. Soap and water, or waterless hand cleaner should be used.

➡**For this procedure, either a Special Tool C-4852 (Engine Support), or equivalent, will be necessary or the timing belt covers and timing belt must be removed. The engine support tool is used to hold the camshaft**

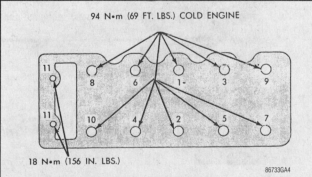

Fig. 81 Tighten the cylinder head bolts in the sequence shown—to loosen the head bolts, simply reverse the order

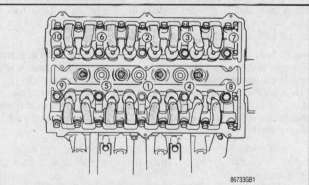

Fig. 82 Make sure to tighten the cylinder head mounting bolts in the sequence shown—2.2L Turbo III engines

sprocket in place with the adequate amount of tension to prevent the timing belt form skipping crankshaft teeth or from falling off of the crankshaft sprocket.

1. Relieve fuel system pressure, as described in Section 5.
2. Disconnect the negative battery cable and detach it from the head.
3. Remove the intake and exhaust manifolds. For more details, refer to the intake and exhaust manifold procedure earlier in this section.
4. Remove the turbocharger, as described earlier in this section.
5. Perform one of the following procedures:
   a. Remove the timing belt covers and timing belt. For more information, refer to the timing belt removal and installation procedure located later in this section. OR . . .
   b. Use the engine support tool C-4852, or equivalent, to suspend the timing sprocket and belt in position. Removal and installation of the cylinder head requires separation of the camshaft sprocket from the camshaft. To maintain camshaft, intermediate shaft and crankshaft timing during service procedures, the timing belt is left indexed on the sprocket while the assembly is "suspended" under light tension by Special Tool C-4852. When removing the sprocket from the camshaft, you must maintain adequate tension on the sprocket and belt assembly to prevent the belt from disengaging from the intermediate or crankshaft timing sprockets. For camshaft sprocket removal and installation directions, refer to the appropriate procedure later in this section.

✳✳ WARNING

Failure to maintain adequate tension on the camshaft, intermediate shaft and crankshaft sprocket belt can result in lost engine timing. If the timing is lost, the timing belt must be removed and reinstalled according to the procedures later in this section.

6. For 2.2L Turbo III engines with A/C, remove the A/C compressor and mounting bracket completely, as described in Section 6.
7. For all other engines with A/C, remove the upper compressor mounting bolts; the cylinder head can be removed with the compressor and bracket still mounted.
8. Remove the rocker arm cover, as described earlier in this section.
9. Remove the cylinder head bolts, then lift the cylinder head off of the engine.

To install:

➡**Since the cylinder heads are tightened using a new procedure, they should be examined before reuse. If the threads are necked down the bolts should be replaced.**

10. Check the cylinder head bolts for necking by holding a scale or straightedge against the threads. If all the threads do not contact the scale, the bolt should be replaced. Lubricate the bolt threads with clean engine oil.

➡**The 2.5L Turbo I engine head gasket is NOT the same as that used for the prior 2.2L Turbo I engine.**

11. Clean the cylinder head gasket mating surfaces and inspect the cylinder head and related components, as described later in this section.

➡**Except 2.2L Turbo III engines—Head bolt diameter is 11mm. These bolts are identified with the number "11" on the head of the bolt. The 10mm bolts used on previous vehicles will thread into an 11mm bolt hole, but will permanently damage the cylinder block. Make sure the correct bolts are used when replacing head bolts.**

➡**2.2L Turbo III engines—The head gasket used on the Turbo III engine is unique to the engine. Make sure the replacement head gasket is identical to the original gasket before installation. Head bolt diameter is 11mm and the head bolts are unique to this engine. These bolts are identified with the number 11 on the head of the bolt and are not interchangeable with other engines. Make sure the correct bolts are used when replacing head bolts.**

12. Using new gaskets and seals, install the cylinder head to the engine. Tighten the cylinder head bolts, following the sequence shown in the accompanying illustrations, in the following steps:
- Step 1—45 ft. lbs. (61 Nm)
- Step 2—65 ft. lbs. (88 Nm)

- Step 3—once again 65 ft. lbs. (88 Nm)
- Step 4—an additional ¼ turn

➡**Bolt torque after the additional ¼ turn should be over 90 ft. lbs. (122 Nm). If it isn't, replace the bolt.**

13. Install the timing belt and all related items, as described later in this section.
14. Install the intake and exhaust manifolds and turbocharger, if applicable. For more information, refer to these procedures earlier in this section.
15. On 2.2L Turbo III engines, install the air conditioning compressor and bracket to the cylinder head, as described in Section 6.
16. For all other engines (except 2.2L Turbo III), install the 2 upper A/C compressor bracket mounting bolts to the cylinder head. Tighten the bolts to 40 ft. lbs. (54 Nm).
17. Install the rocker arm covers and oil curtain or ignition cable cover, as applicable, then tighten the hold-down bolts to 105 inch lbs. (12 Nm).
18. Install the air cleaner assembly and all ductwork.
19. Refill the cooling system, then connect the negative battery cable.
20. Start the engine and check for leaks.

CLEANING & INSPECTION

▶ **See Figure 83**

1. With the valves installed to protect the valve seats, remove deposits from the combustion chambers and valve heads with a scraper and a wire brush. Be careful not to damage the aluminum cylinder head gasket surface. After the valves are removed, clean the valve guide bores with a valve guide cleaning tool. Using cleaning solvent to remove dirt, grease and other deposits and clean all bolts holes.
2. Using a straightedge, inspect the cylinder head gasket surface for excessive warpage. The cylinder head should be resurfaced if the warpage exceeds 0.004 in. (0.1mm). Inspect the cylinder head from corner-to-corner, side-to-side and end-to-end for warpage.
3. Remove all deposits from the valves with a fine wire brush or buffing wheel.
4. Inspect the cylinder heads for cracks or excessively burned areas in the exhaust outlet ports.
5. Check the cylinder head for cracks and inspect the gasket surface for burrs and nicks. Replace the head if it is cracked.

RESURFACING

▶ **See Figure 83**

When the cylinder head is removed, check the flatness of the cylinder head gasket surfaces. Since the tools required for resurfacing a cylinder head are extremely expensive and the necessary skills are important, refer to a reputable machine shop for cylinder head refinishing specifications and procedures.

1. Place a straightedge across the gasket surface of the cylinder head. Using feeler gauges, determine the clearance at the center of the straightedge.
2. If warpage exceeds 0.004 in. (0.1mm) over the total length, the cylinder head must be resurfaced.

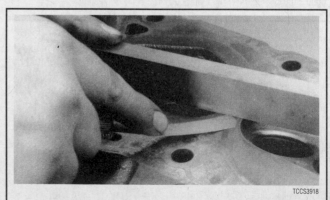

TCCS3918

Fig. 83 Check the cylinder head for flatness across the head surface

Valves

REMOVAL & INSTALLATION

→**Use the following service procedures as a guide for your engine. Machine shop work requires special training and equipment, it is best to send the cylinder head assembly to a reputable machine shop for this kind of repair.**

2.2L and 2.5L Engines

♦ **See Figures 84, 85, 86 and 87**

1. Remove the cylinder head and rocker arms, as described earlier in this section.

2. Label all cylinder head components (i.e. valves and rocker components) so that they can be installed in their original positions.

3. Situate the cylinder head on a clean, flat work area so that the valves will be free to move downward. You'll need a valve spring compressor tool, such as Chrysler Tool No. 4682 (if the camshaft is still installed on the cylinder head) or C-3422-B (if the camshaft is removed from the cylinder head). Tool 4682 hooks around the thinnest diameter sections of the camshaft and pushes downward on either side of each valve spring retainer. Rotate the camshaft so the first rocker arm is under the base circle of the camshaft (the camshaft lobe should point away from the rocker arm). Tool C-3422-B is shaped like a large C, and is designed to compress the valve springs when the camshaft is removed from the cylinder head.

4. Remove all of the hydraulic lash adjusters from the cylinder head, keeping them in order. Support each valve from underneath as you work on it, then depress each valve spring retainer with the special tool. Remove the keepers from either side of the valve stem and then slowly release spring pressure. Remove the spring and spring retainer from the valve stem.

5. Remove the stem seal by gently prying it side-to-side with a small pry-tool blade. Work the seal off the guide post and remove it.

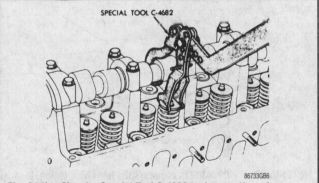

Fig. 84 Use Chrysler Special Tool C-4682 to depress the valve springs so that the spring locks can be removed

6. Repeat Steps 5 and 6 for each valve.

7. Inspect each valve's stem lock grooves for burrs and remove them prior to removing the valve, otherwise the valve guides may be damaged. Pull the valves out of the cylinder head.

To install:

8. Clean the cylinder head and cylinder head components. Inspect the valves, valve guides and valve springs for wear, as described later in this section.

9. Coat the valve stems with clean engine oil, and then insert each valve into the valve guide from the lower side of the cylinder head.

10. Install new valve seals by pushing each firmly and squarely over the guide so that the center bead of the seal lodges in the valve guide groove. The lower edge of the seal must rest on the valve guide boss. Note that if oversize valves have been installed, oversize seals must also be installed. Install the valve springs over the valve stem. Make sure that the springs are seated correctly on the cylinder head.

11. Support the valve you're working on from underneath. Install the valve spring retainer over each spring, depress the spring just enough to expose the grooves for the spring keepers. Make sure to depress the spring squarely so that the spring does not touch the valve stem. Install the keepers securely and raise the retainer slowly, making sure the keepers stay in position. Repeat this step for all valves, as needed.

12. Install each of the hydraulic lash adjusters in its proper position in the cylinder head.

13. Check the valve spring installed height, as described in the following inspection procedures. If it exceeds specifications, valve spring tension will not be adequate. If necessary, install a spring seat under each spring whose height is too great to make it meet specification.

14. Support the head so that the valves will be free to move downward. Install the rockers, each in its original position, in reverse of the removal procedure. Depress the valve spring retainers only enough to install the rockers, and make sure that the keepers remain in position.

15. Check the clearance between the ears of the rocker arm and the spring retainer for each valve with the lash adjuster empty of oil and fully collapsed. The minimum clearance is 0.050 in. (1.25mm). If the minimum clearance is not met, the rocker will have to be machined to create it.

16. After clearance specifications are met, remove the rockers and adjusters, immerse the adjusters in clean engine oil and pump them to prime them with oil.

17. Reinstall the adjusters and rockers.

→**Make sure to allow 10 minutes for the hydraulic lash adjusters to bleed down before installing the cylinder head on the engine, otherwise the hydraulic lash adjusters or valve stems may be damaged.**

2.6L Engine

♦ **See Figures 88, 89 and 90**

1. Remove the cylinder head as described above.

2. Label all of the cylinder head components so that they can be assembled into their original positions.

3. Remove the camshaft bearing caps and rocker shafts as an assembly. For more details, refer to the camshaft removal and installation and rocker arms/shafts removal and installation procedures in this section. Leave the bolts in the front and rear bearing caps.

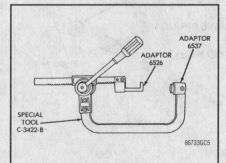

Fig. 85 Special Tool C-3422-B can also be used to depress the valve springs for spring lock removal

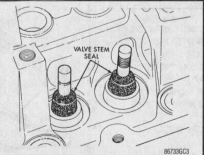

Fig. 86 Once the springs, spring retainers and spring locks are removed, the valve stem seals can be removed from the cylinder head

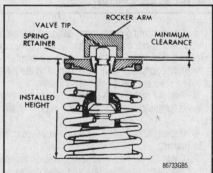

Fig. 87 Check the clearance between the valve rocker ears and spring retainers—minimum clearance is 0.050 in. (1.25mm)

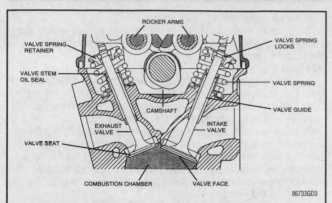

Fig. 88 Cross-section view of the intake and exhaust valves, valve springs, spring retainers, valve stem locks and rocker arms installed on the cylinder head

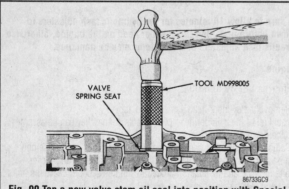

Fig. 89 Once the valves, springs, retainers and locks are removed, the valve stem seals can be removed from the cylinder head with a pair of pliers

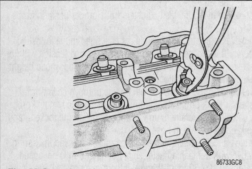

Fig. 90 Tap a new valve stem oil seal into position with Special Tool MD998005 and a hammer

4. Using a spring compressor designed for use on overhead cam engines with inclined valves, depress each valve spring, remove keepers, spring retainer, and spring, then remove each valve from the combustion chamber of the cylinder head. Support each valve while removing the valve keepers so that you do not have to depress the spring unnecessarily.

5. Remove each jet valve by unscrewing it with a special socket wrench designed for this purpose. Pull out the used valve stem seals with a pair of pliers.

6. Repeat Steps 2 and 3 for all of the valves in the cylinder head.

To install:

7. Clean the cylinder head and related components with a suitable solvent. Inspect the valves, valve springs, and valve guides, as described later in this section.

8. Valve stems should be coated with oil before each valve is installed.

9. Assemble the cylinder head, as follows:

a. Slide the valve into the cylinder head.

b. Install new valve seals onto the cylinder head by tapping them lightly with a special installer such as Chrysler part No. MD998005.

c. Set the valve spring over the valve stem so that it sits flush on the cylinder head.

d. Position the spring retainer on the spring.

e. Depress the valve spring and retainer, while supporting the valve from underneath.

f. Install the valve keepers in the grooves in the end of the valve stem.

g. Slowly release the valve spring until the keepers are held in place. Make sure you do not depress the retainers unnecessarily.

h. Check installed height and compare it with specification. If installed height is excessive, install a thicker spring seat until specifications are met by disassembling the valves, springs, and retainers again. Position the spring seats on the cylinder head, then reassemble the cylinder head components.

10. If equipped, install the jet valves by screwing them in. Tighten the jet valves to 14 ft. lbs. (19 Nm). The jet valves themselves have springs, retainers, keepers, and seals. Refer to the following procedure for jet valve disassembly.

11. Make sure in final assembly to set the jet valve clearance after the head bolts are tightened and before setting intake valve clearance. Both must finally be set with the engine hot.

12. Install the rocker arms and camshaft on the cylinder head, then install the cylinder head onto the engine.

JET VALVE DISASSEMBLY AND ASSEMBLY

▶ See Figures 91, 92 and 93

✳✳ WARNING

Make certain that the Jet Valve Socket wrench is not tilted with respect to the centerline of the jet valve. Any misalignment may bend the valve stem.

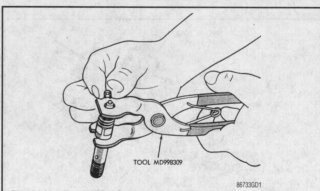

Fig. 91 Use Tool MD998309 to compress the jet valve's spring, then remove the spring keepers

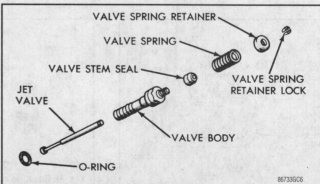

Fig. 92 Exploded view of the jet valve—make sure to coat all components with clean engine oil prior to reassembly

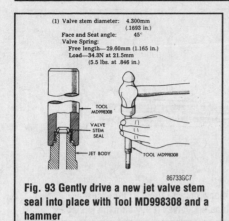

(1) Valve stem diameter: 4.300mm
(.1693 in.)
Face and Seat angle: 45°
Valve Spring:
Free length—29.60mm (1.165 in.)
Load—34.3N at 21.5mm
(5.5 lbs. at .846 in.)

TOOL MD998308
VALVE STEM SEAL
JET BODY
TOOL MD998308

86733GC7

Fig. 93 Gently drive a new jet valve stem seal into place with Tool MD998308 and a hammer

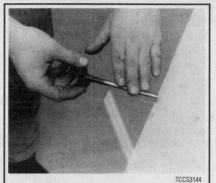

TCCS3144

Fig. 94 Valve stems may be rolled on a flat surface to check for bends

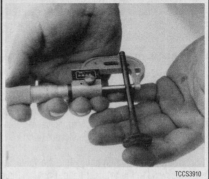

TCCS3910

Fig. 95 Use a micrometer to check the valve stem diameter

1. Remove the jet valve from the cylinder head by loosening it with a socket wrench.

2. Using Tool MD998309 to compress the spring, remove the retainer lock and retainer.

➡**Do not mix the parts of the jet valve assemblies.**

3. Pull the valve stem and seal off with a pair of pliers.

4. When assembling, use engine oil to lubricate all of the parts of the jet valve assembly.

5. Using Tool MD998309 to compress the spring, install the retainer and retainer lock.

6. Install a new O-ring lubricated with engine oil on the jet valve.

7. Install the jet valve in the cylinder head and tighten it to 14 ft. lbs. (19 Nm).

INSPECTION

♦ **See Figures 94 and 95**

2.2L (Except Turbo III) and 2.5L Engines

♦ **See Figure 96**

1. Clean the valves thoroughly and discard burned, warped, or cracked valves.

2. If the valve face is only lightly pitted, the valve may be refaced to the correct angle by a qualified machine shop.

3. Measure the valve stem for wear at various points and check it against the specifications shown in the "Valve Specifications" chart.

4. Once the valve face has been cleaned up, the margin must also be checked. This is the thickness of the valve head below the face. Valves must also meet standards as to head diameter and length. If the valves do not match specifications, new valves must be purchased.

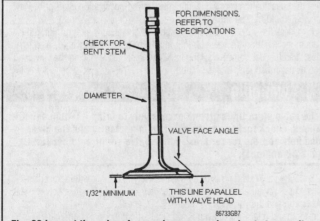

FOR DIMENSIONS, REFER TO SPECIFICATIONS

CHECK FOR BENT STEM

DIAMETER

VALVE FACE ANGLE

1/32" MINIMUM
THIS LINE PARALLEL WITH VALVE HEAD

86733GB7

Fig. 96 Inspect the valves for any damage, such as bent stems, pitting or scratching, nicks or incorrect face angle

VALVE STEM-TO-GUIDE CLEARANCE

♦ **See Figure 97**

1. Clean the valve stem with lacquer thinner or a similar solvent to remove all gum and varnish. Clean the valve guides using solvent and an expanding wire-type valve guide cleaner (a rifle cleaning brush works well here).

2. Use a dial indicator to measure the lateral movement of the valve head (stem-to-guide clearance) with the valve installed in its guide and with the valve head approximately 0.40 in. (10mm) off the valve seat, as follows:

   a. Position a dial indicator so that the indicator shaft is seated against the side of the valve head above the combustion chamber.

   b. Push the head as far away from the dial indicator as it will travel, then zero the dial indicator.

   c. Push the valve head toward the dial indicator as far as it will go and read the measurement on the indicator.

   d. Position the dial indicator against the valve head 90 degrees around the head from its original position and repeat Steps 7b and 7c.

3. Refer to the Valve Specifications chart for the correct clearance allowable. If indicated movement exceeds the correct specification, have the valve guide reamed by a reputable machine shop to accommodate an oversized valve stem. Also, if the 2 measurements are different, this indicates the extent of out-of-roundness in the valve guide.

➡**Valve seats should be reground after reaming the valve guides to ensure that the valve seat is concentric to the valve guide.**

86733GC4

Fig. 97 To measure the valve-to-guide clearance, move the valve head toward and away from the dial indicator and read the fluctuation

2.2L Turbo III Engine

♦ **See Figure 96**

1. Clean all carbon deposits from the combustion chambers, valve ports, valve stems, valve stem guides and cylinder head.

2. Clean all grime and gasket material from the cylinder head gasket surface.

3. Inspect for cracks in the combustion chambers and valve ports.

4. Inspect for cracks in the gasket surface at each coolant passage.
5. Inspect valves for burned, cracked or warped heads. Inspect for scuffed or bent valve stems.
6. Replace the valves if any such damage is evident.

VALVE STEM-TO-GUIDE CLEARANCE

▶ **See Figure 98**

1. Remove the valve from the cylinder head.
2. Clean the valve stem with lacquer thinner or a similar solvent to remove all gum and varnish. Clean the valve guides using solvent and an expanding wire-type valve guide cleaner (a rifle cleaning brush works well here).
3. Insert a telescoping gauge into the valve stem guide bore, with contacts crosswise to the cylinder head. Position the gauge at the top of the valve guide bore. Remove and measure the telescoping gauge with a micrometer.
4. Insert the telescoping gauge into the valve stem guide bore so that it is at the mid-point of the valve guide. Remove and measure the telescoping gauge with a micrometer.
5. Once again, insert the telescoping gauge into the valve stem guide bore. Position the gauge at the very bottom of the valve guide bore. Remove and measure the telescoping gauge with a micrometer.
6. Repeat all 3 measurements with the gauge turned perpendicular (90 degrees) from the first positions.
7. Compare the crosswise-to-lengthwise measurements to determine out-of-roundness. Compare the 3 measurements (top, mid-point and bottom) for valve guide taper or unevenness. If the measurements differ excessively (refer to the Valve Specifications chart), have the guide bore reamed by a reputable automotive machine shop to accommodate an oversized valve stem.
8. Compare the measured valve guide bore diameter with specifications. If the measurement differs from specifications, have the guide bore reamed by a reputable machine shop to accommodate an oversized valve stem.

➡Valve seats should be reground after reaming the valve guides to ensure that the valve seat is concentric to the valve guide.

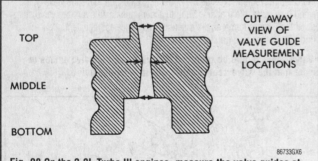

Fig. 98 On the 2.2L Turbo III engines, measure the valve guides at the positions shown

2.6L Engine

▶ **See Figure 99**

1. Clean all carbon deposits from the combustion chambers, valve ports, valve stems, valve stem guides and cylinder head.
2. Clean all grime and gasket material from the cylinder head gasket surface.
3. Inspect for cracks in the combustion chambers and valve ports. Inspect for cracks in the gasket surface at each coolant passage. Inspect valves for burned, cracked or warped heads. Inspect for scuffed or bent valve stems. Replace the valves if any such damage is evident.
4. Check the tip of the stem for pitting (A).
5. Check the stem-to-guide clearance (B). It must meet the specifications in the Valve Specifications chart.
6. Check the valve head margin, which must meet specifications.
7. If the valves are deemed reusable, have the valves refaced by a reputable, competent automotive machine shop.

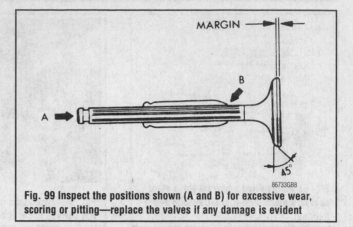

Fig. 99 Inspect the positions shown (A and B) for excessive wear, scoring or pitting—replace the valves if any damage is evident

REFACING

➡Because of the high cost of equipment and the high level of skill required for valve and valve seat refacing, it is recommended that you should have the valves and seats refaced by a reputable automotive machine shop.

1. The intake and exhaust valves and seats should be refaced until they exhibit the angle shown in the Valve Specification chart. Have a reputable automotive machine shop perform this work.
2. Inspect the remaining margin after the valves are refaced. If the margin does not meet the specifications in the Valve Specification chart, the valves should be disposed of and new ones acquired.
3. When refacing the valve seats, it is important that the correct size valve guide pilot be used for reseating stones. A true and complete surface must be obtained.
4. Measure the concentricity of the valve seat using a valve seat dial indicator. Total runout should not exceed the value shown in the Valve Specifications or Engine Rebuilding Specifications charts.
5. Inspect the valve seat with Prussian blue to determine where the valve contacts the seat. To do this, perform the following:
    a. Coat the valve seat **lightly** with Prussian blue, then set the valve in place in the cylinder head.
    b. Rotate the valve with light pressure applied to the valve head.
    c. Remove the valve from the cylinder head.
    d. Inspect the valve seat. If the blue is transferred to the center of the valve face, contact is satisfactory. If the blue is transferred to the top edge of the valve face, lower the valve seat with a 15 degree stone. If the blue is transferred to the bottom edge of the valve face, raise the valve seat with a 65 degree stone.

➡Valve seats which are worn or burned can be reworked, provided that correct angle and seat width are maintained. Otherwise the cylinder head must be replaced.

6. When the seat is properly positioned, the width of the intake seats should meet the specifications shown in either the Valve Specification chart or the Engine Rebuilding Specifications chart.
7. Check the valve tip-to-valve spring seat dimensions after grinding the seats or faces, Grind the valve tip to bring the measurements within specifications. Also inspect the valve spring installed height after refacing the valve and seat, as described later in this section.

❊❊❊ WARNING

If the valve stem tip is ground excessively to bring it within specifications, check rocker arm-to-valve stem geometry and the clearance between the rocker arm and the valve spring retainer (2.2L and 2.5L engines).

8. If the valve stem tip is ground excessively to bring it within specifications, check rocker arm-to-valve stem geometry and the clearance between the rocker arm and the valve spring retainer (2.2L and 2.5L engines). If the rocker arm-to-spring retainer clearance is too small, grind the rocker arm ears to provide the correct amount of space.

Valve Stem Seals

REMOVAL & INSTALLATION

▶ **See Figures 100, 101, 102 and 103**

Cylinder Head Removed From Engine

For the complete removal and installation procedure of the valve stem oil seals, please refer to the valve procedures earlier in this section.

Cylinder Head Installed On Engine

➡**To perform this procedure a compressor and air hose with a spark plug hole adapter fitting is necessary.**

1. Remove the rocker arms, as described earlier in this section.
2. With the air hose attached to the spark plug adapter tool and installed in the spark plug hole, apply 90–120 psi (620–827 kPa) air pressure to the cylinder. This amount of air pressure should hold the valves against their seats; if this does not hold the valves against their seats, the seats and/or valves should be machined.
3. Use Spring Compressor Tool C-4682, or equivalent, to compress the valve springs only enough to remove the spring keepers. Make sure to compress only the spring, not the valve itself. If the valve stem is pushed into the cylinder the air pressure will be lost and will need to be reapplied before commencing with the procedure.
4. Once the spring keepers are removed, slowly release the compression on the valve spring. Remove the valve spring retainer and valve spring.
5. Tie a piece of string or wrap a rubber band around the valve stem tip to prevent it from accidentally falling into the cylinder, which would require removal of the cylinder head to retrieve.
6. Remove the old valve seal from the cylinder head with a pair of pliers or by gently prying side-to-side on the valve seal with a small prytool. Make sure not to accidentally push the valve down.

➡Since only one air hose is being used, only one cylinder can be serviced at one time.

To install:

7. Install new valve seals by pushing each firmly and squarely over the guide so that the center bead of the seal lodges in the valve guide groove. The lower edge of the seal must rest on the valve guide boss. Note that if oversize valves have been installed, oversize seals must also be installed.
8. Install the valve springs over the valve stem. Make sure that the springs are seated correctly on the cylinder head.
9. Install the valve spring retainer over each spring, depress the spring just enough to expose the grooves for the spring keepers. Make sure to depress the spring squarely so that the spring does not touch the valve stem.
10. Install the keepers securely and raise the retainer slowly, making sure the keepers stay in position.
11. Remove the air hose and spark plug adapter from the spark plug hole.
12. Once both the intake and exhaust valve springs, retainers and keepers are in position, proceed to the next cylinder requiring servicing. Perform this procedure for each cylinder, one-at-a-time.
13. Install the rocker arms, as described earlier in this section.

Valve Springs

REMOVAL & INSTALLATION

The valve springs are removed and installed as described under the Valve Stem Seal Removal and Installation procedures. Please refer to those procedures.

INSPECTION

▶ **See Figure 104**

1. Place the valve spring on a flat surface next to a carpenter's square. Measure the height of the spring, and rotate the spring against the edge of the

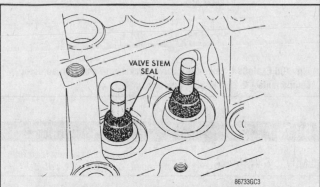

Fig. 100 Once the valve springs, locks, and retainers are removed from the cylinder head the valve stem oil seals can be removed

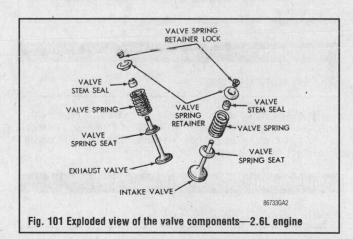

Fig. 101 Exploded view of the valve components—2.6L engine

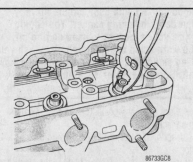

Fig. 102 On 2.6L engines, use a pair of pliers to remove the old valve stem seals—make sure to avoid pushing the valve down into the cylinder head

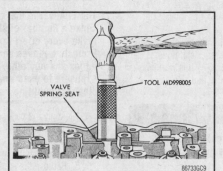

Fig. 103 Use the Tool MD998005 to install new valve stem oil seals onto the cylinder head on 2.6L engines

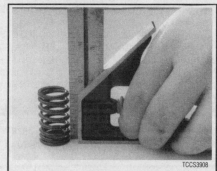

Fig. 104 Check the valve spring for squareness on a flat surface; a carpenter's square can be used

square to measure distortion. If the spring height varies (by comparison) by more than ⅟₁₆ in. (1.6mm) or if the distortion exceeds ⅟₁₆ in. (1.6mm), replace the spring.

2. Test the valve springs for correct spring pressure at the installed and compressed (installed height minus valve lift) height using a valve spring tester. Springs should be within one pound, plus or minus, of each other. Replace springs if they do not meet the specifications shown in either the Valve Specification or Engine Rebuilding Specifications charts.

Valve Spring Installed Height

▶ See Figure 105

After installing the valve spring, measure the distance between the spring mounting pad and the lower edge of the spring retainer. Compare the measurement to the specifications shown in either the Valve Specification or Engine Rebuilding Specifications charts. If the installed height is not within specification, add shim washers between the spring mounting pad and the spring. Use only washers designed for valve springs.

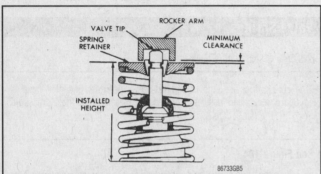

Fig. 105 After the valve springs are installed, check the spring height—add washers under the spring to bring the height down to specification

Valve Seats

REMOVAL & INSTALLATION

The seats are integral with the aluminum cylinder head on all engines and can only be machined to specification, not replaced. If a seat is too worn to be brought to specification, the head must be replaced. Refer to the valve refacing procedures earlier in this section for more information.

Valve Guides

REMOVAL & INSTALLATION

Valve guides are replaceable, but it is necessary to first make sure the valve seats can be brought to specification. If the valve seats cannot be refaced, the head must be replaced anyway.

Worn guides should be pressed out from the combustion chamber side and new guides pressed in as far as they will go. In some cases, existing guides can be "knurled" to restore the inside diameter to specifications. All this work must be performed by a reputable machine shop, as special skills and extremely sophisticated special equipment are required.

✳✳ WARNING

Service valve guides have a shoulder. Once the guide is seated, do not use more than 1 ton (8896 N) pressure or the guide shoulder could break.

Valve Lifters

REMOVAL & INSTALLATION

▶ See Figure 106

➡**When removing valve train components, make sure to keep the parts in order so that they can be installed in their original positions.**

The 2.6L engines do utilize valve lifters. These engines use a solid adjuster screw to adjust the valve lash.

The removal and installation procedures for the valve lifters, also known as hydraulic valve lash adjusters, utilized in the other Chrysler engines is included in with the rocker arms/shafts procedures earlier in this section. Please refer to these procedures for the applicable procedure.

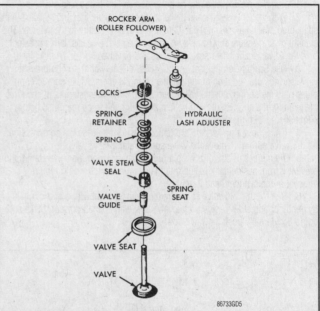

Fig. 106 Exploded view of the valve, rocker arm and lash adjuster components—2.2L and 2.5L engines

Oil Pan

REMOVAL & INSTALLATION

▶ See Figures 107 thru 112

✳✳ CAUTION

The EPA warns that prolonged contact with used engine oil may cause a number of skin disorders, including cancer! You should make every effort to minimize your exposure to used engine oil. Protective gloves should be worn when changing the oil. Wash your hands and any other exposed skin areas as soon as possible after exposure to used engine oil. Soap and water, or waterless hand cleaner should be used.

1. Apply the parking brake, block the rear wheels, then raise and safely support the front of the vehicle on jackstands.
2. Drain the engine oil, as described in Section 1. This would also be a good time to change the oil filter.
3. Remove the engine-to-transaxle struts, if so equipped. These struts prohibit access to the oil pan mounting bolts.

Fig. 107 After raising the vehicle, remove the oil pan attaching bolts . . .

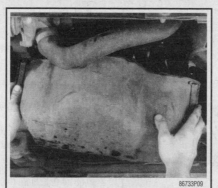

Fig. 108 . . . then lower the oil pan from the engine block

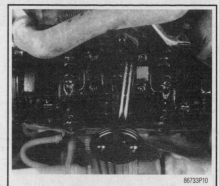

Fig. 109 Once the oil pan is removed, access to the oil pump can be gained

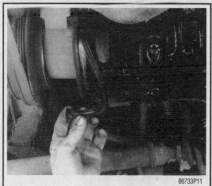

Fig. 110 Remove the old oil pan end gaskets from the engine block

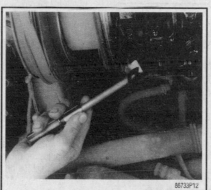

Fig. 111 Use a scraper, if necessary, to remove the old side gaskets

Fig. 112 Apply sealant to the ends of the new oil pan end seals at the junction of the cylinder block pan rail gasket— 1988–95 2.2L and 2.5L engines

4. Remove the torque converter or clutch inspection cover.
5. Support the oil pan and remove the mounting bolts.
6. Lower the pan and remove the old gasket, if so equipped.

To install:

7. Clean all gasket surfaces thoroughly.
8. For 2.6L engines, position a new gasket on the oil pan using a sealer to hold it in place.

➡**1981–87 2.2 and 2.5 Liter engine uses a liquid form-in-place type gasket. Chrysler Part Number 4205918, or equivalent RTV gasket material must be used.**

9. For 1981–87 2.2 and 2.5L engines, install new end seals and apply the form-in-place gasket sealant. The RTV gasket material should be applied in a continuous bead approximately ⅛ in. (3mm) in diameter. All mounting holes must be circled. Uncured RTV may be removed with a rag. The oil pan should be tightened in place while the RTV is still wet to the touch (within 10 minutes). The usage of a locating dowel is recommended during assembly to prevent smearing of the material off location. Make sure to apply sealer where the end seals meet the block.

➡**1988–95 2.2L and 2.5L engines utilize end seals and side gaskets, not liquid gasket as with 1981–87 models.**

10. On 1988–95 2.2L and 2.5L engines, install new end seals and side gaskets. Apply RTV sealant to the parting lines between the end and side seals on these engines. If necessary, use a little grease or RTV sealant to hold the side seals in place.
11. Tighten the pan bolts in a crisscross fashion, starting from the center of the oil pan and working toward the ends, to the following torque values:
- 2.6L engine—53–61 inch lbs. (5.9–6.8 Nm)
- 1981–87 2.2L and 2.5L engines—16 ft. lbs. (22 Nm)
- 1988–95 2.2L and 2.5L engines—M8 bolts, 16 ft. lbs. (22 Nm); M6 bolt, 105 inch lbs. (12 Nm)
12. Allow the oil pan to sit for 15 minutes to ensure that the RTV sealant has completely set.
13. Install the oil drain plug and a new oil filter, if equipped, then lower the vehicle.

14. Refill the engine with oil, as described in Section 1.
15. Start the engine and check for oil leaks.

Oil Pump

REMOVAL

✳✳ CAUTION

The EPA warns that prolonged contact with used engine oil may cause a number of skin disorders, including cancer! You should make every effort to minimize your exposure to used engine oil. Protective gloves should be worn when changing the oil. Wash your hands and any other exposed skin areas as soon as possible after exposure to used engine oil. Soap and water, or waterless hand cleaner should be used.

2.2L and 2.5L Engines

◗ See Figures 113, 114 and 115

➡**Many of the following steps pertain to engines with a distributor. Disregard these steps when working on Turbo III engine. Since that engine does not have a distributor, the oil pump can be installed without timing the distributor gear. The oil pump on all other engines must be properly timed.**

1. Position the engine so that the No. 1 piston is at TDC of its compression stroke, as follows:
   a. Remove the upper timing belt cover.
   b. Turn the engine until the timing marks on the flywheel are aligned with the timing mark on the transaxle housing, and the timing mark on the camshaft sprocket is aligned with the timing mark on the cylinder head; this will position the engine so that the No. 1 piston is at TDC of its compression stroke.

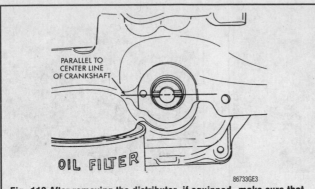

Fig. 113 After removing the distributor, if equipped, make sure that the oil pump shaft groove is positioned as shown

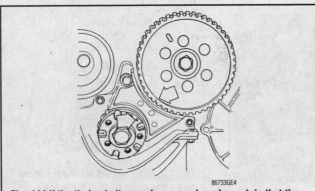

Fig. 114 If the timing belt cover is removed, make certain that the crankshaft and intermediate shaft timing marks are aligned

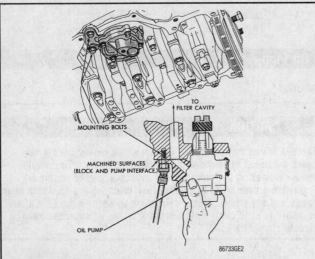

Fig. 115 Remove the oil pump retaining bolts, then remove the pump from the engine

2. Disconnect the negative battery cable.

3. If equipped, remove the distributor, as described in Section 2. Look down the distributor mounting hole and make sure that the oil pump shaft groove is parallel to the centerline of the engine block (crankshaft axis).

4. Remove the engine oil dipstick.

5. Apply the parking brake, block the rear wheels, then raise and safely support the front of the vehicle on jackstands.

6. Drain the engine oil. For more information, refer to Section 1.

7. Remove the oil pan, as described earlier in this section.

8. Remove the oil pick-up by removing the screw on the pump cover holding the oil pick-up tube to the oil pump.

9. Remove the 2 mounting bolts, then remove the oil pump from the engine.

2.6L Engine

For the removal and installation of the oil pump for these engines, refer to the auxiliary (silent shafts) procedure later in this section.

INSPECTION

2.2L and 2.5L Engines

▶ **See Figures 116, 117 and 118**

1. Inspect rotor end clearance with a feeler gauge. Place straightedge across the ends of the gears and the rotors. Select a feeler gauge that fits snugly, but freely between the straightedge and the pump body. Correct clearance is 0.0010–0.0035 in. (0.03–0.09mm).

2. With both gears in position, measure the inner rotor-to-outer rotor clearance by inserting a feeler gauge between the gear tooth and the pump outer rotor inner wall directly opposite the point of gear mesh. Select a feeler gauge which fits snugly, but freely. Rotate the gears to measure each tooth-to-body clearance in this manner.

3. Correct clearance is 0.008 in. (0.20mm) maximum.

4. Insert a feeler gauge between the outer rotor and the oil pump housing. Select a feeler gauge which fits snugly, but freely. Rotate the gears to measure each tooth-to-body clearance in this manner.

5. Correct clearance is 0.014 in. (0.35mm) maximum.

6. Inspect the oil pump cover for flatness by placing a straightedge on the underside of the pump cover. Use feeler gauges to determine if the cover is warped or not. The maximum amount of warpage allowed is 0.003 in. (0.076mm).

7. If the rotor end clearance or gear-to-body clearance is more than specified, replace the oil pump assembly.

8. Inspect the oil pressure relief valve spring as follows:
   a. Remove the cotter pin from the relief valve spring housing.
   b. Slide the cup, spring and relief valve out of the housing.
   c. Clean the relief valve, spring and cup with a suitable solvent.
   d. Measure the oil pressure relief valve spring free-length. The free length should be 1.95 in. (49.5mm).
   e. If the free-length is not the specified length, replace the spring.
   f. Install the relief valve, spring and cup into the pump housing, then install a new cotter pin.

2.6L Engine

▶ **See Figures 119, 120, 121, 122 and 123**

1. Inspect drive gear and driven gear end clearance with a feeler gauge. Place straightedge across the ends of the gears and the pump body. Select a feeler gauge that fits snugly, but freely between the straightedge and the drive gear. Correct clearance is 0.0020–0.0043 in. (0.05–0.11mm). Select a feeler gauge that fits snugly, but freely between the straightedge and the driven gear. Correct clearance is 0.0016–0.0039 in. (0.04–0.10mm).

2. With both gears in position, measure the driven gear-to-body clearance by inserting a feeler gauge between the driven gear tooth and the pump body inner wall directly opposite the point of gear mesh. Select a feeler gauge which fits snugly, but freely. Rotate the gears to measure each driven gear tooth-to-body clearance in this manner. Correct clearance is 0.0043–0.0059 in. (0.11–0.15mm) maximum.

3. With both gears in position, measure the drive gear-to-body clearance by inserting a feeler gauge between the drive gear tooth and the pump body inner wall directly opposite the point of gear mesh. Select a feeler gauge which fits snugly, but freely. Rotate the gears to measure each drive gear tooth-to-body clearance in this manner. Correct clearance is 0.0043–0.0059 in. (0.11–0.15mm) maximum.

4. If the rotor end clearance or gear-to-body clearance is more than specified, replace the oil pump assembly.

5. Inspect the oil pressure relief valve spring as follows:
   a. Remove the spring hole plug.
   b. Slide the spring and relief valve out of the housing.
   c. Clean the relief valve and spring with a suitable solvent.
   d. Measure the oil pressure relief valve spring free-length. The free length should be 1.850 in. (47mm).
   e. If the free-length is not the specified length, replace the spring.

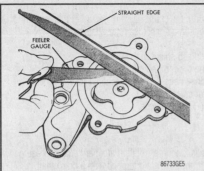

Fig. 116 Check the rotor end clearance with a straightedge and a feeler gauge as shown

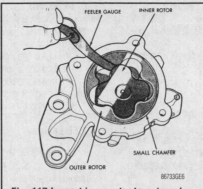

Fig. 117 Inspect inner rotor-to-outer rotor clearance as shown

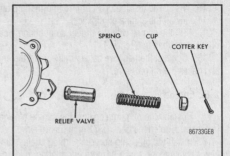

Fig. 118 The spring cup, spring and relief valve are held in the pump housing by a cotter pin—make certain to clean all components before reassembly

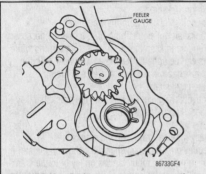

Fig. 119 Use feeler gauge to measure the driven gear-to-pump housing clearance, as shown

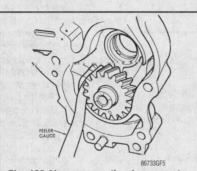

Fig. 120 Also measure the clearance of the drive gear to the pump housing—the clearance should be 0.0043–0.0059 in. (0.11–0.15mm)

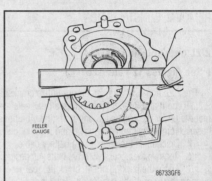

Fig. 121 Use a straightedge and feeler gauges to measure the driven (shown) and drive gear (similar) end-play

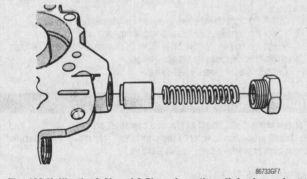

Fig. 122 Unlike the 2.2L and 2.5L engines, the relief valve spring on 2.6L engines is held into the pump housing by a screw-in plug

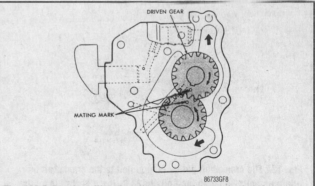

Fig. 123 Before installing the oil pump, make certain that the mating marks on the 2 gears are aligned as shown

f. Install the relief valve and spring into the pump housing, then install the spring hole plug.

6. Align the drive and drive gear mating marks as shown.

7. Fill the oil pump assembly with 0.34 fl. oz. (10cc) of clean engine oil before installing it onto the engine.

INSTALLATION

2.2L and 2.5L Engines

1. Prime the pump by pouring fresh oil into the pump intake and turning the driveshaft until oil comes out the pressure port. Repeat a few times until no air bubbles are present.

2. Apply Loctite® 515, or equivalent, to the pump body-to-block machined surface.

3. Lubricate the oil pump and distributor driveshaft with clean engine oil.

4. Align the slot so it will be in the same position as when it was removed (parallel to the engine centerline). If it is not, the distributor will not be timed correctly.

5. Slide the oil pump shaft into the engine hole, push the pump against the engine block fully while rotating the pump back and forth to ensure proper positioning between the pump mounting surface and the machined surface of the block.

6. Install the mounting bolts finger-tight.

7. From above the engine, look down the distributor mounting hole to ensure that the oil pump shaft groove is properly positioned. If the slot is not properly positioned, raise the vehicle and move the gear as required. If the slot is correct, hold the pump firmly against the block and tighten the mounting bolts to 17 ft. lbs. (23 Nm).

8. Clean out the oil pick-up or replace it, as required. Install the oil pick-up O-ring, then install the pick-up to the pump.

9. Install the oil pan, as described earlier in this section.

10. Install the distributor. For more information, refer to Section 2.

11. Install the engine oil dipstick.

12. Fill the engine with the proper amount and type of clean, fresh engine oil, as described in Section 1.

13. Connect the negative battery cable, start the engine, check the timing and check the oil pressure.

2.6L Engine

1. Position the oil pump against the engine block and install the mounting fasteners. Tighten the bolts to 71 inch lbs. (8 Nm).

2. Install the oil pump sprocket, timing chains, timing chain cover and a new front cover oil seal. For more information, refer to the timing chain cover and seal and timing chain removal and installation procedures later in this section.

Crankshaft Damper/Pulley

REMOVAL & INSTALLATION

2.2L and 2.5L Engines

▶ See Figures 124 and 125

The 2.2L and 2.5L engines do not utilize crankshaft mounted dampers. The 2.2L Turbo II and 2.5L engines utilize a dual-balance shaft system which mounts under the engine to control engine vibrations. This procedure will describe crankshaft pulley removal and installation.

1. Disconnect the negative (-) battery cable.

2. Remove the accessory drive belts, as described in Section 1.

3. Apply the parking brake, block the rear wheels, then raise and safely support the front of the vehicle on jackstands.

4. Remove the right inner splash shield from the wheel well.

5. Loosen and remove the retaining bolts holding the pulley to the crankshaft. Pull the pulley off of the crankshaft flange.

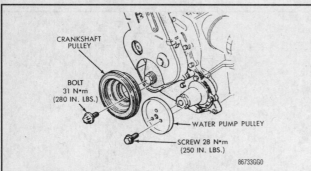

Fig. 124 The crankshaft pulley is mounted to the crankshaft by retaining bolts—tighten the bolts to 23 ft. lbs. (31 Nm) in a crisscross pattern—except 2.2L Turbo III engines

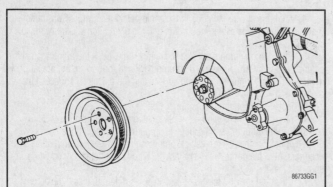

Fig. 125 The 2.2L Turbo III engines use 5 pulley-to-crankshaft flange mounting bolts, which are also tightened to 23 ft. lbs. (31 Nm)

To install:

6. Slide the pulley back onto the crankshaft and secure in place with the attaching bolts. Tighten the bolts in a crisscross (star-shaped) pattern to 23 ft. lbs. (31 Nm).

7. Install the right inner splash shield in the wheel well.

8. Lower the vehicle to the ground and remove the wheel blocks.

9. Install the accessory drive belts. Refer to Section 1 for the procedures on tightening the drive belts for correct tension.

10. Connect the negative (-) battery cable.

2.6L Engine

Since the 2.6L engine utilizes 2 counter-rotating auxiliary shafts to dampen the vibrations of the crankshaft, they are not equipped with a crankshaft mounted damper. This procedure will cover removal and installation of the crankshaft pulley.

1. Disconnect the negative (-) battery cable.

2. Remove the accessory drive belts, as described in Section 1.

3. Apply the parking brake, block the rear wheels, then raise and safely support the front of the vehicle on jackstands.

4. Remove the right inner splash shield from the wheel well.

5. Remove the center crankshaft pulley retaining bolt. It may be necessary to have an assistant hold the engine to keep the crankshaft from turning while loosening the center bolt. This can be done by having an assistant hold the flywheel/flexplate stable with a wrench, a breaker bar or even a C-clamp.

6. Pull the pulley off of the crankshaft.

7. After the pulley is removed, make certain to locate the crankshaft key (if equipped). This key will be needed upon installation.

To install:

8. Install the crankshaft key into the groove on the crankshaft.

9. Slide the crankshaft pulley onto the crankshaft after aligning the slot in the pulley with the key on the crankshaft. Lightly tap the pulley onto the crankshaft with a rubber or plastic mallet. Tap the center of the pulley, not the outer edges.

10. After the pulley is installed slightly onto the crankshaft, install the center bolt and slowly tighten the bolt until the pulley seats itself completely onto the crankshaft.

11. Tighten the center bolt to 87 ft. lbs. (118 Nm) while your assistant holds the engine from turning.

12. Install the right inner splash shield in the wheel well.

13. Lower the vehicle to the ground and remove the wheel blocks.

14. Install the accessory drive belts. Refer to Section 1 for the procedures on tightening the drive belts for correct tension.

15. Connect the negative (-) battery cable.

Timing Belt Cover and Seal

➡️For the crankshaft, silent shafts and camshaft oil seals removal and installation procedures, refer to the crankshaft, camshaft and intermediate sprocket procedure later in this section

REMOVAL & INSTALLATION

▶ See Figures 126, 127, 128, 129 and 130

➡️The 2.2L and 2.5L engines do not use a timing belt cover oil seal since the timing belt runs dry. These engines also utilize timing chains to synchronize the crankshaft, auxiliary and balance shafts. For the front crankshaft oil seal, refer to the timing chain procedure later in this section.

➡️The 2.6L engines are equipped with timing chains.

2.2L and 2.5L Engines

▶ See Figures 131, 132 and 133

1. Disconnect the negative battery cable.

2. Remove the accessory drive belts. For more information, refer to Section 1.

3. Remove the nuts and bolts that attach the upper cover to the valve cover, block or cylinder head.

4. Remove the bolt that attaches the upper cover to the lower cover.

Fig. 126 Remove the upper timing belt attaching nuts and screws, then . . .

Fig. 127 . . . lift the upper cover off of the engine

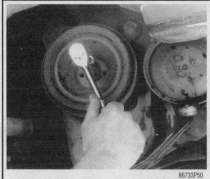

Fig. 128 Loosen and remove the crankshaft pulley attaching bolts, then . . .

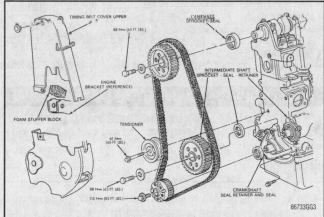

Fig. 129 . . . pull the pulley off of the crankshaft

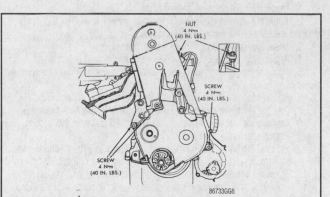

Fig. 130 Remove the lower timing belt cover attaching fasteners and remove the cover

Fig. 131 Exploded view of the timing belt and the upper and lower timing belt covers—2.2L (except Turbo III) and 2.5L engines

Fig. 132 Timing belt cover attaching fasteners for non-Turbo III models

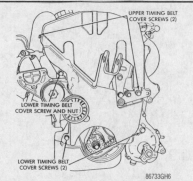

Fig. 133 Upper and lower timing belt cover fasteners for 2.2L Turbo III models

5. Remove the upper cover.

6. Apply the parking brake, block the rear wheels, then raise and safely support the front of the vehicle on jackstands.

7. Remove the right, front wheel, then remove the right-hand inner splash shield.

8. Remove the bolts from the crankshaft and water pump pulleys, then remove both pulleys.

9. Remove the lower timing cover retaining fasteners from the engine block and cylinder head.

10. Remove the lower timing belt cover from the engine.

To install:

11. Position the lower timing belt cover on the engine, then install the retaining fasteners. Make sure that the spacers and washers are installed in their original positions.

12. Tighten the fasteners until snug.

13. Install the water pump and crankshaft pulleys, as described earlier in this section.

14. Install the splash shield and front wheel.

15. Lower the vehicle and remove the wheel blocks.

16. Position the upper cover on the engine, then install the mounting fasteners until snug.

17. Install the accessory drive belts.

18. Connect the negative battery cable.

Timing Chain Cover and Seal

REMOVAL & INSTALLATION

✳✳ CAUTION

When draining the coolant, keep in mind that cats and dogs are attracted by the ethylene glycol antifreeze, and are quite likely to drink any that is left in an uncovered container or in puddles on the ground. This will prove fatal in sufficient quantity. Always drain the coolant into a sealable container. Coolant should be reused unless it is contaminated or several years old.

2.6L Engine

▶ See Figure 134

➥All 2.6 engines are equipped with 2 balance shafts which cancel the vertical vibrating force of the engine and the secondary vibrating forces, which include the sideways rocking of the engine due to the turning direction of the crankshaft and other rolling parts. The shafts are driven by a duplex chain and are turned by the crankshaft. The silent shaft chain assembly is mounted in front of the timing chain assembly and must be removed to service the timing chain.

1. Disconnect the negative battery cable.

2. Apply the parking brake, block the rear wheels, then raise and safely support the front of the vehicle on jackstands.

3. Drain the radiator and remove it from the vehicle.

4. Remove the cylinder head, as described earlier in this section.

5. Remove the cooling fan, spacer, water pump pulley and accessory drive belts.

6. Remove the alternator. For more information, refer to Section 2.

7. Remove the water pump, as described earlier in this section.

8. Remove the oil pan and screen, as described earlier in this section.

9. Remove the crankshaft pulley.

10. Remove the bolts holding the timing indicator and the mounting plate. Remove the timing indicator and mounting plate from the timing chain cover.

11. Remove the timing case cover by removing the mounting bolts.

12. Position the timing chain cover on a clean work space with the outer face of the cover facing down. Arrange wooden blocks under the cover so that

there is room under the oil seal so that it can be driven out of the cover. Use an oil seal driver tool, or a socket which is sized so that it sits on the oil seal, to gently drive the oil seal out of the cover.

To install:

13. Clean the gasket surfaces on the timing chain cover and engine block of all oil, grime and old gasket material.

14. Lightly coat the outer diameter of the oil seal with Loctite® Stud N' Bearing Mount (PN-4057987), or equivalent.

15. Set the timing chain cover on the work space with the outer face of the cover facing up. Position a new oil seal in the oil seal bore, then gently drive the oil seal into the cover with an oil seal installer too or aptly sized socket. Make certain that the oil seal does not become cocked in the bore and that it is seated fully in the bore. Lubricate the oil seal lip with clean engine oil.

16. Clean the oil seal-to-crankshaft portion of the crankshaft stub.

17. Fit new chain cover gaskets to the chain case. Trim the gaskets as required to assure correct fit at the top and bottom.

18. Coat the cover gaskets with Chrysler Sealant 3419115, or equivalent, and install the coated gaskets and chain cover onto the engine block. Make sure not to damage the oil seal. Tighten the mounting bolts until snug.

19. Install the cylinder head and tighten the cylinder head-to-timing chain cover bolts to 13 ft. lbs. (18 Nm).

20. Install the oil screen and the oil pan, as described earlier in this section.

21. Install the crankshaft pulley, as described earlier in this section. Tighten the pulley mounting bolt to 87 ft. lbs. (118 Nm).

22. Install the alternator and the distributor. For more information, refer to Section 2.

23. Install the accessory drive belts, as described Section 1.

24. Connect the negative battery cable.

25. Install the cooling fan and radiator. For more information, refer to the procedures earlier in this section.

26. Fill the system with coolant, start the engine and check for coolant, oil and fuel leaks.

OIL SEAL REPLACEMENT WITH TIMING CASE COVER INSTALLED

1. Remove the crankshaft drive pulley, as described earlier in this section under vibration damper removal and installation procedures.

2. Pry the oil seal out of the cover, taking care not to nick or damage the sealing surfaces.

To install:

3. Install a new oil seal. Lightly coat the outside diameter with Loctite® Stud N' Bearing Mount (PN-4057987) or equivalent.

4. Install the crankshaft drive pulley. Tighten the bolt to 87 ft. lbs. (118 Nm).

Timing Belt

Of the three available 4-cylinder engines (2.2L, 2.5L and 2.6L), the 2.2L and 2.5L engines are equipped with timing belts. The engine comes equipped with timing chains.

INSPECTION

The timing chains generally do not need routine replacement or inspection, unless engine repairs are being done and inspection would be easy to do at the time. Timing belts do, however, need to be inspected at the 60,000 mile (96,000 km) mark. If the timing belt shows signs of wear or defects, the belt should be replaced at that time. If the timing belt is not replaced with a new one at 60,000 miles (96,000 km), the belt MUST be replaced at the 90,000 mile (144,000 km) mark.

Inspection of the timing belt is vitally important to prevent expensive repairs or extensive engine damage because of interference in the valvetrain. Often engine manufacturers design engines to such close tolerances that the relationship between the valves and the pistons is extremely precise. If the timing belt is slightly off or breaks, the valves and the pistons could actually strike each other. Engines designed like this are known as interference motors. The damage created when the valves and pistons hit at high, or even very low, engine speeds can be quite extensive. Often a valve head can be thrust right through the crown of the piston. Chrysler does not indicate that the 2.2L or the 2.5L engines are interference motors (therefore, if the belt breaks the valves and pistons allegedly will not come in contact), however it is still very important to inspect and replace, if necessary, the timing belt.

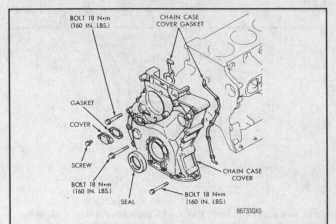

BOLT 18 N•m
(160 IN. LBS.)

CHAIN CASE
COVER GASKET

GASKET

COVER

SCREW

BOLT 18 N•m
(160 IN. LBS.)

SEAL

BOLT 18 N•m
(160 IN. LBS.)

CHAIN CASE
COVER

86733GK5

Fig. 134 Exploded view of the timing chain case cover and fasteners

Inspect both sides of the timing belt. For inspection the front timing belt cover will need removal, refer to Section 3 for this procedure. Replace the belt with a new one if any of the following conditions exist:

• Hardening of black rubber back side is glossy without resilience and leaves no indent when pressed with a fingernail.
• Cracks on rubber backing.
• Cracks or peeling of the canvas.
• Cracks on rib root.
• Cracks on belt sides.
• Missing teeth.
• Abnormal wear of belt sides. The sides are normal if they are sharp as if cut by a knife.

If none of these conditions exist, the belt does not need replacement (until it reaches 90,000 miles/144,000 km). The belt MUST be replaced at this interval.

REMOVAL & INSTALLATION

2.2L (Except 2.2L Turbo III) and 2.5L Engines

♦ See Figures 132, 135 thru 143

➡To perform this procedure, you will need a special tool No. C4703, or equivalent, to apply specified tension to the timing belt. Be careful not to allow the timing belt to come in contact with oil or any solvent, otherwise the teeth will be weakened.

1. Disconnect the negative battery cable.
2. Remove the timing belt cover, as described earlier in this section.
3. Remove the A/C compressor with the fluid lines attached. For more information, refer to Section 6. Set the compressor aside.
4. Remove the alternator pivot bolt and remove the alternator.
5. Remove the A/C compressor belt idler unit.
6. Position a hydraulic floor jack under the engine. Place a long block of wood between the floor jack lifting pad and the oil pan to spread the load of the engine in such a way that the oil pan will not be damaged. Raise the engine only until its weight is taken up by the floor jack, then remove the main through-bolt from the right engine mount—the one that is situated near the timing cover.

7. Remove the five A/C solid mount bracket side mounting bolts (No. 1, 4, 5, 6, and 7). Remove the front mounting nut (No. 2) and remove the front bolt (No. 3). Remove the front mounting bolt and strut, rotate the solid mount bracket away from the engine and slide the bracket on stud until free. Remove the spacer from the stud.

8. Raise the engine slightly more for access to the crankshaft sprocket.

9. Using the larger bolt on the crankshaft pulley, turn the engine until the No. 1 cylinder is at TDC of the compression stroke. At this point the valves for the No. 1 cylinder will be closed and the timing mark will be aligned with the pointer on the flywheel housing. Make sure that the dots on the camshaft sprocket and cylinder head are aligned.

10. Loosen the tensioner pulley center nut. Then, rotate the large hex counterclockwise to reduce belt tension. Now, slide the belt off the tensioner pulley, then the crankshaft, auxiliary shaft and camshaft pulleys.

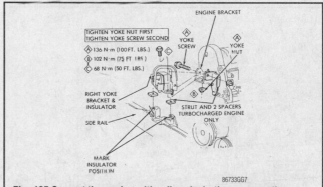

Fig. 135 Support the engine with a floor jack, then remove the engine mount through-bolt

Fig. 136 Rotate the crankshaft until the engine is at TDC for No. 1 cylinder, then matchmark the sprockets

Fig. 137 When at TDC, the camshaft sprocket hole should be at 12 o'clock

Fig. 138 Loosen the timing belt idler pulley, then remove the belt

Fig. 139 After the belt is removed, the idler pulley can also be removed

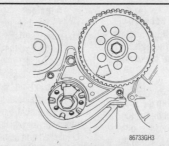

Fig. 140 Before installing the timing belt, make sure that the engine block and sprockets' timing marks are aligned—the crankshaft and intermediate shaft timing marks should be aligned as shown

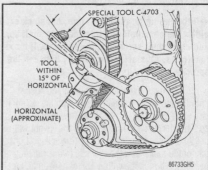

Fig. 141 Use Special Tool C-4703 to tension the timing belt—the tool should drop to within 15 degrees of the horizontal

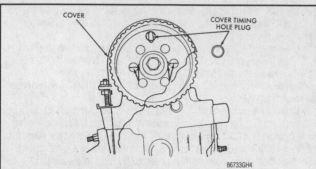

Fig. 142 To check timing, the small hole in the sprocket must be centered in the timing belt cover hole (with No. 1 at TDC of compression)

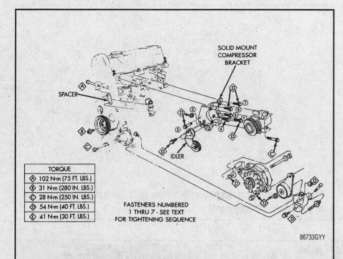

TORQUE	
◇	102 N·m (75 FT. LBS.)
◆	31 N·m (280 IN. LBS.)
◈	28 N·m (250 IN. LBS.)
◉	54 N·m (40 FT. LBS.)
◐	41 N·m (30 FT. LBS.)

Fig. 143 Exploded view of the solid mount compressor bracket and related torque values

To install:

11. Check that the V-notch or dot on the crankshaft pulley aligns with the dot mark or line on the intermediate shaft. Check also that the arrows on the hub of the camshaft are in line with the No. 1 camshaft cap-to-cylinder head line.

➡**If the timing marks are not perfectly aligned, poor engine performance and probable engine damage will result!**

12. Install the belt on the pulleys with the teeth located so as to perfectly maintain the alignment off all pulleys described in the removal procedure. Install the timing belt on the camshaft sprocket first, then, while keeping the belt taut, around the intermediate shaft sprocket. Finally wrap the belt under the crankshaft sprocket. All slack in the belt should be between the camshaft and crankshaft sprocket on the tensioner side.

➡**If the timing marks are in line, but slack exists in the belt between either the camshaft and intermediate shaft sprockets or the intermediate and crankshaft sprockets, the timing will be incorrect when the belt is tensioned. All slack must be only between the crankshaft and camshaft sprockets.**

13. Adjust the tensioner by installing special tool C-4703, or equivalent, onto the large hex. Install the tool with the weight hanging away from the auxiliary shaft drive pulley and allow its weight to tension the belt. Position the tool so that after its tension is applied, the weight will be as close as possible to the height of the center of the pulley (the lever is horizontal). Reset the position of the tool to make sure the tool sits in this position after its tension is applied, if necessary. It must be within 15° of horizontal. Finally, tighten the tensioner locknut to 32 ft. lbs. (44 Nm) for 1981–88 models, or to 45 ft. lbs. (61 Nm) for 1989–95 models. Do not tighten the tensioner tool too tight, otherwise it could cause the belt to howl or possibly break.

14. Rotate the engine 2 full revolutions by the center crankshaft pulley bolt and recheck that the timing marks on the camshaft, crankshaft and intermediate sprockets are correctly aligned as during the removal procedure. If necessary, alter the position of the belt teeth to correct timing and reset the tension.

15. For vehicles with A/C and solid mount compressors, install the solid mount compressor bracket as follows:

   a. Position the spacer onto the stud, then install the bracket on the front (2 nut) mounting stud and slide the bracket over the timing belt cover into position.

   b. Loosen the assembly bracket-to-engine fasteners (numbered 1 through 7—refer to the accompanying illustration).

✷✷ WARNING

The bracket fasteners must be tightened in the proper sequence and to the specified torque values.

   c. Tighten the fasteners in the following sequence: 1) bolt 1 to 30 inch lbs. (3.3 Nm), 2) nut 2 and bolt 3 to 40 ft. lbs. (54 Nm), 3) bolts 1, 4 and 5 to 40 ft. lbs. (54 Nm), 4) bolts 6 and 7 to 40 ft. lbs. (54 Nm).

   d. Install the alternator and compressor to the bracket. Tighten the compressor mounting bolts to 40 ft. lbs. (54 Nm).

16. Install the timing belt cover and pulleys.

17. Lower the engine and reassemble the engine mount, tightening the through-bolt to 70 ft. lbs. (95 Nm).

18. Remove the floor jack from under the engine.

19. Install the timing belt covers, as described earlier in this section.

20. Connect the negative battery cable.

21. Adjust the ignition timing, if necessary.

2.2L Turbo III Engine

◆ **See Figures 143 thru 148**

1. Disconnect the negative battery cable.

2. Apply the parking brake, block the rear wheels, then raise and safely support the front of the vehicle on jackstands.

3. Remove the timing belt covers, as described previously in this section.

4. Remove the A/C compressor with the fluid lines attached. For more information, refer to Section 6. Set the compressor aside.

5. Remove the alternator pivot bolt and remove the alternator.

6. Remove the A/C compressor belt idler unit.

7. Position a hydraulic floor jack under the engine. Place a long block of wood between the floor jack lifting pad and the oil pan to spread the load of the engine in such a way that the oil pan will not be damaged. Raise the engine only until its weight is taken up by the floor jack, then remove the main through-bolt from the right engine mount—the one that is situated near the timing cover.

8. Remove the five A/C solid mount bracket side mounting bolts (No. 1, 4, 5, 6, and 7). Remove the front mounting nut (No. 2) and remove the front bolt (No. 3). Remove the front mounting bolt and strut, rotate the solid mount bracket away from the engine and slide the bracket on stud until free. Remove the spacer from the stud.

9. Remove the lower accessory drive belt idler pulley bracket assembly.

10. Loosen the timing belt tensioner, then remove the timing belt and idler pulley.

To install:

11. Remove the air cleaner fresh air duct, ignition cable cover, spark plugs and rocker arm covers, as described earlier in this section and in Section 1.

12. Loosen the rocker arm retaining bolts about 3 turns in the proper sequence. Check all lash adjusters and replace any that are damaged.

13. Align and pin both camshaft sprockets with ³⁄₁₆ in. drill bits or pin punches to hold them steady while installing the timing belt.

14. Install a dial indicator so that the plunger extends down into the No. 1 spark plug hole. Rotate the crankshaft until the No. 1 piston is at TDC (the dial indicator will register the highest position of the crankshaft). Matchmark crankshaft and camshaft sprockets to the engine block for reference.

➡**Since there is no distributor, the intermediate shaft sprocket does not need to be timed.**

15. Install the timing belt and idler pulley starting at the crankshaft and working counterclockwise. Make sure there is no slack between any sprockets,

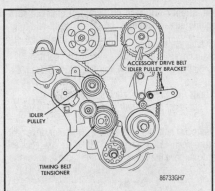

Fig. 144 Timing belt and some related components for the 2.2L Turbo III engine

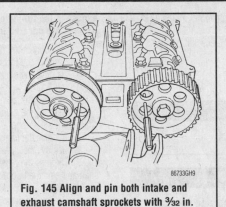

Fig. 145 Align and pin both intake and exhaust camshaft sprockets with ³⁄₃₂ in. drill bits or punches

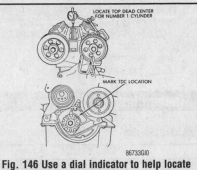

Fig. 146 Use a dial indicator to help locate Top Dead Center (TDC), then matchmark the crankshaft sprocket to the engine block for reference

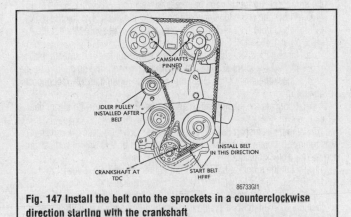

Fig. 147 Install the belt onto the sprockets in a counterclockwise direction starting with the crankshaft

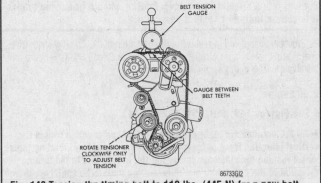

Fig. 148 Tension the timing belt to 110 lbs. (445 N) for a new belt, or to 70 lbs. (311 N) for a used belt

except for the camshaft and crankshaft pulleys on the idler pulley side, when installing. All timing belt slack should be on the idler pulley side of the engine.

16. Install a suitable belt tension gauge on the timing belt between the camshaft sprockets. Remove the pins from the camshaft sprockets.

※※ WARNING

The belt tension gauge must be installed between the belt teeth to get an accurate reading.

17. Rotate the tensioner clockwise to adjust the belt tension to 110 lbs. (445 N). for a new belt, or to 70 lbs. (311 N) for an old belt. Tighten the tensioner bolt 39 ft. lbs. (53 Nm).

18. Rotate the crankshaft clockwise 2 revolutions and recheck that the timing marks on the camshaft and crankshaft sprockets align with the timing marks on the engine. Also double-check belt tension, adjust as required.

19. Remove the dial indicator from the cylinder head valley.

20. Tighten the rocker arm bolts in sequence to 18 ft. lbs. (24 Nm).

21. For vehicles with A/C and solid mount compressors, install the solid mount compressor bracket as follows:

 a. Position the spacer onto the stud, then install the bracket on the front (2 nut) mounting stud and slide the bracket over the timing belt cover into position.

 b. Loosen the assembly bracket-to-engine fasteners (numbered 1 through 7—refer to the accompanying illustration).

※※ WARNING

The bracket fasteners must be tightened in the proper sequence and to the specified torque values.

 c. Tighten the fasteners in the following sequence: 1) bolt 1 to 30 inch lbs. (3.3 Nm), 2) nut 2 and bolt 3 to 40 ft. lbs. (54 Nm), 3) bolts 1, 4 and 5 to 40 ft. lbs. (54 Nm), 4) bolts 6 and 7 to 40 ft. lbs. (54 Nm).

 d. Install the alternator and compressor to the bracket. Tighten the compressor mounting bolts to 40 ft. lbs. (54 Nm).

22. Install engine mount and timing belt covers.

23. Install the spark plugs, rocker arm covers, ignition cable cover and air duct.

24. Connect the negative battery cable, start the engine and check for leaks.

ADJUSTMENT

➡Use these procedure to adjust the timing belt if it was not removed from the engine.

2.2L (Except 2.2L Turbo III) and 2.5L Engines

1. Disconnect the negative battery cable.

2. Apply the parking brake, block the rear wheels, then raise and safely support the front of the vehicle on jackstands.

3. Remove the right front inner splash shield.

4. Remove the timing belt tensioner cover.

5. Position Special Tensioning Tool C-4703, or equivalent, on the hex of the tensioner so that its weight is approximately at the 10 o'clock position, then loosen the bolt.

6. The tensioner should drop to the 9 o'clock position. Reposition the tool as required in order to have it end up at the 9 o'clock position (parallel to the ground, hanging toward the rear of the vehicle) with a range to approximately 15° above and below the 9 o'clock position.

7. Hold the tensioning tool in position and tighten the bolt. Do not pull the tool past the 9 o'clock position or the belt will be too tight and will cause howling or possible breakage. Tighten the tensioner locknut to 32 ft. lbs. (44 Nm) for 1981–88 models, or to 45 ft. lbs. (61 Nm) for 1989–95 models.

8. Install the tensioner cover and the splash shield.

9. Lower the vehicle and remove the wheel blocks.

10. Connect the negative battery cable.

2.2L Turbo III Engine

1. Disconnect the negative battery cable.

2. Remove the timing covers.

3. Install a suitable belt tension gauge on the timing belt between the camshaft sprockets.

4. Rotate the tensioner clockwise to adjust the belt tension to 70 lbs. (311 N). This tensioning value is for a used timing belt.

5. Rotate the crankshaft clockwise 2 revolutions and recheck the tension. Readjust as required.

6. Install the timing covers.

7. Connect the negative battery cable.

Timing Chain

REMOVAL & INSTALLATION

❋❋ CAUTION

When draining the coolant, keep in mind that cats and dogs are attracted by the ethylene glycol antifreeze, and are quite likely to drink any that is left in an uncovered container or in puddles on the ground. This will prove fatal in sufficient quantity. Always drain the coolant into a sealable container. Coolant should be reused unless it is contaminated or several years old.

Procedures applying to removal and installation of the auxiliary shaft drive chains are located under Auxiliary (Intermediate or Silent) Shafts Removal and Installation, later in this section.

2.6L Engine

▸ **See Figures 149, 150, 151, 152 and 153**

➟All 2.6 engines are equipped with 2 silent shafts which cancel the vertical vibrating force of the engine and the secondary vibrating forces, which include the sideways rocking of the engine due to the turning direction of the crankshaft and other rolling parts. The shafts are driven by a duplex chain and are turned by the crankshaft. The silent shaft chain assembly is mounted in front of the timing chain assembly and must be removed to service the timing chain. Because of the inter-relatedness of the timing chains, silent shafts and oil pump all of these components are covered under this one procedure.

1. Disconnect the negative battery terminal.

2. Remove the timing chain cover, as described earlier in this section.

3. Remove the silent shaft chain guides, side **A**, top **B**, bottom **C**, from the silent shaft **B** chain.

4. Remove the sprocket bolts from the silent shaft sprockets.

5. Remove the crankshaft sprocket, silent shaft sprockets and the outer chain from the engine.

6. Remove the camshaft sprocket bolt, then remove the distributor drive gear.

7. Remove the camshaft sprocket holder and right and left timing chain guides.

8. Depress the tensioner to remove the timing chain and remove the crankshaft and camshaft sprockets.

To install:

9. Clean all components of old oil, grime and gasket material with a suitable solvent. Inspect the components as follows:

a. Inspect the silent chain guides, the chain tensioner rubber shoe, and the sprocket teeth for damage or excessive wear.

b. Check the chain tensioner spring for deterioration. The free length of the spring should be 2.587 in. (65.7mm) and the load should be 4.4 lbs. (19.6 N) at 1.453 in. (36.9mm).

c. Inspect the silent shaft sprocket cushion ring for free and smooth rotation.

d. Inspect the silent shaft sprocket cushion ring and ring guide for damage.

e. Check the silent shaft chain for roller play, wear, damage, disconnected links, etc.

f. Lubricate the silent shaft chain and the timing chain with clean, new engine oil.

10. With the camshaft bearing caps tightened down (in case the camshaft was removed), rotate the camshaft so that the dowel hole is on the vertical centerline (12 o'clock position).

11. Install the sprocket holder and the right and left chain guides.

12. Rotate the crankshaft until the No. 1 piston is at TDC (since the camshaft is already correctly positioned, this will automatically bring the engine in position so that the No. 1 piston is at TDC on its compression stroke, which is exactly what you want).

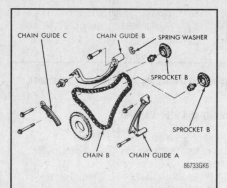

Fig. 149 Exploded view of the silent shaft drive chain and related components

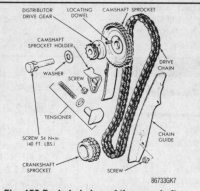

Fig. 150 Exploded view of the camshaft timing drive chain and related components

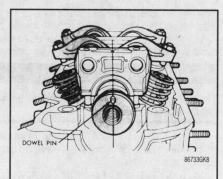

Fig. 151 When installing the timing chain, position the camshaft so that the dowel pin is at the 12 o'clock position

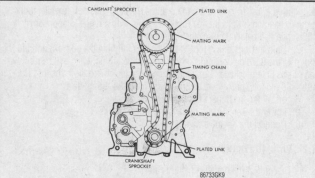

Fig. 152 Make sure to align the sprocket timing marks with the plated links on the timing chain

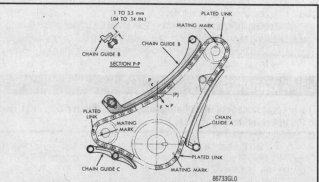

Fig. 153 When installing the silent shaft timing chain, make certain that the plated links and sprocket marks are aligned as shown

13. Install the tensioner spring and shoe on the oil pump body.

14. Install the timing chain on the camshaft and crankshaft sprockets. Make sure that the timing marks are aligned. The timing marks on the sprockets are the punch marks on the teeth, while those on the chain are the plated links (different color from the regular links).

15. Holding the sprockets and chain assembled as in Step 14 with both hands, align the crankshaft sprocket to the crankshaft keyway and slide it into place. Align the camshaft sprocket dowel hole to the camshaft dowel hole, then slide the camshaft sprocket onto the camshaft.

➡The sprocket timing mark and the plated chain link should be at the 2 to 3 o'clock position when correctly installed.

16. Install to dowel pin and install the distributor drive gear. Install the sprocket bolt on the camshaft and tighten it to 40 ft. lbs. (54 Nm).

✴✴ CAUTION

The chain must be aligned in the right and left chain guides with the tensioner pushing against the chain. The tension for the inner chain is determined by spring tension.

17. Install the silent shaft chain drive pulley onto the crankshaft.

18. Install the silent shaft chain onto the oil pump sprocket and onto the silent shaft sprocket. Make sure that the timing marks are aligned. The timing marks on the sprockets are the punch marks on the teeth while those on the chain are the plated links.

19. Holding the parts assembled in Step 18 with both hands, align the crankshaft sprocket plated link with the punch mark on the sprocket.

20. With the chain installed on the crankshaft sprocket, install the oil pump sprocket and silent shaft chain sprocket on their respective bolts.

21. Install the oil pump and silent shaft sprocket bolts and tighten them to 25 ft. lbs. (34 Nm).

22. Loosely install the 3 chain guides.

23. Adjust the silent shaft chain tension, as follows:

 a. Tighten chain guide **A** mounting bolts to 13 ft. lbs. (18 Nm).

 b. Tighten chain guide **C** mounting bolts to 13 ft. lbs. (18 Nm).

 c. Shake the oil pump and silent shaft sprockets to collect chain slack at point **P**.

 d. Adjust the position of chain guide **B** so that when the chain is pulled in the direction of arrow **F** with your finger tips, the clearance between chain guide **B** and the chain links will be between 0.04–0.14 in (1.0–3.5mm). Tighten chain guide **B** mounting bolts to 13 ft. lbs. (18 Nm).

24. Install the timing chain cover, as described earlier in this section.

25. Connect the negative battery cable.

ADJUSTMENT

▶ See Figure 154

The timing chain can be adjusted on the 2.6L engine without removing the timing chain cover, as follows:

1. Remove the cover on the access hole in the chain case cover.

2. Loosen Special Bolt **B**.

3. Apply finger pressure on the boss, as shown in the accompanying illustration. Do **NOT** use a prytool or other implement to apply tension.

4. Tighten Special Bolt **B** to 13 ft. lbs. (18 Nm).

Crankshaft, Camshaft and Intermediate Shaft Sprockets

REMOVAL & INSTALLATION

2.2 and 2.5L Engines

▶ See Figures 140, 155 thru 164

➡Special Tools C-4687, C-4687–1 (2.5L), C-4685, C-4679 (2.2L), C-4991 (2.5L), C-4680 (2.2L), L-4524, Thrust Bearing/Washer, a 5.9 in. (15cm) long bolt and C-4992 (2.5L), or their equivalents, will be necessary for this procedure.

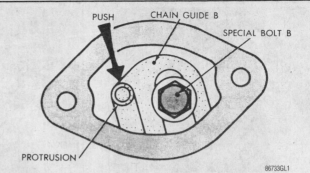

Fig. 154 Remove the small timing chain tensioner cover plate to access the tensioner for adjustments—2.6L engine

1. Disconnect the negative battery cable.

2. Remove the timing belt covers and timing belt, as described earlier in this section.

3. Remove the crankshaft sprocket bolt, then use Special Tool C-4685, Insert and a 5.9 in. (15cm) long bolt to remove the crankshaft sprocket.

4. Either use Special Tool C-4679 for the 2.2L engine, or C-4991 for the 2.5L engine, or their equivalents, to remove the crankshaft oil seal from the engine block, or remove the oil seal retainer. Remove the oil seal from the retainer.

5. Unbolt and remove the camshaft and intermediate shaft sprockets. To hold the camshaft sprocket stationary while it is removed, use Special Tool C-4687 and, for 2.5L engines, Adapter Tool C-4687–1, or equivalents.

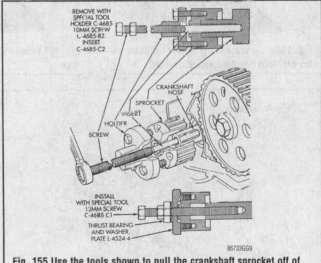

Fig. 155 Use the tools shown to pull the crankshaft sprocket off of the crankshaft

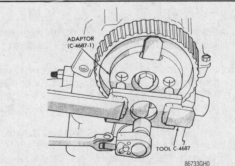

Fig. 156 Use Tool C-4687 and, for 2.5L engines, Adapter C-4687–1, or their equivalents, to hold the camshaft sprocket(s) steady while loosening or tightening the attaching bolt(s)

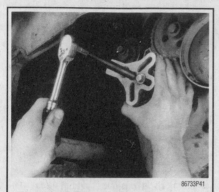

Fig. 157 Install a gear puller onto the crankshaft timing belt sprocket, then . . .

Fig. 158 . . . remove the sprocket

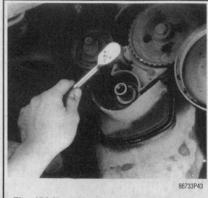

Fig. 159 If equipped, loosen and . . .

Fig. 160 . . . remove the spacer between the crankshaft and intermediate shaft

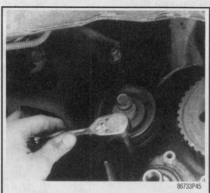

Fig. 161 Loosen the mounting fasteners, then . . .

Fig. 162 . . . remove the oils seal retainer from the engine block

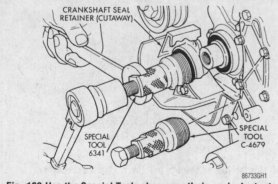

Fig. 163 Use the Special Tools shown, or their equivalents, to remove the crankshaft, intermediate shaft and camshaft oil seals

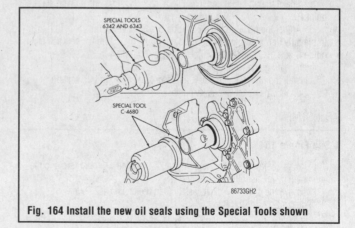

Fig. 164 Install the new oil seals using the Special Tools shown

To install:

6. If removed, apply liquid gasket to the oil seal retainer, then install it onto the engine block. Install the retaining bolts and tighten to 105 inch lbs. (12 Nm).

7. To install a new crankshaft oil seal, first polish the crankshaft with 400 grit emery paper. If the seal has a steel case, lightly coat the outside diameter of the seal with Loctite® Stud N' Bearing Mount, or its equivalent. If the seal case is rubber coated, generously apply a soap and water solution to help facilitate installation.

8. Install the seal with a seal driver. Use C-4680 on the 2.2L engine and C-4992 on the 2.5L engine, or their equivalents.

9. Install the sprockets making sure that the timing marks are aligned as illustrated. Install the crankshaft sprocket using plate L-4524, Thrust Bearing/Washer and a 5.9 in. (15cm) long bolt. When installing the camshaft

sprocket, make certain the arrows on the sprocket are in line with the No. 1 camshaft bearing cap-to-cylinder head line.

10. The small hole in the camshaft sprocket must be at the top and in line with the vertical center line of the engine.

11. Install the timing belt and timing belt covers, as described earlier in this section.

12. Connect the negative battery cable.

2.6L Engine

Refer to the procedures under timing chain cover and oil seal removal and installation procedure and the auxiliary shaft procedures for the 2.6L engine. On all engines that use a timing chain rather than a timing belt assembly always replace the timing gears (sprockets) whenever replacing the timing chain.

Camshaft and Bearings

REMOVAL & INSTALLATION

2.2L (Except Turbo III) and 2.5L Engines

▶ See Figures 165 thru 176

➡Since the 2.2L and 2.5L engines are designed with overhead camshafts, they are not equipped with removable camshaft bearings.

1. Disconnect the negative battery cable.
2. Remove the timing belt covers and timing belt, as described earlier in this section.
3. Remove the rocker arm cover. For more information, please refer to the procedure in this section.

4. Label or mark all valve train components (rocker arms, etc.) for reassembly.
5. Loosen the camshaft bearing cap nuts several turns each in the sequence shown.
6. Using a wooden or rubber mallet, tap the rear of the camshaft a few times to break it loose.
7. Remove the cap nuts and caps, being very careful that the camshaft does not cock. Cocking the camshaft could cause irreparable damage to the bearings.

To install:

8. Install the camshaft followers in the correct order as removed.
9. Lubricate the camshaft with clean engine oil, then set the camshaft onto the cylinder head.
10. Install the bearing caps with No. 1 at the timing belt end and No. 5 at the transaxle end. Caps are numbered and have arrows facing forward. The arrows on caps No. 1, No. 2, No. 3 and No. 4 **must** point toward the timing belt to prevent cap breakage. Tighten the cap nuts in the opposite order of the removal sequence. Tighten the cap nuts to 14 ft. lbs. (19 Nm).

Fig. 165 Once the rocker arm cover is removed the camshaft can be serviced

Fig. 166 Remove the camshaft sprocket attaching bolt and . . .

Fig. 167 . . . remove the camshaft sprocket

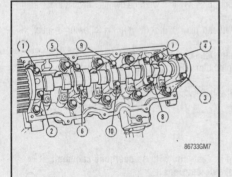

Fig. 168 Loosen the camshaft bearing caps in the sequence shown

Fig. 169 Camshaft bearing cap identification markings—(A) direction, (B) position number

Fig. 170 Remove the front camshaft oil seal, then . . .

Fig. 171 . . . lift the camshaft off of the cylinder head

Fig. 172 After the camshaft is removed, the rocker arms . . .

Fig. 173 . . . and the hydraulic lash adjusters can be removed

Fig. 174 Make sure to tighten the camshaft bearing caps with a torque wrench

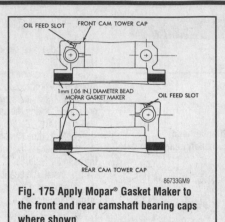

Fig. 175 Apply Mopar® Gasket Maker to the front and rear camshaft bearing caps where shown

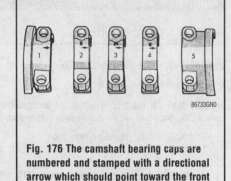

Fig. 176 The camshaft bearing caps are numbered and stamped with a directional arrow which should point toward the front of the engine

11. Apply Mopar® Gasket Maker, or equivalent RTV silicone gasket material, to No. 1 and No. 5 bearing cap as shown in the accompanying illustration.

➡Install the bearing caps BEFORE the seals are installed.

12. Install the rocker arm cover, as described earlier in this section.

13. Install the timing belt and timing belt covers. For more information, please refer to the procedure in this section.

14. Connect the negative battery cable.

2.2L Turbo III Engines

▶ See Figures 177, 178 and 179

➡Since the 2.2L Turbo III engine is designed with an overhead camshaft, it is not equipped with removable bearings.

➡Since the camshafts must be slid out of the cylinder head, the cylinder head must be removed from the engine for this procedure.

1. Disconnect the negative battery cable.

2. Remove the cylinder head. For more information, please refer to the procedure in this section.

3. Label the rocker arms and shafts for reinstallation in the same positions.

4. Remove the rocker arms/shafts, as described earlier in this section.

5. Remove the thrust plates from the rear of the camshafts. The intake camshaft uses a wider thrust plate than exhaust camshaft.

✳✳ WARNING

The thrust plates are not the same thickness and cannot be interchanged.

6. Before the camshaft can be removed from the cylinder head, the rear camshaft seal must be removed first.

7. Using a flat prytool, place it against the side of the camshaft lobe, then pry the camshaft out of the head. The camshaft seal will be pushed out by the camshaft.

8. Slide the camshaft out of the cylinder head. Be careful not to scratch the bearing surfaces in the cylinder head.

✳✳ WARNING

The intake and exhaust camshafts are not interchangeable.

9. Remove the second camshaft in the same manner.

To install:

10. Lubricate the camshaft journals with clean engine oil. Carefully install the camshafts into the cylinder head.

✳✳ WARNING

The camshafts are not interchangeable. The intake camshaft has a wider thrust plate groove.

11. Install the thrust plates and tighten the retaining nuts to 55 inch lbs. (6 Nm).

12. Install new camshaft oil seals flush with the cylinder head surface using Chrysler Tool C-4680.

13. Inspect the camshaft end-play as described in the following inspection procedures.

14. Install the rocker arms/shafts onto the cylinder head, then install the cylinder head onto the engine block. For more information, please refer to the procedure in this section.

15. Connect the negative battery cable.

2.6L Engine

▶ See Figure 180

➡Since the 2.6L engine is designed with an overhead camshaft, it is not equipped with removable bearings.

1. Disconnect the negative battery cable.

2. Remove the rocker arms/shafts, as described earlier in this section.

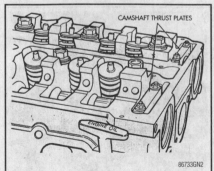

Fig. 177 The intake camshaft utilizes a wider thrust plate than the exhaust camshaft

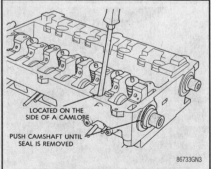

Fig. 178 Use a flat-bladed prytool against a camshaft lobe to pry the camshaft from the cylinder head

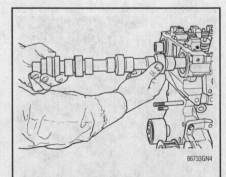

Fig. 179 Once the camshaft is started out of the engine, pull it out of the cylinder head cautiously

Fig. 180 Use Chrysler Tool C-4848 to drive the new oil seals into place

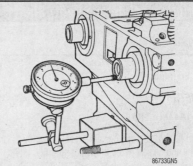

Fig. 181 Position a dial indicator with a magnetic base, as shown, to measure the end-play of the camshaft(s)—2.2L Turbo III engine shown, other engines similar

3. Remove the water pump drive pulley attaching bolt, then remove the pulley itself.

4. Remove and discard the camshaft end bearing cap seals. Remove the seal as follows:

   a. On the back end of the camshaft, remove the water pump drive pulley cover screws, then lift the cover off of the cylinder head.

   b. On the rear end of the camshaft, remove the water pump drive belt. Remove the water pump attaching bolt, then slide the pulley off of the end of the camshaft.

   c. Remove the camshaft end seal with Chrysler Tool C-4847–1.

❊❊ WARNING

Do not nick the camshaft seal surface or bore.

5. Remove the camshaft from the cylinder head.

To install:

6. Lubricate the camshaft lobes and bearings, then set the camshaft onto the cylinder head.

7. Install the assembled rocker arm shaft assembly, as described earlier in this section.

8. The camshaft should be positioned so that the dowel pin on the front end of the cam is in the 12 o'clock position and in line with the notch in the top of the front bearing cap.

9. Install the rocker arm cover.

10. Install a new rear camshaft seal. Lubricate the new seal lip with clean engine oil and carefully position the seal over the camshaft and into the bore.

11. Tap the seal into the bore with Tool C-4848. Seal depth in the bore is correct when the tool bottoms against the camshaft.

12. Install the water pump pulley and tighten the retaining bolt to 40 ft. lbs. (54 Nm).

13. Install the water pump pulley drive belt, then install the water pump pulley cover.

14. Connect the negative battery cable.

INSPECTION

Camshaft End-Play Check

▶ **See Figure 181**

1. Install the camshaft, thrust plates and new oil seals.

2. Position a dial indicator with a magnetic base as shown in the accompanying illustration to measure the end-play.

3. Move the camshaft as far forward as possible, then "zero" the dial indicator.

4. Push the camshaft back and forth as far as possible, while watching the dial indicator for maximum end-play. Maximum end-play is shown in the Camshaft Specification chart in this section.

5. Remove the dial indicator and continue installing the camshaft.

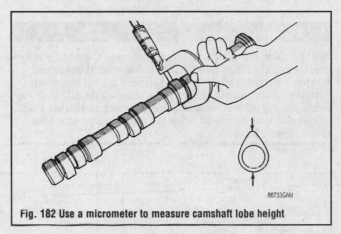

Fig. 182 Use a micrometer to measure camshaft lobe height

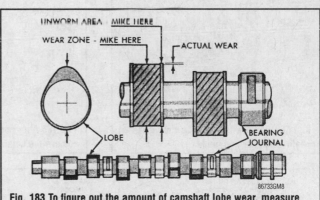

Fig. 183 To figure out the amount of camshaft lobe wear, measure the camshaft lobes at the positions shown

Inspecting The Camshaft

▶ **See Figures 182 and 183**

Measure cam lobe height at the nose or thickest point. Measure at the very edge of the lobe, where there is no wear, and at the center, where wear is at a maximum. On the 2.2 and 2.5 liter engines, 0.010 in. (0.254mm) wear is permitted, while on the 2.6, the figure is 0.020 in. (0.508mm). Replace the camshaft if it is worn excessively.

➡**Use the above procedures as a guide for your engine. Machine shop work requires special training and equipment, it is best to send the camshaft assembly to a reputable machine shop for this kind of repair.**

Auxiliary (Intermediate or Silent) Shafts

REMOVAL & INSTALLATION

2.2L and 2.5L Engines

BALANCE SHAFTS

◆ **See Figures 184 thru 189**

The 2.2L Turbo III and 2.5L engines are equipped with 2 balance shafts, mounted under the engine and in the oil pan, in addition to the intermediate shaft.

➡️To complete this procedure, you will need Tool C-4916, or a shim 0.039 in. (1mm) thick and 2.75 in. (70mm) long.

1. Drain and remove the oil pan, as described earlier in this section.
2. Remove the attaching bolts and remove the pick-up from the oil pump.

❋❋ CAUTION

The EPA warns that prolonged contact with used engine oil may cause a number of skin disorders, including cancer! You should make every effort to minimize your exposure to used engine oil. Protective gloves should be worn when changing the oil. Wash your hands and any other exposed skin areas as soon as possible after exposure to used engine oil. Soap and water, or waterless hand cleaner should be used.

3. Remove the timing belt cover, belt, and crankshaft sprocket, as described earlier in this section. Remove the front crankshaft oil seal retainer, as described earlier in this section.
4. Remove its 3 mounting bolts and remove the chain cover.
5. Remove the mounting bolt from the chain guide and remove the guide from the engine block.
6. Remove the mounting bolt from the tensioner, then remove the tensioner unit.
7. Remove the bolts which retain the balance shaft gear and chain sprocket (the chain sprocket is retained by Torx® bolts). Remove both sprockets and the chain as an assembly.
8. Remove the gear cover retaining stud with a deep well socket. Then, remove the gear cover. Remove the gears from the shafts.
9. Unbolt and remove the carrier rear cover. Then, slide the balance shafts out of the carrier.
10. If it is necessary to remove the balance shaft carrier, remove the six carrier-to-crankcase attaching bolts and remove the carrier.

To install:

11. Clean all components and mating surfaces with a suitable solvent.
12. Installation the reverse of the removal order. Start by installing the carrier onto the crankcase and tightening the mounting bolts to 40 ft. lbs. (54 Nm).
13. Lubricate the bearing surfaces with clean engine oil, then install the shafts. Install the rear cover and tighten the bolts to 105 inch lbs. (12 Nm).
14. Turn both balance shafts until the keyways are parallel to the vertical centerline of the engine and above the shafts (12 o'clock position). Turn the timing gears so the timing marks align at the center point between the 2 shafts. Install the drive gear with the shorter hub onto the shaft which is driven by the crankshaft-to-balance shaft chain (the left shaft when viewing the front of the

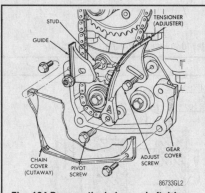

Fig. 184 Remove the balance shaft drive chain tensioner and guide

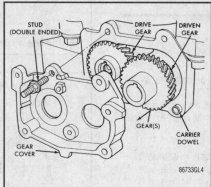

Fig. 185 After removing the drive chain, remove the balance shaft gear cover

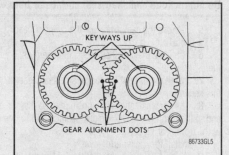

Fig. 186 Position the balance shafts so that their keyways are at the 12 o'clock position, then install the gears so that the timing marks are aligned as shown

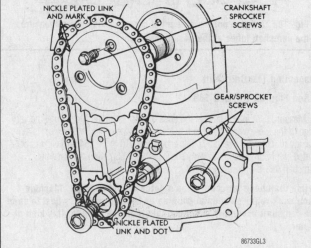

Fig. 187 Assemble and install the drive chain and chain sprockets with the marks and plated links aligned

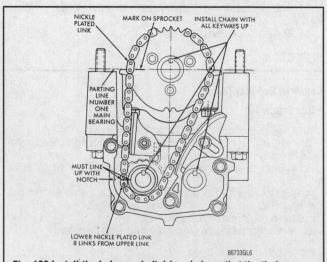

Fig. 188 Install the balance shaft drive chain so that the timing marks are aligned as shown

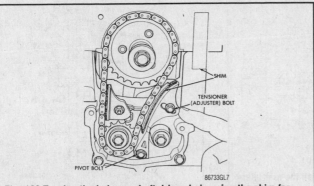

Fig. 189 Tension the balance shaft drive chain using the shim for correct adjustment

engine). Install the gear with the longer hub onto the other shaft (the right-hand one when viewing the engine from the front).

15. Install the gear cover and tighten the stud to 105 inch lbs. (12 Nm).

16. Install the crankshaft-to-balance shaft chain sprocket on the left-hand shaft, then tighten the Torx® bolts to 130 inch lbs. (14.5 Nm). Turn the crankshaft until the No. 1 cylinder is at Top Dead Center (TDC) on the compression stroke. The timing marks on the chain sprocket should line up with the parting line on the left side of No. 1 main bearing cap.

17. Place the chain over the crankshaft sprocket in such a way that the nickel plated link of the chain fits over the timing mark on the crankshaft sprocket.

18. Engage the balance shaft sprocket with the timing chain so that the yellow dot on the sprocket mates with the chain link that is painted yellow or nickel plated.

19. With both balance shaft keyways pointing up, slide the balance shaft sprocket onto the nose of the balance shaft. If necessary, push the nose of the balance shaft in slightly to allow the sprocket to clear the chain cover, when it is installed.

➡ **The timing marks on the sprocket, the painted link, and the arrow on the side of the gear cover must all line up with their corresponding marks. If not, rearrange the shafts so that timing is correct, because improper timing will result in severe engine vibration!**

20. If the sprockets are all timed correctly, install the balance shaft bolts. Position a wooden block between the crankcase and a crankshaft counterweight to prevent rotation, then tighten the balance shaft bolts to 21 ft. lbs. (28 Nm).

21. Install the chain tensioner with bolts just finger tight.

22. Install Tool C-4916, or a shim 0.039 in. (1mm) thick and 2.75 in. (70mm) long between the tensioner and chain. Then, apply pressure to the tensioner directly behind the adjustment slot to push the tensioner and shim up against the chain. The shim must contact the shoe of the tensioner from the bottom almost all the way to the top and all slack must be removed.

23. Hold the tension and tighten the top tensioner bolt, then tighten the pivot bolt to 105 inch lbs. (12 Nm).

24. Remove the shim or tool.

25. Install the chain guide onto the double-ended stud. Make sure the tab on the guide fits into the slot on the gear cover. Install the nut and washer, then tighten the nut to 105 inch lbs. (12 Nm).

26. Install the carrier covers and tighten the bolts to 105 inch lbs. (12 Nm).

27. Install the oil seal retainer, crankshaft timing belt sprocket, timing belt and timing belt covers.

28. Install the oil pump pick-up and the oil pan.

✴✴ WARNING

Do NOT start the engine without first filling the engine with clean engine oil.

29. Fill the engine with the proper type and amount of engine oil. For more details, refer to Section 1.

30. Connect the negative battery cable.

INTERMEDIATE SHAFT

▶ **See Figures 190, 191, 192, 193 and 194**

1. Disconnect the negative battery cable.

2. Rotate the crankshaft so that the No. 1 piston is at Top Dead Center (TDC) of its compression stroke.

3. Remove the timing belt covers to confirm that all timing marks on the camshaft, crankshaft and intermediate sprockets are aligned with the engine block timing marks.

4. Remove the distributor, if equipped. Looking down the distributor shaft at the oil pump, make sure that the slot in the shaft is parallel with the center line of the engine block (runs the same direction as the crankshaft).

5. Remove the oil pan and oil pump.

6. Remove the timing belt, as described earlier in this section.

7. Remove the intermediate shaft sprocket.

8. Remove the shaft retainer bolts and remove the retainer from the engine block.

9. Slide the intermediate shaft out of the engine.

10. If necessary, remove the front bushing using Chrysler Tool C-4697-2, or equivalent, and the rear bushing using Chrysler Tool C-4686-2, or equivalent.

To install:

11. Clean all components and mating surfaces of dirt, grease and grime.

12. Install the front bushing using Tool C-4697-1, or equivalent, until the tool is flush with the engine block. Install the rear bushing using tool C-4686-1, or equivalent, also until the tool is flush with the block.

13. Lubricate the distributor drive gear, if equipped, then install the intermediate shaft into the engine block.

14. Install a new seal in the retainer and apply silicone sealer to the mating surface of the retainer. Install the retainer onto the engine block, then tighten the bolts to 105 inch lbs. (12 Nm).

15. Install the intermediate shaft sprocket, the timing belt and the timing belt covers, as described earlier.

16. With the timing belt properly installed, install the oil pump so the slot is parallel to the center line of the crankshaft. If equipped, install the distributor so that the rotor is aligned with the No. 1 spark plug wire tower on the cap.

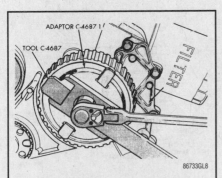

Fig. 190 Use the tools shown to hold the intermediate shaft sprocket stable while loosening the attaching bolt

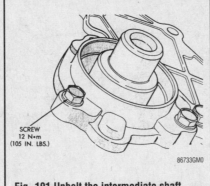

Fig. 191 Unbolt the intermediate shaft retainer from the engine block

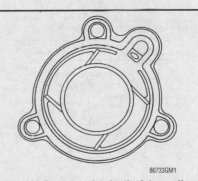

Fig. 192 Form a gasket for the intermediate shaft retainer using Mopar® Gasket Maker, as shown

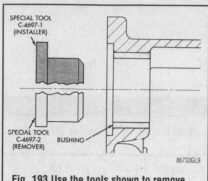

Fig. 193 Use the tools shown to remove and install the front intermediate shaft bushing

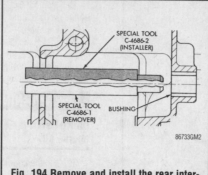

Fig. 194 Remove and install the rear intermediate shaft bushing with tools C-4686–2 and C-4686–1, or their equivalents

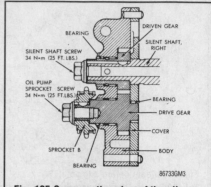

Fig. 195 Cross-section view of the oil pump and lower silent shaft assembly

17. Fill the engine with the proper amount and type of engine oil. Refer to Section 1 for more details.

✳✳ WARNING

Do NOT start the engine without first filling the engine with clean engine oil.

18. Connect the negative battery cable.
19. Start the engine, check for leaks and adjust the ignition timing, as required.

2.6L Engine

▸ **See Figures 195, 196, 197 and 198**

➡The 2.6L engines are equipped with 2 silent shafts, one of which drives the oil pump.

1. Disconnect the negative battery cable.
2. Remove the timing chain cover and timing chains, as described earlier in this section.
3. Remove the sleeve from the oil pump. Remove the oil pump by first removing the bolt locking the oil pump driven gear and the right silent shaft, then remove the oil pump mounting bolts.
4. Slide the silent shaft out of the engine block.

➡If the bolt locking the oil pump and the silent shaft is difficult to loosen, remove the oil pump and the shaft as a unit.

5. Remove the left silent shaft thrust washer and slide the shaft out of the engine block.
To install:
6. Install the right silent shaft into the engine block.
7. Install the oil pump assembly onto the engine block. Do not lose the woodruff key from the end of the silent shaft. Tighten the oil pump mounting bolts to 73–85 inch lbs. (8.2–9.5 Nm).
8. Tighten the silent shaft and oil pump driven gear mounting bolt.

➡The silent shaft and the oil pump can be installed as a unit, if necessary.

9. Install the left silent shaft into the engine block.
10. Install a new O-ring on the thrust plate and install the unit into the engine block, using a pair of bolts without heads, as alignment guides.

✳✳ CAUTION

If the thrust plate is turned to align the bolt holes, the O-ring may be damaged.

11. Remove the guide bolts and install the regular bolts into the thrust plate and tighten securely.
12. Install the timing chains and timing chain cover, as described earlier in this section.
13. Fill the engine with the proper amount and type of engine oil, if the engine oil was drained during the removal procedure. For more details, refer to Section 1.

✳✳ WARNING

Do not start the engine without first filling it with clean engine oil.

14. Connect the negative battery cable.

Pistons and Connecting Rods

IDENTIFICATION

▸ **See Figures 199 and 200**

The pistons used in the 2.2L and 2.5L engines have notches in them to indicate the proper installed position. The notch faces the front of the engine, when installed. Connecting rods have markings to indicate proper assembly of the rod to the cap.

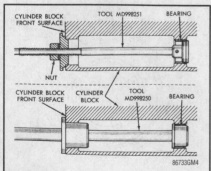

Fig. 196 Remove and install the silent shaft bearings with Tools MD998250 and MD998251, as shown

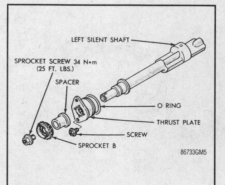

Fig. 197 Exploded view of the left silent shaft

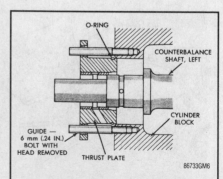

Fig. 198 Cross-section view of installing the thrust plate with 2 alignment dowels fabricated from 2 old bolts

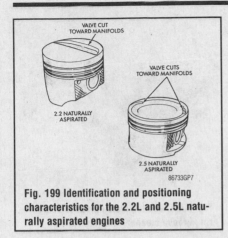

Fig. 199 Identification and positioning characteristics for the 2.2L and 2.5L naturally aspirated engines

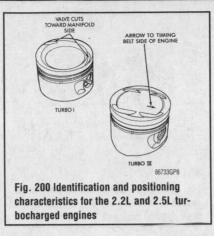

Fig. 200 Identification and positioning characteristics for the 2.2L and 2.5L turbocharged engines

Fig. 201 Use rubber hose over the connecting rod studs to protect the crankshaft and cylinders

2.6L engines have arrows on the pistons. These arrows must face front when installed in the engine. The connecting rods are numbered for easy identification.

➡**This procedure requires removal of the cylinder head and oil pan. It is much easier to perform this work with the engine removed from the vehicle and mounted on a stand. These procedures require certain hand tools which may not be in your tool box. A cylinder ridge reamer, a numbered punch set, piston ring expander, snapring tools and piston installation tool (ring compressor) are all necessary for correct piston and rod repair.**

REMOVAL

▶ **See Figures 201, 202, 203, 204 and 205**

1. Remove the cylinder head, following correct procedures listed earlier in this section.

2. Remove the oil pan, following correct procedures listed earlier in this section.

3. For 2.2L Turbo III and 2.5L engines, remove the balance shafts and carrier. For more information, refer to the correct procedure earlier in this section.

4. Note the identification of the pistons, as described earlier in the identification section of the piston and connecting rod procedures.

5. The connecting rods are marked to indicate which surface faces front, but the bearing caps should be matchmarked with numbers (front to rear) before disassembly. Use a marking punch and a small hammer; install the number over the seam of the rod and cap so that each piece will be reused in its original location.

6. Remove the connecting rod cap bolts, pull the caps off the rods, and place them on a bench in order.

7. Inspect the upper portions of the cylinder (near the head) for a ridge formed by ring wear. If there is a ridge, it must be removed by first pushing the piston down in the cylinder and then covering the piston top completely with a clean rag. Use a ridge reamer to remove metal at the lip until the cylinder is smooth. If this is not done, the rings will be damaged during piston removal.

8. Once the ridges have been removed, the pistons and rods may be pushed upward and out of the cylinders. Place pieces of rubber tubing over the rod bolts to protect the cylinder walls. Use a piece of wood or a hammer handle under the piston to tap it upward. If you're working under an engine that's still installed in the vehicle (with the crankshaft still in position) turn the crankshaft until the crankpin for each cylinder is in a convenient position. Be careful not to subject the piston and/or rod to heavy impact and do not allow the piston rod to damage the cylinder wall on the way out. The slightest nick in the metal can cause problems after reassembly.

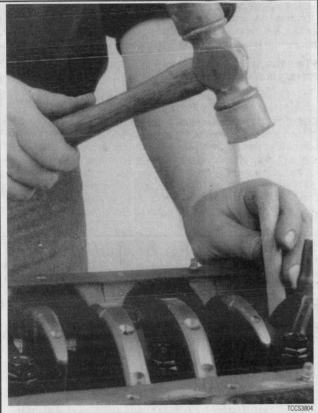

Fig. 202 Carefully tap the piston out of the bore using a wooden dowel

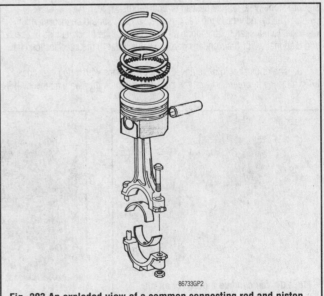

Fig. 203 An exploded view of a common connecting rod and piston assembly

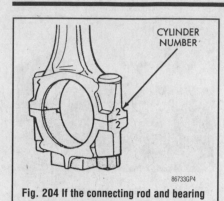

Fig. 204 If the connecting rod and bearing cap are not already matchmarked, use a steel stamp and hammer to do so

Fig. 205 Label the pistons if they are to be reused so that they can be installed in their original positions

Fig. 206 Clean the piston grooves using a ring groove cleaner—all engines

CLEANING & INSPECTION

♦ See Figures 206, 207, 208, 209 and 210

1. Clean the pistons, rings and rods in parts solvent with a bristle brush. Do not use a wire brush, even to remove heavy carbon. The metal may be damaged.

2. Measure the bore of the cylinder at 3 levels and in 2 dimensions (fore-and-aft and side-to-side). That's six measurements for each cylinder. By comparing the 3 vertical readings, the taper of the cylinder can be determined and by comparing the front–rear and left–right readings the out-of-round can be determined. The block should be measured: at the level of the top piston ring at the top of piston travel; in the center of the cylinder; and at the bottom of the cylinder bore. The measurements are located in the specification charts in this section.

3. If the cylinder bore is not within specification for taper and out-of-round, or the wall is scored or scuffed, according to Chrysler the block must be replaced with a new one. However, in most cases it is possible to have the cylinders bored oversize to correct the problem. Under these circumstances, the block should be taken to a machine shop for proper boring by a qualified machinist using the specialized equipment required.

➡️ If the cylinder is bored, oversize pistons and rings must be installed. Since all pistons must be the same size (for correct balance within the engine) ALL cylinders must be re-bored if any one is out of specification.

4. Even if the cylinders do not need to be bored, they should be fine honed for proper break-in by a qualified machine shop. A de-glazing tool may be used in a power drill to remove the glossy finish on the cylinder walls. Use only the smooth stone type, not the beaded or bottle–brush type.

5. The cylinder head top deck (gasket surface) should be inspected for warpage. Run a straightedge along all four edges of the block, across the center, and diagonally. For the standard warpage value, refer to the specification charts in this section.

6. The rings should be removed from the pistons with a ring expander. Keep all rings in order and with the piston from which they were removed. The rings and piston ring grooves should be cleaned thoroughly with solvent and a brush as deposits will alter readings of ring wear. The piston ring grooves should also be cleaned with a groove cleaning tool or a piece of piston ring as shown in the illustrations.

7. Before any measurements are begun, visually examine the piston for any signs of cracks, particularly in the skirt area, or for scratches in the metal. Anything other than light surface scoring disqualifies the piston from further use. The metal will become unevenly heated and the piston may break apart during use.

8. Piston diameter should be measured at the skirt, at right angles to the piston pin. Compare either with specified piston diameter or subtract the diameter from the cylinder bore dimension to get clearance, depending upon the information in the specifications. If clearance is excessive, the piston should be replaced. If a new piston still does not produce piston-to-wall clearance within specifications, use an oversize piston and bore out the cylinder accordingly. Refer to the specification charts for the specific values for the various engines.

9. Ring end-gap must be measured for all 3 rings in the cylinder by using a piston top (upside down) to press the ring squarely into the top of the cylinder. First wipe the cylinder bore clean. The rings must be at least 0.63 in. (16mm) from the bottom of the bore. Use a feeler gauge to measure the end-gap and compare it with specifications. If cylinder bore wear is very slight, you may use new rings to bring the end-gap to specification without boring the cylinder.

➡️ For piston ring specifications, refer to the Piston and Ring Specification chart in this section.

10. Compression ring side clearance should be measured by using a ring expander to put cleaned rings back in their original positions on the pistons. Measure side clearance on one side by attempting to slide a feeler gauge of the thickness specified between the ring and the edge of the ring groove. If the gauge will not pass into the groove, the ring may be re-used. If the gauge will pass, but a gauge of slightly greater thickness representing the wear limit will not, the piston may be re-used, but new rings must be installed.

11. The connecting rods must be free from wear, cracking and bending. Visually examine the rod, particularly at its upper and lower ends. Look for any sign of metal stretching or wear. The piston pin should fit cleanly and tightly

Fig. 207 You can use a piece of an old ring to clean the ring grooves, but be CAREFUL the ring is sharp—all engines

Fig. 208 Measure the piston's outer diameter using a micrometer

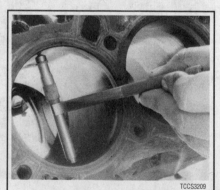

Fig. 209 A telescoping gauge is the best way to measure in the cylinder bore

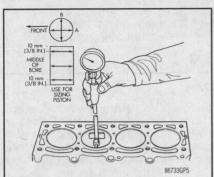

Fig. 210 Use the telescoping gauge to measure the cylinder bore diameter in the six directions shown

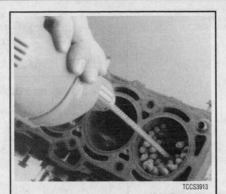

Fig. 211 Using a ball type cylinder hone is an easy way to hone the cylinder bore

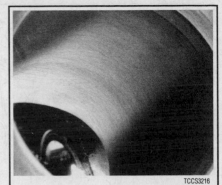

Fig. 212 A properly cross-hatched cylinder bore

through the upper end, allowing no side-play or wobble. The bottom end should also be an exact half-circle, with no deformity of shape. The bolts must be firmly mounted and parallel. The rods may be taken to a machine shop for exact measurement of twist or bend.

12. If removal of the pistons from the connecting rods is necessary or desired, have the pins pressed out and the new pins heated and pressed back in by a qualified automotive machine shop. This procedure requires extreme heat and pressures which are not available to the general mechanic without the special tools needed.

RIDGE REMOVAL & HONING

Ridge Removal

Inspect the upper portions of the cylinder (near the head) for a ridge formed by ring wear. If there is a ridge, it must be removed by first shifting the piston down in the cylinder and then covering the piston top completely with a clean rag. Use a ridge reamer to remove metal at the lip until the cylinder is smooth. If this is not done, the rings will be damaged during removal of the piston.

Honing

▶ See Figures 211 and 212

Before honing the cylinders, stuff plenty of clean shop towels under the bores and over the crankshaft (if still in the engine) to keep the abrasive materials from entering the crankcase area.

1. Used carefully, the cylinder bore resizing hone C-823 equipped with 220 grit stones, or equivalent, is the best tool for this job. In addition to deglazing, it will reduce taper and out-of-round as well as removing light scuffing, scoring or scratches. Usually a few strokes will clean up a bore and maintain the required limits.

2. Deglazing of the cylinder walls may be done using a cylinder surfacing hone (or equivalent), Tool C-3501, equipped with 280 grit stones (C-3501–3810) if the cylinder is already straight and round. 20–60 strokes depending on the bore condition will be sufficient to provide a satisfactory surface. Inspect the cylinder walls after each 20 strokes, using a light honing oil available from an automotive parts store.

➡Do not use engine or transaxle oil, mineral spirits or kerosene.

3. Honing should be done by moving the hone up and down fast enough to get a cross-hatch pattern. When hone marks intersect at 50–60°, the cross-hatch angle is most satisfactory for proper seating of the rings.

4. A controlled hone motor speed between 200–300 rpm is necessary to obtain the proper cross-hatch angle. The number of up and down strokes per minute can be regulated to get the desired 50–60° angle. Faster up and down strokes increase the cross-hatch angle.

5. After honing, it will be necessary to clean the block to remove all traces of abrasive.

✳✳ WARNING

Be sure that all abrasive is removed from the engine parts after honing. It is recommended that a solution of soap and hot water be

used with a brush and the parts then thoroughly dried. The bore is considered clean when it can be wiped with a white cloth and the cloth remains clean. Oil the bores after cleaning to prevent rust.

PISTON PIN REPLACEMENT

Except 2.2L Turbo III and 2.5L Turbo I Engines

The piston pins in all of these engines are press-fit into the piston/connecting rod assemblies. The piston pin must be heated up to an extreme temperature (often as high as 1500°F/815°C or higher) and then the pin must be pressed into the piston and connecting rod with a special press. Therefore, because of the special machinery and specific skills needed to either remove the old piston pin or to install the new piston pin, the piston, connecting rod and piston pin should be taken to a qualified machine shop.

2.2L Turbo III and 2.5L Turbo I Engines

▶ See Figures 213, 214 and 215

The turbocharged engine piston/pin/connecting rod assemblies should not be disassembled unless a malfunction is present or a damaged assembly component is to be replaced.

✳✳ CAUTION

Approved safety glasses must be worn during piston lockring removal or installation to prevent possible injury from flying parts.

1. Carefully remove the piston pin lockrings from the piston using a small prytool in the removal notch.
2. Discard the used lockring.

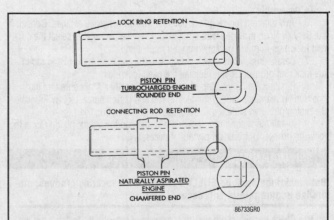

Fig. 213 Unlike other engines which use interference fit piston pins, the 2.2L Turbo III and 2.5L Turbo I engines use full floating piston pins and lockrings

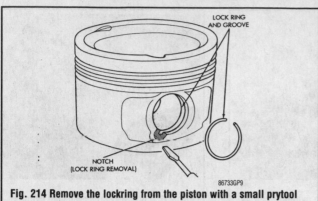

Fig. 214 Remove the lockring from the piston with a small prytool through the notch

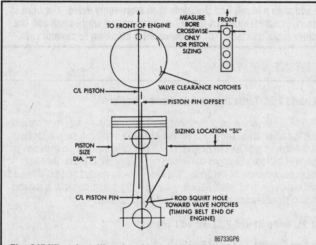

Fig. 215 When installing the piston to the rod, make sure to position the piston valve clearance notches on the same side as the rod oil squirt hole

3. Following lockring removal, attempt to slide the pin out of the piston. If the pin does not slide freely by hand, check for a burr on the outer edge of the lockring groove. If a burr is present, carefully scrape the burr away with a knife or other hand tool, being careful not to damage the lockring retaining groove.

4. Slide the piston pin out to complete disassembly.

5. Inspect the components, discard damaged or excessively worn parts.

➡ **If a new piston is being installed, a new piston pin should also be installed.**

To assemble:

6. Two different lockrings are used for the turbocharged engines. Consult the Service Note, provided with the lockring service package, to select the correct lockrings from the package for your application.

7. Careful install one new lockring with the gap toward the piston top in the lock ring groove. Do not reinstall the used lockrings.

8. Position the connecting rod and piston together. Make sure that the positioning markings on the connecting rod and piston agree. Lightly lubricate the piston pin, then slide it into the piston and connecting rod.

9. Install the second new lockring with the gap toward the piston top in the lockring groove. Use a small prytool, if necessary.

❋ WARNING

Both lockrings must be FULLY SEATED in the lockring grooves, otherwise engine failure will occur.

10. Check the piston pin end-play movement between the lockrings in the assembly. The piston pin end-play specifications are as follows:
- 2.5L Turbo I—new part, 0.000–0.035 in. (0.00–0.88mm)

- 2.5L Turbo I—used component wear limit, 0.047 in. (1.20mm)
- 2.2L Turbo III—new part, 0.0015–0.0400 in. (0.04–1.02mm)
- 2.2L Turbo III—used component wear limit, 0.047 in. (1.20mm)

PISTON RING REPLACEMENT

▶ **See Figures 216 thru 222**

1. Use a ring expander to remove the old rings from the pistons. Chances are that new piston rings will be used upon installation so it doesn't matter if the rings break during disassembly. Be careful though, the broken ring edges are extremely sharp. If the old piston rings are to be reused, be careful when removing the old rings and only expand them far enough to remove them from the piston.

2. Clean the piston and ring grooves. Refer to the previous cleaning procedures.

Fig. 216 Use a ring expander tool to remove the piston rings

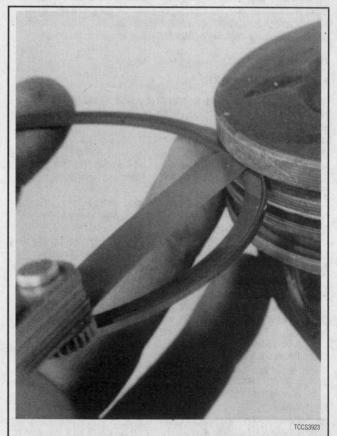

Fig. 217 Checking the ring-to-ring groove clearance

Fig. 218 Most rings are marked to show which side should face up

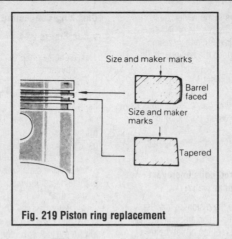

Fig. 219 Piston ring replacement

Fig. 220 Install the 2 oil ring side rails by hand

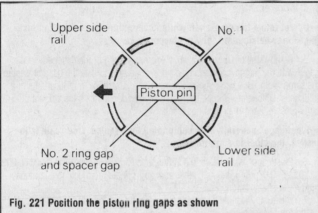

Fig. 221 Position the piston ring gaps as shown

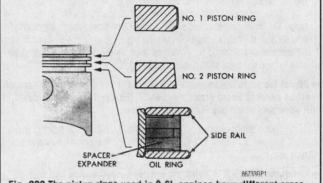

Fig. 222 The piston rings used in 2.6L engines have different cross-sections, which can be used for identification purposes

To assemble:

3. The No. 1 and No. 2 piston rings have a different cross-section. Install the rings with manufacturers mark and size mark facing up (toward the top of the piston).

➡**Install the pistons rings in the following order: a) oil ring expander, b) upper oil ring side rail, c) lower oil ring side rail, d) No. 2 intermediate (compression) piston ring, e) No. 1 upper (compression) piston ring.**

4. Install the oil ring expander by hand into its groove (bottom groove).

5. Install the upper side rail first, then the lower side rail by placing one end between the piston ring groove and the expander ring. Hold the end firmly while pressing the portion of the ring to be installed down (working along the side rail) until the ring is in position.

➡**Do not use a piston ring expander for the oil expander ring or either of the 2 side rail rings.**

6. Use a piston ring expander tool to install the No. 2 intermediate compression ring, then the No. 1 piston compression ring.

7. Position the piston ring end-gaps as shown in the illustration.

8. Position the oil ring expander gap at least 45° from the side rail gaps, but NOT on the piston pin center or on the thrust direction.

CONNECTING ROD BEARINGS

Out-of-Vehicle Replacement

▶ See Figure 223

1. Remove the connecting rod and piston assemblies from the engine, as described earlier in this section.

2. Remove the old bearings from the connecting rod large end and the connecting rod bearing cap.

3. Clean and inspect the connecting rod and bearing cap. Refer to the procedures found previously.

4. Install the new bearings into the bearing cap and connecting rod large end. To install the bearings, push the bearings into the cap or rod so that the bearing is flush with the flat cap/rod mounting surface. The side of the bearing with the groove tang goes on the same side of the rod or cap that has the groove in it. The tang sides of the upper and lower bearings are installed on the same side of the rod journal.

5. Coat the bearing surface with assembly lube. Engine oil can also be used, but it is recommended that assembly lube be used to help the break-in of the bearings.

6. Install the piston/connecting rod assemblies back into the engine.

In-Vehicle Replacement

▶ See Figure 223

This procedure can be accomplished with either the engine in the vehicle with the pistons and crankshaft installed or with the pistons removed from the engine.

Fig. 223 A notch on the connecting rod bearing surface matches a groove on the insert

1. If the bearings need to replaced while the engine is in the vehicle, disconnect the negative battery cable. Raise and safely support the vehicle on jackstands. Removal of the oil pan will be necessary, refer to the procedure in this section.

2. For 2.2L Turbo III engines and 2.5L engines, remove the balance shafts and carrier, as described earlier in this section.

3. Matchmark the bearing caps with their cylinder number for ease of assembly.

4. Perform the following procedure to each connecting rod, one at a time.

    a. Rotate the crankshaft until the connecting rod being worked on is at the lowest point in its stroke.

    b. Remove the bearing cap retaining nuts and remove the bearing cap from the crankshaft.

➡ **Use pieces of rubber hose over the connecting rod bolts to prevent scratching the crankshaft bearing surfaces or cylinder walls.**

    c. Using a piece of wood or a hammer handle, tap the piston up into the engine until the connecting rod bottom end comes off of the crankshaft journal.

    d. Using a small punch or prytool push the old bearings out of the bearing cap and the end of the connecting rod large end.

    e. Using a micrometer check the crankshaft journal for out-of-round and taper. The limits for either are shown in the Crankshaft Specifications chart in this section. If the crankshaft exhibits too much taper or out-of-round it must be replaced or machined by a machine shop. Undersized bearings are available in case the crankshaft needs machining.

➡ **Do not lubricate the bearings at this time. First the bearing clearance must be checked using Plastigage® and if the bearings are lubricated, it will adversely affect the Plastigage® process.**

    f. Install the new bearings into the cap and rod end. The bearing shells must be installed with the tangs inserted into the machined grooves in the rods and caps.

➡ **Install the bearings in pairs. Do not use a new bearing half with an old bearing half. Do not file the rods or bearing caps.**

    g. Clean the crankshaft journal of all oil, dirt or all other contaminants.

    h. Pull the piston back down until the connecting rod is once again seated on the crankshaft journal.

    i. Apply the Plastigage® to the crankshaft journal. Refer to the Plastigage® procedures following this procedure before commencing.

    j. Install the bearing cap onto the crankshaft journal. When the bearing caps are installed, install the cap with the tangs on the same side as the rod.

    k. Tighten the connecting rod nuts to specifications (shown in the Torque Specifications chart in the beginning of this section).

➡ **Do not turn the crankshaft while the Plastigage® is being used. Refer to the Plastigage® procedures following this procedure.**

    l. Remove the bearing caps again. Using the gauge which came with the Plastigage® read the clearance of the connecting rod bearing. The connecting rod bearing clearances are shown in the Crankshaft and Connecting Rod Specifications chart earlier in this section. If the connecting rod bearing clearance is too great, the crankshaft must be machined by a machine shop and undersized bearings used.

    m. Clean the Plastigage® off of the crankshaft journal or connecting rod bearings.

    n. The rod bolts must be examined before reuse. If the threads are necked down (stretched) the bolts will have to be replaced with new bolts. Necking can be checked by holding a ruler or straightedge against the threads. If all of the threads do not contact the scale, the bolt is exhibiting necking.

    o. If the clearance is within specification, lubricate the connecting rod bearings with assembly lube or clean engine oil (assembly lube is preferred by the manufacturer). Install the connecting rod bearing cap onto the crankshaft again. Tighten the cap to the designated torque, as described previously.

5. Repeat the procedure with all of the other connecting rods, one at a time.

6. If the pistons and crankshaft are removed from the engine, install the crankshaft and pistons to the engine block before tightening the bearing caps and checking for clearance. However, the new bearings can be inserted into the connecting rod ends and bearing caps prior to installation.

7. For 2.2L Turbo III and 2.5L engines, install the balance shafts and carrier.

8. Install the oil pan, lower the vehicle and connect the negative battery cable.

9. Fill the engine with the proper amount of oil.

Checking Connecting Rod Bearing Clearance With Plastigage®

◆ **See Figure 224**

The engine crankshaft and connecting rod bearing clearances can be determined by the use of Plastigage® or a similar product. The following is the recommended procedure for the use of Plastigage®:

1. Rotate the crankshaft until the connecting rod boss to be checked is at the bottom of its stroke.

2. With the connecting rod and the connecting rod bearing cap removed from the crankshaft, remove the oil film from the surface to be checked. Plastigage® is soluble in oil.

3. Place a piece of Plastigage® across the entire width of the bearing shell in the bearing cap approximately ¼ in. (6.35mm) off center and away from the oil hole. In addition, suspect areas can be checked by placing Plastigage® in the suspect area.

4. Before assembling the rod bearing cap with the Plastigage® in place, the crankshaft must be rotated until the connecting rod being checked starts moving toward the top of the engine. Only then should the cap be assembled and tightened to specifications.

➡ **Do not rotate the crankshaft while assembling the cap or the Plastigage® may be smeared, giving inaccurate results.**

5. Remove the bearing cap and compare the width of the flattened Plastigage® with the metric scale provided on the package. Locate the band closest to the same width. This band shows the amount of clearance in thousandths of a millimeter. Differences in readings between the ends indicate the amount of taper present. Record all readings taken.

➡ **Plastigage® generally is accompanied by 2 scales. One scale is in inches, the other is a metric scale.**

6. Plastigage® is available in a variety of clearance ranges. The 0.001–0.003 in. (0.025–0.076mm) is usually the most appropriate for checking engine bearing proper specifications.

7. Clean the Plastigage® from the connecting rod journal or from the connecting rod bearing shell.

TCCS3912

Fig. 224 Use the gauge supplied with the Plastigage® to check the bearing clearance

INSTALLATION

◆ **See Figure 225**

1. Have a machine shop reassemble the pistons to the connecting rods, unless servicing the 2.2L Turbo III or 2.5L Turbo I engines. If repairing either of these engines, assemble the pistons, connecting rods and piston pins, as described earlier in this section.

✳✳ WARNING

Do not use a piston ring expander for the oil expander ring or either of the 2 side rail oil rings.

2. Install the rings onto the pistons as follows:

    a. The No. 1 and No. 2 piston rings have a different cross section. Install the rings with manufacturer's mark and size mark facing up (toward the top of the piston).

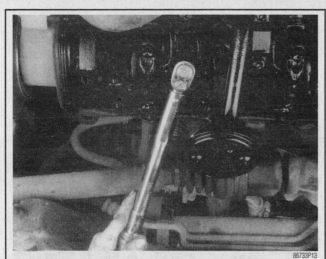

Fig. 225 Always make sure to tighten the connecting rod attaching nuts with a torque wrench

➡ **Install the pistons rings in the following order: a) oil ring expander, b) upper oil ring side rail, c) lower oil ring side rail, d) No. 2 intermediate (compression) piston ring, e) No. 1 upper (compression) piston ring.**

   b. Install the oil ring expander by hand into its groove (bottom groove).

   c. Install the upper side rail first, then the lower side rail by placing one end between the piston ring groove and the expander ring. Hold the end firmly while pressing the portion of the ring to be installed down (working along the side rail) until the ring is in position.

   d. Use a piston ring expander tool to install the No. 2 intermediate compression ring, then the No. 1 piston compression ring.

   e. Position the piston ring end-gaps as shown in the illustration.

   f. Position the oil ring expander gap at least 45° from the side rail gaps, but NOT on the piston pin center or on the thrust direction.

  3. All the pistons, rods and caps must be reinstalled in the correct cylinder. Make certain that all labels and stamped numbers are present and legible. Double check the piston rings; make certain that the ring gaps DO NOT line up.

  4. Reinstall the protective rubber hose pieces on the connecting rod bolts.

  5. Liberally coat the cylinder walls and the crankshaft journals with clean, fresh engine oil.

  6. Install each piston/connecting rod into its respective cylinder bore one at a time as follows:

   a. Identify the front mark on each piston/connecting rod assembly and position the piston loosely in its cylinder with the marks facing the front (pulley end) of the motor.

✳ WARNING

Failure to observe the applicable markings and the pistons' correct placements can lead to sudden engine failure.

   b. Install a ring compressor (piston installation tool) around one piston and tighten it gently until the rings are compressed almost completely.

   c. Gently push down on the piston top with a wooden hammer handle or similar soft-faced tool and drive the piston into the cylinder bore. Once all 3 rings are within the bore, the piston will move with some ease.

✳ WARNING

If any resistance or binding is encountered during the installation, DO NOT apply excessive force. Tighten or adjust the ring compressor and/or reposition the piston. Brute force will break the ring(s) or damage the piston.

   d. From underneath, pull the connecting rod into place on the crankshaft. Remove the rubber hoses from the bolts. Check the rod cap to confirm that the bearing is present and correctly mounted.

   e. At this time check the connecting rod bearing clearance. Refer to the connecting rod bearing instructions with Plastigage® for this procedure. After checking the clearance do not completely tighten the connecting rod bearing caps to their final torque yet.

   f. If all of the bearing clearances are within specifications continue with this procedure. Otherwise the crankshaft or connecting rods will need to be either machined or replaced with new ones. If out of specification, have them checked by a reputable automotive machine shop.

   g. Install the rod cap (observing the correct number and position) and its nuts. Leaving the nuts finger-tight will make installation of the remaining pistons and rods easier.

  7. Assemble the remaining pistons in the same fashion, repeating Step 6.

  8. With all the pistons installed and the bearing caps secured finger-tight, the retaining nuts may be tightened to their final setting. Refer to the Torque Specifications chart at the beginning of this section for the correct torque for the engine in your vehicle. For each pair of nuts, make 3 passes alternating between the 2 nuts on any given rod cap. The 3 tightening steps should each be about one third of the final torque. The intent is to draw each cap up to the crankshaft straight and under even pressure at the nuts.

  9. Turn the crankshaft through several clockwise rotations, making sure everything moves smoothly and there is no binding. With the piston rods connected, the crank may be stiff to turn. Try to turn it in a smooth continuous motion so that any binding or stiff spots may be felt.

  10. At this time, use a feeler gauge to measure the connecting rod side clearance. Refer to the specifications chart for the correct amount of side clearance allowed. If the side clearance is too great, the connecting rods will have to be replaced with new ones. If the side clearance to is too small, the connecting rods will have to be removed and machined by a reputable automotive machine shop.

  11. For 2.2L Turbo III and 2.5L engines, install the balance shafts and carrier. For more information, refer to the procedure earlier in this section.

  12. Reinstall the oil pan. Even if the engine is to remain apart for other repairs, install the oil pan to protect the bottom end and tighten the bolts to the correct specification; this eliminates one easily overlooked mistake during future reassembly.

  13. If the engine is to remain apart for other repairs, pack the cylinders with crumpled newspaper or clean rags (to keep out dust and grit) and cover the top of the motor with a large rag. If the engine is on a stand, the whole block can be protected with a large plastic trash bag.

  14. If no further work is to be performed, continue reassembly by installing the cylinder head, timing belt or chains, and all other components.

Rear Main Oil Seal

REMOVAL & INSTALLATION

2.2L and 2.5L Engines

▶ **See Figures 226, 227 and 228**

➡ **Use these procedures as a guide for all other engines. Modify service steps as required.**

  1. Remove the transaxle. For more information, refer to Section 7.

  2. Remove the flywheel/flexplate from the engine, as described later

➡ **On some early models, before removing the transaxle, align the dimple on the flywheel with the pointer on the flywheel housing. The transaxle will not mate with the engine during installation unless this alignment is observed.**

  3. Very carefully, pry the oil seal out of the support ring. Be careful not to nick or damage the crankshaft flange seal surface or retainer bore.

To install:

  4. Position Special Tool C-4681, or its equivalent, on the crankshaft.

  5. Lightly coat the outside diameter of the new rear main seal with Loctite® Stud N' Bearing Mount, or its equivalent. Also coat the inside of the seal with clean engine oil.

  6. Place the seal over Tool C-4681 and gently tap it into place with a plastic hammer.

  7. Remove Tool C-4681 from the crankshaft.

  8. Install the flywheel/flexplate and transaxle.

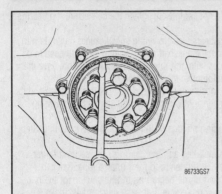

Fig. 226 Use a flat-bladed prytool to pry the used oil seal out of the housing

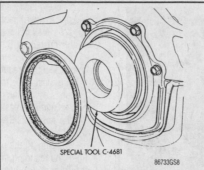

Fig. 227 Use Special Tool C-4681 to install the new rear main oil seal into the seal housing

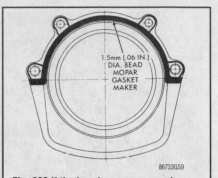

Fig. 228 If the housing was removed, apply sealant as shown when installing onto the engine block

2.6L Engine

▶ See Figure 229

The rear main oil seal is located in a housing on the rear of the block. To replace the seal, remove the transaxle and flywheel or flexplate and do the work from underneath the vehicle or remove the engine and do the work on the bench.

1. Remove the bolts holding the crankshaft rear oil seal case to the engine block, then remove the case.
2. Remove the separator from the case and remove the oil seal.

To install:

3. Lightly oil the inner lip of the new oil seal.
4. Install the oil seal so that the seal plate fits into the inner contact surface of the seal case. Make certain it is flush and level in the case.
5. Install the separator with the oil hole at the bottom.

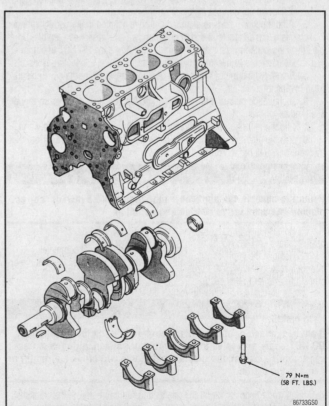

Fig. 230 Always tighten the main bearing nuts with a torque wrench

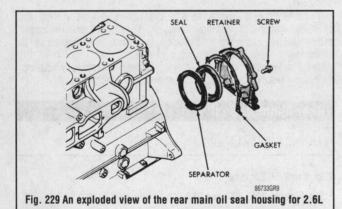

Fig. 229 An exploded view of the rear main oil seal housing for 2.6L engines

Crankshaft and Main Bearings

REMOVAL & INSTALLATION

▶ See Figure 230

➡Although the following procedure is presented as if the engine is removed from the vehicle and installed on an engine stand, it may also be possible to service the crankshaft when the engine is still installed in the vehicle.

All Engines

▶ See Figures 231, 232 and 233

➡This is a general procedure which is applicable to all engines covered by this manual. However, slight variations may arise; alter the procedure accordingly.

Fig. 231 An exploded view of a common crankshaft and main bearing cap set-up—2.6 L engine shown, however the other engines are very essentially the same

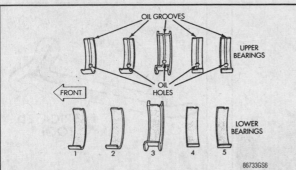

Fig. 232 The bearing halves vary based on their installed positions—grooved shells are installed in the block and smooth shells go in the caps

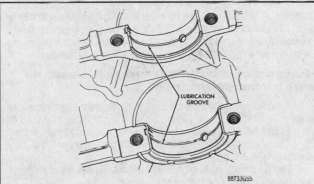

Fig. 233 Be sure the bearings are not cocked and their edges are flush with the block or bearing cap (as applicable)

The crankshaft is supported in five main bearings. All upper bearing shells in the crankcase have oil grooves. All lower bearing shells are not equipped with oil grooves. Crankshaft end-play is controlled by the thrust bearing on the number 3 main bearing journal.

1. Remove the engine from the vehicle and install it onto an engine stand.
2. Remove the upper end components (intake manifold, cylinder heads, timing belt and cover, etc.). Refer to the particular procedures in this section.
3. Remove the oil pan and oil pump. Refer to the particular procedure in this section.
4. Flip the engine upside-down on the engine stand.
5. Remove the rear oil seal retainer and seal as an assembly from the engine block. Refer to the particular procedure in this section.
6. If equipped, remove the balance shafts and carrier, as described earlier in this section.

➡Bearing caps are not interchangeable and should be marked at removal to ensure correct reassembly.

7. Release the crankshaft main bearing cap bolts evenly. Remove the lower bearing shells and identify them for ease of reassembly.
8. Remove the connecting rod bearing caps and push the pistons down into their respective cylinder bores. For more information, refer to the proper procedures earlier in this section.
9. Lift the crankshaft out and remove the upper crankshaft main bearing shells.

To install:

➡Upper and lower bearing halves are NOT interchangeable. The lower main bearing halves 1, 2, 4 and 5 are interchangeable and upper main bearing halves 1, 2, 4 and 5 are also interchangeable.

10. Install the upper main bearing shells making certain the oil holes are in alignment, and the bearing tabs seat in the block tabs. All upper bearings have oil grooves. The crankshaft thrust bearing is installed in journal No. 3 for the 2.2L, 2.5L 2.6L engines.
11. Wipe any oil from the crankshaft journals and bearing shells.
12. Set the crankshaft into the engine.

13. Cut pieces of Plastigage® to the same length as the width of the bearing and place a piece on each of the journals parallel with the journal axis.
14. Install the lower main bearing shells (without oil grooves) in the crankshaft bearing caps.
15. Install the main bearing caps carefully and tighten the bolts to the specified torque value, as shown in the Torque Specifications chart in the beginning of this section.

➡Do not rotate crankshaft or the Plastigage® will be smeared.

16. Carefully remove the bearing caps and measure the width of the various pieces of the Plastigage® at their widest points using the scale on the Plastigage® package. If the clearances are not within specifications, either different bearing shells will be needed or the crankshaft must be machined by a reputable automotive machine shop.
17. Wipe the Plastigage off of the crankshaft or bearing shell. Remove the crankshaft from its position in the engine.
18. Oil the bearings and journals. Reinstall the crankshaft to the engine.
19. Carefully install the bearing caps with the arrows toward the timing belt end.
20. Oil the bearing cap bolt threads, install and tighten the bolts progressively to the torque specification. On the 2.2L and 2.5L engines, tighten the crankshaft main bearing cap bolts first only finger-tight, then tighten them to 30 ft. lbs. (41 Nm) plus an additional ¼ turn. On the 2.6L engine, tighten the crankshaft main bearing bolts to 58 ft. lbs. (79 Nm) in 3 even steps, such as 20 ft lbs. (27 Nm), 40 ft. lbs. (54 Nm) and 58 ft. lbs. (79 Nm).
21. Rotate the crankshaft to check for binding or any other problems.
22. Mount a dial indicator to the front of the engine, locating the probe on the nose of the crankshaft.
23. Move the crankshaft all the way to the rear of its travel.
24. Set the dial indicator to zero.
25. Move the crankshaft all the way to the front and read the dial indicator. Refer to the engine charts for the proper end-play specification.
26. Scrape clean or wire brush the gasket surface of the oil seal retainer to remove all lose material. Inspect the housing to ensure that the gasket surface is flat.
27. Clean the surface of all oil and residual dirt. Make sure all of the old gasket material is removed from any bolt holes or housing surfaces.
28. Set the retainer on a flat, hard, clean work surface with the inside face resting down. Install a new oil seal, as described earlier in this section.
29. Apply Mopar Silicone Rubber Adhesive Sealant® or the equivalent to the oil seal housing in a continuous bead of 0.120 in. (3mm) diameter or less, as shown. Be certain that the sealing material surrounds each mounting bolt hole. Excess material can easily be wiped off. The oil seal retainer should be installed and tightened to its specified torque within 10 minutes (still wet to the touch).
30. Apply a light coating of engine oil to the entire circumference of the oil seal lip.
31. Install the seal retainer onto the cylinder block. For more information, refer to the rear main oil seal procedures in this section.
32. Pull the pistons and connecting rods back up and install them onto the crankshaft, as described earlier in this section.
33. Install a new front oil seal. For more information, refer to the crankshaft, camshaft and intermediate shaft sprocket procedure in this section.
34. Install the oil pan, oil pump and related components. Refer to the procedures in this section.
35. Reassemble the engine and install it back into the vehicle.

CLEANING & INSTALLATION

Clean all components in a solvent to remove oil, dirt or caked on grime.
The crankshaft main journals should be checked for excessive wear, taper and scoring. Limits of taper or out-of-round on any crankshaft journals are shown in the Engine Rebuilding Specification charts at the end of this section. Do not grind the thrust faces of No. 3 main bearing. Do not nick the crankshaft pin or bearing fillets. After grinding, remove all rough edges from the crankshaft oil holes and clean out all passages.

Crankshaft End-Play

◆ See Figures 234 and 235

1. Rotate the crankshaft to check for binding or any other problems.
2. Mount a dial indicator to the front of the engine, locating the probe on the nose of the crankshaft.

Fig. 234 A dial gauge should be positioned as shown to measure crankshaft end-play

Fig. 235 Carefully pry the shaft back and forth while reading the dial gauge for play

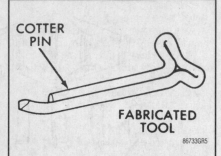

Fig. 236 A roll-out pin can be fabricated from a cotter pin—simply bend it as shown

3. Pry the crankshaft all the way to the rear of its travel with a prybar.

4. Set the dial indicator to zero.

5. Move the crankshaft all the way to the front and back again while reading the dial indicator. Pry the crankshaft back and forth several times. The amount of variation measured by the dial indicator is the end-play. Refer to the engine charts for the proper end-play specification.

6. If end-play is not within specification, inspect the crankshaft thrust faces for wear. If no wear is evident, replace the thrust bearing and measure end-play again. If end-play is still not within specification, replace the crankshaft.

Main Bearing Oil Clearance

➡Perform this procedure if only the crankshaft oil bearing clearance must be measured, otherwise refer to either the crankshaft removal and installation procedure or the crankshaft main bearing replacement procedure.

1. Remove cap from the bearing to be checked. Using a clean, dry rag, thoroughly clean all oil from crankshaft journal and bearing insert.

➡Plastigage® is soluble in oil; therefore, oil on the journal or bearing could result in erroneous readings.

2. Place a piece of Plastigage® along the full width of the insert, reinstall cap, and torque to specifications.

3. Remove bearing cap, and determine clearance by comparing width of Plastigage® to the scale on Plastigage® envelope. Journal taper is determined by comparing width of the Plastigage® strip near its ends. Remove the Plastigage®, rotate the crankshaft 90 degrees and retest, to determine journal concentricity.

➡Do not rotate crankshaft with Plastigage® installed.

4. If the bearing insert and journal appear intact, and are within tolerances, no further main bearing service is required. Just make sure to oil the bearing and crankshaft journal surfaces thoroughly and reassemble caps to the specified torque. If the bearing or journal appear defective, the cause of failure should be determined before replacement.

BEARING REPLACEMENT

▶ See Figure 236

This procedure explains how to replace the crankshaft bearings without removing the crankshaft from the engine. If the crankshaft must be removed for some other reason, refer to the previous removal and installation procedure.

➡Use these procedures as a guide for all engines. Modify service steps, if required.

1. Rod bearings can be installed when the pistons have been removed for servicing (rings etc.) or, in most cases, while the engine is still in the car. Bearing replacement, however, is far easier with the engine out of the car and disassembled.

2. For in-car service, remove the oil pan, oil pump, balance shafts and carrier (if equipped—2.2L Turbo III and 2.5L engines), spark plugs and front cover, as necessary.

3. Main bearings may be replaced while the engine is still in the car by "rolling" them out and in.

4. A special roll-out pin is available from Chrysler (Tool C-3059), from automotive parts houses or can be fabricated from a cotter pin (refer to the illustration). The roll out pin fits in the oil hole of the main bearing journal on the crankshaft. When the crankshaft is rotated opposite the direction of the bearing lock tab, the pin engages the end of the bearing and rolls out the insert.

➡Bearing caps are not interchangeable and should be marked at removal to ensure correct reassembly.

5. Remove one main bearing cap and roll out the upper bearing insert, as follows:

a. Insert the roll-out pin into the oil hole of the crankshaft main journal.

b. Slowly rotate the crankshaft clockwise, forcing the upper half of the bearing shell out of the engine block.

6. Remove the bearing insert from the main bearing cap. Clean the inside of the bearing cap and crankshaft journal.

➡Upper and lower bearing halves are NOT interchangeable. Lower main bearing halves 1, 2, 4 and 5 are interchangeable and upper main bearing halves 1, 2, 4 and 5 are also interchangeable. Only one main bearing should be selectively fitted while all other main bearing caps are properly tightened.

➡If servicing main bearing No. 3 (middle main bearing), make sure to install the thrust bearing (bearing with the folded over edges).

7. Lubricate only the upper bearing shell with assembly lube or clean engine oil (assembly lube is preferred by the manufacturer) and roll the upper insert into position in the crankshaft main, make sure the lock tab is anchored in the groove of the main journal and the insert is not cocked. Remove the bearing roll-out tool.

❊❊ WARNING

Make sure to remove the roll-out pin tool, otherwise extensive crankshaft and/or engine block damage will occur.

8. Check the main bearing oil clearance, as follows:

a. Wipe any oil from the bottom half of the crankshaft journal and bearing shells.

b. Cut a piece of Plastigage® to the same length as the width of the bearing and place a piece on the journal parallel with the journal axis.

c. Install the lower main bearing shell (without oil grooves) dry in the crankshaft bearing cap.

d. Install the main bearing cap carefully and tighten the bolts to the specified torque value, as shown in the Torque Specifications chart in the beginning of this section.

➡Do not rotate crankshaft or the Plastigage® will be smeared.

e. Carefully remove the bearing cap and measure the width of the Plastigage® at its widest point using the scale on the Plastigage® package; this is the minimum oil clearance for this journal. Measure the thinnest section of Plastigage® and subtract this number from the widest section, this is the amount of taper of the crankshaft journal or it indicates that the bearings may be slightly cocked. Double check that the bearings are mounted flush in their bores. If the clearances measured are not within specifications, either different bearing shells must be acquired or the crankshaft must be machined by a reputable automotive machine shop. Remove the crankshaft and inspect it with a micrometer, or have a reputable machine shop inspect it.

    f. Wipe the Plastigage off of the crankshaft or bearing shell.

   9. Oil the lower bearing half and lower half of the journal with assembly lube or clean engine oil (assembly lube is preferred by the manufacturer).

  10. Install the lower bearing insert into the main cap. Lubricate it with assembly lube or engine oil as with the upper bearing, then install it on the engine. Make sure the main bearing cap is installed facing in the correct direction. Make sure the oil holes line up with those in the block and that the grooved bearing shell is located in the block (rather than in the cap). The thrust bearing (the bearing with folded up sides) must be installed in the No. 3 main.

  11. Oil the bearing cap bolt threads. Check the cap bolts for "necking down". This is a condition that would prevent the right size nut from being run down until it touches the cap or would cause some threads not to touch a straightedge run along the side of the bolt.

  12. Tighten the crankshaft main bearing cap bolts until slightly looser than snug.

  13. Repeat Steps 5 through 11 for all main bearings which are to be replaced (all of the bearings should be replaced at the same time).

  14. Once all replacement bearings are installed, install and tighten the bolts progressively to the torque specification. On the 2.2L and 2.5L engines, tighten the crankshaft main bearing cap bolts first only finger-tight, then tighten them to 30 ft. lbs. (41 Nm) plus an additional ¼ turn. On the 2.6L engine, tighten the crankshaft main bearing bolts to 58 ft. lbs. (79 Nm) in 3 even steps, such as 20 ft lbs. (27 Nm), 40 ft. lbs. (54 Nm) and 58 ft. lbs. (79 Nm).

  15. Rotate the crankshaft to ensure that there is no binding. If binding, or other problems, are evident, the crankshaft should be completely removed from the engine and inspected for defects.

  16. Mount a dial indicator to the front of the engine, locating the probe on the nose of the crankshaft.

  17. Move the crankshaft all the way to the rear of its travel.

  18. Set the dial indicator to zero.

  19. Move the crankshaft all the way to the front and read the dial indicator. Refer to the engine charts for the proper end-play specification.

  20. Install the components removed earlier. For more information, refer to the applicable procedures.

BREAK-IN PROCEDURE

Start the engine, and allow it to run at low speed for a few minutes, while checking for leaks. Stop the engine, check the oil level, and fill as necessary. Restart the engine, and fill the cooling system to capacity. Check and adjust the ignition timing. Run the engine at low to medium speed (800–2,500 rpm) for approximately ½ hour, and retighten the cylinder head bolts. Road test the car, and check again for leaks.

EXHAUST SYSTEM

Inspection

▶ See Figures 237 thru 243

➡ Safety glasses should be worn at all times when working on or near the exhaust system. Older exhaust systems will almost always be covered with loose rust particles which are more than a nuisance and could injure your eye.

✳✳ CAUTION

DO NOT perform exhaust repairs or inspection with the engine or exhaust hot. Allow the system to cool completely. Exhaust systems are noted for sharp edges, flaking metal and rusted bolts. Gloves and eye protection are required. A healthy supply of penetrating oil and rags is highly recommended.

Your vehicle must be raised and supported safely at four points to inspect the exhaust system properly. Start the inspection at the exhaust manifold where the header pipe is attached and work your way to the back of the vehicle. On dual exhaust systems, remember to inspect both sides of the vehicle. Check the com-

➡ Some gasket manufacturers recommend not retightening the cylinder head(s) due to the composition of the head gasket. Follow the directions in the gasket set.

Flywheel/Flexplate and Ring Gear

REMOVAL & INSTALLATION

The flywheel on manual transaxle cars serves as the forward clutch engagement surface. It also serves as the ring gear with which the starter pinion engages to crank the engine. The most common reason to replace the flywheel is broken teeth on the starter ring gear.

On automatic transaxle cars, the torque converter actually forms part of the flywheel. It is bolted to a thin flexplate which, in turn, is bolted to the crankshaft. The flex plate also serves as the ring gear with which the starter pinion engages in engine cranking. The flex plate occasionally cracks; the teeth on the ring gear may also break, especially if the starter is often engaged while the pinion is still spinning. The torque converter and flex plate are separated so the converter and transaxle can be removed together.

   1. Remove the transaxle from the vehicle. For more information, refer to Section 7.

   2. On vehicles equipped with manual transaxles, remove the clutch assembly from the flywheel, as described in Section 7.

   3. Support the flywheel in a secure manner (the flywheel on manual transaxle-equipped vehicles can be heavy).

   4. Matchmark the flywheel/flexplate to the rear flange of the crankshaft.

   5. Remove the attaching bolts and pull the flywheel/flexplate from the crankshaft.

To install:

   6. Clean the flywheel/flexplate attaching bolts, the flywheel/flexplate and the rear crankshaft mounting flange.

   7. Position the flywheel/flexplate onto the crankshaft flange so that the matchmarks align.

   8. Coat the threads of the attaching bolts with Loctite® Thread Locker 271, or equivalent, to help ensure that the attaching bolts will not work loose. Install the bolts finger-tight.

   9. Tighten the attaching bolts in a crisscross fashion in 3 even steps until the following torque values are reached:
- 1986–95 Chrysler Manual and Automatic transaxles—70 ft. lbs. (95 Nm)
- 1981–85 Automatic transaxles—65 ft. lbs. (88 Nm)
- 1984–85 Manual transaxles—65 ft. lbs. (88 Nm)
- 1981–83 Manual transaxles—50 ft. lbs. (68 Nm)

  10. For manual transaxle-equipped vehicles, install the clutch assembly. For more information, refer to Section 7.

  11. Install the transaxle, as described in Section 7.

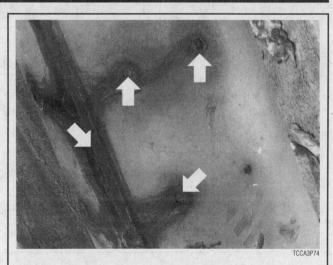

TCCA3P74

Fig. 237 Check the muffler for rotted spot welds and seams

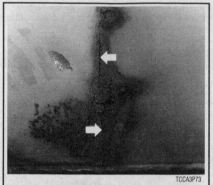

Fig. 238 Cracks in the muffler are a guaranteed leak

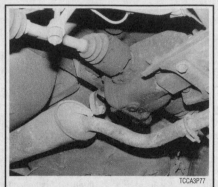

Fig. 239 Make sure the exhaust does contact the body or suspension

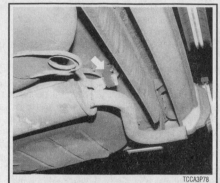

Fig. 240 Check for overstretched or torn exhaust hangers

Fig. 241 Example of a badly deteriorated exhaust pipe

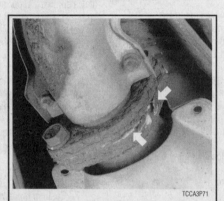

Fig. 242 Inspect flanges for gaskets that have deteriorated and need replacement

Fig. 243 Some systems, like this one, use large O-rings (donuts) in between the flanges

plete exhaust system for open seams, holes, loose connections, or other deterioration which could permit exhaust fumes to seep into the passenger compartment. Inspect all mounting brackets and hangers for deterioration, some may have rubber O-rings that can become overstretched and non-supportive (and should be replaced if worn). Many technicians use a pointed tool to poke up into the exhaust system at rust spots to see whether or not they crumble. Most models have heat shield(s) covering certain parts of the exhaust system, it is often necessary to remove these shields to visually inspect those components.

REPLACEMENT

◆ **See Figures 244 thru 252**

There are basically two types of exhaust systems. One is the flange type where the component ends are attached with bolts and a gasket in-between. The other exhaust system is the slip joint type. These components slip into one another using clamps to retain them together.

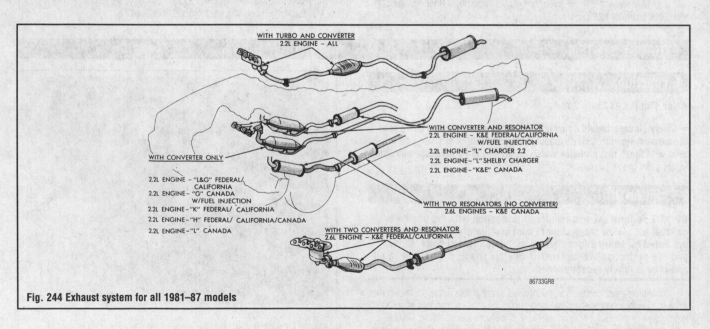

Fig. 244 Exhaust system for all 1981–87 models

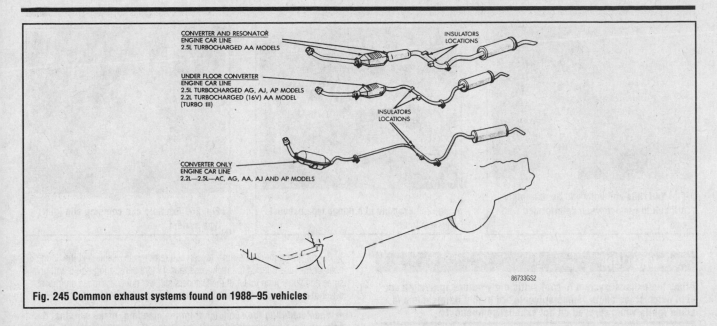

Fig. 245 Common exhaust systems found on 1988–95 vehicles

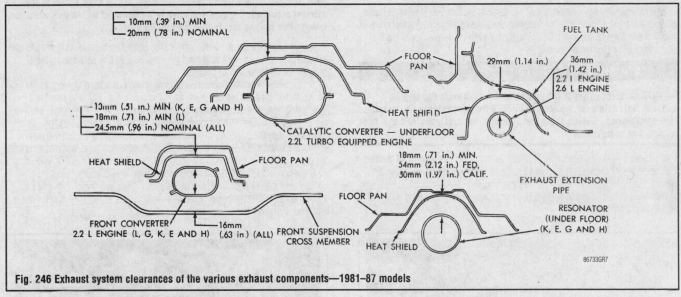

Fig. 246 Exhaust system clearances of the various exhaust components—1981–87 models

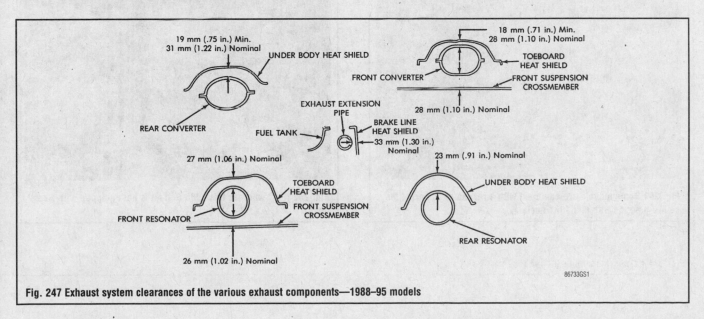

Fig. 247 Exhaust system clearances of the various exhaust components—1988–95 models

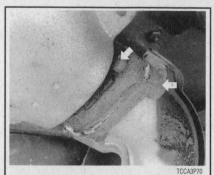

Fig. 248 Nuts and bolts will be extremely difficult to remove when deteriorated with rust

Fig. 249 Example of a flange type exhaust system joint

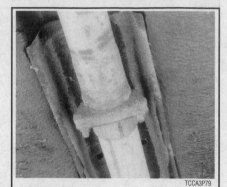

Fig. 250 Example of a common slip joint type system

> ※※ **CAUTION**
>
> Allow the exhaust system to cool sufficiently before spraying a solvent exhaust fasteners. Some solvents are highly flammable and could ignite when sprayed on hot exhaust components.

Before removing any component of the exhaust system, ALWAYS squirt a liquid rust dissolving agent onto the fasteners for ease of removal. A lot of knuckle skin will be saved by following this rule. It may even be wise to spray the fasteners and allow them to sit overnight.

> ※※ **CAUTION**
>
> Do NOT perform exhaust repairs or inspection with the engine or exhaust hot. Allow the system to cool. Exhaust systems are noted for sharp edges, flaking metal and rusted bolts. Gloves and eye protection are required.

1. Raise and support the vehicle safely, as necessary for access. Remember that some longer exhaust pipes may be difficult to wrestle out from under the vehicle if it is not supported high enough.
2. If you haven't already, apply a generous amount of penetrating oil or solvent to any rusted fasteners.

3. On flange joints, carefully loosen and remove the retainers at the flange. If bolts or nuts are difficult to break loose, apply more penetrating liquid and give it some additional time to set. If the fasteners still will not come loose an impact driver may be necessary to jar it loose (and keep the fastener from breaking).

➡ **When unbolting the headpipe from the manifold, make sure that the bolts are free before trying to remove them. If you snap a stud in the exhaust manifold, the stud will have to be removed with a bolt extractor, which often means removal of the manifold itself.**

4. On slip joint components, remove the mounting U-bolts from around the exhaust pipe you are extracting from the vehicle. Don't be surprised if the U-bolts break while removing the nuts.
5. Loosen the exhaust pipe from any mounting brackets retaining it to the floor pan and separate the components. Slight twisting and turning may be required to remove the component completely from the vehicle. You may need to tap on the component with a rubber mallet to loosen it. If all else fails, use a hacksaw to separate the parts. An oxy-acetylene cutting torch may be faster but the sparks are DANGEROUS near the fuel tank, and at the very least, accidents could happen, resulting in damage to the under-vehicle parts, not to mention yourself.
6. When installing exhaust components, you should loosely position all components before tightening any of the joints. Once you are certain that the system is run correctly, begin tightening the fasteners at the front of the vehicle and work your way back.

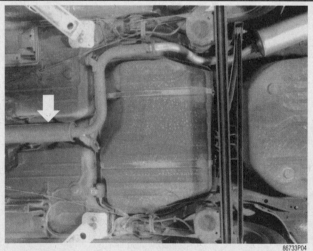

Fig. 251 Some models are equipped with a resonator as part of the center pipe, as with this 1991 Acclaim . . .

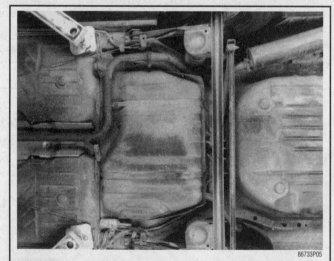

Fig. 252 . . . whereas this 1986 Reliant is not equipped with a resonator

ENGINE REBUILDING SPECIFICATIONS
2.2L and 2.5L Chrysler Engines

Description		Standard Dimension	
		English	Metric
Type			
	Except 2.2L Turbo III	In line SOHC	
	2.2L Turbo III	In line DOHC	
Number of Cylinders		4	
Bore		3.44 in.	87.5mm
Stroke			
	2.2L Engines	3.62 in.	92mm
	2.5L Engines	4.09 in.	104mm
Compression ratio			
	2.2L Standard	9.5:1	
	2.2L Turbo III	8.1:1	
	2.5L Standard	8.9:1	
	2.5L Turbo I	7.8:1	
	2.2L Turbo I and Turbo II	8.5:1	
Firing order		1–3–4–2	
Valve timing			
2.2L Standard	Intake Open	0° TDC	
	Close	55° ABDC	
	Exhaust Open	44° BBDC	
	Close	8° ATDC	
2.2L Turbo III	Intake Open	25° ATDC	
	Close	35° ABDC	
	Exhaust Open	16° BBDC	
	Close	75° ATDC	
2.5L Standard	Intake Open	4° BTDC	
	Close	60° ABDC	
	Exhaust Open	40° BBDC	
	Close	12° ATDC	
2.5L Turbo I	Intake Open	8° ATDC	
	Close	56° ABDC	
	Exhaust Open	40° BBDC	
	Close	8° ATDC	
2.2L Turbo I and Turbo II	Intake Open	10° BTDC	
	Close	50° ABDC	
	Exhaust Open	50° BBDC	
	Close	10° ATDC	
Valve Overlap			
	2.2L Standard	8°	
	2.2L Turbo III	NA	
	2.5L Standard	8°	
	2.5L Turbo I	0°	
	2.2L Turbo I and Turbo II	20°	

86733C1

ENGINE REBUILDING SPECIFICATIONS
2.2L and 2.5L Chrysler Engines

Description		Standard Dimension	
		English	Metric
Intake Valve Duration			
	2.2L Standard	236°	
	2.2L Turbo III	NA	
	2.5L Standard	236°	
	2.5L Turbo I	228°	
	2.2L Turbo I and Turbo II	240°	
Exhaust Valve Duration			
	2.2L Standard	232°	
	2.2L Turbo III	NA	
	2.5L Standard	232°	
	2.5L Turbo I	228°	
	2.2L Turbo I and Turbo II	240°	
Compression pressure			
	1981-86 models	130-150 psi [1]	896-1034 kPa [1]
	Maximum variation between cylinders	20 psi	138 kPa
	1987-95 models	100 psi @ 130 RPM [1]	689.5 kPa @ 130 RPM [1]
	Maximum variation between cylinders	25%	
Valve clearance — hot engine		Hydraulic lash adjusters	
Camshaft			
Journal diameter	Except 2.2L Turbo II		
	Standard	1.395-1.396 in.	34.939-34.960mm
	Oversize	1.395-1.396 in.	35.439-35.460mm
	2.2L Turbo III	1.886-1.887 in.	47.925-47.950mm
Camshaft end-play	Except 2.2L Turbo III	0.005-0.013 in.	0.13-0.33mm
	Service limit	0.010 in.	0.25mm
	2.2L Turbo III	0.001-0.008 in.	0.025-0.200mm
	Service limit	0.020 in.	0.50mm
Cylinder Head			
	Flatness of gasket surface	0.004 in.	0.1mm
	Cylinder head gasket (thickness compressed)	0.068 in.	1.73mm
Valves			
Thickness of valve head (margin)	Except 2.2L Turbo III		
	Intake	0.060 in.	1.5mm
	Service limit	0.030 in.	0.793mm
	Exhaust	0.060 in.	1.5mm
	Service limit	0.050 in.	1.19mm
2.2L Turbo III	Intake	0.041 in.	1.06mm
	Exhaust	0.042 in.	1.07mm
Valve stem-to-guide clearance	Except 2.2L Turbo III		
	Intake	0.0009-0.0026 in.	0.022-0.065mm
	Exhaust	0.0030-0.0047 in.	0.076-0.119mm

86733C17

ENGINE REBUILDING SPECIFICATIONS
2.2L and 2.5L Chrysler Engines

Description	Standard Dimension	
	English	Metric
Valves (continued)		
Valve stem-to-guide clearance (continued)		
2.2L Turbo III		
Intake	0.0010–0.0023 in.	0.03–0.06mm
Service limit	0.004 in.	0.1mm
Exhaust	0.0020–0.0031 in.	0.05–0.08mm
Service limit	0.004 in.	0.1mm
Intermediate shaft		
Large journal	1.679–1.680 in.	42.670–42.703mm
Bushing (large) inside diameter	1.682–1.683 in.	42.720–42.750mm
Small journal	0.774–0.775 in.	19.670–19.703mm
Bushing (small) inside diameter	0.776–0.777 in.	19.720–19.750mm
Valve Springs		
Free height		
2.2L and 2.5L Standard	2.39 in.	60.8mm
2.5L Turbo I	2.28 in.	57.9mm
2.2L Turbo III	2.094 in.	53.2mm
2.2L Turbo I and Turbo II	2.28 in.	57.9mm
Valve spring load—intake and exhaust		
1981-86 2.2L and 2.5L Standard		
Open	144–156 lbs. @ 1.22 in.	640–694 N @ 31mm
Closed	90–108 lbs. @ 1.65 in.	442–482 N @ 41.9mm
2.2L Turbo I and Turbo II		
Open	168–182 lbs. @ 1.22 in.	748–806 N @ 31mm
Closed	90–108 lbs. @ 1.65 in.	442–482 N @ 41.9mm
2.2L Turbo III		
Open	255–275 lbs. @ 1.344 in.	1133–1227 N @ 34.2mm
Closed	115–127 lbs. @ 1.73 in.	513–567 N @ 44mm
1987-95 2.2L and 2.5L Standard		
Open	195–215 lbs. @ 1.22 in.	890–961 N @ 31mm
Closed	108–120 lbs. @ 1.65 in.	480–534 N @ 41.9mm
Perpendicularity		
2.2L and 2.5L Standard	0.079 in.	2.0mm
2.2L Turbo I and Turbo II	0.06 in.	1.5mm
2.2L Turbo III	0.065 in.	1.65mm
Pistons		
Outside diameter		
2.2L Standard	3.443–3.445 in.	87.442–87.507mm
2.5L Standard	3.443–3.444 in.	87.442–87.481mm
2.2L Turbo I and Turbo II	3.4416–3.4441 in.	87.416–87.481mm
2.2L Turbo III	3.441–3.443 in.	87.407–87.472mm
2.5L Turbo I	3.443–3.445 in.	87.453–87.492mm
Piston pin end-play (Turbocharged engines only)		
2.5L Turbo I		
Standard	0.000–0.035 in.	0.000–0.088mm
Service limit	0.047 in.	1.20mm
2.2L Turbo III	0.0015–0.0400 in.	0.04–1.02mm

86733C18

ENGINE REBUILDING SPECIFICATIONS
2.2L and 2.5L Chrysler Engines

Description	Standard Dimension	
	English	Metric
Pistons (continued)		
Ring side clearance		
No. 1 compression ring		
Except 2.5L Turbo I and 2.2L Turbo III	0.0015–0.0031 in.	0.038–0.078mm
2.5L Turbo I and 2.2L Turbo III	0.0016–0.0030 in.	0.040–0.075mm
No. 2 compression ring		
Except 2.5L Turbo I and 2.2L Turbo III	0.0015–0.0037 in.	0.038–0.093mm
2.5L Turbo I	0.0016–0.0035 in.	0.040–0.090mm
2.2L Turbo III	0.0016–0.0030 in.	0.040–0.075mm
Oil control ring		
Except 2.2L Turbo III	0.000–0.008 in.	0.000–0.200mm
2.2L Turbo III	0.0007–0.0020 in.	0.020–0.055mm
Ring end-gap		
No. 1 compression ring		
1981-89 2.2L and 2.5L Standard	0.011–0.021 in.	0.28–0.53mm
1990-95 2.2L and 2.5L Standard	0.010–0.020 in.	0.25–0.51mm
2.5L Turbo I	0.010–0.020 in.	0.25–0.51mm
2.2L Turbo I and Turbo II	0.010–0.020 in.	0.25–0.51mm
2.2L Turbo III	0.014–0.020 in.	0.35–0.50mm
No. 2 compression ring		
1981-89 2.2L and 2.5L Standard	0.011–0.021 in.	0.28–0.53mm
1990-95 2.2L and 2.5L Standard	0.011–0.021 in.	0.28–0.48mm
2.5L Turbo I	0.009–0.019 in.	0.23–0.48mm
2.2L Turbo I and Turbo II	0.009–0.018 in.	0.23–0.48mm
2.2L Turbo III	0.014–0.020 in.	0.35–0.50mm
Oil control ring		
Except 2.2L Turbo III	0.015–0.055 in.	0.38–1.40mm
2.2L Turbo III	0.010–0.020 in.	0.25–0.50mm
Connecting Rods		
Parallelism and twist combined	0.003 in.	0.08mm
Connecting rod side clearance		
Standard	0.005–0.013 in.	0.13–0.32mm
Service limit	0.004 in.	0.10mm
Bearing clearance		
1981-89 2.2L and 2.5L Standard	0.0008–0.0034 in.	0.019–0.087mm
2.2L Turbo I and Turbo II	0.0008–0.0031 in.	0.019–0.079mm
1990-95 models	0.0008–0.0030 in.	0.019–0.075mm
Crankshaft		
Connecting rod journal outside diameter	1.968–1.969 in.	49.979–50.005mm
Main bearing journal outside diameter		
1982-86 2.2L turbo I	2.3622–2.3627 in.	60.000–60.013mm
Except 1982-86 2.2L Turbo I	2.362–2.363 in.	59.987–60.013mm
Bearing surface out-of-round		
1981-86 models		
Standard	0.0005 in.	0.013mm
Service limit	0.012 in.	0.03mm
1987-95 models		
Standard	0.0003 in.	0.008mm
Service limit	0.005 in.	0.013mm

86733C19

ENGINE REBUILDING SPECIFICATIONS
2.2L and 2.5L Chrysler Engines

Description	Standard Dimension	
	English	Metric
Crankshaft (continued)		
Bearing surface taper		
1981-86 2.2L and 2.5L Standard		
Standard	0.0003-0.0031 in.	0.007-0.080mm
Service limit	0.004 in.	0.10mm
1981-86 2.2L Turbo I		
Standard	3.0004-0.0023 in.	0.011-0.54mm
1987-95 models		
Standard	0.0003 in.	0.008mm
Service limit	0.004 in.	0.01mm
Main bearing oil clearance		
Standard	0.0004-0.0029 in.	0.011-0.072mm
Service limit	0.004 in.	0.10mm
End-play		
Standard	0.002-0.007 in.	0.05-0.18mm
Service limit	0.014 in.	0.35mm
Cylinder Bore		
Out-of-round	0.002 in.	0.050mm
Bore taper	0.005 in.	0.125mm
Oil Pump		
Relief valve opening pressure		
Standard	60 psi	414 kPa
Service limit	80 psi	560 kPa
Outer rotor-to-housing bore clearance		
Standard	0.010 in.	0.26mm
Service limit	0.014 in.	0.36mm
Outer rotor thickness		
1981-86 models		
Standard	0.826-0.827 in.	20.96-21.00mm
Service limit	0.825 in.	20.96mm
1987-95 models		
Standard	0.944-0.945 in.	23.96-24.00mm
Service limit	0.9435 in.	23.96mm
Inner rotor-to-outer rotor tip clearance		
1981-86 models		
Standard	0.010 in.	0.26mm
1987-95 models		
Standard	0.004 in.	0.10mm
Service limit	0.008 in.	0.20mm
Inner and Outer rotor-to-housing clearance		
Standard	0.001-0.003 in.	0.03-0.08mm
Service limit	0.0035 in.	0.09mm
Pump cover flatness		
1981-86 models		
Standard	0.010 in.	0.26mm
Service limit	0.015 in.	0.39mm
1987-95 models		
Standard	0.002 in.	0.05mm
Service limit	0.03 in.	0.076mm

86733C20

ENGINE REBUILDING SPECIFICATIONS
2.2L and 2.5L Chrysler Engines

Description	Standard Dimension	
	English	Metric
Oil Pump (continued)		
Relief spring free length	1.95 in.	49.5mm
Relief spring load	20 lbs. @ 1.34 in.	89 N @ 34mm
Oil pressure		
At curb idle	4 psi [2]	30 kPa [2]
At 3000 RPM	25-80 psi [2]	170-550 kPa [2]

1 – This is the minimum allowable value at minimum cranking speed (130 RPM)
2 – Minimum values with the engine fully warmed

86733C21

ENGINE REBUILDING SPECIFICATIONS
2.6L Engine

Description	Standard Dimension	
	English	Metric
Type	In line OHV	
Number of Cylinders	4	
Bore	3.59 in.	91.1mm
Stroke	3.86 in.	98mm
Compression ratio	8.7:1	
Firing order	1-3-4-2	
General Engine		
Compression pressure	149 psi	1026.61 kPa
Maximum variation between cylinders	15 psi	103.35 kPa
Valve clearance—Hot engine		
Intake valve	0.006 in.	0.15mm
Exhaust valve	0.010 in.	0.25mm
Jet valve	0.010 in.	0.25mm
Camshaft		
Valve timing		
Intake Open	25° BTDC	
Close	59° ABDC	
Exhaust Open	64° BBDC	
Close	20° ATDC	
Jet Valve Open	25° BTDC	
Close	59° ABDC	
Valve overlap	45°	
Valve duration		
Intake	264°	
Exhaust	264°	
Jet valve	264°	
End-play	0.004-0.008 in.	0.1-0.2mm
Bearing clearance	0.002-0.004 in.	0.05-0.09mm
Camshaft lobe height	1.6614 in.	42.2mm
Service limit (minimum allowable height)	1.6414 in.	41.7mm
Connecting Rods		
Bearing clearance	0.0008-0.0028 in.	0.02-0.07mm
Side clearance	0.004-0.010 in.	0.10-0.25mm
Maximum twist	0.0039 in. in 3.937 in.	0.1mm in 100mm
Maximum bend	0.002 in. in 3.937 in.	0.05mm in 100mm
Crankshaft		
End-play	0.002-0.007 in.	0.05-0.18mm
Main bearing journal diameter	2.3622 in.	60mm
Connecting rod journal diameter	2.0866 in.	53mm
Main bearing clearance	0.0008-0.0028 in.	0.02-0.07mm
Maximum out-of-round (all journals)	0.004 in.	0.01mm
Maximum taper (all journals)	0.004 in.	0.01mm
Cylinder Block		
Cylinder block flatness	less than 0.002 in.	less than 0.05mm
Service limit	0.004 in.	0.10mm
Oil Pressure		
At idle speed	6 psi	40 kPa
At 3000 RPM	45-90 psi	300-600 kPa

86733C25

ENGINE REBUILDING SPECIFICATIONS
2.6L Engine

Description	Standard Dimension	
	English	Metric
Oil Pump		
Relief valve opening pressure	49.8-64.0 psi	343-441 kPa
Gear-to-housing clearance	0.0043-0.0069 in.	0.11-0.15mm
Driven gear-to-bearing clearance	0.0008-0.0020 in.	0.02-0.05mm
Driven gear-to-bearing clearance (oil pump body)	0.0008-0.0020 in.	0.02-0.05mm
Driven gear-to-bearing clearance (oil pump cover)	0.0016-0.0028 in.	0.04-0.07mm
Gear end-play		
Drive gear	0.0020-0.0043 in.	0.05-0.11mm
Driven gear	0.0016-0.0039 in.	0.04-0.10mm
Relief spring free-length	1.850 in.	47mm
Relief spring load	9.5 lbs. @ 1.575 in.	42.2 N @ 40mm
Oil pressure switch minimum actuating pressure	4 ps. or less	28 kPa or less
Silent Shaft		
Front bearing journal outside diameter	0.906 in.	23mm
Front bearing clearance	0.0006-0.0024 in.	0.02-0.06mm
Rear bearing journal outside diameter	1.393 in.	43mm
Rear bearing clearance	0.0020-0.0035 in.	0.05-0.09mm
Pistons		
Outside diameter	3.5866 in.	91.1mm
Piston ring end-gap clearance		
Compression rings	0.010-0.018 in.	0.25-0.45mm
Service limit	C.039 in.	1.0mm
Oil control rails	0.0078-0.0350 in.	0.2-0.9mm
Service limit	0.059 in.	1.5mm
Piston ring side clearance		
No. 1 compression ring	0.0024-0.0039 in.	0.06-0.10mm
Service limit	.006 in.	0.15mm
No. 2 compression ring	0.008-0.0024 in.	0.02-0.06mm
Service limit	0.0039 in.	0.1mm
Piston pin press-in pressure	1,614-3,659 lbs.	7,350-17,100 N
Valves		
Valve head thickness (margin)		
Intake	0.047 in.	1.2mm
Service limit	0.028 in.	0.7mm
Exhaust	0.079 in.	2.0mm
Service limit	0.039 in.	1.0mm
Stem-to-guide clearance		
Intake valve	0.0012-0.0024 in.	0.03-0.06mm
Service limit	0.004 in.	0.1mm
Exhaust valve	0.0020-0.0035 in.	0.05-0.09mm
Service limit	0.006 in.	0.15mm
Valve spring perpendicularity	1.5°	
Service limit	3°	
Valve spring installed height	1.590 in.	40.4mm
Service limit	1.629 in.	41.4mm
Valve springs free-length	1.869 in.	47.5mm
Service limit	1.479 in.	46.5mm
Valve spring load	61 lbs. @ 1.59 in.	270 N @ 40.4mm

86733C26

ENGINE REBUILDING SPECIFICATIONS

2.6L Engine

Description	Standard Dimension	
	English	Metric
Valves (continued)		
Jet valve		
Stem outside diameter	0.1693 in.	4.30mm
Seat angle	45°	
Spring free-length	1.1654 in.	29.60mm
Spring load	6.5 lbs. @ 0.846 in.	34.3 N @ 21.5mm

1 – At cranking speed (250 RPM).

86733C27

TORQUE SPECIFICATIONS

Components	Torque	
	ft. lbs.	Nm
2.2L and 2.5L Engines (continued)		
Balance shaft carrier components—2.2L Turbo III and 2.5L engines		
Front chain cover bolt	105 inch lbs.	12
Chain tensioner adjustment bolt	105 inch lbs.	12
Chain tensioner pivot bolt	105 inch lbs.	12
Chain snubber stud and washer	105 inch lbs.	12
Chain snubber nut	105 inch lbs.	12
Gear cover bolt	105 inch lbs.	12
Gear and sprocket-to-balance shaft	21	28
Sprocket-to-crankshaft—Torx drive cap bolt	130 inch lbs.	15
Rear cover bolt	105 inch lbs.	12
Carrier-to-engine block bolts	40	54
Additional 2.2L Turbo III engine block components		
Camshaft thrust plate retaining nut	53 inch lbs	2
Connecting rod bearing cap nuts	50	68
Camshaft sprocket bolts	47	65
Crankshaft sprocket bolt	85	115
Intermediate shaft sprocket bolt	65	89
Lower timing belt cover	72 inch lbs	8
Intake manifold bolts	18	24
Exhaust manifold studs	18	24
Rocker arm shaft retaining bolts	18	24
Rocker arm cover bolts	105 inch lbs.	12
Thermostat housing bolts	18	24
Timing belt idler pulley bolt	40	54
Timing belt tensioner pulley bolt	40	54
2.6L Engine		
Spark plug	18	25
Intake manifold nut	150 inch lbs.	17
Exhaust manifold nut	150 inch lbs.	17
Water pump mounting bolt	17	23
Water pump drive pulley bolt	40	54
Rocker arm cover bolts	53 inch lbs.	6
Camshaft bearing cap bolt	160 inch lbs.	18
Cylinder head-to-engine block bolt (cold engine)	69	94
Cylinder head-to-engine block bolt (hot engine)	76	103
Cylinder head-to-timing chain case cover bolt	160 inch lbs.	18
Jet valve	168 inch lbs.	19
Engine mounting plate bolt	160 inch lbs.	18
Timing chain case cover bolt	160 inch lbs.	18
Oil pan bolt	53 inch lbs.	6
Camshaft sprocket bolt	40	54
Timing chain guide bolt	160 inch lbs.	18
Silent chain sprocket bolt	25	34
Oil pump sprocket bolt	25	34
Silent chain guide bolt	160 inch lbs.	18
Main bearing cap bolt	58	79
Connecting rod bearing cap bolt	34	46
Oil pump mounting bolt	71 inch lbs.	8
Crankshaft sprocket bolt	87	118

Note: All fasteners should be cleaned and lubricated prior to tightening them to the specified values.

① — Except 2.2L Turbo III engines.

86733C30

TORQUE SPECIFICATIONS

Components	ft. lbs.	Nm
2.2L and 2.5L Engines (continued)		
Balance shaft carrier components—2.2L Turbo III and 2.5L engines		
Front chain cover bolt	105 inch lbs.	12
Chain tensioner adjustment bolt	105 inch lbs.	12
Chain tensioner pivot bolt	105 inch lbs.	12
Chain snubber stud and washer	105 inch lbs.	12
Chain snubber nut	105 inch lbs.	12
Gear cover bolt	105 inch lbs.	12
Gear and sprocket-to-balance shaft	21	28
Sprocket-to-crankshaft—Torx drive cap bolt	130 inch lbs.	15
Rear cover bolt	105 inch lbs.	12
Carrier-to-engine block bolts	40	54
Additional 2.2L Turbo III engine components		
Camshaft thrust plate retaining nut	53 inch lbs.	2
Connecting rod bearing cap nuts	50	68
Camshaft sprocket bolts	47	65
Crankshaft sprocket bolt	85	115
Intermediate shaft sprocket bolt	65	89
Lower timing belt cover	72 inch lbs.	8
Intake manifold bolts	18	24
Exhaust manifold studs	18	24
Rocker arm shaft retaining bolts	18	24
Rocker arm cover bolts	105 inch lbs.	12
Thermostat housing bolts	18	24
Timing belt idler pulley bolt	40	54
Timing belt tensioner pulley bolt	40	54
2.6L Engine		
Spark plug	18	25
Intake manifold nut	150 inch lbs.	17
Exhaust manifold nut	150 inch lbs.	17
Water pump mounting bolt	17	23
Water pump drive pulley bolt	40	54
Rocker arm cover bolts	53 inch lbs.	6
Camshaft bearing cap bolt	160 inch lbs.	18
Cylinder head-to-engine block bolt (cold engine)	69	94
Cylinder head-to-engine block bolt (hot engine)	76	103
Cylinder head-to-timing chain case cover bolt	160 inch lbs.	18
Jet valve	168 inch lbs.	19
Engine mounting plate bolt	160 inch lbs.	18
Timing chain case cover bolt	160 inch lbs.	18
Oil pan bolt	53 inch lbs.	6
Camshaft sprocket bolt	40	54
Timing chain guide bolt	160 inch lbs.	18
Silent chain sprocket bolt	25	34
Oil pump sprocket bolt	25	34
Silent chain guide bolt	160 inch lbs.	18
Main bearing cap bolt	58	79
Connecting rod bearing cap bolt	34	46
Oil pump mounting bolt	71 inch lbs.	8
Crankshaft sprocket bolt	87	118

Note: All fasteners should be cleaned and lubricated prior to tightening them to the specified values.

① — Except 2.2L Turbo III engines.

86733C31

TORQUE SPECIFICATIONS

Components	ft. lbs.	Nm
2.5L Premier Engine		
Front support bracket-to-engine block	45	61
Front support cushion-to-mount (through-bolt)	48	65
Front support cushion-to-sill bracket	30	40
Fuel pump bolts	16	22
Oil pan bolts		
1/4-20	7	9
5/16-18	11	15
Oil pan drain plug	25	34
Oil pan-to-timing case cover bolts	11	13
Oil pump attaching bolts (short)	10	14
Oil pump attaching bolts (long)	17	23
Oil pump cover bolts	70 inch lbs.	8
Power steering pump pressure hose nut	38	52
Rear support cushion-to-bracket bolts	32	43
Rocker arm assembly-to-cylinder head bolts	19	26
Starter motor-to-engine block bolts	33	45
Timing case cover-to-engine block bolts	62 inch lbs.	7
Vibration damper bolt	80	108
2.6L Engine		
Spark plug	18	25
Intake manifold nut	150 inch lbs.	17
Exhaust manifold nut	150 inch lbs.	17
Water pump mounting bolt	17	23
Water pump drive pulley bolt	40	54
Rocker arm cover bolts	53 inch lbs.	6
Camshaft bearing cap bolt	160 inch lbs.	18
Cylinder head-to-engine block bolt (cold engine)	69	94
Cylinder head-to-engine block bolt (hot engine)	76	103
Cylinder head-to-timing chain case cover bolt	160 inch lbs.	18
Jet valve	168 inch lbs.	19
Engine mounting plate bolt	160 inch lbs.	18
Timing chain case cover bolt	160 inch lbs.	18
Oil pan bolt	53 inch lbs.	6
Camshaft sprocket bolt	40	54
Timing chain guide bolt	160 inch lbs.	18
Silent chain sprocket bolt	25	34
Oil pump sprocket bolt	25	34
Silent chain guide bolt	160 inch lbs.	18
Main bearing cap bolt	58	79
Connecting rod bearing cap bolt	34	46
Oil pump mounting bolt	71 inch lbs.	8
Crankshaft sprocket bolt	87	118

Note: All fasteners should be cleaned and lubricated prior to tightening them to the specified values.

① — Except 2.2L Turbo III engines.

86733C32

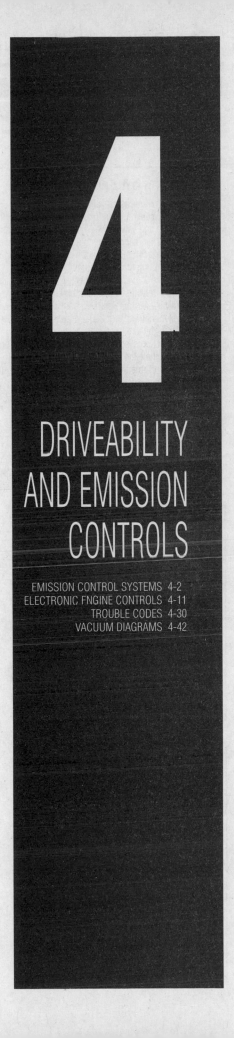

4

DRIVEABILITY AND EMISSION CONTROLS

EMISSION CONTROL SYSTEMS

Positive Crankcase Ventilation System

OPERATION

♦ See Figures 1, 2, 3, 4 and 5

The Positive Crankcase Ventilation (PCV) system is used to draw the incompletely burned air/fuel mixture that passes the piston rings and valve guides out of the crankcase and valve cover. This mixture contains a great deal of unburned hydrocarbons. The PCV system conducts it to the engine's air intake system for burning with the fresh mixture in the combustion chambers. In this way, total emissions of unburned fuel are greatly reduced.

The system's PCV valve is connected, via a short hose, to the rocker arm cover. The PCV valve itself controls total flow to the system so that, regardless of engine intake vacuum, a stable amount of air will enter the system. The Chrysler system is unique in that it draws fresh air into the PCV circuit without passing it through the engine crankcase.

The fuel injection system, or carburetor system is precisely calibrated to compensate for the extra air the system introduces into the engine's combustion chambers. At the same time, because of the high vacuum the system operates under, the potential exists for it to bleed a great deal of excess air into the system and disturb the mixture. If the engine runs poorly, especially at idle speeds (when vacuum is highest), inspect the PCV system thoroughly for leaks and the PCV valve for clogging or sticking. The valve may be clogged (stuck partly open), so that too much excess air can enter the system, which creates a lean mixture.

Since the PCV system removes vapors from the crankcase that, if left there, could condense and contribute significantly to engine wear, effective maintenance can improve both engine performance and longevity. If there are other-wise unexplained oil leaks through seals or if crankcase vapors are expelled into the engine compartment, check the system for clogged hoses or a PCV valve that is stuck shut or clogged. See Section 1 for basic maintenance and PCV valve tests.

➡ **With the engine idling, remove the PCV valve from the engine. If the valve is operating properly, a hissing noise will be heard and a strong vacuum felt when a finger is placed over the valve inlet. With the engine OFF, the valve should rattle when it is shaken. If the valve is not operating properly it must be REPLACED. Do not attempt to clean the old PCV valve.**

SYSTEM TESTING

♦ See Figures 6 and 7

To inspect the PCV valve, remove the valve from the rocker arm cover and shake it. If the valve rattles, it is probably fine; if there is no sound, it must be replaced and the PCV hose cleaned by spraying solvent (such as a carburetor cleaner type of solvent) through it.

If the valve rattles, you should still check the PCV valve with the engine idling. Pull it out of the rocker arm cover and place your finger or thumb over the end to stop air flow. You should feel some suction, and the engine speed should drop slightly. If there is no suction, or if the engine idle speeds up and smoothes out considerably, replace the valve. Remove the PCV hose from the engine, then inspect it and, if the inside is coated with gum and varnish, clean it by spraying solvent through it.

Check the vacuum at the PCV inlet (from the rocker arm cover to the air cleaner) tube, as well. Disconnect this tube from the air cleaner and loosely hold a piece of paper over the tube. After a few seconds (10–15 seconds), enough

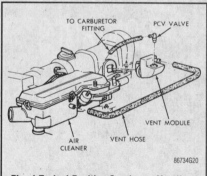

Fig. 1 Typical Positive Crankcase Ventilation (PCV) system used on 1981–86 non-turbocharged 2.2L engines

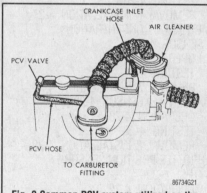

Fig. 2 Common PCV system utilized on the 1981–85 2.6L engines

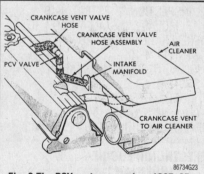

Fig. 3 The PCV systems used on 1987–95 non-turbocharged 2.2L and 2.5L engines are the same

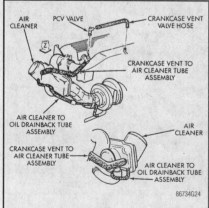

Fig. 4 The PCV system used on the 2.5L Turbo I engine

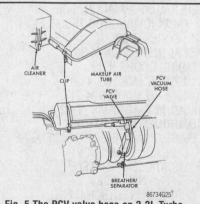

Fig. 5 The PCV valve hose on 2.2L Turbo III engines is routed directly into one of the intake manifold runners

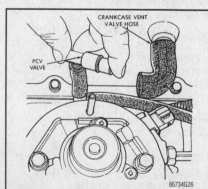

Fig. 6 To test the PCV valve, position a finger against its opening while the engine idles to test for vacuum—1987–95 2.2L and 2.5L engine shown

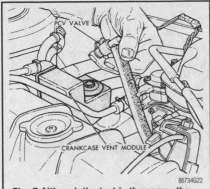

Fig. 7 Although the test is the same, the PCV valve is mounted in a vent module on 1981–86 2.2L engines

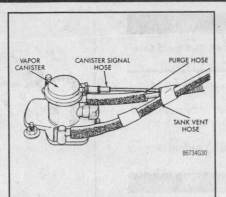

Fig. 8 The fuel vapors drawn out of the fuel tank are stored in a vapor (charcoal) canister

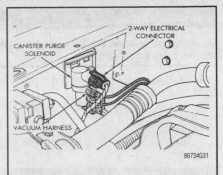

Fig. 9 The canister purge solenoid keeps vacuum from reaching the vacuum canister during and shortly after the engine start-up period

vacuum should build up to cause the paper to be sucked against the opening with a noticeable amount of force. This test proves whether or not the suction side of the system is clear.

Evaporation Control System

OPERATION

▶ **See Figures 8 and 9**

The evaporation control system prevents the emission of fuel tank vapors into the atmosphere. When fuel in the tank evaporates, the vapors pass through vent hoses or tubes to a charcoal canister. The canister temporarily holds the vapors. The Powertrain Control Module (PCM) allows intake manifold vacuum to draw vapors into the combustion chambers during certain operating conditions. The PCM uses the canister purge solenoid to regulate vapor flow.

On all 2.2L and 2.5L Chrysler EFI engines, the manifold vacuum purges the vapors at idle as well as off idle. These engines use a bi-level purge system. The system uses 2 sources of vacuum to remove fuel vapors from the canister.

The 2.2L Turbo III and 2.5L Turbo I engines utilize a tri-level canister purge system. In this system, fuel vapors are drawn into the engine through the throttle body and air cleaner. Fuel vapors are drawn in at closed throttle, part throttle, and Wide Open Throttle (WOT) in boost.

❋❋ WARNING

The evaporative system uses specially manufactured hoses. If they need replacement, only use fuel resistant hose.

➡ **All vehicles are equipped with a Vehicle Emission Control Information (VECI) label which is located in the engine compartment. The label contains emission specifications and vacuum hose routing. All hoses must be connected and routed as shown on the label.**

Pressure Relief/Rollover Valve

All vehicles have a combination pressure relief and rollover valve. The dual function valve relieves fuel tank pressure and also prevents fuel flow through the fuel tank vent valve hoses if the vehicle accidentally rolls over. All vehicles pass a 360° rollover test.

The pressure relief valve opens at a certain pressure. When the fuel tank pressure increases above the calibrated pressure, the valve opens to release fuel tank vapor pressure. The evaporative (charcoal) canister stores the vapors.

Evaporative Canister

▶ **See Figure 8**

All vehicles use a sealed, maintenance free evaporative (charcoal) canister. The canister mounts to the inner wheel well area of the engine compartment.

Fuel tank pressure vents into the canister. The canister temporarily holds the fuel vapors until the intake manifold vacuum draws them into the combustion

chamber. The canister purge solenoid purges vapors from the canister at predetermined intervals and engine conditions.

Canister Purge Solenoid

▶ **See Figure 9**

The 2.2L and 2.5L Chrysler EFI, 2.5L Turbo I and 2.2L Turbo III engine-equipped vehicles are equipped with a canister purge solenoid. The engine PCM operates the canister purge solenoid. During warm-up and for a specified period after hot starts, the PCM grounds the purge solenoid causing it to energize. When the PCM grounds the solenoid, vacuum does not reach the charcoal canister valve.

When the engine reaches a specified operating temperature and the time delay interval has occurred, the PCM de-energizes the solenoid, vacuum flows to the canister purge valve. Intake manifold vacuum purges fuel vapors through the throttle body. The PCM also energizes the purge solenoid during certain idle conditions to update the fuel delivery calibration.

Duty Cycle Evaporation (EVAP) Purge Solenoid

The 2.5L Chrysler Flex Fuel engines use a duty cycle purge system. The PCM controls vapor flow by operating the duty cycle EVAP purge solenoid. The duty cycle EVAP purge solenoid regulates the rate of vapor flow from the EVAP canister to the throttle body.

During the cold start warm-up period and the hot start time delay, the engine computer does not energize the solenoid. When de-energized, no vapors are purged. The engine computer de-energizes the solenoid during open loop operation.

The engine enters closed loop operation after it reaches a specified temperature and the time delay ends. During closed loop operation, the engine computer energizes and de-energizes the solenoid approximately 5–10 times per second, depending upon operating conditions. The engine computer varies the vapor flow rate by changing solenoid pulse width. Pulse width is the amount of time the solenoid energizes. The engine computer adjusts solenoid pulse width based on engine air flow.

A rubber boot covers the duty cycle EVAP purge solenoid. The solenoid attaches to a bracket mounted to the right engine mount. The top of the solenoid has the word TOP on it. The solenoid will not operate unless it is installed correctly.

REMOVAL & INSTALLATION

Fuel Tank Pressure Relief and Rollover Valve

❋❋ CAUTION

Release the fuel system pressure before servicing the fuel system components. Service the vehicle in a well ventilated area and avoid ignition sources. Never smoke while servicing the vehicle.

1. Remove the fuel tank. Refer to Section 5 for this procedure.
2. Wedge the blade of a thin prytool between the rubber grommet and the fuel tank where the support rib is located.

※※ WARNING

Do not wedge between the valve and the grommet. This could damage the valve during removal.

3. Use a second prytool as a support to pry the valve and grommet assembly from the tank.

4. Place the valve upright on a flat surface. Push down on the grommet and peel it off of the valve.

To install:

5. Install the rubber grommet in the fuel tank by working it around the curled lip of the tank.

※※ WARNING

Only use power steering fluid to lubricate the pressure relief/rollover valve grommet.

6. Lightly lubricate the grommet with power steering fluid only and push the valve downward into the grommet. Twist the valve until properly positioned.

7. Install the fuel tank. Refer to Section 5 for this procedure.

8. Connect the negative battery cable.

9. Start the vehicle and check for any fuel leaks.

➡ When starting the vehicle after servicing any part of the fuel system, it will take longer for the engine to start because the system will need to repressurize itself.

Exhaust Gas Recirculation System

OPERATION

1981–88 Models

▶ See Figures 10 thru 19

This system reduces the amount of oxides of nitrogen in the exhaust by allowing a predetermined amount of exhaust gases to recirculate and dilute the incoming fuel/air mixture. The principal components of the system are the EGR valve and the Coolant Control Exhaust Gas Recirculation Valve (CCEGR) used on 1981–86 models or the Coolant Vacuum Switch Cold Closed (CVSCC) used on 1986–88 models. The EGR valve is located in the intake manifold and directly regulates the flow of exhaust gases into the intake. The latter is located in the thermostat housing and overrides the EGR valve when coolant temperature is below 125°F (52°C).

Exhaust system backpressure tends to increase the rate at which the EGR valve flows exhaust gas back into the engine. For this reason, on fuel injected and turbocharged engines, an Exhaust Backpressure Transducer is used to regulate the vacuum that opens the EGR valve. When backpressure increases, the transducer will decrease vacuum in such a way that the valve opening will be reduced and gas flow rate will remain correct in spite of that backpressure increase.

2.6L engines use a Sub EGR Control Valve. This valve is an integral part of the carburetor, and is directly opened and closed by linkage connected to the throttle valve. In conjunction with the standard EGR system the sub EGR more closely modulates EGR flow in response to the throttle valve opening.

1989–95 Models

▶ See Figures 20 and 21

➡ The turbocharged engines do not utilize an EGR system.

This system reduces the amount of oxides of nitrogen (NOx) in the exhaust by allowing a predetermined amount of exhaust gases to recirculate and dilute the incoming fuel/air mixture. The diluted air/fuel mixture reduces peak flame temperature during combustion, which in turn inhibits the production of Nitrogen oxides.

The principal components of the system are:
- EGR tube (connects a passage in the intake manifold to the exhaust manifold)
- EGR valve

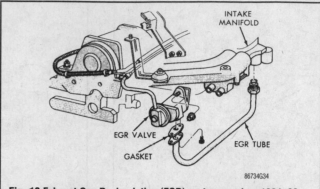

Fig. 10 Exhaust Gas Recirculation (EGR) system used on 1981–86 2.2L carbureted engines

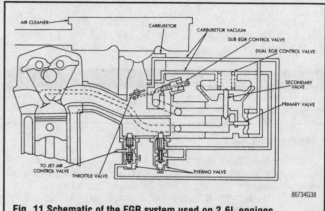

Fig. 11 Schematic of the EGR system used on 2.6L engines

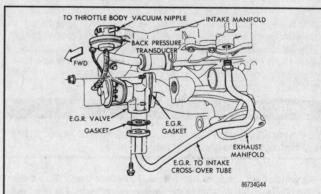

Fig. 12 Exploded view of the EGR system used on 1984–88 2.2L and 2.5L EFI engines

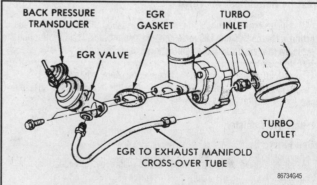

Fig. 13 The system components are placed differently for the 2.2L Turbo I engine than for the EFI 2.2L engine

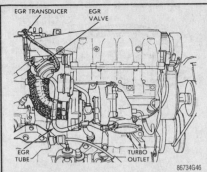

Fig. 14 The EGR system on 2.2L Turbo II engines is different from the one used on Turbo I engines

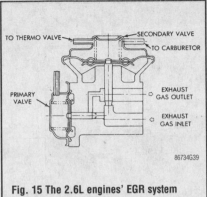

Fig. 15 The 2.6L engines' EGR system uses a dual EGR control valve

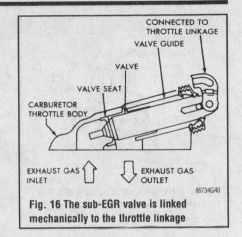

Fig. 16 The sub-EGR valve is linked mechanically to the throttle linkage

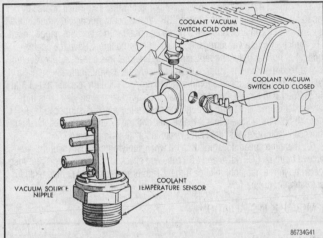

Fig. 17 The Coolant Vacuum Switch Cold Closed (CVSCC) and the Coolant Vacuum Switch Cold Open (CVSCO) are mounted in the water box, near the thermostat housing—1986-88 models

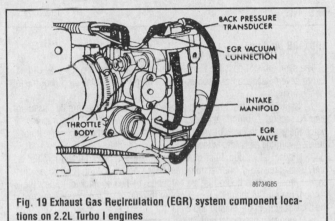

Fig. 19 Exhaust Gas Recirculation (EGR) system component locations on 2.2L Turbo I engines

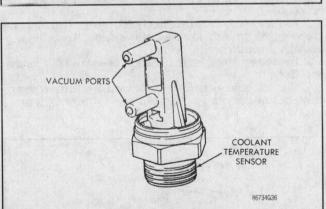

Fig. 18 The CVSCC on 1981–85 models is equipped with 2 vacuum ports, while the 1986–88 CVSCC's have 3

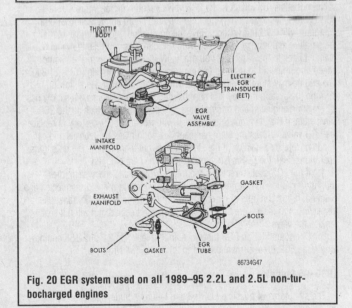

Fig. 20 EGR system used on all 1989-95 2.2L and 2.5L non-turbocharged engines

- Electronic EGR Transducer (EET)
- Vacuum hoses

The EET contains an electrically operated solenoid and a back-pressure transducer. The Powertrain Control Module (PCM) operates the solenoid. The PCM determines when to energize the solenoid. Exhaust system backpressure controls the transducer.

When the PCM grounds the solenoid, which causes it to energize, vacuum does not reach the transducer. Vacuum flows to the transducer when the PCM de-energizes the solenoid.

When the exhaust system backpressure becomes high enough, it fully closes a bleed valve in the transducer. When the PCM de-energizes the solenoid and backpressure closes the transducer bleed valve, vacuum flows through the transducer to operate the EGR valve.

De-energizing the solenoid, but not fully closing the transducer bleed hole (because of low backpressure), varies the strength of vacuum applied to the EGR valve. Varying the strength of the vacuum changes the amount of EGR supplied to the engine. This provides the correct amount of exhaust gas recirculation for different operating conditions.

These systems do not allow EGR at idle. The system operates at all engine temperatures.

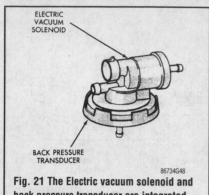

Fig. 21 The Electric vacuum solenoid and back pressure transducer are integrated into one component

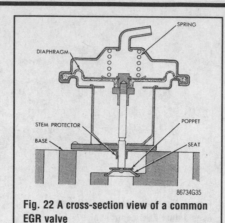

Fig. 22 A cross-section view of a common EGR valve

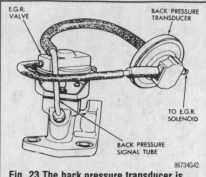

Fig. 23 The back pressure transducer is linked to the EGR valve by two vacuum hoses

TESTING

1981–88 Models

The symptoms of possible EGR system failure include: spark knock, engine sag or severe hesitation on acceleration, or rough idle or stalling. Check the following items:

1. Start the engine and allow it to idle in neutral with the throttle closed, for over 70 seconds. Abruptly accelerate the engine to 2,000–3,000 rpm as you watch the groove in the EGR valve stem. The stem should move visibly. If not, proceed with the tests that follow.

2. Inspect all vacuum hose connections between the carburetor/throttle body, intake manifold, and vacuum transducer. All connections and hoses must be leak-free. Replace hoses that are hardened, melted or cracked. Inspect the vacuum passage in the carburetor body or throttle body. If necessary, remove the assembly from the engine and clean it.

3. Connect a hand operated vacuum pump or other confirmed source of vacuum that can be valved to the EGR valve vacuum motor, via rubber hose connections. Tee a vacuum gauge into the line, if you are not using a pump equipped with a vacuum gauge. Have the engine running at normal operating temperature and normal idle speed. Apply vacuum as you read the vacuum gauge. Listen to the engine as you gradually increase vacuum. The engine speed should begin to drop as vacuum reaches 2.0–3.5 in. Hg (6.75–11.8 kPa). The engine may stumble or even stall. This means exhaust gas is flowing through the system the way it is supposed to. If a separate vacuum supply has no effect on engine speed or smoothness, repeat the test, watching the EGR valve stem. If the stem does not move, it will probably be necessary to replace the EGR valve. Unless the stem has been frozen in place by deposits and can be freed up, replace the valve. If the stem moves, but there is no effect on engine operation, clean the EGR system passages—they are clogged.

4. If the EGR system recycles too much exhaust and the system idles roughly, try idling the engine with the EGR valve vacuum line disconnected and plugged. If this has little or no effect, try removing the EGR valve/transducer and inspecting it to make sure the EGR valve poppet is seated. If it will not seat, replace the valve.

5. Check also for an EGR tube-to-manifold leak. On 2.2 and 2.5L engines, torque the EGR tube-to-manifold nut to 25 ft. lbs. (34 Nm).

1989–95 Models

The symptoms of possible EGR system failure include: spark knock, engine hesitation on acceleration, or rough idle or stalling. Check the following items:

1. Inspect all vacuum hose connections between the carburetor/throttle body, intake manifold, and vacuum transducer. All connections and hoses must be leak-free. Replace hoses that are hardened, melted or cracked. Inspect the vacuum passage in the throttle body. If necessary, remove the assembly from the engine and clean it.

2. Start the engine and allow it to warm-up to the point when the engine coolant is at least 150°F (65°C). Idle the engine in Neutral with the throttle closed, for over 70 seconds. Abruptly accelerate the engine to 2000–3000 rpm as you watch the groove in the EGR valve stem. Repeat the test several times to confirm that the system is operating normally. The stem should move visibly. If not, proceed with the tests that follow.

3. Connect a hand-operated vacuum pump or other confirmed source of vacuum that can be connected to the EGR valve vacuum motor, via rubber hose connections. If you are not using a pump equipped with a vacuum gauge, insert a "T" junction with a vacuum gauge attached into the line, . Have the engine running at normal operating temperature and normal idle speed. Apply vacuum as you read the vacuum gauge. Listen to the engine as you gradually increase vacuum. The engine speed should begin to drop as vacuum reaches 2.0–3.5 in. Hg (6.75–13.18 kPa). Engine speed may drop quickly or even stall. This indicates exhaust gas is flowing through the system the way it is supposed to.

4. If both the acceleration of the vehicle and the externally applied vacuum show satisfactory results, the EGR system is functioning properly.

5. If engine speed does not drop off when applying external vacuum, remove both the EGR valve and EGR tube and check for plugged passages. Also check the intake manifold inlet passage. Clean or replace these components for restoration of proper flow.

REMOVAL & INSTALLATION

EGR Valve

▶ See Figures 22, 23 and 24

1. On newer vehicles, unplug the electrical connectors from the Electric EGR Transducer (EET).

2. Remove the vacuum connectors from the EET. Inspect the vacuum lines for cracking, poor sealing due to hardness, or other damage. Replace the vacuum hoses, if necessary.

3. Remove the bolts attaching the EGR valve to the intake manifold. Remove the EGR valve.

4. Clean both gasket surfaces and check for any signs of leakage or cracks. Replace the components if any such damage is found or if the valve fails the tests.

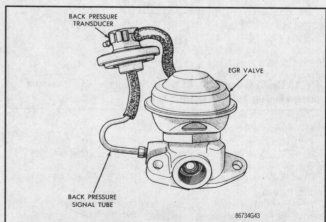

Fig. 24 With the exception of vacuum hose routing, the EGR valve and back pressure transducer used on turbocharged engines (shown) is the same as that used on non-turbocharged applications

To install:

5. Install a new gasket and the EGR valve onto the manifold. Install the two attaching bolts and torque to 16 ft. lbs. (22 Nm).

6. Reconnect the vacuum lines and electrical wires to the electrical EGR transducer.

EGR Tube

1. Remove the EGR tube attaching bolts from the intake and exhaust manifolds.

2. Remove the EGR tube from the engine.

3. Clean all gasket surfaces. Inspect gasket surfaces for signs of cracking and replace the EGR tube or manifolds if cracking is found. Discard old gaskets and supply new ones.

To install:

4. Assemble the tube and gaskets into place, installing the attaching bolts only loosely.

5. Tighten the attaching bolts at the intake manifold to 16 ft. lbs. (22 Nm).

6. Tighten the mounting fasteners at the exhaust manifold to 16 ft. lbs. (22 Nm).

Catalytic Converter

OPERATION

The catalytic converter, standard equipment in all newer vehicles, has the job of altering pollutants in the car's exhaust gas. The catalytic converters do this by chemically altering the harmful chemicals present in exhaust gases, such as oxides of nitrogen (NO_x), unburned hydrocarbons (HC), carbon monoxide (CO) and oxides of sulfur (SO_x) into harmless variants of these chemicals, such as carbon dioxide (CO_2) and water (H_2O). For a more in-depth description of the chemical reactions in exhaust gases, refer to the beginning of this section.

Two things can to destroy the catalyst: the use of leaded gas and excessive heat. The use of leaded fuel was the most common cause of catalyst destruction. The lead coats the thin layer of platinum and palladium (that actually promotes final combustion of the almost completely burned hydrocarbons that enter the catalytic converter). The coating keeps the mixture from actually contacting the noble metals. The lead may also cause the passages of the "substrate"—the material that carries the noble metal coating—to clog. This would cause the car to run at reduced power or even stop altogether.

Excessive heat results in the converter when raw fuel and air with a high oxygen content enter the catalytic converter, which greatly accelerates the combustion process. This most often occurs when a spark plug wire is disconnected. Excessive heat during misfiring due to poor vehicle maintenance and prolonged testing with the ignition system wires disconnected are two common ways a catalyst may be rendered ineffective. Test procedures should be accomplished as quickly as possible. The car should be shut off whenever misfiring is noted. Misfiring due to extremely lean or extremely rich mixtures will also damage the catalyst.

While the catalyst itself is a maintenance-free item, it should be understood that long life depends completely on proper fueling and good maintenance. The car should be tuned as required, and the fuel and air filters, as well as the oxygen sensor, should be changed as specified in the maintenance intervals chart in Section 1. Ignition wires and the distributor cap and rotor should be inspected/tested and replaced if necessary to prevent misfire.

Two catalysts are used on each car on model years through 1985. On dual catalyst systems, a small one located just after the exhaust manifold ignites early in the engine warm-up cycle, and a larger one located under the car body completes the clean-up process during warmed-up operation of the car. If the unit should be damaged, it must be replaced—no service is possible.

1986 and later models employ a 3-way catalyst. Two converters, working under different fuel/air mixture conditions are used. The first catalyst is fed exhaust from the engine that is at the chemically correct mixture ratio of 14.7:1. At this point, the exhaust gases contain oxygen that has combined with the nitrogen in the air to form nitrogen oxides (a pollutant); and unburned (or oxygen-short) hydrocarbons and carbon monoxide (another pollutant). This converter creates conditions which cause the oxygen in the nitrogen oxides to combine with the unburned material. This is called "reduction" of the nitrogen oxides. Once the nitrogen oxides have been reduced, the air pump adds extra air

(and oxygen). The second converter uses this extra oxygen to complete the job of oxidizing the unburned material.

REMOVAL & INSTALLATION

For the removal and installation of the catalytic converter, refer to the end of Section 3.

Pressure-Vacuum Filler Cap

✳✳ WARNING

Remove the fuel filler cap to relieve the fuel tank pressure. Remove the cap before disconnecting the fuel system components or servicing the fuel tank.

OPERATION

A pressure-vacuum relief cap seals the fuel tank. Tightening the cap on the fuel filler tube forms a seal between them. The relief valves in the cap are a safety feature. They prevent possible excessive pressure or vacuum in the tank. Excessive fuel tank pressure could be caused by a malfunction in the system or damage to the vent lines.

The seal between the cap and filler tube breaks when the cap is removed. Removing the cap breaks the seal and relieves the fuel tank pressure. If the filler cap needs to be replaced, only use new filler cap with the same pressure rating.

Heated Air Inlet System

OPERATION

♦ See Figures 25, 26, 27, 28 and 29

All 2.2L, 2.5L Chrysler and 2.6L carbureted and EFI engines are equipped with a vacuum device located in the air cleaner air intake. A small door is operated by a vacuum diaphragm and a thermostatic spring. When the air temperature outside is 65°F (18°C) or lower on carbureted engines, or 115°F (46°C) or lower on throttle body injected engines, the door will block off air entering from outside and allow air channeled from the exhaust manifold area to enter the intake. This air is heated by the hot manifold. At 90°F (32°C) or above on carbureted engines and 140°F (60°C) or above on TBI engines, the door fully blocks off the heated air. At temperatures in between, the door is operated in intermediate positions. During heavy acceleration the door is controlled by engine vacuum to allow the maximum amount of air to enter the carburetor.

This system is critically important to the operation of carbureted and throttle body injected cars because, when the carburetor or throttle body handles cold air, mixture calibration will become incorrect (too lean). The result will be lean

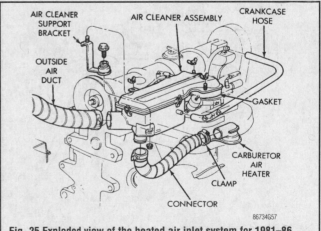

Fig. 25 Exploded view of the heated air inlet system for 1981–86 carbureted 2.2L engines

running (misfire and hesitation). Engine performance will deteriorate even more during warm up in cold weather. The carburetor will also be more likely to ice up in cool, damp weather. There may also be high emissions of hydrocarbons, as revealed by emissions testing.

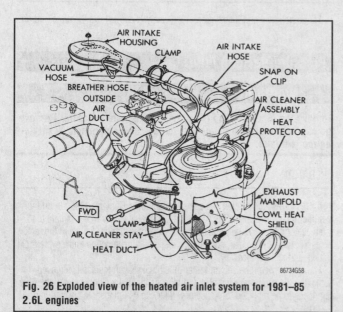

Fig. 26 Exploded view of the heated air inlet system for 1981–85 2.6L engines

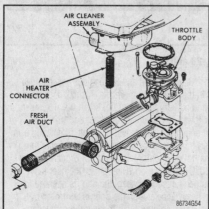

Fig. 27 The heated air inlet system used on all Electronic Fuel Injected (EFI) 2.2L and 2.5L engines

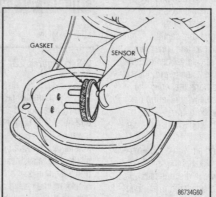

Fig. 28 The air temperature sensor for the carbureted engines is mounted on the inside of the air cleaner housing, as shown

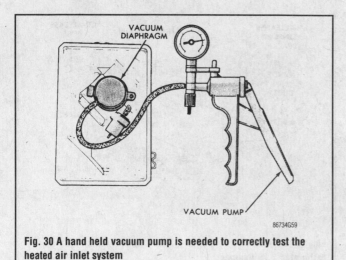

Fig. 30 A hand held vacuum pump is needed to correctly test the heated air inlet system

TESTING

▶ See Figure 30

➡You'll need a hand vacuum pump or other source of measurable vacuum for this test.

1. Remove the air cleaner from the engine and allow it to cool to 65°F (18°C) on carbureted engines and 115°F (46°C), or below, on fuel injected engines.

2. Inspect all the vacuum lines associated with the system and replace them if they are cracked or broken or if they do not seal tightly at the connections.

3. Apply 20 in. Hg (67.5 kPa) of vacuum to the inlet side of the temperature sensor, a small round device with two vacuum ports, one of which was connected to the intake manifold. Apply the vacuum to the port that was connected to the manifold. Observe the temperature door—it should close.

4. If the door remains open, connect the vacuum source to the vacuum diaphragm on the temperature door. The door should close and then retest the system.

5. If the door now closes, replace the temperature sensor. If the door still does not close, replace the air cleaner, as the temperature door vacuum diaphragm and door are integral parts of it.

REMOVAL & INSTALLATION

Temperature Sensor

▶ See Figure 28

1. Remove the air cleaner. Note routing and then disconnect both vacuum hoses from the sensor.

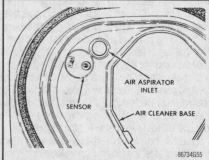

Fig. 29 Newer models, equipped with fuel injection, also have the sensor mounted in the air cleaner housing—some models, if equipped with an air aspirator system, are equipped with the aspirator inlet next to the temperature sensor

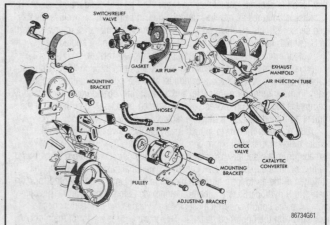

Fig. 31 Exploded view of the air injection system on the 2.2L engine—U.S. models

2. Pry the retaining clips off the sensor connections and discard them. Pull the sensor and gasket out of the wall of the air cleaner.

3. Install the new sensor and gasket and fasten the sensor in place by forcing the new retaining clips all the way onto the vacuum connectors. Make sure to hold the sensor against the air cleaner by its outside diameter as you install the clips so as to compress the gasket.

4. Reconnect the vacuum hoses securely and reinstall the air cleaner.

Air Injection System

OPERATION

▶ **See Figures 31 and 32**

This system is used on all 1981–87 2.2L carburetor-equipped engines. Its job is to reduce carbon monoxide and hydrocarbons to required levels. It adds a controlled amount of air to exhaust gases, causing oxidation of the gases and a reduction in carbon monoxide and hydrocarbons.

The air injection system on the 2.2L engine also includes an air switching system. It has been designed so that air injection will not interfere with the EGR system to control NO_x emissions, and on vehicles equipped with an oxygen sensor, to insure proper air-fuel distribution for maximum fuel economy.

The vehicles produced for sale in the 50 states pump air into the base of the exhaust manifold and into the catalytic converter body. The Canadian system pumps air through the cylinder head at the exhaust port.

The air injection system consists of a belt-driven air pump, a diverter valve (Canadian engines only), a switch-relief valve, rubber hoses, and check valve tube assemblies to protect the hoses and other components from high temperature exhaust gases in case the air pump fails.

Diverter Valve

The purpose of the diverter valve is to prevent backfire in the exhaust system during sudden deceleration. Sudden throttle closure at the beginning of deceleration temporarily creates an air-fuel mixture too rich to burn. This mixture becomes burnable when it reaches the exhaust area and combines with injector air. The next firing of the cylinder will ignite this air-fuel mixture. The valve senses the sudden increase in manifold vacuum, causing the valve to open, allowing air from the pump to pass through the valve into the atmosphere.

A pressure relief valve incorporated in the same housing as the diverter valve controls pressure within the system by diverting excessive pump output to the atmosphere at high engine speed.

Switch/Relief Valve

The purpose of this valve, an integral part of all U.S. air injection systems, is two-fold. First of all, it directs the air injection flow to either the exhaust port location or to the down-stream injection point. Second, the valve regulates system pressure by controlling the output of the air pump at high speeds. When the

pressure reaches a certain level, some of the output is vented to the atmosphere through the silencer.

Check Valve

A check valve is located in the injection tube assemblies that lead to the exhaust manifold and the catalyst injection points on the 50 state engines and to the exhaust port area, through four hollow bolts on the Canadian engines.

This valve has a one-way diaphragm which prevents hot exhaust gases from backing up into the hose and pump. It also protects the system in the event of pump belt failure, excessively high exhaust system pressure, or air hose ruptures.

DIAGNOSIS AND TESTING

The most common problem with the air pump system is air pump noise. It first must be understood that a small amount of rattling or chirping noise comes from an air pump in perfect mechanical condition. It should also be understood that, if the air pump requires replacement, the new pump will be extra noisy until it has been broken in. Operate the new pump for 1,000 miles (1,600 km) before condemning it as noisy.

If the air pump belt suddenly becomes noisy, first check that tension is correct. If the belt is slipping, noise will often be the result. Retension the belt or, if it is glazed (with smooth, glassy wear surfaces), replace it, making sure to tension the new belt properly and to readjust it a week or two later.

Check also that the pump rotates freely by removing the belt and turning the pump drive pulley by hand. There is normally some slight roughness and rattling when turning the drive pulley. A frozen pump's pulley will be impossible or extremely hard to turn.

If the car is in generally good tune and mechanical condition, and runs well but exhibits high CO and hydrocarbon emissions, the air pump system may not be supplying air to the catalytic converter (or exhaust manifold on Canadian cars). In this case, the best procedure is to disconnect the outlet hose passing from the switch/relief valve to the converter and check for airflow. If there is no flow at idle speed, and noticeable flow above idle speed, which increases when the engine is accelerated, the air pump system is okay and the problem may be in the oxygen sensor or fuel system. If air does not flow at this point in the system, disconnect the hose at the air pump side of the switch/relief valve and repeat the test. If there is air at this point now, and no vacuum actuating the switch/relief valve, replace it.

Check also that all hoses are free of cracks, breaks and clogs and that they are tightly and fully connected.

REMOVAL & INSTALLATION

Air Pump

1. Disconnect the negative battery cable.
2. Disconnect the hoses at the air pump.
3. Disconnect the air and vacuum hoses at the switch/relief valve.
4. Remove the air pump drive pulley shield from the engine.
5. Loosen the air pump pivot and adjusting bolts and remove the air pump drive belt.
6. Remove the air pump attaching bolts and remove the pump and switch/relief valve as an assembly.
7. Remove the switch/relief valve and gasket from the pump.

To install:

8. Clean both gasket surfaces. Install a new gasket and the relief valve and tighten the mounting bolts to 125 inch lbs. (14 Nm).
9. Install the drive pulley on the new air pump and tighten the mounting bolt to 12 inch lbs. (1.3 Nm) or less.
10. Position the air pump onto the engine and install the mounting bolts loosely. Loosen the bolts attaching the rear air pump bracket to the transmission housing.
11. Install the drive belt onto the air pump drive pulley. Then apply force with a torque wrench to the adjusting bracket. Use 80–100 ft. lbs. (109–136 Nm) to obtain the proper tension. **Do not apply force to the pump body!** Hold this figure and tighten the bracket-to-transmission bolts to 40 ft. lbs. (54 Nm) maximum.

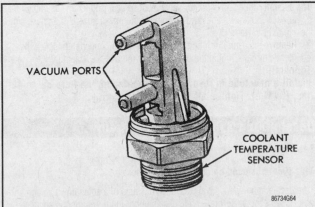

VACUUM PORTS

COOLANT TEMPERATURE SENSOR

86734G64

Fig. 32 Coolant Vacuum Switch Cold Open (CVSCO) is installed into a coolant passage in the intake manifold

Pulse Air Feeder System

OPERATION

▶ **See Figure 33**

➡ **This system is used only 2.6L engines.**

Pulse Air Feeder (PAF) is used for supplying secondary air into the exhaust system between the front and rear catalytic converters, for the purpose of promoting oxidation of exhaust emissions in the rear converter.

The PAF consists of a main reed valve and a sub reed valve. The main reed valve is actuated in response to movement of a diaphragm, which is activated by pressure generated when the piston is in the compression stroke. The sub reed valve is opened on the exhaust stroke.

SYSTEM INSPECTION

To inspect the system, remove the hose connected to the air cleaner and check for vacuum, with the engine running. If vacuum is not present, check the lines for leaks and evidence of oil leaks. Periodic maintenance of this system is not required.

Air Aspiration System

OPERATION

▶ **See Figures 34 and 35**

Some 1983 and later cars with the 2.2 and 2.5L Chrysler engines use an air aspiration system in place of an air pump. This system operates off the pulses

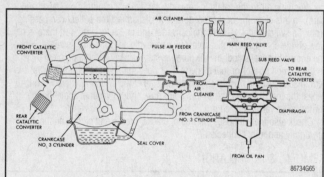

Fig. 33 Schematic view of the pulse air feeder system used on Canadian 2.6L engines

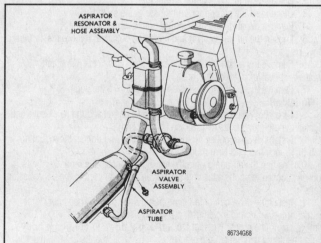

Fig. 34 Air aspirator system used on fuel injected U.S. 2.2L and 2.5L Chrysler engines

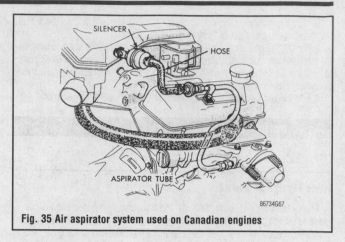

Fig. 35 Air aspirator system used on Canadian engines

generated in the exhaust system when the exhaust valves open and close. Canadian carbureted engines and U.S. 50 States EFI engines are the most common applications.

INSPECTION & TESTING

The aspirator valve is not repairable and, if necessary, should be replaced with a new valve.

The most common part of this system to fail is the aspirator valve. Symptoms of failure are excessive exhaust system noise under the hood at idle speed and hardening of the rubber hose leading from the valve to the air cleaner. If there is excessive exhaust system noise, first check the aspirator tube/exhaust manifold assembly joint and hose connections at the aspirator valve and the air cleaner for leakage. If the aspirator tube/exhaust manifold assembly joint is leaking, retighten the aspirator tube and the adapter tube to 50 ft. lbs. (68 Nm). If either hose connection is leaking and the hose has not hardened, install hose clamps.

To determine whether or not the system has failed, disconnect the aspirator system intake hose from the at the air cleaner. Start the engine and allow it to idle in neutral.

✳✳ CAUTION

Hot exhaust gases may be emitted from the system if the valve has failed.

Cautiously and gradually place your hand near the open end of the aspirator system intake hose. If the valve is operating, the system will be drawing in fresh air, the area around the valve will be cool and you will be able to feel pulses when you touch the open end of the inlet. If the valve has failed, there will be no pulses that can be felt and hot exhaust gas will be emitted.

REMOVAL & INSTALLATION

The aspirator tube and aspirator valve must be replaced as an assembly.

1. Loosen the hose clamp and disconnect the intake hose at the intake side of the aspirator valve.

2. Remove the aspirator tube bracket screw at the converter, unscrew the flared connector collar nut at the converter and remove the assembly.

To install:

Install a new tube in reverse order, tightening the flare nut to 40 ft. lbs. (54 Nm). Tighten all hose clamps securely.

Deceleration Spark Advance System

▶ **See Figure 36**

➡ **This system is used on carbureted engines.**

The deceleration spark advance system consists of a solenoid valve and an engine speed sensor. During vehicle deceleration, ignition timing is advanced by intake manifold vacuum acting on the distributor advance through the solenoid valve. However, when the engine speed sensor detects engine speed at or

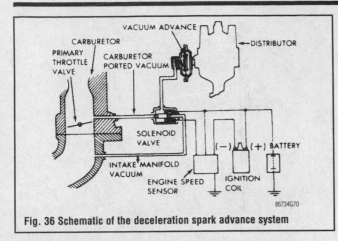

Fig. 36 Schematic of the deceleration spark advance system

below 1,300 rpm the vacuum acting on the vacuum advance is changed from the intake manifold to carburetor ported vacuum. This is performed by the movement of the Deceleration Spark Advance System Solenoid Valve in order to maintain smooth vehicle operation.

High Altitude Compensation System

♦ See Figure 37

➡ This system is used only on carbureted vehicles.

A high altitude compensation system is installed on California vehicles. This modification affects the primary metering system as follows:

A small cylindrical bellows chamber mounted on the body panel in the engine compartment and connected to the carburetor with hoses, is vented to

the atmosphere at the top of the carburetor. Atmospheric pressure expands and contracts the bellows.

A small brass tapered-seat valve regulates air flow when it is raised off its seat by expanding the bellows.

If the car travels to a mountainous area, rarefied atmosphere is encountered, producing a rich air/fuel mixture. At a predetermined atmospheric pressure, the bellows opens, allowing additional air to enter the main air bleeds. The auxiliary air, along with the air normally inducted by the carburetor provides the system with the proper amount of air necessary to maintain the correct air/fuel mixture.

Throttle Opener (Idle-Up System)

➡ This system is used only on carbureted vehicles.

This system consists of a throttle opener assembly, a solenoid valve, an engine speed sensor and a compressor switch for the air conditioner unit.

When the compressor switch is turned on and the speed sensor detects engine speed at or below its present level, the solenoid valve is opened slightly by the throttle opener. Consequently, the engine idle speed increases to compensate for the compressor load. When the compressor switch is turned off, the throttle stops working and returns to normal idle.

Jet Air Control Valve (JACV)

♦ See Figure 38

➡ This system is used only on carbureted vehicles.

The jet air control valve system consists of a jet air control valve, which is an integral part of the carburetor, and a thermo-valve which is controlled by coolant temperature. Its purpose is to help decrease hydrocarbons and carbon monoxide during engine warm-up while the choke is operating.

Carburetor vacuum opens the valve thereby allowing air to flow into the jet air passage preventing an overly rich air-fuel mixture. There is also a thermo-valve in the system. The function of the thermo-valve is to stop jet valve operation when the coolant temperature is above or below a pre-set value.

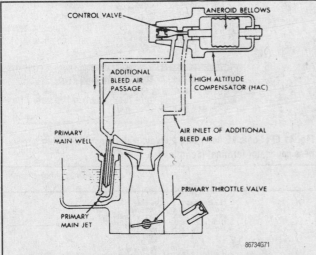

Fig. 37 System schematic for the high altitude compensation system found on California carbureted engines

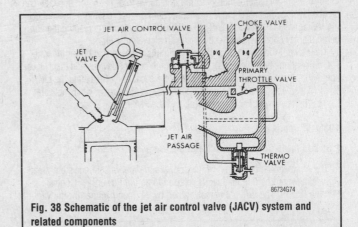

Fig. 38 Schematic of the jet air control valve (JACV) system and related components

ELECTRONIC ENGINE CONTROLS

Diagnosis and Testing

Diagnosis of a driveability problem requires attention to detail and following the diagnostic procedures in the correct order. Resist the temptation to begin extensive testing before completing the preliminary diagnostic steps. The preliminary or visual inspection must be completed in detail before diagnosis begins. In many cases this will shorten diagnostic time and often cure the problem without electronic testing.

VISUAL INSPECTION

This is possibly the most critical step of the diagnosis. Many fault codes or apparent failures are caused by loose, damaged or corroded electrical connectors. A detailed examination of all connectors, wiring and vacuum hoses can often lead to a repair without diagnosis. Performance of this step relies on the skill of the person performing it; a careful inspector will check the undersides of hoses as well as the integrity of the hard-to-reach hoses blocked by the air cleaner or other components.

Wiring should be checked carefully for any sign of strain, burning, crimping or terminal pull-out from a connector. Checking connectors at components or in harnesses is required; usually, pushing them together will reveal a loose fit. Pay particular attention to ground circuits, making sure they are not loose or corroded. Remember to inspect connectors and hose fittings at components not mounted on the engine, such as the evaporative canister or relays mounted on the fender aprons. Any component or wiring in the vicinity of a fluid leak or spillage should be given extra attention during inspection.

Additionally, inspect maintenance items such as belt condition and tension, battery charge and condition and the radiator cap carefully. Any of these very simple items may effect the system enough to set a fault code. **The self-diagnostic system will not operate properly if the battery is low on charge.**

Powertrain Control Module (PCM)

➡**Depending on the particular fuel or ignition system on your vehicle, the engine control computer may have several designations, such as: Engine Control Unit (ECU), Single Board Engine Controller (SBEC), Single Module Engine Controller (SMEC), Logic Module (LM), Power Module (PM). The term "Powertrain Control Module" or PCM will be used in this manual as a generic term meaning any of the aforementioned electronic engine controllers.**

OPERATION

1981–87 Models

▶ **See Figures 39 thru 49**

The fuel-injection systems on 1981–87 models do not use a single PCM to control the engine functions; these vehicles utilize two computers: the Logic Module (LM) and the Power Module (PM).

The LM is a digital computer containing a microprocessor. The module receives input signals from various switches, sensors and components. It then computes the fuel injector pulse width, spark advance, ignition coil dwell, idle speed, purge and EGR control cycles, cooling fan and alternator.

The LM test many of its own input and output circuits. If a fault is found in a major system, this information is stored in the LM. Information on this fault can be displayed by means of the instrument panel power loss lamp or by connecting a Diagnostic Read-out Box (DRB or DRB-II) scan tool and reading the numbered display code, which directly relates to a general fault.

The Power Module (PM) contains the circuits necessary to power the ignition coil and the fuel injector(s). These are high current devices and their power supply has been isolated to minimize any "electrical noise" reaching the LM. The PM also energizes the Automatic Shut Down (ASD) relay, which activates the fuel pump, ignition coil, injector(s), and the PM itself.

1988–95 Models

▶ **See Figures 50, 51, 52, 53 and 54**

The main engine computer, which controls the fuel injection system on all vehicles covered by this manual, is referred to as the Powertrain Control Module (PCM). The original names coined by the manufacturer for the vari-

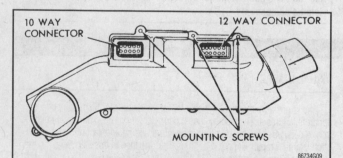

Fig. 39 One of the easiest ways to distinguish between the Power Module (PM) and the PCM is that the PM is equipped with two wiring connectors—a 10-way and a 12-way connector

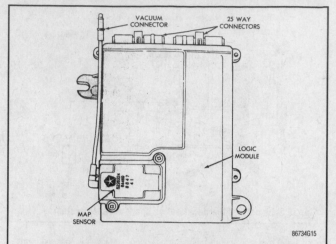

Fig. 40 The Logic Module (LM) is mounted behind the right-hand side, lower kick panel in the passenger's compartment—note that the MAP sensor is mounted on it

Pin	Circuit	Color	Function
1	—	—	5 Volt Supply
2	K16	20 VT/YL	Injector Control
3	—	—	Not Used
4	—	—	Not Used
5	R31	20 DG/OR	Alternator Field Control
6	K15	20 YL	Dwell Control
7	K14	18 DB	Fused J2
8	K14	18 DB	Fused J2
9	—	—	Not Used
10	N 7	18 GY	Distributor Reference
11	DK21	20 PK	SCI Interface Transmit
12	T21	20 GY/LB	Tachometer Signal
13	DK20	20 LG	SCI Interface Receive
14	Z 6	20 LB	Fuel Monitor
15	U 3	20 OR/LG	Shift Indicator Light
16	—	—	Not Used
17	K19	20 DB/YL	ASD Relay Control
18	N 1	18 GY/RD	AIS Motor Open
19	—	—	Not Used
20	—	—	Not Used
21	C27	20 DB/PK	Radiator Fan Relay
22	N 2	18 BR	AIS Motor Close
23	N 6	18 OR	7.5 Volts Input
24	K 5	18 BK	Signal Ground
25	K 5	18 BK/LB	Sensor Return

WHITE CONNECTOR (NO. 1)

Fig. 41 EFI Logic Module (LM) 25-way, white electrical wiring harness connector terminal identification

Pin	Circuit	Color	Function
1	K 6	18 OR/WT	TPS 5 Volts
2	J11	20 RD/WT	Battery Standby
3	N13	20 DB/OR	A/C Cut-out Relay
4	K 3	20 BK/OR	Power Loss Lamp
5	K 1	20 PK	Purge Solenoid
6	S 6	—	Not Used
7	K 9	18 LB/RD	Power Ground
8	K 9	18 LB/RD	Power Ground
9	—	—	Not Used
10	—	—	Not Used
11	C 2B	18 BR	A/C Clutch
12	S 4	20 BR/YL	P/N Switch
13	D 4	18 WT/TN	Brake Switch
14	G 7	20 WT/OR	Distance Sensor
15	—	—	Not Used
16	—	—	Not Used
17	—	—	Not Used
18	N11	18 BK	Oxygen Sensor
19	—	—	Not Used
20	K22	20 RD/BK	Battery Temperature Signal
21	K 7	18 OR/DB	TPS
22	J11	20 RD/WT	Battery Sense
23	K10	20 TN	Coolant Sensor
24	—	—	Not Used
25	—	—	Not Used

BLACK CONNECTOR (NO. 2)

Fig. 42 EFI Logic Module (LM) 25-way, black electrical wiring harness connector terminal identification

Pin	Circuit	Color	Function
1	J 5	18 BK/YL	Coil (−) Terminal
2	J 2	14 DB	Ignition Switch Input
3	K14	18 DB	Fused J2 Output
4	J 1	12 PK	Direct Battery
5	K18	18 TN	Injector
6	Z 1	14 DG/BK	Switched Battery
7	K17	18 WT	Injector
8	R 3	18 DG	Alternator Field
9	J 9	14 BK	Power Ground
10	J 9	14 BK	Power Ground

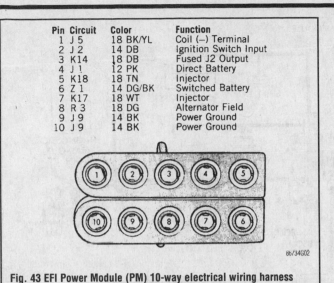

Fig. 43 EFI Power Module (PM) 10-way electrical wiring harness connector terminal identification

Pin	Circuit	Color	Function
1	K 6	18 OR/WT	TPS 5 Volts
2	J11	20 RD/WT	Battery Standby
3	N13	20 DB/OR	A/C Cutout Relay
4	K 3	20 BK/OR	Power Loss Lamp
5	K 1	20 PK	Purge Solenoid
6	S 6	20 GY/YL	EGR Solenoid
7	K 9	18 LB/RD	Power Ground
8	K 9	18 LB/RD	Power Ground
9	—	—	Not Used
10	—	—	Not Used
11	C 2	18 BR	A/C Clutch
12	S 4	20 BR/YL	P/N Switch
13	D 4	18 WT/TN	Brake Switch
14	G 7	20 WT/OR	Distance Sensor
15	—	—	Not Used
16	—	—	Not Used
17	Y 7	18 TN/YL	Distributor Synch
18	N11	18 BK	Oxygen Sensor
19	—	—	Not Used
20	K22	20 RD/BK	Battery Temperature Signal
21	K 7	18 OR/DB	TPS
22	J11	20 RD/WT	Battery Sense
23	K10	20 TN	Coolant Sensor
24	N12	18 BK/LG	Detonation Sensor
25	K13	18 BK/RD	Charge Sensor

BLUE CONNECTOR (NO. 2)

Fig. 46 MFI Logic Module (LM) 25-way, blue electrical wiring harness connector terminal identification

Pin	Circuit	Color	Function
1	K16	20 VT/YL	Injector Control
2	Y 5	18 BK/LB	Signal Ground
3	K22	20 RD/BK	Battery Temperature Sensor
4	—	—	Not Used
5	K19	20 DB/YL	ASD Relay Control
6	J11	20 RD/WT	Battery Sense and Standby
7	—	—	Not Used
8	—	—	Not Used
9	—	—	Not Used
10	K15	20 YL	Dwell Control
11	R31	20 DG/OR	Alternator Field Control
12	N 6	18 OR	8 Volts Output

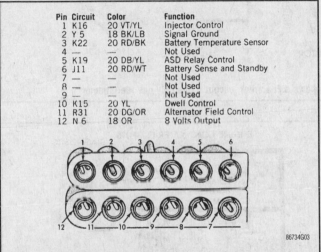

Fig. 44 EFI Power Module (PM) 12-way electrical wiring harness connector terminal identification

Pin	Circuit	Color	Function
1	J 5	18 BK/YL	Coil (−) Terminal
2	J 2	14 DB	Ignition Switch Input
3	K14	18 DB	Fused J2 Output
4	J 1	12 PK	Direct Battery
5	Y11	18 WT	Injector
6	Z 1	14 DG/BK	Switched Battery
7	Y12	18 TN	Injector
8	R 3	18 DG	Alternator Field
9	J 9	14 BK	Power Ground
10	J 9	14 BK	Power Ground

Fig. 47 MFI Power Module (PM) 10-way electrical wiring harness connector terminal identification

Pin	Circuit	Color	Function
1	—	—	5 Volt Supply
2	K16	20 VT/YL	Injector Control
3	Y 1	20 GY/WT	Injector on Signal
4	U 3	OR/LG	Fuel Pacer Lamp
5	R31	20 DG/OR	Alternator Field Control
6	K15	20 YL	Dwell Control
7	K14	18 DB	Fused J2
8	K14	18 DB	Fused J2
9	—	—	Not Used
10	N 7	18 GY	Distributor Reference
11	DK21	20 PK	SCI Interface Transmit
12	T 21	20 GY/LB	Tachometer Signal
13	DK20	20 LG	SCI Interface Receive
14	Z 6	20 LB	Fuel Monitor
15	Y 4	20 LB	Barometric Read Solenoid
16	—	—	Not Used
17	K19	20 DB/YL	ASD Relay Control
18	N 1	18 GY/RD	AIS Motor Open
19	Y 6	20 LG	Wastegate Solenoid Signal
20	—	—	Not Used
21	C27	20 DB/PK	Radiator Fan Relay
22	N 2	18 BR	AIS Motor Close
23	N 6	18 OR	7.5 Volts Input
24	K 5	18 BK	Signal Ground
25	K 5	18 BK/LB	Sensor Return

RED CONNECTOR (NO. 1)

Fig. 45 MFI Logic Module (LM) 25-way, red electrical wiring harness connector terminal identification

Pin	Circuit	Color	Function
1	K16	20 VT/YL	Injector Control
2	Y 5	18 BK/LB	Signal Ground
3	K22	20 RD/BK	Battery Temperature Sensor
4	—	—	Not Used
5	K19	20 DB/YL	ASD Relay Control
6	J11	20 RD/WT	Battery Sense and Standby
7	—	—	Not Used
8	Y 1	20 GY/WT	Injector Control
9	—	—	Not Used
10	K15	20 YL	Dwell Control
11	R31	20 DG/OR	Alternator Field Control
12	N 6	18 OR	8 Volts Output

Fig. 48 MFI Power Module (PM) 12-way electrical wiring harness connector terminal identification

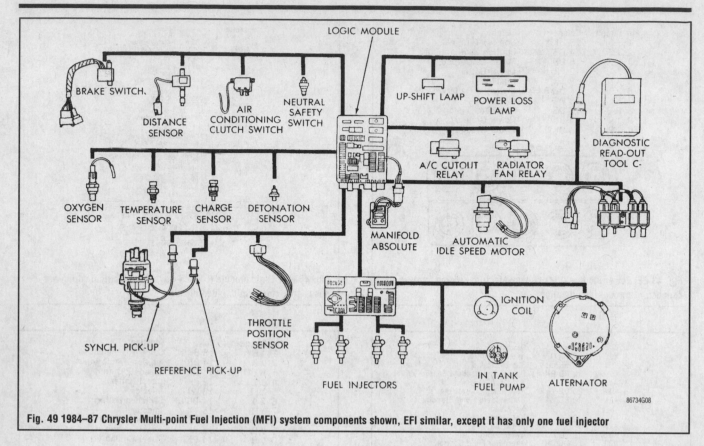

Fig. 49 1984–87 Chrysler Multi-point Fuel Injection (MFI) system components shown, EFI similar, except it has only one fuel injector

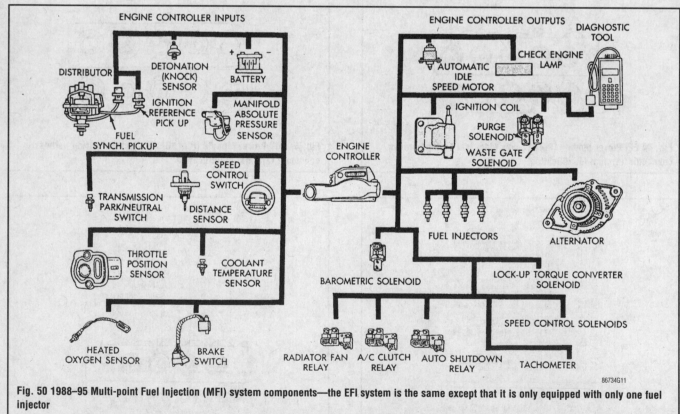

Fig. 50 1988–95 Multi-point Fuel Injection (MFI) system components—the EFI system is the same except that it is only equipped with only one fuel injector

ous engine computers differ greatly from year-to-year or model-to-model. The PCM is also known as the following: Logic Module (LM). Power Module (PM), Engine Control Unit (ECU), Single-Board Engine Controller (SBEC),

Single Module Engine Controller (SMEC). Throughout this manual these various computers will be referred to as simply the Powertrain Control Module (PCM).

CAV	WIRE COLOR	DESCRIPTION	CAV	WIRE COLOR	DESCRIPTION
1	DG/RD*	MAP SENSOR SIGNAL	37		
2	TN/BK*	COOLANT SENSOR	38		
3	RD	DIRECT BATTERY VOLTAGE	39	GY/RD*	AIS STEPPER #3 DRIVER
4	BK/LB*	SENSOR RETURN	40	BR/WT*	AIS STEPPER #1 DRIVER
5	BK/WT*	SIGNAL GROUND	41	BK/DG*	OXYGEN SENSOR SIGNAL
6	VT/WT*	5.0 VOLT OUTPUT (MAP AND TPS)	42		
7	OR	9.0 VOLT OUTPUT (DISTRIBUTOR PICK-UP AND DISTANCE SENSOR)	43	GY/LB*	TACHOMETER SIGNAL OUTPUT
8	WT	B1 VOLTAGE SENSE (START SIGNAL)	44		
9	DB	A21 SUPPLY (IGNITION START/RUN)	45	LG	SCI RECEIVE
10			46	WT/BK*	CCD (-) BUS
11	BK/TN*	POWER GROUND	47	WT/OR*	DISTANCE SENSOR SIGNAL
12	BK/TN*	POWER GROUND	48		
13			49		
14			50		
15			51	DB/YL*	AUTO SHUTDOWN RELAY AND FUEL PUMP RELAY
16	WT/DB*	INJECTOR DRIVER	52	PK/BK*	PURGE SOLENOID
17			53	LG/RD*	SPEED CONTROL VENT SOLENOID
18			54	OR/BK*	PART THROTTLE UNLOCK SOLENOID
19	BK/GY*	IGNITION COIL	55		
20	DG	ALTERNATOR FIELD CONTROL	56		
21			57	DG/OR*	A142 CIRCUIT VOLTAGE SENSE
22	OR/DB*	THROTTLE POSITION SENSOR	58		
23	RD/LG*	SPEED CONTROL SENSE	59	VT/BK*	AIS STEPPER #4 DRIVER
24	GY/BK*	IGNITION REFERENCE PICK-UP	60	YL/BK*	AIS STEPPER #2 DRIVER
25	PK	SCI TRANSMIT			
26	VT/BR*	CCD (+) BUS			
27	BR	A/C SWITCH SENSE			
28					
29	WT/PK*	BRAKE SWITCH			
30	BR/YL*	PARK/NEUTRAL SWITCH (AUTO TRANS.)			
31	DB/PK*	RADIATOR FAN RELAY			
32	BK/PK*	CHECK ENGINE LAMP			
33	TN/RD*	SPEED CONTROL VACUUM SOLENOID			
34	DB/OR*	A/C CLUTCH RELAY			
35	GY/YL*	EGR SOLENOID			
36					

WIRE COLOR CODES

BK	BLACK	LB	LIGHT BLUE	VT	VIOLET
BR	BROWN	LG	LIGHT GREEN	WT	WHITE
DB	DARK BLUE	OR	ORANGE	YL	YELLOW
DG	DARK GREEN	PK	PINK	*	WITH TRACER
GY	GRAY	RD	RED	TN	TAN

CONNECTOR TERMINAL SIDE SHOWN

86734G12

Fig. 51 1988–95 EFI Powertrain Control Module (PCM) 60-way connector terminal identification

CAV	WIRE COLOR	DESCRIPTION	CAV	WIRE COLOR	DESCRIPTION
1	DG/RD*	MAP SENSOR	37		
2	TN/BK*	COOLANT SENSOR	38		
3	RD	DIRECT BATTERY VOLTAGE	39	GY/RD*	AIS STEPPER DRIVER #3
4	BK/LB*	SENSOR RETURN	40	BR/WT*	AIS STEPPER DRIVER #1
5	BK/WT*	SIGNAL GROUND	41	BK/DG*	OXYGEN SENSOR SIGNAL
6	VT/WT*	5-VOLT OUTPUT (MAP AND TPS)	42	BK/LG*	DETONATION SENSOR SIGNAL
7	OR	9-VOLT OUTPUT (DISTRIBUTOR PICK-UP AND DISTANCE SENSOR)	43	GY/LB*	TACHOMETER SIGNAL OUTPUT
8			44	TN/YL*	FUEL SYNC. PICK-UP
9	DB	A21 SUPPLY (IGNITION START/RUN)	45	LG	SCI RECEIVE
10			46		
11	BK/TN*	POWER GROUND	47	WT/OR*	DISTANCE SENSOR SIGNAL
12	BK/TN*	POWER GROUND	48		
13	LB/BR	INJECTOR DRIVER #4	49		
14	YL/WT*	INJECTOR DRIVER #3	50		
15	TN	INJECTOR DRIVER #2	51	DB/YL*	AUTO SHUTDOWN (ASD) RELAY AND FUEL PUMP RELAY
16	WT/DB*	INJECTOR DRIVER #1	52	PK/BK*	PURGE SOLENOID
17			53	LG/RD*	SPEED CONTROL VENT SOLENOID
18			54	LG/WT*	PART THROTTLE UNLOCK SOLENOID
19	BK/GY*	IGNITION COIL DRIVER #1	55	LB	BARO. PRESS. READ SOLENOID
20	DG	ALTERNATOR FIELD CONTROL	56		
21			57	DG/OR*	A142 CIRCUIT VOLTAGE SENSE
22	OR/DB*	THROTTLE POSITION SENSOR (TPS)	58		
23	RD/LG*	SPEED CONTROL SENSE	59	VT/BK*	AIS STEPPER DRIVER #4
24	GY/BK*	IGNITION REFERENCE PICK-UP	60	YL/BK*	AIS STEPPER DRIVER #2
25	PK	SCI TRANSMIT			
26					
27	BR	A/C SWITCH SENSE			
28					
29	WT/PK*	BRAKE SWITCH			
30	BR/YL*	PARK/NEUTRAL SWITCH (AUTO TRANS.)			
31	DB/PK*	RADIATOR FAN RELAY			
32	BK/PK*	CHECK ENGINE LAMP			
33	TN/RD*	SPEED CONTROL VACUUM SOLENOID			
34	DB/OR*	A/C CLUTCH RELAY			
35	GY/YL*	EGR SOLENOID (CALIFORNIA ONLY)			
36	LG/BK*	WASTEGATE SOLENOID			

WIRE COLOR CODES

BK	BLACK	LB	LIGHT BLUE	VT	VIOLET
BR	BROWN	LG	LIGHT GREEN	WT	WHITE
DB	DARK BLUE	OR	ORANGE	YL	YELLOW
DG	DARK GREEN	PK	PINK	*	WITH TRACER
GY	GRAY	RD	RED	TN	TAN

CONNECTOR TERMINAL SIDE SHOWN

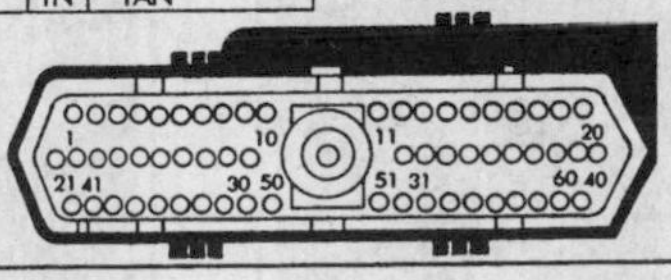

86734G13

Fig. 52 1988–95 MFI Powertrain Control Module (PCM) 60-way connector terminal identification

The PCM is a digital computer containing a microprocessor. The engine computer receives input signals from various switches and sensors that are referred to as engine computer inputs. Based on these inputs, the engine computer adjusts various engine and vehicle operations through devices referred to as engine computer outputs.

The possible engine computer inputs are as follows:
- Air conditioning controls
- Battery voltage
- Brake switch
- Carburetor switch
- Closed throttle switch
- Coolant temperature sensor or switch
- Crankshaft Position Sensor (CKPS)
- Camshaft Position Sensor (CPS)
- Detonation (knock) sensor
- Engine speed sensor
- Distributor reference pick-up
- Manifold Absolute Pressure (MAP) sensor
- Manifold Air Temperature (MAT) sensor
- Methanol concentration sensor
- Oxygen (O_2) sensor
- Speed control system controls
- Throttle position sensor
- Throttle body temperature sensor
- Park/Neutral switch (automatic transaxle)
- Vehicle Speed Sensor (VSS)

The possible engine computer outputs are:
- Air conditioning clutch relay
- Alternator field
- Idle Air Control Motor (IACM)
- Auto Shutdown (ASD) and fuel pump relays
- Canister purge solenoid
- Malfunction indicator lamp
- Data link connector
- Electric EGR Transducer (EET)
- Fuel injectors
- Ignition coil
- Torque converter clutch solenoid
- Radiator fan relay
- Speed control solenoids
- Tachometer output

Based on inputs it receives, the engine computer adjusts fuel injector pulse width, idle speed, ignition spark advance, ignition coil dwell and canister purge operation. The engine computer regulates the cooling fan, air conditioning and speed control systems. The engine computer changes the alternator charge rate by adjusting the generator field.

On systems equipped with distributors, the distributor pick-up signal or, for systems without distributors, Crankshaft Position Sensor (CKPS)/Camshaft Position Sensor (CPS) is sent to the engine computer. If the engine computer does not receive a signal within approximately one second of engine cranking, the ASD relay and fuel pump relay are deactivated. When these relays are deactivated, power is shut off to the fuel injector, ignition coil, oxygen sensor heating element and fuel pump.

The engine computer contains a voltage converter that changes battery voltage to a regulated 8.0 volts. The 8.0 volts power the distributor pick-up and Vehicle Speed Sensor (VSS). The engine computer also provides a 5.0 volt supply for the coolant temperature sensor, manifold absolute pressure sensor and throttle position sensor.

REMOVAL & INSTALLATION

1981–87 Models—Power Module

▶ See Figures 55, 56 and 57

The removal and installation procedure is the same as that for the PCM in 1988–95 models; please refer to that procedure later in this section.

1981–87 Models—Logic Module

▶ See Figure 40

➡The LM is located behind the right-hand side (passenger's side), front kick panel.

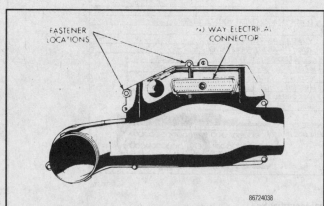

Fig. 53 The PCM in 1988–95 models is equipped with a 60-way connector, rather than two connectors as with 1981–87 models

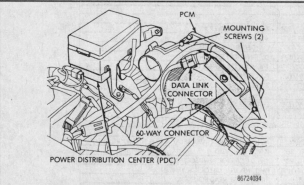

Fig. 54 The PCM is mounted on the inner left-hand fender, next to the battery

Fig. 55 For 1981–87 models, remove the battery and detach the air inlet tube . . .

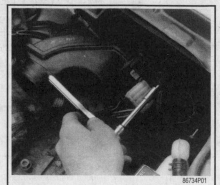

Fig. 56 . . . detach the electrical connectors and remove the attaching screws

Fig. 57 Remove the PM from the inner left-hand fender—note the two electrical connections

1. Raise the hood and disconnect the negative battery cable.
2. Remove the right-hand side, lower kick panel.
3. Remove the LM mounting screws.
4. Remove the harness connectors from the LM, then remove it from the vehicle.

To install:

5. Attach the harness connectors to the LM.
6. Place the LM in its original position.
7. Install the mounting screws until secure.
8. Install the kick panel.
9. Connect the negative battery cable.
10. Close the hood.

1988–95 Models

▶ **See Figures 58, 59, 60, 61 and 62**

1. Remove the air cleaner duct or air cleaner assembly from the engine.
2. Remove the battery from the vehicle as described in Section 2.
3. Remove the engine computer mounting screws.
4. Remove the connector(s) from the engine computer. Remove the engine computer from the vehicle.

To install:

5. Plug the connector(s) into the engine computer.
6. Install the PCM on the inside left front fender. Install and tighten the mounting screws.
7. Install the battery into the vehicle.
8. Install the air cleaner duct or air cleaner assembly.

Fig. 58 As with the PM, first detach the air inlet hose from the computer housing to remove the PCM

Fig. 59 After removing the battery and tray, loosen the center bolt from the 60-way harness connector

Fig. 60 Pull the 60-way connector out of the PCM and make sure all of the connector holes are clean

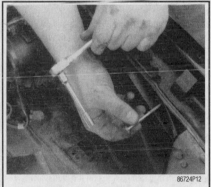

Fig. 61 Loosen and remove the mounting screws from the PCM . . .

Fig. 62 . . . then lift the PCM out of the engine bay—1988–95 models

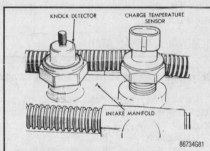

Fig. 63 The air intake charge temperature sensor is mounted in the intake manifold or air cleaner assembly—as shown on this MFI engine, the temperature sensor is located next to the detonation sensor

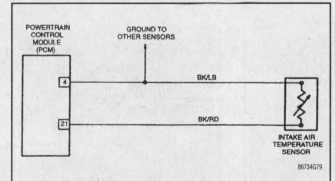

Fig. 64 Air intake charge temperature sensor circuit schematic for 1988–95 models, other models similar

Air Intake Charge Temperature Sensor

OPERATION

▶ **See Figures 63 and 64**

Chrysler Electronic Spark Control (ESC) System

➡ The ESC system is used only on 2.2L carbureted engines.

➡ Make certain to properly identify all switches and sensors, before attempting to test any temperature sensing component.

The charge temperature sensor supplies a signal to the computer indicating the engine temperature. This information is required to prevent changing of the air/fuel ratio until the engine reaches operating temperature. It also controls the amount of spark advance with a cold engine.

Chrysler Mikuni Feedback Carburetor System

➡ **The Mikuni feedback carburetor system is used only on 2.6L engines.**

The air temperature sensor is a resistor-based sensor used to detected the intake air temperature. Since air density is proportional to temperature, the PCM uses this data to adjust the air/fuel ratio.

TESTING

Chrysler Electronic Spark Control (ESC) System

1. Turn the ignition switch **OFF** and disconnect wire from temperature sensor.
2. Connect one lead of an ohmmeter to one terminal of sensor.
3. Connect the other lead of the ohmmeter to the remaining terminal of the sensor.
4. Check for the following ohmmeter readings:
    a. With the engine at room temperature (approximately 70°F/21°C)—Resistance should be more than 6000 ohms.
    b. Hot engine (normal operating temperature, approximately 200°F/93°C)—Resistance should be less than 2500 ohms.
5. If the sensor fails to perform as specified, replace the sensor and retest.

Chrysler Mikuni Feedback Carburetor System

1. Disconnect the electrical connector from the air temperature sensor.
2. Connect an ohmmeter across the sensor terminals and measure the resistance as follows:
    • With the engine cold—resistance should be above 6000 ohms
    • With the engine at room temperature—resistance should be 1300–2500 ohms
    • With engine at normal operating temperature—resistance should be 100–1300 ohms
3. If the resistance deviates from these standard values greatly, replace the sensor and retest.

REMOVAL & INSTALLATION

Chrysler Electronic Spark Control (ESC) System

The air intake charge temperature sensor is located in the throttle body adapter below the throttle body and behind the fitting for the brake vacuum booster.
1. Disconnect the negative battery cable.
2. Unplug the electrical connector from the sensor.
3. Unscrew the sensor from the adapter.
To install:
4. Install the sensor in the throttle body adapter.
5. Tighten the sensor to 21 ft. lbs. (28 Nm) and the charge Temperature sensor to 50 inch lbs. (6 Nm).

6. Plug the electrical connector back into the sensor.
7. Connect the battery cable.

Chrysler Mikuni Feedback Carburetor System

The air intake charge temperature sensor is located in the air cleaner.
1. Disconnect the negative battery cable.
2. Unplug the electrical connector from the sensor.
3. Remove the sensor from the air cleaner housing.
To install:
4. Install the sensor in the air cleaner housing.
5. Attach the electrical connector to the sensor.
6. Connect the battery cable.

Camshaft Position Sensor (CPS)

OPERATION

Chrysler Multi-Point Fuel Injection (MFI) System

➡ **The MFI system is used on 2.2L and 2.5L turbocharged and flex fuel engines.**

2.2L TURBO III ENGINE

▶ See Figures 65, 66 and 67

The CPS provides cylinder identification to the PCM. The sensor generates pulses as groups of notches on the camshaft sprocket pass underneath it. The PCM keeps track of the crankshaft rotation and identifies each cylinder by the pulses generated by the notches on the camshaft sprocket. Four crankshaft pulses follow each group of camshaft pulses.

When the PCM receives two camshaft pulses followed by the long flat spot on the camshaft sprocket, it knows that the crankshaft timing marks for cylinder one are next (on the drive plate). When the PCM receives one camshaft pulse after the long flat spot on the sprocket, cylinder No. 2 crankshaft timing marks are next. After three camshaft pulses, the PCM knows cylinder four crankshaft timing marks follow. One camshaft pulse after the three pulses indicates cylinder five. The two camshaft pulses after cylinder No. 5 signals cylinder No. 6. The PCM can synchronize on cylinders No. 1 or No. 4.

When metal aligns with the sensor, voltage goes low (less than 0.5 volts). When a notch aligns with the sensor, voltage spikes high (5.0 volts). As a groups of notches pass under the sensor, the voltage switches from low to high then back to low again. The number of notches determine the amount of pulses. If available, an oscilloscope can display the square wave patterns of each timing event.

Top Dead Center (TDC) does not occur when notches on the camshaft sprocket pass below the sensor. TDC occurs after the camshaft pulse (or pulses) and after the 4 crankshaft pulses associated with the particular cylinder. The

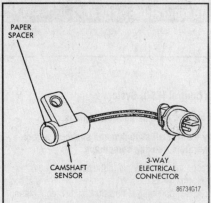

Fig. 65 The Camshaft Position Sensor (CPS)—using a new paper spacer during installation is a must

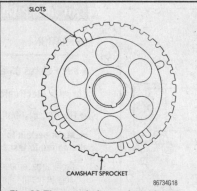

Fig. 66 The camshaft gear is equipped with specifically positioned holes, which activate the CPS and inform the PCM of engine timing

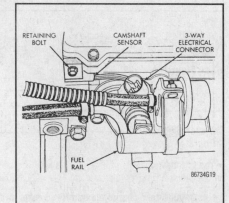

Fig. 67 The CPS is mounted onto the cylinder head, next to the fuel rail and fuel supply lines

arrows and cylinder call in the illustration represent which cylinder the flat spot and notches identify, they do not indicate the TDC position.

The camshaft position sensor is mounted to the top of the timing case cover. The bottom of the sensor is positioned above the camshaft sprocket.

➡**The distance between the bottom of sensor and the camshaft sprocket is critical to the operation of the system.**

2.5L ENGINES

The 2.5L engines with MFI utilize distributor reference signals, like the Chrysler EFI system, to keep track of the camshaft and crankshaft positions. The 2.5L Flex Fuel engines do not use separate CPS or CKPS sensors.

TESTING

Chrysler Multi-Point Fuel Injection (MFI) System

2.2L TURBO III ENGINE

1. With ignition **ON** and engine **OFF**, measure voltage between terminals **1** and **2** of the camshaft position sensor harness connector. If the voltage reading is about 8V, the power circuit to the sensor is OK.
2. While varying the engine rpm, measure the voltage between terminals **3** and **2** of the CMP sensor with a DVOM on AC scale (to monitor less than 5.0V). If the reading varies more than 0.1V AC, the sensor is OK

REMOVAL & INSTALLATION

Chrysler Multi-Point Fuel Injection (MFI) System

2.2L TURBO III ENGINE

1. Disconnect the negative battery cable.
2. Unplug the camshaft position sensor electrical connector from the wiring harness.
3. Loosen the camshaft position sensor retaining bolt enough to allow the slot in the sensor to slide past the bolt.
4. Pull the sensor up and out of the chain case cover. **Do not pull on the sensor wires.** There is an O-ring on the sensor case and may make the removal slightly difficult. A light tap on the top of the sensor prior to removal may reduce the force needed for removal.

To Install:
5. If installing the original sensor, clean off the old spacer on the sensor face. A new spacer must be attached to the face before installation. Inspect the O-ring for damage (cuts, tears, etc.), replace with a new O-ring if any damage is found. If the sensor is being replaced with a new one, confirm that the paper spacer is attached to the face and O-ring is positioned in the groove of the new sensor.
6. Apply a couple drops of clean engine oil to the O-ring prior to installation. Install the sensor into the chain case cover and push the sensor down until contact is made with the camshaft gear. While holding the sensor in this position, install and tighten the retaining bolt to 108 inch lbs. (12 Nm).
7. Plug the sensor's connector back into the engine wiring harness. Position the connector away from the accessory drive belt.
8. Connect the negative battery cable.

Carburetor Switch

◆ **See Figure 68**

OPERATION

Chrysler Electronic Spark Control (ESC) and Mikuni Feedback Carburetor Systems

➡**The ESC system is used only on 2.2L carbureted engines. The Mikuni feedback carburetor system is used only on 2.6L engines.**

The carburetor switch is located at the end of the idle stop solenoid. The primary purpose of the switch is to inform the computer when the engine is at idle or off-idle. When the carburetor switch is closed at idle, the computer cancels the spark advance and the idle control circuit adjusts the air/fuel ratio.

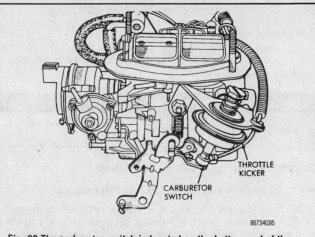

Fig. 68 The carburetor switch is located on the bottom end of the throttle kicker, as shown

TESTING

Chrysler Electronic Spark Control (ESC) System

➡**Grounding carburetor switch eliminates all spark advance on most systems.**

1. With ignition key in **OFF** position, disconnect 10-way connector from Spark Control Computer.
2. With throttle completely closed, check continuity between pin **7** of disconnected 10-way connector and a good engine ground. Continuity should exist.
   • If continuity does not exists, check the wiring between the ESC computer and carburetor switch.
   • If continuity does exist, proceed to the next step.
3. With throttle open, check continuity between pin **7** of disconnected 10-way connector and a good engine ground. There should be no continuity.
4. If the switch fails to perform as specified, replace the switch and retest.

Chrysler Mikuni Feedback Carburetor System

1. Disconnect the electrical connector from the carburetor switch.
2. Connect an ohmmeter between the switch connector and a known good engine ground.
3. Operate the throttle linkage while observing the ohmmeter.
   • With the throttle plates opened continuity should **NOT** exist
   • With the throttle plates fully closed continuity should exist
4. If the sensor did not operate as specified, replace the switch and retest.

REMOVAL & INSTALLATION

➡**The carburetor switch is located on the end of the idle stop solenoid. If the carburetor switch is deemed faulty, the entire idle stop solenoid must be replaced.**

1. Disconnect the negative battery cable.
2. Disengage the electrical wiring harness connectors from the carburetor switch.
3. Loosen and remove the idle stop solenoid bracket mounting bolt.
4. Remove the solenoid from the carburetor.

To install:
5. Place the idle stop solenoid against the carburetor in its original position.
6. Install the mounting bolt and tighten it until secure.
7. Attach the electrical wiring harness connectors to the carburetor switch and idle stop solenoid.
8. Connect the negative battery cable.
9. Adjust the carburetor switch as follows:
   a. Check the ignition timing and adjust, if necessary.
   b. With the engine fully warmed up, place the transaxle in Neutral and set the parking brake. Turn all electrical accessories **OFF**.

c. Ground the idle stop carburetor switch with a jumper wire.

d. Remove the red wire from the 6-way connector on the carburetor side of the connector.

e. Adjust the throttle stop screw until the engine speed reaches 700 rpm.

f. Reattach the wire at the connector and remove the jumper wire from the idle stop carburetor switch.

Coolant Temperature Sensor

OPERATION

Chrysler Electronic Spark Control (ESC) System

➡ **The ESC system is used only on 2.2L carbureted engines.**

The coolant temperature sensor supplies a signal to the computer indicating the engine temperature. The sensor resistance is inversely related to the temperature of the coolant; therefore, the hotter the coolant, the lower the sensor's resistance. This information is required to prevent changing of the air/fuel ratio until the engine reaches normal operating temperature. It also controls the amount of spark advance during cold engine operation.

Chrysler Mikuni Feedback Carburetor System

➡ **The Mikuni feedback carburetor system is used only on 2.6L engines.**

The engine coolant temperature sensor installed in the engine coolant passage of the intake manifold is a resistor based sensor. The PCM determines engine warm-up state through the sensor output voltage, and adjusts the air/fuel mixture to provide optimum fuel enrichment.

Chrysler Electronic Fuel Injection (EFI) and Multi-Point Fuel Injection (MFI) Systems

➡ **The MFI system is used on 2.2L and 2.5L turbocharged and flex fuel engines.**

The coolant temperature sensor is a thermistor (a temperature controlled variable resistor with a range of −40°F (−40°C) to 265°F (129°C) mounted in the engine coolant stream. Engine controller uses the temperature input to adjust the fuel mixture slightly richer and raise the idle speed, until normal operating temperatures are reached. All models equipped with electric cooling fans use this sensor to control the cooling (radiator) fan operation.

TESTING

Chrysler Electronic Spark Control (ESC) System

1. Turn ignition switch **OFF** and disconnect wire from temperature sensor.
2. Connect one lead of an ohmmeter to one terminal of sensor.
3. Connect other lead of ohmmeter to remaining terminal of sensor.
4. Check for following ohmmeter readings:

a. Engine at room temperature (approximately 70°F/21°C): Resistance should be 5000–6000 ohms. If not, replace the sensor.

b. Hot engine (normal operating temperature, approximately 200°F/93°C): Resistance should be less than 2500 ohms. If not, replace the sensor.

5. If the sensor fails to perform as specified, replace the sensor and retest.

Chrysler Mikuni Feedback Carburetor System

1. Disconnect the negative battery cable.
2. Disengage the electrical connector from the coolant temperature sensor.
3. Connect an ohmmeter to the sensor terminals and measure the resistance as follows:

• With the engine cold, the resistance should be between 3000–17,000 ohms

• With the engine warmed up to approximately room temperature, the sensor's resistance should be between 1000–3000 ohms

• With the engine warmed up to normal operating temperature, the resistance should be between 100–1000 ohms

4. If the resistance deviates from these standard values greatly, replace the sensor and retest.

Chrysler Electronic Fuel Injection (EFI) and Multi-Point Fuel Injection (MFI) Systems

◆ **See Figures 69 and 70**

1. Disconnect the electrical connector from the coolant temperature sensor.
2. Connect an ohmmeter across the terminals of the sensor. The sensor resistance should be as follows:

• With the engine cold (approximately. 70°F/21°C) the sensor resistance should be between 7,000–13,000 ohms.

• With the engine at normal operating temperature (approximately. 200°F/93°C) the sensor resistance should be between 700–1000 ohms.

3. If the resistance readings are not within specifications, replace the sensor and retest.

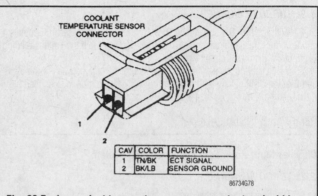

Fig. 69 Engine coolant temperature sensor connector terminal identification

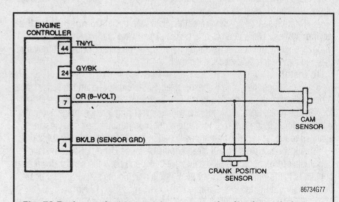

Fig. 70 Engine coolant temperature sensor circuit schematic for 1988–95 models—earlier models are similar

REMOVAL & INSTALLATION

◆ **See Figures 71, 72, 73 and 74**

✳✳ WARNING

It is essential that coolant does not contact the accessory drive belt or pulleys because it may cause the belt to slip and/or squeak. Cover the belt and pulleys with shop rags to protect them from coolant spillage. If coolant contacts the belt or pulleys, flush them with clean water.

1. Disconnect the negative battery cable.
2. Unplug the electrical connector from the coolant temperature sensor.
3. Drain the coolant system until it is below the level of the sensor. Make certain to drain the fluid into a large, clean vessel so that it may be used later.

4. Unscrew the sensor from the thermostat housing or waterbox (next to the thermostat housing).

To install:

5. Start the sensor into its hole slowly, making sure that the threads do not crossthread. Screw the sensor in as far as possible by hand.

6. Tighten the sensor to 21 ft. lbs. (28 Nm).

7. Connect the coolant temperature sensor's electrical plug to the wiring harness.

8. Remove the shop towels from the pulleys and drive belts.

9. Connect the negative battery cable.

10. Refill and bleed the coolant system. For more details, refer to Section 1.

11. Start the vehicle and check for coolant leaks.

Fig. 71 After disconnecting the battery, detach the sensor wiring connector . . .

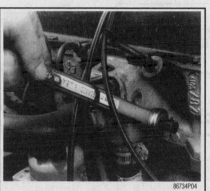

Fig. 72 . . . then remove the sensor with a wrench—Chrysler EFI engine

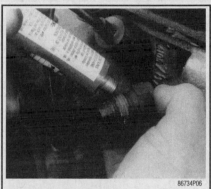

Fig. 73 Apply sealant to threads after they are cleaned . . .

Fig. 74 . . . and reinstall the sensor into the water box

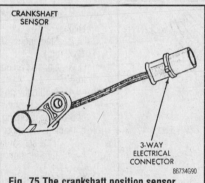

Fig. 75 The crankshaft position sensor used on 2.2L Turbo III engines is a Hall-effect device

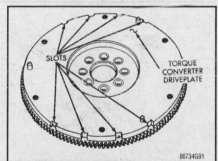

Fig. 76 The CKPS, since it is a Hall-effect device, can sense the slots cut into the outer edge of the torque converter drive-plate or flywheel

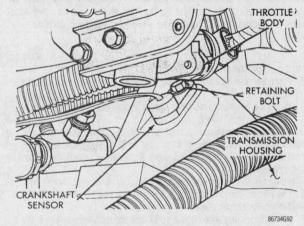

Fig. 77 The CKPS is mounted in the transaxle housing beneath the throttle body assembly

Crankshaft Position Sensor (CKPS)

OPERATION

2.2L Turbo III Engine

▶ **See Figures 75, 76 and 77**

Only the 2.2L Turbo III engine utilizes separate crankshaft and camshaft position sensors; the other engines use distributor reference signals to perform the same functions.

The Crankshaft Position Sensor (CKPS) perceives slots cut into the transaxle drive plate extension. There are 2 sets of slots, each set containing 4 slots, for a total of 8 slots. Basic timing is determined by the position of the last slot in each group. Once the PCM senses the last slot, it determines crankshaft position (which piston will next be at Top Dead Center/TDC) from the Camshaft Position Sensor (CPS) input. It may take the PCM one engine revolution to determine crankshaft position during cranking.

The PCM uses the CKPS to determine fuel injector sequence and ignition timing. Once the crankshaft position has been determined, the PCM begins energizing the injectors in sequence.

The CKPS is located in the transaxle housing, below the throttle body. The bottom of the sensor is positioned next to the drive plate.

➡ **The distance between the bottom of the sensor and the drive plate is critical to the operation of the system.**

2.5L Flexible Fuel And Turbo I Engines

The 2.5L Flex Fuel and Turbo I engines utilize distributor reference signals, like the EFI system. For the proper service procedures for the distributor pick-up sensors, refer to those procedures later in this section.

TESTING

2.2L Turbo III Engine

⬥ See Figures 78 and 79

1. With ignition **ON** and engine **OFF**, measure voltage between terminals 1 and 2 of the camshaft position sensor harness connector. If the voltage reading is approximately 8V, the power circuit to the sensor is OK.

2. While varying the engine rpm, measure the voltage between terminals **3** and **2** of the CMP sensor with a DVOM on AC scale (to monitor less than 5.0V). If the reading varies more than 0.1V AC, the sensor is OK.

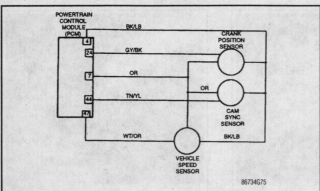

Fig. 78 Crankshaft position sensor circuit wiring schematic for 2.2L Turbo III engines

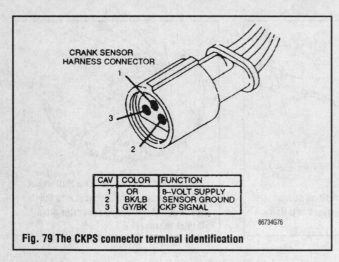

Fig. 79 The CKPS connector terminal identification

REMOVAL & INSTALLATION

2.2L TURBO III ENGINE

1. Disconnect the negative battery cable.
2. The sensor is located on the side of the transaxle (front of vehicle).
3. Unplug the CKPS electrical connector from the wiring harness.
4. Unscrew the CKPS retaining bolt.
5. Pull the sensor straight out of the transaxle housing.

To install:

6. If installing the original sensor, clean off the old spacer from the sensor face. A new spacer **must** be attached to the sensor face before installation. If the sensor is being replaced with a new one, confirm that the paper spacer is attached to the face of the new sensor.

7. Slide the sensor into the hole in the transaxle and push the sensor in until contact is made with the drive plate. While holding the sensor in this position, install and tighten the retaining bolt to 108 inch lbs. (12 Nm).

8. Plug the CKPS wiring connector into the wiring harness.
9. Connect the negative battery cable.

OPERATION

Chrysler Electronic Spark Control (ESC) System

➡**The ESC system is used only on 2.2L carbureted engines.**

The detonation sensor is tuned to the frequency characteristic of engine knocking ("spark knock" or "ping"). When detonation occurs, the sensor sends a low voltage signal to the computer, which retards ignition timing in proportion to the strength and frequency of the signal. The maximum amount of retard is 20 degrees. When the detonation condition is no longer detected, the computer advances timing to the original value.

Chrysler Multi-Point Fuel Injection (MFI) System

➡**The MFI system is used on 2.2L and 2.5L turbocharged and flex fuel engines.**

EXCEPT 2.5L FLEX FUEL ENGINE

The detonation sensor is a device that generates a signal when spark knock occurs in the combustion chamber(s). It is mounted at a position on the intake manifold where detonation in each cylinder can be detected. The sensor provides information used by the engine controller to modify spark advance and boost schedules in order to eliminate detonation.

TESTING

Chrysler Electronic Spark Control (ESC) System

1. Connect an adjustable timing light or magnetic timing unit light to engine.
2. Start engine and run it on second highest step of fast idle cam (at least 1200 rpm).
3. Connect an auxiliary vacuum supply to vacuum transducer and set on 16 in. Hg.
4. Tap lightly on the intake manifold near sensor with a small metal object.
5. Using the timing light, look for a decrease in spark advance. The amount of decrease in timing should be directly proportional to strength and frequency of tapping. The most decrease in timing will be 20 degrees.
6. If the sensor fails to perform as specified, replace the sensor and retest.
7. Turn ignition switch to **OFF** position and disconnect timing light.

Chrysler Multi-Point Fuel Injection (MFI) System

EXCEPT 2.5L FLEX FUEL ENGINE

⬥ See Figure 80

➡**A DRB scan tool is required for this test procedure. If a scan tool is not available, the test procedure for the ESC system can be used as a general procedure for this system as well; alter the procedure as needed.**

1. Connect Chrysler Diagnostic Readout Box (DRB II) or an equivalent scan tool to the diagnostic connector.
2. Place the scan tool into **Sensor Test Mode** to observe the knock sensor operation.
3. Warm the engine to normal operating temperature.
4. Raise the engine speed above 1000 rpm and using a metal object, lightly tap around the knock sensor. The scan tool should indicate knock is occurring. The DRB scan tool will do this by displaying an **8** in the readout box.
   - If the scan tool is displaying a knock signal has occurred, the system is operating properly.
   - If the scan tool is not displaying a knock signal, proceed to the next step.
5. Disconnect the electrical connector from the knock sensor.
6. Connect a jumper wire to the harness connector.
7. Raise the engine speed above 1000 rpm and momentarily touch the jumper wire to the positive battery terminal. The scan tool should indicate knock has occurred.

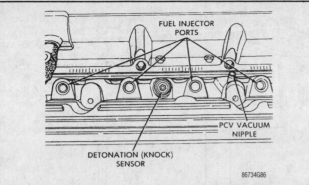

Fig. 80 The detonation (knock) sensor on 2.5L Turbo I engines is located in the cylinder head between the center two fuel injector ports

- If the system does not perform as indicated, the problem is not the knock sensor. Check the sensor wiring and the engine controller operation.
- If the system now indicates a knock signal, replace the knock sensor and retest.

REMOVAL & INSTALLATION

Chrysler Electronic Spark Control (ESC) and Multi-point Fuel Injection (MFI) Systems

EXCEPT 2.5L FLEX FUEL ENGINE

➡The detonation sensor is located in the cylinder head, behind the PCV breather/separator unit.

1. Disconnect the negative battery cable.
2. Disengage the detonation sensor electrical wiring connector.
3. Use a wrench or socket and ratchet wrench to remove the detonation sensor from the cylinder head.

To install:

4. Apply anti-seizing compound to the sensor threads, then carefully start the sensor into the cylinder head by hand. Make sure that the sensor does not crossthread in the cylinder head.
5. Tighten the sensor until secure.
6. Attach the electrical connectors to the sensor.
7. Connect the negative battery cable.

Distance Sensor (Vehicle Speed Sensor)

OPERATION

Chrysler Electronic Spark Control (ESC) System

➡The ESC system is used only on 2.2L carbureted engines.

The distance sensor is located in series with the speedometer cable and transmission. This is a reed-switch type sensor which produces a specific number of switch closures per cable rotation. The number of switch closures is calculated by the PCM to determine vehicle speed or motion.

Chrysler Electronic Fuel Injection (EFI) and Multi-Point Fuel Injection (MFI) Systems

◆ See Figures 81 and 82

➡The MFI system is used on 2.2L and 2.5L turbocharged and flex fuel engines.

The speed sensor is located in the transaxle extension housing to sense vehicle motion. This sensor generates 8 pulses per axle shaft revolution. These signals are interpreted, in conjunction with other sensor inputs by the engine controller to adjust engine operation.

TESTING

Chrysler Electronic Spark Control (ESC) System

1. Remove the distance sensor from the transaxle.
2. Connect an ohmmeter across the terminals of the sensor.
3. Rotate the sensor shaft while observing the ohmmeter. For each complete rotation there should be 8 distinct pulses. Each pulse should not exceed 0.5 ohms.
   - If sensor failed to perform as specified, replace the sensor and retest.
   - If sensor was within specifications, check for a fault in the wiring, cable or drive mechanism.

Chrysler Electronic Fuel Injection (EFI) and Multi-Point Fuel Injection (MFI) Systems

1. Remove the distance sensor from the transaxle.
2. Connect an ohmmeter across the terminals of the sensor.
3. Rotate the sensor shaft while observing the ohmmeter. For each complete rotation there should be eight distinct pulses. Each pulse should not exceed 0.5 ohms.
   - If sensor failed to perform as specified, replace the sensor and retest.
   - If sensor was within specifications, check for a fault in the wiring, cable or drive mechanism.

REMOVAL & INSTALLATION

Chrysler Electronic Spark Control (ESC) System

➡The distance sensor is located in series with the speedometer cable and transmission.

1. Disconnect the negative battery cable.
2. Apply the parking brake, block the rear wheels, then raise and safely support the front of the vehicle on jackstands.
3. Disengage the electrical wiring connectors from the sensor.
4. Disconnect the front and rear speedometer cables from the sensor.
5. If equipped, remove the sensor mounting bolts or nuts.

To install:

6. If equipped, install the sensor on its mounting bracket and install the mounting fasteners. Tighten the fasteners until secure.
7. Attach the front and rear speedometer cables to the sensor.
8. Attach the wiring connectors to the sensor.
9. Lower the vehicle and remove the wheel blocks.
10. Connect the negative battery cable.

Chrysler Electronic Fuel Injection (EFI) and Multi-Point Fuel Injection (MFI) Systems

➡When the vehicle speed sensor is removed for any reason, a new O-ring must be installed on its outside diameter.

1. Disconnect the negative battery cable.
2. Raise and support the front of the vehicle safely on jackstands.
3. Remove the speedometer cable (if so equipped) from the transaxle.
4. Unplug the harness connector from the sensor. Make sure that the weatherseal stays on the harness connector.
5. Remove the bolt securing the sensor in the extension housing or unscrew the sensor from the transaxle.
6. Place a pan under the sensor to catch any transaxle fluid which may leak out of the sensor mounting hole (not much, if any, will leak out unless the vehicle is now moved).
7. Carefully pull the sensor and pinion gear assembly out of the extension housing.
8. Remove the pinion gear from the sensor.

To install:

9. Clean the extension housing and sensor flange mounting surfaces. Install a new O-ring to the sensor.
10. Install the pinion gear back onto the sensor.
11. Carefully slide the sensor/pinion gear assembly back into the transaxle housing. Make certain that the pinion gear engages the gear inside of the transaxle correctly.

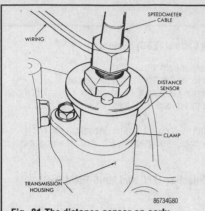

Fig. 81 The distance sensor on early (1981–87 models) is mounted on the transaxle housing—the speedometer cable is installed into the sensor

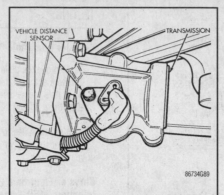

Fig. 82 The distance sensor used on later models (1988–95 models) is also mounted on the transaxle housing, however a speedometer cable is no longer used for the speedometer

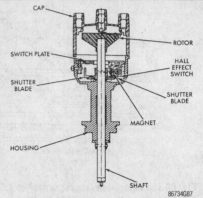

Fig. 83 Cross-section view of the distributor used in all Chrysler fuel injected (EFI and MFI) and Electronic Spark Control (ESC) equipped engines

12. Install and tighten the retaining bolt, or sensor itself, to 60 inch lbs. (7 Nm).

13. Plug the sensor connector back into the wiring harness.

14. Install the speedometer cable and tighten the cable nut to 35 inch lbs. (4 Nm).

15. Lower the vehicle.

16. Connect the negative battery cable.

Distributor Reference Pick-up

OPERATION

Chrysler Electronic Fuel Injection (EFI) and Multi-Point Fuel Injection (MFI) Systems

▶ See Figure 83

➡The MFI system is used on 2.2L and 2.5L turbocharged and flex fuel engines.

The distributor uses a hall effect switch to produce reference pick-up signals. These signals are used to provide crankshaft position and speed to the engine controller. The engine controller uses this information to control both fuel and ignition timing.

Distributors on turbocharged models have two Hall-effect switches. The reference signal is used for ignition timing, and a second signal (sync pick-up) to control fuel synchronization.

TESTING

Chrysler Electronic Fuel Injection (EFI) System

1. Connect Chrysler Diagnostic Readout Box (DRB II) or an equivalent scan tool to the diagnostic connector.

2. Check for stored trouble codes and proceed as follows:
- Fault code 11—proceed to the next step.
- No Fault code 11—the problem is intermittent, proceed with visual inspection.

➡Before proceeding, verify that a minimum of 12.4 battery volts is available for operation of cranking and ignition systems.

3. Test the distributor pick-up signal reference circuit as follows:
   a. Turn the ignition switch to the **OFF** position.
   b. Disconnect the distributor pick-up connector.
   c. Remove the coil wire from the distributor cap and place it ¼ from a good engine ground.
   d. Turn the ignition switch to the **ON** position.
   e. Connect a jumper wire between the harness connector cavities **2** and

3. Make and break the connection several times, while observing the coil wire.
- If there is spark from the coil wire proceed to the next step
- If there is no spark from the coil wire, the problem is in the engine controller or wiring

4. Check the power supply to the distributor reference pick-up as follows:
   a. Turn the ignition switch to the **ON** position.
   b. Connect a voltmeter between harness connector cavity **1** and a known good ground.
- If the reading on the voltmeter is at 7 volts, replace the distributor pick-up coil assembly
- If the reading is 0 volts, check for an open in the wiring harness between the reference connector and the engine controller

Chrysler Multi-Point Fuel Injection (MFI) System

1. Connect Chrysler Diagnostic Readout Box (DRB II) or an equivalent scan tool to the diagnostic connector.

2. Check for stored troubles and proceed as follows:
- Fault code 11—proceed to the next step
- Fault code 54—proceed to step **5**

3. Test the distributor pick-up signal reference circuit as follows:
   a. Clear all stored trouble codes.
   b. Turn the ignition switch to the **OFF** position.
   c. Disconnect the distributor reference pick-up coil (black connector).
   d. Turn the ignition switch to the **ON** position.
   e. Connect a jumper wire between harness terminals **2** and **3**. Make and break the connection several times.
   f. Recheck for stored trouble codes.
- If code 11 no longer exists, proceed to the next step
- If code 11 still exists, the problem is in the engine controller or wiring

➡This step may produce other fault codes. Ignore all codes except code 11.

4. Check the power supply to the distributor reference pick-up as follows:
   a. Turn the ignition switch to the **OFF** position.
   b. Disconnect the distributor reference pick-up coil (black connector).
   c. Turn the ignition switch to the **ON** position.
   d. Connect a voltmeter between connector cavity number **1** and a known good ground.
- If the reading on the voltmeter is at 7 volts, replace the distributor reference pick-up coil
- If the reading is 0 volts, check for an open in the wiring harness between the reference connector and the engine controller

5. Check for fault code 54 (No distributor sync pick-up signal) as follows:
   a. Turn the ignition switch to the **OFF** position.
   b. Disconnect the distributor sync pick-up coil (gray connector).
   c. Turn the ignition switch to the **ON** position.
   d. Connect a voltmeter negative lead to harness connector cavity number **3**.

e. Connect the positive lead of a voltmeter to both cavities **1** and **2** of the harness connector. Compare the readings to the chart below.

6. If the readings at harness cavity number **2** were not within specifications, check wiring between the distributor harness connector and the engine controller. If wiring is okay, replace the engine controller and retest.

REMOVAL & INSTALLATION

▶ **See Figures 84, 85 and 86**

1. Disconnect the negative battery cable.
2. Remove the distributor from the engine as described in Section 2.
3. Remove the distributor cap retaining screws.
4. Remove the distributor cap and inspect for flashover, cracked carbon button, cracked cap, or burned terminals. If any of these conditions exist, replace the cap with a new one.
5. Pull the rotor off of the distributor shaft. Inspect the rotor for cracks or burned electrodes. If any of these conditions exist, replace the rotor.
6. Remove the two Hall-effect device hold-down screws, or, on earlier models, the hold-down clamps. Lift the Hall-effect device off of the distributor body.

To install:

7. Place the Hall-effect pick-up unit onto the distributor housing. Make sure to route the pick-up wires as when disassembled.

➡ **The distributor pick-up wires may be damaged if not properly routed.**

8. Install the protective cover into the distributor housing.
9. Install the rotor onto the distributor shaft so that the aligning groove in the shaft is aligned with the tab in the hole of the rotor.
10. Install the distributor cap and secure it in place with the screws.
11. Install the distributor into the vehicle as described in Section 2.
12. Connect the negative battery cable.

The throttle body has an air bypass passage that provides air for the engine at idle (the throttle blade is closed). The idle air control motor pintle protrudes into the air bypass passage and regulates air flow through it.

The engine computer adjusts engine idle speed by moving the idle air control motor pintle in and out of the bypass passage. The adjustments are based on inputs the engine computer receives. The inputs are from the throttle position sensor, engine speed sensor (distributor pick-up coil), coolant temperature sensor, and various switch operations (brake, park/neutral, air conditioning). Deceleration die-out is also prevented by increasing airflow when the throttle is closed quickly after a driving (speed) condition.

TESTING

Chrysler Electronic Fuel Injection (EFI) and Multi-point Fuel Injection (MFI) Systems

➡ **For this test, a Diagnostic Readout Box (DRB or DRB-II) or an equivalent diagnostic tool in order to actuate the IACM pintle, while it is removed from the throttle body.**

1. Allow the engine to warm up to normal operating temperature, then idle at normal engine speed.
2. Unplug the IACM connector.
3. Using a voltmeter, measure each of the four terminals of the connector (wiring harness side) to engine ground (one at a time). While probing each terminal to ground, momentarily open and close the throttle.
   a. If any one, or more, of the terminal circuits registers below 1.0 volt, refer to Step 8.
   b. If all of the terminal circuits registered above 1.0 volt, proceed to the next step.
4. Turn the engine **OFF**.

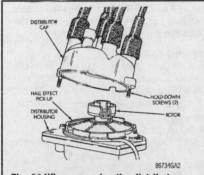

Fig. 84 When removing the distributor cap, do not attempt to detach the spark plug wires from the outside of the cap—they are retained to the inside of the distributor cap by retaining clips

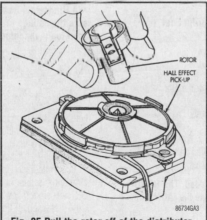

Fig. 85 Pull the rotor off of the distributor shaft

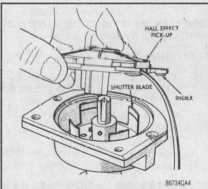

Fig. 86 Remove the two hold-down screws (earlier models may use hold-down clamps) and lift the Hall-effect pick-up off of the distributor housing

Idle Air Control Motor

OPERATION

Chrysler Electronic Fuel Injection (EFI) and Multi-point Fuel Injection (MFI) Systems

▶ **See Figure 87**

➡ **The MFI system is used on 2.2L and 2.5L turbocharged and flex fuel engines.**

The Idle Air Control Motor (IACM) or Automatic Idle Speed (AIS) motor (for newer models) is found on all fuel injected vehicles covered by this manual. The IACM is mounted on the throttle body and is controlled by the PCM. The engines computer adjusts engine idle speed through the idle air control motor to compensate for engine load or ambient conditions.

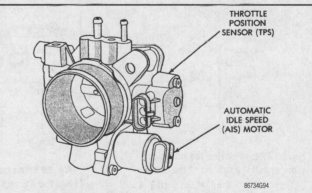

Fig. 87 On 2.2L Turbo III and 2.5L Turbo I models, the TPS and AIS are mounted on throttle body next to each other

5. Disconnect the PCM connector and check to make certain that all of the terminals are clean and tightly installed in the connectors.

6. Using an ohmmeter, test the resistance of each of the four circuits from the oxygen sensor connector to the PCM connector as follows:

    a. Oxygen sensor connector terminal 1 (gray/red wire)—PCM terminal 39 (gray/red wire).

    b. Oxygen sensor connector terminal 2 (yellow/black wire)—PCM terminal 60 (yellow/black wire).

    c. Oxygen sensor connector terminal 3 (brown/white wire)—PCM terminal 40 (brown/white wire).

    d. Oxygen sensor connector terminal 4 (violet/black wire)—PCM terminal 59 (violet/black wire).

7. If the resistance of any of the circuits is below 10.0 ohms, replace the PCM. If any of the circuits register resistance above 10.0 ohms, repair the wire circuit with the high resistance.

8. Inspect the engine for any vacuum leaks.

    a. If any leaks are found, repair them and retest the IACM from the beginning.

    b. Otherwise, continue to the next step.

➡For the next couple of steps the DRB scan tool or equivalent is required.

9. Remove the IACM from the throttle body; leave the harness connected to it.

10. Plug the scan tool into the data link connector, and actuate the IACM.

    a. If the IACM pintle extends and retracts, the IACM is fine and should be reinstalled.

    b. If the IACM does not extend or retract, the IACM is defective and a new one should be installed.

11. After any repairs, make sure to retest the system to located numerous trouble spots.

REMOVAL & INSTALLATION

Chrysler Electronic Fuel Injection (EFI) and Multi-point Fuel Injection (MFI) Systems

▶ See Figures 88 and 89

1. Disconnect the negative cable from the battery.
2. Remove the electrical connector from the idle air control motor.
3. Remove the idle air control motor mounting screws.
4. Remove the idle air control motor from the throttle body. Ensure that the O-ring is removed with the motor.

To install:

5. New idle air control motors have a new O-ring installed on them. If the pintle measures more than 1 in. (25.4mm), it must be retracted.

➡To retract the pintle the DRB-II scan tool will be needed. The DRB-II scan tool is expensive, therefore, you may need to take the IACM to a qualified Chrysler dealer to have the pintle retracted.

6. Carefully place the idle air control motor into the throttle body.

7. Install the mounting bolts and tighten them to 17 inch lbs. (2 Nm).
8. Plug the electrical connector back into the idle air control motor.
9. Connect the negative cable to the battery.

Manifold Absolute Pressure (MAP) Sensor

OPERATION

Chrysler Electronic Fuel Injection (EFI) and Multi-Point Fuel Injection (MFI) Systems

▶ See Figure 90

➡The MFI system is used on 2.2L and 2.5L turbocharged and flex fuel engines.

The manifold absolute pressure (MAP) sensor is a device which monitors manifold vacuum. It is connected to a vacuum nipple on the throttle body and electrically to the engine controller. The sensor transmits manifold vacuum conditions and barometric pressure changes to the engine controller. The MAP sensor data is used along with data from other sensors to determine the correct air/fuel mixture.

TESTING

Chrysler Electronic Fuel Injection (EFI) and Multi-Point Fuel Injection (MFI) Systems

➡This test should be performed with the engine cold (room temperature).

1. Backprobe the dark green/red tracer wire from the MAP sensor connector with a voltmeter (do not unplug the MAP connector).

➡A Diagnostic Read-out Box (DRB or DRB-II) can also be used to measure the voltage of the MAP sensor. For more information, refer to the scan tool's manufacturer's instructions.

2. If a DRB scan tool is being used, set it up as follows:

    a. Connect Chrysler DRB II or an equivalent scan tool to the diagnostic connector.

    b. Place the scan tool into **Sensor Test Mode** number **8**.

3. Disconnect the vacuum hose from the map sensor and connect a hand-held vacuum pump to the sensor vacuum port.

4. Turn the ignition key **ON**, but do not start the engine.

5. Apply 5 in. Hg (17 kPa) of vacuum to the sensor and record the reading on the voltmeter/scan tool.

6. While observing the voltmeter/scan tool, continue to slowly apply vacuum to the sensor until 20 in. Hg. (68 kPa) is reached. The voltage should decrease smoothly without any interruptions.

• If the sensor does not perform as specified, replace the sensor and retest
• If the sensor performs as specified proceed to the next step

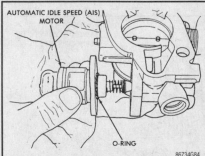

Fig. 88 After removing the retaining screws, pull the AIS out of the throttle body—make certain that the O-ring is still on the AIS motor; if it is not, check the AIS bore in the throttle body for it

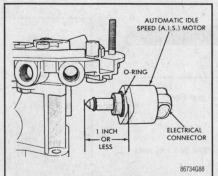

Fig. 89 When installing the AIS, ensure that the AIS motor is in the retracted mode—if the pintle's length is as shown, the motor is retracted

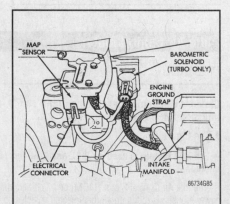

Fig. 90 The MAP sensor is mounted on the fire wall in the engine compartment

7. Record the voltmeter/scan tool reading with 20 in. Hg (67.5 kPa) of vacuum applied to the sensor. Subtract the second reading from the first reading (i.e. reading at 5 in. Hg.-reading at 20 in. Hg=difference).

• If the difference is between 2.3–2.9 volts, the sensor is okay. Check the wiring and vacuum supply to the sensor.

• If the difference is not between 2.3–2.9 volts, replace the sensor with a new one, then retest.

REMOVAL & INSTALLATION

Chrysler Electronic Fuel Injection (EFI), Multi-point Fuel Injection (MFI)

1. Disconnect the negative battery cable.
2. Unplug the electrical connector from the sensor.
3. If so equipped, disconnect the vacuum hose from the sensor.
4. Remove the MAP sensor mounting fasteners.
5. Remove the sensor from the vehicle.

To install:

6. Install the MAP sensor into its position and secure in place with the mounting screws. Tighten the screws until snug.
7. Connect the vacuum hose, if so equipped.
8. Plug the electrical connector back into the sensor. Make certain that the connector is clean and snug fitting.
9. Connect the battery cable.

Methanol Concentration Sensor

OPERATION

♦ See Figure 91

➡This sensor is only used on 2.5L Flexible Fuel engines.

The methanol concentration sensor contains a microprocessor that determines the percentage of gasoline and methanol in the fuel system. From the methanol concentration sensor input, the PCM determines the amount of methanol in the fuel. The vehicle can operate on mixtures up to 85% methanol, 15% gasoline.

The PCM supplies 8 volts to the methanol concentration sensor. The methanol concentration sensor output voltage varies with the percent of methanol in the fuel system. The sensor output voltage (input for the PCM) ranges from 0.5 volt for pure gasoline to 4.50 volts for 85% methanol. For two seconds at key **ON**, when the operator starts the vehicle, the sensor calibrates the PCM. During the calibration period the sensor sends 4.45 volts to the PCM as a correction factor.

The methanol concentration sensor attaches to a bracket at the rear of the fuel tank, next to the fuel filler tube.

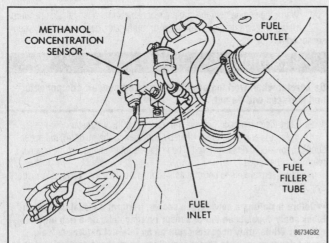

Fig. 91 The Methanol Concentration sensor (Flex Fuel Sensor) is mounted under the back end of the vehicle, near the fuel tank

TESTING

♦ See Figures 92 and 93

➡The Methanol concentration sensor, because of the increasing complexity of today's advanced fuel injection systems, especially concerning the Flexible Fuel system, direct diagnostic inspection cannot be performed on this sensor without expensive and Chrysler specific diagnostic equipment. If, after testing the supply circuit, the sensor is still malfunctioning, have the system inspected by a qualified and reputable automotive technician.

1. Disengage the flexible fuel (methanol) sensor connector.
2. With the ignition **ON** and the engine **OFF**, measure the voltage between terminals **1** and **3** of the sensor's harness connector.

a. If the reading is approximately 8 volts, the power circuit to the sensor is functioning properly; have the system inspected by a reputable mechanic familiar with Chrysler MFI systems.

b. If the reading is not approximately 8 volts, there is a problem with the sensor's supply circuit. Correct the circuit before having the system tested by an automotive technician.

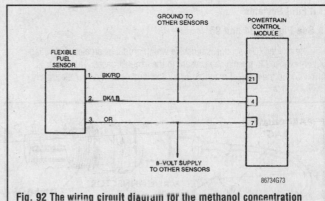

Fig. 92 The wiring circuit diagram for the methanol concentration sensor

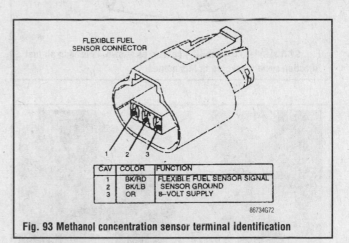

Fig. 93 Methanol concentration sensor terminal identification

REMOVAL & INSTALLATION

✳✳ CAUTION

Release the fuel system pressure before servicing fuel system components. When servicing flexible fuel vehicles, wear methanol resistant gloves and eye protection and avoid breathing the fumes. Do not allow methanol/gasoline mixtures to contact skin. Service vehicles in well ventilated areas and avoid ignition sources. never smoke while servicing the vehicle.

➥Quick-disconnect fuel line fittings attach the fuel tubes to the methanol concentration sensor. Refer to Section 5 for more information regarding quick-disconnect fittings.

1. Relieve the fuel system pressure, as described in Section 5.
2. Disconnect the negative battery cable.
3. Disconnect the fuel tubes from the sensor. For more information, refer to Section 5.
4. Disengage the electrical connector from the sensor.
5. Remove the mounting nuts, then remove the sensor.

To install:

6. Position the sensor onto its bracket.
7. Install and tighten the mounting nuts until secure.
8. Attach the electrical connector to the sensor.
9. Connect the fuel tubes to the sensor.
10. Connect the negative battery cable.

Oxygen (O₂) Sensor

OPERATION

All Fuel Systems

◗ **See Figures 94 and 95**

The oxygen (O₂) sensor is a device which produces an electrical voltage when exposed to the oxygen present in the exhaust gases. The sensor is mounted in the exhaust manifold or turbocharger outlet and is electrically

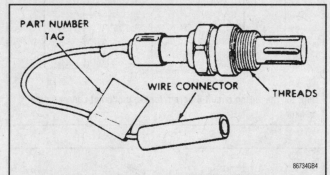

Fig. 94 A standard oxygen (O₂) sensor, as shown, is used in all fuel injection system covered in this manual

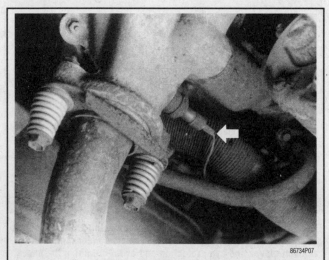

Fig. 95 On non-turbocharged engines, the oxygen sensor (arrow) is mounted in the exhaust manifold

heated internally for faster switching when the engine is running. When there is a large amount of oxygen present (lean mixture), the sensor produces a low voltage. When there is a lesser amount present (rich mixture) it produces a higher voltage. By monitoring the oxygen content and converting it to electrical voltage, the sensor acts as a rich-lean switch. The voltage is transmitted to the engine controller which changes the fuel injector's pulse width. The injector changes the mixture.

TESTING

Chrysler Electronic Spark Control (ESC), Electronic Fuel Injection (EFI), and Multi-Point Fuel Injection (MFI) Systems

➥The EFI system is also known as the Single-Point Fuel Injection, or as Throttle-body Fuel Injection. The ESC system is used on 1981–86 2.2L carbureted engines.

1. Start the engine and allow it to reach operating temperature. Turn the engine **OFF**.
2. Connect the positive lead of a multimeter (set to measure voltage) to the O₂sensor signal wire and the negative lead to the engine ground. Backprobe the O₂sensor connector to attach the multimeter to the circuit.
3. Start the engine and run at 2000 rpm for two minutes.
4. Return the engine to idle and read the voltage displayed by the multimeter. The voltage reading should fluctuate between 100–900 millivolts, as the O₂sensor detects varying levels of oxygen in the exhaust stream.

➥Under normal conditions the O₂ sensor should fluctuate high and low. If the O₂ sensor voltage does not fluctuate, the sensor may be defective or the air/fuel mixture could be extremely out of range.

5. Prior to condemning the O₂ sensor, check the sensor response to changes in the fuel mixture as follows:
   a. Force the system rich by closing the choke plate for carbureted engines, or by using propane or another approved method for EFI and MFI engines. If the O₂ sensor reads now reads above 550 millivolts, the sensor is operating properly and the problems is elsewhere in the system. If the sensor fails to respond, replace the sensor and retest.
   b. Force the system lean by removing a vacuum line. If this causes the oxygen sensor voltage to read below 350 millivolts the sensor is operating properly and the problem is elsewhere in the system. If the sensor fails to respond, replace the sensor and retest.

➥Before installing a new oxygen sensor, perform a visual inspection. Black sooty deposits on the O₂ sensor tip may indicate a rich air/fuel mixture. White gritty deposits could be an internal antifreeze leak. Brown deposits indicate oil consumption. All of these contaminants can damage a new sensor.

Chrysler Mikuni Feedback Carburetor System

➥The Mikuni carburetor system is used only on 2.6L engines.

1. Warm the engine until the coolant reaches normal operating temperature.
2. Using an accurate digital voltmeter or multimeter, backprobe the oxygen sensor connector.

✳✳ CAUTION

Be careful when working around the oxygen sensor; components and surfaces will be hot.

3. Start the engine and observe the reading on the voltmeter.
4. When the engine is raced (thereby enrichening the mixture), the meter should show approximately 1 volt. The voltage should change as the engine returns to idle speed.
5. If the sensor fails to perform as specified, replace the sensor and recheck system operation.

➥Before installing a new oxygen sensor, perform a visual inspection. Black sooty deposits on the O₂ sensor tip may indicate a rich air/fuel mixture. White gritty deposits could be an internal antifreeze leak. Brown deposits indicate oil consumption. All of these contaminants can damage a new sensor.

REMOVAL & INSTALLATION

➡To remove the oxygen sensor, a special removal tool is needed. There are two types of sensors: standard and heated. Heated sensors have a multi-prong electrical terminal with three wires, and standard sensors have only a single wire connector. For standard sensors, use tool C-4589 or an equivalent from the aftermarket; for heated sensors, use C-4907 or equivalent. It is necessary to be able to adapt this tool to a torque wrench. Also needed is a thread tap to clean the sensor mounting threads.

1. Make sure the engine has been turned off for several hours so all parts will have cooled sufficiently for safe handling.
2. Disconnect the negative battery cable.
3. Pulling on the plug and not the wiring, disconnect the oxygen sensor electrical lead.
4. Install the special tool and unscrew the sensor from the exhaust manifold.
5. Oil the threads in the exhaust manifold or turbocharger outlet, then turn the tap into the sensor threads to chase any corrosion or dirt out.

To install:
6. If installing a new sensor, make sure to get the proper replacement parts. Sensors used with turbocharged vehicles have a terminal boot not used on other sensors. As previously mentioned, 1988 and later models use a heated sensor with a multi-prong plug.
7. If the sensor is to be reinstalled, coat the threads with an anti-seizing compound (new O_2 sensors come already coated with an anti-seizing compound).
8. Install the sensor and tighten it to 20 ft. lbs. (27 Nm).
9. Reattach the electrical connector securely.
10. Connect the negative battery cable.

Throttle Position Sensor (TPS)

OPERATION

Chrysler Mikuni Feedback Carburetor System

➡The Mikuni feedback carburetor system is used only on 2.6L engines

The Throttle Position Sensor (TPS) is a rotation type variable resistor that rotates together with the carburetor throttle shaft to sense the throttle valve angle. As the throttle shaft rotates, the TPS output voltage changes and the PCM detects the throttle valve opening based on the change of the voltage.

Using the TPS output signal, engine speed signal and other signals, the PCM judges the engine operating mode and controls the air-fuel ratio, etc. for an optimum air-fuel mixture in that mode.

Chrysler Electronic Fuel Injection (EFI) and Multi-Point Fuel Injection (MFI) Systems

▶ See Figure 96

➡The MFI system is used on 2.2L and 2.5L turbocharged and flex fuel engines.

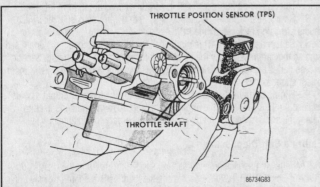

86734G83

Fig. 96 Remove the two retaining screws, then slide the TPS off of the throttle shaft

The Throttle Position Sensor (TPS) is a variable resistor which is activated by the movement of the throttle shaft. It is mounted on the throttle body and senses the angle of the throttle blade opening. The voltage that the sensor produces increases or decreases according to the throttle blade opening. This voltage is transmitted to the engine controller where it is used along with data from other sensors to adjust the air/fuel ratio to varying conditions and during acceleration, deceleration, idle, and wide open throttle operations.

TESTING

Chrysler Mikuni Feedback Carburetor System

1. Disengage the TPS connector.
2. Check resistance with a circuit tester (ohm range) between the orange wire and the light green/red wire.
3. Check to ensure that when throttle valve is slowly operated from closed to wide open position, resistance changes smoothly. Resistance should be:
   - Closed throttle—Approximately 3500–6500 ohms
   - Wide Open Throttle (WOT)—Approximately 100–1000 ohms
4. If the TPS resistance is not within the specifications, replace the TPS sensor with a new one.

Chrysler Electronic Fuel Injection (EFI) and Multi-Point Fuel Injection (MFI) Systems

1. Before testing the TPS, check the terminals at the TPS and PCM to ensure good connections (tight and clean).
2. If available, connect Chrysler Diagnostic Readout Box (DRB II) or an equivalent scan tool to the diagnostic connector.
3. If using a scan tool, place it into **Sensor Test Mode** number 5.
4. Turn the ignition switch to the **ON** position.
5. If a DRB scan tool is not available, perform the following. While the throttle is completely closed, check the output voltage at the orange/dark blue tracer wire of the connector by backprobing the connector with a multimeter set to measure voltage. Make certain not to pierce the wire insulation to take a reading, use only the backprobe method. (for more information on testing methods of circuits, refer to Section 6.)

   a. If the voltage is ½–1½ volts for the MFI system, or lower than 1 volt for the EFI system with the throttle completely closed, proceed to the next step.

   b. If the voltage is above 1½ volts (MFI system) or 1 volt (EFI system) with the throttle completely closed, the TPS is defective and must be replaced with a new one.

6. While slowly opening the throttle to wide open, watch the voltage reading.

   a. If the voltage change was a smooth transition, proceed to the next step.

   b. If the voltage was irregular or no voltage change was detected, the TPS is defective and must be replaced with a new one.

7. With the throttle completely open (wide open throttle), read the voltage again.

   a. If the maximum voltage detected was at least 3.5 volts with the throttle completely open, proceed to the next step.

   b. If the maximum voltage was not 3.5 volts or more, the TPS is defective and must be replaced with a new one.

8. The TPS is functioning correctly if it passed all steps in this test.

REMOVAL & INSTALLATION

1. Disconnect the negative battery cable.
2. Remove the electrical connector from the throttle position sensor.
3. Remove the throttle position sensor mounting screws.
4. If necessary, remove the wire harness mounting bracket screws.
5. Lift the throttle position sensor off of the throttle shaft.

To install:
6. Install the throttle position sensor on the throttle shaft and install the mounting screws. Tighten the screws to 17 inch lbs. (2 Nm).

➡When installing the throttle position sensor, ensure that the TPS lever is on top of the throttle lever.

7. Plug electrical connector back into the throttle position sensor.
8. Connect the negative battery cable.
9. Tighten the retaining screws until snug once the TPS has been adjusted correctly.

TROUBLE CODES

General Information

➡The fault codes can be checked with either a scan tool or the CHECK ENGINE lamp in the dashboard.

The Chrysler fuel injection systems combine electronic spark advance and fuel control. At the center of these systems is a digital, pre-programmed computer, known as the Powertrain Control Module (PCM). The PCM (refer to the electronic engine control portion of this section) as engine computer in this section) regulates ignition timing, air-fuel ratio, emission control devices, cooling fan, charging system, idle speed and speed control. It has the ability to update and revise its commands to meet changing operating conditions.

Various sensors provide the input necessary for the engine computer to correctly regulate fuel flow at the injectors. These include the Manifold Absolute Pressure (MAP), Throttle Position Sensor (TPS), oxygen sensor, coolant temperature sensor, charge temperature sensor and vehicle speed sensors.

In addition to the sensors, various switches are used to provide important information to the engine computer. These include the neutral safety switch, air conditioning clutch switch, brake switch and speed control switch. These signals cause the engine computer to change either the fuel flow at the injectors or the ignition timing or both.

FAULT (DIAGNOSTIC TROUBLE) CODES

The engine computer is designed to test its own input and output circuits. The engine computer monitors the input and output signals coming from and going to the various sensors. The computer then compares the in-coming and outgoing signals to specific parameters, which are written into the computer's memory at the factory. If a sensor's signal is showing operation of the sensor to be out of the given range, the computer stores a fault code. The fault code (a 2 digit number) is stored in the engine computer for eventual display to the person performing the readout procedure. The fault code does not indicate which component is faulty, rather which circuit was perceived as functioning out of the given parameters. Therefore, once a fault code is known, the entire circuit must be checked for problems, rather than simply replacing the main sensor of the circuit.

The fault codes can be displayed by means of the instrument panel CHECK ENGINE light or by connecting a Diagnostic Readout Box (DRB or DRB-II) and reading a numbered display code, which indicates the circuit in question. Some inputs and outputs are checked continuously and others are checked under certain conditions.

➡If the problem is repaired or no longer exists, the PCM cancels the fault code after 50–100 key ON/OFF cycles.

When a fault code is detected, it appears as either a flash of the "CHECK ENGINE" on the instrument panel or by watching the Diagnostic Readout Box II (DRB II). This indicates that an abnormal signal in the system has been recognized by the engine computer.

➡Fault codes DO indicate that a circuit has performing outside of pre-established parameters, but DO NOT identify the faulty components directly.

Visual Inspection

➡This is a general procedure and the specific steps may differ from vehicle-to-vehicle; adjust the procedure as necessary.

When a fault code is exhibited by the engine computer it is a good idea to perform this general inspection to make sure that the cause is not a loose wire or a dirty connection.

Perform a visual inspection for loose, disconnected or mis-routed wires and hoses before diagnosing or servicing the fuel injection system. A visual check saves unnecessary test and diagnostic time. A thorough visual inspection includes the following:

1. Check for correct spark plug cable routing. Ensure the cables are completely connected to the spark plugs and distributor.
2. Check ignition coil electrical connections.
3. Verify the electrical connector is attached to the purge solenoid.
4. Verify vacuum connection at the purge solenoid is secure and not leaking.
5. Verify the electrical connector is attached to the MAP sensor.

6. Check the MAP sensor hose (if so equipped) at the MAP sensor assembly and at the vacuum connection at the intake plenum fitting.
7. Check the alternator wiring connections. Ensure the accessory drive belt has proper tension.
8. Verify the hoses are securely attached to the vapor canister.
9. Verify the engine ground strap is attached at the engine and dash panel.
10. Ensure the heated oxygen sensor connector is attached to the wiring harness.
11. Verify that the distributor connector (if so equipped) is connected to the harness connector.
12. Verify that the coolant temperature sensor connector is attached to the wiring harness.
13. Check that the vacuum hose connection at the fuel pressure regulator and intake plenum.
14. Ensure that the harness connector is securely attached to each fuel injector.
15. Check the oil pressure sending unit electrical connection.
16. Check the hose connections at the throttle body.
17. Check the throttle body electrical connections.
18. Check the PCV system hose connections.
19. If equipped, check the EGR system vacuum hose connections.
20. If equipped, check the EGR tube to intake plenum connections.
21. Inspect the electronic EGR transducer solenoid electrical connector.
22. Ensure that the vacuum connections at the electronic EGR transducer is secure and not leaking.
23. Check the power brake booster and speed connections.
24. Inspect the engine harness to main harness connections.
25. Check all automatic transaxle electrical connections, if so equipped.
26. Check the vehicle speed sensor electrical connector.
27. Inspect the PCM electrical connector(s) for damage or spread terminals. Verify that the 60-way connector is fully inserted into the socket of the PCM. Ensure wires are not stretched or pulled out of the connector.
28. Check the air conditioning, starter, automatic shutdown relay, fuel pump, and radiator fan relay connections.
29. Check the battery cable connections.
30. Check the hose and electrical connections at the fuel pump. Ensure that the connector is making contact with the terminals on the pump.

Reading Codes

1981–87 MODELS

▶ See Figure 97

Test Modes

There are 5 modes of testing required for the proper diagnosis of the system. They are as follows:

1. Diagnostic Test Mode—This mode is used to access the fault codes from the PCM memory.
2. Circuit Actuation Test Mode (ATM Test)—This mode is used to turn a certain circuit on and off in order to test it. ATM test codes are used in this mode.
3. Switch Test Mode—This mode is used to determine is specific switch inputs are being received by the PCM.
4. Sensor Test Mode—This mode looks at the output signals of certain sensors as they are received by the PCM when the engine is not running. Sensor access codes are read in this mode. Also this mode is used to clear PCM memory of stored codes.
5. Engine Running Test Mode—This mode looks at sensor output signals as seen by the PCM when the engine is running. Also this mode is used to determine some specific running conditions necessary for diagnosis.

Entering Self-Diagnostics

The following service procedures are intended for use with the Diagnostic Readout Box II (DRB II). Since each available diagnostic readout box may differ in its interpretation and display of the sensor results, refer to the instructional procedure that accompanies each tester unit.

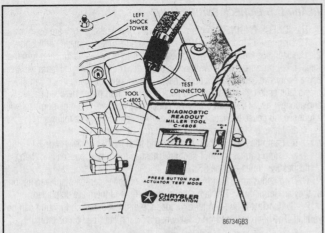

Fig. 97 Using a Diagnostic Readout Box (DRB or DRB-II) scan tool is one method for reading the diagnostic trouble codes

Obtaining Fault Codes

1. Connect the readout box to the diagnostic connector located in the engine compartment near the PCM unit.
2. Start the engine, if possible, cycle the transmission selector and the A/C switch if applicable. Shut off the engine.
3. Turn the ignition switch ON, OFF, ON, OFF, ON within 5 seconds to access the read fault code data.
4. Record all the fault code messages displayed on the readout box.
5. Observe the CHECK ENGINE LIGHT on the instrument panel. The CHECK ENGINE LIGHT should illuminate for 3 seconds and then go out.

Switch Test

The PCM only recognizes 2 switch input states—HI and LOW. For this reason the PCM cannot tell the difference between a selected switch position and an open circuit, short circuit or an open switch. However, if one of the switches is toggled, the controller does have the ability to respond to the change of state in the switch. If the change is displayed, it can be assumed that entire switch circuit to the PCM is operational.

Obtaining Circuit Actuation Test Mode (ATM Test)

The purpose of the circuit actuation mode test is to check for proper operation of the output circuits that the PCM cannot internally recognize. The PCM can attempt to activate these outputs and allow the technician to affirm proper operation. Most of the tests performed in this mode issue a audible click or visual indication of component operation (click of relay contacts, injector spray etc.) Except for intermittent conditions, if a component functions properly when it is tested, it can be assumed that the component, attendant wiring and driving circuit are functioning properly.

Obtaining Sensor Read Test Mode Display Codes

The sensor mode allows the output of the 7 sensors and the state of 3 switches to be displayed on the readout box while the engine is not running. This provides a vehicle for testing each individual sensor and switch including harness wiring and PCM circuitry.

Engine Running Test Mode

The engine running test mode monitors the sensors on the vehicle which check operating conditions while the engine is running. The engine running test mode can be performed with the engine idling in Neutral and with parking brake set or under actual driving conditions. With the diagnostic readout box READ/HOLD switch in the READ position, the engine running test mode is initiated after the engine is started.

Select a test code by switching the READ/HOLD switch to the READ position and pressing the actuator button until the desired code appears. Release actuator button and switch the READ/HOLD switch to the HOLD position. The logic module will monitor that system test results will be displayed.

Exiting Diagnostic Test

By turning the ignition switch to the **OFF** position, the test mode system is exited. With a Diagnostic Readout Box attached to the system and the ATM control button not pressed, the computer will continue to cycle the selected circuits for 5 minutes and then automatically shut the system down.

1988–95 MODELS

There are two methods for obtaining or reading the diagnostic trouble codes from the vehicles covered in this manual: with a Diagnostic Readout Box (DRB or DRB-II) or the equivalent type of scan tool, or with the CHECK ENGINE light, located in the instrument panel. Both methods will be covered in the following sections.

Diagnostic Readout Box (DRB or DRB-II)

▶ See Figures 97 thru 109

➡ Make sure to follow the manufacturer's instructions when using a scan tool.

1. Attach the DRB-II scan tool, or equivalent, to the data link connector located in the engine compartment near the powertrain control module (an L shaped connector with 8 terminals—refer to the engine compartment component location illustrations earlier in this section).
2. Start the engine, if possible, cycle the transaxle selector and the A/C switch (if applicable). Shut the engine **OFF**.
3. Turn the ignition switch **ON**, access Read Fault Screen. Record all of the fault messages shown on the DRB-II or other scan tool. Observe the malfunction indicator lamp (CHECK ENGINE lamp on the instrument panel). The lamp should light for 3 seconds, then go out (bulb check).

STATE DISPLAY TEST MODE

The switch inputs used by the PCM have only 2 recognized states, high and low. For this reason, the PCM cannot recognize the difference between a selected switch position versus an open circuit, a short circuit, or a defective switch. If the change is displayed, it can be assumed that the entire switch circuit to the PCM is functional. From the state display screen access either State Display Inputs and Outputs or State Display Sensors.

State Display Inputs and Outputs—
Connect the DRB-II scan tool, or equivalent, to the vehicle (data link connector). access the State Display screen, then access Inputs and Outputs. Select one of the engine control system functions displayed in the Input and Output screen.

State Display Sensors—
Connect the DRB-II scan tool, or the equivalent, to the vehicle (data link connector) and access the State Display screen. Access the Sensor Display and select one of the engine control system functions available in this window.

CIRCUIT ACTUATION TEST MODE

The circuit actuation test mode checks for proper operation of output circuits or devices which the PCM cannot internally recognize. The PCM can attempt to

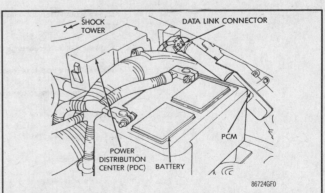

Fig. 98 The data link connector is located behind the battery, next to the 60-way PCM connector

activate these outputs and allow an observer to verify proper operation. Most of the tests provide an audible or visual indication of device operation (click of relay contacts, spray fuel, etc.). Except for intermittent conditions, if a device functions properly during testing, assume the device, its associated wiring and the driver circuit are working correctly.

Obtaining Circuit Actuation Test

Connect the DRB-II scan tool , or the equivalent, to the vehicle and access the Actuators screen. Select one of the numerous engine control system functions accessible through this screen.

Check Engine Light

The CHECK ENGINE light has 2 modes of operation: diagnostic mode and switch test mode. If a DRB II diagnostic tester is not available, the PCM can show the technician fault codes by flashing the CHECK ENGINE light on the instrument panel in the diagnostic mode. In the switch test mode, after all codes are displayed, switch function can be confirmed. The light will turn on and off when a switch is turned ON and OFF. Even though the light can be used as a diagnostic tool, it has the following restrictions:

• Once the light starts to display fault codes, it cannot be stopped. If the technician loses count, the must start the test procedure again

• The light cannot tell the technician if the oxygen feed-back system is lean or rich and if the idle motor and detonation system are operational

• The light cannot perform the actuation test mode, sensor test mode or engine running test mode

➡ Be advised that the CHECK ENGINE light can only perform a limited amount of functions and it is a good idea to have the system checked with a scan tool to double-check the circuit function.

READING THE CHECK ENGINE LIGHT

The "CHECK ENGINE" lamp has two modes of operation. They are as follows:
1. Diagnostic Mode—The PCM can show fault codes by means of flashing the check engine lamp on the instrument cluster. To activate this function turn the ignition key on-off-on-off-on within five seconds. The check engine lamp will then come on for two seconds as a bulb check. Immediately following this it will display a fault code by flashing on and off. There is a short pause between flashes and a longer pause between digits. All codes displayed are two digit numbers with a four second pause between codes. An example of a code is as follows:

    a. Lamp on for two seconds, then turns off—lamp check.

    b. Lamp flashes 5 times, pauses, and then flashes once—code 51.

    c. Lamp pauses for four seconds, flashes five times, pauses and then flashes five times—code 55.

The two codes are 51 and 55. Any number of codes can be displayed as long as they are in memory. The lamp will flash until all of them are displayed.

2. Switch Test Mode—After all codes are displayed, switch function can be verified. The lamp will turn on or off when a switch is turned on or off.

➡ After the component failure has been repaired, the engine computer will erase the fault codes after 50–100 ON/OFF turns of the ignition key.

Limp-In Mode

The limp-in mode is the attempt by the PCM to compensate for the failure of certain components by substituting information from other sources. If the engine computer senses incorrect data or no data at all from the MAP sensor, throttle position sensor or coolant temperature sensor, the system is placed into limp-in mode and the CHECK ENGINE light on the instrument panel is activated. Although at the expense of performance and emission control efficiency, this mode will keep the vehicle driveable until service is obtained.

DIAGNOSTIC TROUBLE CODE DESCRIPTION

Diagnostic Trouble Code	Description of Diagnostic Trouble Code
00 . . .	Indicates that the diagnostic readout box (DRB) is receiving power
11 . . .	Indicates a problem in the Oxygen solenoid control circuit
13 . . .	Indicates a problem in the canister purge solenoid circuit
14 . . .	Indicates the battery has been disconnected
16 . . .	Indicates a problem in the radiator fan control relay circuit
17 . . .	Indicates a problem in the electronic throttle control vacuum solenoid system
18 . . .	Indicates a problem in the vacuum operated secondary control solenoid system
21 . . .	Indicates a problem in the distributor pick-up system
22 . . .	Indicates that the Oxygen system is stuck in either the full lean or full rich position
24 . . .	Indicates a problem in the PCM
25 . . .	Indicates a problem in the radiator fan coolant sensor portion of the engine temperature dual sensor system
26 . . .	Indicates a problem in the engine temperature portion of the engine temperature dual sensor system
28 . . .	Indicates a problem in the distance sensor system on engines equipped with manual transaxles
31 . . .	Indicates that the engine has not been cranked since the battery was disconnected
32 . . .	Indicates a problem in the PCM
33 . . .	Indicates a problem in the PCM
55 . . .	Indicates end of message
88 . . .	Indicates start of message

86734GI1

Fig. 99 Diagnostic trouble codes—1981–85 2.2L engines

DIAGNOSTIC TROUBLE CODE DESCRIPTION

Diagnostic Trouble Code	DRB Scan Tool Display	Description of Diagnostic Trouble Code
11*	No Crank Reference Signal at PCM	No crank reference signal detected during engine cranking.
12*	Battery Disconnect	Direct battery input to PCM was disconnected within the last 50 Key-on cycles.
13***	Slow Change in Idle MAP Signal **or** No Change in MAP From Start to Run	MAP output change is slower and/or smaller than expected. No difference recognized between the engine MAP reading and the barometric (atmospheric) pressure reading at start-up.
14***	MAP Sensor Voltage Too Low **or** MAP Sensor Voltage Too High	MAP sensor input below minimum acceptable voltage. MAP sensor input above maximum acceptable voltage.
15**	No Vehicle Speed Sensor Signal	No vehicle distance (speed) sensor signal detected during road load conditions.
17*	Engine Is Cold Too Long	Engine coolant temperature remains below normal operating temperatures during vehicle travel (thermostat).
21**	O2S Stays at Center **or** O2S Shorted to Voltage	Neither rich or lean condition detected from the oxygen sensor input. Oxygen sensor input voltage maintained above the normal operating range.
22***	ECT Sensor Voltage Too High **or** ECT Sensor Voltage Too Low	Engine coolant temperature sensor input above maximum acceptable voltage. Engine coolant temperature sensor input below minimum acceptable voltage.
24**	Throttle Position Sensor Voltage High **or** Throttle Position Sensor Voltage Low	Throttle position sensor input above the maximum acceptable voltage. Throttle position sensor input below the minimum acceptable voltage.
25**	Idle Air Control Motor Circuits	A shorted condition detected in one or more of the idle air control motor circuits.
27***	Injector Control Circuit	Injector output driver does not respond properly to the control signal.
31**	EVAP Solenoid Circuit	An open or shorted condition detected in the purge solenoid circuit.

*   Check Engine Lamp will not illuminate at all times if this Diagnostic Trouble Code was recorded. Cycle Ignition key as described in manual and observe code flashed by Check Engine lamp.

**   Check Engine Lamp will illuminate during engine operation if this Diagnostic Trouble Code was recorded.

86734G87

Fig. 101 Diagnostic trouble codes—1988-95 2.2L and 2.5L Chrysler EFI engines

DIAGNOSTIC TROUBLE CODE DESCRIPTION

Diagnostic Trouble Code	Description of Diagnostic Trouble Code
00	Indicates that the diagnostic readout box (DRB) is receiving power.
11	Indicates a problem in the Oxygen solenoid control circuit
12	Indicates a problem in the transaxle unlock relay
13	Indicate a problem in the vacuum operated secondary control solenoid circuit
14	Indicates the battery has been disconnected
17	Indicates a problem in the electronic throttle control vacuum solenoids system (2.2L engine only)
18	Indicates a problem in the canister purge solenoid system (2.2L engine only)
21	Indicates a problem in the distributor pick-up system
22	Indicates that the Oxygen system is stuck in the full lean position
23	Indicates that the Oxygen system is stuck in the full rich position
24	Indicates a problem in the PCM
25	Indicates a problem in the radiator fan coolant sensor portion of the engine temperature dual sensor system (2.2L engine only)
26	Indicates a problem in the engine temperature portion of the engine temperature dual sensor system (2.2L engine only)
28	Indicates a problem in the distance sensor system on engines equipped with manual transaxles
31	Indicates that the engine has not been cranked since the battery was disconnected
32	Indicates a problem in the PCM
33	Indicates a problem in the PCM
55	Indicates end of message
88	Indicates start of message

8673-GI2

Fig. 100 Diagnostic trouble codes—1986-87 2.2L and 2.5L EFI engines

FAULT CODE DESCRIPTION

FAULT CODE	DRB II DISPLAY	DESCRIPTION
11	No reference Signal During Cranking	No distributor reference signal detected during engine cranking.
13**	Slow change in Idle MAP signal or No change in MAP from start to run	MAP output change is slower and/or smaller than expected. / No difference recognized between the engine MAP reading and the barometric (atmospheric) pressure reading at start-up.
14**	MAP voltage too low or MAP voltage too High	MAP sensor input below minimum acceptable voltage. / MAP sensor input above maximum acceptable voltage.
15**	No vehicle speed signal	No vehicle distance (speed) sensor signal detected during road load conditions.
17	Engine is cold too long	Engine coolant temperature remains below normal operating temperatures during vehicle travel (thermostat).
21**	O2 signal stays at center or O2 signal shorted to voltage	Neither rich or lean condition detected from the oxygen sensor input. / Oxygen sensor input voltage maintained above the normal operating range.
22+**	Coolant sensor voltage too high or Coolant sensor voltage too low	Coolant temperature sensor input above the maximum acceptable voltage. / Coolant temperature sensor input below the minimum acceptable voltage.
23	Charge Temperature voltage low or Charge Temperature voltage high	Charge temperature sensor input below the minimum acceptable voltage. / Charge temperature sensor input above the maximum acceptable voltage.
24+**	Throttle position sensor voltage high or Throttle position sensor voltage low	Throttle position sensor input above the maximum acceptable voltage. / Throttle position sensor input below the minimum acceptable voltage.
25**	Automatic idle speed motor circuits	An open or shorted condition detected in one or more of the AIS control circuits.
27	Injector control circuit (DRB II)	Injector output driver does not respond properly to the control signal (DRB II specifies the injector by cylinder number).
31**	Purge solenoid circuit	An open or shorted condition detected in the purge solenoid circuit.

+ Check Engine Lamp On
** Check Engine Lamp On (California Only)

Fig. 103 Diagnostic trouble codes—2.2L turbocharged engines

DIAGNOSTIC TROUBLE CODE DESCRIPTION

Diagnostic Trouble Code	DRB Scan Tool Display	Description of Diagnostic Trouble Code
32**	EGR Solenoid Circuit or EGR System Failure	An open or shorted condition detected in the EGR transducer solenoid circuit. / Required change in air/fuel ratio not detected during diagnostic test.
33*	A/C Clutch Relay Circuit	An open or shorted condition detected in the A/C clutch relay circuit.
34*	Speed Control Solenoid Circuits	An open or shorted condition detected in the speed control vacuum or vent solenoid circuits.
35*	Radiator Fan Relay CTRL Circuits	An open or shorted condition detected in the radiator fan circuit.
37*	Torque Convertor Clutch Solenoid CKT	An open or shorted condition detected in the torque convertor clutch solenoid circuit (automatic transaxle).
41**	Generator Field Not Switching Properly	An open or shorted condition detected in the generator field control circuit.
42*	Auto Shutdown Relay Control Circuit or No ASD Relay Output Voltage at PCM	An open or shorted condition detected in the auto shutdown relay circuit. / PCM did not detect ASD sense signal after grounding the ASD relay.
46**	Charging System Voltage Too High	Battery voltage sense input above target charging voltage during engine operation.
47**	Charging System Voltage Too Low	Battery voltage sense input below target charging during engine operation. Also, no significant change detected in battery voltage during active test of generator output.
51**	O2S Signal Stays Below Center (Lean)	Oxygen sensor signal input indicates lean air/fuel ratio condition during engine operation.
52**	O2S Signal Stays Above Center (Rich)	Oxygen sensor signal input indicates rich air/fuel ratio condition during engine operation.
53*	Internal Controller Failure	Powertrain Control Module internal fault condition detected.
62*	PCM Failure SRI Mile Not Stored	Unsuccessful attempt to update SRI Mileage.
63*	PCM Failure EEPROM Write Denied	Unsuccessful attempt to write to an EEPROM location by the Powertrain Control Module.
55	N/A	Completion of fault code display on Check Engine lamp.

* Check Engine Lamp will not illuminate at all times if this Diagnostic Trouble Code was recorded. Cycle Ignition key as described in manual and observe code flashed by Check Engine lamp.
** Check Engine Lamp will illuminate during engine operation if this Diagnostic Trouble Code was recorded.

Fig. 102 Diagnostic trouble codes—1988-95 2.2L and 2.5L Chrysler EFI engines (continued)

FAULT CODE DESCRIPTION

Fault Code	DRB II Display	Description
11	No reference Signal During Cranking	No distributor reference signal detected during engine cranking.
13+**	No change in MAP from start to run	No difference recognized between the engine MAP reading and the barometric (atmospheric) pressure reading at start-up.
14+**	MAP voltage too low *or* MAP voltage too High	MAP sensor input below minimum acceptable voltage. / MAP sensor input above maximum acceptable voltage.
15**	No vehicle speed signal	No vehicle distance (speed) sensor signal detected during road load conditions.
17	Engine is cold too long	Engine coolant temperature remains below normal operating temperatures during vehicle travel (thermostat).
21**	O₂ signal stays at center *or* O₂ signal shorted to voltage	Neither rich or lean condition detected from the oxygen sensor input. / Oxygen sensor input voltage maintained above the normal operating range.
22+**	Coolant sensor voltage too high *or* Coolant sensor voltage too low	Coolant temperature sensor input above the maximum acceptable voltage. / Coolant temperature sensor input below the minimum acceptable voltage.
24+**	Throttle position sensor voltage high *or* Throttle position sensor voltage low	Throttle position sensor input above the maximum acceptable voltage. / Throttle position sensor input below the minimum acceptable voltage.
25**	Automatic idle speed motor circuits	An open or shorted condition detected in one or more of the AIS control circuits.
27	Injector control circuit (DRB II)	Injector output driver does not respond properly to the control signal (DRB II specifies the injector by cylinder number).
31**	Purge solenoid circuit	An open or shorted condition detected in the purge solenoid circuit.
33	A/C clutch relay circuit	An open or shorted condition detected in the A/C clutch relay circuit
34	Speed control solenoid circuits	An open or shorted condition detected in the speed control vacuum or vent solenoid circuits.

+ Check Engine Lamp On
** Check Engine Lamp On (California Only)

Fig. 105 Diagnostic trouble codes—2.5L Turbo I engines

86734GC4

FAULT CODE DESCRIPTION (CON'T)

FAULT CODE	DRB II DISPLAY	DESCRIPTION
33	A/C clutch relay circuit	An open or shorted condition detected in the A/C clutch relay circuit.
34	Speed control solenoid circuits	An open or shorted condition detected in the speed control vacuum or vent solenoid circuits.
35	Radiator fan relay circuits	An open or shorted condition detected in the radiator fan circuit
36+**	Wastegate solenoid circuit	An open or shorted condition detected in the turbocharger wastegate solenoid circuit.
41+**	Alternator field not switching properly	An open or shorted condition detected in the alternator field control circuit.
42	Auto shutdown relay control circuit	An open or shorted condition detected in the auto shutdown relay circuit.
43	Ignition coil #1 primary circuit *or* Ignition coil #2 primary circuit	Peak primary circuit current not achieved with maximum dwell time. / Peak primary circuit current not achieved with maximum dwell time.
45	Turbo boost limit exceeded	MAP sensor reading above overboost limit detected during engine operation.
46+**	Charging system voltage too high	Battery voltage sense input above target charging voltage during engine operation.
47+**	Charging system voltage too low	Battery voltage sense input below target charging during engine operation. Also, no significant change detected in battery voltage during active test of alternator output.
51**	O₂ signal stays below center (lean)	Oxygen sensor signal input indicates lean air/fuel ratio condition during engine operation.
52**	O₂ signal stays above center (rich)	Oxygen sensor signal input indicates rich air/fuel ratio condition during engine operation.
53	Internal controller	Engine controller internal fault condition detected.
54	No sync pick-up signal	No fuel sync signal detected during engine rotation.
61**	Baro read solenoid circuit	An open or shorted condition detected in the baro read solenoid circuit.

+ Check Engine Lamp On
** Check Engine Lamp On (California Only)

86734GC3

Fig. 104 Diagnostic trouble codes—2.2L turbocharged engines (continued)

DIAGNOSTIC TROUBLE CODE DESCRIPTION

Diagnostic Trouble Code	DRB Scan Tool Display	Description of Diagnostic Trouble Code
11*	No Crank Reference Signal at PCM	No crank reference signal detected during engine cranking.
12*	Battery Disconnect	Direct battery input to PCM was disconnected within the last 50 Key-on cycles.
13**	Slow Change in Idle MAP Signal or No Change in MAP From Start to Run	MAP output change is slower and/or smaller than expected. / No difference recognized between the engine MAP reading and the barometric (atmospheric) pressure reading at start-up.
14**	MAP Sensor Voltage Too Low or MAP Sensor Voltage Too High	MAP sensor input below minimum acceptable voltage. / MAP sensor input above maximum acceptable voltage.
15**	No Vehicle Speed Sensor Signal	No vehicle distance (speed) sensor signal detected during road load conditions.
17*	Engine Is Cold Too Long	Engine coolant temperature remains below normal operating temperatures during vehicle travel (thermostat).
21*	O2S Stays at Center or O2S Shorted to Voltage	Neither rich or lean condition detected from the oxygen sensor input. / Oxygen sensor input voltage maintained above the normal operating range.
22**	ECT Sensor Voltage Too High or ECT Sensor Voltage Too Low	Engine coolant temperature sensor input above maximum acceptable voltage. / Engine coolant temperature sensor input below minimum acceptable voltage.
24**	Throttle Position Sensor Voltage High or Throttle Position Sensor Voltage Low	Throttle position sensor input above the maximum acceptable voltage. / Throttle position sensor input below the minimum acceptable voltage.
25**	Idle Air Control Motor Circuits	A shorted condition detected in one or more of the idle air control motor circuits.
27**	Injector Control Circuit	Injector output driver does not respond properly to the control signal.
31**	EVAP Solenoid Circuit	An open or shorted condition detected in the duty cycle purge solenoid circuit.

* Check Engine Lamp will not illuminate at all times if this Diagnostic Trouble Code was recorded. Cycle Ignition key as described in manual and observe code flashed by Check Engine lamp.

** Check Engine Lamp will illuminate during engine operation if this Diagnostic Trouble Code was recorded.

Fig. 107 Diagnostic trouble codes—2.5L Chrysler Flex Fuel MFI engines

FAULT CODE DESCRIPTION (CON'T)

FAULT CODE	DRB II DISPLAY	DESCRIPTION
35	Radiator fan relay circuits	An open or shorted condition detected in the radiator fan circuit
36**	Wastegate solenoid circuit	An open or shorted condition detected in the turbocharger wastegate solenoid circuit.
37	Torque convertor unlock solenoid CKT	An open or shorted condition detected in the torque convertor port throttle unlock solenoid circuit (automatic transmission).
41+**	Alternator field not switching properly	An open or shorted condition detected in the alternator field control circuit.
42	Auto shutdown relay control circuit	An open or shorted condition detected in the auto shutdown relay circuit.
45	Turbo boost limit exceeded	MAP sensor reading above overboost limit detected during engine operation.
46+**	Charging system voltage too high	Battery voltage sense input above target charging voltage during engine operation.
47+**	Charging system voltage too low	Battery voltage sense input below target charging during engine operation. Also, no significant change detected in battery voltage during active test of alternator output.
51**	O2 signal stays below center (lean)	Oxygen sensor signal input indicates lean air/fuel ratio condition during engine operation.
52**	O2 signal stays above center (rich)	Oxygen sensor signal input indicates rich air/fuel ratio condition during engine operation.
53	Internal controller	Engine controller internal fault condition detected.
54	No sync pickup signal	No fuel sync signal detected during engine rotation.
61**	Baro read solenoid circuit	An open or shorted condition detected in the baro read solenoid circuit.
62	Controller Failure EMR miles not stored	Unsuccessful attempt to update EMR milage in the controller EEPROM.
63	Controller Failure EEPROM write denied	Unsuccessful attempt to write to an EEPROM location by the engine controller.
55	N/A	Completion of fault code display on Check Engine lamp.

+ Check Engine Lamp On

** Check Engine Lamp On (California Only)

Fig. 106 Diagnostic trouble codes—2.5L Turbo I engines

DIAGNOSTIC TROUBLE CODE DESCRIPTION (CONTINUED)

Diagnostic Trouble Code	DRB Scan Tool Display	Description of Diagnostic Trouble Code
64**	Flex Fuel Sensor Volts Too Low or Flex Fuel Sensor Volts Too High	Methanol concentration sensor input below the minimum acceptable voltage. / Methanol concentration sensor input above the maximum acceptable voltage.
	Loss of Flex Fuel Calibration Signal	PCM did not detect a flex fuel calibration signal from the methanol concentration sensor at Key-On.
55	N/A	Completion of fault code display on Check Engine lamp.

* Check Engine Lamp will not illuminate at all times if this Diagnostic Trouble Code was recorded. Cycle Ignition key as described in manual and observe code flashed by Check Engine lamp.

** Check Engine Lamp will illuminate during engine operation if this Diagnostic Trouble Code was recorded.

86734GC1

Fig. 109 Diagnostic trouble codes—2.5L Chrysler Flex Fuel MFI engines (continued)

DIAGNOSTIC TROUBLE CODE DESCRIPTION (CONTINUED)

Diagnostic Trouble Code	DRB Scan Tool Display	Description of Diagnostic Trouble Code
33*	A/C Clutch Relay Circuit	An open or shorted condition detected in the A/C clutch relay circuit.
34*	Speed Control Solenoid Circuits	An open or shorted condition detected in the speed control vacuum or vent solenoid circuits.
35*	Radiator Fan Relay CTRL Circuits	An open or shorted condition detected in the radiator fan circuit.
37*	Torque Convertor Clutch Solenoid CKT	An open or shorted condition detected in the torque convertor clutch solenoid circuit (automatic transaxle).
41**	Generator Field Not Switching Properly	An open or shorted condition detected in the generator field control circuit.
42*	Auto Shutdown Relay Control Circuit or No ASD Relay Output Voltage at PCM	An open or shorted condition detected in the auto shutdown relay circuit. / PCM did not detect ASD sense signal after grounding the ASD relay.
46**	Charging System Voltage Too High	Battery voltage sense input above target charging voltage during engine operation.
47**	Charging System Voltage Too Low	Battery voltage sense input below target charging during engine operation. Also, no significant change detected in battery voltage during active test of generator output.
51**	O2S Signal Stays Below Center (Lean)	Oxygen sensor signal input indicates lean air/fuel ratio condition during engine operation.
52**	O2S Signal Stays Above Center (Rich)	Oxygen sensor signal input indicates rich air/fuel ratio condition during engine operation.
53*	Internal Controller Failure	Powertrain Control Module internal fault condition detected.
62*	PCM Failure SRI Mile Not Stored	Unsuccessful attempt to update SRI Mileage.
63*	PCM Failure EEPROM Write Denied	Unsuccessful attempt to write to an EEPROM location by the Powertrain Control Module.

* Check Engine Lamp will not illuminate at all times if this Diagnostic Trouble Code was recorded. Cycle Ignition key as described in manual and observe code flashed by Check Engine lamp.

** Check Engine Lamp will illuminate during engine operation if this Diagnostic Trouble Code was recorded.

86734GC0

Fig. 108 Diagnostic trouble codes—2.5L Chrysler Flex Fuel MFI engines (continued)

COMPONENT LOCATIONS

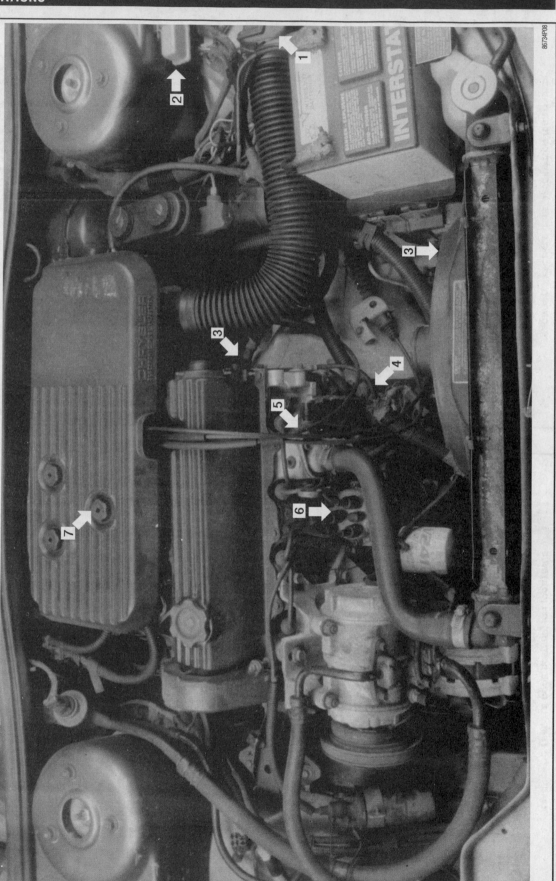

EMISSION AND ELECTRONIC ENGINE CONTROL COMPONENT LOCATIONS—CHRYSLER EFI ENGINES

1. Powertrain Control Module (PCM)
2. Relay cluster
3. Distance sensor (lower right or left-hand side of transaxle)
4. Oil pressure sending unit/switch
5. Engine coolant temperature sensor
6. Distributor reference pick-up sensor (Hall-effect device)
7. EGR solenoid, Throttle Position Sensor (TPS), fuel injector, Automatic Idle Speed (AIS) motor (mounted on, or near the throttle body—under the air cleaner assembly)

CHRYSLER ELECTRONIC FUEL INJECTION (EFI) THROTTLE BODY COMPONENTS

1. Fuel injector
2. Automatic Idle Speed (AIS) motor
3. PCV valve and hose
4. Throttle Position Sensor (TPS)
5. EGR valve

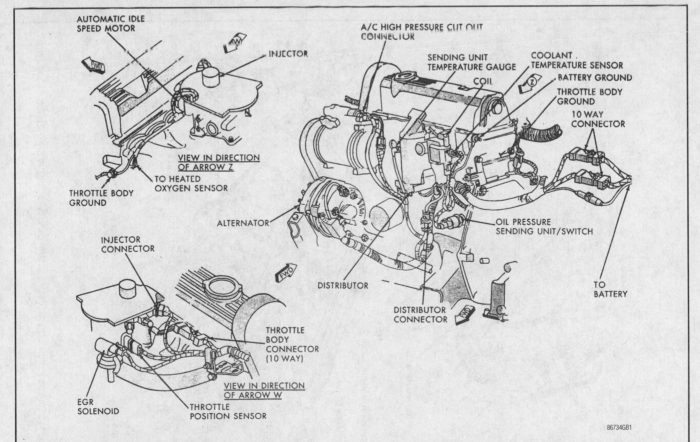

Fig. 110 Emission and electronic engine control component locations—1989–95 2.2L and 2.5L Chrysler EFI engines (earlier models similar)

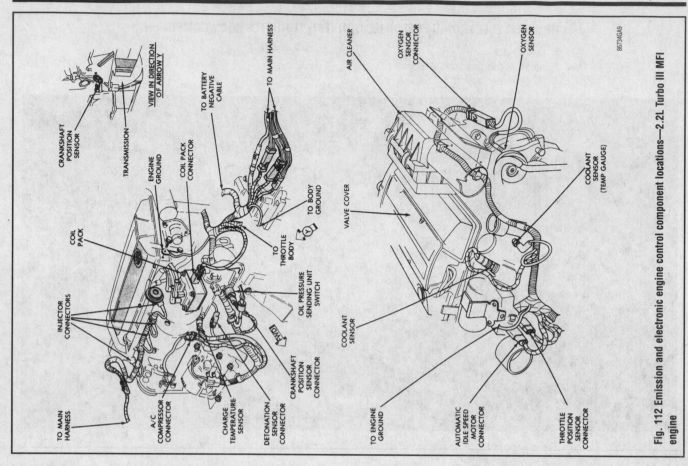

Fig. 112 Emission and electronic engine control component locations—2.2L Turbo III MFI engine

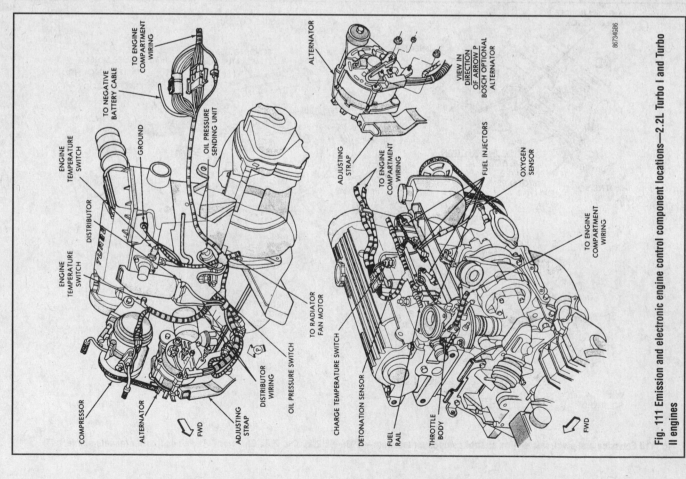

Fig. 111 Emission and electronic engine control component locations—2.2L Turbo I and Turbo II engines

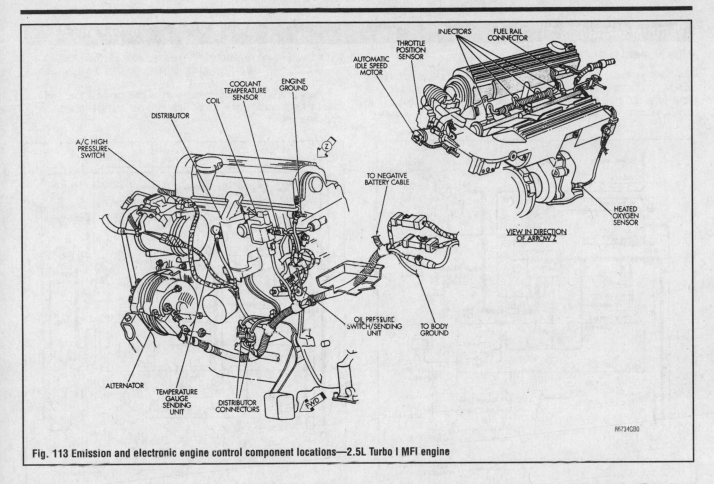

Fig. 113 Emission and electronic engine control component locations—2.5L Turbo I MFI engine

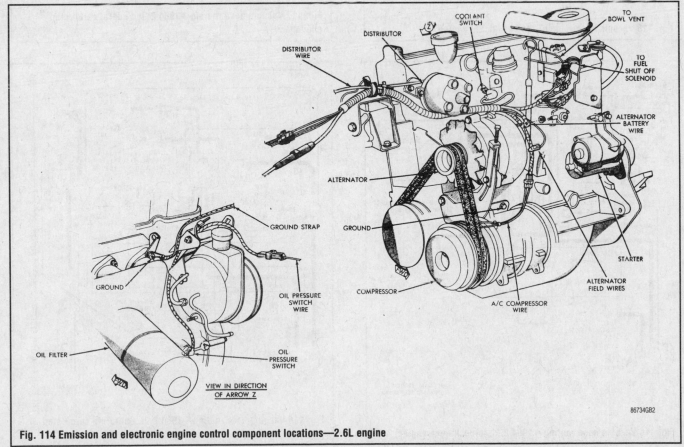

Fig. 114 Emission and electronic engine control component locations—2.6L engine

VACUUM DIAGRAMS

♦ **See Figures 115 thru 163**

Following are vacuum diagrams for most of the engine and emissions package combinations covered by this manual. Because vacuum circuits will vary based on various engine and vehicle options, always refer first to the Vehicle Emission Control Information (VECI) label, if present. Should the label be miss-

ing, or should vehicle be equipped with a different engine from the vehicle's original equipment, refer to the diagrams below for the same or similar configuration.

If you wish to obtain a replacement emissions label, most manufacturers make the labels available for purchase. The labels can usually be ordered from a local dealer.

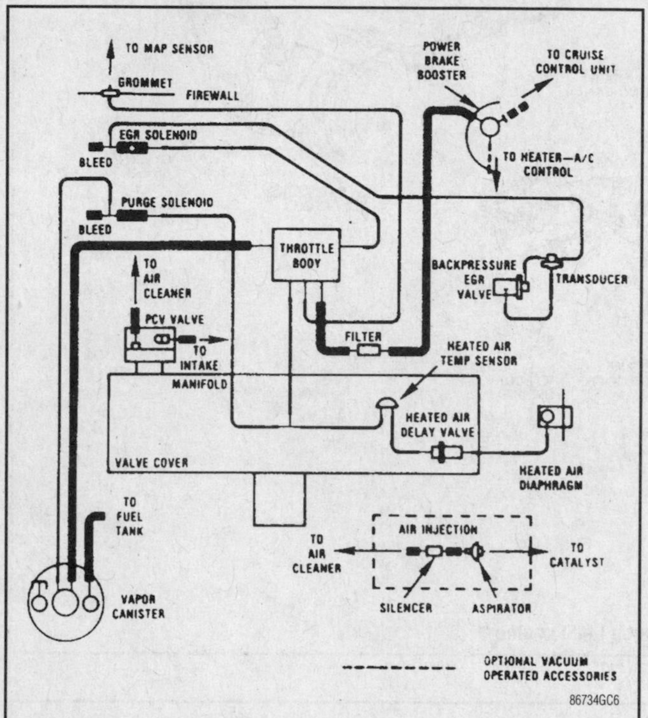

Fig. 115 Vacuum hose routing—1984 2.2L EFI engine

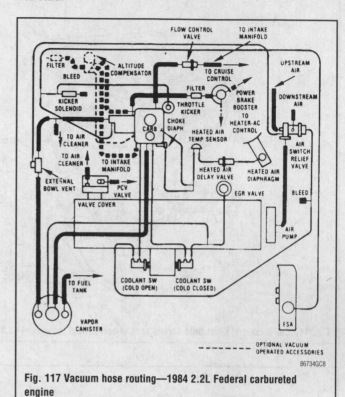

Fig. 117 Vacuum hose routing—1984 2.2L Federal carbureted engine

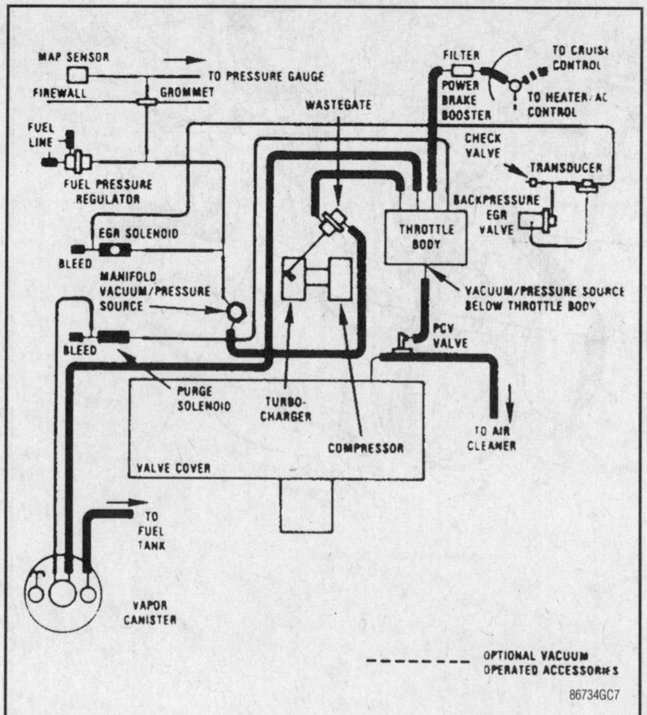

Fig. 116 Vacuum hose routing—1984 2.2L turbocharged engine

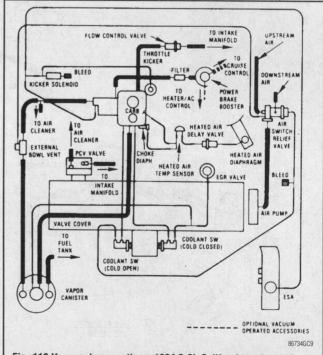

Fig. 118 Vacuum hose routing—1984 2.2L California carbureted engine

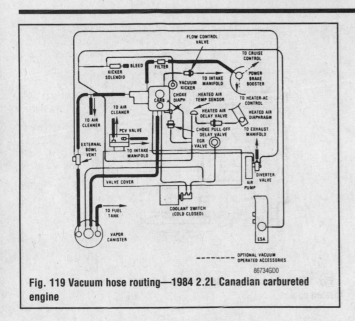

Fig. 119 Vacuum hose routing—1984 2.2L Canadian carbureted engine

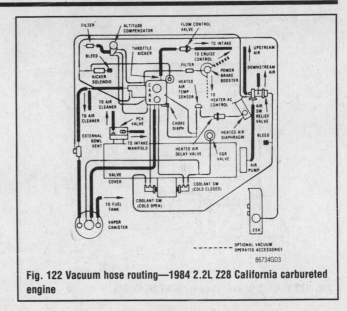

Fig. 122 Vacuum hose routing—1984 2.2L Z28 California carbureted engine

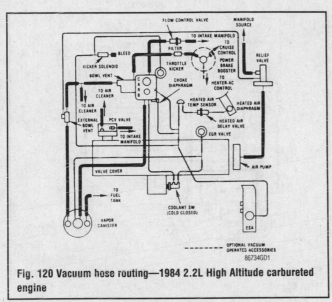

Fig. 120 Vacuum hose routing—1984 2.2L High Altitude carbureted engine

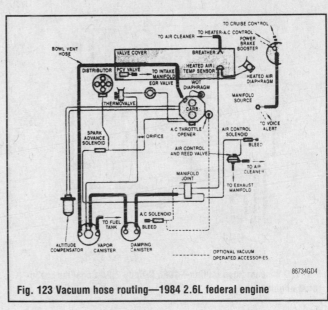

Fig. 123 Vacuum hose routing—1984 2.6L federal engine

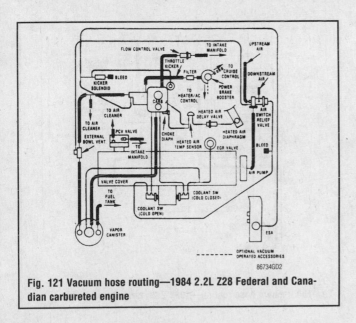

Fig. 121 Vacuum hose routing—1984 2.2L Z28 Federal and Canadian carbureted engine

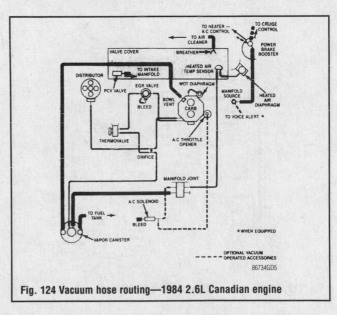

Fig. 124 Vacuum hose routing—1984 2.6L Canadian engine

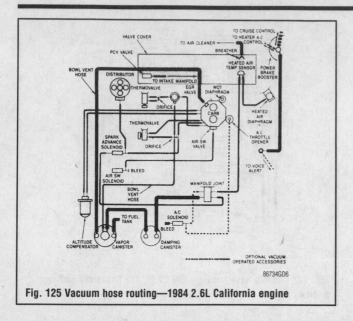

Fig. 125 Vacuum hose routing—1984 2.6L California engine

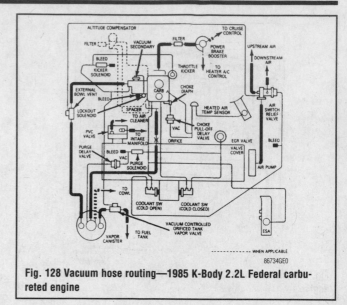

Fig. 128 Vacuum hose routing—1985 K-Body 2.2L Federal carbureted engine

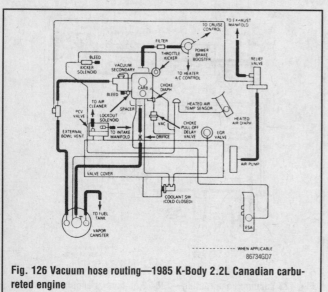

Fig. 126 Vacuum hose routing—1985 K-Body 2.2L Canadian carbureted engine

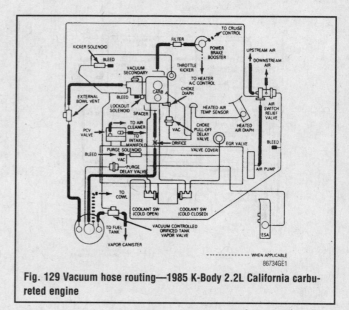

Fig. 129 Vacuum hose routing—1985 K-Body 2.2L California carbureted engine

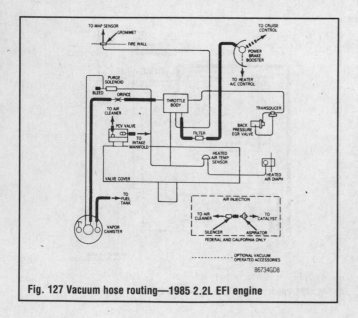

Fig. 127 Vacuum hose routing—1985 2.2L EFI engine

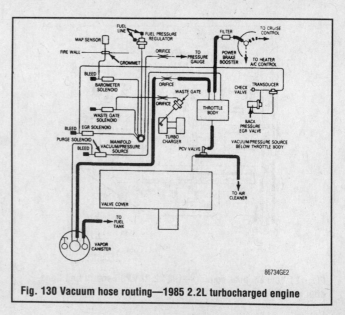

Fig. 130 Vacuum hose routing—1985 2.2L turbocharged engine

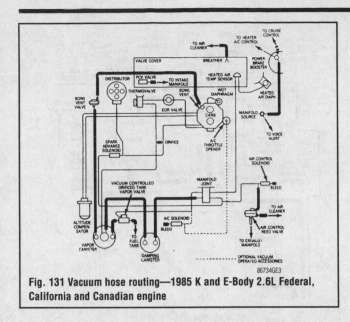

Fig. 131 Vacuum hose routing—1985 K and E-Body 2.6L Federal, California and Canadian engine

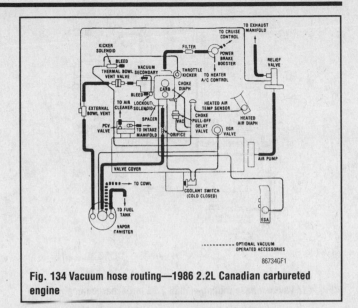

Fig. 134 Vacuum hose routing—1986 2.2L Canadian carbureted engine

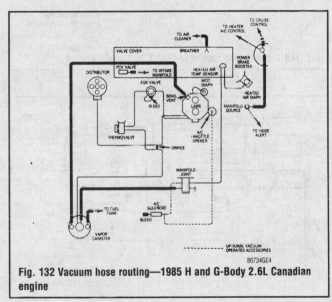

Fig. 132 Vacuum hose routing—1985 H and G-Body 2.6L Canadian engine

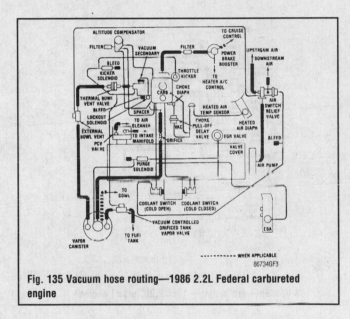

Fig. 135 Vacuum hose routing—1986 2.2L Federal carbureted engine

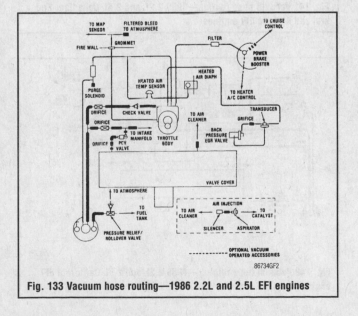

Fig. 133 Vacuum hose routing—1986 2.2L and 2.5L EFI engines

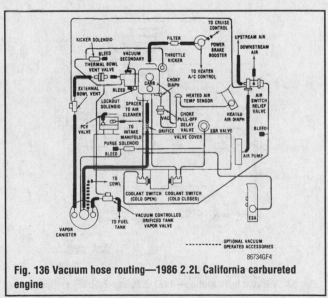

Fig. 136 Vacuum hose routing—1986 2.2L California carbureted engine

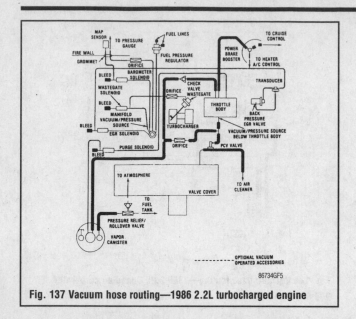

Fig. 137 Vacuum hose routing—1986 2.2L turbocharged engine

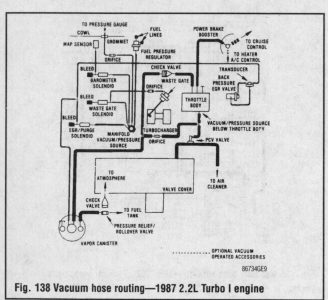

Fig. 138 Vacuum hose routing—1987 2.2L Turbo I engine

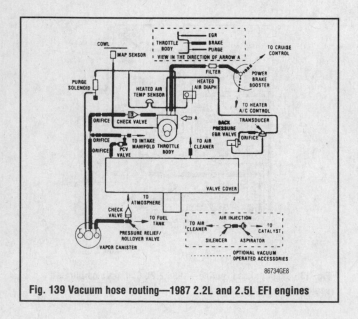

Fig. 139 Vacuum hose routing—1987 2.2L and 2.5L EFI engines

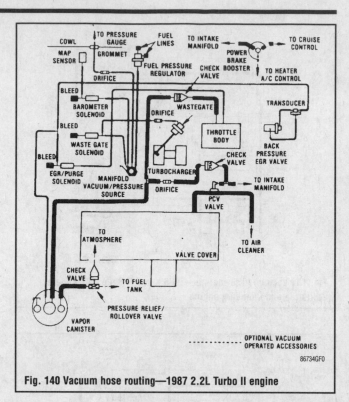

Fig. 140 Vacuum hose routing—1987 2.2L Turbo II engine

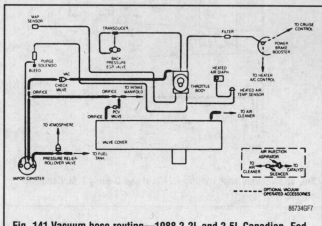

Fig. 141 Vacuum hose routing—1988 2.2L and 2.5L Canadian, Federal and Altitude EFI engines

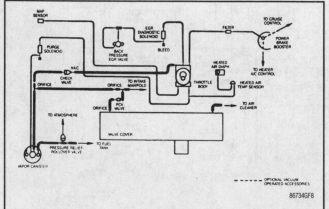

Fig. 142 Vacuum hose routing—1988 2.2L and 2.5L California EFI engines

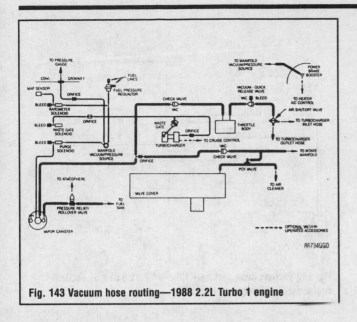

Fig. 143 Vacuum hose routing—1988 2.2L Turbo 1 engine

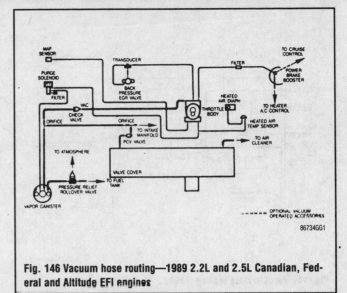

Fig. 146 Vacuum hose routing—1989 2.2L and 2.5L Canadian, Federal and Altitude EFI engines

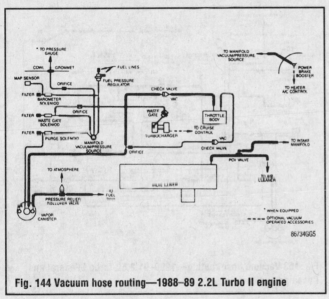

Fig. 144 Vacuum hose routing—1988–89 2.2L Turbo II engine

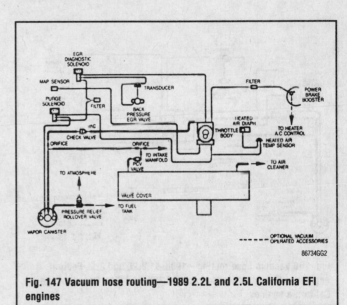

Fig. 147 Vacuum hose routing—1989 2.2L and 2.5L California EFI engines

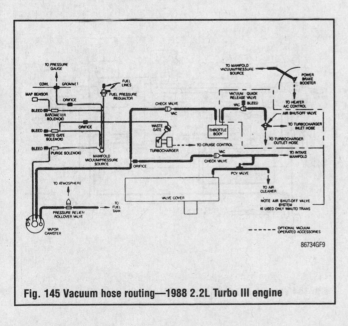

Fig. 145 Vacuum hose routing—1988 2.2L Turbo III engine

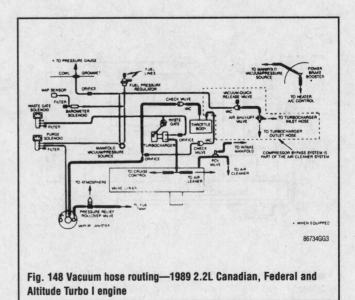

Fig. 148 Vacuum hose routing—1989 2.2L Canadian, Federal and Altitude Turbo I engine

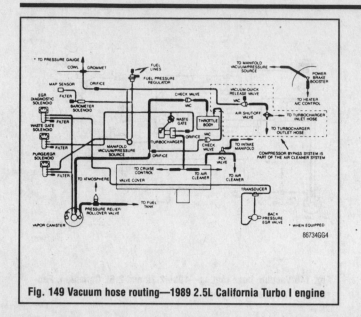

Fig. 149 Vacuum hose routing—1989 2.5L California Turbo I engine

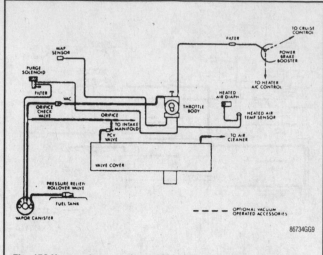

Fig. 152 Vacuum hose routing—1990–91 2.2L and 2.5L Federal engines with automatic transaxles

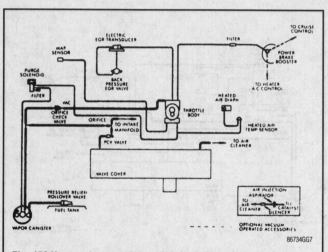

Fig. 150 Vacuum hose routing—1990–91 2.2L and 2.5L Federal engines with manual transaxles, and 2.2L and 2.5L Canadian and California engines

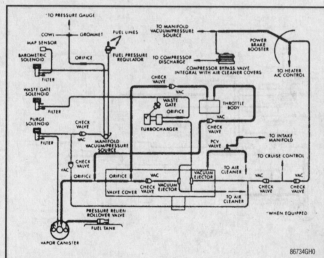

Fig. 153 Vacuum hose routing—1990–91 2.5L Turbo I Federal and Canadian engines

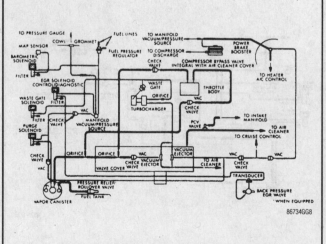

Fig. 151 Vacuum hose routing—1990–91 2.5L Turbo I California engines

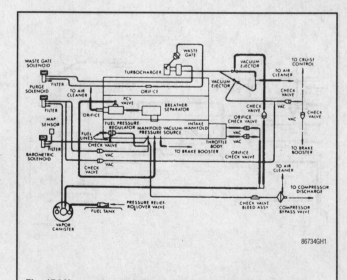

Fig. 154 Vacuum hose routing—1990–91 2.2L Turbo III engines

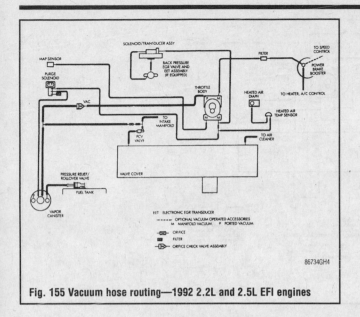

Fig. 155 Vacuum hose routing—1992 2.2L and 2.5L EFI engines

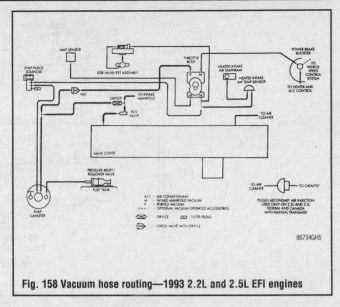

Fig. 158 Vacuum hose routing—1993 2.2L and 2.5L EFI engines

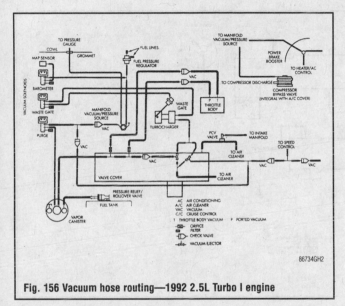

Fig. 156 Vacuum hose routing—1992 2.5L Turbo I engine

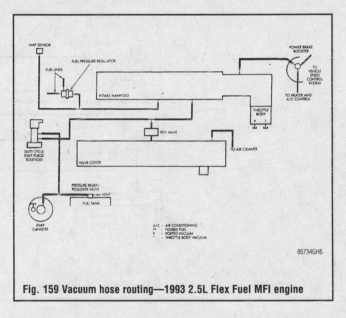

Fig. 159 Vacuum hose routing—1993 2.5L Flex Fuel MFI engine

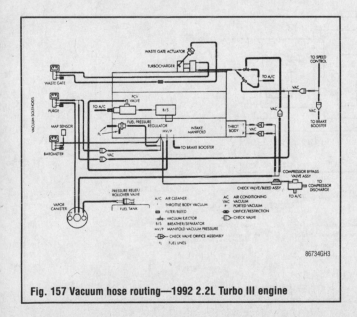

Fig. 157 Vacuum hose routing—1992 2.2L Turbo III engine

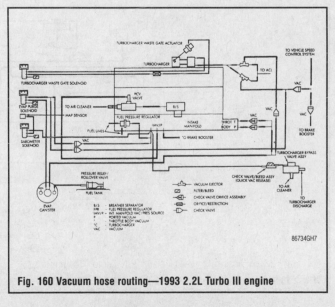

Fig. 160 Vacuum hose routing—1993 2.2L Turbo III engine

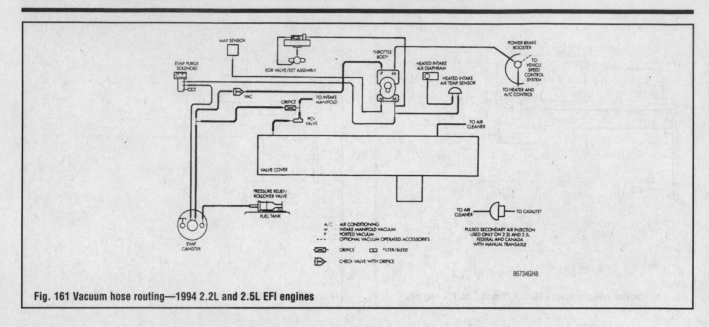

Fig. 161 Vacuum hose routing—1994 2.2L and 2.5L EFI engines

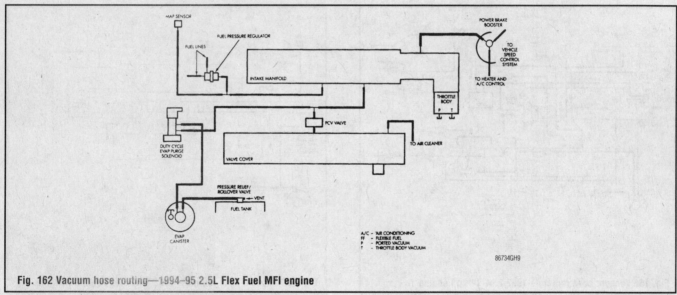

Fig. 162 Vacuum hose routing—1994–95 2.5L Flex Fuel MFI engine

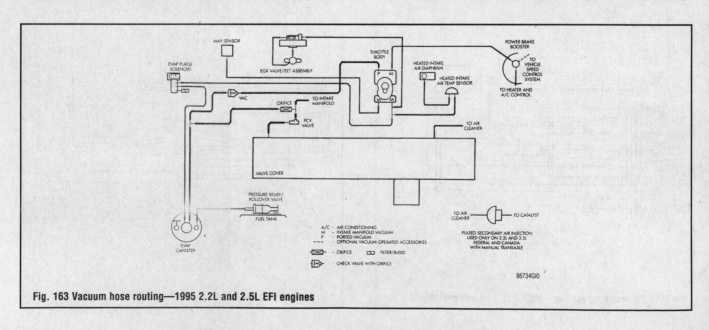

Fig. 163 Vacuum hose routing—1995 2.2L and 2.5L EFI engines

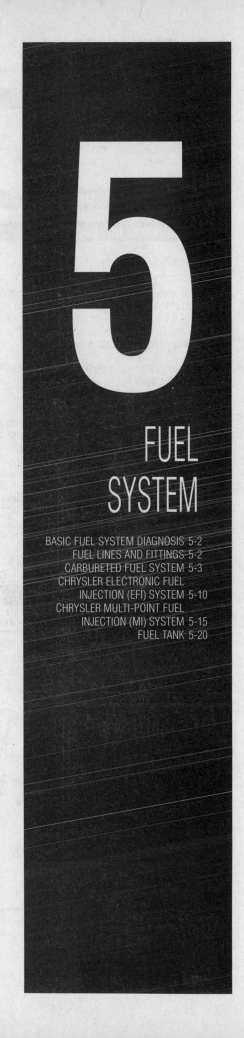

5

FUEL
SYSTEM

BASIC FUEL SYSTEM DIAGNOSIS

When there is a problem starting or driving a vehicle, two of the most important checks involve the ignition and the fuel systems. The questions most mechanics attempt to answer first, "is there spark?" and ``is there fuel?" will often lead to solving most basic problems. For ignition system diagnosis and testing, please refer to the information on engine electrical components and ignition systems found earlier in this manual. If the ignition system checks out (there is spark), then you must determine if the fuel system is operating properly (is there fuel?).

FUEL LINES AND FITTINGS

Quick-Connect Fittings

REMOVAL & INSTALLATION

Note that whenever replacing any fuel lines, it is necessary to use hoses marked ``EFI/EFM," or an equivalent product from the aftermarket. Whenever replacing hose clamps, use clamps incorporating a rolled edge to prevent hose damage, rather than standard aviation-type clamps. This will prevent damage to the hoses that could produce dangerous leaks.

Chrysler Electronic Fuel Injection (EFI) and Multi-point Fuel Injection (MFI) Systems

▶ See Figures 1, 2 and 3

The fuel systems on 1990–95 model vehicles utilize plastic fuel tubes with quick-connect fittings that have sealed O-rings; these O-rings do not have to be replaced when the fittings are disconnected. The quick-connect fitting consists of the O-rings, a retainer and the casing.

When the fittings are disconnected, the retainer will stay on the nipple of the component that the tube is being disconnected from. A fuel tube should never be inserted into a quick-connect fitting without the retainer being either on the tube or already in the quick-connect fitting. In either case, care must be taken to ensure that the retainer is locked securely into the quick-connect fitting.

1. Perform the appropriate fuel system pressure release procedure found later in this section.
2. Disconnect the negative battery cable, if not already done.
3. Remove any loose dirt from the quick-connect fittings.

✷✷ CAUTION

Wrap shop towels around the hoses to catch any fuel spillage.

4. Push the quick-connect fitting toward the fuel tube while depressing the built-in release tool. Then twist the fitting slightly and pull it off the fuel tube.
5. Cover the fitting to prevent contaminants from entering the fuel system.

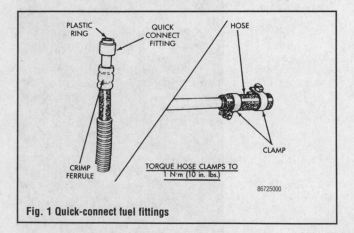

Fig. 1 Quick-connect fuel fittings

To install:

➡The fuel tube nipples must first be lubricated with clean SAE 30 weight engine oil prior to reconnecting the quick-connect fitting.

6. Insert the fuel tube nipple into the quick-connect fitting. The shoulder of the nipple is locked in place by the retainer, and the O-rings seal the tube.
7. The fuel line should be fully seated in the fittings.
8. If the quick-connect fitting has windows in the side of the casing, the retainer locking ears and the shoulder (stop bead) on the tube must be visible in the windows, or the retainer is not properly installed.
9. After fastening a quick-connect fitting, the connection should be verified by pulling on the lines to ensure that the lock is secure.

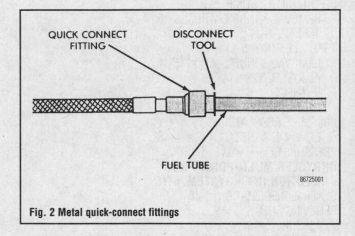

Fig. 2 Metal quick-connect fittings

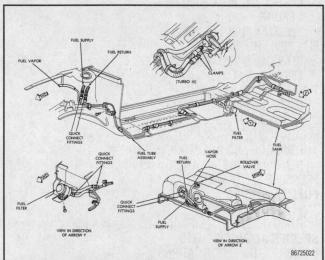

Fig. 3 Fuel delivery system—Chrysler EFI and MFI systems, carburetor and Flex Fuel systems similar

CARBURETED FUEL SYSTEM

Mechanical Fuel Pump

OPERATION

The fuel pump used with carburetor-equipped engines is located on the left-hand side of the engine. It is a mechanical type with an integral vapor separator for better performance during hot weather. The pump is driven by an eccentric cam lobe that is cast onto the accessory driveshaft.

REMOVAL & INSTALLATION

▶ **See Figure 4**

1. Make sure the negative battery cable is disconnected. Have a metal cup handy to collect any fuel that may spill.
2. Place a drain pan under the oil filter, then remove the filter with a strap wrench or equivalent.
3. Disconnect the fuel and vapor lines, catching fuel that spills. Dispose of any spilled fuel safely.
4. Plug the fuel lines to prevent leaks
5. Remove the attaching bolts and remove the fuel pump.

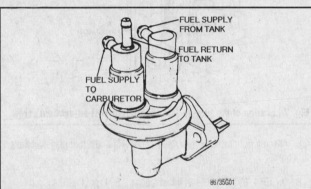

Fig. 4 Identification of the mechanical fuel pump inlet and outlet tubes

➡ **The fuel pump is not repairable. It must be replaced as a complete unit. Always use a new gasket when installing the pump and make certain that the gasket surfaces are clean.**

To install:

6. Clean the fuel pump and engine block gasket surfaces of all old gasket material or dirt.
7. Position a new fuel pump gasket against the engine block, then situate the pump in position over the gasket with bolt holes lined up squarely. Install the retaining bolts and tighten them to 21 ft. lbs. (28 Nm).
8. Connect the fuel lines to the pump (always start fuel line connections by hand—before using a wrench to tighten) and tighten the fittings to 175 inch lbs. (20 Nm).
9. Clean the block surface, check the gasket, then install the oil filter, tightening it by hand only. If the gasket is damaged, replace the filter. Refer to Section 1 for the proper service procedures regarding oil filters.
10. Start the engine and check for leaks. Check the crankcase oil level and refill as necessary.

TESTING

The fuel pump may be tested three different ways—for volume, vacuum and pressure. While it is best to test in all three ways, a pressure test will most often reveal a defective pump. Only if pressure meets specifications and there are still fuel supply problems is it necessary to complete all three tests.

➡ To perform these tests, a pressure gauge capable of reading 1–10 psi (6.89–68.90 kPa), a vacuum gauge that will read 025 in. Hg (4.22 kPa), a metal container of just over 1 qt. (0.046L), several plugs the right diameter for the engine's fuel lines, a watch, and a supply of new fuel hose clamps.

Pressure Test

1. Using a metal cup to collect spilled fuel, disconnect the fuel pump outlet hose at the bottom of the filter and plug it. Connect a pressure gauge into the line.
2. Disconnect the coil-to-distributor high tension wire so that the engine will not start. Have a helper crank the engine as you watch the pressure gauge.
3. Read the gauge and compare the pressure to the range shown in the Tune-Up Specifications chart in Section 1. If the pressure is either too high or too low, replace the pump. If the pump passes this test and you still have doubts about its performance, proceed with the tests that follow.
4. Remove the pressure gauge from the fuel pump discharge. Disconnect the fuel pump suction line and plug it, collect any spilled fuel, and then connect a vacuum gauge to the suction side of the fuel pump.
5. Again have a helper crank the engine while you watch the pressure gauge. The fuel pump should produce a minimum of 11 in. Hg (37 kPa)—readings may go as high as 22 in. Hg (74 kPa).
6. If the pump passes these tests, but there is still some question about its ability to produce adequate flow (poor high rpm full throttle performance in spite of a clean filter), proceed with the volume test.

Volume Test

✳ CAUTION

This test must be performed very carefully! It is necessary to run the engine while checking the volume of flow. The potential for spilling and igniting gasoline is very great. Proceed very carefully or, if you are not sure you can perform the test safely, have it performed professionally.

➡ A watch will be necessary for this test.

1. Make sure both fuel filters are clean.
2. Start the engine and allow it to idle a few seconds to stabilize the fuel supply to the carburetor. Make sure the engine is warmed up and off the choke (at normal idle speed). Stop the engine.
3. Disconnect the fuel line at the inlet of the filter-reservoir on the carburetor.
4. Collect any fuel that drains out of the fuel supply line in a metal container and dispose of it safely.
5. Tightly seal or plug the fuel supply line.
6. Position the carburetor end of the fuel supply line over a large metal container (at least 1 qt./0.946L capacity) so that when the fuel line plug is removed, it will drain into the container.
7. With the supply line plugged, start the engine and allow it to idle for a few seconds to stabilize the fuel supply to the carburetor. Make sure the engine is warmed up and at normal idle speed. Have a watch available so you can time the test.
8. If not already performed, position the 1 qt. (0.946L) container under the fuel line.
9. Unplug the fuel supply line and allow the fuel to spray into the metal container as the engine continues to idle. Run the engine for about 15 seconds, and then stop the engine (before the carburetor begins to run out of fuel).
10. Connect the line to the fuel filter, start the engine, and run it for 15–20 seconds to restore full fuel level to the carburetor.
11. Stop the engine, and repeat Steps 3 through 10. There should be a total of four 15second cycles in which you idle the engine on the fuel in the carburetor and drain the fuel pump output into the container.
12. After four cycles, if the pump has moved 1 qt. (0.946L) or more into the container, it is working within specifications and is functioning normally. Otherwise, replace it, even if pressure and vacuum are satisfactory.

Carburetor

ADJUSTMENTS

Idle Speed

HOLLEY 5220/6520

▶ **See Figure 5**

➡ **The Holley 5220/6520 carburetors are used only on the 2.2L engine. This procedure is prformed while the carburetor is installed on the engine.**

1. Install a tachometer on the engine following the manufacturer's instructions.
2. Put the transaxle in Neutral and set the parking brake securely.
3. Turn all accessories OFF.
4. Allow the engine to warm up on the lowest step of the fast idle cam.
5. Make the following preparations for adjustment, depending on the year:

   a. Disconnect and plug the vacuum connector at the CVSCC (Coolant Vacuum Switch Cold Closed) on 1981–84 engines, so equipped.

   b. Pull the PCV valve out of the vent module and allow it to breathe underhood air.

   c. Disconnect the oxygen feedback system test connector located on the left fender shield, if working on a 6520 carburetor.

   d. Disconnect the wiring from the kicker solenoid located on the left fender shield on 1986 models. On 1981–85 models so-equipped, ground the carburetor switch with a jumper wire.

6. If the tachometer indicates the rpm is not set to specifications, turn the idle speed screw, located on the top of the idle solenoid, until the correct rpm is achieved. Refer to the underhood sticker on the vehicle or to the Gasoline Engine Tune-up chart in Section 1 for correct idle speed.

7. Restore the PCV system and other vacuum and electrical connections. Road test the vehicle for proper operation.

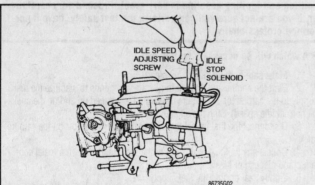

Fig. 5 To adjust the idle speed, turn the screw on the top of the idle stop solenoid

MIKUNI

▶ **See Figures 6 and 7**

➡ **The Mikuni carburetor is used only on the 2.6L engine. This procedure is performed while the carburetor is installed on the engine.**

1. Place the transaxle in Neutral, set the parking brake, and turn OFF all accessories.
2. Disconnect the radiator fan.
3. Run the engine until it reaches operating temperature. On 1981–83 models, allow the engine to idle for one minute to stabilize the rpm.
4. On 1984 models, turn the engine **OFF**. Disconnect the negative battery cable for three seconds, then reconnect it.
5. Detach the engine wiring harness lead from the O₂sensor at the bullet connector. Don't pull on the sensor wire in doing this; only pull on the connector boot.

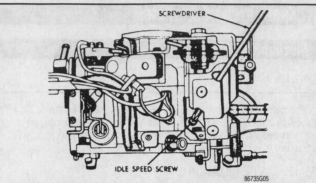

Fig. 6 Adjust the idle speed screw with a long, slender screwdriver as shown

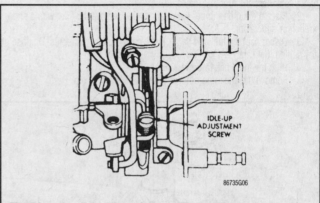

Fig. 7 Location of the idle-up (air conditioner ON) adjustment screw

6. Attach a tachometer to the engine according to the tool manufacturer's instructions.
7. Restart the engine.
8. On 1984–85 vehicles, run the engine at 2,500 rpm for 10 seconds. Then, wait two minutes before checking idle speed.
9. Check the idle speed with the tachometer. If the idle rpm is not within specifications:

   a. On 1983–84 models—disconnect idle switch connector, if the idle speed must be adjusted. Adjust the idle speed with the idle screw.

   b. On A/C models—turn on the air conditioning with the temperature control lever set to the coldest setting. If the rpm is not approximately 900, turn the idle-up screw to obtain this reading.

10. Turn the engine **OFF** and reattach all connectors. Road test the vehicle for proper operation.

Air Conditioning Idle Speed

HOLLEY 5220/6520

▶ **See Figure 8**

➡ **This adjustment is required on 1981–82 2.2L engines only. On later models, just verify that the A/C idle speed kicker works. This procedure is performed while the carburetor is installed on the engine.**

1. Turn the air conditioner ON and set the blower on low. Disconnect and plug the EGR valve vacuum hose.
2. Remove the adjusting screw and spring from the top of the air conditioning solenoid.
3. Insert a ⅛ in. Allen wrench into the solenoid and adjust to obtain the correct idle speed, as indicated on the underhood sticker.
4. Make sure that the air conditioning clutch is operating during the speed adjustments.
5. Reinstall the adjusting screw and spring onto the solenoid and turn the air conditioner OFF.

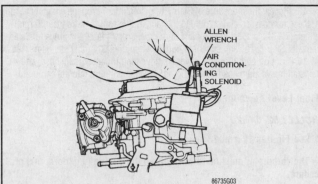

Fig. 8 To adjust the idle speed for when the A/C is engaged, turn to the recessed screw with an Allen wrench

Fast Idle Speed

HOLLEY 5220/6520

♦ See Figure 9

➡This procedure is performed while the carburetor is installed on the engine.

1. On 1981–82 cars, disengage the two-way electrical connector at the carburetor (red and tan wires).
2. On all years, disconnect the jumper wire at the radiator fan and install a jumper wire so that the fan runs continuously.
3. On 1983–86 models, pull the PCV valve out of the valve cover and allow it to draw underhood air.
4. Disengage the oxygen sensor system connector located on the left fender shield near the shock tower.
5. Ground the carburetor switch with a jumper wire.
6. Open the throttle slightly and place the adjustment screw on the slowest speed step of the fast idle cam.
7. With the choke fully open, adjust the fast idle speed to comply with the value indicated on the underhood sticker.
8. Return the vehicle to curb idle, then reposition the adjusting screw on the slowest speed step of the fast idle cam to verify fast idle speed. Re-adjust as necessary.
9. Turn the engine **OFF**, remove the jumper wire and reconnect the fan.
10. Reinstall the PCV valve and remove the tachometer. On 1983–86 models, reattach the oxygen sensor system connector, and remove the jumper wire from the carburetor.

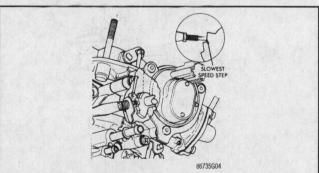

Fig. 9 Turn the adjusting screw with a screwdriver to raise or lower the fast idle speed—make sure that the adjusting screw is resting against the lowest speed step

Fast Idle Opening

MIKUNI

1. Before adjustment, leave the carburetor alone for approximately one hour at 73°F (23°C).
2. Adjust the fast idle opening by turning the fast idle adjusting screw to the following specified values (drill diameter):

- 2.6L engines equipped with manual transaxles—0.028 in.
- 2.6L engines equipped with automatic transaxles—0.031 in.

Choke Valve Setting

MIKUNI

♦ See Figure 10

➡This procedure need only be performed if the carburetor is disassembled.

1. Fit the strangler spring to the choke lever.
2. Assemble the choke valve, aligning the inscribed line or black painted line on the tooth of the choke pinion with the inscribed line on the cam lever.
3. Temporarily tighten the new lockscrews.
4. Set the choke valve by moving the pinion arm up or down, align a punched mark on the float chamber cover at the center of the three inscribed lines, and secure the pinion arm with the lockscrews.
5. Install the choke cover and tighten the lockscrews.
6. Cut off the heads off of lockscrews **A**.
7. Stake the heads of lockscrews **B** using a blunt punch.

Fig. 10 After tightening the choke cover lockscrews, cut the heads off of lockscrews A (total of 3 screws) and stake the heads of lockscrews B (total of 2 screws) with a blunt punch

Vacuum Kick

HOLLEY 5220/6520

➡This procedure is performed while the carburetor is installed on the engine.

If the vacuum kick is adjusted to open the choke too far, the engine may stall or idle very roughly just after cold start. If it is adjusted so that the choke does not open enough, there may be black smoke in the exhaust.

➡To perform this procedure, you will need a hand held vacuum pump capable of producing at least 15 in. Hg (50.6 kPa) of vacuum. The vacuum kick diaphragm may be damaged if you attempt to retract it manually. You will also need a drill or dowel which has a diameter equivalent to the specification for Vacuum Kick in the Carburetor Specifications Chart.

1. Remove the air cleaner. Open the throttle, close the choke and hold it in the closed position, and then release the throttle to trap the fast idle cam in the choke-closed position.
2. Disconnect the vacuum hose at the choke vacuum kick diaphragm. Connect a vacuum pump and apply 15 in. Hg (50.6 kPa) or more of vacuum.
3. Gently move the choke blade toward the closed position just until play is eliminated from the vacuum kick linkage (so that the vacuum kick is determining choke blade position).
4. Insert the drill or dowel into the gap between the upper edge of the choke blade and the air horn wall, toward the center of the gap. The dowel or drill should just fit into the gap. If necessary, rotate the Allen head screw in the center of the diaphragm housing to create the proper gap and then recheck with the measuring device.
5. Restore all vacuum connections and reinstall the air cleaner.

Air/Fuel Mixture Adjustment

♦ **See Figure 11**

➡**Always refer to Vehicle Emission Control Information (VECI) label in the engine compartment as a specification guide. The sticker information reflects running changes made by the manufacturer during production of the vehicle.**

Chrysler recommends the use of propane enrichment procedure to adjust the mixture. The equipment needed for this procedure is not readily available to the general public. The procedure is included here for reference purposes.

➡**Mixture screws are sealed under tamperproof plugs. The only time mixture adjustments are necessary is during a major carburetor overhaul. Refer to the instructions supplied with the overhaul kit.**

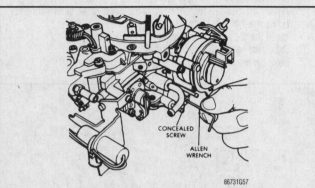

Fig. 11 The location of the idle speed mixture adjusting screw for the 2.2L carbureted engines

1. Remove the concealment plug located under the choke housing.
2. Set the parking brake. As applicable, place either the manual transaxle in Neutral or the automatic transaxle in Park.
3. Connect a tachometer to the engine. Then, start it and allow it to run on the bottom step of the fast idle cam until it has reached operating temperature. Open the throttle so the engine will run at normal idle speed.
4. Unplug the radiator fan electrical connector and install a jumper wire so the fan runs continuously.
5. Pull the PCV valve out of the crankcase vent module so it will draw underhood air.
6. Disconnect the oxygen feedback system test connector located on the left fender shield.
7. Disconnect the vacuum harness from the CVSCC valve and plug both hoses. On the 2.2L engine only, disconnect the wiring from the single solenoid kicker vacuum control solenoid, which is located on the left fender shield.
8. Disconnect the vacuum hose which leads to the heated air sensor at the three-way connector and install the supply hose from the propane bottle where it was connected. Make sure the propane valves are fully closed and that the bottle is in a safe and secure position that will maintain it upright.
9. Open the propane main valve. Leaving the air cleaner in place, slowly and very steadily open the propane metering valve while you watch the tach, until maximum rpm is reached. You will note that there will be an optimum mixture, after which further addition of propane will cause the engine rpm to begin falling. Note what this rpm is and carefully adjust the propane valve to produce this exact rpm.
10. Adjust the idle speed screw on top of the solenoid kicker (without changing the propane setting) so that the tach reads the propane enrichment rpm shown on the engine compartment sticker.
11. Increase the engine speed to 2500 rpm for 15 seconds and then return it to idle. Read the rpm and, if it has changed, readjust the idle speed to give the specified rpm.
12. Turn off the propane system main valve and allow the engine speed to stabilize. With the air cleaner in place, slowly adjust the mixture screw to achieve the specified idle set rpm with an Allen wrench. Work very slowly and pause after slight adjustment increments to allow the engine rpm to stabilize. Again, increase the engine speed to 2500 rpm for 15 seconds and then return it to idle. Recheck the rpm.

13. Repeat the procedure of Step 7 to get optimum propane enrichment rpm at these new basic settings. Reread the tach. If this rpm is more than 25 rpm either side of the specified propane enrichment rpm, repeat the procedure starting with Step 7. The adjustment is correct when the test in this step is passed.
14. Turn off both propane valves, remove the propane supply hose, and reinstall the vacuum hose. Reinstall the concealment plug into the carburetor.

Float Level Adjustment

HOLLEY 5220/6520

♦ **See Figures 12 and 13**

➡**The carburetor must be removed from the engine to perform this procedure.**

1. Remove the air horn from the carburetor body.
2. Invert the air horn and remove the gasket.
3. Insert a gauge or drill bit 12mm in diameter between the air horn and float. The gauge must lay flat along the gasket surface.
4. If the float's position is not correct, bend the tang, which actuates the needle valve, to correct it. Bend the tang up toward the floats to decrease the measurement and downward to increase it.
5. Check float drop with a float drop gauge or using a ruler and straightedge. Float drop must be 1.87 in. (47.5mm).
6. Bend the tang on the outer end of the float hinge outward to increase float drop and inward to decrease it.
7. Install the air horn onto the carburetor body.

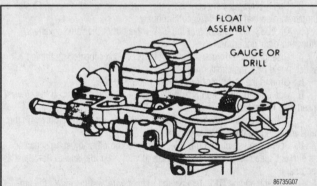

Fig. 12 Adjust the float level on Holley 5220/6520 carburetors with a properly-sized gauge or drill bit as shown

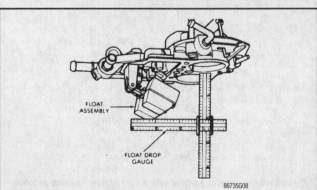

Fig. 13 Use two rulers or straightedges affixed at a right angle to correctly measure the amount of float drop

MIKUNI

♦ **See Figures 14 and 15**

➡**The Mikuni carburetor is used only on the 2.6L engine. The carburetor must be removed from the engine to perform this procedure. Also,**

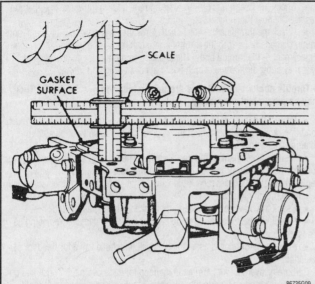

Fig. 14 Measure the float level with two rulers or straightedges as shown

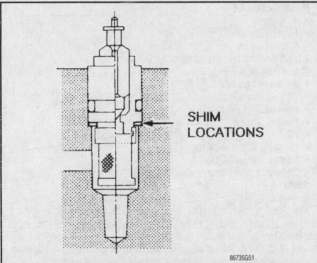

Fig. 15 The shims, which adjust the height of the float, are located under the needle seat

before attempting to adjust float level, acquire shim pack (part No. MD606952) or equivalent. These shims are placed under the float needle seat to change its position and, therefore, the float level.

1. Remove the air horn from the carburetor.
2. Invert the air horn and remove the gasket.
3. Measure the distance from the bottom of the float to the surface of the air horn. The dimension must be 0.75–0.83 in. (19–21mm).
4. If the dimension is incorrect, disassemble the float, remove the needle and unscrew the float needle seat. Change the shim under the seat or add or subtract shims as necessary. Shims are 0.30mm, 0.40mm and 0.50mm thick. Adding a shim of 0.30mm will lower the float level by three times that amount (0.90mm).

5. Reassemble the seat, needle and float and recheck the level. Repeat the process until the float level is within the required range.
6. Install the air horn onto the carburetor body.

Carburetor

REMOVAL & INSTALLATION

▶ **See Figures 16 and 17**

➡**When removing the carburetor on 2.2L engines, it should not be necessary to disturb the isolator (check it for cracks), unless it has been determined that there is a leak in it.**

1. Disconnect the negative battery terminal. Allow the engine to cool thoroughly.
2. Remove the air cleaner.
3. Remove the fuel filler cap.
4. Position a clean coffee can or similar metal container to catch fuel when the lines are disconnected. Detach the fuel inlet line and all necessary wiring from the carburetor.

➡**It is necessary to drain the coolant on the 2.6L engine before removing the coolant lines at the carburetor.**

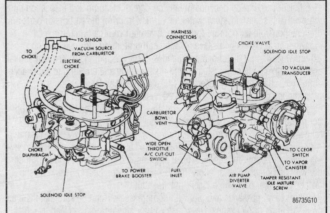

Fig. 16 Identification of Holley 5220/6250 carburetor components—2.2L engine only

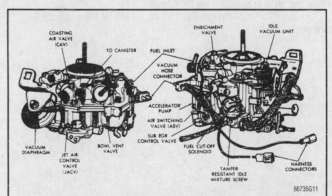

Fig. 17 Identification of the Mikuni carburetor components—2.6L engine only

5. For 2.6L engines, drain the cooling system until the level of coolant is below the carburetor. For more information on draining the engine coolant, refer to Section 1. Disconnect the coolant lines from the carburetor.

6. Disconnect the throttle linkage and all vacuum hoses from the carburetor.

7. Remove the mounting nuts and lift the carburetor off of the isolator (carburetor-to-intake manifold adapter) and intake manifold. Hold the carburetor level to avoid spilling fuel from the bowl.

8. Drain the fuel from the carburetor bowl into the fuel can used earlier.

To install:

9. Clean the carburetor, isolator and, if the isolator was removed, the intake manifold gasket surfaces.

10. Lightly lubricate the carburetor mounting studs and nuts with clean engine oil or a spray lubricant.

11. Along with a new gasket, position the carburetor onto the isolator and mounting studs. Make sure that the carburetor is mounted facing the proper direction.

12. Install and tighten the carburetor mounting nuts evenly until secure.

13. The remainder of installation is the reverse order of removal.

14. Start the engine and make all necessary carburetor adjustments, as described earlier in this section.

15. Road test the vehicle for proper operation.

OVERHAUL

Efficient carburetion depends greatly on careful cleaning and inspection during overhaul, since dirt, gum, water, or varnish in or on the carburetor parts are often responsible for poor performance. Overhaul your carburetor in a clean, dust-free area. Carefully disassemble the carburetor, referring often to the exploded views and directions packaged with the rebuilding kit. Keep all similar and look-alike parts segregated during disassembly and cleaning to avoid accidental interchange during assembly. Make a note of all jet sizes.

When the carburetor is disassembled, wash all parts (except diaphragms, electric choke units, pump plunger, and any other plastic, leather, fiber, or rubber parts) in clean carburetor solvent. Do not leave parts in the solvent any longer than is necessary to sufficiently loosen the deposits. Excessive cleaning may remove the special finish from the float bowl and choke valve bodies, leaving these parts unfit for service. Rinse all parts in clean solvent and blow them dry with compressed air or allow them to air dry. Wipe clean all cork, plastic, leather, and fiber part with a clean, lint-free cloth.

Blow out all passages and jets with compressed air and be sure that there are no restrictions or blockages. Never use wire or similar tools to clean jets, fuel passages, or air bleeds. Clean all jets and valve separately to avoid accidental interchange.

Check all parts for wear or damage. If wear or damage is found, replace the defective parts. Especially check the following.

• Check the float needle and seat for wear. If wear is found, replace the complete assembly.

• Check the float hinge pin for wear and the float(s) for dents or distortion. Replace the float if fuel has leaked into it.

• Check the throttle and choke shaft bores for wear or an out-of-round condition. Damage or wear to the throttle arm, shaft, or shaft bore will often require replacement of the throttle body. These parts require a close tolerance of fit; wear may allow air leakage, which could affect starting and idling.

➡**Throttle shafts and bushings are not included in overhaul kits. They may be purchased separately.**

• Inspect the idle mixture adjusting needles for burrs or grooves. Any such condition requires replacement of the needle, since you will not be able to obtain a satisfactory idle.

• Test the accelerator pump check valves. They should pass air one way but not the other. Test for proper seating by blowing and sucking on the valve. Replace the valve as necessary. If the valve is satisfactory, wash the valve again to remove breath moisture.

• Check the bowl cover for warped surfaces with a straightedge.

• Closely inspect the valves and seats for wear and damage, replacing as necessary.

• After the carburetor is assembled, check the choke valve for freedom of operation.

Carburetor overhaul kits are recommended for each overhaul. These kits contain all gaskets and new parts to replace those which deteriorate most rapidly. Failure to replace all parts supplied with the kit (especially gaskets) can result in poor performance later.

Some carburetor manufacturers supply overhaul kits of three basic types: minor repair; major repair; and gasket kits. Basically, they contain the following:

Minor Repair Kit—
• All gaskets
• Float needle valve
• All diaphragms
• Spring for the pump diaphragm

Major Repair Kit—
• All jets and gaskets
• All diaphragms
• Float needle valve
• Pump ball valve
• Float
• Complete intermediate rod
• Intermediate pump lever
• Some cover hold-down screws and washers

Gasket Kit—
• All gaskets

After cleaning and checking all components, reassemble the carburetor, using new parts and referring to the exploded view. When reassembling, make sure that all screws and jets are tight in their seats, but do not overtighten as the tips will be distorted. Tighten all screws gradually, in rotation. Do not tighten needle valves into their seats; uneven jetting will result. Always use new gaskets. Be sure to adjust the float level when reassembling.

CARBURETOR SPECIFICATIONS
Holley 5220/6520

Year	Carb. Part No.	Dry Float Setting (in.)	Solenoid Idle Stop (rpm)	Fast Idle Speed (rpm)	Vacuum Kick (in.)
1981	R9060A R9061A	.480	850	1100	.030
	R9125A R9126A	.480	850	1200	.030
	R9052A R9053A	.480	850	1400	.070
	R9054A R9055A	.480	850	1400	.040
	R9602A R9603A	.480	850	1500	.065
	R9604A R9605A	.480	850	1600	.065
1982	R9824A	.480	900	1400	.065
	R9503A R9504A R9750A R9751A	.480	850	1300	.085
1983	R-40003A	.480	775	1400	.070
	R-40004A	.480	900	1500	.080
	R-40005A	.480	900	1350	.080
	R-40006A	.480	850	1275	.080
	R-40007A	.480	775	1400	.070
	R-40008A	.480	900	1600	.070
	R-40010A	.480	900	1500	.080
	R-40012A	.480	900	1600	.070
	R-40014A	.480	850	1275	.080
	R-40080A	.480	850	1400	.045
	R-40081A	.480	850	1400	.045
1984	R-40060-1A	.480	see	see	.055
	R-40085-1A	.480	underhood	underhood	.040
	R-40170A R-40171A	.480	sticker	sticker	.060
	R-40067-1A R-40068-1A R-40058-1A	.480	see underhood sticker	see underhood sticker	.070
	R-40107-1A	.480			.055
	R-40064-1A R-40065-1A R-40081-1A R-40082-1A R-40071A R-40122A	.480	see underhood sticker	see underhood sticker	.080
1985	R40058A	.480	see	see	.070
	R40060A	.480	underhood	underhood	.055
	R40116A R40117A	.480	sticker	sticker	.095
	R40134A R40135A R40138A R40139A	.480	see underhood sticker	see underhood sticker	.075
1986	U.S.	.480	see	see	.075
	Canada	.480	underhood sticker	underhood sticker	.095

86735C00

CHRYSLER ELECTRONIC FUEL INJECTION (EFI) SYSTEM

✳✳ CAUTION

Whenever replacing fuel lines, it is necessary to utilize fuel hoses marked EFI/EFM or an equivalent product from the aftermarket. Whenever replacing hose clamps, use clamps incorporating a rolled edge to prevent hose damage, rather than standard aviation type clamps. This will prevent damage to the hoses that could produce dangerous leaks.

➡Experience has shown that many complaints that may occur with EFI can be traced to poor wiring or hose connections. A visual and ``wiggle'' check will help spot these most common faults and save unnecessary test and diagnosis time.

General Information

▸ See Figures 18 and 19

The computer regulated, Electronic Fuel Injection (EFI) system provides a precise air/fuel mixture ratio for all driving conditions. The fuel injection system is controlled by the Powertrain Control Module (PCM).

➡For complete explanation of the electrical aspect of the EFI system, refer to Sections 2 and 4.

The fuel system consists of the fuel tank, fuel pump, fuel filter, throttle body, fuel injector, fuel tubes and vacuum tubes. The fuel system is kept under a constant pressure of 14.5 psi (100 kPa) for 1984–90 and early 1991 Shadow and Sundance models and 39 psi (265 kPa) for 1991–95 models (except early 1991 Shadow and Sundance). **Make sure to relieve the fuel system pressure before servicing any EFI component.**

Relieving Fuel System Pressure

▸ See Figure 20

✳✳ CAUTION

Before servicing the fuel pump, fuel lines, fuel filter, throttle body, or fuel injector, release the fuel system pressure.

1. Loosen the fuel filler cap to release any built-up fuel tank pressure.
2. Detach the injector wiring harness connector at the edge of the throttle body.
3. Connect a jumper wire between terminal No. 1 of the injector harness and a good engine ground.
4. Connect a second jumper wire between terminal No. 2 of the injector harness and touch the battery positive post **for no longer than 5 seconds**—this will release the fuel system pressure.
5. Remove the jumper wires.
6. Continue with the fuel system service.

Electric Fuel Pump

REMOVAL & INSTALLATION

▸ See Figures 19 and 21

An electric fuel pump is used with fuel injection systems in order to provide higher and more uniform fuel pressures. It is located in the fuel tank.

1. Relieve the fuel system pressure, as described earlier in this section.
2. Disconnect the negative battery cable.
3. Remove the fuel tank, as described at the end of this section.
4. Using a hammer and a brass or non-metallic punch, tap the fuel pump lockring counterclockwise to release it.
5. Remove the fuel pump and old O-ring seal from the fuel tank. Discard the old seal.

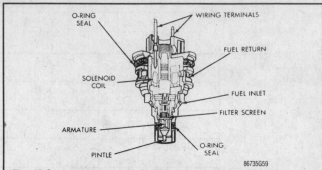

Fig. 18 Cut-away view of the inside of the single fuel injector used in the EFI system

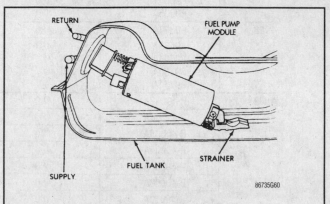

Fig. 19 The electric fuel pump is mounted in the fuel tank

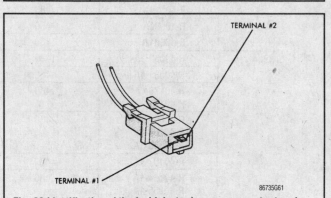

Fig. 20 Identification of the fuel injector harness connector terminals

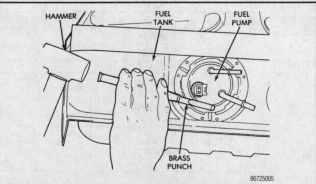

Fig. 21 Use a brass or non-metallic punch and mallet to loosen (counterclockwise) the retaining lockring

To install:

6. Wipe the seal area of the tank clean and install a new O-ring seal.

7. Replace the filter (sock) on the end of the pump if it appears to be damaged.

8. Position the pump in the fuel tank and install the locking ring. Tighten the ring in the same manner in which it was loosened, however tap the ring clockwise to tighten it

✳✳ WARNING

Do not overtighten the lockring, as this can cause fuel leakage.

9. Install the fuel tank, as described at the end of this section.

10. Connect the negative battery cable.

TESTING

♦ **See Figures 22 and 23**

➡**To perform this test, you will need a pressure gauge capable of reading pressures above 55 psi (379 kPa). The gauge must have a connection that will fit the fuel rail service valve. The gauge must be the equivalent of Chrysler pressure gauge No. C-4799 and the connector fitting compatible with pressure test adapter 6539. You may also need a T and the fittings necessary to connect the gauge into the fuel supply line at the tank, as well as a 2 gallon container suitable for collecting fuel.**

1. Release the fuel system pressure as described in Section 1.

2. Remove fuel hose quick-connect fitting from the chassis fuel line.

3. Install the adapter between the fuel supply hose and chassis fuel line assembly.

4. Hold the gauge and have someone start the engine. Run the engine at idle speed in Neutral (manual transaxles) or Park (automatic transaxles).

✳✳ CAUTION

Exercise extreme caution while under the hood with the engine running. Keep clear of all moving belts, fans, exhaust manifolds, etc.

5. Read the pressure. It should be 39 psi (265 kPa) for 1991–95 models or 14.5 psi (100 kPa) for 1984–90 and early 1991 Shadow and Sundance models. If it is not at the specified value, note the fuel pressure.

6. Stop the engine.

7. Once again depressurize the system, disconnect the gauge and replace the protective cover.

8. If the pressure is correct, the test is complete. If the pressure is below the range, proceed with the next step; if it is too high, skip to Step 12.

✳✳ WARNING

In the next step, note that fuel may drain from the lines as you disconnect them. Make sure all surrounding exhaust system parts are cool and that all sources of ignition are removed from the area. Collect fuel and dispose of it safely.

9. Connect the gauge into the fuel supply line running between the tank and the filter which is located at the rear of the vehicle.

✳✳ WARNING

Make sure all connections are secure.

10. Have an assistant start the engine, then read the pressure gauge.

a. If the pressure has risen more than 5 psi (35 kPa), replace the fuel filter.

b. If the pressure is now within range, allow the engine to cool and remove all sources of ignition; depressurize the system; disconnect the gauge from the lines; replace the fuel filter; and restore all connections.

11. If the pressure is still too low, gently and gradually pinch the fuel return line closed as you watch the gauge.

a. If the pressure increases, the fuel pressure regulator is at fault.

b. If there is no change, the problem is either clogging of the filter sock mounted on the pump or a defective pump itself.

12. If the pressure is too high, follow this procedure:

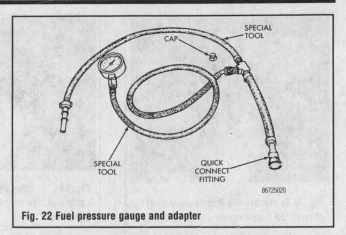

Fig. 22 Fuel pressure gauge and adapter

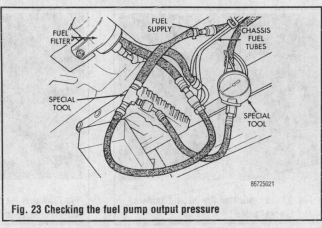

Fig. 23 Checking the fuel pump output pressure

a. Shut **OFF** the engine and allow it to cool.

b. Depressurize the fuel system, then disconnect the fuel return hose at the chassis, near the fuel tank.

c. Connect a 3 ft. (91cm) length of hose to the open end of the line running along the chassis (from the engine). Position the open end of the line into a container suitable for collecting fuel.

d. Have a helper start the engine, then check the pressure again. If it is now correct, check the in-tank fuel return hose for kinking.

e. If the in-tank fuel return hose is okay, and the system still exhibits excessive pressure with the tank half full or more, the fuel pump reservoir check valve or aspirator jet may be obstructed and the assembly must be replaced.

13. If the pressure is still too high, perform the following:

a. Shut the engine **OFF**, and allow it to cool.

b. Depressurize the system once again and reconnect the fuel lines at the rear.

c. Disconnect the fuel return hose but this time at the pressure regulator. Collect all fuel that drains.

d. Run the open connection into a large metal container.

e. Reconnect the fuel gauge to the fuel rail.

f. Start the engine and repeat the test. If the fuel pressure is now correct, clean a clogged return line or replace pinched or kinked sections of the return line. If no such problems exist, replace the fuel pressure regulator.

Throttle Body

REMOVAL & INSTALLATION

♦ **See Figures 24 thru 36**

➡**To perform this operation, you'll need a new throttle body-to-manifold gasket and new original equipment-type fuel hose clamps (with rolled edges).**

1. Allow the engine to cool completely.

2. Perform the fuel system pressure release procedure, as described earlier in this section.

Fig. 24 To remove the throttle body, first remove the return spring . . .

Fig. 25 . . . then disconnect the throttle cable and transaxle kickdown cable, if equipped

Fig. 26 Remove the cable bracket bolts, then . . .

Fig. 27 . . . position the throttle cable(s) and bracket aside

Fig. 28 Label the fuel lines and remove the air cleaner-to-throttle body gasket

Fig. 29 Detach all of the vacuum lines and electrical harness connectors . . .

Fig. 30 . . . then remove the fuel line-to-rocker arm cover retaining clamp

Fig. 31 Loosen the fuel line clamps (older models—newer models use quick-connect fittings)

Fig. 32 Remove the throttle body hold-down bolts . . .

Fig. 33 . . . then lift the throttle body off of the intake manifold

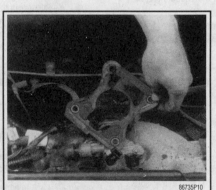

Fig. 34 Remove the old throttle body-to-intake manifold gasket and . . .

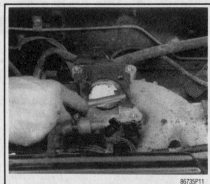

Fig. 35 . . . scrape any residual gasket material off of the mating surfaces

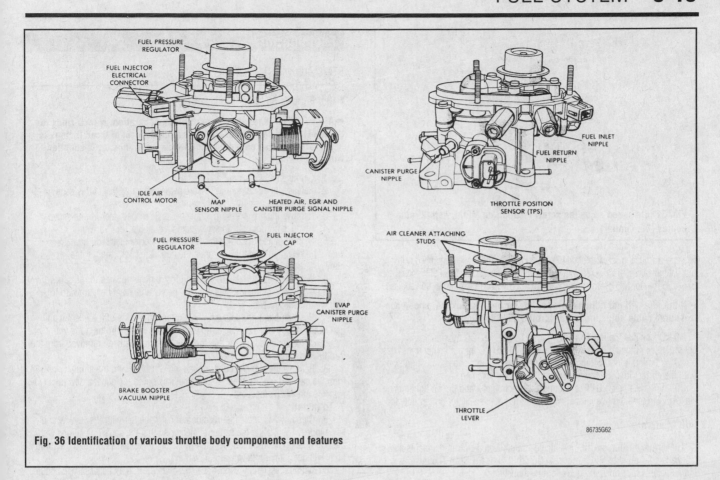

Fig. 36 Identification of various throttle body components and features

86735G62

3. Disconnect the negative battery cable.

4. Remove the air cleaner and any air hoses which may restrict access to the throttle body.

5. Label and detach all vacuum hoses and electrical harness connectors from the throttle body.

6. Disconnect the throttle cable and, on automatic transmission-equipped cars the transmission kickdown cable.

7. Remove the throttle return spring.

8. Loosen the fuel tube clamp on the rocker arm cover, if equipped.

9. Wipe the quick-connect fittings, if equipped, to remove any dirt.

10. On models not equipped with quick-connect fittings on the fuel lines, disconnect the fuel supply and return hoses by loosening the tube clamp, wrapping a rag around the hose and twisting. Collect any fuel that drains in a metal can. Remove and discard the old copper washers.

11. On models equipped with quick-connect fittings, place a shop rag under the fittings to soak up any spilled fuel, then disengage the fittings as described earlier in this section.

12. Remove the throttle body mounting bolts and lift the throttle body from the manifold. Remove the old gasket and clean both gasket surfaces.

To install:

13. Install the new gasket and carefully set the throttle body into position on the intake manifold.

14. Install the mounting bolts and torque them alternately and evenly to 160–200 inch lbs. (20–22 Nm).

15. For engines equipped with quick-connect fuel lines, lubricate the ends of the fuel supply and return tubes with clean 30 weight oil. Connect the fuel lines to the quick-connect fittings. For more information, refer to the fuel line procedures earlier in this section.

After the fuel lines are connected to the fittings, pull on the tubes to ensure that they are fully inserted and locked into position.

16. For earlier models without quick-connect fittings, reconnect the fuel supply hose to the supply connection on the throttle body using a new copper washer. Reconnect the return hose to the return connection with a new copper washer as well. Use new clamps and tighten the clamp screws to 10 inch lbs. (1.1 Nm).

17. If equipped, tighten the fuel tube clamp on the rocker arm cover.

18. Install the throttle return spring. Reconnect the throttle and, if necessary, the transaxle kickdown cable.

19. Reattach all wiring connectors and vacuum hoses removed earlier.

20. Install the air cleaner and hoses.

21. Reconnect the negative battery cable.

22. Start the engine and check for fuel leaks.

ADJUSTMENTS

Idle Speed

▶ **See Figure 37**

➡ **This procedure applies to vehicles built through 1986. The idle speed is controlled automatically by the PCM on 1987–95 models. 1987–95 models require a "Throttle Body Minimum Airflow Check Procedure" to inspect the throttle body if any idling problems are evident. This cannot be performed without utilizing an expensive electronic test system. If airflow is incorrect on 1987–95 models, the entire throttle body must be replaced.**

1. Before adjusting the idle on an electronic fuel injected vehicle the following items must be checked.

a. AIS motor has been checked for operation.

b. Engine has been checked for vacuum or EGR leaks.

c. Engine timing has been checked and set to specifications.

d. Coolant temperature sensor has been checked for operation.

2. Connect a tachometer and timing light to engine.

3. Detach the throttle body 6-way connector. Remove the brown with white tracer AIS wire from the connector, then reattach the connector.

4. Connect one end of a jumper wire to the AIS wire and the other end to the battery positive post for 5 seconds.

5. Connect a jumper to radiator fan so that it will run continuously.

6. Start and run the engine for 3 minutes to allow idle speed to stabilize.

7. With the transaxle is Neutral and using tool C-4804 or equivalent, turn the

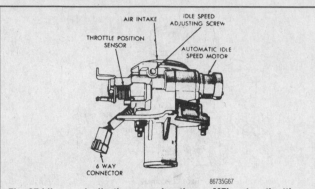

Fig. 37 Idle speed adjusting screw location on MFI system throttle bodies (EFI similar)

idle speed adjusting screw to obtain 790–810 rpm for EFI models equipped with manual transaxles, to 715–735 rpm for automatic transaxle equipped EFI models, to 675–725 rpm for MFI green engines, and or to 750–800 rpm for other MFI engines.

➡ If the idle will not adjust down, check for binding linkage, speed control servo cable adjustments, or throttle shaft binding.

8. Check that the ignition timing is at 16°–20° BTDC for vehicles equipped with manual transaxles, or at 10°–14° BTDC for automatic transaxles.

9. If timing is not within specifications, turn the idle speed adjusting screw until the correct idle speed and ignition timing are obtained.

10. Turn the engine **OFF**, disconnect the tachometer and timing light, reinstall AIS wire and remove jumper wire. Road test the vehicle for proper operation.

Idle Mixture

The air/fuel mixture on all fuel-injected cars covered by this manual is automatically controlled by the Powertrain Control Module (PCM). The mixture is not adjustable, nor does it require routine adjusting.

Fuel Injector

REMOVAL & INSTALLATION

♦ See Figures 38, 39, 40, 41 and 42

➡ A Torx® driver is required to perform this operation. New O-rings for the injector and cap should also be supplied. A set of three O-rings is necessary to re-use an old injector, while a new injector is supplied with new O-rings.

1. Remove the air cleaner and air hoses.
2. Release the fuel system pressure as described earlier in this section, then disconnect the negative battery cable.
3. Remove the fuel pressure regulator, as described later in this section.
4. Remove the Torx® head screw using a suitable Torx® driver.
5. Using pointed prytool, remove the fuel injector electrical harness connector retaining clip, then separate the connector from the throttle body.
6. With two appropriate blunt prying instruments located in the screwdriver slot on either side of the fuel injector cap, gently and evenly pry upward to remove the injector cap.
7. Position blunt prytools into the slot on either side of the injector and gently and evenly pry the injector upward and out of the throttle body unit. Once the injector is removed, check that the lower O-ring has been removed from the throttle body unit.
8. Remove the two O-rings from the injector body and the single O-ring from the cap and replace them. If the injector is being replaced, a new upper O-ring will already be installed.

To install:

9. Carefully assemble the injector and cap together with the keyway and key aligned. Then, align the cap and injector so that the cap's hole aligns with the bolt hole in the throttle body. Start the injector/cap assembly into the throttle body without applying downward pressure.
10. With the assembly almost seated, rotate the cap as necessary to ensure

Fig. 38 After removing the pressure regulator, remove the Torx® hold-down screw

Fig. 39 Remove the wiring connector retaining clip . . .

Fig. 40 . . . then separate the connector from the throttle body

Fig. 41 Lift the cap off of the fuel injector . . .

Fig. 42 . . . then lift the fuel injector out of the throttle body

perfect alignment of the cap and throttle body. Then apply gentle, downward pressure on both sides to seat the injector and cap.

11. Install the Torx® screw and tighten it to 30–35 inch lbs. (3.4–3.9 Nm).
12. Install the fuel pressure regulator, as described later in this section.
13. Connect the negative battery cable.
14. Start the engine and check for leaks with the air cleaner off, then install the air cleaner and hoses. Road test the vehicle for proper operation.

Pressure Regulator

REMOVAL & INSTALLATION

▶ See Figures 43, 44, 45 and 46

➡**Make sure to have a towel or rag on hand to absorb fuel. Supply a new O-ring and gasket for the pressure regulator.**

1. Remove the air cleaner and air hoses.
2. Release the fuel system pressure as described earlier in this section, then disconnect the negative battery cable.
3. Remove the 3 fuel pressure regulator hold-down screws, then **quickly** place a rag over the fuel inlet chamber to absorb any fuel that remains in the system. When fuel is absorbed, safely dispose of the rag.
4. Pull the pressure regulator from the throttle body. Carefully remove the old O-ring and gasket.

To install:

5. Carefully install a new O-ring and gasket onto the regulator.
6. Position the pressure regulator onto the throttle body. Press it into place squarely so as to properly seat the O-ring and gasket.
7. Install the 3 hold-down screws and tighten them to 40 inch lbs. (4.5 Nm).
8. Connect the negative battery cable.
9. Start the engine and check for fuel leaks with the air cleaner off, then install the air cleaner and hoses.

Pressure Relief Valve

The pressure relief valve on all vehicles covered by this manual is incorporated with the rollover valve into one assembly. For procedures pertaining to this component, refer to Section 4.

Fig. 44 . . . then lift the regulator off of the throttle body

Fig. 45 Remove the old gasket . . .

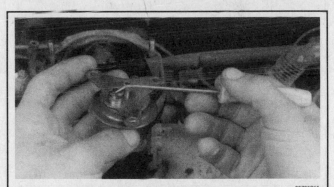

Fig. 46 . . . as well as the old O-ring from the underside of the regulator

Fig. 43 After removing the air cleaner unit, remove the regulator hold-down screws . . .

CHRYSLER MULTI-POINT FUEL INJECTION (MFI) SYSTEM

✳✳ **CAUTION**

Whenever replacing fuel lines, it is necessary to utilize fuel hoses marked EFI/EFM or an equivalent product from the aftermarket. Whenever replacing hose clamps, use clamps incorporating a rolled edge to prevent hose damage, rather than standard aviation type clamps. This will prevent damage to the hoses that could produce dangerous leaks.

➡**Experience has shown that many complaints that may occur with EFI can be traced to poor wiring or hose connections. A visual and "wiggle"** check (grasp the wiring plugs and wiggle them to check for a loose connection) will help spot these most common faults and save unnecessary test and diagnosis time.

✳✳ **CAUTION**

Before servicing any component of the Flex Fuel system make certain to read the warnings and cautions provided in Section 1. This is very important since the methanol fuel used in this system can cause severe physical injury.

General Information

▶ See Figures 47 and 48

The computer regulated, Multi-Point Fuel Injection (MFI) system provides a precise air/fuel mixture ratio for all driving conditions. The fuel injection system is controlled by the Powertrain Control Module (PCM).

➡ For complete explanation of the electrical aspect of the MFI system, refer to Sections 2 and 4.

The fuel system consists of the fuel tank, fuel pump, fuel filter, throttle body, 4 fuel injectors, fuel tubes and vacuum tubes. The fuel system is kept under a constant pressure of 53–57 psi (366–394 kPa) for all MFI engines (2.5L Flex Fuel, 2.5L Turbo I and 2.2L Turbo I, II, III, and IV engines). **Make sure to relieve the fuel system pressure before servicing any MFI component.**

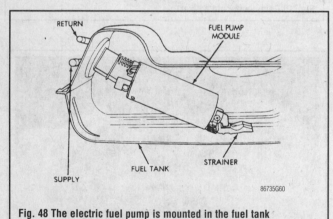

Fig. 47 Fuel supply system components which are mounted on the engine

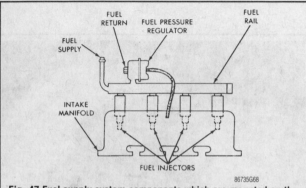

Fig. 48 The electric fuel pump is mounted in the fuel tank

Relieving Fuel System Pressure

EXCEPT 2.5L FLEX FUEL ENGINE

▶ See Figure 49

✳✳ CAUTION

Before servicing the fuel pump, fuel lines, fuel filter, throttle body, or fuel injectors, release the fuel system pressure.

1. Loosen the fuel filler cap to release any built-up fuel tank pressure.
2. Detach the injector wiring harness connector from the engine or main harness.
3. Connect a jumper wire between terminal No. 1 of the injector harness and a good engine ground.

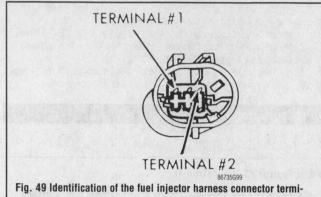

Fig. 49 Identification of the fuel injector harness connector terminals

4. Connect a second jumper wire between terminal No. 2 of the injector harness and touch the battery positive post **for no longer than 5 seconds**—this will release the fuel system pressure.
5. Remove the jumper wires.
6. Continue with the fuel system service.

2.5L FLEX FUEL ENGINE

▶ See Figures 50 and 51

✳✳ CAUTION

Before servicing any component of the Flex Fuel system make certain to read the warnings and cautions provided in Section 1 under Oil and Fuel Recommendations. This is paramount since the methanol fuel used in this system can cause severe physical injury.

1. Disconnect the negative battery cable.

✳✳ CAUTION

Service the vehicle in a well ventilated area and avoid ignition sources. Never smoke while servicing the vehicle.

2. Remove the fuel filler cap.
3. Remove the protective cap from the fuel pressure test port on the fuel rail.

➡ Fuel gauge C-4799-A contains hose C-4799–1.

4. Place the open end of the fuel pressure release hose, tool C-4799–1, into an approved gasoline container. Connect the other end of the hose C-4799–1 to the fuel pressure test port. Fuel pressure will bleed off through the hose into the gasoline container.

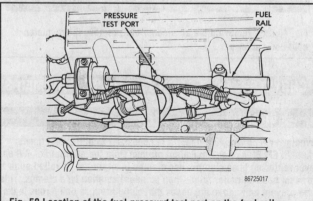

Fig. 50 Location of the fuel pressure test port on the fuel rail

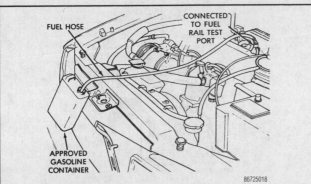

Fig. 51 Using a hose and fuel container to release the fuel system pressure on Flex Fuel engines

Electric Fuel Pump

REMOVAL & INSTALLATION

▶ See Figures 48 and 52

An electric fuel pump is used with fuel injection systems in order to provide higher and more uniform fuel pressures. It is located in the fuel tank.

1. Relieve the fuel system pressure, as described earlier in this section.
2. Disconnect the negative battery cable.
3. Remove the fuel tank, as described at the end of this section.
4. Using a hammer and a brass or non-metallic punch, tap the fuel pump lockring counterclockwise to release it.
5. Remove the fuel pump and old O-ring seal from the fuel tank. Discard the old seal.

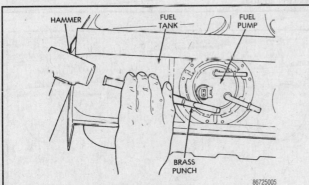

Fig. 52 Use a brass or non-metallic punch and mallet to loosen (counterclockwise) the retaining lockring

To install:

6. Wipe the seal area of the tank clean and install a new O-ring seal.
7. Replace the filter (sock) on the end of the pump if it appears to be damaged.
8. Position the pump in the fuel tank and install the locking ring. Tighten the ring in the same manner in which it was loosened, however tap the ring clockwise to tighten it

✳✳ WARNING

Do not overtighten the lockring, as this can cause fuel leakage.

9. Install the fuel tank, as described at the end of this section.
10. Connect the negative battery cable.

TESTING

▶ See Figures 53 and 54

➡To perform this test, you will need a pressure gauge capable of reading pressures above 60 psi (414 kPa). The gauge must have a connection that will fit the fuel rail service valve. The gauge will be compatible with Chrysler part No. C-3292 and the connector fitting compatible with C-4805. You may also need a Tee and fittings necessary to Tee the gauge into the fuel supply line at the tank, and a 2 gallon container suitable for collecting fuel.

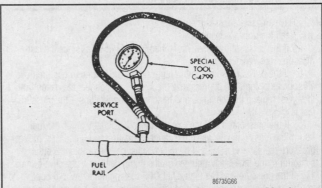

Fig. 53 A fuel pressure gauge capable of reading at least 60 psi (414 kPa) is necessary to test the fuel pump

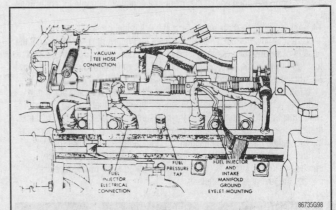

Fig. 54 To test the fuel pump, connect the fuel pressure gauge to the fuel pressure tap shown at the center of the illustration

1. Release the fuel system pressure as described earlier in this section.
2. Remove the protective cover from the service valve on the fuel rail or remove the fuel hose quick-connect fitting from the chassis line (newer models), if so equipped.
3. Connect the gauge to the pressure tap on the fuel rail or to the disconnected fuel line with a Tee.
4. While holding the gauge, have an assistant start the engine.
5. Run the engine at idle speed in Neutral (manual transaxles) or Park (automatic transaxles).
6. Read the fuel pressure; it should be 53–57 psi (365–393 kPa). If it is not within specifications, take note of it.
7. Stop the engine, depressurize the fuel system again, disconnect the gauge and replace the protective cover; attach the fuel lines if necessary.
   a. If the fuel pressure was correct, the test is complete.
   b. If the pressure was below the range proceed with the following steps.
   c. If it was too high, proceed to Step 12.

In the next step, note that fuel may drain from the lines as you disconnect them. Make sure all surrounding exhaust system parts are cool and that all sources of ignition are removed from the area. Collect fuel and dispose of it safely.

8. Tee the gauge into the fuel supply line running between the tank and the filter which is located at the rear of the vehicle.

Make sure all connections are secure.

9. Have an assistant start the engine.
10. Read the pressure gauge.
   a. If the pressure has risen more than 5 psi (34.5 kPa) since the last measurement, replace the filter.
   b. If the pressure is now within range: allow the engine to cool, remove all sources of ignition, depressurize the system, disconnect the gauge from the lines, replace the fuel filter, and restore the connections—the pressure test is complete.
   c. If the pressure is still too low, gently and gradually pinch the fuel return line closed as you watch the gauge. If the pressure increases, the fuel pressure regulator is at fault. If there is no change, the problem is either clogging of the filter sock mounted on the pump itself or a defective pump.
11. If the pressure was too high, shut **OFF** the engine, allow it to cool, depressurize the system and then disconnect the fuel return hose at the chassis, near the fuel tank.
12. Connect a 3 foot length of hose to the open end of the line running along the chassis.
13. Position the open end of the line into a container suitable for collecting fuel.
14. Ask a helper start the engine and check the fuel pressure.
   a. If it is now correct, check the in-tank fuel return hose for kinking. If the hose is okay, and the system still exhibits excessive pressure with the tank half full or more, the fuel pump reservoir check valve or aspirator jet may be obstructed and the assembly must be replaced.
   b. If the pressure is still too high, shut the engine **OFF**, and allow it to cool. Depressurize the system and then reconnect the fuel lines at the rear. Disconnect the fuel return hose at the pressure regulator. Collect all fuel that drains. Then, run the open connection into a large metal container. Connect the fuel gauge back into the fuel rail. Start the engine and repeat the test. If the fuel pressure is now correct, clean a clogged return line or replace pinched or kinked sections of the return line. If no such problems exist, replace the fuel pressure regulator.

Throttle Body

REMOVAL & INSTALLATION

▶ See Figures 55, 56 and 57

➡ The following procedure can be used on all years and models. Slight variations may occur due to extra connections, etc., but the basic procedure remains the same.

1. Disconnect the negative battery cable.
2. Remove the nuts attaching the air cleaner adapter to the throttle body, loosen the hose clamps, and remove the air cleaner adapter.
3. Remove the three control cables—accelerator, automatic transaxle kickdown (if equipped) and cruise control (if equipped) cables. Then remove the throttle cable bracket from the throttle body.
4. Label, then disengage all wiring harness connectors and vacuum hoses from the throttle body.
5. Remove the throttle body-to-intake manifold retaining nuts, then remove the throttle body and its gasket.
To install:
6. Clean the gasket surfaces and install a new gasket. Install the throttle body-to-intake manifold retaining nuts and tighten them alternately and evenly to 15 ft. lbs. (20 Nm).

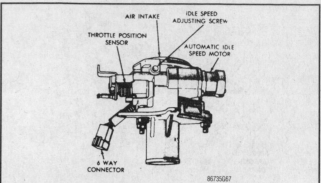

Fig. 55 Identification of throttle body related components—2.2L Turbo I and Turbo II engines

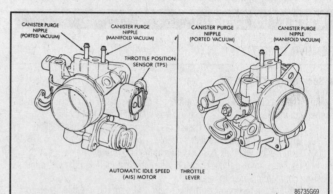

Fig. 56 Throttle body and related components—2.5L Turbo I and Flex Fuel engines

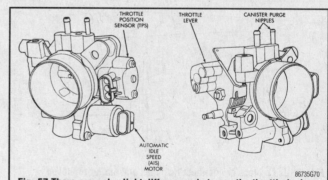

Fig. 57 There are only slight differences between the throttle body on the 2.2L Turbo III engines (shown here) and the 2.5L Turbo I and Flex Fuel engines

7. Reattach all vacuum hoses and wiring harness connectors, checking that their routing is correct and that their connections are secure.
8. Install the throttle body cable bracket. Tighten the retaining nuts until secure.
9. Attach all of the applicable throttle body cables (accelerator, transaxle kickdown and cruise control).
10. Install the air cleaner adapter and air inlet hose to the throttle body.
11. Connect the negative battery cable.
12. Road test the vehicle for proper operation.

ADJUSTMENTS

Idle Speed

The MFI system idle speed adjustment is the same as the EFI system adjustment; refer to the throttle body procedure under the Chrysler EFI system instructions earlier in this section.

Idle Mixture

The air/fuel mixture on all fuel-injected cars covered by this manual is automatically controlled by the Powertrain Control Module (PCM). The mixture is not adjustable, nor does it require routine adjusting.

Fuel Rail, Fuel Pressure Regulator and Injectors

REMOVAL & INSTALLATION

▶ See Figures 58 thru 63

✳✳ CAUTION

Before servicing any component of the Flex Fuel system make certain to read the warnings and cautions provided in Section 1. This is very important since the methanol fuel used in this system can cause severe physical injury.

➡A set of four injector nozzle protective caps and a set of new O-rings should be purchased prior to removing the fuel injectors.

1. Release fuel system pressure as described earlier in this section
2. Disconnect the negative battery cable.
3. On earlier models, loosen the hose clamp on the fuel supply hose at the fuel rail inlet and disconnect it; on newer models, unfasten the quick-connect fitting and disconnect the fuel supply hose. Collect any fuel that may drain out into a metal cup and dispose of it safely.
4. Disconnect the fuel pressure regulator vacuum hose, if equipped, from the intake manifold vacuum tree.
5. Remove the 2 fuel pressure regulator-to-intake manifold bracket screws.
6. Loosen the clamp, or unfasten the quick-connect fitting (whichever applies), at the rail end of the fuel rail-to-pressure regulator hose, then remove the regulator and hose. Collect any fuel that may drain out into a metal cup and dispose of it safely.

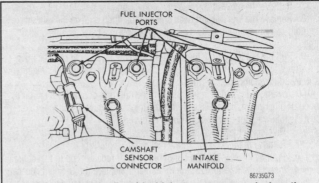

Fig. 60 Once the fuel rail and fuel injectors are removed, clean the injector bores of all dirt and grime

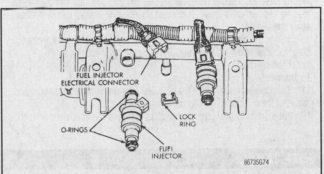

Fig. 61 The fuel injector wiring harness connector is secured to the injector with a lockring—the lockring must be removed before the injector and wiring connector can be separated

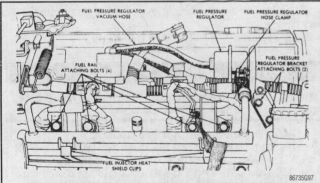

Fig. 58 The fuel rail and related components used with 2.2L Turbo I and Turbo II engines

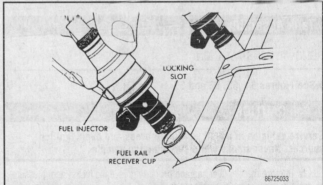

Fig. 62 Apply a drop of engine oil to the new O-ring on the injector inlet end, then gently install it to the fuel rail

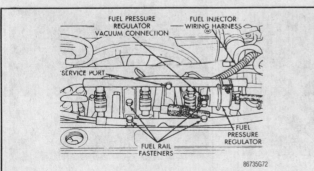

Fig. 59 The fuel rail and related components used with the newer MFI engines—2.2L Turbo III, 2.5L Turbo I and 2.5L Flex Fuel engines

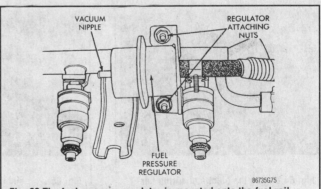

Fig. 63 The fuel pressure regulator is mounted onto the fuel rail with 2 attaching nuts

7. Remove the fuel rail-to-rocker arm cover bracket bolt.

8. Remove the fuel injector head shield clips, then remove the four intake manifold-to-rail mounting bolts. Note that one bolt retains an engine ground strap.

9. Pull the rail away from the manifold in such a way as to pull the injectors straight out of their mounting holes. They should be pulled out straight so as to avoid damaging their O-rings.

10. To remove individual injectors from the rail, first position the rail on a bench or other clean, flat surface so that the injectors are easily attached. Perform the following for each injector to be removed:

   a. Disengage the wiring connector.

   b. Remove the lockring from the fuel rail and injector.

   c. Pull the injector straight out of the injector receiver cup in the fuel rail.

   d. Inspect the injector O-rings for damage. Replace the O-ring if necessary. If the injector will be re-used and will remain off the rail while other work is performed, install a protective cap over the nozzle.

   e. Lubricate the O-ring that seals the upper end of the fuel injector with a drop of clean engine oil. Then, install the inlet end carefully into the fuel rail receiver cup. Proceed slowly and insert the injector straight in to avoid damaging the O-ring.

   f. Slide the open end of the injector lockring down over the injector and onto the ridge in the receiver cup. The lockring must lock into the slot on the top of the injector.

To install:

11. Remove all protective covers installed over the injector tips. Make sure the bores of the injector mounting holes are clean.

12. Put a drop of clean engine oil on the O-ring at the nozzle end of each injector. Then position the rail with the injectors positioned squarely in their mounting holes, then gently, and evenly, slide all four injectors into place.

13. Install the four rail mounting bolts and tighten them to 21 ft. lbs. (28 Nm). Make sure to reconnect the ground strap removed earlier.

14. Connect each wiring harness plug to its corresponding injector. Install each wiring harness into its clips. Connect the injector wiring harness to the main harness.

15. Install the heat shield clips. Install the bolt fastening the rail mounting bracket to the rocker arm cover.

16. Connect the vacuum line for the fuel pressure regulator to the vacuum tree on the manifold, then connect the fuel return hose to the fuel pressure regulator (on models not equipped with quick-connect fittings, use a wrench to hold the fuel pressure regulator while tightening the fuel tube nut), then position and tighten the clamp. On newer models, make sure that the quick-connect fitting is properly engaged. Install the bolts fastening the regulator bracket to the intake manifold.

17. Attach the fuel supply hose to the fuel rail and, if applicable, position and tighten the clamp.

18. Recheck all wiring and hose connections for routing and tightness.

19. Connect the negative battery cable, start the engine, and check for fuel leaks.

Pressure Relief Valve

The pressure relief valve on all vehicles covered by this manual is incorporated with the rollover valve into one assembly. For procedures pertaining to this component, refer to Section 4.

FUEL TANK

> ※※ **CAUTION**
>
> **Always exercise caution when servicing the fuel tank assembly as fuel vapors are extremely flammable.**

Tank Assembly

REMOVAL & INSTALLATION

▶ See Figures 64, 65, 66 and 67

> ※※ **CAUTION**
>
> **Service vehicles in a well ventilated areas and avoid ignition sources. Never smoke while servicing the vehicle.**

1. Remove the fuel filler cap and properly relieve the fuel system pressure, as described earlier in this section.

2. Disconnect the negative battery cable.

3. Loosen the lug nuts on the right rear wheel, then raise and support the rear of the vehicle using jackstands.

4. Remove the rubber cap from the drain tube. The tube is located on the rear of the fuel tank. Connect either a portable holding tank or a siphon hose to the drain tube.

5. Drain the fuel tank into a holding tank or a properly labeled gasoline safety container.

6. Remove the fuel filler tube-to-quarter panel screws.

7. Remove the right rear tire and wheel assembly.

> ※※ **CAUTION**
>
> **Keep rags handy to wipe any gasoline which may be spilled during separation of the various fuel lines and tubes.**

8. Unplug the pump and sending unit wire connectors.

9. Disconnect the fuel supply and return hoses from the fuel pump. Refer to the procedures describing fuel line removal earlier in this section.

10. Support the fuel tank with a transmission jack. Loosen the mounting straps and lower the tank slightly. Remove the hose from the pressure relief/rollover valve.

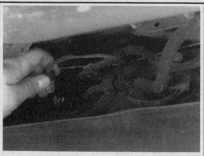

Fig. 64 Unplug the electrical wiring harness connectors from the fuel pump and sending unit . . .

Fig. 65 . . . and make sure that the connectors are clean for better electrical contact

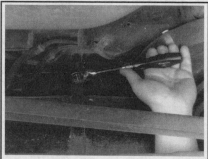

Fig. 66 Use a ratchet and socket for ease and speed when loosening the fuel tank strap bolt

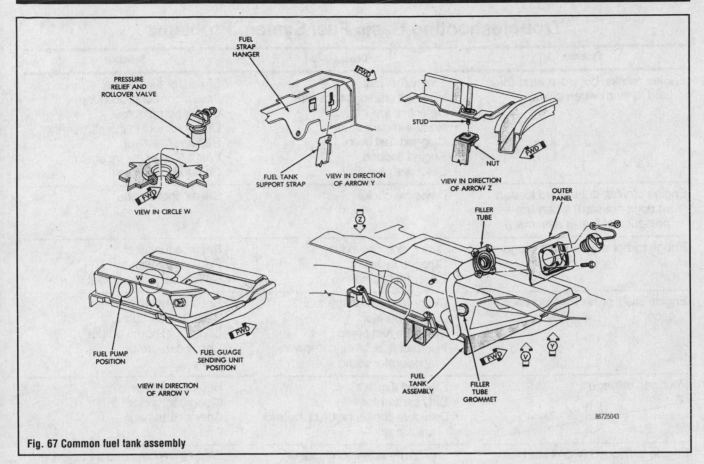

Fig. 67 Common fuel tank assembly

11. Carefully work the fuel filler tube from the tank.
12. Remove the tank mounting straps and lower the tank.

To install:

13. Position the tank on the transmission jack. Connect the vapor separator/rollover valve hose and place the insulator pad on the fuel tank. Position the vapor vent so it will not be pinched between the tank and floor pan.

14. Raise the tank and fuel filter tube carefully into position. Use a light coating of power steering fluid to ease the fuel filler tube installation. Ensure that the filler tube grommet is not damaged. Verify that the tube is installed correctly.

15. Make sure the straps are not twisted or bend, then tighten the fuel tank strap nuts to 17 ft. lbs. (23 Nm). Remove the transmission jack.

16. Lubricate the metal tubes on the fuel pump with clean SAE 30 weight engine oil. Install the quick-connect fuel fittings. Refer to the fuel fitting procedures located earlier in this section.

17. Attach the electrical connector to the fuel pump module and level sensor unit.

18. Install the rear wheel and tighten the lug nuts until snug.

19. Lower the vehicle.

20. Tighten the lug nuts on the right rear wheel.

21. Attach the filler tube to the filler neck opening in the quarter panel. Tighten the quarter panel screws to 17 inch lbs. (2 Nm).

22. Fill the fuel tank, install the filler cap, and connect the negative battery cable.

23. Start the vehicle and check for fuel leaks.

➡**When starting the engine, allow extra time for the system to pressurize itself.**

Troubleshooting Basic Fuel System Problems

Problem	Cause	Solution
Engine cranks, but won't start (or is hard to start) when cold	• Empty fuel tank • Incorrect starting procedure • Defective fuel pump • No fuel in carburetor • Clogged fuel filter • Engine flooded • Defective choke	• Check for fuel in tank • Follow correct procedure • Check pump output • Check for fuel in the carburetor • Replace fuel filter • Wait 15 minutes; try again • Check choke plate
Engine cranks, but is hard to start (or does not start) when hot— (presence of fuel is assumed)	• Defective choke	• Check choke plate
Rough idle or engine runs rough	• Dirt or moisture in fuel • Clogged air filter • Faulty fuel pump	• Replace fuel filter • Replace air filter • Check fuel pump output
Engine stalls or hesitates on acceleration	• Dirt or moisture in the fuel • Dirty carburetor • Defective fuel pump • Incorrect float level, defective accelerator pump	• Replace fuel filter • Clean the carburetor • Check fuel pump output • Check carburetor
Poor gas mileage	• Clogged air filter • Dirty carburetor • Defective choke, faulty carburetor adjustment	• Replace air filter • Clean carburetor • Check carburetor
Engine is flooded (won't start accompanied by smell of raw fuel)	• Improperly adjusted choke or carburetor	• Wait 15 minutes and try again, without pumping gas pedal • If it won't start, check carburetor

TCCA5C01

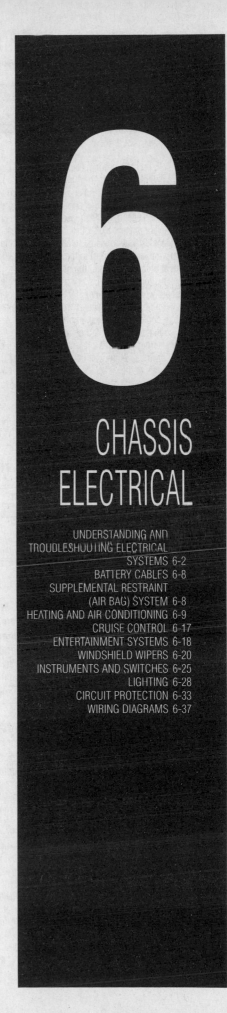

6

CHASSIS ELECTRICAL

UNDERSTANDING AND TROUBLESHOOTING ELECTRICAL SYSTEMS

Basic Electrical Theory

♦ See Figure 1

For any 12 volt, negative ground, electrical system to operate, the electricity must travel in a complete circuit. This simply means that current (power) from the positive (+) terminal of the battery must eventually return to the negative (-) terminal of the battery. Along the way, this current will travel through wires, fuses, switches and components. If, for any reason, the flow of current through the circuit is interrupted, the component fed by that circuit will cease to function properly.

Perhaps the easiest way to visualize a circuit is to think of connecting a light bulb (with two wires attached to it) to the battery—one wire attached to the negative (-) terminal of the battery and the other wire to the positive (+) terminal. With the two wires touching the battery terminals, the circuit would be complete and the light bulb would illuminate. Electricity would follow a path from the battery to the bulb and back to the battery. It's easy to see that with longer wires on our light bulb, it could be mounted anywhere. Further, one wire could be fitted with a switch so that the light could be turned on and off.

The normal automotive circuit differs from this simple example in two ways. First, instead of having a return wire from the bulb to the battery, the current travels through the frame of the vehicle. Since the negative (-) battery cable is attached to the frame (made of electrically conductive metal), the frame of the vehicle can serve as a ground wire to complete the circuit. Secondly, most automotive circuits contain multiple components which receive power from a single circuit. This lessens the amount of wire needed to power components on the vehicle.

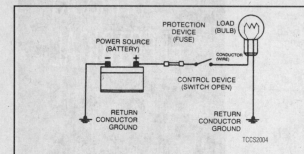

Fig. 1 This example illustrates a simple circuit. When the switch is closed, power from the positive (+) battery terminal flows through the fuse and the switch, and then to the light bulb. The light illuminates and the circuit is completed through the ground wire back to the negative (-) battery terminal. In reality, the two ground points shown in the illustration are attached to the metal frame of the vehicle, which completes the circuit back to the battery

HOW DOES ELECTRICITY WORK: THE WATER ANALOGY

Electricity is the flow of electrons—the subatomic particles that constitute the outer shell of an atom. Electrons spin in an orbit around the center core of an atom. The center core is comprised of protons (positive charge) and neutrons (neutral charge). Electrons have a negative charge and balance out the positive charge of the protons. When an outside force causes the number of electrons to unbalance the charge of the protons, the electrons will split off the atom and look for another atom to balance out. If this imbalance is kept up, electrons will continue to move and an electrical flow will exist.

Many people have been taught electrical theory using an analogy with water. In a comparison with water flowing through a pipe, the electrons would be the water and the wire is the pipe.

The flow of electricity can be measured much like the flow of water through a pipe. The unit of measurement used is amperes, frequently abbreviated as amps (a). You can compare amperage to the volume of water flowing through a pipe. When connected to a circuit, an ammeter will measure the actual amount of current flowing through the circuit. When relatively few electrons flow through a circuit, the amperage is low. When many electrons flow, the amperage is high.

Water pressure is measured in units such as pounds per square inch (psi);

The electrical pressure is measured in units called volts (v). When a voltmeter is connected to a circuit, it is measuring the electrical pressure.

The actual flow of electricity depends not only on voltage and amperage, but also on the resistance of the circuit. The higher the resistance, the higher the force necessary to push the current through the circuit. The standard unit for measuring resistance is an ohm. Resistance in a circuit varies depending on the amount and type of components used in the circuit. The main factors which determine resistance are:

• Material—some materials have more resistance than others. Those with high resistance are said to be insulators. Rubber materials (or rubber-like plastics) are some of the most common insulators used in vehicles as they have a very high resistance to electricity. Very low resistance materials are said to be conductors. Copper wire is among the best conductors. Silver is actually a superior conductor to copper and is used in some relay contacts, but its high cost prohibits its use as common wiring. Most automotive wiring is made of copper.

• Size—the larger the wire size being used, the less resistance the wire will have. This is why components which use large amounts of electricity usually have large wires supplying current to them.

• Length—for a given thickness of wire, the longer the wire, the greater the resistance. The shorter the wire, the less the resistance. When determining the proper wire for a circuit, both size and length must be considered to design a circuit that can handle the current needs of the component.

• Temperature—with many materials, the higher the temperature, the greater the resistance (positive temperature coefficient). Some materials exhibit the opposite trait of lower resistance with higher temperatures (negative temperature coefficient). These principles are used in many of the sensors on the engine.

OHM'S LAW

There is a direct relationship between current, voltage and resistance. The relationship between current, voltage and resistance can be summed up by a statement known as Ohm's law.

Voltage (E) is equal to amperage (I) times resistance (R): $E = I \times R$

Other forms of the formula are $R = E/I$ and $I = E/R$

In each of these formulas, E is the voltage in volts, I is the current in amps and R is the resistance in ohms. The basic point to remember is that as the resistance of a circuit goes up, the amount of current that flows in the circuit will go down, if voltage remains the same.

The amount of work that the electricity can perform is expressed as power. The unit of power is the watt (w). The relationship between power, voltage and current is expressed as:

Power (w) is equal to amperage (I) times voltage (E): $W = I \times E$

This is only true for direct current (DC) circuits; The alternating current formula is a tad different, but since the electrical circuits in most vehicles are DC type, we need not get into AC circuit theory.

Electrical Components

POWER SOURCE

Power is supplied to the vehicle by two devices: The battery and the alternator. The battery supplies electrical power during starting or during periods when the current demand of the vehicle's electrical system exceeds the output capacity of the alternator. The alternator supplies electrical current when the engine is running. Just not does the alternator supply the current needs of the vehicle, but it recharges the battery.

The Battery

In most modern vehicles, the battery is a lead/acid electrochemical device consisting of six 2 volt subsections (cells) connected in series, so that the unit is capable of producing approximately 12 volts of electrical pressure. Each subsection consists of a series of positive and negative plates held a short distance apart in a solution of sulfuric acid and water.

The two types of plates are of dissimilar metals. This sets up a chemical reaction, and it is this reaction which produces current flow from the battery when its positive and negative terminals are connected to an electrical load .

The power removed from the battery is replaced by the alternator, restoring the battery to its original chemical state.

The Alternator

On some vehicles there isn't an alternator, but a generator. The difference is that an alternator supplies alternating current which is then changed to direct current for use on the vehicle, while a generator produces direct current. Alternators tend to be more efficient and that is why they are used.

Alternators and generators are devices that consist of coils of wires wound together making big electromagnets. One group of coils spins within another set and the interaction of the magnetic fields causes a current to flow. This current is then drawn off the coils and fed into the vehicles electrical system.

GROUND

Two types of grounds are used in automotive electric circuits. Direct ground components are grounded to the frame through their mounting points. All other components use some sort of ground wire which is attached to the frame or chassis of the vehicle. The electrical current runs through the chassis of the vehicle and returns to the battery through the ground (-) cable; if you look, you'll see that the battery ground cable connects between the battery and the frame or chassis of the vehicle.

➡It should be noted that a good percentage of electrical problems can be traced to bad grounds.

PROTECTIVE DEVICES

♦ See Figure 2

It is possible for large surges of current to pass through the electrical system of your vehicle. If this surge of current were to reach the load in the circuit, the

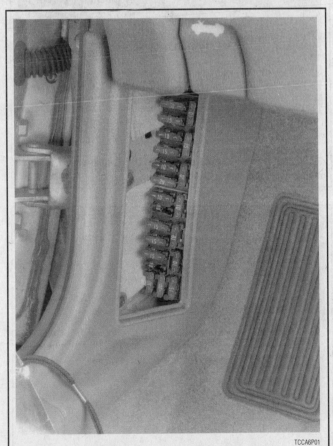

Fig. 2 Most vehicles use one or more fuse panels. This one is located on the driver's side kick panel

surge could burn it out or severely damage it. It can also overload the wiring, causing the harness to get hot and melt the insulation. To prevent this, fuses, circuit breakers and/or fusible links are connected into the supply wires of the electrical system. These items are nothing more than a built-in weak spot in the system. When an abnormal amount of current flows through the system, these protective devices work as follows to protect the circuit:

• Fuse—when an excessive electrical current passes through a fuse, the fuse "blows" (the conductor melts) and opens the circuit, preventing the passage of current.

• Circuit Breaker—a circuit breaker is basically a self-repairing fuse. It will open the circuit in the same fashion as a fuse, but when the surge subsides, the circuit breaker can be reset and does not need replacement.

• Fusible Link—a fusible link (fuse link or main link) is a short length of special, high temperature insulated wire that acts as a fuse. When an excessive electrical current passes through a fusible link, the thin gauge wire inside the link melts, creating an intentional open to protect the circuit. To repair the circuit, the link must be replaced. Some newer type fusible links are housed in plug-in modules, which are simply replaced like a fuse, while older type fusible links must be cut and spliced if they melt. Since this link is very early in the electrical path, it's the first place to look if nothing on the vehicle works, yet the battery seems to be charged and is properly connected.

✳✳ CAUTION

Always replace fuses, circuit breakers and fusible links with identically rated components. Under no circumstances should a component of higher or lower amperage rating be substituted.

SWITCHES & RELAYS

♦ See Figures 3 and 4

Switches are used in electrical circuits to control the passage of current. The most common use is to open and close circuits between the battery and the various electric devices in the system. Switches are rated according to the amount of amperage they can handle. If a sufficient amperage rated switch is not used in a circuit, the switch could overload and cause damage.

Some electrical components which require a large amount of current to operate use a special switch called a relay. Since these circuits carry a large amount of current, the thickness of the wire in the circuit is also greater. If this large wire were connected from the load to the control switch, the switch would have to carry the high amperage load and the fairing or dash would be twice as large to accommodate the increased size of the wiring harness. To prevent these problems, a relay is used.

Relays are composed of a coil and a set of contacts. When the coil has a current passed though it, a magnetic field is formed and this field causes the contacts to move together, completing the circuit. Most relays are normally open, prevent-

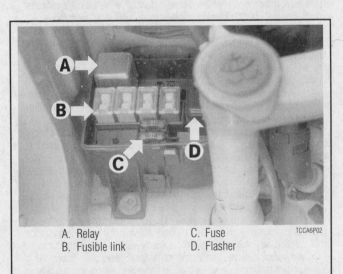

A. Relay
B. Fusible link
C. Fuse
D. Flasher

TCCA6P02

Fig. 3 The underhood fuse and relay panel usually contains fuses, relays, flashers and fusible links

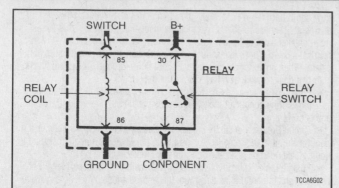

Fig. 4 Relays are composed of a coil and a switch. These two components are linked together so that when one operates, the other operates at the same time. The large wires in the circuit are connected from the battery to one side of the relay switch (B+) and from the opposite side of the relay switch to the load (component). Smaller wires are connected from the relay coil to the control switch for the circuit and from the opposite side of the relay coil to ground

ing current from passing through the circuit, but they can take any electrical form depending on the job they are intended to do. Relays can be considered "remote control switches." They allow a smaller current to operate devices that require higher amperages. When a small current operates the coil, a larger current is allowed to pass by the contacts. Some common circuits which may use relays are the horn, headlights, starter, electric fuel pump and other high draw circuits.

LOAD

Every electrical circuit must include a "load" (something to use the electricity coming from the source). Without this load, the battery would attempt to deliver its entire power supply from one pole to another. This is called a "short circuit." All this electricity would take a short cut to ground and cause a great amount of damage to other components in the circuit by developing a tremendous amount of heat. This condition could develop sufficient heat to melt the insulation on all the surrounding wires and reduce a multiple wire cable to a lump of plastic and copper.

WIRING & HARNESSES

The average vehicle contains meters and meters of wiring, with hundreds of individual connections. To protect the many wires from damage and to keep them from becoming a confusing tangle, they are organized into bundles, enclosed in plastic or taped together and called wiring harnesses. Different harnesses serve different parts of the vehicle. Individual wires are color coded to help trace them through a harness where sections are hidden from view.

Automotive wiring or circuit conductors can be either single strand wire, multi-strand wire or printed circuitry. Single strand wire has a solid metal core and is usually used inside such components as alternators, motors, relays and other devices. Multi-strand wire has a core made of many small strands of wire twisted together into a single conductor. Most of the wiring in an automotive electrical system is made up of multi-strand wire, either as a single conductor or grouped together in a harness. All wiring is color coded on the insulator, either as a solid color or as a colored wire with an identification stripe. A printed circuit is a thin film of copper or other conductor that is printed on an insulator backing. Occasionally, a printed circuit is sandwiched between two sheets of plastic for more protection and flexibility. A complete printed circuit, consisting of conductors, insulating material and connectors for lamps or other components is called a printed circuit board. Printed circuitry is used in place of individual wires or harnesses in places where space is limited, such as behind instrument panels.

Since automotive electrical systems are very sensitive to changes in resistance, the selection of properly sized wires is critical when systems are repaired. A loose or corroded connection or a replacement wire that is too small for the circuit will add extra resistance and an additional voltage drop to the circuit.

The wire gauge number is an expression of the cross-section area of the conductor. Vehicles from countries that use the metric system will typically describe the wire size as its cross-sectional area in square millimeters. In this method, the larger the wire, the greater the number. Another common system for

expressing wire size is the American Wire Gauge (AWG) system. As gauge number increases, area decreases and the wire becomes smaller. An 18 gauge wire is smaller than a 4 gauge wire. A wire with a higher gauge number will carry less current than a wire with a lower gauge number. Gauge wire size refers to the size of the strands of the conductor, not the size of the complete wire with insulator. It is possible, therefore, to have two wires of the same gauge with different diameters because one may have thicker insulation than the other.

It is essential to understand how a circuit works before trying to figure out why it doesn't. An electrical schematic shows the electrical current paths when a circuit is operating properly. Schematics break the entire electrical system down into individual circuits. In a schematic, usually no attempt is made to represent wiring and components as they physically appear on the vehicle; switches and other components are shown as simply as possible. Face views of harness connectors show the cavity or terminal locations in all multi-pin connectors to help locate test points.

CONNECTORS

▶ See Figures 5 and 6

Three types of connectors are commonly used in automotive applications—weatherproof, molded and hard shell.

• Weatherproof—these connectors are most commonly used where the connector is exposed to the elements. Terminals are protected against moisture and dirt by sealing rings which provide a weathertight seal. All repairs require the use of a special terminal and the tool required to service it. Unlike standard blade type terminals, these weatherproof terminals cannot be straightened once they are bent. Make certain that the connectors are properly seated and all of the sealing rings are in place when connecting leads.

Fig. 5 Hard shell (left) and weatherproof (right) connectors have replaceable terminals

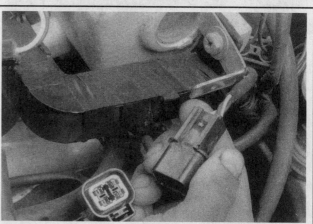

Fig. 6 Weatherproof connectors are most commonly used in the engine compartment or where the connector is exposed to the elements

• Molded—these connectors require complete replacement of the connector if found to be defective. This means splicing a new connector assembly into the harness. All splices should be soldered to insure proper contact. Use care when probing the connections or replacing terminals in them, as it is possible to create a short circuit between opposite terminals. If this happens to the wrong terminal pair, it is possible to damage certain components. Always use jumper wires between connectors for circuit checking and NEVER probe through weatherproof seals.

• Hard Shell—unlike molded connectors, the terminal contacts in hard-shell connectors can be replaced. Replacement usually involves the use of a special terminal removal tool that depresses the locking tangs (barbs) on the connector terminal and allows the connector to be removed from the rear of the shell. The connector shell should be replaced if it shows any evidence of burning, melting, cracks, or breaks. Replace individual terminals that are burnt, corroded, distorted or loose.

Test Equipment

Pinpointing the exact cause of trouble in an electrical circuit is most times accomplished by the use of special test equipment. The following describes different types of commonly used test equipment and briefly explains how to use them in diagnosis. In addition to the information covered below, the tool manufacturer's instructions booklet (provided with the tester) should be read and clearly understood before attempting any test procedures.

JUMPER WIRES

✳✳ CAUTION

Never use jumper wires made from a thinner gauge wire than the circuit being tested. If the jumper wire is of too small a gauge, it may overheat and possibly melt. Never use jumpers to bypass high resistance loads in a circuit. Bypassing resistances, in effect, creates a short circuit. This may, in turn, cause damage and fire. Jumper wires should only be used to bypass lengths of wire or to simulate switches.

Jumper wires are simple, yet extremely valuable, pieces of test equipment. They are basically test wires which are used to bypass sections of a circuit. Although jumper wires can be purchased, they are usually fabricated from lengths of standard automotive wire and whatever type of connector (alligator clip, spade connector or pin connector) that is required for the particular application being tested. In cramped, hard-to-reach areas, it is advisable to have insulated boots over the jumper wire terminals in order to prevent accidental grounding. It is also advisable to include a standard automotive fuse in any jumper wire. This is commonly referred to as a "fused jumper". By inserting an in-line fuse holder between a set of test leads, a fused jumper wire can be used for bypassing open circuits. Use a 5 amp fuse to provide protection against voltage spikes.

Jumper wires are used primarily to locate open electrical circuits, on either the ground (-) side of the circuit or on the power (+) side. If an electrical component fails to operate, connect the jumper wire between the component and a good ground. If the component operates only with the jumper installed, the ground circuit is open. If the ground circuit is good, but the component does not operate, the circuit between the power feed and component may be open. By moving the jumper wire successively back from the component toward the power source, you can isolate the area of the circuit where the open is located. When the component stops functioning, or the power is cut off, the open is in the segment of wire between the jumper and the point previously tested.

You can sometimes connect the jumper wire directly from the battery to the "hot" terminal of the component, but first make sure the component uses 12 volts in operation. Some electrical components, such as fuel injectors or sensors, are designed to operate on about 4 to 5 volts, and running 12 volts directly to these components will cause damage.

TEST LIGHTS

▶ **See Figure 7**

The test light is used to check circuits and components while electrical current is flowing through them. It is used for voltage and ground tests. To use a 12 volt test light, connect the ground clip to a good ground and probe wherever

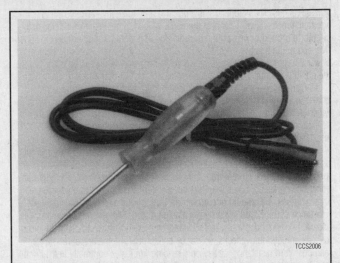

TCCS2006

Fig. 7 A 12 volt test light is used to detect the presence of voltage in a circuit

necessary with the pick. The test light will illuminate when voltage is detected. This does not necessarily mean that 12 volts (or any particular amount of voltage) is present; it only means that some voltage is present. It is advisable before using the test light to touch its ground clip and probe across the battery posts or terminals to make sure the light is operating properly.

✳✳ WARNING

Do not use a test light to probe electronic ignition, spark plug or coil wires. Never use a pick-type test light to probe wiring on computer controlled systems unless specifically instructed to do so. Any wire insulation that is pierced by the test light probe should be taped and sealed with silicone after testing.

Like the jumper wire, the 12 volt test light is used to isolate opens in circuits. But, whereas the jumper wire is used to bypass the open to operate the load, the 12 volt test light is used to locate the presence of voltage in a circuit. If the test light illuminates, there is power up to that point in the circuit; if the test light does not illuminate, there is an open circuit (no power). Move the test light in successive steps back toward the power source until the light in the handle illuminates. The open is between the probe and a point which was previously probed.

The self-powered test light is similar in design to the 12 volt test light, but contains a 1.5 volt penlight battery in the handle. It is most often used in place of a multimeter to check for open or short circuits when power is isolated from the circuit (continuity test).

The battery in a self-powered test light does not provide much current. A weak battery may not provide enough power to illuminate the test light even when a complete circuit is made (especially if there is high resistance in the circuit). Always make sure that the test battery is strong. To check the battery, briefly touch the ground clip to the probe; if the light glows brightly, the battery is strong enough for testing.

➡ **A self-powered test light should not be used on any computer controlled system or component. The small amount of electricity transmitted by the test light is enough to damage many electronic automotive components.**

MULTIMETERS

Multimeters are an extremely useful tool for troubleshooting electrical problems. They can be purchased in either analog or digital form and have a price range to suit any budget. A multimeter is a voltmeter, ammeter and ohmmeter (along with other features) combined into one instrument. It is often used when testing solid state circuits because of its high input impedance (usually 10 megaohms or more). A brief description of the multimeter main test functions follows:

• Voltmeter—the voltmeter is used to measure voltage at any point in a circuit, or to measure the voltage drop across any part of a circuit. Voltmeters usually have various scales and a selector switch to allow the reading of different voltage ranges. The voltmeter has a positive and a negative lead. To avoid damage to the meter, always connect the negative lead to the negative (-) side of the circuit (to ground or nearest the ground side of the circuit) and connect the positive lead to the positive (+) side of the circuit (to the power source or the nearest power source). Note that the negative voltmeter lead will always be black and that the positive voltmeter will always be some color other than black (usually red).

• Ohmmeter—the ohmmeter is designed to read resistance (measured in ohms) in a circuit or component. Most ohmmeters will have a selector switch which permits the measurement of different ranges of resistance (usually the selector switch allows the multiplication of the meter reading by 10, 100, 1,000 and 10,000). Some ohmmeters are "auto-ranging" which means the meter itself will determine which scale to use. Since the meters are powered by an internal battery, the ohmmeter can be used like a self-powered test light. When the ohmmeter is connected, current from the ohmmeter flows through the circuit or component being tested. Since the ohmmeter's internal resistance and voltage are known values, the amount of current flow through the meter depends on the resistance of the circuit or component being tested. The ohmmeter can also be used to perform a continuity test for suspected open circuits. In using the meter for making continuity checks, do not be concerned with the actual resistance readings. Zero resistance, or any ohm reading, indicates continuity in the circuit. Infinite resistance indicates an opening in the circuit. A high resistance reading where there should be none indicates a problem in the circuit. Checks for short circuits are made in the same manner as checks for open circuits, except that the circuit must be isolated from both power and normal ground. Infinite resistance indicates no continuity, while zero resistance indicates a dead short.

❄ WARNING

Never use an ohmmeter to check the resistance of a component or wire while there is voltage applied to the circuit.

• Ammeter—an ammeter measures the amount of current flowing through a circuit in units called amperes or amps. At normal operating voltage, most circuits have a characteristic amount of amperes, called "current draw" which can be measured using an ammeter. By referring to a specified current draw rating, then measuring the amperes and comparing the two values, one can determine what is happening within the circuit to aid in diagnosis. An open circuit, for example, will not allow any current to flow, so the ammeter reading will be zero. A damaged component or circuit will have an increased current draw, so the reading will be high. The ammeter is always connected in series with the circuit being tested. All of the current that normally flows through the circuit must also flow through the ammeter; if there is any other path for the current to follow, the ammeter reading will not be accurate. The ammeter itself has very little resistance to current flow and, therefore, will not affect the circuit, but it will measure current draw only when the circuit is closed and electricity is flowing. Excessive current draw can blow fuses and drain the battery, while a reduced current draw can cause motors to run slowly, lights to dim and other components to not operate properly.

Troubleshooting Electrical Systems

When diagnosing a specific problem, organized troubleshooting is a must. The complexity of a modern automotive vehicle demands that you approach any problem in a logical, organized manner. There are certain troubleshooting techniques, however, which are standard:

• Establish when the problem occurs. Does the problem appear only under certain conditions? Were there any noises, odors or other unusual symptoms? Isolate the problem area. To do this, make some simple tests and observations, then eliminate the systems that are working properly. Check for obvious problems, such as broken wires and loose or dirty connections. Always check the obvious before assuming something complicated is the cause.

• Test for problems systematically to determine the cause once the problem area is isolated. Are all the components functioning properly? Is there power going to electrical switches and motors. Performing careful, systematic checks will often turn up most causes on the first inspection, without wasting time checking components that have little or no relationship to the problem.

• Test all repairs after the work is done to make sure that the problem is fixed. Some causes can be traced to more than one component, so a careful verification of repair work is important in order to pick up additional malfunctions that may cause a problem to reappear or a different problem to arise. A blown fuse, for example, is a simple problem that may require more than another fuse to repair. If you don't look for a problem that caused a fuse to blow, a shorted wire (for example) may go undetected.

Experience has shown that most problems tend to be the result of a fairly simple and obvious cause, such as loose or corroded connectors, bad grounds or damaged wire insulation which causes a short. This makes careful visual inspection of components during testing essential to quick and accurate troubleshooting.

Testing

OPEN CIRCUITS

▶ **See Figure 8**

This test already assumes the existence of an open in the circuit and it is used to help locate the open portion.

1. Isolate the circuit from power and ground.
2. Connect the self-powered test light or ohmmeter ground clip to the ground side of the circuit and probe sections of the circuit sequentially.
3. If the light is out or there is infinite resistance, the open is between the probe and the circuit ground.
4. If the light is on or the meter shows continuity, the open is between the probe and the end of the circuit toward the power source.

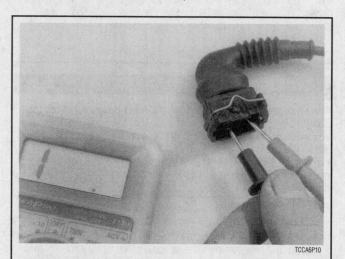

TCCA6P10

Fig. 8 The infinite reading on this multimeter indicates that the circuit is open

SHORT CIRCUITS

➡ **Never use a self-powered test light to perform checks for opens or shorts when power is applied to the circuit under test. The test light can be damaged by outside power.**

1. Isolate the circuit from power and ground.
2. Connect the self-powered test light or ohmmeter ground clip to a good ground and probe any easy-to-reach point in the circuit.
3. If the light comes on or there is continuity, there is a short somewhere in the circuit.
4. To isolate the short, probe a test point at either end of the isolated circuit (the light should be on or the meter should indicate continuity).
5. Leave the test light probe engaged and sequentially open connectors or switches, remove parts, etc. until the light goes out or continuity is broken.
6. When the light goes out, the short is between the last two circuit components which were opened.

VOLTAGE

This test determines voltage available from the battery and should be the first step in any electrical troubleshooting procedure after visual inspection. Many electrical problems, especially on computer controlled systems, can be caused by a low state of charge in the battery. Excessive corrosion at the battery cable terminals can cause poor contact that will prevent proper charging and full battery current flow.

1. Set the voltmeter selector switch to the 20V position.

2. Connect the multimeter negative lead to the battery's negative (-) post or terminal and the positive lead to the battery's positive (+) post or terminal.

3. Turn the ignition switch **ON** to provide a load.

4. A well charged battery should register over 12 volts. If the meter reads below 11.5 volts, the battery power may be insufficient to operate the electrical system properly.

VOLTAGE DROP

▶ **See Figure 9**

When current flows through a load, the voltage beyond the load drops. This voltage drop is due to the resistance created by the load and also by small resistances created by corrosion at the connectors and damaged insulation on the wires. The maximum allowable voltage drop under load is critical, especially if there is more than one load in the circuit, since all voltage drops are cumulative.

1. Set the voltmeter selector switch to the 20 volt position.

2. Connect the multimeter negative lead to a good ground.

3. Operate the circuit and check the voltage prior to the first component (load).

4. There should be little or no voltage drop in the circuit prior to the first component. If a voltage drop exists, the wire or connectors in the circuit are suspect.

5. While operating the first component in the circuit, probe the ground side of the component with the positive meter lead and observe the voltage readings. A small voltage drop should be noticed. This voltage drop is caused by the resistance of the component.

6. Repeat the test for each component (load) down the circuit.

7. If a large voltage drop is noticed, the preceding component, wire or connector is suspect.

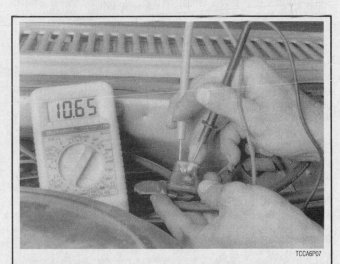

Fig. 9 This voltage drop test revealed high resistance (low voltage) in the circuit

RESISTANCE

▶ **See Figures 10 and 11**

✳✳ WARNING

Never use an ohmmeter with power applied to the circuit. The ohmmeter is designed to operate on its own power supply. The normal 12 volt electrical system voltage could damage the meter!

1. Isolate the circuit from the vehicle's power source.

2. Ensure that the ignition key is **OFF** when disconnecting any components or the battery.

3. Where necessary, also isolate at least one side of the circuit to be checked, in order to avoid reading parallel resistances. Parallel circuit resistances will always give a lower reading than the actual resistance of either of the branches.

4. Connect the meter leads to both sides of the circuit (wire or component) and read the actual measured ohms on the meter scale. Make sure the selector switch is set to the proper ohm scale for the circuit being tested, to avoid misreading the ohmmeter test value.

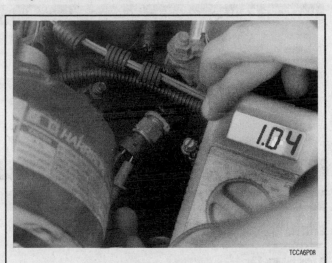

Fig. 10 Checking the resistance of a coolant temperature sensor with an ohmmeter. Reading is 1.04 kilohms

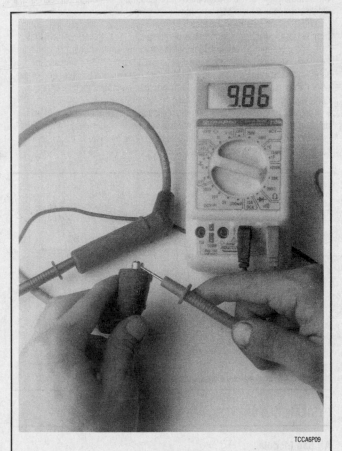

Fig. 11 Spark plug wires can be checked for excessive resistance using an ohmmeter

Wire and Connector Repair

Almost anyone can replace damaged wires, as long as the proper tools and parts are available. Wire and terminals are available to fit almost any need. Even the specialized weatherproof, molded and hard shell connectors are now available from aftermarket suppliers.

Be sure the ends of all the wires are fitted with the proper terminal hardware and connectors. Wrapping a wire around a stud is never a permanent solution and will only cause trouble later. Replace wires one at a time to avoid confusion. Always route wires exactly the same as the factory.

➡**If connector repair is necessary, only attempt it if you have the proper tools. Weatherproof and hard shell connectors require special tools to release the pins inside the connector. Attempting to repair these connectors with conventional hand tools will damage them.**

BATTERY CABLES

When detaching the battery cables from the battery it is important to remove the cables in a particular order to minimize the chance of personal injury and component damage. The negative (-) battery cable should be removed first to stop the body of the car from being an active ground. After the negative cable is removed and set aside, the positive cable can be removed from the battery. The cables, once removed, can be cleaned with a solution of water and baking soda to remove any corrosion.

If the positive (+) battery cable is detached first, the chance of grounding the positive terminal against the negatively charged car body with a wrench or other metal tool is much greater. If the battery is so grounded, the battery, alternator, PCM or other fragile electronic components may be damaged by electrical surges, or any flammable gases may be ignited by the sparks produced by the electrical arcing, leading to possible fatal personal injury.

The battery cables should also not be detached with the ignition in the **ON** position. The sudden removal of the electric current can cause numerous electrical surges throughout the electrical system. These surges can damage any of the various voltage sensitive components such as the PCM. Always make certain that the ignition switch is turned **OFF**.

SUPPLEMENTAL RESTRAINT (AIR BAG) SYSTEM

General Information

SYSTEM OPERATION

◗ **See Figure 12**

The Supplemental Restraint System (SRS) is designed to work in concert with the seat belts to further prevent personal injury during a head-on collision with another object. The SRS utilizes an air bag module, front impact sensors, a clockspring, and a diagnostic module.

With the battery cables connected, the SRS system is energized and monitoring the front impact sensors and the safing sensor for collision confirmation messages. When the vehicle strikes, or is struck by, another object (such as a tree, wall, another vehicle, etc.), the front impact sensors and safing sensor send impulses to the diagnostic module, which determines the force and direction of the impact. Based on this information the diagnostic module either deploys or does not deploy the air bag.

The only time that the SRS is completely disarmed with no chance of accidental deployment is when the battery cables have been detached from the battery and set aside, and at least 2 minutes have gone by to allow the system capacitor to discharge any residual energy.

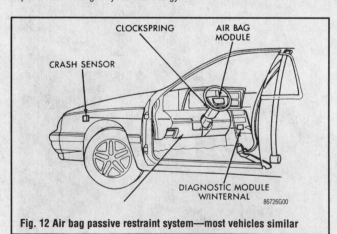

Fig. 12 Air bag passive restraint system—most vehicles similar

SYSTEM COMPONENTS

Air Bag Module

The air bag module is the most visible part of the system. It contains the air bag cushion and its supporting components. The air bag module contains a housing to which the cushion and inflator are attached and sealed.

The inflator assembly is mounted to the back of the module housing. When supplied with the proper electrical signal, the inflator assembly produces a gas which discharges directly into the cushion. A protective cover is fitted to the front of the air bag module and forms a decorative cover in the center of the steering wheel. The air bag module is mounted directly to the steering wheel.

Front Impact Sensors

The driver air bag system is a safety device designed to reduce the risk of fatality or serious injury, caused by a frontal impact of the vehicle.

The impact sensors provide verification of the direction and severity of the impact. Three impact sensors are used. One is called a safing sensor. It is located inside the diagnostic module which is mounted on the floor pan, just forward of the center console. The other two sensors are mounted on the upper crossmember of the radiator closure panel on the left and right side of the vehicle under the hood.

The impact sensors are threshold sensitive switches that complete an electrical circuit when an impact provides a sufficient G force to close the switch. The sensors are calibrated for the specific vehicle and react to the severity and direction of the impact.

Clockspring

The clockspring is mounted on the steering column behind the steering wheel and is used to maintain a continuous electrical circuit between the wiring harness and the driver's air bag module. This assembly consists of a flat ribbon-like electrically conductive tape which winds and unwinds with the steering wheel rotation.

Diagnostic Module

The Air Bag System Diagnostic Module (ASDM) contains the safing sensor and energy reserve capacitor. The ASDM monitors the system to determine the system readiness. The ASDM will store sufficient energy to deploy the air bag for only two minutes after the battery is detached. The ASDM contains on-board diagnostics and will illuminate the AIR BAG warning lamp in the cluster when a fault occurs.

SERVICE PRECAUTIONS

When working on the SRS or any components which require the removal of the air bag, adhere to all of these precautions to minimize the risks of personal injury or component damage:

• Before attempting to diagnose, remove or install the air bag system components, you must first detach and isolate the negative (-) battery cable. Failure to do so could result in accidental deployment and possible personal injury.

• When an undeployed air bag assembly is to be removed from the steering wheel, after detaching the negative battery cable, allow the system capacitor to discharge for two minutes before commencing with the air bag system component removal.

• Replace the air bag system components only with Chrysler Mopar® specified replacement parts, or equivalent. Substitute parts may visually appear interchangeable, but internal differences may result in inferior occupant protection.

• The fasteners, screws, and bolts originally used for the SRS have special coatings and are specifically designed for the SRS. They must never be replaced with any substitutes. Anytime a new fastener is needed, replace with the correct fasteners provided in the service package or fasteners listed in the parts books.

Handling A Live Air Bag Module

At no time should any source of electricity be permitted near the inflator on the back of the module. When carrying a live module, the trim cover should be pointed away from the body to minimize injury in the event of accidental deployment. In addition, if the module is placed on a bench or other surface, the plastic trim cover should be face up to minimize movement in case of accidental deployment.

When handling a steering column with an air bag module attached, never place the column on the floor or other surface with the steering wheel or module face down.

Handling A Deployed Air Bag Module

The vehicle interior may contain a very small amount of sodium hydroxide powder, a by-product of air bag deployment. Since this powder can irritate the skin, eyes, nose or throat, be sure to wear safety glasses, rubber gloves and long sleeves during cleanup.

If you find that the cleanup is irritating your skin, run cool water over the affected area. Also, if you experience nasal or throat irritation, exit the vehicle for fresh air until the irritation ceases. If irritation continues, see a physician.

Begin the cleanup by putting tape over the two air bag exhaust vents so that no additional powder will find its way into the vehicle interior. Then remove the air bag and air bag module from the vehicle.

Use a vacuum cleaner to remove any residual powder from the vehicle interior. Work from the outside in so that you avoid kneeling or sitting in an uncleaned area.

Be sure to vacuum the heater and A/C outlets as well. In fact it's a good idea to run the blower on low and to vacuum up any powder expelled from the plenum. You may need to vacuum the interior of the car a second time to recover all of the powder.

Check with the local authorities before disposing of the deployed bag and module in your trash.

After an air bag has been deployed, the air bag module and clockspring must be replaced because they cannot be reused. Other air bag system components should be replaced with new ones if damaged.

DISARMING THE SYSTEM

To disarm the SRS, simply detach the negative battery cable from the battery. Isolate the battery cable by taping up any exposed metal areas of the cable. This will keep the cable from accidentally contacting the battery and causing accidental deployment of the air bag. Allow the system capacitor to discharge for at least 2 minutes, although 10 minutes is recommended to allow the dissipation of any residual energy.

ARMING THE SYSTEM

To arm the SRS, reconnect the negative battery cable. This will automatically enable the air bag system.

HEATING AND AIR CONDITIONING

Blower Motor

REMOVAL & INSTALLATION

1981–86 MODELS WITHOUT A/C

The blower motor is located under the instrument panel on the left side of the heater assembly.

1. Disconnect the negative battery terminal.
2. Disconnect the motor wiring.
3. Remove the two attaching screws and remove the left outlet duct.
4. Remove the motor retaining screws and the motor.
5. Installation is the reverse of the removal procedure.
6. Connect the negative battery cable and check the blower motor for proper operation.

1981–86 MODELS WITH A/C

♦ See Figures 13 thru 21

1. Disconnect the negative battery cable.
2. Remove the three screws securing the glove box to the instrument panel.

3. Disconnect the wiring from the blower and case.
4. Remove the blower vent tube from the case.
5. Loosen the recirculating door from its bracket and remove the actuator from the housing. Leave the vacuum lines attached.
6. Remove the seven screws attaching the recirculating housing to the air conditioning unit and remove the housing.
7. Remove the three mounting flange nuts and washers.
8. Remove the blower motor from the unit.

To install:

9. Position the motor into the housing and install the mounting flange nuts and washers. Tighten the nuts evenly until secure.
10. The remainder of installation is the reverse of the removal procedure.
11. Connect the negative battery cable and check the blower motor for proper operation.

1987–95 MODELS

♦ See Figures 22 thru 29

1. Disconnect the negative battery cable.
2. Remove the glove box assembly, lower right side instrument panel trim cover and right cowl trim panel, as required. Detach the blower lead wire connector.

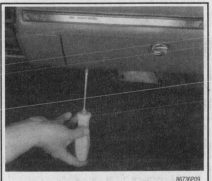

Fig. 13 Remove the glove box-to-instrument panel retaining screws . . .

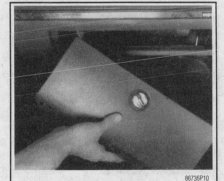

Fig. 14 . . . then remove the glove box from the panel

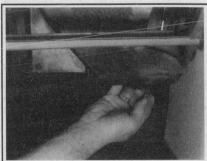

Fig. 15 Detach all vacuum hoses and wiring harness connections from the housing . . .

Fig. 16 . . . remove all housing attaching fasteners . . .

Fig. 17 . . . and remove the housing from under the instrument panel

Fig. 18 Remove the fan retaining clamp with a pair of pliers . . .

Fig. 19 . . . and slide the fan off of the motor shaft

Fig. 20 Remove the motor attaching screws . . .

Fig. 21 . . . pull the motor out of the housing and detach any wires—1981–88 A/C models

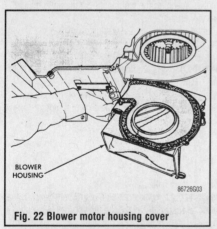

Fig. 22 Blower motor housing cover

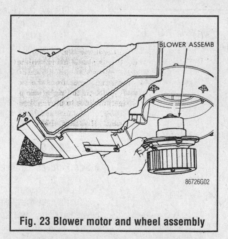

Fig. 23 Blower motor and wheel assembly

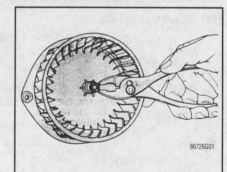

Fig. 24 Remove the spring-type retaining clip to separate the wheel from the blower motor

Fig. 25 To gain access to the blower motor, unplug the electrical connectors from the glove box lamp, . . .

Fig. 26 . . . then remove the glove box assembly from the dash panel

Fig. 27 Remove all of the retaining screws, then extract the motor housing from under the dash panel

Fig. 28 Unfasten the three blower motor assembly mounting screws and remove the blower motor

Fig. 29 Compress and slide the spring clip off the drive shaft, then remove the fan from the motor

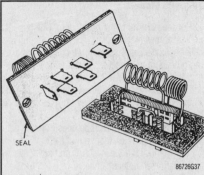

Fig. 30 A common blower motor resistor block

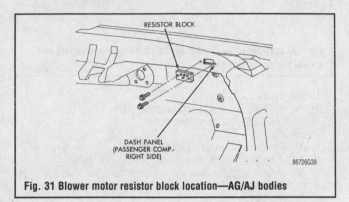

Fig. 31 Blower motor resistor block location—AG/AJ bodies

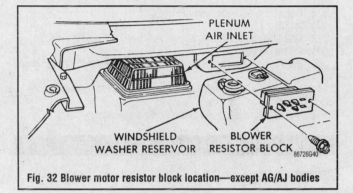

Fig. 32 Blower motor resistor block location—except AG/AJ bodies

3. If the vehicle is equipped with air conditioning, detach the 2 vacuum lines from the recirculating door actuator and position the actuator aside.

4. Remove the 2 screws at the top of the blower housing that secure it to the unit cover.

5. Remove the 5 screws from around the blower housing and separate the blower housing from the unit.

6. Remove the 3 screws that secure the blower assembly to the heater or air conditioning housing and remove the assembly from the unit. Remove the fan from the blower motor by removing the spring-type retaining ring from the center of the blower wheel. Note the location of the fan-to-blower motor assembly for correct installation.

To install:

7. Slide the blower wheel onto the new blower motor shaft and install the spring type retaining ring to hold it in place. Make certain to position the wheel on the motor in the same place as before removal.

8. Position the blower motor in the heater/air conditioning unit and secure in place with the 3 screws.

9. Install the blower housing onto the unit and secure in place with the 5 retaining screws.

10. Install the 2 screws at the top of the blower housing, securing it to the unit cover.

11. Attach the blower lead wire connector and the two vacuum hoses (vehicles with A/C).

12. Install the glove box.

13. Connect the negative battery cable and check the blower motor for proper operation.

Blower Motor Resistor

REMOVAL & INSTALLATION

♦ See Figures 30, 31 and 32

❊❊ CAUTION

Stay clear of the blower motor and resistor block (hot) when the battery is connected.

1. Disconnect the negative battery cable.

2. Remove the glove box, if necessary. Locate the resistor block and detach the wire harness. On LeBaron (AG body) and Daytona models, the resistor block is located above and to the front of the glove box opening on the dash panel. On all other models, the resistor block is located under the front cowl grille and windshield wiper arms.

❊❊ WARNING

Do not operate the blower motor with the resistor block removed from the heater-A/C housing. Air must move over the hot coils.

3. Remove the attaching screws and remove the resistor from the housing.

4. Installation is the reverse of the removal procedure. Make sure there is no contact between any of the coils before installing.

5. Connect the negative battery cable and check the blower system for proper operation.

Heater Core

REMOVAL & INSTALLATION

1981–84 Models

1. Remove the heater assembly, as described later in this section.

2. Remove the padding from around the heater core outlets and remove the upper core mounting screws.

3. Pry loose the retaining snaps from around the outer edge of the housing cover.

➡**If a retaining snap should break, the housing cover has provisions for mounting screws.**

4. Remove the housing top cover.

5. Remove the bottom heater core mounting screw.

6. Slide the heater core out of the housing.

7. Installation is the reverse of the removal procedure.

8. Install the heater assembly, as described later in this section.

1985–95 Models

For the removal of the heater core, which is located inside the heater-A/C unit assembly, first remove the heater-A/C unit assembly from the vehicle as described later in this section. Once the unit has been removed, use the following procedure to extract the heater core:

1. Place the heater-A/C unit on a suitable work surface.
2. Locate and remove one retaining nut from the blend-air door pivot shaft.
3. To remove the top cover from the heater-A/C case, the crank arm must be removed.
4. Disconnect the vacuum lines from the defroster and panel mode vacuum actuators and position them out of the way.
5. Remove the 3 heater-A/C unit cover attaching screws, fastened upward at the defroster outlet chamber.
6. Remove the 2 heater-A/C unit cover attaching screws, fastened upward at the air inlet plenum.
7. Remove the 11 heater-A/C unit cover attaching screws, fastened downward into the housing. Then lift the cover from the heater-A/C unit.
8. Remove the old heater core from the case.

To install:

9. Install the new heater core into the heater-A/C unit case in the same position as the old one.
10. Place the cover onto the case and secure in place with the 11 retaining screws.
11. Install the remaining components in the reverse of the removal procedure.
12. Install the heater-A/C unit assembly into the vehicle.

Heater-A/C Unit Assembly and Core

REMOVAL & INSTALLATION

☀☀ CAUTION

When draining the coolant, keep in mind that cats and dogs are attracted by the ethylene glycol antifreeze, and are quite likely to drink any that is left in an uncovered container or in puddles on the ground. This will prove fatal in sufficient quantity. Always drain the coolant into a sealable container. Coolant should be reused unless it is contaminated or several years old.

1981–84 Models

WITHOUT AIR CONDITIONING

♦ See Figure 33

1. Disconnect the negative battery cable and drain the radiator.
2. Detach the blower motor wiring connector.
3. Reach under the unit, depress the tab on the mode door and temperature control cables, pull the flags from the receivers, and remove the self-adjust clip from the crank arm.
4. Remove the glove box assembly.
5. Disconnect the heater hoses to the unit on the engine side and seal the heater core tube openings and hoses.
6. Through the glove box opening, remove the screw attaching the hanger strap to the heater assembly.
7. Remove the nut attaching the hanger strap to the dash panel and remove the hanger strap.
8. Remove the two nuts attaching the heater assembly to the dash panel. The nuts are on the engine side.
9. Pull out the bottom of the instrument panel and slide out the heater assembly.
10. Remove the padding from around the heater core outlets and remove the upper core mounting screws.
11. Pry loose the retaining snaps from around the outer edge of the housing cover.

➡If a retaining snap should break, the housing cover has provisions for mounting screws.

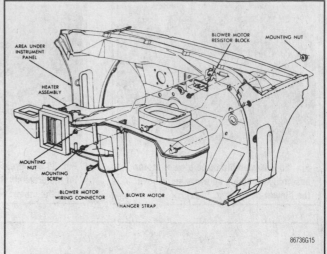

Fig. 33 Locations of the heater assembly mounting fasteners and blower motor resistor block

12. Remove the housing top cover.
13. Remove the bottom heater core mounting screw.
14. Slide the heater core out of the housing.

To install:

15. Slide the heater core into the housing.
16. Install the bottom heater core mounting screw until secure.
17. Install the housing top cover and engage the retaining snaps around the outer perimeter of the housing. If the snaps were damaged during removal, install mounting screws.
18. The remainder of installation is the reverse of the removal sequence.
19. Install the glove box assembly.
20. Attach the blower motor wiring.
21. Fill the cooling system, as described in Section 1.
22. Connect the negative battery cable.

WITH AIR CONDITIONING

Removal of the Heater-Evaporator Unit is required for heater core removal. Two people will be required to perform the operation.

➡It is vital to have the A/C system discharged by a reputable automotive technician utilizing a recovery/recycling machine before detaching the A/C system. Refer to the A/C system precautions presented in Section 1.

1. Have the A/C system discharged, as described in Section 1.
2. Disconnect the negative battery ground.
3. Drain the engine coolant, as described in Section 1.
4. Disconnect the temperature door cable from the heater-evaporator unit.
5. Disconnect the temperature door cable from the retaining clips.
6. Remove the glove box.
7. Detach the vacuum harness from the control head.
8. Disconnect the blower motor lead and anti-diesel relay wire.
9. Remove the seven screws fastening the right trim bezel to the instrument panel. Starting at the right side, swing the bezel clear and remove it.
10. Remove the three screws on the bottom of the center distribution duct cover and slide the cover rearward and remove it.
11. Remove the center distribution duct.
12. Remove the defroster duct adapter.
13. Remove the H-type expansion valve, located on the right side of the fire wall:
    a. Remove the ⅝ in. bolt in the center of the plumbing sealing plate.
    b. Carefully pull the refrigerant lines toward the front of the car, taking care to avoid scratching the valve sealing surfaces.
    c. Remove the two Allen head capscrews and remove the valve.
14. Cap the pipe openings at once. Wrap the valve in a plastic bag.
15. Disconnect the hoses from the core tubes.
16. Disconnect the vacuum lines at the intake manifold and water valve.
17. Remove the unit-to-firewall retaining nuts.

18. Remove the panel support bracket.
19. Remove the right cowl lower panel.
20. Remove the instrument panel pivot bracket screw from the right side.
21. Remove the screws securing the lower instrument panel at the steering column.
22. Pull back the carpet from under the unit as far as possible.
23. Remove the nut from the evaporator-heater unit-to-plenum mounting brace and blower motor ground cable. While supporting the unit, remove the brace from its stud.
24. Lift the unit, pulling it rearward to allow clearance. These operations may require two people.
25. Slowly lower the unit taking care to keep the studs from hanging-up on the insulation.
26. When the unit reaches the floor, slide it rearward until it is out from under the instrument panel.
27. Remove the unit from the car.
28. Place the unit on a workbench. On the inside-the-car-side, remove the nut from the mode door actuator on the top cover and the two retaining clips from the front edge of the cover. To remove the mode door actuator, remove the two screws securing it to the cover.
29. Remove the screws attaching the cover to the assembly and lift off the cover. Lift the mode door out of the unit.
30. Remove the screw from the core retaining bracket and lift out the core.
To install:
31. Place the core in the unit and install the bracket.
32. Install the actuator arm.

➡**When installing the unit in the car, care must be taken that the vacuum lines to the engine compartment do not hang-up on the accelerator or become trapped between the unit and the fire wall. If this happens, kinked lines will result and the unit will have to be removed to free them. Proper routing of these lines will require two people. The portion of the vacuum harness which is routed through the steering column support MUST be positioned BEFORE the distribution housing is installed. The harness must be routed ABOVE the temperature control cable.**

33. Place the unit on the floor as far under the panel as possible.
34. Raise the unit carefully, at the same time pull the lower instrument panel rearward as far as possible.
35. Position the unit in place and attach the brace to the stud.
36. Install the lower ground cable and attach the nut.
37. Install and tighten the unit-to-firewall nuts.
38. Reposition the carpet and install, but do not tighten the right instrument panel pivot bracket screw.
39. Place a piece of sheet metal or thin cardboard against the evaporator-heater assembly to center the assembly duct seal.
40. Position the center distributor duct in place making sure that the upper left tab comes in through the left center air conditioning outlet opening and that each air take-off is properly inserted in its respective outlet.

➡**Make sure that the radio wiring connector does not interfere with the duct.**

41. Install and tighten the screw securing the upper left tab of the center air distribution duct to the instrument panel.
42. Remove the sheet metal or cardboard from between the unit and the duct.

➡**Make sure that the unit seal is properly aligned with the duct opening.**

43. Install and tighten the two lower screws fastening the center distribution duct to the instrument panel.
44. Install the remaining components in the reverse of the removal procedure. When installing the H-valve, position the valve against the evaporator sealing plate surface and install the two through-bolts. Tighten to 6–10 ft. lb. Tighten the refrigerant line connector bolt to 14–20 ft. lb. (19–27 Nm).
45. Have the A/C system evacuated, recharged and leak tested by a reputable automotive technician utilizing a recovery/recycling apparatus.

1985–86 Models

➡**Modify the service steps as necessary for vehicles not equipped with air conditioning.**

➡**It is vital to have the A/C system discharged by a reputable automotive technician utilizing a recovery/recycling machine before detaching the A/C system. Refer to the A/C system precautions presented in Section 1.**

1. Have the air conditioning system discharged by a reputable automotive technician utilizing a refrigerant recovery/recycling machine.
2. Disconnect the negative battery cable.
3. Drain the engine cooling system, as described in Section 1.
4. Disconnect the heater hoses at the core and plug the core openings with a cork or cap.
5. Label, then detach the vacuum lines for the heater/air conditioning system at the intake manifold and water valve.
6. Remove the right side scuff plate and the cowl side trim panel.
7. Remove the glove box.
8. Remove the air conditioning control head, as described later in this section.
9. If the car has a console, remove it.
10. Remove the two bolts and two screws which fasten the forward console mounting bracket to the body and remove it.
11. Remove the center distribution duct.
12. Remove the side window demister adapter on those models so-equipped. Pull the defroster adapter from the bottom of the defroster duct.
13. Remove the drain tube clamp, then remove the L-shaped condensate drain tube. Disengage the heater/air conditioning unit from the wiring harness at the connector.
14. Disconnect the control cable at the receiver, located near the evaporator assembly. To do this, depress the tab on the red flag and pull the flag out of the receiver.
15. Remove the right side cowl-to-plenum brace. Pull the carpet out from under the unit and fold it back.
16. Remove the screw holding the hanger strap to the unit, then remove the 4 mounting nuts for the unit which are located on the engine compartment side of the cowl. Finally, pull the unit toward the rear of the car until the studs clear the dash liner. Allow it to drop down until it rests on the catalytic converter tunnel.
17. Turn the unit so as to clear the lower instrument panel reinforcement without moving it too far to either side, then remove the unit from the car and place it on a workbench, standing behind it just as a front seat passenger would.
18. Disconnect the actuator arm at the mounting shaft by squeezing it with a pair of pliers to release it. **Be careful to avoid prying the mounting clips, as they can easily be broken.** When the arm is free, remove the retaining clips from the front edge of the cover.
19. Remove the two screws mounting the mode door actuator to the cover and remove it.
20. Remove the 15 screws attaching the cover to the housing and remove it, then lift the mode door out.
21. Remove the screw from the heater core tube retaining bracket and lift the core out of the unit.
To install:
22. Slide the new heater core into position and then install the screw into the retaining bracket.
23. Install the mode door. Install the cover to the heater/air conditioning housing and install the 15 attaching screws.
24. Install the mode door actuator and its two attaching screws.
25. Connect the actuator arm at the mounting shaft by squeezing it with a pair of pliers to permit it to be installed over the shaft (again be careful not to squeeze the mounting clips). Install the retaining clips on the front edge of the cover.
26. Install the unit back into the car, working it around the instrument panel reinforcement. Raise it until the mounting studs line up with the holes in the cowl and position it so the studs pass through the cowl. Install the four mounting nuts from the engine compartment side.
27. Install the screw attaching the hanger strap to the unit. Work the carpet back into position under the unit. Install the right side cowl-to-plenum brace.
28. Connect the control cable at the receiver. Install the L-shaped condensate drain tube. Attach the heater/air conditioning unit wiring harness connector.
29. Install the remaining components in the reverse of the removal procedure.
30. Fill the engine cooling system, as described in Section 1.

31. Connect the negative battery cable, then start the engine and check for coolant leaks. Refill the cooling system after the engine has reached operating temperature and cooled back off.

32. Have the A/C system evacuated, recharged and leak tested by a reputable automotive technician using a recovery/recycling machine.

1987 Models

➡️Modify the service steps as necessary on vehicles not equipped with air conditioning. To complete this procedure, make sure to have suitable caps or plastic sheeting and tape to cover and seal open refrigerant lines. Also needed are caps or plugs for the heater core tubes.

➡️It is vital to have the A/C system discharged by a reputable automotive technician utilizing a recovery/recycling machine before detaching the A/C system. Refer to the A/C system precautions presented in Section 1.

1. Have the air conditioning system discharged by a reputable automotive technician utilizing a refrigerant recovery/recycling machine.
2. Disconnect the negative battery cable.
3. Drain the engine cooling system.
4. Remove the right side cowl cover. Remove the trim panel from the door opening scuff plate.
5. There is a roll down bolt located behind the instrument panel to the right of the glove box. Loosen this bolt so that the instrument panel can be shifted later on in the procedure.
6. Remove the four instrument cluster center bezel attaching screws, open the glove box door and remove the bezel.
7. Remove the lower instrument panel module cover, if so equipped.
8. Remove the center console assembly. Position the accessory wiring harness so it will be out of the way when removing the heater/air conditioning unit.
9. Remove the instrument panel center support braces and brackets.
10. Remove the radio, as described later in this section.
11. Remove the ash tray, then remove its mounting bracket.
12. Remove the cigarette lighter and socket. Remove the glove box.
13. Remove the heater/air conditioning control, as described later in this section.
14. Disconnect the temperature cable attaching flag and vacuum harness from the control assembly.
15. Remove the two attaching screws and remove the center air duct.
16. Disconnect the blower motor relay module and wiring lead from the harness and position both so the heater/air conditioning unit can be removed later.
17. The defroster duct adapter is located between the heater/air conditioning unit and the defroster duct. Pull it downward from its installed position and remove it.
18. Remove the attaching nut and 4 screws from the heater/air conditioning unit support bracket and remove it.
19. Remove the 3 attaching screws from the heat outlet duct (located under the unit) and remove the duct.
20. Slide the front passenger's seat as far to the rear as it will go, then roll the carpet out from under the unit.
21. Disconnect the lines from the refrigerant expansion H-valve, and immediately and tightly cover the openings.
22. Disconnect both heater hoses and plug the core tubes.
23. Remove the condensate drain tube.
24. Remove the four heater/air conditioning unit attaching nuts from the engine compartment side of the cowl. Remove the heater/air conditioning unit support brace lower attaching bolt, then swing the brace out of the way to the left and behind the dash panel.
25. Pull the unit directly away from the dash panel (do not twist or turn it, so as to avoid damaging the seals). Once the studs clear both the dash panel and liner, allow it to drop down until it rests on the floor tunnel.
26. Remove the demister adapter duct from the top of the unit to provide working clearance.
27. Then, keeping the unit upright, slide it from under the instrument panel and out the right side door opening.
28. Place the unit on a workbench or in some similar spot where you can work on it effectively. Remove the retaining nut from the blend-air door pivot shaft, then position a pair of pliers so that the upper jaw rests against the top of the pivot shaft and the lower jaw will tend to pry the crank lever upward. Gently pry the crank lever off the pivot shaft.

29. Disconnect the vacuum lines from the defrost mode and panel mode vacuum actuators and position them out of the way.
30. Remove the two heater/air conditioning unit cover attaching screws located above the cover in the air inlet plenum. Remove the 11 heater/air conditioning unit cover attaching screws located downward from the cover in the housing. Lift the cover off the heater/air conditioning unit.
31. Remove the heater core-to-dash panel seal from the tubes of the core, then pull the core out of the unit.

To install:

32. Slide the core into the unit and install the seal. Then install the unit cover and all 13 attaching screws.
33. Connect the vacuum lines going to the defrost and panel vacuum actuators. Reinstall the blend air door crank lever onto the pivot shaft.
34. Put the unit back into the car. Install the demister adapter duct, then raise the unit until the mounting studs are lined up with the holes in the cowl and work the studs through the holes. Install the support brace and attaching bolt. Install the mounting nuts from the other side of the cowl.
35. Install the condensate drain tube. Install the heater hoses.
36. Reinstall the expansion H-valve. Uncap the openings and immediately reconnect the refrigerant lines.
37. Install the carpet back under the unit, then install the heat outlet duct and the 3 attaching screws.
38. Put the heater/air conditioning unit support bracket into position and then install the attaching nut and 4 screws.
39. Installation of the remaining components is the reverse of the removal procedure.
40. Refill the engine cooling system.
41. Connect the battery negative cable. Charge the air conditioning system, utilizing the procedures in Section 1. Operate the engine and check for leaks. After the engine has reached operating temperature and then has cooled back off, bring the coolant level back up to where it belongs.

1988 Models

➡️Modify the service steps as necessary on vehicles not equipped with air conditioning. To complete this procedure, make sure to have suitable caps or plastic sheeting and tape to cover and seal open refrigerant lines. Also needed are caps or plugs for the heater core tubes.

➡️It is vital to have the A/C system discharged by a reputable automotive technician utilizing a recovery/recycling machine before detaching the A/C system. Refer to the A/C system precautions presented in Section 1.

1. Have the A/C system discharged by a reputable automotive technician using a refrigerant recycling/recovery machine.
2. Disconnect the battery negative cable.
3. Drain the engine cooling system. Disconnect the heater hoses at the core and plug the openings.
4. Remove the air conditioner condensate drain. Label and then detach the vacuum lines running from the car body to various components on the heater/air conditioning unit.
5. Disconnect/remove the following items, according to the body style of the car:
  a. On LeBaron (AK body) models, remove the right upper and lower silencers from under the instrument panel.
  b. On LeBaron (AK body) models with passive restraints, remove the right side lower trim panel from under the dashboard.
  c. On Sundance and Shadow models, remove the steering column cover.
  d. On Daytona and LeBaron (AJ body) models with passive restraints, remove the inner steering column cover.
6. Put the bench seat or right individual seat all the way to the rear, then, on Sundance models, remove the right pillar trim.
7. On all cars, remove the right cowl side trim (note that on the LeBaron, this requires pulling the lower end of the right side A-pillar trim outward).
8. Remove the glove box, then perform each of the following procedures on the models indicated:
  a. On Daytona, LeBaron and New Yorker with passive restraints, and on Lancer and LeBaron GTS, remove the right instrument panel reinforcement.
  b. On Sundance and Shadow, Caravelle, 600 and New Yorker Turbo, remove the right instrument panel roll-up screw.

c. On Daytona, LeBaron and New Yorker, remove the forward console bezel, side trim, and lower carpet panels, then loosen the floor console and move it to the rear. Remove the forward console. If the car has passive restraints, remove the instrument panel-to-floor reinforcement.

d. On the Sundance and Shadow, remove the center dashboard bezel, lower center module cover, floor console, and instrument support brace (this brace runs from the steering column opening to the right cowl side at the bottom of the instrument panel). Also remove the bracket linking the instrument panel and its support, located under the glove box. Remove the ashtray. Remove the radio as described later. Remove the instrument panel top cover. Finally, remove the 3 right side panel-to-lower windshield panel attaching screws.

e. On the Caravelle, 600 and New Yorker Turbo, remove the forward console and its mounting bracket.

f. On the Aries, Reliant, LeBaron, New Yorker, and Town & Country, remove the floor console.

g. On the Lancer, remove both front and rear consoles.

h. On the Sundance and Shadow, Aries, Reliant, LeBaron, New Yorker, Town & Country, Caravelle, 600, and New Yorker Turbo pull the right lower side of the instrument panel to the rear.

9. On all models, remove the center distribution and defroster adapter ducts, then perform each of the following procedures on the model indicated:

a. On the Sundance, Shadow and Lancer, remove and detach the relay module.

b. On the Sundance and Shadow, remove the bracket linking the air conditioning unit and instrument panel, then on these models, remove the lower air distribution duct.

c. On the Aries, Reliant, LeBaron, New Yorker, Town & Country, Caravelle, 600 and New Yorker Turbo, remove the audible message center, then on these models, remove the right side cowl-to-plenum brace.

10. On all models, detach the blower motor wire connector, then detach the demister hoses at the top of the heater/air conditioning unit.

11. If the car is equipped with a manual control, rather than the Automatic Temperature Control (ATC), perform the following:

a. Disconnect the temperature control cable flag from the bottom of the heater/air conditioning unit and unclip the cable from the left side of the heat distribution duct, then swing the cable out of the way and to the left.

b. Label, then detach the vacuum lines at the unit.

12. On vehicles equipped with the ATC, detach the instrument panel wiring from the rear face of the ATC unit.

13. On the Lancer, disengage the right side 25-way connector bracket and fuse block from the panel.

14. Remove the antenna cable from the clip on the top or rear face of the unit, where it is so-routed.

15. On all models but Lancer, fold the carpeting back on the right side.

16. Remove the four attaching nuts for the unit from the engine compartment side of the cowl.

17. Remove the lower screw from the unit's hanging strap and then rotate the strap out of the way.

18. Pull the unit to the rear until its studs clear the cowl and liner and then lower it. On the Sundance and Shadow, remove the demister adapter from the top of the unit, then pull the lower right section of the instrument panel rearward and hold it for clearance as you slide the unit out of the car in an upright position. On the other models, rotate the unit as necessary for clearance as it is pulled out from under the instrument panel.

To install:

19. Reverse the step above to get the heater assembly into position under the dash. On the Sundance and Shadow, install the demister adapter, then raise it, line up the four mounting studs with the holes in the cowl, and work the studs through the cowl.

20. Install the four retaining nuts from the engine compartment side of the cowl.

21. Rotate the hanging strap back into position and install the attaching bolt.

22. Reposition the carpeting, if it was moved.

23. Reclip the antenna cable, if it is clipped to the heater/air conditioning unit.

24. The remainder of installation is the reverse of the removal procedure.

25. Refill the cooling system, as described in Section 1.

26. Connect the negative battery cable.

27. Start the engine and check for coolant leaks. Refill the cooling system

once the vehicle has reached normal operating temperate and allowed to cool back down.

28. Have the air conditioning system evacuated, recharged and leak tested by a reputable automotive technician using a recovery/recycling machine, utilizing the procedures in Section 1. Operate the engine and check for leaks.

1989–95 Models

EXCEPT DYNASTY

➡The following procedure can be used on all specified 1989–95 models. Slight variations may occur due to extra connections, etc., but the basic procedure should cover all models. Modify the service steps as necessary. Refer to the supplemental restraint system disarming procedure as necessary.

➡It is vital to have the A/C system discharged by a reputable automotive technician utilizing a recovery/recycling machine before detaching the A/C system. Refer to the A/C system precautions presented in Section 1.

1. If the vehicle is equipped with air conditioning, have the A/C system discharged by a qualified professional mechanic, using an approved recovery/recycling machine.

2. Disconnect the negative battery cable. Drain the cooling system.

3. Clamp off the heater hoses near the heater core and remove the hoses from the core tubes. Plug the hose ends and the core tubes to prevent spillage of coolant.

4. Disconnect the H-valve connection at the valve and remove the H-valve. Remove the condensation tube.

5. Remove the glove box, right side kick and sill panels, and all modules, relay panels and computer components in the vicinity of the heater housing.

6. Remove the lower instrument panel silencers and reinforcements. Remove the radio and other dashboard-mounted optional equipment, as required.

7. Remove the floor console, if equipped. Remove the floor and defroster distribution ducts.

8. Remove the bolt holding the right side instrument panel to the right cowl.

9. Disconnect the blower motor wiring, antenna, resistor wiring and the temperature control cable.

10. On 1990–95 Daytona and LeBaron models, using a suitable cutting device, cut the instrument panel along the indented line on the padded cover to the right of the glove box opening. Cut only plastic, not metal. Remove the reinforcement and the piece of instrument panel that is riveted to it.

11. Disconnect the demister hoses from the top of the housing, if equipped.

12. Disconnect the hanger strap from the package and rotate it aside.

13. Remove the retaining nuts from the package mounting studs at the fire wall.

14. Fold the carpeting and insulation back to provide a little more working room and to prevent spillage from staining the carpeting. Pull the right side of the instrument panel out as far as possible.

15. Remove the heater housing from the dash panel and remove it from the passenger compartment. If the passenger seat is preventing removal, remove it.

16. To disassemble the housing assembly, remove the retaining screws from the cover and remove the cover.

17. Remove the retaining screw from the heater core and remove the core from the housing assembly.

To install:

18. Remove the temperature control door from the housing and clean the unit out with solvent. Lubricate the lower pivot rod and its well, then install. Wrap the heater core with foam tape and place it in position. Secure it with its screw.

19. Assemble the housing, making sure all cover screws were used.

20. Connect the demister hoses. Install the nuts to the fire wall and connect the hanger strap inside the passenger compartment.

21. Fold the carpeting back into position.

22. Install the bolt that attaches the right side of the instrument panel to the cowl.

23. Connect the blower motor wiring, antenna, resistor wiring and the temperature control cable.

24. Install the remaining components in the reverse of the removal procedure.

25. Fill the cooling system.

26. Connect the negative battery cable and check the entire climate control system for proper operation and leakage.

27. Have the air conditioning system evacuated and recharged by a qualified professional mechanic utilizing the proper equipment.

1989–93 DYNASTY

➡**It is vital to have the A/C system discharged by a reputable automotive technician utilizing a recovery/recycling machine before detaching the A/C system. Refer to the A/C system precautions presented in Section 1.**

1. Have the air conditioning system discharged by a qualified professional mechanic using an approved recovery/recycling machine.

2. Disconnect the negative battery cable. Refer to the supplemental restraint system disarming service procedure as necessary.

3. Clamp off the heater hoses near the heater core and remove the hoses from the core tubes. Plug the hose ends and the core tubes to prevent spillage of coolant.

4. Disconnect the H-valve connection at the valve and remove the H-valve. Remove the condensation tube.

5. Disconnect the vacuum lines at the brake booster and water valve, if equipped.

6. Remove the right upper and lower under-panel silencers.

7. Remove the steering column cover and the ashtray.

8. Remove the left side under-panel silencer.

9. Remove the right side cowl trim piece.

10. Remove the glove box assembly and the right side instrument panel reinforcement.

11. Remove the center distribution and defroster adapter ducts.

12. Detach the relay module, blower motor wiring, 25-way connector bracket and fuse block from the panel.

13. Disconnect the demister hoses from the top of the package.

14. Disconnect the temperature control cable and vacuum harness, if equipped. If equipped with Automatic Temperature Control (ATC), detach the instrument panel wiring from the rear of the ATC unit.

15. Disconnect the hanger strap from the package and rotate it out of the way.

16. Remove the retaining nuts from the package mounting studs at the fire wall.

17. Fold the carpeting and insulation back to provide a little more working room and to prevent spillage from staining the carpeting.

18. Move the package rearward to clear the mounting studs and lower.

19. Pull the right side of the instrument panel out as far as possible. Rotate the package while removing it from under the instrument panel.

20. To disassemble the housing assembly, remove the vacuum diaphragm, if equipped, then remove the retaining screws from the cover and remove the cover.

21. Remove the retaining screw from the heater core and remove the core from the housing assembly.

To install:

22. Remove the temperature control door from the housing and clean the unit out with solvent. Lubricate the lower pivot rod and its well, then install. Wrap the heater core with foam tape and place it in position. Secure it with its screw.

23. Assemble the package, making sure all vacuum tubing is properly routed.

24. If equipped, feed the vacuum lines through the hole in the fire wall and install the assembly to the vehicle. Connect the vacuum harness and demister hoses. Install the nuts to the fire wall and fasten the hanger strap inside the passenger compartment.

25. Fold the carpeting back into position.

26. Connect the wiring to the ATC unit, if equipped.

27. Installation of the remaining components is the reverse of the removal procedure.

28. Fill the cooling system, as described in Section 1.

29. Connect the negative battery cable and check the entire climate control system for proper operation and leakage.

30. Have the air conditioning system evacuated and recharged by a qualified professional mechanic utilizing the proper equipment.

REMOVAL & INSTALLATION

▶ **See Figures 34 thru 39**

1. Disconnect the battery negative cable. For Acclaim, Spirit and some LeBaron (AA body) models, isolate or remove fuse No. 2 prior to removing the switch or the wires may short to ground.

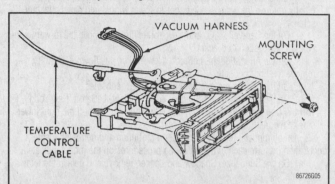

Fig. 34 The heater-A/C control panel in Sundance and Shadow models—other models similar

Fig. 35 Remove the outer trim bezel from over the heater-A/C control panel and radio, . . .

Fig. 36 . . . making sure to detach any wiring from the back of the trim pieces

Fig. 37 If necessary, remove the lower trim piece to gain access to any of the retaining screws

Fig. 38 Loosen and remove the heater-A/C control panel retaining screws, then . . .

Fig. 39 . . . the control panel can be slid out and the cables removed

2. Remove the cover bezel.

3. If applicable, detach the ashtray's lamp socket.

4. Remove the glove box assembly on the LeBaron (AA body), Spirit and Acclaim models, then reach through the glove box hole and detach the vacuum hoses.

5. Remove the two control mounting screws.

6. Slide the heater-A/C control rearward, then detach the cable and any electrical wiring from the control.

7. Remove the unit from the dashboard.

To install:

8. Install the control into the dashboard.

9. Slide the heater-A/C control rearward, then connect the temperature cable and any electrical wiring to the control.

10. Install the two control mounting screws and tighten until snug.

11. On the LeBaron (AA body), Acclaim and Spirit models, reach through the glove box hole and plug the vacuum lines back in. Install the glove box.

12. Connect the ashtray's lamp socket, if so equipped.

13. Install the cover bezel.

14. For Acclaim, Spirit and some LeBaron models, install fuse No. 2 after installing the switch. Connect the negative battery cable.

Blower Switch

REMOVAL & INSTALLATION

This procedure applies to all vehicles covered by this manual; however slight variances may occur and this procedure should be adjusted accordingly.

1. Disconnect the negative battery cable, then remove the heater control panel from the vehicle's dashboard.

➡To protect the cosmetic face plate, place cardboard or a similar material on the face plate while prying.

2. Pry the temperature and blower switch knobs off with a flat blade prytool.

3. Remove the face plate by lifting on the 6 tabs, 3 of which are on the top and 3 on the bottom of the face plate.

➡To protect the cosmetic face plate, place cardboard or a similar material on the face plate while prying.

4. Pry the blower switch off of the heater-A/C control panel with a flat blade prytool.

To install:

5. Line up the blower switch terminals with the holes in the control panel and press firmly until it bottoms out on the housing.

6. Install the face plate onto the control panel and press until all of the tabs engage the panel.

7. Push the temperature and blower switch knobs back onto their respective levers.

8. Install the heater control panel as described in the previous procedure. Attach the negative battery cable.

Air Conditioning Components

REMOVAL & INSTALLATION

Repair or service of air conditioning components is not covered by this manual, because of the risk of personal injury or death, and because of the legal ramifications of servicing these components without the proper EPA certification and experience. Cost, personal injury or death, environmental damage, and legal considerations (such as the fact that it is a federal crime to vent refrigerant into the atmosphere), dictate that the A/C components on your vehicle should be serviced only by a Motor Vehicle Air Conditioning (MVAC) trained, and EPA certified automotive technician.

➡If your vehicle's A/C system uses R-12 refrigerant and is in need of recharging, the A/C system can be converted over to R-134a refrigerant (less environmentally harmful and expensive). Refer to Section 1 for additional information on R-12 to R-134a conversions, and for additional considerations dealing with your vehicle's A/C system.

CRUISE CONTROL

General Information

▸ See Figures 40, 41 and 42

The speed control system is electronically controlled and vacuum operated. The electronic control is integrated into the engine controller, located next to the battery. The controls are located on the steering wheel.

The system is designed to operate at speeds above 35 mph (50 km/h). The use of the speed control is not recommended when driving conditions do not permit maintaining a constant speed, such as in heavy traffic or on roads that are winding, icy, snow covered or slippery.

Diagnostic Procedures

Whenever a speed control malfunction occurs, first verify that the speed control wire harness is properly connected to all connectors before starting repairs. A poor connection can cause a complete or intermittent malfunction and is also the only connection in the circuit that cannot be tested. For this reason, a loose connection may be misdiagnosed as a component malfunction.

Also, check all vacuum connections for tightness and cracked hoses. Road test the vehicle to verify speed control problems. The road test should include attention to the speedometer. Speedometer operation should be smooth and without flutter at all speeds. A flutter in the speedometer indicates a problem

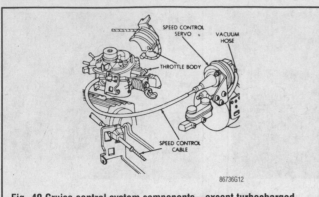

Fig. 40 Cruise control system components—except turbocharged and AC body

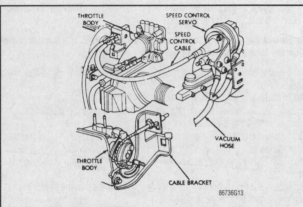

Fig. 41 Cruise control system components—turbocharged engines

which might cause surging in the speed control system. The cause of any speedometer problems should be corrected before any more diagnosis is done.

If the road test verifies an inoperative system with correct speedometer operation, follow these steps:

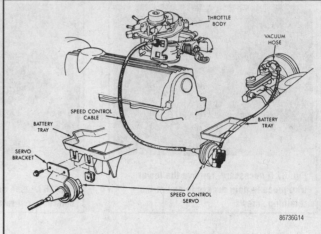

Fig. 42 Cruise control system components—AC body

1. Inspect the cruise control fuse, and replace if it has blown.
2. Check for a loose electrical or vacuum connection at the servo unit.
3. Check for vacuum supply (refer to the tests below) and correct position of the vacuum check valve in the hose from the servo unit to the vacuum source. The word VAC on the valve must point toward the vacuum source.
4. Remove corrosion from all electrical terminals in the speed control system.
5. Verify that both ends of the speed control cable are securely attached. If either end is loose, the speed control system will be inoperative.

VACUUM SUPPLY TEST

1. Disconnect the vacuum hose at the servo and install a vacuum gauge in the hose.
2. Start the engine and observe at idle. The vacuum gauge should read at least 10 in. Hg (33.7 kPa). Shut off the engine; the vacuum should continue to hold to that specification.
3. If the vacuum does not meet this specification, check the vacuum lines, check valve, vacuum reservoir and servo unit. Note that poor engine performance can cause problems with the speed control system.

ENTERTAINMENT SYSTEMS

Radio/Tape Player/CD Player

REMOVAL & INSTALLATION

1981–88 Models

AK BODY VEHICLES

▶ See Figures 43, 44, 45, 46 and 47

➡The AK body vehicles include some LeBaron, all Town & Country, 400, some 600, all Aries, Reliant, Executive and Executive Limousine models.

1. Remove the bezel.
2. If equipped with a mono (single) speaker, remove the instrument panel top cover, speaker, and detach the wires from the radio.
3. Remove the two screws attaching the radio to the base panel.
4. Pull the radio through the front of the base, then detach the wiring harness, antenna lead and ground strap.
5. Installation is the reverse of the removal procedure.
6. Connect the negative battery cable, sit back and enjoy the tunes.

AG AND AJ BODY VEHICLES

➡The AG and AJ body vehicles include some LeBaron and all Daytona models. For more information regarding body designations, refer to Section 1.

1. Remove the two screws from the bottom of the console trim bezel, then lift the bezel out of the console.
2. Remove the two attaching screws fastening the radio to the console.
3. Pull the radio through the front face of the console far enough for access

Fig. 43 Remove the upper bezel retaining screws . . .

Fig. 44 . . . and the lower bezel retaining screws . . .

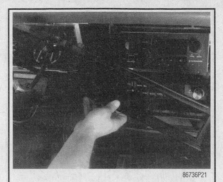

Fig. 45 . . . then remove the bezel from the instrument panel

Fig. 46 Remove the radio retaining bolts, slide the radio out of the panel . . .

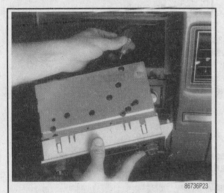

Fig. 47 . . . and detach the antenna lead wire—1981–88 AK body

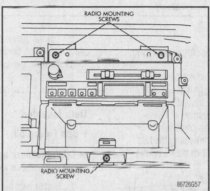

Fig. 48 Typical radio retaining screw locations

Fig. 49 After removing the trim bezels, unscrew the retaining fasteners from the radio unit, . . .

to the wiring, then detach the wiring harness, antenna lead, and ground strap. Remove the radio.

4 Installation is the reverse of the removal procedure.
5 Connect the negative battery cable and crank up the music.

AH BODY VEHICLES

➡The AH body vehicles include all LeBaron GTS and Lancer models.

1. Remove the instrument cluster bezel, then remove the two radio attaching screws.
2. Detach the wiring connectors and antenna cable.
3. Remove the ground strap attaching screw. Remove the radio.
4. Installation is the reverse of the removal procedure.
5. Connect the negative battery cable, turn the radio ON and groove to the music.

AP BODY VEHICLES

➡The AP body vehicles include all Shadow and Sundance models.

1. Remove the center module bezel.
2. If the car has a short console, remove the lower center module cover. If the car has a full-length console, remove the right console sidewall.
3. Remove the two radio mounting screws and pull it out of the dash far enough to reach the wiring. Disconnect the power wiring and the antenna cable. Detach the ground strap and remove the radio.
4. Installation is the reverse of the removal procedure.
5. Connect the negative battery cable, sit back and enjoy the tunes.

1989–95 Models

▶ See Figures 48, 49, 50 and 51

➡On vehicles equipped with a compact disc player or graphic equalizer assembly, removal and installation procedures are the same as for the radio/tape player.

Fig. 50 . . . then slide the radio out of its mounting hole

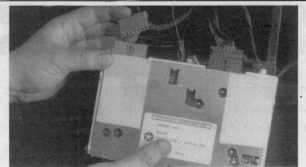

Fig. 51 Unplug and label the electrical connectors from the back of the radio

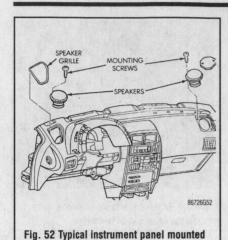

Fig. 52 Typical instrument panel mounted speaker assembly

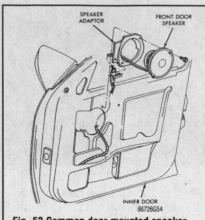

Fig. 53 Common door mounted speaker assembly

Fig. 54 Common rear trim panel mounted speaker assembly

1. Disconnect the negative battery cable.
2. Remove the console, cluster bezel or any trim panels to gain access to the front of the radio, as required.
3. Remove the screws that attach the radio to the instrument panel.
4. Slightly pull the radio out of the dashboard. Unplug and label the electrical wiring connectors, ground cable and antenna. Remove the radio.
5. If the radio is tandem-mounted with a graphic equalizer or CD player, loosen and remove the bracket screws holding the components in the mounting bracket. Unplug any electrical wiring connecting the two components. Remove the radio and other component out of the mounting bracket.
6. Installation is the reverse of the removal procedure.
7. Connect the negative battery cable and check all functions of the radio for proper operation.

Speakers

REMOVAL & INSTALLATION

Instrument Panel Mounted

▶ **See Figure 52**

➡**This procedure applies to all vehicles covered by this manual. Some slight differences may arise; adjust the procedure accordingly.**

1. Disconnect the negative battery cable.
2. Remove the speaker cover grilles by prying upward at the rear corners of the grille with a blunt edge plastic or wooden tool.
3. As the rearward edge of the speaker grille comes free of the pad, insert your fingers under the exposed grille surface and push up to disengage two posts at the forward corners of the grille.
4. Remove the speaker mounting screws.

5. Lift the speaker up and out of its mounting hole. Unplug and label the electrical wiring connectors to the speaker.
6. Remove the speaker.
7. Installation is the reverse of the removal procedure.
8. Connect the negative battery cable.

Door Mounted

▶ **See Figure 53**

➡**This procedure applies to all vehicles covered by this manual. Some slight differences may arise; adjust the procedure accordingly.**

1. Disconnect the negative battery cable.
2. Remove the door trim panel. Refer to Section 10 for this procedure.
3. Remove the speaker retaining screws.
4. Pull the speaker away from the door and unplug the electrical wires from the speaker.
5. Installation is the reverse of the removal procedure.
6. Connect the negative battery cable.

Rear Trim Panel Mounted

▶ **See Figure 54**

➡**This procedure applies to all vehicles covered by this manual. Some slight differences may arise: adjust the procedure accordingly.**

1. Disconnect the negative battery cable.
2. Pull the speaker grille away from the quarter trim panel to disengage the retaining clips.
3. Remove the speaker retaining screws.
4. Pull the speaker away from the body and unplug the electrical wires from the speaker.
5. To install, reverse the removal procedure.
6. Connect the negative battery cable.

WINDSHIELD WIPERS

Windshield Wiper Blade and Arm

REMOVAL & INSTALLATION

Wiper Blade

▶ **See Figures 55 and 56**

1. Lift the wiper arm away from the glass.
2. Depress the coil spring in the wiper blade with a narrow prytool and remove the blade from the wiper arm.

To install:
3. Snap the wiper blade onto the arm by inserting the wiper arm stud through the blade assembly.

Wiper Arm Assembly

▶ **See Figures 57 thru 63**

1. On latch release type: lift the arm (note installation position) so that the latch can be pulled out to the holding position and then release the arm. The arm will remain off the windshield in this position.
2. On the arm attaching nut type: lift the wiper arm (note installation posi-

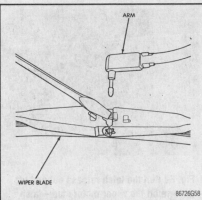

Fig. 55 Press down on the tang with a flat-bladed prytool to release the wiper blade retaining mechanism

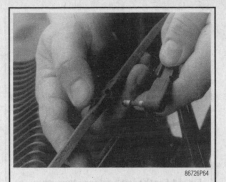

Fig. 56 Press the wiper blade onto the wiper arm mounting stud until it snaps in place

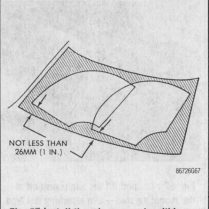

Fig. 57 Install the wiper arms to within these specifications

NOT LESS THAN 26MM (1 IN.)

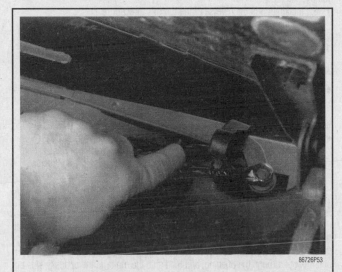

Fig. 58 Remove the wiper arm mounting nut, then . . .

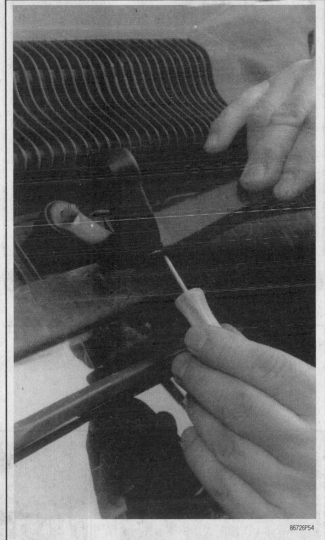

Fig. 59 . . . while holding the wiper arm up, insert a slim tool into the hole near the hinge . . .

tion) and place a ⅛ in. (3mm) pin or equivalent into the arm hole. Lift the head cover and remove the attaching nut.

3. On all types, remove the arm assembly from the mounting stud using a rocking and lifting motion.

To install:

4. When installing the wiper arm, the motor should be in the park position and the tips of the blades ¾–1½ in. (19–38mm) above the bottom of the windshield molding.

5. Position the wiper arm over the mounting stud.

6. Tighten the arm attaching nut to 120 inch lbs. (13 Nm).

7. Install the nut cover.

8. Operate the wipers to check all components for proper operation.

Rear Window Wiper Blade and Arm

REMOVAL & INSTALLATION

Wiper Blade

1. Lift the wiper arm away from the glass.

2. Depress the coil spring in the wiper blade with a narrow prytool and remove the blade from the wiper arm.

To install:

3. Snap the wiper blade onto the arm by inserting the wiper arm stud through the blade assembly.

4. Lower the blade down to the window.

Wiper Arm Assembly

Refer to the procedures for the removal and installation of the windshield wiper arms, described earlier in this section.

Fig. 60 . . . and lift the wiper arm off of the mounting stud—arm attaching nut type

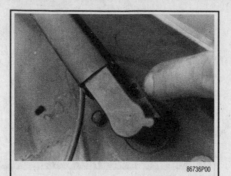

Fig. 61 For the latch release type, the release lever is located on the wiper arm as shown

Fig. 62 Pull the latch release out and lift the arm off the wiper motor stud—latch release type

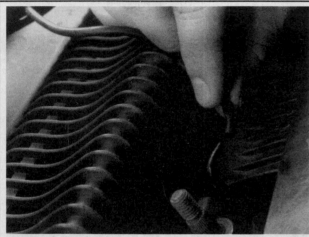

Fig. 63 After removing the wiper arm, detach the washer hose at the cowl panel

Windshield Wiper Motor

REMOVAL & INSTALLATION

1981–85 Models

1. Disconnect the negative battery terminal.
2. Disconnect the linkage from the motor crank arm.
3. Remove the wiper motor plastic cover.
4. Detach the wiring harness from the motor.

5. Remove the three mounting bolts from the motor mounting bracket and remove the motor.
6. Installation is the reverse of the removal procedure.
7. Connect the negative battery cable.

1986–88 Models

AE, AG, AJ, AK, AND AC BODIES

▸ See Figures 64 thru 69

1. With the ignition switch **ON**, turn the wiper switch on until the wipers have run halfway across the windshield and then turn the switch **OFF**. Leave the ignition switch **ON** until the wipers are fully parked and then turn it **OFF**.
2. Remove the wiper arms and blades as described earlier in this section. On the Daytona, detach the washer fluid reservoir hose at the tee connector.
3. Remove the plastic screen from the top of the cowl.
4. Remove the mounting bolts from the two pivots for the wiper arms.
5. Remove the plastic cover for the wiper motor from the cowl. Detach the motor electrical connector. Remove the three motor mounting nuts.
6. Push the pivots down into the plenum chamber behind the cowl, then pull the motor outward, past the point where it clears the mounting studs, and then as far toward the driver's side of the car as it will go. At this point, pull the right pivot and link out through the opening, and then shift the motor to the opposite side of the opening to remove it, the passenger's side link, and that side's pivot.
7. Carefully clamp the motor bracket in a vise and remove the nut from the end of the motor shaft. Separate the linkage from the shaft. If the motor is to be reinstalled, be careful not to turn it out of the PARK position.
8. If the motor's position is disturbed or if installing a new motor that is obviously not in the PARK position: Connect the wiring connector, turn the ignition switch **ON**, turn the wiper switch on briefly, then turn it back off. When the motor has reached the PARK position, turn the ignition switch **OFF**.

To install:

9. Connect the linkage to the motor with the crank by installing the crank so its D-shaped slot fits over the motor shaft. Install the attaching nut and tighten it to 95 inch lbs. (11 Nm).

Fig. 64 Remove the wiper motor cover attaching bolts . . .

Fig. 65 . . . then lift the cover off of the motor

Fig. 66 Disengage the small black wiring harness connector and . . .

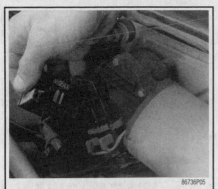

Fig. 67 . . . any other electrical connectors attached to the motor

Fig. 68 Remove the wiper motor retaining bolts . . .

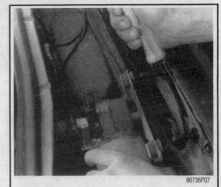

Fig. 69 . . . and, while prying the linkage from the motor arm, remove the motor

10. Maneuver the left pivot and its link into the chamber behind the cowl. Slide the assembly all the way to the left (toward the driver's side of the car) until the motor clears the mounting studs and the crank is positioned behind the sheet metal. Push the right pivot and link through the opening in the cowl; then, maneuver the assembly to the right until the motor is lined up with the mounting studs and install it over those studs.

11. Install the 3 motor mounting nuts and tighten to 55 inch lbs. (6 Nm).

12. Position the pivots and install the pivot mounting bolts, torquing them to 55 inch lbs. (6 Nm). Connect the motor wiring connector.

13. Install the plastic motor cover onto the cowl. On Daytona with passive restraints, connect the washer fluid reservoir hose to the Tee connector. Note that the hoses passes through a special hole in the cowl screen, then mount the screen to the cowl, on these cars.

14. Install the wiper arms and connect their washer hoses to the Tee connectors.

AH AND AP BODY

1. Remove the wiper arms, as described earlier in this section. Open the hood.

2. Remove the cover from the top of the cowl, then remove the 2 or 3 attaching screws from each wiper pivot.

3. Detach the wiper motor wiring connector.

4. Remove the 3 bolts that attach the motor mounting bracket to the body, then remove the motor, its bracket, and the linkage assembly from the cowl plenum.

5. Carefully clamp the motor bracket in a vise and remove the nut from the end of the motor shaft. Separate the linkage from the shaft. If the motor is to be reinstalled, be careful not to turn it out of the PARK position.

6. If the motor's position is disturbed or if installing a new motor that is obviously not in the PARK position, connect the wiring connector, turn **ON** the ignition switch, turn the wiper switch on briefly and then turn it back off. When the motor has reached the PARK position, turn **OFF** the ignition switch.

To install:

7. Connect the linkage to the motor with the crank by installing the crank

so its D-shaped slot fits over the motor shaft. Install the attaching nut and tighten it to 95 inch lbs. (11 Nm).

8. Install the motor, bracket and linkage assembly into the cowl plenum.

9. Loosely install the 3 attaching screws for each pivot, then install the 3 motor mounting bracket attaching bolts. Finally, tighten the pivot attaching screws.

10. Connect the motor electrical connector. Install the cowl cover. Install and adjust the wiper arms as described earlier in this section.

1989–95 Models

♦ See Figures 70 thru 75

1. Disconnect the negative battery cable.

2. If the cowl top plastic cover must be removed to access the motor, first remove the wiper arm and blade assemblies, then and remove the cover.

3. Remove the wiper motor cover and detach the motor wiring harness.

4. Disconnect the linkage drive crank from the output shaft.

5. Remove the motor mounting nuts, then remove the wiper motor and wiper linkage from the vehicle.

➡ Do not rotate the motor output shaft from the park position.

To install:

6. Assemble the linkage to the motor. Make sure that the crank fits over the D slot on the motor shaft. Tighten the mounting nut to 90–100 inch lbs. (10–11 Nm). Be sure the motor is still in the park position before assembling to the linkage; if it is not, temporarily connect the motor to the wiring and operate the switch to park the motor before assembling the linkage.

7. Position the wiper motor and install the retaining nuts until snug.

8. Attach the linkage drive crank to the motor crank arm.

9. Plug the wiper motor wiring back together.

10. Install the wiper motor cover.

11. Install the wiper arms and plastic cowl if removed previously.

12. Connect the negative battery cable and check the wiper motor for proper operation.

Fig. 70 To remove the wiper motor, first remove the cowl panel retaining screws, then . . .

Fig. 71 . . . remove the cowl panel

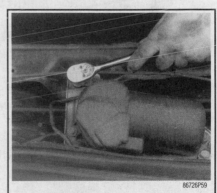

Fig. 72 Remove the three wiper motor cover mounting bolts and . . .

Fig. 73 . . . lift the wiper motor cover off of the motor, then . . .

Fig. 74 . . . label and detach the electrical connectors from the wiper motor

Fig. 75 Lift the wiper motor up and detach the wiper linkage from the motor output shaft

Rear Window Wiper Motor

REMOVAL & INSTALLATION

1981–88 Models

▶ See Figure 76

1. Disconnect the negative battery terminal.
2. Remove the blade and arm assembly. Remove the grommet and escutcheon from the motor driveshaft.
3. Open the liftgate.
4. Remove the trim panel from the inside of the liftgate.
5. Remove the motor cover and disengage the wiring connector.
6. Remove the four bracket retaining screws and remove the motor.
7. Installation is the reverse of the removal procedure.
8. Connect the negative battery terminal.

1989–95 Models

➡ For more information regarding the different body classifications included in this manual, refer to Section 1.

1. Disconnect the negative battery cable.
2. Remove the wiper arm by lifting it against its spring tension and releasing the latch. Lift the arm off of the motor shaft.
3. Open the liftgate and remove the trim panel. Detach the connector from the motor.
4. Remove the grommet from the liftgate glass.
5. Remove the screws that fasten the bracket to the liftgate and remove the motor assembly from the vehicle.

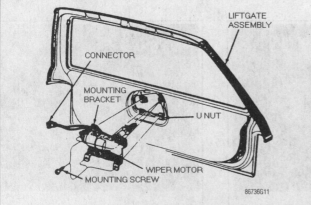

Fig. 76 Location of the rear window wiper motor used on 1986–88 Aries, Sundance and Shadow models

To install:
6. Install a new grommet in the liftgate glass.
7. Position the motor on the liftgate and secure with the screws. Tighten the screws to 60–70 inch lbs. (7–8 Nm).
8. Connect the feed wires to the motor.
9. Install the trim panel.
10. Install and the arm and blade assembly.
11. Tighten the wiper arm nut to 13–14 ft. lbs. (17–19 Nm).
12. Connect the negative battery cable and check the liftgate wiper system for proper operation.

Wiper Linkage

REMOVAL & INSTALLATION

The linkage is removed along with the windshield wiper motor. Refer to the wiper motor procedure earlier in this section.

Windshield Washer Motor

REMOVAL & INSTALLATION

1. Drain the washer fluid from the reservoir.
2. Remove the mounting screws from the reservoir and remove the reservoir/pump assembly from the vehicle.
3. Disconnect the electrical lead and rubber hose from the bottom of the pump.
4. Gently pry the pump away from the reservoir and out of the grommet. Care must be taken not to puncture the reservoir.
5. Remove the rubber grommet from the reservoir and discard.
6. Installation is the reverse of the removal procedure.
7. Fill the reservoir with washer fluid.

Rear Window Washer Motor

REMOVAL & INSTALLATION

1. Remove the washer reservoir and pump assembly.
2. With what Chrysler refers to as "mechanical fingers" (a pair of long needle nose pliers or another suitable tool should work), loosen the pump filter and nut through the liquid filler opening.
3. Disconnect the outside portion of the pump.
4. Remove the inner and outer portions of the pump, then remove the pump from the reservoir.
To install:
5. Install a new rubber grommet into place in the bottom of the reservoir.
6. Position the pump in place, then install the nut through the filler opening and tighten it with the same tool used to loosen it.
7. Install the reservoir and pump assembly.

INSTRUMENTS AND SWITCHES

Instrument Cluster

REMOVAL & INSTALLATION

1981–85 Models

◆ **See Figure 77**

CONVENTIONAL CLUSTER

1. Disconnect the negative battery terminal.
2. Apply the parking brake and block the wheels. Place the gearshift lever in position **1**.
3. Remove the instrument panel trim strip.
4. Remove the left upper and lower cluster bezel screws.
5. Remove the right lower cluster bezel screw and retaining clip.
6. Remove the instrument cluster bezel by snapping the bezel off of the five retaining clips.
7. Remove the seven retaining screws and remove the upper right bezel.
8. Remove the four rear instrument panel top cover mounting screws.
9. Lift the rear edge of the panel top cover and remove the two screws attaching the upper trim strip retainer and cluster housing to the base panel.
10. Remove the trim strip retainer.
11. Remove the two screws attaching the cluster housing to the base panel of the lower cluster.
12. Lift the rearward edge of the panel top cover and slide the cluster housing rearward.
13. Detach the right printed circuit board connector from behind the cluster housing.
14. Detach the speedometer cable connector.
15. Detach the left printed circuit connector.
16. Remove the cluster assembly.

To install:

17. Position the cluster in front of the instrument panel opening, then attach the left printed circuit connector, the speedometer cable connector and the right printed circuit board connector to the back of the cluster.
18. Slide the cluster into position in the instrument panel, then install the retaining screws.
19. The remainder of installation is the reverse of the removal procedure.
20. Position the transaxle in Park (if automatic).
21. Connect the negative battery cable.

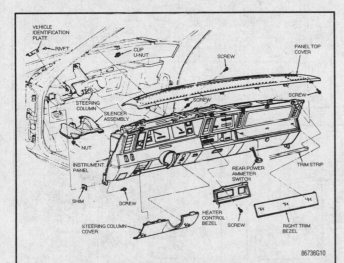

Fig. 77 Exploded view of instrument panels equipped with conventional instrument clusters—1981–85 models

ELECTRONIC CLUSTER

The electronic cluster is removed in the same manner as the conventional cluster, except for that there is no speedometer cable. When replacing the electronic cluster, the odometer memory chip can be removed from the old cluster and placed in the new one. To remove the chip, special tool C-4817 must be used.

1986–88 Except AG and AJ Bodies

➡ **For more information regarding the different body classifications included in this manual, refer to Vehicle Identification in Section 1.**

CONVENTIONAL CLUSTER

1. Disconnect the negative battery cable. Apply the parking brake and block the wheels. If the vehicle is equipped with an automatic transaxle with column shift, position the gearshift lever in the **1** position.
2. Remove the 6 screws from the cluster bezel, then remove the bezel by snapping it off of all 5 retaining clips.
3. Remove the rear-facing screws from the instrument panel upper pad, then lift the rearward edge of the pad and, while holding it up, remove the 2 screws from the top of the cluster.
4. Remove the 2 screws from the bottom of the cluster (these attach it to the dash panel). Lift the rear edge of the pad on top of the dash and hold it upward as you pull the cluster out far enough to reach the wiring.
5. Unscrew the speedometer outer cable retaining collar and then pull the inner cable out of the rear of the speedometer. If necessary, mark the wiring connectors, then detach all of them.
6. Remove the cluster.

To install:

7. To install the cluster, first position it in front of the dash, then reconnect the wiring connectors to their original locations. Insert the square end of the speedometer cable into the rear of the speedometer, turning it slightly to line it up, if necessary. Install and tighten the speedometer cable collar nut.
8. Lift the rear edge of the dash pad and hold it upward as you slide the cluster back into position.
9. Install the 4 cluster attaching screws (2 at the bottom and 2 at the top, under the pad). Install the rear-facing screws into the instrument panel upper pad.
10. Install the bezel so all the retaining clips lock, then install the 6 bezel attaching screws. Return the gearshift lever to Park and reconnect the battery cable.

ELECTRONIC CLUSTER

The electronic cluster is removed in the same manner as the conventional cluster, except for that there is no speedometer cable. When replacing the electronic cluster, the odometer memory chip can be removed from the old cluster and placed in the new one. To remove the chip, special tool C-4817 must be used.

➡ **On some later models the odometer memory is no longer retained in the cluster. This information is stored in the body computer.**

1986–88 AG and AJ Body Vehicles

➡ **For more information regarding the different body classifications included in this manual, refer to Vehicle Identification in Section 1.**

1. Disconnect the battery negative cable. Remove the 5 screws attaching the top of the cluster bezel to the instrument panel.
2. Pull the bezel to the rear to disengage the 3 clips on its bottom surface and then remove it.
3. Remove the four screws attaching the cluster housing to the dash panel.
4. Pull the cluster assembly to the rear to gain clearance to the wiring, then reach underneath it to detach the wiring harness.
5. Remove the cluster from the instrument panel.
6. Installation is the reverse of the removal procedure.
7. Connect the negative battery cable.

1989-95 Models

AP BODY WITH CONVENTIONAL OR ELECTRONIC CLUSTER

♦ See Figures 78, 79 and 80

➡For more information regarding the different body classifications included in this manual, refer to Vehicle Identification in Section 1.

1. Disconnect the negative battery cable.
2. Remove the instrument cluster bezel. Cluster removal is not necessary if just removing gauges.
3. When only removing gauge(s) or the speedometer, remove the trip odometer reset knob, if necessary, followed by the mask and lens assembly, then remove the desired gauge from the cluster. Disconnect the speedometer cable, if equipped, when removing the speedometer.
4. If equipped with an automatic transaxle and column shift, remove the lower column cover and detach the gear indicator cable.
5. Remove the screws attaching the cluster to the instrument panel.
6. Pull the cluster out and detach all wiring harnesses and the speedometer cable, if equipped. Remove the cluster from the vehicle.

To install:

7. Position the cluster and feed the gear indicator cable through its slot.
8. Connect all wiring and install the speedometer cable to the speedometer, if removed; make sure the cable end is securely clicked in place.
9. Install the cluster retaining screws. Connect the gearshift indicator cable.
10. Install the cluster bezel.
11. Connect the negative battery cable, check all gauges and the speedometer for proper operation.
12. Make sure the gearshift indicator is properly aligned.

AA, AG AND AJ BODIES WITH CONVENTIONAL OR ELECTRONIC CLUSTER

♦ See Figure 81

➡For more information regarding the different body classifications included in this manual, refer to Vehicle Identification in Section 1.

1. Disconnect the battery negative cable to assure no air bag system diagnostic codes are stored.

2. Remove the switch pod assembly.
3. Unscrew the tilt column if so equipped.
4. Remove the steering column trim cover.
5. Remove the attaching screws on the cluster and pull the cluster rearward.
6. Tilt the cluster to detach the wiring connections. Remove the cluster.
7. Slide the cluster part way into its opening, then attach the electrical connections.
8. Position the cluster so that the screw holes align, then install the retaining screws.
9. The remainder of installation is the reverse of the removal procedure.
10. Connect the negative battery cable and check all gauges, switches and the speedometer for proper operation.

AB BODY WITH CONVENTIONAL OR ELECTRONIC CLUSTER

♦ See Figure 82, 83, and 84

➡For more information regarding the different body classifications included in this manual, refer to Vehicle Identification in Section 1.

1. Disconnect the negative battery cable.
2. Remove the screws retaining the instrument cluster bezel and remove the bezel.
3. Remove the cluster retaining screws and tilt the cluster forward. Detach the electrical connectors.
4. If necessary, detach the speedometer cable.
5. Remove the lower instrument panel cover and remove the cluster.
6. Installation is the reverse of the removal procedure.
7. Connect the negative battery cable.

Windshield Wiper Switch

REMOVAL & INSTALLATION

The front wiper switch on most vehicles (exceptions follow) is part of the combination turn signal/cruise control/wiper switch or column mounted assembly. Refer to the appropriate procedure in Section 8 or the service procedures below.

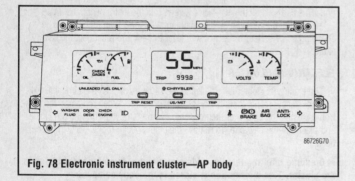

Fig. 78 Electronic instrument cluster—AP body

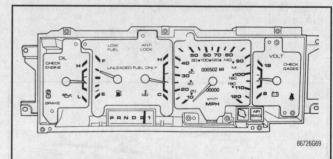

Fig. 79 Conventional instrument cluster—AP body

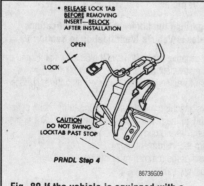

Fig. 80 If the vehicle is equipped with a column shift, detach the PRNDL cable as shown

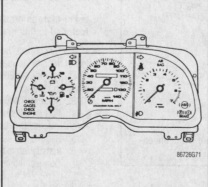

Fig. 81 Conventional instrument cluster with the mask and lens—AA body

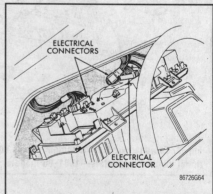

Fig. 82 Remove the upper bezel screws to remove the bezel—AB body

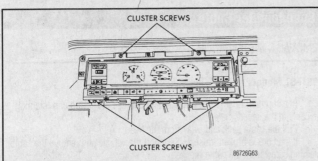

Fig. 83 Remove the cluster screws and pull the cluster part way out of the dashboard—AB body

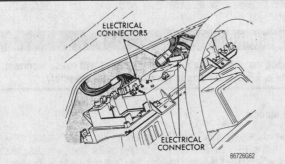

Fig. 84 Unplug the electrical connectors from the rear of the instrument cluster—AB body

AG and AJ Bodies

➡️**For more information regarding the different body classifications included in this manual, refer to Vehicle Identification in Section 1.**

1. Disconnect the negative battery cable.
2. Remove the panel vent grille above the switch pod assembly and remove the 2 revealed pod mounting screws.
3. Remove the 2 remaining screws under the pod and pull the pod out to detach the wiring harnesses. Remove the pod from the instrument panel.
4. Remove the inner panel from the pod. Disconnect the switch linkage from the buttons.
5. Remove the windshield wiper switch mounting screws and remove the entire switch assembly.
6. Installation is the reverse of the removal procedure.
7. Connect the negative battery cable and check the entire wiper system for proper operation.

AB Body

➡️**For more information regarding the different body classifications included in this manual, refer to Vehicle Identification in Section 1.**

Refer to the Headlight (Combination Switch) service procedures in this section.

Rear Window Washer/Wiper Switch

REMOVAL & INSTALLATION

➡️**Use these service procedures as guide. Slight variations may occur due to extra connections, etc., but the basic procedure should work on applicable models.**

Except AG and AJ Bodies

➡️**For more information regarding the different body classifications included in this manual, refer to Vehicle Identification in Section 1.**

1. Disconnect the negative battery cable.
2. Remove the instrument cluster bezel as described earlier in this section.

3. Remove the left lower trim bezel by pulling it off the two attaching clips. Pull it out of the dash just far enough to reach the wiring connectors. Note the wires and their connector locations for easy reinstallation, detach the connectors.
4. Remove the 2 screws attaching the wiper switch to the bezel assembly and pull it off.
5. Installation is the reverse of the removal procedure.

AG and AJ Bodies

➡️**For more information regarding the different body classifications included in this manual, refer to Vehicle Identification in Section 1.**

1. Disconnect the negative battery cable.
2. Lift the console lid. Remove the 2 screws from the console bezel and lift the bezel assembly out of the console.
3. Detach the rear wiper/washer switch connectors.
4. Remove the 2 switch-to-bezel mounting screws and remove the switch from the bezel.
5. Installation is the reverse of the removal procedure.

Headlight Switch

REMOVAL & INSTALLATION

➡️**For more information regarding the different body classifications included in this manual, refer to Vehicle Identification in Section 1.**

1981–88 MODELS—EXCEPT AP BODY MODELS

➡️**For more information regarding the different body classifications included in this manual, refer to Vehicle Identification in Section 1.**

1. Disconnect the negative battery cable.
2. Remove the cluster bezel as necessary.
3. Remove the three screws securing the headlamp switch mounting plate to the base panel.
4. Pull the switch and plate rearward and disengage the wiring connector.
5. Depress the button on the switch and remove the knob and stem.
6. Snap out the escutcheon, then remove the nut that attaches the switch to the mounting plate.
   To install:
7. Position the switch so that the switch protrudes through the mounting plate from the back, then install the attaching nut until snug.
8. Snap the escutcheon into place.
9. Insert the knob and stem into the switch until the switch engages the stem barb. Gently pull out on the knob to ensure that the stem is locked into the switch.
10. Attach the wiring harness connector to the switch, then place the switch in the instrument panel and install the attaching screws. Tighten the screws until snug.
11. Install the cluster bezel if necessary.
12. Connect the negative battery cable.

1987–88 AP BODY MODELS

➡️**For more information regarding the different body classifications included in this manual, refer to Vehicle Identification in Section 1.**

1. Remove the headlamp switch bezel from the instrument panel by unsnapping the attaching tangs.
2. Remove the 3 screws securing the switch mounting plate to the instrument panel, then pull the switch and mounting plate rearward and out of the instrument panel opening.
3. Disengage the electrical connector at the switch. Press the release button on the bottom of the switch and then pull the knob and shaft out of the switch.
4. Detach the headlamp switch escutcheon from the mounting plate by unsnapping the attaching tangs and removing it, then unscrew the switch-to-mounting plate retaining nut and pull the switch off the mounting plate.
5. Installation is the reverse of the removal procedure.

1989–93 AG AND AJ BODY MODELS

➡️**For more information regarding the different body classifications included in this manual, refer to Vehicle Identification in Section 1.**

1. Disconnect the negative battery cable.
2. Remove the panel vent grille above the switch pod assembly and remove the 2 revealed pod mounting screws.
3. Remove the 2 remaining screws under the pod and pull the pod out to detach the wiring harnesses. Remove the pod from the instrument panel.
4. Remove the turn signal switch lever by pulling it straight out of the pod.
5. Remove the inner panel from the pod. Remove the turn signal switch in order to gain access to the headlight switch.
6. Disconnect the switch linkage from the buttons.
7. Remove the switch mounting screws and remove the entire switch assembly.
8. Installation is the reverse of the removal procedure.
9. Connect the negative battery cable and check the system for proper operation.

1989–95 AA, AP AND AQ BODY MODELS

➡For more information regarding the different body classifications included in this manual, refer to Vehicle Identification in Section 1.

1. Disconnect the negative battery cable.
2. Remove the headlight switch bezel or cluster bezel, as required.
3. Remove the screws securing the headlight switch mounting plate to the instrument panel. Pull the assembly out and detach the connectors from the switch.
4. Depress the spring button and remove the headlight switch knob and stem.
5. Remove the escutcheon, if equipped, and remove the nut that attaches the switch to the mounting plate.
6. Installation is the reverse of the removal procedure.
7. Connect the negative battery cable and check the switch for proper operation.

LIGHTING

Headlights

REMOVAL & INSTALLATION

Sealed Beam

➡If vehicle is equipped with headlamp doors turn the headlight switch ON. Open the hood and locate the power distribution center. This center is located in the front of the left front strut tower. Remove the cover from the center and remove the Headlamp Close Relay. This will prevent the headlamp doors from closing to provide easier servicing. Turn the headlight switch to OFF, then perform this repair.

1. Remove the headlight bezel.
2. Unhook the spring from the headlight retaining ring if so equipped.
3. Unscrew the retaining ring and remove it.

➡Do not disturb the two long aiming screws. Conventional and Halogen headlamp sealed beams units are interchangeable in pairs, but it is recommended that they not be mixed together (one halogen and one conventional). It is fine to upgrade from conventional bulbs to halogen, but do not change from halogen bulbs to conventional bulbs, especially if the vehicle came equipped with halogen bulbs.

4. Unplug the old sealed beam from the engine electrical wiring harness.
5. Extract the old bulb from its mounting bracket.
To install:
6. Connect the replacement bulb and install it into the receptacle (check operation of headlight before completing repair).
7. Install the retaining ring and secure it in place with the retaining screws. Connect the spring.
8. Install the headlight bezel.

Aero Headlamp

Aero headlamp systems use replaceable halogen bulbs that are mounted in aerodynamic, molded plastic lens reflector assemblies.

Speedometer Cable

REMOVAL & INSTALLATION

1981–87 Models

1. Reach under the instrument panel and depress the spring clip retaining the cable to the speedometer head.
2. Pull the cable back and away from the head.
3. If the core is broken, raise and support the vehicle and remove the cable retaining screw from the cable bracket.
4. Carefully slide the cable out of the transaxle.
To install:
5. Coat the new core sparingly with speedometer cable lubricant and insert it in the cable.
6. Install the cable at the transaxle, lower the car and install the cable at the speedometer head.

❊❊❊ WARNING

Do not bend the cable or cable housing, a bend will cause incorrect indication or abnormal noise in the speedometer assembly.

1988–95 Models

The front wheel drive, 4-cylinder Chrysler, Dodge, Eagle and Plymouth vehicles from 1988 to 1995 do not utilize speedometer cables. These vehicles use a distance or vehicle speed sensor to measure the speed of the vehicle. This sensor is mounted on the transaxle near the flywheel. Refer to Section 4 for the vehicle speed sensor.

➡Lens fogging is a normal condition and does not require service, as moisture will vent from tubes behind the lens on Aero headlamp-type system.

▶ See Figures 85, 86 and 87

It may be necessary to remove the entire headlamp assembly if enough access cannot be gained otherwise.
1. Locate and remove the wire connector behind the headlamp assembly in the engine compartment. It may be necessary to remove certain items in the engine compartment to gain access to the bulb wires.
2. Rotate the bulb retaining ring counterclockwise ¼ turn and remove the ring, bulb and bulb holder from the lens assembly. The bulb holder has alignment notches.

➡Do not touch the bulb with bare fingers or any possibly oily surface, since reduced bulb life may result!

To install:
3. Wearing gloves or holding the replacement bulb with a cloth rag to keep oil off of the bulb surface, insert the bulb into the rear hole of the headlamp assembly. Make certain that the alignment grooves and tabs line up, push the light bulb into the assembly until seated flush, then turn the bulb clockwise ¼ turn.
4. Plug the electrical light bulb wiring harness into the new light bulb. Install any items removed from the engine compartment.

MANUAL OPERATION OF POWER HEADLAMP DOORS

▶ See Figure 88

A manual over-ride hand wheel permits the power headlamp doors to be opened in case of motor failure or to service the headlamps. The wheel is located on the top of the headlamp door drive motor. To gain access to the wheel, open the hood and go in through the flap located in the sight shield behind the bumper fascia. The wheel must be turned a number of turns to remove play and then open the doors.
1. Disconnect the negative battery cable.

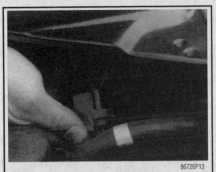

Fig. 85 To remove the light bulb, first unplug the headlight electrical connector, then . . .

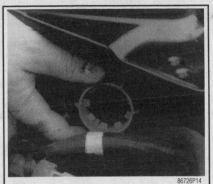

Fig. 86 . . . remove the light bulb socket retaining ring

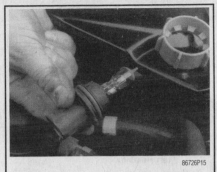

Fig. 87 Rotate the light bulb socket ¼ turn counter-clockwise, then pull it straight out of the lens assembly

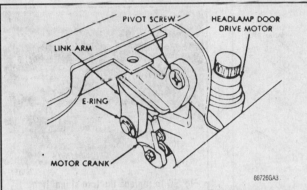

Fig. 88 The power headlamp drive mechanism—note the location of the manual actuating wheel on the top of the drive motor

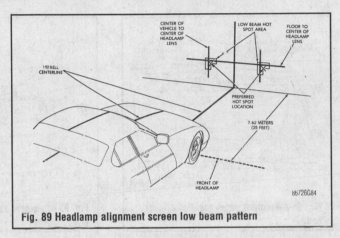

Fig. 89 Headlamp alignment screen low beam pattern

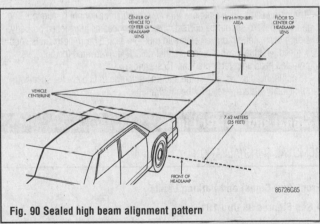

Fig. 90 Sealed high beam alignment pattern

2. Locate the manual override knob. On Daytona, they are located under access shields behind the bumper facia and under the center of the front bumper on LeBaron and other models.

3. Remove the protective cover boot.

4. Rotate the manual override knob to raise the headlight cover(s).

5. Connect the negative battery cable.

ALIGNMENT

Aiming Preparation

➡Headlamps should be adjusted with a special alignment tool, state regulations may vary this procedure, use the following procedure for temporary adjustments only.

Perform the following items before attempting to aim the headlamps:
- Verify the headlamp dimmer and high beam indicator operation
- Inspect and correct all components that could interfere with the proper headlamp alignment
- Verify proper tire inflation on all wheels
- Clean headlamp lenses and make sure that there are no heavy loads in the trunk or hatch luggage area
- The fuel tank should be full. Add 6.5 lbs. (3 kg) of weight over the fuel tank for each estimated gallon of missing fuel.

Alignment Screen Preparation

♦ See Figures 89 and 90

1. Position the vehicle on a level surface perpendicular to a flat wall 25 ft. (7.62 m) away from the front of the headlamp lens.

2. From the floor up 5 ft. (1.3 m), tape a line on the wall at the centerline of the vehicle. Sight along the centerline of the vehicle (from the rear of the vehicle forward) to verify accuracy of the line placement.

3. Rock the vehicle side to side and up and down (on front bumper assembly) a few times to allow the suspension to stabilize.

4. Measure the distance from the center of the headlamp lens to the floor. Transfer measurements to the alignment screen with tape. Use this mark for the up/down adjustment reference.

5. Measure distance from the centerline of the vehicle to the center of each headlamp being aligned. Transfer measurements to screen with tape to each side of the vehicle centerline. Use this mark for left/right adjustment reference.

Headlight Adjustment

♦ See Figures 91, 92, 93, 94 and 95

A properly aimed low beam headlamp will project the top edge of high intensity pattern on the alignment screen from 2 in. (50mm) above to 2 in. (50mm) below the headlamp centerline. The side-to-side outboard edge of high intensity pattern should be from 2 in. (50mm) left to 2 in. (50mm) right of the headlamp centerline.

➡The preferred headlamp alignment is "0" for the up/down adjustment and "0" for the left/right adjustment.

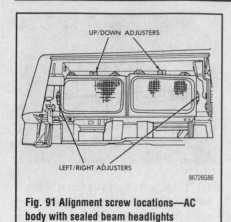

Fig. 91 Alignment screw locations—AC body with sealed beam headlights

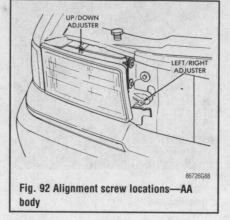

Fig. 92 Alignment screw locations—AA body

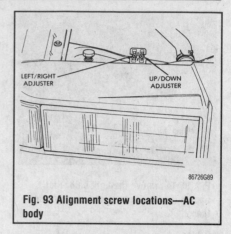

Fig. 93 Alignment screw locations—AC body

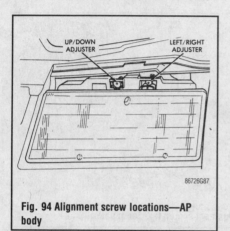

Fig. 94 Alignment screw locations—AP body

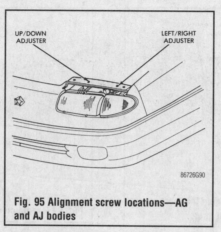

Fig. 95 Alignment screw locations—AG and AJ bodies

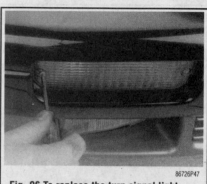

Fig. 96 To replace the turn signal light bulbs, remove the lens assembly retaining screws and . . .

The high beams on a vehicle with a Aero headlamps cannot be aligned. The high beam pattern should be correct when the low beams are aligned properly. The high beam pattern on vehicles with multiple sealed beam headlamps should be aligned with the low beam lamp either detached or covered (do not cover illuminated headlamp for more than 15 seconds).

To adjust headlamps, adjust the alignment screws to achieve the specified high intensity pattern—refer to the illustrations.

Signal and Marker Lights

REMOVAL & INSTALLATION

Front Turn Signal and Parking Lights

▶ See Figures 96 thru 101

The marker lights are replaced with new ones by removing the lamp assembly from the bumper or quarter panel, twisting and pulling the socket out of the assembly, and then twisting the lamp to release it from the socket.

Where the lamp is located in an assembly separate from the headlamp, remove the screws from the lens and pull the assembly out of the bumper fascia.

Where the lamp is located in the side of the headlamp bezel, remove the two nuts from the rear of the turn signal/parking light assembly. These are located in the wall of the bezel, directly in front of the headlight and will also release the lens (catch it and remove it to a safe place to keep it from being damaged).

Remove the lamp by turning it to release it from the socket. Install the new lamp by inserting it into the socket so the prongs line up with the internal grooves, permitting it to be turned and locked easily. If the lamp cannot be fully inserted and turned readily, turn it 180° and try again. Insert the socket into the assembly and turn it tight to lock it, then install the lamp assembly. On separate designs, install the mounting screws. On integral designs, install the lens and then turn the nuts over the threaded studs on the back of the lens.

Side Marker Lights

▶ See Figures 102, 103, 104 and 105

The side marker lights are located in a socket locked into the back of the lamp assembly. Reach in behind the bumper, grasp the socket, turn it to release, and pull it from the lamp. Some newer models may require the removal of the lens assembly from the fender before access to the light bulb socket can be gained.

Remove the lamp by turning it to release it from the socket. Install the new lamp by inserting it into the socket so the prongs line up with the internal grooves, permitting it to be turned and locked easily. If the lamp cannot be fully inserted and turned readily, turn it 180° and try again. Insert the socket into the lamp assembly and turn it tight to lock it.

Rear Turn Signal, Brake, and Parking Lights

▶ See Figures 106 thru 112

For sedans, remove the luggage compartment rear trim cover, then loosen the quarter panel silencer and shift it out of the way. Grasp the appropriate socket and rotate it counterclockwise; then pull it out of the lamp. Rotate the bulb counterclockwise and remove it from the socket.

Install the new lamp by inserting it into the socket so the prongs line up with the internal grooves, permitting it to be turned and locked easily. If the lamp cannot be fully inserted and turned readily, turn it 180° and try again. Insert the socket into the lamp assembly and turn it tight to lock it.

On wagons, depress the flexible bumper fascia and use a socket wrench and extension to remove the two lower attaching nuts for the lamp assembly. Open the hatch to gain access to the two upper nuts and use the same tool to remove them. Pull the lamp assembly off the mounting studs.

Grasp the appropriate socket and rotate it counterclockwise; then pull it out of the lamp. Rotate the bulb counterclockwise and remove it from the socket.

Install the new lamp by inserting it into the socket so the prongs line up with the internal grooves, permitting it to be turned and locked easily. If the lamp

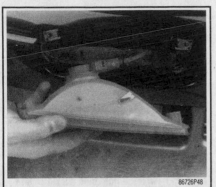

Fig. 97 . . . slide the lens assembly out of the body panel

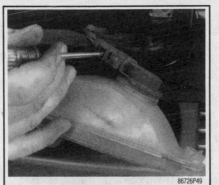

Fig. 98 Use a tool to depress the electrical connector side retaining clips, then . . .

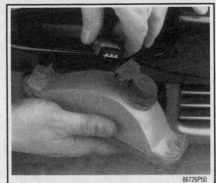

Fig. 99 . . . pull the connector out of the light bulb socket

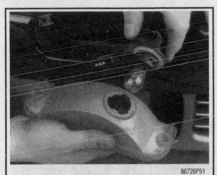

Fig. 100 Twist the socket ¼ turn counter-clockwise, then pull the socket and light bulb out of the lens

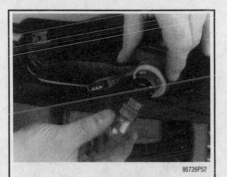

Fig. 101 Unlike the headlight bulbs, the other exterior light bulbs can be removed bare-handed

Fig. 102 Locate and remove the lens assembly retaining screws

Fig. 103 Some retaining screws may be behind weatherstripping—make sure to remove them all

Fig. 104 With the retaining screws removed, you can access the light bulb socket, wiring and light bulb

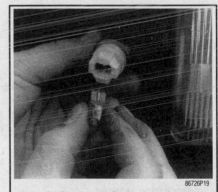

Fig. 105 The light bulb simply pulls out of the light bulb socket

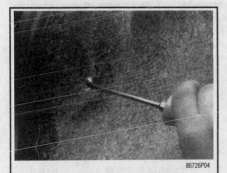

Fig. 106 Locate and remove the luggage compartment rear trim cover retaining screws, then . . .

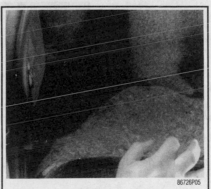

Fig. 107 . . . pull the trim away from the trunk wall

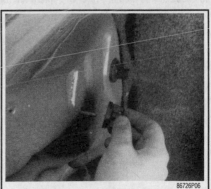

Fig. 108 Remove the plastic lens assembly retaining fasteners and . . .

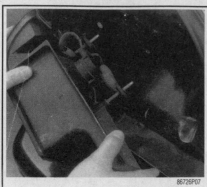

Fig. 109 . . . pull the lens assembly out of its mounting position

Fig. 110 With the lens assembly removed from the vehicle body panel, you can access the light bulbs

Fig. 111 Twist the light bulb socket ¼ turn counter-clockwise, then pull it out of the assembly

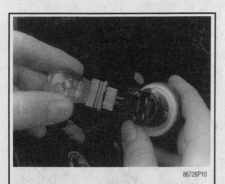

Fig. 112 Remove the light bulb from the socket—make sure that all of the connectors are clean

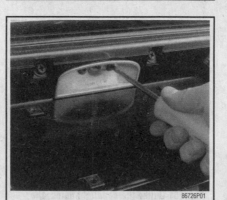

Fig. 113 Remove the license plate light assembly retaining screws, then . . .

Fig. 114 . . . extract the license light assembly from the bumper or rear fascia

cannot be fully inserted and turned readily, turn it 180° and try again. Insert the socket into the lamp assembly and turn it tight to lock it.

High Mounted Brake Light

AC AND AJ BODY MODELS

➡For more information regarding the different body classifications included in this manual, refer to Vehicle Identification in Section 1.

1. Open the trunk.
2. Reach up under the package shelf and turn the light bulb socket counterclockwise to remove it from the light housing.
3. Pull the bulb out of the socket.
4. Installation is the reverse of the removal procedure.

AP BODY SEDAN MODELS

➡For more information regarding the different body classifications included in this manual, refer to Vehicle Identification in Section 1.

1. Raise the trunk lid and remove the attaching screws from the stop light trim cover.
2. Turn the bulb socket counterclockwise to remove it from the housing.
3. Pull the bulb straight out of the socket.
4. Installation is the reverse of the removal procedure.

AA, AE, AK AND AP BODY CONVERTIBLE MODELS

➡For more information regarding the different body classifications included in this manual, refer to Vehicle Identification in Section 1.

1. Remove the two mounting screws and pull the light assembly out to expose the light bulb socket.
2. Turn the bulb socket counterclockwise to remove it from the housing.
3. Pull the bulb straight out of the socket.

To install:

4. Insert the new bulb into the socket.
5. Insert the socket into the light assembly and turn clockwise to lock in place.
6. Install the light assembly and secure in place with the mounting screws.
7. Installation is the reverse of the removal procedure.

AA, AE AND AK BODY SEDAN MODELS

➡For more information regarding the different body classifications included in this manual, refer to Vehicle Identification in Section 1.

1. Remove the stop light cover by pulling it firmly away from the rear window.
2. Turn the bulb socket counterclockwise to remove it from the housing.
3. Pull the bulb straight out of the socket.
4. Installation is the reverse of the removal procedure.

License Plate Lights

REMOVAL & INSTALLATION

▶ See Figures 113, 114 and 115

1. Remove the screws holding the license plate lighting assembly onto the vehicle.
2. Remove the lighting assembly from the rear bumper or fascia body panel.
3. Remove the light bulb socket from the lighting assembly.
4. Pull the used light bulb from the socket.
5. Installation is the reverse of the removal procedure.

Fig. 115 Once the light assembly is removed, the light bulb can be extracted

Dome/Map Lights

REMOVAL & INSTALLATION

AA Body

▶ See Figure 116

➡For more information regarding the different body classifications included in this manual, refer to Vehicle Identification in Section 1.

1. Remove the lens by inserting a large paper clip or wire, with a hook on the end, into the hole in the lens and pull downward.
2. Remove the light bulb by pulling firmly toward the front of the vehicle.
3. Installation is the reverse of the removal procedure.

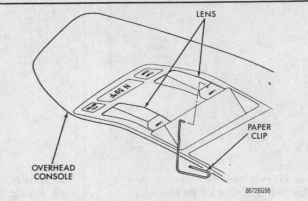

Fig. 116 Use a paper clip shaped into a hook on one end to open the light lens—Spirit, Acclaim and LeBaron sedan

AC Body

➡For more information regarding the different body classifications included in this manual, refer to Vehicle Identification in Section 1.

1. Remove the lens by inserting a flat blade tool between the round end of the lamp lens and housing. Pry the lens from the housing. Pivot the lens and remove it.
2. Pull the used light bulb out of the light socket.
3. Installation is the reverse of the removal procedure.

Except AA and AC Bodies

➡For more information regarding the different body classifications included in this manual, refer to Vehicle Identification in Section 1.

1. Remove the lens by inserting a flat-bladed prytool into the slot located alongside of the lens. Once the prytool is inserted, pry the lens to the side and swing it down as it unhooks from the housing edge.
2. Remove the light bulb by pulling straight down.
3. Installation is the reverse of the removal procedure.

CIRCUIT PROTECTION

Fuses, Fusible Links and Relays

LOCATION

AE and AK Bodies

▶ See Figure 117

➡For more information regarding the different body classifications included in this manual, refer to Vehicle Identification in Section 1.

The fuse block is located behind a removable access panel, below the steering column. The hazard and turn signal flashers along with the time delay and horn relays are also located behind the panel. Additional relays are mounted on the inner fender panel near the battery.

AQ Body

▶ See Figures 117 and 118

➡For more information regarding the different body classifications included in this manual, refer to Vehicle Identification in Section 1.

The fuse block is to the left of the steering column, above the parking brake. The hazard flasher, ignition time delay relay and the horn relay are also located in the fuse block.

Fig. 117 Some relays are mounted on the inner right-hand fender

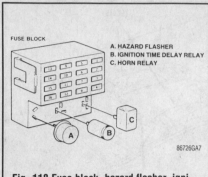

Fig. 118 Fuse block, hazard flasher, ignition time delay relay and the horn relay setup—TC by Maserati

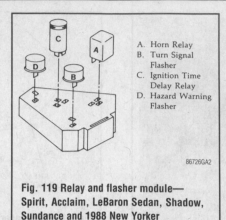

Fig. 119 Relay and flasher module—Spirit, Acclaim, LeBaron Sedan, Shadow, Sundance and 1988 New Yorker

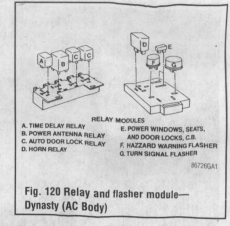

Fig. 120 Relay and flasher module—Dynasty (AC Body)

AA and AP Bodies

▶ See Figures 117 and 119

➡For more information regarding the different body classifications included in this manual, refer to Vehicle Identification in Section 1.

The fuse block is located behind the steering column cover, accessible by removing the fuse access panel above the hood latch release lever. The relay and flasher module is either located behind the fuse panel or behind an access panel in the glove box. Included in the module are the hazard and turn signal flashers along with the time delay and horn relays. Additional relays are mounted on the inner fender panel near the battery.

AH Body

▶ See Figure 117

➡For more information regarding the different body classifications included in this manual, refer to Vehicle Identification in Section 1.

The fuse block is located behind the glove box door, accessible by removing the fuse access panel. The relay and flasher module is located behind the cup holder in the center of the instrument panel. The entire module can be removed by pushing it up and off of its mounting bracket. Included in the module are the hazard and turn signal flashers along with the time delay and horn relays. Additional relays are mounted on the inner fender panel near the battery.

AG and AJ Bodies

▶ See Figure 117

➡For more information regarding the different body classifications included in this manual, refer to Vehicle Identification in Section 1.

The fuse block is located behind a removable access panel to the left of the lower portion of the steering column. On 1988–89 Daytona and LeBaron, the hazard and turn signal flashers along with the time delay and horn relays are also located behind the panel.

On 1990–92 Daytona and LeBaron, a relay bank is located on the left side kick panel. The Power Distribution Center, which contains additional relays and fuses, is located in the engine compartment behind the battery. Each item is identified on the cover.

AC Body

▶ See Figures 117 and 120

➡For more information regarding the different body classifications included in this manual, refer to Vehicle Identification in Section 1.

On vehicles without a Power Distribution Center, fusible links are part of the large wiring harness behind the battery. On vehicles with a Power Distribution Center, fusible links in the form of cartridge fuses, which resemble small relays but serve as fusible links, are located in the Center. Each item is identified on the cover of the Power Distribution Center.

The fuse panel, which contains fuses and circuit breakers, is located behind the glove box door. To remove the panel, pull it out from the bottom and slide the tabs out from the top. Additional fuses are in the Power Distribution Center located near the left side strut tower in the engine compartment. Each item is identified on the cover of the Power Distribution Center.

There is an additional relay module (relay and flasher module) located to the right lower corner of the instrument panel. A relay or flasher can be removed by pulling it straight down from the module.

AB Body

The fuse panel is located above the parking brake release lever, under the instrument panel.

Fusible links are used to prevent major wire harness damage in the event of a short circuit or an overload condition in the wiring circuits which are normally not fused, due to carrying high amperage loads or because of their locations within the wiring harness. Each fusible link is of a fixed value for a specific electrical load and, should a link fail, the cause of the failure must be determined and repaired prior to installing a new fusible link of the same value.

Circuit beakers are an integral part of the headlight switch, the wiper switch and the air conditioning circuit. They are used to protect each circuit from an overload. Other circuit breakers are on the fuse panel.

Relays are used throughout the system in various locations. When replacing a protective electrical relay, be very sure to install the same type of relay. Verify that the schematic imprinted on the original and replacement relays are identical. Relay part numbers may change. Do not rely on them for identification. Instead, use the schematic imprinted on the relay for positive identification.

A relay bank is located on the left side of the engine compartment. Additional relay locations are as follows:

- **Power door lock relay**—is located on the right side kick panel.
- **Passive restraint relays**—are located under the seats.
- **Light outage module**—is located behind the right side speaker in the trunk.
- **Passive restraint control module**—is located on the left side of the trunk.
- **Headlight module**—is located under the left side of the instrument panel.
- **Daytime running light module**—is located in the right front area of the engine compartment.
- **Climate control relays and module**—are located under the right side of the instrument panel.
- **Sun roof relay**—is near the sun roof motor.

The turn signal flasher is located behind the left side of the instrument panel. The hazard flasher is located behind the left side of the instrument panel.

REPLACEMENT

Fuses

▶ See Figures 121, 122, 123, 124 and 125

✳✳ WARNING

When replacing a blown fuse, it is important to use only a fuse having the correct amperage rating. The use of a fuse with a rating

Fig. 121 The fuse box often has a door, which unsnaps from the trim panel, for easy access

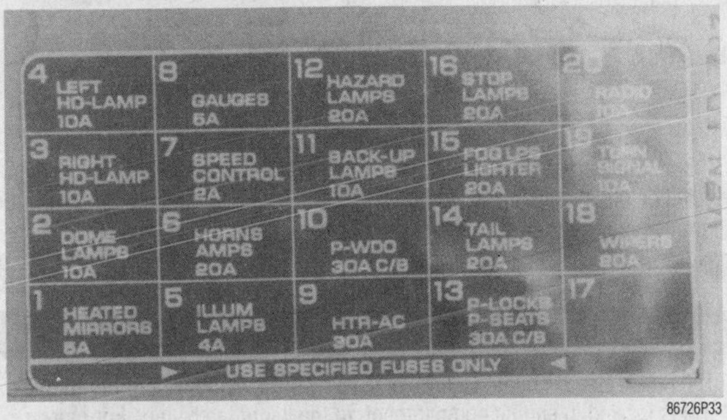

Fig. 122 To help alleviate confusion, most fuse box doors have an I.D. label on the inside

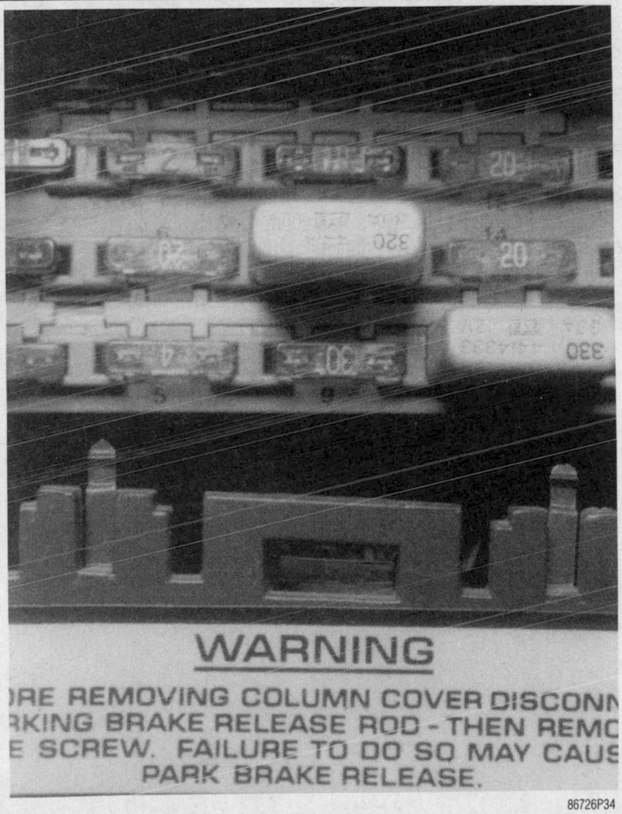

Fig. 124 The newer blade type fuses can easily be pulled from the fuse block by hand

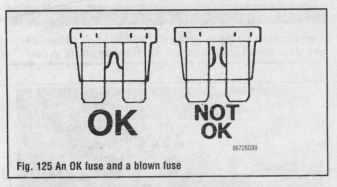

Fig. 125 An OK fuse and a blown fuse

Fig. 123 The fuses are clearly marked as to what amperage rating they are capable of handling

other than indicated may result in a dangerous electrical system overload. If a properly rated fuse continues to blow, it indicates a problem in the circuit that must be corrected.

1981–87 MODELS

1. Disconnect the negative battery cable.
2. Remove the panel by unsnapping the clips at the bottom (pulling out hard).
3. Slide the retaining tabs out at the top.
4. A special fuse removal tool may be located on the back of the access panel, otherwise slide the fuse block to the left and off the retaining bracket to remove it for easy access to the fuses.
5. Pull the fuse out of the retaining clamps.

To install:

➡Standard fuses have the amperage rating stamped on the silver connector at either end. Make sure to note the amperage rating before discarding a blown fuse!

✳ CAUTION

Always replace the fuse with one of exactly the same rating, as use of a rating even slightly higher than standard could result in a dangerous vehicle fire.

6. Clean the metal clamps on the fuse block to ensure a good electrical contact after the new fuse is installed.
7. Push the new fuse into the retaining clamps until fully seated.
8. If the fuse block was removed from the mounting bracket, slide it back onto the bracket.
9. Connect the negative battery cable.

If a circuit continues to blow a fuse of the proper rating, leave the fuse out and check the circuit or the accessories it runs for an electrical short or mechanical overload.

Remember, in replacing the access panel, to insert the tabs at the top first and then to snap the locking tabs at the bottom into place.

1988–95 MODELS

The 1988–95 models covered by this manual use blade type fuses. The fuses have the amperage printed on the outer edge and are also color coded according to amperage rating.

➡**Make sure to note the amperage rating before discarding a blown fuse! Always replace the fuse with one of exactly the same rating, as use of a rating even slightly higher than standard could result in a dangerous vehicle fire.**

If a circuit continues to blow a fuse of the proper rating, leave the fuse out and check the circuit or the accessories it runs for an electrical short or mechanical overload.

Remember, in replacing the access panel, to insert the tabs at the top first and then to snap the locking tabs at the bottom into place.

Fusible Links

▶ **See Figure 126**

The main wiring harnesses are equipped with fusible links to protect against harness damage should a short circuit develop.

✳✳ WARNING

Never replace a fusible link with standard wire. Only fusible link wire of the correct gauge with hypalon insulation should be used.

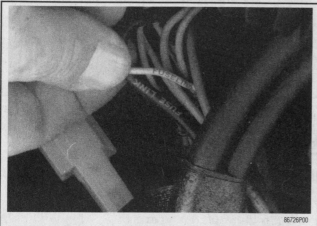

86726P00

Fig. 126 On newer vehicles, the fusible links are easily identified by their markings

When a fusible link blows, it is very important to locate and repair the short. Do not just replace the link to correct the problem.

Always detach battery negative cable when servicing the electrical system.
1. Disconnect the negative battery cable.
2. Cut off the remaining portion of the blown fusible link flush with the multiple connection insulator. Take care not to cut any of the other fusible links.
3. Carefully remove about one inch of insulation from the main harness wire at a point one inch away from the connection insulator.
4. Remove one inch of insulation from the replacement fusible link wire and wrap the exposed area around the main harness wire at the point where the insulation was removed.
5. Heat the splice with a high temperature soldering gun and apply resin type solder until it runs freely. Remove the soldering gun and confirm that a "bright" solder joint has been made. Resolder if "cold" (dull) joint has occurred.
6. Cut the other end of the fusible link off at a point just behind the small single wire insulator. Strip one inch of insulation from fusible link and connection wires. Wrap and solder.
7. After the connections have cooled, wrap the splices with at least three layers of electrical tape.

Flashers

Flashers are located either on the bottom of the fuse block or on a module under the dash. They are replaced by simply pulling them straight out. Note that the prongs are arranged in such a way that the flasher must be properly oriented before attempting to install it. Turn the flasher until the orientation of the prongs is correct and simply push it firmly in until the prongs are fully engaged.

Vehicle Computer Locations

The Single Board Engine Controller (SBEC) or Powertrain Control Module (PCM) is located in engine compartment, to the left of the battery. For more details, refer to Section 4.

If equipped with the A604 automatic transaxle, the transaxle control computer is located in the right front of the engine compartment, mounted to the inside of the fender. For more information, refer to Section 7.

The body control computer, if so equipped, is located inside the passenger compartment, behind the right side kick panel.

The Anti-lock Brake System (ABS) control computer is located depending on the year of the vehicle as follows:
• 1988–90: The Bosch III ABS controller is located behind the rear seat bulkhead trim panel in the trunk.
• 1991–95: The Bendix Type 10 ABS controller is located under the battery tray.
• 1992–95: The Bendix Type 6 ABS controller is located on the inner right-hand fender in the engine compartment.

If the vehicle is equipped with automatic load leveling or automatic air suspension, the control computer is located behind the right side trunk trim panel.

WIRING DIAGRAMS

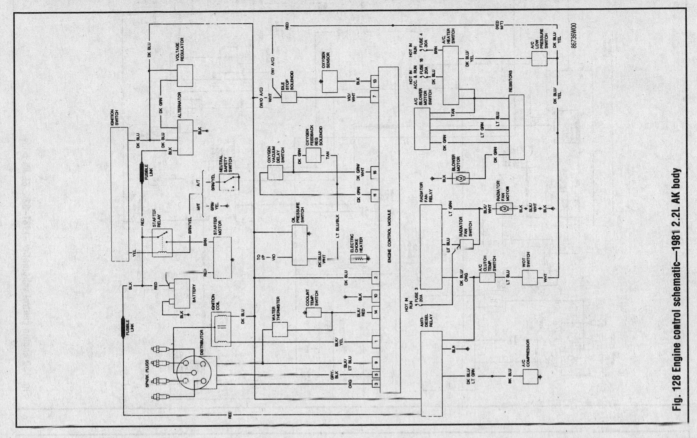

Fig. 128 Engine control schematic—1981 2.2L AK body

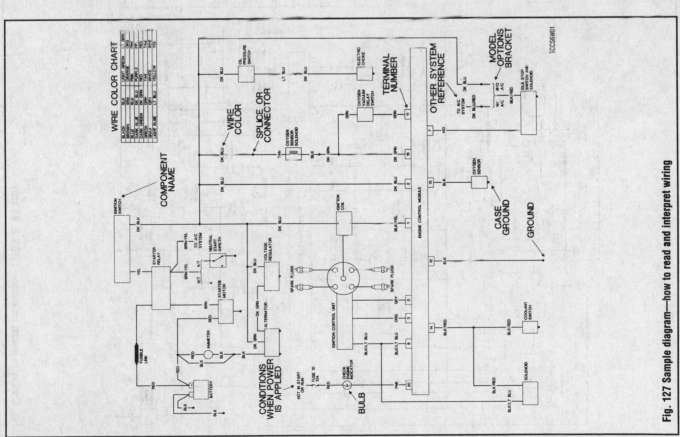

Fig. 127 Sample diagram—how to read and interpret wiring

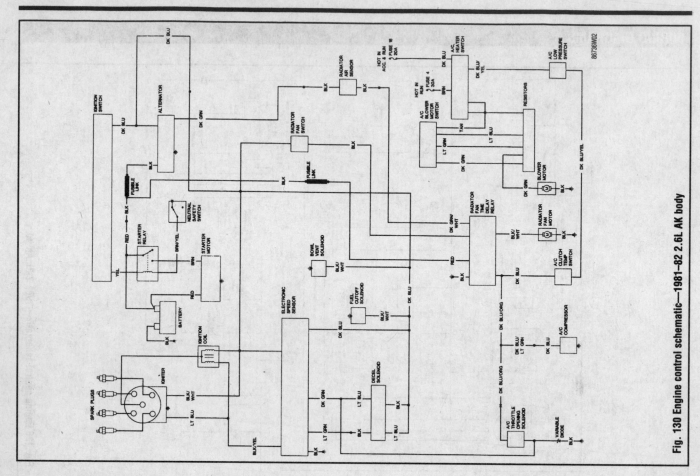

Fig. 130 Engine control schematic—1981–82 2.6L AK body

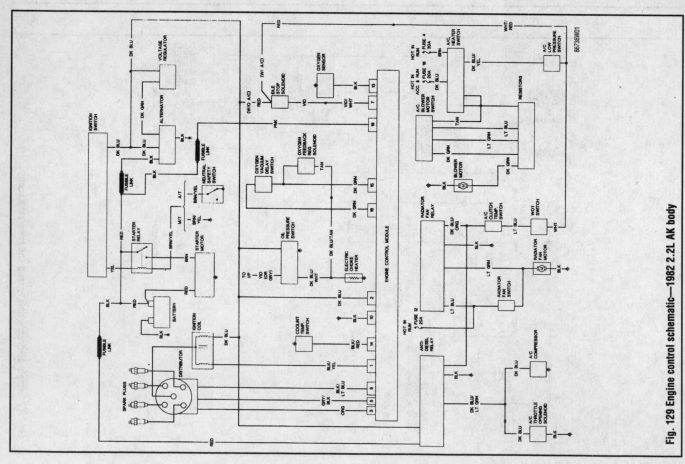

Fig. 129 Engine control schematic—1982 2.2L AK body

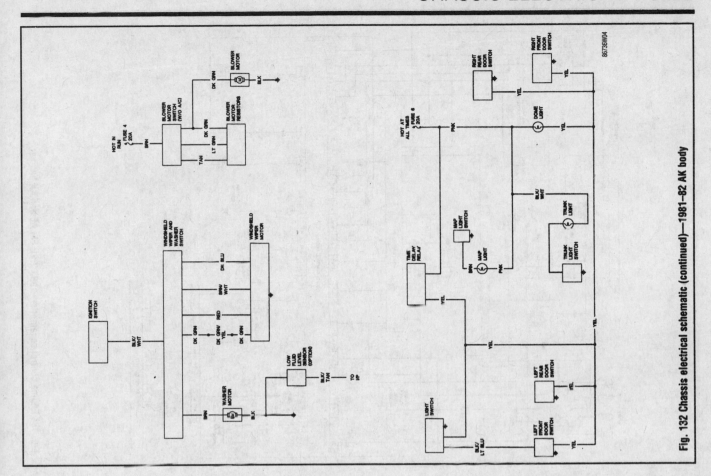

Fig. 132 Chassis electrical schematic (continued)—1981–82 AK body

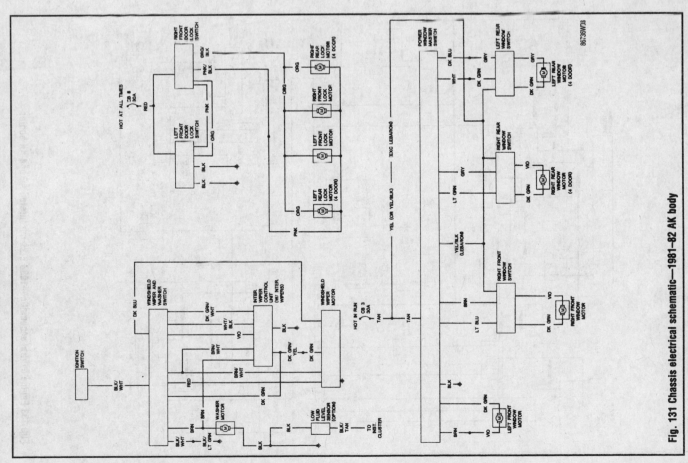

Fig. 131 Chassis electrical schematic—1981–82 AK body

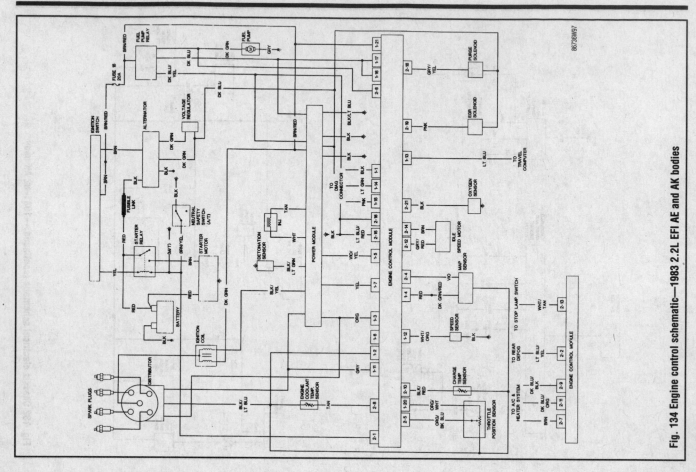

Fig. 134 Engine control schematic—1983 2.2L EFI AE and AK bodies

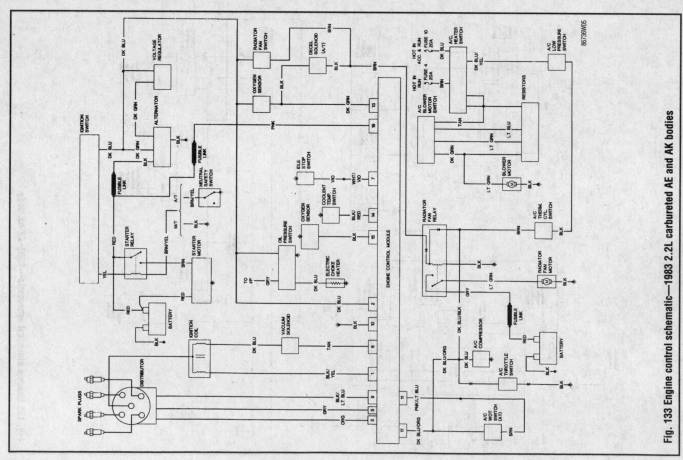

Fig. 133 Engine control schematic—1983 2.2L carbureted AE and AK bodies

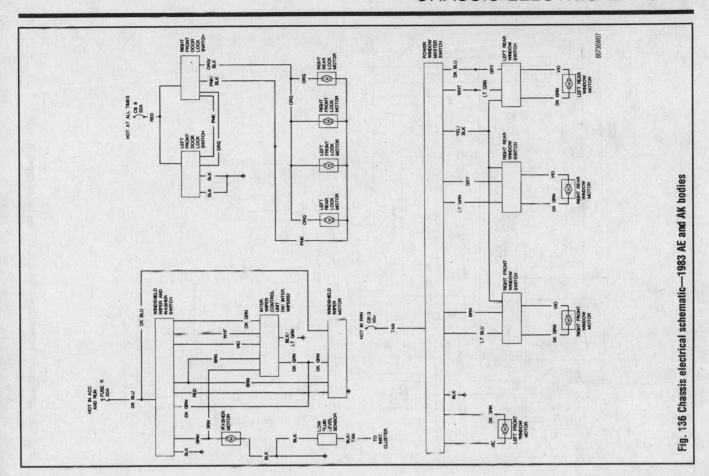

Fig. 136 Chassis electrical schematic—1983 AE and AK bodies

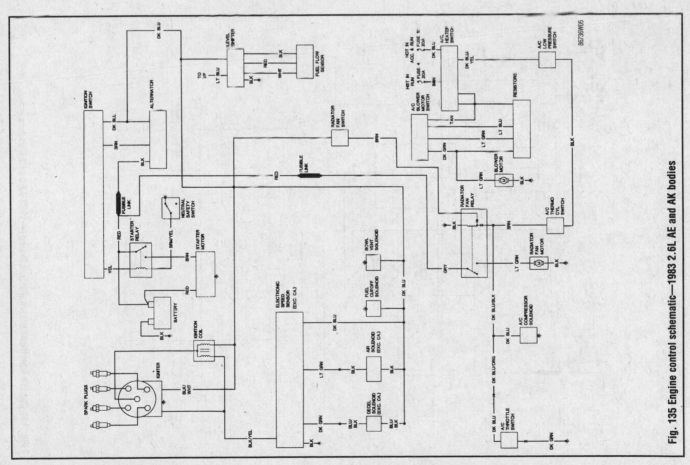

Fig. 135 Engine control schematic—1983 2.6L AE and AK bodies

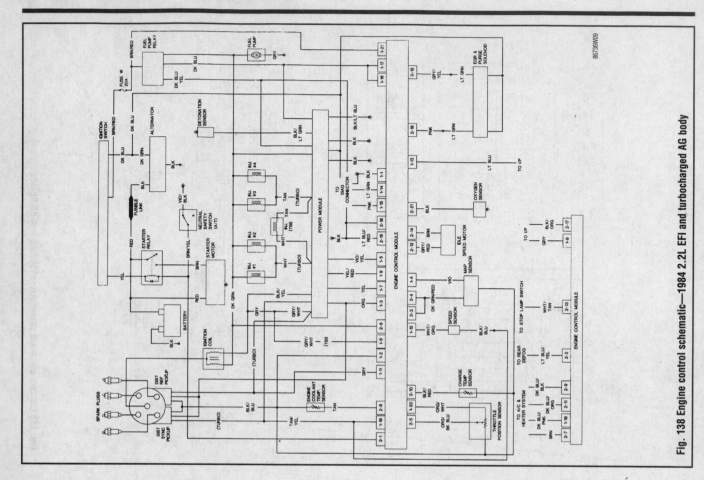

Fig. 138 Engine control schematic—1984 2.2L EFI and turbocharged AG body

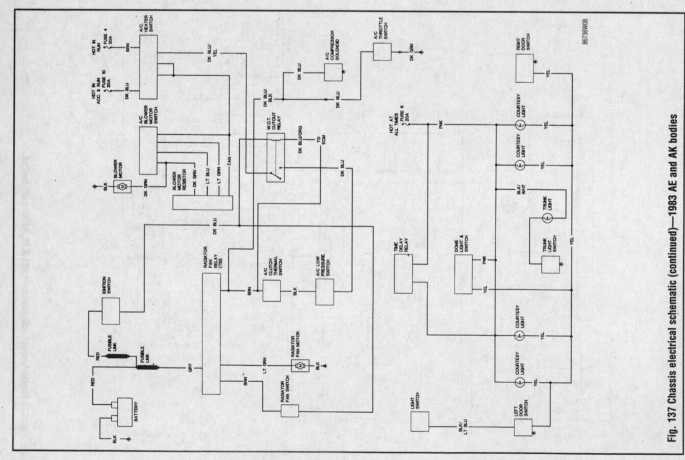

Fig. 137 Chassis electrical schematic (continued)—1983 AE and AK bodies

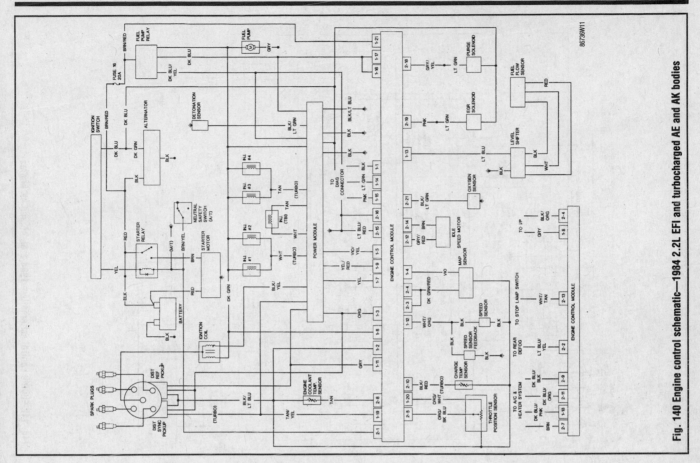

Fig. 140 Engine control schematic—1984 2.2L EFI and turbocharged AE and AK bodies

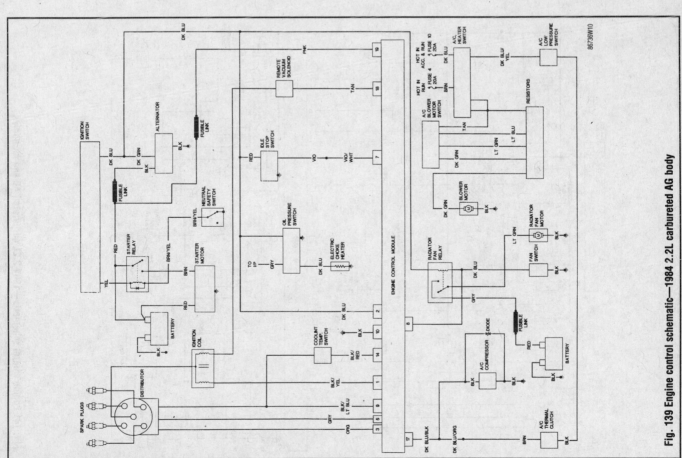

Fig. 139 Engine control schematic—1984 2.2L carbureted AG body

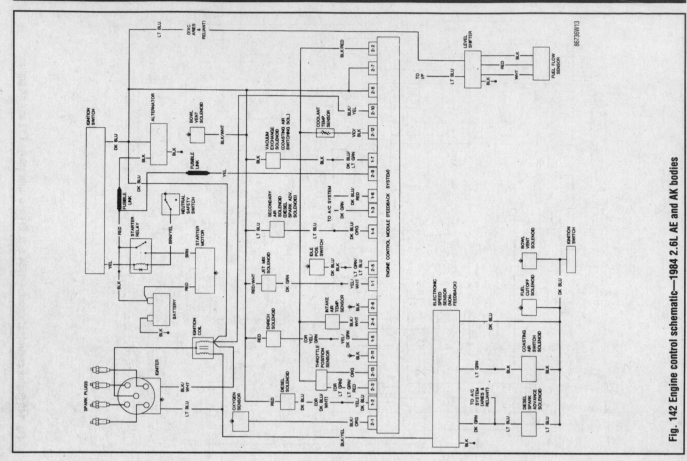

Fig. 142 Engine control schematic—1984 2.6L AE and AK bodies

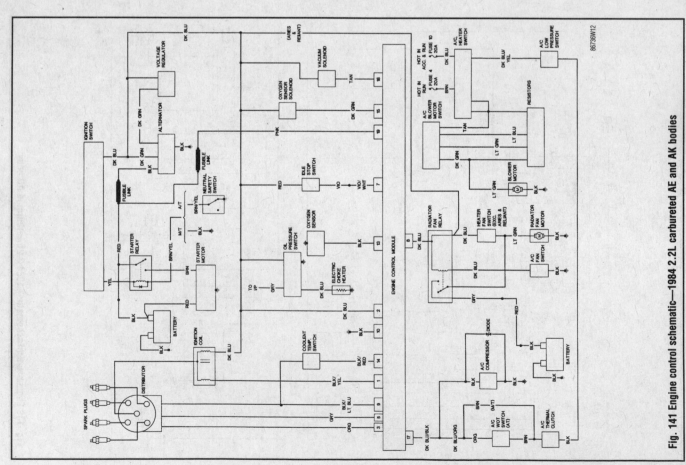

Fig. 141 Engine control schematic—1984 2.2L carbureted AE and AK bodies

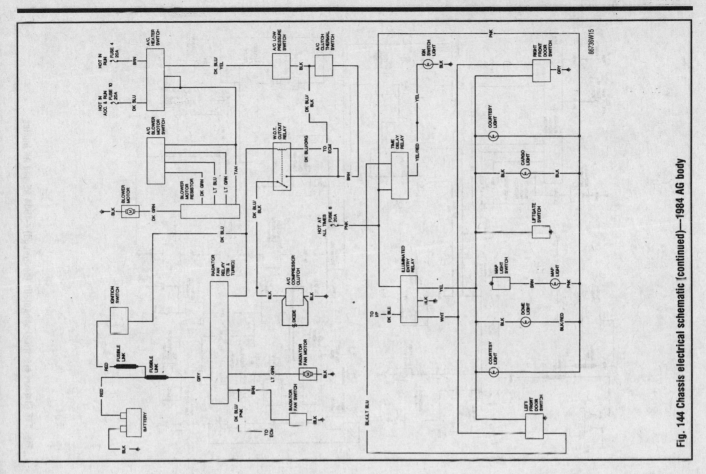

Fig. 144 Chassis electrical schematic (continued)—1984 AG body

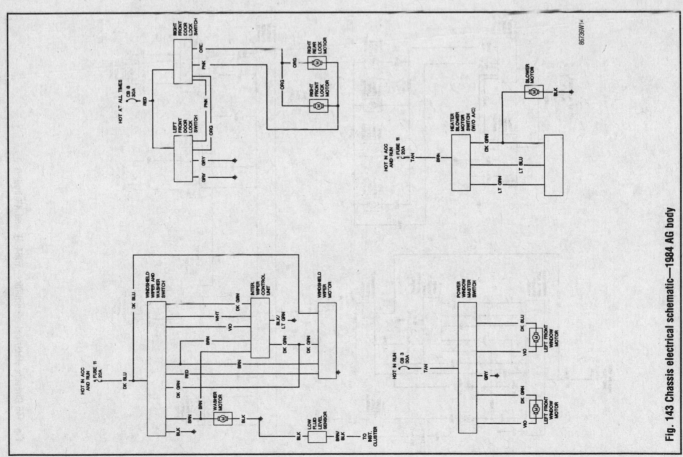

Fig. 143 Chassis electrical schematic—1984 AG body

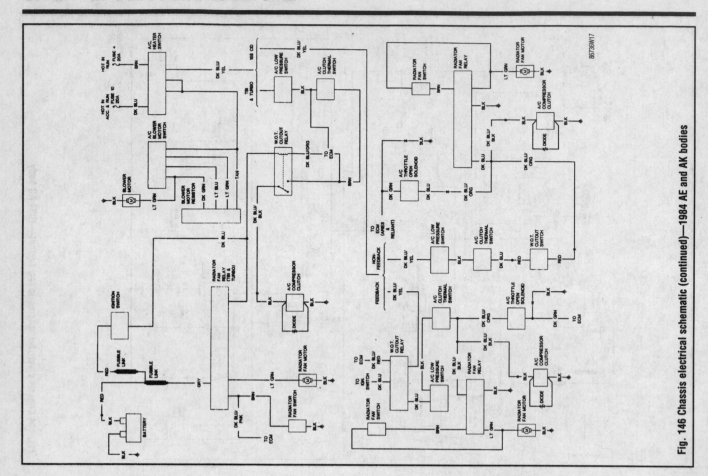

Fig. 146 Chassis electrical schematic (continued)—1984 AE and AK bodies

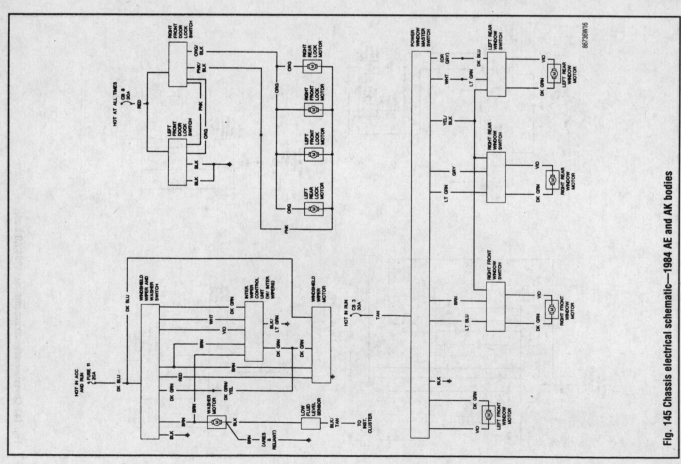

Fig. 145 Chassis electrical schematic—1984 AE and AK bodies

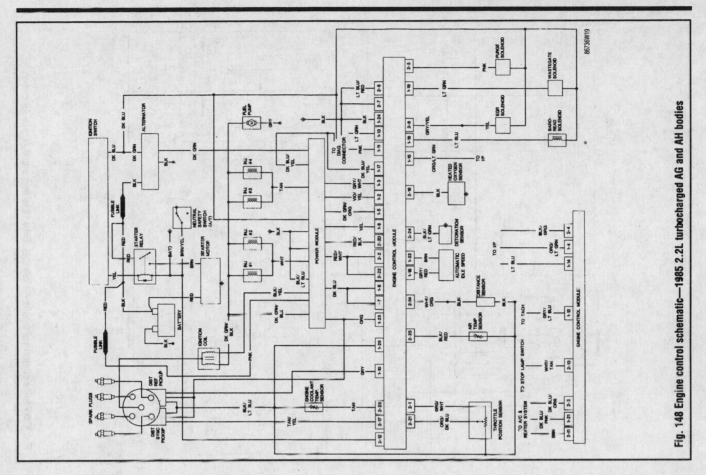

Fig. 148 Engine control schematic—1985 2.2L turbocharged AG and AH bodies

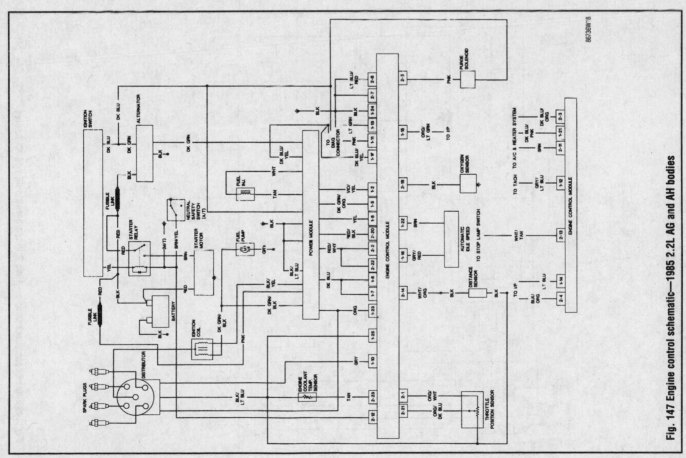

Fig. 147 Engine control schematic—1985 2.2L AG and AH bodies

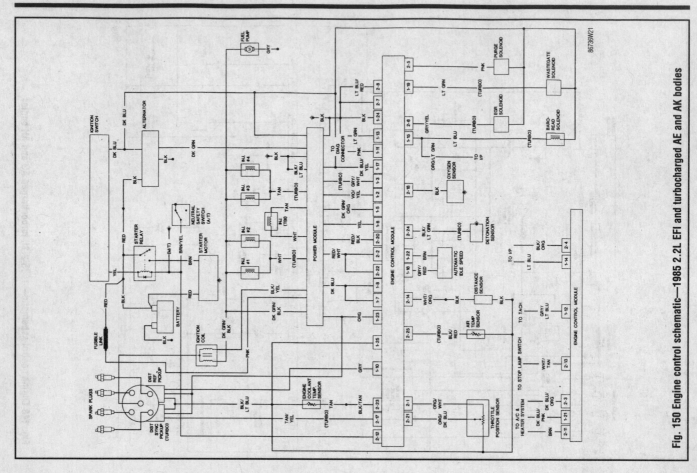

Fig. 150 Engine control schematic—1985 2.2L EFI and turbocharged AE and AK bodies

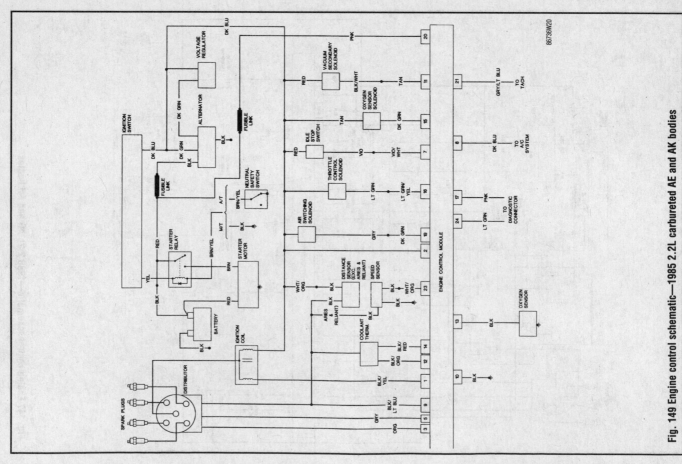

Fig. 149 Engine control schematic—1985 2.2L carbureted AE and AK bodies

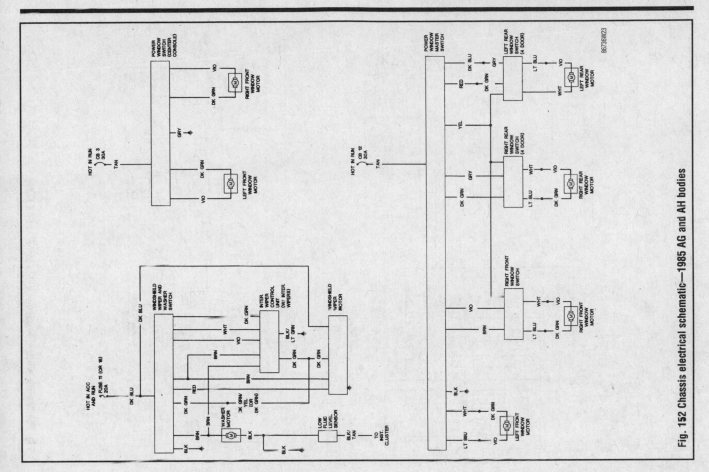

Fig. 152 Chassis electrical schematic—1985 AG and AH bodies

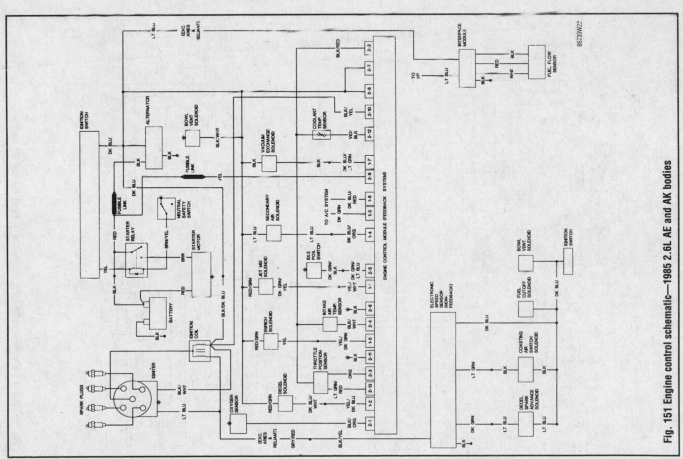

Fig. 151 Engine control schematic—1985 2.6L AE and AK bodies

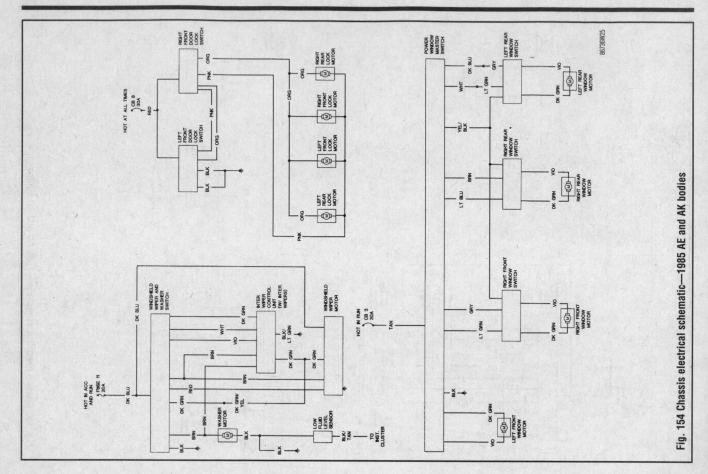

Fig. 154 Chassis electrical schematic—1985 AE and AK bodies

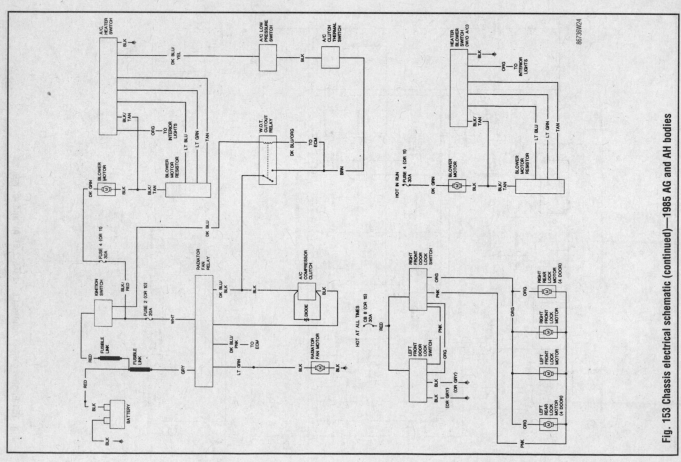

Fig. 153 Chassis electrical schematic (continued)—1985 AG and AH bodies

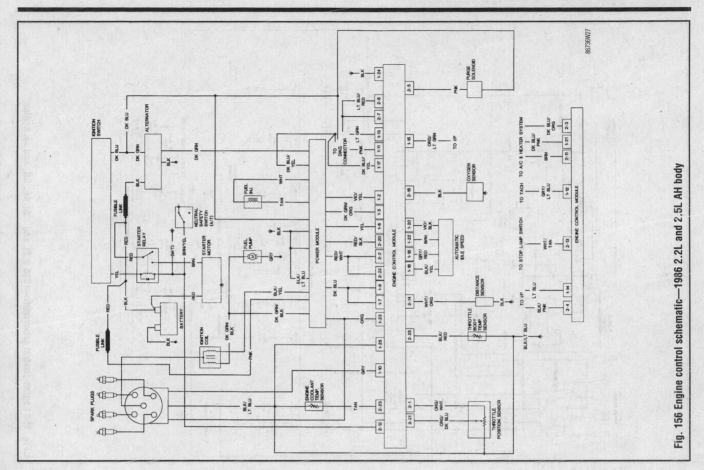

Fig. 156 Engine control schematic—1986 2.2L and 2.5L AH body

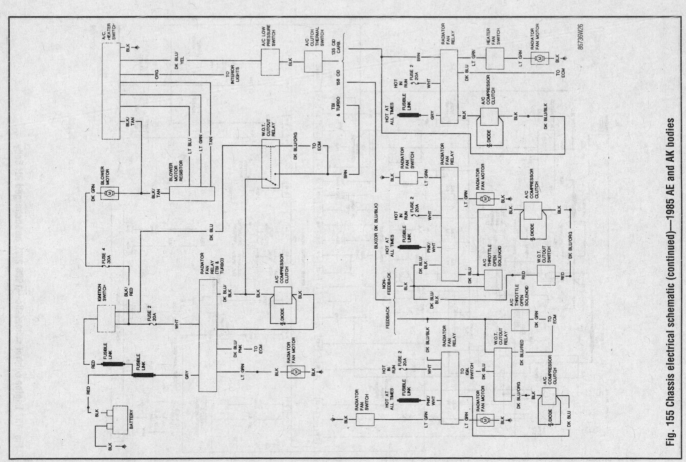

Fig. 155 Chassis electrical schematic (continued)—1985 AE and AK bodies

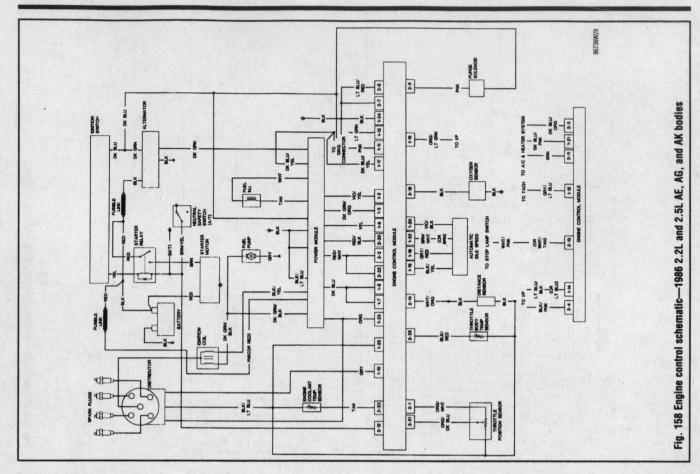

Fig. 158 Engine control schematic—1986 2.2L and 2.5L AE, AG, and AK bodies

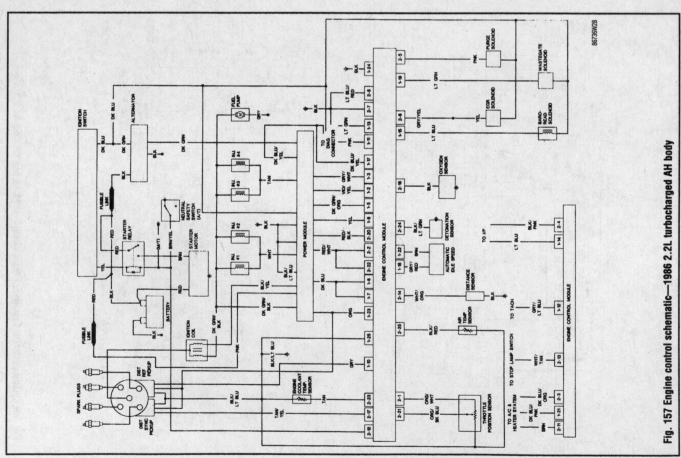

Fig. 157 Engine control schematic—1986 2.2L turbocharged AH body

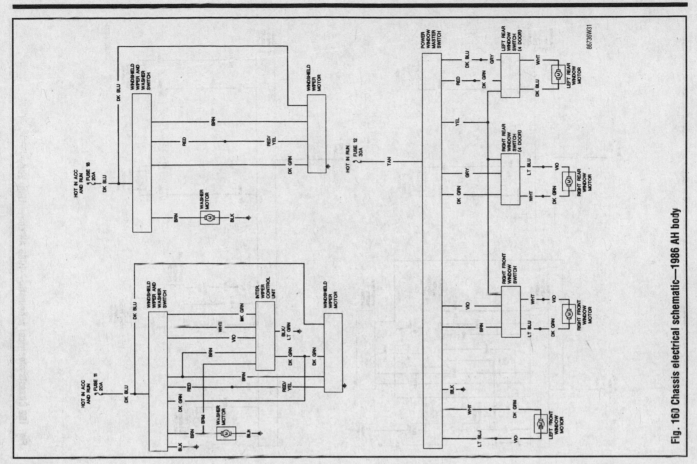

Fig. 160 Chassis electrical schematic—1986 AH body

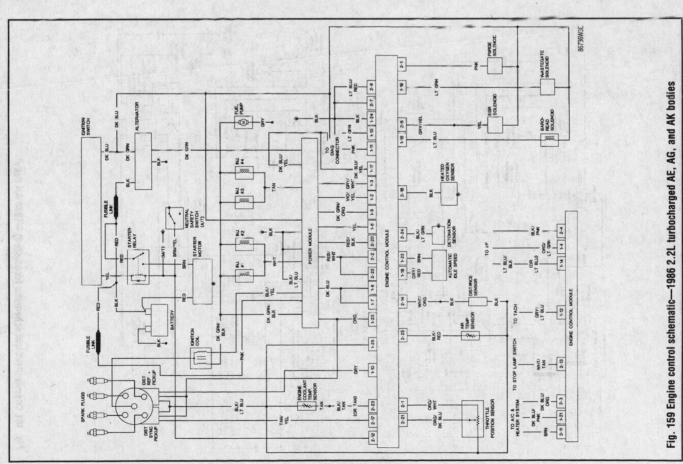

Fig. 159 Engine control schematic—1986 2.2L turbocharged AE, AG, and AK bodies

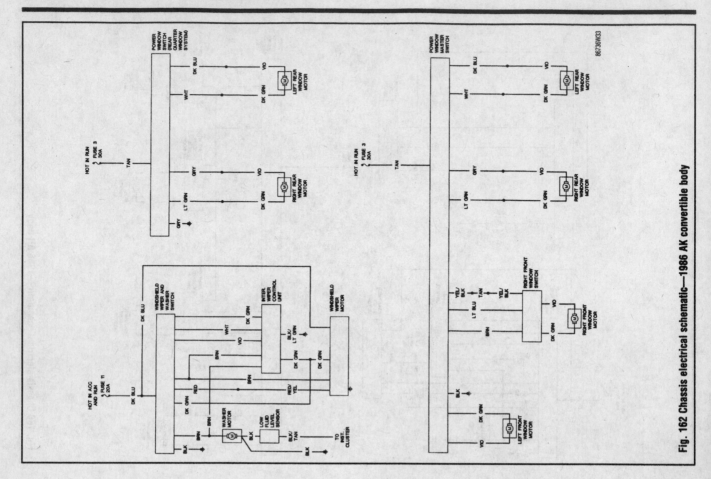

Fig. 162 Chassis electrical schematic—1986 AK convertible body

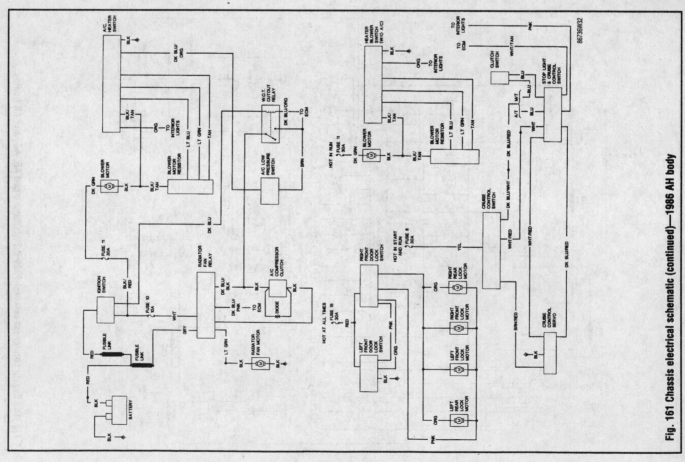

Fig. 161 Chassis electrical schematic (continued)—1986 AH body

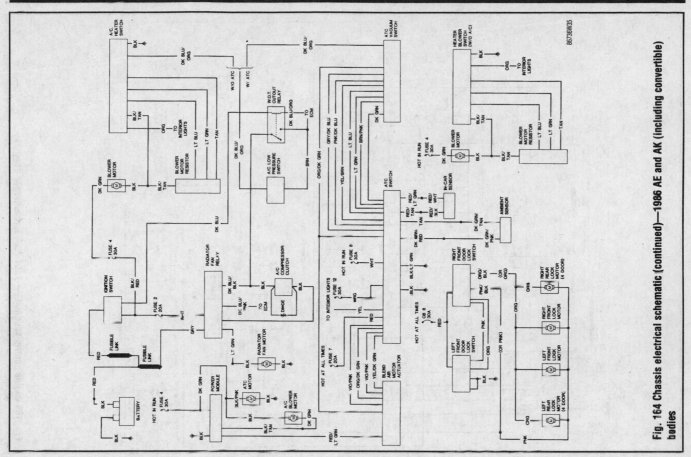

Fig. 164 Chassis electrical schematic (continued)—1986 AE and AK (including convertible) bodies

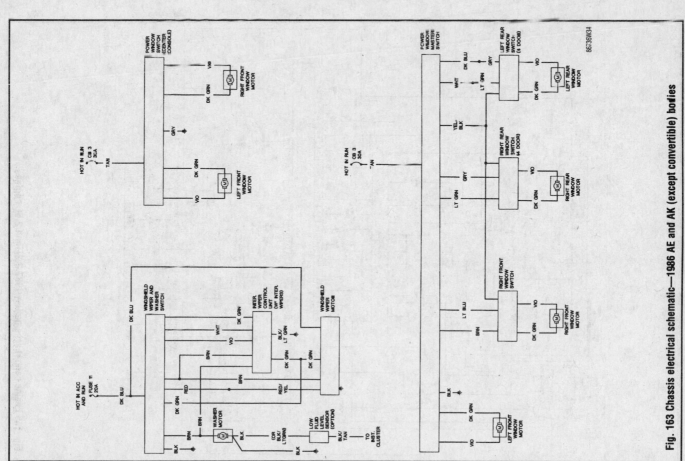

Fig. 163 Chassis electrical schematic—1986 AE and AK (except convertible) bodies

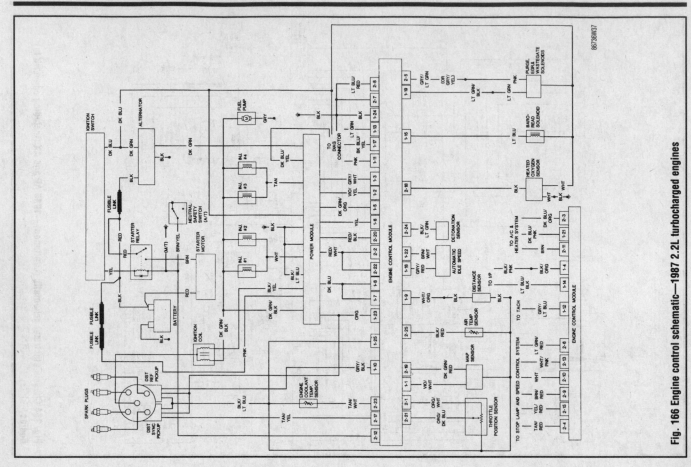

Fig. 166 Engine control schematic—1987 2.2L turbocharged engines

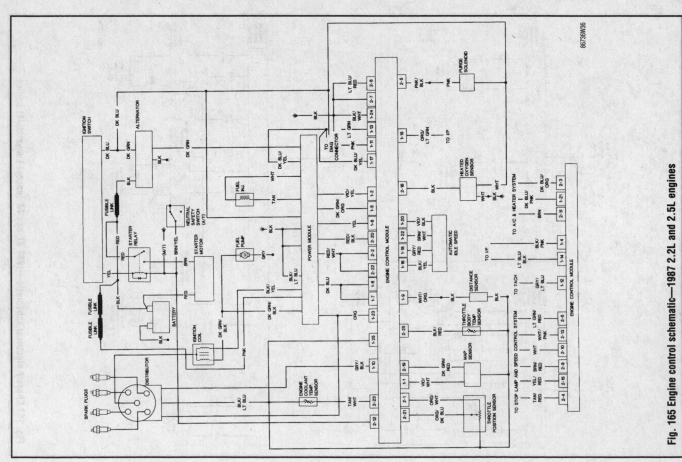

Fig. 165 Engine control schematic—1987 2.2L and 2.5L engines

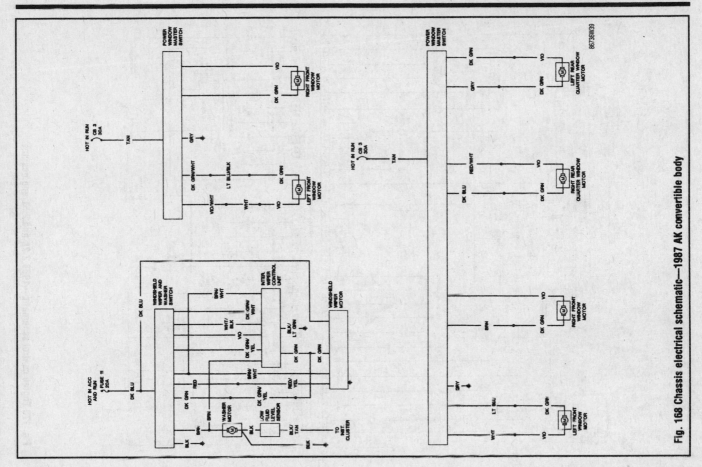

Fig. 168 Chassis electrical schematic—1987 AK convertible body

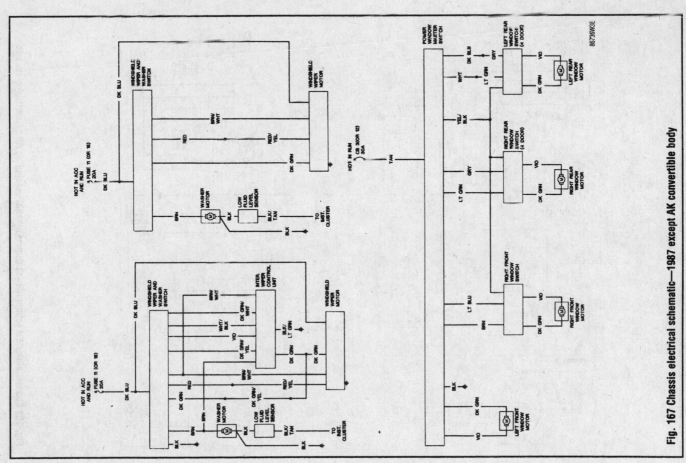

Fig. 167 Chassis electrical schematic—1987 except AK convertible body

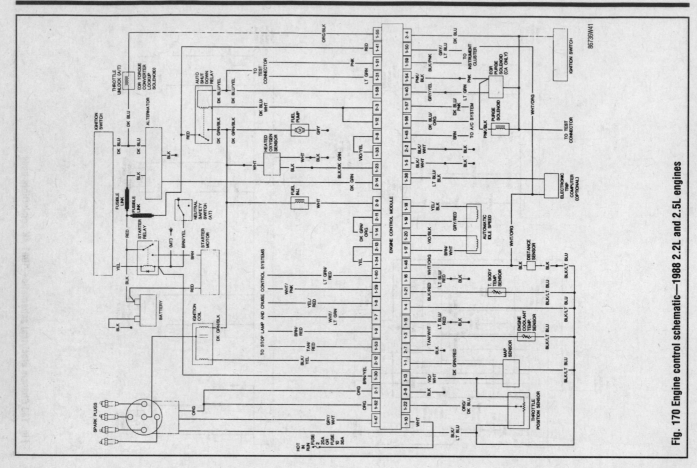

Fig. 170 Engine control schematic—1988 2.2L and 2.5L engines

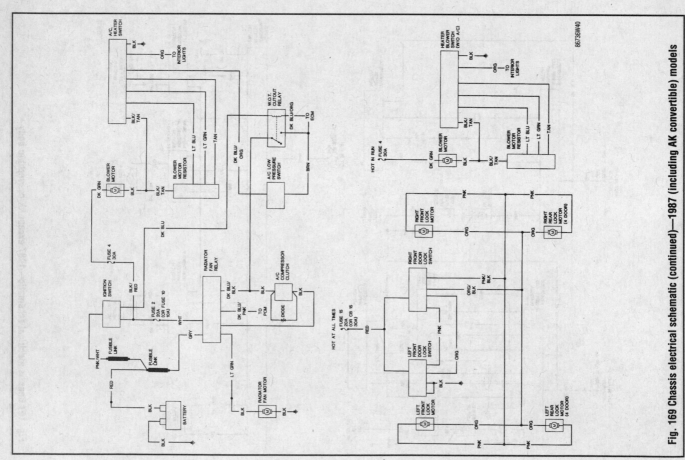

Fig. 169 Chassis electrical schematic (continued)—1987 (including AK convertible) models

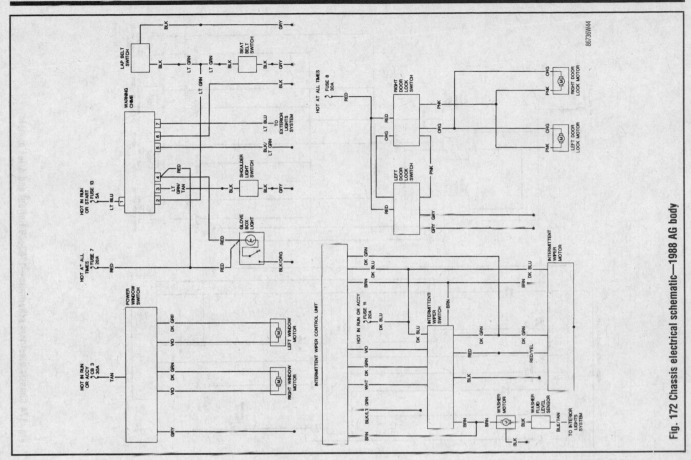

Fig. 172 Chassis electrical schematic—1988 AG body

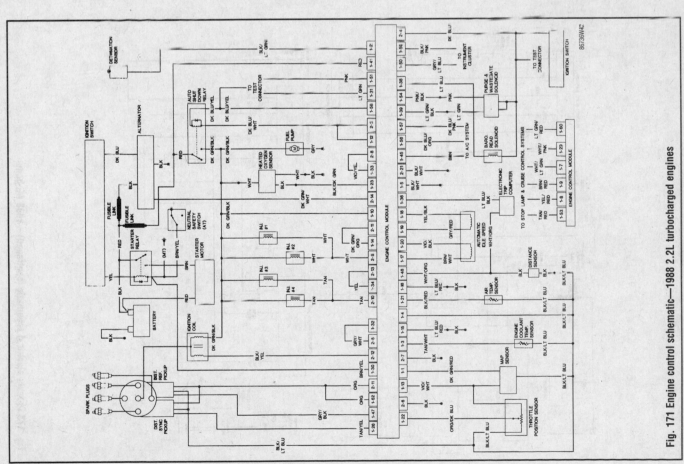

Fig. 171 Engine control schematic—1988 2.2L turbocharged engines

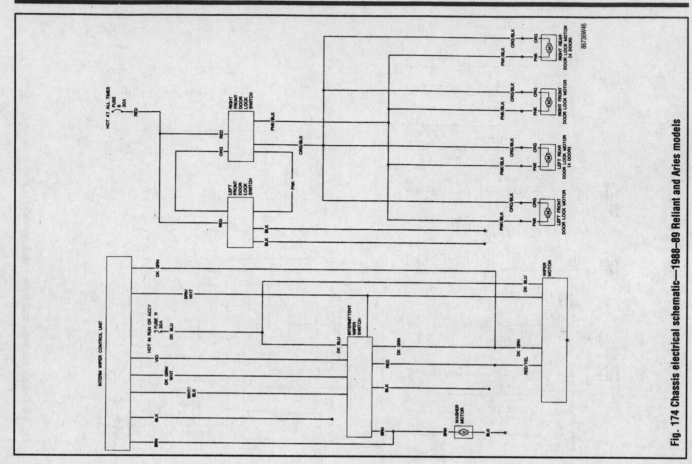

Fig. 174 Chassis electrical schematic—1988-89 Reliant and Aries models

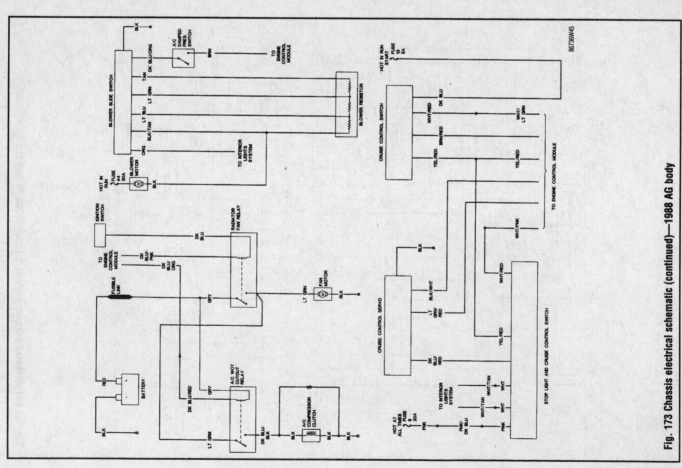

Fig. 173 Chassis electrical schematic (continued)—1988 AG body

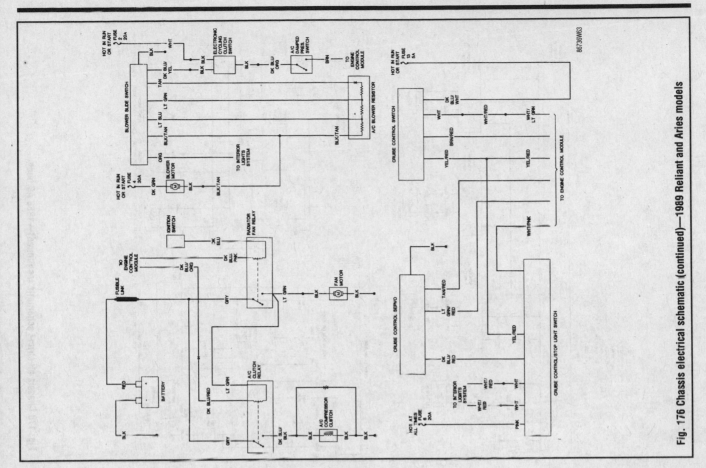

Fig. 176 Chassis electrical schematic (continued)—1989 Reliant and Aries models

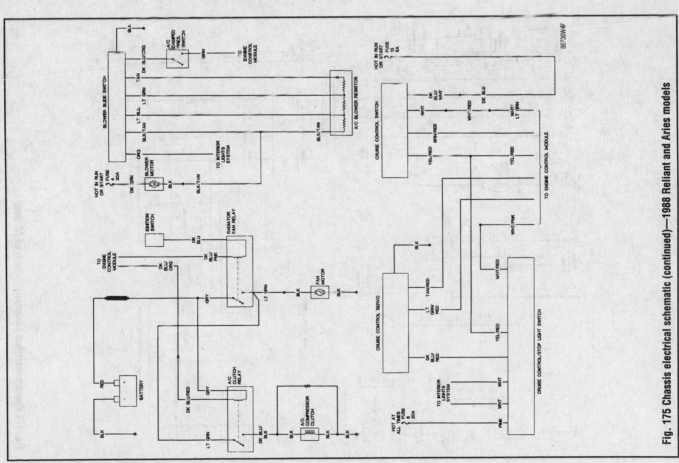

Fig. 175 Chassis electrical schematic (continued)—1988 Reliant and Aries models

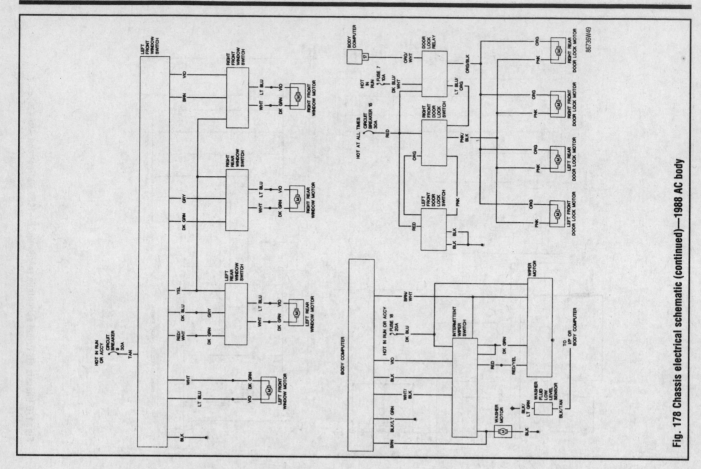

Fig. 178 Chassis electrical schematic (continued)—1988 AC body

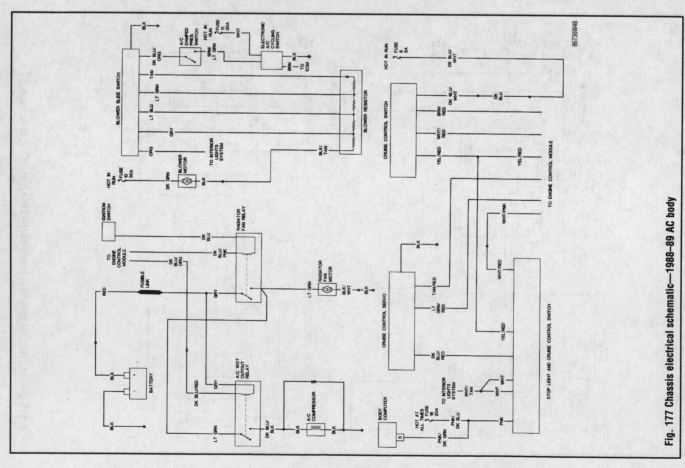

Fig. 177 Chassis electrical schematic—1988-89 AC body

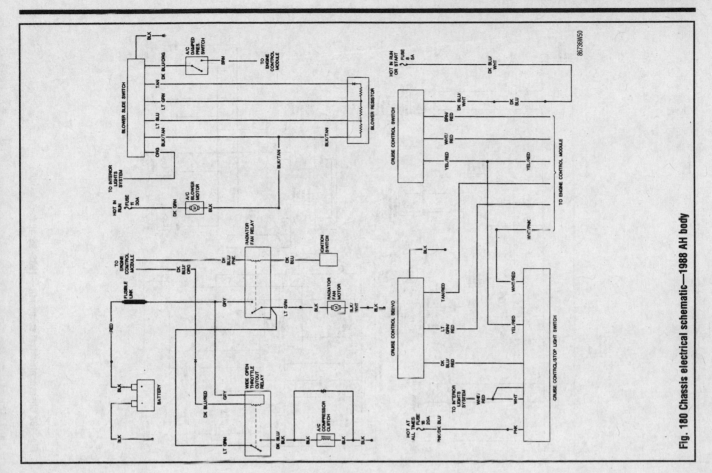

Fig. 180 Chassis electrical schematic—1988 AH body

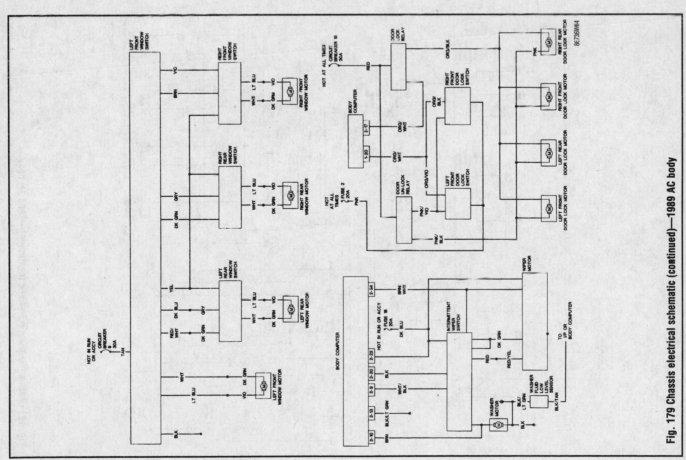

Fig. 179 Chassis electrical schematic (continued)—1989 AC body

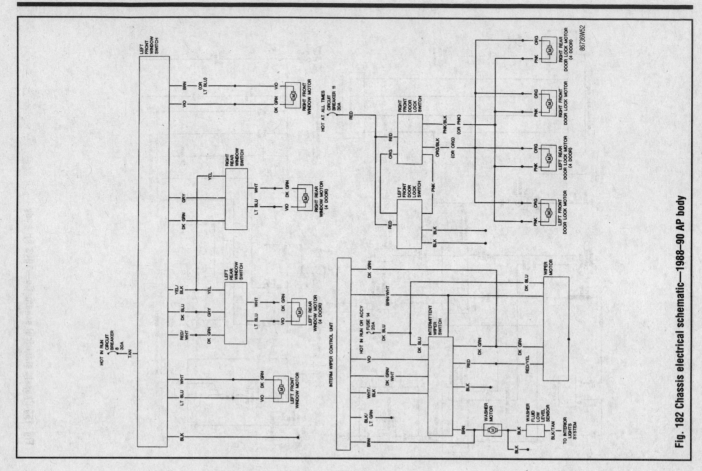

Fig. 182 Chassis electrical schematic—1988-90 AP body

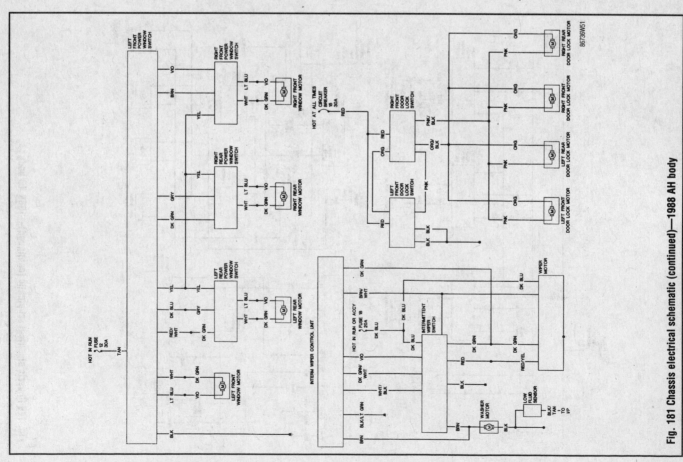

Fig. 181 Chassis electrical schematic (continued)—1988 AH body

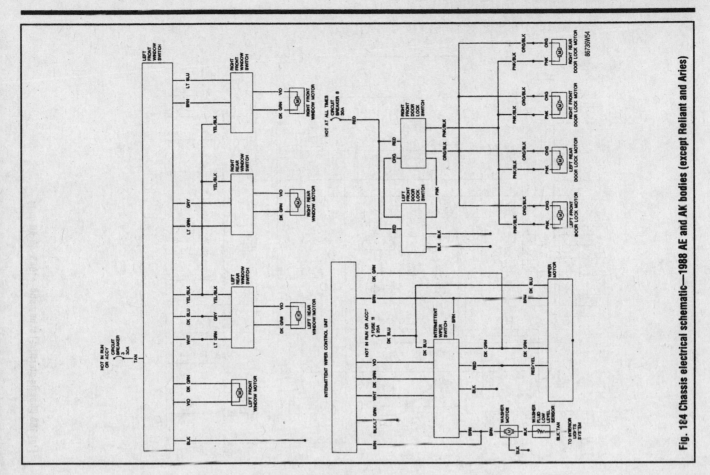

Fig. 184 Chassis electrical schematic—1988 AE and AK bodies (except Reliant and Aries)

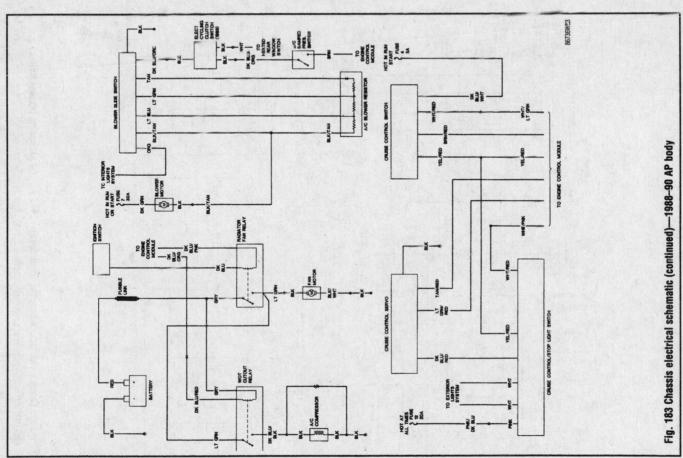

Fig. 183 Chassis electrical schematic (continued)—1988–90 AP body

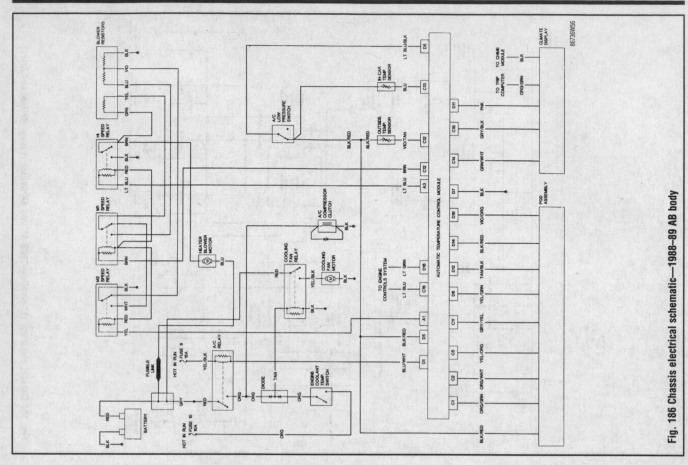

Fig. 186 Chassis electrical schematic—1988-89 AB body

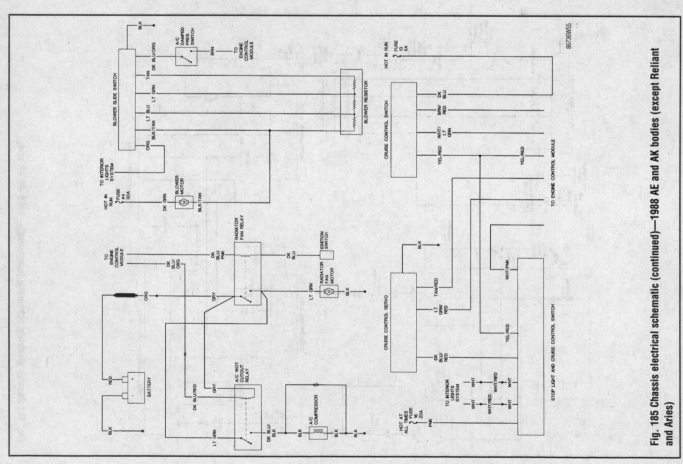

Fig. 185 Chassis electrical schematic (continued)—1988 AE and AK bodies (except Reliant and Aries)

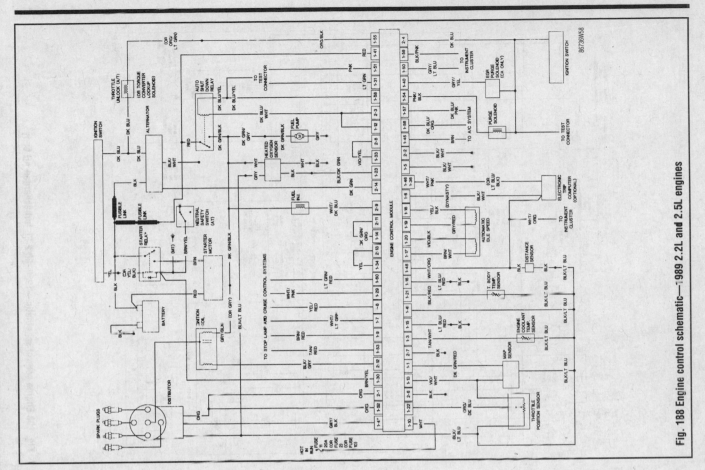

Fig. 188 Engine control schematic—1989 2.2L and 2.5L engines

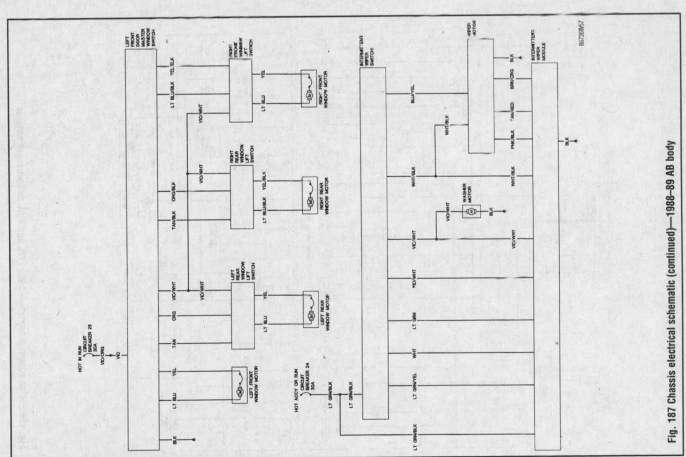

Fig. 187 Chassis electrical schematic (continued)—1988-89 AB body

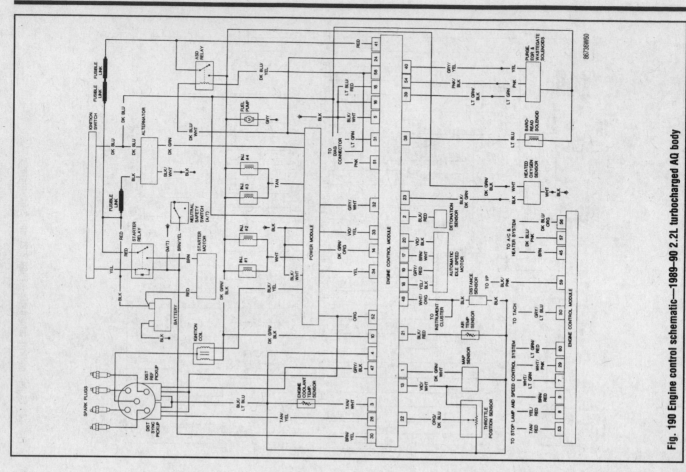

Fig. 190 Engine control schematic—1989-90 2.2L turbocharged AQ body

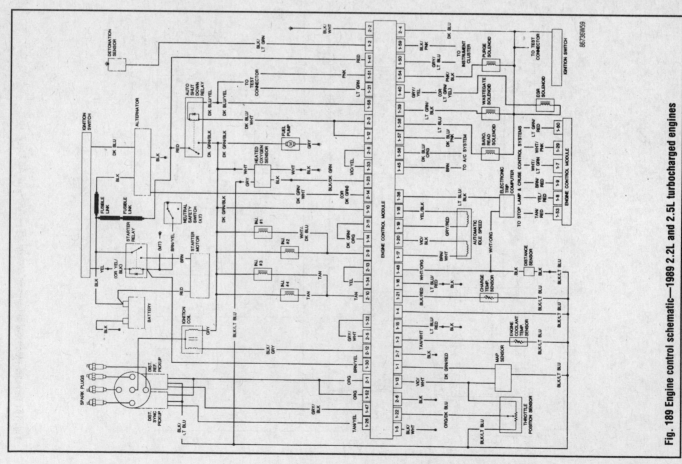

Fig. 189 Engine control schematic—1989 2.2L and 2.5L turbocharged engines

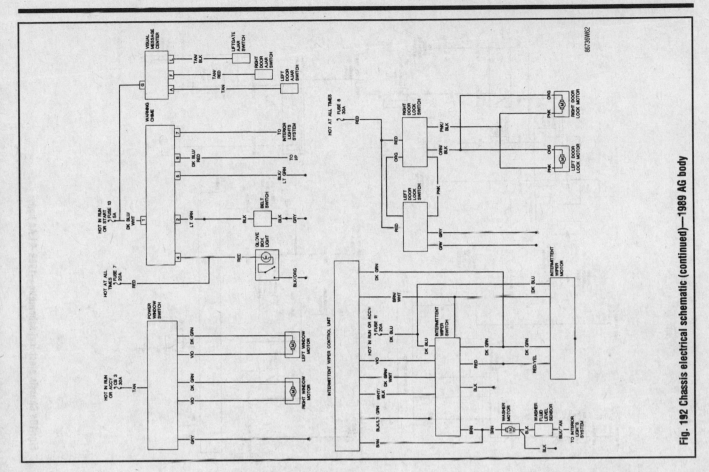

Fig. 192 Chassis electrical schematic (continued)—1989 AG body

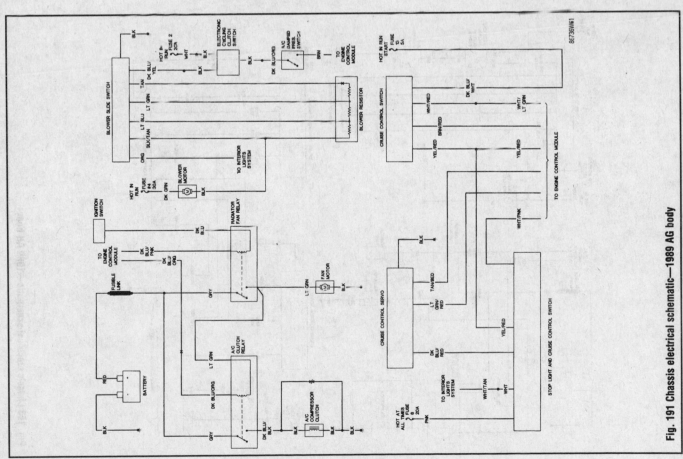

Fig. 191 Chassis electrical schematic—1989 AG body

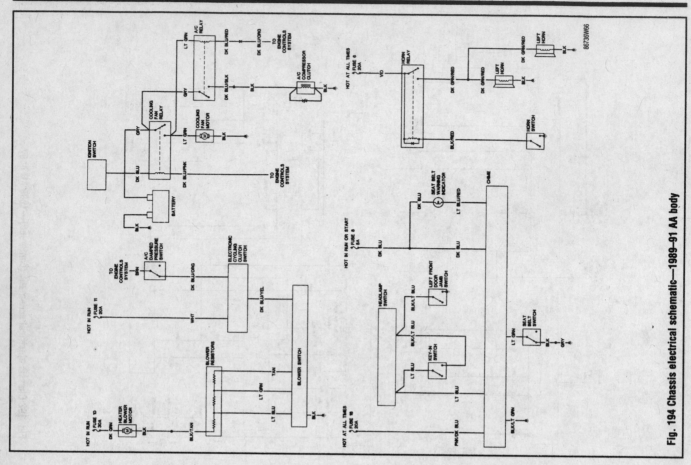

Fig. 194 Chassis electrical schematic—1989-91 AA body

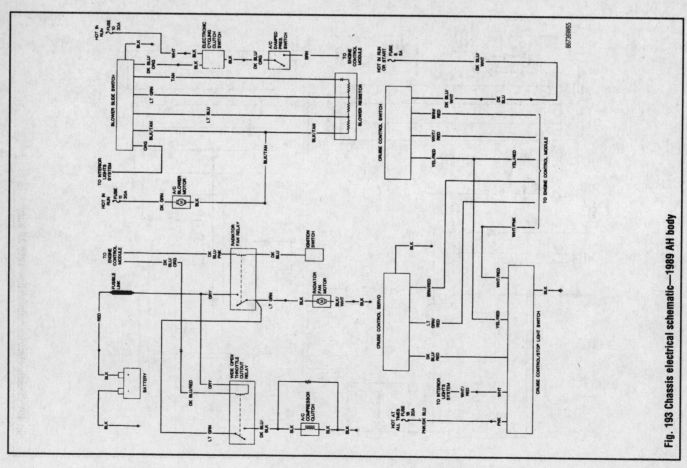

Fig. 193 Chassis electrical schematic—1989 AH body

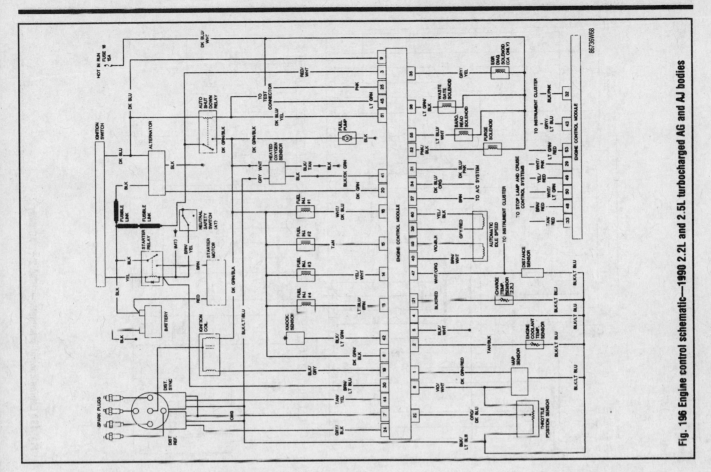

Fig. 196 Engine control schematic—1990 2.2L and 2.5L turbocharged AG and AJ bodies

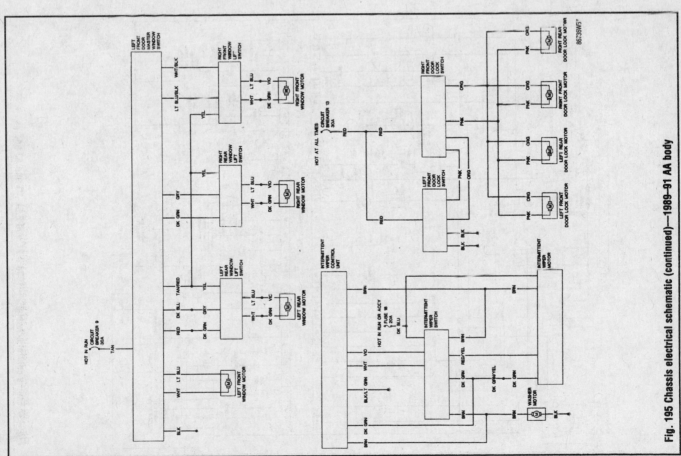

Fig. 195 Chassis electrical schematic (continued)—1989–91 AA body

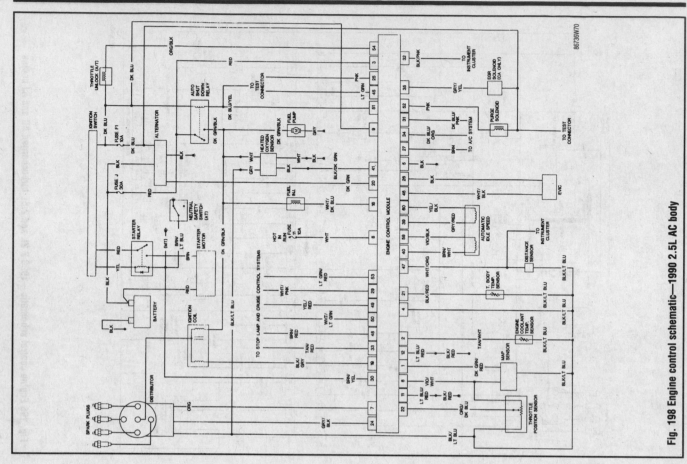

Fig. 198 Engine control schematic—1990 2.5L AC body

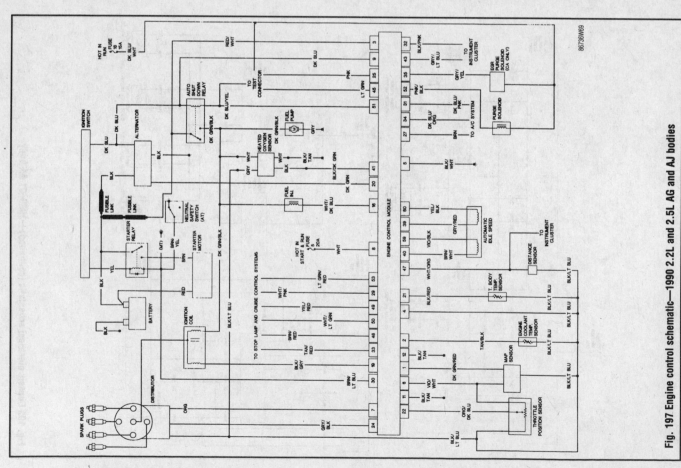

Fig. 197 Engine control schematic—1990 2.2L and 2.5L AG and AJ bodies

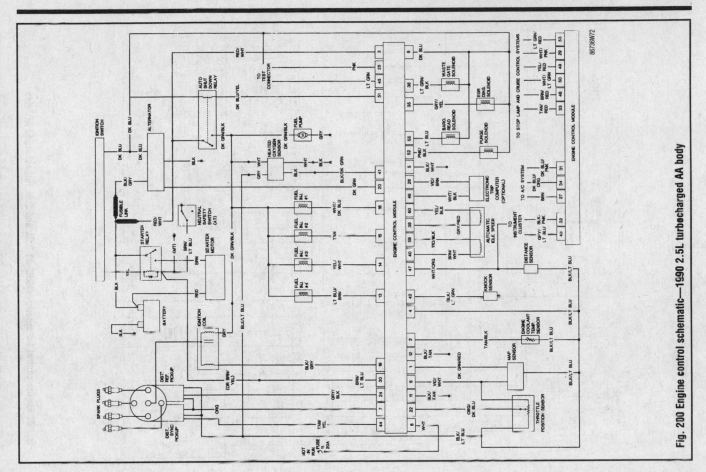

Fig. 200 Engine control schematic—1990 2.5L turbocharged AA body

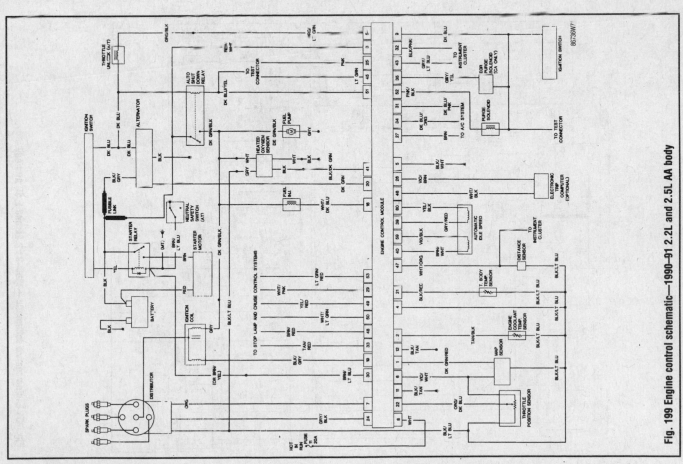

Fig. 199 Engine control schematic—1990–91 2.2L and 2.5L AA body

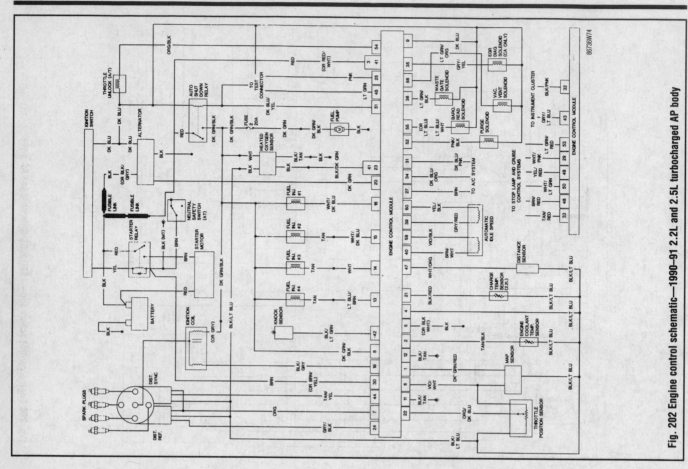

Fig. 202 Engine control schematic—1990–91 2.2L and 2.5L turbocharged AP body

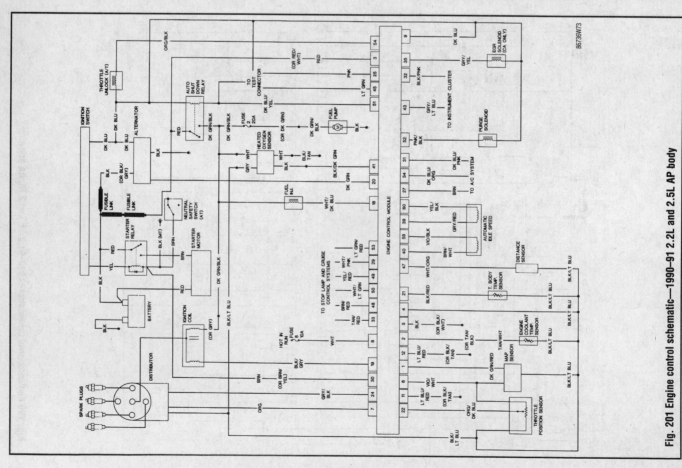

Fig. 201 Engine control schematic—1990–91 2.2L and 2.5L AP body

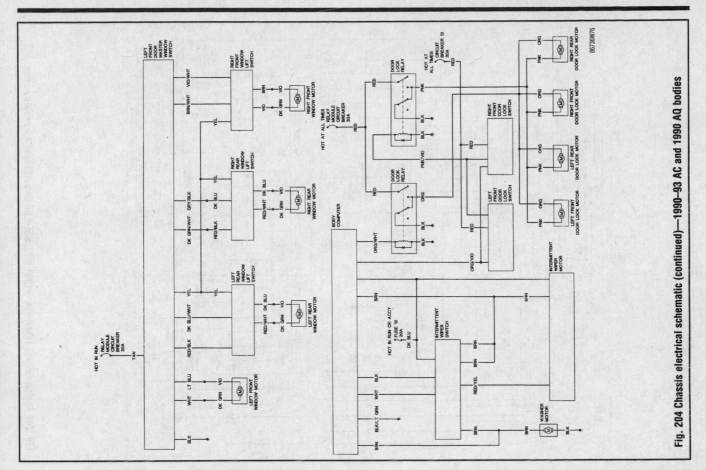

Fig. 204 Chassis electrical schematic (continued)—1990-93 AC and 1990 AQ bodies

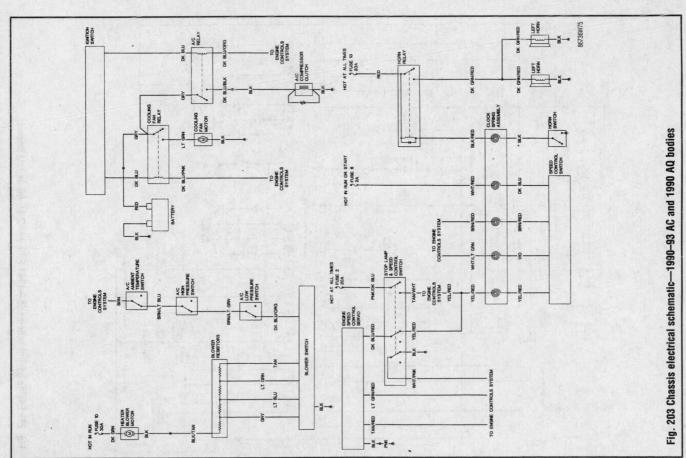

Fig. 203 Chassis electrical schematic—1990-93 AC and 1990 AQ bodies

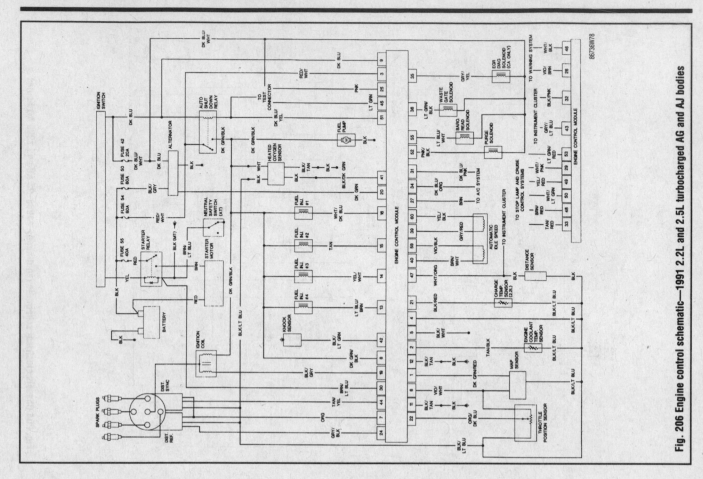

Fig. 206 Engine control schematic—1991 2.2L and 2.5L turbocharged AG and AJ bodies

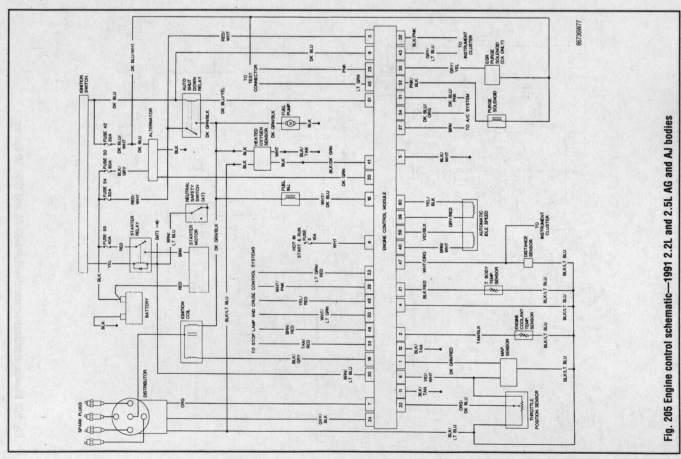

Fig. 205 Engine control schematic—1991 2.2L and 2.5L AG and AJ bodies

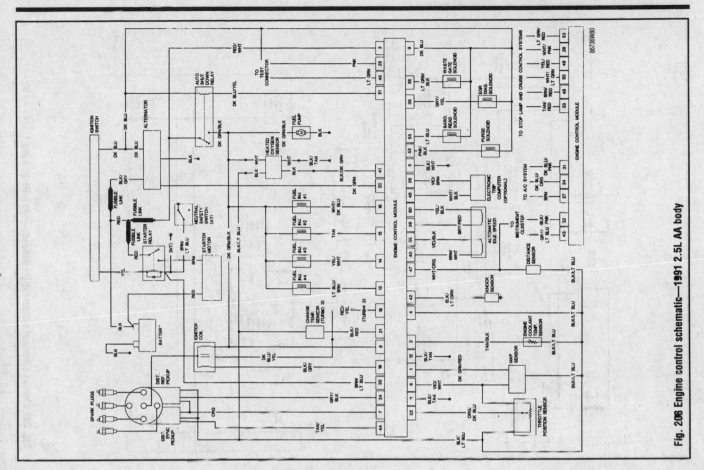

Fig. 206 Engine control schematic—1991 2.5L AA body

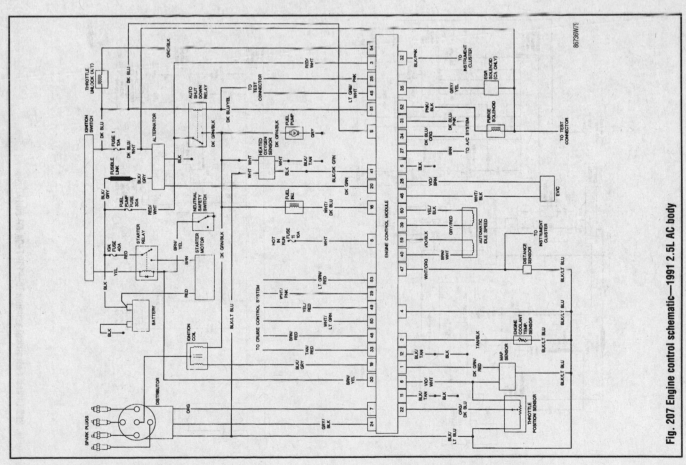

Fig. 207 Engine control schematic—1991 2.5L AC body

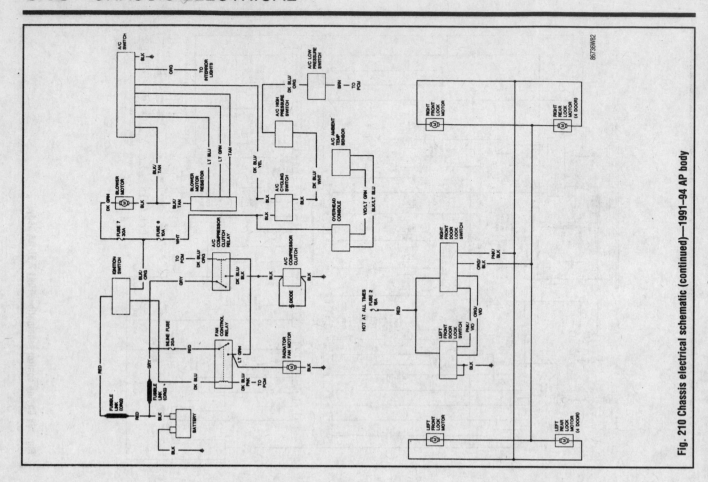

Fig. 210 Chassis electrical schematic (continued)—1991-94 AP body

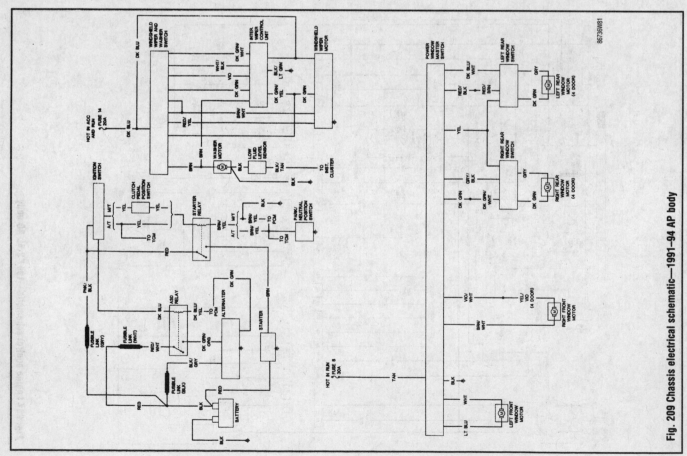

Fig. 209 Chassis electrical schematic—1991-94 AP body

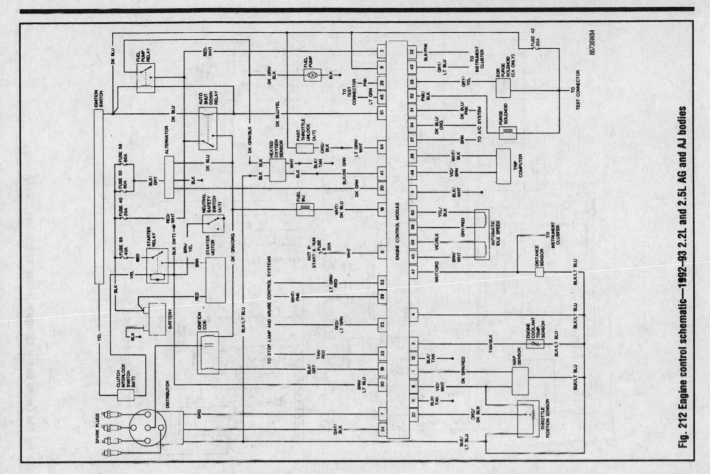

Fig. 212 Engine control schematic—1992-93 2.2L and 2.5L AG and AJ bodies

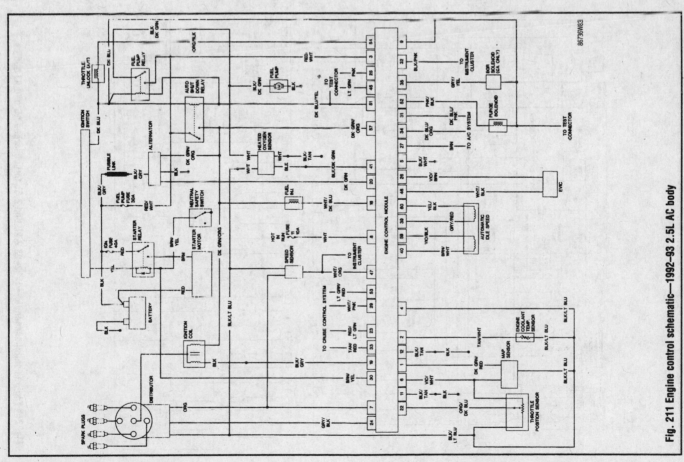

Fig. 211 Engine control schematic—1992-93 2.5L AC body

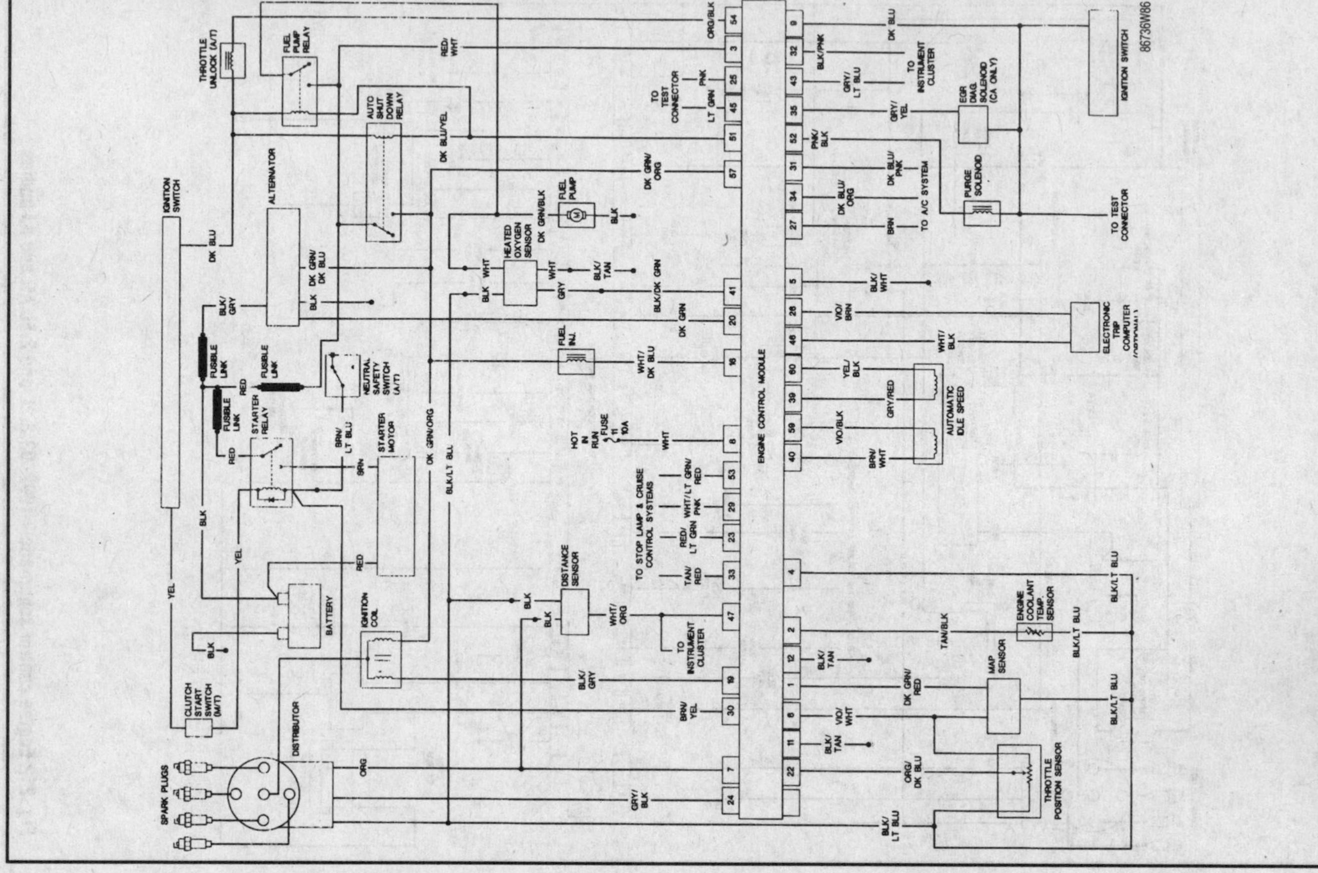

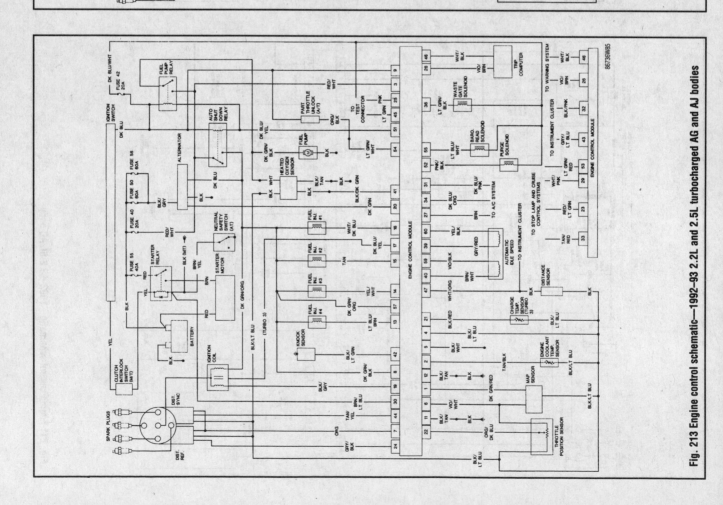

Fig. 214 Engine control schematic—1992–95 2.2L and 2.5L AA body

Fig. 213 Engine control schematic—1992–93 2.2L and 2.5L turbocharged AG and AJ bodies

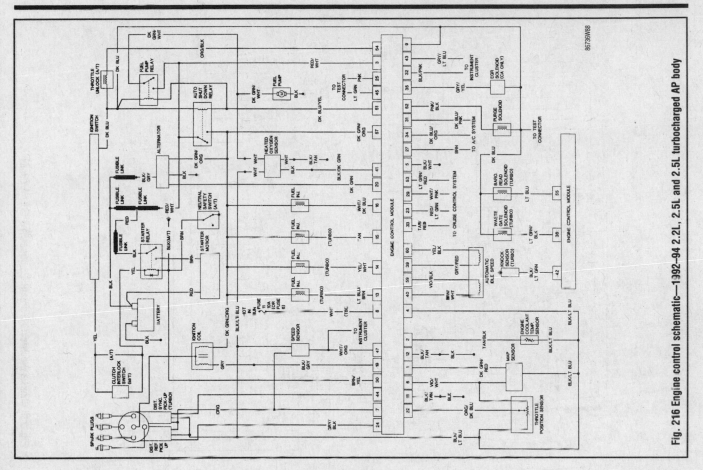

Fig. 216 Engine control schematic—1992-94 2.2L, 2.5L and 2.5L turbocharged AP body

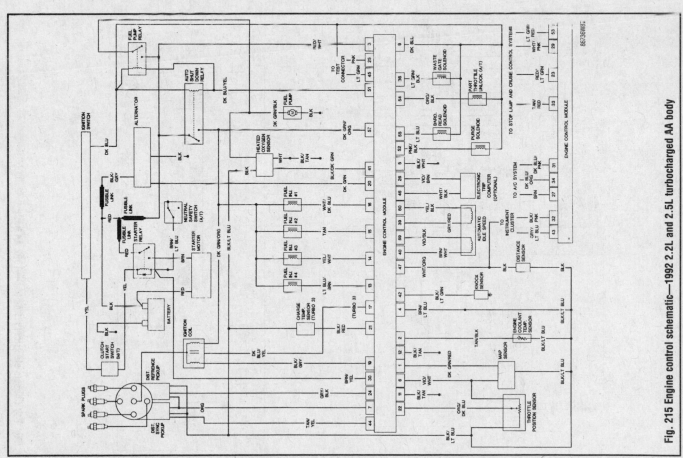

Fig. 215 Engine control schematic—1992 2.2L and 2.5L turbocharged AA body

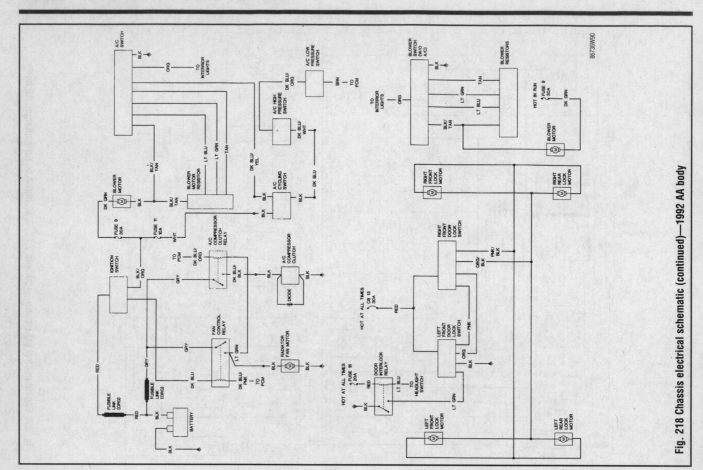

Fig. 218 Chassis electrical schematic (continued)—1992 AA body

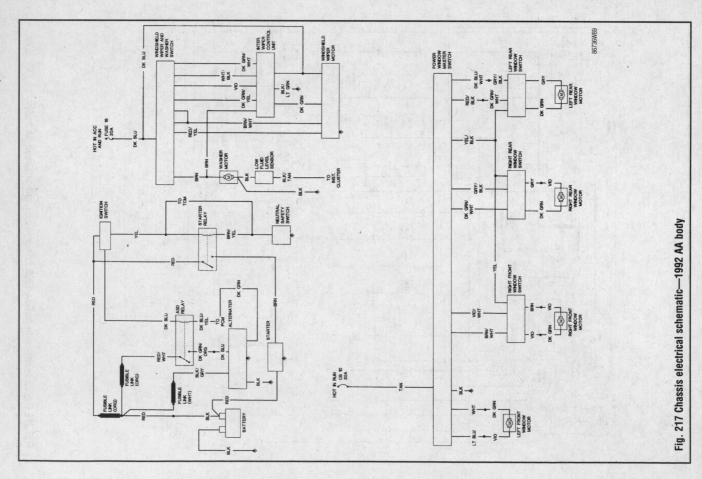

Fig. 217 Chassis electrical schematic—1992 AA body

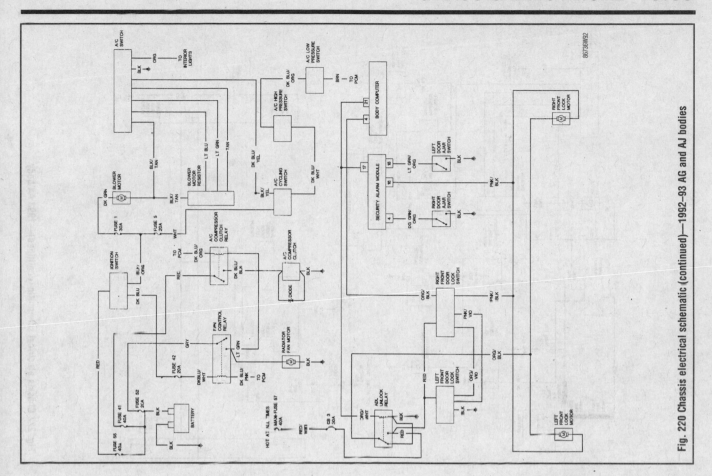

Fig. 220 Chassis electrical schematic (continued)—1992–93 AG and AJ bodies

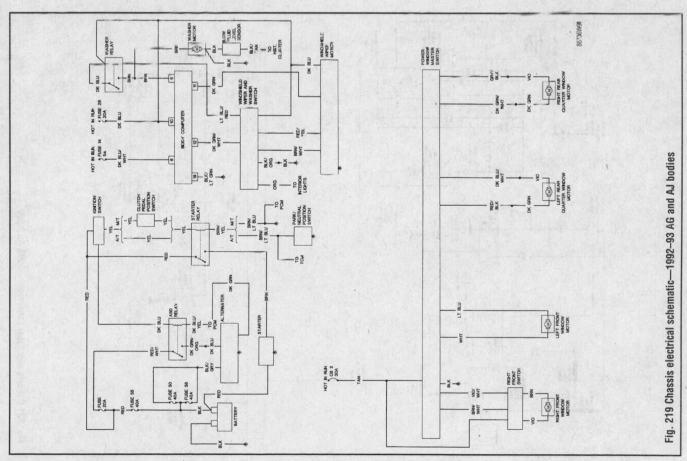

Fig. 219 Chassis electrical schematic—1992–93 AG and AJ bodies

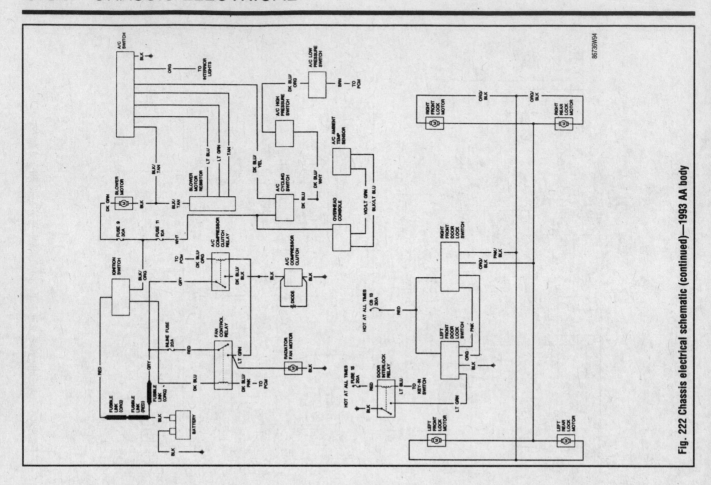

Fig. 222 Chassis electrical schematic (continued)—1993 AA body

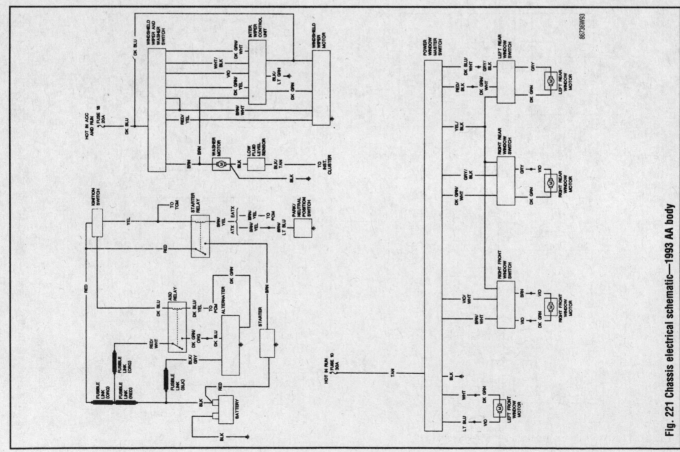

Fig. 221 Chassis electrical schematic—1993 AA body

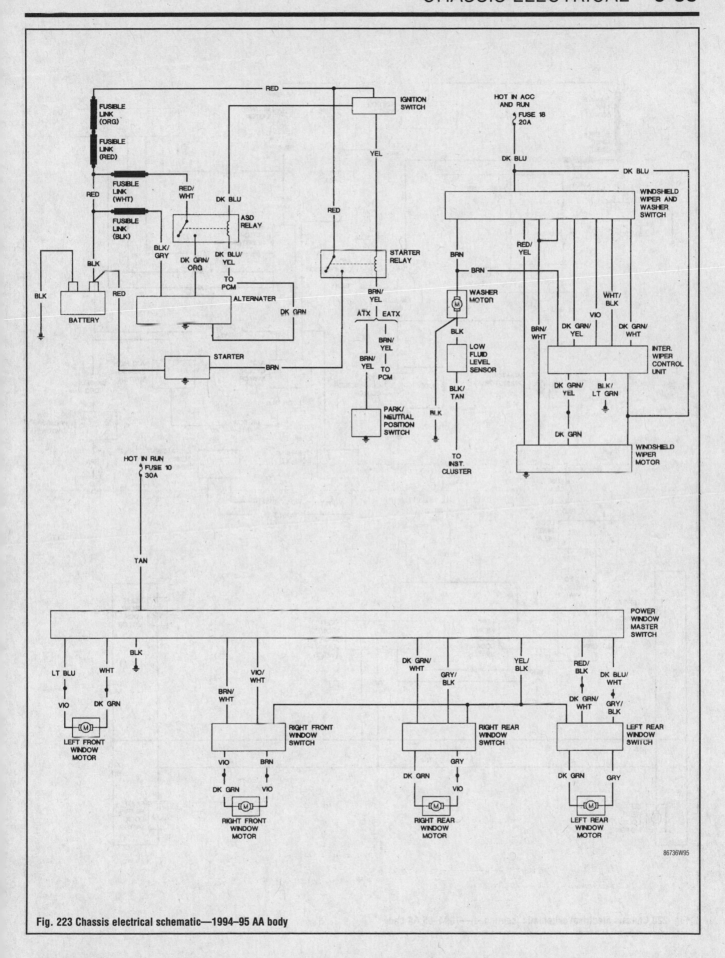

Fig. 223 Chassis electrical schematic—1994–95 AA body

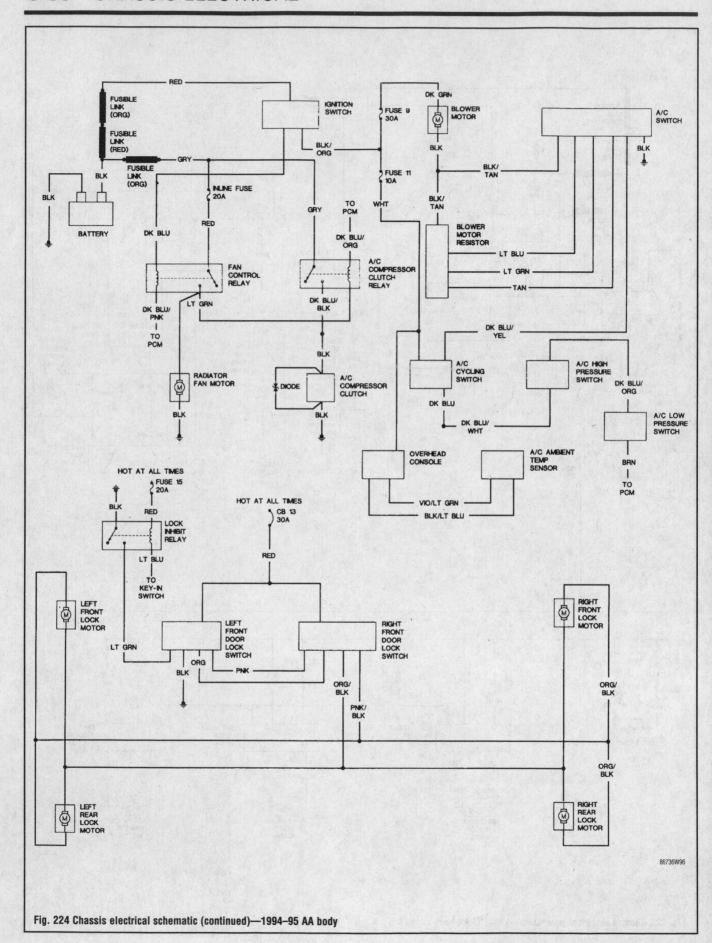

Fig. 224 Chassis electrical schematic (continued)—1994–95 AA body

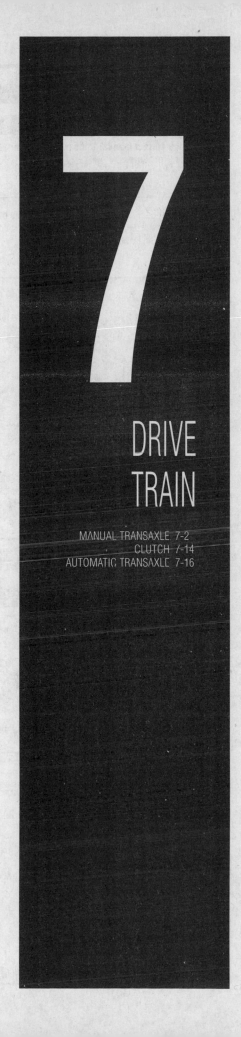

7

DRIVE
TRAIN

MANUAL TRANSAXLE

Adjustments

➡️**Identify the correct manual transaxle model for your vehicle before starting this procedure.**

LINKAGE

The cables used for shifting the transaxles can only be adjusted at their shifter connections. If the cables are defective they must be replaced with new ones. Refer to the shifter adjustment procedures.

SHIFTER

Shift Rod Operated Type

▶ **See Figures 1 and 2**

1. From the left side of the car, remove the lockpin from the transaxle selector shaft housing.
2. Reverse the lockpin and insert it in the same threaded hole while pushing the selector shaft into the selector housing. A hole in the selector shaft will align with the lockpin, allowing the lockpin to be screwed into the housing. This will lock the selector shaft in the 1–2 neutral position.
3. Raise and support the vehicle on jackstands.
4. Loosen the clamp bolt that secures the gearshift tube to the gearshift connector.
5. Make sure that the gearshift connector slides and turns freely in the gearshift tube.
6. Position the shifter mechanism connector assembly so that the isolator is contacting the standing flange and the rib on the isolator is aligned front and back with the hole in the block-out bracket. Hold the connector in this position while tightening the clamp bolt on the gearshift tube to 14 ft. lbs. (19 Nm).

7. Lower the car.
8. Remove the lockpin from the selector shaft housing and install it the original way in the housing.
9. Tighten the lockpin to 105 inch lbs. (12 Nm).
10. Check the shifter action.

Shift Cable Operated Type

1981–89 VEHICLES

▶ **See Figures 3 thru 9**

Before replacing the gearshift selector cable or crossover cable for a hard-shifting problem, disconnect both cables from the transaxle. Then, from the driver's seat, manually operate the gearshift lever through all of the gear ranges. If the gearshift lever moves smoothly, the cable(s) should not be replaced with new ones. The problem lies elsewhere.

➡️**To adjust the shift cable, two 140mm lengths of rod (except Daytona and K-body LeBarons) and an inch-pound torque wrench are required. The rod stock should be 5mm diameter for Aries, Reliant, LeBaron, Town & Country, Sundance and Shadow; for Lancer and LeBaron GTS, it should be 4mm.**

1. Working over the left front fender and remove the lockpin from the transaxle selector shaft housing.
2. Turn the lockpin so the long end faces downward. Gently attempt to insert it into the same threaded hole while you gradually push the selector shaft into the selector housing. When the pin fits into the selector shaft, stop sliding the shaft into the housing and screw the pin into the housing. If done correctly, this will lock the selector shaft into the neutral fore and aft position and into the 1–2 shift plane. Make sure that these conditions are met.
3. Remove the gearshift knob. Coat the shift shaft with a soap and water solution, then pull the shift boot up and over the pull-up ring.

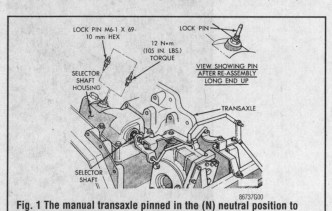

Fig. 1 The manual transaxle pinned in the (N) neutral position to adjust gearshift—cable or rod type

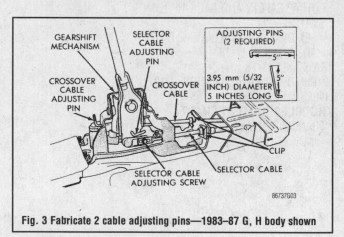

Fig. 3 Fabricate 2 cable adjusting pins—1983–87 G, H body shown

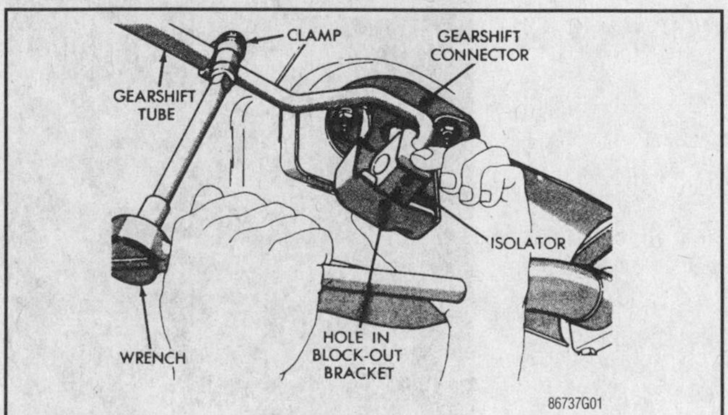

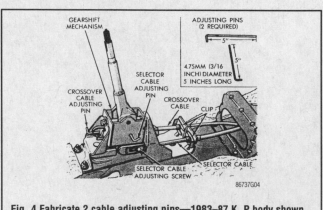

Fig. 4 Fabricate 2 cable adjusting pins—1983–87 K, P body shown

Fig. 2 Adjusting the gearshift rod

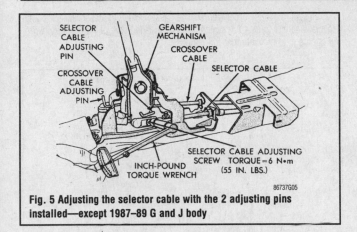

Fig. 5 Adjusting the selector cable with the 2 adjusting pins installed—except 1987–89 G and J body

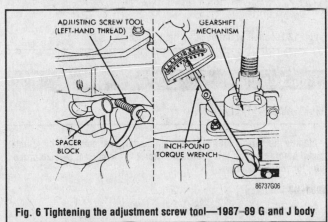

Fig. 6 Tightening the adjustment screw tool—1987–89 G and J body

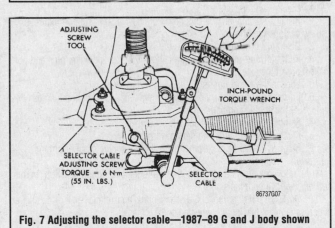

Fig. 7 Adjusting the selector cable—1987–89 G and J body shown

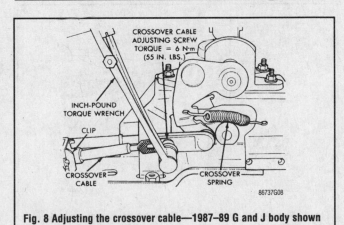

Fig. 8 Adjusting the crossover cable—1987–89 G and J body shown

Fig. 9 The gear shift mechanism and exploded view of entire linkage system

4. Remove the console if so equipped, by referring to Section 10 for the correct procedure.

5. The selector (fore and aft) and crossover (side-to-side) shift cables, located on either side of the shifter, each have slotted slides. A bolt locks the position of the slide to the gear lever mechanism. Loosen both bolts enough so that the slides can move freely.

6. On all except 1987–89 A, G and J-Body vehicles, bend the end of each of the two lengths of rod so the longer portion is just 127mm long. On 1987–89 A, G and J-Body vehicles, pull the adjusting screw tool off the shifter support bracket (it's taped there).

7. On all except 1987–89 A, G and J-Body vehicles, move the gearshift in the fore and aft plane while attempting to insert the rod into the side of the shifter support bracket until it locks the gearshift in place. Repeat the operation in the side-to-side plane, attempting to insert the other rod into the rear of the shifter support bracket. On 1987–89 A, G and J-Body vehicles, pass the bolt portion of the adjusting screw tool through the spacer block and then insert the tool through the shifter support bracket. Move the gearshift until you can turn the bolt and thread it into the shifter, locking it in place. Torque the bolt to 20 inch lbs. (2.3 Nm).

8. Once the shifter is properly locked in place, tighten both the lockbolts for the shift cable slide and crossover cable slide to 55 inch lbs. (6 Nm). Then, remove the fabricated rod pins or the adjusting screw tool. Unscrew the adjusting screw tool and tape it back where it was.

9. Unscrew and remove the lock pin from the transaxle, turn it around, and reinstall it, tightening again to 105 inch lbs. (12 Nm). Check to make sure the transaxle shifts smoothly and effectively into 1st and reverse. Make sure reverse is properly blocked out until the shift ring is raised.

10. Install the gearshift knob and boot. Install the console as described in Section 10.

1990–95 VEHICLES

♦ See Figures 10 and 11

Before replacing the gearshift selector cable or crossover cable for a hard-shifting problem, disconnect both cables from the transaxle. Then, from the driver's seat, manually operate the gearshift lever through all of the gear ranges. If the gearshift lever moves smoothly, the cable(s) should not be replaced with new ones. The problem lies elsewhere.

→To adjust the shift cable an inch pound and foot pound torque wrench will be required.

1. Working over the left front fender, remove the lock pin from the transaxle selector shaft housing.

2. Reverse the lock pin so the long end is down and insert it into the same threaded hole while pushing the selector shaft into the selector housing. A hole in the selector shaft will align with the lock pin, allowing the lock pin to be screwed into the housing. This operation locks the selector shaft in the **N** position between 3rd and 4th gears.

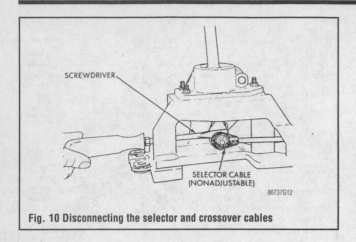

Fig. 10 Disconnecting the selector and crossover cables

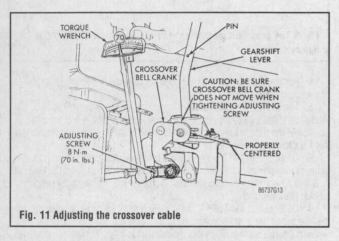

Fig. 11 Adjusting the crossover cable

3. Remove the gearshift knob from the gearshift lever.

4. If necessary, remove the shift lever boot and console to expose the gearshift linkage. The selector cable is not adjustable.

➡**Be certain that the crossover bell crank does not move when tightening the adjusting screw. Proper torque to the crossover cable adjusting screw is very important.**

5. Loosen the crossover cable adjusting screw and allow the cable to move in the slot. Center the shifter bracket (**N** position), then tighten the screw to 70 inch lbs. (8 Nm). Do not allow the shifter lever or crossover bell crank (pivot shifter arm to which the crossover cable is attached). The selector cable is not adjustable.

❊❊ WARNING

Proper torque to the crossover cable and adjusting screw is extremely important.

6. Remove the lock pin from the selector shaft housing and reinstall the lock pin, with the long end up, in the selector shaft housing. Tighten the lock pin to 105 inch lbs. (12 Nm) for 1990 vehicles or 70 inch lbs. (8 Nm) for 1991–95 vehicles..

7. Check the first/reverse shifting and blockout into reverse.

8. Reinstall the console, boot, pull-up ring, retaining nut and knob.

Back-Up Light Switch

REMOVAL & INSTALLATION

▶ **See Figure 12**

The back-up light switch is located on the top of the transaxle.

1. Detach the electrical connector, then unscrew the switch by engaging the flats with an open-end wrench.

2. Install in reverse order (replace the gasket or O-ring as necessary), being especially careful to start the switch into the threaded bore of the transaxle without forcing it, to prevent cross-threading.

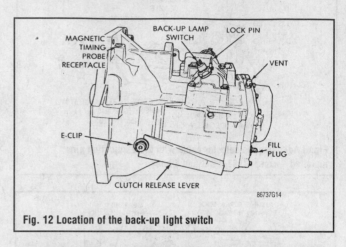

Fig. 12 Location of the back-up light switch

Transaxle

REMOVAL & INSTALLATION

➡**Identify the correct manual transaxle model, year coverage or vehicle model before starting this procedure. Refer to the correct service procedure for your vehicle.**

1981–88 Vehicles

▶ **See Figures 13, 14, 15, 16 and 17**

1. Disconnect the battery.

2. Install a suitable engine support fixture device. This support fixture is usually designed to fit across the engine compartment.

3. Disconnect the shift linkage.

4. With the vehicle on the ground, remove the axle end cotter pins and nut locks. Loosen the axle hub nuts.

5. Loosen the wheel lug nuts.

6. Raise and support the vehicle safely high enough to work underneath and inside the engine compartment.

7. Remove both front wheel and tire assemblies.

8. Remove the axle nuts and spring washers.

9. Remove the left front splash shield, and left engine mount from the transaxle.

10. Follow the procedures under "Halfshaft Removal and Installation" in this section. Remove both halfshafts.

11. On 1987 and later models, disconnect the anti-rotation link or damper at the crossmember, leaving it connected at the transaxle.

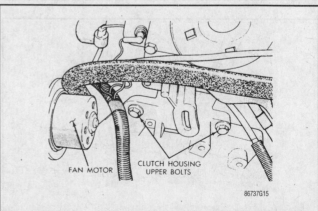

Fig. 13 Removal or installation of the clutch housing upper bolts

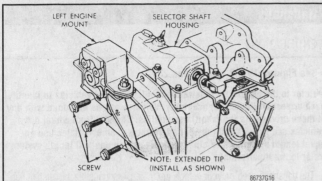

Fig. 14 Removal or installation of the left engine mount-to-transaxle bolts

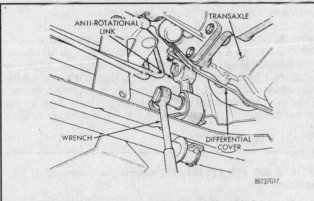

Fig. 15 Removal or installation of the ant-rotational link

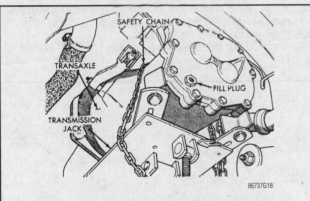

Fig. 16 Positioning the transaxle jack under the transaxle

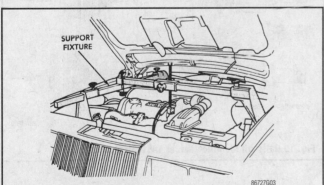

Fig. 17 A special support fixture should be used, however a second floor jack can also be used

12. Remove all necessary components, wiring and or cables to gain removal and installation access clearance to the transaxle assembly.

13. If working with the use of a lift, make sure the vehicle is properly placed on the lift. Raise the vehicle to standing level. If using a floor transmission jack, raise and support the vehicle safely, yet high enough to permit the removal of the transaxle.

14. Position a suitable transmission jack under the transaxle a secure it properly to the transaxle.

15. Remove all transaxle retaining bolts. Slowly, slide the transaxle directly away from the engine so the input shaft will slide smoothly out of the clutch release bearing and clutch/pressure plate assembly. Lower the transaxle (transaxle assembly must be properly supported with transmission jack) from the engine compartment.

➡To make transaxle mounting and alignment to the engine block easier, fabricate two bell housing locating pins. Install the locating pins at the top of the engine block. After the transaxle is in place, remove the locating pins and install the bell housing bolts. To fabricate the pins: Buy two extra bolts. Hacksaw the heads off the bolts. Then, cut slots in the ends of the bolts for a flat-bladed screwdriver. Finally, remove all burrs with a grinding wheel. Before installing the transaxle onto the engine block, install the two locating pins into tho top two engine block holes.

To install:

16. Prior to placing the transaxle on the transmission jack, apply a light coating of grease on the input shaft.

17. Support the transaxle unit securely and raise it into precise alignment with the engine block. Then, move it toward the engine block, inserting the transaxle input shaft into the release bearing and clutch/pressure plate assembly onto the transaxle mounting guide pins.

18. Complete the remaining part of installation by reversal of the removal procedures.

19. Make all necessary adjustments and fill thc transaxle if necessary with the specific fluid to the correct level. Road test the vehicle for proper operation.

1989–95 Vehicles

▶ See Figures 17 and 18

➡If the vehicle is going to be rolled while the transaxle is out of the vehicle, obtain 2 outer CV-joints to install in the hubs. If the vehicle is rolled without the proper torque applied to the front wheel bearings, the bearings will no longer be usable. Different transaxles are used according to application. It is important to use the round identification tag screwed to the top of the case when obtaining parts for exact parts matching. The tag should be reinstalled for future reference.

1. Disconnect the negative battery cable.

2. Install a suitable engine support fixture device. This support fixture is usually designed to fit across the engine compartment.

3. Remove the air cleaner assembly with all ducts. Remove the upper bell housing bolts. Disconnect the reverse light switch and the ground wire.

4. Remove the starter attaching nut and bolt at the top of the bell housing.

5. With the vehicle on the ground, remove the axle end cotter pins and nut locks. Loosen the axle hub nuts.

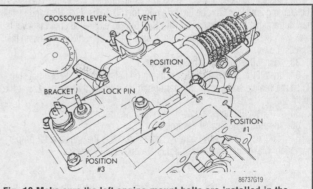

Fig. 18 Make sure the left engine mount bolts are installed in the proper locations

6. Loosen the wheel lug nuts.

7. Raise and support the vehicle safely high enough to work underneath and inside the engine compartment.

8. Remove both front wheel and tire assemblies.

9. Remove the axle nuts and spring washers.

10. Remove the ball joint retaining bolts and pry the control arm from the steering knuckle. Position a drain pan under the transaxle where the axles enter the differential or extension housing.

11. Remove the axles from the transaxle or center bearing. Unbolt the center bearing and remove the intermediate axle from the transaxle, if equipped. Follow the procedures under "Halfshaft Removal and Installation" in this section. Remove both halfshafts.

12. Remove the engine left mount from the transaxle.

13. Remove the anti-rotation link from the crossmember. Disconnect the shifter cables from the transaxle and unbolt the cable bracket.

14. Remove the speedometer gear adapter bolt and remove the adapter from the transaxle.

15. Unbolt the starter and position it aside.

16. Using the proper equipment, support the weight of the engine.

17. Position a suitable transaxle jack under the transaxle.

18. Remove the lower bell housing bolts.

19. Remove the left side splash shield. Remove the transaxle mount bolts.

20. Carefully pry the transaxle from the engine.

21. Slide the transaxle rearward until the input shaft clears the clutch disc.

22. Pull the transaxle completely away from the clutch housing and remove it from the vehicle.

23. To prepare the vehicle for rolling, support the engine with a suitable support or reinstall the front motor mount to the engine. Then reinstall the ball joints to the steering knuckle and install the retaining bolt. Install the obtained outer CV-joints to the hubs, install the washers and torque the axle nuts to 180 ft. lbs. (244 Nm). The vehicle may now be safely rolled.

To install:

24. Lubricate the pilot bushing and input shaft splines very lightly with high temperature lubricant.

25. Mount the transaxle securely on a suitable jack. Lift it in place until the input shaft is centered in the clutch housing opening. Roll the transaxle forward until the input shaft splines fully engage with the clutch disc and install the transaxle to clutch housing bolts.

26. Raise the transaxle and install the left side mount bolts.

27. Remove the engine and transaxle support fixtures.

28. Install the starter to the transaxle and install the lower bolt finger-tight.

29. Install a new O-ring to the speedometer cable adapter and install to the extension housing; make sure it snaps in place. Install the retaining bolt.

30. Install the shift cable bracket and snap the cable ends in place. Install the anti-rotation link.

31. Install the left engine mount to the transaxle.

✳✳ WARNING

On some later transaxles, the left engine mounting bolts used in position No. 1 and No. 3 are the same length. The bolt in No. 2 position is longer. If bolt No. 2 is used in position No. 3 it can damage the selector shift housing when the bolt is seated.

32. Install the axles and center bearing, if equipped. Install the ball joints to the steering knuckles. Torque the axle nuts to 180 ft. lbs. (244 Nm) and install new cotter pins. Fill the transaxle with SAE 5W-30 engine oil until the level is even with the bottom of the filler hole. Install the splash shield and install the wheels. Lower the vehicle.

33. Install the upper bell housing bolts.

34. Install the starter attaching nut and bolt at the top of the bell housing. Raise the vehicle and tighten the starter bolt from under the vehicle. Lower the vehicle.

35. Connect the reverse light switch and the ground wire.

36. Install the air cleaner assembly.

37. Connect the negative battery cable and check the transaxle for proper operation. Make sure the reverse lights are on when in Reverse.

Halfshafts

IDENTIFICATION

♦ **See Figures 19, 20, 21, 22 and 23**

➥**Refer to the necessary illustrations on later model vehicles to identify each driveshaft (halfshaft) assembly. Vehicles can be equipped with any of these driveshafts (halfshaft) assemblies. Chrysler front wheel drive vehicles use two different driveshaft systems. Some vehicles use an equal length system while other vehicles use an unequal length system (refer to the illustration).**

The halfshafts used on your vehicle are three-piece units. Each halfshaft has an inner sliding constant velocity (Tripod) joint and an outer constant velocity (Rzeppa) joint with a stub shaft splined into the hub. On 2.2L engines with turbocharger, the shafts are of equal length and both are short and of solid construction. With this setup, there is a short, intermediate shaft with a bearing and bracket on the outer side and a Cardan (U-joint) on the inner side.

On vehicles with the normally aspirated (non-turbocharged) 2.2L and 2.5L engines, the connecting shafts for the CV-joints are unequal in length and construction. The left side is a short solid shaft and the right is longer and tubular.

It is impossible to classify the halfshaft type according to model and year designations. However, each type of shaft is clearly identifiable according to the design features pointed out on the enclosed illustrations. Use these to classify the joint according to brand and type so that if parts are to be replaced, you can order by manufacturer name as well as the year and model of the car.

REMOVAL & INSTALLATION

1981–83 A-460, 465, 525 Manual Transaxle and Automatic Transaxles

♦ **See Figures 24 thru 33**

The inboard CV-joints are retained by circlips in the differential side gears. The circlip tangs are located on a machined surface on the inner end of the stub shaft.

1. Have someone apply the brakes and, with the car still resting on the wheels, loosen the hub nut and the wheel nuts.

2. Remove the axle end cotter pins and nut locks. Loosen the axle hub nuts.

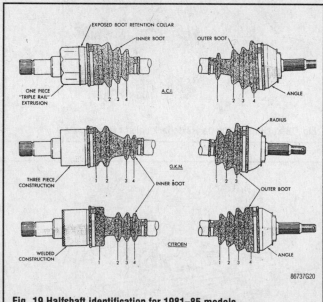

Fig. 19 Halfshaft identification for 1981–85 models

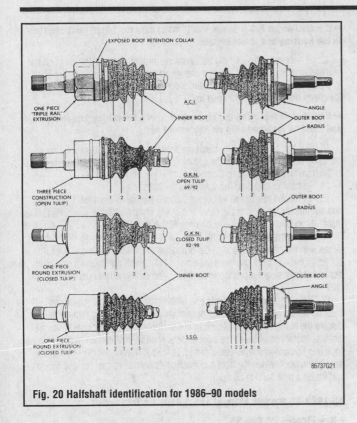

Fig. 20 Halfshaft identification for 1986–90 models

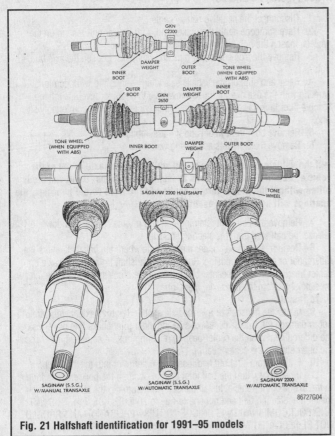

Fig. 21 Halfshaft identification for 1991–95 models

3. Raise and support the vehicle safely high enough to work comfortably. If working with the use of a lift, raise the vehicle to shoulder level. If working using a floor jack, raise the vehicle just high enough to work comfortably sitting.

4. Remove both front wheel and tire assemblies.

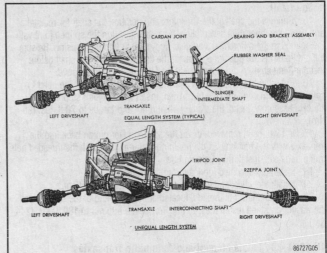

Fig. 22 The 2 types of halfshaft systems can easily be identified by the extra intermediate shaft and Cardan joint

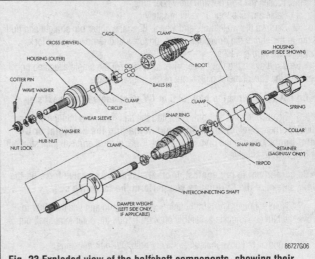

Fig. 23 Exploded view of the halfshaft components, showing their positions relative to one another—typical

5. Remove the axle nuts and spring washers.

6. Remove the ball joint retaining bolts and pry the control arm from the steering knuckle. Position a drain pan under the transaxle where the axles enter the differential or extension housing.

7. Drain the transaxle differential and remove the cover.

➡**Any time the transaxle differential cover is removed, a new gasket should be formed from RTV sealant.**

8. To remove the right hand halfshaft, disconnect the speedometer cable and remove the cable and gear before removing the driveshaft.

9. Rotate the halfshaft to expose the circlip tangs.

10. Compress the circlip with needle nose pliers and push the shaft into the side gear cavity.

11. Remove the clamp bolt from the ball stud and steering knuckle.

12. Separate the ball joint stud from the steering knuckle, by prying against the knuckle leg and control arm.

13. Separate the outer CV-joint splined shaft from the hub by holding the CV-joint housing and moving the hub away. Do not pry on the slinger or outer CV-joint.

14. Support the shaft at the CV-joints and remove the shaft. Do not pull on the shaft.

➡**Removal of the left shaft may be made easier by inserting the blade of a thin prybar between the differential pinion shaft and prying against the end face of the shaft.**

To install:

15. Support the shaft at the CV-joints and position the shaft for reinstallation. Hold the inner joint assembly at the housing. Align the splined joint with the splines in the differential side gear, and guide it into the housing. Be sure the circlip tangs are positioned against the flattened end of the shaft before installing the shaft. A quick thrust will lock the circlip in the groove.

16. Push the hub and knuckle assembly outward and insert the outer splined CV-joint shaft into the hub. Then, insert the ball joint stud into the knuckle assembly. Install the clamp bolt and nut and torque to 70 ft. lbs. (95 Nm).

17. If it has been removed, insert the speedometer pinion back into the transaxle with the bolt hole in the retaining collar aligned with the threaded hole in the transaxle. Install the retaining bolt.

18. Install the specified lubricant into the transaxle.

19. Install the wheel and wheel nuts. Lower the car to the floor.

20. Clean the hub nut threads, located at the outer end of the shaft. Install the washer and then install the hub nut. Torque the hub nut to 180 ft. lbs. (244 Nm).

All 1984–88 Models Manual and Automatic Transaxles

▶ **See Figures 24 thru 33**

1. Drain the transaxle fluid as described in Section 1.

2. Have someone apply the brakes and, with the car still resting on the wheels, loosen the hub nut and the wheel nuts.

3. Raise and support the vehicle safely.

4. Remove the wheel nuts and wheel. Bend the cotter pin straight and pull it out of the end of the driveshaft. Then, unscrew and remove the nut lock. Remove the spring washer.

5. If removing the right side driveshaft, remove the single attaching bolt and pull the speedometer pinion out of the transaxle case.

➡**Do not pry against the ball joint or CV-joint boots in the next step.**

6. Remove the nut and bolt clamping the ball joint stud into the steering knuckle. Then, carefully **so as to avoid damaging the ball joint or CV-joint boots**, use a small prybar to pry the lower control arm ball joint stud out of the steering knuckle.

➡**Be careful not to pry against or otherwise use excessive force on the wear sleeve of the CV-joint as you perform the following step.**

7. Hold the outer CV-joint housing with one hand and use the other to move the hub and knuckle assembly outward to pull the outer joint shaft out of the hub.

8. Support the driveshaft assembly at both CV-joint housings.

➡**The axle must be supported at both CV-joints during this operation to avoid pulling on the shaft. Any stretching forces may damage the U-joints!**

Then, pull on the inner joint housing in order to pull it out of the transaxle.

➡**Note that the driveshaft, when in its normal, installed position, acts to keep the hub/bearing assembly in place. If the vehicle is to be supported by its wheels or moved on them while the driveshaft is out of the car, install a bolt through the hub to ensure the hub bearing assembly cannot loosen.**

To install:

9. Thoroughly clean the seal located between the outer end of the driveshaft and the steering knuckle with a safe solvent. Make sure solvent does not get onto the driveshaft boot. Apply a bead of a lubricant such as Mopar Multipurpose Lubricant Part No. 4318063 or the equivalent. Apply it to the full circumference and make the bead ¼ in. (6mm) wide. Fill the lip-to-housing cavity on the seal around its complete circumference; wet the seal lip with the lubricant, as well.

10. To install the driveshaft assembly, first inspect units on turbocharged cars to make sure the rubber washer seal is in place on the right inner joint. Relocate the seal, if necessary.

11. Support the driveshaft by both CV-joints. Hold the inner joint assembly at the housing. Align the splined joint with the splines in the differential side gear, guide it into the housing, and insert it until it locks.

➡**If installing an A.C.I. brand shaft, make sure the tripod joint engages in the housing and is not twisted.**

12. If necessary, remove the bolt installed through the hub earlier. Push the hub and knuckle assembly outward and insert the outer splined CV-joint shaft into the hub. Then, insert the ball joint stud into the knuckle assembly. Install the clamp bolt and nut and torque to 70 ft. lbs. (95 Nm).

➡**Note that, if replacing the clamp bolt, it is a prevailing torque type and must be replaced with an equivalent part.**

13. If it has been removed, insert the speedometer pinion back into the transaxle with the bolt hole in the retaining collar aligned with the threaded hole in the transaxle. Install the retaining bolt.

14. Install the specified lubricant into the transaxle.

15. Install the wheel and wheel nuts. Lower the car to the floor. Clean the hub nut threads, located at the outer end of the shaft. Install the washer and then install the nub nut. Torque the hub nut to 180 ft. lbs. (244 Nm).

16. Install the lock finger-tight. Then, back it off until the cotter pin slot aligns with the hole in the end of the driveshaft. Install the cotter pin until it is pulled all the way through. Bend the prongs tightly around the outer end of the nut lock. Make sure the prongs wrap tightly. Torque the wheel nuts to 95 ft. lbs. (127 Nm).

17. If the boot on the transaxle end of the shaft is deformed (collapsed), it must be vented and restored to its normal shape. To do so, first remove and discard the clamp on the shaft side (if the shaft has one); then, insert a round, small diameter rod between the boot and the shaft to vent it; then, work the boot back into its normal shape, being careful to keep dirt from getting in or grease from getting out. When the boot has reached its normal shape, remove the rod and install a new service clamp.

All 1989–95 Models Manual and Automatic Transaxles

▶ **See Figures 24 thru 33**

1. Disconnect the negative battery cable.

2. Have someone apply the brakes and, with the car still resting on the wheels, loosen the hub nut and the wheel nuts.

3. Remove the axle end cotter pins and nut locks. Loosen the axle hub nuts.

4. Raise and support the vehicle safely high enough to work comfortably. If working with the use of a lift, raise the vehicle to shoulder level. If working using a floor jack, raise the vehicle just high enough to work comfortably sitting.

5. Remove both front wheel and tire assemblies.

6. Remove the axle nuts and spring washers.

➡**If the vehicle is going to be rolled while the transaxle is out of the vehicle, obtain 2 outer CV-joints to install in the hubs. If the vehicle is rolled without the proper torque applied to the front wheel bearings, the bearings will no longer be usable.**

7. Remove the ball joint retaining bolt and pry the control arm down to release the ball stud from the steering knuckle.

8. Position a drain pan under the transaxle where the halfshaft enters the differential or extension housing. Remove the halfshaft from the transaxle or center bearing. Unbolt the center bearing from the block and remove the intermediate shaft from the transaxle, if equipped.

To install:

9. Install the halfshaft or intermediate shaft to the transaxle, being careful not to damage the side seals. Make sure the inner joint clicks into place inside the differential. Install the center bearing retaining bolts if equipped, then install the outer shaft to the center bearing.

10. Pull the front strut out and insert the outer joint into the front hub.

11. If necessary, turn the ball joint stud to position the bolt retaining indent to the inside of the vehicle. Install the ball joint stud into the steering knuckle. Install the retaining bolt and nut and torque to 70 ft. lbs. (95 Nm). THIS NUT AND BOLT COMBINATION IS UNIQUE TO THIS APPLICATION AND SHOULD NOT BE REPLACED WITH CONVENTIONAL HARDWARE! USE ORIGINAL EQUIPMENT PARTS IF REPLACING!

12. Install the axle nut washer and nut and tighten the nut to 180 ft. lbs. (244 Nm). Install the spring washer, nut lock and a new cotter pin.

13. Install the tire and wheel assembly. Lower the vehicle.

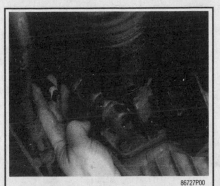

Fig. 24 Before removing the halfshafts, unplug the speed sensor wiring connector . . .

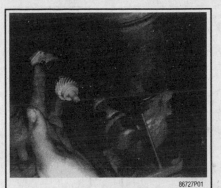

Fig. 25 . . . unbolt the sensor and pull it out of the transaxle, making sure . . .

Fig. 26 . . . to retain the drive gear on the end of the sensor

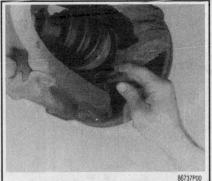

Fig. 27 Remove the lower ball joint cinch bolt . . .

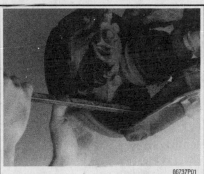

Fig. 28 . . . then pry the lower control arm and ball joint out of the steering knuckle

Fig. 29 Disengage the halfshaft slightly at the transaxle end . . .

Fig. 30 . . . pull the halfshaft from the steering knuckle hub . . .

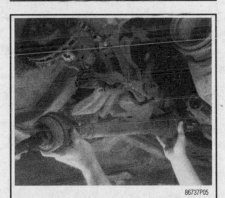

Fig. 31 . . . then remove the halfshaft assembly from the vehicle

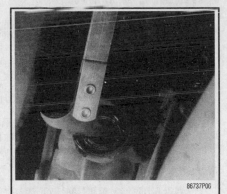

Fig. 32 If necessary, remove the inner seal from the transaxle

Fig. 33 Installing a new inner seal

CV-JOINT OVERHAUL

Inner CV-Joint

DISASSEMBLY

▶ See Figures 23 and 34

With the driveshaft assembly removed from the vehicle, identify the unit type from the illustrations.

1. Remove the boot clamps and pull the boot back to gain access to the tripod retention system, which prevents accidental separation from the CV-joint housing.

→ When removing the housing from the tripod, hold the rollers in place on the trunnion studs to prevent the rollers and needle bearings from falling away. After the tripod is out of the housing, secure the rollers in place with tape.

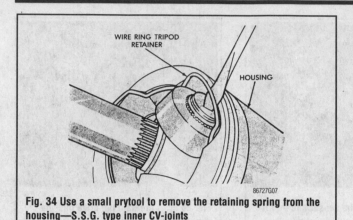

Fig. 34 Use a small prytool to remove the retaining spring from the housing—S.S.G. type inner CV-joints

2. Depending on the type of CV-joint assembly, separate the tripod from the housing as follows:

a. S.S.G.—Utilizes a wire ring tripod retainer which expands into a groove around the top of the housing. Use a flat head pry tool to pry the wire ring out of the groove and slide the tripod from the housing.

➡**Do not mangle or destroy the retainer during disassembly.**

b. G.K.N.—The retention system on this assembly is a integral part of the plastic collar on the inside of the CV-joint housing. Clamp the stub shaft of the CV-joint housing in a vise and use protective caps or the equivalent on the jaws of the vise to prevent damage to the stub shaft. Hold the interconnecting shaft on an angle, while gently pulling on the shaft until one of the tripod bearings is free of the retaining collar. Continue holding the interconnecting shaft on an angle and gently pull on the shaft until all rollers are free of the retaining collar.

TRIPOD REMOVAL FROM INTERCONNECTING BAR

◆ **See Figures 35, 36, 37 and 38**

1. For S.S.G. CV-joints, remove the snapring from the shaft end-groove. Remove the tripod by hand or by tapping the body with a brass punch.

2. For G.K.N. CV-joints, perform the following:

a. Expand the stop ring behind the tripod and slide it back along the shaft.

b. Slide the tripod back along the shaft, either by hand or by tapping the body with a brass drift. This will expose the circlip on the end of the interconnecting bar.

c. Remove the circlip from the end of the interconnecting bar.

d. Remove the tripod from the interconnecting bar. It is not necessary to remove the stop ring from the interconnecting bar unless the bar is being replaced.

INSPECTION OF TRIPOD AND HOUSING

Remove as much grease as possible from the assembly. Inspect the joint housing ball raceway and tripod components for excessive wear, replace if needed.

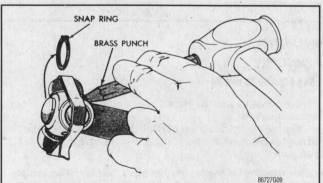

Fig. 35 Carefully use a brass punch or drift to remove the tripod joint from the shaft—S.S.G. type inner CV-joints

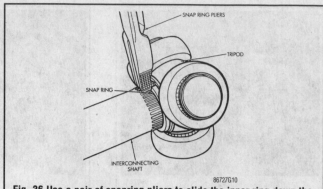

Fig. 36 Use a pair of snapring pliers to slide the inner ring down the shaft, then tap the tripod joint down the shaft . . .

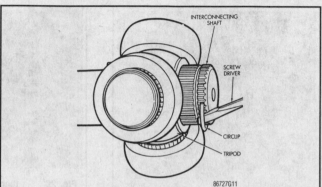

Fig. 37 . . . after which the outer circlip can be removed from the end of the shaft

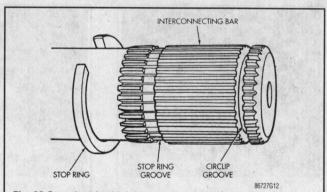

Fig. 38 Once the tripod joint has been removed from the shaft, both the stop ring and circlip grooves can be seen easier

Inspect the spring, spring cup and the spherical end of the connecting shaft for excessive wear or damage, replace with new components if needed.

ASSEMBLY

1. For G.K.N. CV-joints, perform the following:

a. Slide the rubber washer seal over the stub shaft and down into the groove provided. The rubber washer seal is used only on the right inner CV-joint on the equal length drive shaft systems.

b. Fasten the boot to the interconnecting shaft. For more details, refer to the CV-joint boot procedure.

c. Slide the stop ring back into the stop ring groove on the interconnecting bar.

d. Install a new circlip in the circlip groove on the interconnecting bar.

e. With the chamfered end of the tripod facing the stop ring, align the tripod splines and push or tap on the body of the tripod assembly with a soft drift, until the tripod is seated on the shaft. Check to make sure that the tripod is fully installed by attempting to pull the tripod off of the shaft by hand.

2. For S.S.G. CV-joints, perform the following steps:

a. Slide the washer seal over the stub shaft and down into the groove provided. The rubber washer seal is used only on the right inner CV-joint on the equal length drive shaft systems.

b. Fasten the boot to the interconnecting shaft. For more details, refer to the CV-joint boot procedure.

c. Install the first wire ring tripod retainer over the interconnecting shaft, slide the tripod on the shaft (both ends are the same).

d. Install the snapring into the groove on the interconnecting shaft to lock the tripod in position.

3. If the wire ring tripod retainer is not suitable for reuse and a new one is not available, the following procedure should be used:

a. Install the tripod on the interconnecting shaft.

b. Install the spring and cup assembly into the inner joint housing.

c. Position the small end of the boot in the locating grooves on the interconnecting shaft.

d. Clamp the small end of the boot clamp onto the boot, thereby retaining the boot to the interconnecting shaft.

e. Distribute ½ packet of the CV-joint rebuild grease into the boot and ½ into the housing.

f. Install the tripod into the housing.

g. Place the large clamp over the shaft.

h. Install the halfshaft into the vehicle.

i. Position the large end of the boot into the locating groove.

j. Slide the large clamp into position.

k. For boot clamping instructions, refer to the CV-joint boot procedure later in this section.

INNER CV-JOINT HOUSING INSTALLATION

1. For the G.K.N. CV-joints, perform the following steps:

a. Distribute ½ of the lubricant provided in the CV-joint rebuild kit into the housing and the remaining amount into the boot.

b. Position the spring in the housing spring pocket with the spring cup attached to the exposed end of the spring. Place a small amount of grease on the concave surface of the spring cup.

➡**Care must be taken to ensure proper spring positioning. The spring must remain centered in the housing spring pocket when the tripod is installed and seated in the spring cup.**

c. Clamp the stub shaft of the housing in a vise. Use protective caps (or the equivalent) on the jaws of the vise so that the stub shaft does not get damaged by the vise. Position the interconnecting shaft and the tripod assembly on top of the plastic retaining collar. Carefully insert each of the tripod rollers into the retaining collar, one at a time while holding the interconnecting shaft on an angle. Carefully push down on the shaft until the rollers are locked into the retaining collar in the housing.

d. Position the boot over the boot retaining groove in the housing and clamp in place. For more details, refer to the CV-joint boot installation procedure later in this section.

2. For the S.S.G. type CV-joints, use the following steps:

a. Distribute ½ of the lubricant provided in the CV-joint rebuild kit into the housing and the remaining amount into the boot.

b. Position the spring in the housing spring pocket with the spring cup attached to the exposed end of the spring. Place a small amount of grease on the concave surface of the spring cup.

➡**Care must be taken to ensure proper spring positioning. The spring must remain centered in the housing spring pocket when the tripod is installed and seated in the spring cup.**

c. Slip the tripod into the housing and install the tripod wire retaining ring into position. Check for the ability of the retaining ring to hold the tripod in the housing.

d. Position the boot over the boot retaining groove in the housing and clamp in place. For more details, refer to the CV-joint boot installation procedure later in this section.

Outer CV-Joint

DISASSEMBLY

▶ **See Figures 39 and 40**

1. Remove the boot clamps and boot, then discard the old boot.

2. Wipe away the grease to expose the joint.

3. For G.K.N. type CV-joints, remove the CV-joint from the shaft by supporting the interconnecting shaft in a vise. Use protective caps (or the equivalent) on the jaws of the vise so that the stub shaft does not get damaged by the vise. Give a sharp tap with a rubber or plastic mallet to the top of the housing to dislodge the joint from the internal circlip installed in a groove at the outer end of the shaft.

4. In S.S.G. type CV-joints, a single circlip located in a groove on the cross and is used to retain the cross to the shaft. Loosen the damper weight bolts and slide it and the boot toward the inner CV-joint. Expand the circlip and with snapring pliers and slide the joint off of the shaft. Reinstall the damper weight onto the shaft.

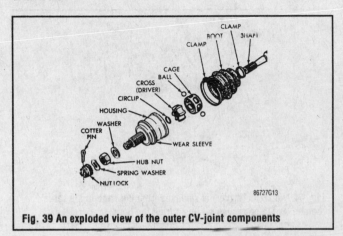

Fig. 39 An exploded view of the outer CV-joint components

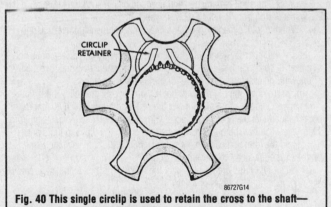

Fig. 40 This single circlip is used to retain the cross to the shaft— use snapring pliers to expand the circlip

WEAR SLEEVE

▶ **See Figures 41, 42, 43 and 44**

A wear sleeve installed on the outer CV-joint housing provides a wipe surface for the hub bearing seal (installed in the steering knuckle).

1. If bent or damaged, carefully pry the wear sleeve from the CV-joint machined ledge.

2. Remove the circlip from the shaft groove and discard. A replacement boot package should include a new circlip.

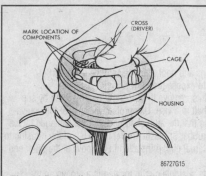

Fig. 41 Before disassembly, make certain to matchmark the housing, the cage and the cross (driver) for reassembly

Fig. 42 Remove each ball, one at a time, until all have been removed . . .

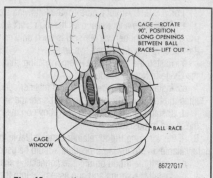

Fig. 43 . . . then remove the cage by turning it 90° on its side and pulling it out of the housing

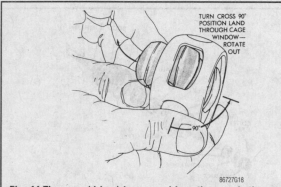

Fig. 44 The cross (driver) is removed from the cage in the same manner as the cage was removed from the housing

3. Unless the shaft is damaged and needs to be replaced, do not remove the heavy spacer ring from the shaft (G.K.N. types only).

4. With the joint separated from the interconnecting shaft proceed as follows:

a. If the outer CV-joint was operating satisfactorily and grease does not appear to be contaminated, just replace the boot with a new one. Bypass the following disassembly procedure for the CV-joint assembly.

b. If the outer joint is noisy or badly worn, bypass the following disassembly procedure and replace the entire unit with a new one. It is also recommended that the boot be replaced with a new one. The boot package from Chrysler includes the boot, clamps, retaining ring (circlip) and lubricant.

5. Hold the joint vertically in a vise by clamping the splined shaft, using soft jaws (or equivalent) to prevent damage.

6. Wipe off surplus grease and mark the relative position of the inner cross, cage and housing with a dab of paint.

7. Press down on one side of the inner race to tilt the cage and remove the ball from the opposite side. If the joint is tight, use a hammer and brass drift to tap the inner race. **Do not hit the cage.** Repeat this step until all 6 balls are removed. A small pry tool may be used to pry the balls loose.

8. Tilt the cage and inner race assembly vertically and position the two opposing cage windows in the area between the ball grooves. Remove the cage and inner race assembly by pulling upward and away from the housing.

9. Turn the inner cross (driver) 90° to the cage and align one of the race spherical lands with the cage window. Raise the land into the cage window and remove the inner race by swinging it out.

INSPECTION

Check the grease for contamination and all parts for defects as follows:
1. Wash all parts in a suitable solvent and dry, preferably with compressed air.
2. Inspect the housing ball races for excessive wear and scratching.
3. Check the splined shaft and nut threads for damage.
4. Inspect all 6 balls for pitting, cracks, scoring and wear. Dulling of the balls' surface is normal.

5. Inspect the cage for excessive wear on the inside and outside spherical surfaces, surface ripples on the cage window, cracks and chipping.
6. Inspect the inner race (cross) for excessive wear or scoring of the ball races.

➡️**Any of the previous defects warrants the replacement of the CV-joint assembly as a unit.**

Polished areas in races (cross and housing) and on cage spheres are normal and do not indicate need for joint replacement.

ASSEMBLY

♦ **See Figure 45**

➡️**If neither the outer joint was disassembled nor the wear sleeve damaged, go to Step 9.**

1. Position the new wear sleeve on the joint housing machined ledge. Assemble the installation tool (Special Tool C-4698 or the equivalent), which is provided with a handle and dual purpose drive head for installing the wear sleeve onto the CV-joint housing and seal into the knuckle.
2. Install the wear sleeve with the installation tool.
3. Lightly oil all components before assembling the outer joint.
4. Align all components according to the paint markings.
5. Insert one of the inner race (cross) lands into the cage window and feed the race into the cage. Pivot the cross 90° to complete the cage assembly.
6. Align the opposing cage windows with the housing land and feed the cage assembly into the housing. Pivot the cage 90° to complete the installation.

When properly assembled, the large counterbore in the cross should be facing outward from the joint on the G.K.N. units. On the S.S.G. joint the internal circlip in the cross will be facing outward from the housing.

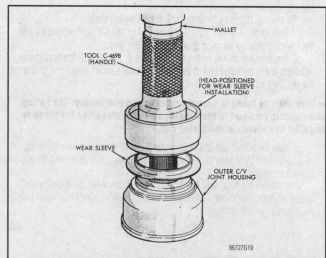

Fig. 45 This tool (or the equivalent) is necessary for the installation of the wear sleeve—do not try to install it with a hammer and drift

7. Apply lubricant to the ball races from the packet provided in the boot kit and distribute equally between all sides of the ball grooves. One packet is sufficient to lubricate the joint.

8. Insert the balls into the raceway by tilting the cage and inner race assembly.

9. Fasten the boot to the shaft. For more details, refer to the boot installation procedure later in this section.

10. On G.K.N. units, insert the new circlip, provided with the kit, in the shaft groove. Do not over expand or twist the circlip during installation. The S.S.G. unit has a reusable circlip retainer that is an integral part of the driver assembly.

11. Position the outer joint on the splined end with the hub nut on the stub shaft. Engage the splines, then tap sharply with the plastic or rubber mallet.

12. Check that the circlip is properly seated by attempting to pull the joint from the shaft.

13. Locate the large end of the boot over the joint housing checking that the boot is not twisted.

14. Fasten the boot to the housing. For more details, refer to the boot installation procedure.

CV-Joint Boots

HANDLING AND CLEANING

It is vitally important during any service procedures requiring boot handling, that care be taken not to puncture or tear the boot by over tightening the clamps, misuse of tools or pinching the boot. Pinching can occur by rotating the CV-joint beyond normal working angles.

The halfshaft boots are not compatible with oil, gasoline or cleaning solvents. Care must be taken that boots never come in contact with any of these liquids.

➡**The only acceptable cleaning agent for the halfshaft boots is soap and water. After washing, the boots must be thoroughly rinsed and dried before reusing.**

INSPECTION

Noticeable amounts of grease on areas adjacent to or on the exterior of the CV-joint boot, is the first indication that a boot is punctured, torn or that a clamp has loosened. When a CV-joint is removed for servicing of the joint. The boot should be properly cleaned and inspected for cracks, tears and scuffed areas on the interior surfaces. If any of these conditions exist, boot replacement is necessary.

INSTALLATION—RUBBER BOOTS

▶ **See Figures 46 thru 53**

✳✳ WARNING

The hard plastic boots require approximately 100 times the clamping force of the rubber boot. The clamps used on the rubber boots do not have the type of load capacity required to seal the hard plastic boots and should not be used for this purpose.

Rubber boots appear only on the inner joints of certain halfshafts. The rubber boots must be serviced with the strap and buckle clamp. Use the clamp installation tool (Special tool C–4653 or the equivalent).

1. Slide the small end of the boot over the shaft. Position the boot to the edge of the locating mark or groove, whichever is appropriate.

2. Install the CV-joint. For more details, refer to the CV-joint installation procedures earlier in this section.

3. Slide the large diameter of the boot into the locating groove.

4. Wrap the binding strap around the boot twice, plus an additional 2½ in. (63mm).

5. Pass the strap through the buckle and fold it back about 1⅛ in. (29mm) on the inside of the buckle.

6. Put the strap around the boot with the eye of the buckle toward you. Wrap the strip around the boot once and pass it through the buckle, then wrap it around a second time also passing it through the buckle.

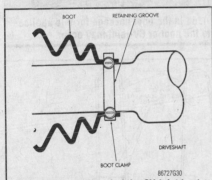

Fig. 46 The small end of the CV-joint boot should be positioned as shown—G.K.N. type CV-joints

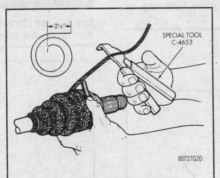

Fig. 47 Wrap the strap around the large end of the boot 2 times, plus an additional 2½ in. (63mm) and cut off the excess

Fig. 48 Unwrap the strap from the boot, then install the buckle over one end of the strap as shown

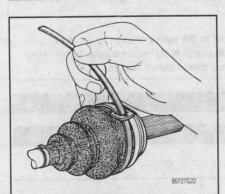

Fig. 49 Wrap the strap around the boot once and insert it through the buckle, then . . .

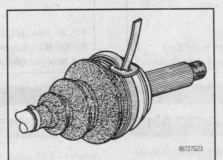

Fig. 50 . . . wrap it around the boot and insert it through the buckle once again, then fold the strap back slightly to hold its position

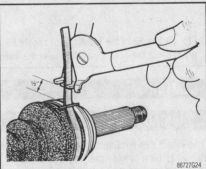

Fig. 51 Position the tightening tool ½ in. (13mm) above the buckle (with the strap in the narrow slot of the tool), . . .

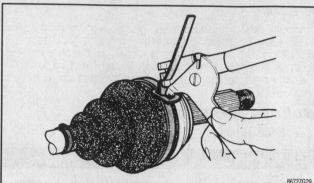

Fig. 52 . . . push the tool forward and insert the lower tang into the buckle notch, then . . .

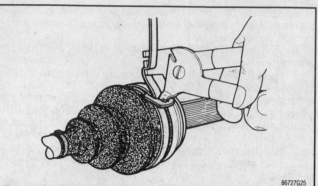

Fig. 53 . . . tighten the strap by squeezing the tool handles together

7. Fold the strip back slightly to prevent it from slipping backwards.

8. Open the tool all the way and place the strip in the narrow slot approximately ½ in. (13mm) from the buckle.

9. Hold the binding strip with the left hand and push the tool forward and slightly upward. Then fit the hook of the tool into the eye of the buckle.

10. Tighten the strip by closing the tool handles. Rotate the tool (handles) downward while slowly releasing the pressure on the tool handles. Allow the tool (handles) to open progressively. Then open the tool entirely and remove it sideways.

11. If the strip is not tight enough, engage the tool a second or even a third time, always about ½ (13mm) from the buckle. When tightening always be careful to see that the strap slides in a straight line and without resistance in the buckle. An effective grip will be obtained only by following the above instructions.

✳✳ WARNING

Never fold the strap back or bring the tool down while tightening, as this action will break the strap.

12. When the strap is finally tight enough, remove the tool sideways and cut the strap off ⅛ in. (3mm) so that it does not overlap the edge of the buckle. Complete the installation by folding the strip back neatly.

INSTALLATION—PLASTIC BOOT

▶ **See Figures 54 and 55**

1. Slide the small clamp onto the shaft.

2. Position the small end of the boot over the interconnecting shaft with the clip of the boot in the third groove, toward the center of the interconnecting shaft.

3. Position the clamp evenly over the boot. Place the clamp installation tool (C-4975 or the equivalent) over the bridge of the clamp and tighten the nut until the jaws of the tool are closed completely, face-to-face.

4. After attaching the boot to the shaft, install the CV-joint following the procedure earlier in this section.

5. Position the large end of the boot on the housing and install the clamp by crimping the bridge of the clamp with the crimping tool (Special tool C-4975 or equivalent).

✳✳ WARNING

Use only the clamps provided in the boot package for this application, otherwise damage to the boot or CV-joint may occur.

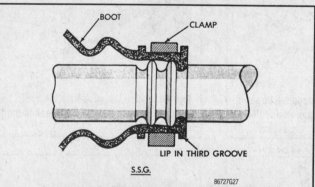

Fig. 54 The lip of the plastic boot should be settled in the third groove and the clamp installed over the second groove as shown

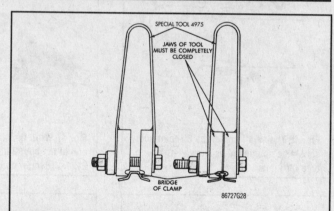

Fig. 55 This special tool (or the equivalent) will be needed to tighten the clamps—the plastic boots require a much higher clamping force, so rubber boot clamps cannot be used

CLUTCH

✳✳ CAUTION

The clutch driven disc may contain asbestos, which has been determined to be a cancer-causing agent. Never clean clutch surfaces with compressed air! Avoid inhaling any dust emitted from any clutch surface! When cleaning clutch surfaces, use a commercially available brake cleaning fluid.

Adjustments

LINKAGE/PEDAL HEIGHT/FREE-PLAY

The manual transaxle clutch release system has a unique self-adjusting mechanism to compensate for clutch disc wear. This adjuster mechanism is located within the clutch pedal. The preload spring maintains tension on the cable. This tension keeps the clutch release bearing continuously loaded against the fingers of the clutch cover assembly. Therefore no adjustment is necessary.

Clutch Cable

REMOVAL & INSTALLATION

1. Remove the retainer from the clutch release lever at the transaxle by pulling on the tail of the ball stud after removing the retainer.

2. Pry out the ball end of the cable from the positioner adjuster and remove the cable, passing it through the hoop in the shock tower mounting bracket.

To install:

3. Inspect the cable for wear and contamination. The inner cable strand should move smoothly inside the cable housing. If the cable is worn or damaged, replace the cable with a new one.

➡**Do not lubricate the cable.**

4. Inspect the clutch pedal and adjuster mechanism for wear.

5. Route the clutch cable as when removed, and press the ball end of the cable into the positioner adjuster.

6. Insert the transaxle end of the cable into the clutch release lever, then install the retainer.

7. After installation, push and lift the clutch pedal 2 or 3 times to allow the adjuster mechanism to function.

Driven Disc and Pressure Plate

REMOVAL & INSTALLATION

▶ **See Figures 56 and 57**

➡**Chrysler recommends the use of special tool C-46/6 for disc alignment. Clean the flywheel face with crocus cloth or fine sandpaper (400–600 grade), then wipe the surface with mineral spirits. If the flywheel surface is severely scored, heat cracked or warped, replace the flywheel. Always replace the clutch assembly, pressure plate and release bearing as a matched set.**

1. Disconnect the negative battery cable. Remove the transaxle as described earlier in this section.

2. Matchmark the clutch cover and flywheel for installation in the same positions.

3. Insert special tool C-4676 (or its equivalent) through the clutch disc hub to prevent the clutch disc from falling and damaging the facings.

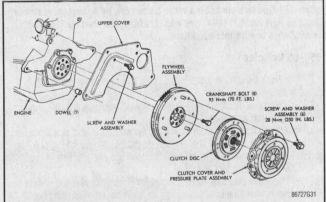

Fig. 56 Exploded view of the clutch plate and flywheel, showing their positions relative to each other

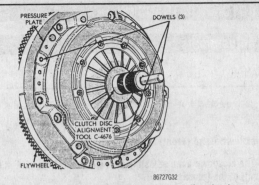

Fig. 57 The clutch disc alignment tool (C-4676) keeps the clutch disc from being damaged when it is removed from the flywheel

4. Loosen the cover attaching bolts. Do this in a crosswise pattern, a few turns at a time to prevent warping the cover.

❊❊ WARNING

Do not touch the clutch disc facing with oily or dirty hands. Oil or dirt transferred from your hands onto the clutch disc facing may cause clutch chatter.

5. Remove the cover assembly and disc from the flywheel. Be careful to keep any dirt or other contamination off the friction surfaces.

6. Remove the clutch release shaft and slide the release bearing off the input shaft seal retainer.

7. Remove the fork from the release bearing thrust plate.

To install:

8. Inspect the rear main seal for leakage. Repair the seal at this point, if there is leakage, perform the following:

a. Make sure the friction surfaces of both the flywheel and the pressure plate are uniform in appearance. If there is evidence of heavy contact at one point and very light contact 180° away, the flywheel or pressure plate may be improperly mounted (tightened) or sprung due to mechanical damage.

b. If there is evidence that the flywheel may not be true, it should be checked with a dial indicator or replaced (always replace the flywheel retaining bolts-with new bolts coated with Loctite® sealant-tighten to specifications).

c. The indicator must be mounted so that its plunger is in contact with the flywheel wear circle. In a full turn, the indicator should read no more than 0.003 in. (0.076mm).

d. Make sure to push forward on the flywheel before you begin taking the reading, zeroing the indicator and continuously as you turn it (to keep any crankshaft end-play out of the reading—refer to a local machine shop if necessary, because the flywheel assembly can be machined if still in specifications).

9. With a straightedge, check the pressure plate for flatness. The inner surface of the pressure plate should be straight within 0.020 in. (0.5mm). It should also be free of discoloration, cracks, grooves, or ridges. Otherwise, replace it.

10. Spin the clutch bearing to make sure it turns freely and smoothly.

11. Install the fork, release bearing, and clutch release shaft in the reverse order of the removal procedure.

12. Install the clutch assembly onto the flywheel, carefully aligning the dowels on the flywheel with the holes in the assembly. Make sure the alignment marks made earlier also align. Then, apply pressure to the clutch alignment tool to precisely center it as you snug the clutch attaching bolts sufficiently to hold the clutch disc in the proper position.

13. Tighten the clutch cover bolts alternately and evenly until they all are seated. Then, tighten to 21 ft. lbs. (29 Nm). Remove the disc alignment tool.

14. Install the transaxle as described earlier in this section.

AUTOMATIC TRANSAXLE

Adjustments

BANDS

Only the A–404, A–413, A–415, A–470 and A–670 transaxles have easily adjustable bands.

Kickdown Band (Front)

➡**The kickdown band adjusting screw is located on the left side (top front) of the transaxle case.**

1. Loosen the locknut and back the nut off approximately five complete revolutions. Test the adjusting screw for free turning in the transaxle case.
2. Using a special wrench (Tool C-3880-A with the adapter Tool C-3705, or equivalent), tighten the band adjusting screw to 47–50 inch lbs. (5 Nm). If the adapter C-3705 is not used, tighten the adjusting screw to 72 inch lbs. (8 Nm) which is the true torque amount.
3. Back the adjusting screw off 3 revolutions for A–404 and A–415 to 2½ revolutions for all other transaxles.
4. Tighten the locknut to 35 ft. lbs. (47 Nm).
5. The band should now be completely adjusted.

Low/Reverse Band (Front)

1. Loosen the locknut and back the nut off approximately five complete revolutions. Test the adjusting screw for free turning in the transaxle case.
2. Tighten the adjusting screw to 41 inch lbs. (5 Nm).
3. Back the adjusting screw off 3½ revolutions. A–404 and A–415 is non-adjustable.
4. Tighten the locknut to 10 ft. lbs. (14 Nm).
5. The band should now be completely adjusted.

2–4 Band

▶ **See Figures 58 and 59**

This band adjustment is used only on the ZF-4 transaxle.
1. Remove the pan and valve body.
2. Remove the existing band adjusting shim.
3. Measure and record the thickness of the adjusting shim.
4. Measure the clearance between the band pin and case. Clearance should be 0.049–0.059 in. (1.25–1.50mm).
5. If clearance must be adjusted, install a thicker or thinner shim to obtain the required clearance.
6. Install the valve body and pan. Use a new pan gasket.

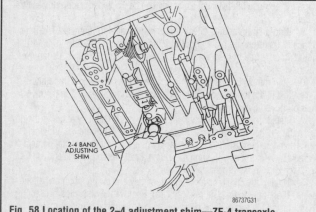

Fig. 58 Location of the 2–4 adjustment shim—ZF-4 transaxle

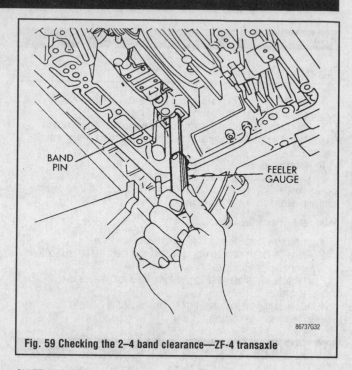

Fig. 59 Checking the 2–4 band clearance—ZF-4 transaxle

SHIFT LINKAGE

1981–83 Vehicles

➡**When it is necessary to disassembly the linkage cable from the lever, which uses plastic grommets as retainers, the grommets should be replaced with new ones.**

1. Make sure that the adjustable swivel block is free to slide on the shift cable.
2. Place the shift lever in PARK.
3. With the linkage assembled, and the swivel lock bolt loose, move the shift arm on the transaxle all the way to the front detent.
4. Hold the shift arm in this position with a force of about 10 ft. lbs. (14 Nm) and tighten the adjust swivel lock bolt to 8 ft. lbs. (11 Nm).
5. Check the linkage action.

➡**The automatic transaxle gear selector release button may pop up in the knob when shifting from PARK to DRIVE. This is caused by inadequate retention of the selector release knob retaining tab. The release button will always work but the loose button can be annoying. A sleeve (Chrysler Part No. 5211984) and washers (Chrysler Part No. 6500380) are available to cure this condition.**

1984–95 Vehicles

1. Put the gearshift in **P**. Loosen the clamp bolt located on the gearshift cable bracket.
2. On column shifts, make sure that the preload adjustment spring engages the fork on the transaxle bracket.
3. Pull the shift lever (on the transaxle) all the way to the front detent position (which puts the transaxle in **P**). Then, tighten the lockbolt to 90 inch lbs. (10.2 Nm) (on 1984–87 models and 100 ft. lbs. (135 Nm) on 1988 and later model cars.
4. Check the adjustment as follows:
   a. The detent positions of the transaxle shift lever for **N** and **D** should be within the limits of the corresponding gate stops on the hand shift lever.
   b. The starter must operate with the key only if the shift lever is in **P** or **N** position.

THROTTLE PRESSURE CABLE

1981–85 Vehicles

♦ See Figure 60

➡This adjustment should be performed while the engine is at normal operating temperature. Make sure that the carburetor is not on fast idle by disconnecting the choke.

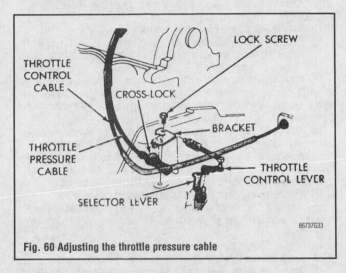

Fig. 60 Adjusting the throttle pressure cable

1. Loosen the adjustment bracket lock screw.
2. To insure proper adjustment, the bracket must be free to slide on its slot.
3. Hold the throttle lever firmly to the left (toward the engine) against its internal stop and tighten the adjusting bracket lock to 105 inch lbs. (8¾ ft. lbs.).
4. Reconnect the choke. Test the cable operation by moving the throttle lever forward and slowly releasing it to confirm it will return fully rearward.

1986–95 Vehicles

1. Make sure the engine is at operating temperature. On carbureted cars, disconnect the choke to make sure the throttle is completely off the fast idle cam.
2. Loosen the bracket lock screw that is mounted on the cable.
3. The bracket should be positioned with both its alignment tabs touching the surface of the transaxle. If not, position it that way. Then tighten the lock bolt to 105 inch lbs. (12 Nm).
4. Release the cross-lock on the cable assembly by pulling it upward. Make sure that the cable is then free to slide all the way toward the engine (until it is against its stop).
5. Now turn the transaxle throttle control lever fully clockwise until it hits its internal stop. Press the cross lock downward and into its locked position. This will automatically remove all cable backlash.
6. Reconnect the choke, if it has been disconnected. Turn the transaxle throttle lever forward (or counterclockwise) and then slowly release it. It should return to the full clockwise position, indicating that the cable operates freely.

Upshift and Kickdown Learning Procedure

A-604 ULTRADRIVE TRANSAXLE

In 1989, the A-604 4-speed, electronic transaxle was introduced; it is the first to use fully adaptive controls. The controls perform their functions based on real time feedback sensor information. Although, the transaxle is conventional in design, functions are controlled by its ECM.

Since the A-604 is equipped with a learning function, each time the battery cable is disconnected, the ECM memory is lost. In operation, the transaxle must be shifted many times for the learned memory to be re-input to the ECM; during this period, the vehicle will experience rough operation. The transaxle must be at normal operating temperature when learning occurs.

1. Maintain constant throttle opening during shifts. Do not move the accelerator pedal during upshifts.

2. Accelerate the vehicle with the throttle ⅛–½ open.
3. Make fifteen to twenty 1st–2nd, 2nd–3rd and 3rd–4th gear upshifts. Accelerating from a full stop to 50 mph (80 km/h) each time at the aforementioned throttle opening is sufficient.
4. With the vehicle speed below 25 mph (40 km/h), make 5–8 wide open throttle kickdowns to 1st gear from either 2nd or 3rd gear. Allow at least 5 seconds of operation in 2nd or 3rd gear prior to each kickdown.
5. With the vehicle speed greater than 25 mph (40 km/h), make 5 part throttle-to-wide open throttle kickdowns to either 3rd or 2nd gear from 4th gear. Allow at least 5 seconds of operation in 4th gear, preferably with load throttle prior to performing the kickdown.

Neutral Safety and Back-up Lamp Switch

REMOVAL & INSTALLATION

♦ See Figures 61 and 62

1. Disconnect the negative battery cable.
2. Remove the wiring connector from the switch.

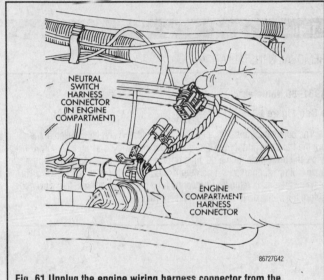

Fig. 61 Unplug the engine wiring harness connector from the switch, . . .

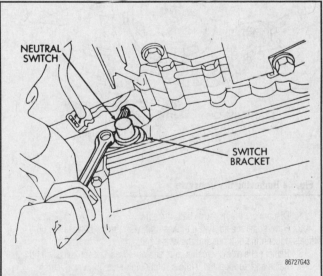

Fig. 62 . . . then remove the switch retaining bolt, and pull the switch out of the transaxle case

3. Place a drain pan under the switch to catch any fluid which might escape through the switch hole, then unscrew the switch from the case.

To install:

4. Install the new switch with a new seal and tighten it to 24 ft. lbs. (33 Nm).

5. Top off the transaxle fluid to compensate for any lost fluid.

6. Attach the electrical wiring to the switch.

7. Connect the negative battery cable.

ADJUSTMENT

The neutral safety switch is the center terminal of the three terminal switch, located on the transaxle. The back-up light switch uses the two outside terminals. The center terminal provides a ground for the starter solenoid circuit through the selector lever in the **P** and **N** positions only.

1. Disconnect the negative battery terminal.

2. Unscrew the switch from the transaxle, and allow the fluid to drain into a pan.

3. Move the selector lever to see that the switch operating lever fingers are centered in the switch opening.

4. Install the new switch and new seal. Tighten the switch assembly to 24 ft. lbs. (33 Nm). Check for proper operation.

Transaxle

REMOVAL & INSTALLATION

1981–88 Vehicles

▶ **See Figure 63**

The automatic transaxle can be removed with the engine installed in the car, but the transaxle and torque converter must be removed as an assembly. Otherwise, the drive plate, pump bushing or oil seal could be damaged. The drive plate will not support a load no weight should be allowed to rest on the drive plate as the unit is removed; it must be fully disconnected from the converter before the transaxle is shifted out of its normal position.

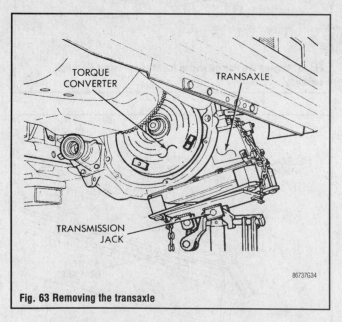

Fig. 63 Removing the transaxle

1. Disconnect the negative battery cable.

2. Have someone apply the brakes and, with the car still resting on the wheels, loosen the hub nut and the wheel nuts.

3. Remove the axle end cotter pins and nut locks. Loosen the axle hub nuts.

4. Raise and support the vehicle safely high enough to work comfortably.

Raise the vehicle just high enough to work under the vehicle and inside the engine compartment.

5. Remove both front wheel and tire assemblies.

6. Remove the axle nuts and spring washers.

7. Disconnect the throttle and shift linkage from the transaxle.

8. Put a drain pan underneath and then disconnect both the upper and lower oil cooler hoses. If the car has a lockup converter, unplug the electrical connector, which is located near the dipstick.

9. Install a suitable engine support fixture device.

10. Remove the upper bolts those that are accessible from above from the bell housing.

11. Remove both front wheel and tire assemblies.

12. Remove the left splash shield, and left engine mount from the transaxle.

13. Follow the procedures under "Halfshaft Removal and Installation" in this section. Remove both halfshafts.

14. If working with the use of a lift, make sure the vehicle is properly placed on the lift. Raise the vehicle to standing level. If using a floor transmission jack, raise and support the vehicle safely, yet high enough to permit the removal of the transaxle.

15. Remove the dust cover from under the torque converter. Remove the access plug in the right splash shield to rotate the engine. Matchmark the torque converter and drive plate. Then, remove the torque converter mounting bolts, rotating the engine after each bolt is removed for access to the next one.

16. Disconnect the plug for the neutral safety/backup light switch.

17. Remove the engine mount bracket from the front crossmember.

18. Support the transaxle from underneath. It must be supported in a positive manner and without the weight resting on the pan; it should be supported by its corners.

19. Remove the front mount insulator through-bolts.

20. Remove the long through-bolt from the left hand engine mount.

21. Remove the starter. Then, remove any bell housing bolts that are still in position.

22. Pry the transaxle away from the engine to ensure that the torque converter will clear the drive plate. Lower the transaxle and remove it from the engine compartment.

To install:

23. To install the transaxle, first support the unit securely and raise it into precise alignment with the engine block. Then, move it toward the block. Make sure to align the lower bolt holes in the transaxle bell housing with those in the block.

24. Install the lower bell housing bolts and the starter. Bell housing bolts are torqued to 105 inch lbs. (12 Nm)

25. Turn the engine via the crankshaft pulley bolt as necessary to align the torque converter bolt holes with those in the drive plate. Make sure the matchmarks made prior to disassembly are aligned. Install each bolt and torque it to 40 ft. lbs. (54 Nm) on 1981–85 models, and 55 ft. lbs. (75 Nm) on 1986–88 models. Then, turn the crank for access to the next set of bolt holes and install the bolt in that position.

26. Install the long through-bolt into the left hand engine mount.

27. Install the front mount insulator through-bolts.

28. Remove the jack supporting the transaxle. Then, install the engine mount bracket onto the front crossmember.

29. Reconnect the electrical connector for the backup light/neutral safety switch.

30. Install the dust cover under the torque converter. Install the access plug in the right splash shield.

31. Install the driveshafts by reversing the removal procedure. Install the left side splash shield.

32. With the wheels remounted and the car back on the floor, install the remaining bell housing bolts and torque them to 105 inch lbs.

33. Remove the engine support fixture.

34. Connect both the upper and lower oil cooler hoses. If the car has a lockup converter, replug the electrical connector.

35. Reconnect the throttle and shift cables and adjust them.

36. Install the differential cover on those transaxles from which it was removed. Form a new gasket from RTV sealant when installing the cover. See Section 1. Fill the differential or combined transaxle and differential with the approved automatic transaxle fluid. Reconnect the battery.

1989–95 Vehicles

♦ See Figure 63

➡ If the vehicle is going to be rolled while the transaxle is out of the vehicle, obtain 2 outer CV-joints to install in the hubs. If the vehicle is rolled without the proper torque applied to the front wheel bearings, the bearings will no longer be usable.

1. Disconnect the negative battery cable.

2. Remove the air cleaner assembly if it is preventing access to the upper bell housing bolts. Remove the upper bell housing bolts and water tube, where applicable. Unplug all electrical connectors from the transaxle.

3. Remove the starter attaching nut and bolt at the top of the bell housing.

4. Have someone apply the brakes and, with the car still resting on the wheels, loosen the hub nut and the wheel nuts.

5. Remove the axle end cotter pins and nut locks. Loosen the axle hub nuts.

6. Raise and support the vehicle safely high enough to work comfortably. Raise the vehicle just high enough to work under the vehicle and inside the engine compartment.

7. Remove both front wheel and tire assemblies.

8. Remove the axle nuts and spring washers.

9. Remove the ball joint retaining bolts and pry the control arm from the steering knuckle.

10. Remove the halfshafts and center bearing. Follow the procedures under "Halfshaft Removal and Installation" in this section. Remove both halfshafts.

11. Position a drain pan under the transaxle where the axles enter the differential or extension housing.

12. Unbolt the center bearing and remove the intermediate axle from the transaxle, if equipped.

13. Drain the transaxle. Disconnect and plug the fluid cooler hoses. Disconnect the shifter and kickdown linkage from the transaxle, if equipped.

14. Remove the speedometer cable adapter bolt and remove the adapter from the transaxle.

15. Remove the starter. Remove the torque converter inspection cover, matchmark the torque converter to the driveplate and remove the torque converter bolts.

16. Using the proper equipment, support the weight of the engine.

17. Remove the front motor mount and bracket.

18. Position a suitable transaxle jack under the transaxle.

19. Remove the lower bell housing bolts.

20. Remove the left side splash shield. Remove the transaxle mount bolts.

21. Carefully pry the transaxle from the engine.

22. Slide the transaxle rearward until dowels disengage from the mating holes in the transaxle case.

23. Pull the transaxle completely away from the engine and remove it from the vehicle.

24. To prepare the vehicle for rolling, support the engine with a suitable support or reinstall the front motor mount to the engine. Then reinstall the ball joints to the steering knuckle and install the retaining bolt. Install the obtained outer CV-joints to the hubs, install the washers and torque the axle nuts to 180 ft. lbs. (244 Nm). The vehicle may now be safely rolled.

To install:

25. Install the transaxle securely on the transmission jack. Rotate the converter so it will align with the positioning of the driveplate.

26. Apply a coating of high temperature grease to the torque converter pilot hub.

27. Raise the transaxle into place and push it forward until the dowels engage and the bell housing is flush with the block. Install the transaxle to bell housing bolts.

28. Raise the transaxle and install the left side mount bolts. Install the torque converter bolts and torque to 55 ft. lbs. (74 Nm).

29. Install the front motor mount and bracket. Remove the engine and transaxle support fixtures.

30. Install the starter to the transaxle. Install the bolt finger-tight.

31. Install a new O-ring to the speedometer cable adapter and install to the extension housing; make sure it snaps in place. Install the retaining bolt.

32. Connect the shifter and kickdown linkage to the transaxle, if equipped.

33. Install the axles and center bearing, if equipped. Install the ball joints to the steering knuckles. Torque the axle nuts to 180 ft. lbs. (244 Nm) and install new cotter pins. Install the splash shield and install the wheels. Lower the vehicle. Install the dipstick.

34. Install the upper bell housing bolts and water pipe, if removed.

35. Install the starter attaching nut and bolt at the top of the bell housing. Raise the vehicle again and tighten the starter bolt from under the vehicle. Lower the vehicle.

36. Connect all electrical wiring to the transaxle.

37. Install the air cleaner assembly, if removed. Refill all fluid levels. Fill the transaxle with the proper amount of the specified fluid to the correct level.

38. Connect the negative battery cable and check the transaxle for proper operation. Refer to the upshift and kickdown learning procedure in the adjustment portion of this section.

Halfshafts

Removal and installation procedures for all halfshafts, whether used with automatic or manual transaxles, are covered under the appropriate portions of the manual transaxle portion of this section. Refer to the necessary service procedures in this section.

Transmission Fluid Indications

The appearance and odor of the transmission fluid can give valuable clues to the overall condition of the transmission. Always note the appearance of the fluid when you check the fluid level or change the fluid. Rub a small amount of fluid between your fingers to feel for grit and smell the fluid on the dipstick.

If the fluid appears:	It indicates:
Clear and red colored	• Normal operation
Discolored (extremely dark red or brownish) or smells burned	• Band or clutch pack failure, usually caused by an overheated transmission. Hauling very heavy loads with insufficient power or failure to change the fluid, often result in overheating. Do not confuse this appearance with newer fluids that have a darker red color and a strong odor (though not a burned odor).
Foamy or aerated (light in color and full of bubbles)	• The level is too high (gear train is churning oil) • An internal air leak (air is mixing with the fluid). Have the transmission checked professionally.
Solid residue in the fluid	• Defective bands, clutch pack or bearings. Bits of band material or metal abrasives are clinging to the dipstick. Have the transmission checked professionally.
Varnish coating on the dipstick	• The transmission fluid is overheating

TCCA7C02

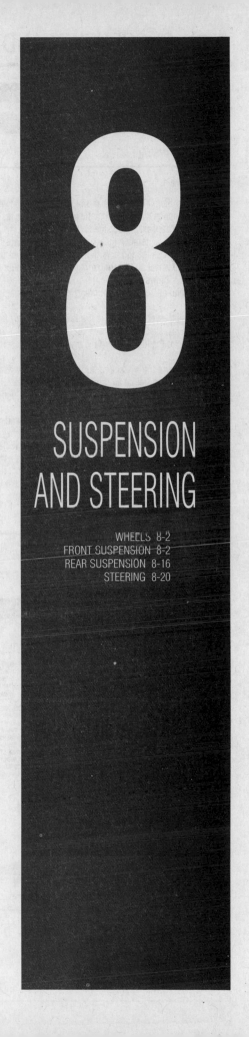

8

SUSPENSION
AND STEERING

WHEELS

Wheel Assembly

REMOVAL & INSTALLATION

▶ **See Figure 1**

1. Apply the parking brake and block the opposite wheel.
2. If equipped with an automatic transaxle, place the selector lever in **P**; with a manual transaxle, place the shifter in Reverse.
3. If equipped, remove the wheel cover or hub cap.
4. Break loose the lug nuts. If a nut is stuck, never use heat to loosen it or damage to the wheel and bearings may occur. If the nuts are seized, one or 2 heavy hammer blows directly on the end of the bolt head usually loosens the rust. Be careful as continued pounding will likely damage the brake drum or rotor.
5. Raise the vehicle until the tire is clear of the ground. Support the vehicle safely using jackstands.
6. Remove the lug nuts and the tire and wheel assembly.

To install:

7. Make sure the wheel and hub mating surfaces as well as the wheel lug studs are clean and free of all foreign material. Always remove rust from the wheel mounting surfaces and the brake rotors/drums. Failure to do so may cause the lug nuts to loosen in service.
8. Position the wheel on the hub or drum and hand-tighten the lug nuts. Tighten all the lug nuts, in a crisscross pattern, until they are snug.
9. Remove the supports, if any, and lower the vehicle. Tighten the lug nuts, in a crisscross pattern to 95 ft. lbs. (129 Nm). Always use a torque wrench to achieve the proper lug nut torque and to prevent stretching the wheel studs.
10. Repeat the torque pattern to assure proper wheel tightening.
11. If equipped, install the hub cab or wheel cover.

INSPECTION

The wheel assemblies should be checked for the following problems:
- Excessive run-out (wobble)
- Bends or dents

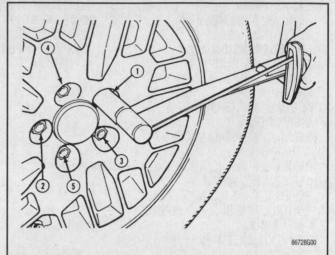

Fig. 1 Make certain to tighten the wheel lug nuts in the sequence shown

- Air leakage through the rim welds
- Damaged bolt holes (rusty or worn oversized)

Wheel repairs employing hammering, heating or welding are not allowed.

Original equipment replacement wheels are available through a Chrysler dealer. When obtaining wheels from any other source, the replacement wheels should be equivalent in load carrying capacity. Failure to use equivalent replacement wheels may adversely affect the safety and handling of your vehicle.

➡**Replacement with used wheels is not recommended as their service history may have included severe treatment or very high mileage and they could fail without warning.**

FRONT SUSPENSION

▶ **See Figure 2**

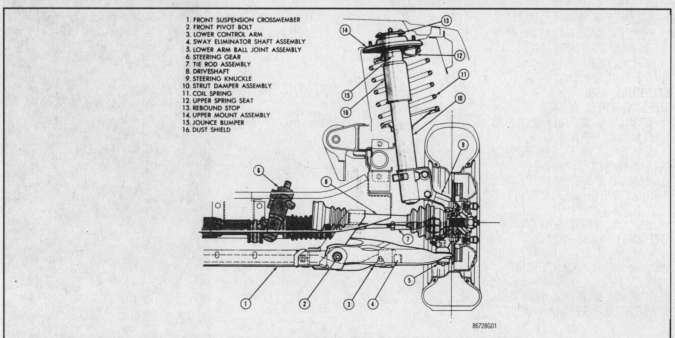

1. FRONT SUSPENSION CROSSMEMBER
2. FRONT PIVOT BOLT
3. LOWER CONTROL ARM
4. SWAY ELIMINATOR SHAFT ASSEMBLY
5. LOWER ARM BALL JOINT ASSEMBLY
6. STEERING GEAR
7. TIE ROD ASSEMBLY
8. DRIVESHAFT
9. STEERING KNUCKLE
10. STRUT DAMPER ASSEMBLY
11. COIL SPRING
12. UPPER SPRING SEAT
13. REBOUND STOP
14. UPPER MOUNT ASSEMBLY
15. JOUNCE BUMPER
16. DUST SHIELD

Fig. 2 The front suspension components are similar on all Chrysler front wheel drive vehicles covered by this manual

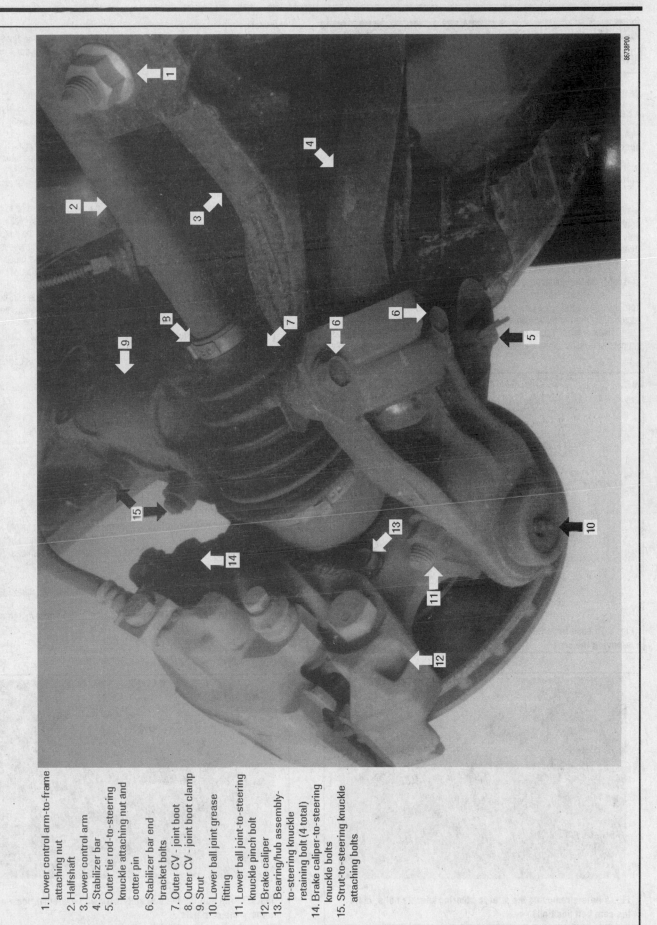

CHRYSLER FRONT WHEEL DRIVE FRONT SUSPENSION COMPONENTS

1. Lower control arm-to-frame
   attaching nut
2. Halfshaft
3. Lower control arm
4. Stabilizer bar
5. Outer tie rod-to-steering
   knuckle attaching nut and
   cotter pin
6. Stabilizer bar end
   bracket bolts
7. Outer CV - joint boot
8. Outer CV - joint boot clamp
9. Strut
10. Lower ball joint grease
    fitting
11. Lower ball joint-to-steering
    knuckle pinch bolt
12. Brake caliper
13. Bearing/hub assembly-
    to-steering knuckle
    retaining bolt (4 total)
14. Brake caliper-to-steering
    knuckle bolts
15. Strut-to-steering knuckle
    attaching bolts

86738P00

MacPherson Struts

REMOVAL & INSTALLATION

Without Air Suspension

▶ **See Figures 3 thru 11**

➡ **A 4 in. (10cm) or larger C-clamp is needed to properly perform this operation.**

1. Loosen the wheel lug nuts. Raise and safely support the vehicle with jackstands.
2. Remove the wheel.

➡ **When the original strut assembly is going to be reused, mark the cam adjusting bolt to the lower strut on Spirit, Acclaim and LeBaron models only. Mark the outline of the strut on the steering knuckle on New Yorker, Dynasty, Daytona, Sundance, Shadow, Imperial and Fifth Ave. models.**

3. Remove the cam bolt, knuckle bolt(s), washer plate(s), and brake hose-to-damper bracket retaining screw.
4. On vehicles equipped with variable damping, detach the electrical lead from the upper strut rod by pinching the 2 latching arms and pulling the connector straight off of the rod end. Do not rotate the connector.
5. Have someone support the strut from underneath. Remove the strut mounting nuts and washers from the fender well. Lower and remove the strut assembly.

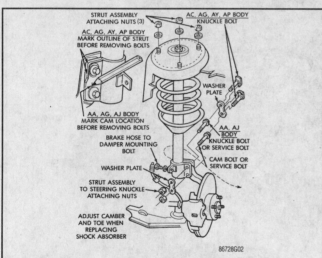

Fig. 3 To ease installation, keep track of all components when removing the strut

Fig. 4 Before removing the strut-to-steering knuckle bolts, mark the cam bolt position

➡ **Inspect strut assembly for fluid leakage, actual leakage will be a stream of fluid running down the side and dripping off of the lower end of the unit. A slight amount of seepage is not unusual and does not affect performance.**

To install:

6. Install the strut assembly by raising it into position and then supporting it from underneath. Have someone support the strut at the bottom as you do this and hold it until it can be bolted to the knuckle. Install the washers and nuts, then tighten the 3 nuts to 20 ft. lbs. (27 Nm).
7. Position the neck of the knuckle in between the strut brackets, then install the cam bolt(s), knuckle bolt(s) and any washers. Attach the brake hose retainer to the damper and tighten the mounting bolt to 10 ft. lbs. (13 Nm).
8. Index the strut to align the mark made on the knuckle neck at disassembly with the edge of the strut bracket.
9. Install a 4 in. (10cm) C-clamp (or larger) onto the strut so as to pull the strut onto the knuckle neck. The rotating part of the clamp should rest against the neck. While tightening the clamp, constantly check the fit of the knuckle neck into the strut, feeling for looseness. At the point where looseness is just eliminated, stop tightening the clamp. Make sure the index marks made earlier are aligned. If necessary, loosen the clamp and change the position of the strut to align them, and then retighten the clamp.
10. Tighten the bolts to 45 ft. lbs. (61 Nm) on 1981–83 models, or to 75 ft. lbs. (100 Nm) on 1984–95 models, then tighten them another ¼ turn beyond the specified torque. Remove the C-clamp.
11. For the vehicles equipped with variable damping assembly, attach the electrical connector to the top of the strut rod, being careful to align the key-way (wire should point toward the vehicle centerline). The connector is correctly seated when both latching fingers engage in the strut stem.
12. Install the wheel and tire and tighten the bolts to 95 ft. lbs. (129 Nm). Have the front wheel alignment checked, if necessary.

With Air Suspension

▶ **See Figures 12, 13 and 14**

1. Disconnect the negative battery cable.
2. Raise the vehicle and support safely. Remove the wheel and tire assembly.
3. To disconnect the air line, pull back on the plastic ring and pull the air line from the fitting.
4. Disconnect the electrical leads from the solenoid and the height sensor.
5. The solenoid has a molded square tang that fits into stepped notches in the air spring housing to provide for exhaust and a retaining positions. To vent the air spring:
   a. Release the retaining clip.
   b. Rotate the solenoid to the first step in the housing and allow the air pressure to vent.
   c. Rotate the solenoid farther to the release slot and remove it from the housing.
6. Matchmark the assembly to the knuckle.

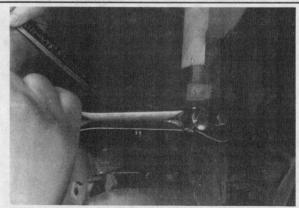

Fig. 5 While holding the bolt stationary with a wrench, loosen and remove the cam nuts . . .

Fig. 6 . . . then remove the cam bolt washer/spacer

Fig. 7 Disconnect the brake line bracket from the steering knuckle

Fig. 8 Separate the lower strut end from the steering knuckle

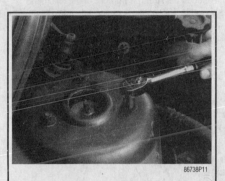

Fig. 9 While an assistant holds the strut lower end, remove the strut-to-fender nuts . . .

Fig. 10 . . . then extract the strut from the vehicle

Fig. 11 Use a C-clamp to hold the steering knuckle to the strut during installation

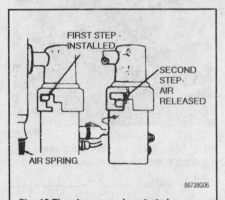

Fig. 12 The air suspension struts have various solenoid positions which release the built-up air pressure

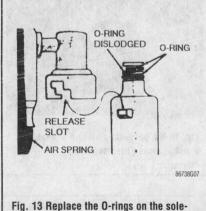

Fig. 13 Replace the O-rings on the solenoid if any damage is evident

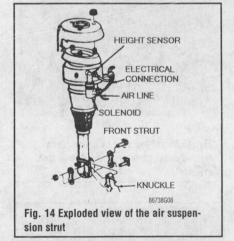

Fig. 14 Exploded view of the air suspension strut

7. Remove cam bolt, knuckle bolt, and washers. Disconnect the brake hose bracket retaining bolt.

8. Hold or support the strut. Remove the upper nuts from the shock tower. Remove the strut assembly.

➡**Disassembly is restricted to the upper mount and bearing housing. The strut, air spring, height sensor, solenoid and wiring harness cannot be disassembled or serviced. They are replaced as a unit.**

To install:

9. Install the strut assembly into the fender reinforcement, then install the retaining nuts and washers. Tighten to 20 ft. lbs. (27 Nm).

10. Position the knuckle into strut. Install washers with cam and knuckle bolts.

11. Attach brake hose retainer and tighten to 10 ft. lbs. (13 Nm).

12. Index the strut to the marks made during removal.

13. Use C-clamp to hold strut and knuckle. Tighten the clamp just enough to eliminate any looseness between the knuckle and the strut.

14. Check alignment of matchmarks. Tighten the nuts on the cam and knuckle bolts to 75 ft. lbs. (100 Nm) plus ¼ turn.

15. Remove the C-clamp.

16. Install the solenoid to the top step in the housing.

17. Connect the electrical leads to the solenoid and height sensor.

18. Connect the air line by pushing it into place; it will lock in place.

19. Connect the negative battery cable.

20. To recharge the air spring:

a. To activate the left front spring solenoid, ground **Pin 7** (dark green with orange tracer) to **Pin 19** (gray with black tracer) of the controller connector.

b. To activate the right front spring solenoid, ground **Pin 6** (dark blue with orange tracer) to **Pin 19** of the controller connector.

c. Run the compressor for 60 seconds by jumping from **Pin 9** (black wire with red tracer) to **Pin 19** of the controller connector.

d. The air suspension controller is located behind the right side trunk trim panel.

21. Install the wheel and tire.
22. Check the system for proper operation.

OVERHAUL

Without Air Suspension

▶ See Figures 15 thru 26

➡To perform this procedure, a special spring compressor such as Tool C-4838 or equivalent is required. Also needed is a special large socket and adapter L-4558 and L-4558–1, or Tool 6430 (or equivalent) for variable damping struts, which must be used to produce correct torque on the strut rod retaining nut.

This service repair requires above average mechanical ability or skill and special tools. Extreme care should be exercised when performing this operation.
1. Remove the strut, as described earlier in this section.
2. Compress the spring, using a reliable coil spring compressor.

✳✳ CAUTION

Make sure the spring is locked securely into the compressor and that all tension has been removed before beginning the next step.

3. Install a large box or open-end wrench onto the rod nut and a smaller wrench onto the end of the strut rod. Hold the strut rod stationary with the small box wrench and use the larger wrench to remove the rod nut.

4. Remove the isolator, dust shield, jounce bumper, spacer (if used), and spring seat.
5. Remove the spring. Mark the spring as RIGHT or LEFT side of the vehicle as they are not interchangeable from side to side.

To assemble:

6. Inspect the strut damper mount assembly for severe deterioration of the rubber isolator, cracked retainers, and distorted retainers and isolators or those with a failure of the bond holding rubber and metal parts together. Inspect the bearings for noise, roughness, or looseness. Pull the shock through its full stroke to make sure its resistance is even. Replace all defective parts.
7. If the spring is being replaced, carefully unscrew and then remove the compressor. Compress the new spring in the same manner as the original: until it will fit onto the strut and permit assembly of all parts without interference. Install the spring with the single small coil at the top. The end of the lower coil must line up with the recess in the seat.
8. Struts with variable resistance require strut rod alignment for the electrical connection. Align the flat spot on the strut rod with one of the retaining studs on the mount assembly (within 15°) on the opposite side from the spring seat alignment notch.
9. Install the spring seat, spacer (if used), jounce bumper, dust shield, and isolator.
10. For normal struts, tighten (using the special tool L-4558 or equivalent) the rod nut to 55 ft. lbs. (75 Nm) plus ¼ turn (1991–95 models) before removing the spring compressor. Be sure the lower coil end of the spring is seated in the recess. Use a crow's foot adapter L-4558–1 to tighten the nut while holding the rod with an open end wrench. For variable resistance struts, use Special Tool 6430, or equivalent, to hold the retaining plate and strut rod position, then tighten the nut to 75 ft. lbs. (102 Nm).

➡The use of the adapter is necessary to ensure the proper torque is actually applied to the nut.

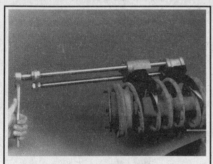

Fig. 15 Mount the strut in a vise, then relieve upper plate pressure with a compressor

Fig. 16 If a pneumatic air gun is available, use it to loosen the upper nut, otherwise . . .

Fig. 17 . . . a box wrench and socket wrench should be used to loosen the shaft nut

Fig. 18 Remove the upper shaft nut and rebound retainer . . .

Fig. 19 . . . then slide the strut mount assembly and washer from the strut shaft

Fig. 20 Remove the upper spring seat and dust shield . . .

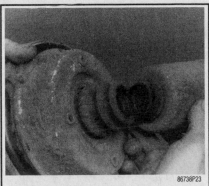

Fig. 21 . . . which can be separated after they are removed

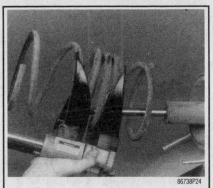

Fig. 22 Remove the spring from the strut and label it left or right for reassembly

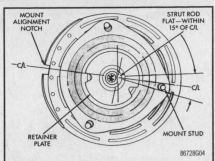

Fig. 23 For variable resistance struts, make sure that the retainer plate, alignment notch, flat spot and mount stud are installed in the proper positions

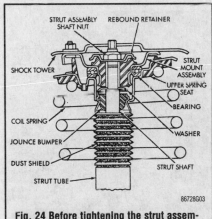

Fig. 24 Before tightening the strut assembly shaft nut to the full torque specification, make sure that all of the components are situated correctly on the strut

Fig. 25 Use the special tool L-4558 or equivalent to properly tighten the strut shaft nut—non-variable resistance struts

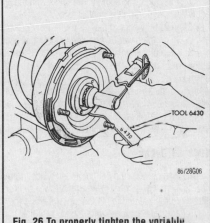

Fig. 26 To properly tighten the variable resistance strut shaft nut, use special tool 6430 or equivalent

11. Release the tension on the spring compressor. Install the strut back into the vehicle as described earlier in this section.

With Air Suspension

On this system disassembly is restricted to the upper mount and bearing housing. The strut, air spring, height sensor, solenoid and wiring harness cannot be disassembled or serviced. They are replaced as a unit.

Lower Ball Joints

INSPECTION

▶ See Figure 27

The lower front suspension ball joints operate with no free play. The ball joint housing is pressed into the lower control arm with the joint stud retained in the steering knuckle with a (clamp) bolt.

With the weight of the vehicle resting on the ground, grasp the ball joint grease fitting with the fingers, and attempt to move it. If the ball joint is worn, the grease fitting will move easily. If movement is noted, replacement of the ball joint is necessary.

REMOVAL & INSTALLATION

Except 1988–91 Dynasty

▶ See Figures 28, 29 and 30

1. Remove the lower control arm from the vehicle as described later in this section.

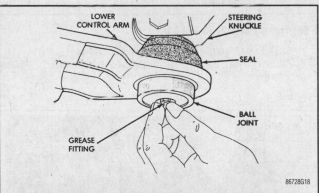

Fig. 27 If the grease fitting moves in the ball joint, the ball joint is defective and must be replaced

2. Pry off the ball joint grease seal.
3. Position a receiving cup, special tool C-4699–2 or equivalent, to support the lower control arm while pressing the old ball joint out of the lower control arm.
4. Install the Remover/Installer Special tool (C-4699–1 or equivalent) over the ball joint stud and against the ball joint upper housing.
5. Using and arbor press, push against the upper housing, to remove the ball joint from the arm.

To install:

6. By hand, position the ball joint housing into the ball joint bore of the lower control arm. Be sure the ball joint assembly is not cocked in the bore of the control arm, which could cause binding of the ball joint assembly.

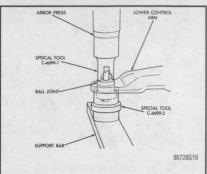

Fig. 28 Press the old ball joint out and the new ball joint in with special tool C-4699-1 or equivalent

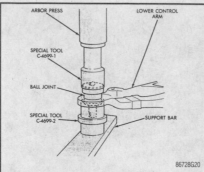

Fig. 29 When pressing the ball joint out or in, use special tool C-4699-2 or equivalent to support the control arm

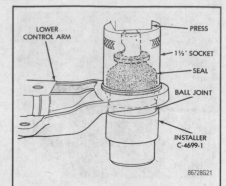

Fig. 30 Use a high impact socket to install the new ball joint grease seal

7. Position the assembly in a press with the special tool C-4699-2 or equivalent supporting the control arm.

8. Install the special tool C-4699-1 or equivalent over the ball joint stud and down on the lower body of the ball joint assembly.

9. Carefully align all of the ball joint components, then install it (using an arbor press) until the housing ledge stops against the control arm cavity down flange.

10. To install a new seal, support the ball joint housing with tool C-4699-1 and place a new seal over the stud, against the housing.

11. With a 1½ in. (38mm) socket, press the seal onto the ball joint housing until it is squarely seated against the top surface of the control arm.

1988–91 Dynasty

On these models, the ball joints are welded to the lower control arms. This necessitates replacement of the entire lower control arm assembly. Do not attempt to replace ball joints that are welded to the control arm; replacement control arms are equipped with a new ball joint.

Sway Bar

REMOVAL & INSTALLATION

♦ **See Figures 31, 32, 33 and 34**

1. Raise the vehicle and safely support it with jackstands.

2. Remove the nuts, bolts, and retainers at the ends of the sway bar—where it meets the control arms.

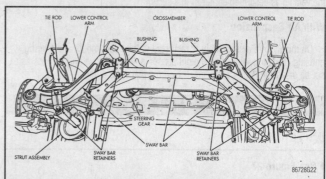

Fig. 32 . . . then remove the inner bracket bolts and remove the sway bar

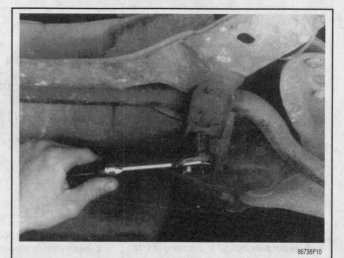

Fig. 33 Make sure that the weight of the vehicle is resting on the wheels before tightening the sway bar fasteners to the specified torque

3. Remove the bolts from the mounting clamps attached to the crossmember and remove the sway bar from the vehicle.

To install:

➡ **Lubricate the sway bar rubber bushings liberally with suitable grease before assembling.**

4. Put the bushings that attach the sway bar to the crossmember into position on the sway bar with the slit facing forward.

5. Raise the sway bar into position and install the mounting clamps and their bolts.

Fig. 31 Remove the sway bar end mounting bracket retaining bolts (arrows) . . .

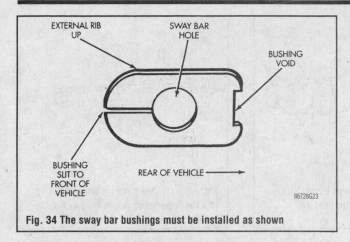

Fig. 34 The sway bar bushings must be installed as shown

6. Position the outboard retainers at the control arms, and install the bolts and nuts.

7. Lower the vehicle to the ground and make sure it is at design height by loading it normally. Then, tighten all retaining bolts evenly to 50 ft. lbs. (68 Nm).

Lower Control Arm

REMOVAL & INSTALLATION

➡**Ball joints and pivot bushings that are welded to the control arms must be serviced by replacement of the complete control arm assembly.**

1. Jack up your vehicle and support it with jackstands.
2. Remove the ball joint stud-to-steering knuckle clamp nut and bolt.
3. Remove the sway bar-to-lower control arm retainer on both sides of the vehicle. Then rotate the sway bar down and away from the lower control arms.
4. Separate the ball joint stud from the steering knuckle by prying between the ball stud retainer on the knuckle and the lower control arm.

➡**Pulling the steering knuckle out from the vehicle after releasing it from the ball joint can separate the inner CV-joint.**

5. Remove the front and rear control arm pivot bushing-to-crossmember attaching nuts and bolts. Then remove the lower control arm from the crossmember.

➡**The substitution of fasteners other than those of the grade originally used is not recommended.**

6. Inspect the lower control arm for distortion. Check the bushings for severe deterioration.

To install:

7. Position the lower control arm into the crossmember. Install the front and ear pivot bushing-to-crossmember attaching bolts. Then loosely assemble the nuts to the bolts.

8. Install the ball joint stud into steering knuckle and install the clamp bolt. Tighten the clamp bolt to 105 ft. lbs. (143 Nm).

9. Position the sway bar and bushings against the lower control arms. Install the sway bar-to-control arms. Install the retainer bolts and tighten them to 50 ft. lbs. (68 Nm).

10. Lower the car so that it is resting on the wheels. On 1981–87 models, tighten the front pivot bolt to 105 ft. lbs. (143 Nm). On 1988–90 models, tighten the front pivot bolt to 95 ft. lbs. (129 Nm). On 1991–95 vehicles, tighten the pivot bolts to 125 ft. lbs. (169 Nm) with the suspension supporting the vehicle (control arm at design height). Tighten the stub strut nut to 70 ft. lbs. (95 Nm).

CONTROL ARM BUSHING REPLACEMENT

➡**When performing the replacement procedure on the lower control arm pivot bushings, the following steps must be performed in the sequence in which they are presented.**

When removing the pivot bushings, the large bushing must be removed first, then the small bushing. The small bushing must be installed first, then the large bushing must be installed. This sequence is vital when using the Bushing Remover/Installer Special Tool 6602 or the equivalent.

Large Bushing Removal

▶ **See Figures 35 and 36**

1. Remove the lower control arm from the vehicle as described previously.
2. Position the lower control arm in a vise.
3. Assemble the washer, thrust bearing and large bushing disk (special tool 6602–5) onto the threaded rod from the bushing removal and installation tool (6602 or equivalent).
4. Install the tools assembled in Step 2 into the large bushing of the lower control arm. Then assemble the remaining special tools (cup 6602–2, thrust bearing, washer and long nut) onto the threaded rod as shown in the illustration.
5. Hold the long nut stationary. Using a deep socket, turn the long threaded rod until the large pivot bushing is pushed out of the lower control arm.

Small Bushing Removal

▶ **See Figures 37 and 38**

1. Remove the tools from the lower control arm that were used for the removal of the large bushing.
2. Remove the large bushing disc (special tool 6602–5 or equivalent) from the threaded rod. Leave the thrust bearing and washer on the rod. Install the small bushing disc (special tool 6602–3 or equivalent) on the threaded rod and against the thrust bearing.
3. Install the tools assembled in the lower control arm from where the large bushing was removed. Assemble the cup (special tool 6602–2), thrust bearing, washer and long nut onto the threaded rod. The cup, thrust bearing, washer and long nut should be installed on the rod with the cup facing out and undercut in the large bushing hole of the lower control arm.
4. Hold the threaded rod stationary and turn the long nut until the small pivot bushing is pulled out of the lower control arm.

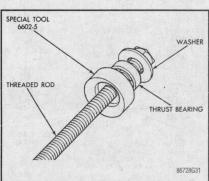

Fig. 35 For large bushing removal, install the components shown on the threaded rod . . .

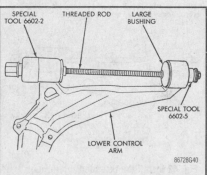

Fig. 36 . . . then install it in the control arm and tighten the long nut to pull the bushing out of the control arm

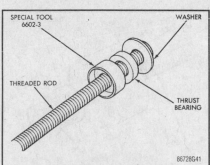

Fig. 37 To remove the small bushing, install special tool 6602-3 (or equivalent), the thrust bearing and washer onto the threaded rod, then . . .

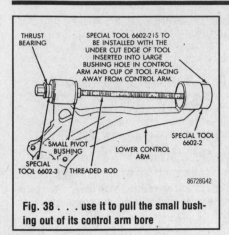

Fig. 38 . . . use it to pull the small bushing out of its control arm bore

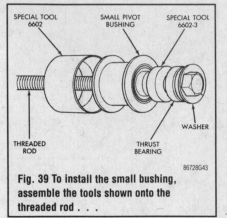

Fig. 39 To install the small bushing, assemble the tools shown onto the threaded rod . . .

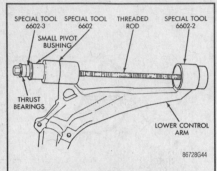

Fig. 40 . . . then push the small bushing into the lower control arm bore by tightening the long nut on the threaded rod

Small Bushing Installation

▶ **See Figures 39 and 40**

1. Remove the special tools from the lower control arm that were used for the removal of the small pivot bushing.

2. On the threaded rod from the removal and installation tool, assemble the following pieces, in this order: washer, thrust bearing, small bushing disc, new small pivot bushing and small bushing sizer (special tool 6602 or equivalent).

3. Install the pieces assembled through the small and large pivot bushing holes in the lower control arm. At the large pivot bushing holes in the lower control arm, assemble the cup, thrust bearing, washer and nut. The cup is to be installed on the threaded rod with the cup facing out and the undercut in the large bushing hole of the lower control arm. Lubricate the installer cone and new bushing using a silicone spray lube.

4. Hold the threaded rod stationary and turn the long nut until the small pivot bushing is fully installed into the lower control arm. Be sure that the flanges of the bushing are fully expanded around the control arm bushing holes.

Large Bushing Installation

▶ **See Figures 41, 42 and 43**

1. Remove the special tools from the lower control arm that were used for the installation of the small pivot bushing.

2. On the threaded rod from the removal and installation tool, assemble the following pieces, in this order: washer, thrust bearing and cup.

3. Install the pieces assembled in Step 2 through the hole in the small pivot bushing and the large pivot bushing hole in the lower control arm. At the large pivot bushing hole in the lower control arm, assemble the large bushing sizer (special tool 6602–4 or equivalent), large lower control arm bushing, large bushing disc (special tool 6602–5 or equivalent), thrust bearing, washer and nut. Lubricate the installer cone and new bushing using a silicone spray lube.

4. Hold the threaded rod stationary and turn the long nut until the large pivot bushing is fully installed into the lower control arm. Be sure that the flanges of the bushing are fully expanded around the control arm bushing holes.

5. Install a nut and bolt through the bushing sleeve and tighten it down.

Using a wrench rotate the bolt until the bushing arrow marking faces the direction shown in the illustration.

Steering Knuckle and Spindle

REMOVAL & INSTALLATION

▶ **See Figures 44 thru 55**

✳✳ CAUTION

Depress the brake pedal several times to seat the brake pads before moving the vehicle.

1. Remove the cotter pin, nut lock and spring washer from the threaded outer end of the front axle.

2. The car should be resting on the floor with brakes applied. Loosen the hub nut and lug nuts.

3. Raise and safely support the vehicle on jackstands. Remove the front wheel(s).

4. Remove the hub nut.

5. Remove the bolts and washers attaching the brake caliper to the steering knuckle. Slide the caliper off the knuckle and support it (with strong wire or cord) in a position that will not put excessive pressure on the brake hose.

6. Slide the rotor off the wheel studs.

7. Remove the cotter pin and nut from the tie rod stud. Press the tie rod end off the steering arm with an appropriate tool (C-3894 or equivalent).

8. Disconnect the brake hose retainer from the strut damper. Then, remove the pinch bolt which secures the ball joint stud in the steering knuckle.

9. Remove the outer sway bar mounting brackets and rotate the sway bar down and out of the way.

10. Push the lower control arm down to remove the ball joint stud from the bottom of the steering knuckle.

11. Pull the steering knuckle assembly out and away from the driveshaft.

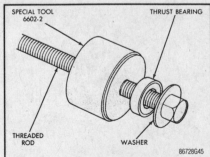

Fig. 41 For installation of the large bushing, install special tool 6602–2 or equivalent, the thrust bearing and washer onto the threaded rod

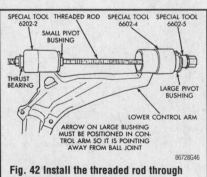

Fig. 42 Install the threaded rod through the hole in the small bushing and the large bushing bore hole, then install the large bushing

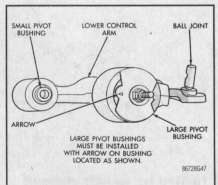

Fig. 43 Make certain to position the large pivot bushing as shown

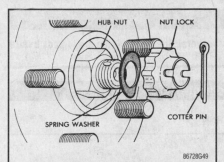

Fig. 44 With the vehicle still on the ground, remove the cotter pin, nut lock and spring washer from the end of the axle

Fig. 45 Remove the cotter pin and nut from the tie rod, then use a puller to remove the tie rod end

Fig. 46 Loosen, then remove the pinch bolt and . . .

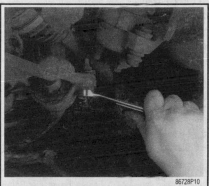

Fig. 47 . . . disconnect the outer ends of the sway bar from the control arms

Fig. 48 Pry the lower control arm down and remove the ball joint stud from the knuckle

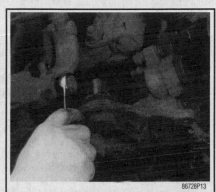

Fig. 49 Remove the brake caliper bracket for access to the front hub-to-knuckle bolts

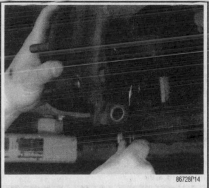

Fig. 50 Remove the 4 hub-to-steering knuckle attaching bolts . . .

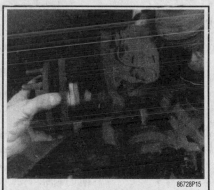

Fig. 51 . . . and remove the hub assembly from the steering knuckle

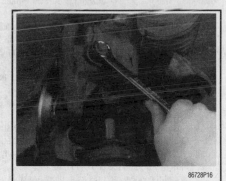

Fig. 52 Unfasten the 2 strut-to-steering knuckle bolts, then remove the steering knuckle

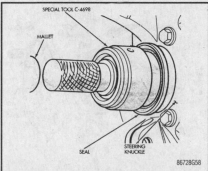

Fig. 53 Use the special installation tool to insert the new seal into the steering knuckle until flush, and . . .

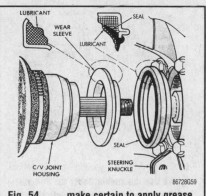

Fig. 54 . . . make certain to apply grease to the wear sleeve and seal as shown

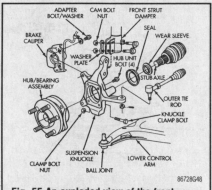

Fig. 55 An exploded view of the front steering knuckle and related components

→Care must be taken not to separate the inner CV-joint during this operation. Do not allow the driveshaft to hang by the inner CV-joint; the driveshaft must be supported.

12. Remove the steering knuckle-to-strut damper attaching bolt and cam bolt.

→Note the location of the cam bolt, it must be installed in the same location and position when the steering knuckle is installed back onto the strut damper.

To install:

✳✳ WARNING

The knuckle and bearing mounting surfaces must be smooth and completely free of foreign material or nicks.

13. Install the hub and bearing assembly into the steering knuckle, if removed. Install the 4 hub and bearing assembly-to-steering knuckle attaching bolts and tighten them in a crisscross sequence to 45 ft. lbs. (65 Nm).

14. Position a new seal in the recess on the back of the steering knuckle. Assemble the Installer Tool (C-4698 or equivalent), then install the seal into the steering knuckle until it is fully seated in the recess. Inspect the wear sleeve on the CV-joint housing and replace it if necessary.

15. Install the knuckle back on the strut damper. Install the strut damper-to-steering knuckle attaching bolt, cam bolt, washer plate and nuts. Tighten the bolts to 75 ft. lbs. (100 Nm) plus an additional ¼ turn. Be sure that the cam bolt is installed in the same position it was removed from.

16. Lubricate the full circumference of the seal (and wear sleeve) with Mopar® Multi-Purpose Lubricant or equivalent.

17. Slide the driveshaft back into the hub and bearing assembly and install the steering knuckle onto the ball joint stud.

18. Install the original (or equivalent) steering knuckle-to-ball joint stud, pinch bolt and nut. Tighten the pinch bolt to 105 ft. lbs. (145 Nm) for 1992–95 vehicles and to 70 ft. lbs. (95 Nm) for 1988–91 models.

19. Install the tie rod end into the arm of the steering knuckle. Install the tie rod end-to-steering knuckle attaching nut, then tighten to 35 ft. lbs. (47 Nm). Install a new cotter pin into the tie rod end.

20. Install the brake disc over the wheel studs. Then, install the brake caliper over the disc. Position the caliper adapter over the steering knuckle. Install the caliper adapter-to-steering knuckle attaching bolts and tighten them to 160 ft. lbs. (217 Nm).

21. Attach the brake hose retainer to the strut damper and tighten its mounting screw to 10 ft. lbs. (14 Nm).

22. Clean the axle threads, then install the washer and axle hub nut.

23. While having an assistant sit in the vehicle and apply the brakes, tighten the axle hub nut to 180 ft. lbs. (244 Nm). Install the spring washer, nut lock, and a new cotter pin (the nut lock has a slot in the outer edge which must line up with the hole through the end of the driveshaft). Finally, wrap the 2 ends of the cotter pin tightly around the end of the nut lock.

24. Install the wheel lug nuts as tight as possible with the vehicle still off of the ground.

25. Lower the vehicle until some of its weight is resting on the tires, then tighten the lug nuts to 95 ft. lbs. (129 Nm).

✳✳ CAUTION

Depress the brake pedal several times to seat the brake pads before moving the vehicle.

Front Hub and Bearing

REMOVAL & INSTALLATION

1981–88 Vehicles

♦ See Figures 56, 57 and 58

→It is not necessary to disassemble and repack wheel bearings. In fact, the bearings must be broken to disassemble them. This procedure is for replacement of damaged or worn bearings only. This procedure requires a set of special tools (C-4811 or equivalent).

1. Remove the knuckle assembly from the car as previously described.

2. Back one of the bearing retainer screws out of the hub and install bracket C-4811–17 or equivalent between the head of the screw and the retainer. Then, insert the thrust button C-4811–6 or equivalent into the bore of the hub.

3. Position tool C-4811–14 so its 2 bolts will screw into the caliper mounting threads on the knuckle, passing through the tapped brake adapter extensions. Install the tool's nut and washer onto the bracket bolt of the tool. Then, tighten the bolt to pull the hub off the bearing.

4. If the outboard race stays on the hub, use a C-clamp and universal puller to remove it. Use the thrust button and the fabricated washer from tool C-4811–6 or equivalent; use the C-clamp to keep the puller jaws over the edges of the outboard inner race.

5. Remove the tool and attach the bolts from the steering knuckle.

6. Remove its three retaining screws and remove the bearing retainer from the steering knuckle.

7. Pry the bearing seal out of the machined recess in the knuckle, being careful not to scratch the surfaces of the recess.

8. Install a tool set such as C-4811 through the knuckle hub. Hold the nut with one wrench as you turn the bolt with another to pull the bearing out of the knuckle and into the ring. Then, be sure to discard both the bearing and seal, as they **are not** reusable.

To install:

9. Inspect the inner surfaces of the hub (where the bearing interfaces with the outside of the bearing). **If these surfaces are rough or damaged in any way, the knuckle must be replaced.**

10. Turn the bearing so that the **Red** seal will face outward and be located near the brake disc.

✳✳ WARNING

Failure to do this would cause heat from the brakes to damage the type of seal used on the opposite side.

Then, with C-4811 or an equivalent tool set, press the new bearing into the

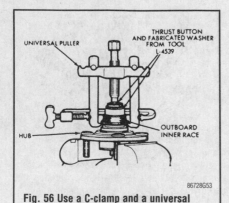

Fig. 56 Use a C-clamp and a universal puller to remove the inner bearing race

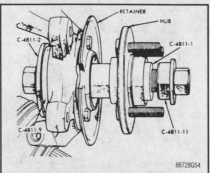

Fig. 57 Use the special tools (or equivalents) to press a new bearing into the knuckle

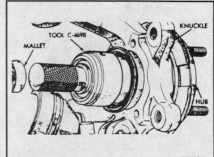

Fig. 58 Use special tool C-4698, or equivalent, to install the new seal into the bearing recess

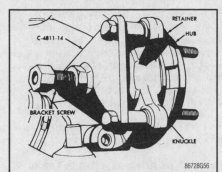

Fig. 59 Remove the hub from the steering knuckle with special tool C-4811-14, or equivalent

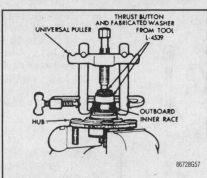

Fig. 60 The C-clamp and universal puller tools can also be used to pull the inner race from the hub assembly

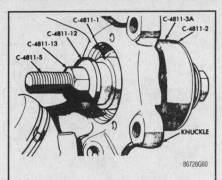

Fig. 61 Use these special tools, or their equivalents, to pull the bearing out of the steering knuckle

knuckle until it seats. Install a new seal and the bearing retainer and then tighten the retainer bolts to 20 ft. lbs.

11. Press the hub into the bearing with C-4811-1, -2, -9 and -11 or equivalent.

12. Position a new seal into the recess and then install Tool C-4698: Note that this tool has a handle and dual-purpose drive head provided for installing the seal into the knuckle and for installing the wear sleeve into the CV-Joint housing. Assemble the tool as shown, make sure it and the seal are positioned squarely, and then lightly tap the seal into place with a lightweight mallet.

13. Lubricate the entire circumference of the seal and wear sleeve with Multi-Purpose grease.

14. Install the driveshaft into the knuckle and install the knuckle back into the car as described above.

1989–90 Models (With Pressed-in 2-piece Hub and Bearing)

▶ See Figures 59, 60 and 61

➡The 1989–90 Chrysler vehicles were equipped with a either one of 2 possible hub and bearing assemblies: a pressed-in hub and bearing assembly or a bolt-in hub and bearing assembly. All of the 1991–95 Chrysler vehicles covered in this manual use the bolt-in hub and bearing assembly. Both the press-in and bolt-in hub and bearing assemblies are replaced as a unit; disassembly of the hub is not recommended or necessary.

1. Loosen the wheel lug nuts and axle hub nut.
2. Raise the vehicle and support safely on jackstands.
3. Remove the tire and wheel assembly from the hub.
4. Remove the brake caliper from the adapter, then remove the adapter. Slide the brake disc off of the hub assembly. For more details, refer to the procedure in Section 9.
5. Remove the halfshaft(s). For more details, refer to the installation and removal procedure located in Section 7.

➡Knuckle removal is not necessary for bearing and hub replacement.

6. Disconnect the tie rod from the knuckle.
7. If knuckle removal is desired, matchmark the lower strut mount to the knuckle. Remove the 2 strut clamp bolts and remove the knuckle from the vehicle.
8. Attach the hub removal tool C-4811, or equivalent, and the triangular adapter to the 3 rear threaded holes of the steering knuckle housing with the thrust button situated inside the hub bore.
9. Tighten the bolt in the center of the tool, to press the hub from the steering knuckle. Remove the special tools from the steering knuckle.
10. Remove the bolts and bearing retainer from the outside of the steering knuckle.
11. Carefully pry the bearing seal from the machined recess of the steering knuckle and clean the recess of all dirt and grease.
12. Insert tool C-4811, or equivalent, through the hub bearing (in the steering knuckle) and install the bearing removal adapter to the outside of the steering knuckle. Tighten the tool to press the hub bearing from the steering knuckle. Discard the bearing and the seal.

To install:

13. Use tool C-4811, or equivalent, and the bearing installation adapter to press the hub bearing into the steering knuckle.

➡For high temperature durability, the red seal on the bearing is positioned outboard toward the bearing retainer.

14. Install a new gasket, the bearing retainer and the bolts to the steering knuckle. Tighten the bearing retainer bolts to 20 ft. lbs. (27 Nm).

15. Press the hub into the bearing with Special Tools C-4811-1, C-4811-2, C-4811-9 and C-4811-11 as shown in the illustrations.

16. Position the new seal in the recess and assemble the installer tool C-4698 (tool is provided with a handle and dual purpose drive head for installing the seal into the knuckle or for installing the wear sleeve into a CV-joint housing). Install the new seal.

✳✳ WARNING

During any service procedures when the knuckle and driveshaft are separated, thoroughly clean the seal and wear sleeve, then relubricate both components.

17. Lubricate the full circumference of the seal and wear sleeve with Mopar® Multi-Purpose Lubricant, Part Number 4318063, or equivalent.

18. Install the driveshaft through the hub, then install the steering knuckle assembly to the lower control arm ball joint stud.

19. Install the original, or equivalent, ball joint-to-knuckle pinch bolt and nut. Tighten the nut to 70 ft. lbs. (95 Nm).

20. Install the tie rod end to the steering knuckle, then tighten the tie rod nut to 35 ft. lbs. (47 Nm). Install a new cotter pin.

21. Install the brake rotor onto the hub.

22. Install the brake caliper assembly over the brake rotor and position the adapter onto the steering knuckle. Tighten the adapter-to-knuckle bolts to 160 ft. lbs. (216 Nm).

23. Attach the brake hose retainer-to-strut damper bolt, then tighten to 10 ft. lbs. (13 Nm).

24. Install the washer and hub nut to the end of the axle shaft.

25. Have an assistant apply the brakes, then tighten the hub nut to 180 ft. lbs. (245 Nm).

26. Install the spring washer, nut lock and a new cotter pin. Bend the ends of the cotter pin tight against the nut lock.

27. Install the wheel and tire assembly. Tighten the lug nuts to 95 ft. lbs. (129 Nm).

28. Lower the vehicle to the ground.

29. Have the front end aligned.

1989–95 Models (With Bolt-in 1-piece Hub and Bearing)

▶ See Figures 62 thru 71

➡The 1989–90 Chrysler vehicles were equipped with a either one of 2 possible hub and bearing assemblies: a pressed-in hub and bearing assembly or a bolt-in hub and bearing assembly. All of the 1991–95 Chrysler vehicles covered in this manual use the bolt-in hub and bearing assembly. Both the press-in and bolt-in hub and bearing assemblies are replaced as a unit; disassembly of the hub is not recommended or necessary.

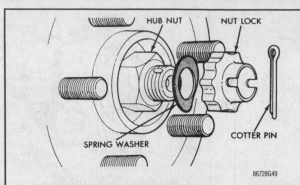

Fig. 62 With the vehicle still on the ground, remove the cotter pin, nut lock and spring washer from the end of the axle

The Unit III Front Hub and Bearing is used on all 1991–95 and some 1988–90 front wheel drive Chrysler vehicles. All hub and bearing assemblies mount to the steering knuckle in the same fashion, but vary by the wheel size on the vehicle. Vehicles equipped with 14 in. wheels have a 4 in. (10.2cm) wheel mounting stud pattern. Vehicles equipped with 15 in. wheels have a 4½ in. (11.4cm) wheel mounting stud pattern. If the hub and bearing assembly is to be replaced with a new one, be sure that the replacement assembly has the same size wheel mounting stud pattern as the original assembly.

These units are serviced only as a complete assembly. It is mounted to the steering knuckle by 4 mounting bolts that are removed from the rear of the steering knuckle.

1. Remove the cotter pin, nut lock and spring washer from the threaded outer end of the front axle.

2. The car should be resting on the floor with brakes applied. Loosen the hub nut and lug nuts.

Fig. 63 Remove the cotter pin and nut, then pull the tie rod end from the knuckle

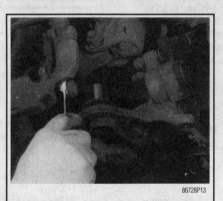

Fig. 64 Loosen, then remove the pinch bolt and . . .

Fig. 65 . . . disconnect the outer ends of the sway bar from the control arms

Fig. 66 Pry the lower control arm down to remove the ball joint from the steering knuckle

Fig. 67 Remove the brake caliper bracket for access to the front hub-to-knuckle bolts

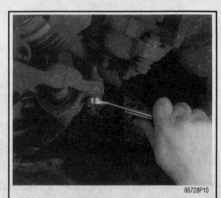

Fig. 68 Remove the 4 hub-to-steering knuckle attaching bolts . . .

Fig. 69 . . . and remove the hub assembly from the steering knuckle

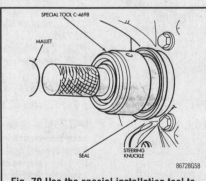

Fig. 70 Use the special installation tool to insert the new seal into the steering knuckle until flush, and . . .

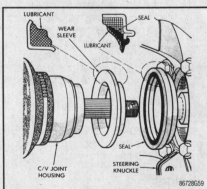

Fig. 71 . . . make certain to apply grease to the wear sleeve and seal as shown

3. Raise and safely support the vehicle on jackstands. Remove the front wheel(s).

4. Remove the hub nut.

5. Remove the bolts and washers attaching the brake caliper to the steering knuckle. Slide the caliper off the knuckle and support it (with strong wire or cord) in a position that will not put excessive pressure on the brake hose.

6. Slide the rotor off the wheel studs.

7. Remove the cotter pin and nut from the tie rod stud. Press the tie rod end off the steering arm with an appropriate tool (C-3894 or equivalent).

8. Disconnect the brake hose retainer from the strut damper. Then, remove the pinch bolt which secures the ball joint stud in the steering knuckle.

9. Remove the outer sway bar mounting brackets and rotate the sway bar down and out of the way.

10. Push the lower control arm down to remove the ball joint stud from the bottom of the steering knuckle.

11. Pull the steering knuckle assembly out and away from the driveshaft.

➥**Care must be taken not to separate the inner CV-joint during this operation. Do not allow the driveshaft to hang by the inner CV-joint; the driveshaft must be supported.**

12. Remove the 4 hub and bearing assembly mounting bolts from the rear of the steering knuckle.

13. Remove the hub and bearing assembly from the steering knuckle. Be careful, the hub will simply fall out of the knuckle once the bolts have been removed.

➥**Replacement of the grease seal is recommended whenever this service is performed.**

To install:

✳ WARNING

The knuckle and bearing mounting surfaces must be smooth and completely free of foreign material or nicks.

14. Install the new hub and bearing assembly into the steering knuckle, if removed. Install the 4 hub and bearing assembly-to-steering knuckle attaching bolts and tighten them in a crisscross sequence to 45 ft. lbs. (65 Nm).

15. Position a new seal in the recess on the back of the steering knuckle. Assemble the Installer Tool (C-4698 or equivalent), then install the seal into the steering knuckle until it is fully seated in the recess. Inspect the wear sleeve on the CV-joint housing and replace it if necessary.

✳ WARNING

During any required service procedures that require the steering knuckle and driveshaft to be separated, both the seal and wear sleeve must be thoroughly cleaned and relubricated.

16. Lubricate the full circumference of the seal (and wear sleeve) with Mopar® Multi-Purpose Lubricant or equivalent.

17. Slide the driveshaft back into the hub and bearing assembly and install the steering knuckle onto the ball joint stud.

18. Install the original (or equivalent) steering knuckle-to-ball joint stud, pinch bolt and nut. Tighten the pinch bolt to 105 ft. lbs. (145 Nm) for 1992–95 vehicles and to 70 ft. lbs. (95 Nm) for 1988–91 models.

19. Install the tie rod end into the arm of the steering knuckle. Install the tie rod end-to-steering knuckle attaching nut, then tighten to 35 ft. lbs. (47 Nm). Install a new cotter pin into the tie rod end.

20. Install the brake disc over the wheel studs. Then, install the brake caliper over the disc. Position the caliper adapter over the steering knuckle. Install the caliper adapter-to-steering knuckle attaching bolts and tighten them to 160 ft. lbs. (217 Nm).

21. Attach the brake hose retainer to the strut damper and tighten its mounting screw to 10 ft. lbs. (14 Nm).

22. Clean the axle threads, then install the washer and axle hub nut.

23. While having an assistant sit in the vehicle and apply the brakes, tighten the axle hub nut to 180 ft. lbs. (244 Nm). Install the spring washer, nut lock, and a new cotter pin (the nut lock has a slot in the outer edge which must line up with the hole through the end of the driveshaft). Finally, wrap the 2 ends of the cotter pin tightly around the end of the nut lock.

24. Install the wheel lug nuts as tight as possible with the vehicle still off of the ground.

25. Lower the vehicle until some of its weight is resting on the tires, then tighten the lug nuts to 95 ft. lbs. (129 Nm).

Front End Alignment

◆ **See Figures 72 and 73**

If the tires are worn unevenly, if the vehicle is not stable on the highway or if the handling seems uneven in spirited driving, wheel alignment should be checked. If an alignment problem is suspected, first check tire inflation and look for other possible causes such as worn suspension and steering components, accident damage or unmatched tires. Repairs may be necessary before the wheels can be properly aligned. Wheel alignment requires sophisticated equipment and can only be performed at a properly equipped shop.

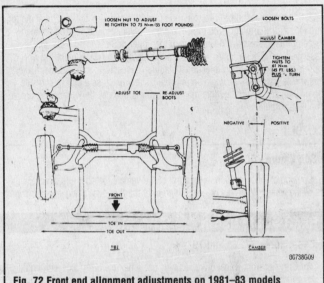

Fig. 72 Front end alignment adjustments on 1981–83 models

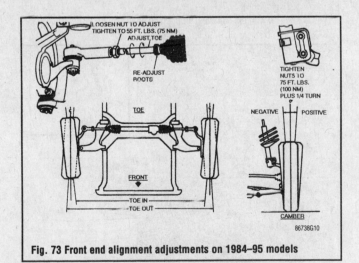

Fig. 73 Front end alignment adjustments on 1984–95 models

CASTER

◆ **See Figure 74**

Wheel alignment is defined by three different adjustments in three planes. Looking at the vehicle from the side, caster angle describes the steering axis

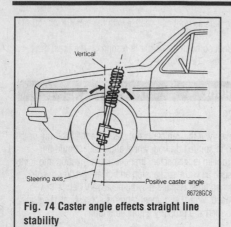

Fig. 74 Caster angle effects straight line stability

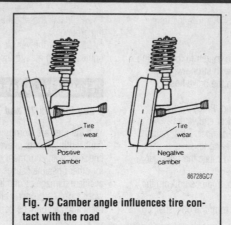

Fig. 75 Camber angle influences tire contact with the road

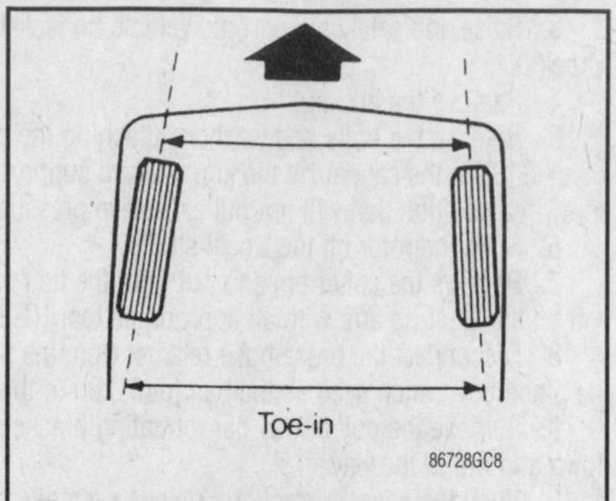

Fig. 76 Toe-in means the distance between the wheels is closer at the front than at the rear of the wheels

rather than a wheel angle. The steering knuckle is attached to the strut at the top and the control arm at the bottom. The wheel pivots around the line between these points to steer the vehicle. When the upper point is tilted back, this is described as positive caster. Having a positive caster tends to make the wheels self-centering, increasing directional stability. Excessive positive caster makes the wheels hard to steer, while an uneven caster will cause a pull to one side. On all vehicles covered by this manual, caster is fixed by body geometry and it is not adjustable.

CAMBER

▶ **See Figure 75**

Looking at the wheels from the front of the vehicle, camber adjustment is the tilt of the wheel. When the wheel is tilted in at the top, this is negative camber.

In a turn, a slight amount of negative camber helps maximize contact of the outside tire with the road. Too much negative camber makes the vehicle unstable in a straight line.

TOE-IN

▶ **See Figure 76**

Looking down at the wheels from above the vehicle, toe alignment is the distance between the front of the wheels relative to the distance between the back of the wheels. If the wheels are closer at the front, they are said to be toed-in or to have a negative toe. A small amount of negative toe enhances directional stability and provides a smoother ride on the highway. On most front wheel drive vehicles, standard toe adjustment is either zero or slightly positive. When power is applied to the front wheels, they tend to toe-in naturally.

REAR SUSPENSION

▶ **See Figures 77, 78 and 79**

All Chrysler front wheel drive vehicles use a flexible beam axle with trailing links and coil (or air) springs. The blade type trailing arms, attached to body mounted pivots, provide fore and aft location of the suspension while a Track Bar provides lateral location.

Located in line with the spindles, an open channel section beam axle assures

that the rear tires remain parallel to each other and essentially perpendicular to the road surface. While being able to twist as one wheel moves vertically with respect to the other.

Roll resistance is provided partly by the axle's resistance to twist. But primarily by a torque tube or rod depending (on the rear suspension) running through the channel and attached rigidly to its end plates by welding. Because the torque tube or rod is an integral part of the axle assembly, it cannot be individually replaced.

One shock absorber on each side is mounted outside the coil spring and attached to the body and the beam axle. Wheel spindles are bolted to the outer ends of the axle and can be individually replaced if necessary.

Rear wheel alignment changes require the use of shims between the spindle and the axle end plates.

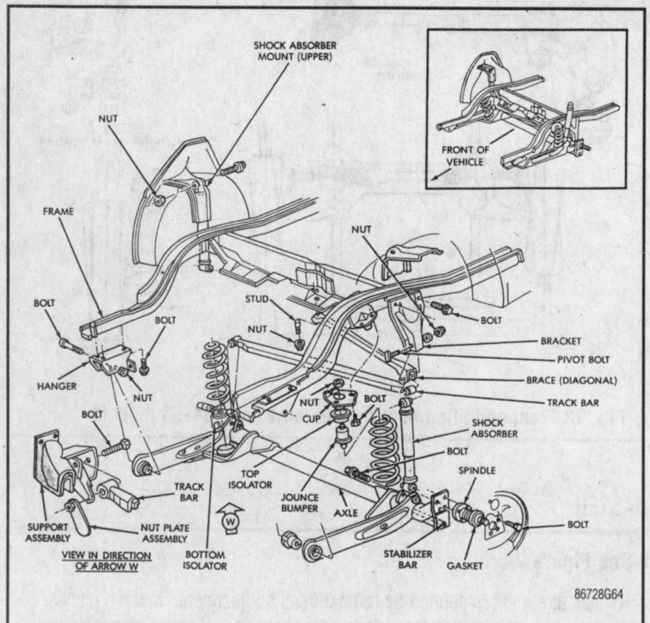

Fig. 77 Exploded view of the trailing arm rear suspension

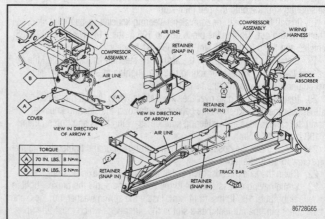

Fig. 78 The supplemental automatic air load leveling system enhances the trailing arm rear suspension

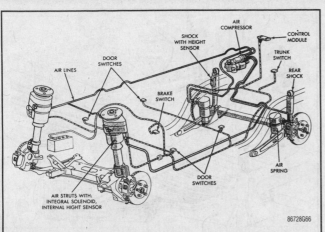

Fig. 79 The optional automatic air suspension is a completely different system from the regular trailing arm rear suspension system

Coil Springs

REMOVAL & INSTALLATION

1. Raise the vehicle and support it with jackstands.
2. Support the rear axle with a floor jack.
3. Remove the bottom bolt from both rear shock absorbers.
4. Lower the axle assembly until the spring and support isolator can be removed.

➡**Do not stretch the brake hoses.**

5. Remove the spring and isolator. Note the position of spring and isolator for correct installation.

To install:
6. Install the isolator over the jounce bumper and install the spring.
7. Raise the axle and loosely assemble both shock absorber-to-axle mounting bolts. Remove the axle support (floor jack) and lower the vehicle.
8. With suspension supporting the weight of the vehicle, tighten the lower shock absorber mounting bolts to 45 ft. lbs. (61 Nm).

Air Springs

REMOVAL & INSTALLATION

▶ **See Figures 80, 81 and 82**

1. Disconnect the negative battery cable.
2. Loosen the lug nuts on the rear wheel(s).
3. Raise the entire vehicle (no vehicle weight can be on any of the wheels) and support it safely on jackstands. Remove the rear wheel(s).

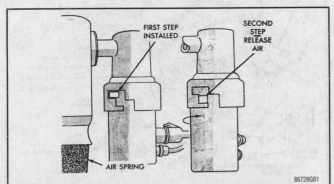

Fig. 80 The solenoids have three different positions (installed, air release and removal) for the tab on the solenoid body

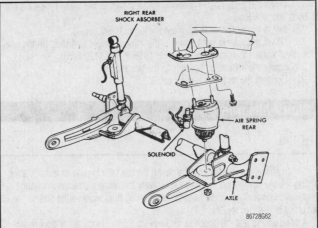

Fig. 81 Exploded view of the air spring mounting orientation and related components

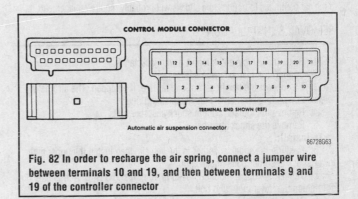

Fig. 82 In order to recharge the air spring, connect a jumper wire between terminals 10 and 19, and then between terminals 9 and 19 of the controller connector

4. Disconnect the air line by pulling back on the plastic ring, then pulling the air line from the fitting.
5. Disconnect the electrical leads from the solenoid and the height sensor.
6. The solenoid (attached to the shock absorber) has a molded square tang that fits into stepped notches in the air spring housing. The notches provide an air relief position and a retaining position. The retaining position is locked with a retaining clip. To vent the air spring:
   a. Release the retaining clip.
   b. Rotate the solenoid to the first step in the housing and allow the air pressure to vent.
   c. Rotate the solenoid to the release slot and remove it from the housing.
7. Release the upper air spring alignment/retaining clips.
8. Remove the nut that attaches the lower portion of the spring to the axle.
9. Pry the assembly down, pull the alignment studs through the retaining clips and remove the assembly from the vehicle.

To install:
10. Position the lower stud into its seat in the axle and the upper alignment pins through the frame rail adapter. Install the upper retaining clips.
11. Loosely install the lower mounting nut.
12. Install the solenoid to the top step in the housing.
13. Connect the electrical lead to the solenoid.
14. Connect the air line by pushing it into place: it will lock in place.
15. Connect the negative battery cable.
16. To recharge the air spring:
    a. Unplug the air suspension controller connector.

➡**The controller is located behind the right side trunk trim panel.**

   b. To activate the right rear spring solenoid, ground Pin 10 (light green with orange tracer) to Pin 19 (gray with black tracer) of the controller connector.
   c. Run the compressor for 60 seconds by jumping from Pin 9 (black wire with red tracer) to Pin 19 of the controller connector.
   d. Attach the connector back to the air suspension controller.

17. When the air spring is properly inflated, tighten the lower mounting nut to 50 ft. lbs. (68 Nm).

18. Install the wheel(s) and tighten the lug nuts until snug.

19. Lower the vehicle until some of the vehicle weight is resting on the rear tires, then tighten the rear wheel lug nuts to 95 ft. lbs. (129 Nm).

20. Lower the vehicle completely to the ground.

21. Connect the negative battery cable.

Shock Absorbers

TESTING

Shock absorbers require replacement if the car fails to recover quickly after hitting a large bump or if it sways excessively following a directional change.

Always check shock absorbers for signs of oil fluid leaks; if the shock absorber is leaking, replace it.

A good way to test the shock absorbers is to intermittently apply downward pressure to the side of the car until it is moving up and down for almost its full suspension travel. Release it and observe its recovery. If the car bounces once or twice after having been released and then comes to a rest, the shocks are all right. If the car continues to bounce, the shocks will probably require replacement.

REMOVAL & INSTALLATION

1. Raise the vehicle and support it with jackstands.

2. Support the rear axle with a floor jack.

3. Disconnect the height sensor and air line, if equipped. The air line is released by pulling back on the plastic retaining ring.

4. Remove the top and bottom shock absorber bolts.

5. Remove the shock absorber.

To install:

6. Position the shock absorber in the vehicle, then install the upper and lower shock absorber bolts finger-tight.

7. Tighten the upper mounting bolts to 40 ft. lbs. (55 Nm). At this time do not tighten the lower mounting bolt.

8. Attach the height sensor wire and air line (simply push it in until it snaps in place) to the shock absorber.

9. Make sure that the lower shock absorber mounting nut is finger-tight, then remove the floor jack from under the rear axle.

10. Lower the vehicle to the ground, then tighten the lower shock absorber mounting bolt to 40 ft. lbs. (55 Nm).

Track Bar and Diagonal Brace

REMOVAL & INSTALLATION

▶ **See Figure 83**

1. Raise the vehicle and support it securely by the body. Then, raise the rear axle to approximately its normal curb height and support it securely with a jackstand.

2. If the car has a load-leveling system, disconnect the link from the sensor to the track bar.

3. Remove the track bar-to-axle pivot bolt and the track bar-to-frame pivot bolt. Then, remove the track bar.

4. Remove the diagonal brace-to-underbody stud nut. Remove the diagonal brace from the vehicle.

5. Remove the 2 track bar bracket-to-frame rail bolts. Remove the bracket.

To install:

6. Position the support bracket on the frame rail, then install and tighten the 2 bolts to 40 ft. lbs. (54 Nm).

7. Fit the diagonal brace into the support bracket and over the underbody stud. Tighten the stud nut to 55 ft. lbs. (75 Nm).

8. Fit the track bar to the diagonal brace, then loosely install the pivot bolt, the washer and the nut. Attach the other end of the track bar-to-bracket on the axle and tighten it to 70 ft. lbs. (95 Nm). Tighten the nut on the track bar-to-frame bolt to 55 ft. lbs. (75 Nm).

9. Install the link onto the track bar, if equipped.

10. Lower the vehicle to the ground.

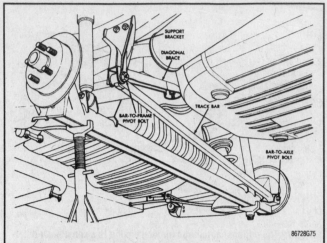

Fig. 83 The track bar, diagonal brace and support bracket simply bolt to the vehicle frame and crossmember

Rear Crossmember/Axle Assembly

REMOVAL & INSTALLATION

▶ **See Figure 84**

1. Loosen the rear wheel lug nuts.

2. Raise the vehicle and support safely.

3. Remove the rear wheels.

4. Disconnect the parking brake cable from the rear brake assembly.

5. Disconnect the brake tubes from the hoses and unclip the brake tubes from the axle housing. Make sure to plug the brake lines, otherwise brake fluid will continue to leak out of the system and the remaining fluid could become tainted. Disconnect the rear wheel speed sensors, if equipped with anti-lock brakes.

6. If equipped, disconnect the link from the suspension leveling sensor from the track bar. Remove the rear air spring, if so equipped.

7. Using a floor jack, support the weight of the axle.

8. Unbolt the shock absorbers and remove the track bar-to-axle pivot bolt. Suspend the track bar with a wire.

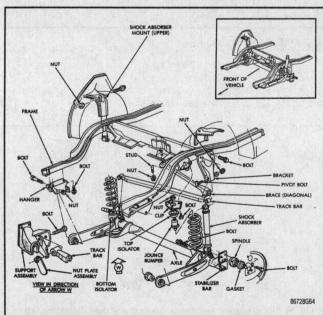

Fig. 84 Exploded view of the rear crossmember assembly

9. Lower the axle until the spring and isolator assemblies can be removed, then remove them from the vehicle.

10. Carefully pull the axle out from under the vehicle.

11. At this point in time, the brake assemblies can be removed from the axle assembly. For more details, refer to Section 9.

To install:

12. Position the axle under the vehicle, then raise the axle with a floor jack. Be careful to not allow the axle to fall off of the floor jack.

13. Attach the pivot bushing hanger brackets-to-frame rail. Tighten the bolts to 45 ft. lbs. (61 Nm).

14. Install the springs and isolators. For more details, refer to the spring installation procedure located earlier in this section.

15. Raise the axle and loosely install the shock absorber and track bar through bolts.

16. Install the brake assemblies onto the rear axle.

17. Attach the brake hose and parking brake cable to the rear caliper (disc brakes), or rear brake cylinder (drum brakes), and suspension arm. Install the brake hose mounting bracket to the caliper support.

18. Route the parking brake cable through the hanger bracket and lock the housing end into the bracket. Install the cable end into the intermediate connector.

19. Install the brake hose and fitting into the bracket and install the lock. Attach the brake tube assembly to the hose fitting and tighten it to 12 ft. lbs. (16 Nm).

20. Install the wheels and tighten the lug nuts until snug.

21. Lower the vehicle until some of its weight is resting on the tires, then tighten the lug nuts to 95 ft. lbs. (129 Nm).

22. Lower the vehicle completely to the ground. Tighten the lower shock absorber bolts to 45 ft. lbs. (61 Nm). Tighten the track bar bolt to 70 ft. lbs. (95 Nm).

23. Bleed the brake system. For more details, refer to Section 9.

Rear Wheel Bearings

REPLACEMENT

♦ See Figure 85

Removal

❊❊ CAUTION

Brake linings may contain asbestos. Avoid using compressed air or any other means to remove dust from the drum or brake shoes or areas nearby. Failure to heed this warning could cause inhalation of asbestos fibers, a known carcinogen!

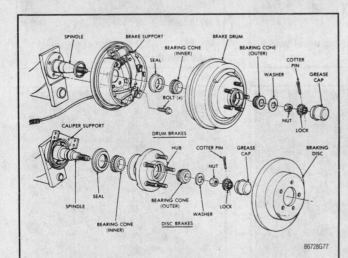

Fig. 85 Exploded view of the drum (above) and disc (below) brake and bearing assemblies

1. Loosen the rear wheel lug nuts.

2. Raise the car and support it securely. Remove the wheel(s).

3. On rear disc brake-equipped vehicles, remove the caliper and rotor. Support the caliper out of the way with strong wire or cord. Do not allow the caliper to hang by the hydraulic hose. For more details, refer to the rear disc brake caliper removal procedure in Section 9.

4. Remove the grease cap, cotter pin, nut lock, retaining nut and outer wheel bearing.

5. Carefully pull the brake drum and outer bearing off the spindle. Do not drag the inner bearing or grease seal over the stub axle (the thread bearing and oil seal may be damaged.) Using an appropriate tool, remove the grease seal and inner bearing from the drum or hub. Discard the old grease seal—a new seal should be used when reinstalling the inner bearing.

Cleaning and Inspection

1. Thoroughly clean all old grease from the outer and inner bearings, bearing cups and hub cavity.

   a. To clean the bearings, soak them in an appropriate cleaning solvent.

   b. Strike the flat surface of the bearing inner race against a hardwood block several times.

   c. Immerse the bearings in solvent between the blows to jar grease loose and wash old particles of hardened grease from the bearings.

   d. Repeat this procedure until the bearings are clean.

   e. Bearings can be dried using compressed air, but do not spin the bearings.

   f. After cleaning, oil the bearings with engine oil.

2. Check the old bearings for damage as follows:

   a. Insert the previously oiled bearing into its appropriate cup, apply pressure to the bearing while rotating it to test them for pitting and roughness.

   b. Replace all worn or defective bearings with new ones.

   c. If the bearings show signs of pitting or roughness, they should be replaced.

   d. Bearings must be replaced as a set; both the cup and the bearing need to be replaced at the same time.

   e. If the used bearings are suitable for further use, remove the engine oil from the bearings using an appropriate solvent, then dry the bearings.

3. To repack the bearings, use a Multi-Purpose NLGI Grade 2 EP Grease such as Mopar® or equivalent. Place the bearings in a clean covered container until ready for installation. If a bearing packer is not available, hand pack the grease into all cavities between the cage and rollers. Make sure to completely fill the bearings with grease (when hand packing the bearings, you can never have too much grease packed into it).

4. If the bearings and cups are to be replaced, remove the cups from the drum or hub using a brass drift or suitable removal tool.

5. Install the new bearing cups with the an appropriate bearing cup installation tool.

Installation

1. Install the inner bearing in the grease coated hub and bearing cup; then install new grease seals (inner and outer) using an appropriate seal installation tool.

2. Coat the hub cavity and cup with grease.

3. Before installing the hub or drum assembly, inspect the stub axle and seal surface for burrs or roughness. Smooth out all rough surfaces with emery paper.

4. Coat the stub axle with the bearing grease.

5. Carefully slide the hub or the drum assembly over the stub axle.

➥**Do not drag the seal or inner bearing over the threaded area of the stub axle.**

6. Install the outer bearing, thrust washer and nut.

7. Tighten the wheel bearing adjusting nut to 20–25 ft. lbs. (27–34 Nm) while rotating the hub or drum assembly. This seats the bearings.

8. Back off the adjusting nut ¼ turn (90°), then tighten the adjusting nut only finger-tight.

9. Position the nut lock over the bearing adjusting nut with one pair of slots in line with the cotter pin hole in the stub axle, and install a new cotter pin.

10. Install the grease caps.

11. Install the wheels and tighten the lug nuts until snug.

12. Lower the vehicle to the ground.

13. Tighten the lug nuts to 95 ft. lbs. (129 Nm).

Rear End Alignment

Just as the front end of the front wheel drive Chrysler vehicles needs to be periodically aligned to reduce irregular tire wear and deteriorating ride comfort, so too must the rear end of the vehicles be aligned. The rear axle assemblies of the vehicles covered by this manual have provisions built-in to allow the rear end to be aligned. Aligning the rear axles also helps to reduce tire wear and improve driving characteristics of the vehicle. Aligning the rear end of the vehicle, although a simple task, requires complex tools be used to accurately align the vehicle. Thus, the vehicle should be aligned by a qualified automotive service facility.

STEERING

Steering Wheel

REMOVAL & INSTALLATION

❋❋ CAUTION

On vehicles equipped with an air bag, the negative battery cable must be disconnected, isolated and a period of at least 2 minutes allowed to pass before working on the system. Failure to do so may result in deployment of the air bag and possible personal injury. Read all air bag precautions in Section 6 before servicing this component.

Without Air Bag System

▶ **See Figures 86 thru 93**

1. Disconnect the negative battery cable.
2. Straighten the steering wheel so the front tires are pointing straight forward.
3. Remove the horn pad. Label, then disconnect any electrical wire leads (horn, cruise control, etc.).
4. Remove the steering wheel hold-down nut and remove the damper, if equipped. Matchmark the steering wheel to the shaft.
5. Using a suitable steering wheel puller (Special Tool C-3428-B or equivalent), pull the steering wheel off of the shaft.

➡ **Do not bump or hammer on the steering column shaft to remove the wheel.**

To install:

6. Place the steering wheel on the steering column shaft with the master splines and the matchmarks aligned.
7. Install the steering wheel-to-column shaft retaining nut. Tighten the nut to 45 ft. lbs. (61 Nm).

➡ **Do not force the steering wheel onto the shaft by driving it on with a heavy object. Pull the steering wheel down onto the column shaft using only the steering wheel retaining nut.**

8. Install the horn pad onto the steering wheel.
9. Connect the battery.

With Air Bag System

▶ **See Figures 94 thru 102**

❋❋ CAUTION

On vehicles equipped with an air bag, the negative battery cable must be disconnected, isolated and a period of at least 2 minutes allowed to pass before working on the system. Failure to do so may result in deployment of the air bag and possible personal injury. Read all air bag precautions in Section 6 before servicing this component.

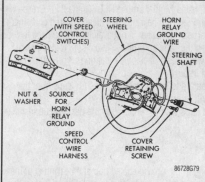

Fig. 86 Exploded view of the steering wheel and electrical connectors

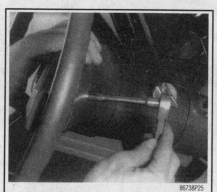

Fig. 87 Remove the steering wheel pad-to-wheel retaining screws . . .

Fig. 88 . . . lift the pad off of the wheel and detach the horn wires

Fig. 89 Loosen the center steering wheel retaining nut . . .

Fig. 90 . . . remove the retaining nut . . .

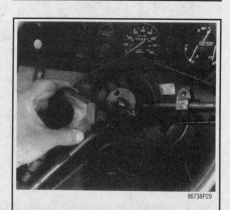

Fig. 91 . . . then remove the spacer block

Fig. 92 Use a steering wheel puller to break the steering wheel loose . . .

Fig. 93 . . . then remove the steering wheel from the column shaft

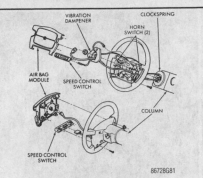

Fig. 94 Exploded view of the steering wheel, air bag module and electrical connectors

Fig. 95 Disconnect the battery, wait at least 2 minutes, then remove the air bag retaining bolts . . .

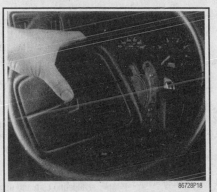

Fig. 96 . . . then lift the air bag module off of the steering wheel and . . .

Fig. 97 . . . unplug the electrical connector from the back of the module

Fig. 98 Remove the speed control panel switch (if equipped) and unplug the connector

Fig. 99 Unplug and label all wiring connectors which interfere with steering wheel removal

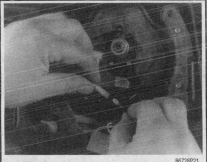

Fig. 100 Loosen and remove the steering wheel-to-steering column retaining bolt . . .

➡A steering wheel puller (Special Tool C-3428-B or equivalent) and a scan tool (DRB II or equivalent) will be needed for this procedure.

1. Disconnect the negative battery cable.
2. Straighten the steering wheel so the front tires are pointing straight forward.
3. Remove the 4 nuts located on the back side of the steering wheel that attach the air bag module to the steering wheel.
4. Lift the module off of the wheel, then detach the electrical connectors. Remove the speed control switch, if equipped.

➡All columns except for the Acustar are equipped with a clockspring set screw held by a plastic tether on the steering wheel. Acustar-mounted clocksprings are auto-locking. If the steering column is not an Acustar and is lacking the set screw, obtain one before proceeding.

5. If equipped with the set screw, place it in the clockspring to ensure proper positioning when the steering wheel is removed.

6. Remove the steering wheel hold-down nut and remove the damper, if equipped. Matchmark the steering wheel to the shaft.
7. Using a suitable steering wheel puller (Special Tool C-3428-B or equivalent), pull the steering wheel off of the shaft.

To install:

8. Position the steering wheel on the steering column. Make sure the flats on the hub of the steering wheel are aligned with the formations on the clockspring.
9. Pull the air bag and speed control connectors through the lower, larger hole in the steering wheel and pull the horn wire through the smaller hole at the top. Make sure the wires are not pinched anywhere.
10. Install the damper, if equipped.
11. Install the hold-down nut and tighten it to 45 ft. lbs. (60 Nm).
12. If equipped with a clockspring set screw, remove the screw and place it in its storage location on the steering wheel.
13. Connect the horn wire.

Fig. 101 . . . then remove the steering wheel using a steering wheel puller

Fig. 102 Do not hammer on the steering wheel to install it—doing so could damage the column

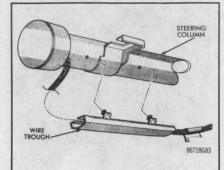

Fig. 103 Remove the wire channel from under the steering column—new channel clips may be needed upon installation

14. Connect the speed control wire and install the speed control switch.

15. Connect the clockspring lead wire to the air bag module and install module to steering wheel.

➡Do not allow anyone to enter the vehicle from this point on, until this procedure is completed.

16. Connect the negative battery cable.

17. Connect the DRB II to the Air bag System Diagnostic Module (ASDM) connector located to the right of the console.

18. From the passenger side of the vehicle, turn the key to the **ON** position.

19. Check to make sure nobody has entered the vehicle. Connect the negative battery cable.

20. Using the DRB II, read and record any active fault data or stored codes.

21. If any active fault codes are present, perform the proper diagnostic procedures before continuing.

22. If there are no active fault codes, erase the stored fault codes; if there are active codes, the stored codes will not erase.

23. From the passenger side of the vehicle, turn the key **OFF**, then **ON** and observe the instrument cluster air bag warning light. It should come on for 6–8 seconds, then go out, indicating the system is functioning normally. If the warning light either fails to come on, or stays lit, there is a system malfunction and further diagnostics are needed.

Turn Signal Switch

REMOVAL & INSTALLATION

1981–87 Vehicles

WITHOUT TILT WHEEL

1. Disconnect the negative battery terminal.

2. Remove the steering wheel as described earlier.

3. On vehicles equipped with intermittent wipe or intermittent wipe with speed control, remove the 2 screws that attach the turn signal lever cover to the lock housing and remove the turn signal lever cover.

4. Remove the wash/wipe switch assembly.

5. Pull the hider up the control stalk and remove the 2 screws that attach the control stalk sleeve to the wash/wipe shaft.

6. Rotate the control stalk shaft to the full clockwise position and remove the shaft from the switch by pulling straight out of the switch.

7. Remove the turn signal switch and upper bearing retainer screws. Remove the retainer and lift the switch up and out.

To install:

8. Position the switch in place and install the retainer. Install the retaining screws until snug.

9. Install the shaft into the turn signal switch by pushing it into the switch until it is fully engaged.

10. The remainder of installation is the reverse of the removal procedure.

11. Install the steering wheel, as described earlier in this section.

12. Connect the negative battery cable.

WITH TILT WHEEL

1. Disconnect the negative battery terminal.

2. Remove the steering wheel as previously described.

3. Remove the tilt lever and push the hazard warning knob in and unscrew it to remove it.

4. Remove the ignition key lamp assembly.

5. Pull the knob off the wash/wipe switch assembly.

6. Pull the hider up the stalk and remove the 2 screws that attach the sleeve to the wash/wipe switch and remove the sleeve.

7. Rotate the shaft in the wiper switch to the full clockwise position and remove the shaft by pulling straight out of the wash/wipe switch.

8. Remove the plastic cover from the lock plate. Depress the lock plate with tool C-4156 and pry the retaining ring out of the groove. Remove the lock plate, canceling cam and upper bearing spring.

9. Remove the switch actuator screw and arm.

10. Remove the three turn signal switch attaching screws and place the shift bowl in low position. Wrap a piece of tape around the connector and wires to prevent snagging, then remove the switch and wires.

To install:

11. Route the wires in their original position and situate the switch against the column. Install the 3 turn signal switch attaching screws. Remove the tape from the connector.

12. Install the switch actuator screw and arm.

13. The remainder of installation is the reverse of the removal procedure.

14. Install the steering wheel, as described earlier in this section.

15. Connect the negative battery cable.

1988–89 Models

WITH STANDARD COLUMN

▶ **See Figures 103, 104, 105 and 106**

✸✸ CAUTION

On vehicles equipped with an air bag, the negative battery cable must be disconnected, isolated and a period of at least 2 minutes allowed to pass before working on the system. Failure to do so may result in deployment of the air bag and possible personal injury. Read all air bag precautions in Section 6 before servicing this component.

1. Disconnect the negative battery cable.

2. Remove the lower steering column cover, if equipped.

3. Straighten the steering wheel so the tires are pointing straight-ahead.

➡If equipped with an air bag, it is imperative that the steering wheel removal and installation procedure in this section be followed.

4. Remove the steering wheel. For more details, refer to the steering wheel removal procedure located earlier in this section.

5. Remove the plastic wiring channel from the under the steering column and unplug the turn signal switch connector.

6. Remove the hazard switch knob. Remove the slotted hex-head screw that attaches the wiper switch to the turn signal switch.

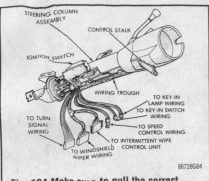

Fig. 104 Make sure to pull the correct wiring harness out of the steering column when removing the turn signal switch

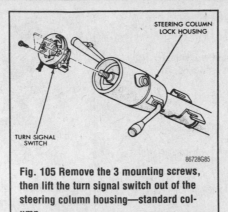

Fig. 105 Remove the 3 mounting screws, then lift the turn signal switch out of the steering column housing—standard column

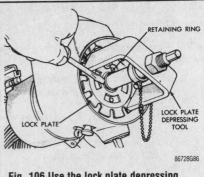

Fig. 106 Use the lock plate depressing tool (C-4156 or equivalent) to remove the retaining ring from the steering column

7. Remove the 3 mounting screws and pull the turn signal switch out of the column.

To install:

8. Lubricate the turn signal switch pivot (entire 360° around the depth of the column hole through which it must be installed.) Use a film of Lubriplate® or the equivalent.

9. Run the wiring through the opening and down the steering column.

10. Position the switch on the upper bearing housing. Install the 3 mounting screws and tighten until snug. Position the turn signal lever (control stalk) to the turn signal switch pivot, then install the screw through the pivot and tighten securely. Be sure that the dimmer switch rod is in the control stalk pocket.

11. Install the upper bearing spring, cancelling cam and lock plate. Using tool C-4156, or equivalent, compress the lock plate and install a new retaining ring. Install the hazard warning knob with the screw.

12. Connect the turn signal wires and install the wiring channel.

13. Install the steering wheel and tighten the retaining nut to 45 ft. lbs. (61 Nm).

14. Install the horn pad.

15. Connect the negative battery cable and check the turn signal switch and dimmer switch for proper operation.

16. Install the lower column cover, if equipped.

WITH TILT COLUMN

♦ See Figures 103, 104, 105 and 106

❊❊ CAUTION

On vehicles equipped with an air bag, the negative battery cable must be disconnected, isolated and a period of at least 2 minutes allowed to pass before working on the system. Failure to do so may result in deployment of the air bag and possible personal injury. Read all air bag precautions in Section 6 before servicing this component.

1. Disconnect the negative battery cable.

2. Remove the lower steering column cover, if equipped, then remove the plastic wiring channel from under the steering column. If the wiring channel retainers were damaged during removal, new ones will be needed for installation.

3. Straighten the steering wheel so that the tires are pointing straight-ahead.

➡ If equipped with an air bag, it is imperative that the steering wheel removal and installation procedure under in this section is followed.

4. Remove the steering wheel. For more details, refer to the steering wheel removal procedure earlier in this section.

5. While pushing the lockplate down with the depressing tool (Tool C-4156 or equivalent), pry out the retaining ring from its groove and remove the tool, ring, lockplate, cancelling cam and spring.

6. Position the turn signal lever in the right turn position. Remove the screw which attaches the link between the turn signal switch and the wiper-washer switch pivot. Remove the screw which attaches the hazard warning switch knob. Remove the 3 screws attaching the turn signal switch to the steering column.

7. Remove the hazard switch and turn signal switch assembly by gently pulling the switch up from the column while straightening and guiding the wires up through the column opening.

To install:

8. Run the wiring through the opening and down the steering column.

9. Position the switch in the upper steering column housing. Place the switch in the right turn position, then install the 3 mounting screws and tighten until snug. Place the link in position between the turn signal switch and the wiper-washer switch pivot, then secure it in place with the retaining screw.

10. Install the upper bearing spring, cancelling cam and lock plate. Using tool C-4156, or equivalent, compress the lock plate and install a new retaining ring. Install the hazard warning knob with the screw.

11. Connect the turn signal wires and install the wiring channel.

12. Install the steering wheel and tighten the retaining nut to 45 ft. lbs. (61 Nm).

13. Install the horn pad.

14. Connect the negative battery cable and check the turn signal switch and dimmer switch for proper operation.

15. Install the lower column cover, if equipped.

Combination Switch

REMOVAL & INSTALLATION

1990–95 Models

❊❊ CAUTION

On vehicles equipped with an air bag, the negative battery cable must be disconnected, isolated and a period of at least 2 minutes allowed to pass before working on the system. Failure to do so may result in deployment of the air bag and possible personal injury. Read all air bag precautions in Section 6 before servicing this component.

The New Yorker, Dynasty, Imperial, Fifth Ave., LeBaron sedan, Spirit, Acclaim, Shadow, Sundance and TC by Maserati vehicles have turn signals which are part of the multi-function switch (combination switch). The multi-function switch contains electrical circuitry for the turn signals, cornering lamps (if equipped), hazard warning lights, headlamp beam selection, headlamp optical horn (if equipped), windshield wiper, pulse wipe (if equipped) and windshield washer system. This integrated switch assembly is mounted to the left-hand side of the steering column.

The LeBaron coupes and convertibles, as well as the Daytona models are equipped with a turn signal switch (named the dual-function switch), which also functions for the hazard warning light system. These vehicles also utilize a second switch, called the remote turn signal switch, which actually contains the actuating lever to work the turn signals. The dual function switch receives the message from the remote turn signal switch and controls the turn signal system accordingly. Both types of switches, multi-function and turn signal (not the remote switch), are, however, removed from and installed into the 1990–95 models in essentially the same fashion.

MULTI-FUNCTION AND DUAL-FUNCTION SWITCH

▶ See Figures 107 and 108

➡This procedure covers all steering column mounted turn signal switches (multi-function and dual-function switches—all models).

1. Disconnect the negative battery cable.
2. Remove the tilt lever, if so equipped.
3. Remove the steering column covers.
4. Remove the combination switch tamper-proof mounting screws and pull the switch away from the steering column.
5. Loosen the connector screw; the screw will remain in the connector. Unplug the connector from the switch.

To install:

6. Attach the connector back into the switch, then tighten the connector retaining screw until snug.
7. Position the switch on the steering column, then install and tighten the mounting screws until snug.
8. Install the steering column covers.
9. Install the tilt lever, if equipped.
10. Connect the negative battery cable and check all functions of the combination switch for proper operation.

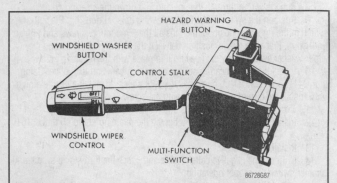

Fig. 107 The multi-function switch controls many of the vehicle's systems, such as the windshield wipers, hazard lights, headlamps and turn signals

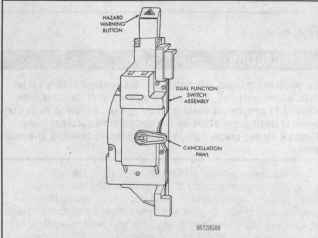

Fig. 108 The dual-function switch found on Daytona and LeBaron coupe/convertible models, controls the turn signals and hazard lights only

REMOTE TURN SIGNAL SWITCH

▶ See Figure 109

➡Only the Daytona and LeBaron coupe (AJ Body) and convertible models are equipped with this second turn signal switch, which is mounted in the switch pod.

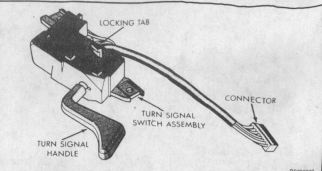

Fig. 109 The Daytona and LeBaron coupe and convertible models utilize a second turn signal switch to activate the primary switch (dual-function switch)

1. Disconnect the negative battery cable.
2. Remove the panel vent grille above the switch pod assembly and remove the 2 revealed pod mounting screws.
3. Remove the 2 remaining screws under the pod and pull the pod out to disconnect the wiring harnesses. Remove the pod from the instrument panel.
4. Remove the turn signal switch lever by pulling it straight out of the pod.
5. Remove the inner panel from the pod. Unplug the switch from the printed circuit board.
6. Remove the turn signal switch mounting screws and slide the switch out of the slot.

To install:

7. Slide the new switch into the slot, then install the turn signal mounting screws.
8. Attach the new switch to the printed circuit board.
9. Install the inner panel of the pod.
10. Push the turn signal lever into the switch.
11. Install the pod to the instrument panel, after attaching the wiring harness connector.
12. Install the 2 lower mounting screws and the 2 upper pod mounting screws.
13. Install the panel vent grille into the switch pod assembly.
14. Connect the negative battery cable and check the turn signal switch and dimmer function for proper operation.

Ignition Switch and Lock Cylinder

REMOVAL & INSTALLATION

Non-Acustar® Column

➡1981–89 front wheel drive 4-cylinder Chrysler vehicles, were equipped with either a non-Acustar® standard or tilt steering column. 1990 models were equipped with either a non-Acustar® standard column or an Acustar® tilt column. 1991–95 vehicles came equipped with the Acustar® (tilt or standard) steering column, which can be identified by the "halo" light around the ignition key cylinder.

STANDARD COLUMN

▶ See Figure 110

✳✳ CAUTION

On vehicles equipped with an air bag, the negative battery cable must be disconnected, isolated and a period of at least 2 minutes allowed to pass before working on the system. Failure to do so may result in deployment of the air bag and possible personal injury. Read all air bag precautions in Section 6 before servicing this component.

1. Remove the steering wheel and turn signal switch from the steering column. For more details, refer to the turn signal switch removal procedure located earlier in this section.

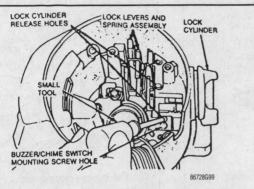

Fig. 110 Removing the ignition lock cylinder on standard steering columns

2. Unplug the horn and key light ground wires.

3. Remove the retaining screw and move the ignition key lamp assembly aside.

4. Remove the 4 screws that hold the bearing housing to the lock housing.

5. Remove the snapring from the upper end of the steering shaft.

6. Remove the bearing housing from the shaft.

7. Remove the lock plate spring and lock plate from the steering shaft.

8. Remove the ignition key, then remove the screw and lift out the buzzer/chime switch.

9. Remove the 2 screws attaching the ignition switch to the column jacket.

10. Remove the ignition switch by rotating the switch 90 degrees on the rod then sliding off the rod.

11. Remove the 2 mounting screws from the dimmer switch and disengage the switch from the actuator rod.

12. Remove the 2 screws that mount the bell crank and slide the bell crank up in the lock housing until it can be disconnected from the ignition switch actuator rod.

13. To remove the lock cylinder and lock lever, place the cylinder in the lock position and remove the key.

14. Insert a small diameter prytool or similar tool into the lock cylinder release holes and push in the release spring loaded lock retainers. At the same time pull the lock cylinder out of the housing bore.

15. Grasp the lock lever and spring assembly and pull straight out of the housing.

16. If necessary the lock housing may be removed from the column jacket by removing the hex head retaining screws.

To install:

17. If the lock housing was removed, install it and tighten the lock housing screws to 90 inch lbs. (10 Nm).

18. To install the dimmer switch, firmly seat the push rod into the switch. Compress the switch until two $FR3/32 in. drill shanks (or equivalent) can be inserted into the alignment holes. Reposition the upper end of the push rod in the pocket of the washer/wiper switch. With a light rearward pressure on the switch, install the 2 screws until snug.

19. Grease and assemble the 2 lock levers, lock lever spring and pin.

20. Install the lock lever assembly in the lock housing. Seat the pin firmly into the bottom of the slots and make sure the lock lever spring leg is firmly in place in the lock casting notch.

21. Install the ignition switch actuator rod from the bottom through the oblong hole in the lock housing and attach it to the bell crank. Position the bell crank assembly into the lock housing while pulling the ignition switch rod down the column, install the bell crank onto its mounting surface. The gearshift lever should be in the Park position.

22. Place the ignition switch on the ignition switch actuator rod and rotate it 90 degrees to lock the rod into position.

23. To install the ignition lock, turn the key to the lock position and remove the key. Insert the cylinder far enough into the housing to contact the switch actuator. Insert the key and press inward and rotate the cylinder. When the parts align the cylinder will move inward and lock into the housing.

24. With the key cylinder in the lock position and the ignition switch in the lock position (second detent from top) tighten the ignition switch mounting screws.

25. Feed the buzzer/chime switch wires behind the wiring post and down

through the space between the housing and the jacket. Remove the ignition key and position the switch in the housing and tighten the mounting screws. The ignition key should be removed.

26. Install the lock plate on the steering shaft.

27. Install the upper bearing spring, then the upper bearing housing.

28. Install the upper bearing snapring on the steering shaft, locking the assembly in place.

29. Install the 4 screws attaching the bearing housing to the lock housing.

30. Install the turn signal switch and steering wheel, following the procedure given previously.

TILT COLUMN—LOCK CYLINDER

▶ See Figure 111

On vehicles equipped with an air bag, the negative battery cable must be disconnected, isolated and a period of at least 2 minutes allowed to pass before working on the system. Failure to do so may result in deployment of the air bag and possible personal injury. Read all air bag precautions in Section 6 before servicing this component.

1. Remove the steering wheel and turn signal switch. For more details, refer to the turn signal removal procedure earlier in this section.

2. Place the lock cylinder in the lock position.

3. Insert a thin tool into the slot next to the switch mounting screwing boss (right-hand slot) and depress the spring latch at the bottom of the slot and remove the lock.

To install:

4. Turn the ignition lock to the **LOCK** position and remove the key. Insert the cylinder into the steering column lock mounting hole until the spring loaded retainer snaps into place.

5. Install the turn signal and steering wheel. For more details, refer to the turn signal installation procedure earlier in this section.

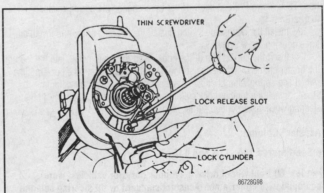

Fig. 111 Use a thin tool to depress the lock release pin, then slide the lock cylinder out of the steering column

TILT COLUMN—IGNITION SWITCH

▶ See Figures 112 and 113

1. Remove the steering wheel and turn signal switch, as described earlier in this section. Remove the ignition lock cylinder as described above.

➡ **If the wedge spring described in the next step is dropped, it could fall into the column, requiring complete disassembly. Follow the directions and work carefully to avoid dropping it.**

2. Bend a paper clip or similar type of wire into a hook. Insert the curved end of the hook into the exposed loop of the buzzer/chime switch wedge spring. Pull the wire hook straight up to remove both the buzzer/chime switch and the spring.

3. Remove the three housing cover screws and remove the housing cover. Then, remove the wash/wipe switch.

4. Adjust the column into the full up position. Then, to remove the tilt

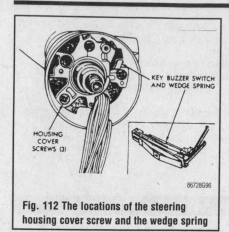

Fig. 112 The locations of the steering housing cover screw and the wedge spring

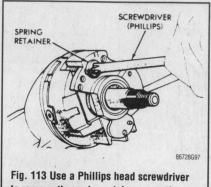

Fig. 113 Use a Phillips head screwdriver to remove the spring retainer mounting screws

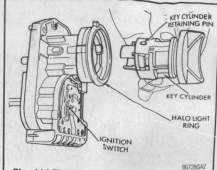

Fig. 114 The key cylinder slides out of the ignition switch when the retaining pin is depressed

spring retainer, insert a large Phillips screwdriver into the tilt spring opening, press the lockscrew in about ³⁄₁₆ in. (5mm) and turn it approximately ¹⁄₈ turn counterclockwise to align the ears with the grooves in the housing. Remove the spring and guide.

5. Pull the actuating rod out of the dimmer switch. Remove the dimmer switch mounting screws and remove the switch.

6. Push the upper steering shaft inward far enough to remove the inner race and inner race seat, and remove both.

7. Turn the ignition switch to the **ACCESSORY** position, remove its mounting screws, and remove it.

To install:

8. Turn the new ignition switch to the **ACCESSORY** position and slide it into place in the steering column. Install the mounting screws.

9. Hold the steering shaft inward and replace the inner race seat and inner race.

10. Hold the dimmer switch in position and install its retaining screws until snug. Install the actuating rod.

11. Install the tilt spring and guide. Set the tilt spring retainer into position. Then, use a Phillips screwdriver to re-engage the spring retainer lockscrew.

12. Install the wash/wipe switch. Install the housing cover and install the three housing cover screws.

13. Insert the curved end of the hook, used during removal, into the loop of the buzzer/chime switch wedge spring. Use it to install both the buzzer/chime switch and spring without allowing the spring to drop into the column.

14. Install the ignition lock cylinder as previously described. Install the steering wheel as described earlier in this section.

Acustar® Column

▶ **See Figures 114, 115 and 116**

➡1981–89 front wheel drive 4-cylinder Chrysler vehicles, were equipped with either a non-Acustar® standard or tilt steering column. 1990 models were equipped with either a non-Acustar® standard column or an Acustar® tilt column. 1991–95 vehicles came equipped with the Acustar® (tilt or standard) steering column, which can be identified by the "halo" light around the ignition key cylinder.

✳✳ CAUTION

On vehicles equipped with an air bag, the negative battery cable must be disconnected, isolated and a period of at least 2 minutes allowed to pass before working on the system. Failure to do so may result in deployment of the air bag and possible personal injury. Read all air bag precautions in Section 6 before servicing this component.

1. Disconnect the negative battery cable.

2. If the vehicle is equipped with a tilt column, remove the tilt lever by turning it counterclockwise.

3. Remove the upper and lower column covers.

4. Remove the 3 ignition switch mounting screws. These bolts have tamper proof Torx® heads and the appropriate Torx® tool should be used.

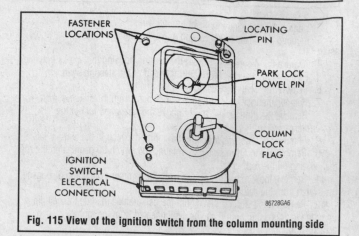

Fig. 115 View of the ignition switch from the column mounting side

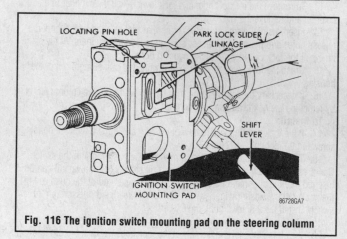

Fig. 116 The ignition switch mounting pad on the steering column

5. Gently pull the switch away from the column. Release the retainer locks on the 2 wiring connectors and unplug them from the switch.

6. Remove the key lock cylinder from the ignition switch, as follows:

a. Insert the ignition key into the switch, then turn the switch to the **LOCK** position. Using a suitable small tool, depress the key cylinder retaining pin until it is flush with the key cylinder surface.

b. Rotate the key clockwise to the **OFF** position to unseat the key cylinder from the ignition switch assembly. The cylinder bezel should be about ¹⁄₈ in. (3mm) above the ignition switch halo light ring. **Do not attempt to remove the key cylinder yet.**

c. With the key cylinder in the unseated position, rotate the key counterclockwise to the **LOCK** position and remove the key.

d. Remove the key cylinder from the ignition switch.

To install:

7. If the vehicle is equipped with a floor mounted gear shifter, place the selector in the **PARK** position.

8. Attach the wiring connectors to the ignition switch. Make sure that the switch locking tabs are fully seated in the wiring connectors.

9. Mount the ignition switch to the column:

a. Position the shifter in **PARK** position. The park lock dowel pin on the ignition switch assembly must engage with the column park lock slider linkage.

b. Verify that the ignition switch is in the **LOCK** position; the flag should be parallel to the ignition switch terminals. Apply a small amount of grease to the flag and pin.

c. Position the park lock link to mid-travel.

d. Align the locating pin hole and its pin, position the ignition switch against the lock housing face and make sure the pin is inserted into the park lock link contour slot. Tighten the retaining screws to 17 inch lbs. (2 Nm).

10. With the key cylinder and ignition switch in the **LOCK** position, key not in cylinder, gently insert the key cylinder into the ignition switch until it bottoms.

11. Insert the key. Simultaneously, push in on the cylinder and rotate the key to the **RUN** position. This action should fully seat the cylinder in the ignition switch.

12. Install the column covers and the tilt lever, if equipped.

13. Connect the negative battery cable and check the push-to-lock and park lock functions, halo lighting and all ignition switch positions for proper operation.

Steering Linkage

REMOVAL & INSTALLATION

Outer Tie Rod End

♦ See Figures 117 thru 125

1. Raise the vehicle and support it with jackstands.
2. Loosen the jam nut which connects the tie rod end to the rack.
3. Mark the tie rod position on the threads.
4. Remove the tie rod cotter pin and nut.
5. Using a puller, remove the tie rod from the steering knuckle.

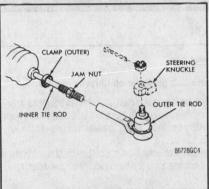

Fig. 117 Exploded view of the outer tie rod assembly

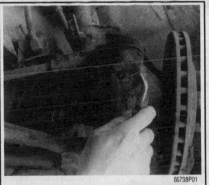

Fig. 118 Remove the outer tie rod cotter pin . . .

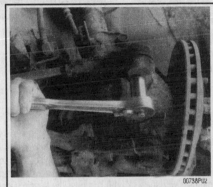

Fig. 119 . . . then loosen the tie rod retaining nut

Fig. 120 Slightly loosen the outer tie rod jam nut while the tie rod is installed on the knuckle

Fig. 121 Use Tool C-3894-A, or equivalent, to remove the tie rod from the steering knuckle

Fig. 122 Count the rotations necessary to remove the tie rod for reassembly . . .

Fig. 123 . . . and measure the position of the jam nut

Fig. 124 If the inner CV-joint boot will be removed, clean the shaft of all dirt and rust . . .

Fig. 125 . . . then continue with the CV-joint boot removal

6. Unscrew the tie rod end from the rack. Count the number of complete turns it takes to remove the tie rod end from the rack assembly.

To install:

7. Install a new tie rod end assembly (install new grease fitting, if so equipped) the same of number of turns it took to remove the old one. Tighten the jam nut to 55 ft. lbs. (75 Nm).

✳✳ WARNING

Do not allow the steering gear boot to become twisted.

8. Insert the tie rod stud into the lower steering knuckle hole. Install the tie rod stud nut and tighten to 38 ft. lbs. (52 Nm).

9. Install a new cotter pin through the tie rod stud. Bend the cotter pin ends tightly against the tie rod stud.

10. Have the wheel alignment checked by a qualified automotive service facility.

Manual and Power Steering Gears

REMOVAL & INSTALLATION

▶ **See Figure 126**

➡ **An assistant will be needed to perform this procedure.**

1. Loosen the wheel nuts. Raise the vehicle and support it securely with jackstands.

2. Detach the tie rod ends from the steering knuckles, as previously described.

3. Support the lower front suspension crossmember securely with a jack. Then, remove all 4 suspension crossmember attaching bolts. Lower the crossmember with the jack until it is possible to gain access to the steering gear and the lower steering column. Disconnect the gear from the steering column coupling.

4. Remove the splash shields and boot seal shields, if applicable.

5. If the car has power steering, remove the fasteners from the hose locating bracket attachment points. Disconnect both hoses at the opening nearest the steering gear and drain them into a large container. Discard the O-rings.

6. Remove the bolts attaching the power steering unit to the crossmember.

7. Remove the steering gear from the crossmember.

To install:

8. Install the steering gear to the crossmember, tightening the mounting bolts to 21 ft. lbs. (28 Nm) on 1988 vehicles, to 50 ft. lbs. (68 Nm) on 1989–90 vehicles and to 90 ft. lbs. (122 Nm) on 1991–95 vehicles.

9. Raise the crossmember into position with the floor jack, lining up the steering column coupling and the corresponding fitting on the end of the steering rack pinion shaft. Have an assistant inside the car help to position the column. If the car has manual steering, make sure the master serrations are lined up. Then, maneuver the crossmember/rack assembly so as to engage the column coupling and pinion shaft.

10. Position the crossmember so that the mounting bolt holes will line up. Install the bolts, but do not tighten them—only start the threads. Tighten the

right rear bolt, which serves as a pilot bolt to properly locate the crossmember. Then, tighten all 4 bolts to 90 ft. lbs. (122 Nm).

➡ **Proper torque for these crossmember bolts is very important.**

11. Attach the tie rod ends to the steering knuckle, as described earlier in this section.

12. Clean the ends of the power steering pump hoses and the ports in the steering gear with a clean shop towel or rag. Install new O-rings on the hose tube ends and coat them with power steering fluid. Then, route the hose carefully in all clips and in such a way as to avoid kinks or close proximity to any exhaust system parts.

13. Install the hose connections and tighten them to 25 ft. lbs. (34 Nm). Refill the power steering pump with the approved fluid.

14. Bleed the steering system procedure, located later in this section, and check for any system leaks.

15. Have the front end aligned by a qualified automotive service facility.

Power Steering Pump

REMOVAL & INSTALLATION

▶ **See Figures 127, 128 and 129**

➡ **Use this service procedure as a guide for all Chrysler models.**

1. Disconnect the negative battery cable, then, on vehicles equipped with an air bag system, cover the cable terminal with electrical tape to isolate it from accidentally contacting the battery terminal; this is important to prevent the air bag from accidentally being deployed.

2. Disconnect the vapor separator hose from the carburetor/throttle body. If the car has air conditioning, disconnect the 2 wires from the air conditioning clutch cycling switch.

3. Remove the accessory drive belt, as described in Section 1.

4. Apply the parking brake, block the rear wheels, then raise and safely support the front of the vehicle on jackstands.

5. Place a drain pan under the pump. Disconnect the return hose from the tube on the steering gear and lower the end of the hose into the pan to drain the fluid from the pump (fluid will continue to drain during the next step).

6. Remove the right side splash shield (this protects the drive belts).

7. Remove the power steering pressure line from the pump. Drain excess power steering fluid from the line.

8. Loosen, but do not remove the unit holding the back of the power steering pump to its mounting bracket. Remove the bolt attaching the pulley side of the power steering pump to the mounting bracket.

9. Lower the front of the vehicle.

10. Remove the bolt retaining the pump in the adjusting slot of the mounting bracket.

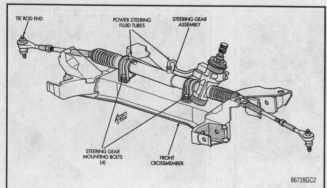

Fig. 126 Power steering gear and related components—manual gear similar

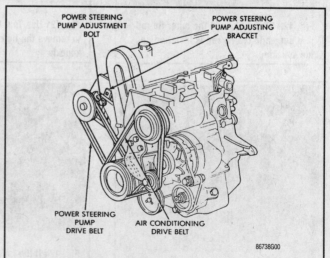

Fig. 127 The power steering pump is located on the left side of the engine (between the engine and the dash panel)

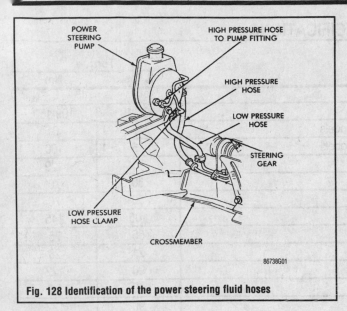

Fig. 128 Identification of the power steering fluid hoses

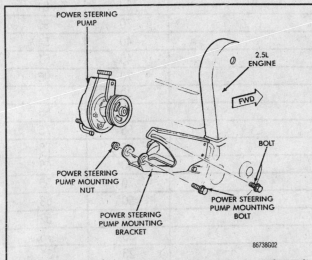

Fig. 129 Exploded view of the power steering pump mounting and fasteners

11. Remove the pump from the top of the engine compartment, using the following procedure:
    a. Lift the pump out of the mounting bracket.
    b. Rotate the pump 90°.
    c. Remove the pump from between the engine and dash panel.

12. Transfer the required parts from the removed power steering pump to the replacement pump.

To install:

13. Install the power steering pump into the vehicle by sliding it down between the engine and the dash panel, then rotate the pump 90° to install it onto its mounting bracket.

14. Install the pump onto the bracket, being sure that the stud on the backside of the pump is engaged in the slotted bracket hole. Install the pump-to-adjusting slot bolt, but do not tighten the nut or bolt.

15. Raise the front of the vehicle and support it securely on jackstands.

16. Install the bolt attaching the pulley side of the power steering pump to the pump mounting bracket. **Do not fully tighten the power steering pump mounting bolts at this time.**

17. Install the pump fluid pressure line into the output fitting on the pump. Tighten the fluid line tube nut to 23 ft. lbs. (31 Nm). **Before connecting the pressure line to the steering pump, inspect the O-ring on the pressure line for damage; replace it with a new one if required.**

18. Install the power steering low pressure return hose onto the steering pump low pressure fitting. Install the hose clamp onto the low pressure hose, being sure that the hose clamp is installed on the hose past the upset bead on the pump tube.

19. Lower the vehicle to the ground and connect the vapor separator and vent hoses to the carburetor/throttle body. Connect the 2 wires to the air conditioning cycling switch, if the car has air conditioning.

20. Install and adjust the accessory drive belt, as described in Section 1. Tighten the bolt at the power steering pump mounting bracket adjusting slot to 40 ft. lbs. (54 Nm). tighten the pump-to-bracket pivot nut and bolt to 40 ft. lbs. (54 Nm).

✳✳ WARNING

Do not use automatic transmission fluid in the power steering system. Only use Mopar® Power Steering Fluid, or the equivalent.

21. Fill the pump reservoir with the proper amount of fluid, as described in Section 1.

22. Remove the tape from the negative battery cable, if necessary, and connect the battery cable.

23. Start the engine and turn the steering wheel several times from stop-to-stop to bleed air from the fluid in the system.

24. Stop the engine, check the fluid level and inspect the system for leaks.

BLEEDING THE SYSTEM

1. Check the fluid level in the reservoir and fill to the correct level with the approved power steering fluid.

2. Start the engine and allow it to idle with the transaxle in Neutral (manual) or Park (automatic).

3. Slowly turn the steering wheel all the way to the left and then all the way to the right. Turn it from lock to lock several times. Then, refill the fluid reservoir.

TORQUE SPECIFICATIONS

Components	Torque	
	ft. lbs.	Nm
All Vehicles		
Wheel lug nut	80-110	109-150
Strut assembly lower end-to-steering knuckle leg—1981-83 models	45 [1]	61 [1]
Strut assembly lower end-to-steering knuckle leg—1984-95 models	75 [1]	100 [1]
Lower control arm pivot nut and bolt	95	129
Sway bar cushion bracket bolts	50	70
Sway bar end bushing bracket bolts	50	70
Ball joint stud-to-steering knuckle bolt and nut	105	145
Strut damper rod-to-upper strut mount nut	55	75
Upper strut mount-to-shock tower nuts	21	28
Front crossmember-to-frame rail bolts	90	122
Crossmember-to-frame rail studs	40	54
Crossmember attaching nut-to-frame rail stud	90	122
Spring hanger bracket-to-frame rail mounting bolts	60	81
Trailing arm-to-hanger bracket nuts	70	95
Shock absorber upper mounting bolts	40	54
Shock absorber lower mounting bolts	45	61
Track bar-to-rear axle attaching bolts	70	95
Track bar mounting bracket-to-frame rail bolts	40	55
Track bar brace-to-body mounting stud	40	55
Track bar-to-mounting bracket nut	55	75
Track bar brace-to-body stud nut	55	75
Jounce bumper-to-cup attaching nuts	40	55
Jounce bumper cup-to-frame rail attaching bolts	70	95
Steering gear-to-crossmember bolts	50	68
Tie rod end-to-steering knuckle attaching nut	35	52
Outer tie rod-to-inner tie rod locknut	55	75
Power steering pressure hose tube nuts	23	31
Power steering pump adjusting bolt	40	54
Power steering pump pivot bolt and nut	40	54
Steering wheel-to-shaft nut	45	61
Track bar-to-mounting bracket nut	55	75

1 – Plus an additional 1/4 (90°) turn.

86738C03

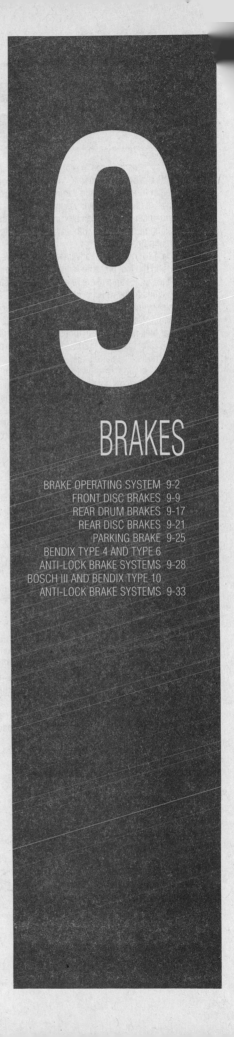

9

BRAKES

BRAKE OPERATING SYSTEM

Basic Operating Principles

▶ **See Figure 1**

Hydraulic systems are used to actuate the brakes of all automobiles. The system transports the power required to force the frictional surfaces of the braking system together from the pedal to the individual brake units at each wheel. A hydraulic system is used for two reasons.

First, fluid under pressure can be carried to all parts of an automobile by small pipes and flexible hoses without taking up a significant amount of room or posing routing problems.

Second, a great mechanical advantage can be given to the brake pedal end of the system, and the foot pressure required to actuate the brakes can be reduced by making the surface area of the master cylinder pistons smaller than that of any of the pistons in the wheel cylinders or calipers.

The master cylinder consists of a fluid reservoir and a double cylinder and piston assembly. Double type master cylinders are designed to separate the front and rear braking systems hydraulically in case of a leak.

Steel lines carry the brake fluid to a point on the vehicles frame near each of the vehicles wheels. The fluid is then carried to the calipers and wheel cylinders by flexible tubes in order to allow for suspension and steering movements.

In drum brake systems, each wheel cylinder contains two pistons, one at either end, which push outward in opposite directions.

In disc brake systems, the cylinders are part of the calipers. One cylinder in each caliper is used to force the brake pads against the disc.

All pistons employ some type of seal, usually made of rubber, to minimize fluid leakage. A rubber dust boot seals the outer end of the cylinder against dust and dirt. The boot fits around the outer end of the piston on disc brake calipers, and around the brake actuating rod on wheel cylinders.

The hydraulic system operates as follows: When at rest, the entire system, from the piston(s) in the master cylinder to those in the wheel cylinders or calipers, is full of brake fluid. Upon application of the brake pedal, fluid trapped in front of the master cylinder piston(s) is forced through the lines to the wheel cylinders. Here, it forces the pistons outward, in the case of drum brakes, and inward toward the disc, in the case of disc brakes. The motion of the pistons is opposed by return springs mounted outside the cylinders in drum brakes, and by spring seals, in disc brakes.

Upon release of the brake pedal, a spring located inside the master cylinder immediately returns the master cylinder pistons to the normal position. The pistons contain check valves and the master cylinder has compensating ports drilled in it. These are uncovered as the pistons reach their normal position. The piston check valves allow fluid to flow toward the wheel cylinders or calipers as the pistons withdraw. Then, as the return springs force the brake pads or shoes into the released position, the excess fluid reservoir through the compensating ports. It is during the time the pedal is in the released position that any fluid that has leaked out of the system will be replaced through the compensating ports.

Dual circuit master cylinders employ two pistons, located one behind the other, in the same cylinder. The primary piston is actuated directly by mechanical linkage from the brake pedal through the power booster. The secondary pis-

ton is actuated by fluid trapped between the two pistons. If a leak develops in front of the secondary piston, it moves forward until it bottoms against the front of the master cylinder, and the fluid trapped between the pistons will operate the rear brakes. If the rear brakes develop a leak, the primary piston will move forward until direct contact with the secondary piston takes place, and it will force the secondary piston to actuate the front brakes. In either case, the brake pedal moves farther when the brakes are applied, and less braking power is available.

All dual circuit systems use a switch to warn the driver when only half of the brake system is operational. This switch is located in a valve body which is mounted on the fire wall or the frame below the master cylinder. A hydraulic piston receives pressure from both circuits, each circuit's pressure being applied to one end of the piston. When the pressures are in balance, the piston remains stationary. When one circuit has a leak, however, the greater pressure in that circuit during application of the brakes will push the piston to one side, closing the switch and activating the brake warning light.

In disc brake systems, this valve body also contains a metering valve and, in some cases, a proportioning valve. The metering valve keeps pressure from traveling to the disc brakes on the front wheels until the brake shoes on the rear wheels have contacted the drums, ensuring that the front brakes will never be used alone. The proportioning valve controls the pressure to the rear brakes to lessen the chance of rear wheel lock-up during very hard braking.

Warning lights may be tested by depressing the brake pedal and holding it while opening one of the wheel cylinder bleeder screws. If this does not cause the light to go on, substitute a new lamp, make continuity checks, and, finally, replace the switch as necessary.

The hydraulic system may be checked for leaks by applying pressure to the pedal gradually and steadily. If the pedal sinks very slowly to the floor, the system has a leak. This is not to be confused with a springy or spongy feel due to the compression of air within the lines. If the system leaks, there will be a gradual change in the position of the pedal with a constant pressure.

Check for leaks along all lines and at wheel cylinders. If no external leaks are apparent, the problem is inside the master cylinder.

DISC BRAKES

Instead of the traditional expanding brakes that press outward against a circular drum, disc brake systems utilize a disc (rotor) with brake pads positioned on either side of it. Braking effect is achieved in a manner similar to the way you would squeeze a spinning phonograph record between your fingers. The disc (rotor) is a casting with cooling fins between the two braking surfaces. This enables air to circulate between the braking surfaces making them less sensitive to heat buildup and more resistant to fade. Dirt and water do not affect braking action since contaminants are thrown off by the centrifugal action of the rotor or scraped off the by the pads. Also, the equal clamping action of the two brake pads tends to ensure uniform, straight line stops. Disc brakes are inherently self-adjusting. There are three general types of disc brake:

1. A fixed caliper.
2. A floating caliper.
3. A sliding caliper.

The fixed caliper design uses two pistons mounted on either side of the rotor (in each side of the caliper). The caliper is mounted rigidly and does not move.

The sliding and floating designs are quite similar. In fact, these two types are often lumped together. In both designs, the pad on the inside of the rotor is moved into contact with the rotor by hydraulic force. The caliper, which is not held in a fixed position, moves slightly, bringing the outside pad into contact with the rotor. There are various methods of attaching floating calipers. Some pivot at the bottom or top, and some slide on mounting bolts. In any event, the end result is the same.

All the vehicles covered in this book employ the sliding caliper design.

DRUM BRAKES

Drum brakes employ two brake shoes mounted on a stationary backing plate. These shoes are positioned inside a circular drum which rotates with the wheel assembly. The shoes are held in place by springs. This allows them to slide toward the drums (when they are applied) while keeping the linings and drums in alignment. The shoes are actuated by a wheel cylinder which is mounted at the top of the backing plate. When the brakes are applied, hydraulic pressure

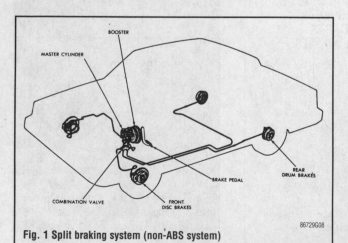

Fig. 1 Split braking system (non-ABS system)

86729G08

forces the wheel cylinder's actuating links outward. Since these links bear directly against the top of the brake shoes, the tops of the shoes are then forced against the inner side of the drum. This action forces the bottoms of the two shoes to contact the brake drum by rotating the entire assembly slightly (known as servo action). When pressure within the wheel cylinder is relaxed, return springs pull the shoes back away from the drum.

Most modern drum brakes are designed to self-adjust themselves during application when the vehicle is moving in reverse. This motion causes both shoes to rotate very slightly with the drum, rocking an adjusting lever, thereby causing rotation of the adjusting screw.

✳✳ WARNING

Clean, high quality brake fluid is essential to the safe and proper operation of the brake system. You should always buy the highest quality brake fluid that is available. If the brake fluid becomes contaminated, drain and flush the system and fill the master cylinder with new fluid. Never reuse any brake fluid. Any brake fluid that is removed from the system should be discarded.

Adjustments

DRUM BRAKES

▶ **See Figures 2, 3 and 4**

The brakes are self-adjusting and require no periodic adjustment. If the pedal is low and there are no apparent hydraulic problems, the rear drum brake linings are excessively worn or the automatic adjusters may be defective.

The brakes are adjusted (the automatic adjusters are actuated) after drum removal or lining replacement. First, pump the pedal through its full stroke and with firm pressure repeatedly until the adjusters bring the linings out to fit the drum (the pedal comes up to a normal level). Then, adjust the parking brake cable as described later in this section. Finally, drive the car and stop normally several times to allow the adjusters to reach their final position.

When the rear brake drums must be removed, it may be necessary to loosen the rear brake shoes to pull the drum off of the brake assembly.

Loosening Rear Brake Shoes

1. Loosen the rear wheel lug nuts.
2. Raise and safely support the rear of the vehicle with jackstands.
3. Remove the rear wheels.
4. Make sure that the parking brake is fully released.
5. Using a small prytool, remove the adjusting hole plug from the back of the drum brake backing plate.
6. Insert a flat bladed prytool or brake adjuster tool (C-3784 or equivalent) into the adjusting hole to engage the teeth of the drum brake shoe adjuster piston.
7. On the right side rear drum assembly, turn the adjusting cylinder down to loosen the brake shoes. On the left side of the vehicle, turn the cylinder up to loosen the shoes.

8. Continue to loosen the cylinder until the drum slides off of the assembly (the axle hub nut must be removed first).

Adjusting Rear Brake Shoes

All though the rear brakes are self-adjusting, perform this procedure after servicing the rear brake assemblies to speed up the adjusting time.
1. Loosen the rear wheel lug nuts.
2. Raise and safely support the rear of the vehicle with jackstands.
3. Remove the rear wheels.
4. Make sure that the parking brake is fully released.
5. Using a small prytool, remove the adjusting hole plug from the back of the drum brake backing plate.
6. Insert a flat bladed prytool or brake adjuster tool (C-3784 or equivalent) into the adjusting hole to engage the teeth of the drum brake shoe adjuster piston.
7. Tighten the adjuster cylinder until a slight drag is felt when the brake drum is rotated.
8. Insert a thin prytool into the brake adjusting hole along with the first tool. Using this second tool, push the adjusting lever out of engagement with the adjusting cylinder. Care should be taken so as not to bend the adjusting lever or distort the lever spring. While holding the adjusting lever out, back off the adjuster cylinder to ensure free wheeling with no brake shore drag.
9. Repeat the procedure on the other rear wheel.
10. Install the access hole rubber plugs back into the backing plate.
11. Adjust the parking brake **after** the wheel brake adjustment. Refer to the parking brake procedure later in this section.

➡ **It is important to follow the above sequence to avoid the possibility of the parking brake system causing brake drag. This could occur if the parking brakes are adjusted before the service brakes.**

Brake Light Switch

REMOVAL & INSTALLATION

▶ **See Figure 5**

➡ **The brake light switch is mounted to the brake pedal bracket assembly, under the instrument panel. The stop lamp switch attached to the mounting bracket.**

1. Disconnect the negative battery cable.
2. Unplug the two brake switch wiring harness connectors.
3. Remove the wiring harness for the switch from the clip on the brake pedal bracket assembly. Remove the nut and washer from the switch and bracket assembly stud and remove the switch and bracket assembly.
   To install:
4. Position the switch and bracket assembly to the brake pedal bracket assembly, then install the nut and lockwasher. Tighten the retaining nut for the bracket until finger-tight (loose enough to allow movement of the bracket).
5. Attach the electrical wiring harness connectors and route the wire through the retainer clip.

Fig. 2 Remove the adjusting access hole plug to gain access to the adjuster cylinder . . .

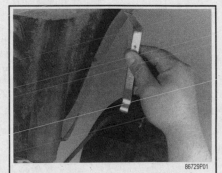

Fig. 3 . . . then use either a brake tool or a small prytool to adjust the brake shoe adjuster cylinder

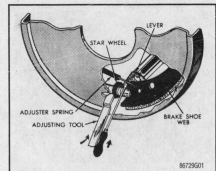

Fig. 4 To loosen the brake shoes, use a second thinner prytool to push the lever off of the adjuster cylinder star wheel

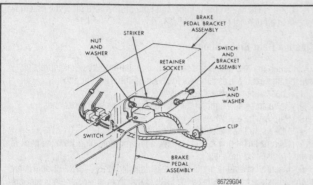

Fig. 5 Switch and bracket assembly mounting position on the brake pedal bracket

6. Push the switch forward (toward the front of the vehicle) as far as it will go (this will cause the brake pedal to move forward slightly).

7. Gently pull backward (toward the rear of the vehicle) on the brake pedal until the pedal lever rests against the its stop. This will ratchet the switch back to its properly adjusted position.

8. Tighten the switch and bracket assembly mounting bracket nut securely.

Master Cylinder

REMOVAL & INSTALLATION

✳✳ WARNING

On vehicles equipped with a Bendix Type 6 Anti-lock Brake System (ABS), a Diagnostic Readout Box (DRB or DRB II) is necessary for brake system bleeding. Failure to use a DRB to bleed the system will lead to system failure. Refer to the ABS portion of this section for bleeding procedures and precautions.

Non-Power Brakes

1. Disconnect the primary and secondary brake lines and install plugs in the master cylinder openings.

2. Disconnect the stoplight switch mounting bracket from under the instrument panel. Pull the stop light switch out of the way to prevent switch damage.

3. Pull the brake pedal backward to disengage the pushrod from the master cylinder piston.

➡The grommet will break during removal. Be sure to use a new grommet during installation.

4. Remove the master cylinder-to-firewall nuts.

5. Slide the master cylinder out and away from the fire wall. Be sure to remove all pieces of the broken grommet.

To install:

6. Install the boot on the pushrod.

7. Install a new grommet on the pushrod.

8. Apply a soap and water solution to the grommet and slide it firmly into position in the primary piston socket. Move the pushrod from side to side to make sure it's seated.

9. From the engine side, press the pushrod through the master cylinder mounting plate and align the mounting studs with the holes in the cylinder.

10. Install the nuts and torque them to 250 inch lbs.

11. From under the instrument panel, place the pushrod on the pin on the pedal and install a new retaining clip. Be sure to lubricate the pin.

12. Install the brake lines on the master cylinder.

13. Bleed the system.

Power Brakes—Without ABS

▶ See Figures 6, 7, 8 and 9

1. Disconnect the primary and secondary brake lines from the master cylinder. Plug the openings.

2. Remove the nuts attaching the master cylinder to the power brake booster.

3. Slide the master cylinder straight out, away from the booster.

To install:

4. Before installing the replacement master cylinder on the vehicle, it is a good idea to bench bleed the master cylinder. This will reduce the amount of system bleeding needed after installation is complete.

5. Position the master cylinder onto the power booster studs, align the push rod with the master cylinder piston, then install the mounting nuts.

6. Tighten the mounting nuts to 21 ft. lbs. (28 Nm).

7. Connect the brake tubes to the master cylinder primary and secondary ports. Tighten the fittings to 13 ft. lbs. (17 Nm).

8. Bleed the brake system. For more details, refer to the brake system bleeding procedure located later in this section.

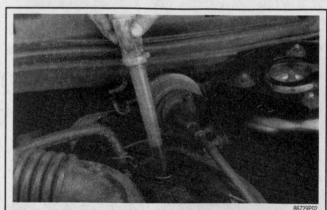

Fig. 6 Before removing the master cylinder, withdraw as much of the brake fluid as possible, . . .

Fig. 7 . . . then loosen and remove the brake line fittings from the master cylinder outlet ports

Fig. 8 Remove the master cylinder mounting nuts from the vacuum booster studs and . . .

Fig. 9 . . . pull the master cylinder off of the vacuum booster

Power Brakes—With ABS

For the removal and installation of the ABS-equipped master cylinder (hydraulic assembly), refer to the ABS portion of this section.

BLEEDING

▶ See Figure 10

➡A master cylinder bleeding kit or 2 pieces of brake tubing (with a fitting on at least one end) will be needed for this procedure.

1. Place the removed master cylinder in a bench-mounted vise.
2. If using the master cylinder bleeding kit, install the two hoses into the master cylinder outlet ports. Position the other ends in the master cylinder reservoir.

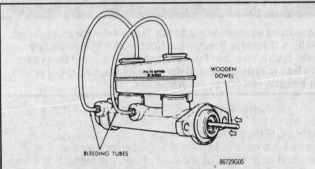

Fig. 10 When bleeding the master cylinder, make sure that the outlet fittings are tight and that the hoses are below the fluid level—use a dowel to depress the master cylinder plunger

3. If using the two pieces of brake line, bend the brake lines so that when installed to the outlet ports of the master cylinder, the other ends of the tubing will be positioned about ¼ in. (6mm) from the floor of the reservoir (the ends are in the reservoir). The tubes will almost form a complete circle shape (as shown in the illustration). Install the tubes to the master cylinder and tighten the fittings.
4. Fill the reservoir with brake fluid. The fluid level must be above the ends of the tubing in the reservoir.
5. Using a wooden dowel, depress the pushrod slowly, then allow the pistons to return to its resting position. Perform this several times (it may take a while) until ALL of the air bubbles are all expelled.
6. Remove the bleeding tubes from the master cylinder and quickly plug the master cylinder outlets.
7. Install the cylinder into the vehicle.
8. Make sure to bleed the entire brake system after master cylinder installation.

Power Brake Booster

REMOVAL & INSTALLATION

✷✷ WARNING

On vehicles equipped with a Bendix Type 6 Anti-lock Brake System (ABS), a Diagnostic Readout Box (DRB or DRB II) is necessary for brake system bleeding. Failure to use a DRB to bleed the system will lead to system failure. Refer to the ABS portion of this section for bleeding procedures and precautions.

▶ See Figures 11 and 12

1. Remove the brake lines from the master cylinder.
2. Remove the nuts attaching the master cylinder to the brake booster, and remove the master cylinder. For more details, refer to the master cylinder removal procedure earlier in this section.

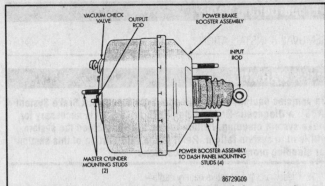

Fig. 11 The power brake vacuum booster is a sealed component, which does not require any adjustments

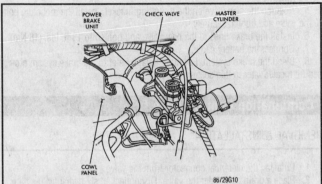

Fig. 12 The master cylinder is mounted to the booster, which, in turn, is mounted to the fire wall of the vehicle

3. Release its tension with a pair of pliers and slide the vacuum hose retaining clamp back from the check valve. Then, disconnect the vacuum line supplying the brake booster at the check valve. **Do not remove the check valve.** On models with manual transaxles; remove the clutch cable mounting bracket, then pull the wiring harness up and away from the strut tower.
4. Working underneath the instrument panel, remove the retainer clip from the brake pedal pin. To do this, position a small, bladed instrument between the center tang of the retainer clip and the pin on the brake pedal and twist it. Use this method to cause the tang on the clip to pass over the end of the brake pedal pin. Discard the retainer clip because it will no longer lock safely.
5. Remove the brake light switch and striker plate.
6. Remove the four power booster attaching nuts.
7. Remove the booster from the car. The power brake booster is not repairable. Do not attempt to disassemble it.

To install:

8. Position the booster on its mounting bracket and install its four mounting nuts. Torque them to 21 ft. lbs. (28 Nm).
9. Coat the load bearing surface of the brake pedal pin with Lubriplate® or equivalent to reduce wear. Then, connect the pushrod to the pedal pin and install a new retaining clip through the end. Lock the retaining clip securely.
10. Position the master cylinder onto the brake booster, install the mounting nuts and torque them to 21 ft. lbs. (28 Nm).
11. Route the vacuum hose carefully to the booster, ensuring that it is not kinked or pinched. Then, position its retaining clamp carefully.
12. Install each brake hydraulic tube into its correct master cylinder opening and torque the retaining flare nut to 12 ft. lbs. (16 Nm)
13. Slide the wiring harness down over the strut tower and reinstall the retaining clips. On models equipped with manual transaxles, install the clutch cable mounting bracket.
14. Bleed the brake system, making sure to keep the master cylinder full of the approved brake fluid throughout the procedure. Make sure the unit is filled to the correct level when bleeding is completed. Road test the vehicle for proper operation.

Proportioning Valve

REMOVAL & INSTALLATION

✳ WARNING

On vehicles equipped with a Bendix Type 6 Anti-lock Brake System (ABS), a Diagnostic Readout Box (DRB or DRB II) is necessary for brake system bleeding. Failure to use a DRB to bleed the system will lead to system failure. Refer to the ABS portion of this section for bleeding procedures and precautions.

1. Disconnect the negative battery cable.
2. Disconnect and plug the brake lines from the proportioning valve.
3. Remove the bolt and nut attaching the valve to the bracket.
4. Remove the valve from the vehicle.

To install:

5. Position the new valve on the mounting bracket. Install the mounting bolt to the valve and tighten securely.
6. Install the brake lines to the new valve and tighten to 13 ft. lbs. (18 Nm).
7. Connect the battery cable.
8. Bleed the brake system. For more details, refer to the brake system procedure located later in this section.

Combination Control Valve

REMOVAL & INSTALLATION

1. Unfasten the electrical connector from the valve.
2. Place a drain pan under the valve. Disconnect all six hydraulic line flare nuts.
3. Remove the mounting bolt and remove the valve from the fender well.

To install:

4. Bolt the new valve onto the fender well.
5. Reconnect all six flare nut fittings. Tighten the flare nuts to 145 inch lbs. (16 Nm).
6. Reattach the electrical connector.
7. Thoroughly bleed the brake system as described later in this section. Then, repeatedly stop the vehicle with firm application on the pedal to center the warning switch spool valve and extinguish the brake light.

Brake Hoses and Pipes

REMOVAL & INSTALLATION

▶ **See Figures 13, 14 and 15**

✳ WARNING

On vehicles equipped with a Bendix Type 6 Anti-lock Brake System (ABS), a Diagnostic Readout Box (DRB or DRB II) is necessary for brake system bleeding. Failure to use a DRB to bleed the system will lead to system failure. Refer to the ABS portion of this section for bleeding procedures and precautions.

It is important to use quality brake hose intended specifically for the application. Hose of less than the best quality, or hose not made to the specified length will tend to fatigue and may therefore create premature leakage and, consequently, a potential for brake failure. Note also that the brake hoses differ from one side of the car to the other and should, therefore, be ordered by specifying the side on which it will be installed.

Make sure hose end mating surfaces are clean and free of nicks and burrs, which would prevent effective sealing. Use new copper seals on banjo fittings. Tighten the brake tubing fittings to 10–14 ft. lbs. (13–19 Nm), hose-to-caliper connections to 19–29 ft. lbs. (26–40 Nm) and front brake hose-to-intermediate bracket fittings to 75–115 inch lbs. (9–13 Nm).

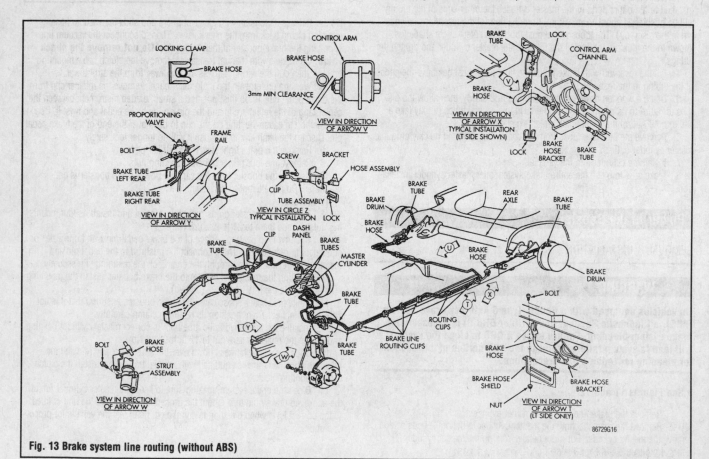

Fig. 13 Brake system line routing (without ABS)

86729G16

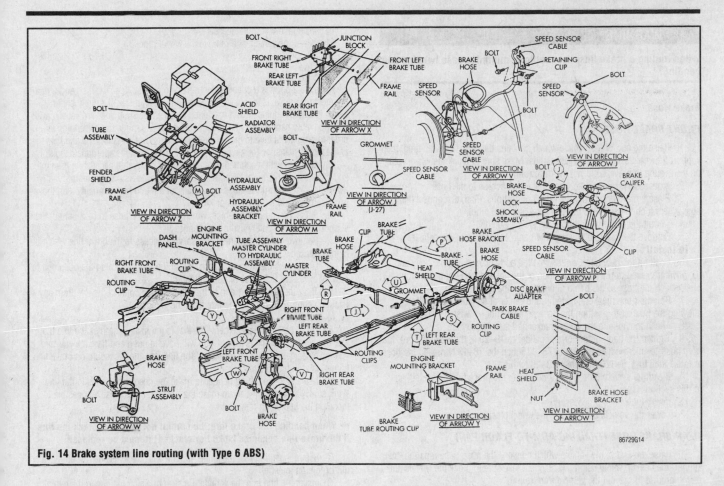

Fig. 14 Brake system line routing (with Type 6 ABS)

86729G14

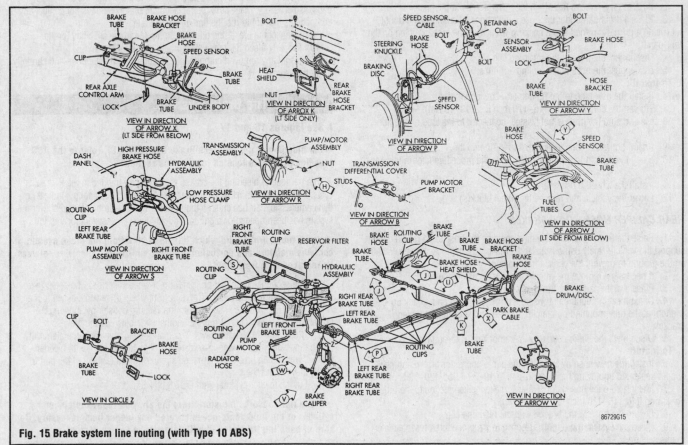

Fig. 15 Brake system line routing (with Type 10 ABS)

86729G15

When routing a brake hose to a vehicle, minimize hose twisting and bending.

Brake Hose

FRONT BRAKE HOSE

1. Raise the end of the vehicle which contains the hose to be repaired, then support the vehicle safely using jackstands. Make sure to block the wheels still on the ground to prevent the vehicle from rolling.
2. If necessary, remove the wheel for easier access to the hose.
3. Place a drain pan under the hose connections. First, disconnect the hose where it connects to the body bracket and steel tube.
4. Unbolt the hose bracket from the strut assembly.
5. Remove the bolt to disengage the banjo connection at the caliper.

To install:

6. Position the new hose, noting that the body bracket and the body end of the hose are keyed to prevent installation of the hose in the wrong direction. First, attach the hose to the banjo connector on the caliper.
7. Bolt the hose bracket, located in the center of the hose, to the strut, allowing the bracket to position the hose so it will not be twisted.
8. Attach the hose to the body bracket and steel brake tube.
9. Tighten the banjo fitting on the caliper to 19–29 ft. lbs. (26–39 Nm), the front hose-to-intermediate bracket to 75–115 inch lbs. (8–13 Nm), and the hose to brake tube to 115–170 inch lbs. (13–19 Nm).
10. Bleed the system thoroughly, referring to the procedure presented later in this section.
11. Install the wheel, if necessary.
12. Lower the vehicle and remove the wheel block(s).

REAR BRAKE HOSE (TRAILING ARM-TO-FLOOR PAN)

1. Raise the end of the vehicle which contains the hose to be repaired, then support the vehicle safely using jackstands. Make sure to block the wheels still on the ground to prevent the vehicle from rolling.
2. If necessary, remove the wheel for easier access to the hose.
3. Place a drain pan under the hose connections. Disconnect the double nut (using a primary wrench and a back-up wrench) at the tube mounted on the floor pan.
4. Disconnect the hose at the retaining clip.
5. Disconnect the hose at the trailing arm tube.

To install:

6. Install the new tube to the trailing arm connection first.
7. Tighten the connection to 115–170 inch lbs. (13–19 Nm).
8. Making sure the hose is not twisted, connect it to the tube on the floor pan.
9. Again, tighten the connection to 115–170 inch lbs. (13–19 Nm).
10. Bleed the system thoroughly, referring to the procedure later in this section.
11. Install the wheel, if necessary.
12. Lower the vehicle and remove the wheel block(s).

REAR CALIPER HOSE—DISC BRAKES

1. Raise the end of the vehicle which contains the hose to be repaired, then support the vehicle safely using jackstands. Make sure to block the wheels still on the ground to prevent the vehicle from rolling.
2. If necessary, remove the wheel for easier access to the hose.
3. Place a drain pan under the hose connections.
4. Disconnect the double nut (using a primary wrench and a back up wrench) at the tube mounted on the clip, located on the caliper-mounted bracket.
5. Disconnect the banjo connector by removing the through-bolt.

To install:

6. Install the new hose by attaching the banjo connector first, using new copper seals and tightening the through-bolt to 19–29 ft. lbs. (26–39 Nm).
7. Making sure the hose is not twisted, make the connection to the tube, tightening it to 115–170 inch lbs. (13–19 Nm).
8. Secure the hose to the bracket with the retaining clip.
9. Bleed the system thoroughly, referring to the procedure presented later in this section.

10. Install the wheel, if necessary.
11. Lower the vehicle and remove the wheel block(s).

Brake Line

There are 2 options available when replacing a brake line. The first, and probably most preferable, is to replace the entire line using a line of similar length which is already equipped with machined flared ends. Such lines are usually available from auto parts stores and usually require only a minimum of bending in order to properly fit then to the vehicle. The second option is to bend and flare the entire replacement line (or a repair section of line) using the appropriate tools.

Buying a line with machined flares is usually preferable because of the time and effort saved, not to mention the cost of special tools if they are not readily available. Also, machined flares are usually of a much higher quality than those produced by hand flaring tools or kits.

1. Raise the end of the vehicle which contains the hose to be repaired, then support the vehicle safely using jackstands.
2. Remove the components necessary for access to the brake line which is being replaced.
3. Disconnect the fittings at each end of the line, then plug the openings to prevent excessive fluid loss or contamination.
4. Trace the line from 1 end to the other and disconnect the line from any retaining clips, then remove the line from the vehicle.

To install:

5. Try to obtain a replacement line that is the same length as the line that was removed. If the line is longer, you will have to cut it and flare the end, or if you have decided to repair a portion of the line, see the procedure on brake line flaring, later in this section.
6. Use a suitable tubing bender to make the necessary bends in the line. Work slowly and carefully; try to make the bends look as close as possible to those on the line being replaced.

➡ **When bending the brake line, be careful not to kink or crack the line. If the brake line becomes kinked or cracked, it must be replaced.**

7. Before installing the brake line, flush it with brake cleaner to remove any dirt or foreign material.
8. Install the line into the vehicle. Be sure to attach the line to the retaining clips, as necessary. Make sure the replacement brake line does not contact any components that could rub the line and cause a leak.
9. Connect the brake line fittings and tighten to the specified torque.
10. Properly bleed the brake system and check for leaks.
11. Install any removed components, then remove the supports and carefully lower the vehicle.

Bleeding The Brake System

▶ **See Figures 16 and 17**

➡**For bleeding of the Anti-lock Brake System (ABS), refer to the ABS bleeding procedure located later in this section.**

The purpose of bleeding the brakes is to expel air trapped in the hydraulic system. The system must be bled whenever the pedal feels spongy, indicating that compressible air has entered the system. It must also be bled whenever the system has been opened or repaired. You will need an assistant for this job.

➡**Never reuse brake fluid which has been bled from the brake system. It contains moisture and corrosion products and should, therefore, always be replaced with fresh fluid.**

1. The sequence for bleeding is right rear wheel, left front wheel, left rear wheel, then right front wheel for Chrysler front wheel drive vehicles without an ABS system. Remove the vacuum from the vacuum booster by applying the brakes several times. Do not run the engine while bleeding the brakes.
2. Clean all the bleeder screws. You may want to give each one a shot of penetrating solvent to loosen it; seizure is a common problem with bleeder screws, which then break off, sometimes requiring replacement of the part to which they are attached.
3. Fill the master cylinder with DOT 3 brake fluid.

➡**Brake fluid absorbs moisture from the air. Don't leave the master cylinder or the fluid container uncovered any longer than necessary. Be careful handling the fluid—it will damage the vehicle's paint.**

Fig. 16 Use a bottle of clean brake fluid and a clear hose when bleeding the brakes

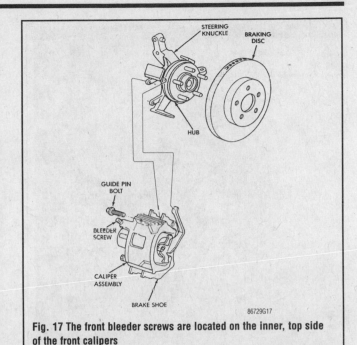

Fig. 17 The front bleeder screws are located on the inner, top side of the front calipers

Check the level of the fluid often when bleeding, and refill the reservoirs as necessary. Don't let them run dry, or you will have to repeat the process.

4. Attach a length of clear vinyl tubing to the bleeder screw on the wheel cylinder. Insert the other end of the tube into a clear, clean jar half filled with brake fluid.

5. Have your assistant slowly depress the brake pedal. As this is done, open the bleeder screw until the brake fluid starts to flow through the tube. Then, close the bleeder screw before the brake pedal reaches the end of its travel. After the bleeder valve is fully closed, have your assistant slowly release the pedal. Repeat this process until no air bubbles appear in the expelled fluid.

6. Repeat the procedure on the other three brake cylinders/calipers, checking the level of brake fluid in the master cylinder reservoir often.

After finishing, there should be no feeling of sponginess in the brake pedal. If there is, either there is still air in the line, in which case the process must be repeated, or there is a leak somewhere, which, of course, must be corrected before the car is moved. After all repairs and service work is finished, road test the vehicle for proper operation.

FRONT DISC BRAKES

✳✳ CAUTION

Brake shoes may contain asbestos, which has been determined to be a cancer-causing agent. Never clean the brake surfaces with compressed air! Avoid inhaling any dust from any brake surface! When cleaning brake surfaces, use a commercially available brake cleaning fluid.

Brake Pads

INSPECTION

♦ **See Figure 18**

Measure lining wear by measuring the combined thickness of the pad and pad backing plate at the thinnest point. It must measure at least 5/16 in. (8mm) thick on all vehicles covered by this manual.

Some vehicles are equipped with a wear sensor on the outboard pad of the front disc brake assemblies. This sensor, when emitting a squealing sound, signals that the brake linings should be inspected and may require replacement.

Always replace both front brake pad assemblies (inboard and outboard

pad) on both front wheels whenever necessary. The specifications given above on front disc brake lining wear should be used as the guide for replacement.

REMOVAL & INSTALLATION

✳✳ WARNING

On vehicles equipped with a Bendix Type 6 Anti-lock Brake System (ABS), a Diagnostic Readout Box (DRB or DRB II) is necessary for brake system bleeding. Failure to use a DRB to bleed the system will lead to system failure. Refer to the ABS portion of this section for bleeding procedures and precautions.

ATE-Type Brake Caliper

♦ **See Figures 19, 20, 21 and 22**

This non-family caliper is used on some 1981–87 models. This caliper, unlike the later non-family caliper, does utilize an adapter. During the period between 1981–87, this is the only dual-pin caliper used; the single pin caliper is a Kelsey-Hayes type and is covered later in this section.

1. Apply the parking brake, block the rear wheels, then raise and securely support the front of the vehicle on jackstands.

2. Remove the front wheels.

3. Remove the caliper hold-down spring by pushing in on the center of the spring and pushing outward.

4. Loosen, but do not remove the guide pins, until the caliper is free. Remove the guide pins only if the bushings are being replaced.

5. Lift the caliper away from the rotor. The inboard pad will remain with the caliper. Remove the pad by pulling it away from the caliper piston to unsnap the retaining clip.

6. Remove the outboard pad by simply pulling it away from the caliper adapter.

7. If the caliper is being removed, disconnect and cap the brake line. If only the pads are being removed, support the caliper with wire in such a way that the brake line will not be stressed.

To install:

8. Lubricate both bushing channels with silicone lubricant.

9. Remove the protective backing from the noise suppression gasket on the inner pad assembly.

10. Install the new inboard pad in the caliper, centering the retainer in the piston bore.

11. Remove the protective backing from the noise suppression gasket on the outboard pad and position the pad on the adapter.

12. Carefully lower the caliper over the rotor and inboard pad.

13. Install the guide pins and tighten to 18–22 ft. lbs. (25–30 Nm).

➡️ **It is easy to crossthread the guide pins. Start them carefully, turning them gently by hand and allowing them to find their own angle.**

14. Install the hold-down spring.

15. Install the wheels and tighten the lugs to 461 inch lbs. (61 Nm) in a star pattern, then tighten them to the full torque of 961 inch lbs. (129 Nm).

16. If the brake hose was disconnected from the caliper, bleed the system thoroughly, as described earlier in this section.

17. Pump the brake pedal several times to ensure that the brake pads seat against the rotor. **The pedal must give resistance at the normal position before attempting to drive the car.** Drive the car at moderate speeds in an isolated area in order to apply the brakes several times to test the system and seat the new linings.

Double Pin Non-Family Caliper

▸ See Figure 23

This front brake caliper was available on some of the 1991–93 vehicles covered by this manual. The exact models equipped with these calipers, in contrast to the other double pin Kelsey-Hayes caliper, is not known. This caliper is characterized by the lack of an adapter, to which the caliper is mounted. The non-family double pin caliper, therefore, mounts directly to the steering knuckle with 2 through-bolts.

1. Remove the master cylinder reservoir lid and remove some of the brake fluid from the master cylinder.

2. Slightly loosen the front wheel lug nuts.

3. Raise and support the front end on jackstands.

4. Remove the front wheels.

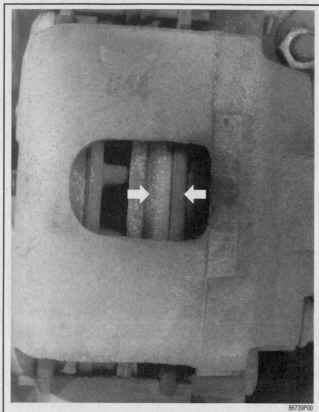

Fig. 18 When inspecting the pads, measure the pad and backing plate together (between the arrows)

Fig. 19 After removing the attaching bolts, remove the retaining spring . . .

Fig. 20 . . . then lift the caliper off of the adapter

Fig. 21 Remove the outboard brake pad from the adapter and . . .

Fig. 22 . . . remove the inboard pad from the caliper—suspend the caliper with strong wire or cord

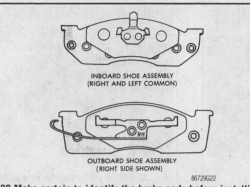

Fig. 23 Make certain to identify the brake pads before installing them on the vehicle

5. Remove the brake caliper assembly-to-steering knuckle attaching guide pin bolts.

6. Pull the lower end of the brake caliper out from the machined abutment on the steering knuckle. Then roll the caliper out and away from the rotor. The pads will remain on the caliper.

➡ **Support the caliper with strong wire or cord from the vehicle frame to prevent the weight of the caliper from damaging the flexible hose.**

7. Remove the outboard brake pad by prying between the top of the outboard shoe and the top of the caliper assembly.

8. Remove the inboard pad by simply pulling it away from the caliper piston.

To install:

9. Thoroughly clean and lubricate both steering knuckle/brake pad contacting surfaces with a liberal amount of Mopar® Multi-purpose lubricant or equivalent.

10. Lubricate both bushing channels with silicone grease.

11. Using a large C-clamp, slowly press the caliper piston back into the caliper (until fully seated).

12. The inboard brake shoes are common. The outboard brake shoes are marked with either LH (left hand side) or RH (right hand side) to denote which side of the vehicle to be installed on.

13. Remove the protective backing from the noise suppression gasket on the inboard pad assembly.

14. Install the new inboard pad in the caliper, centering the retainer in the piston bore.

15. Remove the protective backing from the noise suppression gasket on the outboard pad and position the pad on the brake caliper.

16. Carefully lower the caliper over the rotor and guide hold-down spring under the machined abutment on the knuckle assembly.

17. Install the guide pins and torque to 18–261 inch lbs. (24–34 Nm).

➡ **It is easy to crossthread the guide pins. Start them carefully, turning them gently by hand and allowing them to find their own angle.**

18. Install the wheels. For more details refer to Section 8.

19. Lower the vehicle.

20. Pump the brake pedal several times to ensure that the brake pads seat against the rotor. The pedal must give resistance at the normal position before attempting to drive the car. Drive the car at moderate speeds in an isolated area in order to apply the brakes several times to test the system and seat the new linings.

Single and Double Pin Family Caliper

▶ See Figures 24 thru 32

✳✳✳ WARNING

On vehicles equipped with a Bendix Type 6 Anti-lock Brake System (ABS), a Diagnostic Readout Box (DRB or DRB II) is necessary for brake system bleeding. Failure to use a DRB to bleed the system will lead to system failure. Refer to the ABS portion of this section for bleeding procedures and precautions.

Fig. 24 After removing the wheels, loosen the caliper slide pin bolts . . .

Fig. 25 . . . then remove the bolts from the caliper

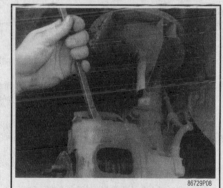

Fig. 26 Pry the caliper loose from the brake rotor, then . . .

Fig. 27 . . . carefully lift the caliper off of the brake rotor

Fig. 28 Remove the outboard brake pad from the brake adapter and . . .

Fig. 29 . . . slide the brake rotor off of the axle hub

Fig. 30 The brake rotor must be removed before the inboard pad can be removed from the adapter

Fig. 31 Remove the inboard brake pad from the brake adapter, along with the retaining spring

Fig. 32 Before installing the new pads, push the piston back into the caliper with a large C-clamp

The Kelsey-Hayes single pin family front brake caliper was available on some 1981–87 vehicles, whereas the double pin Kelsey-Hayes caliper was available on 1988–95 models. The exact models equipped with these calipers is not known. These calipers are characterized by the use of an adapter, to which the caliper is mounted. The Kelsey-Hayes calipers, therefore, mount to adapters with 2 through-bolts, which is mounted to the steering knuckle. The 1981–87 single pin caliper is characterized by the single pin; all other calipers used at that time utilize a dual pin design.

1. Remove the master cylinder reservoir lid and remove some of the brake fluid from the master cylinder.
2. Slightly loosen the wheel lug nuts.
3. Raise and support the front end of the vehicle on jackstands.
4. Remove the front wheels.
5. Remove the caliper guide pin bolt(s), by loosening them until they are free from the threads then pull them out of the caliper adapter.
6. Using a small prybar, gently wedge the caliper away from the rotor, breaking the adhesive seals.
7. Slowly slide the caliper away from the rotor and off the caliper adapter. Support the caliper securely by hanging it from the body with wire (this is necessary to keep its weight from damaging the brake hose).
8. Slide the outboard pad off the caliper adapter. Then remove the disc by simply sliding it off the wheel studs.
9. Remove the inboard pad by sliding it off the caliper adapter.
To install:
10. Lubricate both bushing channels with silicone grease.
11. Using a large C-clamp, slowly press the caliper piston back into the caliper (until fully seated).
12. Remove the protective paper backing from the anti-squeal surfaces on both pads. Install the inboard pad on the adapter. Be careful to keep grease from the bushing channels from getting onto the pad as you do this.
13. Install the rotor onto the wheel studs of the steering knuckle. Install the outboard pad in the caliper.
14. Remove the caliper from the hanger. Lower the caliper into position over the rotor and pads. Install the guide pin bolt(s) and torque them to 361 inch lbs. (48 Nm).

➡It is easy to crossthread the guide pin. Start it carefully, turning it by hand gently and allowing it to find its own angle.

15. Install the wheels.
16. Lower the vehicle.
17. Pump the brake pedal several times to ensure that the brake pads seat against the rotor. The pedal must give resistance at the normal position before attempting to drive the car. Drive the car at moderate speeds in an isolated area in order to apply the brakes several times to test the system and seat the new linings.

Calipers

REMOVAL & INSTALLATION

➡When replacing the front disc brake pads, remove some of the brake fluid from the master cylinder first, then after removing the caliper use a large C-clamp or equivalent and slowly compress the piston back into the caliper bore to aid installation. On vehicles equipped with an ABS system, refer to the necessary service procedures.

ATE-Type Brake Caliper

◆ See Figures 33 thru 41

➡This procedure is for removal of the caliper and adapter together; if the brake pads must be removed as well, refer to the brake pad procedure earlier in this section.

This non-family caliper is used on some 1981–87 models. This caliper, unlike the later non-family caliper, does utilize an adapter. During the period between 1981–87, this is the only dual-pin caliper used; the single pin caliper is a Kelsey-Hayes type and is covered later in this section.

1. Apply the parking brake, block the rear wheels, then raise and securely support the front of the vehicle on jackstands.

Fig. 33 After removing the front wheel, loosen the upper brake adapter retaining bolt . . .

Fig. 34 . . . then remove it from the adapter bracket

Fig. 35 Remove the lower caliper adapter bracket retaining bolt as well

Fig. 36 Install a hose clamp onto the hydraulic brake hose . . .

Fig. 37 . . . clean all dirt and grime from the hose-to-caliper mounting area . . .

Fig. 38 . . . loosen the brake hose banjo bolt . . .

Fig. 39 . . . and separate the brake hose from the caliper

Fig. 40 Remove the brake caliper and adapter as one unit

Fig. 41 If necessary, the brake rotor can now easily be removed from the axle hub

2. Remove the front wheels.

3. Remove the caliper adapter bracket retaining bolts.

4. Disconnect and cap the brake line. If only the pads are being removed, support the caliper with wire in such a way that the brake line will not be stressed.

5. Lift the caliper and adapter assembly away from the rotor.

To install:

6. Slide the caliper and adapter assembly over the brake rotor and into position against the hub.

7. Install the adapter-to-hub mounting bolts and tighten them to 130–190 ft. lbs. (176–258 Nm).

8. Install the brake hose to the caliper along with new copper washers and install the banjo bolt. Tighten the banjo bolt to 19–29 ft. lbs. (26–40 Nm).

9. Install the wheels and tighten the lugs to 461 inch lbs. (61 Nm) in a star pattern, then tighten them to the full torque of 961 inch lbs. (129 Nm).

10. If the brake hose was disconnected from the caliper, bleed the system thoroughly, as described earlier in this section.

11. Pump the brake pedal several times to ensure that the brake pads seat against the rotor. **The pedal must give resistance at the normal position before attempting to drive the car.** Drive the car at moderate speeds in an isolated area in order to apply the brakes several times to test the system and seat the new linings.

Double Pin Non-Family Caliper

♦ See Figure 42

⁂ WARNING

On vehicles equipped with a Bendix Type 6 Anti-lock Brake System (ABS), a Diagnostic Readout Box (DRB or DRB II) is necessary for brake system bleeding. Failure to use a DRB to bleed the system will lead to system failure. Refer to the ABS portion of this section for bleeding procedures and precautions.

This front brake caliper was available on some of the 1991–93 vehicles covered by this manual. The exact models equipped with these calipers in contrast to the other double pin Kelsey-Hayes caliper is not known. This caliper is characterized by the lack of an adapter, to which the caliper is mounted. The non-family double pin caliper, therefore, mount directly to the steering knuckle by 2 through-bolts.

1. Remove the master cylinder reservoir lid and remove some of the brake fluid from the master cylinder.

2. Slightly loosen the front wheel lug nuts.

3. Raise and support the front end on jackstands.

4. Remove the front wheels.

5. Remove the brake caliper assembly-to-steering knuckle attaching guide pin bolts.

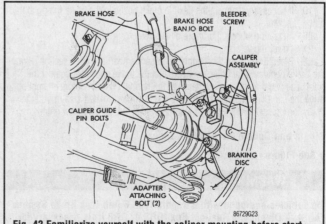

Fig. 42 Familiarize yourself with the caliper mounting before starting the repairs

6. Pull the lower end of the brake caliper out from the machined abutment on the steering knuckle. Then roll the caliper out and away from the rotor. The pads will remain on the caliper.

➡Support the caliper with strong wire or cord from the vehicle frame to prevent the weight of the caliper from damaging the flexible hose.

7. If the caliper is to be overhauled, perform the following:
   a. Place a small piece of wood between the piston and caliper fingers.
   b. Carefully depress the brake pedal to hydraulically push the piston out of the bore. The brake pedal will fall away when the piston has passed the bore opening. Then prop the brake pedal to any position below the first inch (25mm) of pedal travel (in other words, the brake pedal should be held in the down position); this will prevent the loss of brake fluid from the master cylinder.
   c. If both front calipers are to be removed, disconnect the flexible brake line at the frame bracket after removing the piston. Plug the brake tube and remove the piston from the opposite caliper, using the same process as above for the first piston removal.

CAUTION

Under no condition should air pressure be used to remove the piston from the caliper bore. Personal injury could result.

   d. Disconnect the flexible brake hose from the caliper.
   e. For the overhaul, mount the caliper in a bench-mounted vise.
8. If the caliper is simply going to be replaced with a new one, disconnect the flexible brake hose from the caliper. Immediately plug the brake hose, to stop any brake fluid leakage and keep the fluid from becoming contaminated.

To install:

9. Thoroughly clean and lubricate both steering knuckle/brake pad contacting surfaces with a liberal amount of Mopar® Multi-purpose lubricant or equivalent.
10. Lubricate both bushing channels with silicone grease.
11. If necessary, use a large C-clamp to slowly press the caliper piston back into the caliper (until fully seated).
12. The inboard brake shoes are common. The outboard brake shoes are marked with either LH (left hand side) or RH (right hand side) to denote which side of the vehicle to be installed on.
13. Remove the protective backing from the noise suppression gasket on the inboard pad assembly.
14. Install the new inboard pad in the caliper, centering the retainer in the piston bore.
15. Remove the protective backing from the noise suppression gasket on the outboard pad and position the pad on the brake caliper.
16. Carefully lower the caliper over the rotor and guide hold-down spring under the machined abutment on the knuckle assembly.
17. Install the guide pins and torque to 18–261 inch lbs. (24–34 Nm).

➡It is easy to crossthread the guide pins. Start them carefully, turning them gently by hand and allowing them to find their own angle.

18. Install the flexible brake hose to the caliper. Make sure to use new seal washers. Tighten the banjo fitting to 24 ft. lbs. (33 Nm).
19. If necessary, connect the flexible brake hoses to the brake tubing at the frame bracket.
20. Install the wheels. For more details refer to Section 8.
21. Lower the vehicle.
22. Bleed the system thoroughly, as described earlier in this section. Pump the brake pedal several times to ensure that the brake pads seat against the rotor. The pedal must give resistance at the normal position before attempting to drive the car. Drive the car at moderate speeds in an isolated area in order to apply the brakes several times to test the system and seat the new linings.

Single and Double Pin Family Caliper

➧ See Figures 23 thru 32

WARNING

On vehicles equipped with a Bendix Type 6 Anti-lock Brake System (ABS), a Diagnostic Readout Box (DRB or DRB II) is necessary for brake system bleeding. Failure to use a DRB to bleed the system will lead to system failure. Refer to the ABS portion of this section for bleeding procedures and precautions.

The Kelsey-Hayes single pin family front brake caliper was available on some 1981–87 vehicles, whereas the double pin Kelsey-Hayes caliper was available on 1988–95 models. The exact models equipped with these calipers is not known. These calipers are characterized by the use of an adapter, to which the caliper is mounted. The Kelsey-Hayes calipers, therefore, mount to adapters with 2 through-bolts, which is mounted to the steering knuckle. The 1981–87 single pin caliper is characterized by the single pin; all other calipers used at that time utilize a dual pin design.

1. Raise and support the front end on jackstands.
2. Remove the front wheels.
3. Remove the caliper guide pin bolt(s). To do this, unscrew it until it is free from the threads and then pull them out of the caliper adapter.
4. Using a small prybar, gently wedge the caliper away from the rotor, breaking the adhesive seals.
5. Slowly slide the caliper away from the rotor and off the caliper adapter. Support the caliper securely by hanging it from the body with wire (this is necessary to keep its weight from damaging the brake hose).
6. Slide the outboard pad off the caliper adapter. Then remove the disc by simply sliding it off the wheel studs.
7. Remove the inboard pad by sliding it off the caliper adapter.

➡Support the caliper with strong wire or cord from the vehicle frame to prevent the weight of the caliper from damaging the flexible hose.

8. If the caliper is to be overhauled, perform the following:
   a. Place a small piece of wood between the piston and caliper fingers.
   b. Carefully depress the brake pedal to hydraulically push the piston out of the bore. The brake pedal will fall away when the piston has passed the bore opening. Then prop the brake pedal to any position below the first inch (25mm) of pedal travel: this will prevent the loss of brake fluid from the master cylinder.
   c. If both front calipers are to be removed, disconnect the flexible brake line at the frame bracket after removing the piston. Plug the brake tube and remove the piston from the opposite caliper, using the same process as above for the first piston removal.

CAUTION

Under no condition should air pressure be used to remove the piston from the caliper bore. Personal injury could result.

   d. Disconnect the flexible brake hose from the caliper.
   e. For the overhaul, mount the caliper in a bench-mounted vise.
9. If the caliper is simply going to be replaced with a new one, disconnect the flexible brake hose from the caliper. Immediately plug the brake hose, to stop any brake fluid leakage and keep the fluid from becoming contaminated.

To install:

10. Lubricate both bushing channels with silicone grease.
11. Using a large C-clamp, slowly press the caliper piston back into the caliper (until fully seated).
12. Remove the protective paper backing from the anti-squeal surfaces on both pads. Install the inboard pad on the adapter. Be careful to keep grease from the bushing channels from getting onto the pad as you do this.
13. Install the rotor onto the wheel studs of the steering knuckle. Install the outboard pad in the caliper.
14. Remove the caliper from the hanger. Lower the caliper into position over the rotor and pads. Install the guide pin bolt(s) and torque them to 361 inch lbs. (48 Nm).

➡It is easy to crossthread the guide pin. Start it carefully, turning it by hand gently and allowing it to find its own angle.

15. Install the flexible brake hose to the caliper. Make sure to use new seal washers. Tighten the banjo fitting to 24 ft. lbs. (33 Nm).
16. If necessary, connect the flexible brake hoses to the brake tubing at the frame bracket.
17. Install the wheels.
18. Lower the vehicle.
19. Pump the brake pedal several times to ensure that the brake pads seat against the rotor. The pedal must give resistance at the normal position before attempting to drive the car. Drive the car at moderate speeds in an isolated area in order to apply the brakes several times to test the system and seat the new linings.

OVERHAUL

♦ **See Figures 43 thru 48**

➡Use this service procedure as a guide for overhaul of the caliper assembly for all years/models. If in doubt about overhaul condition or service procedure REPLACE the complete assembly.

1. Remove the caliper as previously outlined, leaving the brake line connected.

2. Carefully have a helper depress the brake pedal to hydraulically push the piston out of the bore. When the piston has passed out of the bore, fluid and pedal pressure will drop. As soon as pedal pressure drops, hold the pedal in position with the foot and then devise a means to keep it there during work—this will minimize fluid loss and difficulty bleeding the system later.

✷✷ CAUTION

Under no condition should air pressure be used to remove the piston. Personal injury could result from this practice.

3. Disconnect the flexible brake line at the frame bracket and immediately plug the open end of the line. If the piston from the caliper on the opposite side of the car must now be removed, it can be removed in the same way. When the piston has been removed, disconnect and plug the other flexible line.

4. Place the caliper in a vise which has soft jaws, clamping it as lightly as possible.

➡**Excessive vise pressure will cause bore distortion and piston binding.**

5. Remove the dust boot and discard it.

6. Use a plastic rod to work the piston seal out of its groove in the piston bore. Discard the old seal.

➡**Do not use a metal tool for this procedure, because of the possibility of scratching the piston bore or damaging the edges of the seal.**

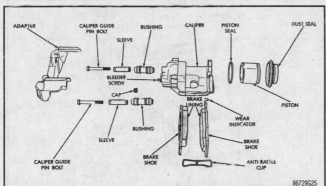

Fig. 43 Exploded view of the Kelsey-Hayes Double Pin Family caliper

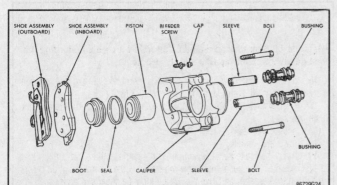

Fig. 44 Exploded view of the Kelsey-Hayes Double Pin Non-Family caliper

Fig. 45 Remove the protruding piston from the brake caliper . . .

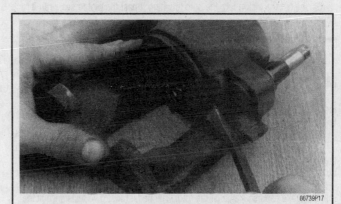

Fig. 46 . . . then gently pry the piston boot loose from the caliper

Fig. 47 Remove the boot, then . . .

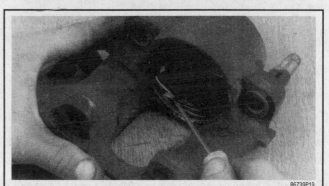

Fig. 48 . . . remove the piston seal from the groove in the caliper bore

7. Remove the bushings from the caliper by pressing them out, using a suitable tool. Discard the old bushings. If a Teflon® sleeve is used, discard this also.

8. Clean all parts using alcohol and blow dry with compressed air.

➡**Whenever a caliper has been disassembled, a new boot and seal must be installed.**

9. Inspect the piston bore for scoring or pitting. Bores with light scratches can be cleaned up. If the bore is scratched beyond repair, the caliper should be replaced.

10. Dip the new piston seal in clean brake fluid and install it in the bore groove.

➡**Never use an old piston seal.**

11. Coat the new piston with clean brake fluid, leaving a generous amount inside the boot.

12. Position the dust boot over the piston.

13. Install the piston into the bore, pushing it past the piston seal until it bottoms in the bore.

➡**Force must be applied uniformly to avoid cocking the piston.**

14. Position the dust boot in the counterbore.

15. Using tools C-4689 and C-4171 or their equivalents install the dust boot.

16. Remove the Teflon® sleeves from the guide pin bushings before installing the bushings into the caliper. After the new bushings are installed in the caliper, reinstall the Teflon® sleeves into the bushings.

17. Be sure the flanges extend over the caliper casting evenly on both sides.

18. When reinstalling the calipers use new seal washers and torque the brake hose connections to the specified torque. Follow the installation procedure above.

19. Bleed the brake system. Pump the brake pedal several times to ensure that the brake pads seat against the rotor. The pedal must give resistance at the normal position before attempting to drive the car. Drive the car at moderate speeds in an isolated area in order to apply the brakes several times to test the system.

Brake Disc (Rotor)

REMOVAL & INSTALLATION

✳✳ WARNING

On vehicles equipped with a Bendix Type 6 Anti-lock Brake System (ABS), a Diagnostic Readout Box (DRB or DRB II) is necessary for brake system bleeding. Failure to use a DRB to bleed the system will lead to system failure. Refer to the ABS portion of this section for bleeding procedures and precautions.

1. Raise and support the front end on jackstands.
2. Remove the caliper from the rotor, but do not disconnect the brake line.
3. Suspend the caliper out of the way with wire. Do not put stress on the brake hose.
4. Remove the rotor (some applications have 2 hold down in the brake disc or rotor screws that must be removed) from the drive flange studs.

To install:

5. Coat both sides of the rotor with alcohol or equivalent (to clean assembly) and slide it onto the studs.
6. Install the caliper. For more details, refer to the caliper installation procedure earlier in this section.
7. Install the wheels. Tighten the lug nuts until snug.
8. Lower the vehicle.
9. Tighten the lug nuts to the specified torque in the torque specifications chart in Section 8.
10. Pump the brake pedal several times to ensure that the brake pads seat against the rotor. The pedal must give resistance at the normal position before attempting to drive the car. Drive the car at moderate speeds in an isolated area in order to apply the brakes several times to test the system and seat the new linings.

INSPECTION

♦ See Figures 49, 50 and 51

Whenever the brake calipers are removed, the brake pads are replaced, or any front axle work is performed to the vehicle, inspect the rotors for defects. The brake rotor is an extremely important component of the brake system. Cracks, large scratches or warpage can adversely affect the braking system, and at times, to the point of becoming very dangerous.

Light scoring is acceptable. Heavy scoring or warping will necessitate refinishing or replacement of the disc. The brake disc must be replaced if cracks or burned marks are evident.

Check the thickness of the disc. Measure the thickness at 12 equally spaced points 1 in. (25mm) from the edge of the disc. If thickness varies more than 0.0005 in. (0.013mm) the disc should be refinished, provided equal amounts are out from each side and the thickness does not fall below 0.882 inch (22.4mm) on Chrysler front wheel drive vehicles.

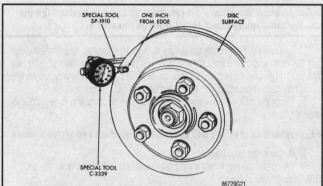

Fig. 49 Use Special Tool C-3339 or its equivalent to measure the run-out (warpage/wobble) of the front disc brake rotors

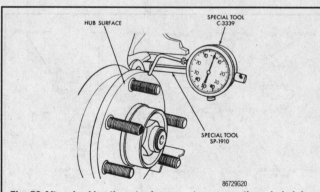

Fig. 50 After checking the rotor for run-out, measure the axle hub in the same manner

Fig. 51 The minimum allowable thickness of the brake rotors is stamped on a flat on the rotor itself

Check the run-out (warpage) of the disc. Total run-out of the disc installed on the car should not exceed 0.005 in. (0.013mm). The disc can be resurfaced to correct minor variations; as long as equal amounts are cut from each side and the thickness is at least 0.882 inch (22.4mm) on Chrysler front wheel drive vehicles after resurfacing.

Check the run-out of the hub (disc removed). It should not be more than 0.002–0.003 inch (0.050–0.076mm) on Chrysler front wheel drive vehicles If so, the hub should be replaced.

All brake discs or rotors have markings for MINIMUM allowable thickness cast on an unmachined surface or an alternate surface. **Always use this specification as the minimum allowable thickness or refinishing limit.** Refer to a local auto parts store or machine shop, if necessary, shop where brake disc or rotors are resurfaced.

If the brake disc or rotor needs to be replaced with a new part, the protective coating on the braking surface of the rotor must be removed with an appropriate solvent before installing the rotor to the vehicle.

REAR DRUM BRAKES

❋❋ CAUTION

Brake shoes may contain asbestos, which has been determined to be a cancer-causing agent. Never clean the brake surfaces with compressed air! Avoid inhaling any dust from any brake surface! When cleaning brake surfaces, use a commercially available brake cleaning fluid.

Brake Drums

REMOVAL & INSTALLATION

▶ **See Figures 52 thru 58**

❋❋ WARNING

On vehicles equipped with a Bendix Type 6 Anti-lock Brake System (ABS), a Diagnostic Readout Box (DRB or DRB II) is necessary for brake system bleeding. Failure to use a DRB to bleed the system will lead to system failure. Refer to the ABS portion of this section for bleeding procedures and precautions.

1. Slightly loosen the rear wheel lug nuts.
2. Raise the car and safely support it with jackstands.
3. Remove the rear wheels.
4. Loosen the parking brake cable adjustment by backing off the adjusting nut.
5. Remove the access hole plug from the rear brake backing plate, then insert a brake spoon or similar prytool and release the brake shoe drag (to gain further clearance for brake drum removal, if necessary). For more details, refer to the rear brake adjustment procedure located in the beginning of this section.
6. Remove the grease cap covering the end of the axle shaft and hub nut.
7. Remove the cotter pin, locknut, retaining nut and washer from the stub axle.
8. Pull the brake drum and bearings off of the axle stub.

❋❋ WARNING

Be careful not to allow the bearings to drag across the threaded portion of the stub axle, otherwise new bearings may be needed upon installation.

To install:

➡Since the rear drum is off of the axle, this would be an excellent opportunity to regrease the rear wheel bearings. For more details, refer to Section 8.

Fig. 52 Use a small prytool to remove the grease cap from the brake drum . . .

Fig. 53 . . . then remove the old cotter pin with pliers

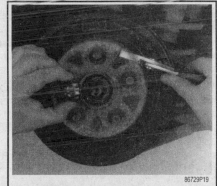
Fig. 54 Remove the nut lock from the end of the axle shaft, then . . .

Fig. 55 . . . loosen the axle shaft hub nut

Fig. 56 Remove the axle nut and washer from the axle shaft, then . . .

Fig. 57 . . . pull the brake drum and outboard bearing off of the axle together

Fig. 58 Once the brake drum is removed, the outboard bearing is easily removed

9. Slide the hub onto the stub axle, making sure that the inboard bearing is installed in the drum.

10. Install the outboard bearing over the axle shaft, then install the hub nut.

11. Tighten wheel bearing adjusting nut (hub nut) to 20–261 inch lbs. (27–34 Nm) while rotating the drum—this seats the bearings on the axle shaft. Back off (loosen) the adjusting nut ¼ turn (90°), then tighten the adjusting nut finger-tight.

12. Install the locknut on the axle shaft, then tighten against the hub nut until the locknut is snug and aligned with the hole in the axle shaft.

13. Install a new cotter pin and bend the cotter pin ends tightly against the axle tip.

INSPECTION

▶ **See Figure 59**

Whenever the rear brake drums are removed from the rear hubs, they should be inspected for damage or irregularities. Periodic inspection can help prevent dangerous conditions from developing to the point of personal injury, and can help maintain the quality of the vehicle's driving characteristics.

➡**Refer to the brake specification chart in this section for the model-specific specifications of the brake components.**

Measure drum run-out and diameter. If the drum is not to specifications, have the drum resurfaced. All brake drums will show markings of the maximum allowable diameter. All brake drums have markings for MINIMUM allowable thickness. Always use this specification as the minimum allowable thickness or refinishing limit. Refer to a local auto parts store or machine shop if necessary shop where brake drums are resurfaced.

Once the drum is removed from the axle shaft, clean the shoes and springs with a damp rag to remove the accumulated brake dust.

Fig. 59 The maximum allowable inside drum diameter is stamped on the outside

Do not use compressed air to blow brake dust off the linings or other brake system parts. Brake dust may contain asbestos, a known cancer causing agent.

Grease on the shoes can be removed with alcohol or fine sandpaper. After cleaning, examine the brake shoes for glazed, oily, loose, cracked or improperly (unevenly) worn linings. Light glazing is common and can be removed with fine sandpaper. Linings that are worn improperly or below specification (refer to the specification chart) should be replaced. A good "eyeball" test is to replace the linings when the thickness is the same as or less than the thickness of the metal backing plate (shoe).

Wheel cylinders are a vital part of the brake system and should be inspected carefully. Gently pull back the rubber boots; if any fluid is visible, it's time to replace the wheel cylinders. Boots that are distorted, cracked or otherwise damaged, also point to the need for service. Check the flexible brake lines for cracks, chafing or wear.

Check the brake shoe retracting and hold-down springs; they should not be worn or distorted. Be sure that the adjuster mechanism moves freely. The points on the backing plate where the shoes slide should be shiny and free of rust. Rust in these areas suggests that the brake shoes are not moving properly.

Brake Shoes

INSPECTION

For the inspection procedure for the rear brake shoes, refer to the inspection procedure of the rear brake drum portion of this section.

REMOVAL & INSTALLATION

1981–83 Models

1. Remove the brake drum. See the procedure earlier in this section.

2. Unhook the parking brake cable from the secondary (trailing) shoe.

3. Remove the shoe-to-anchor springs (retracting springs). They can be gripped and unhooked with a pair of pliers.

4. Remove the shoe hold down springs: compress them slightly and slide them off of the hold down pins.

5. Remove the adjuster screw assembly by spreading the shoes apart. The adjuster nut must be fully backed off.

6. Raise the parking brake lever. Pull the secondary (trailing) shoe away from the backing plate so pull-back spring tension is released.

7. Remove the secondary (trailing) shoe and disengage the spring end from the backing plate.

8. Raise the primary (leading) shoe to release spring tension. Remove the shoe and disengage the spring end from the backing plate.

9. Inspect the brakes (see procedures under Brake Drum Inspection).

To install:

10. Lubricate the six shoe contact areas on the brake backing plate and the web end of the brake shoe which contacts the anchor plate. Use a multi-purpose lubricant or a high temperature brake grease made for this purpose.

11. Chrysler recommends that the rear wheel bearings be cleaned and repacked whenever the brakes are renewed. Be sure to install a new bearing seal. Refer to the illustration in this section.

12. With the leading shoe return spring in position on the shoe, install the shoe at the same time as you engage the return spring in the end support.

13. Position the end of the shoe under the anchor.

14. With the trailing shoe return spring in position, install the shoe at the same time as you engage the spring in the support (backing plate).

15. Position the end of the shoe under the anchor.

16. Spread the shoes and install the adjuster screw assembly making sure that the forked end that enters the shoe is curved down.

17. Insert the shoe hold down spring pins and install the hold down springs.

18. Install the shoe-to-anchor springs.

19. Install the parking brake cable onto the parking brake lever.

20. Replace the brake drum and tighten the nut to 20–25 ft. lbs. (27–34 Nm) while rotating the wheel.

21. Back off the nut enough to release the bearing preload and position the locknut with one pair of slots aligned with the cotter pin hole. Refer to service procedures in this section.

22. Install the cotter pin. The end-play should be 0.001–0.003 in. (0.025–0.076mm).

23. Install the grease cap.

1984–95 Models

◆ See Figures 60 thru 66

✳✳ WARNING

On vehicles equipped with a Bendix Type 6 Anti-lock Brake System (ABS), a Diagnostic Readout Box (DRB or DRB II) is necessary for brake system bleeding. Failure to use a DRB to bleed the system will lead to system failure. Refer to the ABS portion of this section for bleeding procedures and precautions.

➡️If you are not thoroughly familiar with the procedures involved in brake replacement, disassemble and assemble one side at a time, leaving the other wheel intact, as a reference. This will reduce the risk of assembling the brakes incorrectly. Special brake tools are available to make this repair easier.

1. Remove the brake drum as described above. Remove the automatic adjuster spring by disconnecting the upper hook with a pair of pliers and then disconnecting it at the bottom. Then, remove the automatic adjuster lever.

2. Rotate the adjuster screw assembly to move each shoe out far enough to be free of the wheel cylinder boots.

3. Disconnect the parking brake cable from the parking brake actuating lever located at the brake mounting plate.

4. Remove the two shoe hold-down springs (use special brake tool if possible) by depressing and then turning each mounting washer so the narrow cut in the center of the clip is lined up with the locking bar. When the washer is properly lined up, slowly remove the tension and then remove the washer and spring.

5. Rock the shoes away from the wheel cylinder at the top and then loosen the adjustment on the automatic adjuster until tension is removed from the brake return spring (linking the tops of the shoes). Then, unhook and remove this spring. Unhook the shoe-to-shoe spring from the bottoms of the shoes, too.

6. Pull the shoes down and away from the support plate and remove them. In the case of the trailing shoe, use a suitable small lever to pull the C-clip off the retaining post. Remove the C-clip and the wave washer underneath, and then disconnect the parking brake lever at the shoe.

7. Clean the metal parts of the brake shoes and inspect them to ensure that they are not bent or severely worn. Inspect the lining to make sure it contacts the drum evenly. Also inspect it to make sure that the minimum lining thickness requirement shown in the Brake Specifications chart and any applicable state inspection standards for lining thickness are met. Always use these specifica-

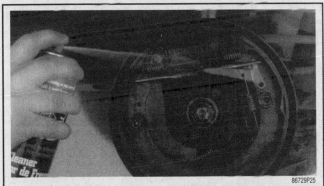

Fig. 60 Use an approved brake parts spray cleaner to remove the dust and dirt

Fig. 61 At this time, the brake shoes can be checked for wear. If deemed defective . . .

Fig. 62 . . . remove the brake shoes by first removing the adjuster lever spring . . .

Fig. 63 . . . then disconnect the parking brake cable from the parking brake lever

Fig. 64 Remove the 2 lower brake shoe retaining springs—special pliers make this job much easier

Fig. 65 At this point, the brake shoes and adjuster cylinder can be removed as an assembly

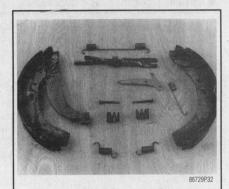

Fig. 66 To help ease installation, lay the parts out as you disassemble them

tions as a guide. Replace the brake shoes before damage to the brake drum starts.

To install:

8. Clean and inspect the brake support plate and the self-adjuster threads. Apply Multipurpose grease to the threads. Replace the self-adjuster if the threads are corroded. Inspect the springs for overheating (signs are burned paint or distorted end coils) and replace as necessary.

9. Lubricate all 8 contact areas of the support plate with Multipurpose grease. Insert the post of the parking brake lever through the trailing shoe. Install the wave washer and a new C-clip.

10. Attach the return (upper) spring between the two shoe assemblies; then install the brake automatic adjuster with the two stepped sides of the forks facing to the front or outboard sides of the shoes. The longer fork must face toward the rear.

11. Connect the shoe-to-shoe spring to the bottoms of the shoes. Then, expand the automatic adjuster assembly by turning the screw until the shoes are far enough apart that they will not disturb the wheel cylinder boots when installing them. Move the shoes upward and into position on the support plate, sliding the bottoms under the retaining clip at the bottom of the plate.

12. Install the hold-down springs by forcing the locks over the retainers and then turning them 90° to ensure they lock positively.

13. Install the automatic adjuster lever and its retaining spring. Connect the parking brake cable to the parking brake actuating lever on the mounting plate.

14. Adjust the automatic adjuster well inward so the brake drum can be installed without resistance.

➡ **Make sure the adjuster nut stays in contact with the tubular strut of the adjuster when you do this.**

15. Install the brake drum. Readjust the wheel bearings as described in Section 8 and install a new cotter pin. Install the wheel and torque the bolts.

16. After lowering the car, pump the brake pedal several times to adjust the brakes. When there is adequate pedal, road test the car in an isolated area at lower speeds applying the brakes repeatedly to ensure that they are performing well and to complete the adjustment. Refer to the necessary service procedures in this book.

Wheel Cylinders

INSPECTION

For the inspection procedure for the rear brake wheel cylinders, refer to the inspection procedure of the rear brake drum portion of this section.

REMOVAL & INSTALLATION

✳✳ WARNING

On vehicles equipped with a Bendix Type 6 Anti-lock Brake System (ABS), a Diagnostic Readout Box (DRB or DRB II) is necessary for brake system bleeding. Failure to use a DRB to bleed the system will lead to system failure. Refer to the ABS portion of this section for bleeding procedures and precautions.

1. Raise and safely support the vehicle on jackstands.
2. Remove the brake drums, as described earlier in this section.
3. Visually inspect the wheel cylinder boots for signs of excessive leakage. Replace any boots that are torn or broken.

➡ **A slight amount of fluid on the boots may not be a leak but may be preservative fluid used at the factory.**

4. If a leak has been discovered, remove the brake shoes and check for contamination. Replace the linings if they are soaked with grease or brake fluid.
5. Disconnect the brake line from the wheel cylinder.
6. Remove the wheel cylinder attaching bolts, then pull the wheel cylinder out of its support.

To install:

7. Position the wheel cylinder onto the backing plate and install the retaining nuts to 75 inch lbs. (8.4 Nm).
8. Attach the brake line to the wheel cylinder. Start the fitting by hand to

prevent crossthreading it in the wheel cylinder. Tighten the brake line fitting to 115–170 inch lbs. (13–19 Nm).

9. Install the brake drums and adjust the brake shoes, as described earlier in this section.

10. Bleed the brake system, as described earlier in this section.

Brake Backing Plate

REMOVAL & INSTALLATION

▶ **See Figure 67**

✳✳ WARNING

On vehicles equipped with a Bendix Type 6 Anti-lock Brake System (ABS), a Diagnostic Readout Box (DRB or DRB II) is necessary for brake system bleeding. Failure to use a DRB to bleed the system will lead to system failure. Refer to the ABS portion of this section for bleeding procedures and precautions.

1. Slightly loosen the rear lug nuts.
2. Raise and safely support the rear of the vehicle on jackstands.
3. Remove the drum cap, cotter pin, washer, locknut and adjusting nut, then remove the brake drum.
4. Disconnect the adjuster lever spring.
5. Disconnect the brake line from the rear brake cylinder. Plug the brake line to keep the brake fluid from becoming contaminated.
6. Disconnect the parking brake cable from the brake lever. Compress the parking brake cable clip (using a 14mm box wrench over the clip compresses all three retaining fingers). Pull the cable out of the backing plate, then remove the backing plate from the vehicle.
7. Remove the backing plate attaching bolts and washers, then separate the backing plate and spindle from the rear support trailing arm.

To install:

8. Lubricate the brake shoe contact points on the backing plate with brake lubricant or moly grease.
9. Insert the parking brake cable into the backing plate.
10. Install the backing plate, gasket and spindle onto the rear suspension member. Tighten the backing plate bolts to 53 ft. lbs. (71 Nm).
11. Attach the parking brake cable to the brake lever.
12. Connect the brake tube to the rear wheel cylinder. Tighten the brake fitting to 13 ft. lbs. (17 Nm).
13. Install the brake drum. For more details, refer to the brake drum installation procedure located earlier in this section.
14. Adjust and bleed the brake system before driving anywhere.
15. Adjust the parking brake **after** adjusting the service brakes.
16. Install the wheels and tighten the lug nuts until snug.
17. Lower the vehicle.
18. Tighten the lug nuts to the specified value in the torque chart in Section 8.

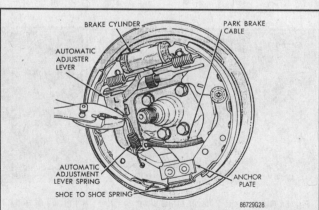

Fig. 67 The backing plate and stub axle is attached to the trailing arm by 4 bolts

REAR DISC BRAKES

✳ CAUTION

Brake shoes may contain asbestos, which has been determined to be a cancer-causing agent. Never clean the brake surfaces with compressed air! Avoid inhaling any dust from any brake surface! When cleaning brake surfaces, use a commercially available brake cleaning fluid.

Brake Pads

REMOVAL & INSTALLATION

1988 Models

◆ See Figures 68, 69, 70, 71 and 72

✳ WARNING

On vehicles equipped with a Bendix Type 6 Anti-lock Brake System (ABS), a Diagnostic Readout Box (DRB or DRD II) is necessary for brake system bleeding. Failure to use a DRB to bleed the system will lead to system failure. Refer to the ABS portion of this section for bleeding procedures and precautions.

➡You'll need a metric size Allen wrench (4mm) to perform this operation.

1. Slightly loosen the rear wheel lug nuts.
2. Raise rear of the vehicle and support it securely on jackstands.

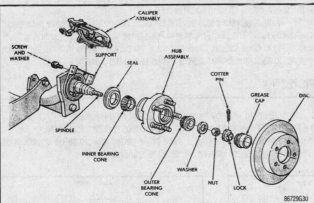

Fig. 68 Exploded view of the rear disc brake assembly—1988 models

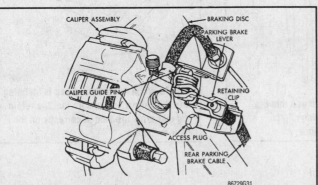

Fig. 69 Before disassembling the caliper components, familiarize yourself with their location and mounting position

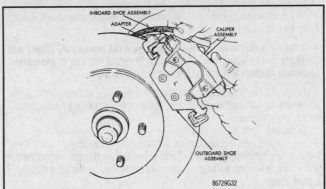

Fig. 70 When the caliper is lifted off of the rear disc, the outboard pad will remain on the brake adapter

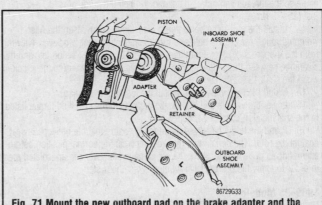

Fig. 71 Mount the new outboard pad on the brake adapter and the new inboard pad on the caliper

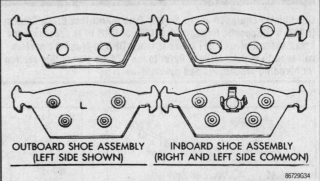

Fig. 72 The brake pads are easily identifiable by their backside markings

3. Remove the rear wheels.
4. There is an access plug on the inboard side of the caliper that looks like an ordinary bolt. It is located just under the parking brake cable lever. Clean the plug and the area around it to keep dirt out of the caliper and then remove it.
5. Install the 4mm Allen wrench into the access hole and turn it counterclockwise to retract the pads from the disc. Turn the retractor a few turns: just until there is daylight between the disc and the pads.
6. Remove the anti-rattle spring by prying it off the outside of the caliper with a small, blunt instrument. Be careful to pry outward on the spring only far enough to release it; if the spring is pried excessively, it may be damaged.
7. Clean the guide pin heads and the areas around them of dirt, then loosen them. Pull them out just far enough to free the caliper from the adapter, if it is not necessary to replace the caliper bushings. If the bushings are to be replaced, remove the guide pins completely.

8. Lift the caliper (and the inboard pad, which will remain with it) upward and away from the braking disc and then suspend it securely on a piece of wire to prevent putting excessive stress on the brake hose.

9. Pull the inboard pad away from the caliper piston to remove it. Pull the outboard pad off of the caliper adapter.

➡In the following step, be careful to retract the piston very slowly and carefully and by using only a minimum of force. The use of excessive force will damage the retraction and actuation shafts.

10. Insert the Allen wrench into the rear access hole and retract the piston all the way by turning the wrench very gently and only until the rotating effort very slightly increases.

To install:

11. Install a new inboard brake pad to the bore of the caliper piston. Then, install a new outboard pad, marked with either an **L** or **R**, according to the side of the vehicle you are working on. This pad is installed by sliding it onto the caliper adapter.

12. Lower the caliper over the disc and outboard pad. Gently and cautiously turn the guide pins in order to start them in their threads without cross-threading them. Use a minimum amount of force and allow the pins to find their own angle so the threads will not be damaged. Tighten the guide pins to 18–26 ft. lbs. (25–35 Nm).

13. Install the anti-rattle spring onto the caliper. Then, insert the Allen wrench through the access hole and turn the retraction shaft clockwise (viewing from the inboard side) just until there is a slight amount of tension felt, and the clearance between the pads and disc is removed. Then, loosen (counterclockwise) the shaft ⅓ (120°) turn.

14. Install the rear wheels and install the lug nuts until snug.

15. Lower the vehicle and tighten the lug nuts to the specified torque listed in the specification chart in Section 8.

16. Pump the brake pedal several times to ensure that the brake pads seat against the rotor. The pedal must give resistance at the normal position before attempting to drive the car. Drive the car at moderate speeds in an isolated area in order to apply the brakes several times to test the system.

1989–95 Models

▶ **See Figures 73, 74 and 75**

> ❋❋ **WARNING**
>
> On vehicles equipped with a Bendix Type 6 Anti-lock Brake System (ABS), a Diagnostic Readout Box (DRB or DRB II) is necessary for brake system bleeding. Failure to use a DRB to bleed the system will lead to system failure. Refer to the ABS portion of this section for bleeding procedures and precautions.

➡All brake pins, shims and other parts removed must be reinstalled in the proper location. Record their locations before removing any brake hardware. On vehicles equipped with ABS, refer to the necessary service procedures later in this section.

1. Remove some of the fluid from the master cylinder.
2. Slightly loosen the rear wheel lug nuts.
3. Raise the vehicle and support safely on jackstands.
4. Remove the rear wheels.
5. Remove the hold-down spring, if equipped.
6. Remove the caliper mounting pin bolts. Lift the caliper off the rotor assembly.
7. Remove the outboard pad by prying the shoe retaining clip over the raised area of the caliper. Slide the pad down and off of the caliper.
8. Pull the inboard pad away from the piston until the retaining clip is free from the piston cavity.

➡Support the caliper with strong wire or cord from the vehicle frame to prevent the weight of the caliper from damaging the flexible hose.

To install:

9. Use a large C-clamp, slowly compress the piston back into the caliper bore.

10. Install the inner pad to the caliper by centering the retaining clamp in the caliper piston bore and seating the pad against the piston.

11. Install the outer pad by sliding the retaining clip over the caliper fingers. Be sure that the brake pad is installed on the caliper so that the retaining clip is past the raised area on the caliper fingers.

12. Position the caliper over the rotor so the caliper engages the adapter correctly (the lower tabs on the brake pads and the casting projections on the caliper are under the adapter rail). Tighten the guide pin bolts to 16 ft. lbs. (22 Nm).

13. Install the hold-down spring, if removed.
14. Refill the master cylinder as necessary.
15. Install the rear wheels and install the lug nuts until snug.
16. Lower the vehicle and tighten the lug nuts to the specified torque listed in the specification chart in Section 8.
17. Pump the brake pedal several times to ensure that the brake pads seat against the rotor. The pedal must give resistance at the normal position before attempting to drive the car. Drive the car at moderate speeds in an isolated area in order to apply the brakes several times to test the system.

INSPECTION

Measure lining wear by measuring the combined thickness of the shoe and the lining at its thinnest point. Refer to the brake specifications chart for the minimum brake lining thickness. If the brake pads are worn below specification, or is excessively worn uneven, replace the rear brake pads.

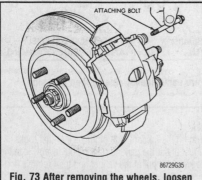

Fig. 73 After removing the wheels, loosen and remove the 2 attaching bolts from the caliper assembly

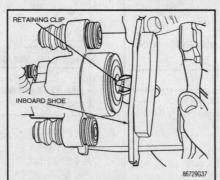

Fig. 74 Install the inboard pad into the caliper so that the retaining clip is inserted into the piston bore

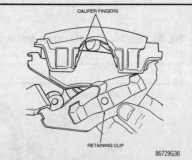

Fig. 75 When the outboard pad is installed into the caliper, make sure that the retaining clip arms are seated correctly on the caliper fingers

➡Whenever the disc brake pad is to be replaced, replace the pads on both rear wheels as a set.

Brake Caliper

REMOVAL & INSTALLATION

1988 Models

◆ See Figures 68, 69, 70, 71 and 72

❊❊ WARNING

On vehicles equipped with a Bendix Type 6 Anti-lock Brake System (ABS), a Diagnostic Readout Box (DRB or DRB II) is necessary for brake system bleeding. Failure to use a DRB to bleed the system will lead to system failure. Refer to the ABS portion of this section for bleeding procedures and precautions.

➡You'll need a metric size Allen wrench (4mm) to perform this operation.

1. Slightly loosen the rear wheel lug nuts.
2. Raise rear of the vehicle and support it securely on jackstands.
3. Remove the rear wheels.
4. There is an access plug on the inboard side of the caliper that looks like an ordinary bolt. It is located just under the parking brake cable lever. Clean the plug and the area around it to keep dirt out of the caliper and then remove it.
5. Install the 4mm Allen wrench into the access hole and turn it counter-clockwise to retract the pads from the disc. Turn the retractor a few turns; just until there is daylight between the disc and the pads.
6. Remove the anti-rattle spring by prying it off the outside of the caliper with a small, blunt instrument. Be careful to pry outward on the spring only far enough to release it; if the spring is pried excessively, it may be damaged.
7. Clean the guide pin heads and the areas around them of dirt, then loosen them. Pull them out just far enough to free the caliper from the adapter, if it is not necessary to replace the caliper bushings. If the bushings are to be replaced, remove the guide pins completely.
8. Lift the caliper (and the inboard pad, which will remain with it) upward and away from the braking disc and then suspend it securely on a piece of wire to prevent putting excessive stress on the brake hose.
9. Pull the inboard pad away from the caliper piston to remove it. Pull the outboard pad off of the caliper adapter.

➡In the following step, be careful to retract the piston very slowly and carefully and by using only a minimum of force. The use of excessive force will damage the retraction and actuation shafts.

10. Insert the Allen wrench into the rear access hole and retract the piston all the way by turning the wrench very gently and only until the rotating effort very slightly increases.
11. Disconnect the brake line from the caliper, then immediately plug the brake line.
12. Remove the brake caliper from the vehicle.

To install:

13. Install a new inboard brake pad to the bore of the caliper piston. Then, install a new outboard pad, marked with either an **L** or **R**, according to the side of the vehicle you are working on. This pad is installed by sliding it onto the caliper adapter.
14. Lower the caliper over the disc and outboard pad. Gently and cautiously turn the guide pins in order to start them in their threads without cross-threading them. Use a minimum amount of force and allow the pins to find their own angle so the threads will not be damaged. Tighten the guide pins to 18–26 ft. lbs. (25–35 Nm).
15. Install the anti-rattle spring onto the caliper. Then, insert the Allen wrench through the access hole and turn the retraction shaft clockwise (viewing from the inboard side) just until there is a slight amount of tension felt, and the clearance between the pads and disc is removed. Then, loosen (counterclockwise) the shaft ⅓ (120°) turn.
16. Attach brake line to the rear brake caliper. Tighten the rear brake line fitting to 16 ft. lbs. (22 Nm). Bleed the brake system.

➡New seal washers must always be used when installing the brake hose to the caliper.

17. Install the rear wheels and install the lug nuts until snug.
18. Lower the vehicle and tighten the lug nuts to the specified torque listed in the specification chart in Section 8.
19. Pump the brake pedal several times to ensure that the brake pads seat against the rotor. The pedal must give resistance at the normal position before attempting to drive the car. Drive the car at moderate speeds in an isolated area in order to apply the brakes several times to test the system.

1989–95 Models

◆ See Figures 73, 74 and 75

❊❊ WARNING

On vehicles equipped with a Bendix Type 6 Anti-lock Brake System (ABS), a Diagnostic Readout Box (DRB or DRB II) is necessary for brake system bleeding. Failure to use a DRB to bleed the system will lead to system failure. Refer to the ABS portion of this section for bleeding procedures and precautions.

➡All brake pins, shims and other parts removed must be reinstalled in the proper location. Record their locations before removing any brake hardware. On vehicles equipped with ABS, refer to the necessary service procedures later in this section.

1. Remove some of the fluid from the master cylinder.
2. Slightly loosen the rear wheel lug nuts.
3. Raise the vehicle and support safely on jackstands.
4. Remove the rear wheels.
5. Remove the hold-down spring, if equipped.
6. Remove the caliper mounting pin bolts. Lift the caliper off the rotor assembly.
7. Remove the outboard pad by prying the shoe retaining clip over the raised area of the caliper. Slide the pad down and off of the caliper.
8. Pull the inboard pad away from the piston until the retaining clip is free from the piston cavity.

➡Support the caliper with strong wire or cord from the vehicle frame to prevent the weight of the caliper from damaging the flexible hose.

9. If the caliper is to be overhauled (rebuilt), perform the following:
   a. Place a small piece of wood between the piston and caliper fingers.
   b. Carefully depress the brake pedal to hydraulically push the piston out of the bore. The brake pedal will fall away when the piston has passed the bore opening. Then prop the brake pedal to any position below the first inch (25mm) of pedal travel: this will prevent the loss of brake fluid from the master cylinder.
   c. If both rear calipers are to be removed and overhauled, disconnect the flexible brake line at the frame bracket after removing the piston. Plug the brake tube and remove the piston from the opposite caliper, using the same process as above for the first piston removal.

❊❊ CAUTION

Under no condition should air pressure be used to remove the piston from the caliper bore. Personal injury could result.

   d. Disconnect the flexible brake hose from the caliper.
   e. For the overhaul, mount the caliper in a bench-mounted vise.
10. If the caliper is simply going to be replaced with a new one, disconnect the flexible brake hose from the caliper. Immediately plug the brake hose, to stop any brake fluid leakage and keep the fluid from becoming contaminated.

To install:

11. Connect the brake tube to the caliper. Tighten the brake hose-to-caliper banjo bolt to 24 ft. lbs. (33 Nm).

➡New seal washers must always be used when installing the brake hose to the caliper.

12. Use a large C-clamp, slowly compress the piston back into the caliper bore.
13. Install the inner pad to the caliper by centering the retaining clamp in the caliper piston bore and seating the pad against the piston.

14. Install the outer pad by sliding the retaining clip over the caliper fingers. Be sure that the brake pad is installed on the caliper so that the retaining clip is past the raised area on the caliper fingers.

15. Position the caliper over the rotor so the caliper engages the adapter correctly (the lower tabs on the brake pads and the casting projections on the caliper are under the adapter rail). Tighten the guide pin bolts to 16 ft. lbs. (22 Nm).

16. Install the hold-down spring, if removed.

17. Refill the master cylinder as necessary.

18. Install the rear wheels and install the lug nuts until snug.

19. Lower the vehicle and tighten the lug nuts to the specified torque listed in the specification chart in Section 8.

20. Pump the brake pedal several times to ensure that the brake pads seat against the rotor. The pedal must give resistance at the normal position before attempting to drive the car. Drive the car at moderate speeds in an isolated area in order to apply the brakes several times to test the system.

OVERHAUL

▶ See Figures 76 and 77

Rear disc brake calipers are not overhauled, but are replaced on most vehicles. Check with local Auto Supply store or Dealership for the availability of service related parts. Only the dust boots and guide pin bushings are serviced, as described here. If a new caliper assembly complete with dust boots and guide pin bushings is to be installed, make sure to transfer usable pads and related parts and replace those which are worn.

1. Disconnect and plug the brake line. Disconnect the parking brake cable retaining clips from the hanger bracket and caliper. Disconnect the cable at the parking brake lever. Then, remove the caliper.

2. Check the caliper dust boot and inboard pad area for piston seal leaks. If there is a visible leak, the caliper must be replaced (they are not serviceable).

3. Inspect the dust boot and the caliper pin bushings. Replace them if they are damaged, dry, or brittle.

4. Clean the area around the dust boot with alcohol or a suitable solvent and wipe it dry. Remove the dust boot retainer with a finger or a blunt instrument and remove the dust boot from the caliper and piston grooves and discard it.

5. Clean the grooves in the piston and caliper and then coat a new boot with clean brake fluid, leaving a heavy coating inside. Position the boot over the piston and into the grooves of both piston and caliper. Install a boot retainer over the groove in the caliper.

6. Pry the bushings from the caliper with a small, dull tool. Discard the bushings and Teflon® sleeves.

7. Remove the Teflon® sleeves from new bushings. Install the bushings by putting pressure on their flanges with the fingers to press them in until seated. Reinstall the Teflon® sleeves.

8. Install the caliper as described above. Connect the brake hose, torquing the banjo bolt to 19–29 ft. lbs. (26–39 Nm).

9. Bleed the brake system. Pump the brake pedal several times to ensure that the brake pads seat against the rotor. The pedal must give resistance at the normal position before attempting to drive the car. Drive the car at moderate speeds in an isolated area in order to apply the brakes several times to test the system.

Brake Disc (Rotor)

REMOVAL & INSTALLATION

▶ See Figure 78

1. Remove the brake caliper and pads as described earlier in this section.

➡ Do not disconnect the rear brake hose and make sure to hang the caliper from the vehicle's frame with strong wire or cord.

2. The rear brake rotor is held in place by the wheel and wheel nuts. In some cases, the rotor is also held onto the rear axle hub with 2 or 3 retaining nuts (on the wheel lug studs).

3. 1988 models have a rear brake adapter which must be removed before the rotor can be pulled off of the hub. Remove the 2 mounting bolts from the rear and separate the adapter from the brake assembly.

4. Before removing the rotor, matchmark it and one adjacent wheel stud so it may be installed in the same position.

5. After removing the retaining nuts, if applicable, the rotor can simply be pulled off the studs.

To install:

6. Slide the new rotor onto the hub studs so that the matchmarks line up. If retaining nuts were used to retain the rotor, install the retaining nuts until snug.

7. If applicable, install the brake adapter. Tighten the adapter mounting bolts to 130–190 ft. lbs. (176–258 Nm).

8. Install the brake caliper and pads. For more details, refer to the caliper installation procedure located earlier in this section.

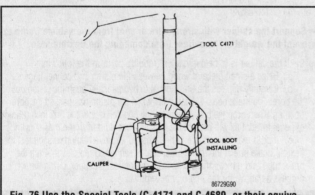

Fig. 76 Use the Special Tools (C-4171 and C-4689, or their equivalents) to install the new dust boot

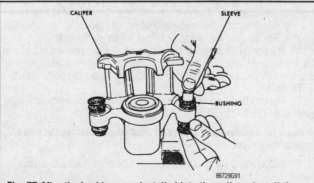

Fig. 77 After the bushings are installed into the caliper, install the Teflon® sleeves into the bushings

Fig. 78 Some rotors are held onto the axle flanges by retaining washers

INSPECTION

♦ **See Figures 79, 80 and 81**

Inspect the disc for scoring, rust, impregnated lining material and ridges, and replace or machine it if serious problems in these areas are visible. Take the following specific measurements:

1. With the wheel removed, install the lug nuts to hold the disc snugly in place against the hub. Then, mount a dial indicator so it will read run-out about 1 in. (25.4mm) from the outer edge of the rotor. Zero the indicator, rotate the disc, and read the maximum reading. Compare the reading with the specification in the brake specification chart located at the end of this section.

2. If the specification is excessive, remove the rotor and repeat the process, this time mounting the indicator so as to measure the run-out of the hub. This must not exceed 0.003 in. (0.076mm). If it does, the hub requires replacement. If hub run-out meets the specification and disc run-out does not, replace the disc or have it machined, if it can be trued up while maintaining minimum thickness specifications (stamped on an unmachined surface). Note that this specification includes 0.030 in. (0.76mm) wear beyond the maximum machining limit of 0.030 in. (0.76mm) from original thickness.

3. Use a micrometer to measure disc thickness at 4 locations. Thickness variation must not exceed 0.0005 in. (0.013mm). If thickness variation can be corrected by machining the disc while maintaining maximum thickness limits, this may be done.

All brake discs or rotors have markings for MINIMUM allowable thickness cast on an unmachined surface or an alternate surface. Always use this specification as the minimum allowable thickness or refinishing limit. Refer to a local auto parts store or machine shop if necessary shop where brake disc or rotors are resurfaced.

If the brake disc or rotor needs to be replaced with a new part, the protective coating on the braking surface of the rotor must be removed with an appropriate solvent.

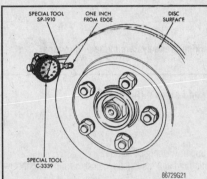

Fig. 79 Use Special Tool SP-1910, or a similar dial indicator, to check the disc for run-out (warpage/wobble), but . . .

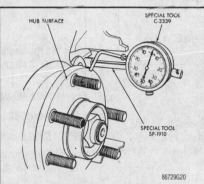

Fig. 80 . . . before condemning the disc as defective, also check the hub for run-out in a similar manner

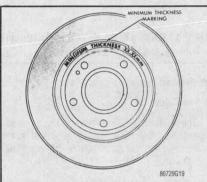

Fig. 81 The rear disc brake rotors have the minimum allowable thickness stamped right on them

PARKING BRAKE

Cable

ADJUSTMENT

With Foot Lever

♦ **See Figures 82 and 83**

➡The rear service brakes must be properly adjusted before adjusting the parking brake. For more details, refer to the brake adjusting procedures in the beginning of this section.

1. Release the parking brake lever.
2. Raise and safely support the rear of the vehicle on jackstands.
3. Back off the parking brake cable adjuster nut so that there is slack in the cable. Before loosening cable adjusting nut, clean and lubricate the threads.

➡The parking brake cable adjuster nut is located under the passenger's side of the vehicle, approximately at the vehicle's mid-point.

4. Tighten the parking brake adjuster nut (after service brake adjustment, if necessary) until a slight drag is felt while rotating the rear wheels.
5. Loosen the cable adjuster nut until the rear wheels can be rotated freely (no brake drag is felt or heard), then back the cable adjuster nut off 2 full turns.
6. Apply and release the parking brake several times.
7. Test the parking brake. The rear wheels should rotate freely without dragging when parking brake is released, and the parking brake should hold the vehicle on a slight incline (transaxle in Neutral).

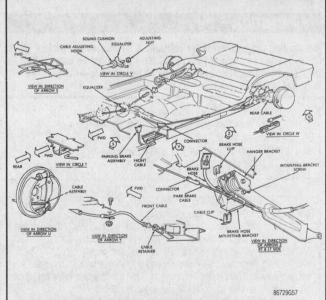

Fig. 82 Routing of the parking brake system cables—LeBaron Sedan, Spirit, Acclaim, Sundance and Shadow

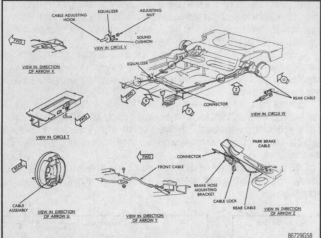

Fig. 83 Routing of the parking brake system cables—New Yorker, Dynasty, Imperial and Fifth Ave.

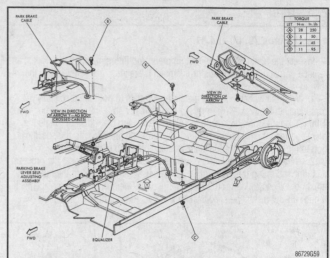

Fig. 84 Routing of the parking brake system cables—Daytona, LeBaron (AJ Body)

With Hand Lever

▶ See Figure 84

The parking brake hand lever contains a self-adjusting loaded clock spring feature. Routine parking brake adjustment is not required. Refer to the parking brake cable removal and installation procedure later in this section for additional information.

REMOVAL & INSTALLATION

➡ The 1990–95 Daytona, LeBaron Coupe and LeBaron Convertible utilize a one-piece cable rather than several cables (as with all of the other vehicles).

1990–93 Daytona and LeBaron (AJ Body)

▶ See Figure 84

☀ CAUTION

The parking brake hand lever contains a self-adjusting loaded clock spring loaded to about 30 lbs. (133 N). Care must be taken when handling components in the vicinity of the hand lever or serious personal injury may result.

1. Disconnect the negative battery cable.
2. Disengage the cable from the equalizer bracket in the console.
3. Lift the carpet and floor matting and remove the floor pan seal.
4. Separate the cable from the rear parking brake shoes lever.
5. Pull the cable through the hole and remove.

To install:

6. Install the cable and connect to the rear shoes and equalizer bracket. Install the floor pan seal and position the carpet.
7. To reload, lockout and adjust the system:
   a. Pull on the equalizer output cable with at least 30 lbs. (133 N) pressure to wind up the spring. Continue until the self-adjuster lockout pawl is positioned about midway between the self-adjuster sector.
   b. Rotate the lockout pawl into the self-adjuster sector by turning the Allen screw clockwise. This action requires very little effort; do not force the screw.
   c. Adjust the rear drum-in-hat parking brake shoes.
   d. Turn the Allen screw counterclockwise about 15 degrees. When turning the lockout device, self-adjuster release is a snapping noise followed by a detent that should be felt. Very light effort is required to seat the lockout device into the detent. Make sure to follow through into the detent.
   e. Cycle the lever a few times to complete the adjustment. The wheels should rotate freely.
8. Connect the negative battery cable and check the parking brakes for proper operation.

Except 1990–93 Daytona and LeBaron (AJ Body)

▶ See Figures 82 and 83

FRONT CABLE

1. Jack up your car and support it with jack stands.
2. Loosen the cable adjusting nut and disengage the cable from the connectors.
3. Lift the floor mat for access to the floor pan.
4. Remove the floor pan seal panel.
5. Pull the cable end forward and disconnect it from the clevis.
6. Pull the cable assembly through the hole.
7. Installation is the reverse of removal.
8. Adjust the service and parking brakes.

REAR CABLE (DRUM BRAKES)

1. Jack up your vehicle and support it with jack stands.
2. Remove the rear wheels.
3. Remove the brake drums.
4. Back off the cable adjuster to provide slack in the cable.
5. Compress the retainers on the end of the cable and remove the cable from the brake backing plate or support plate. A worm gear type hose clamp can be used for this procedure (remove the clamp before removing the brake cable assembly from the support plate).
6. Disconnect the cable from the brake shoe lever.
7. Remove the clip from brake cable at support bracket. Pull the brake cable from the trailing arm.
8. Installation is the reverse of removal. Adjust the service and parking brakes.

REAR CABLE (DISC BRAKES)

1. Jack up your vehicle and support it with jack stands. Back off the cable adjuster to provide slack in the cable.
2. Remove the rear wheels.
3. Remove the brake caliper and disc assembly.
4. Compress the retainers on the end of the cable and remove the cable from the adapter. A worm gear type hose clamp can be used for this procedure (remove the clamp before removing the brake cable assembly from the adapter).
5. Remove the clip from brake cable at support bracket. Pull the brake cable from the trailing arm.
6. Installation is the reverse of removal. Be sure that the retainers on the brake cable are expanded around the mounting hole in adapter. Adjust the parking brake shoe diameter to 6.75 in. (171.5mm). Install the brake disc, caliper and wheel/tire assembly.

Parking Brake Shoes

REMOVAL, INSTALLATION & ADJUSTMENT

▶ See Figures 85, 86, 87, 88 and 89

This procedure only refers to vehicle equipped with rear disc brakes. The drum brake shoes do function also as the parking brake shoes, but the removal of the drum brake shoes is covered in the rear drum brake portion of this section.

1. Remove the caliper from the disc assembly. Refer to the necessary service procedures in this section.
2. Remove the brake disc from the hub assembly. Refer to the necessary service procedures in this section.

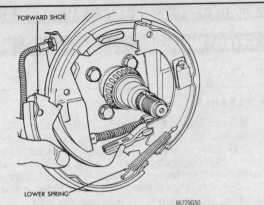

Fig. 88 Remove the forward brake shoe and the lower spring from the rearward brake shoe

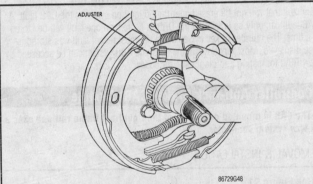

Fig. 85 Use a pair of pliers to remove the brake shoe hold-down clip, then . . .

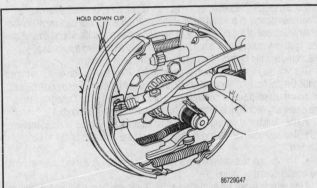

Fig. 86 . . . remove the adjuster assembly from in between the two brake shoes

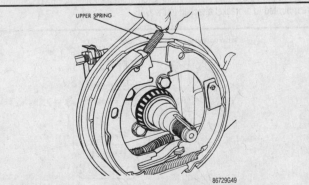

Fig. 87 Remove the upper spring after the adjuster assembly is removed

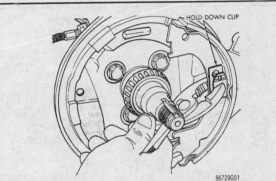

Fig. 89 Use the pliers to remove the hold-down clip on the rearward brake shoe, then remove the shoe from the backing plate

3. Remove the grease cap, cotter pin, lock nut, retaining nut and washer.
4. Remove the hub and bearing assembly.
5. Remove the forward hold down clip on brake shoes.
6. Turn adjuster wheel until adjuster is at shortest length. Remove the adjuster assembly.
7. Remove the upper shoe to shoe spring. Pull front shoe away from anchor and remove the front shoe and lower spring.
8. Remove the rear hold-down clip and shoe.

To install:

9. Install rear shoe and hold-down clip.
10. Install the lower shoe to shoe spring. Pull forward shoe over anchor block until properly located on adapter.
11. Install upper shoe to shoe spring. Install adjuster assembly (grease threads with suitable grease before installation) with star wheel forward.
12. Install front hold-down clip.
13. Adjust parking brake shoe diameter to 6.75 inch (171mm). Install hub assembly on the spindle.
14. Install outer bearing, thrust washer and nut. Tighten wheel bearing adjusting nut to 20–261 inch lbs. (27–34 Nm) while rotating hub this seats the bearing.
15. Back off adjusting nut ¼ turn or 90° then tighten adjusting nut finger tight.
16. Position locknut with a pair of slots in line with cotter pin. Install cotter pin, always use a NEW cotter pin upon installation.
17. Install grease cap, brake disc, caliper and wheel/tire assemblies.
18. Test the parking brake. The rear wheels should rotate freely without dragging when parking brake is released. To check operation, make sure the parking brake holds on an incline.

BENDIX TYPE 4 AND TYPE 6 ANTI-LOCK BRAKE SYSTEMS

General Information

SYSTEM IDENTIFICATION

▶ See Figure 90

The Bendix Type 4 Anti-lock Brake System (ABS) was an option on the 1993½–95 LeBaron, Spirit, Acclaim, Daytona, Sundance and Shadow. The 1988–93½ LeBaron, Daytona, Spirit, Acclaim, Shadow and Sundance had an option of coming equipped with the Bendix Type 6 ABS. The Dynasty came equipped with one of two systems, depending on the model-year of the vehicle: 1988–90 models came with Bosch III ABS, 1991–93 models came with Bendix Type 10 ABS. For the Dynasty ABS procedures, refer to the Bosch III ABS/Bendix Type 10 ABS portion of this section.

All procedures presented should be considered applicable for both the Type 4 and Type 6 systems, unless otherwise noted.

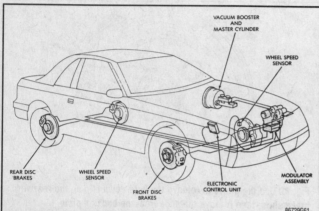

Fig. 90 Four wheel Anti-lock Brake System (ABS) on 1988–93½ LeBaron, Spirit, Acclaim and Daytona

SYSTEM OPERATION

When conventional brakes are applied in an emergency stop or on ice, one or more wheels may lock. This may result in loss of steering control and vehicle stability. The purpose of the Bendix Type 4 Anti-lock Brake System (ABS) is to prevent lock up under heavy braking conditions. This system offers the driver increased safety and control during braking. Anti-lock braking operates only at speeds above 3 mph (5 km/h).

Under normal braking conditions, the ABS functions the same as a standard brake system with a diagonally split master cylinder and conventional vacuum assist.

If wheel locking tendency is detected during application, the system will enter anti-lock mode. During anti-lock mode, hydraulic pressure in the four wheel circuits is modulated to prevent any wheel from locking. Each wheel circuit is designed with a set of electrical valves and hydraulic line to provide modulation, although for vehicle stability, both rear wheel valves receive the same electrical signal. The system can build or reduce pressure at each wheel, depending on signals generated by the Wheel Speed Sensors (WSS) at each wheel and received at the Controller Anti-lock Brake (CAB).

PRECAUTIONS

Failure to observe the following precautions may result in system damage:
• Before performing electric arc welding on the vehicle, disconnect the control module and the hydraulic unit connectors.
• When performing painting work on the vehicle, do not expose the control module to temperatures in excess of 185°F (85°C) for longer than 2 hours. The system may be exposed to temperatures up to 200°F (95°C) for less than 15 minutes.

• Never disconnect or connect the control module or hydraulic modulator connectors with the ignition switch ON.
• Never disassemble any component of the Anti-Lock Brake System (ABS) which is designated unserviceable; the component must be replaced as an assembly.
• When filling the master cylinder, always use brake fluid which meets DOT-3 specifications; petroleum-based fluid will destroy the rubber parts.
• Working on ABS system requires extreme amount of mechanical ability, training and special tools. If you are not familiar have your vehicle repaired by a certified mechanic or refer to a more advanced publication on this subject.

SYSTEM/COMPONENT TESTING

For the proper diagnostic procedure for either the entire ABS system or a single component of the system, a scan tool (DRB, DRB II or equivalent) is necessary. Because of the complexity of the ABS system and the importance of correct system functioning, it is a good idea to have a qualified automotive mechanic test the system if any problems have been detected.

The self-diagnostic ABS start up cycle begins when the ignition switch is turned to the **On** position. An electrical check is completed on the ABS components, such as the wheel speed sensor continuity and other relay continuity. During this check the amber anti-lock light is turned on for approximately 1–2 seconds.

Further functional testing is accomplished once the vehicle is set in motion.
• The solenoid valves and the pump/motor are activated briefly to verify function
• The voltage output from the wheel speed sensors is verified to be within the correct operating range

If the vehicle is not set in motion within 3 minutes from the time the ignition switch is set in the **ON** position, the solenoid test is bypassed, but the pump/motor is activated briefly to verify that it is operating correctly.

Fault codes are kept in a non-volatile memory until either erased by the DRB II or erased automatically after 50 ignition cycles (key **ON-OFF** cycles). The only fault that will not be erased after the 50 ignition cycles is the CAB fault. A CAB fault can only be erased by the DRB II. More than one fault can be stored at a time. The number of key cycles since the most recent fault was stored is also displayed. Most functions of the CAB and ABS system can be accessed by the DRB II for testing and diagnostic purposes.

Controller Anti-lock Brake (CAB) Module

➡The CAB is mounted on the top of the right front frame rail and uses a 60-way system connector.

REMOVAL & INSTALLATION

▶ See Figure 91

1. Turn the ignition switch **OFF**.
2. Disconnect the negative battery cable.
3. Unplug the wiring harness connectors from the Anti-Lock relays, which are mounted to a bracket attached to the CAB.

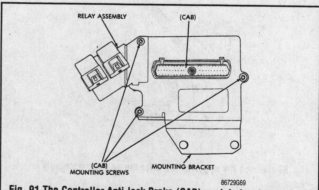

Fig. 91 The Controller Anti-lock Brake (CAB) module has two anti-lock relays mounted to it

4. Detach the wiring harness connector 60-way connector from the CAB.

5. Remove the 2 CAB module mounting bracket-to-frame rail bolts.

6. Remove the CAB from the vehicle.

7. Remove the 3 CAB module-to-bracket mounting screws, then remove the CAB module from the bracket.

8. Installation is the reverse of the removal procedure.

9. Connect the battery cable.

Pump/Motor Assembly

REMOVAL & INSTALLATION

The pump and motor assembly used on the Bendix Anti-lock 6 brake system is integral to the modulator and is not separately removable. If the pump or motor fails, the entire modulator assembly must be replaced.

Modulator Assembly

REMOVAL & INSTALLATION

◆ **See Figures 92 thru 97**

1. Remove the battery, battery tray and the protective cover from the modulator.

2. Disconnect the electrical connector from the Delta P switch (see illustration).

3. Remove the top bolt holding the modulator bracket to the fender shield.

4. Disconnect the 2 master cylinder supply tubes at the modulator. Loosen (but do not remove) the other end of the tubes at the master cylinder; swing the tubes aside without kinking them.

5. Elevate and safely support the front of the vehicle.

6. From below, disconnect the modulator 10-pin electrical connector. Remove the remaining 4 brake tubes from the modulator assembly.

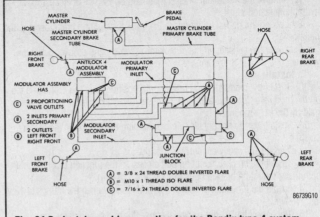

Fig. 94 Brake tube and hose routing for the Bendix type 4 system

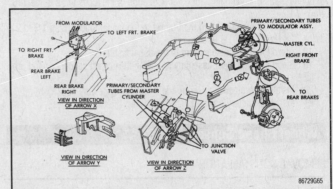

Fig. 95 Brake tube and hose routing at the modulator assembly—Bendix Type 6

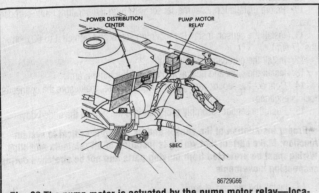

Fig. 92 The pump motor is actuated by the pump motor relay—location on vehicles equipped with power distribution center

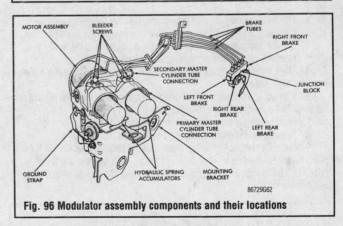

Fig. 96 Modulator assembly components and their locations

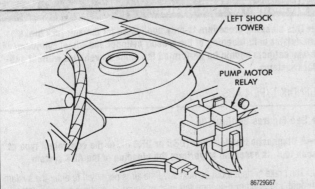

Fig. 93 Pump motor relay location on vehicles equipped with out power distribution center

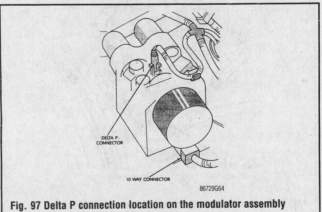

Fig. 97 Delta P connection location on the modulator assembly

7. Remove the modulator bracket mounting bolt which is closest to the hydraulic junction block.

8. Loosen but do not fully remove the bracket mounting bolt closest to the radiator.

9. Lower the vehicle; lift the modulator assembly and bracket out of the vehicle.

To install:

10. Install the modulator and bracket into position. Use the protruding tab on the modulator to locate and hold the assembly. Make certain the bracket is held by the front mounting bolt.

11. Install, but do not tighten, the bolt holding the bracket to the fender shield.

12. Elevate and safely support the vehicle.

13. Install the bracket mounting bolt closest to the junction block. Tighten both lower mounting bracket bolts to 21 ft. lbs. (28 Nm).

14. Install the 4 hydraulic lines at the modulator; tighten the fittings to 12 ft. lbs. (16 Nm).

15. Reconnect the 10-pin electrical connector to the modulator.

16. Lower the vehicle. Connect the 2 supply tubes from the master cylinder to the modulator. Tighten the fittings at both ends of the tubes to 12 ft. lbs. (16 Nm).

17. Tighten the bolt holding the bracket to the fender shield (Step 11) to 21 ft. lbs. (28 Nm).

18. Bleed the base brake system in the usual fashion.

19. Bleed the modulator assembly following the correct sequences and procedure.

20. Install the protective cover on the modulator assembly.

21. Install the battery tray and battery. Connect the battery cables.

Wheel Speed Sensors (WSS)

REMOVAL & INSTALLATION

Front Wheel

◆ **See Figure 98**

1. Elevate and safely support the vehicle. Remove the wheel and tire.
2. Remove the clip holding the wiring grommet to the fender well.
3. Remove the screws holding the sensor wiring tube to the fender well.
4. Carefully remove the grommet from the fender shield.
5. Make certain the ignition switch is **OFF**. Disconnect the sensor wiring from the ABS harness.
6. If so equipped, remove the triangular retaining clip from the bracket on the strut. Not all vehicles have this clip.
7. Remove the sensor wiring grommets from the bracket.
8. Remove the fastener holding the sensor head.
9. Carefully remove the sensor head from the steering knuckle. Do not use pliers on the sensor head; if it is seized in place, use a hammer and small punch to tap the edge of the sensor ear. The tapping and side-to-side motion will free the unit.

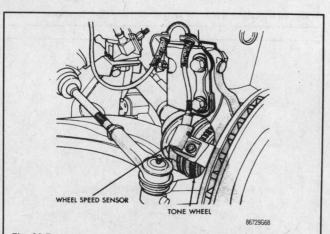

WHEEL SPEED SENSOR

TONE WHEEL

86729G68

Fig. 98 Front wheel speed sensor location and cable routing

To install:

10. Connect the speed sensor to the ABS harness.

11. Push the sensor assembly grommet into the hole in the fender shield. Install the retainer clip and screw.

12. Install the sensor wiring tube and tighten the retaining bolts to 35 inch lbs. (4 Nm).

13. Install the sensor grommets into the brackets on the fender shield and strut. Install the retainer clip at the strut.

14. Install the sensor to the knuckle. Install the retaining screw and tighten it to 60 inch lbs. (7 Nm).

➡ **Proper installation of the sensor and its wiring is critical to system function. Make certain that wiring is installed in all retainers and clips. Wiring must be protected from moving parts and not be stretched during suspension movements.**

15. Install the tire and wheel. Lower the vehicle to the ground.

Rear Wheel

1. Elevate and safely support the vehicle. Remove the wheel and tire.
2. Remove the sensor assembly grommet from the underbody and pull the harness through the hole in the body.
3. Make certain the ignition switch is **OFF**. Disconnect the sensor wiring from the ABS harness.
4. Remove the clip retaining screw from the bracket just forward of the trailing arm bushing.
5. Remove the sensor and brake tube assembly clip from the inboard side of the trailing arm.
6. Remove the sensor wire retainer from the rear brake hose bracket.
7. Remove the outboard sensor assembly nut. This nut is also used to hold the brake tube clip.
8. Remove the fastener holding the sensor head.
9. Carefully remove the sensor head from the adapter assembly. Do not use pliers on the sensor head; if it is seized in place, use a hammer and small punch to tap the edge of the sensor ear. The tapping and side-to-side motion will free the unit.

To install:

10. Before installation, coat the sensor with high temperature multi-purpose grease.

11. Install the sensor; install the retaining screw and tighten it to 60 inch lbs. (7 Nm).

12. Install the outboard retaining nut.

13. Install the clips and nuts at and around the trailing arm.

14. Connect the sensor wiring to the ABS harness; make sure the connector lock is engaged.

15. Push the sensor assembly grommet into the hole in the underbody.

➡ **Proper installation of the sensor and its wiring is critical to system function. Make certain that wiring is installed in all retainers and clips. Wiring must be protected from moving parts and not be stretched during suspension movements.**

16. Install the tire and wheel.
17. Lower the vehicle to the ground.

Bleeding The ABS System

➡ **This bleeding procedure is only applicable for the anti-lock brake modulator unit; bleeding of the master cylinder and wheel cylinders/ brake calipers should be performed the same as vehicles without anti-lock systems.**

BENDIX TYPE 4 ABS

◆ **See Figures 99 thru 104**

➡ **A Diagnostic Readout Box (DRB or DRB II), or the equivalent type of scan tool, is essential to perform the bleeding of the ABS system.**

The brake system must be bled any time air is permitted to enter the system through loosened or disconnected lines or hoses, or anytime the modulator is removed. Excessive air within the system will cause a soft or spongy feel in the brake pedal.

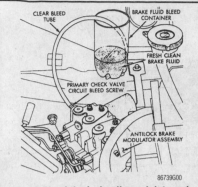

Fig. 99 Bleed the hydraulic modulator primary check valve circuit first . . .

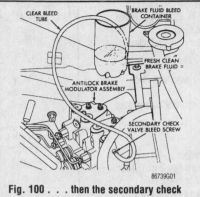

Fig. 100 . . . then the secondary check valve circuit

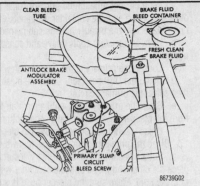

Fig. 101 Step 3 requires bleeding the primary sump circuit . . .

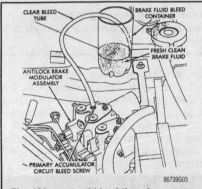

Fig. 102 . . . and bleed the primary accumulator circuit as the 4th step

Fig. 103 When bleeding the secondary sump circuit, as well as all of the other circuits, make sure to open the correct bleeder valve

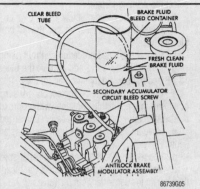

Fig. 104 Finally bleed the secondary accumulator circuit

When bleeding any part of the system, the reservoir must remain as close to full as possible at all times. Check the level frequently and top off fluid as needed.

❊❊ WARNING

The base brake and ABS systems can NOT be bled using any type of pressure bleeding equipment. This type of bleeding equipment does not develop the pressure required in the brake hydraulic system to adequately bleed all trapped air. The only method which should be used for bleeding the base brake hydraulic system is the manual procedure of pressurizing the hydraulic system using constant moderate-to-heavy foot pressure on the brake pedal.

The Bendix Anti-lock 4 brake system must be bled as 2 separate brake systems. Proper procedures must be followed if the system is to work correctly. The normal portion of the brake system is bled in the usual fashion with either pressure or manual bleeding equipment and must be fully and properly bled before bleeding the modulator.

To bleed the ABS system, the battery must be relocated outside the vehicle and connected to the vehicle with jumper cables. This allows access to the 4 bleeder screws on top of the modulator assembly. Additionally, the DRB II must be connected to the diagnostic plug before bleeding begins; the DRB II is used to activate the system(s) during the procedure. The 4 components to be bled within the modulator are (in order) the secondary sump, the primary sump, the primary accumulator and the secondary accumulator. The following procedure **MUST** be used to bleed the modulator assembly.

❊❊ CAUTION

Wear eye protection when bleeding the modulator assembly and always use a hose on the bleed screw to direct the flow of fluid away from painted surfaces. Bleeding the modulator may result in the release of very high pressure fluid.

➡**To bleed the hydraulic circuits of the brake system modulator assembly, the aid of an assistant will be required to pump the brake pedal.**

The Bendix 4 anti-lock brake system modulator does not need to be bled when doing normal servicing procedures such as caliper, hose or wheel cylinder replacement. The modulator does need to be bled when the modulator is removed or the lines are disconnected from the modulator. When servicing this system use DOT 3 brake fluid.

1. Remove the battery and connect a suitable set of jumper cables from the battery to the vehicle.
2. Remove the acid shield covering the modulator.
3. Fill the master cylinder reservoir to the proper level.
4. Bleed the primary check valve circuit as follows.
   a. Put a bleeder tube on the primary check valve circuit bleeder screw and place the other end into a suitable container with approximately 2 in. (51mm) of brake fluid. Make sure the bleeder hose is submerged in brake fluid.
   b. Have an assistant apply heavy and constant pressure on the brake pedal.
   c. Loosen the primary check valve circuit screw.
   d. Bleed the primary check valve circuit until a clear air free flow of brake fluid comes from the bleeder hose or the brake pedal bottoms.
   e. Close bleeder valve and remove the bleeder hose.
5. Bleed the secondary check valve circuit as follows.
   a. Put a bleeder tube on the secondary check valve circuit bleeder screw and place the other end into a suitable container with approximately 2 in. (51mm) of brake fluid. Make sure the bleeder hose is submerged in brake fluid.
   b. Have an assistant apply heavy and constant pressure on the brake pedal.
   c. Loosen the secondary check valve circuit bleeder screw.
   d. Bleed the secondary check valve circuit until a clear air free flow of brake fluid comes from the bleeder hose or the brake pedal bottoms.
   e. Close bleeder valve and remove the bleeder hose.
6. Bleed the primary sump as follows.

a. Put a bleeder tube on the primary sump bleeder screw and place the other end into a suitable container with approximately 2 in. (51mm) of brake fluid. Make sure the bleeder hose is submerged in brake fluid.

b. Have an assistant apply heavy and constant pressure on the brake pedal.

c. Loosen the primary sump bleeder screw.

d. Using the DRB scan tool select the bleed ABS hydraulic unit mode then select the primary circuit.

e. Bleed the primary sump until a clear air free flow of brake fluid comes from the bleeder hose or the brake pedal bottoms.

f. Close bleeder valve and remove the bleeder hose.

7. Bleed the primary accumulator as follows.

a. Put a bleeder tube on the primary accumulator bleeder screw and place the other end into a suitable container with approximately 2 in. (51mm) of brake fluid. Make sure the bleeder hose is submerged in brake fluid.

b. Have an assistant apply heavy and constant pressure on the brake pedal.

c. Using the DRB scan tool select bleed ABS hydraulic unit mode then select the primary circuit.

d. Loosen the bleeder screw.

e. Bleed the until a clear air free flow of brake fluid comes from the bleeder hose.

f. Repeat the bleed procedure without using the DRB scan tool.

g. Close bleeder valve and remove the bleeder hose.

8. Bleed the secondary sump as follows.

a. Put a bleeder tube on the secondary sump bleeder screw and place the other end into a suitable container with approximately 2 in. (51mm) of brake fluid. Make sure the bleeder hose is submerged in brake fluid.

b. Have an assistant apply light and constant pressure on the brake pedal.

c. Loosen the secondary sump bleeder screw.

d. Using the DRB scan tool select the bleed ABS hydraulic unit mode then select the secondary circuit valves.

e. Bleed the secondary sump until a clear air free flow of brake fluid comes from the bleeder hose or the brake pedal bottoms.

f. Close bleeder valve and remove the bleeder hose.

9. Bleed the secondary accumulator as follows.

a. Put a bleeder tube on the secondary accumulator bleeder screw and place the other end into a suitable container with approximately 2 in. (51mm) of brake fluid. Make sure the bleeder hose is submerged in brake fluid.

b. Have an assistant apply heavy and constant pressure on the brake pedal.

c. Loosen the secondary sump bleeder screw.

d. Using the DRB scan tool select bleed ABS hydraulic unit. Then select secondary circuit valves.

e. Bleed the secondary sump until a clear air free flow of brake fluid comes from the bleeder hose or the brake pedal bottoms.

f. Repeat the bleeding procedure without using the DRB scan tool.

g. Close bleeder valve and remove the bleeder hose.

10. Fill the master cylinder to the proper level.

11. Install the acid shield and the battery.

12. Road test the vehicle to check for proper brake system operation.

BENDIX TYPE 6 ABS

♦ **See Figure 105**

➡**A Diagnostic Readout Box (DRB or DRB II), or the equivalent type of scan tool, is essential to perform the bleeding of the ABS system.**

The brake system must be bled any time air is permitted to enter the system through loosened or disconnected lines or hoses, or anytime the modulator is removed. Excessive air within the system will cause a soft or spongy feel in the brake pedal.

When bleeding any part of the system, the reservoir must remain as close to full as possible at all times. Check the level frequently and top off fluid as needed.

The Bendix Anti-lock 6 brake system must be bled as 2 separate brake systems. Proper procedures must be followed if the system is to work correctly. The normal portion of the brake system is bled in the usual fashion with either pressure or manual bleeding equipment and must be fully and properly bled before bleeding the modulator.

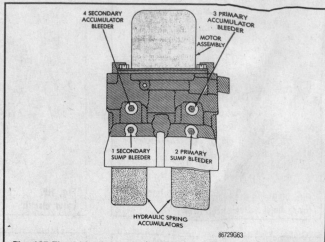

Fig. 105 The 4 bleeder valves (primary accumulator, secondary accumulator, primary sump and secondary sump) are necessary for system bleeding

To bleed the ABS system, the battery must be relocated outside the vehicle and connected to the vehicle with jumper cables. This allows access to the 4 bleeder screws on top of the modulator assembly. Additionally, the DRB II must be connected to the diagnostic plug before bleeding begins; the DRB II is used to activate the system(s) during the procedure. The 4 components to be bled within the modulator are (in order) the secondary sump, the primary sump, the primary accumulator and the secondary accumulator. Use the following procedure to bleed the modulator assembly.

❈❈ CAUTION

Wear eye protection when bleeding the modulator assembly and always use a hose on the bleed screw to direct the flow of fluid away from painted surfaces. Bleeding the modulator may result in the release of very high pressure fluid.

➡**To bleed the hydraulic circuits of the brake system modulator assembly, the aid of an assistant will be required to pump the brake pedal.**

1. Connect a clear hose to the secondary sump bleeder screw and route the hose to a clear container.

2. Either install and pressurize the pressure bleeding equipment at the master cylinder or have an assistant provide light and constant pressure on the brake pedal.

3. Open the bleeder screw about ½–¾ turn. Use the DRB II to select the ACTUATE VALVES test; actuate the left front build/decay valve.

4. Bleed until the fluid flows free of air bubbles or until the brake pedal bottoms.

5. Tighten the bleeder screw and release the brake pedal if it was being held.

6. Repeat Steps 2 through 5 until the fluid is free of air bubbles. Remember to check the fluid reservoir level periodically.

7. Select and actuate the right rear build/decay valve and perform Steps 2–5 until the fluid flows without air bubbles.

8. Move the bleeder tube to the primary sump bleeder screw.

9. Pressurize the pressure bleeding equipment at the master cylinder or have an assistant provide light and constant pressure on the brake pedal.

10. Open the bleeder screw about ½–¾ turn. Using the DRB II, actuate the right front build/decay valve.

11. Bleed until the fluid flows free of air bubbles or until the brake pedal bottoms.

12. Tighten the bleeder screw and release the brake pedal if it was being held.

13. Repeat Steps 2 through 5 until the fluid is free of air bubbles. Remember to check the fluid reservoir level periodically.

14. Select and actuate the left rear build/decay valve. Perform Steps 2–5 until the fluid runs free of air bubbles.

15. Move the bleeder tube to the primary accumulator bleeder screw.

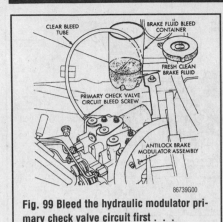

Fig. 99 Bleed the hydraulic modulator primary check valve circuit first . . .

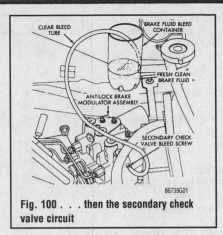

Fig. 100 . . . then the secondary check valve circuit

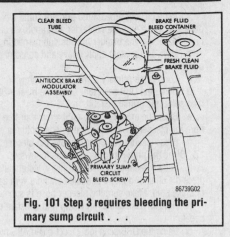

Fig. 101 Step 3 requires bleeding the primary sump circuit . . .

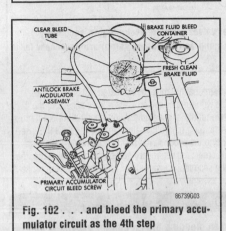

Fig. 102 . . . and bleed the primary accumulator circuit as the 4th step

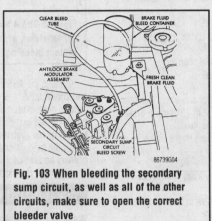

Fig. 103 When bleeding the secondary sump circuit, as well as all of the other circuits, make sure to open the correct bleeder valve

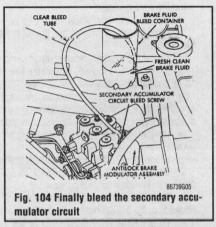

Fig. 104 Finally bleed the secondary accumulator circuit

When bleeding any part of the system, the reservoir must remain as close to full as possible at all times. Check the level frequently and top off fluid as needed.

※※ WARNING

The base brake and ABS systems can NOT be bled using any type of pressure bleeding equipment. This type of bleeding equipment does not develop the pressure required in the brake hydraulic system to adequately bleed all trapped air. The only method which should be used for bleeding the base brake hydraulic system is the manual procedure of pressurizing the hydraulic system using constant moderate-to-heavy foot pressure on the brake pedal.

The Bendix Anti-lock 4 brake system must be bled as 2 separate brake systems. Proper procedures must be followed if the system is to work correctly. The normal portion of the brake system is bled in the usual fashion with either pressure or manual bleeding equipment and must be fully and properly bled before bleeding the modulator.

To bleed the ABS system, the battery must be relocated outside the vehicle and connected to the vehicle with jumper cables. This allows access to the 4 bleeder screws on top of the modulator assembly. Additionally, the DRB II must be connected to the diagnostic plug before bleeding begins; the DRB II is used to activate the system(s) during the procedure. The 4 components to be bled within the modulator are (in order) the secondary sump, the primary sump, the primary accumulator and the secondary accumulator. The following procedure **MUST** be used to bleed the modulator assembly.

※※ CAUTION

Wear eye protection when bleeding the modulator assembly and always use a hose on the bleed screw to direct the flow of fluid away from painted surfaces. Bleeding the modulator may result in the release of very high pressure fluid.

→**To bleed the hydraulic circuits of the brake system modulator assembly, the aid of an assistant will be required to pump the brake pedal.**

The Bendix 4 anti-lock brake system modulator does not need to be bled when doing normal servicing procedures such as caliper, hose or wheel cylinder replacement. The modulator does need to be bled when the modulator is removed or the lines are disconnected from the modulator. When servicing this system use DOT 3 brake fluid.

1. Remove the battery and connect a suitable set of jumper cables from the battery to the vehicle.

2. Remove the acid shield covering the modulator.

3. Fill the master cylinder reservoir to the proper level.

4. Bleed the primary check valve circuit as follows.

a. Put a bleeder tube on the primary check valve circuit bleeder screw and place the other end into a suitable container with approximately 2 in. (51mm) of brake fluid. Make sure the bleeder hose is submerged in brake fluid.

b. Have an assistant apply heavy and constant pressure on the brake pedal.

c. Loosen the primary check valve circuit screw.

d. Bleed the primary check valve circuit until a clear air free flow of brake fluid comes from the bleeder hose or the brake pedal bottoms.

e. Close bleeder valve and remove the bleeder hose.

5. Bleed the secondary check valve circuit as follows.

a. Put a bleeder tube on the secondary check valve circuit bleeder screw and place the other end into a suitable container with approximately 2 in. (51mm) of brake fluid. Make sure the bleeder hose is submerged in brake fluid.

b. Have an assistant apply heavy and constant pressure on the brake pedal.

c. Loosen the secondary check valve circuit bleeder screw.

d. Bleed the secondary check valve circuit until a clear air free flow of brake fluid comes from the bleeder hose or the brake pedal bottoms.

e. Close bleeder valve and remove the bleeder hose.

6. Bleed the primary sump as follows.

a. Put a bleeder tube on the primary sump bleeder screw and place the other end into a suitable container with approximately 2 in. (51mm) of brake fluid. Make sure the bleeder hose is submerged in brake fluid.

b. Have an assistant apply heavy and constant pressure on the brake pedal.

c. Loosen the primary sump bleeder screw.

d. Using the DRB scan tool select the bleed ABS hydraulic unit mode then select the primary circuit.

e. Bleed the primary sump until a clear air free flow of brake fluid comes from the bleeder hose or the brake pedal bottoms.

f. Close bleeder valve and remove the bleeder hose.

7. Bleed the primary accumulator as follows.

a. Put a bleeder tube on the primary accumulator bleeder screw and place the other end into a suitable container with approximately 2 in. (51mm) of brake fluid. Make sure the bleeder hose is submerged in brake fluid.

b. Have an assistant apply heavy and constant pressure on the brake pedal.

c. Using the DRB scan tool select bleed ABS hydraulic unit mode then select the primary circuit.

d. Loosen the bleeder screw.

e. Bleed the until a clear air free flow of brake fluid comes from the bleeder hose.

f. Repeat the bleed procedure without using the DRB scan tool.

g. Close bleeder valve and remove the bleeder hose.

8. Bleed the secondary sump as follows.

a. Put a bleeder tube on the secondary sump bleeder screw and place the other end into a suitable container with approximately 2 in. (51mm) of brake fluid. Make sure the bleeder hose is submerged in brake fluid.

b. Have an assistant apply light and constant pressure on the brake pedal.

c. Loosen the secondary sump bleeder screw.

d. Using the DRB scan tool select the bleed ABS hydraulic unit mode then select the secondary circuit valves.

e. Bleed the secondary sump until a clear air free flow of brake fluid comes from the bleeder hose or the brake pedal bottoms.

f. Close bleeder valve and remove the bleeder hose.

9. Bleed the secondary accumulator as follows.

a. Put a bleeder tube on the secondary accumulator bleeder screw and place the other end into a suitable container with approximately 2 in. (51mm) of brake fluid. Make sure the bleeder hose is submerged in brake fluid.

b. Have an assistant apply heavy and constant pressure on the brake pedal.

c. Loosen the secondary sump bleeder screw.

d. Using the DRB scan tool select bleed ABS hydraulic unit. Then select secondary circuit valves.

e. Bleed the secondary sump until a clear air free flow of brake fluid comes from the bleeder hose or the brake pedal bottoms.

f. Repeat the bleeding procedure without using the DRB scan tool.

g. Close bleeder valve and remove the bleeder hose.

10. Fill the master cylinder to the proper level.

11. Install the acid shield and the battery.

12. Road test the vehicle to check for proper brake system operation.

BENDIX TYPE 6 ABS

♦ **See Figure 105**

➡**A Diagnostic Readout Box (DRB or DRB II), or the equivalent type of scan tool, is essential to perform the bleeding of the ABS system.**

The brake system must be bled any time air is permitted to enter the system through loosened or disconnected lines or hoses, or anytime the modulator is removed. Excessive air within the system will cause a soft or spongy feel in the brake pedal.

When bleeding any part of the system, the reservoir must remain as close to full as possible at all times. Check the level frequently and top off fluid as needed.

The Bendix Anti-lock 6 brake system must be bled as 2 separate brake systems. Proper procedures must be followed if the system is to work correctly. The normal portion of the brake system is bled in the usual fashion with either pressure or manual bleeding equipment and must be fully and properly bled before bleeding the modulator.

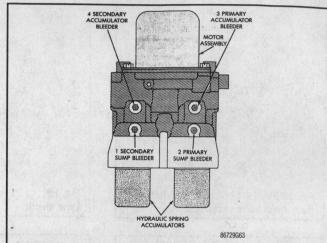

Fig. 105 The 4 bleeder valves (primary accumulator, secondary accumulator, primary sump and secondary sump) are necessary for system bleeding

To bleed the ABS system, the battery must be relocated outside the vehicle and connected to the vehicle with jumper cables. This allows access to the 4 bleeder screws on top of the modulator assembly. Additionally, the DRB II must be connected to the diagnostic plug before bleeding begins; the DRB II is used to activate the system(s) during the procedure. The 4 components to be bled within the modulator are (in order) the secondary sump, the primary sump, the primary accumulator and the secondary accumulator. Use the following procedure to bleed the modulator assembly.

✳ CAUTION

Wear eye protection when bleeding the modulator assembly and always use a hose on the bleed screw to direct the flow of fluid away from painted surfaces. Bleeding the modulator may result in the release of very high pressure fluid.

➡**To bleed the hydraulic circuits of the brake system modulator assembly, the aid of an assistant will be required to pump the brake pedal.**

1. Connect a clear hose to the secondary sump bleeder screw and route the hose to a clear container.

2. Either install and pressurize the pressure bleeding equipment at the master cylinder or have an assistant provide light and constant pressure on the brake pedal.

3. Open the bleeder screw about ½–¾ turn. Use the DRB II to select the ACTUATE VALVES test; actuate the left front build/decay valve.

4. Bleed until the fluid flows free of air bubbles or until the brake pedal bottoms.

5. Tighten the bleeder screw and release the brake pedal if it was being held.

6. Repeat Steps 2 through 5 until the fluid is free of air bubbles. Remember to check the fluid reservoir level periodically.

7. Select and actuate the right rear build/decay valve and perform Steps 2–5 until the fluid flows without air bubbles.

8. Move the bleeder tube to the primary sump bleeder screw.

9. Pressurize the pressure bleeding equipment at the master cylinder or have an assistant provide light and constant pressure on the brake pedal.

10. Open the bleeder screw about ½–¾ turn. Using the DRB II, actuate the right front build/decay valve.

11. Bleed until the fluid flows free of air bubbles or until the brake pedal bottoms.

12. Tighten the bleeder screw and release the brake pedal if it was being held.

13. Repeat Steps 2 through 5 until the fluid is free of air bubbles. Remember to check the fluid reservoir level periodically.

14. Select and actuate the left rear build/decay valve. Perform Steps 2–5 until the fluid runs free of air bubbles.

15. Move the bleeder tube to the primary accumulator bleeder screw.

16. Pressurize the pressure bleeding equipment at the master cylinder or have an assistant provide light and constant pressure on the brake pedal.

17. Open the bleeder screw about ½–¾ turn. Using the DRB II, actuate the right front/left rear isolation valve.

18. Bleed until the fluid flows free of air bubbles or until the brake pedal bottoms.

19. Tighten the bleeder screw and release the brake pedal if it was being held.

20. Repeat Steps 2 through 5 until the fluid is free of air bubbles. Check the fluid reservoir level periodically.

21. Select and actuate the right front build/decay valve. Perform Steps 2–5 until the fluid runs free of air bubbles.

22. Move the bleeder tube to the secondary accumulator bleeder screw.

23. Pressurize the pressure bleeding equipment at the master cylinder or

have an assistant provide light and constant pressure on the brake pedal.

24. Open the bleeder screw about ½–¾ turn. Using the DRB II, actuate the left front/right rear isolation valve.

25. Bleed until the fluid flows free of air bubbles or until the brake pedal bottoms.

26. Tighten the bleeder screw and release the brake pedal if it was being held.

27. Repeat Steps 2 through 5 until the fluid is free of air bubbles. Check the fluid reservoir level periodically.

28. Select and actuate the left front build/decay valve. Perform Steps 2–5 until the fluid runs free of air bubbles.

29. Remove the bleeding apparatus; fill the brake fluid reservoir to the correct level and install the cap.

BOSCH III AND BENDIX TYPE 10 ANTI-LOCK BRAKE SYSTEMS

General Information

SYSTEM IDENTIFICATION

▶ See Figure 106

The Dynasty came equipped with one of two systems, depending on the model year of the vehicle: 1988–90 vehicles were equipped with Bosch III ABS, and 1991–93 vehicles were equipped with Bendix Type 10 ABS.

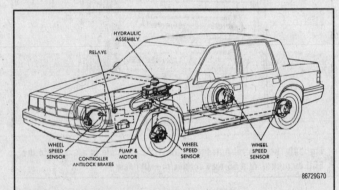

Fig. 106 Four wheel Anti-lock Brake System (ABS) component locations—Dynasty

SYSTEM OPERATION

▶ See Figures 107 and 108

The purpose of the Anti-lock Brake System (ABS) is to prevent wheel lock-up under heavy braking conditions on virtually any type of road surface. ABS is desirable because a vehicle which is topped without locking the wheels will retain directional stability and some steering capability. This allows the driver to retain greater control of the vehicle during heavy braking.

Under normal braking conditions, the ABS functions the same as a standard brake system with a diagonally split master cylinder and conventional vacuum assist.

If wheel locking tendency is detected during application, the system will enter anti-lock mode. During anti-lock mode, hydraulic pressure in the four wheel circuits is modulated to prevent any wheel from locking. Each wheel circuit is designed with a set of electrical valves and hydraulic line to provide modulation, although for vehicle stability, both rear wheel valves receive the same electrical signal. The system can build or reduce pressure at each wheel, depending on signals generated by the Wheel Speed Sensors (WSS) at each wheel and received at the Controller Anti-lock Brake (CAB).

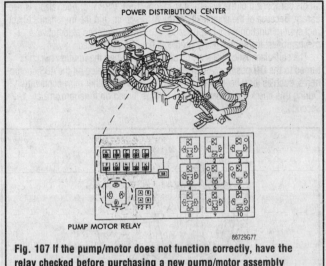

Fig. 107 If the pump/motor does not function correctly, have the relay checked before purchasing a new pump/motor assembly

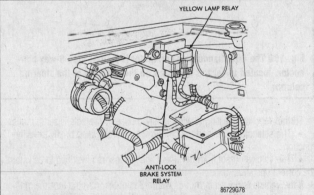

Fig. 108 The ABS relay and yellow lamp relay are the other 2 relays in the ABS system

PRECAUTIONS

Failure to observe the following precautions may result in system damage:

• Before performing electric arc welding on the vehicle, disconnect the control module and the hydraulic unit connectors.

• When performing painting work on the vehicle, do not expose the control module to temperatures in excess of 185°F (85°C) for longer than 2 hours. The system may be exposed to temperatures up to 200°F (95°C) for less than 15 minutes.

• Never disconnect or connect the control module or hydraulic modulator connectors with the ignition switch **ON**.

• Never disassemble any component of the Anti-Lock Brake System (ABS) which is designated unserviceable; the component must be replaced as an assembly.

• When filling the master cylinder, always use brake fluid which meets DOT-3 specifications; petroleum-based fluid will destroy the rubber parts.

• Working on ABS system requires extreme amount of mechanical ability, training and special tools. If you are not familiar have your vehicle repaired by a certified mechanic or refer to a more advanced publication on this subject.

SYSTEM/COMPONENT TESTING

▶ See Figure 109

For the proper diagnostic procedure for either the entire ABS system or a single component of the system, a scan tool (DRB, DRB II or equivalent) is necessary. Because of the complexity of the ABS system and the importance of correct system functioning, it is a good idea to have a qualified automotive mechanic test the system if any problems have been detected.

The self-diagnostic ABS start up cycle begins when the ignition switch is turned to the **ON** position. An electrical check is completed on the ABS components, such as the wheel speed sensor continuity and other relay continuity. During this check the amber anti-lock light is turned on for approximately 1–2 seconds.

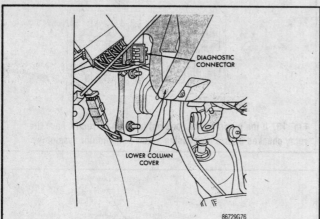

Fig. 109 The ABS diagnostics connector is a light blue 6-way connector, located under the dash and on the left side of the steering column

Further functional testing is accomplished once the vehicle is set in motion.

• The solenoid valves and the pump/motor are activated briefly to verify function

• The voltage output from the wheel speed sensors is verified to be within the correct operating range

If the vehicle is not set in motion within 3 minutes from the time the ignition switch is set in the **ON** position, the solenoid test is bypassed, but the pump/motor is activated briefly to verify that it is operating correctly.

Fault codes are kept in a non-volatile memory until either erased by the DRB II or erased automatically after 50 ignition cycles (key **ON-OFF** cycles). The only fault that will not be erased after the 50 ignition cycles is the CAB fault. A CAB fault can only be erased by the DRB II. More than one fault can be stored at a time. The number of key cycles since the most recent fault was stored is also displayed. Most functions of the CAB and ABS system can be accessed by the DRB II for testing and diagnostic purposes.

Depressurizing the Hydraulic Accumulator

➡**Unless otherwise specified, the hydraulic accumulator should be depressurized before disassembling any portion of the hydraulic brake system.**

1. With the ignition **OFF**, pump the brake pedal a minimum of 40 times, using approximately 50 lbs. (222 N) pedal force. A noticeable change in pedal feel will occur when the accumulator is discharged.

2. When a definite increase in pedal effort is felt, stroke the pedal a few additional times. This should remove all hydraulic pressure from the system.

Controller Anti-lock Brake (CAB) Module

➡**The CAB is mounted on the top of the right front frame rail and uses a 60-way system connector.**

REMOVAL & INSTALLATION

▶ See Figures 110

1. Turn the ignition switch **OFF**.
2. Disconnect the negative battery cable.
3. Detach the wiring harness connector 60-way connector from the CAB.
4. Remove the CAB module mounting bracket-to-inner fender bolts.
5. Remove the CAB from the vehicle.
6. Installation is the reverse of the removal procedure.
7. Connect the battery cable.

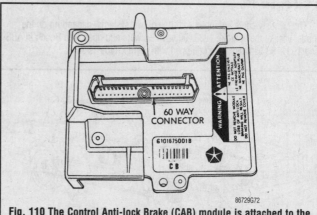

Fig. 110 The Control Anti-lock Brake (CAB) module is attached to the ECU by means of a 60-way connector—Dynasty

Pump/Motor Assembly

REMOVAL & INSTALLATION

1989–90 Models

1. Disconnect the negative battery cable. Depressurize the hydraulic accumulator.

✴✴ CAUTION

Failure to depressurize the hydraulic accumulator, prior to performing this operation may result in personal injury and/or damage to the painted surfaces.

2. Remove the fresh air intake ducts.
3. Disconnect all electrical connectors to the pump motor.
4. Disconnect the high and low pressure hoses from the hydraulic assembly. Cap the spigot on the reservoir.
5. Disconnect the shift selection cable bracket from the transaxle and move it aside.
6. Loosen the nuts on the 2 studs that position the pump/motor to the transaxle differential cover.
7. Remove the retainer bolts that are used to mount hose bracket and pump/motor. The engine inlet water extension pipe is also held in position by these bolts.

➡**Do not disturb the inlet water extension pipe, or engine coolant will leak out.**

8. Disconnect the wiring harness retaining clip from the hose bracket.

9. Lift the pump/motor assembly off of the studs and out of the vehicle.

10. Remove the heat shield from the pump/motor, if equipped and discard.

To install:

11. Place a new heat shield onto the pump/motor bracket, using fasteners provided.

12. Install the pump/motor assembly onto the studs.

13. Install the wiring harness retaining clip onto the hose bracket.

14. Install the retainer bolts to the hose bracket and pump/motor. Tighten securely.

15. Tighten the 2 nuts until secure.

16. Install the shift selection cable bracket onto the transaxle.

17. Connect the high and low pressure hoses to the hydraulic assembly and tighten to 13 ft. lbs. (17 Nm).

18. Attach all electrical connectors to the pump/motor.

19. Install the air ducts.

20. Readjust the gearshift linkage, if it was disturbed.

21. Connect the negative battery cable and check the assembly for proper operation.

1991–93 Models

◆ **See Figures 111 and 112**

1. Disconnect the negative battery cable.

✳✳ CAUTION

Failure to depressurize the hydraulic accumulator, prior to performing this operation may result in personal injury and/or damage to the painted surfaces.

2. Depressurize the brake system.

3. Remove the fresh air intake ducts from the engine.

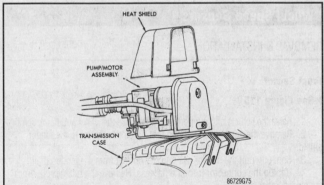

Fig. 111 The pump/motor assembly mounts to the top of the transaxle case and is covered by a heat shield

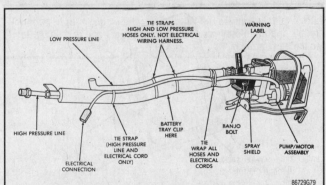

Fig. 112 When reinstalling the high and low pressure tie straps, make sure to position them in the correct places

4. Remove the clip holding the high pressure line to the battery tray.

5. Disconnect the electrical connectors running across the engine compartment in the vicinity of the pump/motor high and low pressure hoses. One of these connectors is the one for the pump/motor assembly.

6. Disconnect the high and low pressure hoses from the hydraulic assembly. Cap or plug the reservoir fitting.

7. Disconnect the pump/motor electrical connector from the engine mount.

8. Remove the heat shield bolt from the front of the pump bracket. Remove the heat shield.

9. Lift the pump/motor assembly from the bracket and out of the vehicle.

To install:

10. Fit the pump motor assembly onto the bracket; install the heat shield and its retaining bolt.

11. Install the pump/motor electrical connector to the engine mount.

12. Connect the high and low pressure hose to the hydraulic assembly. Tighten the high pressure line to 145 inch lbs. (16 Nm). Tighten the hose clamp on the low pressure hose to 10 inch lbs. (1 Nm).

13. Connect the electrical connectors which were removed for access.

14. Install the high pressure line retaining clip to the battery tray if it was removed.

15. Install the fresh air intake ducts.

16. Bleed the brake system.

Hydraulic Assembly

REMOVAL & INSTALLATION

◆ **See Figures 113 and 114**

1. Disconnect the negative battery cable. Depressurize the hydraulic accumulator.

✳✳ CAUTION

Failure to depressurize the hydraulic accumulator, prior to performing this operation may result in personal injury and/or damage to the painted surfaces.

2. Remove the fresh air intake ducts.

3. Disconnect all electrical connectors from the hydraulic unit and pump/motor.

4. Remove as much of the fluid as possible from the reservoir on the hydraulic assembly.

5. Remove the pressure hose fitting (banjo bolt) from the hydraulic assembly. Use care not to drop the 2 washers used to seal the pressure hose fitting to the hydraulic assembly inlet.

6. Disconnect the return hose from the reservoir nipple. Cap the spigot on the reservoir.

7. Disconnect all brake tubes from the hydraulic assembly.

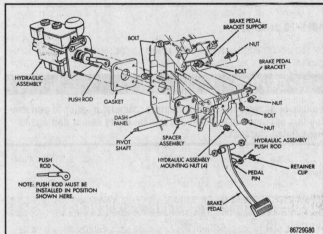

Fig. 113 Exploded view of the hydraulic assembly mounting components—make sure that the pushrod is correctly positioned

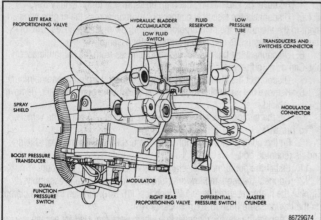

Fig. 114 The hydraulic assembly is a complex unit, comprised of many of the ABS components

8. Remove the driver's side sound insulation panel.

9. Disconnect the pushrod from the brake pedal by using a small, flat tool to release the retainer clip on the brake pedal pin. The center tang on the clip must be moved back enough to allow the lock tab to clear the pin. Disconnect the pushrod from the pedal pin.

10. Remove the 4 underdash hydraulic assembly mounting nuts.

11. Remove the hydraulic assembly.

To install:

12. Position the hydraulic assembly on the vehicle.

13. Install and torque the mounting nuts to 21 ft. lbs. (28 Nm).

14. Using Lubriplate® or equivalent, coat the bearing surface of the pedal pin.

15. Connect the pushrod to the pedal and install a new retainer clip.

16. Install the brake tubes. If the proportioning valves were removed from the hydraulic assembly, reinstall valves and tighten to 20 ft. lbs. (27 Nm).

17. Install the return hose to the nipple on the reservoir.

18. Install the pressure hose to the hydraulic assembly; be sure the 2 washers are in there proper position. Tighten the banjo bolt to 13 ft. lbs. (18 Nm).

19. Fill the reservoir to the top of the screen.

20. Connect all electrical connectors to the hydraulic assembly.

21. Bleed the entire brake system.

22. Install the cross-car brace, if disturbed. Install the fresh air intake duct.

23. Connect the negative battery cable and check the assembly for proper operation.

Sensor Block

REMOVAL & INSTALLATION

1989–90 Vehicles

1. Disconnect the negative battery cable. Depressurize the hydraulic accumulator.

✳✳ CAUTION

Failure to depressurize the hydraulic accumulator, prior to performing this operation may result in personal injury and/or damage to the painted surfaces.

2. Disconnect all electrical connectors from the reservoir on the hydraulic assembly.

3. Working from under the dash, disconnect the pushrod from the brake pedal.

4. Remove the driver's side sound insulator panel.

5. Remove the 4 hydraulic assembly mounting nuts.

6. Working from under the hood, pull the hydraulic assembly away from the dash panel and rotate the assembly enough to gain access to the sensor block cover.

➠The brake lines should not be removed or deformed during this procedure.

7. Remove the sensor block cover retaining bolt and remove the sensor block cover. Care should be used not to damage the cover gasket during removal.

8. Disengage the locking tabs and disconnect the valve block connector (12 pin) from the sensor block.

9. Disengage the reed block connector, marked **PUSH**, by carefully pulling outward on the orange connector body. The connector is partially retained by a plastic clip and will only move outward approximately ½ in. (13mm).

10. Remove the 3 block retaining bolts.

11. Carefully disengage the sensor block pressure port from the hydraulic assembly and remove the sensor block from the vehicle. The sensor block pressure port is sealed with an O-ring and extra care should be taken to prevent damage to the seal.

12. Inspect the sensor block pressure port O-ring for damage. Replace the O-ring if cut or damaged. Check the sensor block wiring for incorrect positioning or damage. Correct any damage or replace the sensor block, if damage cannot be corrected.

To install:

13. Pull the reed block connector (2 pin) outward to the disengage position prior to installing the sensor block on the hydraulic unit.

14. Thoroughly lubricate the sensor block pressure port O-ring with fresh, clean brake fluid. Carefully insert the pressure port into the hydraulic assembly's orifice, taking care not to cut or damage the O-ring. Position the sensor block for installation of the mounting bolts.

15. Install the sensor block mounting bolts. Tighten to 11 ft. lbs. (15 Nm).

16. Engage the reed block connector by pressing on the orange connector body marked **PUSH**.

17. Connect the valve block connector (12 pin) to the sensor block.

18. Install the sensor block cover, gasket and mounting bolt.

19. Connect the sensor block and control pressure switch connectors.

20. Install the hydraulic assembly by reversing the removal procedure.

21. Connect the negative battery cable and check the sensor block for proper operation.

Wheel Speed Sensors

REMOVAL & INSTALLATION

Front Sensor

▶ **See Figure 115**

1. Raise the vehicle and support safely. Remove the wheel and tire assembly.

2. Remove the screw from the clip that holds the sensor to the fender shield.

3. Carefully pull the sensor assembly grommet from the fender shield.

4. Unplug the connector from the harness. Remove the retainer clip from the strut damper bracket.

5. Remove the sensor mounting screw.

6. Carefully remove the sensor.

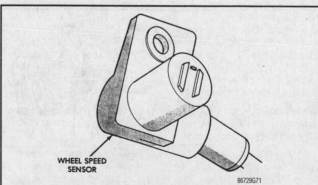

WHEEL SPEED SENSOR

Fig. 115 The Wheel Speed Sensors (WSS) are very sensitive devices—make sure that their cables are routed correctly

To install:

7. Coat the sensor with high temperature multi-purpose anti-corrosion compound before installing into the steering knuckle. Install the screw and tighten to 60 inch lbs. (7 Nm).

8. Connect the sensor connector to the harness and install the sensor connector lock.

9. Install the sensor assembly grommet and attach the clip to the fender shield.

➡**Proper installation of the wheel speed sensor cables is critical to continued system operation. Be sure the cables are installed in retainers. Failure to install the cables in the retainers may result in contact with moving parts and/or overextension of the cables, resulting in an open circuit.**

10. Install the wheel.

Rear Sensor

1. Raise the vehicle and support safely. Remove the wheel and tire assembly.

2. Carefully pull the sensor assembly grommet from the underbody and pull the harness through the hole.

3. Unplug the connector from the harness. Remove the retainer clip from the strut damper bracket.

4. Remove the sensor spool grommet clip retaining screw from the body hose bracket, located in front of the inside of the trailing arm.

5. Remove the outboard sensor assembly retaining nut and sensor mounting screw.

6. Carefully remove the sensor.

To install:

7. Coat the sensor with high temperature multi-purpose anti-corrosion compound before installing into the steering knuckle. Install the screw and tighten to 60 inch lbs. (7 Nm). Install the retaining nut.

8. Install the sensor spool grommet clip retaining screw.

9. Feed the sensor connector wire through the grommet and connect to the harness.

10. Install the sensor assembly grommet.

11. Install the wheel.

Bleeding The ABS System

BOOSTER BLEEDING

Bosch III ABS

➡**Only the Bosch III ABS system might require bleeding of the booster.**

1. The hydraulic accumulator must be depressurized.

2. Connect all pump/motor and hydraulic assembly electrical connections, if previously disconnected. Be sure all brake lines and hose connections are tight.

3. Fill the reservoir to the full level.

4. Connect a transparent hose to the bleeder screw location on the right side of the hydraulic assembly. Place the other end of the hose into a clear container to receive brake fluid.

5. Open the bleeder screw ½–¾ of a turn.

6. Turn the ignition switch to the **ON** position. The pump/motor should run, discharging fluid into the container. After a good volume of fluid has been forced through the hose, an air-free flow in the plastic hose and container will indicate a good bleed.

7. Turn the ignition switch **OFF**.

➡**If the brake fluid does not flow, it may be due to a lack of priming the pump/motor. Try shaking the return hose to break up air bubbles that may be present within the hose.**

8. Should the brake fluid still not flow, turn the ignition switch to the OFF position. Remove the return hose from the reservoir and cap nipple on the reservoir. Manually fill the return hose with brake fluid and connect to the reservoir. Repeat the bleeding process.

9. Remove the hose from the bleeder screw. Tighten the bleeder screw to 7.61 inch lbs. (10 Nm). Do not overtighten.

10. Top off the reservoir to the correct fluid level.

11. Turn the ignition switch to the **ON** position. Allow the pump to charge the accumulator, which should stop after approximately 30 seconds.

PRESSURE BLEEDING

➡**This procedure is applicable to both the Bosch III and Bendix Type 10 ABS systems.**

The brake lines may be pressure bled, using a standard diaphragm type pressure bleeder. Only diaphragm type pressure bleeding equipment should be used to bleed the system.

1. The ignition should be turned **OFF** and remain **OFF** throughout this procedure.

2. Depressurize the hydraulic accumulator.

✳✳ **CAUTION**

Failure to depressurize the hydraulic accumulator, prior to performing this operation may result in personal injury and/or damage to the painted surfaces.

3. Remove the electrical connector from fluid level sensor on the reservoir cap(s) and remove the reservoir cap(s).

4. Install the pressure bleeder adapter.

5. Attach the bleeding equipment to the bleeder adapter. Charge the pressure bleeder to approximately 20 psi (138 kPa).

6. Connect a transparent hose to the caliper bleed screw. Submerge the free end of the hose in a clear glass container, which is partially filled with clean, fresh brake fluid.

7. With the pressure turned **ON**, open the caliper bleed screw ½–¾ turn and allow fluid to flow into the container. Leave the bleed screw open until clear, bubble-free fluid slows from the hose. If the reservoir has been drained or the hydraulic assembly removed from the vehicle prior to the bleeding operation, slowly pump the brake pedal 12 times while the bleed screw is open and fluid is flowing. This will help purge air from the hydraulic assembly. Tighten the bleeder screw to 7.61 inch lbs. (10 Nm).

8. Repeat Step 7 at all calipers. Calipers should be bled in the following order:

    a. Left rear

    b. Right rear

    c. Left front

    d. Right front

9. After bleeding all 4 calipers, remove the pressure bleeding equipment and bleeder adapter by closing the pressure bleeder valve and slowly unscrewing the bleeder adapter from the hydraulic assembly reservoir. Failure to release pressure in the reservoir will cause spillage of brake fluid and could result in injury or damage to painted surfaces.

10. Using a syringe or equivalent method, remove excess fluid from the reservoir to bring the fluid level to full level.

11. Install the reservoir cap and connect the fluid level sensor connector. Turn the ignition **ON** and allow the pump to charge the accumulator.

MANUAL BLEEDING

➡**This procedure is applicable to both the Bosch III and Bendix Type 10 ABS systems.**

1. Depressurize the hydraulic accumulator.

✳✳ **CAUTION**

Failure to depressurize the hydraulic accumulator, prior to performing this operation may result in personal injury and/or damage to the painted surfaces.

2. Connect a transparent hose to the caliper bleed screw. Submerge the free end of the hose in a clear glass container, which is partially filled with clean, fresh brake fluid.

3. Slowly pump the brake pedal several times, using full strokes of the pedal and allowing approximately 5 seconds between pedal strokes. After 2 or 3 strokes, continue to hold pressure on the pedal, keeping it at the bottom of its travel.

4. With pressure on the pedal, open the bleed screw ½–¾ turn. Leave the bleed screw open until fluid no longer flows from the hose. Tighten the bleed screw and release the pedal.

5. Repeat this procedure until clear, bubble-free fluid flows from the hose.

6. Repeat all steps at each of the calipers. Calipers should be bled in the following order:
   a. Left rear.
   b. Right rear.
   c. Left front.
   d. Right front.

7. Install the reservoir cap and connect the fluid level sensor connector. Turn the ignition **ON** and allow the pump to charge the accumulator.

BRAKE SPECIFICATIONS
All measurements in inches unless noted

Year	Model	Master Cylinder Bore	Brake Disc Original Thickness	Brake Disc Minimum Thickness	Brake Disc Maximum Runout	Brake Drum Diameter Original Inside Diameter	Brake Drum Diameter Max. Wear Limit	Brake Drum Diameter Maximum Machine Diameter	Minimum Lining Thickness Front	Minimum Lining Thickness Rear
1981	Aries	0.875	0.940	0.882	0.005	7.87	④	NA	0.300	③
	Reliant	0.875	0.940	0.882	0.005	7.87	④	NA	0.300	③
1982	400	0.875	0.940	0.882	0.005	7.87	④	NA	0.300	③
	600	0.875	0.940	0.882	0.005	7.87	④	NA	0.300	③
	Aries	0.875	0.940	0.882	0.005	7.87	④	NA	0.300	③
	LeBaron	0.875	0.940	0.882	0.005	7.87	④	NA	0.300	③
	Reliant	0.875	0.940	0.882	0.005	7.87	④	NA	0.300	③
	Town & Country	0.875	0.940	0.882	0.005	7.87	④	NA	0.300	③
1983	400	0.827	0.940	0.882	0.005	7.87 ⑤	④	NA	0.300	③
	600	0.827	0.940	0.882	0.005	8.66	④	NA	0.300	③
	Aries	0.827	0.940	0.882	0.005	7.87 ⑤	④	NA	0.300	③
	E-Class	0.827	0.940	0.882	0.005	8.66	④	NA	0.300	③
	LeBaron	0.827	0.940	0.882	0.005	7.87 ⑤	④	NA	0.300	③
	New Yorker	0.827	0.940	0.882	0.005	8.66	④	NA	0.300	③
	Reliant	0.827	0.940	0.882	0.005	7.87 ⑤	④	NA	0.300	③
	Town & Country	0.827	0.940	0.882	0.005	7.87 ⑤	④	NA	0.300	③
1984	600	0.827	0.940	0.882	0.005	8.66	④	NA	0.300	③
	Aries	0.827	0.940	0.882	0.005	7.87 ⑤	④	NA	0.300	③
	Daytona	0.827	0.940	0.882	0.005	8.66	④	NA	0.300	③
	E-Class	0.827	0.940	0.882	0.005	8.66	④	NA	0.300	③
	Laser	0.827	0.940	0.882	0.005	8.66	④	NA	0.300	③
	LeBaron	0.827	0.940	0.882	0.005	7.87 ⑤	④	NA	0.300	③
	New Yorker	0.827	0.940	0.882	0.005	8.66	④	NA	0.300	③
	Reliant	0.827	0.940	0.882	0.005	7.87 ⑤	④	NA	0.300	③
	Town & Country	0.827	0.940	0.882	0.005	7.87 ⑤	④	NA	0.300	③
1985	600	0.827	0.940	0.882	0.005	8.66	④	NA	0.300	③
	Aries	0.827	0.940	0.882	0.005	7.87 ⑤	④	NA	0.300	③
	Caravelle	0.827	0.940	0.882	0.005	8.66	④	NA	0.300	③
	Daytona	0.827	0.940	0.882	0.005	8.66	④	NA	0.300	③
	Lancer	0.827	0.940	0.882	0.005	7.87 ⑤	④	NA	0.300	③
	Laser	0.827	0.940	0.882	0.005	8.66	④	NA	0.300	③
	LeBaron	0.827	0.940	0.882	0.005	7.87 ⑤	④	NA	0.300	③
	LeBaron GTS	0.827	0.940	0.882	0.005	7.87 ⑤	④	NA	0.300	③
	LeBaron Limo	0.827	0.940	0.882	0.005	7.87 ⑤	④	NA	0.300	③
	New Yorker	0.827	0.940	0.882	0.005	8.66	④	NA	0.300	③
	Reliant	0.827	0.940	0.882	0.005	7.87 ⑤	④	NA	0.300	③
	Town & Country	0.827	0.940	0.882	0.005	7.87 ⑤	④	NA	0.300	③
1986	600	0.827	0.940	0.882	0.005	8.66	④	NA	0.313	③
	Aries	0.827	0.940	0.882	0.005	7.87 ⑤	④	NA	0.313	③
	Caravelle	0.827	0.940	0.882	0.005	8.66	④	NA	0.313	③
	Daytona	0.827	0.940	0.882	0.005	8.66	④	NA	0.313	③
	Lancer	0.827	0.940	0.882	0.005	7.87 ⑤	④	NA	0.313	③
	Laser	0.827	0.940	0.882	0.005	8.66	④	NA	0.313	③
	LeBaron	0.827	0.940	0.882	0.005	7.87 ⑤	④	NA	0.313	③
	LeBaron GTS	0.827	0.940	0.882	0.005	7.87 ⑤	④	NA	0.313	③
	New Yorker	0.827	0.940	0.882	0.005	8.66	④	NA	0.313	③
	Reliant	0.827	0.940	0.882	0.005	7.87 ⑤	④	NA	0.313	③
	Town & Country	0.827	0.940	0.882	0.005	7.87 ⑤	④	NA	0.313	③

86739C00

BRAKE SPECIFICATIONS
All measurements in inches unless noted

Year	Model			Master Cylinder Bore	Brake Disc Original Thickness	Brake Disc Minimum Thickness	Brake Disc Maximum Runout	Brake Drum Original Inside Diameter	Brake Drum Max. Wear Limit	Brake Drum Maximum Machine Diameter	Min. Lining Thickness Front	Min. Lining Thickness Rear
1989	Sundance			0.827	0.940	0.882	0.005	7.87	④	NA	0.313	③
	TC Maserati			NA	0.348	0.291	0.005	-	-	-	0.313	-
1990	Acclaim		F	0.827	0.940	0.882	0.005	-	-	NA	0.313	0.281 ⑥
			R	-	0.468	0.409	0.005	8.66	④	-	-	
	Daytona		F	0.827	0.940	0.882	0.005	-	-	NA	0.313	0.281 ⑥
			R	-	0.468	0.409	0.003	8.66	④	-	-	0.281 ⑥
	Dynasty	①	F	0.827	0.940	0.882	0.005	-	-	NA	0.313	
		②	R	-	0.356	0.797	0.005	-	-	-	-	0.281 ⑥
	LeBaron		F	0.827	0.358	0.339	0.005	8.66	④	NA	0.313	
		①	R	0.827	0.940	0.882	0.005	7.87 ⑤	④	NA	0.313	0.281 ⑥
		②		-	0.468	0.409	0.005	7.87	-	-	-	0.281
1991	Shadow		F	0.827	0.940	0.882	0.005	7.87	④	NA	0.313	③
	Spirit		R	0.827	0.940	0.882	0.005	8.66	④	NA	0.313	⑥
	Sundance			0.827	0.940	0.882	0.005	7.87	④	NA	0.313	0.281 ⑥
	TC Maserati			NA	0.348	0.291	0.005	-	-	-	0.313	
	Acclaim	①	F	0.827	0.940	0.882	0.005	-	-	NA	0.313	0.281 ⑥
		②	R	-	0.468	0.409	0.005	8.66	④	-	-	0.281
	Daytona		F	0.827	0.940	0.882	0.003	-	-	NA	0.313	0.281 ⑥
		①	R	-	0.368	0.409	0.005	8.66	④	-	-	0.281
		②		-	0.356	0.797	0.003	-	-	-	-	
	Dynasty		F	0.827	0.940	0.882	0.005	-	-	NA	0.313	
			R	-	0.358	0.339	0.003	8.66	④	-	-	
	LeBaron		F	0.827	0.540	0.882	0.005	-	-	NA	0.313	
		①	R	-	0.468	0.409	0.005	7.87 ⑤	④	-	-	0.281 ⑥
		②		-	0.356	0.797	0.003	-	-	-	-	0.281
1992	Shadow		F	0.827	0.940	0.882	0.005	7.87	④	NA	0.313	③
	Spirit		R	0.827	0.940	0.882	0.005	8.66	④	NA	0.313	0.281 ⑥
	Sundance			0.827	0.448	0.409	0.005	8.66	④	NA	0.313	0.281
				0.827	0.856	0.797	0.003	7.87	④	NA	0.313	
	Acclaim	①	F	0.827	0.940	0.882	0.005	-	-	NA	0.313	0.281 ⑥
		②	R	-	0.468	0.409	0.003	8.66	④	-	-	0.281
	Daytona		F	0.827	0.856	0.797	0.005	-	-	NA	0.313	0.281 ⑥
			R	-	0.854	0.797	0.003	8.66	④	-	-	
	Dynasty		F	0.827	0.934	0.882	0.005	-	-	NA	0.313	0.281 ⑥
			R	-	0.468	0.409	0.005	8.66	④	-	-	
	LeBaron		F	0.827	0.940	0.882	0.005	-	-	NA	0.313	0.281 ⑥
			R	-	0.468	0.409	0.005	7.87 ⑤	④	-	-	0.281
	Shadow			0.827	0.940	0.882	0.005	7.87	④	NA	0.313	③

86739C02

BRAKE SPECIFICATIONS
All measurements in inches unless noted

Year	Model		Master Cylinder Bore	Brake Disc Original Thickness	Brake Disc Minimum Thickness	Brake Disc Maximum Runout	Brake Drum Original Inside Diameter	Brake Drum Max. Wear Limit	Brake Drum Maximum Machine Diameter	Min. Lining Thickness Front	Min. Lining Thickness Rear
1987	600		0.827	0.940	0.882	0.005	8.66	④	NA	0.313	③
	Aries		0.827	0.940	0.382	0.005	7.87 ⑤	④	NA	0.313	③
	Caravelle		0.827	0.940	0.882	0.005	8.66	④	NA	0.313	③
	Daytona	F	0.827	0.940	0.882	0.005	-	-	NA	0.313	
		R	-	0.348	0.291	0.005	8.66	④	-	-	0.281 ⑥
	Lancer		0.827	0.940	0.882	0.005	7.87	④	NA	0.313	③
	LeBaron		0.827	0.940	0.882	0.005	7.87 ⑤	④	NA	0.313	③
	LeBaron GTS		0.827	0.940	0.882	0.005	7.87	④	NA	0.313	③
	New Yorker		0.827	0.940	0.832	0.005	8.66	④	NA	0.313	③
	Reliant		0.827	0.940	0.882	0.005	7.87 ⑤	④	NA	0.313	③
	Shadow		0.827	0.940	0.882	0.005	7.87	④	NA	0.313	③
	Sundance		0.827	0.940	0.882	0.005	7.87	④	NA	0.313	③
	Town & Country		0.827	0.940	0.882	0.005	7.87 ⑤	④	NA	0.313	③
1988	600		0.827	0.940	0.882	0.005	8.66	④	NA	0.313	③
	Aries		0.827	0.940	0.382	0.005	7.87 ⑤	④	NA	0.313	③
	Caravelle		0.827	0.940	0.882	0.005	8.66	④	NA	0.313	③
	Daytona	F	0.827	0.940	0.882	0.005	-	-	NA	0.313	
		R	-	0.348	0.291	0.005	8.66	④	-	-	0.281 ⑥
	Dynasty	F	0.827	0.940	0.882	0.003	-	-	NA	0.313	
		R	-	0.358	0.339	0.005	8.66	④	-	-	0.281 ⑥
	Lancer		0.827	0.940	0.882	0.005	7.87	④	NA	0.313	③
	LeBaron		0.827	0.940	0.882	0.005	7.87	④	NA	0.313	③
	LeBaron GTS	F	0.827	0.940	0.882	0.005	-	-	NA	0.313	
		R	-	0.348	0.291	0.005	8.66	④	-	-	0.281 ⑥
	New Yorker		0.827	0.940	0.882	0.005	8.66	④	NA	0.313	③
	Reliant		0.827	0.940	0.882	0.005	7.87 ⑤	④	NA	0.313	③
	Shadow		0.827	0.940	0.882	0.005	7.87	④	NA	0.313	③
	Sundance		0.827	0.940	0.882	0.005	7.87	④	NA	0.313	③
	Town & Country		0.827	0.940	0.882	0.005	7.87 ⑤	④	NA	0.313	③
1989	Acclaim		0.827	0.940	0.882	0.005	8.66	④	NA	0.313	⑥
	Aries		0.827	0.940	0.882	0.005	7.87 ⑤	④	NA	0.313	③
	Daytona	F	-	0.940	0.882	0.005	-	-	NA	0.313	0.281 ⑥
		R	0.827	0.468	0.409	0.003	8.66	④	-	0.313	0.281
	Dynasty	F	0.827	0.358	0.339	0.003	-	-	NA	0.313	0.281 ⑥
		R	-	0.940	0.882	0.005	8.66	④	-	-	
	Lancer		0.827	0.940	0.882	0.005	7.87	④	NA	0.313	③
	LeBaron	F	0.827	0.940	0.882	0.005	-	-	NA	0.313	0.281 ⑥
		R	-	0.468	0.409	0.005	7.87	④	-	-	0.281
	LeBaron GTS	F	0.827	0.856	0.797	0.005	-	-	NA	0.313	0.281 ⑥
		R	-	0.940	0.882	0.005	7.87 ⑤	④	NA	-	
	Reliant		0.827	0.348	0.291	0.005	7.87	④	NA	0.313	③
	Shadow		0.827	0.940	0.882	0.005	7.87 ⑤	④	NA	0.313	③
	Spirit		0.827	0.940	0.882	0.005	8.66	④	NA	0.313	③

86739C00

BRAKE SPECIFICATIONS

All measurements in inches unless noted

Year	Model			Master Cylinder Bore	Brake Disc			Brake Drum Diameter			Minimum Lining Thickness	
					Original Thickness	Minimum Thickness	Maximum Runout	Original Inside Diameter	Max. Wear Limit	Maximum Machine Diameter	Front	Rear
1992	Spirit		F	0.827	0.940	0.882	0.005	-	-	-	0.313	-
		①	R	-	0.468	0.409	0.005	8.66	④	NA	-	0.281 ⑥
		②	R	-	0.856	0.797	0.003	-	-	-	-	0.281
	Sundance			0.827	0.940	0.882	0.005	7.87	④	NA	0.313	③
1993	Acclaim		F	0.827	0.940	0.882	0.005	-	-	-	0.313	-
		①	R	-	0.468	0.409	0.005	8.66	④	NA	-	0.281 ⑥
		②	R	-	0.856	0.797	0.003	-	-	-	-	0.281
	Daytona		F	0.827	0.940	0.882	0.005	-	-	-	0.313	-
			R	-	0.856	0.797	0.003	8.66	④	NA	-	0.281 ⑥
	Dynasty		F	0.827	0.940	0.882	0.005	-	-	-	0.313	-
			R	-	0.468	0.409	0.005	8.66	④	NA	-	0.281 ⑥
	LeBaron		F	0.827	0.940	0.882	0.005	-	-	-	0.313	-
			R	-	0.468	0.409	0.005	7.87 ⑤	④	NA	-	0.281 ⑥
	Shadow		F	0.827	0.940	0.882	0.005	-	-	-	0.313	-
			R	-	0.468	0.409	0.005	7.87	④	NA	-	0.281 ⑥
	Spirit		F	0.827	0.940	0.882	0.005	-	-	-	0.313	-
		①	R	-	0.468	0.409	0.005	8.66	④	NA	-	0.281 ⑥
		②	R	-	0.856	0.797	0.003	-	-	-	-	0.281
	Sundance		F	0.827	0.940	0.882	0.005	-	-	-	0.313	-
			R	-	0.468	0.409	0.005	7.87	④	NA	-	0.281 ⑥
1994	Acclaim		F	0.827	0.940	0.882	0.005	-	-	-	0.313	-
		①	R	-	0.468	0.409	0.005	8.66	④	NA	-	0.281 ⑥
		②	R	-	0.856	0.797	0.003	-	-	-	-	0.281
	Shadow		F	0.827	0.940	0.882	0.005	-	-	-	0.313	-
			R	-	0.468	0.409	0.005	7.87	④	NA	-	0.281 ⑥
	Spirit		F	0.827	0.940	0.882	0.005	-	-	-	0.313	-
		①	R	-	0.468	0.409	0.005	8.66	④	NA	-	0.281 ⑥
		②	R	-	0.856	0.797	0.003	-	-	-	-	0.281
	Sundance		F	0.827	0.940	0.882	0.005	-	-	-	0.313	-
			R	-	0.468	0.409	0.005	7.87	④	NA	-	0.281 ⑥
1995	Acclaim		F	0.827	0.940	0.882	0.005	-	-	-	0.313	-
		①	R	-	0.468	0.409	0.005	8.66	④	NA	-	0.281 ⑥
		②	R	-	0.856	0.797	0.003	-	-	-	-	0.281
	Spirit		F	0.827	0.940	0.882	0.005	-	-	-	0.313	-
		①	R	-	0.468	0.409	0.005	8.66	④	NA	-	0.281 ⑥
		②	R	-	0.856	0.797	0.003	-	-	-	-	0.281

F - Front
R - Rear
① Solid rear disc
② Vented rear disc
③ Bonded lining use 0.062 in.
　 Riveted lining use 0.030 in. over rivet head

④ Maximum diameter is stamped on drum
⑤ Optional: 8.66
⑥ For rear disc brakes, combined shoe and lining thickness is shown.
　 For drum brakes: 0.062 in. for bonded lining
　　　　　 0.030 in. over rivet head for riveted lining

86739C03

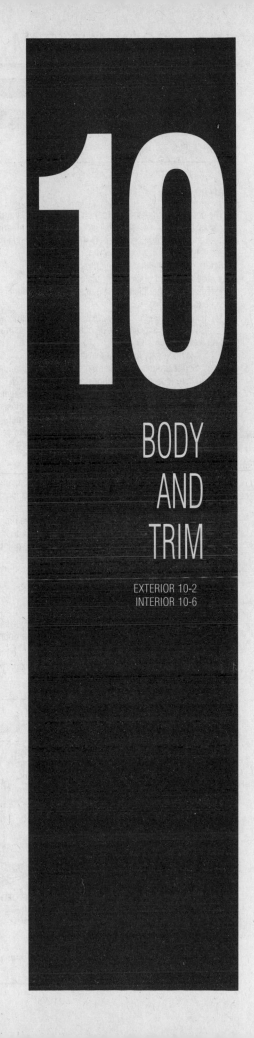

10

BODY AND TRIM

EXTERIOR

Doors

ADJUSTMENT

1981–90 Models

The door hinges are welded to both the door panels and door pillars. Because of this fact, adjustments can be performed only through the use of a special door hinge adjusting tool (C-4736), which bends the hinges in a controlled way.

Before adjusting either hinge, check these items:
- The alignment of the striker plate. Is it correct?
- The fit and condition of the hinge roll pins. If there is looseness, they must be replaced.
- The installation of the door seal. Sealing problems which may seem to be door misalignment may actually be due to irregular/incorrect positioning of the seal on the body.

1. If it is necessary to adjust the striker plate:
   a. Scribe around the striker plate to mark its location against the door jamb. Then, loosen the mounting screws just slightly.
   b. Open and close the door slowly to watch engagement of the door with the striker. The door should not rise or fall as it is closed. Reposition the striker vertically to ensure that this requirement is met.
   c. Close the door and inspect its outer surface to see if it is flush with adjacent sheet metal. If not, adjust the striker inward or outward until the door rests in a flush position.
   d. Tighten the striker adjustments securely.
2. If these other checks fail to resolve door alignment problems, it is necessary to bend the hinges. Keep in mind that this process must be done gradually to fine tune the door position. First, determine the exact angle/area of misalignment.
3. Slip the hinge bending tool completely over the hinge to be bent. Then, slowly and gradually apply pressure so the change in door position can be monitored accurately. Stop the process and check the point of misalignment frequently.

1991–95 Models

▶ See Figure 1

If the hinges are not removed from the pillar the door should not need adjusting. If, however, the hinges were removed or the door does need adjusting, perform the following:
1. Scribe around the striker plate to mark its location against the door jamb. Then, loosen the mounting screws just slightly.

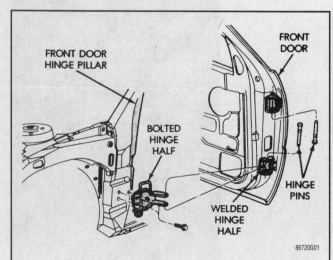

Fig. 1 One half of the hinges are bolted to the door pillar, the other is welded to the door itself

Figure labels: FRONT DOOR HINGE PILLAR, FRONT DOOR, BOLTED HINGE HALF, HINGE PINS, WELDED HINGE HALF, 86720G01

2. Open and close the door slowly to watch engagement of the door with the striker. The door should not rise or fall as it is closed. Reposition the striker vertically to ensure that this requirement is met.
3. Close the door and inspect its outer surface to see if it is flush with adjacent sheet metal. If not, adjust the striker inward or outward until the door rests in a flush position.
4. Close the door and inspect the gap around the door. The gap should be approximately ¼ in. (6mm) wide and even all the way around the door. Adjust the hinges up or down, or install shims to the hinges, to adjust the gap.
5. After the door is correctly adjusted, tighten the striker adjustments securely.

LATCH ADJUSTMENT

The latch adjustment affects both the smoothness of door latch operation and the door handle-to-skin position.
1. Insert a 5⁄32 in. (4mm) Allen wrench through the access hole in the end of the door and engage it with the Allen screw in the latch mechanism. Slide the screw up or down in the slot to adjust the latch position and then tighten the Allen screw to 30 inch lbs. (4 Nm). Remove the wrench.
2. Close the door and check the operation of the latch, as well as the door handle position.
3. Readjust as described in Steps 1 and 2 until the door closes smoothly and the door handle is flush.

Hood

REMOVAL & INSTALLATION

▶ See Figures 2 thru 7

➡ To perform this procedure a cover that will protect both the windshield and the two fenders is required, as well as an assistant.

1. Disconnect the negative battery cable.
2. If applicable, unplug all electrical connectors on the hood, then remove the wiring harness from the hood.
3. Scribe a mark around each hinge where it connects to the underside of the hood for reinstallation with a minimum of adjustment.
4. Protect the windshield and fenders with a cover. Then, place blocks of wood behind the hood—between it and the windshield to protect the windshield in case the hood should slide to the rear.
5. While an assistant supports the hood, remove the hood bolts. With one person on either side, remove the hood from the car. If the hood is being replaced with a new one, transfer the latch striker and safety catch by removing the attaching bolts and reinstalling these components onto the new hood with them.
   To install:
6. To install the hood, first position it as precisely as possible—with the bolt holes of the upper hinge and the hood lined up. Then, with the assistant both supporting the front of the hood and keeping the assembly from sliding back toward the windshield, install the bolts until their heads are just a turn or two below the lower hinge surface.
7. Shift the hood on both sides to align the matchmarks and hinges precisely. Tighten one bolt on either side gradually, checking that the hood remains in position and shifting it to maintain alignment (refer to the following service procedure) as necessary. Tighten one bolt on either side to hold the hood in position.
8. Have the assistant hold the hood up as you tighten all the remaining bolts.
9. Install the hood support pistons, if removed.
10. Route the wiring harness into the hood and attach all electrical connectors.
11. Connect the negative battery cable.
12. Remove the cover and blocks.

ALIGNMENT

1. Inspect the gap between the hood edges in relation to the cowl, fenders and grille panel. The desired clearance is 0.16 in. (4mm).
2. If the hood requires adjustment, loosen the mounting bolts located on the underside of the hood (the hinge-to-hood attaching bolts).

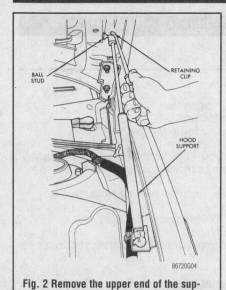

Fig. 2 Remove the upper end of the support piston by prying the retaining clip off of the ball stud

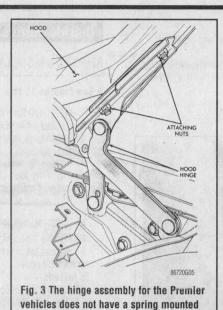

Fig. 3 The hinge assembly for the Premier vehicles does not have a spring mounted to it . . .

Fig. 4 . . . whereas all other models have a spring-equipped hinge unit

Fig. 5 Scribe a mark around each hinge for reinstallation

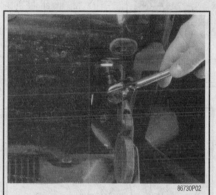

Fig. 6 Removing the hinge-to-hood mounting bolts

Fig. 7 It may be necessary to remove part of the hood insulation to gain access to some electrical connectors

3. Shift the hood forward or rearward to change the dimension between the grille and cowl first, if necessary. Once this is correct, shift the hood right or left, as needed.

4. Tighten all bolts evenly and tightly.

Bumpers

ADJUSTMENT

It is possible to adjust the bumper's side-to-side or vertical location. Loosen the bumper-to-energy absorber (outer) attaching nuts or bolts. Shift the bumper as necessary. Using a helper or an adjustable floor jack to hold the bumper in position, tighten the mounting bolts to 21 ft. lbs. (28 Nm) on all models.

REMOVAL & INSTALLATION

▶ See Figures 8, 9 and 10

✳ CAUTION

Energy absorbing units may become stuck in the retracted position because of an impact. Do not drill the absorber to remove pressure This would result in the release of the built-up pressure. If loosening the bolts or nuts at either end to relieve torque on the energy absorber does not cause it to expand, it MUST BE DISCARDED.

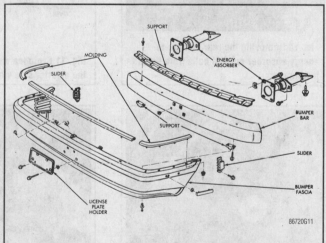

Fig. 8 Exploded view of a common bumper assembly—most vehicles similar

1. Place supports under the bumper. If the bumper is equipped with a fascia, remove the retaining nuts and remove it.

2. Remove the bumper-to-energy absorber (outer end) retaining nuts or bolts. Then, lower the bumper assembly to the floor.

To install:

3. To install the bumper, raise it into its normal position and install the retaining nuts/bolts loosely.

4. Shift the bumper as necessary to achieve proper alignment. While using an assistant or an adjustable floor jack to hold the bumper in position, tighten the attaching nuts or bolts to 21 ft. lbs. (28 Nm).

5. Install the bumper fascia and retaining nuts.

Fig. 9 Removing the front bumper-to-energy absorber nut and bolts from behind the bumper

Outside Mirrors

REMOVAL & INSTALLATION

♦ **See Figures 11 thru 16**

1. Disconnect the negative battery cable.
2. Remove the front door trim panel.
3. Remove the side view mirror remote adjusting knob cover, if equipped.
4. Remove the screws holding the mirror bezel to the door frame. Separate the bezel from the door. Loosen the setscrew holding the bezel to the mirror adjuster cable, if equipped.
5. Remove the silencer seal from the door frame behind the mirror bezel.
6. Unplug the power mirror wire connector, if equipped.
7. Remove the access hole cover.
8. Remove the nuts holding the mirror to the door frame, then separate the mirror from the door.

To install:

9. Position the mirror against the door frame, then install the retaining nuts. Tighten the nuts until snug.
10. Install the access hole cover.
11. Attach the wire connector to the mirror, if applicable.
12. Install the silencer seal to the door frame.
13. Install the bezel over the mirror adjuster cable (if equipped) and install the bezel to the door frame. Tighten the bezel setscrew to hold the mirror adjuster cable in position.
14. Install the side view mirror remote adjusting knob cover, if equipped.
15. Install the door trim panel.
16. Connect the negative battery cable.

Fig. 10 Removing the rear bumper-to-energy absorber nut and bolts from behind the bumper

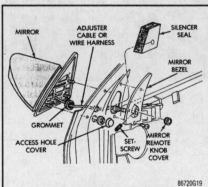

Fig. 11 Exploded view of the mounting of the exterior side view mirror

Fig. 12 Loosening the mirror remote control knob set screw—1991 Acclaim shown

Fig. 13 Removing the mirror remote control knob

Fig. 14 Removing the mirror access cover retaining screws

Fig. 15 With the mirror access cover removed, unfasten the mirror retaining nuts

Antenna

REPLACEMENT

Manual Antenna

◆ See Figures 17, 18 and 19

➡To perform this operation, a special antenna cap nut (much like a socket wrench), Tool C-4816, is required. On some vehicles the radio must be remove to gain access to the antenna connection. Some vehicles use a two piece cable do not remove the radio, but disconnect the cable at harness connection.

1. The radio may have to be removed from the car to gain access to the antenna connection. Remove the radio, if necessary. Then, unplug the antenna lead at the radio or harness connection.

2. Use an open-end wrench of appropriate size across the flats at the bottom of the antenna mast to unscrew the mast from the antenna adapter. Then, remove the mast.

3. Use the special tool to unscrew the antenna cap nut from the fender. Then, remove the cap nut and the adapter and gasket underneath it.

4. If access to the antenna body from underneath the fender is blocked by an inner fender shield, remove the 3 screws from the rear of the shield and bend it away to gain access.

5. Then, remove the antenna lead and body assembly.

To install:

6. To install the antenna, first insert the antenna body and cable through the hole in the fender from underneath. Then, Install the gasket, adapter and cap nut. Tighten the cap nut to 10 ft. lbs. (14 Nm) with the special tool.

7. Screw the antenna mast into the antenna body. Tighten it with the open-end wrench until its sleeve bottoms on the antenna body.

8. Route the antenna cable to the radio, connect it to the radio (or harness connection) and then reinstall the radio if necessary. Check the radio for proper operation.

Power Antenna

◆ See Figures 20 and 21

1. Disconnect the negative battery cable.

2. Remove the right front fender splash shield fasteners and pull the shield away from the wheel housing.

3. Detach the motor leads at the connector.

4. Separate the lead-in cable by twisting at the connector.

5. Remove the one screw attaching the antenna to the antenna brace.

6. Remove the cap nut on the fender surface with the Antenna Nut Wrench C-4816, or equivalent.

7. Extract the antenna from under the fender.

To install:

8. Position the antenna under the fender and through the fender adapter.

9. Install and tighten the cap nut to 10 ft. lbs. (14 Nm) with the antenna nut wrench.

10. Position the antenna on the antenna brace, then install the attaching screw to 40 inch lbs. (4 Nm).

11. Attach the antenna lead at the twist connector.

12. Install the motor leads at the connector.

13. Position the right front fender splash shield and install the attaching fasteners.

14. Connect the negative battery cable and test the operation of the antenna.

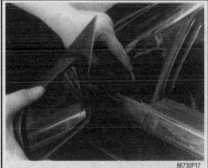

Fig. 16 With the inside retaining nuts removed, separate the mirror from the door

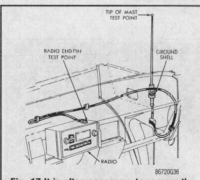

Fig. 17 It is often necessary to remove the radio unit to gain access to the antenna cable

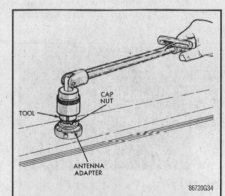

Fig. 18 Use the special tool (C-4816) to removal and install the antenna cap nut

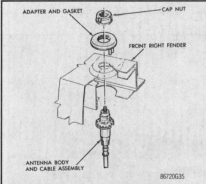

Fig. 19 Exploded view of the antenna cable-to-fender mounting junction

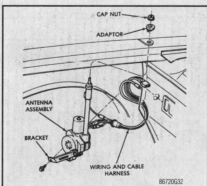

Fig. 20 The power antenna mounts to the underside of the front right fender

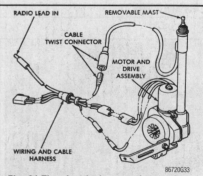

Fig. 21 The electrical connections and components of the power antenna assembly

INTERIOR

Instrument Panel and Pad

✱✱ CAUTION

On vehicles equipped with air bags, it is important to disarm the system to prevent accidental deployment of the air bag and avoiding possible injury. To disarm the air bag system, simply detach the negative battery cable from the battery. Isolate the battery cable by taping up any exposed metal areas of the cable. This will keep the cable from accidentally contacting the battery and causing accidental deployment of the air bag. Allow the system capacitor to discharge for at least 2 minutes, although 10 minutes is recommended to allow the dissipation of any residual energy. To arm the air bag system, reconnect the negative battery cable. This will automatically enable the air bag system.

REMOVAL & INSTALLATION

Aires, Reliant, 400, 600, E-Class, Caravelle, Spirit, Acclaim, LeBaron Sedan and TC by Maserati Models

▶ See Figures 22 thru 30

1. Disconnect the negative battery cable.
2. Remove the left and right A-pillar trim.
3. Remove left and right cowl side trim.
4. Remove the glove box assembly.
5. Remove all necessary electrical relays above the glove box assembly area.
6. Reach through glove box opening and disconnect A/C control vacuum lines, radio noise suppressor wires and blower motor/cycling switch wires.
7. Remove hood release handle.
8. Remove the lower steering column cover.
9. Remove lower left instrument panel silencer and reinforcement.
10. Remove instrument panel center bezel.
11. Remove the floor console assembly, as outlined in this section.
12. Remove the radio, A/C control, lighter assembly and message center/traveler if so equipped.
13. Disconnect defroster hoses.
14. Remove the instrument panel top cover.
15. Remove the instrument cluster assembly.
16. Remove the radio and rear window defogger bezels.
17. Lower steering column.
18. Loosen instrument panel pivot bolts.
19. Remove screws which attach instrument panel to windshield fence line.
20. Allow panel to roll down slightly and disconnect all remaining electrical connections. Remove the panel pivot bolts and remove instrument panel assembly from vehicle.

To install:

21. Position the instrument panel assembly in the vehicle and reconnect all necessary electrical connections. Install and evenly tighten the instrument panel pivot bolts.
22. Install and tighten the screws which attach the instrument panel to the windshield fence line.
23. Install the steering column.
24. To install the remaining components, reverse the removal procedure.
25. Reconnect the A/C control vacuum lines, radio noise suppressor wires and blower motor/cycling switch wires through the glove box opening, and install all necessary relays at this time.
26. Reconnect the negative battery cable.

Fig. 22 Removing the A-pillar trim on either side of the door openings—1991 Acclaim shown

Fig. 23 Remove the two hood release handle retaining screws

Fig. 24 Remove the lower steering column cover

Fig. 25 Remove lower left instrument panel silencer and reinforcement retaining screws

Fig. 26 Remove the lower left instrument panel silencer and reinforcement

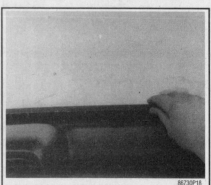

Fig. 27 Remove the instrument panel top cover

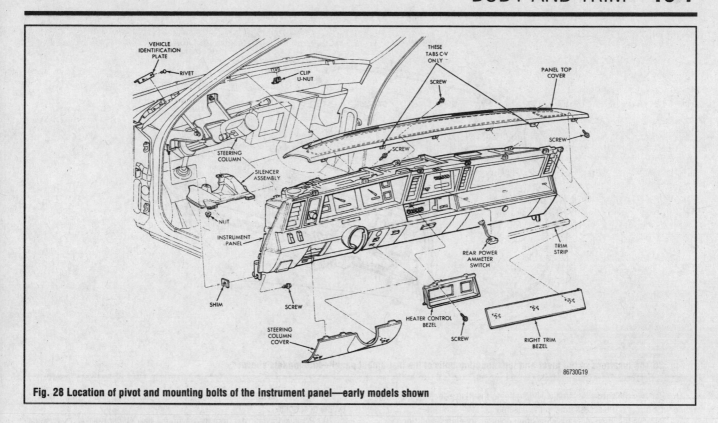

Fig. 28 Location of pivot and mounting bolts of the instrument panel—early models shown

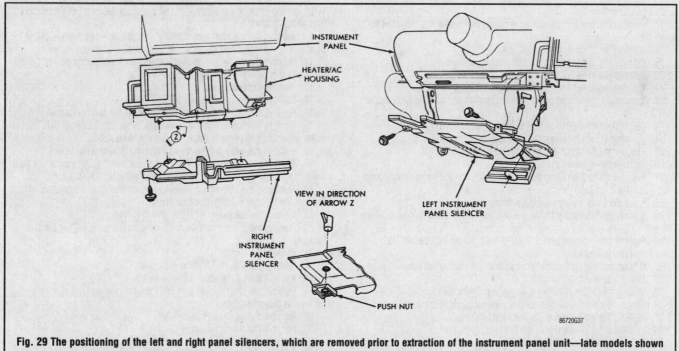

Fig. 29 The positioning of the left and right panel silencers, which are removed prior to extraction of the instrument panel unit—late models shown

New Yorker and Dynasty

1. Disconnect the negative battery cable.
2. Remove the left instrument panel silencer.
3. Remove the right and left cowl side and scuff plate trim molding.
4. Remove the right and left A-pillar trim molding.
5. Remove the panel top cover by pushing forward and prying up.
6. Unplug the bulkhead connector at the brace under the instrument panel left side.
7. Remove the glove box/ashtray module and right instrument panel silencer.

8. Remove the center panel support brace and air bag diagnostic module assembly.
9. Disconnect the wiring to the air bag module.
10. Remove the upper and lower cluster bezels.
11. Remove the steering column cover.
12. Remove the steering column mounting nuts and lower the steering column.
13. Unhook the shift indicator cable eyelet from the steering column actuator.
14. Unlatch the lock tab in the shift indicator column insert and squeeze the legs together to remove from the steering column.

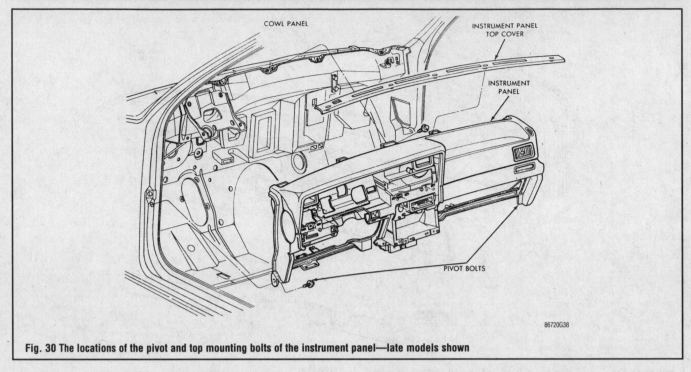

Fig. 30 The locations of the pivot and top mounting bolts of the instrument panel—late models shown

15. Remove the cluster assembly while guiding the transaxle range indicator guide tube through the access hole in the base panel.

16. Remove the instrument panel steering column opening support/hood release handle assembly.

17. Remove the steering column upper studs and loosen the side cowl tie-down bolts.

18. Remove the steering column tilt lever.

19. Remove the upper and lower lock housing shroud.

20. Remove the lower fixed shroud.

21. Remove the upper fixed shroud (snaps in place).

22. Disconnect the air bag pigtail, ignition switch and halo light/key buzzer switch wiring.

23. Disconnect the multi-function switch.

24. Disconnect the air bag pigtail from the wiring trough housing.

25. Remove the wiring trough from the steering column.

26. Remove the defroster ducts.

27. Remove the screws along the fence line and roll the panel down. Attach a hook to hold it in place.

28. Open the hood and remove the plenum grille.

29. Disconnect the washer bottle, resistor block and underhood lamp wiring. The washer bottle must be removed to gain access.

30. Remove the grommet and pull the plenum wiring into the vehicle through the plenum panel.

31. Disconnect the right defroster hose from the instrument panel.

32. Disconnect the antenna cable.

33. Unplug all electrical wiring from the instrument panel.

34. Disconnect the A/C-heater control cables and vacuum hoses.

35. Remove the instrument panel from the vehicle.

36. Installation is the reverse of the removal procedure.

37. Connect the negative battery cable.

Daytona, LeBaron Coupe and LeBaron Convertible Models

▶ **See Figure 31**

1. Disconnect the negative battery cable.

2. Remove the instrument panel center bezel.

3. Remove the upper and lower steering column covers.

4. Remove the left under panel silencer.

5. Set the parking brake.

6. Remove the console side carpet panels.

7. Remove the center console.

8. Remove the transmission range clip and cable loop end from the post on the gear shifter.

9. Remove the adjuster from the tab on the gear shifter bracket, by pushing in the locking knob on the adjuster and sliding the adjuster off of the tab on the gear shifter bracket.

10. Remove the 2 screws and slide the air bag diagnostic module out of the right side of the instrument panel center stack area. Disconnect the wiring.

11. Remove the screw from the instrument panel dimmer module at the left of the steering column and lower module.

12. Remove the fuse block.

13. Remove the hood release handle.

14. Remove the flasher relay from the bracket on the center distribution duct.

15. Remove the screw from the Automatic Temperature Control (ATC) sensor motor assembly and unhook it from the bracket, if equipped.

16. Remove the radio ground screw above the flasher relay mount.

17. Remove the center distribution duct screw from the left instrument panel lower brace, then remove the 4 screws to remove the left lower brace.

18. Remove the 5 nuts on the steering column and drop the column. Remove the 2 upper column attaching studs.

19. Remove the CD player or cubby box.

20. Remove the Electronic Vehicle Information Center (EVIC) or Electronic Navigator.

21. Remove the radio.

22. Remove the ATC or A/C-heater controls.

23. Remove the rear window defogger switch.

24. Remove the cluster lower trim bezel, switch pod vent grille, speaker grilles and defroster grilles.

25. Remove the switch pod assembly.

26. Remove the cluster assembly.

27. Remove the dash speakers.

28. Snap out the bezel with or without the message center, then disconnect the wiring.

29. Open the glove box door, squeeze the sides and roll the glove box completely open. Remove the glove box light switch and disconnect the wiring.

30. Loosen the right side cowl pivot bolt through the glove box opening, then close the glove box.

31. Loosen the left cowl side pivot bolt.

32. Remove the four screw attachments at the top of the instrument panel and roll the panel out.

33. Pull the wiring, antenna cable, A/C cable and vacuum lines out of the instrument panel. Disconnect the defroster hose and remove the instrument panel with the ducts still attached.

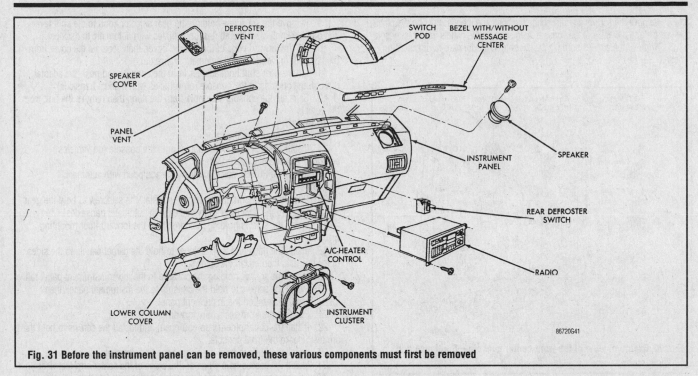

Fig. 31 Before the instrument panel can be removed, these various components must first be removed

To install:

34. Transfer the ducts and brackets onto the new panel.
35. Position the new instrument panel in the vehicle.
36. Route the wiring, antenna cable, A/C cable and vacuum lines into the new instrument panel. Connect the defroster hose.
37. Roll the panel up, then install the four screw attachments at the top of the instrument panel.
38. Install the remaining components in the reverse of the removal procedure.
39. Connect the negative battery cable.

Sundance and Shadow Models

1. Disconnect the negative battery cable.
2. Remove the windshield wiper arms.
3. Open the hood and remove the cowl top plastic cover.
4. Remove the windshield washer reservoir.
5. Pull the connector loose from the A/C resistor block, then push the wiring and grommet through the bulkhead into the passenger compartment.
6. Remove the center console assembly.
7. Remove the passive restraint seat belt logic control module wiring.
8. Remove the attaching nuts securing the instrument panel to the console support brace.
9. Remove the instrument panel-to-console support brace with the air bag system diagnostic module attached.
10. Remove the right and left cowl side and scuff plate trim moldings.
11. Remove the left and right A-pillar trim moldings.
12. Remove the instrument panel top cover.
13. Remove the steering column cover.
14. Unplug the steering column wiring at the 25-way connector.
15. Disconnect the parking brake, brake light and the speed control wiring.
16. Remove the 5 steering column support nuts and lower the steering column. Then remove the 2 steering column attaching studs.
17. Detach the engine harness wiring at the 18-way and 16-way connectors located on the left side panel support bracket.
18. Remove the glove box assembly.
19. Remove the panel top cover.
20. Loosen the panel roll down pivot bolts.
21. Remove the defroster duct adapter from the defroster duct.
22. Remove the screws which attach the instrument panel to the windshield fence line.
23. Roll the panel down, attach a heavy wire to hold it in position and remove the defroster duct retaining screws.

24. Detach the body wiring at the right side 18-way connector and the left side 25-way connector.
25. Separate the temperature mode cable at the in-line connector.
26. Unplug the resistor block and blower motor wiring connectors.
27. Detach the antenna cable.
28. Disconnect the left and right defroster hoses from the defroster outlets on the panel.
29. Remove the instrument panel from the vehicle.

To Install:

30. Position the instrument panel into the vehicle.
31. Connect the left and right defroster to from the defroster outlets on the panel.
32. Attach the antenna cable.
33. Attach the resistor block and blower motor wiring connectors.
34. Install the temperature mode cable at the in-line connector.
35. Attach the body wiring at the right side 18-way connector and the left side 25-way connector.
36. Install the defroster duct retaining screws, then position the panel up.
37. Install the screws to attach the instrument panel to the windshield fence line.
38. To install the remaining components, reverse the removal procedure.
39. Connect the negative battery cable.

Front Center Console

REMOVAL & INSTALLATION

▶ **See Figures 32, 33 and 34**

➡**This is a general procedure and applies to all models covered by this manual. Because of slight year-to-year variances, adjust the procedure to fit your vehicle as necessary.**

1. Position the front seats fully forward.
2. Remove the access hole plugs on the sides of the center arm rest riser and remove the bolts holding the riser to the floor bracket.
3. Remove the coin holder (if equipped) and remove the screws holding the armrest riser to the front console.
4. Position the front seats fully rearward.
5. Remove the radio bezel from the instrument panel. Remove the screws holding the console to the instrument panel.
6. Remove the screws holding the console to the lower instrument panel rail.

7. Remove the screws and disengage the hook and loop fastener holding the carpet panels to the sides of the console, then separate the panels from the console.

8. Remove the screws holding the console to the forward floor mounting bracket.

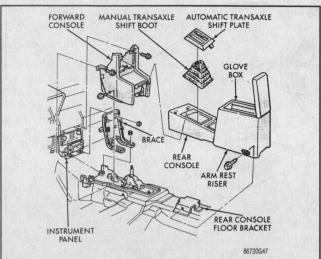

Fig. 32 Exploded view of the front center console—Sundance and Shadow models

86720G47

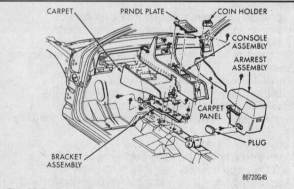

Fig. 33 Exploded view of the LeBaron Sedan, Spirit and Acclaim models' center console

86720G45

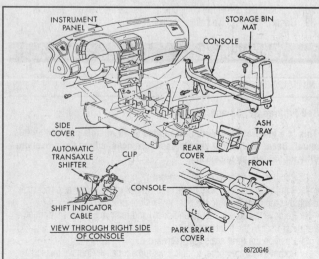

Fig. 34 The center console unit on Daytona, LeBaron Coupe and LeBaron Convertible models

86720G46

9. Remove the set screw holding the gear selector knob to the shift lever and pull the knob off of the shifter (on vehicles with automatic transaxles).

10. Lift the forward edge of the PRNDL cover, then separate the cover from the console (on vehicles with automatic transaxle).

11. Lift the gear shift boot adapter from the console and push the adapter through the opening in the console (on vehicles with manual transaxle).

12. Separate the console assembly from the floor, then remove the unit from the vehicle.

To install:

13. Install the unit in the vehicle.

14. Install the gear shift boot adapter onto the console (on vehicles equipped with manual transaxles).

15. Install the PRNDL cover (on vehicles equipped with automatic transaxles).

16. Push the knob onto the shifter, then install the setscrew to hold the gear selector knob to the shift lever (on vehicles with automatic transaxles).

17. Install the screws holding the console to the forward floor mounting bracket.

18. Install the hook and loop fastener to hold the carpet panels to the sides of the console, then install the screws.

19. Install the screws holding the console to the lower instrument panel rail.

20. Install the screws to hold the console to the instrument panel, then install the radio bezel on the instrument panel.

21. Position the front seats fully forward.

22. Install the coin holder (if so equipped) and install the screws to hold the armrest riser to the front console.

23. Install the bolts to hold the riser to the floor bracket.

24. Install the access hole plugs on the sides of the center arm rest riser.

25. On vehicles with automatic transaxles, verify gear selector indicator adjustment and check all necessary items for proper operation.

Overhead Console

REMOVAL & INSTALLATION

▶ **See Figure 35**

1. Disconnect the negative battery cable.
2. Remove the screws holding overhead console to reinforcement bracket.
3. Slide the overhead console rearward to separate the reinforcement bracket retainer tab from the console.
4. Lower the console assembly from the roof and disconnect electrical connections.
5. Installation is the reverse of the removal procedure.
6. Connect the negative battery cable.

Door Panels

REMOVAL & INSTALLATION

➡ **Use these service procedures as a guide to all years/models. Adjust the procedure for your particular vehicle as necessary.**

Except Daytona, LeBaron Coupe and LeBaron Convertible Models

▶ **See Figures 36 thru 50**

➡ **If the water shield must be removed to work on the window mechanism or other items mounted inside the door, you will need RTV sealant to retain the water shield to the door metal. Since rain water that gets into the window slit drains down inside the door, it is necessary to seal the water shield carefully so there will not be leakage inside the car.**

1. Unsnap the plastic appliquÇs (decorative covers) from the door pull strap and the remote bezel. Then, pull the front edge of the bezel outward and push the bezel backward to release it.

2. Remove the mounting screws at either end of the pull strap and remove it from the door panel.

3. Note the installation angle of the window crank handle and then remove it. To do this, use an Allen wrench to remove the Allen screw from the center of the window mechanism shaft.

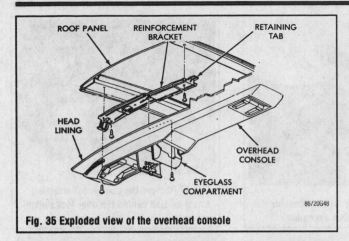

Fig. 35 Exploded view of the overhead console

Labels: ROOF PANEL, REINFORCEMENT BRACKET, RETAINING TAB, HEAD LINING, OVERHEAD CONSOLE, EYEGLASS COMPARTMENT

4. Remove the retaining screws from the lower side of the door handle and remove it.

5. There are spring clips mounted to the door panel which slip into holes drilled into the door metal. Using a flat stick, gently pry the panel off the door at front, back and bottom to release the clips.

6. Lift the panel straight upward to release clips which retain it to the inside of the door by running down into the window slot.

7. If the water shield must be removed, carefully pull it off the retaining material.

To install:

8. To install the panel, first run new sealer around the door metal under the water shield and then stick the water shield to the door.

9. Hook the panel over the door at the window slit and hang it down over the door. Make sure the retaining clips line up with their corresponding holes and then press the panel inward directly over each clip to engage it with the door.

10. Install the door handle with the retaining screws if the car has one.

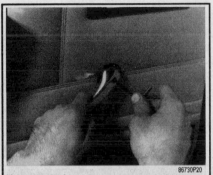

Fig. 36 Use an Allen wrench to remove the Allen screw from the center of the window mechanism shaft—1986 Reliant shown

Fig. 37 After removing the Allen screw remove the handle and spacer from the center of the window mechanism shaft

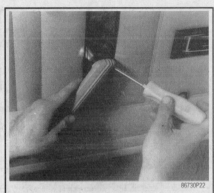

Fig. 38 Removing the upper retaining screw for the pull handle and armrest

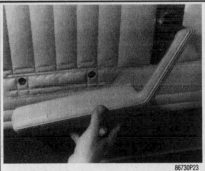

Fig. 39 After removing the remaining two retaining screws remove the pull handle and armrest

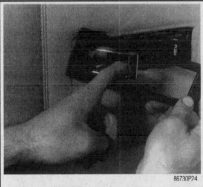

Fig. 40 Unsnap the door handle bezel from the trim panel

Fig. 41 Unsnap the bezel around the power window switch control panel—1991 Acclaim shown

Fig. 42 Unplug the electrical connector from the power window control switch assembly

Fig. 43 The speaker grille unsnaps from the door panel

Fig. 44 Pry the plastic appliquç from the door lock switch

Fig. 45 Remove the retaining screws and remove the door lock switch and plastic bezel from the trim panel

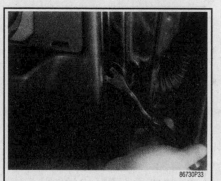

Fig. 46 Unplug the electrical connector from the door lock switch assembly

Fig. 47 Remove the door panel retaining screw located behind the door lock switch assembly

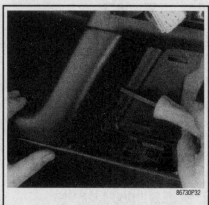

Fig. 48 Pry the door panel from the retaining clip

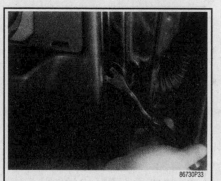

Fig. 49 Pry the around the perimeter of the door panel to release retaining clips with the use of a special trim tool—1991 Acclaim shown, other models similar

Fig. 50 After releasing the retaining clips, lift up and detach the trim panel from the door

11. Install the window crank handle at the same angle by engaging its internal splines with those on the window mechanism shaft. Then, install the retaining screw and tighten it with the Allen wrench.

12. Install the pull strap, its retaining screws and the bezels.

13. Install the remote bezel.

Daytona Model

♦ **See Figure 51**

1. Lower the window all the way. Disconnect the battery negative cable.

2. If the car has manual windows, remove the Allen screw from the end of the window mechanism shaft and remove the crank handle.

3. With a piece of thin, relatively soft material (such as a strip of wood), gently pry the electric mirror/door lock bezel out of the armrest. Then, detach the wiring connectors for the electric mirror and the door lock switch.

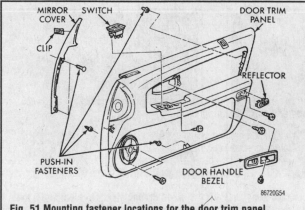

Fig. 51 Mounting fastener locations for the door trim panel

4. Remove the bezel surrounding the remote lock/latch release switches.

5. Disconnect the 4 armrest electrical plugs at the armrest. Remove the screw located behind each plug and the single screw in the opening of the switch bezel.

6. Rotate the armrest to release and remove it.

7. Remove the one remaining trim panel retaining screw from the area of the door near the body pillar.

8. There are spring clips mounted in the door panel which slip into holes drilled into the door metal. Using a flat stick, gently pry the panel off the door at the front, back and bottom to release the clips.

9. Detach the wire connector at the courtesy lamp.

10. Lift the panel straight upward to release the clips which retain it to the inside of the door.

11. If the water shield must be removed, carefully pull it off the retaining material.

To install:

12. To install the panel, first run new sealer around the door metal under the water shield and then stick the water shield to the door.

13. Hook the panel over the door at the window slit and hang it down over the door. Make sure the retaining clips line up with their corresponding holes and then press the panel inward directly over each clip to engage it with the door. Attach the wire connector at the courtesy lamp.

14. Install the trim panel retaining screw located in the area of the door near the body pillar.

15. Rotate the armrest into position.

16. Install the screw located behind the location of each plug in the armrest and the single screw in the opening of the switch bezel. Connect the 4 armrest electrical plugs.

17. Install the bezel surrounding the remote lock/latch release switches.

18. Install the wiring connectors for the electric mirror and the door lock switch. Then, install the electric mirror/door lock bezel into the armrest.

19. If the car has manual windows, install the crank handle, then install the Allen screw into the end of the window mechanism shaft.

20. Reconnect the negative battery cable.

LeBaron Coupe and Convertible Models

▶ See Figure 52

1. Lower the window all the way.
2. Remove the switch bezel and the radio speaker from the door.
3. Remove the screw from the opening in which the switch bezel was located.
4. Remove the 2 mounting screws from the through-slits in the carpeted area of the map pocket.
5. If the car has manually operated windows, remove the retaining Allen screw for the regulator handle from the center of the window regulator shaft. Note the installation angle of the regulator handle and then remove it. Remove the spacer behind the handle.
6. Pull the bottom of the trim panel outward carefully to disengage the lower clips. Pull it out just far enough to gain access to the courtesy lamp connection. Then, reach behind the panel and disconnect the courtesy lamp wire.
7. Pull the panel in order to remove the remaining clips from the door. Lift the panel straight upward to release clips which retain it to the inside of the door.
8. If the water shield must be removed, carefully pull it off the retaining material.

To install:

9. To install the panel, first run new sealer around the door metal under the water shield and then stick the water shield to the door.
10. Hook the panel over the door at the window slit and hang it down over the door. Attach the wire connector at the courtesy lamp. Make sure the retaining clips line up with their corresponding holes and then press the panel inward directly over each clip to engage it with the door.
11. Reinstall the regulator handle at its original installation angle.
12. Install the 2 screws attaching the door panel, working through the slits in the carpeted area of the map pocket.
13. Install the panel retaining screw in the opening in which the switch bezel was located.
14. Install the switch bezel and the radio speaker in the door.

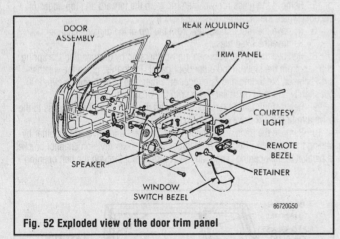

Fig. 52 Exploded view of the door trim panel

Door Locks

REMOVAL & INSTALLATION

Except Daytona

▶ See Figures 53 and 54

➡ On Sundance and Shadow, a Torx® screwdriver is required to remove the lock mechanism mounting screws.

1. Raise the glass until it is up all the way.
2. Remove the trim panel and plastic air shield as previously described.
3. Disconnect the outside handle link and key cylinder link from the lock mechanism.
4. Disconnect the remote control link, remote latch lock link and, if the car has electric locks, the electric motor link.

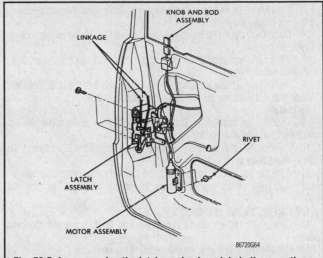

Fig. 53 Before removing the latch mechanism, label all connecting rods/links and electrical cables

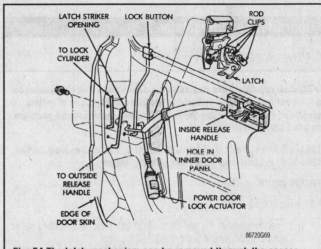

Fig. 54 The latch mechanism can be removed through the access hole in the door

5. Remove the 3 lock attaching screws, then extract the lock through the access hole.

To install:

6. Reposition the lock inside the door through the access hole. Install the 3 attaching screws.
7. Reconnect the remote control link, remote latch lock link and, if the car has electric locks, the electric motor link.
8. Reconnect the outside handle link and key cylinder link to the lock mechanism.
9. Install the water shield and trim panel as previously described.
10. Adjust the latch as described in the door adjusting procedure earlier in this section.

Daytona

➡ If the car has electric door locks, you will need 2 short ¼–20 bolts and corresponding nuts.

1. Roll the window down all the way.
2. Disconnect the negative battery cable.
3. Remove the door panel as described earlier in this section. Peel the water shield away at the top/rear to gain access to the hole located on the inside of the door and near the lock mechanism.
4. Raise the window all the way (if the car has electric windows, reconnect the battery to do this and then disconnect it again).

5. Disconnect the lock cylinder-to-lock link. Disconnect the outside handle-to-lock mechanism link.

6. Disconnect the inside handle-to-lock link and the inside remote lock actuator-to-lock link.

7. If the car is equipped with electric door locks, drill out the 2 rivets that retain the locking motor.

8. Remove the 3 bolts attaching the lock mechanism to the door. Remove the lock and, if the car has electric locks, the locking motor.

To install:

9. To install the mechanism, first transfer the locking motor to the new mechanism (on cars with electric locks).

10. Position the latch assembly on the door and install the 3 attaching bolts. Tighten these bolts to 75 inch lbs. (9 Nm).

11. If the car has electric locks, attach the locking motor to the door with 2 short ¼–20 bolts and corresponding nuts. Tighten the bolts to 90 inch lbs. (10 Nm).

12. Connect the lock cylinder to the latch link.

13. Connect the outside handle to the latch link. Do the same with the inside handle.

14. Connect the inside lock remote switch to the latch link.

15. Lower the window all the way (temporarily connecting the battery on cars equipped with electric windows to do so). Then, install the air shield, water shield and trim panel as described earlier in this section.

16. Reconnect the battery.

Door Glass and Regulator

REMOVAL & INSTALLATION

➡**Window regulators are riveted to the door frame. The rivets must be drilled out and replaced by bolts or bolt/nut combinations of certain specification. Read through the procedure and make sure all parts are on hand before beginning work.**

1981–88 Aries, Reliant, Town and Country, Caravelle, New Yorker, 400, 600, E-Class and 1988–90 LeBaron Sedan

FRONT DOOR

▶ **See Figure 55**

1. Lower the glass all the way. Remove the trim panel as described earlier.

2. Gently pull the air and water shields off the door.

3. Remove the 3 nuts that attach the glass to the regulator channel. Then, lower the glass all the way.

4. Remove the outer glass-sealing weatherstrip by disengaging the spring clip tabs from the slots in the outer door panel. To do this, grasp the weather-

strip between the thumb and forefinger on either side of each spring clip. Pull out slightly and then up at each clip until the weatherstrip is free.

5. Work the glass off the mounting studs and remove it through the slot in the top of the lower door.

6. To remove the regulator, drive the center pin of each regulator mounting rivet out with a hammer and drift punch. Then, drill the rivets out with a ¼ in. (6mm) drill.

7. Disengage the regulator arm from the lift plate and then remove the regulator through the access hole in the inside of the door.

To install:

8. Load the new regulator in through the access hole and engage the access arm with the lift plate. Then, bolt the regulator to the door with ¼–20 nuts and short screws, making sure these screws will not interfere with regulator operation. Tighten the screws and nuts to 90–115 inch lbs. (10–13 Nm).

9. Install the new glass by lowering it into the door. Position the glass on the mounting studs.

10. Install the outer weatherstrip by sliding the clips into the door panel slots and sliding them downward until they lock.

11. Raise the glass to the top of its travel, then loosely install the 3 retaining nuts. Seat the glass fully in the upper glass run to adjust it, and then tighten the mounting nuts gently.

12. Install the air and water shields and the trim panel as described earlier in this section.

REAR DOOR

▶ **See Figures 56 and 57**

1. Remove the trim panel as described earlier in this section.

2. Remove the water shield and air shield. Remove the end seals from the front and rear of the door at the belt line.

3. Remove its 2 mounting bolts and remove the support bracket from underneath the fixed glass at the rear of the door.

4. Remove, from inside the door, the 2 brackets that attach the "division" channel (dividing the moveable and stationary glass sections).

5. Remove the glass run weatherstrip from the forward and top edges of the door where the movable glass contacts it.

6. Remove the mounting screw from the top of the division channel.

7. Remove the fixed glass.

8. Remove the outer glass-sealing weatherstrip by disengaging the spring clip tabs from the slots in the outer door panel. To do this, grasp the weatherstrip between the thumb and forefinger on either side of each spring clip. Pull out slightly and then up at each clip until the weatherstrip is free.

9. Remove the bolt (it has a shoulder on it) which attaches the glass to the drive arm of the flex drive mechanism.

10. Remove the division channel, movable glass and drive arm together by raising the assembly. Rotate it 90 degrees, so the lower division channel bracket is parallel to the opening. Then, lift the assembly out through the belt opening.

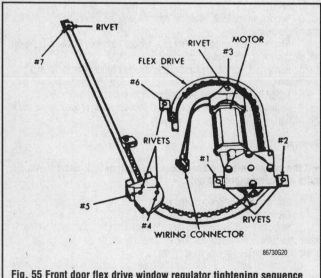

Fig. 55 Front door flex drive window regulator tightening sequence

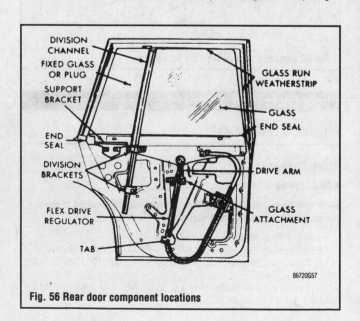

Fig. 56 Rear door component locations

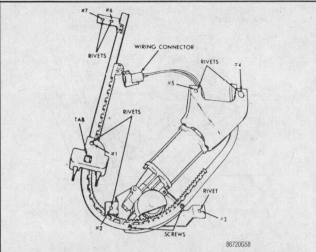

Fig. 57 When tightening the regulator mounting bolts, make certain to follow the numerical sequence as shown

11. Drive the center pins from the 6 mounting rivets (7 with electric windows) from the regulator using a hammer and drift pin. Then drill the rivets out with a ¼ in. (6mm) drill. Then, rotate the regulator as necessary for clearance and remove it through the access hole in the door.

To install:

12. If reusing the same regulator, clean and lubricate the flex drive teeth. Then, orient the regulator so it can be installed through the access hole and locate it inside the door with its locating tab engaging the appropriate hole.

➡ **The tightening sequence specified for the following step must be followed to prevent binding of the flex drive unit for the window.**

13. Use ¼–20 bolts and nuts to remount the regulator, tightening the nuts as specified in the illustration. Tighten to 90 inch lbs. (10 Nm).

14. To install the new glass, start the bottom of the division channel, the glass, and the drive arm assembly into the belt opening. With the lower bracket parallel to the opening, lower the assembly into the door until the upper division channel bracket is near the belt opening.

15. Rotate the assembly 90 degrees to bring it into its normal orientation. Then, rest the channel on the bottom of the door.

16. Raise the glass by hand. Then, position the drive arm onto the flex drive and secure it using the bolt with the shoulder on it.

17. Install the outer glass-sealing weatherstrip.

18. Install the fixed-glass bracket, but do not tighten the bolts. Then, position the fixed-glass into the opening and rock it into position. Allow it to rest lightly on the support bracket.

19. Fit the rear edge of the division channel over the front edge of the fixed-glass. Then, install the mounting screw into the top of the division channel.

20. Install the glass run weatherstrip into the forward and top door channels.

21. Install the upper bracket retaining the division channel. Then, install the lower bracket retaining the division channel.

22. Push the fixed glass bracket upward and secure it in place.

23. Install the end seals at the belt opening. Install the air and water shields.

24. Install the door trim panel as described earlier in this section.

Daytona

✳✳ CAUTION

If the glass has shattered, wear gloves and work cautiously. Use a protective, heavy cloth to cover all painted surfaces, plastic parts, and interior trim near the glass. Remove the glass from the window frame before removing the gloves.

1. Roll the window all the way down.
2. Disconnect the battery.
3. Remove the trim panel and air and water shields as described earlier in this section. Then, raise the glass until it is possible to work on the glass

mounting nuts through the lower access hole (reconnecting the battery temporarily to operate the window motor, if the car has electric windows).

✳✳ WARNING

If the glass is still in position, make sure to support it during the next step.

4. Remove the 3 lift plate-to-glass attaching nuts.
5. Remove the 2 glass stabilizers. If the glass is intact, remove it through the window frame.

✳✳ CAUTION

If the glass has been shattered, wear gloves/goggles and use a heavy duty shop-vacuum to carefully remove all glass particles from the door and glass run at this point.

6. Remove the lift plate-to-regulator screw and remove the lift plate from the door.

7. Using a hammer and drift punch, drive out the center pin in each of the 6 rivets (7 on cars with electric windows) that mount the regulator to the door. Then, drill out each rivet with a ¼ in. (6mm) drill.

8. Turn the regulator as necessary and then remove it through the access hole in the door.

To install:

9. Remove the flex window drive and install it onto the new regulator. Clean and lubricate the teeth.

10. Work the assembly back into the door through the access hole, and position it so its mounting holes line up with the holes where rivets where installed. Install ¼x20 bolts and corresponding nuts to mount the regulator. Tighten the bolts to 90 inch lbs. (10 Nm).

11. Attach the lift plate to the regulator with an M6x25 bolt.

12. Attach the 3 glass-to-lift plate mounting studs to the new glass. Then, install the glass through the window opening. It must initially be cocked to the rear to work it into position and then leveled. Install the retaining nuts without tightening them.

13. Attach the 2 inner stabilizers without tightening them. Then, loosen the 3 glass track mounting screws.

14. Connect the battery if the car has electric windows and install the crank handle if it has manually operated windows. Then, guiding the glass, move the window up carefully until it has reached its uppermost position.

15. Tighten the 3 lift plate-to-glass attaching nuts, starting with the one in the middle, to 85 inch lbs. (9 Nm).

16. Tighten the 3 glass track mounting screws to 115 inch lbs. (13 Nm).

17. Adjust the inner glass stabilizers so they just touch the glass and then tighten them to 115 inch lbs. (13 Nm).

18. Lower the glass and disconnect the battery or remove the window regulator handle. Install the door trim panel as described earlier in this section.

19. Connect the negative battery cable.

1989–90 Models Except Daytona and LeBaron Sedan

FRONT DOOR WITH MANUAL REGULATOR

➡ **A special tool must be used to remove the glass, or the glass-run channel may be damaged. Use Miller Tool No. C–4867 or equivalent.**

1. Remove the door trim panel as described earlier. Carefully remove the water shield as described there also.

2. Lower the glass to gain the best possible access to the rear glass sliders. Then, use the special tool to disengage the sliders from the rear glass guide, holding the glass to keep it from rotating and falling.

3. Rotating the glass on the regulator roller, slide it rearward and lower the rear until it reaches a 45° angle. Then, remove it.

4. Temporarily install the regulator handle and set the position of the unit for easy access to the regulator mounting rivets (just below the position where the window would normally be all the way up).

5. Drill out the three rivets on the regulator with a ¼ in. (6mm) drill. Then, slide the regulator off the glass lift channel. Cock the regulator to an appropriate angle and remove it through the access hole.

To install:

6. Angle and position the regulator appropriately and work it through the access hole in the door.

7. Line up the regulator mounting and rivet holes and then install short ¼–20 bolts and nuts (it may be easier to install the bolts if you reset the position of the regulator by temporarily installing the handle). Tighten the bolts to 90–115 inch lbs. (10–13 Nm) and make sure they are short enough so that they will not interfere with the moving parts as the window is raised and lowered.

8. Transfer the lift channel and sliders to the new glass. Then, slide the glass back into the door at the angle at which it was removed.

9. Rotate the glass to its normal position and slide it forward on the regulator roller in reverse of the removal procedure.

10. Position the glass for best possible access to the rear sliders, holding it to keep it from rotating and falling. Then, use the special tool to engage the sliders with the rear glass guide.

11. Install the water shield and trim panel as described earlier in this section.

12. Connect the negative battery cable.

FRONT DOOR WITH ELECTRIC REGULATOR

➡**A special tool must be used to remove the glass, or the glass-run channel may be damaged. Use Miller Tool No. C–4867 or equivalent.**

1. Disconnect the negative battery cable.

2. Remove the door trim panel as described earlier in this section. Carefully remove the water shield as described there also.

3. Lower the glass (temporarily attach the battery cable) to gain the best possible access to the rear glass sliders. Then, use the special tool to disengage the sliders from the rear glass guide, holding the glass to keep it from rotating and falling.

4. Rotating the glass on the regulator roller, slide it rearward and lower the rear until it reaches a 45° angle. Then, remove it.

5. Adjust the position of the regulator until there is access to all the regulator mounting rivets (this is just below the position where the glass is all the way up.

6. Disconnect the negative battery cable. Then, detach the window motor electrical connector.

7. Drill out the 6 regulator mounting rivets with a ¼ in. (6mm) drill. Then, slide the regulator off the glass channel.

8. Remove the motor from the regulator. Then, remove the regulator from the door, turning it as necessary so it will fit easily through the access hole.

To install:

9. If the regulator is being re-used, clean and lubricate the teeth on the flex drive rack. Then, load the regulator assembly through the door access panel.

10. Install the motor onto the regulator. Then, engage the regulator roller with the lift channel.

11. Line up the regulator mounting and rivet holes, then install short ¼–20 bolts and nuts (it may be easier to install the bolts if you reset the position of the regulator by temporarily installing the handle). Tighten the bolts to 90–115 inch lbs. (10–13 Nm) and make sure they are short enough that they will not interfere with the moving parts as the window is raised and lowered.

12. Attach the regulator wiring connector and the negative battery cable.

13. Transfer the lift channel and sliders to the new glass. Then, slide the glass back into the door at the angle at which it was removed.

14. Rotate the glass to its normal position and slide it forward on the regulator roller in reverse of the removal procedure.

15. Position the glass for best possible access to the rear sliders, holding it to keep it from rotating and falling. Then, use the special tool to engage the sliders with the rear glass guide.

16. Install the water shield and trim panel as described earlier.

REAR DOOR WITH MANUAL REGULATOR

Follow the previous front door with manual regulator procedure, noting that there are only 3 or 4 mounting rivets for the regulator assembly.

REAR DOOR WITH ELECTRICAL REGULATOR

Follow the previous front door with electric regulator procedure through Step 4. Remove the regulator-to-regulator arm bolt; then proceed with the remaining steps of the procedure. Note that the rear door electric window regulator is retained by only 5 mounting rivets.

1991–95 Spirit, Acclaim, LeBaron Sedan, Sundance and Shadow

▸ See Figures 58, 59 and 60

1. Remove the door trim panel, silencer pad and water shield.

2. Position the door glass half way up pin the door glass opening.

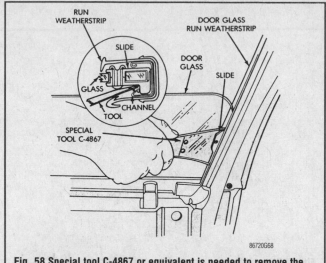

Fig. 58 Special tool C-4867 or equivalent is needed to remove the window glass from the door

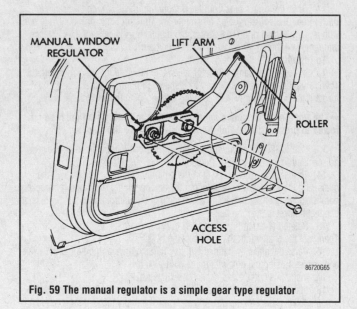

Fig. 59 The manual regulator is a simple gear type regulator

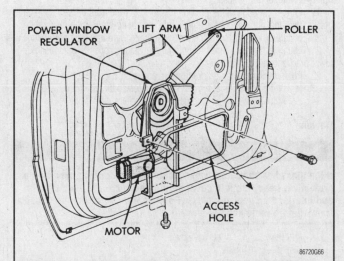

Fig. 60 The power window regulator is also a gear type regulator, but it driven by the power motor rather than the hand crank

3. Insert the door glass removal tool C-4867 (or equivalent) between the glass slide and channel retaining lip at approximately 2 in. (51mm) down from the top rearward corner of the glass. Push the handle of the tool toward the glass to open the channel. Push downward at the front of the glass to separate the slide from the channel.

4. Insert the door glass removal tool C-4867 (or equivalent) between the glass slide and channel retaining lip at approximately 2 in. (51mm) up from the bottom rearward corner of the glass through the opening in the inner door panel. Push the handle of the tool toward the glass to open the channel. Pull upward at the front of the glass to separate the slide from the channel. Do not allow the upper slide to snap back into the channel.

5. Rotate the front of the glass downward and slide the glass forward to separate the glass lift channel from the regulator lift arm roller.

6. Remove the door glass through the opening at the top of the door.

7. On vehicles with power windows, disconnect the negative battery cable.

8. Detach all electrical connectors from the power window motor, if applicable.

9. Remove the bolts holding the window regulator to the inner door panel.

10. Slide the roller from the window lift channel. Rotate the regulator to bring the lift arm through the access hole first.

11. Remove the regulator assembly from the door

To install:

12. Position the regulator in the door in its original position, then install and tighten the regulator mounting bolts until snug. Make sure that the roller is situated in the window lift channel.

13. Connect the electrical wiring to the window motor, if applicable.

14. Lower the door glass into the opening at the top of the door.

15. Tip the rear of the glass downward and insert the window channel regulator arm roller into the glass lift channel, if not already done.

16. Guide the door glass into the glass run weatherstrip at the front of the door.

17. Push the top of the glass rearward to snap the top slide into the glass run channel.

18. Push downward at the front of the glass to snap the bottom slide into the glass run channel.

19. Install the water shield, silencer pad and trim panel.

20. Connect the negative battery cable.

1991–95 Dynasty

▶ See Figures 61 and 62

1. Disconnect the negative battery cable.
2. Remove the door trim panel.
3. Remove the silencer pad and water shield.
4. Remove the side view mirror trim cover and door frame trim molding.
5. Remove the front door speaker.
6. Move the glass to the down position and remove the glass-to-lift plate fasteners.

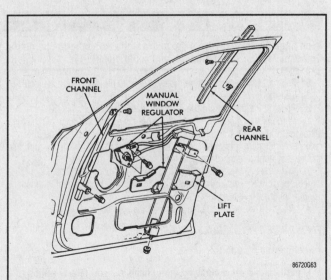

Fig. 61 Manual window regulator orientation in the door unit

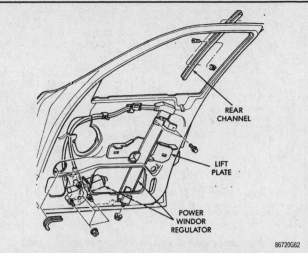

Fig. 62 The power window regulator is positioned the same as the manual type, but the power motor is mounted in the bottom of the door

7. Loosen the door glass slam bumpers.

8. Lift the glass upward through the opening at the top of the door.

9. Remove the nut holding the cable retainer to the inner door panel and slip the cables from behind the retainer.

10. Disengage the push-in retainer holding the cables to the inner door panel above the speaker on vehicles with power windows.

11. Remove the bolts holding the top of the glass lift bar to the inner door panel.

12. Remove the nut holding the bottom of the lift bar to the bottom panel of the door.

13. Remove the bolts holding the window crank regulator to the inner door panel on vehicles with manual windows.

14. Remove the nuts holding the motor and regulator to the inner door panel on vehicles with power windows.

15. Separate the window regulator and power motor, if applicable, from the door.

To install:

16. Position the window regulator and power motor, if applicable, in the door.

17. Install the nuts to hold the motor and regulator to the inner door panel on vehicles with power windows.

18. Install the bolts to hold the window crank regulator to the inner door panel on vehicles with manual windows.

19. Install the nut to hold the bottom of the lift bar to the bottom panel of the door.

20. Install the bolts to hold the top of the glass lift bar to the inner door panel.

21. Engage the push-in retainer to hold the cables to the inner door panel above the speaker on vehicles with power windows.

22. Slip the cables in behind the retainer and remove the nut to hold the cable retainer to the inner door panel.

23. Lower the glass down through the opening at the top of the door.

24. Tighten the door glass slam bumpers.

25. Install the glass-to-lift plate fasteners.

26. Install the front door speaker, if applicable.

27. Install the side view mirror trim cover and door frame trim molding.

28. Install the silencer pad and water shield.

29. Install the door trim panel.

30. Connect the negative battery cable.

1990–91 TC by Maserati; 1991–93 Daytona, LeBaron Coupe and LeBaron Convertible

▶ See Figures 63 and 64

1. Remove the door trim panel.
2. Remove the silencer pad and water shield.
3. Raise the door glass to 4 in. (10cm) above the down position.

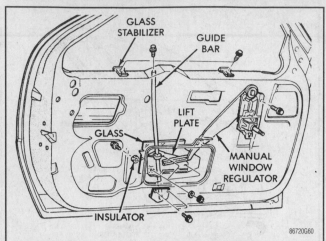

Fig. 63 Familiarize yourself with the various components and their locations before dismantling the regulator from the door

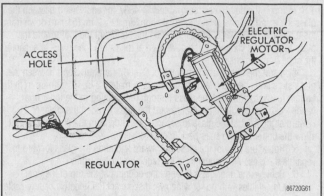

Fig. 64 The electric power window regulator, as well as the manual regulator, should be removed through the access hole in the door

4. Disconnect the negative battery cable, if the vehicle is equipped with power windows.

5. Loosen the bolts holding the glass stabilizers and guide hook receiver to the top of the inner door frame.

6. Remove the nuts holding the door glass to the lift plate.

7. Separate the glass from the lift plate and lift the glass upward from the opening at the top of the door.

8. Remove the bolts holding the regulator to the inner door panel.

9. Remove the nuts holding the lift plate to the glass.

10. Remove the regulator assembly through the access hole in the door.

To install:

11. Install the regulator assembly through the access hole in the door.

12. Install the nuts to hold the lift plate to the glass.

13. Install the bolts to hold the regulator to the inner door panel.

14. Lower the glass down through the opening at the top of the door, then install the glass to the lift plate.

15. Install the nuts to hold the door glass to the lift plate.

16. Tighten the bolts to hold the glass stabilizers and guide hook receiver to the top of the inner door frame.

17. Connect the negative battery cable, if disconnected.

18. Install the silencer pad and water shield.

19. Install the door trim panel.

Electric Window Motor

REMOVAL & INSTALLATION

1981–90 Models

CONVENTIONAL (GEAR TYPE) REGULATORS

▶ See Figure 65

✻✻ CAUTION

The regulator incorporates a very powerful spring which forces the window toward the top of the window frame at all times. Raise the window to the full up position and keep it there at all times while replacing the motor.

1. Remove the trim panel as described in the appropriate procedure above. Raise the window until it is in the full up position. Then, securely prop the window in this position.

2. Disconnect the negative battery cable. Then, detach the electric window motor electrical connector located about 11 in. (28cm) away from the motor in the wiring harness.

3. Remove the 3 mounting screws which attach the motor gearbox to the window regulator. On most models, there are 3 holes in the inner panel to pro-

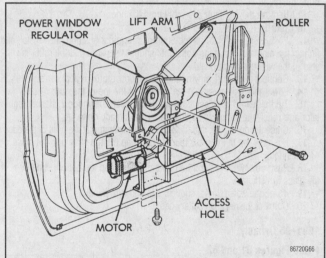

Fig. 65 Although older models retain the regulator with rivets, newer models use attaching bolts

vide access to these screws. On the LeBaron coupe and convertible models, access can be gained through the opening in the inner panel, then reach around to the rear of the regulator to gain access to these screws.

4. Remove the motor from the regulator by grabbing the motor housing and pulling it toward either the inner or outer panel.

✻✻ CAUTION

Keep fingers well away from the gears while disengaging the motor. Gears may turn a small amount, and could pinch!

5. Rock or twist the motor as necessary to get it to disengage from the regulator.

To install:

6. Position the motor onto the regulator, gaining access as during removal. Work the motor into a position that will ensure the motor gear engages the regulator sector teeth and the center post on the motor gearbox enters the pilot hole in the mounting plate. As the motor approaches its final position, rock it to ensure easy engagement of the gear teeth.

7. Align the motor screw holes with those in the mounting plate. Install the 3 motor gearbox screws and the single tie-down bracket screw. Tighten them to 50–60 inch lbs. (6–7 Nm).

8. Attach the multi-prong connector and then the battery.

FLEX-DRIVE TYPE REGULATORS

▶ See Figures 66 and 67

➡To perform this procedure, a center punch, a ¼ in. (6mm) drill, and 7 size #8 (¼ x 32) in. screws are required.

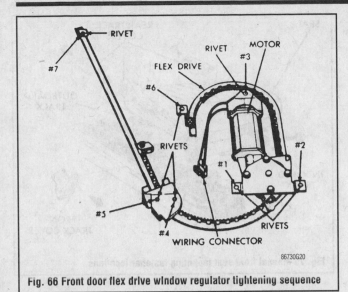

Fig. 66 Front door flex drive window regulator tightening sequence

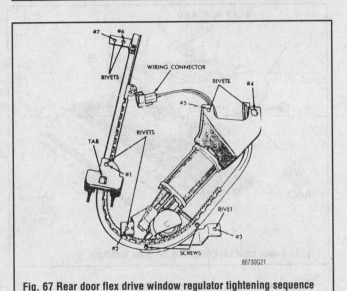

Fig. 67 Rear door flex drive window regulator tightening sequence

1. Remove   the trim panel as described in the appropriate procedure above. Then, the screw that attaches the flexible rack to the drive arm must be removed. Adjust the position of the window up and down until the position is right for access to this screw and then remove it. Securely prop the window in this position. If the motor will not operate on its own, try assisting it cautiously. If this fails, see the note below.

2. Disconnect the battery. Disconnect the motor electrical connector.

3. Remove the regulator/motor attaching rivets by knocking out the rivet center mandrels with a hammer and the center punch. Then, drill the rivets out with the ¼ in. (6mm) drill.

4. Start the motor end of the flex drive regulator out through the largest access hole in the door panel, maneuvering and rotating the unit out. Remove the screws attaching the motor to the flexible track.

➡If the motor will not move, it will be necessary follow Steps 2 and 3 to drill out the attaching rivets. Then, move the motor/flexible drive assembly as necessary to gain access to the screws mounting the motor to the flex drive. Manually lift the window upward until it is possible to access the screw that attaches the flexible rack to the drive arm and then remove it.

5. Remove the 2 screws attaching the motor to the flex drive.

To install:

6. Feed the top of the flexible drive track into the access hole and then rotate it toward the door pillar until the motor is horizontal. Then, rotate the assembly (about ¼ turn) in the opposite direction to align the bracket tab with the slot in the inner door panel.

7. Install the mounting screws and tighten in sequence to 40 inch lbs. (4 Nm). Refer to the illustrations in this section.

8. Connect the motor electrical connector. Reconnect the battery. Position the window drive so the flex rack fitting lines up with the window drive arm. Install the screw and tighten to 40 inch lbs. (4 Nm). Remove the window prop.

1991–95 Models

CABLE AND SLIDE TYPE REGULATORS

▶ See Figure 68

➡This type of regulator is found on all Dynasty models.

The electric window motor cannot be replaced separately from the regulator assembly. If either the motor or regulator becomes defective, both components must be replaced together. For the removal and installation instructions, refer to the regulator and door glass procedure earlier in this section.

CONVENTIONAL (GEAR TYPE) REGULATORS

This procedure is the same for 1981–95 vehicles. Therefore, refer to the 1981–90 procedure, located earlier in this section, for this type of regulator.

FLEX-DRIVE TYPE REGULATORS

▶ See Figure 69

1. Remove the regulator and motor, as described earlier in this section.
2. Remove the electric motor attaching screws.
3. Remove the motor from the flex-drive bracket.

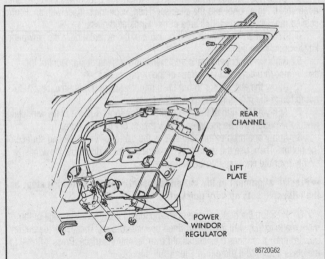

Fig. 68 The complete cable and slide type regulator assembly must be replaced with a new one if the power motor is defective

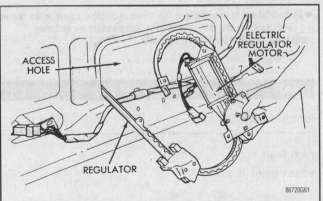

Fig. 69 The electric power window regulator, flex-drive and electric motor must all be removed together

To install:

4. Position the new motor onto the flex-drive bracket.

5. Install the attaching screws until snug.

6. Install the regulator, flex-drive and new motor into the door. For more details, refer to the door glass and regulator installation procedure earlier in this section.

Inside Rear View Mirror

REPLACEMENT

The mirror is mechanically attached to the mirror button, and if it should become cracked or develop a mechanical problem which prevents easy adjustment, it can be replaced very simply by disconnecting it from the button. The button, in turn, serves to mount the mirror to the windshield. If it should be damaged or the adhesive bond should become partly broken, it can be removed and replaced after the mirror is detached. Note that removal of the button and/or remaining adhesive requires the use of a controllable electric heat gun. Also needed, if the button must be replaced, are a rag soaked in alcohol, ordinary kitchen cleanser, and fine-grit sandpaper. The new button is installed using a special adhesive kit 4054099 or an equivalent available in the aftermarket.

1. Loosen the setscrew with a standard screwdriver until all tension is removed. Slide the base of the mirror upward and off the mounting button.

2. If the mirror mounting button must be removed, first mark the location of the button on the outside of the windshield with a wax pencil. Then, apply low heat with the electric heat gun to soften the vinyl. When it is soft, peel the button off the glass.

3. Clean the surface of the windshield where the button was mounted with a rag soaked in alcohol and the cleanser. Then, wipe the surface with an alcohol soaked rag. Do not touch this area of the windshield glass!

4. Crush the vial in the plastic housing of the accelerator in the new button kit to saturate the applicator.

5. Remove the paper sleeve and then apply a generous amount of the accelerator to the mounting surface of the mirror button.

6. Allow the accelerator to dry for 5 minutes; during this time, be careful not to touch the mounting surface of the button.

7. Apply a thin film of the accelerator to the inner surface of the windshield where the button will be mounted. Allow this to dry for 1 minute.

8. Apply one drop of the adhesive to the center of the mounting surface of the button. Then, use the bottom of the adhesive tube, distribute the adhesive evenly over the entire button bonding surface.

➥**Precise alignment of the button is essential in the following step, as the adhesive sets up very quickly!**

9. Position the bottom edge of the button against the lower edge of the mark made earlier with the button lined up side-to-side. Then, rock the button upward until it touches the windshield over its entire surface. Press it firmly to the glass and hold it there firmly for 1 full minute.

10. Remove the pressure, but allow 5 minutes more time for the button mounting adhesive to dry.

11. With an alcohol-dampened cloth, remove any adhesive which may have spread beyond the mounting surface of the button.

➥**Be careful not to over-tighten the mirror mounting screw in the following procedure, as the mirror mounting button could be distorted, destroying its bond with the windshield.**

12. Slide the mirror downward and over the mount. Tighten the screw gently!

Seats

REMOVAL & INSTALLATION

Front Seats

▶ **See Figures 70 and 71**

1. Position the seat fully forward.

2. Remove the screws holding the rear track riser covers and separate the covers from the tracks.

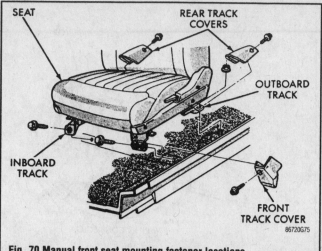

Fig. 70 Manual front seat mounting fastener locations

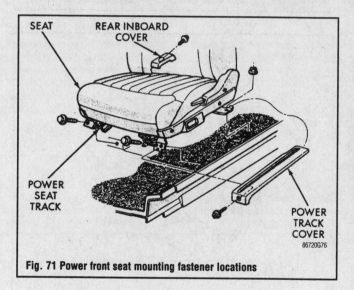

Fig. 71 Power front seat mounting fastener locations

3. On power seats, remove the outboard track cover.

4. Remove the inboard seat belt attaching bolt from the floor.

5. Remove the nuts holding the seat track to the floor.

6. Position the seat fully rearward.

7. On power seats, remove the door sill scuff plate and unplug the wire connector.

8. Remove the bolts holding the seat track to the crossmember.

9. Remove the seat from the vehicle.

To install:

10. Install the seat into the vehicle.

11. Install the bolts to hold the seat track to the crossmember.

12. On power seats, install the door sill scuff plate and attach the wire connector.

13. Position the seat fully forward.

14. Install the nuts to hold the seat track to the floor.

15. Install the inboard seat belt attaching bolt to the floor.

16. On power seats, install the outboard track cover.

17. Install the covers onto the tracks, then install the screws to hold the rear track riser covers.

Rear Seats

ARIES, RELIANT TOWN & COUNTRY, CARAVELLE, 400, 600, E-CLASS AND 1982–85 LEBARON

1. To remove the rear seat cushion, perform the following:

a. Remove the 2 screws from the underside of the front of the rear seat cushion.

b. Remove the cushion from the vehicle.

2. Remove the seat back by performing the following:

a. Remove the screws from the bottom/rear of the seatback. Then unsnap the 2 seatbelt retainers.

b. Lift the seat back upward to disengage the seat back wires from the support pockets.

To install:

3. Install the seat back as follows:

a. Position the seat back in the vehicle, then push the seat back inward to engage the inboard pivot.

b. Install the bolts to hold the outboard hinge pivot bracket to the seat back.

c. Engage the push-in fasteners to hold the carpet backing to the trunk floor. Swing the seat back rearward.

4. To install the rear seat cushion, perform the following:

a. Install the cushion into the vehicle.

b. Route the center occupant seat belts through the openings in the cushion.

c. Install the bolts to hold the cushion to the floor.

ACCLAIM, SPIRIT, SUNDANCE, SHADOW AND 1986–95 LEBARON

♦ **See Figure 72**

1. To remove the rear seat cushion, perform the following:

a. Remove the bolts holding the cushion to the floor.

b. Push the center occupant seat belts through the openings in the cushion.

c. Remove the cushion from the vehicle.

2. Remove the seat back by performing the following:

a. Hinge the seat back forward and disengage the push-in fasteners holding the carpet backing to the trunk floor.

b. Remove the bolts holding the outboard hinge pivot bracket to the seat back.

c. Pull the seat back outward to disengage the inboard pivot and remove it from the vehicle.

To install:

3. Install the seat back as follows:

a. Position the seat back in the vehicle, then push the seat back inward to engage the inboard pivot.

b. Install the bolts to hold the outboard hinge pivot bracket to the seat back.

c. Engage the push-in fasteners to hold the carpet backing to the trunk floor. Swing the seat back rearward.

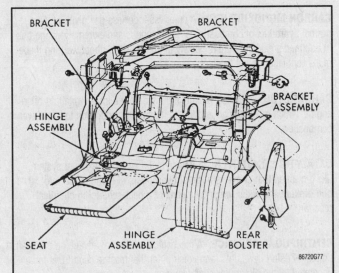

Fig. 72 Exploded view of the rear seat cushion and back mounting

BRACKET
BRACKET
BRACKET ASSEMBLY
HINGE ASSEMBLY
SEAT
HINGE ASSEMBLY
REAR BOLSTER

86720G77

4. To install the rear seat cushion, perform the following:

a. Install the cushion into the vehicle.

b. Route the center occupant seat belts through the openings in the cushion.

c. Install the bolts to hold the cushion to the floor.

NEW YORKER AND DYNASTY

1. To remove the rear seat cushion, perform the following:

a. Remove the bolts holding the cushion to the floor.

b. Push the center occupant seat belts through the openings in the cushion.

c. Remove the cushion from the vehicle.

2. Remove the seat back by performing the following:

a. Remove the bolts holding the seat back to the rear floor kick-up.

b. Lift the seat back upward to disengage the upper hooks from the shelf support panel.

c. Separate the seat back from the vehicle.

To install:

3. Install the seat back as follows:

a. Position the seat back in the vehicle.

b. Slide the seat back down to engage the upper hooks to the shelf support panel.

c. Install the bolts to hold the seat back to the rear floor kick-up.

4. To install the rear seat cushion, perform the following:

a. Install the cushion into the vehicle.

b. Route the center occupant seat belts through the openings in the cushion.

c. Install the bolts to hold the cushion to the floor.

DAYTONA

1. Hinge the seat backs forward.

2. Remove the bolts holding the rear seat frame to the floor on the sides of the center floor hump near the luggage compartment kick-up.

3. Pull the seat forward to disengage the retaining hooks from the floor.

4. Remove the seat from the vehicle.

To install:

5. Install the seat into the vehicle:

6. Push the seat rearward to engage the retaining hooks to the floor.

7. Install the bolts to hold the rear seat frame to the floor on the sides of the center floor hump near the luggage compartment kick-up.

8. Hinge the seat backs rearward.

Power Seat Motor

REMOVAL & INSTALLATION

1. Move the seat adjuster as required for easy access to the mounting bolts, if possible. Remove the adjuster mounting bolts/nuts from the floor pan.

2. Disconnect the battery negative cable. Detach the wiring harness motor connector at the carpet. Then, remove the seat from the car as described earlier in this section.

3. Lay the seat on its back on a clean surface. Then, remove the motor mounting screws from the motor bracket and the single mounting bolt from the adjuster.

4. Note the routing of the cable to the motor. Then, carefully disconnect the housing and cables from the motor assembly. Remove the motor from the seat bottom.

To install:

5. To install the motor, first position it in its mounted position.

6. Connect the cables and the housing to the motor.

7. Install the motor mounting screws. Install the bolt fastening the motor to the adjuster.

8. Install the seat as described earlier in this section.

9. Attach the wiring harness connector and the battery negative cable. Check the seat for proper operation.

GLOSSARY

AIR/FUEL RATIO: The ratio of air-to-gasoline by weight in the fuel mixture drawn into the engine.

AIR INJECTION: One method of reducing harmful exhaust emissions by injecting air into each of the exhaust ports of an engine. The fresh air entering the hot exhaust manifold causes any remaining fuel to be burned before it can exit the tailpipe.

ALTERNATOR: A device used for converting mechanical energy into electrical energy.

AMMETER: An instrument, calibrated in amperes, used to measure the flow of an electrical current in a circuit. Ammeters are always connected in series with the circuit being tested.

AMPERE: The rate of flow of electrical current present when one volt of electrical pressure is applied against one ohm of electrical resistance.

ANALOG COMPUTER: Any microprocessor that uses similar (analogous) electrical signals to make its calculations.

ARMATURE: A laminated, soft iron core wrapped by a wire that converts electrical energy to mechanical energy as in a motor or relay. When rotated in a magnetic field, it changes mechanical energy into electrical energy as in a generator.

ATMOSPHERIC PRESSURE: The pressure on the Earth's surface caused by the weight of the air in the atmosphere. At sea level, this pressure is 14.7 psi at 32°F (101 kPa at 0°C).

ATOMIZATION: The breaking down of a liquid into a fine mist that can be suspended in air.

AXIAL PLAY: Movement parallel to a shaft or bearing bore.

BACKFIRE: The sudden combustion of gases in the intake or exhaust system that results in a loud explosion.

BACKLASH: The clearance or play between two parts, such as meshed gears.

BACKPRESSURE: Restrictions in the exhaust system that slow the exit of exhaust gases from the combustion chamber.

BAKELITE: A heat resistant, plastic insulator material commonly used in printed circuit boards and transistorized components.

BALL BEARING: A bearing made up of hardened inner and outer races between which hardened steel balls roll.

BALLAST RESISTOR: A resistor in the primary ignition circuit that lowers voltage after the engine is started to reduce wear on ignition components.

BEARING: A friction reducing, supportive device usually located between a stationary part and a moving part.

BIMETAL TEMPERATURE SENSOR: Any sensor or switch made of two dissimilar types of metal that bend when heated or cooled due to the different expansion rates of the alloys. These types of sensors usually function as an on/off switch.

BLOWBY: Combustion gases, composed of water vapor and unburned fuel, that leak past the piston rings into the crankcase during normal engine operation. These gases are removed by the PCV system to prevent the buildup of harmful acids in the crankcase.

BRAKE PAD: A brake shoe and lining assembly used with disc brakes.

BRAKE SHOE: The backing for the brake lining. The term is, however, usually applied to the assembly of the brake backing and lining.

BUSHING: A liner, usually removable, for a bearing; an anti-friction liner used in place of a bearing.

CALIPER: A hydraulically activated device in a disc brake system, which is mounted straddling the brake rotor (disc). The caliper contains at least one piston and two brake pads. Hydraulic pressure on the piston(s) forces the pads against the rotor.

CAMSHAFT: A shaft in the engine on which are the lobes (cams) which operate the valves. The camshaft is driven by the crankshaft, via a belt, chain or gears, at one half the crankshaft speed.

CAPACITOR: A device which stores an electrical charge.

CARBON MONOXIDE (CO): A colorless, odorless gas given off as a normal byproduct of combustion. It is poisonous and extremely dangerous in confined areas, building up slowly to toxic levels without warning if adequate ventilation is not available.

CARBURETOR: A device, usually mounted on the intake manifold of an engine, which mixes the air and fuel in the proper proportion to allow even combustion.

CATALYTIC CONVERTER: A device installed in the exhaust system, like a muffler, that converts harmful byproducts of combustion into carbon dioxide and water vapor by means of a heat-producing chemical reaction.

CENTRIFUGAL ADVANCE: A mechanical method of advancing the spark timing by using flyweights in the distributor that react to centrifugal force generated by the distributor shaft rotation.

CHECK VALVE: Any one-way valve installed to permit the flow of air, fuel or vacuum in one direction only.

CHOKE: A device, usually a moveable valve, placed in the intake path of a carburetor to restrict the flow of air.

CIRCUIT: Any unbroken path through which an electrical current can flow. Also used to describe fuel flow in some instances.

CIRCUIT BREAKER: A switch which protects an electrical circuit from overload by opening the circuit when the current flow exceeds a predetermined level. Some circuit breakers must be reset manually, while most reset automatically.

COIL (IGNITION): A transformer in the ignition circuit which steps up the voltage provided to the spark plugs.

COMBINATION MANIFOLD: An assembly which includes both the intake and exhaust manifolds in one casting.

COMBINATION VALVE: A device used in some fuel systems that routes fuel vapors to a charcoal storage canister instead of venting them into the atmosphere. The valve relieves fuel tank pressure and allows fresh air into the tank as the fuel level drops to prevent a vapor lock situation.

COMPRESSION RATIO: The comparison of the total volume of the cylinder and combustion chamber with the piston at BDC and the piston at TDC.

CONDENSER: 1. An electrical device which acts to store an electrical charge, preventing voltage surges. 2. A radiator-like device in the air conditioning system in which refrigerant gas condenses into a liquid, giving off heat.

CONDUCTOR: Any material through which an electrical current can be transmitted easily.

CONTINUITY: Continuous or complete circuit. Can be checked with an ohmmeter.

COUNTERSHAFT: An intermediate shaft which is rotated by a mainshaft and transmits, in turn, that rotation to a working part.

CRANKCASE: The lower part of an engine in which the crankshaft and related parts operate.

CRANKSHAFT: The main driving shaft of an engine which receives reciprocating motion from the pistons and converts it to rotary motion.

CYLINDER: In an engine, the round hole in the engine block in which the piston(s) ride.

CYLINDER BLOCK: The main structural member of an engine in which is found the cylinders, crankshaft and other principal parts.

CYLINDER HEAD: The detachable portion of the engine, usually fastened to the top of the cylinder block and containing all or most of the combustion chambers. On overhead valve engines, it contains the valves and their operating parts. On overhead cam engines, it contains the camshaft as well.

DEAD CENTER: The extreme top or bottom of the piston stroke.

DETONATION: An unwanted explosion of the air/fuel mixture in the combustion chamber caused by excess heat and compression, advanced timing, or an overly lean mixture. Also referred to as "ping".

DIAPHRAGM: A thin, flexible wall separating two cavities, such as in a vacuum advance unit.

DIESELING: A condition in which hot spots in the combustion chamber cause the engine to run on after the key is turned off.

DIFFERENTIAL: A geared assembly which allows the transmission of motion between drive axles, giving one axle the ability to turn faster than the other.

DIODE: An electrical device that will allow current to flow in one direction only.

DISC BRAKE: A hydraulic braking assembly consisting of a brake disc, or rotor, mounted on an axle, and a caliper assembly containing, usually two brake pads which are activated by hydraulic pressure. The pads are forced against the sides of the disc, creating friction which slows the vehicle.

DISTRIBUTOR: A mechanically driven device on an engine which is responsible for electrically firing the spark plug at a predetermined point of the piston stroke.

DOWEL PIN: A pin, inserted in mating holes in two different parts allowing those parts to maintain a fixed relationship.

DRUM BRAKE: A braking system which consists of two brake shoes and one or two wheel cylinders, mounted on a fixed backing plate, and a brake drum, mounted on an axle, which revolves around the assembly.

DWELL: The rate, measured in degrees of shaft rotation, at which an electrical circuit cycles on and off.

ELECTRONIC CONTROL UNIT (ECU): Ignition module, module, amplifier or igniter. See Module for definition.

ELECTRONIC IGNITION: A system in which the timing and firing of the spark plugs is controlled by an electronic control unit, usually called a module. These systems have no points or condenser.

END-PLAY: The measured amount of axial movement in a shaft.

ENGINE: A device that converts heat into mechanical energy.

EXHAUST MANIFOLD: A set of cast passages or pipes which conduct exhaust gases from the engine.

FEELER GAUGE: A blade, usually metal, or precisely predetermined thickness, used to measure the clearance between two parts.

FIRING ORDER: The order in which combustion occurs in the cylinders of an engine. Also the order in which spark is distributed to the plugs by the distributor.

FLOODING: The presence of too much fuel in the intake manifold and combustion chamber which prevents the air/fuel mixture from firing, thereby causing a no-start situation.

FLYWHEEL: A disc shaped part bolted to the rear end of the crankshaft. Around the outer perimeter is affixed the ring gear. The starter drive engages the ring gear, turning the flywheel, which rotates the crankshaft, imparting the initial starting motion to the engine.

FOOT POUND (ft. lbs. or sometimes, ft.lb.): The amount of energy or work needed to raise an item weighing one pound, a distance of one foot.

FUSE: A protective device in a circuit which prevents circuit overload by breaking the circuit when a specific amperage is present. The device is constructed around a strip or wire of a lower amperage rating than the circuit it is designed to protect. When an amperage higher than that stamped on the fuse is present in the circuit, the strip or wire melts, opening the circuit.

GEAR RATIO: The ratio between the number of teeth on meshing gears.

GENERATOR: A device which converts mechanical energy into electrical energy.

HEAT RANGE: The measure of a spark plug's ability to dissipate heat from its firing end. The higher the heat range, the hotter the plug fires.

HUB: The center part of a wheel or gear.

HYDROCARBON (HC): Any chemical compound made up of hydrogen and carbon. A major pollutant formed by the engine as a byproduct of combustion.

HYDROMETER: An instrument used to measure the specific gravity of a solution.

INCH POUND (inch lbs.; sometimes in.lb. or in. lbs.): One twelfth of a foot pound.

INDUCTION: A means of transferring electrical energy in the form of a magnetic field. Principle used in the ignition coil to increase voltage.

INJECTOR: A device which receives metered fuel under relatively low pressure and is activated to inject the fuel into the engine under relatively high pressure at a predetermined time.

INPUT SHAFT: The shaft to which torque is applied, usually carrying the driving gear or gears.

INTAKE MANIFOLD: A casting of passages or pipes used to conduct air or a fuel/air mixture to the cylinders.

JOURNAL: The bearing surface within which a shaft operates.

KEY: A small block usually fitted in a notch between a shaft and a hub to prevent slippage of the two parts.

MANIFOLD: A casting of passages or set of pipes which connect the cylinders to an inlet or outlet source.

MANIFOLD VACUUM: Low pressure in an engine intake manifold formed just below the throttle plates. Manifold vacuum is highest at idle and drops under acceleration.

MASTER CYLINDER: The primary fluid pressurizing device in a hydraulic system. In automotive use, it is found in brake and hydraulic clutch systems and is pedal activated, either directly or, in a power brake system, through the power booster.

MODULE: Electronic control unit, amplifier or igniter of solid state or integrated design which controls the current flow in the ignition primary circuit based on input from the pick-up coil. When the module opens the primary circuit, high secondary voltage is induced in the coil.

NEEDLE BEARING: A bearing which consists of a number (usually a large number) of long, thin rollers.

OHM: (Ω) The unit used to measure the resistance of conductor-to-electrical flow. One ohm is the amount of resistance that limits current flow to one ampere in a circuit with one volt of pressure.

OHMMETER: An instrument used for measuring the resistance, in ohms, in an electrical circuit.

OUTPUT SHAFT: The shaft which transmits torque from a device, such as a transmission.

OVERDRIVE: A gear assembly which produces more shaft revolutions than that transmitted to it.

OVERHEAD CAMSHAFT (OHC): An engine configuration in which the camshaft is mounted on top of the cylinder head and operates the valve either directly or by means of rocker arms.

OVERHEAD VALVE (OHV): An engine configuration in which all of the valves are located in the cylinder head and the camshaft is located in the cylinder block. The camshaft operates the valves via lifters and pushrods.

OXIDES OF NITROGEN (NOx): Chemical compounds of nitrogen produced as a byproduct of combustion. They combine with hydrocarbons to produce smog.

OXYGEN SENSOR: Use with the feedback system to sense the presence of oxygen in the exhaust gas and signal the computer which can reference the voltage signal to an air/fuel ratio.

PINION: The smaller of two meshing gears.

PISTON RING: An open-ended ring with fits into a groove on the outer diameter of the piston. Its chief function is to form a seal between the piston and cylinder wall. Most automotive pistons have three rings: two for compression sealing; one for oil sealing.

PRELOAD: A predetermined load placed on a bearing during assembly or by adjustment.

PRIMARY CIRCUIT: the low voltage side of the ignition system which consists of the ignition switch, ballast resistor or resistance wire, bypass, coil, electronic control unit and pick-up coil as well as the connecting wires and harnesses.

PRESS FIT: The mating of two parts under pressure, due to the inner diameter of one being smaller than the outer diameter of the other, or vice versa; an interference fit.

RACE: The surface on the inner or outer ring of a bearing on which the balls, needles or rollers move.

REGULATOR: A device which maintains the amperage and/or voltage levels of a circuit at predetermined values.

RELAY: A switch which automatically opens and/or closes a circuit.

RESISTANCE: The opposition to the flow of current through a circuit or electrical device, and is measured in ohms. Resistance is equal to the voltage divided by the amperage.

RESISTOR: A device, usually made of wire, which offers a preset amount of resistance in an electrical circuit.

RING GEAR: The name given to a ring-shaped gear attached to a differential case, or affixed to a flywheel or as part of a planetary gear set.

ROLLER BEARING: A bearing made up of hardened inner and outer races between which hardened steel rollers move.

ROTOR: 1. The disc-shaped part of a disc brake assembly, upon which the brake pads bear; also called, brake disc. 2. The device mounted atop the distributor shaft, which passes current to the distributor cap tower contacts.

SECONDARY CIRCUIT: The high voltage side of the ignition system, usually above 20,000 volts. The secondary includes the ignition coil, coil wire, distributor cap and rotor, spark plug wires and spark plugs.

SENDING UNIT: A mechanical, electrical, hydraulic or electro-magnetic device which transmits information to a gauge.

SENSOR: Any device designed to measure engine operating conditions or ambient pressures and temperatures. Usually electronic in nature and designed to send a voltage signal to an on-board computer, some sensors may operate as a simple on/off switch or they may provide a variable voltage signal (like a potentiometer) as conditions or measured parameters change.

SHIM: Spacers of precise, predetermined thickness used between parts to establish a proper working relationship.

SLAVE CYLINDER: In automotive use, a device in the hydraulic clutch system which is activated by hydraulic force, disengaging the clutch.

SOLENOID: A coil used to produce a magnetic field, the effect of which is to produce work.

SPARK PLUG: A device screwed into the combustion chamber of a spark ignition engine. The basic construction is a conductive core inside of a ceramic insulator, mounted in an outer conductive base. An electrical charge from the spark plug wire travels along the conductive core and jumps a preset air gap to a grounding point or points at the end of the conductive base. The resultant spark ignites the fuel/air mixture in the combustion chamber.

SPLINES: Ridges machined or cast onto the outer diameter of a shaft or inner diameter of a bore to enable parts to mate without rotation.

TACHOMETER: A device used to measure the rotary speed of an engine, shaft, gear, etc., usually in rotations per minute.

THERMOSTAT: A valve, located in the cooling system of an engine, which is closed when cold and opens gradually in response to engine heating, controlling the temperature of the coolant and rate of coolant flow.

TOP DEAD CENTER (TDC): The point at which the piston reaches the top of its travel on the compression stroke.

TORQUE: The twisting force applied to an object.

TORQUE CONVERTER: A turbine used to transmit power from a driving member to a driven member via hydraulic action, providing changes in drive ratio and torque. In automotive use, it links the driveplate at the rear of the engine to the automatic transmission.

TRANSDUCER: A device used to change a force into an electrical signal.

TRANSISTOR: A semi-conductor component which can be actuated by a small voltage to perform an electrical switching function.

TUNE-UP: A regular maintenance function, usually associated with the replacement and adjustment of parts and components in the electrical and fuel systems of a vehicle for the purpose of attaining optimum performance.

TURBOCHARGER: An exhaust driven pump which compresses intake air and forces it into the combustion chambers at higher than atmospheric pressures. The increased air pressure allows more fuel to be burned and results in increased horsepower being produced.

VACUUM ADVANCE: A device which advances the ignition timing in response to increased engine vacuum.

VACUUM GAUGE: An instrument used to measure the presence of vacuum in a chamber.

VALVE: A device which control the pressure, direction of flow or rate of flow of a liquid or gas.

VALVE CLEARANCE: The measured gap between the end of the valve stem and the rocker arm, cam lobe or follower that activates the valve.

VISCOSITY: The rating of a liquid's internal resistance to flow.

VOLTMETER: An instrument used for measuring electrical force in units called volts. Voltmeters are always connected parallel with the circuit being tested.

WHEEL CYLINDER: Found in the automotive drum brake assembly, it is a device, actuated by hydraulic pressure, which, through internal pistons, pushes the brake shoes outward against the drums.

MASTER

INDEX